LOOK FOR THESE OTHER TITLES IN THE
FODOR'S GAY GUIDE SERIES

Fodor's Gay Guide to Amsterdam

Fodor's Gay Guide to Los Angeles and Southern California

Fodor's Gay Guide to New York City

Fodor's Gay Guide to the Pacific Northwest

Fodor's Gay Guide to San Francisco and the Bay Area

Fodor's Gay Guide to South Florida

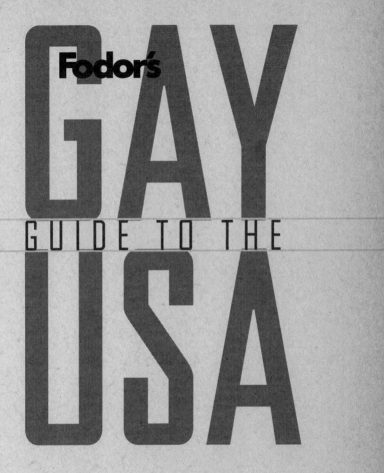

Fodor's GAY GUIDE TO THE USA

BY ANDREW COLLINS

FODOR'S TRAVEL PUBLICATIONS, INC.
NEW YORK • TORONTO • LONDON • SYDNEY • AUCKLAND

Fodor's Gay Guide to the USA

EDITORS: Jeff Boswell, Matthew Lore, Daniel Mangin

Fodor's Gay Guides Project Editor: Daniel Mangin
Editorial Contributors: Stephanie Adler, Kaline J. Carter, Deborah Carroll, Fionn Davenport, Karen Huber, James Sinclair, Russell Stockman
Map Editor: Robert P. Blake
Production Editors: Laura Kidder, Linda Schmidt
Creative Director: Fabrizio La Rocca
Cartographer: David Lindroth; Eureka Cartography
Cover Design: Tigist Getachew
Text Design: Between the Covers

Copyright © 1998 by Andrew Collins

Second Edition

ISBN 0–679–03374–2

Special Sales

Fodor's Travel Publications are available at special discounts for bulk purchases for sales promotions or premiums. Special editions, including personalized covers, excerpts of existing guides, and corporate imprints, can be created in large quantities for special needs. For more information, contact your local bookseller or write to Special Markets, Fodor's Travel Publications, 201 East 50th Street, New York, NY 10022. Inquiries from Canada should be directed to your local Canadian bookseller or sent to Random House of Canada, Ltd., Marketing Department, 2775 Matheson Blvd. E, Mississauga, Ontario L4W 4P7. Inquiries from the United Kingdom should be sent to Fodor's Travel Publications, 20 Vauxhall Bridge Road, London SW1V 2SA, England.

PRINTED IN THE UNITED STATES OF AMERICA

10 9 8 7 6 5 4 3 2 1

CONTENTS

Maps

AUTHOR'S NOTE

BEING GAY OR LESBIAN influences our choice of accommodations, nightlife, dining, shopping, and perhaps even sightseeing. This book will enable you to plan your trip confidently. On the following pages I've tried to provide ideas for every segment of our community, giving you the skinny on everything from bars and clubs to gay beaches, from the best shopping in New York City to the top restaurants in Chicago. You'll also find a wide selection of accommodations, from exclusively gay resorts to mainstream hotels. And you'll be shown which properties are closest to downtown businesses and which are near gay nightlife. Two dozen new destinations and many new maps have been added to this second edition of *Fodor's Gay Guide to the USA*.

About Me

I'm a gay male in my late 20s. I grew up in Wilton, Connecticut, graduated from Wesleyan University, have lived briefly in London and Atlanta, and currently split my time between a small house in New Hampshire's Monadnock mountains and an apartment in New York City's East Village.

How I Researched This Book

Since the day first edition was published, I've been crisscrossing the country, revisiting places I've seen before and discovering hundreds of new ones. In every community I interviewed local gays and lesbians—newspaper editors, activists, innkeepers, barflies, and people on the street. I spent between 5 and 15 days in most cities, and a couple of days in smaller resort towns.

On the road, I often I slept in the living rooms of friends . . . or friends of friends . . . or acquaintances, who soon became new friends. Sometimes I paid for hotel rooms and in some cases hoteliers extended their hospitality on the house. More than once I slept in my car. Without the generosity of friends and many hotels, I couldn't have written the book. But I never included a property or wrote favorably about one in exchange for a room.

And I personally paid for every other expense, from airfare and car rentals to meals and club covers. I made all my own travel arrangements. In short, I attempted to experience these destinations in the same manner you will.

This is an opinionated book. I don't hesitate to say what I think—I'm prone to describe certain neighborhoods as characterless, resorts as touristy or uppity, restaurants as dumpy or over-the-top. My intention is always to relate what I've observed and what I've heard locals say. For the most part I traveled without announcing myself—the majority of the businesses in this book had no idea I was writing about them when I visited. I've described everything as I've seen it—or as it has been reported to me. In the end, *Fodor's Gay Guide to the USA* is a service not to hotels and guest houses, or to gay bars and restaurants, or to anybody in the travel industry. It is a resource for you, the traveler.

Language and Voice

I've written this book in a casual, personal voice, using terms such as "faggy," "dyke," and "queer" the way my friends and I do in general conversation. I know that for some people these words are painful reminders of more repressive times—be assured that no offense is intended. Also, unless the context suggests otherwise, when I use the terms "gay" or "homosexual," I'm referring to gay men and lesbians. I specify gender only as needed for clarity.

Content

Each chapter has several sections. Here's a quick rundown:

The Lay of the Land

If you're looking for a quick summation of each destination's geography, its neighborhoods and major attractions, and its shopping, you'll want to read this carefully. At the end of each section are tips on getting around.

Eats

I'm a restaurant junkie, so I've included a broad range of options. The places I investigated were suggested by gay and lesbian locals, advertised in gay publications, or were reviewed positively in local newspapers and magazines. I stopped by almost every restaurant (and ate at as many as I could) to study the menu, check out the ambience, and observe the crowd.

I've tried to include choices for every budget. Many recommendations are in or near gay-oriented neighborhoods. A few establishments get a nod less for the food than the overtly festive atmosphere. Conversely, some places are listed simply because they represent some of the destination's finest or most unusual dining. The omission of your personal favorite may be more because it was similar to a place I did include than because I think it's not up to snuff. Unless otherwise noted, any restaurant in this book is at least somewhat popular with the community.

The Eats section ends with a sampling of area coffeehouses. Unless I describe the food, assume that each place offers only coffee and light snacks.

The following charts explain the price categories used for restaurants throughout this guide:

CHART A

CATEGORY	COST*
$$$$	over $20
$$$	$15–$20
$$	$10–$15
$	under $10

*Cost of dinner entrée

CHART B

CATEGORY	COST*
$$$$	over $16
$$$	$12–$16
$$	$7–$12
$	under $7

*Cost of dinner entrée

Scenes

I checked out nearly every bar reviewed in this book. If a place opened after my visit to the city, I telephoned an employee and also got a report from a knowledgeable local resource to ensure an accurate review.

The most popular spots are listed under the heading "Prime Suspects." I've also written short reviews about neighborhood bars, roving parties, weekly events, and straight hangouts with queer followings. I've bulleted the most popular clubs, bars,

and other nightlife options on the dining maps, which appear in the Eats section of each chapter.

Male-oriented places outnumber those that cater mostly to women by about 10 to 1. This is a reflection of America's gay-bar culture—it's overwhelmingly young and male. Still, don't assume that a bar described as 80% male or mostly young doesn't welcome lesbians or older guys. Descriptions of each bar's crowd and its "cruise factor" are based on my own observations and interviews and are provided simply to give you a profile of what's typical.

Under the heading "Action," I've listed a few bathhouses, adult theaters, and the like. I'd be remiss if I didn't tell you what's where. (I would also be remiss if I didn't encourage you to play safely and observe local regulations.)

Sleeps

In most chapters I've included gay-specific establishments that I felt confident recommending. I visited most of the B&Bs and small inns (usually anonymously), though I stayed in only a handful. If the establishment was straight-owned and I had no knowledge of its gay-friendliness, I checked with the owners to verify their interest in being covered in a gay publication. My descriptions of the clientele, compiled without the owners' input, are there to give you a general sense of the place.

When I discuss larger hotels, particularly those in cities, don't assume that they are gay-friendly (or otherwise) unless the reviews specifically state so. Obviously the degree of tolerance you encounter at a large property with many employees will depend largely on who happens to assist you. I've favored mainstream properties that are in and near gay neighborhoods and those that have a strong reputation with the community.

The following charts explain the price categories used for lodging establishments throughout this guide:

CHART A

CATEGORY	COST*
$$$$	over $180
$$$	$130–$180
$$	$90–$130
$	under $90

*Cost of double-occupancy room in high season

CHART B

CATEGORY	COST*
$$$$	over $150
$$$	$115–$150
$$	$75–$115
$	under $75

Cost of double-occupancy room in high season

The Little Black Book

This is your quick resource guide. If some establishments have closed by the time you read about them—bars and restaurants are unpredictable—try the contacts here to get the latest scoop. Local tourist boards can be helpful, and lesbigay bookstores and community centers are tremendous resources, as are alternative weeklies, many of which have Web sites with up-to-the-minute arts and entertainment information. I've included a few gay-popular gyms, the phone numbers of AIDS, health, and women's clinics and resources, and in most chapters the numbers of local transit systems and cab companies.

Disclaimer

This is where I'm to remind you that time brings changes, and that neither I nor the publisher can accept responsibility for errors. An incredible amount of time and effort has been spent ensuring the accuracy of this book's information, but businesses move and/or close and restaurants and bars change. Always call an establishment before you go to make sure that it will be open when you get there.

The mention of any business, attraction, or person in this book is in no way an indication of sexual orientation or attitudes about sexual orientation. Unless specifically stated, no business in this book is implied or assumed to be gay-owned or operated.

Send Letters

Whatever your reaction to this book—delight, excitement, unbridled rage—your feedback is greatly appreciated. I'd love to hear about your experiences, both good and bad, and about establishments you'd like me to include or exclude in future editions. Send your letters to me c/o Fodor's Travel Publications, 201 East 50th Street, New York, New York 10022, or e-mail me via my Web site, http://members.aol.com/Gay-Fodors/index.html.

In the meantime, I hope you have as much fun using this guide as I had writing it.

Andrew Collins

Andrew Collins
January 1998

ACKNOWLEDGMENTS

SINCE I BEGAN this project, hundreds of you have assisted me with this book by offering insights, opinions, suggestions, and advice. Some of you gave me your names, and I have thanked you personally below. Just as many of you either had no idea I was interviewing you for a book (surprise!) or drifted off before introducing yourselves—please accept my warmest gratitude.

Many members of Fodor's staff worked tirelessly on this book. Particular thanks goes to gay guides project editor Daniel Mangin, who slaved over this edition as he has over each of the gay pocket guides that preceded it, finessing the book's many rough edges, drawing on his considerable knowledge of travel and gay history, and going to astounding lengths to accommodate his verbose, tardy, demanding, and frequently AWOL author (this would be me). Editors Jeff Boswell and Matthew Lore also worked wonders on the many chapters assigned to them, Stephanie Adler spent long hours tracking down obscure and elusive minutiae without which the book would have countless gaps and shortcomings, and Bob Blake coordinated all of the book's maps and continues to act as my unofficial spiritual adviser. Former Fodor's editors Craig Seligman and Chris Billy were instrumental in helping me get the first edition of this guide off the ground and continue to lend their support and friendship.

For more than a year, Kaline J. Carter accompanied me, both in my travels and back at home. It was the best year of my life.

Special thanks also go to the following:

Wonderful friends who have helped along the way: Valerie Aaronoff, Noel Ambery, Steven Amsterdam, D. Keller Beasley, Forrest H. "Woody" Bennett, Dan Bial, Michelle Bouchard, Leigh Bucknam, Susan Cross, Nancy Duran and Jason Jercinovik, Thomas R. Harris, Caroline Hickson, Edie Jarolim, Peter Johnson, Jeffrey Kazin and Christopher Pennington, Rick Kleczkowski, Deborah Knapp, Christina Knight, Mark Kollar, Rebecca Miller and Jim Ffrench, Silvana Nova and Craig Seligman, Laura Prichard, Craig Pritchard, Marcy Pritchard, Julius Roberge, Ruth Scovill, Andrew Spurgin, Todd Whitley.

Colleagues, readers, and friends on the road: Ty Accornero, Garbo Afarian, Kyle Amdahl, Taylor Andrews, Chris Arrott, Wayne Beers and Mike Bobo, Gregory Bennett, David Berry, David Bianco, Stephanie Blackwood, Christopher Brandmeir, Mark Breckenridge, Graham Brown, Kenneth Burrell, Caroline Butler, Jeff Canham, W.A. Casey, Mary Casiano, Chris Cerullo, John Cochie, William Colbrunn, Pat Colognesi, Albert Colombo, Renée T. Coulombe, Steve Crohn, Tim Cusick, Sam Donato, Cliff Edge and Les Howell, Rees Erwin, Sandy Ferlisi, Robert Frankl, Lucy Friedland, Brian Gosh, Mark Haile, Michael Igram, Wesley Kashiwagi, the late Jim Kepner, Brent Kirby, Steve Knight, Lance Lattig, Matthew Link, Jack Levin, Larry J. Loyer, Jon C. Martin, Tom Mayak, Renee McBride, Robert Minor, Mahrya Monson, Christopher A. Moore, Charles Morvant and Bill Shimp, Fred Mutter and Andy Velez-Rivera, Jason Oliver Nixon, Kerry O'Quinn, Conrad Paulus, Tony Potter, Lois Reborne, Douglas C. Reilly, Joe Rio, Eric Rockey and Steve Sickenberger, Amy Rosenberg, Arich Sanchez, Jose dos Santos, Todd Savage, Chase Schade, Thomas F. Schulz, Mickey Sery, John Shore, Mike Silverman, Ken Slavin, Paul K. Smith, Trae Smith, Amy Adams Squires Strongheart, Carol Ann Susi, Jim Vivyan, Nick Welyhorskyj, Dan Woog.

Newspaper editors, innkeepers and hoteliers, and business owners: Joseph S. Amster (*Orange County Blade*), Lee Azus (Get Lost Bookstore, San Francisco), Larry Bailey and Ron Grantz (The Open Book, Sacramento) Rob Boyd (B&W Courtyards B&B, New Orleans), Cathy Bugliari and Trish Pyke (Hummingbird Ranch, Santa Fe), Richard D. Burns and Benjamin Stilp (NYC Gay and Lesbian Center), Kit and Bill Christopher (Cottonwood Inn, Taos), Antonio Cintra (Capitol Hill Guesthouse, Washington, D.C.), Chip Conley and Rob Delamater (Joie De Vivre Hotels, San Francisco), Martin Contreras and Keith Orr (Aut Bar, Ann Arbor), Allen Cook (*Triangle Journal News*, Memphis),

Robert Cotillo (Holiday Inn Emerald Springs, Las Vegas), Paul Crowley (Beachcomber Hotel, Miami Beach), Peter Ian Cummings (*XY Magazine,* San Francisco), Richard DiCusati (Citywide Reservation Service, Boston), Glenn Dixon (Highland Dell Inn, Russian River), Dave and Nancy Eshelman (Morning Glory Inn, Pittsburgh), Richard J. Fasenmyer and Lawrence Wald (Club Cathode Ray, Fort Lauderdale), John Frazier (representing Wyndham hotels), Tom Fricke and Bruce Burgner (Lovett Inn, Houston), Robert Frost and Ralph Bolton (Turquoise Bear, Santa Fe), Nancy Geary (A Room of One's Own, Madison), Kay and Charles Giddens (Little Tree, Taos), Rawley Grau (*Baltimore Alternative*), Dale Gray (Villa Toscana, Chicago), Richard Gray (Royal Palms Inn, Fort Lauderdale), Bob Guilmartin (South Florida Hotel Network, Miami Beach), Aaron Happel and Harvey Hertz (A Brother's Touch, Minneapolis), Gary Hackney and Tony Jenkins (Prospect Hill B&B, Cincinnati), Randy Hartley (Hartley House, Sacramento), Ed Hermance (Giovanni's Room, Philadelphia), Fred Holdridge (Columbus B&B), Bruce Kerschner and the staff (Obelisk Bookstore, San Diego), Carolyn Larson (*Houston Voice*), Brent Lawyer and Steve Vittum (Lamplighter Inn, Provincetown), Steve Levicki and Urban Jupena (Bunn-Pher Hill B&B, Ann Arbor), Michael Lindsay and Doug Motz (An Open Book, Columbus), Dilia Loe (Gay and Lesbian Center of Fort Lauderdale), Michael MacIntyre (Brass Key, Provincetown/Key West), Penny McCord (Peabody Orlando), Anne Davis Mulford (Aid for AIDS of Nevada), Jody Ohrazda and Austin Wallace (Obelisk Bookstore, Phoenix), David Oshinski (Ramada West Hollywood), Cleo Pelleteri (Claiborne Mansion, New Orleans), Steve Smith (Key West Business Guild), Gary Trosclair (Cabana Suites, Rehoboth Beach), Erik Wolf (Big Blue Marble Productions, New York), Trevor Wright and Steven Mascilo (Beaconlight Inn, Provincetown).

Tourism officials and public relations specialists who assisted in arranging many of my trips: Laurie Allison (San Diego), R. J. Bélanger, Michelle Fusco, and Renée Monforton (Detroit), Amy Blyth (Charleston), Christine DeCuir and Beverly Gianna (New Orleans), Myram Borders (Las Vegas), Michael Doughman and Cheryl Lewis (Dallas), Beth Ervin (Columbus), Tom Garrity (Albuquerque), Vincent Grandinetti, R.C. Staab, and Deirdre Wright (Philadelphia), Richard Grant (Denver), Heidi Kooi (Chicago), Stacey Krauszer (Houston), Melissa Libby (Atlanta/Charleston), Anne Lucke (Madison), Francine Mason (Fort Lauderdale), Jason Mathius (Salt Lake), Laura McCarthy (Minneapolis), Marla Meyer (Pittsburgh), Diane Milton (Aspen), Nancy Milton (St. Louis), Rick Murphy (Eureka Springs), Scott Owings and Gwen Spain (Austin), Dee Dee Poteete (San Antonio), Cindy Sanders (Nashville), Marsha Meyer Sculatti and Haley Powers (West Hollywood), David Serino (Ann Arbor), Gil Stotler and Mindy Schneeberger (Baltimore), Lois Smith (Cincinnati), Susan Solari (Portland), Lucy Steffens (Sacramento), Jenny Stacy (Savannah), Tracy Stockwell and Miles Carson (Milwaukee).

The United States

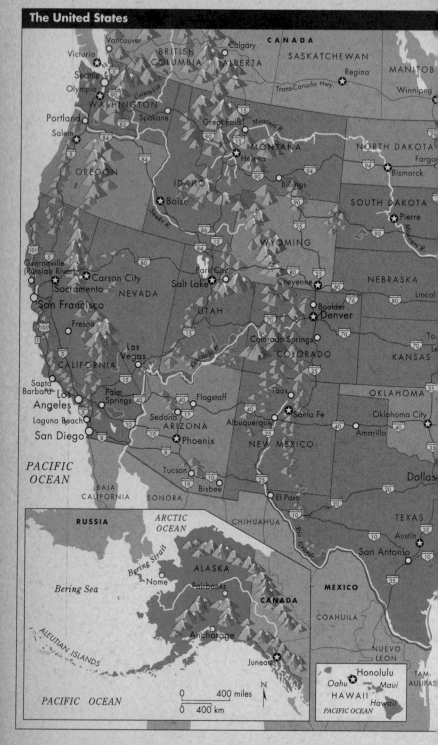

1 *Out in Atlanta*

With Charleston, South Carolina and Savannah, Georgia

ATLANTA IS THE ULTIMATE MELTING POT of southern cultures, tainted—or spiced up, depending on how you look at it—by myriad northern influences. It is not the land of Rhetts and Scarletts, nor are residents mired in the Old South mentality commonly attributed to them. Atlanta is as sophisticated and tolerant as most major urban centers. *And* it's extremely gay: More cars have pink triangle and rainbow decals than in any city in America (granted, there also seem to be more cars). In the last couple of years, business interest in the gay dollar has risen radically; hundreds of mainstream advertisers place ads in the gay papers.

Circling Atlanta is a six-lane beltway called I–285, and though much of what lies inside this ring—Atlanta proper—possesses a refreshingly enlightened outlook toward lesbians and gays, much of what lies outside it despises us. If you were to draw a new ring around I–285 every mile out indefinitely, each band in the resultant tree-ring pattern would represent roughly a one-year step back in time. Head 30 miles outside I–285, and you'll enter pre–civil rights Georgia; here, in places like virulently antigay Cobb County, it feels as if the presence of gay symbols on your car is an invitation to have your tires slashed or your windows smashed.

To be sure, even in Atlanta proper things are not perfect. Early in 1997, one of the city's top lesbian and gay nightclubs, the Otherside, was bombed. Although nobody inside the crowded club was killed, several patrons were injured. Gay Atlantans have always lived with the knowledge that such violently unfriendly forces live in their midst, but the community never seems to back away from its quest for acceptance and equality. Within weeks, the Otherside was back and better than ever, with extremely tight security, mandatory valet parking—and record crowds.

On a more positive note, the southeast Atlanta suburb of Decatur has been a foil to Cobb County. When Cobb announced its resolution, the straight mayor of Decatur invited gays and lesbians to come live peacefully in his city. Indeed, Decatur attracts lesbians and gay men who have reached the point where vegetable gardens are more important than beer gardens—no surprise, then, the city is the home of the Digging Dykes of Decatur, the hottest social club in Georgia. This sapphic garden club is said to know relatively little about tulip bulbs and topsoil; on gossiping, however, they're experts.

Atlanta has always been a city of stereotypical southern hospitality, a warm place with a friendly outlook and a genuine interest in newcomers. But these traits are changing as development booms and outsiders begin to make up a significant chunk of the population. The under-30 gay crowd is made up largely of men and women from neighboring states who have left their small, backward towns and discovered a climate where they are welcome. And so, in many of the new discos and bars you encounter equal numbers of friendly Southerners and image-conscious newcomers. Today, in every respect, Atlanta is a world-class city with both the benefits and the problems that come with the territory.

THE LAY OF THE LAND

Though Downtown, specifically Five Points, is Atlanta's official center, other symbolic centers have evolved over the past few years: the intersection of Highland and Virginia avenues, Little Five Points, Buckhead's intersection of Piedmont Avenue and Peachtree Road, Midtown's 14th and Peachtree streets. Atlanta is the land of shopping centers, and sidewalk culture is nonexistent but for a handful of neighborhoods. In many places you can park and wander, but to travel among neighborhoods you need to drive. This continuous sprawl is a bane of Atlanta existence—sitting in traffic all day can put an edge on people. On the other hand, there's no shortage of greenery, rolling hills, attractive houses, or stunning commercial architecture.

Should the city's emphasis on automobiles frustrate you, keep one phenomenal resource in mind: The **Atlanta Preservation Center** (☎ 404/876–2040) gives outstanding walking tours of several historic neighborhoods, including Ansley Park, Inman Park, Sweet Auburn, and Piedmont Park, and the Fox Theatre. Tours focus on historic architecture, cost $5 for adults, run typically early spring through late fall, and are usually offered once or twice weekly.

Downtown

Although it possesses a fascinating mix of early and late-20th-century buildings, Atlanta's **Downtown** provides little you can't find in safer, cleaner, and greener parts of the metro area. The 1996 Olympics spurred several massive civic rebuilding programs, but it's unclear how much these new stadiums, housing units, and improved thoroughfares have permanently enhanced downtown.

Five Points, where Edgewood Avenue and Peachtree, Marietta, and Decatur streets converge, is the commercial and spiritual center of the city—as it has been since 1837, when it marked the terminus of Atlanta's railways. Now the site of Downtown's most central MARTA (Metropolitan Atlanta Rapid Transit Authority) station, Five Points is just north of a large shopping and entertainment district called **Underground Atlanta,** a relatively unsuccessful three-level (two of them underground) network of avenues packed with somewhat cheesy shops and restaurants. It's worth a quick visit, but you'll find better options elsewhere.

A short walk south is the campy **World of Coca-Cola** (⊠ 55 Martin Luther King Jr. Dr., ☎ 404/676–5151), a shameless but amusing promotional tribute to Coke's history, with tastings, memorabilia, and gifts relevant to the Atlanta-born soft drink.

The blocks just north contain most of Downtown's earliest prominent buildings, including historic churches, the neoclassical **Georgia State Capitol** (1889; ⊠ Washington St. and Capitol Ave.), the neo-Gothic **Atlanta City Hall** (1930; ⊠ 68 Mitchell St.), the Beaux-Arts **Fulton County Courthouse** (1913; ⊠ 136 Pryor St.), the original **NationsBank Building** (1901; ⊠ 35 Broad St.), the art deco **William Oliver Building** (1930; ⊠ 32 Peachtree St.), the neo-Gothic **Hurt Building** (1913; ⊠ 45 Edgewood Ave.), the **Flatiron Building** (1897; ⊠ 84 Peachtree St.), and the ornate **Candler Building** (1906; ⊠ 127 Peachtree St.). On Downtown's western edge stands Ted Turner's **CNN Center** (⊠ International Blvd. and Marietta St., ☎ 404/827–2300); 45-minute studio tours are available.

Heading up Peachtree Street, you begin to see the buildings that make up today's dramatic modern skyline. The most striking towers are the 52-story, pyramid-crowned **Georgia-Pacific Building** (⊠ 133 Peachtree St.); Philip Johnson's and John Burgee's neoclassical 50-story **191 Peachtree Tower;** the 73-story **Westin Peachtree Plaza Hotel** (⊠ 210 Peachtree St.); and the 60-story gray-granite **One Peachtree Center** (⊠ 303 Peachtree St.). This stretch of Peachtree is the liveliest bit of Downtown; there are several stores and restaurants here, most notably a dramatic old **Macy's** (⊠ 180 Peachtree St.), whose grand exterior dates from 1927. Note also the Jetsonesque and somewhat silly-looking **Hyatt Regency Hotel** (⊠ 265 Peachtree St.). When it opened in 1967, its glowing blue rooftop restaurant permitted unobstructed views of Atlanta. Today, from many parts of town, you can't even see it.

Just east of Downtown is the **Sweet Auburn** historic district, a series of landmarks—most of them relating to the city's rich African-American history—stretching along Auburn Avenue from about Peachtree Street to Jackson Street. The western span of Auburn is where blacks conducted business in segregated Atlanta earlier in this century; the eastern span, beyond the I–75/85 overpass, comprises the **Martin Luther King Jr. National Historic Site** (visitor center, ⊠ 450 Auburn Ave., ☎ 404/331–5190), which documents the life and times of the civil rights leader who grew up and lived here. The **Ebenezer Baptist Church** (⊠ 407 Auburn Ave., ☎ 404/688–7263), the site for many years of King's sermons and ultimately his funeral; the **Martin Luther King Jr. Center for Nonviolent Social Change** (⊠ 449 Auburn Ave., ☎ 404/524–1956); and **Dr. King's Birthplace** (⊠ 501 Auburn Ave., ☎ 404/331–3920) are among the many moving stops on this tour.

Midtown and Ansley Park

To the north, **Midtown,** where the counterculture nested three decades ago, has Atlanta's highest concentration of gays and lesbians. The neighborhood has become expensive and less queer recently, as many gays have migrated toward southeastern Atlanta, where several historic neighborhoods remain affordable. Most of Midtown's popular gay bars and several of its restaurants are on or near Peachtree Street, from about 6th to 14th streets. Also here is the South's tallest structure, the 55-story **NationsBank Plaza Tower** (⊠ 600 Peachtree St.). History buffs might stop by the quirky **Atlanta Museum** (⊠ 537 Peachtree St., ☎ 404/872–8233); performing arts supporters should check out the esteemed **Woodruff Arts Center** (⊠ 1280 Peachtree St., ☎ 404/733–4200), which is home to the Alliance Theatre and the Atlanta Symphony Orchestra; and fine-art lovers should see the adjacent **High Museum of Art** (⊠ 1280 Peachtree St., ☎ 404/733–4444), whose respectable collection (including 19th-century European painting, Hudson River School paintings, American decorative arts, and a fine array of Alfred Uhry prints) competes with the walls that contain it—the striking, white-porcelain-paneled building designed by Richard Meier.

One of the most distinctive buildings in Atlanta, the Moorish- and Egyptian-inspired **Fox Theatre** (⊠ 660 Peachtree St., ☎ 404/817–8700) was built as a Shriners' temple in 1916, converted into a theater in the late '20s, nearly demolished to make way for an office building in 1978, and now presents touring musicals, shows, and performers.

Budding Scarletts mustn't miss the nearby **Road to Tara Museum** (⊠ 659 Peachtree St., ☎ 404/897–1939), which contains enough *Gone with the Wind* memorabilia and costumes to satisfy even the most dedicated groupie. Up the street is the **Margaret Mitchell House** (⊠ Peachtree and 10th Sts., ☎ 404/249–7012), the former home of the book's author; it has faced constant obstacles in its journey to becoming a museum. After having nearly been razed in 1988, it suffered devastating fires in 1994 and 1996; it's now finally open to the public and contains a wealth of information on Mitchell's tragically short but unusual life (in 1949 she was struck and killed by a car as she crossed Peachtree Street a few blocks north of her home).

On the eastern edge of Midtown, **Piedmont Park,** one of the loveliest urban parks in America, feels miles away from city life, except for its views of Atlanta's skyline. It's common to see dykes and queens merrily blading, jogging, sunning, reading, and cruising just about everywhere. At night, the park is notoriously cruisy but heavily policed and fairly dangerous. The park's northern edge is bordered by Atlanta's spectacular 60-acre **Botanical Garden** (⊠ 1345 Piedmont Ave., ☎ 404/876–5859).

In northern Midtown you'll find the rather tony and quite gay residential neighborhood of **Ansley Park,** where many houses date from the early part of the century. Here, at the intersection of Piedmont Avenue and Monroe Drive, is a small but concentrated gay entertainment district, anchored by the **Ansley Square shopping center** (⊠ 1492–1510 Piedmont Ave.), which is packed with community-oriented shops, bars, and eateries. Just down Piedmont from Ansley Square is a great little gay-male fashion boutique, **Boy Next Door** (⊠ 1447 Piedmont Ave., ☎ 404/873–2664).

Buckhead

In the northern reaches of the city, posh **Buckhead** is far removed from Downtown, both geographically and psychologically. Residential Buckhead encompasses a rather huge area—everything west of Peachtree Road and east of the Northwest Expressway (I–75) up to the **Perimeter** (an expanse of office buildings, restaurants, and malls), where Highway 400 runs over I–285. A great sunny-day activity is to drive around Buckhead's winding, wooded roads gawking at the hundreds of mansions; West Paces Ferry Road and Northside Drive are two of the better routes. A highlight is the **Atlanta History Center** (⊠ 130 W. Paces Ferry Rd., ☎ 404/814–4000), a 32-acre wooded spread with several historic buildings, including the sumptuous **Swan House,** a furnished 1928 Palladian mansion.

Commercial Buckhead is where the chic go to see and be seen. Most of the nightclubs, restaurants, and shops are along Paces Ferry and Pharr roads, between Peachtree and Piedmont roads. On weekend nights, this section is overrun with yuppies and college students. It's not particularly gay, although Elton John owns a high-rise condo nearby. The gays who live here tend to be older, settled, wealthy, and male, but a more diverse gay and lesbian presence gets stronger every day. The two most popular—and fashionable—malls in Atlanta are on Peachtree Road, north of where it intersects with Piedmont Road. **Lenox Square Mall** (⊠ 3393 Peachtree Rd.) is officially the most visited site in Atlanta—it's the larger of the two, and has the most mainstream selection of shops. The snazzy **Phipps Plaza** (⊠ 3500 Peachtree Rd.) has the sorts of boutiques and department stores you'd find on Manhattan's 5th Avenue. Both have enough homo traffic to qualify unofficially as America's two fanciest gay community centers.

Virginia-Highland

Monroe Drive is the boundary between Midtown and **Virginia-Highland,** a funky yet gentrified residential and commercial neighborhood that's hot with guppies and yuppies. There are several good shops and restaurants where Monroe hits 10th Street from the west. The true hub, however, is a short drive east, at the intersection of Highland and Virginia avenues, where galleries and offbeat home-furnishings stores abound. Just south of Virginia-Highland, the **Dekalb Farmer's Market** (⊠ 3000 E. Ponce de

Leon Ave., ☎ 404/377–6400) is the best dyke-cruising ground in the Atlanta metro area—maybe even in the whole Southeast.

Little Five Points and Inman Park

Atlanta does well when it comes to outrageousness. The city teems with young counterculturists; most congregate in a tiny district southeast of Virginia-Highland. **Little Five Points** is centered, aptly, at a five-street intersection anchored most prominently by Moreland and Euclid avenues. What to see? Grungers, goths, Deadheads, the tattooed and pierced, boys in ski hats in summer, girls in fishnet tights in winter, loiterers, poets, actors, artists, slackers, ruffians, poseurs, curiosity-seekers, you name it. It's not necessarily a gay scene, but everybody is welcome. Bumble into **Village Coffee House** (✉ 420 Seminole Ave., ☎ 404/688–3176), where Atlanta's headbangers like to bang heads. There are also several experimental theaters, **Charis Books** (*see* Bookstores, *below*), and the lesbian-popular **Sevananda Natural Food Co-op** (✉ 1111 Euclid Ave., ☎ 404/681–2831).

The heart of **Inman Park** is just south of here. This neighborhood, Atlanta's first suburb, was abandoned and run-down before gay and African-American gentrification took hold in the early '80s, with the restoration of many of its elaborate Victorian houses. It's now a great place to wander.

Ormewood Park, Grant Park, and East Atlanta Village

As recently as the early '90s, the southeast Atlanta neighborhoods of **Ormewood Park** and **Grant Park** were undesirable places to live. But as gays and lesbians have sought bigger houses and more acreage for moderate prices, they've moved east to the gay-friendly suburb of Decatur or headed to these now-promising areas. Perhaps most significant is that whites are slowly settling into a predominantly African-American area—this in a city whose racial spheres still rarely overlap. The movement first began in Grant Park, which is best known as the site of Atlanta's zoo. It has only recently begun spreading to Ormewood. And most recently a small but hip grouping of funky shops and eateries has opened in **East Atlanta Village** around the intersection of Glenwood and Flat Shoals avenues.

GETTING AROUND

Atlanta's extensive but often-criticized mass-transit system was improved for the 1996 Olympics, but you still need a car to see most of the city. Parking is fairly easy in Midtown but can be tough in Buckhead and Downtown. The layout is confusing, the traffic horrendous, and the roads always under construction. Nevertheless, a car is still a better weapon than a map of the **MARTA** bus and subway system, which is limited in coverage and geared more toward commuters. People don't take a lot of taxis here, either.

EATS

Atlantans are justly proud of their dining scene, which is among the nation's best. That there are dozens of first-rate restaurants here is not in question; the trick is separating the stars from the impostors. Especially in Buckhead and Midtown, just about every new eatery has indirect or track lighting, gobs of contemporary paintings, tables and chairs in surreal shapes and colors, pretty (but often absentminded) waitrons, and a menu that draws from an almost interchangeable battery of froufrou ingredients. After a while, these places begin to look and taste alike.

Most restaurants in Atlanta have something of a gay following. Those Downtown are the least gay, and those in Buckhead (a few of which feel like extensions of sororities and fraternities) are usually packed with straight yuppies and are the trendiest. In Midtown, Virginia-Highland, Little Five Points, and Inman Park it's gays galore. Anyplace where the see-and-be-seen factor is high, you're likely to have trouble parking, getting a table, and being served promptly. Be patient: You're in the South.

For price ranges, *see* dining Chart A at the front of this guide.

Midtown and Virginia-Highland

$$$–$$$$ ✕ **The Abbey.** An Atlanta institution since 1968, this is the place to go for special occasions. The stained-glass windows and ecumenical mood of this former church command a certain reverence—as though you should be extra careful not to dribble béarnaise sauce down your front. Food is traditional Continental, the sort of rich meals you'd expect the White House to serve to visiting French dignitaries. ⊠ *163 Ponce de Leon Ave.,* ☎ *404/876–8532.*

$$–$$$$ ✕ **South City Kitchen.** A nirvana for yuppies on the fairly queer mini-restaurant row along Crescent Avenue, this airy sleek dining room draws a well-heeled bunch for creative "New Southern" cooking. Crab hash with poached eggs and cedar plank trout with crayfish succotash are a couple of the delicious possibilities. ⊠ *1144 Crescent Ave.,* ☎ *404/873–7358.*

$$–$$$$ ✕ **South of France.** The words RESTAURANT AND LOUNGE on the sign out front (and the location in a tacky shopping center) belie the authenticity of this fine French restaurant, which has been feeding Francophiles since 1977. The wine overfloweth and the country-style pâtés are plentiful in the refined dining room. ⊠ *2345 Cheshire Bridge Rd.,* ☎ *404/325–6963.*

$$–$$$ ✕ **Cowtippers.** Just about everything here but the tap water is char-grilled, making Cowtippers one of the best steak houses in town—and easily the faggiest. Set in a low ranch-style house on Piedmont Road, just up from Ansley Square, it's a rollicking place with an authentic roadhouse atmosphere. ⊠ *1600 Piedmont Ave.,* ☎ *404/874–3751.*

$$–$$$ ✕ **Indigo Coastal Grill.** One of the major brunch spots in Virginia-Highland, Indigo is a seafood restaurant with a Caribbean kick. Sample the faintly sweet conch fritters, the rich lobster corn chowder, or the goat cheese enchiladas. At any meal, you're likely to see some of the gay community's movers and shakers. ⊠ *1397 N. Highland Ave.,* ☎ *404/876–0676.*

$$–$$$ ✕ **Tiburon Grille.** Although slightly pretentious, with high ceilings, indirect lighting, and rather affected contemporary decor, this stalwart along Highland Avenue's restaurant row churns out fresh California-inspired cuisine. You might try the hefty Caesar salad with fried oysters or the shiitake miso halibut. ⊠ *1190-B N. Highland Ave.,* ☎ *404/892–2393.*

$$ ✕ **Camille's.** No surprises here: just an old-fashioned, family-style Italian restaurant without too many families. Both the bright dining room and the covered patio have candles and red-check tablecloths on the tables. Expect good, filling pastas, chicken, veal, and seafood—and a nice selection of wines by the glass. ⊠ *1186 N. Highland Ave.,* ☎ *404/872–7203.*

$$ ✕ **Colonnade Restaurant.** Blue-haired old ladies and bleached-blond fags: two great things that go well together. Yes, the Colonnade is practically a caricature of itself; it's been serving fattening but beloved southern fare since 1927. Gussied up with hunting prints and floral carpeting, it really does draw a mix of gays and old Southern Baptists (and who says you can't be both?). The chicken potpie will warm your heart and clog your arteries. ⊠ *1879 Cheshire Bridge Rd.,* ☎ *404/874–5642.*

$$ ✕ **Einstein's.** Set in two adjacent old southern bungalows on Juniper Street, Einstein's is one of the gayest of Atlanta's restaurants; it's famous for its

Eats ●
The Abbey, **19**
Babette's Cafe, **24**
Bacchanalia, **2**
Bangkok, **9**
Buckhead Diner, **3**
Café Diem, **22**
Café Tu Tu Tango, **1**
Camille's, **13**
Caribou, **8**
Casbah, **23**
Cheyenne Grill, **4**
Colonnade Restaurant, **6**
Cowtippers, **5**
Dusty's, **10**
Einstein's, **17**
Flying Biscuit Café, **21**
Gallettos Espresso, **14**
Indigo Coastal Grill, **11**
Mary Mac's Tea Room, **18**
Outwrite Books, **20**
Patio, **25**
South City Kitchen, **16**
South of France, **7**
Tiburon Grille, **12**
Vickery's, **15**

Scenes ○
The Armory, **11**
Atlanta Eagle, **16**
Backstreet, **12**
Blake's, **14**
Buddies Midtown, **15**
Bulldog, **10**
Burkhart's, **7**
Coronet Club, **1**
Fusion, **8**
Guys and Dolls, **19**
Heretic, **4**
Hoedown's, **17**
Loretta's, **13**
Metro, **9**
Moreland Tavern, **20**
New Order Lounge, **3**
The Otherside, **2**
Phoenix, **18**
Revolution, **5**
Scandals, **6**

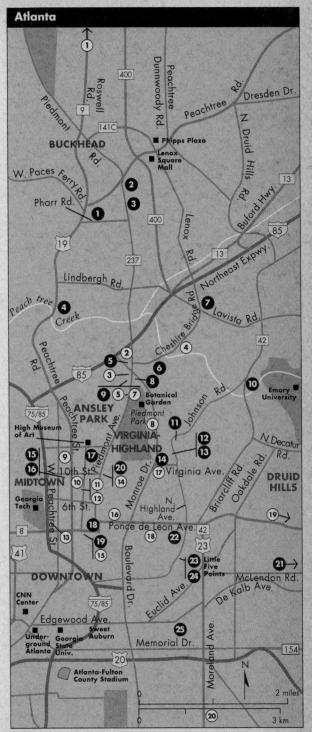

lively Sunday brunches. Getting a patio seat is tough but worth the wait. The crowd is cruisy, loud, and vivacious. Try the black bean and goat cheese quesadilla or the spicy chicken tandoori salad. ⊠ *1077 Juniper St.,* ☎ *404/876–7925.*

$$ ✕ **Vickery's.** This lively restaurant in the heart of Midtown is as cruisy as any bar but also has a dandy kitchen. It's a casual place, serving traditional American food with a few Cuban and Caribbean overtones (black bean cakes, jerk chicken). Great for brunch. ⊠ *1106 Crescent Ave.,* ☎ *404/881–1106.*

$–$$ ✕ **Dusty's.** You are in the South, after all, so at least once you should do as the natives do and hit an authentic barbecue. This rustic place near Emory University is noted for its North Carolina–style preparation (lots of vinegar and spices, no tomatoes). ⊠ *1815 Briarcliff Rd.,* ☎ *404/320–6264.*

$–$$ ✕ **Mary Mac's Tea Room.** A throwback to a quaint and traditional side of Atlanta rarely seen today, this sentimentally sweet eatery has great local cooking (fried chicken, baked catfish, sweet potato soufflé) and delicious desserts. It's always packed with southern belles (both authentic and ersatz). ⊠ *224 Ponce de Leon Ave.,* ☎ *404/876–1800.*

$ ✕ **Bangkok.** Of several good Thai restaurants around town, this one in Ansley Square has the gayest following—it's just steps from three bars. But convenience to nightlife isn't the only reason to come. The staff is friendly, the dining room attractive, and such dishes as deep-fried whole fish with ground pork, onions, and spicy sauce are consistently good. ⊠ *1492 Piedmont Ave.,* ☎ *404/874–2514.*

Buckhead

$$$–$$$$ ✕ **Bacchanalia.** This unassuming pale green house on Piedmont Road is home to some of Buckhead's most creative cooking, borrowing from many cultures—the south of France to Thailand. The menu changes weekly but might feature horseradish-crusted sea bass with roasted shiitake mushrooms. ⊠ *3125 Piedmont Rd.,* ☎ *404/365–0410.*

$–$$$ ✕ **Buckhead Diner.** It's becoming a popular trick: You build a fancy chrome restaurant; jazz up the dining room with marble, neon, and leather; flood the menu with nouveau takes on traditional favorites; and then call it a "diner." The first-rate food, such as barbecued mahimahi with roasted poblano grits and veal-and-wild-mushroom meat loaf, ensures that the trick works. ⊠ *3073 Piedmont Rd.,* ☎ *404/262–3336.*

$–$$ ✕ **Cheyenne Grill.** This cavernous Wild West–style restaurant has more than a few ways to fill you up. The huge, delicious burgers come with a variety of toppings. Also terrific are the seasoned shrimp or chicken kebabs and the filling appetizers, such as salmon pâté. You can eat on the spacious patio or have a drink in the swank martini bar. ⊠ *2391 Peachtree Rd.,* ☎ *404/842–1010.*

$ ✕ **Café Tu Tu Tango.** Packed most nights with beautiful people, this clever theme restaurant in Buckhead often requires a 90-minute wait. Artists and musicians are actually at work inside the restaurant—their oeuvres dot the walls and fill the air. But the real draw is some 50 varieties of tapas, along with great pizza, rosemary flatbread, artichoke dip, and pot stickers. The upstairs seating is quieter and has better ambience. ⊠ *220 Pharr Rd.,* ☎ *404/841–6222.*

Inman Park and Little Five Points

$$–$$$ ✕ **Babette's Café.** Famous for seasonal, prix-fixe Babette's Feasts, Babette's is a modest storefront bistro that captures the essence of southern European farmhouse cooking with favorites like artichoke and olive ravioli and grilled lamb loin with a fresh herb crust and red wine reduction. Also expect plenty of pâté and red wine. ⊠ *471 N. Highland Ave.,* ☎ *404/523–9121.*

$$ ✕ **Casbah.** With North African fine and decorative arts, exotic music, and belly dancers, this gay-popular Inman Park eatery offers a festive slice of Morocco with delicious food to boot. The lamb dishes, such as *maasal* (lamb dipped in a honey-nutmeg sauce, then roasted and garnished with almonds and sesame seeds), are tops. Also consider the fragrant couscous dishes. ⊠ *465 N. Highland Ave.,* ☎ *404/524–5777.*

$$ ✕ **Patio.** The funky ambience and trendy crowd at this Inman Park café contrast with what is essentially down-home Italian cooking. You can choose from fettuccine, penne, or capellini served with any of five fresh sauces. Several pizzas are also available; the bianca has provolone, ricotta, romano, fresh garlic, basil, and sun-dried tomatoes. ⊠ *1029 Edgewood Ave.,* ☎ *404/584–8945.*

$–$$ ✕ **Café Diem.** What originated as a largely queer coffeehouse has developed into an affordable but full-scale bistro with excellent food, including chicken in red wine, and linguine with shrimp, scallops, and mussels. You can also still curl up on a sofa and enjoy steamed milk and biscuits. ⊠ *640 N. Highland Ave.,* ☎ *404/607–7008.*

$ ✕ **Flying Biscuit Café.** Down the road from Little Five Points, this off-beat café is a fave with everyone from hip alternateens to dykes with tykes. Breakfast, served all day, is the main draw. Try the rich orange French toast with honey and caramelized bananas. For lunch don't miss turkey meat loaf with *pudge* (mashed red potatoes, sun-dried tomatoes, basil, and olive oil). ⊠ *1655 McLendon Ave.,* ☎ *404/687–8888.*

Coffeehouse Culture

In addition to the coffeehouses listed below, **Outwrite Books** (*see* Bookstores, *below*) has a charming and always-packed espresso bar.

Caribou. One of the many glitzy coffeehouses to open in Midtown in the past couple of years, Caribou has quickly developed a gay following because of its location across from Ansley Mall and Ansley Square. It's a bright, contemporary place with some outdoor tables. ⊠ *1551 Piedmont Ave.,* ☎ *404/733–5539.*

Gallettos Espresso. With great muffins, bagels, and lots of designer coffees and espressos, this amber-lighted, traditionally furnished coffeehouse is in a small shopping center near the southeast corner of Piedmont Park. Gets a somewhat collegiate crowd. ⊠ *Corner of Monroe Dr., Virginia Ave., and 10th St.,* ☎ *404/724–0204.*

SCENES

Atlantans love to party. Saturday is the big night out on the town, while Fridays are relatively quiet—more like other weeknights than a traditional weekend night. But no matter what the night, there's always something going on at most bars here. You can always find a drag show (Ru Paul got her start here)—everything from serious, traditional shows put on by female impersonators to campy, outrageous productions. Big, glitzy dance clubs are also common (Backstreet and the Armory are among the biggest).

Don't overlook the city's budding music scene. Some of the rock world's biggest bands hail from Atlanta and environs, including R.E.M., Indigo Girls, Hootie and the Blowfish, the B-52s, and Arrested Development. You may not find any all-gay bands, but a ton of them have one or two gay members and substantial followings in the community. **Eddie's Attic** (⊠ *515-B N. McDonough St.,* ☎ *404/377–4976*) in Decatur gets the younger crowd by frequently featuring acoustic women's groups.

Prime Suspects

The Armory. Because the Armory is almost adjacent to Backstreet, lots of guys wind up hitting both. If you find the guys at Backstreet too piss-elegant for words, head here where the booze is cheap and a gotta-get-laid attitude prevails. There are several bars and dance floors, one of which is sometimes country-western. The best assets are the patio (with a gurgling fountain) and the pleasant roof deck. ⊠ *836 Juniper St.*, ☎ *404/881–9280. Crowd: male, mostly under 35, similar to Backstreet's but looser and trashier, mixed racially, cruisy.*

Backstreet. Just about everybody ends up here on a Saturday night—it's one of four Atlanta bars (but the only gay one) that never closes or stops serving alcohol on weekends. A good number of straight folks join the dykes and fags in the upstairs lounge to catch the notoriously bawdy drag act of Charlie Brown and Lily White (and friends). Visitors must buy a $10 membership (good for three months). ⊠ *845 Peachtree St.*, ☎ *404/873–1986. Crowd: 75/25 m/f, mostly under 35, white, guppie, often stuck-up, gym boys; best mix on Saturdays.*

Blake's. Of stand-and-model bars, Blake's has the most uppity reputation in the South. But, in fact, because this is such a friendly city, it's not truly all that stuck-up—it's just a bit of a scene. You enter through a front room, which is cozy, crowded, and pubby; it has a pressed-tin ceiling and walls covered with license plates and odd signs. There are some bar stools, but these guys are known to bare claws and fangs to capture them. A flight of stairs leads to a second, quieter video bar in back, off which you'll find a sunporch and, off that, a patio. ⊠ *227 10th St.*, ☎ *404/892–5786. Crowd: mostly male (but for a few fag hags), clonish and cliquey, starched-shirt, attitudy, uniformly chiseled and beautiful.*

Bulldog. While Loretta's is the most popular space among most gay African-Americans, Bulldog draws black and white guys who want to hang out together. It's along the busy stretch of Peachtree Street clubs and, thanks to a recent remodeling, looks better than ever. You enter through an attractive deck in the back of the building and continue inside to several small cocktail bars and an even smaller dance floor that's packed many nights. Very cruisy bathrooms. This is a members-only club—you pay a nominal fee at the door to gain entrance. ⊠ *893 Peachtree St.*, ☎ *404/872–3025. Crowd: male, mostly 30s to 50s, mixed racially, some leather, very butch, low-key, horny and fun.*

Burkhart's. The crown jewel of Ansley Square, Burkhart's is one of the nicest bars in town—the kind of place where you can walk up and talk to somebody, where they spin classic and current dance tunes, where a stranger is welcome to jump in and play pool with the regulars. The whole place has a warm, taverny feel; downstairs has several small rooms and bars. Upstairs, an open interior balcony encircles the main room below, allowing for prime ogling; a second room has pool tables. ⊠ *Ansely Sq.*, *1492 Piedmont Ave.*, ☎ *404/872–4403. Crowd: mostly male, 20s and 30s, similar to guys at Blake's but less attitude; cruisy and friendly.*

Heretic. Many leather devotees swear by the Eagle, but the Heretic has more character and exudes machismo. The first hint is a parking lot absolutely packed with monster pick-up trucks and Cadillac Eldorados. A strict leather dress code is enforced on Wednesday and Sunday, and suggested the rest of the time. Inside, the place lives up to expectations—it's so dark and smoky you honestly can't see a thing, except the occasional bear belting down a vat of Jack Daniels. ⊠ *2069 Cheshire Bridge Rd.*, ☎ *404/325–3061. Crowd: male, 30s and 40s, dangerous-looking but warm and fuzzy underneath, leathered up.*

Hoedown's. Formerly located in a tacky barnlike structure on Cheshire Bridge Road, Hoedown's is now a slick contemporary space with upscale decor (albeit in a shopping center in Highland Park), but it's still the top gay country-western dance club in Atlanta. The impressive sound system helps fill the dance floor with devoted hoofers. ⊠ *Midtown Promenade*, *931 Monroe Dr.*, ☎ *404/876–0001. Crowd: about 50/50 cowboys and cowgirls; mixed ages, friendly, down-to-earth.*

March. This trendy bar and disco on the lower level of Midtown Outlets, off Monroe Drive, is right by the equally trendy Fitness Factory. The crowds vary somewhat according to the theme and drink specials, but Fusion is gay on Friday and Saturday. Expect high-energy dance music. Loungy nooks and a catwalk offer time-outs from the spacious dance floor. ⊠ *550C Amsterdam Ave.,* ☎ *404/872–6411. Crowd: 75/25 m/f, quite a few straights, 20s and 30s, I'm beautiful and I know it, toned and well-heeled.*

Metro. After moving to fancier digs up the street in 1996, the Metro seems somewhat less sleazy than its former self (don't worry, though, there are still plenty of gyrating bar-top dancers to stare at). Particularly appealing is the landscaped deck at the back of the building. Inside is a large club with a dance floor and very dim lighting. Depending on the night, the Metro can be dead or pulsing with offbeat characters. Monday's amateur strip night packs in the crowds. ⊠ *1080 Peachtree St.,* ☎ *404/874–9869. Crowd: male, 30s to 50s, a colorful blend of daddies, good-time guys, club kids, hustlers, guppies, and the occasional transsexual.*

The Otherside. Long one of the most inviting discos in the South, the Otherside quickly bounced back from its 1997 bombing, reopening with an even more dedicated following. Inside what was once a cheesy steak house are several fireplaces, a mix of retro restaurant furnishings and cozy lounge areas, a glassed-in patio with pool tables and other games, and a large dance floor where you'll find disco or country-western music depending on the night. Valet parking is now mandatory. ⊠ *1924 Piedmont Ave.,* ☎ *404/875–5238. Crowd: mixed m/f, fairly mixed in age and race, gals/guys next door, low attitude.*

Revolution. Revolution has continued to grow in popularity since its 1996 move from its snazzy Buckhead space to the ever-queer Ansley Square. It draws a spicy crowd of mostly women on weekends, with a slightly more mixed crowd the rest of the time. Decor is classy and contemporary, with a concrete dance floor on one side and a bar with tables and chairs on the other. There's live music some nights and country-western music from time to time. A good place to meet a hot, young chippie. ⊠ *Ansley Sq., 1492 Piedmont Ave.,* ☎ *404/874–8455. Crowd: 80/20 f/m, young, stylish, well-heeled and well-dressed.*

Neighborhood Haunts

The **Atlanta Eagle** (⊠ 306 Ponce de Leon Ave., ☎ 404/873–2453) is a favorite with leather men. **Buddies Midtown** (⊠ 239 Ponce de Leon Ave., ☎ 404/872–2655) has plenty of pool tables, a jukebox, and a mixed male/female crowd that spans ages. **Scandals** (⊠ Ansley Sq., 1510 Piedmont Ave., ☎ 404/875–5957) draws a mostly 30s and 40s bunch of men for chatting and cruising. The **Phoenix** (⊠ 567 Ponce de Leon Ave., ☎ 404/892–7871) is a divey country-western bar with a *Deliverance* ambience. The **New Order Lounge** (⊠ Ansley Mall, 1544 Piedmont Rd., ☎ 404/874–8247) is a cheap, dreary lounge set amid several loading docks behind Ansley Mall, but where else is a girl to go for hard drinking at 2 in the afternoon?

West of downtown, **Loretta's** (⊠ 708 Spring St., ☎ 404/874–8125) is a spacious, three-floor, mostly black and mostly gay disco with TV screens, video bars, a dance floor, and a young, hip, and cute crowd (but sometimes very steep covers). Serving the increasingly gay Grant Park and Ormewood Park area, **Moreland Tavern** (⊠ 1196 Moreland Ave., ☎ 404/622–4650) draws both men and women. Among strip clubs, the **Coronet Club** (⊠ 5275 Roswell Rd., ☎ 404/250–1534) has a mostly gay contingent on Sundays—but it's BYOB, and since you can't buy booze on Sundays, plan ahead. Also, **Guys and Dolls** (⊠ 2788 E. Ponce de Leon Ave., Decatur, ☎ 404/377–2956) has the largest all-nude revue in the South; on weekdays you can catch some of the city's premier drag acts.

Action

The **Chamber** (✉ 2115 Faulkner Rd., ☎ 404/248–1612) is a fetish club where you can watch a variety of fascinating, kinky demonstrations representing every conceivable sexual taste. **Flex** (✉ 76 4th St., ☎ 404/815–0456) is the city's bathhouse; it's open 24 hours, has a heated indoor pool, and both lockers and cabins. **Southern Nights** (✉ 2205 Cheshire Bridge Rd., ☎ 404/728–0701) has toys, lube, and tons of porn flicks and magazines.

SLEEPS

The Atlanta metro area has the most impressive selection of contemporary luxury hotels of any American city, although it lacks the splendid, historic grande dames you find in New Orleans, New York, and Chicago. Only a handful of hotels are within walking distance of Midtown bars and restaurants, but since you're probably going to need a car to visit Atlanta for more than a few days, proximity to nightlife isn't all that important. Keep in mind that Downtown is eerily deserted at night, and Buckhead is a traffic nightmare—especially on weekend evenings. Because hotels cater strongly to business travelers, rates at many of the top properties are slashed on weekends.

For price ranges, *see* lodging Chart A at the front of this guide.

Hotels

$$$–$$$$ 🏨 **Four Seasons Hotel Atlanta.** One of the more stunning properties in the nation had remained largely unknown outside the region before the Four Seasons chain took over in 1997. Spanish marble lines the dramatic atrium lobby, which is centered by a sweeping staircase and lit by a large crystal chandelier. Guest rooms are large, sleek, and contemporary with generous use of marble and imported fabrics. ✉ *75 14th St., 30309, ☎ 404/881–9898 or 800/332–3442, FAX 404/873–4692. 263 rooms. Restaurants, pool, health club.*

$$$–$$$$ 🏨 **Grand Hyatt Atlanta.** This 25-story, granite hotel is the most striking structure on Buckhead's skyline. The lobby overlooks a 9,000-square-foot Japanese garden and 35-foot waterfall. Soft colors and Asian designs characterize the guest rooms's dignified decor. ✉ *3300 Peachtree Rd., 30305, ☎ 404/365–8100 or 800/645–5687, FAX 404/233–5686. 471 rooms. Restaurants, pool, health club.*

$$$ 🏨 **Sheraton Colony Square.** Any time there's a gay event in town, this long-time Midtown favorite is packed with family. It's a short walk from Backstreet and other Midtown bars (and two blocks from the Woodruff Arts Center and the High Museum of Art), and the staff is always great to gay guests. Rooms have upscale but typical Sheraton-chain furniture; try to score one on an upper floor—the views are stupendous. ✉ *188 14th St., 30361, ☎ 404/892–6000 or 800/422–7895, FAX 404/872–9192. 461 rooms. Restaurant, pool, exercise room.*

$$–$$$ 🏨 **Biltmore Suites Hotel.** The only historic property in town, the vaunted Georgian-style structure was built in the '20s by Coca-Cola magnate William Candler and has hosted many presidents and Hollywood's Scarlett O'Hara, Vivien Leigh. It's faded some with age, but the price and location are right, and the suites are absolutely enormous. The duplex and triplex penthouse suites, though more costly, have fabulous Jacuzzis and sleep up to four. ✉ *30 5th St., 30308, ☎ 404/874–0824 or 800/822–0824, FAX 404/872–0067. 61 suites.*

$$–$$$ 🏨 **Wyndham Garden Midtown.** With all the enormous convention properties in Atlanta, this 1987 11-floor redbrick hotel is refreshingly intimate and personal. In the center of Midtown, it has touches that please both leisure and business travelers: coffeemakers, extra phones, oversize rooms,

and a 7,000-square-foot fitness center. ⊠ *125 10th St., 30309,* ☎ *404/ 873–4800 or 800/996–3426,* ℻ *404/872–7377. 191 rooms. Restaurant, pool, health club.*

$$ 🛏 **Wyndham Garden Buckhead.** Sandwiched between the Ritz-Carlton and the Grand Hyatt, this business property is one of Buckhead's best values. The large rooms are filled with traditional mahogany hotel furniture. Guests can use the health club next door. ⊠ *3340 Peachtree Rd., 30326,* ☎ *404/231–1234 or 800/822–4200,* ℻ *404/231–3112. 221 rooms. Restaurant, pool.*

$ 🛏 **Quality Inn Midtown.** The exterior of this Midtown budget hotel harks back to the aesthetically challenged 1960s, but it's within steps of many gay bars, has clean and pleasant rooms, and throws gay-friendly pool parties and other events catering to the community. For convenience and value, it's hard to beat. ⊠ *870 Peachtree St., 30308,* ☎ *404/875–5511 or 800/ 221–2222,* ℻ *404/874–3602. Restaurant, pool.*

Guest Houses

$$–$$$$ 🛏 **Ansley Inn.** A block from Piedmont Park and in the heart of Ansley Park, this three-story yellow Tudor mansion is filled with antiques, porcelain, original art, and Persian and Oriental rugs. Many rooms have four-poster beds and whirlpool tubs, and all but the most lavish are reasonably priced. ⊠ *253 15th St., 30309,* ☎ *404/872–9000 or 800/446–5416,* ℻ *404/892–2318. 33 rooms with phone, TV, and private bath. Continental breakfast. Mostly straight.*

$$–$$$ 🛏 **Woodruff Bed & Breakfast Inn.** A short walk from a few of the quieter bars on Ponce de Leon, but also close to Downtown and lower Midtown, this three-story Victorian mansion was once a brothel. Rooms contain mostly British antiques, and two suites have hot tubs. ⊠ *223 Ponce de Leon Ave., 30302,* ☎ *404/875–9449 or 800/473–9449,* ℻ *404/875– 2882. 12 rooms with phone and TV, most with private bath. Full breakfast. Mostly straight.*

$ 🛏 **Magnolia Station B&B.** This antiques-laden B&B is in up-and-coming Inman Park, very close to Little Five Points and a short drive to Midtown. Its best feature is a pool in back. ⊠ *1020 Edgewood Ave., 30307,* ☎ *404/ 523–2005. 3 rooms with TV, some with private bath. Continental breakfast. Pool. Mostly gay male.*

$ 🛏 **Midtown Manor.** The place to be if you're looking for cheap, friendly accommodations within walking distance of Midtown bars. It's not fancy, but the rooms—spread among three linked, Victorian houses—have a smattering of antiques and a simple charm. ⊠ *811 Piedmont Ave., 30308,* ☎ *404/872–5846 or 800/724–4381. 63 rooms with phone and TV, some with private bath. Continental breakfast. Mixed gay/straight.*

THE LITTLE BLACK BOOK

At Your Fingertips

AIDS Hotline for Women (☎ 404/888–9991). **AIDS Atlanta** (☎ 404/872– 0600, Web site www.aidatlanta.org). **AIDS Info-line** (☎ 404/876–9944 or 800/551–2728). **Atlanta Convention and Visitors Bureau** (⊠ 233 Peachtree St., Peachtree Center Mall, Suite 2000, 30300, ☎ 404/222– 6688 or 800/285–2682; visitor centers also at Underground Atlanta, ⊠ 65 Upper Alabama St., and at Lenox Square Mall, ⊠ 3393 Peachtree Rd.). **Atlanta Gay and Lesbian Center** (⊠ 71 12th St., ☎ 404/876–5372, Web site www.aglc.lambda.net/). **Atlanta Gay and Lesbian Visitors Center** (Web site www.altgaylesvisit.w1.com). **Checker Cab** (☎ 404/351– 1111). *Creative Loafing* (alternative weekly, ☎ 404/688–5623, Web site www.creativeloafing.com). **Gay Helpline** (☎ 404/892–0661). **MARTA** (☎ 404/848–4711).

Gay Media

Southern Voice (☎ 404/876–1819, e-mail southvoice@aol.com) is Atlanta's stellar gay and lesbian weekly newspaper. The handy gay entertainment 'zine, ***Etcetera*** (☎ 404/525–3821, Web site www.etcmag.com) also has a smattering of coverage about other parts of the South.

BOOKSTORES

Outwrite Books (✉ 991 Piedmont Ave., ☎ 404/607–0082), one of the nation's best lesbigay bookstores, offers the gamut of books, periodicals, and sidelines; it has a great coffee bar. **Charis Books** (✉ 1189 Euclid Ave., ☎ 404/524–0304) is an excellent feminist and lesbian bookstore in Little Five Points. **Brushstrokes** (✉ 1510 Piedmont Ave., ☎ 404/876–6567), the gay and lesbian variety store in Ansley Square, has a fine selection of books. **Poster Hut** (✉ 2175 Cheshire Bridge Rd., ☎ 404/633–7491) sells books, cards, gifts, fetish wear, and sex stuff.

Working Out

Boot Camp (✉ Ansley Mall, 1544 Piedmont Ave., ☎ 404/876–8686) is big with muscle boys. The **Fitness Factory** (✉ Midtown Outlets, 500 N. Amsterdam Ave., ☎ 404/815–7900) attracts a trendy set. **Mid City Fitness** (✉ 2201 Faulkner Rd., ☎ 404/321–6507), has more of a mainstream following but attracts many lesbians and gay men.

CHARLESTON AND SAVANNAH

Never known as beacons of gay and lesbian tourism, the quintessentially Old South cities of Charleston and Savannah are showing increasing signs of community popularity. Both cities rank among *Condé Nast Traveler* readers' top 10 U.S. destinations (Charleston, in fact, ranks 11th worldwide). With historic homes, many of them open to the public as museums, sophisticated restaurants, scads of galleries, a first-rate lineup of cultural events and festivals, and a few decent nightlife options, these Lowcountry getaways are fast creating a gay following for themselves. With its tangentially gay account of Savannah society, John Berendt's best-seller, *Midnight in The Garden of Good and Evil,* has propelled Savannah's reputation as a hot spot almost singlehandedly.

Outsiders sometimes think of Savannah and Charleston as twins, but they're more like distant cousins—both cities retain distinct personalities. If you've ever spent time in Caribbean islands like Barbados or St. Thomas, you'll recognize Charleston's pastel-hued Colonial homes with their trademark broad piazzas. The city's sunny, palm-lined streets, water views, and nonstop bustle further recall a festive Caribbean village. Historic Savannah owes its ambience and flare more to Europe, with a mix of British- and French-inspired homes, many with ornate wrought-iron balconies and formal gardens.

Savannah and Charleston are just 90 minutes apart by car (via a combination of U.S. 17 and I–95), so you can easily combine a trip to both. Many find that two nights in each city, bracketed by two nights each in Atlanta, make for an engaging and invigorating vacation.

Eats

Charleston and Savannah specialize in Lowcountry cuisine, which blends soul, Creole, and traditional southern recipes and emphasizes the region's bounty of local seafood. Like its Cajun-Creole cousin, the cuisine of New Orleans, Lowcountry cooking has received an infusion of both contemporary American and international influences in recent years.

For price ranges in both cities, *see* dining Chart A at the front of this guide.

Scenes

Charleston and Savannah are somewhat lacking a usually visible segment of the gay and lesbian population: those aged 25 to 40. Gays who live here have typically already done the big-city thing and have decided to return and settle down. Nightlife is dominated by a cliquey but friendly younger crowd (there are colleges in both cities) and older locals, many of them in relationships, out for a night of dancing. The balance are tourists, but again singles are rare hereabouts—thanks to all those expensive but romantic inns that cater primarily to couples. The bar staff and regulars in Savannah's bars are unbelievably friendly and forward, even more so than in Charleston.

Sleeps

The one reason to bypass the authentic Old South experience you'll enjoy at one of the region's fanciful 18th- and 19th-century inns is to save money. For this reason, a few dependable chain budget properties are reviewed. Of the grand old hotels, several are gay-managed or -staffed; despite the conservative sensibility of some of these, you may be surprised at how well you and your honey are welcomed. Wherever you stay, you simply can't appreciate the palpable magnetism of these cities if you're more than a 10-minute walk from their historic areas—if you can, avoid properties on the outskirts.

For price ranges in both cities, *see* lodging Chart A at the front of this guide.

Charleston

The Lay of the Land

Meeting Street, from the run-down northerly reaches of downtown Charleston to the Historic District, contains many of the major attractions. The mostly residential streets on either side of Meeting, below Broad Street, are lined with the historic homes for which the city is known. Charleston has long been a preservation-minded city, and the esteemed **Historic Charleston Foundation** (⊠ 108 Meeting St., ☎ 803/723−1623) is ground zero for information on local architecture and architectural walking tours. From mid-March through mid-April, the foundation sponsors the monthlong **Annual Festival of Houses and Gardens,** during which visitors can take a number of historic home tours. Year-round you can browse the excellent reproduction antiques at the **Historic Charleston Reproductions Shop** (⊠ 105 Broad St., ☎ 803/723−8292) or the books and gifts at the **Historic Charleston Museum Shop** (⊠ 108 Meeting St., ☎ 803/ 724−8484). Also consider touring either of two foundation-operated museums, the 1817 **Aiken-Rhett House** (⊠ 48 Elizabeth St., ☎ 803/724− 8481) and the 1808 **Nathaniel Russell House** (⊠ 51 Meeting St., ☎ 803/ 724−8481).

From the Nathaniel Russell House you can walk a few blocks south to **Waterfront Park,** a grassy tree-filled plot of land with gardens and an adjacent promenade overlooking the confluence of the Ashley and Cooper rivers. Be sure to walk back up toward town by way of **East Bay Street,** which is lined with mansions of every 18th- and 19th-century flavor.

Head back up Meeting Street to see the **Gibbes Museum of Art** (⊠ 135 Meeting St., ☎ 803/722−2706), which opened in 1905; it has one of the nation's foremost collections of miniature portraits. Above Broad Street you'll come upon the full bustle of the Historic District's tony boutiques, fine art galleries, and shops. Dozens of crafts stalls fill the covered **Old City Market,** which runs between North and South Market streets from Meeting to East Bay streets. Many restaurants face the market.

Running parallel to Meeting Street, **King Street** has many newish, hip businesses and is the site of the **Preservation Society of Charleston** (✉ 147 King St., ☎ 803/722–4630), which operates a useful bookshop and sponsors the **Fall Candlelight Tours of Homes and Gardens.**

A few blocks north, back on Meeting Street, are both the **Charleston Visitors Center** (*see* The Little Black Book, *below*) and the **Charleston Museum** (✉ 360 Meeting St., ☎ 803/722–2996), one of the city's must-sees. Opened in 1773, the oldest museum in America houses about a half-million artifacts and decorative objects. It operates the adjacent **Joseph Manigault House** (✉ 350 Meeting St., ☎ 803/723–2926), an 1803 house-museum with local antiques, as well as the **Heyward-Washington House** (✉ 87 Church St., ☎ 803/722–0354), which is in the residential area below Broad Street; it served as the setting of Gershwin's *Porgy and Bess.*

The city played an important role in the American Revolution but is probably best remembered for its early role in the Civil War. Today **Fort Sumter Tour Boats** (☎ 803/722–1691, departures daily Apr.–Oct.) leads excursions out to **Fort Sumter National Monument,** the 19th-century fort on which the first shot of the war was fired on April 12, 1861, leading to a siege by Confederate troops that would end with a Union surrender.

No visit to Charleston is complete without a side trip to a sprawling plantation. Consider the 1740s **Drayton Hall** (✉ 3380 Ashley River Rd., ☎ 803/766–0188), the only extant antebellum mansion along the Ashley River (it's unfurnished, however); and **Middleton Place** (✉ Ashley River Rd., ☎ 803/556–6020), a 1741 spread whose colorful gardens are the oldest in the country; the main home was burned but surviving portions of it have been restored and filled with period-furnishings.

Charleston is humid and hot in summer and sometimes a little raw and rainy in winter, but the city draws large crowds year-round. The busiest time is spring, when the internationally renowned **Spoleto Festival** (☎ 803/723–0402, late May–early June) offers two weeks worth of first-rate opera, dance, theater, music, poetry readings, visual arts exhibitions, and other cultural festivities at venues throughout the area. Simultaneously, the **Piccolo Spoleto Festival** (☎ 803/724–7305), focuses more on regional and local artists and performers.

Getting Around

It can take from five to seven hours to drive from Atlanta to Charleston. Either take I–20 to I–26, which is all interstates but involves the greatest distance; alternatively, hop off I–20 around Aiken, South Carolina, and work your way southeast along state roads (there are several ways, so use a map). The latter plan can shave one to two hours off your journey, but will also subject you to the risk of speeding tickets, as local byways are vigilantly patrolled.

Charleston is an easy city to explore on foot, but you can take advantage of the **DASH** (Downtown Area Shuttle, ☎ 803/747–0922) trolley-style buses, which ply downtown's streets and pass by many sites. If you need a taxi, try **Yellow Cab** (☎ 803/577–6565).

Eats

$$$$ ✕ **Peninsula Grill.** One of the best new restaurants in the South, the dining room at the gay-friendly Planters Inn (*see* Sleeps, *below*) recalls the elegance of a vintage supper club, with a blend of older and contemporary design elements, including glittering chandeliers, velvet, and 19th-century paintings by regional artists. Wild mushroom grits with a Lowcountry oyster stew and pan-seared jumbo scallops with tomato tortilla salad and pecan coulis are among the standouts. ✉ *112 N. Market St.,* ☎ *803/723–0700.*

$$$ ✗ **Anson.** With tall French windows overlooking the historic neighborhood around it, this suave restaurant pulls in a dressy see-and-be-seen crowd for such innovative creations as penne with crawfish, sausage, mushroom, and scallions in a light cracked-black-pepper cream sauce; and seared pork tenderloin and local white shrimp with mustard barbecue sauce, whipped potatoes, and jicama–Granny Smith apple slaw. ✉ *12 Anson St.,* ☎ *803/577–0551.*

$$–$$$ ✗ **Slightly North of Broad.** Affectionately known as "S.N.O.B.," this favorite purveyor of New Southern cooking wows patrons, a few of which are lucky enough to score seats looking into the high-tech kitchen. If you're a beginner, ask for the Lowcountry sampler, comprising grilled quail with cabbage, barbecued smoked sausage with butter beans, and sesame-crusted tuna medallions. Flawless. ✉ *192 E. Bay St.,* ☎ *803/723–3424.*

$$ ✗ **Vickery's.** The Charleston outpost of the très gay Atlanta restaurant is popular with everybody, thanks to a great menu of American and Cuban favorites, including black bean cakes, fried oyster salad, and jerk chicken. Dine in the stunning and spacious dining room or out on the tree-shaded patio. ✉ *15 Beaufain St.,* ☎ *803/577–5300.*

$$ ✗ **Zebo Restaurant and Brewery.** This industriously chic (but noisy) brew pub has towering beer vats visible through a mammoth window. The menu more than complements the great selection of brews. Try seared tuna wasabi or the pizza topped with roasted garlic, crawfish, goat cheese, and spinach. ✉ *275 King St.,* ☎ *803/577–7600.*

$ ✗ **Mickey's.** This 24-hour diner on Market Street is where most fags go after the bars close and where a tremendously varied cross-section of locals and tourists comes for breakfast and lunch. It's a '50s-style diner with posters of Judy, Marilyn, and other icons and dishes with cutesy names like the Four Tops burger (bacon, mushrooms, swiss, and cheddar). ✉ *137 Market St.,* ☎ *803/723–7121.*

Scenes

On the northern edge of the historic district, the **Arcade** (✉ 5 Liberty St., ☎ 803/722–5656) is the city's main event—a rambling entertainment complex with a pulsing dance floor, a few bars, a patio, a small lounge that on certain nights hosts either leather groups or country-western music, and an even smaller room with a couple of pool tables. The crowd is an exact breakdown of the local community, with a mix of students, tourists, and older couples—both male and female, and very mixed racially. The same owners operate a good old-fashioned neighborhood bar around the corner, **Dudley's** (✉ 346 King St., ☎ 803/723–2784), which has antique mirrors, booth and bar seating, and a back room with pool and games—it's friendly to all but caters mostly to men. Both establishments are members-only—guests show I.D., sign in, and pay a small "membership due," which amounts to the price of a typical cover.

Sleeps

$$$–$$$$ ⌂ **John Rutledge House Inn.** Built by a signer of the U.S. Constitution and slept in by George Washington, this 1763 house is one of the most remarkable and romantic inns in the South. The 11 rooms in the Italianate-style main building, which have 13-foot ceilings and elaborate plaster moldings, are the most opulent, but those in two adjoining carriage houses offer more privacy. ✉ *116 N. Broad St., 29401,* ☎ *803/723–7999 or 800/476–9741. 19 rooms with phone, TV, and private bath. Continental breakfast. Mostly straight.*

$$$–$$$$ ⌂ **Planters Inn.** Perhaps the most gay-friendly of the luxury inns in Charleston, the Planters Inn has also grown into one of the most charming after several years of painstaking restoration and the construction of a neighboring wing in 1997. The rooms in both the original and new sections are smartly furnished, but the newer digs have a few more modern amenities, such as whirlpool tubs. The recently opened Peninsula Grill is one of the city's top eateries. ✉ *112 N. Market St., 29401,* ☎ *803/ 722–2345 or 800/845–7082,* FAX *803/577–2125. 62 rooms with phone, TV, and private bath. Continental breakfast. Restaurant, pool. Mostly straight.*

$$–$$$$ 🛏 **Victoria House Inn.** Operated by the owners of the John Rutledge House Inn (*see above*) and two other similarly outstanding properties (the Fulton Lane and Kings Courtyard inns), this Romanesque Revival hotel combines the best of the old and the new. Rooms are filled with antiques and period-style fabrics but also have voice mail and new cable TVs; many have fireplaces and whirlpool tubs. ✉ *208 King St., 29401,* ☎ *803/720– 2944 or 800/933–5464,* FAX *803/720–2930. 16 rooms with phone, TV, and private bath. Continental breakfast. Mostly straight.*

$$ 🛏 **Charleston Columns Guesthouse.** This is the only gay-oriented property in Charleston, and although it's a 10-minute walk north of the true heart of the historic district, it's still in a convenient location, right off King Street. Rooms are either in a restored 1855 house with towering white pillars and a long piazza, or in the cozy adjacent carriage house. It's less fancy than some of the more famous inns, but it's also more affordable. ✉ *8 Vanderhorst St., 29403,* ☎ *803/722–7341, e-mail chs65@aol.com. 5 rooms with TV and private bath. Continental breakfast. Mostly mixed gay male/lesbian.*

$$ 🛏 **Hampton Inn–Historic District.** An excellent budget option that's close to all the historic areas, Hampton has new period-reproduction furnishings and a large pool. ✉ *345 Meeting St., 29403,* ☎ *803/723–4000 or 800/426–7866,* FAX *803/722–3725. 171 rooms. Pool.*

Savannah

The Lay of the Land

The jewel of Georgia's lazily enchanting sea coast, Savannah was founded in 1733 by British General James Oglethorpe, who designed the perfect grid of streets and grassy tree-shaded square for which this city of 150,000 is still famous. Only two of the original 24 squares have been plowed over.

Savannah prospered as a silk exporter during its first century, before developing into one of the world's major cotton suppliers (its protected upriver position and easy access to several southern cities has helped the Port of Savannah remain one of the busiest on the lower East Coast).

Most of the architecture in the Historic District is antebellum, but only by a couple of decades—a mid-19th-century fire destroyed many, but not all, of the beautiful wood-frame Colonial homes that once lined its streets, and the city was quickly rebuilt with elaborate brick and stucco Victorians. Were it not for the fact that General Sherman, strangely, spared Savannah during his notorious and destructive "March to the Sea," most of these structures would also have been destroyed. Supposedly, Sherman presented his glorious conquest to President Lincoln as a Christmas gift in 1864.

Perhaps the greatest threat to the city's architectural heritage, however, occurred during the middle of this century. The prosperous cotton industry had completely bottomed out when World War I began, and by the time of the Depression, Savannah's economy had been brought to its knees. During the '50s, a national trend toward urban renewal reared its ugly head here; it was only the valiant lobbying of several preservation-minded locals that saved many targeted structures from a date with the wrecking ball. The momentum to keep Savannah intact grew, culminating in a 2.5-square-mile chunk of downtown being designated the largest National Historic District in the country.

A good place to begin your explorations is inside the restored 1860s rail terminal that now houses both the **Savannah Visitors Center** (✉ 301 Martin Luther King Jr. Blvd., ☎ 912/944–0455) and the **Savannah History Museum** (✉ 303 Martin Luther King Jr. Blvd, ☎ 912/238–1779). Among the many artifacts on the city's heritage is a tribute to the late lyricist and Savannah native Johnny Mercer, best known for such works as "Moon River" (from *Breakfast at Tiffany's*) and "Satin Doll."

From here it's a short walk north to the one part of Savannah with a significant number of gay-owned and -frequented businesses, **City Market** (✉ between W. Bryan and W. Congress Sts., at Jefferson St.), a three-block pedestrian mall steps from the gay disco, Club One. The funky galleries and shops here occupy part of where the city's food and produce market once stood. Of particular note, drop by **Dream Weaver** (✉ 306 W. St. Julian St., ☎ 912/236–9003), which sells crystals, oils, New Age products, and a few pride items and queer books.

Club One (*see* Scenes, *below*) is the performing home of the Lady Chablis, who figures prominently in "The Book," as *Midnight in The Garden of Good and Evil* is commonly referred to by locals. Between editing and writing stints in New York City, Savannah-born author John Berendt spent five years in his home city sifting through the dirty laundry of colorful residents; hence "The Book," and hence the recent skyrocketing of the city's popularity among the general public, and specifically among gays and lesbians.

Plenty of folks come to Savannah to seek out the sites brought to life in this mesmerizing tale. Of particular note is the **Mercer House** (✉ 429 Bull St.), in which *Midnight*'s central figure, antiques dealer Jim Williams, allegedly shot and killed his young lover, Danny Hansford, in 1981. The private home, in which Williams died in 1990, is now owned by his sister. Several tour companies now offer "The Book" bus excursions, and you can stock up on related souvenirs at **The Book Gift Shop** (✉ 127 E. Gordon St., ☎ 912/233–3867). Also while wandering around town you might try to recognize scenes from the Clint Eastwood film adaption of "The Book," which stars Kevin Spacey, John Cusack, Alison Eastwood, and the Lady Chablis herself, and was shot here in 1997.

Savannah rivals any southern destination for historical architecture and dazzling house museums. If you have time only for one museum, visit the **Owens-Thomas House** (✉ 124 Abercorn St., ☎ 912/233–9743), a splendidly restored 1819 Regency mansion built by the renowned British architect, William Jay. Nearby is the **Isaiah Davenport House** (✉ 324 E. State St., ☎ 912/236–8097), an 1815 Federal beauty. Another favorite, the **Green-Meldrim House** (✉ 14 W. Macon St., ☎ 912/233–3845), was occupied by General Sherman for a time after he assumed command of the city. To view a fine collection of classical sculpture and Impressionist painting, visit the **Telfair Mansion and Art Museum** (✉ 121 Barnard St., ☎ 912/232–1177), a memorable 1819 William Jay structure in its own right.

Savannah's elegant squares merit a leisurely look. Each one has its own personality, usually a monument or fountain commemorating people and events central to local history, and a few benches on which you can sit and catch your breath. **Johnson Square** is the oldest, dating from the city's 1733 inception, but everybody seems to have a favorite. Thanks to their strategic placement, they set Savannah's lovably sleepy pace; because of them, you can't dart across town in an automobile, or even on foot. Every few blocks you're forced gently to cool your heels and marvel at the live oaks and picturesque mansions gracing these squares.

At the north end of the district, the city's **Riverfront** is lined with a beautiful row of restored cotton warehouses and a cobbled lane, which is a full flight of steps lower than the rest of the city. The warehouses now contain a slew of mediocre restaurants and shops and receive a constant parade of mostly straight tourists. The least-crowded time to appreciate it and the views of the bridge and freighters chugging along the river is in the morning.

Before there was John Berendt, there was Flannery O'Connor (1925–1964), whose spellbinding blend of southern Gothic and tortured realism has long captivated readers. Although the late author produced her work while living in the central Georgia town of Milledgeville, she was born in Savannah, and her childhood home, the **Flannery O'Connor House** (⌂ 207 E. Charlton St., ☎ 912/233–6014) is now open to the public; it's filled with exhibits about her life and work.

Savannah's 22 squares are a series of appetizers leading up to 20-acre **Forsyth Park,** at the southern end of the Historic District. Try to take at least a brief stroll through these lush gardens and under the many moss-draped trees. Outdoor plays and concerts are staged here.

Like Charleston, Savannah is most scenic and heavily visited during spring and fall. One of the busiest times is during **St. Patrick's Day;** since the 1860s, Savannah's celebration has been the nation's second-largest, trailing only New York City. One year, feverishly ambitious locals introduced gallons of green dye to the Savannah River—a futile venture that did little to transform the river's naturally murky-brown appearance. Unlike New York, and also Boston, Savannah has yet to see a controversy arise over the inclusion of queer marchers in the St. Patrick's Day parade.

Getting Around

From Atlanta it's a four-hour straight shot along I–75 and I–16 to Savannah. The city is ideal for strolling (*Walking Magazine* rated Savannah one of America's top-10 walking cities), and there's no reason to bother with mass transit, though **Chatham Area Transit** (☎ 912/233–5767) operates buses and shuttles. You might use a car to get between opposite ends of the Historic District, but parking is tight much of the time and you're better off leaving it in one place. If returning to your accommodations late at night, consider a cab; try **Adam Cab Co.** (☎ 912/927–7466).

Eats

$$$$ ✕ **Elizabeth on 37th.** Drive a bit south of the main tourist district to this second neighborhood of restored Victorians for some of the finest—and priciest—cuisine in the South. Such regional fare as sautéed Georgia shrimp with thyme, garlic, vegetables, an eggplant cake, and vinegar butter are subtly sublime. The setting is a refined 19th-century house. ⌂ *105 E. 37th St.,* ☎ *912/236–5547.*

$$–$$$ ✕ **Il Pasticcio.** Despite its charmless modern exterior, the inside of this first-rate northern Italian restaurant is sophisticated and chic, with gold-and-maroon-stripe banquettes and an upstairs art gallery. Standouts include the homemade pastas (a delicious one comes with fresh shrimp, scallops, baby clams, mussels, and calamari) and veal medallions with gorgonzola and a sun-dried tomato demi-glace. ⌂ *2 E. Broughton St.,* ☎ *912/231–8888.*

$$ ✕ **Café at City Market.** Friendly and fast service, seating both inside a simple but handsome dining room and fronting a cheerful pedestrian mall, and reasonably priced American cooking make this fixture of the gay community a regular favorite. The various pastas, grills, and sandwiches use fresh ingredients and are presented with artful aplomb; consider the

parmesan-crusted crab cake sandwich or the piquant black bean soup. ⊠ *224 W. St. Julian St.,* ☎ *912/236–7133.*

$–$$ ✕ **Ogelthorpe Brewing Company.** Locals have slowly—very slowly—taken to this trendy new microbrewery, a former warehouse with hardwood floors, exposed brick, high ceilings, and an ambience that may be a little too slick for this quirky southern city. But the beers are terrific and the New Orleans–influenced pub food tasty. Try red beans and rice with smoky andouille sausage or the spicy crawfish pie. ⊠ *21 W. Bay St.,* ☎ *912/232–0933.*

$ ✕ **Crystal Beer Parlour.** This longtime Savannah institution sits forlornly across from a vacant lot on the southwestern edge of the Historic District. Inside is a festive, old-fashioned tavern abuzz with chatter and redolent of juicy burgers, fried seafood sandwiches, and gooey cheese fries. ⊠ *301 W. Jones St.,* ☎ *912/232–1153.*

Scenes

Although some locals shun the increasingly touristy (and straight) **Club One** (⊠ 1 Jefferson St., ☎ 912/232–0200), the heel-stomping grounds of the Lady Chablis, it's one of the best clubs in the Southeast. At 30,000 square feet, it can accommodate some serious crowds, but only the bar's basement level—with a small disco and an extremely large bar with pool tables and games and a pub with light food—is open daily. On the first floor there's a large disco that's open every night but Monday and Tuesday, and upstairs is the weekends-only cabaret, which usually brims with both straight and gay tourists hoping for a glimpse of the Lady Chablis.

Neighborhood bars include **Felicia's** (⊠ 416 W. Liberty St., ☎ 912/238–4788), a new, large bar and disco with an attractive contemporary interior but a poor location across the street form the Savannah Visitors Center, which is deserted at night. A low-key, mostly over-35 crowd tumbles in regularly to **Faces II** (⊠ 17 Lincoln St., ☎ 912/233–3520), an intimate rustic bar with a low-timber-ceilinged bar and an adjacent patio and pool parlor.

Sleeps

$$$$ 🛏 **Manor House.** The men who run this impeccably decorated and sumptuous 1830s mansion have spared no expense in providing guests with a truly special experience. Fresh flowers adorn the five suites, which have gas fireplaces and museum-quality furnishings. Bathrooms have two-person whirlpool tubs, and at night you'll be treated to turndown with chocolates and brandy. ⊠ *201 W. Liberty St., 31401,* ☎ *912/233–9597 or 800/462–3595,* FAX *912/236–4626. 5 rooms with phone, TV, and private bath. Mostly straight.*

$$$–$$$$ 🛏 **Eliza Thompson House.** This mid-19th-century inn and its expansive landscaped courtyard look much as you might imagine they did when cotton was king of Savannah. Original heart-pine floors and period antiques impart a romantic ambience. ⊠ *5 W. Jones St., 31401,* ☎ *912/236–3620 or 800/348–9378,* FAX *912/238–1920. 12 rooms with TV, phone, and private bath. Continental breakfast. Mostly straight.*

$$$–$$$$ 🛏 **Foley House.** Since charming Danish-born Inge Svensson Moore took over this historic inn a few years back, rooms have received constant refurbishments. Guest rooms contain antiques, Oriental rugs, and four-poster beds; many overlook Chippawa Square and have massive two-person Jacuzzis and gas fireplaces. Behind the inn is a delightful courtyard and garden. Very gay-friendly. ⊠ *14 W. Hull St., 31401,* ☎ *912/232–6622 or 800/647–3708,* FAX *912/231–1218. 19 rooms with phone, TV, and private bath. Continental breakfast. Mostly straight.*

$$–$$$ 🛏 **Hampton Inn.** Filled with high-quality reproduction antiques, the Hampton Inn is centrally located but a bit pricier than other properties in this chain. ⊠ *201 E. Bay St., 31401,* ☎ *912/231–9700 or 800/576–4945,* FAX *912/231–0440. 144 rooms. Restaurant, pool, fitness center.*

$$–$$$　☎ **Joan's on Jones.** If you're planning a long stay or simply want the privacy of your own studio apartment, consider the two suites on the ground level of this stunning 1883 town house. Both units are appointed with period antiques. The front one has a somewhat formal Georgian air while the rear one recalls the airy charm of New Orleans, with large windows overlooking a landscaped patio—it also has a full kitchen. ✉ *17 W. Jones St., 31401,* ☎ *912/234–3863,* FAX *912/234–1455. 2 rooms with phone, TV, and private bath. Continental breakfast. Mostly straight.*

$$　☎ **Days Inn.** Another centrally located option, just steps from City Market and Club One, this typical Days Inn has clean rooms with pleasant but basic furnishings. ✉ *201 W. Bay St., 31401,* ☎ *912/236–4440 or 800/325–2525,* FAX *912/232–2725. 253 rooms. Restaurant, pool.*

$　☎ **912 Barnard.** The only gay-oriented B&B in Savannah, and also one of the least expensive, this dramatic yellow turn-of-the-century house is south of the main tourist district, in a transitional neighborhood that's close to Forsyth Park. It's been handsomely restored to its original splendor, with antiques and authentic colors that fully convey the ambience of the city. Beautiful gardens are in back of the house. ✉ *912 Barnard St., 31401,* ☎ *912/234–9121. 2 rooms with phone, TV, and shared bath. Continental breakfast. Mixed gay male/lesbian.*

The Little Black Book

The **Charleston Convention & Visitors Bureau** (✉ Box 975, 29402, ☎ 803/853–8000 or 800/868–8118; Visitors Center, ✉ 375 Meeting St.) is a one-stop source for Charleston visitor information. The **Savannah Area Convention & Visitors Bureau** (✉ 222 W. Oglethorpe Ave., Suite 100, Box 1628, Savannah, GA 31402, ☎ 912/944–0456) is the source for Savannah visitor info. In the absence of gay papers in the region, check out *UPWITH* (☎ 803/577–5304, Web site www.discovernet.com/upwith) in Charleston and *Creative Loafing Savannah* (☎ 912/231–0250, Web site www.creativeloafing.com) in Savannah for arts and entertainment coverage with a gay-friendly slant.

2 Out in Austin

IF YOU BELIEVE THE MANY MAGAZINE STORIES, Austin is a near-flawless metropolis with nothing but roses in its future. It's the nation's most physically fit city (*Walking*), the fifth-best urban area in which to start a business (*Entrepreneur*), the eighth-best place to live (*Money*), and has the fifth-most-knowledgeable work force (*Fortune*). Its citizens are both literate (the area has the highest per capita bookstore sales in the United States) and computer literate (Apple, Dell, and several other high-tech corporations operate in and around Austin). They support the country's sixth-largest concentration of artists, the most tuneful of which perform in the more than 100 live-music clubs here. It's no wonder, then, that Austin, the hub of Travis County and the capital of Texas, is one of the nation's fastest growing cities.

Its very desirability is Austin's only potential threat. Locals lament the skyrocketing cost of real estate. Rampant development in and around the city has created dense traffic and longer lines at restaurants and grocery checkouts. But despite some growing pains, the quality of life here remains sharply above that of most places in American.

The good life extends to gays and lesbians, who are highly visible and for the most part accepted and respected by the nongay majority—which in Austin is well to the left of the mainstream in the rest of Texas. The greatest worries expressed by queer locals concern how *easy* it is to be gay here, that perhaps an air of complacency prevents the community from recognizing and responding to the malevolence of right-wingers, of which there are plenty, especially in neighboring Williamson County.

The presence of the University of Texas (UT) accounts for much of Austin's appeal. The institution's 50,000 students make up almost 10% of the city's population of 568,000 (1,008,000 people live in the metropolitan area), and many stay here once they graduate. Parking attendants and burger flippers with PhDs are not unheard of—only so many top-level jobs exist, and even well-educated residents often must lower their expectations. Sometimes they do this all too well: Austin became synonymous with the term "slacker" when Richard Linklater's low-budget feature film *Slacker,* about the city's brightest and youngest do-nothings, achieved cult status a few years back.

Stroll by the coffeehouses and restaurants along Guadalupe Street, and you'll see more than a few disillusioned genXers hitting up passersby up for change. Mellower than the scruffians who inhabit San Francisco's Haight-Ashbury or New York's East Village, they lend a '90s countercultural edge to otherwise upstanding Austin. But slackerdom notwithstanding, residents know they've got a good thing going. And visitors, who arrive in ever greater numbers, come to savor cheap meals, catch a few bands, sun themselves along the banks of Barton Creek or Travis Lake, browse through funky shops, and wonder why it is they live some place else.

THE LAY OF THE LAND

Central Austin straddles the banks of the Colorado River—known at this point as Town Lake—which meanders from east to west, due south of downtown. Beyond the central city are hilly, somewhat amorphous neighborhoods anchored by landmarks like Zilker Park, to the west of downtown, and the University of Texas, to the north. Interstate 35 cuts north–south through the east side of downtown, and the Mo-Pac Expressway parallels the interstate a few miles to the west. Lamar Boulevard travels north–south through downtown between the two highways and west of the University of Texas before intersecting with I–35.

Downtown

Austin's walkable **downtown** contains little in the way of sightseeing, but what it lacks in attractions, it makes up for with a bustling street scene, day and especially night. **Sixth Street** (also known as Old Pecan Street) is Austin's equivalent of Bourbon Street in New Orleans. All the street's lively diversions are more than welcoming to gays. **Red River Street**, which intersects 6th, has more of the same between about 4th and 8th streets. This neighborhood has some fine exploring and shopping; you'll find some up-and-coming restaurants and hot clubs (gay and straight) in the vibrant **warehouse district** to the south of 6th Street.

The Renaissance Revival **State Capitol Complex** (✉ 11th St. and Congress Ave., ☎ 512/463–0063) makes for a fascinating excursion. The capitol building was completely restored over the past several years at a cost of $200 million. The **Paramount Theatre** (✉ 713 Congress Ave., ☎ 512/472–5411), another exquisite restoration project, presented vaudeville acts when it opened in 1915. Vintage movies now screen here in summer; the venue presents musicals and top-name music acts at other times of the year. Nearby, the interim space of the **Austin Museum of Art–Downtown** (✉ 823 Congress Ave., ☎ 512/495–9224) hosts special events and stages rotating exhibits.

South of downtown, the **Congress Avenue Bridge** crosses **Town Lake.** From March to November, 1.5 million Mexican free-tailed bats—the nation's largest urban bat colony—hang out beneath it. Curious onlookers gather at dusk on the walkway along the river to watch the creatures emerge from their daytime slumber and take to the skies.

South of Downtown

Barton Springs Road, the site of many slacker-infested shops and eateries, leads west from Congress Avenue to **Barton Springs.** Less prettified than downtown but still engaging, the neighborhood has as its centerpiece 350-acre **Zilker Park** (✉ 2201 Barton Springs Rd., ☎ 512/476–9044); **Barton Creek,** an offshoot of the Colorado River, snakes southwest out of the city through the park. A fine spot to tan your hide on sunny days, Zilker is a good place to meet some of the city's outgoing locals. Spring-fed **Barton Springs Pool,** a popular and enormous swimming hole here, remains an invigorating 68°F year-round.

University of Texas and Environs

North of downtown is the 357-acre campus of the **University of Texas** (☎ 512/475–7348 for tour information), whose attractions include the **Lyndon Baines Johnson Presidential Library and Museum** (✉ 2313 Red River St., ☎ 512/482–5279). The **Texas Memorial Museum** (✉ 2400 Trinity St., ☎ 512/471–1604), also on campus, has exhibits on state history and local flora and fauna. The **Archer M. Huntington Art Gallery** (✉ 21st and Guadalupe Sts., ☎ 512/471–7324) specializes in Latin American art and 20th-century American masterworks. **Guadalupe Street,** known along its border with UT as "The Drag," is another haven of slackerdom as well as *the* place to shop for locally made arts and crafts, Longhorn memorabilia, and other offbeat goods. The **Dobie Cinema** (✉ 2021 Guadalupe St., ☎ 512/472–3456) often plays gay films.

West of the university is **Mount Bonnell** (✉ 3800 Mt. Bonnell Rd.), 785-foot-high mountain (well, hill is more like it) where horny teenagers rendezvous for late-night snogging sessions. By day, locals bring their visiting relatives for a glimpse of the lush countryside. The 99-step climb from the parking area to the beautiful promontory is a handy workout. The nearby Laguna Gloria branch of the **Austin Museum of Art** (✉ 3809 W. 35th St., ☎ 512/458–8191) is in a stately Mediterranean Revival villa at the west end of 35th Street. To satisfy your less cerebral cravings, drive over to **Amy's Ice Cream** (✉ 3500 Guadalupe St., ☎ 512/458–6895), a shrine to fattening dairy treats.

Lake Travis and Points West

A great way to spend a sunny afternoon is to drive out to **Lake Travis.** Pick up the Mo-Pac Expressway (Highway 1) heading north of the Colorado River. Exit to the west at Ranch Road 2222. After several miles, turn left onto Route 620, and a short bit farther take a right on Comanche Trail. This leads to the **Oasis** restaurant (*see* Eats, *below*), which overlooks **Lake Travis.** Farther on is **Hippie Hollow Park,** a gorgeous mecca for gay sunbathers.

Southwest of the city and also worth a tour is the **National Wildflower Research Center** (✉ 4801 La Crosse Ave., ☎ 512/292–4100), which Lady Bird Johnson founded in the early '80s. This 42-acre spread—take the Mo-Pac Expressway south for 10 miles from central Austin and follow the signs—has a visitor center, an observation tower, a nature trail, elaborate stone terraces, and flower-filled meadows.

GETTING AROUND

Austin's downtown is navigable on foot. You can definitely enjoy three or four days in Austin without wheels. But if you want to take advantage of greater Austin—the beautiful countryside west, many of the better restaurants, and the University of Texas—you'll need a car. Public transportation is minimal and basically useless outside downtown, and taxis are inconvenient and too expensive for long distances.

EATS

Downtown has the greatest concentration of memorable and gay-popular eateries, but almost every Austin neighborhood has a few good options. Many places are still hopping past 10 PM, especially on weekends. Mexican (including sophisticated regional fare, not just Tex-Mex) is a prevailing specialty. Slacker culture has developed its own, uniquely Austin style of dining, characterized by divey "alternadiners" with cheap but almost always delicious food, surly and overeducated waitrons, and tragically hip patrons.

For price ranges, *see* dining Chart B at the front of this guide.

Downtown Vicinity

$$$–$$$$ ✕ **Shoreline.** Your overall appreciation of this airy hot spot's perch overlooking the Congress Avenue Bridge may depend on the degree to which bat-watching whets your appetite, but the New American menu should put you in the mood to nosh. Flaky lump crab cakes with grilled shrimp

are served with a piquant mango sauce, and a half rack of ancho-cured lamb comes with caramelized onion potatoes and blackberry cascabel sauce. ✉ 98 San Jacinto Blvd., ☎ 512/477–3300.

$$–$$$ ✗ **Manuel's.** Fancier than most of the Mexican restaurants in town, Manuel's is a sleek space with black leather banquettes, tall mirrors, and a sassy little bar in back. The specials are always a good bet, or try regular favorites like corn sautéed with garlic and roasted onion in a chili pasilla sauce. ✉ 310 Congress Ave., ☎ 512/472–7555.

$$–$$$ ✗ **Mars.** An unprepossessing pale gray clapboard house contains one of Austin's hottest restaurants and bars. The interior walls are fiery red and lined with glittering copper sconces, and the food is fiery hot-bistro versions of Thai, Indian, and Middle Eastern standards, including wonderful nan-bread pizzas. ✉ 1610 San Antonio St., ☎ 512/472–3901.

$$–$$$ ✗ **Mezzaluna.** A trendy darling of the warehouse district, Mezzaluna has black-lacquer chairs and tables and stylish Wedgwood blue walls and tile floors that set the tone for fine northern Italian fare. Delicious pizzas include one with grilled chicken, onions, rosemary, tomatoes, and Gorgonzola. Or try the saffron linguine with garlic, toasted bread crumbs, and caramelized cauliflower. ✉ 310 Colorado St., ☎ 512/472–6770.

$$ ✗ **El Rinconcito.** Specials like jalapeño- and cheese-stuffed shrimp wrapped in bacon and simmered in a smoky chipotle sauce cram the blackboard menu of this little Mexican restaurant. Its intimate dining room, suffused with warm lighting, is decorated with authentic Mexican crafts. ✉ 1014-E N. Lamar Blvd., ☎ 512/476–5277.

$ ✗ **Katz Deli.** Upbeat and contemporary, this busy deli has one of the cutest staffs in town. The half-pound sandwiches—the grilled three-cheese with tomatoes is especially good—are more than most diners can handle in one sitting. Many folks come here for cocktails after work—the martinis are killer. ✉ 618 W. 6th St., ☎ 512/472–2037.

$ ✗ **Momma's Diner.** With a freaky portrait of Joan Crawford in many of its print ads, this diner positions itself as a place for post-clubbing fags to come for a touch of camp and a late-night meal (on weekends it's open 24 hours). Antique mirrors and vintage photos give Momma's a slightly ritzy feel, but the down-home food is affordable and pretty decent. The beer's cheap, too. ✉ 314 Congress Ave., ☎ 512/469–9369.

Greater Austin

$$$$ ✗ **Jeffrey's.** Dark and sexy Jeffrey's has the polish of a big-city supper club and a clientele that ranges from celebs and politicos to college students. The elk loin with roasted red potatoes and juniper-chipotle sauce and the duck and shrimp with black-bean ravioli and shiitake-mushroom sauce draw raves all around. There's also a slightly less pricey bistro menu. ✉ 1204 W. Lynn St., ☎ 512/477–5584.

$$–$$$ ✗ **Granite Café.** This light-filled dining room and inviting terrace, one block east of Lamar Boulevard, is as upscale as Austin gets, but folks still come in jeans. Recent offerings have included sesame mahimahi on Asian noodles, soft-shell crab with banana chutney and black-bean salad, and wood-oven pizzas. ✉ 2905 San Gabriel St. ☎ 512/472–6483.

$–$$ ✗ **Guero's.** A feed store turned divey taqueria, Guero's serves some of the best Mexican fare in town—from standard but artfully seasoned enchiladas and tamales to more innovative creations like marinated grilled pork on a corn tortilla with onions, cilantro, and fresh pineapple. ✉ 1412 S. Congress Ave., ☎ 512/447–7688.

$–$$ ✗ **Hyde Park Bar and Grill.** An enormous silver fork—it must be 20 feet tall—rises from the ground in front of this hoppin' college hangout north of UT. The Grill prides itself on its diverse, healthful, and cheap menu, though the addictive buttermilk-battered Park fries aren't exactly good for you. ✉ 4206 Duval St., ☎ 512/458–3168.

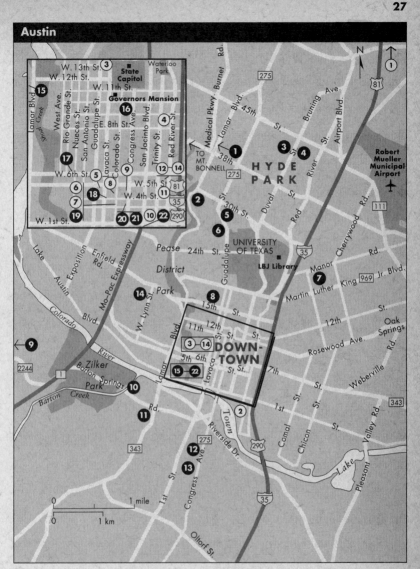

Austin

Eats ●

East Side Cafe, **7**
El Rinconcito, **15**
Flipnotic's, **11**
Granite Café, **2**
Guero's, **12**
Hyde Park Bar and Grill, **3**
Jeffrey's, **14**
Katz Deli, **17**
Kerbey Lane, **1**
Little City, **16**
Magnolia Café, **13**

Manuel's, **20**
Mars, **8**
Mezzaluna, **19**
Mojo's Daily Grind, **6**
Momma's Diner, **21**
Mother's Café and Garden, **4**
Oasis, **9**
Ruby's BBQ, **5**
Ruta Maya Coffee, **18**
Shady Grove, **10**
Shoreline, **22**

Scenes ○

Area 52, **8**
'Bout Time, **1**
Casino El Camino, **14**
Chain Drive, **2**
Charlie's, **3**
Club Deville, **4**
Country Edge, **10**

Edge, **7**
Emo's, **12**
Esther's Follies, **13**
Forum, **9**
Oil Can Harry's, **6**
Paradox, **11**
Rainbow Cattle Co., **5**

$–$$ ✕ **Kerbey Lane.** A late-night fave not far from Mount Bonnell, Kerbey Lane appeals to grungers, bookish types, yuppies, and others who recognize that its menu takes diner-style cooking to superior levels. Fajitas, Portobello mushroom sandwiches, and grilled tuna steaks are among the offerings. From downtown, head north on Lamar and west on 38½ Street; continue west at fork onto 35th. ✉ *3704 Kerbey La.,* ☏ *512/451–1436.*

$ ✕ **East Side Café.** Patronized largely by crunchy peaceniks, the East Side has amazingly well-attended brunches, sunny outdoor seating, and dishes made with fresh produce grown in the café's garden. Try the artichoke manicotti if it's being served. ✉ *2113 Manor Rd.,* ☏ *512/476–5858.*

$ ✕ **Magnolia Café.** The menu at this classic alternadiner scores extra-high marks for breakfast; try the "Solar Landscape" (seasoned grilled potatoes, red onions, and ham topped with queso and chipotle sauce). Russian chicken sandwiches with blackened spices and herb cream cheese, burgers with myriad toppings, and many Mexican specialties round out the hearty fare. ✉ *1920 S. Congress Ave.,* ☏ *512/445–0000.*

$ ✕ **Mother's Café and Garden.** This dyke-popular restaurant in Hyde Park has been drawing UT's veg-heads for years with robust meatless entrées like tofu lasagna, mushroom Stroganoff, and veggie rancheros. The cool staff is very friendly. ✉ *4215 Duval St.,* ☏ *512/451–3994.*

$ ✕ **Oasis.** A multidecked hilltop compound about 20 minutes west of the city center, the Oasis commands glorious views of Lake Travis. It's a little tacky, and the food is mediocre Mexican, but the drinks (especially the margaritas) are great. Everyone—gay, straight, and in between—heads here on weekend afternoons and lingers to admire the best sunset in Texas. ✉ *6550 Comanche Trail, off Rte. 620,* ☏ *512/266–2441.*

$ ✕ **Ruby's BBQ.** Mutton, brisket, and smoked chicken are among the items sold by the pound at this funky spot for real, Texas-style barbecue. For sides, try the delicious tacos, red beans and rice, and other goodies. ✉ *29th and Guadalupe Sts.,* ☏ *512/477–1651.*

$ ✕ **Shady Grove.** Close to Zilker Park, this slacker hangout has been around forever. The patio, gussied up with Christmas lights, odd topiaries, and other kitschy accoutrements, must be seen to be understood. Excellent, down-home southern and Mexican standbys come in gigantic portions. There's an "unplugged" music series on Thursday night from May to October. ✉ *1624 Barton Springs Rd.,* ☏ *512/474–9991.*

Coffeehouse Culture

Flipnotics. This funky coffeehouse is above a terrific clothing boutique across the street from the Shady Grove restaurant. Enter through a rickety porch in back. The desserts are great. Musicians sometimes perform here. ✉ *1601 Barton Springs Rd.,* ☏ *512/322–9750.*

Little City. The crowd at Little City is a little too hot for its own good, but this is a splendid perch from which to observe the rituals of Austin society. Great for a drink after a show at the nearby Paramount Theatre. ✉ *916 Congress Ave.,* ☏ *512/476–2489.*

Mojo's Daily Grind. A major student hangout, Mojo's is on the north side of The Drag. Track lighting, comfy chairs, and ceiling fans lend the place a living-room atmosphere. Parking's a bitch, but there are a few spots in the alley out back. ✉ *2714 Guadalupe St.,* ☏ *512/477–6656.*

Ruta Maya Coffee. The closest thing you'll find to a coffeehouse nightclub, Ruta Maya is in an ancient brick building. The front door was once a loading dock. Assets include live music and a queer, trendy, alternative following. ✉ *218 W. 4th St.,* ☏ *512/472–9637.*

SCENES

Most places here are around Red River Street, 4th Street near Lavaca and Colorado, and 6th Street. The clubs have big dance floors, often host live music, and pull in equally mixed gay and straight (or, at the very least, partially straight) crowds. The bar scene is young and collegiate, a largely hip, nonconformist cadre. The names, locations, and clienteles of bars change at breakneck speed, leaving even the most dedicated club bunnies in a state of confusion; in the past few years, the only constants have been Chain Drive, Charlie's, and Oil Can Harry's.

Prime Suspects

Area 52. This high-tech cruising and voguing ground has a fantastic sound system and lighting, two levels of scaffolds and walkways, a spacious dance floor, an outdoor balcony, and a steamy atmosphere. One of the few 18-and-over clubs in Austin, it's become increasingly straight, and the smug attitude cases who work the door have turned off of former regulars. Still, the place has great music and often stays open for dancing after hours. ⊠ *404 Colorado St.,* ☎ *512/474–4849. Crowd: 60/40 gay/straight, 60/40 m/f, mostly under 25, trendy, dishy, cliquey, stylish.*

Chain Drive. If you're into leather, this is your only choice. Few students come here, which appeals to folks seeking a bearish and rugged experience. The rambling club is dark, even a bit seedy. A leather dress code is enforced on weekends; if you forget your gear, there's a shop on the premises. ⊠ *504 Willow St.,* ☎ *512/480–9017. Crowd: male, 35 and up, butch, cruisy—you know the routine.*

Charlie's. Working-class guys and suits come to Austin's original gay bar for the slightly sleazy and extremely amiable cruise scene; you'll encounter none of the wanna-be attitude that occasionally prevails in the warehouse-district clubs. The music is of the mainstream dance variety, and several video screens keep the patrons amused—that is when they're not catching a drag show or ogling the go-go boys. Charlie's is within the shadow of the capitol building, so you may be able to spot a few polymorphously perverse politicos. ⊠ *1301 Lavaca St.,* ☎ *512/474–6481. Crowd: mostly male, 20s to 60s, high cruise factor.*

Country Edge. A lesbian bar until December 1997 (they just don't seem to last in Austin), this cavernous club plays country-western tunes. Two-steppers and line-dancers ply their trade on the good-size dance floor, and the bar has the full gamut of games and diversions. Some women still get their kicks here, but it's mostly a guy's hang. ⊠ *113 San Jacinto Blvd.,* ☎ *512/457–8010. Crowd: 75/25 m/f, mostly 20s to 40s, some cowboy attire, friendly and approachable, cruisiest later in the evening.*

Forum. A 1997 remodeling of the downstairs dance area of this two-level space re-energized the crowd and seemed to beckon guys who have had enough of Area 52. Hunky guys staff the cozy lounge in back, and a delightful rooftop bar with a long railing commands skyline views. Bring along the breath mints—it's very romantic up here. ⊠ *408 Congress Ave.,* ☎ *512/476–2900. Crowd: 80/20 m/f, 20s to 40s, somewhat mixed racially, a few guppies, plenty of butch boys, edgy and eager, often cruisy.*

Oil Can Harry's. Austin's only true stand-and-model bar attracts a hot collegiate crowd. There are a couple of bars, a patio in back, amber lighting, a good (loud) sound system, a tiny action-packed dance floor, and high stools everywhere. For a guppie cruise bar, Harry's serves amazingly stiff drinks. The management must conduct national talent searches to find waiters so cute and friendly. ⊠ *211 W. 4th St.,* ☎ *512/320–8823. Crowd: 85/15 m/f(ag hags), mostly 20s to mid-30s, professional, buttoned-down, starched-shirt but not stuffed-shirt.*

Rainbow Cattle Co. The cavernous former site of the lesbian disco Nexus has evolved into Austin's prime country-western dance hall. The clientele is now mostly male, though dykes are more than welcome. Below a sea of wagon wheels and Wild West artifacts, two-steppers and line dancers sweep across the elevated dance floor. Chatty regulars sauce it up at the bar or trade tales in the booths. ⊠ *305 W. 5th St.,* ☎ *512/472–5288. Crowd: 80/20 m/f, mostly 30s and 40s, Travis Tritt fans with Nirvana tendencies, eclectic in dress and style, low-attitude.*

Neighborhood Haunts

Occupying an attractive space beside Oil Can Harry's, the **Edge** (⊠ 213 W. 4th St., ☎ 512/480–8686), run by the owners of the Country Edge, attracts a mixed crowd but is one of Austin's few bars with a significant lesbian following. There's a small dance floor, several pool tables, and plenty of games. Austin's only real neighborhood dive, **'Bout Time** (⊠ 9601 N. I–35 Access Rd., ☎ 512/832–5339), well north of downtown (just above Rundberg Street). It has an island bar, good lighting, plenty of seating, and pool tables.

Hangin' with the Hets

The live-music scene in Austin has launched the careers of countless stars, from the late guitar rocker Stevie Ray Vaughan to folksy chanteuse Shawn Colvin. Many of these places have strong followings in the community. Punkish, grungish, stylish, and freakish, **Casino El Camino** (⊠ 517 E. 6th St., ☎ 512/469–9330) has the buzz of Greenwich Village—black-and-white walls, clever music (from punk to acid jazz to Cole Porter), and some pretty good bar food. Dress to impress. **Club Deville** (⊠ 900 Red River St., ☎ 512/457–0900) books popular bands. Some folks find it horribly trendy and buttoned-down, which is exactly why others love it. Red-hot **Emo's** (⊠ 603 Red River St., ☎ 512/477–3667) presents cutting-edge local and national bands. The renowned comedy club **Esther's Follies** (⊠ 525 E. 6th St., ☎ 512/320–0553) has a penchant for drag and queer-theme humor. Sprawling **Paradox** (⊠ 5th and Trinity Sts., ☎ 512/469–7615), a warehouse-style dance club that's neither gay nor straight, plays great house music. Saturday is especially queer.

Action

The **Austin Midtowne Spa** (⊠ 5815 W. Airport Blvd., ☎ 512/302–9696), part of a regional chain, is the all-night spot for bathhouse fun. **Pease Park,** which straddles Shoal Canal northwest of downtown, is reputed to be very cruisy at times. **Hippie Hollow** (*see* Lake Travis and Points West *in* The Lay of the Land, *above*) is *the* spot to sun your buns and show your guns.

SLEEPS

Most bars, shops, and restaurants are close to downtown hotels. Room costs were low in the city until recently, but booming occupancy rates have driven them up. There are no gay-exclusive accommodations, but a couple of guest houses have gay followings.

For price ranges, *see* lodging Chart B at the front of this guide.

Hotels

$$$–$$$$ 🏨 **Four Seasons Austin.** The city's most luxurious hostelry has great views of the Congress Avenue Bridge, where Austin's legendary bats reside in the summer months. Southwestern decorative accents and fabrics lend a laid-back Texan air to the rooms, but the amenities are strictly deluxe. ⊠ *98 San Jacinto Blvd., 78701,* ☎ *512/478–4500 or 800/332–3442,* FAX *512/478–3117. 278 rooms. Restaurant, pool, health club.*

$$$ ⊞ **Hyatt Regency Austin.** A modern business hotel that works closely with the gay community, the Hyatt has classy, spacious rooms, many of which have terrific views of Town Lake and beyond. The pace of this conventioneers' favorite can be hectic—the often ditzy staff reflects this. ⊠ *208 Barton Springs Rd., 78704,* ☎ *512/477–1234 or 800/233–1234,* FAX *512/ 480–2069. 446 rooms. Restaurants, pool, health club.*

$$–$$$ ⊞ **Driskill Hotel.** Austin's gay-hospitable grande dame, an 1886 period piece with a spectacular lobby, attracts celebrities and politicos. The rooms, though not memorable, are some of the largest in town. If opulence matters, pay the extra dough for one of the recently renovated ones. ⊠ *604 Brazos St., between 5th and 6th Sts., 78701,* ☎ *512/474–5911 or 800/527–2008. 177 rooms. Restaurant.*

$$ ⊞ **Radisson Town Lake.** This riverside mid-rise has amiable, efficient service and roomy, well-maintained accommodations—it's tough to beat for value. ⊠ *111 E. 1st St., 78701,* ☎ *512/478–9611 or 800/333–3333,* FAX *512/473–8399. 280 rooms. Restaurant, pool, exercise room.*

$ ⊞ **La Quinta Capital Inn.** A stroll from the capitol building and midway between the bar district and UT, La Quinta is a fine budget hotel with clean, simple rooms. ⊠ *300 E. 11th St., 78701,* ☎ *512/476–1166 or 800/ 531–5900,* FAX *512/476–6044. 148 rooms.*

Guest Houses and Small Hotels

$$$ ⊞ **Citiview Bed & Breakfast.** A Frank Lloyd Wright–inspired compound adorned with sleek '30s furnishings, the Citiview sits amid tree-shaded grounds. There's a huge pool, an exercise solarium, and a sanctuary of llamas, goats, peacocks, wallabies, rabbits, and goats. ⊠ *1405 E. Riverside St., 78714,* ☎ *512/441–2606 or 800/278–8439,* FAX *512/441–2949, Web site www.hyperweb.com/citiview. 8 rooms with phone, TV, and private bath. Full breakfast. Mixed gay/straight.*

$$–$$$ ⊞ **Miller-Crockett House.** This restored 1888 house opened as an inn in 1997, but not before one of its rooms served as a set for the film *The Newton Boys* (starring Ethan Hawke and Matthew McConaughey). The rooms in the main house are furnished with period antiques, pressed-tin ceilings, and bright bathrooms. Two cottages provide more privacy but have a lower quaintness factor. ⊠ *112 Academy Dr., 78704,* ☎ *512/441– 1600, Web site www.earthlink.net/~michelann/mc.html. 5 rooms with private bath, some with TV and phone. Full breakfast. Mixed gay/straight.*

$ ⊞ **Summit House.** An informal gay-hosted property south of downtown, Summit House has the intimacy and personal touch of a European B&B— ideal if you're looking to save money and interact with the friendly owner, who can arrange a tour of downtown attractions and music clubs or point you in the direction of good restaurants and bars. The rooms are modest but characterful, filled with local art and a few antiques. ⊠ *1204 Summit St., 78714,* ☎ *512/445–5304. 3 rooms with phone and TV, one with private bath. Full breakfast. Mixed gay/straight.*

THE LITTLE BLACK BOOK

At Your Fingertips
AIDS Services of Austin Hotline (☎ 512/458–2437). *Austin Chronicle* (☎ 512/454–5766, Web site www.auschron.com). **Austin Convention and Visitors Bureau** (⊠ 201 E. 2nd St., 78701, ☎ 512/474–5171 or 800/926– 2282, Web site www.austintexas.org). **Austin Stonewall Chamber of Commerce** (☎ 512/472–8299). **Capital Metro** (☎ 512/474–1200). **Cornerstone Gay and Lesbian Community Center** (⊠ 1117 Red River St., ☎ 512/708–1515). **Yellow Cab** (☎ 512/472–1111).

Gay Media

The weekly *Texas Triangle* (☎ 512/459–1717), which covers the entire state, is the main source for Austin gay news. *This Week in Texas* (☎ 713/527–9111, e-mail twtmag@aol.com) has the top nightlife coverage.

BOOKSTORES

LOBO (✉ 3204A Guadalupe St., ☎ 512/454–5406), like its Houston branch, specializes in gay-male porn but also carries gay and lesbian titles. **Book Woman** (✉ 918 W. 12th St., ☎ 512/472–2785) is a great feminist bookstore with plenty of lesbian titles and information on the lesbian community. Shop for pride items, gifts, jewelry, and other fun queeriosities at **Sparks** (✉ W. 6th St. at Lamar Blvd., ☎ 512/477–2757). Progressive **Book People** (✉ 603 N. Lamar Blvd., ☎ 512/472–5050), which has been the best general-interest store in town, stocks New Age and gay and lesbian titles. It's next door to the queer-popular **Whole Foods Market** (✉ 601 N. Lamar Blvd., ☎ 512/476–1206). Also a hit with the gay set is **Travelfest** (✉ 1214 W. 6th St., ☎ 512/469–7906), which has an exhaustive selection of travel guides, a full travel agency, seminars, travel gear, and other cool stuff for the inveterate wanderer—if only every city had one of these.

Working Out

World Gym (✉ 115 E. 6th St., ☎ 512/479–0044) has a strong gay and lesbian following.

3 *Out in Baltimore*

JUST AN HOUR FROM WASHINGTON BY CAR and less than two hours from Philadelphia, quiet, unassuming Baltimore has experienced a rebirth in the past two decades, gaining back some of the ground it had lost during this century to flashier East Coast cities. The city's resurgence has been a remarkable urban comeback story. Local political and business leaders undertook a mammoth public and private rehabilitation of the Inner Harbor, converting its dilapidated piers and wharves into museums, shopping centers, restaurants, hotels, and condominiums. By the mid-1980s, Baltimore had virtually reinvented its skyline. Once the butt of jokes, Baltimore is now a legitimate tourist destination.

Fortunately, the city's success hasn't gone to its head. It's hard to find a more genuine and down-to-earth breed of urbanites than the residents of Baltimore, who retain a special affection for their hometown. This civic pride shows up in the works of locally bred filmmakers who set many of their works here. Director Barry Levinson's *Diner* and *The Tin Men,* set in the late-1950s and early 1960s, evoke a small-town sensibility that can still be felt in many Baltimore neighborhoods, and the films of camp queen John Waters, among them *Pink Flamingos* and *Hairspray,* lovingly poke fun at the city's fashion and other foibles.

Though not large, the local lesbian and gay community works hard to keep the city as free as possible from bigotry. You won't find many firebrands on the right or the left, and rare as well are egomaniacs and attention-seekers. Reasonable people used reasonable means to rehabilitate huge sections of the city; gay Baltimoreans employed similar tactics to gain passage of a queer-positive civil rights law, encourage the mayor to set up an efficient gay and lesbian task force, and prompt the police to respond effectively and with sensitivity to gay bashings.

Don't visit Baltimore with expectations of a dazzling gay scene. There are unusual shops and galleries and enough tourist attractions to keep you busy for several days, but it's less in Baltimore's nature to impress you with extremes than it is to charm you with friendly hellos, moderate prices, and low-key pleasures. If you live in any of the East Coast's more intense metropolises, a spell in Baltimore may be just what you need.

THE LAY OF THE LAND

Charles Street and Mount Vernon

Charles Street is the backbone of Baltimore, running from the Inner Harbor north to Johns Hopkins University and continuing into the suburbs of Baltimore County. Earlier this century, the lower stretch of Charles was a fashionable shopping district. Many storefronts that were boarded up as recently as the late 1980s now contain art galleries, bookshops, and unique establishments of the sort you won't find in shopping malls. The best sidewalk strolling begins around Pratt Street and extends almost to Pennsylvania Station, where Charles crosses I–83.

Among the shops worth a peek are **A People United** (⊠ 516 N. Charles St., ☎ 410/727–4470), a women's clothing and arts cooperative; **Nouveau** (⊠ 19 N. Charles St., ☎ 410/962–8248), which has art deco and Art Nouveau furniture and collectibles; the **Zone** (⊠ 813 N. Charles St., ☎ 410/539–2817), known for secondhand duds, grunge garb, and jewelry; and **Louie's** (*see* Eats, *below*), favored by gay and straight locals for its intelligent selection of books and great food and coffee.

The heart of Charles Street bisects **Mount Vernon,** the city's gayest neighborhood. (Queers live throughout the city but are the most visible in Federal Hill and Hampden, both of which are more couples-oriented, and up around Johns Hopkins University, where many lesbians reside. The neighborhood is anchored at Mount Vernon Square by the 178-foot-high **Washington Monument** (you can climb the 228 steps to the top). A grassy lawn, enchanting statuary, and benches surround the small park. South of the monument is the **Walters Art Gallery** (⊠ N. Charles and Centre Sts., ☎ 410/547–9000), whose holdings include many Renaissance and Baroque paintings; jewelry and decorative works; and a strong collection of Byzantine, Islamic, and Oriental works. Be sure to see the dramatic sculpture court. Southeast of the monument, the **Peabody Conservatory of Music** (⊠ N. Charles St. and Mt. Vernon Pl., ☎ 410/659–8124) is the oldest classical music school in the country. The school's neo-Renaissance **library** (☎ 410/659–8179) has stunning marble pillars and floors and intricate iron interior balconies.

Read Street, two blocks north of the square, was a hippie haven during the '60s and now has several vintage-clothing and bric-a-brac shops. North a bit more, the intersection of **Charles and Eager streets** anchors the city's main gay entertainment district. Two blocks west, **Howard Street,** the city's Antiques Row (most shops are between Read and Monument streets), has recently been designated the city's "Avenue of the Arts," a project that will see the construction and renovation of several performing-arts spaces, as well as subsidized arts studios and exhibition venues. Southwest of the square on Lexington Street, locals shop for fresh produce, meats, and seafood at the colorful **Lexington Market,** perhaps the best of Baltimore's several indoor food markets.

The Inner Harbor

A compact wedge of water that cuts directly into the heart of downtown, the **Inner Harbor** was for years a thriving shipping crossroads before falling into a state of filth and disrepair. Its conversion over the past three decades into an entertainment and museum district places it among the most engaging and picturesque harbors in any American city. Popular attractions include the glass-enclosed **Harborplace** pavilions, which occupy the northwest corner of the harbor; here you can browse through more than 100 shops and graze your way through a serious food court. A skywalk connects Harborplace to the upscale **Gallery Mall.** To the east, beside piers jutting into the harbor, are a few historic ships, which together compose the **Baltimore Maritime Museum** (⊠ Piers 2, 3, and 4, ☎ 410/396–3453). You can also visit the tallest pentagonal building in the world, I. M. Pei's **World Trade Center** (⊠ Pier 2, ☎ 410/837–4515), which has a 27th-floor observation deck, and the highly acclaimed **National Aquarium** (⊠ Pier 3, ☎ 410/576–3800). South of Harborplace, along the wharf that borders Light Street, is the kids-oriented **Maryland Science Center** (⊠ 601 Light St., ☎ 410/685–5225).

Federal Hill

The regal grassy knoll south of the harbor was nearly leveled in the 1850s to make a landfill out of the harbor. Fortunately, those plans were scrapped and **Federal Hill Park** rises majestically above downtown and the Inner Harbor. It's an ideal spot to laze under the sun on warm afternoons. The **Federal Hill** neighborhood has gentrified over the past decade, with many young professionals moving in and refurbishing early and mid-19th-century brick homes. West of the actual hill, along Light and Charles streets, are several good ethnic restaurants and quirky shops, plus the bustling **Cross Street Market,** a great place to sample local seafood or grab a sandwich from one of the delis.

North of Federal Hill Park, the **American Visionary Art Museum** (✉ 800 Key Hwy., ☎ 410/244–1900) ingeniously blends two historic warehouses with a striking contemporary structure. The museum contains six exhibition galleries of works by self-taught and other artists working outside the artistic mainstream, a research library, a sculpture garden, and the cutting-edge Joy America Cafe (*see* Eats, *below*).

Fells Point

Fells Point is one of America's best-preserved Colonial waterfront settlements. Perfectly maintained Federal town houses, which date to an era when 16 shipyards bustled nearby, line Thames and Fell streets and nearby blocks. Italian and Eastern European immigrants (Little Italy is just north, around High Street), artsy slackers and genXers, yuppies, and many queers reside in this diverse neighborhood. Many pubs, cafés, and funky shops are along South Broadway or on the blocks just off it. Be sure to poke your head inside **Daily Grind** (✉ 1726 Thames St., ☎ 410/558–0399), an artsy coffeehouse where the cast of *Homicide* often hangs out. Several historic walking tours originate from the **Fells Point Visitors Center** (✉ S. Ann and Thames Sts., ☎ 410/675–6750), an excellent source of information on the neighborhood's history and its current offerings. The wave of Fells Point gentrification has spread east into the adjacent neighborhood of **Canton,** where construction to revitalize more of the harborfront is proceeding briskly.

Outlying Neighborhoods

Lombard Street leads west from downtown past the impressive **Oriole Park at Camden Yards** baseball stadium into a mixed-use area that includes a small garment district, the University of Maryland-Baltimore campus, and a few historic sites. These include the **Westminster Cemetery and Catacombs** (✉ W. Fayette and S. Greene Sts., ☎ 410/706–2072), where you can pay your respects to Edgar Allan Poe; the **Edgar Allan Poe House** (✉ 203 N. Amity St., ☎ 410/396–7932), where you can tour the barebones studio in which the author wrote his first tale of gothic horror (it's in a dicey neighborhood, so call ahead for hours, which vary, and directions); **Babe Ruth's Birthplace** (✉ 216 Emory St., ☎ 410/727–1539); and the **B&O Railroad Museum** (✉ Pratt and Poppleton Sts., ☎ 410/752–2490).

Continue along Lombard to reach up-and-coming **SoWeBo,** which stands for, depending on the resident you talk to, Southwest Baltimore (the "Bo" being a further abbreviation of the town's nickname "Balto") or Southwest Bohemian. In any case, because of its affordable housing and proximity to a few colleges the district has become a small haven of countercultural activity. Most of the action is along **Hollins Street,** around the bustling Hollins food market. The **H. L. Mencken House** (✉ 1524 Hollins St., ☎ 410/396–7997) is where the Sage of Baltimore lived most of his life.

Northwest of Mount Vernon is **Bolton Hill,** a residential neighborhood of Victorian row houses. Continuing north of downtown, taking Charles Street, you'll reach the campuses of Johns Hopkins University, Loyola College, and the College of Notre Dame. Several residential neighborhoods up here, such as **Charles Village, Homewood,** and **Waverly,** are popular with lesbians and, to a lesser extent, gay men. This area was a hotbed of lesbian and gay activism in the '60s; Abell Avenue, which runs through Waverly, is still referred to as Lesbian Lane.

The 140-acre campus of **Johns Hopkins University** is ideal for walking. Hopkins's esteemed medical school was begun with funding from one of America's most illustrious lesbians, Mary Elizabeth Garrett. The daughter of railroad mogul John Work Garrett, Mary Elizabeth inherited one-third of his fortune. When the plans to open a medical school were stalled for lack of funds, the well-educated and highly driven Garrett and her lover, M. Carey Thomas, raised the necessary half-million to open the school. More than $300,000 came from Garrett herself, with the proviso that the school admit women on the same terms that it admitted men. Garrett went on to fund and help found southeastern Pennsylvania's Bryn Mawr School for girls and Bryn Mawr College, of which Thomas later served as president. John Work Garrett's former mansion, **Evergreen** (⊠ 4545 N. Charles St., ☎ 410/516−0895), just off campus, is open for touring.

Adjacent to Johns Hopkins is the **Baltimore Museum of Art** (⊠ N. Charles and 31st Sts., ☎ 410/396−7101), Maryland's largest museum, whose strengths include French Impressionist painting, 18th- and 19th-century American painting, and 20th-century sculpture. A few thousand of the museum's holdings were donated by Baltimore natives Dr. Claribel Cone and Miss Etta Cone, two unmarried sisters who with help from their friends Gertrude and Leo Stein (also Baltimore natives) collected works by Matisse (500 of them), Picasso, Gauguin, and others.

West of Johns Hopkins, **Hampden** is a good old-fashioned Bawl'mer neighborhood, a former mill-workers' community that has recently developed a major funk factor. Along **West 36th Street** (a.k.a. "the Avenue"), you'll find piercing parlors, antiques shops, quirky restaurants, and plain neighborhood businesses. John Waters, who lives in the nearby Tuscany-Canterbury enclave, occasionally strolls the Avenue—he's been known to stop for coffee at Cafe Hon (*see* Eats, *below*). Waters set his 1998 film, *Pecker,* in this slice of retro Baltimore, where sleeveless undershirts and beehive hairdos remain very much in vogue.

GETTING AROUND

Most neighborhoods that are popular with visitors are within walking distance of one another and downtown hotels. Or you can take the bus (the limited subway and light-rail service is of more use to locals). In outlying neighborhoods, you'll need a car but parking is rarely a problem anywhere in town. Cabs are rarely necessary, except perhaps for traveling between Penn Station or the airport and downtown; you phone for them or catch them at hotels. They're fairly easy to hail along Charles Street at night.

EATS

Baltimore's cooking is full of flavor—the city even has its own spice, Old Bay Seasoning, a feisty concoction of 16 seasonings used most often on shellfish but required by some locals on everything but ice cream. Seafood—particularly oysters, clams, and Chesapeake Bay blue crabs—is a regional specialty, as is fried chicken. New American, northern Italian, and even southwestern flavors have been introduced by many of the city's newer kitchens.

For price ranges, *see* dining Chart B at the front of this guide.

Mount Vernon and North Charles Street

$$$–$$$$ ✗ **Brass Elephant.** A terrific place to celebrate a special occasion, the Brass Elephant is set inside an antiques-filled Victorian town house with vast plate-glass windows, polished parquet floors, a carved marble fireplace, brass banisters, chandeliers, and gilt-frame mirrors. Standouts on the sophisticated Continental menu include grilled Angus strip steak with a cabernet demi-glace. ✉ *924 N. Charles St.,* ☎ *410/547–8480.*

$$–$$$$ ✗ **Sotto Sopra.** Inside a storefront with soaring ceilings, dramatic murals, a mosaic floor, and an elegant bar, this Milan-inspired restaurant draws moon-eyed couples, gay and straight. Dishes range from affordable pastas (try the mascarpone, goat cheese, and roasted-red-pepper ravioli) to veal chops and other grills. ✉ *405 N. Charles St.,* ☎ *410/625–0534.*

$$–$$$ ✗ **Ruby Lounge.** Locals love this handsome contemporary space for eclectic fare such as grilled mahimahi with lemon white-wine sauce and pecan-crab relish. Lighter dishes—try the delicious smoked-trout quesadilla—are also served. Local restaurant doyenne Donna Crivello runs Ruby Lounge. ✉ *800 N. Charles St.,* ☎ *410/539–8051.*

$$–$$$ ✗ **Spike & Charlie's.** Close to the Lyric Opera House, the Joseph Meyerhoff Symphony Hall, and several gay clubs, this dapper New American eatery is *the* place to look good and eat well before taking in a concert or a drag show. Prince Edward Island mussels tossed with sweet sausage, oven-cured tomatoes, and green-onion cheese are a good bet, as is the tomato tagliatelle with Portobello mushrooms and feta. ✉ *1225 Cathedral St.,* ☎ *410/752–8144.*

$$ ✗ **Central Station.** The restaurant of the city's most popular gay bar serves decent, affordable grub. It's predictable—crab cakes, pasta primavera, burgers—but competently prepared, and the service is friendly. This is one of the few restaurants along Charles Street with sidewalk seating. ✉ *1001 N. Charles St.,* ☎ *410/752–7133.*

$–$$ ✗ **Gampy's.** The name is an acronym for Great American Melting Pot (chocolate fondue is a specialty), and true to its name Gampy's gets a great mix of real Baltimoreans—including many queers. Red and blue tubes of neon snake along the ceiling and campy disco blares from several speakers. The food is a cut above what you'd find at a good diner: The cholesterol-laden Monte Cristo and the rich chocolate malt are two menu highlights. ✉ *904 N. Charles St.,* ☎ *410/837–9797.*

$–$$ ✗ **Louie's.** You can while away a Sunday afternoon here browsing through the many book racks and plucking favorites off Louie's great brunch menu. The New American options at other times include fried-oyster sandwiches, flavorful crab cakes, and a vegetable pâté. The café is a superb stop for desserts and coffee. Jazz and classical musicians perform from time to time. ✉ *518 N. Charles St.,* ☎ *410/962–1224.*

$–$$ ✗ **Owl Bar.** This over-the-top dining room is decorated with enough Gothic kitsch to impress Poe himself—the blinking-eye owl statuary is particularly memorable. The tasty fare includes wood-fired pizzas and Continental and American favorites like braised lamb shank. The restaurant occupies the former cocktail lounge of the once-fashionable Belvedere Hotel (now a condominium complex), where Tab Hunter, Dinah Shore, Tyrone Power, Barbara Stanwyck, and other pop-culture icons once clinked highballs. ✉ *1 E. Chase St.,* ☎ *410/347–0888.*

$ ✗ **Henry & Jeff's.** A good early-evening rendezvous point before a visit to Mount Vernon's bars, H & J's has mastered the art of quick, filling food. The chefs prepare more than 40 kinds of sandwiches, along with fine pastas and many Mexican goodies. ✉ *1218–1220 N. Charles St.,* ☎ *410/727–3322.*

Elsewhere in Baltimore

$$$–$$$$ ✗ **Joy America Cafe.** The restaurant in the American Visionary Art Museum serves innovative chow—mango and fresh-mint flautas with green

38

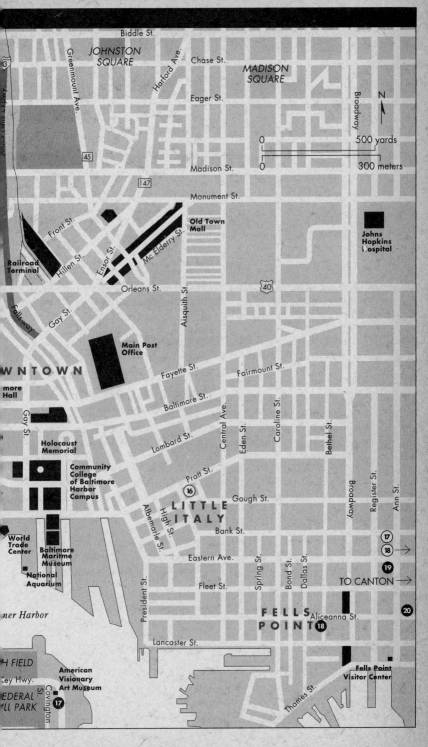

Biddle St.

JOHNSTON SQUARE

Chase St.

MADISON SQUARE

Greenmount Ave.

Harford Ave.

Broadway

Eager St.

N

0   500 yards

45

0   300 meters

147

Madison St.

Monument St.

Old Town Mall

Johns Hopkins Hospital

Front St.

Ensor St.

Mc Elderry St.

Railroad Terminal

Hillen St.

Orleans St.

Aisquith St.

40

Fallsway

Gay St.

Main Post Office

WNTOWN

Fayette St.

Fairmount St.

more Hall

Baltimore St.

Gay St.

Central Ave.

Eden St.

Caroline St.

Bethel St.

Holocaust Memorial

Lombard St.

Community College of Baltimore Harbor Campus

Pratt St.

16

Gough St.

LITTLE ITALY

Broadway

Register St.

Ann St.

Albemarle St.

High St.

Bank St.

17

World Trade Center

Eastern Ave.

Spring St.

Bond St.

Dallas St.

18

Baltimore Maritime Museum

Fleet St.

19

National Aquarium

President St.

TO CANTON

ner Harbor

FELLS POINT

Aliceanna St.

20

18

Lancaster St.

H FIELD

American Visionary Art Museum

Covington St.

Thames St.

Fells Point Visitor Center

Key Hwy.

EDERAL LL PARK

17

pumpkin seeds, farmer's cheese, and bitter chocolate, for instance. The minimalist dining room captures the contemporary sensibility of the adjacent galleries. ✉ *800 Key Hwy.*, ☎ *410/244–6500.*

$$$–$$$$ ✕ **Pierpoint.** Traditional Maryland favorites—dishes such as green tomatoes and braised rabbit, which appeared on city menus a century ago— receive innovative Mediterranean- and California-inspired twists at this popular Fells Point restaurant. The emphasis is on seafood. ✉ *1822 Aliceanna St.,* ☎ *410/675–2080.*

$$ ✕ **Bandaloops.** Baltimore's beautiful people gather for after-work wine and hors d'oeuvres at this Federal Hill favorite. The narrow dining room has a slick pressed-tin ceiling, exposed brick, and contemporary art. Try the cheese board if you're sampling the wines available by the glass. ✉ *1024 S. Charles St.,* ☎ *410/727–1355.*

$–$$ ✕ **Banjara.** The best Indian restaurant in the city is a sedate, softly lit space in Federal Hill. Among the many tandoori specialties are several vegetarian dishes. ✉ *1017 S. Charles St.,* ☎ *410/962–1554.*

$–$$ ✕ **The Kitchen at Peter's Inn.** This old-fashioned pub on the edge of Fells Point serves sophisticated world-beat fare. The menu changes weekly, but you can expect fare like mussel-saffron bisque, marinated roasted vegetables with orzo, and filet mignon with a green-peppercorn mustard cream sauce. ✉ *504 S. Ann St.,* ☎ *410/675–7313. No credit cards.*

$–$$ ✕ **Mencken's Cultured Pearl.** An odd tribute to Baltimore's famed phrasemonger, H. L. Mencken, this Mexican restaurant is in the heart of SoWeBo. The food's just okay—it's the atmosphere that makes Mencken's worth a visit. ✉ *1114 Hollins St.,* ☎ *410/837–1947.*

$ ✕ **Cafe Hon.** Hipsters, fags, and neighborhood characters pass through this Hampden luncheonette that offers up attitude aplenty and terrific home-style cooking. Expect great burgers, sandwiches, salads, and traditional diner fare like "Much Better than Mom's" meat loaf and "Dottie's bread pudding." ✉ *1002 W. 36th St.,* ☎ *410/243–1230.*

Little Italy

The eateries in Baltimore's Little Italy don't have much of a gay following. Among the best are red-saucey **Amicci's** (✉ 231 S. High St., ☎ 410/ 528–1096; also in Canton, ✉ 2903 O'Donnell St., ☎ 410/675–3207; $–$$); the formal **Da Mimmo** (✉ 217 S. High St., ☎ 410/727–6876; $$$– $$$$); and Tuscan-inspired **Germano's** (✉ 300 S. High St., ☎ 410/752– 4515; $$–$$$$).

Coffeehouse Culture

Blue Moon Cafe. Alternateens, guppies, and yuppies mix it up at this Fells Point institution known for its delicious breakfasts, fine coffees, and live music many nights. ✉ *1621 Aliceanna St.,* ☎ *410/522–3940.*

City Cafe. This spacious coffeehouse with art on its walls appeals to an eclectic crowd, from cruisy fags to shoppers fresh from Howard Street's Antiques Row. ✉ *1001 Cathedral St.,* ☎ *410/539–4252.*

Donna's Coffee Bar. Next to the suave Ruby Lounge and with outdoor seating overlooking Washington Monument, this upscale espresso bar serves the best cappuccino in town and fine salads and soups; there are several others throughout the city. ✉ *Madison and Charles Sts.,* ☎ *410/385–0180.*

One World Café. This Federal Hill hangout is as much a popular vegetarian restaurant as a cozy coffeehouse. Come in and chat with locals, listen to music, read the paper, shoot pool, or munch on the rich desserts. ✉ *904 S. Charles St.,* ☎ *410/234–0235.*

SCENES

The most popular hangouts are all close to Charles Street, in either Mount Vernon or north of it, just beyond Penn Station. Exercise caution throughout this area, especially up by the train station and west of Charles along Howard Street and Park Avenue. Baltimoreans complain about how segregated the scene here is, but many places have a stronger racial mix than you'll find in other American cities. The lesbian nightlife has picked up in recent years, with a women-frequented venue downtown and a few neighborhood bars in East Baltimore. Lesbians patronize some of the guys' bars, especially the Stagecoach Saloon.

Prime Suspects

Allegro. The illustrious history of this small disco and cocktail bar dates from the '40s and '50s, when it was Baltimore's main lesbian club (Talullah Bankhead is said to have been a regular). Women maintain a presence and have their own night—Thursday—but the Allegro is mostly male. Its tiny dance floor is especially crowded on Friday and Sunday. A little tough to find, Allegro is on the small, oddly shaped block where Maryland Avenue and a closed-off section of Cathedral Street cut into Chase Street—the bar is down a flight of stairs. ⊠ *1101 Cathedral St.,* ☎ *410/ 837–3906. Crowd: 75/25 m/f, easygoing, the full gamut; from diesel dykes to pretty boys to older guys.*

Central Station. The town's guppie contingent heads to Central Station. Behind an attractively decorated and well-lit front room is a smaller room with pool tables, and beyond that is a small patio. This is a mostly pre-disco spot. ⊠ *1001 N. Charles St.,* ☎ *410/752–7133. Crowd: 80/ 20 m/f, mostly under 35, a bit clonish but very friendly for a stand-and-model bar.*

Club Bunns. The most popular—and largest—of the city's African-American clubs, this lively disco draws women and men, except on Wednesday guys' nights and Saturday women's nights. Happy hour is always bustling, as are Classic Thursdays, when $5 entitles you to all the booze you can swill until 9 PM. ⊠ *606 W. Lexington St.,* ☎ *410/234–2866. Crowd: mixed m/f, all ages, mostly African-American.*

Coconuts Cafe. Other than two local bars in a seedy part of East Baltimore, the city didn't have a good venue for women until Coconuts opened on the fringe of Mount Vernon, a few blocks west of the monument. The cheerfully decorated space contains a bar, pool tables, a restaurant, and a small dance floor. The friendly weekday crowd includes quite a few guys; on weekends the pace picks up. Live music many nights. ⊠ *331 W. Madison St.,* ☎ *410/383–6064. 80/20 f/m, all ages, casual.*

The Eagle. Baltimore's leather bar is like every other Eagle you've ever been to. It has the friendliest bartenders in the city, and there are no dress requirements or pretensions. Favorite events include the full-moon underwear parties. There's a leather shop on the premises. ⊠ *2022 N. Charles St.,* ☎ *410/823–2453. Crowd: mostly male; lots of leather and denim.*

The Gallery. Relaxed and with a real neighborhood feel, the Gallery has a small restaurant, a cocktail bar with relatively quiet music, and a cabaret and pool room; the staff and patrons make newcomers feel right at home. A slight drawback is the bar's dicey location, a block west of 1722 Charles (*see below*). Parking is available across the street, but a cab is advisable late at night. ⊠ *1735 Maryland Ave.,* ☎ *410/539–6965. Crowd: 70/30 m/f, mixed racially, mostly over 35, no attitude.*

Hippo. The city's main disco has a midsize dance floor with lots of standing room around it. Next door is a big cruise bar with video screens and pool tables. Another smaller video bar behind that opens on weekends. Many African-Americans show up on Wednesday; Fridays see more lesbians than other nights. ⊠ *1 W. Eager St.,* ☎ *410/547–0069. Crowd: 80/20 m/f; more white, young, male, and suburban on weekends; more diverse other nights, slightly stand-and-model.*

Leon's. Among the several East Coast clubs that claim to be the oldest continuously operated gay bar in America, Leon's has been around for at least 50 years. Because it's something of a stink hole, few locals admit to coming here. At about 1:30 AM on a Friday or Saturday, the places fairly well hops with desperados from the Hippo and Allegro—they ought to rename it the Last Chance Saloon. Great jukebox. ⊠ *870 Park Ave.,* ☎ *410/539–4993. Crowd: male, scruffy, older.*

Randy's Sportsman's Bar. The most popular African-American cruise bar in the city, Sportsman's is usually jumping from just after work until well into the evening—the drinks at this cozy place are cheap, the music and conversation boisterous, and the staff quite friendly. ⊠ *412 Park Ave.,* ☎ *410/727–8935. Crowd: Mostly male, mostly African-American, 20s and 30s, somewhat cruisy.*

Stagecoach. This place is one of the few reminders that Baltimore is still, in the minds of many locals, a southern city. The best line-dancing and two-stepping club on the East Coast, the Stagecoach, in the heart of Mount Vernon, has a good restaurant that serves burgers, steaks, and southwestern food. A railing around the big dance floor allows full views of all the dancing. The crowd is exceedingly friendly and open to visitors and those unfamiliar with two-stepping. Lessons are given on certain weeknights. ⊠ *1003 N. Charles St.,* ☎ *410/547–0107. Crowd: 60/40 m/f; mixed ages but mostly 30s and up; country-western.*

Neighborhood Haunts

The seedy **Drinkery** (⊠ 201 W. Read St., ☎ 410/669–9820), whose logo is "where Park and Read get forked" makes nearby Leon's look comparatively tame. **Mardi Gras** (⊠ 228 Park Ave., ☎ 410/625–9818) is popular with African-Americans but draws a mellower bunch than Randy's, up the street; it also has more of a mix of races and ages. There's a very popular after-hours club up near the Eagle and the Gallery called **1722 Charles** (⊠ 1722 N. Charles St., ☎ 410/727–7431), which is BYOB, has good dancing, and is about the only Baltimore bar where you stand a chance of getting groped.

The gruff but lovable **Unicorn** (⊠ 2218 Boston St., ☎ 410/342–8344) in Canton is the only gay bar near Fells Point; it draws a mostly male, white, working-class crowd. **Port In A Storm** (⊠ 4330 E. Lombard St., ☎ 410/732–5608) is a women's bar in East Baltimore that's very butch and local; it's recognizable from the Pabst Blue Ribbon signs along the windows.

Hangin' with the Hets

Gays and straights frequent the **Mt. Vernon Stable and Saloon** (⊠ 909 N. Charles St., ☎ 410/685–7427), a hip and noisy little pub that serves good sandwiches, pizzas, and other comfort food. John Waters has been known to hold court at ultratrendy **Club Charles** (⊠ 1726 N. Charles St., ☎ 410/727–8815); you can dine late in the adjacent restaurant, Zodiac. **Club Orpheus** (⊠ 1003 E. Pratt St., ☎ 410/276–5599), which has a similar following, is also very queer on Saturday, when drag shows take place.

Action

Washington, D.C., has the nearest bathhouses, but Baltimore has a couple of gay strip joints. Ten dancers perform nightly at the **Custom House Saloon** (⊠ 18 Custom House Ave., ☎ 410/783–8813). Next door is **Le Salon** (☎ 410/347–7555), a porn shop with videos, magazines, and gay buddy booths. **Atlantis** (⊠ 615 Fallsway, ☎ 410/727–9099) in northern downtown is the other popular strip joint. **Leather Underground** (⊠ 136 W. Read St., ☎ 410/528–0991) in Mount Vernon has leather gear, sex toys, cards, and gifts.

SLEEPS

Many major chains have modern facilities around the Inner Harbor, and some older, grander properties dot the Mount Vernon neighborhood. Most downtown hotels are within walking distance of the gay bars and the restaurants on Charles Street and in Fells Point. The two best B&Bs in town, Mr. Mole and Abacrombie Badger, are gay-owned.

For price ranges, *see* lodging Chart B at the front of this guide.

Hotels

$$$$ ⊞ **Harbor Court Hotel.** A centerpiece of Baltimore's Inner Harbor project, this classy property has a contemporary redbrick facade, but its antiques-filled interior recalls a traditional English country home. Ask for a room overlooking the harbor. ⊠ *550 Light St., 21202,* ☎ *410/234–0550 or 800/824–0076,* ℻ *410/659–5925. 203 rooms. 2 restaurants, pool, exercise room.*

$$$–$$$$ ⊞ **Clarion at Mount Vernon Square.** One of Baltimore's top properties, this 1924 former luxury apartment building overlooks the Washington Monument. Rooms have reproduction antiques and marble baths (some with Jacuzzi tubs). ⊠ *612 Cathedral St., 21201,* ☎ *410/727–7101 or 800/292–5500,* ℻ *410/789–3312. 103 rooms. Restaurant.*

$$$–$$$$ ⊞ **Hyatt Regency Inner Harbor.** Sleek furnishings, wood trim, sparkling baths, and beautiful harbor views from many rooms make this a truly first-rate property. It's a zoo during conventions, but the rooms are terrific. ⊠ *300 Light St., 21202,* ☎ *410/528–1234 or 800/233–1234,* ℻ *410/605–2870. 487 rooms. 2 restaurants, pool, health club.*

$$$ ⊞ **Doubletree Inn at the Colonnade.** Business travelers and academics patronize this European-style hotel across the street from Johns Hopkins University and near the Baltimore Museum of Art. It's about 10 minutes north of downtown, but complimentary transportation to the city center is provided. ⊠ *4 W. University Pkwy., 21218,* ☎ *410/235–5400,* ℻ *410/235–5572. 125 rooms. Restaurant, pool, exercise room.*

$$–$$$ ⊞ **Tremont Hotel.** Built as an apartment house in the 1960s, this all-suites property is perfect for long-term stays; each unit has a fully stocked kitchen and plenty of elbow room. It's midway between the gay district and the Inner Harbor, right off Charles Street. The staff works hard to tend to guests' every need. ⊠ *8 E. Pleasant St., 21202,* ☎ *410/576–1200 or 800/638–6266,* ℻ *410/244–1154. 60 suites. Restaurant.*

$$ ⊞ **Tremont Plaza Suite Hotel.** The kitchens and other amenities at this 37-story property are similar to those at the Tremont Hotel, its sister property around the corner, but the variety of room configurations is greater. ⊠ *222 St. Paul Pl.,* ☎ *410/727–2222 or 800/638–6266,* ℻ *410/685–4215. 193 rooms. Restaurant, pool, exercise room.*

$–$$ ⊞ **Mount Vernon Hotel.** If value is a top priority, consider the hotel run by the Baltimore International Culinary College. The staff, made up of students of hospitality, aims to please, and the Washington Café on the ground floor is outstanding. Rooms in this historic hotel are simply furnished, though a few suites have Jacuzzis. ⊠ *24 W. Franklin St., 21201,* ☎ *410/727–2000 or 800/245–5256,* ℻ *410/576–9300. 115 rooms. Restaurant.*

Small Hotels and Guest Houses

$$–$$$ ⊞ **Abacrombie Badger B&B.** The owners of the delightful Mr. Mole B&B opened this property, which has the grace and ambience of a small European hostelry. The restored 1880s house is steps from the Meyerhoff Symphony Hall and close to gay nightlife, Antiques Row, and other Mount Vernon attractions. Rooms are gorgeously furnished but with the modern conveniences you'd expect in a first-rate inn. ⊠ *58 W. Biddle*

St., *21201*, ☎ *410/244–7227*, ℻ *410/244–8415. 12 rooms with phone, TV, and private bath. Continental breakfast. Mixed gay/straight.*

$$–$$$ 🏠 **Mr. Mole B&B.** This 1870s house in the historic Bolton Hill neighborhood is a five-minute drive from Mount Vernon. Its enormous suites have either canopy or four-poster beds and Victorian antiques and reproductions; some have two bedrooms. Hosts Paul Bragaw and Collin Clarke are extremely helpful. This is an ideal spot for couples (single night owls tend to opt for accommodations closer to Mount Vernon bars or the Inner Harbor). ✉ *1601 Bolton St., 21217*, ☎ *410/728–1179*, ℻ *410/728–3379. 5 suites with phone and private bath. Continental breakfast. Mixed gay/straight.*

$$ 🏠 **Biltmore Suites.** Antiques fill the rooms at one of the most characterful hotels in the city. The small, turn-of-the-century hotel is as popular with leisure travelers as it is with business types, who take advantage of a 24-hour executive business center. A bit worn in places, the Biltmore is nevertheless a nice value. ✉ *205 W. Madison St., 21201*, ☎ *410/728– 6550 or 800/868–5064*, ℻ *410/728–5829. 24 rooms with phone, TV, and private bath. Mostly straight.*

THE LITTLE BLACK BOOK

At Your Fingertips

AIDS Action of Baltimore (☎ 410/837–2437). **African-American Coalition for Sexual Minorities** (☎ 410/462–3026). **Baltimore Area Convention and Visitors Association** (✉ 100 Light St., 12th Floor, 21202, ☎ 410/659– 7300; visitor center: ✉ 301 E. Pratt St., ☎ 410/837–4636 or 800/282– 6632, Web site www.baltconvstr.com). **Chase-Brexton Clinic** (☎ 410/ 837–2050). *City Paper* (☎ 410/523–2300; Web site www.citypaper.com). **Gay and Lesbian Community Center of Baltimore** (✉ 241 W. Chase St., ☎ 410/837–5445). **Gay and Lesbian Switchboard** (☎ 410/837–8888). **Metropolitan Transit Authority** (☎ 410/539–5000). **Royal Cab** (☎ 410/327–0330).

Gay Media

The monthly **Baltimore Alternative** (☎ 410/235–3401, Web site www. baltalt.com) and the biweekly **Baltimore Gay Paper** (☎ 410/837–7748, Web site www.bgp.org) are gay and lesbian news and entertainment rags; both are well written and comprehensive.

BOOKSTORES

Lambda Rising (✉ 241 W. Chase St., ☎ 410/234–0069) has a wide selection of lesbian and gay titles, videos, jewelry, porn and nonporn periodicals and newspapers, and out-of-print titles. In Fells Point, **Adrian's Book Cafe** (✉ 714 S. Broadway, ☎ 410/732–1048) has a decent selection of gay and lesbian titles; you can also catch live acoustic music many nights.

Working Out

The very cruisy **Downtown Athletic Club** (✉ 210 E. Centre St., ☎ 410/ 332–0906) is the city's gayest.

4 *Out in Boston*

With Ogunquit, Maine

THE ONE U.S. METROPOLIS whose brisk pace and dignified countenance compares with many European cities,
Boston yields to few American trends and instead marches
to its own drummer. Bostonians have long supported a liberal social climate, especially on women's issues and gay rights—remarkable given the
city's conservative roots. Local politics and culture, however, are largely
shaped by the intellectuals who inhabit the area's elite colleges and universities and foster a climate of discourse and a groovy egalitarian ethic.

Issues that feed on Boston's sometimes conflicting devotions to tradition
and fairness do make headlines from time to time: Should gays be allowed
to march in the St. Patrick's Day Parade? At the moment, they may not.
Should former first baseman Bill Buckner be forgiven for committing an
error that cost the Red Sox the 1986 World Series? At the moment, he's
not. But on the whole Boston is steady and unflappable, a city with an
unmistakably charming demeanor.

Outsiders sometimes find it difficult to crack a cohesive queer community in which everybody seems to know everybody else. On the other hand,
gays and lesbians permeate not only every civic and corporate echelon
but also the streetscape—it's difficult to walk anywhere and not make
eye contact with others "in the life."

Boston is a culture-vulture's dream. The region's academic vibrancy contributes to a superb fine- and performing-arts scene—tens of thousands
of full- and part-time students display an insatiable appetite for high-brow
diversions, from film and literary festivals to avant-garde art exhibitions.
Neighborhoods are abundant with museums and engaging architecture—
the Back Bay, the South End, Beacon Hill, parts of Cambridge—and thrive
with gay-popular shops, eateries, and hangouts.

THE LAY OF THE LAND

Compact and attractive, Boston is a walker's city. Points north and east
of the famous Common have the broadest appeal to most visitors; here
you'll find notable historic sites, museums, and shopping districts. Beacon Hill is a well-to-do, somewhat conservative residential neighborhood
with a mostly Federal architectural facade. Government Center is corporate on weekdays and always touristy. The North End, the most densely
populated neighborhood in Colonial days, is today the city's Italian
neighborhood. South and west of the Common, late-Victorian Back Bay,
one of the wealthiest areas of Boston, has a younger, hip spirit. The
South End is more modest in scale and appearance, ethnically diverse,
and, despite skyrocketing rents, still extremely gay.

The Common and Environs

The **Boston Common** has been the city hub since 1630. The Boylston and Tremont streets side are dowdier than the stretch along stately Beacon Street, but the whole park merits exploration. The adjacent **Boston Public Garden** (☎ 617/635–4505), with a placid pond traversed in summer by foot pedal–powered swan boats, also contains formal gardens.

One of the nation's earliest urban residential neighborhoods, **Beacon Hill** was settled in the early 1800s by the city's wealthiest merchants and is today the domain of brick sidewalks, town houses, shade trees, and boutiques (the best are on Charles Street). At the corner of Park and Beacon streets, overlooking the Common, stands Charles Bulfinch's golden-domed neoclassical **State House** (☎ 617/727–3676). A bit north, just across the Charles River from the drab West End, are the estimable **Museum of Science** (✉ Science Park, ☎ 617/723–2500), which has more than 400 exhibits, the Charles Hayden Planetarium, and the Mugar Omni Theater.

Northeast of the Common is **Government Center,** a jumble of 1960s-era civic buildings and office blocks. Just east is **Quincy Market,** an extremely touristy complex of specialty food shops, restaurants, bars, and retail stores. The food stalls hawk everything from gelato to fried dough to Italian sausages to steamed clams.

Many popular sights are nearby, most easily visited by walking along the **Freedom Trail,** a mile-and-a-half self-guided historic tour marked with a painted red line along the sidewalk. Note the 1713 **Old State House** (✉ 206 Washington St., ☎ 617/720–3290)**, the site of the Boston Massacre** (in front of the Old State House), and several churches and burial grounds. Just east of Quincy Market, along Central Wharf, is the always-packed **New England Aquarium** (☎ 617/973–5200).

Northwest of Government Center, across the hideous Fitzgerald Expressway, is Boston's **North End,** a network of narrow, crooked streets and 19th-century brick tenements that house one of the nation's most prominent Italian communities. In addition to fine restaurants, you'll find such important Freedom Trail sites as the **Paul Revere House** (✉ 19 North Sq., ☎ 617/523–1676) and the 1723 **Old North Church** (✉ 193 Salem St., ☎ 617/523–6676).

Southeast of Government Center is the closest thing Boston has to a downtown, although you rarely hear Bostonians refer to it as such. High-rise office buildings now dominate this labyrinthine network of streets laid out in Colonial times. Shop among throngs of aggressive bargain seekers along **Washington Street** at the original **Filene's Basement** (✉ 426 Washington St., ☎ 617/542–2011) or nearby **Macy's** (✉ 450 Washington St., ☎ 617/357–3000). Farther south, around Essex and Beach streets, is a small but lively **Chinatown.**

The South End

The **South End's** early flourish as an enclave of gentility was short-lived (hard to believe now). Most of the neighborhood's bowfront redbrick homes, many embellished with elaborate details, were built in the 1850s. By the turn of the century, however, the South End had fallen in stature and been cut off from the rest of Boston by rail lines. Over the next 60 years, middle-class blacks and incoming Middle Easterners, Asians, and Latin Americans moved in. Although wide-scale gentrification here was gradual, the neighborhood did attract students, artists, and young professionals in the '60s. By the early '80s a gay ghetto had been born.

The South End is now better identified as an upscale professional neighborhood than as a predominantly gay one, so much so that its rents and property values have begun to match those of glitzy Back Bay. Still, its main commercial spines, **Columbus Avenue** and **Tremont Street,** are loaded with gay-popular restaurants, cafés, and businesses. Queers are also migrating in a southerly direction, helping rejuvenate the once undesirable blocks around **Shawmut Avenue.** Between Tremont and Shawmut, **Union Square Park** has meticulous gardens and a grand fountain in a center grassy mall. Late at night, locals appear—often under the guise of walking bleary-eyed dogs—to see what's happening (something very often is).

Back Bay and the Fens

Although Beacon Hill and the South End have a distinctly British character, the relatively young **Back Bay** (a tidal flat before the 1860s), with its broad avenues of four-story town houses, its grid layout, and its bustle of sidewalk cafés and swank boutiques, recalls late-19th-century Paris. Although most of the magnificent single-family homes that attracted wealthy families from Beacon Hill have now been gutted and subdivided, it's still one of Boston's preeminent residential neighborhoods.

The Back Bay's long east–west streets are ideal for walking: Beacon and Marlborough streets are predominantly residential and have some of the neighborhood's most impressive single-family homes. Commonwealth Avenue is divided by a gracious grassy mall. Newbury Street is lined with shops and eateries that range from high-end, up by the Public Garden, to funky and collegiate, down toward Mass Ave. Boylston is the most commercial. Both the 62-floor **John Hancock Tower** (✉ Trinity Pl. and St. James Ave., ☎ 617/247–1977) and the 52-story **Prudential Tower** (✉ 800 Boylston St., ☎ 617/859–0648) have phenomenal views for miles around Boston; the latter is surrounded by an indoor shopping mall. Just west of the Pru and southwest of Copley Square is **Copley Place** (✉ 100 Huntington Ave., ☎ 617/375–4400), a larger and more upscale mall anchored by the Westin and the Marriott Copley Place hotels.

West of Mass Ave is **the Fens,** the final piece in Boston's jigsaw puzzle of landfill, an amalgam of residential and shaggy industrial blocks and site of **Northeastern** and **Boston universities.** The topographical feature that defines the neighborhood, however, is the amorphous **Back Bay Fens Park,** the only area of tidal marshlands that was never filled in with gravel as Boston expanded. Landscape architect Frederick Law Olmsted converted this wilderness into a (subtly) manicured park. On its south side is the **Museum of Fine Arts** (✉ 465 Huntington Ave., ☎ 617/267–9300), whose highlights include the Asiatic art and French Impressionists, plus works by John Singleton Copley, Winslow Homer, John Singer Sargent, and Edward Hopper. Two blocks west is the **Isabella Stewart Gardner Museum** (✉ 280 The Fenway, ☎ 617/566–1401), a stunning if idiosyncratic collection of art and furniture (mostly Western European) that began as the private holdings of Mrs. Gardner, an avid, eccentric, Brahmin art collector who stipulated in her will that everything in her palazzo remain just as she left it. On the western side of the park is a small residential enclave of attractive apartment buildings and row houses that is fashionable with young artists and students (it too, however, has experienced a recent rent drive). To the north is quirky **Fenway Park,** one of the smallest and oldest (1912) baseball stadiums in the major leagues, behind which are gay and straight discos.

Cambridge

Often lumped in as just another of Boston's many neighborhoods, **Cambridge** is a small, independent city of 100,000. It was settled in 1630 and six years later became home to the nation's first university, **Harvard** (walking tours, ☎ 617/495–1573), which remains a top tourist draw. Dozens of shops and eateries line the streets around **Harvard Square** (at Mass Ave and John F. Kennedy St.). Within steps of it are such impressive institutions as **Widener Library** (✉ Harvard Yard, ☎ 617/495–

2413), with the country's second-largest book collection; the **Fogg Art Museum** (⌂ 32 Quincy St., ☎ 617/495–9400), whose 80,000 holdings concentrate mostly on European and American painting; the **Arthur M. Sackler Museum** (⌂ 485 Broadway, ☎ 617/495–9400), which emphasizes Asiatic, ancient Greek and Roman, and Egyptian, Buddhist, and Islamic art; and the mammoth **Harvard University Museums of Cultural and Natural History** (⌂ 26 Oxford St., ☎ 617/495–3045).

About 1½ miles southeast is the **Massachusetts Institute of Technology** (MIT; Information Center: ⌂ Building Seven, 77 Massachusetts Ave., ☎ 617/253–4795), which fringes the Charles River near **Kendall Square,** a small dining and shopping hub. Not as exhilarating to tour as Harvard's, MIT's 135-acre campus does have a few small museums and some noteworthy architecture by I. M. Pei and Eero Saarinen.

Cambridge, along with Watertown to the west and Somerville to the east, has a high population of both gay men and women, and in recent years the area around **Central Square**—midway between Harvard and MIT—has become especially popular with lesbians. Right off the Square are several excellent Indian and East Asian restaurants, plus a couple of gay-popular hangouts and bars.

Jamaica Plain

For queers, **Jamaica Plain** is Boston's top "streetcar suburb," known for placid Jamaica Pond and the once-exclusive residential neighborhood around it. This enclave was rediscovered over the past two decades by city dwellers in search of affordable housing. Check out the handful of homo-popular restaurants and coffeehouses, including **Pluto** (⌂ 603 Centre St., ☎ 617/522–0054), a small shop selling gay cards and gifts.

GETTING AROUND

Boston has an extensive bus, trolley, and subway system (referred to as "the T"), but most lines shut down by 1 AM, which can be inconvenient if you're out until the bars close. In fact, the city is *extremely* walkable, and, as it was laid out before the automobile, driving can be nerve-wracking. Find a parking garage and walk or take public transportation to get around. A car is useful to reach the pocket of clubs near Fenway Park (there are garages here). Taxis line up near the busiest clubs around closing time; if you need one at other times, head to a hotel stand.

EATS

The Boston dining scene is exciting and innovative. Young, trendy neighborhood bistros—many of them strung through the South End, the Back Bay, and Beacon Hill—borrow more from San Francisco than they do from Puritan Massachusetts. Boston bistros usually take the form of an intimate, storefront dining room with working a fireplace, exposed brick, indirect lighting, and a menu anchored by that trinity of contemporary Italian dining: designer pizza, risotto, and a fish grill. As with any city, the most touristy areas have the crummiest food, although the stalls at Quincy Market are ideal for snacking. Most kitchens close by 10 PM; for after-hours eating, try the **IHOP** in Kenmore Square (⌂ 500 Commonwealth Ave., ☎ 617/859–0458), not far from the Fenway Park nightspots. In Chinatown, the **Imperial Seafood House** (⌂ 70 Beach St., ☎ 617/426–8439) and **East Ocean City** (⌂ 27 Beach St., ☎ 617/542–2504) entertain legions of hungry disco queens.

For price ranges, *see* dining Chart A at the front of this guide.

Boston

$$$$ ✕ **Biba.** One of Boston's original New American restaurants, Biba is no longer the *in* place it once was, but it's still a hot ticket. The food spans the globe; a favorite is pan-fried oysters on semolina blini. It's a perfect perch from which to watch passersby on Boylston Street. ⊠ *272 Boylston St.,* ☎ *617/426–7878.*

$$$$ ✕ **Hamersley's Bistro.** One of the first restaurants to attract serious diners to the South End, Hamersley's has both a café and a more formal dining room in an elegant but spare space inside the Boston Center for the Arts. Notable dishes include duck confit with a garlic, fennel, and white bean napoleon, and saddle of monkfish with greens, asparagus, a lemon confit, and herb sauce. ⊠ *553 Tremont St.,* ☎ *617/423–2700.*

$$$–$$$$ ✕ **Restaurant Zinc.** This intimate contemporary French bistro near the edge of the South End specializes in healthful seafood dishes and light sauces. Typical is pan-seared Rockport lobster with a succotash of sweet corn, peas, baby turnips, wild mushrooms, and a crispy potato cake. Later in the evening pretty people congregate around the imported zinc bar. ⊠ *35 Stanhope St.,* ☎ *617/262–2323.*

$$$ ✕ **Metropolis.** Local South Enders were skeptical when their neighborhood ice cream parlor was transformed into yet another pricey New American café, but the results have been tremendous. Dishes like herb-crusted pork tenderloin with sweet-onion balsamic mashed potatoes and pear currant chutney are a far cry from ice cream sundaes (which are still offered, by the way). ⊠ *584 Tremont St.,* ☎ *617/247–2931.*

$$–$$$ ✕ **Appetito.** Attractive outgoing waiters; a festive color scheme of mustard yellow, plum, emerald, and cobalt; and well-prepared, reasonably priced food—it all adds up to a terrific restaurant. The northern Italian fare includes such stars as a saffron-infused seafood risotto with marinated swordfish, scallops, shrimp, and calamari. ⊠ *1 Appleton St.,* ☎ *617/338–6777.*

$$–$$$ ✕ **Club Café.** Attached to the gay bar complex of the same name, the Club Café is equally popular with men and women. Expect New American food (such as grilled swordfish with a mango and toasted-almond salsa and a cilantro-lime aioli), a nice wine list, and friendly but sometimes slow service. There's also an affordable café menu with sandwiches and munchies. ⊠ *209 Columbus Ave.,* ☎ *617/536–0966.*

$$–$$$ ✕ **Cottonwood Café.** Both locations—one in Cambridge, another in the Back Bay—are high-profile hangouts. The sleek Southwestern decor fits nicely with offbeat dishes like grilled red chili sausage with cracked black pepper fettucine, sun-dried tomatoes, jalapeños, and mushrooms. ⊠ *222 Berkeley St.,* ☎ *617/247–2225; in Cambridge:* ⊠ *1815 Massachusetts Ave.,* ☎ *617/661–7440.*

$$–$$$ ✕ **Franklin Cafe.** This friendly neighborhood South Ender maintains a loyal following with its attentive waitstaff and excellent, fairly priced New American fare. The menu changes seasonally—you might catch seared soy-marinated chicken liver, and roasted-turkey meatloaf with spiced fig gravy. ⊠ *278 Shawmut Ave.,* ☎ *617/350–0010.*

$$–$$$ ✕ **Giacomo's.** This is as authentic an Italian dining experience as you'll find. In a handsome South End storefront (there's a straighter one in the North End), Giacomo's emphasizes pasta, chicken, and grilled fish; the yellowfin tuna with balsamic and mint vinaigrette, grilled potatoes, and vegetables is especially good. ⊠ *431 Columbus Ave.,* ☎ *617/536–5723; also in the North End,* ⊠ *355 Hanover St.,* ☎ *617/523–9026.*

$$ ✕ **Botolph's on Tremont.** In the heart of the South End, Botolph's is where you go to model designer duds and newly rippled abs. The pretty decor—a high-ceilinged storefront with tile floors—provides a suitable backdrop for posing. The menu emphasizes pastas, pizzas, grains, and grills, with a healthy Tuscan flair. ⊠ *569 Tremont St.,* ☎ *617/424–8577.*

Boston

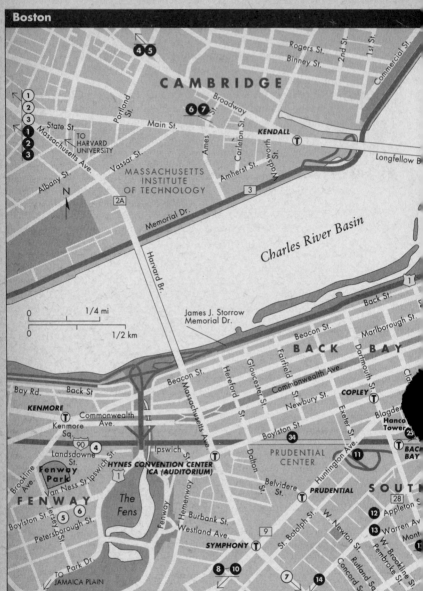

Eats ●

Appetito, **24**
Bertucci's, **25**
Biba, **30**
Blue Diner/
The Artzone, **32**
Blue Room, **6**
Blue Wave Rotisserie
and Grill, **28**
Bob the Chef's, **14**

Botolph's on
Tremont, **15**
Cafe Zinc, **26**
Centre Street Café, **8**
Club Café, **27**
Club Passim
Coffee Shop, **1**
Coffee Cantata
Bistro and Beans, **10**

Cottonwood
Café, **2, 29**
Deluxe Cafe, **23**
East Coast Grill, **5**
Five Seasons, **9**
Franklin Cafe, **22**
Gargoyles, **3**
Geoffrey's, **18**
Giacamos, **12, 33**

Hamersley's
Bistro, **16**
Jae's Café, **4, 13, 31**
Legal Sea
Foods, **7, 11, 34**
Metropolis, **17**
Mildred's, **19**
On the Park, **20**
To Go Bakery, **21**

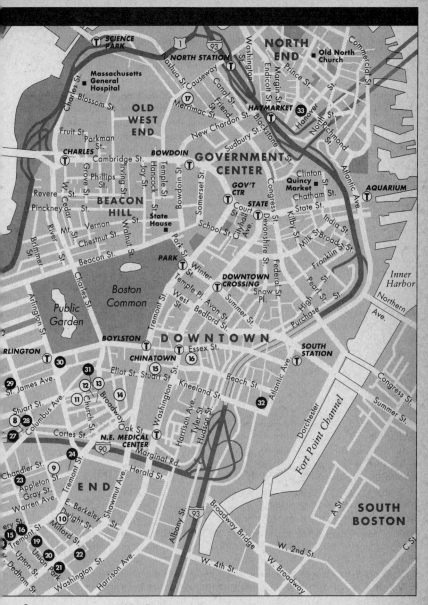

$$ ✕ **On the Park.** Overlooking the lower South End's splendid Union Park, this chic art-filled neighborhood café serves a well-rounded selection of comfort dishes—Chilean sea bass in a lobster broth, hangar steak—at easily digested prices. There can be a long wait for brunch (try the wild-mushroom eggs Benedict). ⊠ *1 Union Park,* ☎ *617/426–0862.*

$–$$ ✕ **Blue Wave Rotisserie and Grill.** With its creatively presented comfort foods—pasta dishes, rotisserie chickens, thick sandwiches, and salads—the Blue Wave is a good place to fill up. Huge floor-to-ceiling storefront windows can make it seem as though you're eating in a window display. Has a big guppie following. ⊠ *142 Berkeley St.,* ☎ *617/424–6711.*

$–$$ ✕ **Delux Café.** Once a frightening dive, Delux is proof of slacker generation-X life in otherwise ungroovy Boston. The inelegant decor, with its crummy Formica tables, strings of lights, and an Elvis shrine on the half shell, is offset by truly delicious and eclectic food like salmon wrapped in parchment paper with new potatoes, carrots, fennel, and peas. The service sucks but that's part of the adventure. ⊠ *100 Chandler St.,* ☎ *617/ 338–5258. No credit cards.*

$–$$ ✕ **Geoffrey's.** Known for hearty breakfasts and lunches, Geoffrey's is one of the gayest restaurants in Boston. Ceiling fans, red walls, and framed prints adorn the completely informal bright dining room. Try the grilled chicken sandwich with corn and black-bean salad, or filling sides like garlic mashed potatoes. ⊠ *578 Tremont St.,* ☎ *617/266–1122.*

$–$$ ✕ **Jae's Café.** This happily bizarre hole-in-the-wall has a few tables on the sidewalk, a sushi bar in the basement, and cute, flirtatious waiters. The basement, with exposed brick, a big fish tank, and a neon clock, is the choice seating area. The Pan-Asian menu offers everything from pad Thai to buckwheat noodles to miso soup. ⊠ *520 Columbus Ave.,* ☎ *617/ 421–9405;* ⊠ *212 Stuart St.,* ☎ *617/451–7788; in Cambridge,* ⊠ *1281 Cambridge St.,* ☎ *617/497–_____.*

$ ✕ **Bertucci's.** On the fringe of the South End, this particular branch of the New England pizza chain has an amazingly queer following. Pies are baked in a brick oven and come with dozens of great toppings. Portions are huge—even for an order of garlic bread or a dinner salad. ⊠ *39–45 Stanhope St.,* ☎ *617/247–6161.*

$ ✕ **Bob the Chef's.** Famed for its Sunday jazz brunch, this soul-food hangout with great sweet-potato pie and authentic Southern-style barbecue is very popular with the community, though the heavy food may render you immobile for several hours after consuming it. ⊠ *604 Columbus Ave.,* ☎ *617/536–6204.*

$ ✕ **Blue Diner/The Artzone.** The Blue Diner dates from 1945, is gay as can be late on weekend nights (it's open 24 hours), and serves the usual blue-plate specials: a great corned-beef hash, a full crab-cake dinner, and gooey baked macaroni and cheese. Art exhibits are held in the back room. ⊠ *150 Kneeland St.,* ☎ *617/338–4639.*

Cambridge, Somerville, and Jamaica Plain

$$–$$$ ✕ **Blue Room.** One of the best restaurants in the area, the Blue Room is hip, funky, informal, smart, and international, with foods from Latin America, Europe, and Asia. The location is convenient to Central Square's nightclubs. The front-counter seating is ideal for mingling. ⊠ *1 Kendall Sq., Cambridge,* ☎ *617/494–9034.*

$$–$$$ ✕ **East Coast Grill.** "Equatorial cuisine" draws crowds to this small, very popular spot. Key tests of your strength: pasta from hell (enlivened with hot sauce); North Carolina barbecue; and ethnic dishes such as grilled tuna with soy, ginger, and wasabi. It's low-key and lots of fun. ⊠ *1271 Cambridge St., Cambridge,* ☎ *617/491–6568.*

$$–$$$ ✕ **Gargoyles.** This artsy neighborhood bistro in Somerville is worth the trip for such New American delicacies as grilled salmon with sweet-pea ravioli, carrot juice, and four-radish slaw, and Maine mussels with polenta

and a chipotle and roasted-corn cream sauce. Hipsters and funkstersjam the snappy contemporary dining room. Live jazz many nights. ⊠ *215 Elm St., Somerville,* ☎ *617/776–5300.*

$$–$$$ ✕ **Legal Sea Foods.** Although locals insist this local chain lacks the authentic feel of a true wharf-side seafood shanty, you can't beat the quality and freshness. Legal is notable for its straightforward preparation of dozens of varieties of fish—broiled, baked, Cajun, or fried. The appetizers of seafood chowder and the smoked bluefish pâté are outstanding. ⊠ *5 Cambridge Center in Kendall Sq.,* ☎ *617/864–3400; in Back Bay:* ⊠ *Copley Place, 100 Huntington Ave.,* ☎ *617/266–7775;* ⊠ *800 Boylston St.,* ☎ *617/266–6800.*

$–$$ ✕ **Centre Street Café.** Jamaica Plain's lesbo central has some great cheap eats—like black-bean burritos, smoked-bluefish cakes, and bountiful veggie sandwiches—and a homey atmosphere that's good for making friends. A bulletin board has tons of information on upcoming readings and meetings. ⊠ *597 Centre St., Jamaica Plain,* ☎ *617/524–9217.*

$–$$ ✕ **Five Seasons Café.** About 80% of the dishes at this crunchy spot are vegetarian, and all use organic ingredients—tofu ravioli with walnut-cilantro pesto was a recent special. Ferns and hanging greenery adorn the bright little dining room. ⊠ *669 Centre St., Jamaica Plain,* ☎ *617/524–9016.*

Coffeehouse Culture

Coffee Cantata Bistro and Beans. Exposed brick walls, varnished wooden tables with Windsor chairs, and a bright red ceiling warm up the atmosphere in this cheerful, earthy coffeehouse, which sometimes seems like a nesting ground for budding lesbian relationships. ⊠ *605 Centre St., Jamaica Plain,* ☎ *617/522–2223.*

Club Passim Coffee Shop. If you expect more than snacks and light lunches from a coffeehouse, this is your place: funky cards, gifts, and jewelry are all also on offer. Good folk and acoustic entertainment many nights attracts lots of cute academics. ⊠ *47 Palmer St., Cambridge,* ☎ *617/492–7679.*

Mildred's. Upbeat Mildred's delights South End straights and queens with great salads, pastas, and sandwiches in a sunny storefront dining room. ⊠ *552 Tremont,* ☎ *617/426–0008.*

To Go Bakery. Opposite Union Square Park, this tiny corner bakery has coffees, salads, and delicious sandwiches and sweets. On sunny days you'll always see a few queers hanging out at one of the sidewalk tables, soaking up the atmosphere. ⊠ *324 Shawmut Ave.,* ☎ *617/482–1015.*

SCENES

Boston's bar scene is chided for being a throwback to the city's Brahmin heritage—blue-blooded white guys in collared shirts chatting, without impiety, about their beloved city. In fact, though Milquetoasts are not uncommon, Boston has a diverse club scene. Crowds may seem a bit aloof, but conversation is not hard to come by—outsiders just have to make the first move. The bar scene is spread among several neighborhoods; only in two pockets—by Fenway Park and in Bay Village near the intersection of Stuart and Church streets—are gay bars clustered. Bars close at 2, and Boston observes the barbaric practice of denying establishments the right to hold happy hours or offer drink specials.

Boston

PRIME SUSPECTS

Boston Eagle. Once a fixture of the city's leather scene, the Eagle has gradually shifted into a low-key cruise-and-chat bar in the South End, drawing a friendly crowd. A few eagle statues and some old posters bear testimony to the bar's bearish past. Otherwise this intimate, if cramped, tavern with a popular pool table is like any other pick-up spot. Cheap and potent drinks are a plus. ⊠ *520 Tremont St.,* ☏ *617/542–4494. Crowd: mostly male, 20s to 40s; local guys; some racial mix; lots of flannel, baseball caps, jeans, T-shirts.*

Boston Ramrod. Sort of a Disneyesque vision of what a leather bar should look like, today's Ramrod is nothing like the rough-and-rowdy club it was in the '80s. It's still seedy, but in a self-conscious way, and on some nights, the linen actually overpowers the leather. On weekends things get serious, when the back room—dimly lit and filled with black-oil-barrel statuary—has a rubber and leather dress code. The rest of the bar is surprisingly well lit and decorated a bit like a frat house rec room. Very big on Thursdays. ⊠ *1254 Boylston St.,* ☏ *617/266–2986. Crowd: male, some hard-core leather men, more often a hodgepodge of curious guppies and overflow from the nearby discos, very mixed in age.*

Chaps. One of New England's longest-running cruise bars, Chaps moved into spacious, slick new digs in the theater district in December 1997. It remains a hot choice for dancing and lounging. Tuesday night's classic disco party is a must-attend for many club kids. ⊠ *100 Warrenton St.,* ☏ *617/695–9500. Crowd: 80/20 m/f, all ages, very cruisy, strong Latino following, mellower than the Club Café but hipper than Luxor.*

Club Café/Moonshine. Despite its dull name, the Club Café is one of the smarter spots in the city. Above the queer Metropolitan Gym, it also has a nice New American restaurant (*see* Eats, *above*). The front end of the bar area is a sophisticated little cocktail lounge and cabaret that's popular with suits after work—this section is 50/50 male/female. In back is a larger, crowded, somewhat attitudy video bar, Moonshine, that's only open Thursday to Saturday. ⊠ *209 Columbus Ave.,* ☏ *617/536–0966. Crowd: 70/30 m/f, guppie, clean-cut, collegiate, generally under 35.*

Luxor/Jox. In the quasi-gay Bay Village neighborhood near Jacques and the Napoleon Club, this two-story compound consists of a downstairs sports bar (Jox) and an upstairs video bar (Luxor). Luxor is the more inviting section, with rows of seats overlooking the many video screens—they play campy movies—and a couple of small bars with lots of room to stand or sit. Great kitschy Egyptian murals on several walls. Gay Bostonians, like their straight counterparts, take their sports seriously, so Jox is packed and lively whenever there's a game on. ⊠ *69 Church St.,* ☏ *617/423–6969. Crowd: mostly male, late 20s to 30s, regular Joes.*

Paragon/The Spike. This new club south of downtown has a hard-core leather bar, the Spike, downstairs, and a large disco, Paragon, upstairs. There are two bars and a snug corner lounge that's ideal for getting to know new friends. Paragon (open Thursday–Saturday) features R&B, soul, and reggae on Thursdays; Latin music on Fridays; and deep house Saturdays. The location is the only drag: well south of even the South End, in a section of Newmarket Square bordering Roxbury—do not try to walk here. ⊠ *965 Massachusetts Ave.,* ☏ *617/427–7807. Crowd: mostly male, young, mixed racially, club kids, leather at the Spike.*

The Spot. A mixed gay/straight club (known as Quest on gay nights, as that was its name for the many years it was a mostly gay bar), the Spot's top attribute is its cool roof deck. The other three (long and narrow) levels aren't bad, either: The third floor is good for dancing; the second floor has a bar, sofas, and video screens; and the basement is a stand-and-pose bar. Friday is the most popular night, when the crowd is similar to that of Avalon (*see below*) on Sundays. ⊠ *1270 Boylston St.,* ☏ *617/424–7747. Crowd: mixed m/f, young, 18-and-over on gay nights, somewhat grungy; officially queer on Monday and Friday, and family-friendly other nights.*

can open. ✉ *47 Huntington Ave., 02116,* ☎ *617/536–9000 or 800/225–7062,* 🆁 *617/267–3547. 132 rooms. Restaurants.*

$$–$$$ 🏨 **Tremont House.** This elegant 1925 hotel, a Theater District bargain, has a spacious lobby with high ceilings, marble columns, a marble stairway, and extensive gold leafing. The compact guest rooms have been jazzed up with reproductions of 18th-century antiques and stately prints from the Museum of Fine Arts. ✉ *275 Tremont St., 02116,* ☎ *617/426–1400 or 800/331–9998,* 🆁 *617/338–7881. 315 rooms.*

$$ 🏨 **John Jeffries.** Owing to its remote location at the end of fashionable Charles Street, this tasteful, turn-of-the-century gem is one the best-kept bargain secrets in the city. Rooms are large and furnished with colonial reproductions and Monet-print fabrics. They all have small kitchens and spacious baths; many have views of the Charles. ✉ *14 Embankment Rd., 02114,* ☎ *617/367–1866,* 🆁 *617/742–0313. 46 rooms.*

$–$$ 🏨 **Buckminster.** This is a good budget choice close to the Fens and Boston University. It feels a bit dormlike—with kitchen and laundry facilities on every floor—but rooms are clean and large. The concierge can usually give a few tips about the gay scene. ✉ *645 Beacon St., 02215,* ☎ *617/236–7050 or 800/727–2825,* 🆁 *617/262–0068. 120 rooms.*

$–$$ 🏨 **Chandler Inn.** With a gay bar on the ground floor, this otherwise unmemorable hostelry is one of the most gay-frequented you'll ever find. The small but clean guest rooms have blond wood furnishings and small writing desks; the baths are very small. You'll be treated like family, usually by "family," and the price is fair. ✉ *26 Chandler St., 02116,* ☎ *617/482–3450 or 800/842–3450,* 🆁 *617/542–3428. 56 rooms.*

Cambridge

$$$ 🏨 **Inn at Harvard.** A favorable Harvard Square location accounts for the tremendous popularity of this refined, discreet hotel that was created to house university visitors but is open to all. Rooms have pieces on loan from the Fogg Art Museum and tasteful, contemporary furnishings. ✉ *1201 Massachusetts Ave., 02138,* ☎ *617/491–2222 or 800/222–8733,* 🆁 *617/491–6520. 113 rooms.*

$ 🏨 **Susse Chalet Inn.** This no-frills chain property is the ideal budget choice in Cambridge, just a short walk from the Red Line T terminus and a 10-minute drive from Harvard Square. ✉ *211 Concord Tpke., 02140,* ☎ *617/661–7800 or 800/524–2538,* 🆁 *617/868–8153. 78 rooms. Exercise room.*

Small Hotels and Guest Houses

Boston

In addition to the inns reviewed below, two women in a historic town house in the South End rent one room, the 🏨 **Victorian Bed and Breakfast** (call for the address, ☎ 617/536–3285) to women only; it's a large room (full breakfast included) with an Oriental rug, simple furnishings, a huge tile bathroom, and bay windows overlooking the street.

$$–$$$ 🏨 **Clarendon Square B&B.** Innkeepers Stephen Gross and Michael Selbst bought a dilapidated South End Victorian town house and have turned it into one of the finest small inns in the city, with open airy rooms, eclectic and stylish furnishings, and a sunny balcony off the back. Though small, the place has the amenities both leisure and business travelers need, including phones with voice mail. ✉ *81 Warren Ave., 02116,* ☎ *617/536–2229, e-mail reservations@clarendonsquare.com. 3 rooms with phone, TV, and private bath. Continental breakfast. Mixed gay/straight.*

$$ 🏨 **Eliot and Pickett Houses.** Not many tourists know about this pair of adjoining historic Beacon Hill mansions with a beautiful deck overlooking the State House and Boston Common. Owned by the gay-friendly Unitarian Universalist Church, the inn has large rooms with modern baths

and a pleasing but simple mix of reproduction antiques and comfy, homey furniture. ⊠ *6 Mt. Vernon Pl. (mail: 25 Beacon St., 02108)*, ☎ *617/248– 8707*, FAX *617/742–1364; Web site www.uua.org/ep. 20 rooms with phone, most with private bath. Continental breakfast. Mostly straight.*

$–$$ 🏠 **463 Beacon Street.** On a lovely tree-lined thoroughfare, this charm-ing town house overlooks, among other things, a frat house across the way. The rooms, unfortunately, could stand a makeover; they have dated functional furnishings, but they're large and several have fireplaces and kitchenettes. ⊠ *463 Beacon St., 02115*, ☎ *617/536–1302*, FAX *617/247– 8876. 20 rooms, most with phone, TV, and private bath. Mixed gay/straight.*

$ 🏠 **Oasis Guesthouse.** This lively, social guest house comprises two ad-joining redbrick buildings about a 15-minute walk from the South End and the bars near Fenway Park. Rooms are small but bright with oak furnishings and a mix of antiques and contemporary pieces. The staff is extremely friendly and helpful. There's a deck for sunning. ⊠ *22 Edgerly Rd., 02115*, ☎ *617/267–2262*, FAX *617/267–1920. 16 rooms, some with private bath, phone, and TV. Continental breakfast. Mostly gay male.*

THE LITTLE BLACK BOOK

At Your Fingertips
AIDS Action Committee (☎ 617/536–7733). **Boston Cab Association** (☎ 617/536–5010). **Boston Living Center** (AIDS resource, ⊠ 29 Stanhope St., ☎ 617/236–1012) is a drop-in center for all persons affected by AIDS and HIV. **Boston Phoenix** (alternative weekly, ☎ 617/536–5390, Web site www.bostonphoenix.com). **Boston Welcome Center** (⊠ 140 Tremont St., 02111, ☎ 617/451–2227 or 800/765–4482). **Cambridge Women's Cen-ter** (46 Pleasant St., Cambridge, ☎ 617/354–8807). **Gay and Lesbian Med-ical Helpline** (☎ 617/267–9001). **Greater Boston Convention and Visitors Bureau** (⊠ Box 490, Prudential Tower, 02199, ☎ 617/536–4100). **Massachusetts AIDS Hotline** (☎ 800/235–2331). **Massachusetts Bay Transportation Authority** (MBTA, ☎ 617/222–3200 or 800/392–6100).

Gay Media
Bay Windows (☎ 617/266–6670, e-mail letters@baywindows.com) is New England's major lesbian and gay newspaper. It has extensive articles, club information, advertisements, and personals. *IN Newsweekly* (☎ 617/723–5130) is similar but more Boston-focused. The best resource for women and lesbians is *Sojourner: The Women's Forum* (☎ 617/524–0415), which includes articles, resources, and fiction. Also look for *Bad Attitude* (☎ 617/395–4849), a bimonthly news and entertainment magazine for lesbians.

BOOKSTORES
The **Glad Day Bookshop** (⊠ 673 Boylston St., ☎ 617/267–3010), di-rectly across from the Public Library, has a great selection of lesbian and gay titles. Toward the back is an extensive porn selection—from books to videos to magazines, new and used. The South End also has a won-derful lesbigay bookstore, **We Think The World Of You** (⊠ 540 Tremont St., ☎ 617/423–1965), which has music, cards, a few mainstream titles, and a helpful staff. **New Words—A Women's Bookstore** (⊠ 186 Hamp-shire St., Cambridge, ☎ 617/876–5310) is the area's premier feminist and lesbian bookstore, with a great selection.

Working Out
The major gay and lesbian guppie gym is the **Metropolitan Health Club** (⊠ 209 Columbus Ave., ☎ 617/536–3006), which is just below the Club Café restaurant and bar complex. It's a major scene. One of the longest-running gay gyms in the Northeast, **Mike's Gym II** (560 Harrison St., ☎ 617/338–6210) gets plenty of big muscle guys.

OGUNQUIT, MAINE

Although it had existed as a village within the town limits of Wells since 1913, tiny Ogunquit (60 miles north of Boston) was not incorporated until 1980. Flanked by a 3-mile beach—one of the most beautiful in the state—and rich with art and theater history, the town has long been a quieter, simpler gay alternative to Provincetown.

Painters first discovered the village in the early part of the century, and the Ogunquit Playhouse, one of the country's first successful summer theaters, opened in 1939. The gay presence grew in the '60s, when a beatnik contingent began summering here, and then boomed in the '70s, when the town finally opened its first gay guest house and a gay disco, Anabelle's (now the Club). Ogunquit now has several more guest houses, and a second bar.

The scene is low-key and the gay and lesbian residents here are content to keep it that way. There will probably never be a gay pride parade or an attempt to pass any gay rights laws—as one local put it, "Many of us are just your average Republicans, except for the time we spend between the sheets."

Lay of the Land

Ogunquit is a tiny village. Most of the gay-popular inns and businesses are in the village center along **U.S. 1**, the main commercial route through town. From here it's a short walk to the beach. The primary tourist months here are July and August, but all weekends from May though October are busy.

Getting Around

You'll need a car to reach Ogunquit; from Boston, take I–95 North into Maine; then take Exit 4 to U.S. 1 and head north 7 miles. Once here the town is easy to navigate on foot; a trolley makes a regular loop between the beach and the few attractions.

Eats

For price ranges, *see* dining Chart B at the front of this guide.

$$$–$$$$ ✕ **Arrows.** This dignified farmhouse restaurant is on every critic's short list of the top restaurants in Maine (if you're planning to dine here on a summer weekend, reserve a week ahead). You may find it stuffy, but if fine food is your goal, persevere. A dinner of lobster risotto followed by grilled salmon and radicchio with marinated fennel and baked polenta is worth dressing up for. ⊠ *Berwick Rd.,* ☎ *207/361–1100.*

$$–$$$$ ✕ **Hurricane.** Arguably the best, though the most touristy, seafood house in town, Hurricane has an unbeatable setting in Perkins Cove, at the end of Marginal Way and overlooking the ocean. The lobster chowder is a much-celebrated starter; a typical main dish is the Cuervo and lime–glazed swordfish. ⊠ *Perkins Cove,* ☎ *207/646–6348.*

$$–$$$ ✕ **Poor Richard's.** This 1788 colonial, a former stagecoach stop, is near Perkins Cove. The chef has yet to succumb to trendy, so you'll generally encounter a selection of true New England classics. It's also a nice place to stop in for a beer and chat with locals, though you should call for dinner reservations. ⊠ *Shore Rd.,* ☎ *207/646–4722.*

$–$$$ ✕ **Front Porch Café.** This is a cheerful little space, decked out with rattan furniture. The dependable traditional American menu includes burgers, grilled chicken, artichoke dip, and a few Mexican munchies such as deep-fried jalapeños and nachos. There's live piano music most afternoons and evenings. ⊠ *Ogunquit Sq. and Shore Rd.,* ☎ *207/646–3976.*

$ ✕ **Fancy That.** Many guests staying at nearby guest houses rub shoulders here for lunch, either while they're dining at one of the simple wooden tables with bright blue chairs or picking up the fixings for a picnic at the beach. Consider more than a dozen creative sandwiches in addition to wines, cheeses, coffees, and sweets. You can also check out the small community bulletin board or pick up some artsy postcards or gifts. ⊠ *7 Main St.,* ☎ *207/646–4118.*

Scenes

Front Porch Café. Known also for its casual restaurant (*see above*), the Front Porch is where many people go early in the evening, for cocktails before or after dinner, or to get warmed up before heading across the street to the Club. The Café, downstairs, has a strong lesbian following early in the evening. Upstairs you can hear piano entertainment nightly in the large, bright room, decorated with white latticework, yellow director's chairs, and bright green walls. ⊠ *Shore Rd.,* ☎ *207/646–3976. Crowd: mixed m/f, older, quieter.*

The Club. Since 1981, the Club has been the town's main gay summer disco (it's also open weekends spring and fall). On the first floor is a mid-size dance floor; upstairs is a video bar. ⊠ *13 Main St.,* ☎ *207/646–6655. Crowd: 80/20 m/f, younger, the disco segment of the town's resort population, but still more conservative and low-key than P-town's.*

Sleeps

Ogunquit's B&Bs are not unlike Provincetown's; most are simply furnished and have small—often shared—baths. Unless otherwise noted, all are open seasonally.

For price ranges, *see* lodging Chart B at the front of this guide.

B&Bs

$$–$$$ 🏠 **Inn at Two Village Square.** Set high on a bluff overlooking downtown and the ocean, this 1886 house has small rooms with quirky furnishings. This is a lively inn with typically chatty guests; activities center around the pool and the sprawling wooden deck. Informal get-togethers are held many nights. ⊠ *135 Rte. 1 (Box 864), 03907,* ☎ *207/646–5779. 18 rooms, some with private bath. Pool, hot tub, exercise room. Continental breakfast. Mixed gay male/lesbian.*

$$ 🏠 **Gazebo.** Although it's a five-minute drive north of town, guests stay here for several reasons: It's open year-round; host Tony Fonts prepares an elaborate breakfast; it's set in a stunning 1865 Greek Revival farmhouse; there's a pool and flagstone patio; and all but one room has a private bath. The decor is heavy on antiques and collectibles. ⊠ *Rte. 1 (Box 668), 03907,* ☎ *207/646–3733. 9 rooms, 8 with private bath. Pool. Full breakfast. Mixed gay/straight.*

$$ 🏠 **Moon Over Maine.** This recent addition to the center of Ogunquit has quickly developed into one of the most popular guest houses, thanks to friendly hosts and a great location. The fully restored 1830s Cape-style house is period-decorated and just a block from the gay bars and restaurants. ⊠ *Berwick Rd. (Box 1478), 03097,* ☎ *207/646–6666 or 800/851–6837. 9 rooms with TV and private bath. Hot tub. Continental breakfast. Mixed gay/straight.*

$–$$ 🏠 **Heritage Inn.** On a quiet residential street and a 15-minute walk from both downtown and Perkins Cove, this gabled Victorian-style house has spacious guest rooms brightened with smart fabrics and hand-stenciling (many of the touches executed by hostess Rica Shepardson). Each room is named after a famous woman, such as Lily Tomlin or Gertrude Stein. ⊠ *14 Marginal Ave. (Box 1295), 03907,* ☎ *207/646–7787. 5 rooms with*

TV, *some with private bath. Hot tub. Continental breakfast. Mostly fe-male (but men are welcome).*

$–$$ ⊞ **The Inn at Tall Chimneys.** Run by amiable host Bob Tosi, this is a sim-ple boardinghouse with small, homey rooms. Continental breakfast is served on an enclosed deck, which also has a Jacuzzi. The attic bedrooms are the coziest and have air-conditioning and private baths. ⊠ *94 S. Main St. (Box 2286), 03907,* ☎ *207/646–8974. 8 rooms with TV, some with private bath. Pool, hot tub, exercise room. Continental breakfast. Mostly mixed gay/lesbian.*

$–$$ ⊞ **Leisure Inn.** This 80-year-old inland complex comprises a house and some cottages and apartments in back. The owner strived for a place that would conjure up memories of visiting your grandmother's house—rooms are informally furnished with old (not antique), comfy pieces. Tends to get a more mature, professional crowd. ⊠ *6 School St. (Box 2113), 03907,* ☎ *207/646–2737. 15 rooms with TV, some with private bath. Continental breakfast. Mostly mixed gay/lesbian.*

$–$$ ⊞ **Ogunquit House.** This converted schoolhouse is within walking dis-tance of the beach and both nightclubs. Rooms have Oriental rugs, che-nille bedspreads, and Victorian wallpaper; most open onto a deck. ⊠ *3 Glen Ave. (Box 1883), 03907,* ☎ *207/646–2967. 6 rooms, 4 cottages, some with TV and private bath. Continental breakfast. Mixed gay/straight.*

The Little Black Book

For tourist information contact the **Ogunquit Chamber of Commerce** (⊠ Box 2289, 03907, ☎ 207/646–2939 or 207/646–5533).

5 Out in Chicago

With Saugatuck and Douglas, Michigan

IN THE 1890S, Chicago was nicknamed "the Windy City" not because the weather was so volatile but because its residents were thought to be a bunch of self-promotional windbags. In a bid to host the World's Columbian Exhibition, city leaders couldn't stop gabbing about how theirs was the greatest town in the world. A century later, Chicago is still one of the world's great destinations. And while certain coastal cousins have caused Chicago's "second city" status to be blown out of proportion by stealing some of the limelight, they have also developed "windy" reputations of their own. Today, Chicago is quietly glorious—with a striking skyline, a dramatic lakeside setting, sophisticated arts and museums, bountiful shopping, and heady dining and nightlife scenes. Its gay and lesbian community is strong and visible.

Chicago's rise to eminence was rapid. Only 150 years ago, this area was a flat, dreary tract of marshland settled by a few spirited pioneers. The completion in 1848 of a canal connecting the Gulf of Mexico (via the Mississippi and its tributaries) with the East Coast (via the Great Lakes and the Erie Canal) instantly turned Chicago into a commercial center. Over the next 40 years, the population mushroomed from roughly 25,000 to more than a million during the city's grandest hour: the 1893 World's Columbian Exhibition. By then Chicago had the world's largest train station and dozens of grand hotels and skyscrapers. For the exhibition, architect Daniel Hudson Burnham constructed a glimmering, electrically lighted "White City" of exhibition halls and civic buildings. His efforts not only elevated Chicago's status, but also lifted the nation's somber spirits during one of its deepest economic depressions.

Chicago has always had a gritty, working-class personality. Many of the city's early immigrants came from central and southern Europe and quickly found work in the city's abundant stockyards, slaughterhouses, and meat-processing plants. The city's scrappy, go-getter mentality has contributed to its history of labor and race problems and political corruption. Infamous are the Haymarket Riot of 1886, the Pullman strike of 1894, and the race riot of 1919. Al Capone, John Dillinger, and other gangsters ran the city in the '20s and '30s. A severe post–World War II housing shortage exacerbated racial strife. By 1957 the Chicago Urban League deemed this the most segregated city in America, and in the late '60s, race riots nearly tore it apart.

Although it still seems a loose collection of neighborhoods, each with its own ethnic traditions and occasional tensions, Chicago is more integrated than ever. The South Side remains a rough patchwork of exclusively black and exclusively white districts, but North Side streets are lined with African, Latin American, eastern and southern European, East Indian, and Southeast Asian shops and restaurants. Here myriad cultures exist peacefully side by side, and this is where most of the city's gays and lesbians have settled.

Although never considered a center of gay activism, Chicago was home to one of the country's first gay rights organizations. The Society of Human Rights was formed by German-American activist Henry Gerber in the mid-'20s—long before the Mattachine Society and the Daughters of Bilitis (DOB). After publishing two issues of an underground journal advocating homosexual rights, it was disbanded when a member's wife alerted police. "Strange Sex Cult Exposed" was how the *Chicago Examiner* billed the episode.

Since then, Chicago's gay and lesbian community has maintained a low national profile. In 1997, however, the city government made international headlines when it moved to beautify and clean up New Town, specifically along Halsted Street, by officially designating it a gay neighborhood—complete with banners and rainbow signage. The move provoked disagreement among gays and straights, and it remains to be seen what sort of compromise will ultimately prevail. Still, the gesture was a clear sign that the city's mainstream has officially recognized the contribution of gays and lesbians to revitalizing a once grim and crime-infested neighborhood.

THE LAY OF THE LAND

Chicago hugs the southwestern shore of Lake Michigan for some 25 miles between the suburb of Evanston, Illinois, and the Indiana border. The city is about 5 miles deep; its streets form an easy-to-navigate grid traversed by a few long diagonals.

Visitors rarely see the city's South Side, an expanse of working-class and, in many places, dicey neighborhoods; Hyde Park, the site of the University of Chicago, and neighboring Kenwood merit detours. Central Chicago—which consists of the South Loop, the Loop, and Near West Side—is the city's geographic hub and was once its commercial and cultural center. Although much of the action has inched north in recent years, the Loop is still the heart of the city.

North of the Loop, above the Chicago River, are a slew of tony residential and shopping districts, beginning with River North and the span of Michigan Avenue known as the Magnificent Mile, moving north through Gold Coast, Old Town, and Lincoln Park. West of here are Wicker Park and Bucktown—fashionable pockets of bohemianism. Uptown Chicago, north of Lincoln Park, is home to the large gay and lesbian neighborhood, New Town (the eastern part of Lakeview); a smaller, more lesbian-based queer community, Andersonville; and such socio-economically diverse neighborhoods as Wrigleyville, Ravenswood, Lincoln Square, and Rogers Park.

In 1997 the Chicago Office of Tourism began organizing **Chicago Neighborhood Tours** (☎ 312/742–1190, e-mail citytour@mcs.net), offering an intimate look at the city's thriving tight-knit neighborhoods. The excellent half-day tours depart on Saturday mornings and rotate among nine neighborhoods: South Shore/Greater Grand Crossing, South Side/Bronzeville, Chinatown/Pilsen, West Side, Near South Side/Prairie Avenue Historic District, Wicker Park/Humboldt Park, Uptown, Andersonville/Lincoln Square, and Devon Avenue. Tours depart by bus at 10 AM from the **Chicago Cultural Center** (✉ 77 E. Randolph St.), but once you arrive in a neighborhood a local guide leads the group (much of the time on foot).

The Loop and South Loop

From the 1880s to the 1950s, people shopped, dined, partied, and worked in the **Loop** (a.k.a. downtown). Today, although it's still the seat of politics and commerce, most big-name shopping has moved north to Michigan Avenue; the nightlife and restaurant scene is now found around Rush and Division streets, in Old Town, and in several North Side neighborhoods.

State Street, which runs north–south, was once the Loop's main commercial strip. Today only a few classic pieces of the golden era remain. The leviathan department store **Marshall Field & Co.** (⊠ 111 N. State St., ☎ 312/781–1000) is a Midwestern monument to conspicuous consumption. Shopping and architecture are the draw at **Carson Pirie Scott** (⊠ 1 S. State St., ☎ 312/641–7000), which is known for its elaborately ornamented facade. **Wabash Avenue,** a block east, provides more opportunities for window shopping, particularly between Randolph Street and Jackson Boulevard.

Consider taking a break from your shopping to visit the **Chicago Cultural Center** (⊠ 78 E. Washington St., ☎ 312/744–6630), an 1897 building in which you'll find the world's largest Tiffany dome. Here you can check out the rotating art exhibits; explore a cultural center that stages daily concerts, films, lectures, and dance performances; or visit the **Museum of Broadcast Communications,** whose interactive exhibits trace the history of radio and television.

The streets that run from just south of the Loop to about Roosevelt Road— a section called the **South Loop** or **Downtown South**—also have a few noteworthy attractions. Perhaps the Loop's greatest attribute is its high concentration of landmark buildings. You can't miss the 110-story **Sears Tower** (Skidmore, Owings & Merrill, 1974; ⊠ 233 S. Wacker Dr.), the world's tallest skyscraper, and the slightly shorter (by only 300 feet) **Amoco Building** (⊠ 200 E. Randolph St.), which was once clad entirely in marble (it began to fall off soon after the building's completion and has since been replaced with granite). Dankmar Adler and Louis Sullivan's elaborate **Auditorium Theatre** (1889; ⊠ 430 S. Michigan Ave.) has almost perfect acoustics and unobstructed sight lines. The **Monadnock Building** (1891–93; ⊠ 53 W. Jackson Blvd.) is the tallest structure built entirely of masonry; the northern half was constructed by Burnham and John Wellborn Root, the southern half by William Holabird and Martin Roche. Mies van der Rohe's sleek, International-style **Federal Center and Plaza** (1964–1975; ⊠ 219–230 S. Dearborn St.) is home to Alexander Calder's famed *Flamingo* stabile. The art deco **Chicago Board of Trade Building** (1930; ⊠ 141 W. Jackson Blvd.) houses the hectic commodities trading market; take in the activity and Holabird and Root's striking interior from the observation deck (☎ 312/435–3590), attached to which is a new visitors gallery. The **Rookery**'s (1886; ⊠ 209 S. LaSalle St.) red-stone masonry and steel-frame construction are by Burnham and Root; the marble and gold-leaf lobby, by Frank Lloyd Wright (1905). The sweeping curve of the postmodern, green-glass-clad **333 W. Wacker Drive** (Kohn Pedersen Fox, 1983) traces the turn in the Chicago River, which flows beside it. Helmut Jahn's **James Thompson Center** (1985; ⊠ 100 W. Randolph St.) is provocative—people either love or hate its unusual mix of plain- and mirrored-glass cladding and its red, white, and blue color scheme. The 35-story **333 N. Michigan Avenue** (1928), an art deco riverfront beauty, complements the dramatic buildings just north of the river.

East of this impressive array of masonry, steel, and glass is **Grant Park,** site of the protests at the 1968 Democratic National Convention. Owing to police paranoia and misconduct (encouraged by then-mayor Richard Daley), the situation escalated to riots involving police brutality, all of it captured vividly on television. Today, peaceful festivals and concerts are frequently staged on the park's lush grounds. Adams Street intersects the park at the dramatic **Art Institute of Chicago** (⊠ S. Michigan Ave. at Adams St., ☎ 312/443–3600), whose 300,000-piece collection spans more than 40 centuries and includes the most impressive display of Impressionist and post-Impressionist works outside of the Louvre, as well as Grant Wood's iconic *American Gothic*. Also check out the Chagall windows and the architectural details from the old Chicago Stock Exchange.

Stroll south through Grant Park to see the **Buckingham Fountain,** the world's largest decorative fountain when it was built in 1927. In the southern half of the park are the **John G. Shedd Aquarium** (⊠ 1200 S. Lake Shore Dr., ☎ 312/939–2438 or 312/939–2426), the world's largest indoor aquarium and largest indoor marine mammal pavilion, the Oceanarium; the **Adler Planetarium** (⊠ 1300 S. Lake Shore Dr., ☎ 312/322–0304); and the humongous **Field Museum of Natural History** (⊠ Lake Shore Dr. at E. Roosevelt Rd., ☎ 312/922–9410), which contains gem rooms, a re-built Pawnee earth-lodge, a comprehensive ancient Egypt exhibit, and a new study of Africa.

Hyde Park and Kenwood

Two South Side neighborhoods worth exploring are **Hyde Park** and, just to its north, **Kenwood.** The World's Columbian Exposition of 1893 was held in Hyde Park. The **University of Chicago,** built a year before the exhibition opened, commands a large social and architectural (Gothic) presence here; this outstanding academic institution counts more than 60 Nobel laureates among its graduates. The 184-acre campus takes up the bulk of the neighborhood, long maintained by strict zoning and urban renewal projects as an island of middle-class living in a sea of poverty. Because this has involved razing bars, artists' studios, and other colorful establishments that once lined 55th Street, the neighborhood is without a vibrant nightlife or interesting shopping strip.

In the lakefront park east of the university is the exposition's Palace of Fine Arts; it now houses the **Museum of Science and Industry** (⊠ 5700 S. Lake Shore Dr., ☎ 773/684–1414), one of the country's first hands-on museums—the museum recently opened a permanent exhibit, "AIDS: The World Within," which discusses the origins, effects, and fights against the epidemic. On or near the campus are several notable sites, including the **David and Alfred Smart Museum of Art** (⊠ 5550 S. Greenwood Ave., ☎ 773/702–0200), whose diverse collection numbers 5,000 items; the **Oriental Institute** (⊠ 1155 E. 58th St., ☎ 773/702–9520), with an outstanding collection of artifacts from the ancient Near East; Frank Lloyd Wright's **Robie House** (⊠ 5757 S. Woodlawn Ave., ☎ 773/702–8374), which you may tour for free daily at noon or by special arrangement; and—a bit west of here in Washington Park, the **Dusable Museum of African-American History** (⊠ 740 E. 56th Pl., ☎ 773/947–0600), which opened in 1961 as the first such museum in the nation and is filled with nearly 100 works of art and thousands of artifacts and documents.

Near North

North of the Loop, between the Chicago River and the lakefront and below North Avenue is a collection of lively neighborhoods—some of them saddled with various combinations of old and new money and others rich with galleries and nightclubs, all of them prosperous. Closest to downtown are River North and Streeterville. North Michigan Avenue (a.k.a. the Miracle Mile) divides these two neighborhoods.

Once heavily industrial, and then virtually abandoned, **River North** had little going for it up until two decades ago, when artisans began buying its inexpensive derelict lofts and warehouse spaces. Now you'll find many galleries, most concentrated around **SuHu** (where *Su*perior and *Hu*ron streets intersect with Orleans and Hudson streets). Interior designers know the area best as the home of the monolithic **Merchandise Mart** (✉ 300 N. Wells St., ☎ 312/527–7600). In America, only the Pentagon has more square footage. Retail shops open to the public line the first two floors. On other floors wholesale showrooms welcome only interior designers. Mart tours are given weekdays at noon.

Architectural landmarks along the northern waterfront include the terra-cotta-clad **Wrigley Building** (1921–24; ✉ 400 N. Michigan Ave.); the twin cylindrical towers of 60-story **Marina City** (1964–67; ✉ 300 N. State St.); the magnificent Gothic Revival **Tribune Tower** (1925; ✉ 435 N. Michigan Ave.); and the imposing limestone-and-granite **NBC Tower** (1989; ✉ 200 E. Illinois St.).

Looming high above all of its neighbors, however, is the 1,107-foot-tall **John Hancock Center** (✉ 875 N. Michigan Ave., ☎ 312/751–3681), whose 94th-floor observation deck has two interactive exhibits. To learn more about Chicago's illustrious architectural history, stop by the **Chicago Architecture Foundation Shop and Tour Center** (☎ 312/922–3432), on the ground floor of the Hancock. The foundation gives excellent "Early Skyscraper" and "Modern and Beyond" walking tours of the Loop, and a similar tour along North Michigan Avenue.

A couple of blocks south is the impressive new home of the **Museum of Contemporary Art** (✉ 220 E. Chicago Ave., ☎ 312/280–2660). Seven times larger than its predecessor, it has added hundreds of permanent works and more space to host important traveling shows. Outdoors are a sculpture garden and café with views of Lake Michigan

The **Magnificent Mile** and **Streeterville** compare with the finest American and European shopping districts. Between the Chicago River and Oak Street, Michigan Avenue is lined with retail giants: Saks Fifth Avenue (✉ 700 N.), Tiffany & Co. (✉ 715 N.), Neiman-Marcus (✉ 737 N.), F.A.O. Schwarz (✉ 840 N.), and Bloomingdale's (✉ 900 N.); new superstores open every month.

Streeterville, a landfill overrun with saloons and whorehouses at the turn of the century, and now a nondescript patch of high-rise apartments, hospital buildings, and office blocks, is home to the small but impressive **Terra Museum of American Art** (✉ 666 N. Michigan Ave., ☎ 312/664–3939), with works by Whistler, Sargent, Homer, Cassatt, and the Wyeths.

East of Streeterville, along the lakefront, is the **Navy Pier**, a former commercial shipping pier that was transformed in 1995 into 50 acres of parks, gardens, shops, and restaurants; it's a bit like San Francisco's Fisherman's Wharf, though not as tacky—yet.

North of Streeterville, brushing the lakefront from Chicago Avenue up to about North Avenue, is that posh and precious chunk of real estate known as the **Gold Coast,** site of grand and exorbitantly priced homes and apartment houses as well as impressive hotels, several good restaurants, and more shopping.

Lincoln Park and Old Town

Lincoln Park is the name for both a lush expanse of green and for one of the city's oldest neighborhoods, settled in the early 1840s by German and Eastern European immigrants. The 1,200-acre park includes the small but impressive **Lincoln Park Zoo** (✉ 2200 N. Cannon Dr., ☎ 773/742–2000); the **Chicago Historical Society** (✉ 1601 N. Clark St., ☎ 773/642–4600), with good displays on the Chicago Fire; and the **Lincoln Park Conservatory** (✉ 2400 N. Stockton Dr., ☎ 773/742–7736). The area around the park is a bit cutesy, but terrific for sidewalk strolling and people-watching, and not as busy as some neighborhoods to the north; many well-heeled, same-sex couples live here. Still hip but increasingly monied, dapper yet daring, it might remind you of Boston's Back Bay or Washington, D.C.'s Woodley Park. Much of the area's dining and shopping is near handsome **DePaul University,** which is at the intersection of Belden and Sheffield avenues. Outside the nearby **Biograph Theater** (✉ 2433 N. Lincoln Ave.), a local landmark that still shows first-run movies, the notorious John Dillinger met his demise.

Lincoln Park's southeast corner, the **Old Town Triangle,** is one of its liveliest sections, with plenty of good shops, restaurants, and nightclubs along Wells Street and its intersecting one-way alleys. Here you'll find **Second City** (✉ 1616 N. Wells St., ☎ 312/337–3992), the famous improvisational comedy club where performers such as Elaine May, Mike Nichols, John Belushi, and Bill Murray earned their comic wings.

Wicker Park and Bucktown

West of Lincoln Park are the newly vibrant neighborhoods of **Wicker Park,** which runs from Division to North avenues, and **Bucktown,** the block of streets stretching above it to Fullerton Avenue. Originally home to immigrant Poles, Ukrainians, and other Eastern Europeans, then later to Puerto Ricans, these areas are a hodgepodge of ethnicities and lifestyles—not particularly gay, but so predominantly countercultural they're sometimes called the "new Seattle." Several restaurants, coffeehouses, bars, and offbeat shops line North Avenue, especially near Milwaukee and Damen avenues.

Lakeview and New Town

Lakeview runs between the lakefront and Ashland Avenue, north of Belmont Avenue up to Irving Park Road. Within this neighborhood is a small triangle east of Belmont Avenue called **New Town** (a.k.a. Boys' Town). Traditionally, while most of Lakeview has been a mix of artsy types, working-class families, and young, not-yet-rolling-in-dough professionals—with a smattering of lesbians and gays—New Town has been overwhelmingly gay and mostly male. Today, New Town draws more straights and lesbians, while homosexuals are now a presence in Lakeview as a whole. Montrose Avenue, on Lakeview's northern outskirts, is fast becoming a dyke enclave second only to Andersonville to the north.

In the heart of Lakeview is **Wrigley Field** (✉ Clark and Addison Sts.), home of baseball's Chicago Cubs. The stadium draws thousands of fans on roughly 80 summer days and—since 1988 when lights were installed (an act still widely regarded as blasphemous)—summer nights. Lakeview is one of the most dynamic entertainment districts you'll find, with throngs of baseball fans mingling with Clark Street's already motley assortment of same-sex couples, straight kids from the 'burbs, yuppies, and the like.

Clark Street, which runs diagonally north–south, is Lakeview's major commercial thoroughfare, with a diverse collection of businesses—from spiffy bistros and simple fast-food joints to sports-cards shops and vintage clothing boutiques. **Halsted Street,** parallel to Clark just one block east, is a strip of shops, restaurants, and bars that cater primarily to gay men. Try **Flashy Trash** (✉ 3524 N. Halsted St., ☎ 773/327–6900) for wigs, drag wear, and make-up; **We're Everywhere** (✉ 3434 N. Halsted St., ☎ 773/404–0590) for the latest gay and lesbian fashions; **Beatnix** (✉ 3436 N. Halsted St., ☎ 773/935–1188) for vintage duds; **Cupid's Treasures** (✉ 3519 N. Halsted St., ☎ 773/348–3884) for fun toys and trinkets; and **Gay Mart** (✉ 3457 N. Halsted St., ☎ 773/929–4272), which has cards, campy decorative arts, and queer curios. East of Halsted, **North Broadway** draws a mixed bag of pedestrians, with its quirky antiques shops, bookstores, and other engaging retail outlets. **Belmont Avenue,** which runs east–west, has scads of cheap eateries and clothing and music shops. Things are gayest along Belmont the closer you are to the lake, but the street is diverse and busy as far west as the El. If you follow Belmont to Lake Michigan, you'll hit what used to be the main gay beach (a.k.a. "Belmont Rocks"). This span has become desolate, as most gays and lesbians now tan their hides at **Hollywood Beach** (across from where Hollywood Road and Bryn Mawr intersect with Sheridan Road).

Uptown

The multiethnic neighborhoods extending north of Lakeview to suburban Evanston are some of Chicago's most up-and-coming. Directly north of Lakeview, from Ashland Avenue west to the Chicago River is **Lincoln Square** (a.k.a. Ravenswood), once heavily German and now populated mainly by Southeast Asians.

From about Ashland Avenue east to the lakefront are a few communities good for exploring. **Argyle Street,** the least touristy of the city's three Asian districts, is lined with restaurants and shops. Most eateries are Thai, Cambodian, Vietnamese, or Chinese; many are extremely inexpensive and BYOB. **Andersonville,** an old Swedish enclave whose main commercial strip is **Clark Street,** is steadily developing into a low-key lesbian and gay residential district. It's nondescript but has some cheap eats and coffeehouses, some friendly neighborhood bars—a couple of them big with the leather crowd—and some good shops, including **Women and Children First** (*see* Bookstores, *below*); **Woman Wild** (✉ 5237 N. Clark St., ☎ 773/878–0300), an arts and crafts gallery devoted to women artists; several original Swedish bakeries and eateries; and the **Swedish-American Museum Center** (✉ 5211 N. Clark St., ☎ 773/728–8111), which displays and sells a variety of crafts and decorative arts. It's possible to drive through this area without registering its true funk factor; spend a few hours poking around to really breathe in its bohemian air.

Chicago's northernmost neighborhood is **Rogers Park,** home to **Loyola University.** Rogers Park has long had a substantial Jewish population but more recently has become a true melting pot: Residents range from down-and-out to upper-middle-class, from college students to retirees, from Indian and West Indian to Russian, African American, and East Asian. Since the '60s, a left-leaning, politically spirited underground of coffeehouses and folk and jazz clubs has thrived here. Although the area is not specifically gay, same-sexers usually feel comfortable here.

Oak Park

One suburb that merits a visit is **Oak Park,** accessible via the Eisenhower Expressway (I–290). One of the city's earliest suburbs, it's where Ernest Hemingway was born and raised and where Frank Lloyd Wright began his career. Stop to visit the **Frank Lloyd Wright Home and Studio** (✉ 951 Chicago Ave., ☎ 708/848–1976) and verse yourself in the ways and means of this legendary architect. Dozens of homes designed by either Wright or his disciples are located around town; a map and self-guided tour is available from the **Oak Park Visitors Center** (✉ 158 N. Forest Ave., ☎ 708/848–1500).

GETTING AROUND

Public transportation in Chicago is not hard to negotiate. The excellent map published by the Chicago Transit Authority is available in many hotels and at fare booths. A network of both elevated ("El") and subway lines traverses the city, and buses usually operate where there's no El. It is not impossible to get around by car, but traffic can be heavy and street parking tough, especially around the Loop and River North. On the North Side, from Lincoln Park to Rogers Park, a car can actually be handy, however; street parking is somewhat easy to find in Lakeview and New

Town, except when the Chicago Cubs have a home game or on weekend evenings when the clubs are hopping (at these times try the 24-hour garage just south of the Treasure Island supermarket on North Broadway). Taxis are metered and can be hailed easily from the busier streets.

EATS

African, Chinese, German, Greek, Israeli, Italian, Mexican, Polish, Russian, Scandinavian, Thai, Ukrainian, and Vietnamese cuisines are all well-represented in Chicago. But over the past two or three years, the dining scene has begun increasingly to rival those in the top culinary cities in the nation, as inventive eateries pop up everywhere. In addition to downtown, Southport Avenue in western Lakeview, North and Damen avenues in Bucktown/Wicker Park, and Halsted Street in ever-queer Boys' Town have seen a constant invasion of hot restaurants.

One great thing about Chicago's restaurant scene is the amount of bang you get for your buck. Even with the new wave of nouvelle eateries, hundreds of Old World diners and cozy pubs still serve up heaps of comfort food. Pizza is a Chicago specialty—the deep-dish version was invented here—and any combination of toppings you can dream up can be found. Even a feast in one of the city's fanciest eateries will generally cost you less than a comparable meal in other big cities.

Gay and lesbian patrons abound just about anywhere you eat in Lakeview and New Town. Andersonville, Wicker Park, and Bucktown restaurants are also quite popular with the community. And when you dine out in other neighborhoods north of North Avenue you're likely to spy at least one or two gay couples, if not some waitrons. Things are straighter as you venture south, through Near North and the Loop.

For price ranges, *see* dining Chart A at the front of this guide.

Lakeview and New Town Vicinity

$$$–$$$$ ✕ **Yoshi's.** The first serious dining spot to open on Halsted's anything-but-serious gay entertainment strip, this intimate international eatery serves such innovative food as soft-shell crab tempura with tomato-cilantro sauce, and rare tuna with basil, garlic, and tomato oil. ✉ *3257 N. Halsted St.,* ☎ *773/248–6160.*

$$$ ✕ **Madame B.** This swank new Asian-fusion restaurant in the heart of Boys' Town has drawn praise from locals who can't seem to get enough of such creative dishes as Thai pesto beef tenderloin with Chinese long beans, sweet potato spring rolls, and a zinfandel glaze. The stylish back-lit dining room offers the right ambience for the dramatic fare. ✉ *3441 Halsted St.,* ☎ *773/248–4040.*

$$–$$$ ✕ **Bella Vista.** This northern Italian restaurant with frescoed ceilings, and servers as stylish as the decor, is one of the most romantic spots in Lakeview. Picture-pretty salads and a long, varied wine list complement a selection of pastas and wood-fired pizzas. Pan-fried gnocchi with braised rabbit, spiced artichokes, arugula, and crimini mushrooms is a standout. ✉ *1001 W. Belmont Ave.,* ☎ *773/404–0111.*

$$–$$$ ✕ **Mia Francesca.** Although numerous imposters have opened nearby, Mia Francesca remains the original and best place for sophisticated but never overwrought northern Italian fare. Feast on such sublime creations as grilled mahimahi with green beans, roasted red pepper vinaigrette, and garlic and roasted red potatoes. ✉ *3311 N. Clark St.,* ☎ *773/281–3310.*

$$–$$$ ✕ **Rhumba.** A hopping gay disco called Fusion after 10 PM (*see Scenes, below*), this Brazilian restaurant has plenty of energy of its own. A Carmen Miranda impersonator typically floats about the space, writhing away on the interior balcony, and handsome waitrons fly in and out of the bustling open kitchen. Consider hearty orange-and-cumin-marinated pork ribs with

Lakeview and New Town

Eats ●
Alonti, **24**
Ann Sather **21, 27**
Archo de
Cuchilleros, **13**
The Bangkok, **5**
Bella Vista, **19**
Buddies, **18**
Café Voltaire, **22**
Charlie Trotter's, **30**
Chicago Diner, **15**
Coffee Chicago, **23**
Cornelia's, **11**
Hi Ricky, **1**
Le Loup, **6**
Leona's, **7**
Madame B, **12**
Mamacita's, **2, 25**
Matsuya, **8**

Melrose Diner, **20, 26**
Mia Francesca, **9**
Nookies Too, **28**
Nookies Tree, **14**
Oo-la-la!, **16**
Penny's Noodle
Soup, **3**
Pepper Lounge, **4**
Relish, **29**
Rhumba, **10**
Yoshi's, **17**

Scenes ○
Annex III, **16**
Berlin, **15**
Big Daddies, **19**
Buck's, **9**
Cell Block, **1**
Charlie's, **4**
The Closet, **14**
Circuit, **5**
Cocktail, **11**
Dandy's, **2**
Fusion, **6**
Gentry on
Halsted, **13**
Girlbar, **20**
Little Jim's, **7**
Lucky Horseshoe, **18**
Manhandler, **21**
Manhole, **8**

The North End, **3**
Roscoe's, **10**
Sidetrack, **12**
Spin, **17**

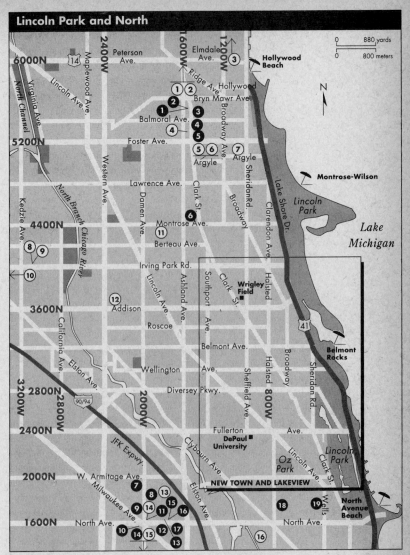

Eats ●

Ann Sather, **5**
Blue Mesa, **18**
Busy Bee, **10**
Café Absinthe, **11**
Coffee Chicago, **2**
Confusion, **9**
Feast, **17**
Hi Ricky, **16**
Kopi Café, **3**
Le Bouchon, **7**
Leo's Lunchroom, **14**
Lolita's, **6**
Nookie's, **19**
Northside Café, **8**
Reza's, **4**
Soul Kitchen, **12**

Starfish, **15**
Tomboy, **1**
Urbus Orbis, **13**

Scenes ○

Artful Dodger, **13**
Big Chicks, **7**
Clark's on Clark, **5**
Crobar, **16**
Eagle, **6**
Friends Pub, **10**
Granville Anvil, **3**
Legacy 21, **8**
Lost & Found, **9**
Madrigal's, **4**
Numbers, **1**
The Other Side, **12**
Rainbo Club, **15**
Red Dog, **14**
Scot's, **11**
Touché, **2**

72

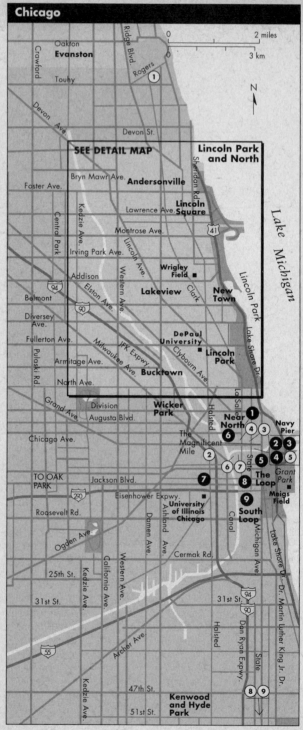

sweet potato mash, or coconut shrimp with peppers, garlic, cashews, and coriander. ✉ *3631 Halsted St.,* ☎ *773/975–2345.*

$$ ✕ **Cornelia's.** Rough-hewn wooden walls make this rustic restaurant feel almost like an old farmhouse. The cuisine has a green-market sensibility. A starter of wild mushrooms is broiled with seasoned bread crumbs and goat cheese; a shrimp entrée is prepared with sun-dried tomatoes, tapenade, and herbs with carrot fettuccine. ✉ *750 W. Cornelia Ave.,* ☎ *773/248–8333.*

$$ ✕ **Matsuya.** A top Japanese choice, Matsuya serves excellent sushi, such spicy starters as deep-fried chicken wings and whitefish with smelt roe, and many tempura, seafood, and teriyaki dishes. A striking wooden screen separates the spare, contemporary dining room from the kitchen. ✉ *3469 N. Clark St.,* ☎ *773/248–2677.*

$$ ✕ **Oo-la-la!** Except for the small shimmering disco ball hung above the center of the dining room, you might think this rustic storefront southern French and northern Italian bistro-cum-trattoria was in Aix-en-Provence. Moon-eyed same-sex couples nuzzle over wine and nosh on tomato pumpkin ravioli and chicken with rosemary in a white wine sauce. ✉ *3335 N. Halsted St.,* ☎ *773/935–7708.*

$$ ✕ **Pepper Lounge.** This hot late-night supper club (serving dinner until 1:30 AM) is decorated in red, from the rich velvet drapes to the lighting—many of the furnishings, including elaborate chandeliers, were salvaged from an old theater. The menu is Continental with contemporary influences; espresso bean–blackened catfish with potato and prosciutto hash drizzled with red currant butter is typical. ✉ *3441 N. Sheffield Ave.,* ☎ *773/665–7377.*

$–$$ ✕ **Archo de Cuchilleros.** This romantic Halsted haunt with whitewashed walls and Spanish paintings offers roughly 20 hot and 20 cold tapas. A highlight is fish cheeks sautéed with garlic, white wine, and cayenne. ✉ *3445 N. Halsted St.,* ☎ *773/296–6046.*

$–$$ ✕ **The Bangkok.** The best of Boys' Town's many good Thai restaurants is filled with museum-quality Thai bibelots and serves rich, fiery cuisine. Sunday buffet brunches are as attractive as they are delicious. ✉ *3542 N. Halsted St.,* ☎ *773/327–2870.*

$ ✕ **Alonti.** Guppies and hipsters swamp this cheap and cheerful newcomer for inexpensive pizzas, sandwiches, and pastas (try the jambalaya pasta with andouille sausage, chicken, peppers, onions, and a spicy Creole sauce). A decent array of wines, beers, and coffees is also served. Not especially atmospheric, but it's a good choice for a quick meal. ✉ *3201 N. Clark St.,* ☎ *773/529–1155.*

$ ✕ **Ann Sather.** You could survive solely on the flaky, freshly baked rolls that accompany every meal at this hallowed Swedish diner with three gay-popular locations. From the fresh pink salmon-salad sandwiches to the fluffy omelets stuffed with crab, spinach, and sour cream, every morsel is memorable. Were it possible to choose your own grandmother, you'd want her to come from the ranks of Ann Sather's doting waitstaff. ✉ *929 W. Belmont Ave.,* ☎ *773/348–2378; 5207 N. Clark St.,* ☎ *773/271–6677;* ✉ *2665 N. Clark St.,* ☎ *773/327–9522.*

$ ✕ **Buddies.** This predominantly queer and always fun restaurant has casual American and Continental food—meatballs marinara, burgers—along with a few fancier dishes such as grilled yellowfin tuna. Now that it's the late '90s, perhaps the management will soon feel inspired to remove the forbidding black paper that currently covers the front windows. ✉ *3301 N. Clark St.,* ☎ *773/477–4066.*

$ ✕ **Chicago Diner.** You won't find meat loaf or baked ham at this diner—everything is vegetarian, and much of it low-fat. Specialties include tempeh burgers, tofu hot dogs, and filling rice-and-bean platters. The storefront dining room has wooden booths and exposed brick, and the staff is friendly and laid back. ✉ *3411 N. Halsted St.,* ☎ *773/935–6696.*

$ ✕ **Hi Ricky.** These two smartly decorated, dirt-cheap Asian eateries serve terrific food in a lively atmosphere. They excel at simple, authentic renditions of such favorite Asian dishes as Thai chicken satays and Chinese stir-fried broccoli rabe with garlic and oyster sauce. ⊠ *3730 N. Southport Ave.,* ☏ *773/388–0000;* ⊠ *1852 North Ave.,* ☏ *773/276–8300.*

$ ✕ **Le Loup.** This "Loup" has nothing to do with Chicago's downtown or the city's elevated railway. *Loup* means "wolf" in French; the place is filled with photos and decorations of the animal. It's a diverting theme for what is an urbane French bistro, where big portions of cassoulet, coq au vin, and ratatouille Niçoise are doled out for bargain prices. ⊠ *3348 N. Sheffield Ave.,* ☏ *773/248–1830.*

$ ✕ **Leona's.** Founded in 1950, Leona's serves delicious pan-, stuffed-, and thin-crust pizzas as well as ridiculously big portions of lasagna. The cozy, dimly lit dining room overlooks Sheffield Avenue. ⊠ *3215 N. Sheffield Ave.,* ☏ *773/327–8861.*

$ ✕ **Mamacita's.** Both branches of this funky Mexican restaurant are notable for their sidewalk seating, understated but classy decor, soft music, friendly staff, and gay followings. The menu may look standard, but the quality of the veggie burritos, steak tacos, and fajitas are second to none. ⊠ *3655 N. Southport Ave.,* ☏ *773/528–2100;* ⊠ *3324 N. Broadway,* ☏ *773/868–6262.*

$ ✕ **Melrose Diner.** This 24-hour diner is big with club-goers and weekend brunchers. Hot turkey with homemade sage dressing and half-pound burgers typify the fare; a bakery on premises turns out an extraordinary cheesecake. ⊠ *930 W. Belmont Ave.,* ☏ *773/404–7901;* ⊠ *3320 N. Broadway,* ☏ *773/327–2060.*

$ ✕ **Nookies Tree.** The gayest of a small group of wonderful diners—the others are named Nookies and Nookies Too (get it?)—this always-busy eatery serves simple but above-average fare, from a filling grilled cheese with avocado and tomatoes to daily entrée specials that come with a soup and salad. Open all night on Friday and Saturday. ⊠ *3334 N. Halsted St.,* ☏ *773/248–9888;* ⊠ *1746 N. Wells St.,* ☏ *312/337–2454;* ⊠ *2112 N. Halsted St.,* ☏ *773/327–1400. No credit cards.*

$ ✕ **Penny's Noodle Shop.** On those raw, windy Chicago days, little warms the soul better than a bowl of piping hot Thai noodles. The pad Thai and beef satay are both excellent. If you're in a hurry, you can count on a simple, quick meal; there's both table and counter seating. ⊠ *3400 N. Sheffield Ave.,* ☏ *773/281–8222.*

Lincoln Park, Bucktown, and Wicker Park

$$$$ ✕ **Charlie Trotter's.** This hallowed institute of creative high-end fare is set in an elegant Lincoln Park brownstone. The restaurant serves two dégustation menus, one vegetarian; these are perfect ways to acquaint yourself with chef Trotter's sublime cooking. À la carte possibilities include mahimahi with leek and sorrel sauce and wild mushroom ravioli. Book at least a few days ahead. ⊠ *816 W. Armitage St.,* ☏ *773/248–6228.*

$$$–$$$$ ✕ **Confusion.** This new addition to Bucktown has several dining rooms, all done with pickled wood floors and spare furnishings. The inventive food is excellent, with such dishes as roasted wild wood pigeon with port wine risotto and black trumpet mushrooms. ⊠ *1616 N. Damen Ave.,* ☏ *773/772–7100.*

$$$ ✕ **Starfish.** One of Bucktown's earliest upscale eateries, Starfish is a slick place, with exposed air ducts and brick, a handsome dark-wood bar, and asterisk-shape light fixtures. The menu offers creative fish fare, but if you're up for a fowl evening, start with roasted quail with goat cheese and move on to the filling smoked duck and lobster tortillas with yellow tomato salsa. ⊠ *1856 W. North Ave.,* ☏ *773/395–3474.*

$$–$$$ ✕ **Café Absinthe.** Directly below the alternative nightclub **Red Dog** (*see* Scenes, *below*), this grungy restaurant has quickly risen to the highest ranks

of Bucktown dining. Scallops in a fennel bouillon and grilled venison loin are just two of the dishes that appeal to an amazing diversity of diners. ⊠ *1954 W. North Ave.,* ☎ *773/278–4488.*

$$–$$$ ✕ **Le Bouchon.** One of those off-the-beaten-path spots that locals bring their friends to only after swearing them to secrecy, this Bucktown bistro provides a real taste of Paris. The diminutive dining room has pressed-tin ceilings, bentwood chairs, and paintings in vintage frames. Expect veal kidneys with mustard sauce, garlicky escargots, and robust monkfish Provençal. ⊠ *1958 N. Damen Ave.,* ☎ *773/862–6600.*

$$–$$$ ✕ **Relish.** The outstanding dessert menu is the most famous attribute of this plant-filled indoor/outdoor café (and the fact that the kitchen serves til 11 PM on weekends). The Chocolate Orgasm entices diners from all over town. All of the New American food, such as lobster-mango que-sadillas, is quite tasty, however. ⊠ *2044 N. Halsted St.,* ☎ *773/868–9034.*

$$ ✕ **Blue Mesa.** Suits and yuppies abound at this Lincoln Park favorite, with an adobe-style dining room complete with kiva fireplace and Santa Fe colors. The cuisine derives from the Southwest, Texas, and Mexico. Try blackened shrimp with tequila butter and the tasty chiles rellenos. ⊠ *1729 N. Halsted St.,* ☎ *312/944–5990.*

$$ ✕ **Feast.** The best attribute of this dapper new North Avenue bistro is the spacious patio in back, half of which is under a tent. The food is New American with a few Pacific Rim touches—homemade Asian chicken ravi-oli with miso broth and ginger is a favorite. ⊠ *1835 W. North Ave.,* ☎ *773/235–6361.*

$$ ✕ **Soul Kitchen.** The chefs at this funky Wicker Park hangout draw on spice-infused recipes from the Caribbean, Louisiana, Asia, the Southwest, and just about everywhere else where hot peppers are a staple. Among the punchy dishes are fresh corn and smoked mushroom tamales with pico de gallo. The orange and black seats with leopard print tables make for a jarring but appropriate setting. ⊠ *1571 N. Milwaukee Ave.,* ☎ *773/ 342–9742.*

$–$$ ✕ **Northside Café.** This former neighborhood hangout now attracts yup-pies from all over the city. The main section, a lively old tavern, has lots of brass and dark wood; a huge greenhouse room with a peaked roof ad-joins it. Traditional American pub food is on tap, and a major weekend brunch scene keeps things busy all day. ⊠ *1635 N. Damen Ave.,* ☎ *773/ 384–3555.*

$ ✕ **Busy Bee.** This traditional Polish diner is in the heart of Wicker Park, which has always had a strong immigrant population. Punks, tourists, dykes and fags, and hefty old Eastern European women feast side-by-side on pierogis, beef barley soup, and blintzes. ⊠ *1546 N. Damen Ave.,* ☎ *773/772–4433.*

$ ✕ **Leo's Lunchroom.** The motley crowd of punky grungers who favor this cool zero-ambience diner give the place the look of a casting office for a Day-Glo hair-dye commercial. The international fare—potato-onion tarts, breakfast burritos—makes the somewhat pretentious ambience worth braving. ⊠ *1809 W. Division St.,* ☎ *773/276–6509. No credit cards.*

Greater Downtown and Near North

$$$–$$$$ ✕ **Printer's Row.** The culinary centerpiece of the revitalized Printer's Row district, this purveyor of creatively updated regional American cui-sine is a popular place for sealing deals and talking futures. Seafood and game dishes are among the many notable offerings. Dressy—save it for special occasions. ⊠ *550 S. Dearborn St.,* ☎ *312/461–0780.*

$$$ ✕ **Shaw's Crab House.** Fresh fish flown in daily from all over the coun-try makes Shaw's the top seafood haunt in Chicago, if not the entire Mid-west. Lots of dark wood, exposed brick, and the aroma of chowder and oyster stew lend this the feel of a New England wharf. ⊠ *21 E. Hubbard St.,* ☎ *312/527–2722.*

$$-$$$ ✕ **The Berghoff.** Waistlines are routinely destroyed by the heavy, classic German dishes churned out at this ancient beer-and-bratwurst hall in a century-old building downtown. The Berghoff has been brewing its own beer since the repeal of Prohibition. The dining room can be stuffy, loud, and touristy, but for a taste of old Chicago, you can't go wrong here. ⊠ *17 W. Adams St.,* ☏ *312/427–3170.*

$$-$$$ ✕ **Frontera Grill.** This sassy Mexican restaurant filled with colorful folk art has redefined Chicago's south-of-the-border dining scene. Run by Rick and Deann Bayless, the authors of *Authentic Mexican,* it offers such regional fare as duck breast in adobo pepper sauce and turkey mole; the menu changes often. ⊠ *445 N. Clark St.,* ☏ *312/661–1434.*

$-$$ ✕ **Santorini.** This is the best of the several fine Greektown favorites—a large, lively tavern with mouthwatering tzatziki dip with pita bread and tender charcoal-grilled octopus. Grilled lamb and seafood dishes are star entrées. ⊠ *800 W. Adams St.,* ☏ *312/829–8820.*

$ ✕ **Heaven on Seven.** What appears to be an ordinary luncheonette on the seventh floor of a nondescript downtown office building is actually one of the city's gems. You can always get good, plain diner food plus many authentically rendered Cajun and Creole dishes. Omelet with habanero peppers, tasso ham, and andouille sausage will wake you right up. Try coming in the midafternoon, when the long lunch lines have disappeared; closes at 5 PM daily. ⊠ *111 N. Wabash Ave.,* ☏ *312/263–6443;* ⊠ *600 N. Michigan Ave.,* ☏ *312/280–7774. No credit cards.*

$ ✕ **Pizzeria Uno.** By now most of America knows about the deep-dish pies at this chain. Even though it looks like all other Unos, this branch is the original. Its pizza seems just a little more flavorful, the crust a hint crispier. ⊠ *29 E. Ohio St.,* ☏ *312/321–1000.*

Andersonville

$$-$$$ ✕ **Tomboy.** This lively bistro with brick walls, white napery, wooden tables, and a heavily queer (especially lesbian, in case the name of the place didn't clue you in) crowd is arguably the best restaurant in Andersonville. Dishes such as pan-seared duck with crimini mushrooms, caramelized shallots, wild rice cakes, and port glaze have inspired considerable accolade. BYOB. ⊠ *5402 N. Clark St.,* ☏ *773/907–0636.*

$-$$ ✕ **Reza's.** This cavernous dining room with varnished wood tables and a large window overlooking the street is a busy Andersonville brunch spot. The Middle Eastern, Mediterranean, and Persian menu emphasizes vegetarian fare such as the *maust museer* (a tangy yogurt with shallots and dill, served with pita bread), but lamb and chicken are available, too. A second branch opened downtown in 1996. ⊠ *5255 N. Clark St.,* ☏ *773/ 561–1898;* ⊠ *downtown at 436 W. Ontario St.,* ☏ *312/664–4500.*

$ ✕ **Lolita's.** Rueben Sanchez and his transgender wife Jennifer run what would be a fairly typical and not particularly atmospheric Mexican restaurant in Andersonville, but for the fact that the place is staffed by lithe and beautiful transgenders. A midnight show runs on weekends. ⊠ *4400 N. Clark St.,* ☏ *773/561–3356.*

Coffeehouse Culture

Café Voltaire. Even before Chicago's coffee bar invasion reached its current fever pitch, this artsy café was staging poetry readings, exhibiting local art, and light munchies (focaccia pizzas, roasted-garlic pâté). Abstract hand-painted tables and brown vinyl seats that appear pilfered from a greasy spoon lend a funky air. ⊠ *3231 N. Clark St.,* ☏ *773/528–3136.*

Coffee Chicago. Less artsy than other neighborhood hangouts, Coffee Chicago is almost upscale and usually filled with pretty people—the kinds of folks who have their own espresso makers at home but come out to hobnob with pals. ⊠ *3323 N. Clark St.,* ☏ *773/477–3323;* ⊠ *5400 N. Clark St.,* ☏ *773/907–8674.*

Kopi Café. This offbeat boutique and coffeehouse in Andersonville sells coffee, travel books, and Asian and New Age jewelry and arts and crafts. In front is a groovy no-shoes parlor with cushions and carpeting. The "kitchen sink" cookies really do contain almost every imaginable ingredient. ⊠ *5317 N. Clark St.,* ☎ *773/989–5674.*

Urbus Orbis. This enormous space occupies a converted Wicker Park warehouse. Amid the big, central coffee bar and a scattering of plush leatherette chairs, acid jazz fans mingle with Beat Generation wannabes. The theater next door is generally hopping with some kind of performance. ⊠ *1934 W. North Ave.,* ☎ *773/252–4446.*

SCENES

Nightlife options in Chicago are as varied and interesting as in any American city. Scads of chummy little bars dot the city's neighborhoods, and several pockets of gay-friendly bars and clubs are big with the grunge and alternative arts set. You'll also find warehouse discos, frisky strip joints, intimate piano bars, and everything in between.

You'll occasionally see risqué club gear and disco duds on Halsted Street, but collared shirts, dressy denims, and other casual sportswear are more common. Compared with smaller Midwest cities such as St. Louis and Milwaukee, Chicago's bar scene is a tad standoffish, but outside of a few stand-and-model clubs most people are still disarmingly forward and friendly. Bar greetings will seldom be met with an East Coast–style snarl or a West Coast–style glance over your shoulder. A perceptible ease is the norm. Still, if you're from either coast and can't stop raving about your home city, you can expect to be pilloried and stoned.

Most Chicago bars close at 2 AM, but about 15% to 20% of them remain open (and still serve liquor) till 4 AM. For a city with an early dining scene, its clubs don't reach their peak till quite late—even on weekdays. Plenty of folks don't even begin to head out till after midnight.

Lakeview and New Town

PRIME SUSPECTS

Berlin. Just west of Halsted's main bar strip, this plain-looking club has been one of Lakeview's premier gay discos for years. Its popularity varies, but after midnight you can almost always count on decent crowds, especially Tuesdays, Thursdays, and weekends. The crowd is noticeably more colorful, funky, and alternative—in many ways a foil to the preppy collared types who haunt Halsted Street. The mood is definitely cruisy, but at the same time cerebral and low-key. Berlin consists of a compact dance area on the left, a long video bar to the right, and often interesting dance music, but it's the people who make the place. ⊠ *954 W. Belmont Ave.,* ☎ *773/348–4975. Crowd: 60/40 m/f, a few straights, mixed racially, mostly under 35, grungers, hipsters, funksters.*

Cell Block. One of the best features of this leather-and-Levi's bar is the facade of huge one-way windows. You get a great view of the guys strolling along Halsted Street without their knowing you can see them—it's especially fun to watch them fix their hair in the reflection of the window. Inside is a large bar with several big video screens, lots of neon beer signs, and a pool table. Has fetish nights from time to time. ⊠ *3702 N. Halsted St.,* ☎ *773/665–8064. Crowd: male, mostly over 30; lots of leather and some Levi's; some uniforms, bears and big daddies; butch and hard-core.*

Charlie's. The city's main country-western dance club, a comfy and friendly place with a neighborhood feel, is smaller and more male-oriented than similar establishments in other cities. A little video bar is off to one side, a dance floor is in the center, and a few rows of seats are behind that. ⊠ *3726 N. Broadway,* ☎ *773/871–8887. Crowd: mostly male, 30s and up, neat mustaches and sideburns; blue denim and flannel shirts, a few 10-gallon hats; low-key.*

Circuit. This new dance club in a converted garage on Halsted has maintained several identities over the past few years. It has become a spot for hot Latin music. Go-go dancers and lithe male dancers please the crowds; the dance floor has a great sound system and plenty of room to cut loose. ⊠ *3641 N. Halsted St.,* ☎ *773/325–2233. Crowd: mostly male, mostly under 35, mixed racially, serious dancers.*

Cocktail. A guy guzzling Bud longnecks and another sipping cosmopolitans can feel right at home together at this cozy upscale cocktail bar. Darkly lit with comfy seating in back and a bar in front, this corner storefront bar feels particularly warm and inviting on cold winter nights and is a great place to meet up with friends before heading out later to larger and louder clubs. More women- and hetero-friendly than most of the other bars along Halsted, and extremely hospitable and fun bartenders. ⊠ *3359 Halsted St.,* ☎ *773/477–1420. Crowd: 80/20 m/f, 20s and 30s, professional but not buttoned-down, friendly, mellow.*

Fusion. The former high-energy disco Vortex has been converted into a restaurant up front, Rhumba (*see* Eats, *above*), which opens into this highly charged and kinetic dance club late in the evening. The staff clears away the tables and chairs from the dining room when the last patrons have finished eating and the metamorphosis is complete. The action officially begins at 10 PM but doesn't really get going until midnight. When many of the other bars in the neighborhood close at 2 AM, it gets another boost. A hot crowd takes to the throbbing dance floor of this post-industrial space, while other revelers jam into the various bars and wander the club's three levels. ⊠ *3631 Halsted St.,* ☎ *773/975–6622. Crowd: 75/25 m/f, mostly 20s to early 30s, mixed racially, club kids, muscle men, voguers and poseurs, intense dancing.*

Gentry on Halsted. This branch of downtown's popular suits bar brings a touch of formality to dressed-down Halsted (though you'll do fine in jeans and a T-shirt). The mood is civil but convivial. When there's not live piano music or a cabaret show, pop music hums in the background. You can sit at the long bar or on bar stools surrounding dainty, candlelit cocktail tables. Ubiquitous exposed brick and indirect lighting round out the decor. Definitely a place you could bring your mom to—there's even valet parking. ⊠ *3320 N. Halsted St.,* ☎ *773/348–1053. Crowd: 80/20 m/f, mostly over 35, a few suits, plenty of sweaters and khakis, artsy but coifed.*

Little Jim's. Of Halsted's bars, this is the one most geared to guys looking to pick up company for the evening—video screens show porn and tight quarters put everyone in a willing mood. It's just a long room with a bar on one side and a long wall on the other—you lean against one side and wait for someone to walk over and punch your dance card. ⊠ *3501 N. Halsted St.,* ☎ *773/871–6116. Crowd: male, diverse in age but mostly mid-20s to late 30s, lots of professional oglers, touchy-feely in a rough sort of way.*

Manhole. Chicago's major leather disco has become more eclectic, especially because it stays open past 2 and is therefore a great option after nearby Cocktail, Sidetrack, and Roscoe's close. The large, rambling place comprises three rooms and is decorated in an under-construction motif (brick walls are cut out in places so as to look like a wrecking ball has passed through). One room has a small dance floor (it can get extremely frisky), and the other two have bars and porn showing on video monitors. The place is famous for its strip shows performed by notable porn stars, "lights out" get-togethers, and underwear parties. ⊠ *3458 N. Halsted St.,* ☎ *773/975–9244. Crowd: mostly male, 20s to 40s, lots of* *leather and Levi's early in evening, eclectic late at night, horny and on the make, fairly butch, gym guys.*

The North End. A massive trophy case presides over this spacious video bar, which is neither a dive nor especially glamorous. Many guys play pool here, and the North End also hosts the local mirth and girth group. Lots of drag, too. ⊠ *3733 N. Halsted St.,* ☎ *773/477–7999. Crowd: male, mostly over 35, laid-back, semicruisy.*

Roscoe's. For several years this guppie bar, a Chicago institution, has been the most reliable option for having fun, dancing, and cruising on the Halsted bar row. The constant crowd makes it easy to mingle and meet. The first room, an old-fashioned saloon, has a large central bar and video screens. Off the middle bar is an outdoor patio. Another tavernlike space fronts Halsted Street next to the first bar. In back there's yet another bar, with two pool tables and a tiny but fun dance floor that doubles as a show space for drag acts and what not. ⊠ *3356 N. Halsted St.,* ☎ *773/281– 3355. Crowd: 80/20 m/f, 20s to 30s, clean-shaven, hair gel galore, same crowd as Sidetrack but less intense.*

Sidetrack. Chicago's classic stand-and-model video bar, Sidetrack's chief asset is the stylish decor, especially the sparkling chrome bar counters and handsome pressed-tin ceilings. The first of its three rooms, large and open with a long L-shaped bar, has lots of room to mingle. The cozy enclosed patio behind it has a handsome little garden and a small center bar—it's quieter here than inside. To your right as you head inside and up a few steps a long platform overlooks the first bar, and off it, an elegant cocktail lounge has a few tables and lots of bar seating. There are different genres of music videos on different nights—Mondays are show tunes, Wednesdays are oldies, etc. ⊠ *3349 N. Halsted St.,* ☎ *773/477–9189. Crowd: mostly male, mostly under 35, guppie, clean-shaven, plenty of attitude, cruisy but with manners.*

Spin. These days, this laid-back, midsize disco is the tame alternative to Fusion—it's neither as stylish, intense, nor urbane. Inside are two distinct halves: The first is a long video bar with several TV screens and a raised platform with two pool tables and big windows overlooking the cruisy intersection of Belmont and Halsted; it's warmly decorated with sconces and fancy light fixtures, and the noise level promotes conversation. The second half has a small dance floor with pink lighting, a great sound system, and a small bar. "Single Dollar Sundays," when all drinks go for a buck, are a good time to come. ⊠ *800 W. Belmont Ave.,* ☎ *773/327– 7711. Crowd: 75/25 m/f; young, white, a mix of guppies and corn-fed queerburbanites, lots of jeans and button-down shirts.*

NEIGHBORHOOD HAUNTS

Annex III (⊠ 3160 N. Clark St., ☎ 773/327–5969) may be the only gay bar with a neon football helmet in the window—it's a place where "bears" like to sit around talking about Bears . . . and Cubs and Bulls and Blackhawks. **Big Daddies** (⊠ 2914 N. Broadway, ☎ 773/929–0922), a festive little tavern, shows adult films and gets a mostly bearish leather crowd, plus a few urban cowboys. **Buck's** (⊠ 3439 N. Halsted St., ☎ 773/525– 1125) is a throwback to the kind of snazzy, inviting, old-fashioned bar you might have expected to find in Chicago in the '20s—the laid-back, mostly male crowd is here to converse and enjoy the old jukebox.

Bathed in pink neon, **Dandy's** (⊠ 3729 N. Halsted St., ☎ 773/525–1200) is a fun piano bar popular for karaoke; there's both bar and table seating. The **Lucky Horseshoe** (⊠ 3169 N. Halsted St., ☎ 773/404–3169) has male strippers nightly and never charges a cover; it's the city's top venue for watching the boys show off their toys. South of Boys' Town in Lincoln Park, the **Manhandler** (⊠ 1948 N. Halsted St., ☎ 773/871–3339) is a favorite spot for leather men, bears, country-western fans, and the like.

Boybar, held on Wednesday at **Girlbar** (*see* Women's Bars, *below*) has become a big to-do, thanks in part to those four-dollar pitchers.

North

PRIME SUSPECTS

Big Chicks. One of Chicago's friendliest and most diverse bars, Big Chicks is a nice neighborhood place with a difference: Fantastic local art hangs on the walls amid art deco touches. Video screens, darts, a minipool table, a small patio, and a great vintage jukebox with every imaginable kind of music also help distinguish it. Folks from the area's many gay and lesbian sports teams are particularly likely to stop in here. If you're alone and looking to make friends or get to know a few locals, you won't find a more genuine, sincere bunch of barflies. ⊠ *5024 N. Sheridan Rd.,* ☎ *773/728–5511. Crowd: mostly gay, mixed m/f, all ages, racially mixed, convivial, dressed-down, not at all cruisy.*

NEIGHBORHOOD HAUNTS

Clark's on Clark (⊠ 5001 N. Clark St., ☎ 773/728–2373), a big, dark, minimalist space, attracts a mix of men and women to shoot pool and hang out. You enter the **Eagle** (⊠ 5015 N. Clark St., ☎ 773/728–0050), which is attached to a bathhouse, through an alley; the dark decor is meant to conjure up a motorcycle garage. It's big with the hard-core leather crowd. You can buy leather gear and accessories next door at **Eagle Leathers** (⊠ 5005 N. Clark St., ☎ 773/728–7228). **Scot's** (⊠ 1829 W. Montrose St., ☎ 773/528–3253), a friendly neighborhood bar popular with both women and men, is good for watching football and shooting pool. **Madrigal's** (⊠ 5316 N. Clark St., ☎ 773/334–3033), a fun neighborhood bar in Andersonville, draws a mixed male/female crowd and serves good pub food.

Numbers (⊠ 6406 N. Clark St., ☎ 773/743–5772), just north of Andersonville, is a popular place to catch strippers and drag performers. Next door, **Touché** (⊠ 6412 N. Clark St., ☎ 773/465–7400) scores with rough-and-tumble leather bears. In Rogers Park, queers head to **Charmers** (⊠ 1502 W. Jarvis St., ☎ 773/465–2811). Just south of Loyola University, the **Granville Anvil** (⊠ 1137 W. Granville Ave., ☎ 773/973–0006) is a chummy hangout that attracts a mix of younger and older guys. West of I–94 on Irving Park Road are **Friends Pub** (⊠ 3432 W. Irving Park Rd., ☎ 773/539–5229), more of a sports bar with darts, pool, and a jukebox; and **Legacy 21** (⊠ 3042 W. Irving Park Rd., ☎ 773/588–9405), a local pub.

Downtown

PRIME SUSPECTS

Gentry. If you think the trading's heavy at the Commodities Exchange, check out the cologne-dipped suits at this downtown institution, which moved from its fancy Rush Street digs to a new space on State Street in November 1997. Handsome bartenders and cocktail waiters saunter about in tuxedo shirts with green bow ties. Early in the evening, about 90% of the guys are in business attire, but as the hours pass things become less dressy. ⊠ *440 N. State St.,* ☎ *312/664–1033. Crowd: 85/15 m/f, all ages, clean-cut, movers and shakers, discreet gentlemen.*

NEIGHBORHOOD HAUNTS

One of the best places to catch drag acts is the **Baton Show Lounge** (⊠ 436 N. Clark St., ☎ 312/644–5269), which has a mixed gay and straight following. It's touristy, but fun just the same. Gay and lesbian African Americans dance til the wee hours at **Generator** (⊠ 306 N. Halsted St., ☎ 312/243–8889). The latest gay bar to open downtown, **Leatherneck** (⊠ 209 W. Lake St., ☎ 312/332–7070) is, as the name suggests, a leather bar, with fetish nights, a dungeon, and a kinky ambience—time will tell whether this place can succeed in luring butch bears downtown. Older guys in suits frequent the **Second Story Bar** (⊠ 157 E. Ohio St., ☎ 312/ 923–9536), a longtime downtown hangout.

ONE-NIGHTERS

Young alternative gen-X guys favor **GLEE Club** at **Crobar** (⊠ 1543 N. King-bury St., ☎ 312/243–2075), a tremendously fun Sunday-night get-to-gether that rocks until the wee hours.

Bucktown and Wicker Park

HANGIN' WITH THE HETS

Most of the hipster-infested lounges and smoky bars in Bucktown and Wicker Park have a moderately queer following, although none are specifically gay. Best bets are the trendy dance loft, **Red Dog** (⊠ 1958 W. North Ave., ☎ 773/278–1009), which is especially queer on Monday nights. You can dance to rock and disco classics at the **Artful Dodger** (⊠ 1734 W. Wabansia, ☎ 773/227–6859), which has strange, colorful drinks and a similar crowd. A former Polish social club, the **Rainbo Club** (⊠ 1150 N. Damen Ave., ☎ 773/489–5999) is now a major hangout for art students, rockers, and neighborhood scenesters.

South Side

PRIME SUSPECTS

Club Escape. The first new African American gay bar to make a major impact on the scene in some time, Club Escape opened in summer 1997. The space, nicely laid-out and well-decorated, has ample seating and chat areas that complement a nice dance floor and an excellent sound system. The extremely personable staff go out of their way to welcome newcomers. The patio out back is a nice spot to cool off. On Wednesday the male dancers pack the place, and Friday and Saturday are the big nights for dancing to house music. Thursday sees more lesbians. A nice alternative to Jeffrey Pub, which can be chaotic, especially on weekends. ⊠ *1530 E. 75th St., ☎ 773/667–6454. Crowd: 75/25 m/f, 20s to 40s, mostly black, social but especially cruisy, low attitude.*

Jeffrey Pub. One of the granddaddies of gay Chicago clubs, Jeffrey Pub is a true mainstay within the South Shore African American community. The patrons and the music make the place, which isn't especially atmo-spheric in terms of decor. It is crowded, dark, and loud—three elements that make this a steamy high-energy night on the town. How good is it? People drive here from all over greater Chicago and even northern Indi-ana. ⊠ *7041 S. Jeffrey St., ☎ 773/363–8555. Crowd: mostly male, mostly 20s to 40s, mostly black, high energy.*

Women's Bars

Although the thriving gay nightlife strip in New Town is mostly male, Chicago has a better scene for lesbians than most cities. There are a few lively video bars, and Lincoln Park has a terrific new dyke disco. Also, of the clubs reviewed above, the Artful Dodger, Berlin, Big Chicks, Madri-gal's, the Rainbo Club, and Red Dog draw a considerable number of women, and the following establishments have a limited dyke presence: Clark's on Clark, Club Escape, Cocktail, Dandy's, Friends, Fusion, Gen-erator, Gentry, Gentry on Halsted, GLEE Club (on Sunday), Jeffrey Pub, Legacy 21, Numbers, Roscoe's, and Spin.

PRIME SUSPECTS

The Closet. Even though this narrow, attractive video bar draws equal num-bers of men and women many nights, it's considered a lesbian hangout.

Almost always packed with neighborhood types, jocks, and regular janes and joes, it has several TV screens, darts, a pool table, warm lighting, and an outgoing staff. Famous for its Bloody Marys on Sunday. ⊠ *3325 N. Broadway,* ☎ *773/477–8533. Crowd: mixed 60/40 f/m, mostly 30s and 40s, low-key, equally popular with couples and singles.*

Girlbar. Since the long-running dyke disco Paris Dance closed in November 1997, the focus of the lesbian social scene has shifted to this hot women's club in Lincoln Park. The mammoth two-level club has a large dance floor on the ground floor and a lounge with pool, darts, and a jukebox upstairs. ⊠ *2625 N. Halsted St.,* ☎ *773/871–4210. Crowd: female, 20s to mid-30s, somewhat mixed racially, professional, lots of lipstick and good hair.*

The Other Side. This small, smoky, unmarked bar on an industrial stretch of Western Avenue has a few tables and chairs, video poker, and darts, plus a small dance floor that rocks to classic dance tunes. It's low-key and draws a local bunch. Has some spicy female go-go dancers on certain nights. ⊠ *3655 N. Western Ave.,* ☎ *773/404–8156. Crowd: female, mostly 30s and 40s, some leather and Levi's, butch.*

NEIGHBORHOOD HAUNTS

On Saturday, lesbians of color convene downtown for dancing and mingling at **Club Intimus** (⊠ 312 W. Randolph St., ☎ 312/901–1703). The **Lost & Found** (⊠ 3058 W. Irving Park Rd., ☎ 773/463–9617) is a mellow old-fashioned pub with a local working-class following.

Action

Baths, strip clubs, video booths, and the like, similar to those in other large cities, can be found all over town. The **Bijou** theater (⊠ 1349 N. Wells St., ☎ 312/943–5397) has several levels and private rooms. The **Ram** (⊠ 3511 N. Halsted St., ☎ 773/525–9528), another popular theater, is in the heart of Boys' Town. A few blocks away is the **Unicorn** (⊠ 3246 N. Halsted St., ☎ 773/929–6081) bathhouse; you can also buy porn and erotica here. Adjacent to Andersonville's Eagle is **Man's Country** (⊠ 5017 N. Clark St., ☎ 773/878–2069), another bathhouse, but with more of a leather scene.

SLEEPS

Unlike the major coastal cities, old-fashioned Chicago has few minimalist, avant-garde hotels. Jumbo cookie-cutter convention properties prevail downtown. North of the Loop, around Michigan Avenue, a mix of stately high-end hotels and smaller European-style boutique establishments prevail. All over town, traditional American and European antiques-inspired furnishings and sedate color schemes are the rule.

Staying in the Loop means putting up with traffic noise and a long trek to Lakeview's nightlife. The farther north you go above the Chicago River, the quieter the neighborhood and the closer to Lakeview. North of North Avenue, options are limited to a handful of smaller, gay-friendly options.

For price ranges, *see* lodging Chart A at the front of this guide.

Hotels

Greater Downtown

$$$$ ⊡ **Ritz-Carlton.** One of the finest hotels in the nation, this Four Seasons–operated Ritz-Carlton (unrelated to the Ritz-Carlton chain) is a true stunner, perched on the floors above the high-end Water Tower Place shopping center. The atmosphere is not as stuffy as some other luxury properties in the city. Afternoon tea is served in the airy, 12th-floor atrium lobby, and rooms have Chippendale-style armoires and stately wing chairs. ✉ *160 E. Pearson St., 60611,* ☎ *312/266–1000 or 800/691–6906,* ℻ *312/266–1194. 431 rooms. Restaurants, pool, exercise room.*

$$$–$$$$ 🏨 **Sutton Place Hotel.** The trendy Sutton Place is tops among performers, models, and European jet-setters. Rather atypical in Chicago, the rooms have state-of-the-art entertainment centers (with VCRs, CD players, and radios) and a crisp black, white, and gray color scheme. Many have original Robert Mapplethorpe photos, too. ✉ *21 E. Bellevue Pl., 60611,* ☎ *312/266–2100 or 800/810–6888,* ℻ *312/266–2141. 247 rooms. Restaurant.*

$$$–$$$$ 🏨 **Westin River North.** Sleek and refined, the former Hotel Nikko invites serenity throughout. A stroll through the granite-and-black-lacquer lobby, which overlooks an ethereal rock garden, is the perfect way to end a back-breaking day of shopping along nearby Michigan Avenue. Rooms come with contemporary American furnishings and marble baths. Nary a dust bunny in sight. ✉ *320 N. Dearborn St., 60610,* ☎ *312/744–1900 or 800/ 937–8641,* ℻ *312/527–2664. 422 rooms. Restaurants, exercise room.*

$$$ 🏨 **Ambassador West.** Across the street from the Omni Ambassador East, this historic hotel has a similar, European-style ambience. Rooms here are smaller and furnished more basically. Still, it's hard to beat the location, and decent weekend rates make it a nice choice. ✉ *1300 N. State Pkwy., 60610,* ☎ *312/787–3700 or 800/300–9378,* ℻ *312/640–2967. 219 rooms. Restaurant, exercise room.*

$$$ 🏨 **Hyatt Regency.** Big, brash, and bustling, this mega-convention hotel has all the warmth of an immigration processing center—if anonymity is your thing, you'll love it. The Wacker Drive location is convenient to Loop and Near North attractions and shopping; rooms are clean and contemporary. ✉ *151 E. Wacker Dr., 60601,* ☎ *312/565–1234 or 800/233– 1234,* ℻ *312/565–2966. 2,019 rooms. Restaurants.*

$$$ 🏨 **Omni Ambassador East.** Just below Lincoln Park, along the tony Gold Coast, this courtly '20s hotel is closer to Lakeview than most downtown properties yet still within walking distance of Michigan Avenue. Rooms are furnished with an eclectic mix of reproduction antiques and newer pieces. The Pump Room restaurant is a favorite gathering spot of celebrities and bigwigs. ✉ *1301 N. State Pkwy., 60610,* ☎ *312/787–7200 or 800/842–6664,* ℻ *312/787–4760. 274 rooms. Restaurant, exercise room.*

$$–$$$ 🏨 **Claridge Hotel.** Free newspapers, Continental breakfast, and complimentary limo service to the Loop and Michigan Avenue are the chief assets of this sedate yet cozy '30s Gold Coast hotel. Rooms are small but tasteful, and the staff is polished and professional. ✉ *1244 N. Dearborn Pkwy., 60610,* ☎ *312/787–4980 or 800/245–1258,* ℻ *312/266–0978. 168 rooms. Restaurant.*

$$–$$$ 🏨 **Raphael.** One of those less-talked-about gems that locals recommend to visiting friends, the Raphael is in the center of the Magnificent Mile. Most guest quarters have separate sitting rooms anchored by long, comfy chaise longues. ✉ *201 E. Delaware Pl., 60611,* ☎ *312/943–5000 or 800/ 821–5343,* ℻ *312/943–9483. 172 rooms. Restaurant.*

North

$–$$ 🏨 **Comfort Inn–Lincoln Park.** A few blocks south of New Town, this surprisingly bright, well-decorated motel boasts a friendly staff, free Continental breakfast, and its own parking lot. ✉ *601 W. Diversey Pkwy., 60614,* ☎ *773/348–2810 or 800/727–0800,* ℻ *773/525–6998. 71 rooms.*

$–$$ 🏨 **Days Inn Lincoln Park North.** This ideally located chain motel has basic clean rooms and a strong gay and lesbian following. ✉ *646 W. Diversey Pkwy., 60614,* ☎ *773/525–7010 or 800/329–7466,* ℻ *773/664–3045. 121 rooms.*

$ ⚏ **City Suites.** Right below the Belmont Street El stop is the rambling old City Suites, one of three properties in the gay-friendly Neighborhood Inns group. It's not fancy—the decor leans toward old-fashioned wallpaper and reproduction antiques—but the place has loads of character and draws a wide range of guests, from visiting grunge rock bands to gays and lesbians who want to be steps from the bar scene. ⊠ *933 W. Belmont Ave., 60657,* ☎ *773/404–3400 or 888/248–9466,* ℻ *773/404–3405. 45 rooms.*

$ ⚏ **Park Brompton Inn.** This affordable European-style hotel is close to Lincoln Park and the lakeshore. Rooms are furnished with reproduction English antiques, and many of the spacious suites have refrigerators, microwaves, and wet bars. A member of the Neighborhood Inn group. ⊠ *528 W. Brompton St., 60657,* ☎ *773/404–3499 or 888/248–9466,* ℻ *773/404–3495. 29 rooms.*

$ ⚏ **Surf Hotel.** The most charming of the three Neighborhood Inns, the Surf sits on a quiet side street just steps from North Broadway's bars and restaurants. Rooms are long and narrow, fitted with spotless modern baths and reproductions of 19th-century French antiques. ⊠ *555 W. Surf St., 60657,* ☎ *773/528–8400 or 888/248–9466,* ℻ *773/528–8483. 55 rooms.*

Guest House

North

$–$$ ⚏ **Villa Toscana.** Set back off hopping Halsted Street and fronted by pretty gardens, this charming 1890s two-story cottage is the only gay-oriented B&B in Chicago. Many gay bars and community-popular restaurants are nearby. The cozy rooms, many with pitched ceilings and characterful corners and nooks, are furnished with a mix of art deco pieces, fluffy beds with down comforters, and reproduction antiques. ⊠ *3447 N. Halsted St., 60657,* ☎ *773/404–2643 or 800/404–2643. 7 rooms, some with phone, TV, and private bath. Continental breakfast. Mostly mixed gay male/lesbian.*

THE LITTLE BLACK BOOK

At Your Fingertips

AIDS Foundation of Chicago (☎ 773/922–2322). **AIDS Hotline (statewide)** (☎ 800/243–2437). **Chicago Black Lesbians & Gays** (☎ 312/409–4917). **Chicago Office of Tourism** (main office: ⊠ 78 E. Washington St., 60602, ☎ 312/744–2400 or 800/226–6632, Web site www.ci.chi.il.us/tourism; visitors centers: ⊠ Old Water Tower, ⊠ 806 N. Michigan Ave.; Chicago Cultural Center, ⊠ 77 E. Randolph St.; Navy Pier, ⊠ 700 E. Grand Ave.). The *Chicago Reader* (alternative weekly, ☎ 312/828–0350, Web site www.chicagoreader.com). **Chicago Transit Authority** (CTA; ☎ 312/836–7000). **Chicago Women's Health Center** (☎ 312/935–6126). **Gay and Lesbian Info Line** (☎ 773/929–4357). **Gerber/Hart Gay and Lesbian Library and Archives** (⊠ 3352 N. Paulina St., ☎ 773/883–3003). **Horizons Lesbian and Gay Community Services** (referrals, support, youth group; ⊠ 961 W. Montana St., ☎ 773/929–4357). *New City* (alternative weekly, ☎ 312/243–8786, Web site www.newcitynet.com). **Yellow Cab Co.** (☎ 312/829–4222).

Gay Media

The *Windy City Times* (☎ 312/397–0025, e-mail wct@wwa.com) is one of the country's best gay and lesbian news weeklies, with strong national and local coverage. *Gay Chicago Magazine* (☎ 773/327–7271, e-mail gaychimag@aol.com) is a hefty entertainment-oriented newsweekly. The monthly newspaper *Outlines* (☎ 773/871–7610, Web site www.suba.com/~outlines) and its weekly pocket-size bar rag, *Nightlines,* are also helpful lesbigay resources. The lesbian coverage in *Outlines* is especially strong; the same publisher also puts out the monthly *Blacklines* for Chicago's black queer community, and *En La Vida* for the Latino queer community. *Gab* (☎ 773/248–4542, e-mail gab@earthlink.net) is a punchy, if irreverent bar 'zine with all of the latest on clubbing and sleazing around town.

BOOKSTORES

The city's only specifically lesbigay bookstore, People Like Us, closed in October 1997, but Lakeview readers still enjoy the presence of the outstanding **Unabridged Bookstore** (⊠ 3251 N. Broadway, ☎ 773/883–9119), which has one of the best selections of lesbian and gay titles in the Midwest; it's also a remarkably well-stocked general-interest store with a friendly, knowledgeable staff. An Andersonville landmark since the early '80s, **Women & Children First Bookstore** (⊠ 5233 N. Clark St., ☎ 773/769–9299) has a vast array of women's titles, plus music videos and magazines.

Working Out

Around the Loop, the seven-floor **Athletic Club Illinois Center** (⊠ 211 N. Stetson St., ☎ 312/616–9000) is terrific, well-equipped, and popular with the gay community. Lakeview's **Body Shop** (⊠ 3246 N. Halsted St., ☎ 773/248–7717), next to the Unicorn bathhouse, is a cruisy fitness center. The **Chicago Sweat Shop** (⊠ 3215 N. Broadway, ☎ 773/871–2789) draws a better mix of men and women for aerobics and Nautilus. Plenty of space for working those buns. **Quad's Gym** (⊠ 3727 N. Broadway, ☎ 773/404–7867) and the **Chicago Health Club** (⊠ 2828 N. Clark St., ☎ 773/929–6900) are also good places to work out. Women should check out **Thousand Waves Spa for Women** (⊠ 1212 W. Belmont St., ☎ 773/549–0700), a dyke-friendly sauna, steam, and massage-therapy center.

SAUGATUCK AND DOUGLAS, MICHIGAN

The sleepy villages of Saugatuck and Douglas comprise the only significant gay vacation spot in the north central United States. A little more than two hours from Chicago and three hours from Detroit, the two towns are separated by Lake Kalamazoo—in fact a wide expanse of the eponymous river, which empties into nearby Lake Michigan.

Douglas, the sleepier of the two communities and the home of the area's main gay lodging and entertainment venue, successfully passed a gay and lesbian civil rights ordinance a few years back. **Saugatuck**—the larger and more commercial of the pair—has sunny boutiques, antiques shops, galleries, fudge shops, and eateries along a compact grid of unassuming, tree-lined streets. Straight yuppies have been and will probably always be the community's bread and butter, and Saugatuck is without rainbow flags or other signs of homo-habitation, despite the fact that gay men and, increasingly, lesbians have been visiting for a few decades. Nonetheless, in 1995 a straight-owned B&B allegedly refused to book one room to a male couple, sparking a mild but controversial civil rights struggle that ended when the city council shot down a proposed antidiscrimination ordinance. Since then, some have debated whether to boycott the area. Despite these rumblings, it's unlikely that you'll encounter negative vibes in either of these quiet and modestly charming towns.

The main tourist season runs from May through September, though many places stay open year-round. Fall is beautiful when the foliage is changing, and winter offers a quiet and romantic (if chilly) respite from Midwest cities.

Lay of the Land

Favorite pastimes are shopping, which is best in downtown Saugatuck, and sunning. Along the sweeping, sandy Lake Michigan shoreline, **Oval Beach** is the main gay and lesbian sun spot. You reach it via downtown Douglas: Take Center Street west; turn right onto Park Street; follow it north, turning left at the Holiday Hill resort and following signs to the beach. The gay and lesbian section is at the north end; parking is $3. Lake Michigan's surf packs a wallop, and the strong winds have formed huge dunes, covered with shrubs, behind the parking lots. Like the area as a whole, Oval Beach has shunned overdevelopment.

Getting Around

You need a car to reach these two towns and to get between them, but once here you can manage on foot (except to get to the beach or the gay nightclub). From Chicago, wind around Lake Michigan on I–94, eventually cutting northward onto I–196 for the final leg of the journey. From Detroit, head west on I–96, cutting southwest onto I–196 just after passing through Grand Rapids.

Eats

Most area restaurants are in the heart of Saugatuck's downtown. These places are mostly gay-friendly, but if you want a predominantly queer ambience, head to the Douglas Dunes Resort.

For price ranges, *see* dining Chart B at the front of this guide.

$$$ ✕ **Toulouse.** Forget that it has a major gay following—Toulouse is one of the finest restaurants in western Michigan. Parisian show posters line the walls of the candlelit, antiques-filled dining room. The food sings, from the vegan platter of pear-stuffed cabbage rolls with bell pepper-infused beurre blanc to the fresh walleye pike with lemon caper butter. The place to go for a special occasion—but it can be tough to get a table on weekends. ✉ *248 Culver St., Saugatuck,* ☎ *616/857–1561.*

$$–$$$ ✕ **Douglas Dunes Resort.** This restaurant at the area's main gay hangout has the look and feel of a standard hotel dining room—wall-to-wall carpeting, jewel tones, and potted plants. In good weather you can dine on a covered patio. The dependable Continental and American menu offers such traditional fare as blackened redfish and chicken Florentine. ✉ *333 Blue Star Hwy., Douglas,* ☎ *616/857–1401.*

$$ ✕ **Chequers.** This festive place could pass for an English pub in the Cotswolds—it's warmly lit and filled with bric-a-brac. A big crowd quaffs pints of imported ales and stouts. Appropriately, the menu offers fish and chips, shepherd's pie, and bangers and mash as well as salads and sandwiches. ✉ *220 Culver St., Saugatuck,* ☎ *616/857–1868.*

$–$$ ✕ **Marro's Italian Restaurant.** With a long, attractive bar that zigzags along one wall and rows of windows looking across the street to Lake Kalamazoo, this rambling pizza-and-pasta house is a lively place to hang out. ✉ *147 Water St., Saugatuck,* ☎ *616/857–4248.*

$ ✕ **Loaf & Mug.** This is a homey, old-fashioned storefront deli with a vast array of hefty sandwiches (several of them vegetarian), a nice selection of wines, and friendly service. Pastrami on rye is a favorite. Breakfast and lunch only. ✉ *236 Culver St., Saugatuck,* ☎ *616/857–2974.*

$ ✕ **Pumpernickles.** This airy bakery and café, open for breakfast and lunch, is a good place to grab supplies for the beach. On a bustling corner in the heart of downtown Saugatuck, it's a good place for people-watching. ✉ *202 Butler St., Saugatuck,* ☎ *616/857–1196.*

$ ✕ **Uncommon Grounds.** One of the only establishments downtown that greets patrons with a big, friendly rainbow flag over the front door, this café has a chatty staff and delicious coffees; the carrot cake is especially tasty. The sunny deck out front is nice for ogling passers-by. ⊠ *127 Hoffman St., Saugatuck,* ☎ *616/857–3333.*

Scenes

The only game in town is the **Douglas Dunes Resort** (⊠ 333 Blue Star Hwy., Douglas, ☎ 616/857–1401); it has a sizable disco, a cocktail lounge and video bar, a huge fenced-in sundeck and bar with a large pool and lush foliage, and a piano cabaret. All kinds mingle—though the crowd is almost entirely gay and lesbian.

Sleeps

Besides the relatively large Douglas Dunes Resort, which is predominantly gay, the area has several gay-oriented inns and B&Bs, from lavish and a bit pricey to moderate. If you want to be within walking distance of downtown restaurants and shopping, pick one of the Saugatuck properties; the ones in Douglas, however, are closer to the beach.

For price ranges, *see* lodging Chart B at the front of this guide.

$$–$$$ ▦ **Kirby House.** This immense 1890 Queen Anne on the edge of downtown Douglas is one of the region's most striking properties. Five fireplaces, myriad stained-glass windows, and fine oak detailing distinguish the interior. Don't miss the big breakfast. ⊠ *294 W. Center St., Douglas, 49406,* ☎ *616/857–2904 or 800/521–6473. 8 rooms with private bath. Pool, hot tub. Full breakfast. Mixed gay/straight.*

$$ ▦ **Lighthouse Motel.** This homo-popular motel within walking distance of the Douglas Dunes disco has pleasant rooms and reasonable rates. ⊠ *130th St. and Blue Star Hwy., Douglas, 49406,* ☎ *616/857–2271. Mixed gay/straight. 27 rooms with phone and TV, most with private bath. Pool. Continental breakfast. Mixed gay/straight.*

$$ ▦ **Moore's Creek Inn.** Close to downtown, this handsome white 1873 farmhouse is hosted by helpful innkeepers Fred Whitman and Clif Taylor, as well as a pair of adorable dogs. Each room has a theme, from Walt Disney memorabilia to Erté prints, and each mixes newish pieces with a smattering of antiques. ⊠ *820 Holland St., Saugatuck, 49453* ☎ *616/ 857–2411 or 800/838–5864. 4 rooms with private bath. Full breakfast. Mixed gay/straight.*

$$ ▦ **Park House.** Built in 1857, this is the oldest inn in Saugatuck (and the most historic: it hosted Susan B. Anthony). Rooms have traditional American furnishings, and if you're truly in search of privacy, you can opt for one of the private cottages out back. Breakfast is served fireside. ⊠ *888 Holland St., Saugatuck, 49453,* ☎ *616/857–4535 or 800/321–4535. 8 rooms with private bath. Continental breakfast. Mostly straight.*

$$ ▦ **Newnham Suncatcher Inn.** This stately brown clapboard inn with a wraparound porch welcomes everyone, but hostesses Barb and Nancy make an especially big effort to encourage lesbians and same-sex couples traveling with children. They treat guests like old friends, yet give them plenty of privacy. The inn is decorated with whimsical touches, such as stuffed animals, toys, and trinkets. ⊠ *131 Griffith St., Box 1106, Saugatuck, 49453,* ☎ *616/857–4249. 7 rooms, some with private bath. Pool, hot tub. Full breakfast. Mixed gay/straight.*

$–$$ ▦ **Douglas Dunes Resort.** A five-minute drive from Oval Beach and Saugatuck's shops and restaurants, this rambling 14-acre resort is the region's gay ground-zero, with four bars, a restaurant, and 64 units ranging from cottages to motel rooms. Accommodations are clean and simple, but some of the cottages have fireplaces and hot tubs. ⊠ *333 Blue Star Hwy., Box 369, Douglas, 49406,* ☎ *616/857–1401. 64 rooms with phone, TV, and private bath. Restaurant, pool, hot tub. Mostly gay male/lesbian.*

$–$$ 🏨 **Grandma's House B&B.** One of the best values in the area, this grand
Victorian is on four secluded acres. Common areas and guest rooms are
comfortably furnished, and full breakfasts are served. Nudity is permitted on the sundeck and in the hot tub. The only drawback is the 10- to
15-minute drive from downtown shops and Oval Beach. ✉ *2135 Blue
Star Hwy., Saugatuck, 49408, ☎ 616/543–4706. 5 rooms with TV and
private bath. Hot tub. Full breakfast. Mixed gay male/lesbian.*

The Little Black Book

For visitor information contact the **Saugatuck Area Business Association**
information booth, (✉ Culver and Butler Sts., Saugatuck, ☎ 616/857–
3133) or the **Saugatuck-Douglas Convention & Visitors Bureau** (✉ 303
Culver St., Box 28, Saugatuck, 49453, ☎ 616/857–1701, Web site
www.saugatuck.com).

6 *Out in Cincinnati*

CINCINNATI HAS EARNED AN INFAMOUS—and somewhat unfair—reputation for being both narrow-minded in its attitudes towards gays and lesbians *and* almost obsessively prudish. In 1990 the city pressed charges against the Cincinnati Contemporary Arts Center for hosting a controversial exhibition of Robert Mapplethorpe photos, many of them with explicit and provocative depictions of nudity and homoeroticism—the official charge was "pandering obscenity." A local jury later acquitted the defendants, but Cincinnati's self-righteous image stuck. Most troubling for the gay community was the passage in 1993 of a city referendum not unlike Colorado's Amendment 2, which sought to prevent the enforcement of an antidiscrimination measure introduced by the City Council a year earlier. Only when the Supreme Court struck down the constitutionality of Amendment 2 did the issue die here.

A few powerful and wealthy corporate and political leaders have led efforts to cleanse the city of any perceived moral shortcomings—the general population has been more often embarrassed than pleased with such efforts. Although Republican politicians control much of the metro region, Cincinnati's mayor, Roxanne Qualls, is a liberal Democrat with extremely close ties to the women's and gay communities. Just recently, during the national controversy within the Presbyterian Church over whether to allow "unrepenting" and openly gay men and lesbians to be ordained as ministers, Cincinnati's 86-church delegation voted pro-gay.

For all the negative publicity certain controversies have generated, Cincinnati's gay community has proven to be coherent and close-knit, with a well-utilized community center and a successful political lobby. Walk through downtown Cincinnati and some of its liveliest neighborhoods, and you'll see a face of the city that appears gay/straight integrated.

THE LAY OF THE LAND

Although metro Cincinnati is geographically immense, most areas of interest to visitors are within a 15-minute drive of downtown, a relatively compact district of office towers on the north bank of the Ohio River. Several bridges, including the majestic Roebling Suspension Bridge (on which the Roebling-created Brooklyn Bridge is based), connect downtown to Covington, Kentucky, and to a network of streets that climb west, north, and east of downtown into the hilly neighborhoods overlooking it. Cincinnati is one of America's hilliest cities, and as its downtown became increasingly industrial toward the end of the 19th century, the city's well-to-do residents fled for these higher points, which today contain beautiful historic homes.

Downtown and Over-the-Rhine

The city's skyline is a bit Jekyll and Hyde: dull and monochromatic by day, glitteringly aglow at night (it was the first city in America to illuminate its buildings with exterior floodlights). Downtown is a vibrant business district with a blend of architectural styles spanning the past century. Alas, most of the newer structures, built in the '60s and '70s, lack the character of the many art deco beauties. Among downtown's countless outdoor sculptures and fountains are the 1871 **Tyler Davidson Fountain,** the majestic anchor of **Fountain Square** (⌧ 6th and Vine. Sts.).

Towering above the city a block away is Cincinnati's tallest building, the art deco **Carew Tower** (⌧ 5th and Race Sts., ☏ 513/241–9743), which has a 49th-floor observation deck. The building is part of a complex that includes the **Omni Netherland Hotel** (*see* Sleeps, *below*) and the **Tower Place** shopping mall, a typically upscale mix of department stores and chain clothiers. A block east of the fountain is the **Cincinnati Contemporary Arts Center** (⌧ 115 E. 5th St., ☏ 513/721–0390); it has no permanent collection but regularly mounts excellent shows. Northeast of the fountain, the Cesar Pelli–designed **Aranoff Center** (⌧ Walnut and 6th Sts.) hosts the acclaimed **Cincinnati Ballet** (☏ 513/621–5219), three performance spaces, and an art gallery with rotating exhibits.

Walk to the eastern edge of downtown to explore the **Taft Museum** (⌧ 316 Pike St., ☏ 513/241–0343), an 1820s home originally owned by Charles Taft (the half-brother of U.S. president William Taft), one of the nation's leading 19th-century art collectors. In addition to priceless decorative arts and fine Chinese porcelains, the house is filled with Taft's astounding cache of old-master paintings, as well as works by Frans Hals, Rembrandt, Goya, Gainsborough, Corot, and many others.

Most of its attractions are geared toward kids, but the **Cincinnati Museum Center** (⌧ 1301 Western Ave., ☏ 513/287–7000 or 800/733–2077) definitely deserves a visit, if for no other reason than to admire one of the finest art deco structures in America, the 1933 Union Terminal. This 500,000-square-foot former rail station has been completely restored and now contains an **Omnimax Theater,** the **Museum of Natural History and Science,** and the **Cincinnati History Museum.** The complex is a short drive west of downtown, not far from the dramatic **Music Hall** (⌧ 1241 Elm St.), an 1878 structure with a nearly 400-foot-tall facade; it's the regular home of the **Cincinnati Opera** (☏ 513/241–2742), the **Cincinnati Symphony Orchestra** (☏ 513/381–3300), and the Erich Kunzel–led **Cincinnati Pops Orchestra** (☏ 513/621–1919).

Quite a few of Cincinnati's queer-popular bars, restaurants, and art galleries are in the northern half of downtown, near or in the **Main Street Historic District.** Between 6th and Court streets, the district is dominated by commercial structures that were built between 1870 and 1930. A few blocks north Main Street leads into the up-and-coming **Over-the-Rhine** neighborhood, which has blossomed in recent years with music clubs, coffeehouses, and microbreweries. It was named in the late 19th century for its location above Central Parkway, a filled-in canal that was once nicknamed "the Rhine" for its huge German-immigrant population. Most of the Over-the-Rhine buildings are Italianate and date from the 1860s to the 1880s; but a few earlier Greek Revival structures are here, too.

Rising above Over-the-Rhine are two historic neighborhoods that are now nesting grounds for gay men and lesbians: **Prospect Hill** and **Mount Auburn.** Although you'll find few businesses or attractions up here, you can tour the **William Howard Taft National Historic Site** (⌧ 2038 Auburn Ave., ☏ 513/684–3262), the 1841 Greek Revival childhood home of our nation's 27th president.

Mt. Adams and Eden Park

One of the prettiest and hilliest urban neighborhoods in the Midwest, **Mt. Adams** rises precipitously above the eastern edge of downtown and comprises a compact jumble of trendy businesses and pricey homes. Most of the shops and eateries are along or near **St. Gregory Street.** It's a quaint yuppified community worth a stroll, but the real draw is adjacent **Eden Park,** where a trail-laced bluff overlooks downtown and the Ohio River. Within this urban oasis are two lakes as well as a number of cultural sites: the **Mt. Adams Observatory** (✉ 3489 Observatory Rd., ☎ 513/321–5186); the **Playhouse in the Park** (☎ 962 Mt. Adams Cir., ☎ 513/421–3888), which presents 11 theatrical works annually; the Classic Revival–style **Cincinnati Art Museum** (✉ Eden Park Dr., ☎ 513/721–5204), known for its fine and decorative arts and its strong Native American and African collections; and the **Krohn Conservatory** (✉ Eden Park Dr., ☎ 513/421–4086), a mammoth, glass-enclosed rainforest with 5,000 varieties of exotic tropical and desert flora.

Mt. Adams is also famous for its association with Rookwood Pottery, which operated a factory here from 1892 to 1967. Around the turn of the century, Rookwood had earned international acclaim. Its pieces now fetch astronomical prices (a Rookwood vase recently sold for $198,000 at a major auction house). The first **Rookwood Pottery Factory** (*see* Eats, *below*) is now a restaurant on whose ground floor you can examine a fine collection of original Rookwood pottery.

Some of Cincinnati's ritziest communities are east of Mt. Adams. Drive west of downtown via the Columbia Parkway (U.S. 50) to **Walnut Hills, Mt. Lookout,** and **Mariemont,** before cutting back inland away from the river through monied **Hyde Park.**

Clifton and Corryville

From Vine Street, head north into the hills above downtown to a pair of colorful neighborhoods, **Corryville** and **Clifton.** The former is home to the **University of Cincinnati** as well as a small student-oriented commercial district with a few funky businesses. Just north of campus is the **Cincinnati Zoo and Botanical Garden** (✉ 3400 Vine St., ☎ 513/281–4700), the second-oldest in the country.

West of Corryville, **Clifton** is on the other side of verdant **Burnet Woods Park,** and best known for its hip and gay-friendly commercial drag, **Ludlow Avenue.** Students and professionals browse these low-key coffeehouses, cheap restaurants, and offbeat retail spaces. The **Esquire Theatre** (✉ 320 Ludlow Ave., ☎ 513/281–8750) shows foreign and independent flicks, many of them queer-themed.

Northside

Ludlow Avenue leads out of Clifton past another of Cincinnati's inviting green spaces, **Mt. Storm Park,** and over I–75 to **Hamilton Avenue,** the main drag of **Northside.** What was for many years a lower-middle-class minority neighborhood began to attract a sizeable lesbian crowd in the late '70s and has recently become trendy among gay men and alternative-minded straights. The few blocks at the foot of Hamilton have gay bars, some cafés, and the long-running feminist/lesbian bookstore, **Crazy Ladies** (*see* Bookstores, *below*).

GETTING AROUND

Interstate highways encircle and cut across Cincinnati, but you can navigate its neighborhoods by sticking to major streets (and perhaps the Memorial Parkway, U.S. 50). Although you'll need a car to get among these areas, you can navigate downtown, Mt. Adams, Clifton, and Northside on foot. Since roughly 75% of the attractions, restaurants, bar, and hotels are within walking distance of downtown, it's possible to get by here without a car (call a taxi for longer journeys).

EATS

Cincinnati has no gay dining district per se, but most spots around downtown's Main Street Historic District, as well as those in Clifton and Northside, are gay-frequented. Less queer but blasé about same-sexers are the eateries in the fashionable neighborhoods east of downtown, such as Mt. Adams and Hyde Park.

The city's intensely German and Irish heritage hasn't infused the local dining scene with sassy specialties. Cincinnati's lucrative pig-processing industry earned the city the rather unbecoming nickname "Porkopolis," and such native delicacies as *goetta* (a gruesome-sounding oatmeal–pork sausage concoction worked into patties and deep fried) and *city chicken* (skewered chunks of fried pork and veal) owe their very existence to this porky legacy. Cincinnati's greatest culinary claim, however, is chili—not the good spicy kind invented in San Antonio but a bland runny hodge-podge of beef, water, and tomato paste jump-started with a seemingly random litany of spices and condiments (vinegar, allspice, Worcestershire sauce, cinnamon, unsweetened chocolate) and then heaped over a mound of spaghetti. There appear to be more chili parlors in Cincinnati than gas stations, if you'll pardon the comparison. You can order chili as just described (a "three way"), with diced onions (a "four way"), with baked beans (a "five way"), or not at all (a "no way")—your stomach may appreciate the latter.

For price ranges, *see* dining Chart B at the front of this guide.

Downtown

$$$$ ✗ **Maisonette.** Could any restaurant live up to the acclaim of this downtown French eatery, the only one in the country to win the Mobil Five Star award 33 years in a row? With a new chef, Jean-Robert de Cavel, coming on board in 1996, the food has only improved and now focuses more on the south of France (and less on heavy, traditional preparations). ✉ *114 E. 6th St.,* ☎ *513/721–2260.*

$$ ✗ **Diner on Sycamore.** This Over-the-Rhine study in neon, vinyl, and stainless steel serves surprisingly sophisticated fare, from the usual steaks, Cobb salads, and BLTs to piquant Caribbean crab chili and baked brie with a tomato-shallot sauce. *1203 Sycamore St.,* ☎ *513/721–1212.*

$$ ✗ **Main Street Brewery.** It's fitting that in a city that supported 40 breweries a century ago, a new brew pub has been integral to the renaissance of one of its oldest neighborhoods, Over-the-Rhine. In addition to the good beers, try such hearty comfort foods as baby back ribs, cheddar ale soup, and beef-and-ale stew. The bar is a big straight singles scene, but a fair number of queers eat here, too. ✉ *1203 Main St.,* ☎ *513/665–4677.*

$–$$ ✗ **Arnold's.** The austere German immigrants who once favored this quaint tavern back in 1861 would hardly recognize it now, filled with loud students and artsy music fans who come for the live jazz and blues, as well as some decent if unadventurous American and Italian food—roast turkey, pasta, salads, and such. ✉ *210 E. 8th St.,* ☎ *513/421–6234. No credit cards.*

$–$$ ✗ **Carol's Corner Café.** This spacious post-industrial space with exposed brick walls hung with avant-garde art is downtown's gayest full-scale restaurant. Although all types of folks eat here, the cocktail bar at one end of the room usually brims with gay trendies. The American menu has towering build-your-own burgers and such goofily named dishes as "Cod Love Ya," which is, seriously, very good. ✉ *825 Main St.,* ☎ *513/651–2667.*

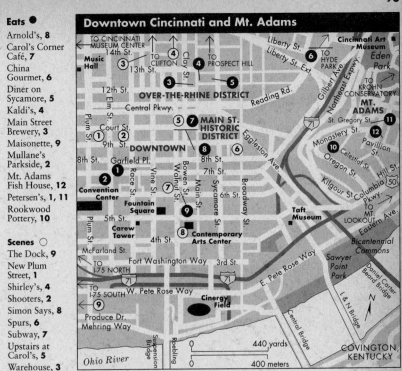

Downtown Cincinnati and Mt. Adams

$ ✕ **Mullane's Parkside.** At this downtown café, you can peruse an art in-stallation, have your cards read by a tarot reader, listen to live music, munch a wide range of salads and light dishes, sip coffee, or cruise the cute vegan at the next table. Steps from several gay bars. ⊠ *723 Race St.,* ☎ *513/ 381–1331. No credit cards.*

Clifton and Northside

$$–$$$ ✕ **Boca.** This airy bistro with a peaceful patio behind it opened in 1997 and helped secure Northside's reputation as a serious dining neighbor-hood. Sample such tantalizing nouvelle international fare as house-smoked double-cut pork chop with wedge of tamale pie on mole black beans and tomatillo salsa. ⊠ *4034 Hamilton Ave.,* ☎ *513/542–2022.*

$–$$ ✕ **Petersen's.** Locals rave about these warmly decorated restaurants—perfect for first dates—with branches downtown, in Clifton, and in Mt. Adams. The eclectic and artfully presented cross-cultural fare ranges from fresh pastas to delicious black burritos; the seafood dishes are al-ways winners, too. ⊠ *308 Ludlow Ave.,* ☎ *513/861–4777; downtown, 700 Elm St.,* ☎ *513/723–1113; Mt. Adams, 1111 St. Gregory St.,* ☎ *513/651–4777.*

$ ✕ **Comet.** This cheap boho-grunge hangout in Northside specializes in rice and beans, mole-marinated beef burritos, and punchy salsas—the kind of grub that always hits the spot and will never set you back more than $7 for a complete meal. With leopard-print walls and scruffy waitrons, Comet caters to an unconventional crowd. ⊠ *4579 Hamilton Ave.,* ☎ *513/541–8900.*

$ ✕ **No Anchovies.** A gritty pizza parlor with no aspirations beyond serv-ing its relentlessly weird clientele of slackers, art students, and counter-culturalists, No Anchovies has tasty pies with silly names. The "Karma" is all veggie, while the "PMS" (pepperoni, mushrooms, and sausage) may or may not ease the condition after which it's named. ⊠ *324 Ludlow Ave.,* ☎ *513/221–2277.*

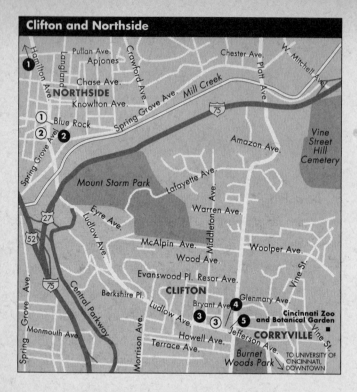

Mt. Adams and Hyde Park

\$\$\$–\$\$\$\$ ✕ **Mt. Adams Fish House.** This elegant bastion of yuppie dining in posh Mt. Adams serves the freshest fish in town, including cedar-plank salmon with a pinot noir glaze and ahi tuna with mango chutney. Sushi is prepared with considerable skill. ⊠ *940 Pavillion St.,* ☎ *513/421–3250.*

\$\$–\$\$\$ ✕ **China Gourmet.** You might end your day of touring the eastern Cincinnati 'burbs with a visit to this stellar upscale Asian restaurant in the heart of Hyde Park. Top dishes include jumbo soft-shell crabs stir-fried in a black bean and scallion sauce with pork, and Mandarin chicken in a spicy sauce of walnuts and green onions. ⊠ *3340 Erie Ave.,* ☎ *513/871–6612.*

\$\$–\$\$\$ ✕ **Rookwood Pottery.** Set in the rambling Tudor-style 1892 Rookwood Pottery Factory, this touristy American restaurant sometimes overflows with noisy kids but is worth a visit if only for the unique experience of dining inside a giant kiln. The entrées are neither special nor affordable, but the Rookwood has terrific burgers and good salads. ⊠ *1077 Celestial St.,* ☎ *513/721–5456.*

Coffeehouse Culture

Kaldi's. This Over-the-Rhine favorite is a great used bookstore with creaky floorboards, pressed-tin ceilings, and comfy chairs, and an inviting coffeehouse and a sophisticated wine bar. The desserts and light food (such as veggie lasagna) are also memorable. A mix of bookish intellectuals and alternaqueers. ⊠ *1204 Main St.,* ☎ *513/241–3070.*

Sitwells. This ultra-cool coffeehouse and Internet café in the basement of a stately old apartment building on Ludlow Avenue feels like an old general store with mismatched furniture, vintage signs, and old books. The mostly student crowd makes for good people-watching. ⊠ *404 Ludlow Ave.,* ☎ *513/281–7487.*

SCENES

With only about a dozen bars serving a metro population of nearly 2 million, the so-called Queen City isn't especially queeny. Indeed, the bar scene is limited, but for this reason it's rewarding if you enjoy meeting and talking with locals. There's one large disco; the other clubs are neighborhood-oriented. Many of the bars are downtown, quite visible and right in the thick of things, and not one could be called a dive. The message Cincinnati's scene seems to send is that gay bars are as respectable and important to the fabric of the city as are any other social institutions.

Prime Suspects

Bullfish's. This playfully named dyke bar in Northside is really no less of a locals's joint than Shirley's (*see below*), but Bullfish's is bigger and draws a greater variety of women—as well as some straights and gay guys. Inside the minimally decorated bar are a pair of pool tables, a dance floor, and plenty of seating. ⊠ *4023 Hamilton Ave.,* ☎ *513/541–9220. Crowd: 80/20 f/m, 20s to 50s, mix of white and blue collar, some students, very friendly, low attitude.*

Colors. Exactly the kind of neighborhood bar every city should have one of, but which most outsiders would never expect to find in white bread Cincinnati. The gays and straights, grungers and yuppies, and college students and settled couples who mingle at this elegant postmodern lounge come for the ambitious selection of beers, fun videos and groovy music, and comfy seating. The cheerful patio gets crowded on warm weekend evenings. ⊠ *4042 Hamilton Ave.,* ☎ *513/681–6969. Crowd: mixed m/f, mixed gay/straight, 20s to 40s, hip but low-attitude, artsy, cute, often collegiate.*

The Dock. In the heart of the club-infested warehouse district, the Dock is the only queer venue in the neighborhood *and* the largest gay disco in Cincinnati. On weekends almost everybody into the dance and cruise scene ends up here, while weeknights range from dead to surprisingly festive. One side of the club is a cavernous video bar, the other has an industrial-style dance floor complete with dim lighting, lasers, strobe lights, and a throbbing sound system. ⊠ *603 Pete Rose Way,* ☎ *513/241–5623. Crowd: 75/25 m/f, mostly under 35, collegiate, preppy, a few folks in club gear.*

New Plum Street. This handsome little video bar is usually packed with a cute stand-and-model crowd that has less of the snootiness you might find in other cities. The pool table leaves limited space for mingling. ⊠ *241 Court St.,* ☎ *513/241–5678. Crowd: mostly male, 20s to early 40s, guppies, students, cruisy, mix of locals and tourists.*

Shooters. Just in case you forgot that Cincinnatians identify as closely with the South as they do the Midwest, pop over to this spirited country-western club with wood paneling, poster- and memorabilia-covered walls, and a small but heavily utilized dance floor. There's also a pool table and games area to one side. Even guys who don't dig country tunes stumble in here on a regular basis. ⊠ *927 Race St.,* ☎ *513/381–9900. Crowd: 80/20 m/f, late 20s to late 40s, some country-western attire, some T-shirts with Levi's, loud, social, easy-going.*

Spurs. Fans of hard-core smutty leather bars may be disappointed with Spurs, which—in keeping with Cincinnati's consistently attractive bar aesthetic—is nicer inside than such clubs elsewhere. Wagon wheels and vintage signs line the walls, and pink lighting lends everyone a rosy, robust cast. Although it's usually mellow, on the third weekend of every July it's transformed into a scene right out of Hurricane Camille: The furnishings are covered with tarp, the overhead sprinklers unleash a torrent of "rain," and fans provide gusts of wind—come dressed in shorts and sandals, or perhaps as Lauren Bacall in *Key Largo*. ⊠ *326 E. 8th St.,* ☎ *513/621–*

2668. Crowd: *mostly male, 30s to 60s, some leather, lots of jeans and flannel, bears, somewhat cruisy.*

Neighborhood Haunts

Despite its location along Clifton's student drag, **Golden Lions** (⊠ 340 Ludlow Ave., ☎ 513/281–4179) appeals to a broad mix of locals—all ages and mixed black and white; it's a nice spot for pool or to chat with friends. **Shirley's** (⊠ 2401 Vine St., ☎ 513/721–8483) is a friendly dyke saloon near the University of Cincinnati. Popular with the after-work set, **Simon Says** (⊠ 428 Walnut St., ☎ 513/381–7577) is a small, slightly upscale cocktail bar with good music and windows overlooking the busy downtown sidewalk—a mostly male mix of ages and races. A sleepy basement bar with a limited following, **Subway** (⊠ 609 Walnut St., ☎ 513/421–1294) is close to several other downtown bars.

Hangin' with the Hets

Attracting a mixed gay/straight crowd, **Upstairs at Carol's** (*see* Carol's Corner Café *in* Eats, *above*), the only cabaret in Cincinnati, has piano sing-alongs and consistently books talented musicians. Up the street, the mostly straight but open-minded **Warehouse** (⊠ 1313 Vine St., ☎ 513/684–9313) rocks to grunge and alternative music most nights—there are always a few fags in this 18-and-over crowd.

SLEEPS

For convenience to nightlife and major attractions, staying at a downtown hotel or the Prospect Hill B&B are your best options. Two other good-value choices outside of downtown are also reviewed.

For price ranges, *see* lodging Chart B at the front of this guide.

Hotels

$$$$ 🏨 **Cincinnatian Hotel.** Fully restored a decade ago, this elegant 1880s hotel is the most exclusive in the city—a perennial favorite of visiting celebrities. Rooms are handsomely appointed, service is personal, and the ambience is intimate. ⊠ *601 Vine St., 45202,* ☎ *513/381–3000 or 800/332–2020,* FAX *513/651–0256. 147 rooms. Restaurant, health club.*

$$$–$$$$ 🏨 **Omni Netherlands Hotel.** Part of the historic Carew Tower, in the heart of downtown and connected to Tower Place shopping mall, the 31-story Omni is a true grande dame. Some rooms are a bit small or slightly faded, but Omni is gradually refurbishing every one to its original splendor. Good weekend deals. ⊠ *35 W. 5th St., 45202,* ☎ *513/421–9100 or 800/843–6664,* FAX *513/421–4291. 621 rooms. Restaurants, pool, health club.*

$$–$$$ 🏨 **Harley Hotel.** It's a bit out of the way, northeast of downtown, but it's also easy driving distance from the Ludlow and Northside neighborhoods and right across the highway from the posh Kenwood Towne Center shopping mall. The clean rooms and good service make it a winner. Quieter than downtown properties. ⊠ *8020 Montgomery Rd., 45236,* ☎ *513/793–4300 or 800/321–2323,* FAX *513/793–1413. 152 rooms. Restaurant, pool, health club.*

$–$$ 🏨 **Holiday Inn Cincinnati.** A location close to downtown bars and nightlife and very low rates make this standard-issue chain property a contender. ⊠ *800 W. 8th St., 45203,* ☎ *513/241–8660 or 800/465–4329,* FAX *513/241–9057. 244 rooms. Restaurant, pool.*

$ 🏨 **Best Western Mariemont.** Book well ahead because plenty of people already know about this quirky old Tudor-style hotel in the heart of Mariemont, a small planned community east of the city but not a long drive from Mt. Adams or even downtown. ⊠ *6880 Wooster Pike, 45227,* ☎ *513/271–2100 or 800/528–1234,* FAX *513/271–1057. 58 rooms. Restaurant.*

Guest House

$$ ⊞ **Prospect Hill B&B.** In a city with so few B&Bs, gays and lesbians are very lucky that one of the nicest ones eagerly welcomes the community. Owners Tony and Gary have done a splendid job decorating this 1867 Italianate town house, giving each room a personal touch—from a book of poems on the nightstand to teddy bears on the pillows. The front rooms have unobstructed views of the city skyline, and the Over-the-Rhine neighborhood is a short drive or 20-minute walk away. First-rate all around. ⊠ *408 Boal St., 45210,* ☎ *513/421–4408. 4 rooms, 2 with private bath. Hot tub. Full breakfast. Mixed gay/straight.*

THE LITTLE BLACK BOOK

At Your Fingertips

AIDS Volunteers of Cincinnati (☎ 513/421–AIDS). **Cincinnati Gay and Lesbian Switchboard** (☎ 513/651–0070). **City Beat** (alternative weekly, ☎ 513/665–4700, Web site www.citybeat.com). **Everybody's News** (arts-and-entertainment weekly, ☎ 513/381–2606, Web site www.everybodys.org). **Greater Cincinnati AIDS Consortium** (☎ 513/558–4259). **Greater Cincinnati Convention and Visitors Bureau** (⊠ 300 W. 6th St., 45202, ☎ 513/621–2142 or 800/246–2987, Web site www.cincyusa.com). **Stonewall Cincinnati Gay and Lesbian Center** (⊠ 214 E. 9th St., 5th floor, ☎ 513/651–0040). **Metro Bus System** (☎ 513/621–4455). **Yellow Cab** (☎ 513/241–2100).

Gay Media

With no local gay newspaper, you can look to the following three queer sources: The best overall option is the Cleveland-based **Gay People's Chronicle** (☎ 216/631–8646, e-mail chronicle@chronoohio.com), which comes out every two weeks. A handy low-budget bar rag, the **Sarj Guide** (☎ 502/495–6350, Web site www.sarjguide.com) has local nightlife coverage, and the monthly **Ohio Word** (☎ 317/725–8840, e-mail www.indword.com), which is the Indianapolis-based *Word* repackaged and distributed in Ohio, is of limited help.

BOOKSTORES

The feminist bookstore **Crazy Ladies** (⊠ 4039 Hamilton Ave., ☎ 513/541–4198), a fixture of the Northside's energetic women's community for years, also carries general gay and gay male titles. For men's titles (and, oddly, a huge selection of vampire books), head downtown to the **Pink Pyramid** (⊠ 907 Race St., ☎ 513/621–7465).

Working Out

Cincinnati is without a specifically gay gym, and there are very few fitness centers near the gay neighborhoods. Your best bet is the **Carew Towers Health and Fitness Club** (⊠ 441 Vine St., ☎ 513/651–1462), which is in the heart of downtown.

7 Out in Cleveland

THE FORMER **"MISTAKE BY THE LAKE"** is riding high after having been named one of *Travel & Leisure* magazine's "10 Hot Spots for 1997," the only North American city to earn such a distinction. Proof that the most-improved metropolis in the Midwest is finally earning major recognition, this hyperbolic kudo might backfire in the immediate future. Cleveland was never as awful as its former reputation suggested, neither is it quite the world-class destination *Travel & Leisure* has made it out to be. The city's potential, however, is unlimited.

A century ago Cleveland was a beacon of industrial prosperity, but the Depression rattled the city's financial stability, and following World War II a bevy of local factories closed or relocated in the South. Cleveland's "suburban flight" during the 1950s and '60s was as severe as in any American city—complete with race riots and urban blight. Even preservation-minded gays and lesbians fled for commuter towns on Cleveland's outskirts. If you could afford to leave Cleveland, by 1975, you had.

The abandonment of downtown actually preserved its bounty of Victorian and turn-of-the-century commercial and residential structures. During a period when many historic areas were plowed under in the name of urban renewal, the city was either too poor or too undesirable to merit a makeover. When the preservation and retrofitting of these buildings became fashionable two decades ago, civic leaders and private investors established an ambitious plan to reinvent Cleveland.

Since 1980 block after block of downtown has been renovated, attracting corporate ventures and drawing suburban dwellers into the city's trendy dining, sports, arts, and entertainment districts. Gays and lesbians have begun to trickle into the once-fashionable blocks south of downtown—most noticeably in the Ohio City neighborhood. If you visit the city, stay downtown to take advantage of the new attractions. But the gayest restaurants are in Cleveland Heights, and the main bars—other than the few in the downtown Warehouse District—are in Western Cleveland and nearby Lakewood. Head to these towns to find the city's core queer communities.

THE LAY OF THE LAND

Cleveland's renaissance has occurred largely downtown, in an area extending from the Flats east through the main business district to about where I–90 slices through the eastern edge of downtown. It's a large but still walkable area. To the north is Lake Erie, which is cut off from downtown by the Memorial Shoreway. University Circle, a district on the east side, contains the top museums, as well as Case Western Reserve

University. The gayified suburbs of Lakewood, to the west, and Cleveland Heights, to the east, are at opposite ends of the city—45 minutes apart by car.

Downtown

Downtown Cleveland hasn't yet recaptured the buzz of 90 years ago, when native son and Standard Oil baron John D. Rockefeller presided over one of America's most formidable business districts. But with a wealth of early 20th-century buildings, entertainment and shopping districts, and renewed tourist interest, the city center is looking snappy.

Action has always revolved around **Public Square** (⊠ Superior and Ontario Sts.), a regal park of fountains and statuary over which looms the focal point of the downtown comeback, **City Tower Center** (⊠ 50 Public Sq.). This 52-story complex serves as a hub for the Greater Cleveland Regional Transit Authority commuter rail system. Above it are three levels of upscale shops and cafés known as the **Avenue at Tower City** (☎ 216/771–0033), and a Ritz-Carlton hotel.

It's a short walk from City Tower Center to the newly completed **Gund Arena,** home to pro basketball's Cleveland Cavaliers, and to the stunning vintage-style **Jacob's Field,** home of baseball's Cleveland Indians.

Walk two blocks east of Public Square to reach the **Cleveland Public Library** (⊠ 325 Superior Ave., ☎ 216/623–2822). Across the street is the 1890 **Arcade** (⊠ Euclid Ave. and 4th St., ☎ 216/621–8500), which has four levels of fine shops. Continue east to reach the **Playhouse Square Theater District** (⊠ 1519 Euclid Ave., ☎ 216/771–4444), a revived complex of five vintage theaters (four of them in use); tours of these structures are available.

The North Coast District

Although not visible from much of downtown, the banks of Lake Erie have recently been touched with the glittering wand of redevelopment. The 1972 Clean Water Act rid the lake of serious pollution and gave investors incentive to create an entertainment district. Although the nightlife and dining aspects of this plan have been executed in the Flats (*see below*), two outstanding museums now anchor lakeside's **North Coast District.**

The pyramidal **Rock and Roll Hall of Fame and Museum** (⊠ 1 Key Plaza, ☎ 216/781–7625 or 800/493–ROLL), designed by I. M. Pei, offers an invigorating tour of music and pop culture during the past half-century, with such colorful memorabilia as Janis Joplin's psychedelically painted Porsche and the original piece of paper on which Jimi Hendrix scrawled "Purple Haze." With apologies to the Polka Hall of Fame in suburban Euclid, this is Cleveland's only certifiable must-see attraction.

The Warehouse District and the Flats

The turnaround of **the Flats,** the district along the Cuyahoga River, has been Cleveland's most awe-inspiring magic trick. The industrial area west of and down a steep slope from downtown was once the domain of grain-processing plants. Some factories still thrive along the river, but the plants and warehouses closest to downtown have been converted into rowdy (and straight) nightclubs and restaurants.

Up the steep hill is the one downtown neighborhood with a homo presence, the **Warehouse District.** In addition to housing three gay nightclubs, these SoHo-like, cast-iron structures now contain good restaurants, funky shops and galleries, and dozens of loft apartments.

University Circle

Three miles east of downtown is **University Circle,** a 500-acre district of turn-of-the-century mansions anchored by grassy Ward Park. Here you'll find Case Western Reserve University, several of the nation's leading research hospitals, and some first-rate museums.

Since it opened in 1916, the 70 galleries within the Georgian-style **Cleveland Museum of Art** (✉ 11150 East Blvd., ☎ 216/421–7340) have earned international attention. The collection spans centuries and cultures but is best known for its Asian and medieval European collections. Within walking distance is the **Cleveland Museum of Natural History** (✉ 1 Wade Oval Dr., ☎ 216/231–4600).

A short drive away are two smaller but also intriguing attractions, the **African-American Museum** (✉ 1765 Crawford Rd., ☎ 216/791–1700) and the **Cleveland Center for Contemporary Art** (✉ 8501 Carnegie Ave., ☎ 216/421–8671).

Cleveland Heights

Continue east from University Circle, turning right onto Mayfield Road (U.S. 322), and you'll cut through the heart of **Little Italy** to picturesque **Cleveland Heights.** Predominantly black or gay or Jewish neighborhoods are often euphemistically described as "diverse," but few towns in the United States can claim the integrated and stable balance of Cleveland Heights, whose population is about 40% nonwhite and includes retirees, yuppies, gays and lesbians, Jews, and families and singles.

This prosperous and neatly laid-out community makes for a pleasurable stroll, the hundreds of early- to mid-20th-century homes offering a lesson in American architecture. Its main shopping district, around the intersection of **Coventry and Mayfield roads,** is abuzz with offbeat boutiques, coffeehouses, and gay-friendly businesses.

West Edge and Lakewood

Many gays live in the communities of **West Edge** (actually part of Cleveland proper) and **Lakewood** (the suburb immediately west) are where many gays live. These neighborhoods, divided at 117th Street, are virtually indistinguishable, although Lakewood has the more stately early 20th-century housing stock (much of it Craftsman-style). The main drags, **Clifton Boulevard** and **Detroit Avenue,** have a few gay businesses; Detroit Avenue is the hub of Cleveland's gay nightlife scene.

When the weather's cooperative, scads of homos drive a mile east of Lakewood to Cleveland's most popular beach, **Edgewater Park** (✉ 6700 Memorial Pkwy.). It's not Waikiki, but it's fun on weekend afternoons.

GETTING AROUND

If you're willing to stick to downtown, and perhaps take a cab to reach University Circle, Cleveland can be managed without a car. Only the North Coast District is slightly out of the way. However, in 1997 Cleveland's **Rapid Transit Authority** inaugurated a new light-rail line (fare $1.50) that begins at City Tower Center, stops at the Flats and Warehouse District, and then wraps around to the North Coast. Existing RTA lines also connect downtown to some suburbs, but do not go directly to Cleveland Heights and Lakewood. You'll need a car if you plan to travel out here. Cleveland has many public parking lots, and although streets can be tricky, traffic is relatively light except during rush hour and pro sporting events.

EATS

Unflashy but dependable, Cleveland's cuisine has strong Eastern European, Greek, and Italian influences. Steak houses and burger joints, as well as home-style eateries known for their good breakfasts, are prevalent, but sophisticated new restaurants have begun opening downtown.

You'll be welcomed anywhere, but the Warehouse District has the queerest scene. The hangouts in the Flats are hetero, but even there the waitrons are pretty cool about same-sex couples. Cleveland Heights has some of the region's most appealing eateries, especially around Coventry Road.

For price ranges, *see* dining Chart B at the front of this guide.

Downtown and the Warehouse District

$$$–$$$$ ✕ **Lira.** For high-profile dining and some of the hottest chow in the city, sample the first-rate northern Italian cuisine of this promising newcomer. Try the carpaccio of smoked salmon with arugula, capers, red onions, and crème fraîche, before moving on to oven-roasted salmon with a fennel-and-potato hash. ✉ *55 Public Sq.,* ☎ *216/348–1955.*

$$–$$$ ✕ **Greek Isles.** This airy, high-ceiling restaurant in the heart of the Warehouse District serves some of the best Greek food in town. Try whole split quail marinated with herbs and char-grilled with oven-roasted potatoes, or *taramosalata,* a creamy caviar dip served with pita bread. Gear up for plate smashing and dancing on weekends. ✉ *500 W. St. Clair Ave.,* ☎ *216/861–1919.*

$ ✕ **Liquid.** Above a small theater and one of those annoyingly trendy cigar lounges the world can't seem to get enough of, Liquid is one of the Warehouse District's best options for good bar food—burgers, lime chicken salad, and a variety of burritolike "wraps." The loud music, saucy waitrons, and sleek industrial decor give it a nightclub ambience. ✉ *1212 W. 6th St.,* ☎ *216/479–7717.*

University Circle

$$$ ✕ **That Place on Bellflower.** This place Case Western students like to take their grandparents is hip and gay-friendly. Tables are scattered among several of this old carriage house's rooms, as well as on a landscaped patio. Typical nouvelle Continental offerings include Atlantic salmon roasted with cracked-peppercorn butter, toasted-almond rice, and fresh asparagus. ✉ *11401 Bellflower Ct.,* ☎ *216/231–4469.*

$$–$$$ ✕ **Club Isabella.** Despite its hard-to-find location, this converted carriage house presents some of the best jazz in the city. The northern Italian cooking is tasty. A great way to end a day of exploring the nearby museums. ✉ *2025 University Hospitals Dr.,* ☎ *216/229–1177.*

Cleveland Heights and Points East

$$–$$$ ✕ **Café Tandoor.** On the east side of Cleveland Heights, this warmly decorated Indian restaurant draws a mix of guppies and yuppies; there's live music some nights. Favorite dishes include *shajahani* curry (curried chicken simmered in a cashew sauce) and tandoori-roasted eggplant with tomatoes, onions, and peas. ✉ *2096 S. Taylor Rd.,* ☎ *216/371–8500.*

$–$$ ✕ **Balaton.** Locals still drive in from all over northern Ohio to fatten up on hearty (but not heart-friendly) Hungarian chow, including goulash, dumplings, and stuffed cabbage. Balaton is in an old neighborhood in Shaker Heights. ✉ *12521 Buckeye Rd.,* ☎ *216/921–9691. No credit cards.*

$ ✕ **Inn on Coventry.** Part of the Coventry Yard shopping complex, which is usually teeming with hipsters and alternateens, this bastion of mom-style comfort food is celebrated foremost for its breakfasts. The meat loaf, burgers, and a cholesterol-laden clump of deep-fried onions known as an "onion brick" are excellent. ✉ *2785 Euclid Heights Blvd.,* ☎ *216/ 371–1811.*

$ ✕ **Lonesome Dove.** Feminists, intellectuals, and neobohemians crowd this general store–inspired vegetarian restaurant, which is housed on the ground-level of Cleveland Heights's distinctive Rockefeller Building. Specialty coffees, deli sandwiches, and fresh salads are served. ✉ *3093 Mayfield Rd.,* ☎ *216/371–9100.*

$ ✕ **Qué Tal.** In a region that's weak on late-night dining, this brightly painted hole-in-the-wall will make you happy should late-night munchies over-

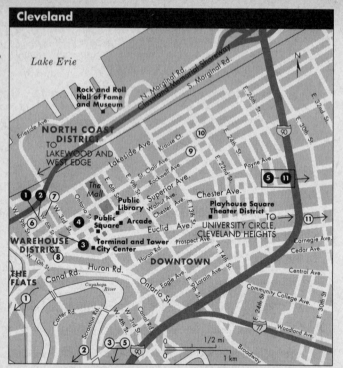

Cleveland

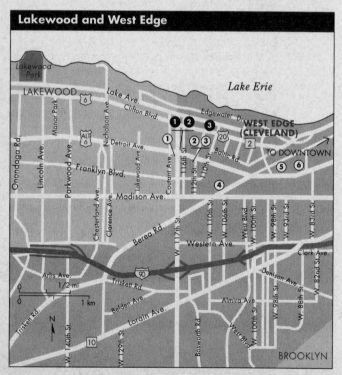

Lakewood and West Edge

come you—it's open til 3 AM. You won't pay more than a few bucks for build-your-own tacos. ☒ *1803 Coventry Rd.,* ☎ *216/932–9800.*

West Edge and Lakewood

$ ✕ **Billy's.** Probably the gayest of Cleveland's restaurants, this casual café serves three meals a day. It's nothing fancy, but the American chow is good, the crowd friendly and dishy, and the staff warm. ☒ *11100 Clifton Blvd.,* ☎ *216/281–7722.*

$ ✕ **My Friend's Restaurant and Deli.** This spacious and attractive 24-hour eatery serves down-home food—the usual sandwiches and home-style dishes you'll find at any diner. It's within walking distance of gay bars. ☒ *11616 Detroit Ave.,* ☎ *216/221–2575.*

Coffeehouse Culture

Drip Stick Coffeehouse. Fags, straight kids from the 'burbs, and slackers head to this elegant Warehouse District café. Improv comedy and live music are featured many nights. Killer desserts. ☒ *1224 W. 6th St.,* ☎ *216/771–3366.*

Red Star Café. A cheerful coffeehouse on up-and-coming Detroit Avenue, Red Star has magazines for sale, poetry readings, open-mike events, and an artsy crowd. Loaded with fun '50s kitsch, it serves terrific desserts, light fare, and coffees. ☒ *11604 Detroit Ave.,* ☎ *216/521–7827.*

SCENES

For such a large a city, Cleveland doesn't have a huge club scene. The few mainstays—some of which are spacious and impressively decorated—still fail to drum up major crowds. The best clubs are downtown in the Warehouse District and in the West Edge/Lakewood area. A few divey dyke bars are in South Cleveland, near the suburb of Brooklyn. Cleveland bars are uniformly friendly and accessible, and draw a racially diverse mix of men and women. Only in the Warehouse District can you walk among a pair of bars; otherwise you'll need a car.

Prime Suspects

The Cage. Many folks start here before heading over to U4ia (*see below*) on weekends; on weekdays it's the most popular dance club and video bar in Lakewood. The interior is done in a true "cage" theme with metal bars and barbed wire around the small dance floor, and other county jail–inspired touches. There's a cozy lounge, a restaurant that serves casual food, and a small room with a pool table. ☒ *9506 Detroit Ave.,* ☎ *216/651–0727. Crowd: 80/20 m/f, 20s to 40s, racially mixed, white and blue collar, low-attitude.*

Code Blue. A gorgeous new disco and lounge that's a hit with both lesbians and gay men, Code Blue is the top option for dykes visiting downtown. With a fun retro-'50s look, the club has dancing downstairs and a video lounge on the second level. A patio will open in summer 1998. ☒ *1946 St. Clair Ave.,* ☎ *216/241–4663. Crowd: mixed male/female, all ages, somewhat mixed racially, a few collegiate types, very diverse and friendly.*

The Grid. The Grid is a lively place with a clever decor. Not large, it's divided into three areas. Up front is a bar with video screens. In back is a small but cool dance floor with a jumble of lasers, lights, and psychedelic designs, and some of the best music in town. And downstairs is a quiet dungeonesque lounge with dark lights. ☒ *1281 W. 9th St.,* ☎ *216/623–0113. Crowd: 80/20 m/f, 20s and 30s, moderately cruisy, mixed bag.*

Leather Stallions. This bar on the edge of downtown has been serving the leather community since 1976—longer than any such bar in Ohio—but the crowd has become more mainstream in recent years. Guys in ordinary attire show up these days. Sunday afternoon is one of the best times to come. There's no dance floor. ⊠ *2205 St. Clair Ave. NE,* ☎ *216/589–8588. Crowd: male, mostly 30s and 40s, mostly leather and Levi's, some hard core, cruisy.*

Legends. With wild music, campy lighting, a tiny but packed dance floor, and a big show stage, Legends is always festive and somewhat unpredictable—the karaoke nights have a cult following. The over-35 crowd keeps the cruising and attitude to a minimum. ⊠ *11719 Detroit Ave.,* ☎ *216/226–1199. Crowd: 60/40 m/f, mostly late 30s to 60s, colorful, loud, outgoing, approachable.*

Numbers. Don't let the dumpy exterior frighten you—this is an absolutely fabulous space, probably the most attractive of the gay bars in the Warehouse District. Numbers is most crowded during its special events: boots and briefs nights, visits from local porn stars. Other times it's quiet, which is a shame because the exposed brick, high ceilings, and ambient lighting deserve to be enjoyed on a regular basis. ⊠ *620 Frankfort Ave.,* ☎ *216/621–6900. Crowd: mostly male, 20s to 40s, mixed racially, high sexual energy.*

Playland. This popular gay bar in the Warehouse District has dozens of TV monitors set throughout the space. In the back is a small dance floor that's only crowded on weekends. Indirect lighting makes everybody look even cuter than they are. ⊠ *1229 W. 6th St.,* ☎ *216/566–0060. Crowd: 80/20 m/f, mostly under 35, stylish, good-looking, slightly attitudy, on the make.*

Rec Room. This lesbian bar is well southwest of downtown, in the suburb of Brooklyn on a dreary strip of auto factories and paint shops. Inside is a merry club with a big central bar, an area with a pool table and games, and a dance floor. ⊠ *15320 Brookpark Rd.,* ☎ *216/433–1669. Crowd: lesbian, all ages, working class, very butch, loud.*

Rockies. Loud and frisky, this guys-oriented dance bar is the city's lone members-only bar. This distinction must carry with it some legal ramifications, but it doesn't seem to affect who they let inside—there's never even a cover charge. There's a dance floor and a cozy patio. Rockies is the only bar in town with a Sunday tea dance. ⊠ *9208 Detroit Ave.,* ☎ *216/961–3115. Crowd: male, 20s to 40s, friendly, cruisy.*

U4ia. This weekends-only megaclub will give any big-city warehouse disco a run for the money. The sound system and music are outstanding, and the space is well laid out. You'll find distinct lounge areas, a stage and dance floor, and an upstairs loft bar that's a good perch from which to watch all the cute folks below. The crowd is diverse but relatively young, with groovy straight friends, as well as a mix of dykes and gay men. ⊠ *10630 Berea Rd.,* ☎ *216/631–7111. Crowd: mostly gay, 70/30 m/f, mostly under 35, club kids, diva dykes, some collegiate types, ranges from preppy to funky to hip, some stand-and-model but low-attitude.*

Neighborhood Haunts

In Ohio City, an old blue-collar neighborhood across downtown from the Flats, the **Ohio City Oasis** (⊠ 2909 Detroit Ave., ☎ 216/574–2203) is normally a mellow bar that appeals to a mix of ages. Country-western music on Sunday attracts a broader following. **Rudy's** (⊠ 2032 W. 25th St., ☎ 216/621–1752), a friendly cocktail lounge in Ohio City, has a jukebox and a decor that's reminiscent of the 1920s. Men and women are welcome.

Regulars frequent **The Hawk** (✉ 11217 Detroit Ave, ☎ 216/521–5443), a good spot to begin a Detroit Avenue barhop. Despite its provocative name, **Sexx** (✉ 11213 Detroit Ave., ☎ 216/221–8576) is a sleepy lounge that occasionally perks up for cabaret.

Cleveland Heights has only one bar, but **Barnaby Lane** (✉ 2619 Noble Rd., ☎ 216/382–2033) is a great little pub that draws a mix of women and men, as well as all ages and races; there's a great jukebox, sweet bartenders, and all the usual games and diversions (but no dance floor).

A small working-class neighborhood in South Cleveland, near the zoo, has lesbian hangouts: **Five Cent Decision** (✉ 4365 State Rd., ☎ 216/661–1314) and the **Paradise Inn** (✉ 4488 State Rd., ☎ 216/741–9819). Neither of these seedy saloons will be showing up on the pages of *Good Housekeeping* anytime soon.

Action

Cleveland's favorite bathhouse, **Flex** (✉ 1293 W. 9th St., ☎ 216/696–0595), is in the Warehouse District, which accounts for its popularity with professionals, guppies, and tourists. Somewhat raunchier and also popular is **The Club Cleveland** (✉ 1448 W. 32nd St., ☎ 216/961–2727), in Ohio City, which is bigger with bears and leather guys.

SLEEPS

Other than the chain motels on the city's outskirts, most hotels are downtown, which puts you within walking distance of several attractions. Unfortunately, it's a short drive from here to the museums around University Circle, and a longer drive to Lakewood and Cleveland Heights. If you must be near Lakewood, opt for one of the chain properties near Cleveland Hopkins International Airport. For easy access to Cleveland Heights, Mayfield Heights and Beachwood are loaded with major chains.

For price ranges, *see* lodging Chart B at the front of this guide.

Hotels

$$$–$$$$ 🏨 **Ritz-Carlton Cleveland.** The Cleveland branch of the Ritz family is attached to the stunning Tower City complex. Rooms have marble baths and the usual chichi furnishings. A highlight is the atrium fitness center and indoor pool. ✉ *1515 W. 3rd St., 44113,* ☎ *216/623–1300,* FAX *216/623–0515. 208 rooms. Restaurant, pool, health club.*

$$–$$$$ 🏨 **Renaissance Cleveland Hotel.** This vintage downtown hotel captures the ambience of Cleveland during its heyday, with lavish public spaces and a suave Mediterranean restaurant (Sans Souci). Rooms are less over-the-top than at the neighboring Ritz-Carlton, but for the price, the Renaissance is a top choice. ✉ *24 Public Sq., 44113,* ☎ *216/696–5600,* FAX *216/696–3102. 491 rooms. Restaurant, pool, exercise room.*

$$$ 🏨 **Wyndham Cleveland Hotel.** One of the most recent additions to downtown, the dramatic Wyndham anchors the city's artsy Playhouse Square and is a short walk from the Warehouse District. A number of visiting actors and musicians stay here. ✉ *1260 Euclid Ave., 44115,* ☎ *216/615–3355,* FAX *216/615–3355. 205 rooms. Restaurant, pool.*

$$ 🏨 **Holiday Inn Lakeside.** A run-of-the-mill high-rise on the lake, the Holiday Inn has been given new life, thanks largely to the redevelopment of the lakeside around it—it's a short walk from the Rock and Roll Hall of Fame and Museum. Rooms have clear views of either Lake Erie or downtown. ✉ *1111 Lakeside Ave., 44114,* ☎ *216/241–5100 or 800/465–4329,* FAX *216/241–7437. 370 rooms. Restaurant, pool.*

$ 🖭 **Days Inn Lakewood.** Although downtown is devoid of budget properties, Lakewood does have a small but dowdy Days Inn. The staff is indifferent and the rooms ordinary, but it's close to gay nightlife, and dirt-cheap. ⊠ *12019 Lake Rd.,* ☎ *216/226–4800 or 800/329–7466,* FAX *216/226–4359. 66 rooms.*

THE LITTLE BLACK BOOK

At Your Fingertips

Cleveland Convention & Visitors Bureau (⊠ 3100 Terminal Tower, 50 Public Sq., 44113, ☎ 216/621–4110 or 800/321–1004). **Cleveland Lesbian/Gay Community Center** (⊠ 1418 W. 29th St., ☎ 216/522–1999). *Free Times* (☎ 216/321–2300, Web site www.freetimes.com). **Lesbian/Gay Hotline** (☎ 216/781–6736). **Rapid Transit Authority** (☎ 216/621–9500). *Scene* (☎ 216/241–7550, Web site www.clevescene.com). **Women's Center of Greater Cleveland** (⊠ 4828 Lorain Ave., ☎ 216/651–1450 or 216/651–4357).

Gay Media

The *Gay People's Chronicle* (☎ 216/631–8646, e-mail chronicle@chronohio.com) carries extensive features, and arts and entertainment coverage. The *Valentine News* (☎ 216/226–1705) is a lively biweekly bar rag.

BOOKSTORES

The general-interest **Bookstore on W. 25th Street** (⊠ 1921 W. 25th St., ☎ 216/566–8897) is not far from the community center and has a lesbigay section. In Cleveland Heights, **Gifts of Athena** (⊠ 2199 Lee Rd., ☎ 216/371–1937) has feminist and lesbian titles. The **Daily Planet News** (⊠ 1842 Coventry Rd., ☎ 216/321–9973) has a few gay books and magazines.

Working Out

The men's bathhouses, **Club Cleveland** and **Flex** (*see* Action, *above*), have well-equipped fitness centers. No mainstream gym has a major queer following but **U.S. Total Fitness of Tower City** (⊠ 1500 W. 3rd St., ☎ 216/861–4040) is an outstanding, centrally located facility.

8 Out in Columbus

FEW VISITORS TO OHIO are surprised to find that Columbus is such a nice place; people expect a city in the center of this laid-back state to be nice. What seems to amaze almost everybody who passes through here, however, is *how* nice Columbus is—it has a great restaurant and bar scene, nationally acclaimed art galleries, a well-educated population, several historic neighborhoods, and a vibrant university. If only it were on a bay and surrounded by hills, Tony Bennett would write a song about it.

But the city's terrain and setting are flat and agrarian—not especially memorable. Cow-lumbus, as it's teasingly known even by loyal supporters, is in the middle of the middle. And so it remains a secret to most people. The *Wall Street Journal* helped let the cat out of the bag by publishing a gushing profile of this city with "a large bowling league for homosexuals, the first Henri Bendel store outside of Manhattan, and the kind of avant-garde art that would pique Jesse Helms's interest." *Newsweek* had named it one of the nation's 10 "hot cities" the year before, and Columbus shows no signs of cooling off. It's the only city in the nation's northeastern quadrant to see population gains during each of the past four census counts.

Lesbians and gay men in Columbus are known for their ability to rally behind important causes—the Human Rights Campaign dinner in Columbus is one of the organization's most financially successful—and for having one of the largest intramural gay and lesbian sports programs in the country. Another claim to fame is the annual Red Party (held in September), which has been going strong for more than two decades, making it one of the nation's longest-running gay-circuit parties.

Perhaps a good bit of Columbus's homo-desirability lies in its all-American personality. Queers who settle in Columbus are rewarded with a tolerant version of the traditional American city. The name of the city's gayest restaurant, Out On Main, captures perfectly what it means to be queer in Columbus: to be comfortably out and open as a gay man or a lesbian while also occupying an important and secure role in the mainstream.

THE LAY OF THE LAND

Greater Columbus covers a huge area, most of it enclosed within the I–270 loop. But visitors tend to stick to a rectangle that extends from just south of downtown, where you'll find German Village and the Brewery District, to several miles north of downtown, past the funky Short North to the campus of Ohio State University. High Street runs north–south, the length of this rectangle.

Downtown

A good place to begin a tour of **downtown** is at the **Columbus Civic Center,** a patch of parkland, government buildings, and memorials on both banks of the Scioto River. You can relax amid the grassy slopes of **Battelle Riverfront Park,** beside a full replica of the *Santa Maria* (⊠ Marconi Blvd. and Broad St., ☎ 614/645–8760), the flagship of Christopher Columbus's fleet.

Broad Street leads east from the river to **High Street,** where you can tour **Capitol Square.** The magnificent **Ohio Statehouse** (⊠ High and State Sts., ☎ 614/466–2125), recently restored, has no dome. The building's funding was depleted shortly after construction was begun in 1839, and by the time money was available, domes were out of fashion.

The Statehouse is in the middle of the burgeoning theater district, whose restored structures include the **Capitol Theatre** (⊠ Vern Riffe Center for Government and the Arts, 77 S. High St., ☎ 614/644–9624), the **Palace Theatre** (⊠ 34 W. Broad St., ☎ 614/461–0022), and the **Ohio Theatre** (⊠ 55 E. State St., ☎ 614/229–4848). The **Columbus City Center** (⊠ 111 S. 3rd St., ☎ 614/221–4900), a mall with about 150 shops, houses big-name department stores like **Marshall Field** (⊠ 225 S. 3rd St., ☎ 614/227–6222) and **Lazarus** (⊠ 141 S. High St., ☎ 614/463–2121).

Columbus, the fast-food capital of the nation, is where franchise restaurants like Bob Evans, White Castle, and the *Ellen*-boycotting Wendy's got their starts. In the future, however, it's possible the city will be better known, in queer circles anyway, for opening the first gay-theme restaurant, **Out On Main** (⊠ 122 E. Main St., ☎ 614/224–9520). Around the corner from the Columbus City Center, this repository of memorabilia and souvenirs, including costumes of Elton John, an African-American lesbian and gay pride mural, a display of homo-pulp novels, and posters celebrating local pride celebrations. Photos of famous queer or bi entertainers, writers, and historical figures cover the walls.

From Capitol Square, Broad Street leads east to **Ohio's Center of Science & Industry** (COSI, ⊠ 280 E. Broad St., ☎ 614/228–2674), and the **Columbus Museum of Art** (⊠ 480 E. Broad St., ☎ 614/228–2674), a respected regional museum. A short walk north, the **Thurber House** (⊠ 77 Jefferson Ave., ☎ 614/464–1032), a museum and bookstore dedicated to the life and work of native son James Thurber, also hosts lectures, and literary picnics.

South of the art museum is one of the more enjoyable and lesser-known attractions in Columbus, the **Topiary Garden** in **Old Deaf School Park** (⊠ E. Town St. and Washington Ave., ☎ 614/645–3350). This unique garden comprises about 60 topiary figures from Georges Seurat's painting "A Sunday Afternoon on the Island of La Grande Jatte"; it's best viewed from mid-July to November.

A short drive east of downtown along Broad Street, toward the yuppi-fied neighborhood of **Bexley,** is one of the most impressive indoor/outdoor botanical gardens in the country, the **Franklin Park Conservatory** (⊠ 1777 E. Broad St., ☎ 614/645–8733), which has a year-round tropical rain forest and fine collections of orchids and bonsais.

The Short North

Bordering downtown north of Maple Street is the **Short North,** a neighborhood that as recently as the mid-'80s harbored crack dens and prostitutes but whose century-old redbrick architecture now support arts community and a substantially gay business and entertainment district. Several blocks of **High Street** north of **North Market** (*see* Eats, *below*) bustle with commercial and sidewalk activity, day and night, and Saturday-night gallery walks draw hordes of visitors. Also here is the lesbigay **An Open Book** (*see* Gay Media, *below*).

To the east is **Victorian Village,** whose streets are lined with restored homes. West of High Street is leafy **Goodale Park** (✉ Goodale and North Park Sts.), which, on warm days, is packed with sunning (and cruising) queens. It's also busy at night. Writer Sam Steward (a.k.a. Phil Andros), in his later life a mentor to John Preston, lived in Columbus and attended OSU. Some of his erotica was set in Goodale Park. It's a quick drive from the Short North west to the diverse **Grandview** neighborhood, whose main drags, **Grandview and 5th avenues,** are lined with funky restaurants and shops.

Ohio State University

Continue north of the Short North along High Street to reach **Ohio State University** (✉ N. High St. and 15th Ave., ☎ 614/292–3980), a virtual city in itself. Tours are available of this immense campus, which is used by about 70,000 faculty, employees, and students. The school's acclaimed sports program has made Columbus one of the country's college football cities. One must-see is the respected **Wexner Center for the Arts** (✉ 15th Ave. and High St., ☎ 614/292–0330), a frequent host of gay exhibits and events. The center was financed largely through the efforts of Les Wexner, who founded The Limited fashion store chain.

North of campus, High Street leads into **Clintonville,** a major lesbian enclave. West of OSU, 5th Avenue will take you to the attractive and somewhat gay-popular neighborhood of **Upper Arlington,** home to the excellent **Ohio Craft Museum** (✉ 1665 W. 5th Ave., ☎ 614/486–4402).

If you've ever watched dry-witted Jack Hanna bring adorably unpredictable animals onto the *Tonight Show,* you probably know about the wonderful **Columbus Zoo** (✉ 9990 Riverside Dr., ☎ 614/645–3550), which is on the banks of the Scioto River in northwestern Columbus.

German Village and the Brewery District

German Village, which is just south of downtown, fell into disrepair in the middle of the century. In the face of plans to demolish the neighborhood, concerned residents created the largest privately funded historical foundation in the nation and preserved this 233-acre haven of cobbled lanes, wrought-iron fences, flower gardens, redbrick cottages, and two-story homes. The Huntington Gardens in beautifully landscaped **Schiller Park** (✉ City Park and Reinhard Aves.) bloom with perennials from spring through fall. Contact the tour director of the **German Village Society** (☎ 614/221–8888) for details about neighborhood tours and events. Oktoberfest is especially popular.

For great German food stop by **Schmidt's Sausage Haus and Restaurant** (✉ 240 E. Kossuth St., ☎ 614/444–6808), and **Katzinger's Deli** (✉ 475 S. 3rd St., ☎ 614/228–3354), which offers around 60 sandwiches. **Deibel's** (✉ 144 Reinhard Ave., ☎ 614/444–1139) is a kitschy German watering hole where Esther Craw, a woman whose name sounds like it came out of a Kurt Vonnegut novel, has been playing the accordion for many years.

West of German Village across High Street is the up-and-coming **Brewery District,** part of which has been completely restored during the past decade. The former breweries now house microbreweries, wine bars, and live-music cafés that draw a straight, fairly rowdy collegiate crowd.

GETTING AROUND

You can manage the most interesting sections of town easily on foot. A wise option, should you arrive by car, is to park wherever you're staying and resist driving again until you've explored central Columbus. It takes

30 minutes to walk from the Short North to German Village, but it's a safe and interesting walk. Parking is relatively easy to come by, even downtown, and the city is not difficult to navigate. Columbus has an extensive bus network, especially to and from OSU.

EATS

Columbus did not take immediately to the invasion in the '80s and '90s of nouvelle cuisine. When sophisticated Rigsby's opened in the Short North more than a decade ago, patrons sent back the rare-seared fish and pâtés, unsure of what to make them. But the scene continues to evolve, and cutting-edge restaurants have opened during the past few years. Foodies should not miss the stalls at **North Market** (⊠ N. Park and Spruce Sts.), which is usually swarming with local queers. The gay dining scene is centered in the Short North, along High Street and to a lesser extent in German Village.

For price ranges, *see* dining Chart B at the front of this guide.

The Short North

$$$–$$$$ ╳ **L'Antibes.** This romantic gay-popular eatery that excels in contemporary and classic French cooking employs a polished yet friendly staff. Loosen your belt to sample rich and tantalizing fare like veal sweetbreads with crème fraîche, brandy, glace de viande, and mushrooms. ⊠ *772 N. High St., Ste. 106,* ☎ *614/291–1666.*

$$$–$$$$ ╳ **Rigsby's Cuisine Volatile.** Rigsby's packs the house every night, offering a regularly revised menu of authentic French-, Italian-, and Spanish-Mediterranean cooking. Recent entrées include cod with potatoes in a faintly sweet saffron-tomato broth; and filet mignon with shallots, and chanterelles. ⊠ *698 N. High St.,* ☎ *614/461–7888.*

$$–$$$ ╳ **K2U.** The hip but rustic ambience sets this Short North hot spot apart from its more chaotic competitors. The eclectic menu borrows ingredients and preparations from around the world to come up with such tantalizing creations as house-smoked pork chops with black beans, salsa fresca, and jalapeño-lime sour cream. ⊠ *641 N. High St.,* ☎ *614/461–4766.*

$$–$$$ ╳ **Tapatio.** Famous for its irresistible fresh-baked bread, this Mexican, Caribbean, and Latin American restaurant concocts such unusual dishes as T-bone steak with roasted corn, sun-dried tomatoes, and shiitake salsa. Great patio, cute staff. ⊠ *491 Park St.,* ☎ *614/221–1085.*

$$ ╳ **Frezno Eclectic Kitchen.** The owners of this Short North mainstay operate two other cool eateries on High Street, Dagwoodz Diner and Carolinaz. These chefs know their way around the kitchen and churn out consistently good wood-fired pizzas, pastas, and other trendy fare. Brunch is a big hit. ⊠ *782 N. High St.,* ☎ *614/298–0031.*

$ ╳ **Frank's Diner at the North Market.** A meal at this lovable greasy spoon in North Market will rarely set you back more than $5 and will usually prove to be as entertaining (in terms of people-watching and gossip-trading) as it is filling. Great omelets. ⊠ *59 Spruce St.,* ☎ *614/621–2233.*

Downtown and German Village

$$$–$$$$ ╳ **Handke's.** The intimate beer-cellar locale of this Brewery District fave may suggest run-of-the-mill pub food, but this is one of the city's most refined restaurants. Regulars cite the veal chops, always-fresh fish grills, and such gamey offerings as buffalo tenderloin. ⊠ *520 S. Front St.,* ☎ *614/621–2500.*

$$$ ╳ **The Clarmont.** This pre-gentrification, retro-furnished steak house is famous for its prime rib, black-tip shark, and French onion soup. Whatever '70s-style outfit you can rustle from the back of your closet will look fabulous here. ⊠ *684 S. High St.,* ☎ *614/443–1125.*

Columbus

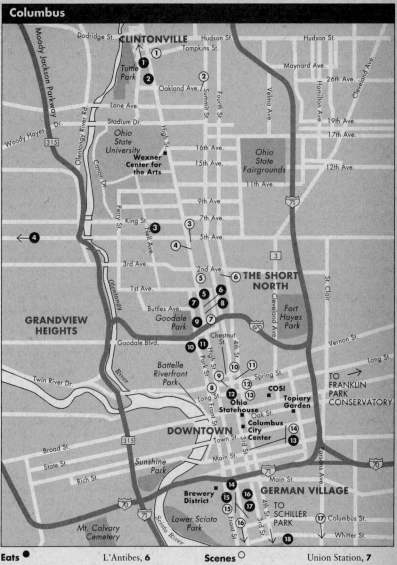

Eats ●

Barcelona, **18**
Blue Nile, **2**
The Clarmont, **15**
Coffee Table, **7**
Cup-O-Joe, **17**
Frank's Diner at the North Market, **11**
Frezno Eclectic Kitchen, **5**
Grand Vu, **4**
The Grapevine Café, **12**
Handke's, **14**
Jimmy's Too & Jimmy's Place Upstairs, **16**
K2U, **9**
King Avenue Coffeehouse, **3**

L'Antibes, **6**
Out On Main, **13**
Rigsby's Cuisine Volatile, **8**
Talita's, **1**
Tapatio, **10**

Scenes ○

Blazer's Pub, **3**
Club 20, **1**
Clubhouse, **14**
Columbus Eagle Bar, **11**
Downtown Connection, **4**
Eagle in Exile, **6**
Garage/Trends, **9**
Garrett's Saloon, **17**
Havana, **5**
Pyramid Nightclub, **13**
Remo's, **16**
Slammer's Pizza Pub, **12**
Summit Station, **2**
Trade Winds II, **10**
Tremont, **15**

Union Station, **7**
Wall Street, **8**

$$–$$$$ ✕ **Jimmy's Too & Jimmy's Place Upstairs.** Occupying different levels of the same German Village building, these gay-popular restaurants offer high-end steak and seafood upstairs, and simpler but still excellent American food (salads, designer pizzas) downstairs. Live jazz many nights. ⊠ *595 S. 3rd St.,* ☎ *614/461–1030.*

$$–$$$ ✕ **Barcelona.** This hot German Village newcomer offers a Mediterranean alternative to the area's sausage houses. A fun, queer-trendy crowd gathers nightly in the long, noisy dining room for inventive tapas like corn-crusted calamari with mint-serrano dipping sauce, and pan-seared walleye with white beans and orzo. ⊠ *263 E. Whittier St.,* ☎ *614/443–3699.*

$$–$$$ ✕ **Out On Main.** This smartly decorated restaurant built around a wonderfully entertaining and informative gay and lesbian archive (*see* Lay of the Land, *above*) also happens to serve first-rate New American food, from vegan risotto to rich chicken Gorgonzola. A final plus is the slick coffee bar (fine desserts) around the corner from the main dining room. ⊠ *122 E. Main St.,* ☎ *614/224–9510.*

$–$$ ✕ **The Grapevine Café.** A casual spot where gaggles of fags congregate for habit-forming munchies (mozzarella sticks, potato skins) and fairly basic but hearty American chow, including lots of pastas, soups, and salads. There's live music some nights. ⊠ *73 E. Gay St.,* ☎ *614/221–8463.*

Elsewhere

$$ ✕ **Grand Vu.** This fun and informal New American star keeps Grandview residents happy with dishes like shrimp bowl (rock shrimp with sugar snap peas, wood-ear mushrooms, cabbage, corn, tomato, basmati rice, and Asian broth). ⊠ *1470 Grandview Ave.,* ☎ *614/487–1001.*

$ ✕ **Blue Nile.** University students flock to this hands-on Ethiopian restaurant, where flatware is replaced with *injera,* spongy bread with which you can scoop up savory and spicy lamb, chicken, beef, and vegetable stews. ⊠ *2361 N. High St.,* ☎ *614/421–2323.*

$ ✕ **Talita's.** This cheap and cheerful hangout in Clintonville is a hit with local college students and neighborhood dykes. The Tex-Mex food is filling and tasty. ⊠ *2977 N. High St.,* ☎ *614/262–6000.*

Coffeehouse Culture

Coffee Table. This long, narrow, and cruisy space with tall windows and sidewalk seating serves good desserts and snacks. Walk by on a busy day and it feels as though the building itself has dozens of piercing eyes locked to your every move. ⊠ *731 N. High St.,* ☎ *614/297–1177.*

Cup-O-Joe. An artsy caffeine joint in a charming section of German Village, Cup-O-Joe draws students, yuppies, and tourists admiring the neighborhood's restored homes and cobbled tree-shaded streets. ⊠ *627 S. 3rd St.,* ☎ *614/221–1563.*

King Avenue Coffeehouse. This crunchy café near OSU is a likely spot to meet politically correct bookish students and to find out the latest about upcoming campus events. The place has a full juice bar, excellent baked goods, and all-organic vegetarian dishes. ⊠ *247 King Ave.,* ☎ *614/294–8287.*

SCENES

Neighborhood bars dominate the Columbus scene, with a few larger clubs—the Garage, the Eagle, and Wall Street—exceptions to this rule. You'll encounter a fairly down-to-earth crowd at most bars, one that is, for the most part, either professional or student. Preppiedom is very much the norm. With so many college students milling around Columbus, it's not surprising that each of the major clubs has an 18-and-older night: the Garage on Friday, the Eagle on Saturday, and Wall Street on Wednesday.

Prime Suspects

Clubhouse. This attractive basement bar beneath the restaurant Out On Main is a nice place for a drink before or after dinner, or before heading out to the clubs. Rare for any bar, especially a gay one, is that the management offers reasonably priced nonalcoholic drinks and coffees. You can carry on a conversation with friends, curl up on one of the cushy lounge chairs, or shoot a game of pool—whatever floats your boat. ⊠ *122 E. Main St.,* ☎ *614/228–5090. Crowd: 75/25 m/f, mostly late 20s to 40s, diverse in appearance and style, not cruisy, easygoing.*

Columbus Eagle Bar. Unlike most Eagles, this one isn't big with leather folks—you have to go to the Eagle in Exile for that. This is the Garage's main competition, and a lot of locals claim to hate one and love the other (all the while sneaking back and forth between the two). A key difference is that the Eagle caters to a broader range of ages and also cultivates a less club-kiddy, more jeans-and-flannel crowd. The club has a mid-size dance floor, a pool hall with vending machines that sell snacks and cassettes of DJ mixes, a large cruisy video bar with several strategic spots from which to ogle, and a chatty lounge in the back. ⊠ *232 N. 3rd St.,* ☎ *614/228–2804. Crowd: mostly male, 20s to 40s, dressed-down, hot to trot, some stand-and-model, low attitude.*

Eagle in Exile. This dark forbidding leather bar enforces a strict dress code every day (it's closed Monday and Tuesday). If you're with somebody dressed in leather or you'd just like to poke your head in and look around, the staff will usually oblige, but to hang out here you'll need to don the right attire. Inside is *dark*—most of the regulars rely heavily on their sense of touch. ⊠ *893 N. 4th St.,* ☎ *614/294–0069. Crowd: male, 30s to 50s, leather, hard-core, raunchy.*

Garage/Trends. Known for hot music and dancing, the Garage is a warehouse space with a large raised dance floor—it's a couple feet above the stand-and-model cruise runway that surrounds it, meaning onlookers are often stuck staring dead at somebody's gyrating abdomen. Off the dance floor are a pair of bars staffed, for the most part, by arrogant beefcakes—but that's part of the fun, if this is your scene. Out back is a spacious patio where pretty boys catch fresh air after drowning their livers. Attached to the frenetic disco, via the patio, is a trendy little neighborhood-style bar named, appropriately, **Trends,** which is fitted with a pool table, cocktail tables, and a jaunty jukebox. ⊠ *40 E. Long St.,* ☎ *614/461–0076. Crowd: mostly male, mostly under 35, students, guppies, some attitude, slaves to club wear, lots of bait but not much biting.*

Havana. Operated by the same folks as Union Station, a few blocks away, Havana is an intimate video bar with a live piano, jazz, and an after-work following. Plenty of folks frequent both bars, which cater more to guys but are extremely female-friendly. Havana, however, is less of a pick-up spot. ⊠ *862 N. High St.,* ☎ *614/421–9697. Crowd: 70/30 m/f, 20s to 50s, very professional, buttoned-down, clean-cut.*

Trade Winds II. This is one of the city's less predictable bars—sometimes there's country-western music, but the very same night they may be playing rock and dance tunes. One local insists it's a popular pick-up bar for straight guys looking to walk on the wild side, others say that bears put off by the leather scene hibernate here. The place consists of several small, well-lighted rooms, the largest of which has a dance floor and a pool table. The rest rooms have cruisy trough urinals. ⊠ *117 E. Chestnut St.,* ☎ *614/461–4110. Crowd: mostly male, mostly late 20s to 40s, butch bears, horn dogs, some country music fans, semi-slutty.*

Union Station. Larger and flashier than its cousin, Havana, Union Station draws a more serious crowd and is a bit less cozy and conversational. Still, it's a great place for drinking, flirting, and chilling out among a consistently nice-looking, well-dressed crowd. The decor is smart, with video screens, tall cocktail tables and bar stools, and a handsome side room with pool tables. This is also a full restaurant with good American food. ✉ *630 N. High St.,* ☎ *614/228–3740. Crowd: 70/30 m/f, 20s to 40s, diverse in look and attire.*

Wall Street. Well-traveled comedienne Suzanne Westenhoffer has called this mostly lesbian nightclub her favorite bar in the country. This spacious two-level club—the second-floor is a loft overlooking the dance floor—is especially appreciated for its theme nights. on Sunday there's drag or stand-up comedy. The hugely successful Wednesday 18-and-over nights render most of the other bars in town nearly empty. This is a hot spot for dancing, scoping out cute femmie dykes, and chattering away with friends. ✉ *144 N. Wall St.,* ☎ *614/464–2800. Crowd: mostly female (except Wed. when it's mixed m/f), all ages, many students, professional, women on the make and a few couples, approachable.*

Neighborhood Haunts

A great queer sports bar with an eclectic jukebox, **Downtown Connection** (✉ 1126 N. High St., ☎ 614/299–4880) draws jocks—young and old—for cheering on the players (or at least discussing their butts). The low-key, semi-butch **Blazer's Pub** (✉ 1205 N. High St., ☎ 614/299–1800) caters to thirty- and fortysomething women and their friends in the northern edge of the Short North. **Summit Station** (✉ 2210 Summit St., ☎ 614/261–9634) is a lively lesbian chat and show bar with a local but loyal following. Both dykes and guys congregate at **Slammer's Pizza Pub** (✉ 202 E. Long St., ☎ 614/221–8880), especially around happy hour, when the cheap beer flows freely and bar food is abundant.

Downtown locals—and few others—frequent the **Pyramid Nightclub** (✉ 196 E. Gay St., ☎ 614/228–6151). During the day **Garrett's Saloon** (✉ Stewart and Parsons Sts., ☎ 614/449–2351) plays country-western tunes; at night there's pop music and strippers—it's always pretty tawdry. At down-home **Club 20** (20 E. Duncan Ave., ☎ 614/261–9111) you're as likely to see dad's foreman from the plant as you are the cute boy from Sunday's softball game. Come here for pinball, pool, darts, and listening to the jukebox. Described by most as a "wrinkle bar," lovable little **Tremont** (✉ 708 S. High St., ☎ 614/445–9365) is a mellow spot that caters to a steady crowd of older guys. Quiet **Remo's** (1409 S. High St., ☎ 614/443–4224) is south of German Village.

SLEEPS

For proximity to gay nightlife and the vibrant German Village and Short North shopping districts, try one of the chain hotels downtown. They offer decent weekend rates and are within walking distance of all the action. A handful of smaller properties are also in these areas, which, though gay-friendly, cater to a mainstream crowd.

A charming, affordable, and highly gay-friendly alternative to a big chain hotel is **Columbus Bed and Breakfast** (☎ 614/443–3680), a small agency run by longtime German Village residents Fred Holdridge and Howard Burns that matches potential guests with hosted B&Bs in this historic neighborhood. Continental breakfast is included.

For price ranges, *see* lodging Chart B at the front of this guide.

$$$–$$$$ 🖬 **Westin Columbus.** This National Historic Landmark was recently restored to its 19th-century character. The two-story lobby with its chandeliers and skylights is particularly remarkable. Rooms have cherry reproduction antiques and are thoroughly modern with voice mail and marble baths. ✉ *310 S. High St., 43215,* ☎ *614/228–3800 or 800/228–3000,* 🗚 *614/228–7666. 196 rooms. Restaurant.*

$$$ ⛨ **Hyatt Regency.** This huge convention hotel is also quite gay-friendly and an easy walk from the Short North. The lobby can be a zoo when conventions are in town, but rooms are comfy and large. ✉ *350 N. High St., 43215,* ☎ *614/463–1234 or 800/233–1234,* ℻ *614/463–1026. 631 rooms. Restaurants, pool.*

$–$$ ⛨ **Holiday Inn City Center.** After a series of renovations, this chain property has clean new furnishings, many in-room amenities (irons, coffeemakers, data ports), and reasonable rates. ✉ *175 E. Town St., 43215,* ☎ *614/221–3281 or 800/367–7870,* ℻ *614/221–2667. 240 rooms. Restaurant, pool.*

$ ⛨ **Clarmont Motor Inn.** If all you need is a roof over your head and clean, basic rooms, try this pleasant motor lodge in German Village. ✉ *650 S. High St., 43215,* ☎ *614/228–6511. 60 rooms. Restaurant.*

THE LITTLE BLACK BOOK

At Your Fingertips

Center For New Directions (women's services and referrals; ✉ 550 E. Spring St., ☎ 614/227–5333). **Central Ohio Transit Authority** (☎ 614/228–1776). **Columbus AIDS Task Force** (☎ 614/488–2437). **Greater Columbus Convention and Visitors Bureau** (✉ 90 N. High St., 43215, ☎ 614/221–CITY or 800/345–4386, Web site www.columbuscvb.org). **Rainbow Pride Hotline** (queer youth resource, ☎ 614/299–8099 or 800/291–9190). **Stonewall Community Center** (✉ 1160 N. High St., ☎ 614/299–7764, Web site www.stonewall-columbus.org). **Women's Health Initiatives** (☎ 614/644–1105). **Yellow Cab** (☎ 614/444–4444).

Gay Media

Biweekly Outlook (☎ 614/268–8525, e-mail outlookpub@aol.com) is a Columbus-based paper with serious news, bar coverage, and good features. The Stonewall Community Center publishes a fine gay and lesbian newspaper, the *Stonewall Journal* (☎ 614/299–7764, Web site www.stonewall-columbus.org). Once a month, give *The Word is OUT!* (☎ 614/784–8146, pfarr83899@aol.com) a look for the latest lesbian point of view. *Gay People's Chronicle* (☎ 216/631–8646, e-mail chronohio@aol.com) is a biweekly Cleveland-based paper with statewide coverage. *Bar Trash* (no phone), a tragic guys-oriented publication, dishes the bar dirt.

BOOKSTORES

In the Short North, **An Open Book** (✉ 761 N. High St., ☎ 614/291–0080) is not only one of the most inviting and elegant lesbigay bookstores in the country, it's also one of the best-stocked, with periodicals, movies, cards, gifts, and general-interest titles. Of mainstream stores, the **Book Loft** (✉ 631 S. Third St., in German Village ☎ 614/464–1774) is your best bet, with bargain books and a good queer section. You can pick up cards, gay gifts, and odds and ends at **Hausfrau Haven** (✉ 769 S. Third St., ☎ 614/443–3680). Try **On the Avenue** (✉ 1415 Grandview Ave., ☎ 614/488–4480) for cards and pride stuff.

Working Out

The downtown **World Gym** (✉ 9 E. Long St., ☎ 614/228–8866) is an impressive facility with a moderately gay following.

9   *Out in Dallas*

A **FEW YEARS BACK THE DALLAS CITY COUNCIL** voted to add sexual orientation and marital status to the city's employment nondiscrimination policy. Of course, votes like this occur regularly across the country, and as many pass as fail. In Dallas, however, the solid 9 to 5 outcome came as a surprise. This is a conservative city, and had this issue been extended to voters, it might never have passed.

With this vote, Dallas's gay community taught the world a few things about how to work in subtle ways for slow but effective change. The two council members who drafted the policy used persuasion and cunning to secure its passage—they concentrated their efforts on the council members they knew were undecided. Suspected opponents weren't apprised of the amendment until shortly before it was brought to a vote. By then, it was too late to rally public support against the amendment.

The gay community's most recent accomplishments have been in the arenas of religion and education. In September 1997 the nation's third high school for gay and lesbian students, the Walt Whitman Community School, opened here. A second headline-grabbing development has been the construction of the nation's largest gay and lesbian church, the 2,000-seat Cathedral of Hope, which will be the new home of the Dallas congregation of the Metropolitan Community Church. It's the creation of gay über–architect Philip Johnson, who, ironically, also designed Dr. Robert Schuller's Crystal Cathedral in Orange County, California.

Dallas maintains a high profile among business travelers, but the city may never be a major vacation destination; attractions are scarce. Gay and lesbian tourists will, however, discover a vibrant bar scene, an internationally acclaimed gay men's chorus, hot restaurants, and enough high-end shopping to wither away the magnetic strips on your credit cards.

THE LAY OF THE LAND

Downtown Dallas sits at the center of a network of highways. Due north, Uptown, which comprises the neighborhoods of Oak Lawn, Highland Park, Turtle Creek, and McKinney Avenue, is where many Dallasites eat, shop, and live, and work.

Oak Lawn, Turtle Creek, and Highland Park

Oak Lawn is for the most part a young, middle-class gay enclave. The hub is Cedar Springs Road, which, from the intersection with Oak Lawn Avenue up to about Knight Road, is lined with gay-supported restaurants, bars, and shops (including a cruisy **Tom Thumb** grocery store). The intersection of Cedar Springs and Throckmorton roads has come to be known as "the Crossroads"; the surrounding area has a strong mix of genders, races, looks, and ages, though on a Saturday night it's overrun with pretty young things on the prowl.

The moneyed gay community extends south into posh **Turtle Creek,** but the condos and housing throughout Uptown have a good share of gay and lesbian residents living in them. To the north of all this gayness is swank **Highland Park,** Dallas's wealthiest residential neighborhood, a land of perfectly manicured lawns and grand mansions. **Highland Park Village** (⊠ Mockingbird La. and Preston Rd.) has upscale clothing stores and boutiques, plus several good restaurants. **McKinney Avenue,** which is in eastern Uptown, has been revitalized in recent years. Dozens of the city's trendiest restaurants are here, and a restored trolley provides access.

Knox–Henderson

In the northeast quadrant of Uptown, many tony shops and restaurants have sprouted along Knox Street, which becomes Henderson Street once it crosses the Central Expressway. **Knox–Henderson** takes in **Travis Walk,** a small complex containing some nifty restaurants and boutiques. The area borders the southern edge of **Southern Methodist University,** and many college types filter through the neighborhood.

Downtown and the West End District

Dallas's downtown feels almost abandoned in the evening, but its space-age skyline is spectacular, with streaks of neon framing many buildings. A growing **arts district** at the northern tip of downtown, near the base of McKinney Avenue, includes the **Dallas Museum of Art** (⊠ 1717 N. Harwood St., ☎ 214/922–1200), which has a collection of pre-Columbian art, as well as a newer wing of North and South American works spanning the past several centuries; and the **Morton H. Meyerson Symphony Center** (⊠ 2301 Flora St., ☎ 214/670–3600), frequent host to the gay Turtle Creek Chorale.

The nearby **West End Historic District,** anchored by the **West End Market Place** (⊠ 603 Munger Ave.), is a series of early 20th-century brick warehouses and factories that have been restored to accommodate mostly touristy and straight-oriented shops, bars, and restaurants.

Just south is **Dealey Plaza,** where President Kennedy was assassinated on November 22, 1963, and where thousands congregate every year on the anniversary of his death. Across Elm Street, along which Kennedy's motorcade traveled, is the so-called **grassy knoll,** from which conspiracy theorists believe a second gunman fired at Kennedy. At the northeast corner of the plaza and Houston Street is the legendary **Texas School Book Depository** (☎ 214/653–6666).

Deep Ellum

Follow either Elm or Main streets east from downtown to about the 3000 block and you'll come to **Deep Ellum** (that's "Deep Elm" with a slow Texas drawl), a haven for nonconformists and alternateens. Dallas's first black neighborhood, Deep Ellum is now a blizzard of low warehouses converted into clubs and eateries, plus a few tattoo shops and art galleries. Gays frequent many of the establishments—or *anti*establishments—in this anything-goes neighborhood.

White Rock Lake

Gays and lesbians tan their hides at **White Rock Lake,** which is a short drive east of Uptown. Bordering the lake is the **Dallas Arboretum and Botanical Gardens** (⊠ 8525 Garland Rd., ☎ 214/327–8263), 65 acres of floral and vegetable gardens and an art- and antiques-filled Spanish Colonial–style mansion. Take I–30 east from downtown, exit north at Grand Avenue, and follow this until it becomes Garland Road.

GETTING AROUND

Outside of downtown, most of Dallas is what a New Yorker or Chicagoan would call the suburbs. Every house has a yard, every commercial establishment is in a shopping center, and everybody gets around by car. People in Dallas rarely use mass transit, but the new commuter-oriented light rail system is slowly catching on. Only downtown is laid out in a grid, and roads often change names between neighborhoods—get a detailed map. Parking near the bars in Oak Lawn can be frustrating.

EATS

Dallas has a sophisticated palate, with trendy bistros dreaming up inventive contemporary creations. You'll also find more familiar comfort food and some pseudo-exotic delicacies—fajitas and frozen margaritas were invented here. Burger joints and barbecues are abundant. Most of the best restaurants are in gay Uptown, in funky Deep Ellum, and in the rapidly gayifying South Dallas neighborhood, Oak Cliff.

If you're planning a picnic at White Rock Lake or looking to stock up on delicious gourmet goods and groceries, check out **Café TuGogh** (⊠ inside Marty's, 3316 Oak Lawn Ave., ☎ 214/526–4070) or, across the street, **Eatzie's** (⊠ 3403 Oak Lawn Ave., ☎ 214/526–1515).

For price ranges, *see* dining Chart A at the front of this guide.

Uptown

$$$$ ✕ **Mansion on Turtle Creek.** There's electricity in the air of this restaurant in a splendid old mansion presided over by New American cooking guru Dean Fearing. His style is complex, and inventions like tortilla soup, warm lobster salad with yellow-tomato salsa, and jicama salad always astonish. ⊠ *2821 Turtle Creek Blvd.,* ☎ *214/559–2100.*

$$$$ ✕ **NorthSouth.** The menu at this ultrachic eatery is divided into two varieties of cooking: South-style (i.e., traditional, high-caloric, and rich) and North-style (i.e., nouvelle, low-fat, and still seemingly rich). The latter is a reflection of chef Larry North's predilection for tasty but healthful fare like tortilla-crusted roasted-corn hash and tomato salsa-verde snapper. ⊠ *Quadrangle, 2800 Routh St.,* ☎ *214/849–0000.*

$$$$ ✕ **Old Warsaw.** This windowless spot has been one of the city's most formal French restaurants for years. Expect fine china and crystal, a piano-and-violin duo, and waiters in tuxedos—it's more than a little retro. Save room (and money) for any of the lavish dessert soufflés. ⊠ *2610 Maple Ave.,* ☎ *214/528–0032.*

$$$–$$$$ ✕ **Star Canyon.** It's tough to land a table at this dining room in the upscale Centrum Sports Complex, the service can be uppity, and some complain it's overrated. But it's hard to argue when the kitchen turns out phenomenal dishes like red snapper on Texas jambalaya. ⊠ *3102 Oak Lawn Ave., Suite 144,* ☎ *214/520–7827.*

$$–$$$ ✕ **Bombay Cricket Club.** In a stately house near the Hotel St. Germain, this elegant Indian restaurant is bright, crisp, and sophisticated, and the menu is impeccably authentic, with every kind of curry, tandoori, and biryani imaginable. Lots of veggie dishes, too. ⊠ *2508 Maple Ave.,* ☎ *214/871–1333.*

$$–$$$ ✕ **Parigi.** This much-discussed trattoria's marble tables, dainty wooden chairs, and lemon-yellow and pale-blue color scheme make for a chic atmosphere. The healthful bistro menu includes many whole-wheat pastas with delicious accents like shallot mashed potatoes and ginger-lime cream sauce. ⊠ *3311 Oak Lawn Ave.,* ☎ *214/521–0295.*

$–$$ ✕ **Bronx.** The best of the Crossroads eateries, the Bronx is inexpensive and untrendy. Come for the mom-style pot roast, London broil, omelets,

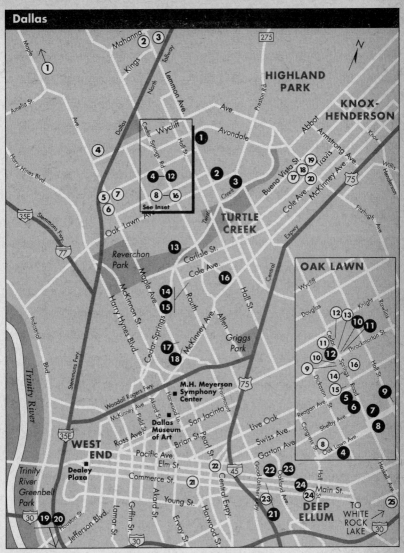

Dallas

Eats ●

Bombay Cricket Club, **18**
Bronx, **6**
Cafe Brazil, **23**
Cosmic Cup, **4**
Dream Café, **15**
Gloria's, **1**
Green Room, **22**
Hunky's, **10**
Java Jones, **7**
Lucky's, **2**
Mansion on Turtle Creek, **13**
Monica Aca y Alla, **24**
NorthSouth, **14**

Old Warsaw, **17**
Parigi, **9**
Sambuca, **21**
Spasso's, **11, 16**
Star Canyon, **8**
That Special Blend, **12**
Tillman, **19**
Vitto, **20**
Zeko's, **5**
ZuZu, **3**

Scenes ○

Anchor Inn/Big Daddy's/Numbers, **12**
Backstreet, **7**
Bamboleo's, **2**
Brick Bar, **5**
Buddies II, **6**
Club Collette's, **21**
Club One, **24**
Crews Inn, **20**
Dallas Eagle, **1**
Gridlock, **23**
Hidden Door, **3**
Hideaway Club, **17**
J. R.'s, **10**
Jugs, **8**
Kolors, **4**
Metro, **22**
Moby Dick's, **11**

Pub Pegasus, **18**
Round-Up Saloon, **16**
Side 2 Bar, **13**
Sue Ellen's, **15**
Throckmorton Mining Co., **9**
The Trestle, **25**
Village Station, **14**
Zipper's, **19**

and chicken cacciatore. It should be called the Bronx Zoo on weekend evenings. ✉ *3835 Cedar Springs Rd.,* ☎ *214/521–5821.*

$–$$ ✕ **Gloria's.** Noisy, cavernous, and unromantic, Gloria's has unfinished concrete floors and green plastic chairs. But the no-frills Mexican and South American menu is fiery and fresh, and the staff is outgoing. Yummy black-bean dip. ✉ *4140 Lemmon Ave., Suite 102,* ☎ *214/521–7576.*

$–$$ ✕ **Lucky's.** At its best late on weekend nights, especially as the bars let out, this well-dressed diner has art deco tables and chairs, a black-and-white tile floor, and judicious use of neon. The food is good if unsurprising. ✉ *3531 Oak Lawn Ave.,* ☎ *214/522–3500.*

$ ✕ **Dream Café.** The place to go for breakfast, this sunny café draws a great mix of people, all of them longing for another crack at the veggie-oriented menu. The buttermilk pancakes topped with ricotta are famous. Between bites, you can toss a Frisbee to your dog or your date on the long green lawn out front. ✉ *Quadrangle, 2800 Routh St.,* ☎ *214/954–0486.*

$ ✕ **Hunky's.** Hunky waitrons skirt around tables of hunky patrons at this gay study in fast food on Cedar Springs Road's bar strip. You'll find the juiciest old-fashioned hamburgers here, but none of the food is overly greasy. ✉ *4000 Cedar Springs Rd.,* ☎ *214/522–1212.*

$ ✕ **Spasso's.** The Crossroads branch of this local chain is the gayest (and it's *quite* gay), but all of them serve mouthwatering pizza—from traditional to white, with both mundane and gourmet toppings (try the pie with goat cheese, spinach, and garlic). ✉ *3227 McKinney Ave.,* ☎ *214/ 520–6000;* ✉ *4000 Cedar Springs Rd.,* ☎ *214/521–1141.*

$ ✕ **Zeko's.** This queer Oak Lawn diner works more because of the funny menu, complete with goofy slogans and oddly named dishes (like the "Sassy Suzy Burger" with hickory sauce, onions, and pickles), than the ordinary grub. The standout here is the ice cream, which comes with an eclectic riot of toppings (Cocoa Puffs are a favorite). ✉ *3847 Cedar Springs Rd.,* ☎ *214/521–8009.*

$ ✕ **ZuZu.** At this ultrabright, cheerful place (part of a regional chain), you order at the counter before plopping down into one of the festive little red chairs. The Mexican food is standard by Texas standards (which means stellar to everybody else); Mexican pizzas and margaritas are a highlight. ✉ *3848 Oak Lawn Ave.,* ☎ *214/521–1290.*

Deep Ellum

$$–$$$ ✕ **Green Room.** Behind a veil of purple crushed-velvet drapes, this triumphantly bizarre eatery is jammed with musical instruments, posters, and alternative-music paraphernalia. Even if you don't have a funky bone in your body, come for such dazzling fare as New Zealand venison with applewood-smoked-bacon mashed potatoes, eggplant-pinot glaze, and bing cherry relish. ✉ *2715 Elm St.,* ☎ *214/748–7666.*

$$–$$$ ✕ **Monica Aca y Alla.** This is the queerest and liveliest of Deep Ellum restaurants. Even yupsters in suits brave the neighborhood's eccentricities for the live music—mostly Latin-flavored jazz, salsa, and mambo—and feisty, somewhat southwestern-inspired fare, from Mexican lasagna to pumpkin ravioli. ✉ *2914 Main St.,* ☎ *214/748–7140.*

$$–$$$ ✕ **Sambuca.** The sign outside says MEDITERRANEAN CUISINE-JAZZ BAH, and that basically sums it up. The seats upholstered in faux-leopard skin are the highlight of the postindustrial interior. Dishes include couscous, pasta, salmon over spinach, and the like. The nightly jazz shows are renowned. ✉ *2618 Elm St.,* ☎ *214/744–0820.*

Oak Cliff

$–$$ ✕ **Tillman.** The cooking at this homey neighborhood restaurant ranges from haute (crab cakes with orange-chipotle sauce) to down-home (bringing to mind the "all you can stands" catfish dinner on Tuesday nights). ✉ *324 W. 7th St.,* ☎ *214/942–0988.*

$ ✕ **Vitto.** Bright and sunny with yellow walls and a huge painting exploding with sunflowers, Vitto is another of Oak Cliff's popular queer hangouts. In addition to great pastas and a mean baked ratatouille, this upbeat café offers an assortment of not-so-conventional pizzas, including a hefty pie with spinach, bacon, pepperoni, and garlic butter (but no red sauce). ✉ *316 W. 7th St.,* ☎ *214/946–1212.*

Coffeehouse Culture

Café Brazil. When the Deep Ellum clubs close, droves of curious-looking slackers and hipsters crowd into this slick coffeehouse, known as much for good sandwiches and salads as for espresso and desserts. By day it attracts a low-key, artsy bunch. ✉ *2815 Elm St.,* ☎ *214/747–2730.*

Cosmic Cup. The dining room is filled with crunchy types perusing the small library of good-for-your-soul, New Age titles. A favorite dish is the "I Hate Eggplant" sandwich, which requires that you eat a good bit of eggplant, along with basil, tomatoes, and mozzarella. Good juice bar. ✉ *2912 Oak Lawn Ave.,* ☎ *214/521–6157.*

Java Jones. Cool and jazzy, with live music some nights, Java Jones collars Oak Lawn's collared-shirt crowd. It's the best spot in the neighborhood for desserts—scrumptious fresh pastries and gelato. The sandwiches and pasta dishes are good, too. ✉ *3211 Oak Lawn Ave.,* ☎ *214/528–2099.*

That Special Blend. Despite its plum location amid a few high-profile bars, this coffee shop doesn't exactly ooze atmosphere. Still, the boys and girls do linger here for hours, hoping to discover other new boys and girls.✉ *4001A Cedar Springs Rd.,* ☎ *214/522–3726.*

SCENES

Gay nightlife in Dallas bubbles in small, dense pockets mostly near Oak Lawn. The bars along the Crossroads are the most heavily frequented by visitors. J.R.'s, Sue Ellen's, the Throckmorton Mining Co., and the Village Station share the same owner, who throws a "Cruising the Crossroads" party on weekend nights: From 9 until 11, these bars pour 50¢ well drinks for a half hour each.

Dallas may be the only city in America where people dress up to go out for a beer. At Moby Dick's or Sue Ellen's, a collared shirt is almost de rigueur. Places outside of the Crossroads are more casual, particularly those around Maple Avenue where it crosses below the Dallas North Tollway (most of these are leather), Fitzhugh Street where it's bisected by Travis and Cole avenues (neighborhood hangouts), and Lemmon Avenue just northwest of the Tollway (mostly Latino bars).

Prime Suspects

Anchor Inn/Big Daddy's/Numbers. The Anchor Inn has strippers, and a loud, fun-loving crowd watching them; Big Daddy's has two drag shows nightly; and Numbers is a hustlery watering hole. Because the compound is technically part of the Crossroads, you see a surprising number of suits and guppies. ✉ *4024 Cedar Springs Rd.,* ☎ *214/526–4098. Crowd: male, generally older, horny, raucous.*

Brick Bar. Everything about the Brick Bar does seem to be brick. It's a brick-shape, painted-red brick building with glass-brick windows. Lots of the men have brick upper bodies—and, some would say, brick brains. The only collars you're gonna see around here are leather with silver spikes—though preppy curiosity-seekers amble through most nights, usually in giggling gaggles. There's a good leather shop inside this labyrinthine complex, which is a short walk from other, slimier, leather bars. Same owners as Moby Dick's (a free shuttle runs between the two bars on weekends). ✉ *4117 Maple Ave.,* ☎ *214/521–2024. Crowd: mostly* *male, all ages, Levi's and leather, get-laid intensity, pretty gym boys and gruff but lovable bears.*

Buddies II. Acclaimed for its swimming pool, spacious deck, and sand vol-leyball court, this down-to-earth dyke bar is packed on weekend after-noons. Every manner of lesbian (and more than a few men) drops by to laze in the sun and mingle. The crowds are fairly large at night, too—there's a main interior bar with videos and a dance floor, and a second, more intimate one that's ideal for conversation and more mingling. ⊠ *4025 Maple Ave.,* ☎ *214/526–0887. Crowd: 70/30 f/m, 20s to 50s, semi-butch but diverse, casual.*

J.R.'s. After falling behind Moby Dick's in popularity, this stand-and-model bar received a slick redo in 1997: A cool upstairs lounge with a balcony overlooking the hunk-infested street below was added. It has high pressed-tin ceilings, brass bar fixtures, and large windows. J.R.'s may not be as happening as it once was, but it's less attitudy. Decent pub food. ⊠ *3923 Cedar Springs Rd.,* ☎ *214/528–1004. Crowd: 70/30 m/f, mixed ages, some suits, starched-shirt.*

Metro. This high-energy disco and drag club in Deep Ellum is the hub of Dallas's black gay scene. You'll find a midsize dance floor with house, disco, and hip-hop blaring most nights; a show lounge with top-name strippers from time to time, and smashing drag and lip-synch shows many nights. The 18-and-older nights, usually Wednesday and Sunday, are a major to-do. ⊠ *2204 Elm St.,* ☎ *214/742–2101. Crowd: mostly male, 20s and 30s, club kids, gym bodies, plenty of drag.*

Moby Dick's. Both floors of this poseurs' perch are decked out with video screens; balconies allow bird's-eye cruising of those down below. And guys do cruise here, so relentlessly that it's rare that anyone lets his guard down long enough to meet somebody. The upstairs patio bar gives a little re-lief from the always-packed interior; from here you can admire the palms bedecked with Christmas lights out front. ⊠ *4011 Cedar Springs Rd.,* ☎ *214/520–6629. Crowd: mostly male, 20s and 30s, buff and beauti-ful, starched-shirt, a bit narcissistic.*

Round-Up Saloon. The friendliest bar in the Crossroads, the Round-Up can still feel a bit intimidating, at least relative to other country-western bars. It may not be the best place to *learn* how to two-step, but if you know what you're doing, join right in—these guys are good. The decor is typical Western (lots of wagon wheels). There's also a nice little room with pool tables off the main dance floor. This place could do a better job welcoming the ladies, who have no country-western club of their own. ⊠ *3912 Cedar Springs Rd.,* ☎ *214/522–9611. Crowd: mostly male, late 20s to early 40s, starched-shirt, country-western.*

Sue Ellen's. In the heart of the Crossroads, this terrific lesbian disco has a big dance floor, booth seating, clear windows showing onto the street, and a patio out back that is packed on weekends and has live music on Friday. The bar is well decorated and thoughtfully laid out—very con-ducive to chatting. Off the main room are pool tables and more seating. ⊠ *3903 Cedar Springs Rd.,* ☎ *214/559–0707. Crowd: 80/20 f/m, mostly under 35, lots of lipstick and mousse.*

Throckmorton Mining Co. Like other "Mining Companies," this one aims for a dark and forbidding leather look, but TMC is smack in the heart of the Crossroads, so it gets a lot of the same guys from neighboring J.R.'s. It is, nevertheless, dark, smoky, and devoid of ambience. One nice touch: peanuts served out of huge beer vats. ⊠ *3014 Throckmorton St.,* ☎ *214/ 521–4205. Crowd: mostly male, all ages, more Levi's than leather but some of both, a few guppies, lots of bears.*

Village Station. It's had other names, it's been burned to the ground, and it's been a shaggy dive. Now rebuilt in concrete, it's more crowded and roomier inside than you might think: There's a room with go-go dancers, the neighborhood's nicest patio bar, and the Rose Room, where you'll find some of the best drag shows in the country. A mob on Saturday, and 18 and over on Wednesday and Thursday. ⊠ *3911 Cedar Springs Rd., ☎ 214/526–7171. Crowd: 80/20 m/f, mostly under 35, well-dressed, mixed racially, just about anybody who parties around the Crossroads.*

Neighborhood Haunts

Near the Crossroads, **Jugs** (⊠ 3810 Congress St., ☎ 214/521–3474) is a racially diverse women's pool hall, and the tiny **Side 2 Bar** (⊠ 4006 Cedar Springs Rd., ☎ 214/528–2026), right next to Hunky's, draws a cross-section of dykes and fags.

East of Oak Lawn, across Turtle Creek, Fitzhugh Avenue leads to a few spots popular with older guys turned off by the Crossroads attitude. The man's-man–oriented **Crews Inn** (⊠ 3215 N. Fitzhugh Ave., ☎ 214/526–9510) is probably the most popular, especially on Tuesday. The **Hideaway Club** (⊠ 4144 Buena Vista St., ☎ 214/559–2966), whose patio is lit with trillions of lights and colors, is the city's gay piano bar (some women attend). It also has drag shows. **Pub Pegasus** (⊠ 3326 N. Fitzhugh Ave., ☎ 214/559–4663), your quintessential dive, has piano entertainment, a lovely neon Pegasus sign inside, and friendly bartenders. **Zipper's** (⊠ 3333 N. Fitzhugh Ave., ☎ 214/526–9519) features male strippers.

Near the Brick Bar (*see above*) are several rough-and-raw bars. **Backstreet** (⊠ 4020 Maple Ave., ☎ 214/522–4814) is across from the Brick. Up the street is **Kolors** (⊠ 2525 Wycliff Ave., ☎ 214/520–2525), a cheesy show and dance bar that is decked in rainbow lights, walls, and curtains. There's usually a steep cover for the shows, which are sometimes good, but often not. A favorite with hard-core leather men, the **Dallas Eagle** (⊠ 2515 Inwood Rd., No. 107, ☎ 214/357–4375) is crowded late on weekend nights.

Bamboleo's (⊠ 5027 Lemmon Ave., ☎ 214/520–1124) has a mixed Hispanic following and some of the best Latin dancing you'll find in any gay club in Texas; the melodramatic drag shows are another reason to visit. Also cultivating a leather scene, the **Hidden Door** (⊠ 5025 Bowser Rd., ☎ 214/526–0620) hosts several area leather groups and has the usual games, dim lighting, and raunchy atmosphere.

Near Deep Ellum, **Club Collette's** (⊠ 2024½ Commerce St., ☎ 214/747–1449) draws primarily an African-American crowd. The **Trestle** (⊠ 412 S. Haskell St., ☎ 214/826–9988), a gnarly hustler bar in a dicey neighborhood, gets raided from time to time. Horny locals swear by it.

Hangin' with the Hets

In Deep Ellum, the **Club One** (⊠ 3025 Main St., ☎ 214/741–1111) is straight though gay-friendly; the queerest night is Friday. Nearby **Gridlock** (⊠ 2612 Commerce St., ☎ 214/712–1721) is another gay-friendly favorite, known for its Saturday-night deep disco and house party called Milk Bar.

Action

Club Dallas (⊠ 2616 Swiss Ave., ☎ 214/821–1990) is the city's bathhouse.

SLEEPS

Dallas has outstanding options close to things queer. Even the stodgiest hotels are used to gay travelers, though discretion is always wise. Thanks to its popularity as a trade-show site, Dallas has from two to five outposts of almost every major hotel chain, and 40,000 hotel rooms. The most interesting and historic hotels (*not* the chains) offer travelers personal attention, individually designed rooms, and great restaurants—though often at a price.

For price ranges, *see* lodging Chart A at the front of this guide.

Hotels

$$$$ ⌷ **Adolphus.** The finest downtown hotel is this 21-story Beaux Arts beauty built by beer baron Adolphus Busch. The only problem with this 1912 structure is that it's a good distance from the grooviest restaurants and nightlife. ⌧ *1321 Commerce St., 75202,* ☎ *214/742–8200 or 800/ 221–9083,* FAX *214/651–3588. 426 rooms. Restaurant, health club.*

$$$$ ⌷ **Mansion on Turtle Creek.** Arguably the top hotel in the country, the Mansion is a 15-minute walk to the Crossroads. It has an amazing restaurant, a state-of-the-art health club, and plush rooms, 50 of which have recently been given sleek makeovers that include whirlpool tubs. ⌧ *2821 Turtle Creek Blvd., 75219,* ☎ *214/559–2100 or 800/527–5432,* FAX *214/528–4187. 141 rooms. Restaurant, pool, health club.*

$$–$$$ ⌷ **Melrose.** It's only about 200 yards from the lobby of this stately hotel to most of the action on Cedar Springs Road and in Oak Lawn. Nearby is the popular Centrum Sports Club, at which guests have privileges. Rooms are nicely appointed. ⌧ *3015 Oak Lawn Ave., 75219,* ☎ *214/521–5151 or 800/637–7200,* FAX *214/521–2470. 184 rooms. Restaurant.*

$$–$$$ ⌷ **Stoneleigh.** A moderately priced historic property, this 70-year-old brick building is where Oliver Stone stayed while filming *JFK.* It's close to Oak Lawn, convenient to many restaurants, and home to the Dallas Press Club. ⌧ *2927 Maple Ave., 75201,* ☎ *214/871–7111 or 800/255–9299,* FAX *214/871–9379. 132 rooms. Restaurant, pool.*

$ ⌷ **La Quinta.** This is the best budget choice, across U.S. 75 from Travis Walk, in the Knox–Henderson area. ⌧ *4440 N. Central Expressway, 75206,* ☎ *214/821–4220 or 800/531–5900. 101 rooms.*

Guest Houses and Small Hotels

$$$$ ⌷ **Hotel St. Germain.** The most luxurious of the city's small inns, this century-old house in southern Oak Lawn contains suites fitted with French and New Orleans antiques. The elaborate touches include canopied featherbeds, rich tapestries, marble bed stands, balconies, fireplaces, and, in two suites, Jacuzzis. ⌧ *2516 Maple Ave., 75201,* ☎ *214/871–2516 or 800/683–2516,* FAX *214/871–0740. 7 rooms with phone, TV, and private bath.*

$$ ⌷ **Inn on Fairmount.** Affordable and attracting a mostly gay crowd, this hotel matches some of Dallas's top hotels for service and amenities. You can walk to bars and restaurants. ⌧ *3701 Fairmount, 75219,* ☎ *214/ 522–2800,* FAX *214/522–2898. 7 rooms with phone, TV, and private bath. Continental breakfast. Hot tub. Mixed gay/lesbian.*

THE LITTLE BLACK BOOK

At Your Fingertips

AIDS Resource Center Hotline (☎ 214/521–5342, e-mail foundgay@on-ramp.net). **Dallas Convention and Visitors Bureau** (⌧ 1201 Elm St., Suite 2000, 75270, ☎ 214/746–6677 or 800/232–5527). **Dallas Gay/Lesbian Line Web site** (www.cyberramp.net/~woofbyte). *Dallas Observer* (☎ 214/ 757–9000, Web site www.dallasobserver.com). **Dallas Visitors Information Center** (⌧ West End Marketplace, 603 Munger Ave., ☎ 214/880–0405). **Gay and Lesbian Community Center** (⌧ 2701 Reagan St., ☎ 214/ 521–5342, Web site www.fhu.org; switchboard, ☎ 214/528–0022). **Gay and Lesbian Information Line** (☎ 214/368–6283). **Lesbian Visionaries** (☎ 214/521–5342, ext. 844). **Stonewall Professional & Business Association** (☎ 214/526–3214). **Women's Business Network** (☎ 214/712–8976).

Gay Media

Dallas has no shortage of gay papers, all of them useful and well-written. The highly regarded *Dallas Voice* (☎ 214/754–8710, Web site www.dallasvoice.com) is a weekly news and entertainment magazine. *This Week in Texas* (☎ 214/521–0622, e-mail twtmag@aol.com), an entertainment-oriented magazine, has plenty of Dallas coverage. The *Texas Triangle* (☎ 214/599–0155) is a news-oriented weekly newspaper. The queer African-American community looks to the *Underground Station* (☎ 972/283–1047, e-mail undrgrdsta@aol.com), not only for club news and local resources and insights, but for news of Texas, Louisiana, and the South.

BOOKSTORES

The lesbigay bookstore **Crossroads Market** (✉ 3930 Cedar Springs Rd., ☎ 214/521–8919) carries lesbian and gay titles, plus gifts, cards, and porn mags.

Working Out

The **Crossroads Gym** (✉ 4001 Cedar Springs Rd., ☎ 214/522–9376) is an incredibly gay scene—some might argue that it's a better place to pick people up than to work out. Bigger and better is the renowned **Centrum Sports Club** (✉ 3102 Oak Lawn Ave., ☎ 214/522–4100).

10 *Out in Denver*

With Aspen and Boulder

EVERYTHING SEEMS BACK TO NORMAL for Denver's lesbian and gay community, for years one of the nation's largest and most visible. In November 1992, Colorado voters approved the antigay Amendment 2, which called for a ban on local and state laws protecting citizens against discrimination in employment, housing, and public accommodation on the basis of sexual orientation. Right-wing think-tanks with headquarters in the city of Colorado Springs had initiated the provision, but its passage tarnished the images of more queer-tolerant towns like Denver, Boulder, and Aspen.

Opponents to the amendment immediately filed a lawsuit challenging its constitutionality. Within a couple of days, local and national gay groups had put into place a comprehensive plan calling for a boycott on travel to Colorado and goods and services provided by Colorado companies. At the beginning of 1993, a Colorado judge postponed the enforcement of the amendment until the constitutional issues had been resolved, and the boycott fizzled out as gays and lesbians resumed traveling to the state. In 1995, the U.S. Supreme Court heard the case regarding Amendment 2, known officially as *Romer v. Evans.* The justices struck down the law in May 1996 by a vote of 6 to 3, ruling that the amendment would have denied gays and lesbians equal protection under the law.

The court's opinion curtailed similar antigay initiatives in other U.S. cities, and made it easier for queer Denverites to enjoy as citizens of equal standing the city's triumphant recovery from the economic bust of the 1980s. New museums, shops, brew pubs, and restaurants have opened all around town in recent years, and the local business community continues to diversify (the city's economic health was previously tied too closely to that of the energy industry).

Gays and lesbians, who played a pivotal role in turning once-dilapidated Lower Downtown (a.k.a. LoDo) into a thriving arts and entertainment district, are helping to reinvigorate other potentially exciting neighborhoods, among them South Broadway. With excellent queer and feminist newspapers and a strong network of social and political organizations, the gay community is accessible to newcomers.

THE LAY OF THE LAND

Most people think Denver is in the Rocky Mountains, but it's actually east of them. Though a mile above sea level, it is nonetheless as flat as can be. The foothills of the Rockies begin their magnificent, sharp ascent immediately west of the city and the mountains are a fixture of the Denver skyline.

As weather systems cross the Rockies from west to east, sometimes dumping several feet of snow along the way, they reach Denver largely worn out and packing little punch. Winters here are milder than in most northern U.S. cities, and though it snows often in late winter and early spring, the flakes usually melt by midday.

Broadway is Denver's major north–south axis; Colfax Avenue, lined with drab carpet stores and auto-parts dealers and possibly the ugliest road in America, is the major east–west axis. Denver's densely populated northwest quadrant is where the city started, when gold was panned in 1859 at the confluence of Cherry Creek and the South Platte River. The streets of this section run at a 45° angle to other city streets. Speer Boulevard, Denver's other major thoroughfare, runs diagonally through the city, for the most part straddling Cherry Creek.

Downtown

Pockets of Victorian and Edwardian residential and commercial architecture grace the city, but on the whole Denver's facade is ordinary. Sixteen skyscrapers, most of them built during the energy boom of the late '70s and early '80s, punctuate the downtown skyline.

Area highlights include the **Brown Palace Hotel** (⊠ 17th St. and Tremont Pl.), which has a great lobby (*see* Sleeps, *below*); the **Museum of Western Art** (⊠ 1727 Tremont Pl., ☎ 303/296–1880), whose holdings include pivotal works by the western genre's greatest practitioners; and the **Trianon Museum and Art Gallery** (⊠ 335 14th St., ☎ 303/623–0739), whose strengths are 18th-century European painting, the decorative arts, and home furnishings.

The mile of 16th Street between Market Street and Broadway was transformed in the early 1980s into the **16th street pedestrian mall.** Most of the shops and restaurants along here are on the touristy side, but city planners hope that the addition (scheduled for late 1998) of the **Denver Pavilions** (⊠ 16th St. between Tremont Pl. and Welton St.), a new center that will house NikeTown, the Hard Rock Cafe, 12 movie screens, six restaurants, and upscale shops, will draw more Denverites and breathe new life into the pedestrian mall. Near the northern end of the mall is the **D&F Tower** (⊠ 16th and Arapahoe Sts.), a 325-foot replica of the campanile of San Marco in Venice. The tower was erected in 1909 as part of the Daniels and Fisher department store. Hip boutiques and restaurants line Victorian **Larimer Square** (⊠ Larimer and 15th Sts.), which attracts a colorful crowd. For one-stop cultural fulfillment, investigate the offerings at the **Denver Performing Arts Complex** (⊠ 14th and Champa Sts., ☎ 303/893–4100), where theater, symphony, opera, and other performances take place.

The **Elitch Gardens** (⊠ Elitch Circle off Speer Blvd., ☎ 303/595–4386) amusement park has all the usual rides and diversions. On Gay Day— the last Sunday in July, an event arranged by Lesbian and Gay Community Center (☎ 303/831–6268)—legions of screaming queens cut loose aboard the *Twister II* roller coaster and other dizzying rides. A bad hair day is enjoyed by all.

Lower Downtown (LoDo)

Larimer Square marks the beginning of dapper **LoDo,** Denver's original shipping and retail center. As recently as 10 years ago this was a district of slums and abandoned redbrick warehouses. When artists began converting the Victorian-era structures into galleries and studios, LoDo's comeback was underway. A flood of restaurants, coffeehouses, and shops followed, but as rents have risen, brew pubs and other more mainstream ventures have edged out many of the offbeat establishments. For a whiff of Victorian grandeur, step into the **Oxford Hotel** (⊠ 17th and Wazee Sts.), which was built in 1891 (*see* Lodging, *below*). **Coors Field** (⊠ Blake and

20th Sts.), a stadium that replicates the quirky old ballparks of years past, is the home of professional baseball's Colorado Rockies.

East and South of Downtown

The **Capitol Hill** neighborhood, which is centered at the intersection of Colfax Avenue and Broadway, is the closest thing Denver has to a gay ghetto. Period-conscious queers here undoubtedly take some of their decorative cues from the **Molly Brown House Museum** (✉ 1340 Pennsylvania St., ☎ 303/832–4092), and not merely because community icon Debbie Reynolds starred in the film about the "unsinkable" survivor of the *Titanic* disaster. A magnificent dome embellished with 200 ounces of gold leafing caps the Federal Revival **State Capitol** (✉ 1475 Sherman St., ☎ 303/866–2604), which overlooks **Civic Center Park,** a grassy, usually flower-filled mall with Greek colonnades. Nearby are the **Colorado History Museum** (✉ 1300 Broadway, ☎ 303/866–3682), which traces the region's gold-mining past, and the **U.S. Mint** (✉ W. Colfax Ave. and Cherokee St., ☎ 303/844–3582), which you can tour for free on weekdays.

Michael Graves, with members of a Denver architectural firm, designed the 10-level **Denver Public Library** (✉ 10 W. 14th Ave. Pkwy., ☎ 303/640–6200), a multicolored postmodern wonder on the south side of Civic Center Park. A 70-panel interior mural by Edward Ruscha reflects on aspects of Colorado's history; the library's art collection also includes originals by Thomas Moran, Frederic Remington, and Albert Bierstadt.

The fortresslike exterior of the library's imposing next-door neighbor, the **Denver Art Museum** (✉ 100 W. 14th Ave., ☎ 303/640–2793), contains 1,000,000 hand-set glass tiles. Italian architect Gio Ponti designed the structure, which was built in 1971. The museum's Native American holdings are the most extensive in the world, but the floor of Asian works also deserves a look.

A gentrified neighborhood of century-old homes surrounds lovely **Cheesman Park,** which is most easily accessed from Race Street, 9th Avenue, or 12th Avenue. The Pavilion, on the east side of the park, has views of the mountains west of Denver (and a cruisy parking lot). Also here is the **Denver Botanic Garden** (✉ 1005 York St., ☎ 303/331–4000).

East of downtown is the **Denver Museum of Natural History** (✉ 2001 Colorado Blvd., ☎ 303/322–7009), whose snappy "Prehistoric Journey" exhibit chronicles the earth's history. Farther east, the **Black American West Museum** (✉ 3091 California St., ☎ 303/292–2566) celebrates the contribution of blacks to America's frontier; it's believed that as many as a third of America's cowboys were black.

Much of the city's commercial gay scene has shifted in recent years from LoDo and Capitol Hill to slightly seedy **South Broadway,** a neighborhood that's on the upswing. In addition to the gay bars and restaurants along this stretch of Broadway south of Cherry Creek are some excellent antiques shops.

GETTING AROUND

Parts of downtown and Capitol Hill are walkable, but a car comes in handy in Denver. The Light Rail System will get you to and from some museums and sights, as will the Cultural Connection Trolley, but neither is extensive. A free shuttle bus runs the length of the 16th Street Mall. For public transportation throughout the metropolitan area and even up to Boulder, you can use the city's Regional Transportation District bus system, but it's inconvenient and slow. Taxis are available by phone or at the major hotels.

EATS

The many ethnic options and a blossoming New American scene are the highlights of Denver dining. LoDo contains some trendy eateries; also try Pearl and Gaylord streets, in South Denver. Informality is the rule, even at the fanciest establishments. The best of the gay bars with restaurants are **Charlie's** and the **SnakePit**.

For price ranges, *see* dining Chart B at the front of this guide.

$$$–$$$$ ✕ **Tante Louise.** Formal Tante Louise is the place to take that special someone for a fabulous meal. The contemporary and traditional French cooking has been winning raves forever; consider the roasted foie gras with shiitakes and goat's-milk cheddar cheese or the roasted rack of New Zealand venison. ✉ *4900 E. Colfax Ave.,* ☎ *303/355–4488.*

$$–$$$$ ✕ **McCormick's Fish House and Oyster Bar.** Part of the Oxford Hotel, McCormick's serves the best seafood in town. At happy hour, several items, including excellent mussels, are available for next to nothing. ✉ *1659 Wazee St.,* ☎ *303/825–1107.*

$$$ ✕ **Barolo Grill.** This slick Tuscan-inspired restaurant is the domain of local power brokers and flashy foodies. The kitchen turns out sterling Mediterranean and New American cooking—delicate rare ahi tuna, tender lamb chops over roasted vegetables, and pizza with yellow beefsteak tomatoes, basil pesto, and walnuts. ✉ *3030 E. 6th Ave.,* ☎ *303/393–1040.*

$$$ ✕ **Denver ChopHouse & Brewery.** The latest megamicrobrewery to satisfy the desires of LoDo beer aficionados, this fancy restored space by Coors Field whips up tantalizing new-frontier American cuisine—hefty steak and veal chops, lobster potpie—and many veggie dishes. ✉ *1735 19th St.,* ☎ *303/296–0800.*

$$–$$$ ✕ **Café Brazil.** A little off the beaten path, this intimate café serves authentic Latin American fare, including black beans with sausage, rice, greens, fresh orange wedges, and plantains. Spicy crowd, too. ✉ *3611 Navajo St.,* ☎ *303/480–1877. No credit cards.*

$$–$$$ ✕ **Hugh's.** Exposed brick, hardwood floors, and warm lighting make this one of Pearl Street's most elegant eateries. The moderately priced New American menu—steaks, seafood, vegetarian entrés—is outstanding, and there's a long wine list. ✉ *1469 S. Pearl St.,* ☎ *303/744–1940.*

$$–$$$ ✕ **Jan Leone.** This swell supper club on Capitol Hill draws gay and straight suits for fine Continental and Italian food. The setting in a stately mansion accounts for much of the restaurant's success. ✉ *1509 Marion St.,* ☎ *303/863–8433.*

$$–$$$ ✕ **Sushi Den.** Come here for fresh sushi and great Japanese steak and chicken dishes. Sushi Den is set in a toasty dining room with exposed brick, high ceilings, contemporary hanging lights, and sleek furnishings. Very trendy. ✉ *1487 S. Pearl St.,* ☎ *303/777–0826.*

$$–$$$ ✕ **Tommy Tsunami's Pacific Diner.** The name may suggest a crummy theme restaurant, but this Larimer Square favorite turns out funky fusion fare—Peking pot stickers of salmon, spinach, and jicama, and a macadamia-crusted sea bass. The decor, chaotic but fun, matches the service and crowd. ✉ *1432 Market St.,* ☎ *303/534–5050.*

$$ ✕ **Aubergine.** This romantic café excels at Mediterranean fare like flatbread with hummus, baby artichokes in a basil sauce, and free-range chicken with couscous. Small paintings and tightly spaced tables with bentwood chairs fill the mustard-hued dining room. ✉ *225 E. 7th Ave.,* ☎ *303/ 832–4778.*

$–$$ ✕ **Basil's Cafe.** A hub of South Broadway's gay social scene, Basil's is equally popular with the rest of the city. Prices are fair, the pasta is made fresh daily, and the staff is lively and outgoing. The cigar room is a big hit with lesbians. ✉ *30 S. Broadway,* ☎ *303/698–1413.*

Denver

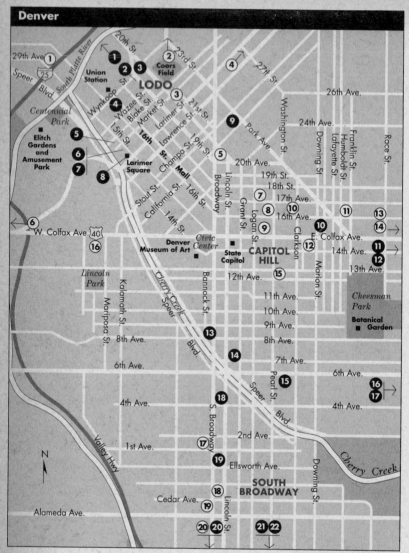

Eats ●
Aubergine, **14**
Barolo Grill, **16**
Basil's Cafe, **19**
Café Brazil, **1**
City Spirit Café, **5**
Club 404, **18**
Denver ChopHouse
& Brewery, **3**
Goodfriends, **12**
Hugh's, **22**
Jan Leone, **10**
Java Creek, **17**
The Market, **8**

McCormick's Fish
House and Oyster
Bar, **4**
Mercury Café, **9**
Newsstand Café, **15**
Pasquinis, **20**
Racine's, **13**
St. Mark's Coffee-
house, **6**
Sushi Den, **21**
Tante Louise, **11**
Tommy Tsunami's Pa-
cific Diner, **7**
Wynkoop Brewing
Company, **2**

Scenes ○
B.J.'s Carousel, **20**
Brick's, **11**
Charlie's, **12**
Club Proteus, **10**
Club Stud, **19**
Club Synergy, **4**
Compound, **17**
Den, **6**
Denver Detour, **9**
Denver Wrangler, **7**

Elle, **16**
The Grand, **8**
Herb's Hideout, **3**
Highland Bar, **1**
Mike's, **18**
Ms. C's, **14**
SnakePit, **15**
Tracks 2000, **2**
The Triangle, **5**
Ye'o Matchmaker, **13**

$–$$ ✕ **City Spirit Café.** Pee Wee Herman would feel at home at this beer hall and pub decorated like his wacked-out Playhouse with bright colors and crudely shaped furnishings. Students, alternateens, and artsy types come here to munch on the cheap pasta dishes and grills. ⊠ *1434 Blake St.,* ☎ *303/575–0022.*

$–$$ ✕ **Club 404.** This is one of the queerest steak houses in America, and while it hasn't got Ruth's Chris or Morton's of Chicago running for cover, it serves up some of the least expensive red meat you'll ever find. The ambience is nothing to write home about—a bit retro, actually. Friendly and queer staff. ⊠ *404 Broadway,* ☎ *303/778–9605.*

$–$$ ✕ **Mercury Café.** The Mercury is equal parts café, coffeehouse, music hall, and theater. Something odd is always going on here, and many of the events are gay-oriented. Crunchy New Age cuisine—tofu, fish grills, salads—is served throughout the day. ⊠ *2199 California St.,* ☎ *303/294–9281.*

$–$$ ✕ **Racine's.** Often referred to as "gay screams"—all you'll hear during the frenetic Sunday brunches—Racine's is also a favorite for power breakfasts and filling lunches. The food is just a cut above standard diner offerings; the few Mexican dishes are your best bet. ⊠ *850 Bannock St.,* ☎ *303/595–0418.*

$–$$ ✕ **Wynkoop Brewing Company.** The most popular of the city's micro-breweries is possibly the most gay-frequented. A huge place with a varied menu (try the green-chili stew or the stick-to-your-bones shepherd's pie), it has an upstairs pool hall and a downstairs viewing area where you can examine the vats. ⊠ *1634 18th St.,* ☎ *303/297–2700.*

$ ✕ **Goodfriends.** Cheap and cheerful, this tavern east of downtown is a good spot for a meal if you're heading toward any of the bars along Colfax or simply looking for a place to meet people and eat. The staff is friendly, and lesbians and gays love it. Try the catfish, burgers, onion rings, or many veggie dishes. ⊠ *3100 E. Colfax Ave.,* ☎ *303/399–1751.*

$ ✕ **Pasquinis.** Near B. J.'s Carousel, this old-fashioned storefront pizza parlor is a South Denver institution (the owners also run the phenomenal Campagna's bakery down the street). Musicians often perform here. ⊠ *1310 S. Broadway,* ☎ *303/744–0917.*

Coffeehouse Culture

St. Mark's Coffeehouse. The young, bookish crowd at this cozy LoDo favorite looks like it's in training to become the "intellectual elite" Dan Quayle rails against. ⊠ *1416 Market St.,* ☎ *303/446–2925.*

Java Creek. A good place to cool your heels after a day of shopping in Cherry Creek, loud and colorful Java Creek has good food, the usual flavored drinks, and great desserts. Musicians perform many nights. ⊠ *287 Columbine St.,* ☎ *303/377–8902.*

The Market. Denver's premier people-watching coffeehouse has a lively front patio devoted to this very activity. A real scene, the Market draws a sophisticated bunch. ⊠ *1445 Larimer St.,* ☎ *303/534–5140.*

Newsstand Café. Here you can buy a magazine (many gay titles), sip a latte, chat up your neighbor, order a turkey and provolone sandwich, and watch the buzz of pedestrian traffic outside on 6th Avenue. There's often a short wait for a seat. ⊠ *630 E. 6th Ave.,* ☎ *303/777–6060.*

SCENES

The queer nightlife in Denver has been in a state of flux throughout the '90s, with new clubs coming or going every few months. One pocket of action is in South Denver, along South Broadway. There are also bars around Capitol Hill, out on East Colfax Avenue, and along trendy East 17th Avenue.

Prime Suspects

B. J.'s Carousel. One of the older bars in Denver, B. J.'s is a campy place with pink walls, Tiffany-style glass, '60s furnishings, pool tables, and a volleyball court out back. There's a light lunch and dinner menu, and shows sometimes occur on weekends. ✉ *1380 S. Broadway,* ☎ *303/777–9880. Crowd: the old male guard—tried and true, beer-bellied, and proud.*

Charlie's. With a large dance floor and great western decor, Charlie's is the best two-stepping place in town. The wild and rowdy crowd welcomes strangers. Thursdays are especially action-packed. A parlor room serves light meals from 11 AM to 4 AM. ✉ *900 E. Colfax Ave.,* ☎ *303/839–8890. Crowd: 80/20 m/f, country-western, mixed ages, lots of 10-gallon hats.*

Club Proteus. The formerly semiqueer Aqua Lounge is now a fully gay club—and a great one at that. You enter a long hallway that leads to a snazzy hardwood dance floor with a polished railing around it. Steps lead to a lower level with tall cocktail tables and chairs and a bar. To the right is a large bright room with four pool tables. The club's intelligent layout encourages mingling and movement. Great theme nights. ✉ *1669 Clarkson St.,* ☎ *303/869–4637. Crowd: 70/30 m/f, good mix, guppies to goatees, not as ageist as at some bars, approachable.*

Compound. Sunday nights at the dark and slightly divey Compound have become something of a tradition in Denver—even preppy boys sneak down here in their denim outfits. Tuesday and Wednesday are also hopping. Let your hair down at this midsize disco and have a scandalously good time—you'll encounter little attitude and plenty of energy. ✉ *145 Broadway,* ☎ *303/722–7977. Crowd: men only, mostly 25 to 35, rough and rarin' to go, racially diverse, flannel shirts, gold chains, and goatees.*

Denver Detour. This is more of a women's bar, but the owners and staff are always friendly to guys. Near the capitol, the Detour is worn and comfy, with an avid pool-shooting crowd and great live music many nights. Folks often meet here for drinks before heading out to the discos and country-western dance halls. ✉ *551 E. Colfax Ave.,* ☎ *303/861–1497. Crowd: 75/25 f/m, mostly thirtysomething, as butch as not, lively.*

Elle. Denver has several women's bars or clubs patronized by gals and guys, and Elle is probably the most mainstream of the bunch. This energetic dance bar rocks on Thursday, Friday, and Saturday (the only nights it's open). The go-go dancers are always a big hit. ✉ *716 W. Colfax Ave.,* ☎ *303/893–3553. Crowd: 70/30 f/m, mostly under 35, fairly professional, hip.*

The Grand. Part of a new generation of gay bars, the supremely elegant Grand is inside an old redbrick building with a huge stone fireplace and tall windows overlooking upscale 17th Avenue. This is where many guys and some women stop on their way home from work or out to dinner. A pianist performs on many nights, and there's a cozy patio in back. ✉ *538 E. 17th Ave.,* ☎ *303/839–5390. Crowd: 80/20 m/f, professional, diverse in age but heavily thirtysomething, down-to-earth, some suits on weekends.*

SnakePit. A Seattle-style bar with high ceilings, purple walls, cool alternative music, and campy accents like the row of silver mannequin legs running along the top of one wall, the SnakePit lures a predictably unpredictable crowd of downwardly and upwardly mobile twenty- and thirty-somethings. It's low-key early in the evening, gets a decent crowd for dinner (casual American cuisine), and often packs in a late-night bunch depending on the night (most evenings there's a theme or event, including some good drag shows). ✉ *608 E. 13th Ave.,* ☎ *303/831–1234. Crowd: mixed gay/straight, mostly under 35, shabby chic, slackers and genXers, not cruisy.*

Tracks 2000. Denver's hottest queer disco in the late '70s and throughout the '80s reopened in the late '90s in a terrific new space behind Coors Field. *The* night to party here is Saturday—past theme nights have included a campy Leather Prom—but Friday and Sunday (the only other nights the club is open) also see fairly wild crowds. The dance floor is massive, and several interesting lounges and bars are ideal for mingling, voguing, and working the crowd. ✉ *2975 Fox St.,* ☎ *303/292–6600. Crowd: 80/20 m/f, young, intense, some stand-and-model, high-energy.*

Neighborhood Haunts

SOUTH BROADWAY

Club Stud (✉ 255 S. Broadway, ☎ 303/733–9398) has well-attended beer busts. **Mike's** (✉ 60 S. Broadway, ☎ 303/777–0193) is a bearish pool-and-darts hall and country-dancing saloon all in one. **The Triangle** (✉ 2036 N. Broadway, ☎ 303/293–9009), a hardcore leather club with a big after-hours following, has a notoriously frisky basement.

EAST OF DOWNTOWN

Brick's (✉ 1600 E. 17th Ave., ☎ 303/377–5400), a nondescript men's bar, has a good lunch and weekend brunch menu. Happy hour lasts from 11 AM until 8 PM at the **Denver Wrangler** (✉ 1700 Logan St., ☎ 303/ 837–1075), a no-nonsense cruise bar for the Levi's set. **Ms. C's** (✉ 7900 E. Colfax Ave., ☎ 303/322–4436), good for country dancing, packs in the k. d. lang and Kathy Mattea wanna-bes. **Tequila Rose's** (✉ 5190 Brighton Blvd., ☎ 303/295–2819), a new hangout northeast of Denver with an outdoor deck, is a great place to catch sporting events on TV and chill with friends. **Ye'o Matchmaker** (✉ 1480 Humboldt St., ☎ 303/ 839–9388) presents outrageous drag shows.

NORTH AND WEST OF DOWNTOWN

Locals in the western side of the city and the 'burbs head to the **Den** (✉ 5110 W. Colfax Ave., ☎ 303/534–9526). Women in northwest Denver frequent the **Highland Bar** (✉ 2532 15th St., ☎ 303/455–9978).

Hangin' with the Hets

Club Synergy (✉ 3240 Larimer St., ☎ 303/296–9515) is a club and coffee-house with events for those 18 and older. It has a huge mixed following on Sunday. For a mellow experience drop by **Herb's Hideout** (✉ 2057 Larimer St., ☎ 303/299–9555), a mostly straight but hip and queer-friendly genXer lounge with live piano many nights.

Action

The **Denver Swim Club** (✉ 6923 E. Colfax Ave., ☎ 303/321–9399) is the sleaziest of the city's gay bathhouses. The **Midtowne Spa** (✉ 2935 Zuni St., ☎ 303/458–8902) is often well-attended. The **Triple C** (✉ 2151 Lawrence St., ☎ 303/297–2601) bathhouse, which is two blocks east of Coors Field, is convenient to downtown and LoDo.

SLEEPS

Most of Denver's hotels are downtown or in LoDo. The city is experiencing an occupancy boom at the moment, so rates have climbed. The Cheesman Park neighborhood contains some gay-friendly inns.

For price ranges, *see* lodging Chart B at the front of this guide.

Hotels

$$$–$$$$ 🏨 **Westin Hotel Tabor Center.** This business-oriented hotel is busiest during the week, which means you can often take advantage of weekend double-room rates that start at around $120 per night; there are also shopping, theater, and skiing packages. An elaborate Sunday brunch unfolds at the Augusta restaurant. ✉ *1672 Lawrence St., 80202,* ☎ *303/572–9100,* FAX *303/572–7288. 420 rooms. Restaurant, pool, health club.*

$$$–$$$$ ⊡ **Brown Palace.** Celebrities and politicians often stay at Denver's best-known luxury hotel, which was built in 1892. The nine-story lobby is crowned by a stained-glass ceiling. The formal rooms have a mix of turn-of-the-century and art deco appointments. ⊠ *321 17th St., 80202,* ☎ *303/297–3111 or 800/321–2599,* ⅎᴀX *303/293–9204. 230 rooms. Restaurants, exercise room.*

$$$ ⊡ **Adam's Mark.** Not everybody is thrilled with the postmodern exterior of the older portion of this downtown high-rise, but a newer wing that opened across the street in 1997 and a overhaul of the old part's interior have given the Mark some of the nicest rooms in town. The high floors in the older wing have stupendous views. The location, right by several museums and convenient to LoDo, is perfect. ⊠ *1550 Court Pl., 80202,* ☎ *303/893–3333 or 800/444-2326,* ⅎᴀX *303/623–0303. 1,230 rooms. Restaurants, pool, health club.*

$$–$$$ ⊡ **Oxford Hotel.** The Oxford's rooms are less sumptuous but no less authentically Victorian than the Brown Palace's, and the public areas are splendid, especially considering the rates. The art deco Cruise Room Bar should not be missed. A wonderful place. ⊠ *1600 17th St., 80202,* ☎ *303/628–5400 or 800/228–5838,* ⅎᴀX *303/628–5413. 81 rooms. Restaurant, health club.*

$–$$ ⊡ **Comfort Inn Downtown.** The best bargain in the city used to be the modern half of the Brown Palace, which is across the street. The hotel has large rooms, and the rates include a Continental breakfast. ⊠ *401 17th St., 80202,* ☎ *303/296–0400 or 800/221–2222,* ⅎᴀX *303/297–0774. 229 rooms.*

Guest Houses

$$–$$$ ⊡ **Castle Marne.** This turreted stone-and-wood Romanesque mansion three blocks from Cheesman Park is one of the more dramatic dwellings in Denver. Period antiques decorate the 1889 structure's ornate rooms. ⊠ *1572 Race St., 80206,* ☎ *303/331–0621 or 800/926–2763,* ⅎᴀX *303/331–0623. 9 rooms with private bath. Continental breakfast. Mostly straight.*

$ ⊡ **Elyria's Western Guest House.** One of the few specifically gay accommodations in Denver, this late-Victorian house with simple furnishings is a short drive north of downtown. ⊠ *1655 E. 47th Ave., 80216,* ☎ *303/291–0915,* ⅎᴀX *303/296–9892. 2 rooms with shared bath and TV. Continental breakfast. Hot tub. Mostly gay male.*

$ ⊡ **Victoria Oaks Inn.** Less fancy than the Castle Marne across the street but equally inviting, this restored century-old Victorian mansion attracts a gayer clientele. Rooms have period furnishings, and many have fireplaces. ⊠ *1575 Race St., 80206,* ☎ *303/355–1818 or 800/662–6257,* ⅎᴀX *303/331–1095, e-mail vicoaksinn@aol.com. 9 rooms with phone and TV, some with private bath. Continental breakfast. Mixed gay/straight.*

THE LITTLE BLACK BOOK

At Your Fingertips

Colorado AIDS Project (☎ 303/837–0166 or 800/333–2437). **Colorado Health Action Project** (☎ 303/837–8214). **Denver Convention and Visitors Bureau** (⊠ 225 W. Colfax Ave., 80202, ☎ 303/892–1112 or 800/888–1990). **Lesbian and Gay Community Center** (⊠ 1245 E. Colfax Ave., ☎ 303/831–6268, Web site www.tde.com/~glbcscc). **Regional Transportation District** (☎ 303/299–6000). **Westword** (☎ 303/296–7744, Web site www.westword.com). **Yellow Cab** (☎ 303/777–7777).

Gay Media

Denver and Colorado have comprehensive and high-quality queer newspapers. **Quest** (☎ 303/722–5965, e-mail questh@aol.com) is a monthly features-oriented gay and lesbian magazine. **Out Front Colorado** (☎ 303/778–7900, e-mail outfrontc@aol.com), a newspaper that covers the whole state, with an emphasis on Denver, comes out biweekly. The bar-oriented **H.** (☎ 303/722–5965, e-mail questh@aol.com) is a biweekly newspaper with dishy writing. **Weird Sisters** (☎ 970/482–4393), a monthly dyke newspaper, is based in Fort Collins but has statewide coverage.

BOOKSTORES

Denver has an excellent gay male bookstore, **Category Six Books** (✉ 42 S. Broadway, ☎ 303/777–0766), and a great feminist one, the **Book Garden** (✉ 2625 E. 12th Ave., ☎ 303/399–2004). **Magazine City** (✉ 200 E. 13th Ave., ☎ 303/861–8249) carries used and new magazines, newspapers, and books, many of them gay. The mainstream **Tattered Cover** (✉ LoDo: 1628 16th St., ☎ 303/436–1070; Cherry Creek shopping mall: ✉ 2955 E. 1st Ave., ☎ 303/322–7727) carries gay titles.

Unique of Denver (✉ 2626 E. 12th Ave., ☎ 303/355–0689) is a big store with pride goods, cards, fashion, and other queer items. **Heaven Sent Me** (✉ 482 S. Broadway, ☎ 303/733–9000), a retail branch of the mega gay mail-order company, sells lesbian and gay pride items, toys, and erotica. Go to **CJ's** (✉ 5 E. Ellsworth Ave., ☎ 303/715–1157) for leather gear.

Working Out

Broadway Bodyworks (✉ 160 S. Broadway, ☎ 303/722–4342) is the queerest gym in the city.

ASPEN

Of the many ski resorts that straddle the Continental Divide, Aspen has the most striking setting and inhabitants. You'll be charmed by the grid of neatly preserved 19th-century buildings. You'll be blown away by the 360° curtain of 14,000-foot mountains. You'll be just as astounded by all the townspeople who are ever so tan, trim, and beautiful. The pages of *GQ* and *Vogue* spring to life here.

Though skiing is Aspen's raison d'être, summer is lush with wildflowers and a perfect time to trade in your ski gear for hiking boots or test your fly-fishing skills on the Roaring Fork and Fryingpan rivers. The season also brings music, food, and dance festivals.

Gays have always felt comfortable in Aspen. The town has had an anti-discrimination law on the books longer than anywhere else in Colorado, and many residents joined their gay neighbors and railed vociferously against Amendment 2. Lesbian icon Martina Navratilova calls Aspen home, and part-time resident Barbra Streisand was a vocal proponent of the state boycott. Other North American ski towns now hold them, but Aspen is home to the original, the fantastic, the coolest (literally) homo gathering in the world, **Gay and Lesbian Ski Week** (☎ 970/925–9249, Web site www.rof.net/yp/skiweek) in late January.

The Lay of the Land

Rows of redbrick buildings and clapboard homes grace delightful Aspen, a former mining town. Compact and easy to see on foot, the restored downtown area is loaded with excellent shopping and dining. The town's famed ski slopes rise sharply from the edge of the commercial district.

Eats

Aspen dining is among the most sophisticated and most expensive of any small town in the world. The international influences, from Mediterranean to Latin American to East Asian, continue to multiply, and brook trout, buffalo, and other regional ingredients are common on menus. Every restaurant in town is gay-friendly; all are within walking distance of each other and Aspen's hotels.

For price ranges, *see* dining Chart A at the front of this guide.

$$$$ ✕ **Syzygy.** Of the many well-regarded expensive restaurants in town, Syzygy is perhaps the hottest spot for drinks, and a big to-do for dinner. With a sleek decor of peach and black, refined service, and an innovative menu that combines the best of Asian, Southwest, and French cuisines, this is a memorable place to cap off Gay Ski Week. ⊠ *520 E. Hyman Ave.,* ☎ *970/925–3700.*

$$$–$$$$ ✕ **Renaissance.** If a special dinner is in order, consider this seductive stunner, an abstract take on a sultan's tent. Chef-owner Charles Dale honed his skills under New York City celebrity chef Daniel Boulud. Dishes like crispy Chilean sea bass with artichokes, shiitakes, and foie gras don't disappoint. ⊠ *304 E. Hopkins St.,* ☎ *970/925–2402.*

$$$ ✕ **Kenichi.** The sushi bar here is a parade of glamorous ski bunnies, but this establishment is celebrated as much for its fresh raw delicacies as for its pretty faces. The tea-smoked duck breast and spicy Japanese rack of lamb are also superb. ⊠ *533 E. Hopkins St.,* ☎ *970/920–2212.*

$$–$$$ ✕ **Campo di Fiori.** Urbane northern Italian bistro fare is generously represented in Aspen, and Campo di Fiori turns out some of the best. In a small courtyard of upscale shops, this warmly lit trattoria is the right spot for swapping ski tales or setting the tone for a romantic evening. Hearty risottos like the one tossed with brandy-flambéed shrimp are recommended. ⊠ *205 S. Mill St.,* ☎ *970/920–7717.*

$$ ✕ **Little Annie's.** In a town whose restaurants strive more for cosmopolitan flair than for ski-bum sincerity, it's refreshing to stumble into this slightly divey, always toasty tavern decked with red-checked tablecloths and wood-panel walls. Burgers, ribs, fresh brook trout, and lamb are the specialties—nothing fancy here. ⊠ *517 E. Hyman Ave.,* ☎ *970/925–1098.*

$–$$ ✕ **Explore Bistro.** Tucked in the second-floor garret amid the stacks of Explore Books, this charming café has an eclectic vegetarian lunch and dinner menu of pastas, sandwiches, and salads. ⊠ *221 E. Main St.,* ☎ *970/925–5336.*

$ ✕ **Café Metropolitan.** Especially gay on Saturday, this elegant but laid-back coffeehouse, restaurant, and bar overlooking and across the street from the Hotel Jerome serves great meals (burgers, salads, et cetera) all day long. Beloved for its breakfasts—try the cinnamon buckwheat pancakes—it stocks more than 70 coffee varieties. ⊠ *325 E. Main St.,* ☎ *970/925–9969.*

Scenes

Though teeming with nightlife opportunities, Aspen has no gay bars, except during Gay Ski Week, when there appear to be no straight bars. Gay and lesbian visitors will feel comfortable just about everywhere.

Faced with high rents, Aspen's bars and clubs change hands and names almost seasonally. It's difficult to guess which après-ski hangouts will be the hottest any given year. **The Tippler** (⊠ 535 E. Dean St., ☎ 970/925–4977) has of late been a favorite of gay night crawlers. Also check out **Double Diamond** (⊠ 450 S. Galena St., ☎ 970/920–6905), a cool spot with high-energy dance music and live bands many nights. The **Tea Room** at the Hotel Jerome (*see* Sleeps, *below*) has a strong queer following on Fridays.

Sleeps

Given the high cost and demand for rooms here, you may want to book through reliable **Aspen Central Reservations** (☎ 970/925–9000 or 800/262–7736), which can also arrange short-term rentals at private homes and condos.

For price ranges, *see* lodging Chart A at the front of this guide.

Hotels

$$$$ ⊞ **Hotel Jerome.** The most charming high-end property in town was built at the height of Aspen's 1880s silver boom. The amenities and decor leave nothing to be desired, yet the hotel retains a warm, old-fashioned air that's reinforced by tile fireplaces in public areas and authentic Victorian papers, fabrics, and fixtures in the unusually big guest rooms. Terrific restaurants, too. ⊠ *330 E. Main St., 81611,* ☎ *970/920–1000 or 800/331–7213,* FAX *970/925–2784. 93 rooms. Restaurants, pool.*

$$$$ ⊞ **Little Nell.** Though relatively new, the Little Nell is just as dignified as the Hotel Jerome. Gas fireplaces, down-filled sofas, VCRs, Belgian wool carpeting, and stunning marble baths are among the standards here at this property at the base of Aspen Mountain. ⊠ *675 E. Durant Ave., 81611,* ☎ *970/920–4600 or 800/525–6200,* FAX *303/920–4670. 92 rooms. Restaurant, pool.*

$$$ ⊞ **Snowmass Lodge & Club.** A 10-minute drive from Aspen in the town of Snowmass, the lodge has rooms with balconies or decks overlooking the slopes. The rates aren't cheap, but you can take advantage of the many facilities, including 11 tennis courts, a championship golf course—on which you can cross-country ski in winter—and a complete fitness center. ⊠ *Snowmass Club Cir., Snowmass Village, 81615,* ☎ *970/923–5600 or 800/525–0710,* FAX *303/923–6944. 76 rooms, 60 villas. Restaurants, pools, fitness center.*

Inns

$$$ ⊞ **Hotel Lenado.** The gay-friendly Lenado feels more like a ski lodge than its nearby cousin, Sardy House, which is owned by the same folks. Rooms have Adirondack furnishings and feather comforters; some have whirlpool tubs. Expect personal service and helpful amenities like heated boot lockers. ⊠ *200 S. Aspen St., 81615,* ☎ *970/925–6246 or 800/321–3457,* FAX *970/925–2784. 19 rooms. Full breakfast. Mostly straight.*

$$$ ⊞ **Sardy House.** This restored redbrick Victorian is one of the most romantic retreats in Aspen. Rooms have antiques and elegant fabrics and prints; some look over a shaded courtyard. Many rooms are in a newer addition behind the original building, but it's almost impossible to tell the difference between the two. ⊠ *128 E. Main St., 81615,* ☎ *970/920–2525,* FAX *970/920–4478. 20 rooms. Restaurant, pool. Full breakfast. Mostly straight.*

$$ ⊞ **Snowflake Inn.** Just steps from the slopes, the Snowflake has cheerfully furnished, cozy (yes, that means small) rooms and is outfitted with the three amenities every tired skier must have: an outdoor heated pool, a sauna, and a Jacuzzi. Many rooms have kitchenettes. ⊠ *221 E. Hyman Ave., 81615,* ☎ *970/925–3221,* FAX *970/925–8740. 38 rooms. Pool.*

$–$$ ⊞ **Skier's Chalet.** If you're on a budget, consider this pleasant inn that's as close to Aspen's skiing action as any property in town. It draws a young, fun-loving crowd. ⊠ *233 Gilbert St., 81615,* ☎ *970/920–2037 or 800/262–7736. 18 rooms.*

The Little Black Book

Aspen Chamber Resort Association (visitor centers: ⊠ 425 Rio Grande Pl., at base of parking garage; Wheeler Opera House, ⊠ 320 E. Hyman Ave.; mail: ⊠ 320 E. Hyman Ave., 81611, ☎ 970/925–1940 or 800/262–7736). **Aspen Gay Community** (☎ 970/925–9249).

Explore Books (✉ 221 E. Main St., ☎ 970/925–5336) stocks gay, lesbian, and feminist books and has a café.

BOULDER

Vibrant **Boulder** is about an hour's drive northwest of Denver; if you have the time, it's worth an excursion. A funky, eco-sensitive college community, the gay-friendly town is a cycling, mountaineering, and hiking mecca—it's an ideal base for a visit to Rocky Mountain National Park and the even closer Eldora Ski Area—and contains as diverse and trendy a collection of shops as any city in Colorado. The University of Colorado Boulder accounts for the politically progressive atmosphere and the strong appreciation residents have for the fine and performing arts. The city's philharmonic orchestra is highly respected, and several music festivals draw thousands throughout the year.

Lay of the Land

Boulder is like Denver, near but not in the Rockies. The western reaches of town sneak up into the foothills, and from most points in town you can see craggy mountains to the west. Many fine examples of Craftsman and Victorian architecture grace Boulder's walkable downtown.

Many of Boulder's most engaging restaurants and shops—including about three dozen art galleries are downtown along **Pearl Street.** From 10th to 15th streets, Pearl and its neighboring blocks compose a landscaped pedestrian mall of high-end chain boutiques (Gap, Body Shop, and the like). Between 15th and 20th streets auto traffic runs freely, and the lower commercial rents accommodate diverse and grass-roots enterprises, from vegetarian restaurants to left-wing bookstores. Small-scale but deserving a visit are the **Boulder Museum of Contemporary Art** (✉ 1750 13th St., ☎ 303/443–2122) and the **Boulder Museum of History** (✉ 1206 Euclid Ave., ☎ 303/449–3464).

Rising slightly above downtown to the south is **University Hill,** the student-infested campus of the University of Colorado. The area has some fine-art galleries and is always a good bet for upcoming theatrical and musical performances. If you're looking for cheap eats and second-hand records and clothes, roam the hill's small commercial district, along **13th Street** from about Penn Street to College Street, and down **College Street** to Broadway.

Eats

Boulder has dozens of terrific ethnic restaurants, organic cafés, and other affordable options. Stock up on picnic and hiking victuals at the **Wild Oats** (✉ 1825 Pearl St., ☎ 303/440–9599) natural-foods market, where the aisles are alive with cruisy New Agers, intellectuals, and crunchy tree huggers.

For price ranges, *see* dining Chart B at the front of this guide.

$$–$$$ ✗ **Little Russian Café.** After a day of hiking or skiing, change into something snappy and treat yourself to hearty and authentic Russian cuisine, from stuffed cabbage to the best borscht in the Rockies (okay, maybe the only borscht in the Rockies). A magnificent chandelier, ruby-red walls, and fine linens impart an intimate Old World ambience. ✉ *1430 Pearl St.,* ☎ *303/449–7696.*

$$–$$$ ✗ **Walnut Brewery.** This redbrick brew pub downtown serves tasty and refreshing beers and some of the most delicious comfort food in town. Start with the Asiago cheese dip, then move onto a burger with hickory-cured bacon, smoked cheddar, and a stout sauce, or try the angel-hair pasta with smoked Roma tomatoes. ✉ *1123 Walnut St.,* ☎ *303/447–1345.*

$$ ✕ **The Mediterranean.** Crowded and always a tad crazy, this cavernous long-time Boulder favorite is the place to come for delicious pan-Mediterranean cooking, including lamb kabobs, wood-fired thin-crust pizzas, calzones, an ever-changing list of tapas, and about 40 wines by the glass. ⊠ *1002 Walnut St.,* ☎ *303/444–5335.*

$–$$ ✕ **Creative Café.** Head to this plant-filled eatery for the best veggie food in town—udon noodles with grilled veggies, Thai curry, whole-wheat pizza with seasoned tempeh, soy, or mozzarella cheese. For dessert the fresh-fruit cobbler is difficult to beat. ⊠ *1837 Pearl St.,* ☎ *303/449–1952.*

$ ✕ **Walnut Café.** It's in a dull strip mall on the western edge of town, but this café that's open for breakfast and lunch is one of the most delightful queer eateries in the Rockies. Sit either in the art-filled dining room or at a sidewalk table outside. Many egg dishes, salads, and sandwiches (try the Santa Fe grilled cheese with green chilies, tomatoes, and cheddar) are prepared, along with great desserts, coffees, and teas. Boost your energy level with the "You Go Girl" steamed chai tea with a shot of chocolate syrup. ⊠ *3073 Walnut St.,* ☎ *303/447–2315.*

Coffeehouse Culture

Penny Lane. Everyone from aging hippies to youthful alternateens drops by this curious place. Decorative touches, including a mysterious hanging casket containing *Sesame Street* icons Bert and Ernie and a lavish collection of crucifixes, establish a mood that's equal parts morbid and fun. At night come for the live music or poetry readings. Light snacks are available, but coffees and teas are the main offerings. ⊠ *1795 Pearl St.,* ☎ *303/443–9516.*

Scenes

Men and women patronize Boulder's lone gay bar, a cozy joint west of downtown called **The Yard of Ale** (⊠ 2690-C 28th St., ☎ 303/443–1987). A loungy area has comfy wicker furniture, and there's a long bar, a pool table, and the usual videos and popular music, but no dance floor.

Sleeps

Many major chains have branches in Boulder, including Marriott, Holiday Inn, Best Western, and Super 8. Among larger properties, the 🏨 **Regal Harvest House** (⊠ 1345 28th St., 80302, ☎ 303/443–3850 or 800/545–6285, FAX 303/443–1480; 270 rooms; $$$), managed by a hospitable staff, has pools, tennis courts, and fitness facilities.

For price ranges, *see* lodging Chart B at the front of this guide.

Guest Houses

$$–$$$ 🏨 **Boulder Victoria.** A couple of blocks off Pearl Street's pedestrian mall, this 1870s painted lady is chock full of dried-flower wreaths and cushy amenities—though the furnishings are slightly less elaborate than the gorgeous exterior might suggest. The afternoon tea is a highlight. ⊠ *1305 Pine St., 80302,* ☎ *303/938–1300. 7 rooms with phone, TV, and private bath. Continental breakfast. Mostly straight.*

$$ 🏨 **Briar Rose Bed & Breakfast.** Laid-back hosts, beautiful grounds, and antiques-filled rooms make this Victorian B&B, conveniently set between University Hill and downtown, one of the best gay-friendly accommodations in Colorado. Several rooms have wood-burning fireplaces. ⊠ *2151 Arapahoe Ave., 80302,* ☎ *303/442–3007. 9 rooms with TV and private bath. Continental breakfast. Mostly straight.*

$$ 🏨 **Pearl Street Inn.** Every room in this 1820s house has a fireplace, antiques, and an unstuffy feel—many overlook a cheerful courtyard in the rear. The inn is within steps of downtown's hip cafés and shops. ⊠ *1820*

Pearl St., 80302, ☎ 303/444–5584 or 800/232–5949. 7 rooms with TV, phone, and private bath. Continental breakfast. Mostly straight.

The Little Black Book

The **Boulder Convention and Visitors Bureau** (✉ 2440 Pearl St., 80302, ☎ 303/442–2911 or 800/444–0447) has general tourist information. **Word Is Out** (✉ 1731 15th St., ☎ 303/449–1415) is primarily a lesbian and feminist bookstore but also carries queer and gay-male titles. The fine general-interest **Boulder Book Store** (✉ 1107 Pearl St., ☎ 303/447–2074) has a great lesbigay section. Boulderites rely on the Denver queer rags for gay news, but mainstream *Boulder Weekly* (☎ 303/494–5511, Web site www.boulderweekly.com) provides some gay coverage.

11 *Out in Detroit*

With Ann Arbor

LONG ASSOCIATED WITH THE WORST of America's urban ills, Detroit is fast remaking its image. The racial riots of the 1960s and subsequent downturn in the auto industry, which flattened the local economy, are now distant memories. Obscured by years of negative publicity is something that even some locals don't realize: Metropolitan Detroit rivals cities like Atlanta and Seattle for museums and engaging attractions. In the Midwest, only Chicago has a more diverse arts and cultural scene.

Detroit sprawled from the start. The automobile culture led to a layout that emphasized roads over public transportation. And because Detroit's early labor force had on average more money than the working class in other cities, residents didn't crowd into urban neighborhoods; they tended to purchase single-family homes and commute by car.

As a result, metropolitan Detroit has a relatively insignificant downtown and a galaxy of satellite communities. When many cities experienced a suburban exodus during the 1950s, Detroit's donut-shaped band of settlements simply widened—those with the greatest means moved to the most remote suburbs. This pattern left Detroit with less potential for gay ghettoizing than other cities, as there weren't many inner-city neighborhoods available to gentrify. The areas most associated with queer migration—Royal Oaks and Ferndale—are suburbs, not inner-city neighborhoods.

Downtown Detroit's rebirth is in its early stage, but you see signs of progress. The riverfront is being restored and the city has an outstanding theater district, north of which is a cultural center anchored by museums and the campus of Wayne State University. Spirited urban pioneers, many of them gay, have begun buying lofts in Harmonie Park and turn-of-the-century homes in the Cass Quarter and Corktown. Filled with architectural masterpieces by Mies van der Rohe, H. H. Richardson, Frank Lloyd Wright, and Albert Kahn, Detroit has the potential for a complete renaissance.

In the meantime, the fifth-largest metropolitan area in the nation has plenty to offer queer visitors. The bar scene is full of energy, gay-popular restaurants continue to open, the city hosts active gay and lesbian sports teams, and a major gay rodeo event is held at the State Fair Grounds every year. Combine the city's strengths with the great gay scene in nearby Ann Arbor, and the region makes for a surprisingly fulfilling getaway.

THE LAY OF THE LAND

Greater Detroit is a rectangle extending north (technically northwest) from the Detroit River, with wealthy conservative shore communities extending to the northeast. To the west is Dearborn, home of the Ford Motor Company. North of downtown, reached via the city's main north–south thoroughfare, Woodward Avenue, are the gay-popular towns of Ferndale and Royal Oak, and beyond them, more posh suburbs. Visiting any one of these areas can take the better part of a day, so plan accordingly.

Downtown

Detroit's **downtown** lacks the high-rise apartments and rows of brick town houses found in many cities. Amid gradual transformation, one block might look dandy and fixed up, but across the street will be an empty lot or a derelict former department store. Interstate highways cut intrusively across downtown. The three features that best define downtown Detroit are the Detroit River, the Renaissance Center, and Woodward Avenue.

The five shiny black cylindrical towers of the **Renaissance Center** (⊠ Jefferson Ave. at Brush St., ☎ 313/568–5600), have been a fixture of the city skyline since 1968. Built following the Detroit riots, the intentionally impenetrable RenCen is badly signed and cold-looking. General Motors bought the place in 1996, launched a $100 million renovation, and moved its headquarters into the office towers, ultimately improving the overall usability of the RenCen's retail areas.

Across Jefferson Avenue, north of the RenCen, is **Greektown,** whose commercial spine, **Monroe Street,** is lined with tavernas and restaurants. Off Monroe is **The Alley** (⊠ 508 Monroe St., ☎ 313/963–5445), a glass-enclosed arcade of shops and eateries inside what used to be fur-trading warehouses and a tannery. Around the corner you'll find the world's largest indoor waterfall (at 103 feet) in the atrium of the **International Center of Apparel Design** (⊠ 1045 Beaubien St., ☎ 313/961–9334), an engaging office and retail space.

West of RenCen, beyond the short tunnel to Windsor, Ontario, is **Hart Plaza,** where important events—including the acclaimed Montreaux–Detroit Jazz Festival and the Freedom Festival fireworks—are held. From here, **Woodward Avenue** begins its northwesterly ascent for miles into the suburbs.

Walk up Woodward a few blocks and you'll come upon **Grand Circus Park,** a green semicircular plaza that marks the beginning of Detroit's **theater district.** Whether to see a show or to appreciate the painstaking preservation, visit the 1927 **Fox Theatre** (⊠ 2211 Woodward Ave., ☎ 313/596–3200), a fantastically elaborate C. Howard Crane creation whose Arabian tent–inspired design incorporates Siamese, Byzantine, and Chinese elements. Within walking distance is the **Bonstelle Theater** (⊠ 3424 Woodward Ave., ☎ 313/577–2960), where Lily Tomlin got her start. Tomlin, who attended Wayne State University, grew up in the suburb of Highland Park, where residents provided the inspiration for some of her wacky characters. At the northern end of the district, the former Paradise Theatre reopened in 1997 after a complete restoration as the **Orchestra Hall** (⊠ Woodward Ave. and Parsons St., ☎ 313/962–1000), home of the Detroit Symphony.

The area west of the span of Woodward between Wayne State and I–75 is known as the **Cass Quarter,** which has many fixer-upper Victorians. Gays have begun buying up older homes here; this looks to be a neighborhood with a bright future.

Across from the Fox Theatre, the construction of an old-style, open-air baseball stadium and a domed football stadium nearly spelled the end of the 1920s **Gem Theatre** (⊠ 333 Madison St., ☎ 313/963–9800). Concerned locals convinced the city to move this intimate performance space a few blocks away. This neighborhood, **Harmonie Park,** is a funky up-

and-coming tract of warehouses, many of which have been refitted into SoHo-style loft apartments. Also here are the **Detroit Opera House** (✉ 1526 Broadway, ☎ 313/874–7850), which boasts one of the world's largest stages, and the historic **Music Hall Center for Performing Arts** (✉ 350 Madison Ave., ☎ 313/963–7622).

Several blocks east of the RenCen is **Rivertown,** another neighborhood whose star is rapidly rising. Many of the structures here have been reinvented from seedy lumber- and shipyards and dilapidated warehouses into restaurants, clubs, and retail spaces. Several blocks north is the **Eastern Market** (✉ Gratiot Ave. and Russell St.), which is open daily and has a terrific outdoor farmers' market on Saturday.

The Cultural Center and the New Center

The **Cultural Center,** along Woodward north of the theater district, is flanked by Wayne State University to the west and excellent museums to the east. The school's **Preservation Wayne** (☎ 313/222–0321) conducts tours of the neighborhood and the theater district, African-American historic sites, and the auto barons' mansions.

The district's top draw is the **Detroit Institute of Arts** (DIA, ✉ 5200 Woodward Ave., ☎ 313/833–7900), whose central courtyard contains Depression-era frescoes by Diego Rivera. Within 100 galleries are works from prehistoric times to the 20th-century and from every continent. DIA is also home to the **Detroit Film Theatre,** which screens new and vintage films.

North of DIA is the **Detroit Historical Museum** (✉ 5401 Woodward Ave., ☎ 313/833–1805), a highlight of which is the Booth-Wilkinson Costume Gallery, which contains some 50,000 garments and accessories. To the south is the **Detroit Science Center** (✉ 5020 John R St., ☎ 313/577–8400). A block east, the **Museum of African-American History** (✉ 315 E. Warren Ave., ☎ 313/833–9800), an immense research facility, mounts exhibitions that trace the culture and contribution of blacks in Africa and the United States.

The **New Center,** a gorgeous complex of '30s art deco office and mixed-use buildings that was the headquarters of General Motors before it moved into the Renaissance Center, has a graceful countenance. Just west is the **Motown Historical Museum** (✉ 2648 W. Grand Blvd., ☎ 313/875–2264), inside two of the original houses owned by Motown Records.

Belle Isle, Indian Village, and Grosse Pointe

Heading out of downtown along Jefferson Avenue, you'll soon come to 1,000-acre **Belle Isle,** an urban retreat in the middle of the Detroit River, little more than a stone's throw from Windsor, Ontario. The park has a fine beach, the nation's oldest freshwater aquarium, and good jogging, biking, and blading paths.

Back on Jefferson, continue east through **Indian Village,** where many of Detroit's first industrial magnates built their homes. Along Jefferson is **Pewabic Pottery** (✉ 10125 E. Jefferson Ave., ☎ 313/822–0954), one of the world's most-respected ceramic-arts centers.

A short distance east is one of the four great homes of the auto barons that are open to the public, the **Fisher Mansion** (✉ 383 Lenox St., ☎ 313/331–6740), built by Lawrence Fisher, founder of Cadillac Motors. The great-grandson of Henry Ford and the daughter of Walter Ruether, who was president of the United Auto Workers, bought the mansion in 1975 and turned it into a Krishna cultural center. Its restaurant, Govinda's, serves good vegetarian food.

Jefferson turns into Lake Shore Drive outside Detroit, and winds alongside **Lake St. Clair** through the five ultrawealthy Grosse Pointe communities. Along this drive are the homes of numerous Dodges, Chryslers, Fords, and Fishers—including unlikely AIDS activist Mary Fisher—as well as singer Anita Baker's mansion.

Serene grounds surround the most remarkable of the auto barons homes, the **Edsel and Eleanor Ford House** (✉ 1100 Lakeshore Rd., Grosse Pointe Shores, ☎ 313/884–4222). The rooms in the Cotswolds-style manor house are decorated with eclectic panache. The excellent café serves lunch and afternoon tea.

The Northern Woodward Corridor

The first suburb you reach along Woodward Avenue is **Ferndale,** a working-class community that has developed increased cachet among gays and lesbians. **Royal Oak,** the next town out, is a bastion of funkiness and alternative culture. It's a very queer community with lefty tendencies. Offbeat boutiques, antiques shops, tattoo parlors, and eateries are along **Main and Washington streets.**

Woodward then passes through **Birmingham,** a tony and aesthetically more conservative community with a pleasant downtown filled with upscale shops and restaurants. Next comes ritzy **Bloomfield Hills,** site of the **Cranbrook Educational Community** (✉ 1221 N. Woodward Ave., Bloomfield Hills, ☎ 248/645–3323), a 315-acre campus with prep schools and the **Cranbrook Academy of Art,** as well as two fine museums. Cranbrook earned international acclaim when Finnish architect Eliel Saarinen moved here in the 1920s to design the compound's buildings and to help lay out the grounds. The **Cranbrook Academy of Art Museum** (☎ 248/645–3312) displays student works and hosts exhibitions of contemporary art. By summer 1998 the **Cranbrook Institute of Science** (☎ 248/645–3323) will have completed a major expansion. You can also tour Saarinen's former home and studio, as well as the **Cranbrook House and Gardens** (☎ 248/645–3149), home of the community's founders, George and Ellen Booth.

Dearborn

Head west from Detroit via I–75 to reach **Dearborn.** Here you can tour the last of the auto barons's homes, Henry Ford's **Fair Lane** (✉ 4901 Evergreen Rd., ☎ 313/593–5590), which is operated by the University of Michigan–Dearborn as a cultural and conference center.

The **Henry Ford Museum and Greenfield Village** (✉ 20900 Oakwood Blvd., Dearborn, ☎ 313/271–1620), a museum and an 81-acre village of historic homes and structures from across the country, holds Thomas Edison's Menlo Park laboratory and the bicycle shop in which the Wright brothers built their first plane. The museum's machines and autos trace the progress of industry during the past 200 years, including a faithfully reconstructed '50s-era Holiday Inn hotel room, and hundreds of automobiles, among them the Lincoln limo in which President Kennedy was assassinated and the phallic Oscar Meyer WienerMobile.

GETTING AROUND

Of the metro area's estimated 2 million commuters, only about 50,000 rely on mass transit—nearly everybody else drives. The city is paved with freeways that lead in every direction. Detroit automakers were the ones who surreptitiously financed the dismantling of America's once first-rate city trolley and bus systems. Ergo, bring along or rent a set of wheels. Downtown you can also hop on the Detroit People Mover, a monorail that loops among 13 stations and is kind of fun for a ride but won't really get you anywhere you can't easily walk. The stations are filled with murals and art installations.

EATS

Detroit's culinary strengths lie both in high-end, expense-account restaurants with glitzy dining rooms and stupendous American and Continental fare, and in bare-bones ethnic eateries—especially those specializing in soul, Greek, Italian, and Middle Eastern food. The most popular downtown restaurant row, Greektown, is no longer home only to Greek establishments—you'll find every kind of food, in every price range. An enclave that retains its culinary heritage is Mexicantown, which falls mostly along Bagley Street in southwestern Detroit. **El Zocalo** (⊠ 3400 Bagley St., ☎ 313/841–3700, $) is the most highly regarded eatery here.

For price ranges, *see* dining Chart B at the front of this guide.

Detroit

$$$$ ✕ **Whitney.** At the least, stop in to marvel at this 1894 Romanesque mansion's frescoed ceilings, carved plaster moldings, mosaic floors, and paneled walls. Don't overlook the New American menu either, which offers such tantalizing fare as roasted venison loin with mushroom sausage, braised fennel, and a red currant sauce. ⊠ 4421 Woodward St., ☎ 313/832–5700.

$$$–$$$$ ✕ **Intermezzo.** This newcomer to hipster-hallowed Harmonie Park dazzles with smooth service, a postindustrial dining area, and traditional, beautifully prepared Italian fare, such as scallops of veal sautéed with mushrooms and marsala wine, and served with risotto and vegetables. ⊠ 1435 Randolph St., ☎ 313/961–0707.

$$$–$$$$ ✕ **Rattlesnake Club.** Foodie-fave Jimmy Schmidt rules this renovated warehouse-district place overlooking the river. His sublime renditions of veal, rack of lamb, and seafood dishes such as swordfish with grapefruit, fried ginger, and chives wow patrons undaunted by the pricey menu. ⊠ 300 Stroh River Pl., ☎ 313/567–4400.

$$–$$$$ ✕ **The Rhinoceros.** Like a big "welcome" sign, a giant rainbow flag wafts over the dining room of this snazzy jazz supper club in the warehouse district. Salmon and shrimp Wellington and soft-shell crabs with garlic and almonds are among the formal offerings. Sandwiches and lighter dishes are also offered. ⊠ 255 Riopelle St., ☎ 313/259–2208.

$$–$$$ ✕ **Fishbones Rhythm Kitchen Café.** The Cajun food at this bustling, old-fashioned restaurant comes awfully close to New Orleans standards. You'll find hot sauces on your table, should you need to turn up the heat of your étouffée or red beans and rice. Wooden booths, tile floors, and Mardi Gras beads convey the warmth of the Big Easy. ⊠ 400 Monroe St., ☎ 313/965–4600.

$$–$$$ ✕ **La Dolce Vita.** Where hip same-sexers come for a night on the town in a deeply romantic setting, this fine Italian restaurant specializes in big, big portions of pastas, salads, and grills—the veal marsala stands out. The conservatory-style dining room and landscaped patio are equally inviting. ⊠ 17546 Woodward Ave., ☎ 313/865–0331.

$$–$$$ ✕ **Majestic Café.** This funky eatery on the edge of the Cultural Center scores high marks for its art exhibits and eclectic food. Try chicken stuffed with apples and mushrooms in an oyster cream sauce. Dinner comes with salad, baguette, and oven-roasted garlic. ⊠ 4124 Woodward Ave., ☎ 313/833–0120.

$$–$$$ ✕ **Très Vite.** This bistro adjacent to the Fox Theatre serves deftly prepared Mediterranean salads, grills, and pastas. It's a perfect place to look sexy, sip martinis, and watch the pretty people sauntering through the theater district. ⊠ 2203 Woodward Ave., ☎ 313/964–4144.

$–$$ ✕ **Murphy's Pub & Grub.** A cozy Irish dive in the shadow of Eastern Market, Murphy's doubles as a semiqueer bar—a place where all types gather for cigars, draft beer, martinis, and arguably the best barbecue sandwiches in Detroit. ⊠ 1408 E. Fisher Service Dr., ☎ 313/567–7990.

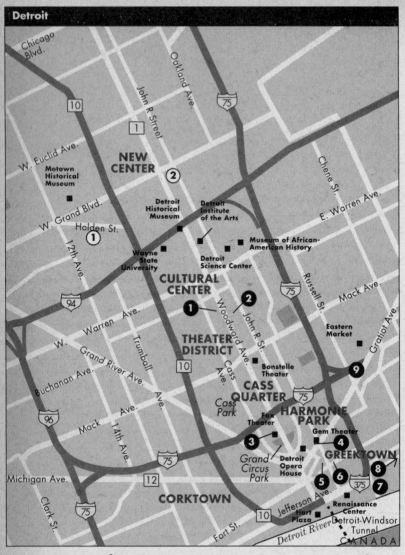

Detroit

[Map labels:]

Chicago Blvd.

Oakland Ave.

John R Street

75

10

1

W. Euclid Ave.

NEW CENTER

2

Motown Historical Museum

Chene St.

Detroit Historical Museum

Detroit Institute of the Arts

E. Warren Ave.

W. Grand Blvd.

Holden St.

1

Museum of African-American History

Wayne State University

Detroit Science Center

94

Russell St.

Mack Ave.

CULTURAL CENTER

1

2

Woodward Ave.

John R St.

Warren Ave.

12th Ave.

Eastern Market

Gratiot Ave.

THEATER DISTRICT

W. Grand River Ave.

Trumball

10

Cass Ave.

Bonstelle Theater

9

Buchanan Ave.

CASS QUARTER

96

Cass Park

HARMONIE PARK

Mack Ave.

14th Ave.

Fox Theater

Gem Theater

GREEKTOWN

75

3

4

8

Grand Circus Park

Detroit Opera House

Michigan Ave.

12

5

6

7

375

CORKTOWN

Renaissance Center

Clark St.

75

Jefferson Ave.

Hart Plaza

10

Fort St.

Detroit-Windsor Tunnel

Detroit River

C A N A D A

Eats ●

Fishbones Rhythm Kitchen Cafe, **5**

Intermezzo, **4**

Majestic Cafe, **2**

Murphy's Pub & Grub, **9**

New Hellas, **6**

Rattlesnake Club, **8**

The Rhinoceros, **7**

Très Vite, **3**

Whitney, **1**

Scenes ○

Eagle, **1**

Woodward Cocktail Lounge, **2**

$–$$ ✕ **New Hellas.** Always-packed, this century-old taverna prepares Hellenic specialties like marinated octopus, broiled monkfish, and hearty moussaka. The waiters are a kick: Listen to them bark orders through windows into the kitchen, or watch them stomp through the dining room bearing plates of flaming *saganaki* (Greek cheese) and yelling "Oopah!" at the top of their lungs. ✉ *583 Monroe St.,* ☎ *313/961–5544.*

Metro Detroit

$$–$$$ ✕ **Sweet Lorraine's Café.** This is a good choice before hitting the Greenfield Road gay bars in nearby west Detroit. The menu crosses cultures with chicken and shrimp Creole, yellowfin tuna Niçoise, and other specialties. ✉ *29101 Greenfield Rd., Southfield,* ☎ *248/559–5985.*

$$ ✕ **Memphis Smoke.** Slick and postmodern, this restaurant in the heart of Royal Oak looks like a northern Italian restaurant in L.A. more than it does a barbecue joint. But walk in and breathe in the fragrances, and you'll detect delicious beef brisket, pulled pork, and blackened rib-eye sandwiches. ✉ *100 S. Main St., Royal Oak,* ☎ *248/543–4300.*

$–$$ ✕ **La Shish.** These cheerful, politely staffed Lebanese restaurants in Dearborn serve up mammoth portions of tabbouleh and baba ganoush. Imported artifacts and art liven up the dining rooms. ✉ *12918 Michigan Ave.,* ☎ *313/584–4477;* ✉ *32401 Van Dyke St.,* ☎ *313/977–2177;* ✉ *22039 Michigan Ave.,* ☎ *313/562–7200.*

$–$$ ✕ **Pronto.** This upscale-looking but affordable café in Royal Oak, attached to the gay video bar of the same name, offers a varied menu of classic American and Continental dishes—chicken potpie, veggie lasagna—and yummy deli items, including huge build-your-own sandwiches. ✉ *608 S. Washington St., Royal Oak,* ☎ *248/544–7900.*

$ ✕ **Mr. B's.** Charbroiled chicken, burgers, and taco salads are the menu mainstays at casual, pub-style Mr. B's. It's a gay-popular spot for brunch, partly because of the ample sidewalk seating. Cheap and cheerful. ✉ *215 S. Main St., Royal Oak,* ☎ *248/399–0017.*

Coffeehouse Culture

Brazil. The original, bizarre genX hangout that has been copied by countless others, this café still manages to draw the biggest crowds, thanks to its bevy of plush sofas, mellow music, and fabulous desserts. The grungy tattooed waitrons can be aloof, but that's part of the ambience. ✉ *305 S. Main St., Royal Oak,* ☎ *248/399-7200.*

SCENES

Detroit's nightlife is lively and fun. Visitors are often surprised by the vitality and the variety—and taken aback by the distances between clubs. Racially, Detroit has one of the most integrated gay bar scenes in the country—not surprising given the city's rich African-American heritage and largest NAACP membership in America. Detroit is a big sports city, with bowling on Sunday a weekly ritual. There are two gay leagues, one favoring **Cloverlanes** (✉ 28900 Schoolcraft Rd., Livonia, ☎ 734/427–6410), the other **Fairlanes** (✉ 29600 Stephenson Hwy., Madison Heights, ☎ 248/548–9333). The leagues always meet on Sunday afternoon from noon to 3. Visitors are welcome to participate.

Prime Suspects

Back Pocket. On Wednesday and Saturday this video bar fills to the rafters after hours (it's open until 4 on those nights), when it offers not only a couple more hours' worth of cruising and conversation, but also a good late-night menu that will cure any case of the munchies. At other times it's a fun but typical neighborhood hang. The place has a big is-

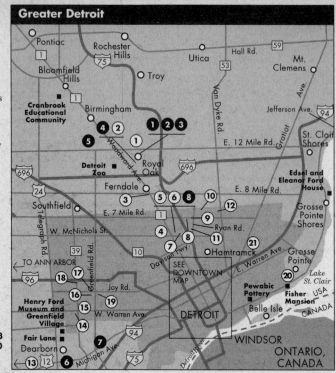

land bar, a great jukebox, and a comfy patio. ⊠ *8832 Greenfield Rd.,*
☎ *313/272–8374. Crowd: mostly male, 20s to 40s (younger and more*
club-kiddie on Wed. and Sat.), casual, conversational.

Backstreet. On Wednesday and Saturday (the only nights it's open) queers
flock to this industrial-style warehouse dance club in West Detroit—one
of the hottest gay scenes in the Midwest. It's not huge, but there's a well-
lit bar with mostly standing room, off of which is a large disco space with
a central dance floor and raised railings along its perimeter. On Saturday an auxiliary bar opens—it's a quiet spot to exchange deep stares and
shallow conversation with that special new someone. ⊠ *15606 Joy Rd.,*
☎ *313/272–8959. Crowd: 80/20 m/f, mostly under 35, mixed racially,*
disco kids, hot numbers, trendy club gear, Madonna legacies.

Club Innuendo. A straight strip club until it was reinvented in September
1997 as a gay disco, Innuendo has a large show stage for male strippers
(and hot ones at that) and drag shows. You can drink at the bar or order
food and take a seat in one of the booths. There are pool tables and a
compact dance floor. The club has loads of potential, but the out-of-the-
way location may hinder it. ⊠ *744 E. Savannah St., off I–75 Service Rd.*
between 6 Mile and 7 Mile Rds., ☎ *313/892–1444. Crowd: 85/15 m/f,*
20s to 30s, mixed racially, catch-all crowd, cruisy.

Eagle. A prototypical Eagle, this one west of New Center has dancing
(often country-western), a dark bar, and a cheerful patio in back with potted flowers (very Martha Stewartesque for such a butch place). Although
it's mostly a guy bar, women pop in on a regular basis. ⊠ *1501 Holden*
St., ☎ *313/873–6969. Crowd: mostly male, 30s to 50s, some leather,*
but more Levi's and T-shirts; bearish; lots of facial hair.

Eclipse. The former Bodyshop, which had been one of the area's most popular clubs, at press time had been bought by the owners of Pronto, who
planned to remodel it into a restaurant and nightclub by mid-1998. This
should continue to be a great place for men and women. ⊠ *22061 Wood-*

ward Ave., Ferndale, ☎ *248/586–0100. Crowd: too early to say for sure, but mostly likely 75/25 m/f, 20s to 40s.*

Male Box. Detroit's No. 1 gay sports bar is also popular for its strippers and its easy pick-up scene. Male Box lures cute, beefy guys with much less attitude than the ones at Pronto or Backstreet. In addition to the main bar are a dance floor and a backroom with pool and darts. ⊠ *3537 E. 7 Mile Rd.,* ☎ *313/892–5420. Crowd: male, 20s to 40s, down-to-earth, regular guys, on the make, outgoing.*

Menjo's. With a glittery but appealing '80s ambience, this landmark dance and video bar hasn't changed much since the days when a young Madonna (who hails from the Detroit suburb of Rochester Hills) used to come and party with one of her gay dance instructors. It's only open Thursday to Sunday, and the best night is Friday, when it draws a trendy crowd not unlike the one at Backstreet. Menjo's is also big with the après-bowling crowd on Sunday. The place consists of a neon-streaked video and dance bar, a room with darts and pool, and a piano area often decked with a big bouquet of flowers. ⊠ *928 W. McNichols St.,* ☎ *313/ 863–3934. Crowd: 80/20 m/f, mostly 20s and 30s, guppies and blue collars, some suits after work, stand-and-model, cruisy.*

Pronto. This Royal Oak video bar, attached to the restaurant of the same name, is Detroit's see-and-be-seen club. The postmodern space has a compact and usually crowded bar, with TV monitors and great music. An ideal place to order cosmos and look suave. ⊠ *608 S. Washington St., Royal Oak,* ☎ *248/544–7900. Crowd: 70/30 m/f, cute, collegiate, some guppies, some grungers, even a few Goths.*

Silent Legacy. The region's most popular lesbian dance club (though men are welcome and make up the majority on Tuesday, when hot male dancers are the night's special) is west of Detroit in the downcast suburb of Inkster. Shooting pool is a big deal, as are the theme nights—from female strip shows to slave/leather parties. ⊠ *1641 Middlebelt Rd., Inkster,* ☎ *734/ 729–8980. Crowd: 80/20 f/m, 20s to 40s, blue collar, UAW dykes, butch.*

Woodward Cocktail Lounge. Having served the community for more than a half-century, this lounge retains the warmth of an old-fashioned city bar, and the jukebox is one of the best in town. Queers who work downtown come for lunch or for dinner after work—the American food is basic but pretty tasty. Park in the rear off Milwaukee Street. ⊠ *6426 Woodward Ave.,* ☎ *313/872–0166. Crowd: mostly male, all ages, mixed racially, some suits early in the evening but otherwise varied.*

Neighborhood Haunts

Zippers (⊠ 6221 E. Davison St., ☎ 313/892–8120), the most popular of the two African-American–oriented clubs, draws men and women. It has a dance floor and a stage. The more male-oriented **Off Broadway** (⊠ 12215 Harper St., ☎ 313/521–0920) is the other. Well regarded for its hot erotic dancers, the club draws a younger crowd.

The standard dance bar **Numbers** (⊠ 17518 Woodward Ave., ☎ 313/ 868–9145) is big with youngish guys; it doesn't really get hopping until 2 AM. **Tiffany's** (⊠ 17436 Woodward Ave., ☎ 313/883–7162), once a popular cruise bar, has slowed down to a dull roar. Hustlers and G-string-wrapped dancers are the main event at the smoky **Club Gold Coast** (⊠ 2971 E. 7 Mile Rd., ☎ 313/366–6135).

Sugarbaker's (⊠ 3800 E. 8 Mile Rd., ☎ 313/892–5203) is a divey but fun girl-jock sports bar on an industrial stretch of 8 Mile Road. A middle-age, working-class men's and women's bar east of the Woodward Corridor, the **Rainbow Room** (⊠ 6640 E. 8 Mile Rd., ☎ 313/891–1020) has some of the area's best drag shows (who can resist the talent of Trixie Deluxxe?), plus good dance music; it's an easy place to meet locals. Grosse Pointe fags swoop down to the slow-paced **Deck** (⊠ 14901 E. Jefferson St., ☎ 313/822–1991) cocktail lounge in East Detroit for cheap drinks and conversation.

Adam's Apple (✉ 18931 W. Warren Ave., ☎ 313/240–8482) is a Cheers-style pub in West Detroit with some serious darts players and a well-attended dyke night on Friday. **Gigi's** (✉ 16920 W. Warren, ☎ 313/584–6525) is a fun mixed male/female drag bar with a devoted transgender following and wonderful, campy shows. The old-school Grayloft—err, **Hayloft** (✉ 8070 Greenfield Rd., ☎ 313/581–8913)—a big hit with over-50s men, usually offers country-western music. The rough-and-tumble **Other Side** (✉ 16801 Plymouth St., ☎ 313/836–2324) is in a dicey location but can be fun, especially on Tuesday when karaoke fans pack the place.

Hangin' with the Hets

The genXer haunt **Groove Club** (✉ 1815 N. Main St., Royal Oak, ☎ 248/589–3344) thinks pink on Vibrator Wednesday and is always gay-friendly; expect deep house and high-energy dance music and a young, trendy crowd.

Over the Border

Fans of racy strippers (the all-nude variety) race over the Canadian border to Windsor, Ontario, to see the boys strut their stuff at **Club Happy Tap** (✉ 1056 Wyandotte St. E, ☎ 519/256–2737); it's not as wild and fun as it used to be, but some Detroiters still make trips to "attend the Windsor Ballet." Another popular spot is **Club Nostalgia** (✉ 634 Chilver Rd., ☎ 519/254–8001), a new lounge and dance club.

Action

The sexually explosive **TNT Health Club** (✉ 13333 W. 8 Mile Rd., ☎ 313/341–5322) is Detroit's favorite all-night playhouse for sex. In Windsor, **Vesuvio** (✉ 563 Brant St., ☎ 519/977–8578) is a frisky bathhouse in the spicy tradition of Canadian sex venues.

SLEEPS

Although attractions, restaurants, and gay clubs are spread out, your best strategy as a visitor is to stay downtown, where you'll find the most inviting properties in each price range—from a gay-friendly, all-suites luxury property to a pair of charming B&Bs. Another good strategy is to stay in Ann Arbor (*see below*).

Hotels

$$$–$$$$ 🏨 **Atheneum Suite Hotel.** A converted warehouse holds Detroit's most distinctive hotel. Rooms open around a central atrium and are outfitted with large sitting areas, two TVs, marble bathrooms (and big hot tubs in many cases). ✉ *1000 Brush St., 48226,* ☎ *313/962–2323 or 800/772–2323,* FAX *313/962–2424. 174 rooms. Restaurant, exercise room.*

$$–$$$ 🏨 **The River Place.** This charming boutique-style hotel in Rivertown is within walking distance of excellent restaurants. Many of the warmly furnished rooms in this five-story structure overlook the Detroit River. ✉ *1000 River Pl., 48207,* ☎ *313/259–9500 or 800/890–9505,* FAX *313/259–3744. 108 rooms. Restaurant, exercise room.*

$ 🏨 **Shorecrest Motor Inn.** A basic motor hotel on the eastern side of downtown, close to Rivertown and Belle Isle, the Shorecrest has clean, functional rooms. ✉ *1316 E. Jefferson Ave., 48207,* ☎ *313/568–3000 or 800/992–9616,* FAX *313/568–3002. 54 rooms.*

Guest Houses and Small Hotels

$$$ 🏨 **Corktown Inn B&B.** Chet Allen and Richard Kokochak run this gem in Detroit's most historic neighborhood, Corktown. The three-story

1850 mansion has four rooms filled with local art, museum-quality antiques, and comfy silk kimonos for guest use. ⊠ *1705 6th St., 48226,* ☎ *313/963–6688,* ℻ *313/964–3883. 4 rooms with TV, phone, and private bath. Full breakfast. Mixed gay/straight.*

$$–$$$ ⊞ **Blanche House Inn and the Castle.** A trio of renovated buildings—a 1905 Colonial Revival mansion, a 19th-century castle-like mansion, and a small cottage with 150 feet of waterfront—this complex contains unusual rooms, from luxury affairs with hot tubs to simpler ones filled with antiques. ⊠ *506 Parkview Dr., 48214,* ☎ *313/822–7090. 13 rooms with phone, TV, and private bath. Full breakfast. Mostly straight.*

THE LITTLE BLACK BOOK

At Your Fingertips
Affirmations Lesbian and Gay Community Center (⊠ 195 W. 9 Mile Rd., Ferndale, ☎ 248/398–7105 or, for the helpline, 800/398–GAYS, e-mail affirmglcc@aol.com). **AIDS Michigan Hotline** (☎ 800/342–AIDS). **Checker Cab** (☎ 313/963–7000). **Department of Transportation** (bus system, ☎ 313/933–1300). **Detroit Community AIDS Library** (⊠ 4325 Brush St., ☎ 313/577–8943). **Detroit People Mover** (☎ 313/962–7245). *Metro Times* (☎ 313/961–4060, Web site www.metrotimes.com). **Metropolitan Detroit Convention and Visitors Bureau** (⊠ 100 Renaissance Center, Suite 1900, 48243, ☎ 313/259–4333 or 800/DETROIT).

Gay Media
The well-written *Between the Lines* (☎ 248/615–7003), which comes out biweekly, has extensive news and entertainment coverage. The Ann Arbor–based *Out Post* (☎ 313/332–0066, e-mail opost@aol.com) provides excellent coverage of the Detroit area and Ann Arbor. *Cruise* (☎ 248/545–9040) and *Metra* (☎ 248/543–3500) are bar and entertainment rags.

BOOKSTORES
A Woman's Prerogative (⊠ 175 W. 9 Mile Rd., Ferndale, ☎ 248/545–5703) is a lesbian and feminist bookstore with new and used books and CDs. The gay-male–oriented **Chosen Books** (⊠ 120 W. 4th St., Royal Oak, ☎ 248/543–5758) has some books and many cards, porn mags, and videos. Nearby **Giggles** (⊠ 309 S. Main St., Royal Oak, ☎ 248/414–6850) sells pride goods and T-shirts.

Working Out
The **Bally's Total Fitness** (⊠ 22340 Michigan Ave., 313/561–3320) franchise in Dearborn is heavily patronized by gay men and women. **TNT Health Club** (*see* Action, *above*) has fitness equipment.

OUT IN ANN ARBOR

Among America's largest educational institutions, the University of Michigan has long been a beacon of liberal politics, high culture, and vibrant campus living. It's not—as is sometimes the case in such cities—the only reason people chose to live in Ann Arbor. But it is the primary attraction for many of the city's 100,000 residents. About 35,000 students are enrolled full time at the University of Michigan, and another 25,000 students in neighboring Ypsilanti attend Eastern Michigan University. For the many gays and lesbians, the sense of community and the overwhelming tolerance of the university, the police, and government officials makes this a wonderful place to call home. The city's human-scale downtown and spirited campus meld together almost imperceptibly, each feeding off the energy of the other. Detroit is only a 45-minute drive away, meaning it's entirely practical to base your explorations of the metro region in Ann Arbor. To the west are the wooded, lake-studded towns of Michigan's Waterloo Recreation Area, an excellent place for boating, cycling, and hiking.

The Lay of the Land

A combination of highways—I–94, U.S. 23, and Route 14—ring Ann Arbor, allowing easy access from Detroit and other Midwest locales. Attractions are mostly downtown and on campus, a rectangular grid of alternating one-way streets that are easily managed on foot.

Once **downtown,** a fine way to get a feel for Ann Arbor is by strolling across that ubiquitous oasis of collegiate living, the campus green—known in these parts as **the Diag** (⊠ N. University Ave. and S. State St.). In the shadows of key **University of Michigan** buildings you'll see students tossing Frisbees, lazing in the sun, sipping lattes, and enjoying themselves.

On the southwestern corner of the Diag, stop by the **U of M Museum of Art** (⊠ 525 S. State St., ☎ 734/764–0395), whose collections span 13,000 years. Across the street to the south is the one campus block whose stately bearing and flamboyant Gothic architecture invites comparisons to Oxford and Cambridge, the **Law Quadrangle** (⊠ S. State St. at S. University Ave.). Across the street to the west is the **Michigan Union** (⊠ 530 S. State St.), an always-bustling student center where you'll find the **M Den** (☎ 734/764–8099), a repository of U of M apparel and paraphernalia. North of the union is the **U of M Kelsey Museum of Archeology** (⊠ 434 S. State St., ☎ 734/764–9304). Shops and cafés line **State Street** north of the Diag. The rest of downtown is characterized by brick sidewalks, old-fashioned gas lamps, diverse architecture, and an abundance of boutiques, art galleries, and restaurants. **Liberty and Washington streets** offer many opportunities to window shop and restaurant hop.

Main Street and parallel 4th Avenue lead north a few more blocks to the most offbeat and gay-identified of the city's neighborhoods, funky **Kerrytown.** Among the best stops at the **Kerrytown Shops** (⊠ N. 4th Ave. and W. Kingsley St., ☎ 734/662–5008) is famous **Zingerman's Deli** (☎ 734/769–1625), ideal for a quick bite. Outside, a farmers' market is held Wednesday and Saturday, and an artisan's market on Sunday.

Getting Around

Ann Arbor has an excellent bus system. Bicycles and rollerblades are also useful. You can drive around greater Ann Arbor, but in the city center parking directly on the street is difficult. It's best to find a garage (large ones are at Fletcher and E. Washington Sts., W. Ann and N. Main Sts., and S. 4th Ave. and E. William St.) and ditch the wheels.

Eats

You might expect a city with thousands of full-time students to be the domain of cheap pizza joints and Chinese restaurants—indeed, such bare-bones purveyors of greasy comfort grub proliferate. But the city also is a bastion of yuppiedom. Upscale eateries play a major role in the local dining scene, with new hot spots constantly opening.

For price ranges, *see* dining Chart B at the front of this guide.

$$$–$$$$ ✕ **Bella Ciao.** The redbrick storefront is the right setting for a romantic candlelight dinner and such tempting northern Italian fare as rigatoni tossed with homemade sausage, rosemary, peas, tomatoes, and Romano cheese. ⊠ *118 W. Liberty St.,* ☎ *734/995–2107.*

$$$–$$$$ ✕ **West End.** This dapper, contemporary bistro has earned kudos for uncomplicated yet richly seasoned New American and Continental ar-

rangements like seared jumbo sea scallops marinated in olive oil and served on a bed of spicy rice. ⊠ *120 W. Liberty St.,* ☎ *734/747–6260.*

$$–$$$ ✕ **Common Grill.** Jiffy Mix may be the claim to fame of Chelsea, a historic village a 30-minute drive west of Ann Arbor, but this outstanding New American restaurant is reason to visit. The blackboard menu changes often but favors fresh seafood grills. Perhaps combine a meal here with a show at Chelsea's innovative **Purple Rose Theater** (⊠ 137 Park St., ☎ 734/475–7902), which was started by hometown boy and Hollywood star Jeff Daniels. ⊠ *112 S. Main St., Chelsea,* ☎ *734/475–0470.*

$$–$$$ ✕ **Zanzibar.** This exotically decorated newcomer delights foodies with "pan-tropical" creations, including Vietnamese barbecue spare ribs and sautéed boneless breast of duck in a robust sauce, with sautéed field greens and poached pears. ⊠ *216 S. State St.,* ☎ *734/994–7777.*

$$ ✕ **Seva.** A vegetarian restaurant with a dedicated gay following, Seva is a great spot to while away a weekend afternoon, noshing on healthful salads, garden burgers, and the like. There's a juice bar, and a full bar known for terrific margaritas. ⊠ *314 E. Liberty St.,* ☎ *734/662–1111.*

$$ ✕ **Sweet Lorraine's.** This Kerrytown branch of the Southfield contemporary American bistro (*see* Eats *in* Detroit, *above*) attracts hip heteros and homos for tasty dining and dishy conversation. The best seating is on the sunken patio. ⊠ *303 Detroit St.,* ☎ *734/665–0700.*

$–$$ ✕ **Grizzley Peak.** Drop by this brewpub for great beers and interesting food. Consult the lengthy menu for frequently appearing new dishes and standbys like goat-cheese pizza and mesquite salmon. ⊠ *120 W. Washington St.,* ☎ *734/741–7325.*

$ ✕ **Angelo's.** A diner-style haunt adjacent to the medical-school campus, Angelo's is a prime spot for filling breakfasts—French toast, raisin bread, and other fresh baked goods. ⊠ *1100 Catherine St.,* ☎ *734/761–8996.*

Coffeehouse Culture

Café Zola. Known first and foremost as a coffeehouse, this funky student hangout also delivers good food morning, noon, and night—from Belgian waffles to savory crepes. Exposed brick and art exhibits add warmth to the space. ⊠ *112 W. Washington St.,* ☎ *734/769–2020.*

Sweetwaters. This smart coffeehouse with hardwood floors, tall windows, a chatty young crowd, and great desserts has live music many nights. ⊠ *123 W. Washington St.,* ☎ *734/769–2331.*

Scenes

Ann Arbor has no shortage of collegiate bars. Because of the high number of undergrad and grad students, the ages of nightlife patrons generally range from the late teens (at certain nondrinking hangouts) to the mid-30s.

Prime Suspects

Aut Bar. A true community melting pot in a converted 1916 house, this bar, coffeehouse, and restaurant attracts everyone from cruisy students to couples having a romantic night out to transgenders. The upstairs level has more of the bar ambience, with a small dance space and video screens to keep you entertained. Downstairs there's seating and a bar; under-21 queers often congregate down here, where they're welcome to sip coffee and Italian sodas. Both levels are decorated with retro '50s and sleek industrial '90s colors and styles. The affordable restaurant serves casual American dishes (with many vegetarian offerings). ⊠ *315 Braun Ct.,* ☎ *734/994–3677. Crowd: 80/20 gay/straight, mixed m/f, all ages and all styles, low-attitude.*

The Flame. This old-style downtown bar has booth seating, amiable bartenders, and mellow music. It's a good place to hang out or cruise. ⊠ *115*

W. *Washington St.,* ☎ *734/662–9680. Crowd: 80/20 m/f, mixed ages, local, some students, more of a smoking and drinking crowd than at Aut Bar.*

One-Nighters

Ann Arbor's favorite high-energy disco, the **Nectarine Ballroom** (⊠ 516 E. Liberty St., ☎ 734/994–5436), has well-attended gay nights on Tuesday and Friday and is community-friendly at other times.

Hangin' with the Hets

The Ark (⊠ 316 S. Main St., ☎ 734/761–1451) is a fantastic music club. The cozy **Del Rio** (⊠ 122 W. Washington St., ☎ 734/761–2530) has live jazz, open-mic poetry nights, and a bohemian mood.

Sleeps

A couple of hotels are downtown, but you pay a premium to be within walking distance of campus and shopping. Chain properties, most of them south of downtown near I–94, are less expensive.

For price ranges, *see* lodging Chart B at the front of this guide.

$$–$$$ 🏨 **Bell Tower.** An impressive on-campus property, the Bell Tower has nicely furnished rooms, including two-bedroom atrium suites that are a great value for friends traveling together. The handsome, preserved building has a European-style mood, complete with formal reproduction antiques. ⊠ *300 S. Thayer St., 48104,* ☎ *734/769–3010 or 800/999–8693,* FAX *734/769–4339. 66 rooms. Restaurant.*

$$–$$$ 🏨 **Crowne Plaza.** This upscale chain is close to the highway and adjacent to the hulking Briarwood shopping center. ⊠ *610 Hilton Blvd., 48108,* ☎ *734/761–7800 or 800/344–7829. 200 rooms. Restaurant, pool, health club.*

$–$$ 🏨 **Bunn-Pher Hill.** A short and pretty drive from Ann Arbor, this wooded retreat is hosted by Steve Levicki and artist Urban Jupena. It's filled with the latter's weavings and leather hangings. The rambling house, built around a 1920s barn, exudes character. Ceramic floors, soaring ceilings, secluded porches, and cozy nooks and lofts are among the unusual touches. ⊠ *11745 Spencer La., Pinckney 48169,* ☎ *734/878–9236. 4 rooms with TV, most with private bath. Full breakfast. Mixed gay/straight.*

$ 🏨 **Motel 6.** Right off the highway, a short drive from downtown Ann Arbor, this budget property is popular with students visiting their sweeties and wanting some privacy. ⊠ *3764 S. State St., 48108,* ☎ *734/665–9900.*

The Little Black Book

Ann Arbor Convention & Visitors Bureau (⊠ 120 W. Huron St., 48104, ☎ 734/995–7281 or 800/888–9487, Web site www.annarbor.org). **Current** (☎ 734/668–4044, Web site www.gisd.com/sgi). **University of Michigan Lesbian, Gay, Bisexual, and Transgender Union** (☎ 734/763–4186, Web site www.umich.edu/~ inqueery).

Gay Media

All the Detroit gay papers cover Ann Arbor, especially the locally based **Out Post.**

BOOKSTORES

Bibliophiles will enjoy Ann Arbor, which has many sources of fine books, including the state's most comprehensive lesbigay bookstore, **Common Language** (⊠ 215 S. 4th Ave., ☎ 734/663–0036), a woman-owned shop with great women's, men's, and general sections; mainstream and adult gay magazines; and many pride items. Two U of M graduates founded what has become the familiar and gay-friendly Borders bookstore chain, whose headquarters remains in Ann Arbor. The large, comfy **Borders** (⊠ 612 E. Liberty St., ☎ 734/668–7652) on the edge of campus has a fine lesbigay selection.

12 *Out on Fire Island*

THE FIRE ISLAND EXPERIENCE—the gay one at least—begins outside two ramshackle ferry terminals in Sayville, Long Island. On every summer weekend morning, island goers begin forming two distinct but harmonious camps. On the left winds the line for the ferry to Cherry Grove—a hodgepodge of creatures representing every gender, age, race, and style. In hand are soiled canvas bags overflowing with sunflower-print beach towels, disposable cameras, and crinkled brown lunch bags. Under buttocks are decade-old Igloo beach coolers packed with canned light beer and 3-liter boxes of Almaden. Frisky bandanna-collared mutts mingle playfully, as their no less frisky owners do. Dykes with tykes change diapers dockside. Drag queens trade dish. The occasional straight couple hops into line—perhaps they have gay friends in the Grove, or maybe they're just mixed up.

Next door winds the line for the ferry to the Pines—a curving band of chiseled bodies, mostly male, white and professional, and wearing at least the appearance of money. Armani sunglasses sparkle in the sunlight. Some guys already have their shirts off, revealing a long off-season's pursuit of the perfectly sculpted figure. Almost everyone is done up in some riff on the Abercrombie & Fitch–Banana Republic–California surfer look (nylon surfer shorts, Tevas, and Adidas anything are the latest rage)—a far cry from the spirit-stifling suits many endure five days a week, but a look that is no less dull and interchangeable. Many carry shopping bags from gourmet food shops like Balducci's and Dean & Deluca, along with cases of Sam Adams beer and creels of fruit and Brie. Yellow labs and Jack Russell terriers wait by their masters. The sight of each bronze Adonis bathing in the glow of the one standing before him is at once breathtaking, heartbreaking, and curious.

Almost simultaneously, the two ferries load up, set sail, and chug along a narrow river from Sayville into Great South Bay, and from there another 5 miles to the north shores of Fire Island's two gay communities: to the east, the Pines; to the west, Cherry Grove. Alike in sexual orientation, they are separated only by a small forest and a strip of white beach. Aesthetically, socially, and, to some extent, ideologically, the gulf between the two towns is much greater. The Pines draws a more image- and beauty-conscious segment of the gay community: nicer digs, bigger pecs, fewer wigs, and hotter sex. Cherry Grove welcomes everybody else and contains none of the Pines's unfortunate narcissism. Lesbians usually prefer Cherry Grove, where they make up nearly half the population, while the Pines is mostly male.

A week in either place will permanently alter your sense of the world. The first time you hop off the boat in Cherry Grove or the Pines and step into these villages of narrow boardwalks, red wagons, and rainbow flags, you feel as though you've just entered Willy Wonka's chocolate factory: An entire kingdom, just for me! Not in Provincetown, not in Manhattan's Greenwich Village, not in San Francisco's Castro are you so completely immersed in gay culture. Here the phrase "10 percent" describes the segment of the population that *isn't* gay. Is it any wonder Andrew Holleran's *Dancer from the Dance* ends with a blowout party here? "Nowhere else on earth was natural and human beauty fused," muses Holleran, "nowhere else on earth could you dance in quite the same atmosphere."

The high season—when most businesses are open, the ferries run full swing, and the island is fully inhabited—is from Memorial Day through Labor Day. Some hotels and businesses are open during all of May and September, fewer in April and October. The ferries run only sporadically in these months. In winter, Fire Island is a ghost town, although the Dune Point rentals in Cherry Grove (*see* Sleeps, *below*) stay open year-round.

THE LAY OF THE LAND

In both communities, your feet are never actually permitted to touch the ground. Each "road" is nothing more than a wooden-plank boardwalk barely wide enough for two people to pass each other. **Cherry Grove** is the senior community of the two—it is both smaller-scale and less uniform in its architecture and ambience. Its most pronounced feature is external: a long ferry dock that juts into Great South Bay from its north shore. The dock turns into the Grove's only true commercial thoroughfare, which twists its way south past the first east-west boardwalk (Bay Walk), around the Cherry Grove Beach Club, past a restaurant and disco, through the second east-west boardwalk (Atlantic Walk), by a couple shops, before finally climbing down a set of wooden stairs to the sandy beach. Virtually every structure east or west of this curving spine is residential—anything from a sprawling contemporary gray-shingle triplex to a modest, white-clapboard Cape. The boardwalk layout is similar to a train track, with Bay and Atlantic walks acting as the two rails, and about 20 short boardwalks running perpendicularly between them.

Cherry Grove's character is playful, a tad rebellious, and decidedly queeny. As you saunter along the boardwalks perusing the sandy "yards" of its seaside retreats, you'll see rainbow wind socks, tatty pink flamingos, gaudy wind chimes, and gardens inhabited by gussied-up Barbie and Ken dolls. Crudely executed signs hang over many front doors, proudly proclaiming the often silly name of each domicile. Foliage-choked wooden fences fringe most properties, and trees tower overhead, encouraged to grow unchecked—you're often forced to duck under or swerve around overgrown branches. The community has a sloppy, cluttered, yet luxuriant feel to it. In a world where co-op boards are known to forbid the draping of rainbow flags from windows, or where condo developments are defined by their rigidly planned and flawlessly manicured flower beds and hedges, it's refreshing to wander through a village that has raised gay tackiness and unkempt landscaping to a respectable, if not empowering, art form.

The neat and tony **Pines** suffers a bit at the hands of Cherry Grove's reverse snobbery. Its distinguishing attribute is internal: a long, narrow harbor bordered on the east bank by clusters of pines and on the west bank by about a dozen shops, a couple of restaurants and the Botel Pines and Dunes Yacht Club. The ferry motors through the harbor and passengers disembark at a wooden-plank town square anchored by a central kiosk that serves as a community bulletin board. Tied up to the docks fringing the harbor on both sides are dozens of enormous and expensive pleasure craft. Seaplanes land and take off on the bay just to the left of the harbor's mouth. Unlike Cherry Grove, business does not extend across the island to the ocean, but ends where the harbor ends. Sitting on the dock you are sucked in by the parade of tan, hairless pecs and tight, retro swimsuits—everybody looks like a runway model. People sometimes make fun of these gaggles of gorgeous gay men, but it's hard not to admire their physical charms.

Away from the harbor, the Pines is largely an enclave of some 600 homes—vastly larger and more often occupied by males than the Grove's. Most of the homes are hulking and quite spectacular—gray, angular, and modern, they rise dramatically from the sand like abstract sculptures, replete with skylights and porticos, pillars and cathedral ceilings, exposed beams and massive windows. Many of the decks have hot tubs, some even full-size swimming pools.

Charity events are organized and attended by folks from both communities. Pines types like to eat at the Grove's restaurants. Grove types like to party at Pines's bars. There is considerable mingling and little animosity—only good-natured rivalry—between the two. And then there is the **"Meat Rack"** (*see* Scenes, *below*), the one section of Fire Island that geographically and spiritually connects the Pines to Cherry Grove, binding the pretty boys unmistakably to the campy queens.

GETTING AROUND

By Plane
There's no direct connection between Sayville and Kennedy or LaGuardia airports, so your best bet is to rent a car if you're arriving in New York by plane. It's faster but more expensive to catch a connecting flight to **MacArthur Airport** (☎ 516/467–3210) in Islip, which is a short taxi ride from Sayville.

North American Flying Services (☎ 201/440–1941) can whisk you by helicopter from the East 23rd Street Marine Terminal in Manhattan to Fire Island Pines in 30 minutes. They take off anywhere from four to seven times a day; the cost: $135 one-way if you pay with cash, $145 on a credit card.

By Train and Bus
Long Island Rail Road (LIRR, ☎ 718/217–5477) trains depart regularly from New York City's Penn Station for the 90-minute trip to Sayville. You might have to change trains; check with your conductor. Shuttle buses and group taxis to the ferry terminal meet almost every train and cost $2. If you're stuck at the station call **Colonial Taxi** (☎ 516/589–7878).

Horizon Coach Islander's Club (☎ 212/255–8014 or 516/654– 2622) runs buses from Manhattan to the ferry terminal Fridays, and Saturdays and from the ferry terminal back to Manhattan on Sundays and Mondays (cost: $20 one-way; $175 for a 12-trip ticket).

By Car
Once on Long Island, head east on the Long Island Expressway (LIE). Take exit 59 (Ocean Avenue South) to Sayville, where signs direct you to the ferry terminal. The huge parking lot across from the terminal costs $7 daily.

By Ferry
No matter how you get to Sayville, you'll need to take the ferry out to the island. The schedule is based on the LIRR schedule, and boats run about every hour from 7 AM to midnight on Friday, until around 10:30 PM on Saturday and Sunday, and every couple of hours from 7 AM to 7 PM on weekdays. Call the **Sayville Ferry Service** (☎ 516/589–0810) for exact times. The round-trip fare is $10 for adults, $5 for kids under 12, and $3 for dogs. Discount commutation tickets are available.

If you miss the ferry and are desperate to get across that day, call **South Bay Water Taxi** (☎ 516/665–8885) which charges anywhere from $100 to $150 for the first group of six people ($10 for each additional person), depending on the hour.

Once on Fire Island

The trek between Cherry Grove and the Pines is not over boardwalk, but rather along the beach, which fringes the entire Atlantic shore of the island, or through the forest, which is laced with poorly marked paths that circuitously connect the two communities. The beach walk takes 20 to 30 minutes; the forest walk can take from 20 minutes to all day, depending on your navigating skills and the degree to which you're distracted by diversions along the way.

Water Taxi

Getting around by water taxi is a way of life. Boats hold from a dozen to three dozen passengers and make frequent stops at all Fire Island communities. They generally run from sunrise to midnight, but when the crowd warrants it, they continue to shuttle people between the Pines and the Grove until as late as 4 AM, when the last bars have closed. If you plan to stay out past midnight, call **Aqualine Water Taxi** (☎ 516/639–9190), which shuttles between Cherry Grove and Ocean Beach or **South Bay Water Taxi** (☎ 516/665–8885), which in addition services the Pines, or ask at the dock how late they're running. If there are enough of you in your party, they'll take a reservation. Be patient: You sometimes have to wait a while dockside. Once aboard, the ride between Cherry Grove and the Pines takes about 10 minutes.

Though the ferry system is informal and dictated largely by supply and demand, you can count on the following. In the Grove, catch the taxi at the foot of the ferry dock just to the left as you face the mainland. In the Pines catch it on the dock just outside the Pines Pantry grocery store. The fare between the two is $4 per person; it's $7 from the Grove to Ocean Beach; $8 from the Pines to Ocean Beach. It is customary to tip a buck or two.

HELPFUL TIPS

Fire Island has no banks and only a handful of ATM machines. Most stores, however, accept ATM or credit cards for payment.

Staples such as groceries, hardware, and household goods cost anywhere from 20% to 50% more than on the mainland, so stock up before coming. The **Pines Pantry** (✉ Harbor Walk, ☎ 516/597–6200) and, in Cherry Grove, the **Associate Too** (✉ Main Walk, ☎ 516/597–9210) are the only grocery stores. The former is better by far: It's twice as large, has a wonderful selection of produce, a fresh fish market and deli, and lots of exotic foods. The two liquor stores in the Pines have a better selection than the one in Cherry Grove. Both communities have hardware stores and florists; the Pines has a pet supply store.

Never walk over the sand dunes. Each year, the fierce and greedy Atlantic Ocean steals precious tons of sand from Fire Island's beaches. Preventing erosion is an ongoing battle. In the Pines little foliage grows on the dunes that separate the homes from the beach, so orange fencing has been set up to bolster them and keep people off. Stay away from these fences.

Cherry Grove's beach is mixed lesbian and gay male, with more dykes to the west of the restaurant (it changes hands and names every year) at Ocean and Lewis walks. It's fine and quite popular to bathe nude. The "no-man's" stretch that abuts the Meat Rack, connecting the Grove to the Pines, gets more nudists. The Pines's beach is mostly male and very few people remove their suits. Swimming can be dangerous along the entire stretch as currents are strong and violent: Exercise caution.

Outside the commercial areas, the boardwalks are quite dark at night. Bring a flashlight to prevent stumbling off a walkway and spraining an ankle on somebody's Flintstones garden diorama.

Fires are a major concern since most of the buildings and walkways are made of wood. Campfires are prohibited, and cigarettes should be completely extinguished before you discard them. Do not toss them off the boardwalk or onto the beach.

Pets are common. You must have them on a leash at all times and clean up after them or be fined. It's against the law to have them on the beach, and although the park service seems to overlook this if they're leashed, it's best not to chance it.

EATS

Every entrée in every Fire Island restaurant costs about 20% more than it would in New York City, which is about 20% more than it would cost anywhere else. Although the quality of the island's cuisine has improved immeasurably in recent years, high prices are due more to the fact that restaurateurs must earn every cent during the short-lived summer season, and every morsel must be hauled over from the mainland.

Cherry Grove has the best restaurants on the entire island—even straight people come here to eat. You're seldom permitted to tip with your credit card, so plan to have extra cash on hand. Typically, restaurant service sucks: it's a bunch of kids trying to subsidize a summer on Fire Island; they party all night, sun themselves all day, and generally resent the time they must spend serving meals. Really, who can blame them? All told, considering the limited personnel and ingredients, Fire Island's restaurants manage very well. But dining is not a reason in itself to visit.

For price ranges, *see* dining Chart A at the front of this guide.

Cherry Grove

$$$$ ✕ **Top of the Bay.** The best restaurant in either community, this second-floor dining room is half indoors, half in a covered porch that overlooks the ferry dock and Great South Bay. The staff is friendly and attentive— rare for Fire Island. There are always about a dozen specials, but you can't go wrong with blue cornmeal–crusted chicken with tomato-basil salsa, and mussels with garlic, shallots, cilantro, tomatoes, and white wine. ⊠ *Dock Walk,* ☎ 516/597–6699.

$$–$$$ ✕ **Michael's.** What used to be a glorified diner now serves serious food: broccoli rabe with white beans and orecchiette, baked snapper with fresh herbs, and a nice array of meat and fish grills. You can still pop in for a light meal, but prices have risen in accordance with the retooled menu. The mood remains casual, the service pleasant and with little attitude. It's open 24 hours on Saturday. Plenty of seating inside and out, but no water views. ⊠ *Dock and Bayview Walk,* ☎ 516/597–6555.

The Pines

$$$ ✕ **Island Club Bistro.** This classy, romantic eatery—fresh flowers on tables and natural white maple floors—serves a fine menu of Continental and northern Italian favorites. The chef is from Florence, and locals swear by his cooking—the pork chops are particularly good. It's below the bar of the same name. ⊠ *Picketty Ruff Walk,* ☎ 516/597–6001.

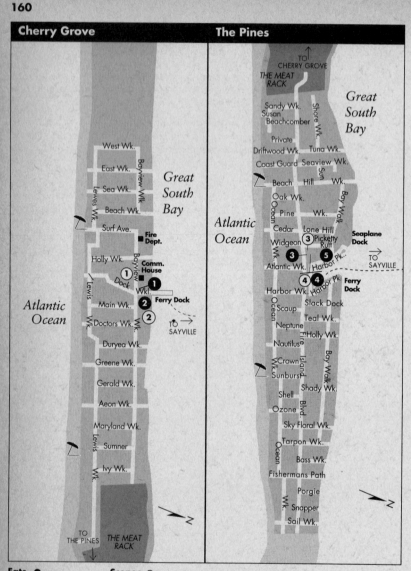

Cherry Grove

The Pines

Great South Bay

Atlantic Ocean

West Wk.
East Wk.
Sea Wk.
Beach Wk.
Surf Ave.
Holly Wk.
Main Wk.
Doctors Wk.
Duryea Wk.
Greene Wk.
Gerald Wk.
Aeon Wk.
Maryland Wk.
Sumner
Ivy Wk.

Bayview Wlk.
Lewes Wk.
Bayview Dock
Lewis
Lewis Wk.

Fire Dept.
Comm. House
Ferry Dock

TO SAYVILLE

TO THE PINES
THE MEAT RACK

TO CHERRY GROVE
THE MEAT RACK

Great South Bay

Sandy Wk.
Susan
Beachcomber
Private
Driftwood Wk.
Coast Guard
Beach
Oak Wk.
Pine
Cedar
Widgeon
Atlantic Wk.
Harbor Wk.
Scaup
Neptune
Nautilus
Crown
Sunburst
Shell
Ozone
Sky Floral Wk.
Tarpon Wk.
Bass Wk.
Fishermans Path
Porgie
Snapper
Sail Wk.

Shore Wk.
Tuna Wk.
Seaview Wk.
Hill Wk.
Sun
Wk.
Lone Hill
Picketty Ruff
Harbor Pk.
Slack Dock
Teal Wk.
Holly Wk.
Shady Wk.
Bay Walk

Bay Walk
Harbor Pk.
Ocean Wk.
Island
Fire Island
Blvd.
Ocean Wk.

Seaplane Dock
TO SAYVILLE
Ferry Dock

Atlantic Ocean

N

Eats ●
Cultured Elephant, **3**
Island Club Bistro, **4**
Michael's, **1**
Top of the Bay, **2**
Yacht Club, **5**

Scenes ○
Cherry's, **2**
Ice Palace Disco, **1**
Island Club Bistro, **4**
The Pavillion, **3**

$$-$$$ ✗ **Yacht Club.** Part of the Botel complex, this spacious restaurant has plenty of indoor and outdoor seating. The food varies in quality: Some love it, but it's a little overrated. The Caesar salad is the best on the island. Also stellar are burgers that come with a wide selection of toppings: sun-dried tomato and watercress, chili, feta cheese, etc. The grilled seafood entrées and steaks are less memorable. ⊠ *Harbor Walk,* ☎ *516/597–6131.*

$$ ✗ **Cultured Elephant.** About as good as the Yacht Club and quite a bit cheaper, it's right on the dock—near the mouth of the harbor—with a deck overlooking passersby. The food's not gourmet but straightforward, with good gazpacho, burgers, mako shark steak, fried seafood platters, and grilled swordfish. ⊠ *Harbor Walk,* ☎ *516/597–6010.*

SCENES

Fire Island is definitely a party playground, especially on weekends when its hot spots are packed. The Pines's clubs draw an expectedly high-profile, at times clonish crowd. Cherry Grove's nightlife is less intense and much more diverse, with good spots for the old and young, male and female. The complaint on this side is that you may meet new friends, but few of them are single.

Cherry Grove

Cherry's. A nice spot to have a drink before hitting the discos, Cherry's is actually two bars. In front of the dining area is a small video bar that's usually not very crowded. Outside, under a red-and-white striped awning and pink-lighted cherry tree branches, is a piano bar with a pool table and a small area for live entertainment—usually pop music or reggae, a cabaret on Thursdays. ⊠ *Bayview Walk,* ☎ *516/597–6820. Crowd: ages 20s to 80s, mixed genders, lots of regulars and here-for-the-week visitors, very friendly, gabby, campy, laid-back.*

Ice Palace Disco. On Saturday nights every kind of person in virtually every kind of outfit—there's even a small straight following—fills this place up. Friday is popular, too, but it's fairly dead the rest of the week (or at least it feels that way because the space is so immense). There's a long, rectangular disco with pool tables, video games, and a bar at one end; a stage in the center; and access to a deck that overlooks an outdoor pool. A bar and porch at the front of the building overlooks the bay. The stage is the frequent host of impersonators, comedians, drag shows, and the famed Miss Fire Island Pageant, held every September. ⊠ *Bayview Walk,* ☎ *516/ 597–6600. Crowd: truly diverse in age, gender, and race; low attitude; plenty of energy; professional partyers.*

The Pines

Island Club. Mellower and less snooty than the Pavillion (*see below*), but with an otherwise similar crowd, the Island Club has plenty of attractions: a small, smartly decorated second-floor bar and disco with a pool table; bartenders whose packages are tied neatly in G-strings; a small dance floor with very hot music; a quieter outdoor terrace; and an elegant piano bar with varnished blond-wood bar. ⊠ *Picketty Ruff Walk,* ☎ *516/ 597–6001. Crowd: young but with many exceptions, 90% male, everyone from pretty boys to hotshot entertainment-industry moguls.*

The Pavillion. On weekends, the tea dances at this urban-warehouse-style disco are impossibly crowded and getting from one end of the balcony to the other—let alone actually meeting somebody—is a tremendous feat. There's a moderately large rectangular dance floor with one mirrored wall, giving it the feel of a much larger club. Adjacent is a long, almost always packed, cruise bar. Upstairs, overlooking the harbor, is an L-shape outdoor balcony, the Loft, where attitudy tea dances are held early each evening. Late nights in the disco are more laid-back—maybe because it's so dark and everybody's so wasted. Best sound system on the island. ⊠ *Fire Island Blvd., no phone. Crowd: young, mostly male, gorgeous but homogeneous, stand-and-model, wired.*

Action

An undeveloped area of sand dunes, pines, shrubs, deer, and other beach flora and fauna, the **"Meat Rack"** is administered by the National Park Service and spans about a mile between the two communities. It is one of the nation's most active cruise grounds, making it a cross between Mutual of Omaha's Wild Kingdom and New York City's Bijou adult theater. Whether you walk through here at noon on a Tuesday or at midnight on a Saturday, you're quite likely to encounter a few discreet (or not so discreet) encounters. Plastic shopping bags filled with condoms dangle strategically from gnarled tree branches (courtesy of Gay Men's Health Crisis) as testimony to the Meat Rack's liveliness. The maze of both clearly and vaguely marked trails is tricky, especially after dark. Enter from Cherry Grove by following either Bay Walk or Atlantic Walk east to the end. From the Pines, follow Coast Guard Walk west to its end. If you head in for a "good time," beware: That soft and fuzzy nose nuzzling at your belt buckle may be that of a white-tail deer foraging for dinner.

SLEEPS

The vast majority of visitors to Fire Island stay in some sort of privately owned or rented house. With the exception of Belvedere Castle, hotels and inns are no more than functional and all are inordinately expensive. If you're planning to stay a week it's more economical to go in with friends and rent a place—properties are listed in most large New York newspapers and magazines and the island has many realtors. If you can't get or don't want a house, be advised that hotel space is limited (there are only about 200 rooms between the two communities) so you should book at least a month ahead for summer weekends; most places begin taking reservations on January 1. Two-night minimums are almost always enforced on weekends, as well as three- and four-day minimums for certain holidays.

For price ranges, *see* lodging Chart A at the front of this guide.

Cherry Grove

$$$–$$$$ ☷ **Belvedere Hotel.** One of the giddiest properties on the East Coast, the Belvedere is patterned immodestly after a Venetian palazzo. Amid the statuary, domes, and terraces, the guest rooms are decorated individually with antiques and reproductions and plenty of quirky touches—many have decks and refrigerators and several have wet bars and VCRs. There's ample room to sun, including a roof deck that's the highest point on the island and about 1,000 feet of private sandy (bay-front) beach. ⊠ *Bayview Walk, Box 4026, 11782,* ☏ *516/597–6448,* 𝔽𝔸𝕏 *516/587–9391. 40 rooms, most with private bath, several with TV. Pool, hot tub, gym. Gay male. Closed October 15–April.*

$$$–$$$$ ☷ **Cherry Grove Beach Hotel.** It has less character than the Belvedere, but higher energy and a more diverse crowd, including lots of dykes. Rooms are small but clean with standard motel furnishings, and overlook a huge sundeck and pool, as well as the popular Ice Palace Disco (*see* Scenes, *above*). Some rooms have VCRs, air-conditioning, kitchenettes, and wet bars. It's the social focal point of Cherry Grove, a true party hotel, and your best bet if getting laid is a priority. ⊠ *Bayview Walk, Box 537, 11782,* ☏ *516/597–6600,* 𝔽𝔸𝕏 *516/597–6651. 58 rooms with private bath, several with phone and TV. Pool. Mixed gay male/lesbian. Closed October–April.*

$$–$$$ ☷ **Carousel Guest House.** The only true B&B on the island is a small, simple, ranch structure that looks like an ordinary beach home. It's surrounded by gardens and adjacent to the Cherry Grove Beach Club. ⊠

185 Holly Walk, Box 4001, 11782, ☎ 516/597–6612. 11 rooms with shared bath. Continental breakfast. Mixed gay male/lesbian.

$–$$ ☎ **Dune Point.** The six apartments and studios (comprising 24 rooms) at this oceanfront complex can work either as weekend retreats or summerlong rentals. Each unit accommodates from two to six people and is fully furnished and quite homey—it has the feel of a share in somebody's home. Open year-round. ✉ *Lewis Walk, Box 78, Cherry Grove, 11782, ☎ 516/597–6261, FAX 516/597–6261. Most units have a private bath and TV. Hot tub. Mixed gay male/lesbian.*

The Pines

$$–$$$$ ☎ **Pines Place.** This contemporary guest house, a somewhat recent and very nice addition to the Pines's otherwise limited accommodations offerings, has spacious, airy rooms that are close to nightlife and the beach but far enough away for peace and quiet. ✉ *Box 5309, Fire Island Pines, 11782, ☎ 516/597–6162. 7 rooms, some with private bath and TV. Hot tub. Continental breakfast. Mostly gay male.*

THE LITTLE BLACK BOOK

At Your Fingertips

Coast Guard: ☎ 516/661–9100. **Community Manager:** Cherry Grove and Pines, ☎ 516/597–6060. **Doctor:** Cherry Grove, Doctor's Walk, ☎ 516/597–6616; Pines, 577 Coast Guard Walk, ☎ 516/597–6160. **Fire:** Cherry Grove, use the alarm boxes along the boardwalks; Pines, dial 0.

Gay Media

Runaway Bay Books (✉ 10 Main St., Sayville, ☎ 516/589–9212), a full-service bookstore, carries lesbian and gay titles. The **Pines Pantry** has a shelf of best-selling novels and gay erotic fiction, as well as gay news magazines (no porn) and a few major newspapers. The **Cherry Grove Grocery** has only the major newspapers.

Working Out

The **Island Gym** (✉ adjacent to Botel, Pines, ☎ 516/597–7867) is open to members and guests ($10 for a one-day pass, $45 for one week). It has a pool and sundeck and free weights under an awning. There's no fitness-training equipment.

13 *Out in* Fort Lauderdale

IT'S BEEN MORE THAN A DECADE since the city of Fort Lauderdale said no to rowdy collegiate spring breakers and began courting a diverse year-round market of business and leisure travelers. The once-famous annual March migration of 350,000 college kids had by the mid-'80s seriously tarnished the city's reputation, earning it the nickname Fort Liquordale. Having had enough of the poorly behaved crowds, local business owners and residents officially banded together in 1985 and discouraged the college set from visiting.

Since then locals have reinvented their city, spending $26 million to refurbish a dreary and dated oceanfront, and countless more dollars on new attractions both downtown and throughout the county. *Money* magazine recently named Fort Lauderdale one of the best cities to live in America, and more than 6.5 million vacationers now visit annually. A key to Fort Lauderdale's success has been its ability to lure new segments of the tourist market. City promoters have concentrated on drawing more foreigners and on appealing to lesbians and gays. Business owners have been quick to take advantage of this favorable climate; in February they organize the city's annual Winter Gayla, a weekend-long pride celebration with numerous beach and dance parties.

Fort Lauderdale offers an alternative to glittery, fast-paced South Beach and touristy and remote Key West (although many lesbian and gay visitors do combine their visit to Florida with a trip to one or both of those destinations). The crowd here tends to be a little older than in South Beach, perhaps in part reflecting the fact that Fort Lauderdale is a desirable gay retirement community. Although the city has no specifically gay neighborhood, many gays and lesbians live in Wilton Manors and Victoria Park. A gay rights ordinance (initially defeated in 1990) was passed in Fort Lauderdale in 1996, and most local politicos are loyal friends of the gay constituency. It's not difficult to see why Fort Lauderdale is said to have one of the highest per-capita lesbian and gay populations in the country.

THE LAY OF THE LAND

Most tourists stick to Route A1A (the beachfront's main thoroughfare), U.S. 1 (the interior's main north–south road), and the several major roads connecting them, including posh Las Olas Boulevard (Route 842). More and more visitors, however, are venturing downtown and into some of the other interior neighborhoods.

Downtown Fort Lauderdale

Downtown is centered at the intersection of **Broward Boulevard** (which runs east–west) and **Federal Highway** (U.S. 1), but the best territory for exploring is along **Riverwalk**, the mile-long pedestrian zone that links parks and museums from Las Olas Boulevard west to the Arts and Science and Historic districts.

Begin by the city's oldest standing structure, **Stranahan House** (✉ 1 Stranahan Pl., ☎ 954/524–4736), which was built in 1901 by an early settler who established a kinship and trading agreement with the area's native Seminole Indians. A few blocks west is the esteemed **Museum of Art** (✉ 1 E. Las Olas Blvd., ☎ 954/525–5500), which houses a fine collection of works by artists of the 1940s CoBrA (as in Copenhagen, Brussels, and Amsterdam) movement, as well as Native American and pre-Columbian art.

From here Riverwalk passes near several new attractions, including the **Brickell Station,** a massive dining, shopping, and entertainment complex; the **New World Aquarium** (☎ 954/522–0076); and **Old Fort Lauderdale,** a living-history interpretive center that debuts in 1998.

Riverwalk continues west into the city's relatively new **Arts and Science District,** a six-block stretch of museums, cafés, and attractions, anchored by the **Broward Center for the Performing Arts** (✉ 201 S.W. 5th Ave., ☎ 954/475–6884), a first-rate venue for theater, classical music, and opera; and the **Museum of Discovery and Science** (✉ 401 S.W. 2nd St., ☎ 954/467–6637).

The Arts and Science District merges with the **Historic District,** which you can start exploring by visiting the **Fort Lauderdale Historical Society Museum** (✉ 219 S.W. 2nd Ave., ☎ 954/463–4431). Museum-led tours take in some of the city's early homes.

Las Olas Boulevard
From the eastern edge of downtown, by the Museum of Art, **Las Olas Boulevard** runs east for about 2 miles before intersecting Route A1A at the ocean. This has long been Fort Lauderdale's fashionable shopping district, on a par with Lincoln Road in South Beach. Stroll down this tree-lined boulevard and you'll pass fine architecture inspired by the Spanish colonial era, buzzing sidewalk cafés, and innovative art galleries and home-furnishings stores.

The Beach
Coastal **Route A1A** is less a scene these days than when it provided the setting for the fluffy 1960 film *Where the Boys Are,* but the sands are still golden, and it's a nice place to plunk down your paunchy, pale, but no less personable body without worrying that a posse of South Beach clones is snickering at you (and so what if they are?). Indeed, despite its fancy refurbishment after two decades of Spring Break fever, the shoreline remains refreshingly attitude-free and laid-back.

Just south of Route A1A's intersection with Las Olas Boulevard, you'll find the **International Swimming Hall of Fame Museum and Aquatic Complex** (✉ 501 Seabreeze Blvd., ☎ 954/468–1580), a massive swimming and diving facility with two floors of exhibits honoring such aquatic luminaries as Olympic diver and gay-rights activist Greg Louganis.

Just north of Las Olas Boulevard, **Beach Place** (which stands on the site of the once famously tacky Marlin Beach Hotel) is a 100,000-square-foot restaurant and shopping complex. To the north is Sunrise Boulevard, where you'll encounter the **Galleria Mall** (✉ 2414 E. Sunrise Blvd.), a cruisy maze of typical retail establishments.

One of the city's most unusual attractions, the **Bonnet House** (✉ 900 N. Birch Rd., ☎ 954/563–5393), is around the corner. This 35-acre estate is the former home of Mrs. Evelyn Fortune Bartlett, who passed away in 1997 at the age of 110. Completed in 1921 by Mrs. Bartlett's late husband, artist Frederic Clay Bartlett, the mansion and grounds contain a museum-quality collection of art and antiques, a fragrant orchid garden, and some resident swans and monkeys.

GETTING AROUND

Even though Fort Lauderdale is laid out in a grid, getting around can prove a challenge. About 300 miles of canals and rivers interrupt the flow of roads, and traffic backs up along the beach road, Route A1A, and at the drawbridges crossing the Intracoastal Waterway. Streets, roads, courts, and drives run east–west, while avenues, terraces, and ways run north–south. Boulevards can (and often do) run in any direction. Best advice: Buy a detailed map, and call for directions whenever you're in doubt. One positive note: Because this is an automobile culture, there's usually ample parking, even near the beaches.

The aforementioned pitfalls notwithstanding, a car is your best way to get around. There are a couple of unusual and interesting alternatives to driving. Buses serve the entire county but aren't a practical way to see the city. Fort Lauderdale's **Water Taxis** (☎ 954/565–5507), 50-passenger boats, will take you anywhere within the 7 miles of Intracoastal Waterway between Port Everglades and Commercial Boulevard, and along the New River into downtown Fort Lauderdale. You can also get around the more touristy parts of town by trolley. The **Downtown Trolley** (free) runs from Las Olas Boulevard to the Arts and Science; the **Waveline Trolley** ($1) runs along Route A1A from the Galleria Mall on Sunrise Boulevard to near the Hyatt Regency Pier Sixty-Six Resort, up by the 17th Street Causeway. A less scenic, more expensive, but more direct way of getting around is to call a cab or catch one from the larger hotels.

EATS

The once run-of-the-mill Fort Lauderdale dining scene has come of age in the past decade. Of the 20 best South Florida restaurants chosen recently by the readers of *Gourmet* magazine, 10 are in Fort Lauderdale. New artsy, trendy eateries—many with beachfront patios, open-air decks, and tropical landscaping—open constantly. Most of the hottest meal tickets have significant queer followings. Wilton Manor has developed into South Florida's only "gay restaurant row," with nearly a dozen options, many doubling as nightclubs or piano lounges.

Head over to the extremely queer-popular **Wild Oats Community Market** (✉ 2501 E. Sunrise Blvd., ☎ 954/566–9333) for natural foods, organic produce, gourmet groceries, and great sandwiches.

For price ranges, *see* dining Chart A at the front of this guide.

Las Olas Boulevard and the Beach

$$$–$$$$ ✕ **East City Grill.** The spacious, open-air patio at this snazzy restaurant adjacent to the Riviera Hotel offers dreamy ocean views. Enjoy the seaside breezes while nibbling on a salad of banana-nut-crusted goat cheese, or while clearing out your sinuses with a sharp Jamaican-shrimp pepper pot with pigeon-pea rice, calabaza squash, chayote, and okra. ✉ *505 N. Atlantic Blvd.,* ☎ *954/565–5569.*

$$$–$$$$ ✕ **Mark's Las Olas.** Run by celebrated chef Mark Militello, this stylish restaurant has the chic decor and A-list clientele you'd expect of such a high-profile place. Ultramod sheet-metal tables fill a room accented with bleached woods and mosaic-tile floors. The menu shows off the likes of oak-rotisserie white duck with a mango-honey glaze, charcoal-grilled vegetables, and sweet potato–vanilla bean purée.✉ *1032 E. Las Olas Blvd.,* ☎ *954/463–1000.*

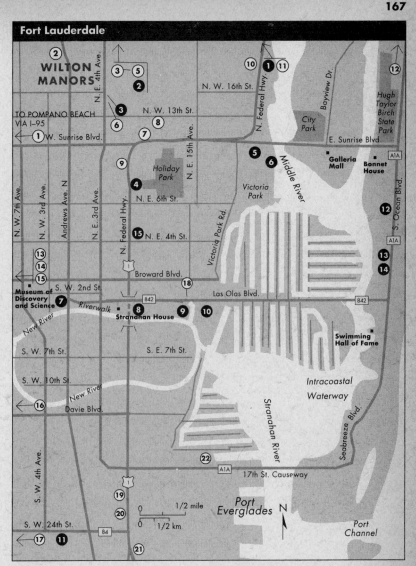

Fort Lauderdale

Eats ●

Casablanca Café, **13**
East City Grill, **12**
Floridian, **10**
Hi-Life Café, **1**
Jalisco, **4**
Legends Café, **3**
Lester's, **11**
Mark's Place, **9**
Pride Factory, **15**
Solo, **7**
Splash, **14**
Sukhothai, **5**
Tropics, **2**
Victoria Park, **6**
Zan(Z)Bar, **8**

Scenes ○

Adventures, **1**
Bill and Jerry's Filling Station, **8**
Boots, **16**
Bus Stop, **20**
Chardees, **4**
Club Cathode Ray, **18**
Club Electra, **22**
The Copa, **21**
Cubby Hole, **9**
825, **7**
End Up, **13**
Everglades, **19**
Georgie's Alibi, **5**
Hideaway, **10**
Johnny's, **14**
Moby Dick, **11**

Ramrod, **6**
Saint, **17**
Sidestreet, **2**
Tropics, **5**
2509 West, **15**
Whale and Porpoise, **12**

$$$–$$$$ ✕ **Zan(Z)Bar.** Offering America's first taste of South African cuisine, Zan(Z)Bar is also a study in safari-style decorating, with leopard-print tablecloths and authentic African masks. The menu changes regularly but might feature crispy broiled African snook from Lake Victoria with a garlic-butter dipping sauce, speckled rice, and vegetables. ⊠ *602 Las Olas Blvd.,* ☎ *954/767–3377.*

$$–$$$ ✕ **Splash.** Set inside the Beach Place shopping center, this noisy, see-and-be-seen eatery offers such distinctive fare as spinach salad with fried oysters, apple-smoked bacon, walnuts, blue cheese, and roasted corn-cranberry dressing; and jerk pork over black bean stew with banana-chili chutney. ⊠ *17 S. Atlantic Blvd.,* ☎ *954/467–3663.*

$$–$$$ ✕ **Victoria Park.** For the price, you won't find a more romantic and gay-friendly top-notch restaurant in Fort Lauderdale. The menu is eclectic but simple; a highlight is spicy Jamaican-style pork loin dipped in Caribbean spices, grilled, and served on a bed of mashed potatoes. ⊠ *900 N.E. 20th Ave.,* ☎ *954/764–6868.*

$–$$ ✕ **Casablanca Café.** This affordable Mediterranean café draws a mix of tourists and locals with its sandwiches, salads, and seafood, and its enticing tropical drinks. Dine either on the brick patio or inside by the long bar. ⊠ *3049 Alhambra St.,* ☎ *954/764–3500.*

$ ✕ **Floridian.** This 24-hour quasi-diner is packed morning, noon, and night with every imaginable type. The chatty waitresses whip around with amazing speed and agility, dishing with the regulars. Even by diner standards, the food can be a little greasy, but when you're starving at 3 AM, you'll be glad this place exists. ⊠ *1410 E. Las Olas Blvd.,* ☎ *954/463–4041. No credit cards.*

Wilton Manors

$$ ✕ **Legends Café.** Near popular bars, Legends is a mostly gay restaurant whose dining rooms immortalize gay icons such as Barbra, Cher, and Madonna. Moderate prices, a cheerful staff, and great food—cashew chicken, mussels in white wine sauce—make this a good choice for both women and men. BYOB. ⊠ *1560 N.E. 4th Ave.,* ☎ *954/467–2233.*

$$ ✕ **Tropics.** A favorite piano cabaret, Tropics also offers better food than most gay restaurants. The menu emphasizes Continental fare, such as a prosciutto pocket starter—a pastry stuffed with prosciutto, apples, walnuts, and mozzarella—or such entrées as chicken breast stuffed with spinach and artichokes. ⊠ *2000 Wilton Dr.,* ☎ *954/537–6000.*

Elsewhere

$$–$$$ ✕ **Solo.** One of the best restaurants in the Arts and Science District, Solo is a classic candlelit trattoria with stucco walls, hand-painted plates, and soft music—very romantic. Of the traditional Italian offerings, try baked ziti with peas and mozzarella or one of the gourmet pizzas. ⊠ *208 S.W. 2nd St.,* ☎ *954/525–7656.*

$$ ✕ **Hi-Life Café.** Of Fort Lauderdale's gay-oriented restaurants, Hi-Life has the most devoted following. Cozy, quaint, and simply decorated, the eatery focuses on sensibly priced fresh pastas, seafood and poultry grills, bountiful salads, and addictive appetizers—try the grilled bacon-wrapped jalapeños stuffed with shrimp and cheese. ⊠ *3000 N. Federal Hwy.,* ☎ *954/563–1395.*

$–$$ ✕ **Sukhothai.** Tucked in the back of the otherwise dull Gateway Shopping Center, in Victoria Park, Sukhothai is a surprisingly chic Thai restaurant with excellent food spiced to order. The house specialty, Siamese lobster with red curry sauce, rarely disappoints. ⊠ *1930 E. Sunrise Blvd.,* ☎ *954/764–0148.*

$ ✕ **Jalisco.** Jalisco specializes in authentic Spanish, Mexican, and Latin cooking; specialties include the Mexican stir fry (chicken strips and veggies with a "secret" ginger sauce over rice) and the chiles rellenos. ⊠ *700 N. Federal Hwy.,* ☎ *954/462–9695.*

$ ✕ Lester's. Fierce club kids, burly truck drivers, and some even burlier drag queens mix it up at this neon '50s-style diner with a fabulous wait-staff right out of an episode of *Alice*. The food (your usual array of burgers, eggs, club sandwiches, shakes) comes in hefty portions. ⊠ *250 Rte. 84,* ☎ *954/525–5641.*

Coffeehouse Culture

Pride Factory. The favorite queer general store of Broward County also has a great coffeehouse that's quite popular with both lesbians and gay men. ⊠ *400 N. Federal Blvd.,* ☎ *954/463–6600.*

SCENES

Fort Lauderdale has nearly 30 gay bars, the majority of them uncrowded neighborhood clones. But you'll also find three big dance clubs, a terrific video bar, a country-western club, a very popular dyke disco, several piano cabarets, a few strip joints, and some of the most popular leather bars in Florida. For the most part, locals are extremely friendly and outgoing and exhibit little of the attitude or intensity common in South Beach.

Besides the clubs and bars listed below, drop by the **Gold Coast Roller Rink** (⊠ 2604 S. Federal Hwy., ☎ 954/523–6783) for the very popular lesbian and gay roller-skating party (Tuesdays from 8 PM until midnight).

Prime Suspects

Adventures. It's only a 15- to 20-minute drive north to Pompano Beach and one of the best gay country-western clubs in southern Florida. This is a big, rowdy place with good music, a laid-back crowd (that usually consists of homesick country guys and gals who have relocated here from parts twangy), and free dance lessons many nights. If you're too chicken to join the fun, mingle away or plop down on a bale of hay and watch the action. The down-home cooking here is pretty decent, too. ⊠ *303 S.W. 6th St., Pompano Beach,* ☎ *954/782–9577. Crowd: 70/30 m/f, mostly 30s and 40s, big cowboy hats, big boots, big belt buckles, and sometimes big hair, very down-to-earth.*

Bill and Jerry's Filling Station. This quintessential neighborhood hang-out is the home of one of the city's top happy hours. The name reflects the owners' affection for old-fashioned filling station memorabilia—vintage gas tanks, spare tires, hubcaps, license plates, and gas company logo flags; even the front door handles are fashioned out of gas pumps. ⊠ *1243 N.E. 11th Ave.,* ☎ *954/525–9403. Crowd: mostly men, 35 to 65, regular joes, unpretentious.*

Chardees. Among older gay men (and to a lesser degree lesbians), Chardees is queen of the hill—the city's unofficial gray gay club (locally poked fun at as "God's Waiting Room"). It looks like the sort of dinner hall your grandparents might love—complete with neon, mirrors, and glass bricks, and handsome, sharply dressed waiters—only here everybody's queer. Adjacent to the large dining room are a comfy piano lounge and a stage offering light music and cabaret. ⊠ *2209 Wilton Dr.,* ☎ *954/563–1800. Crowd: 80/20 m/f, mostly over 40 and many over 60, friendly, lots of golf shirts and checked slacks.*

Club Cathode Ray. In terms of setting, ambience, attitude, and clientele, Cathode Ray is one of the nicest video bars in the state. Smack in the middle of ritzy Las Olas Boulevard, it overlooks a picturesque canal. Inside is a homey, two-tiered tavern, long and narrow with tall mirrors and a few video screens. For a breath of air, head outside to the shaded canal-side patio, a romantic spot for a cup of conversation. Happy hour is a big to-do. ⊠ *1105 E. Las Olas Blvd.,* ☎ *954/462–8611. Crowd: mostly male, 20s and 30s, professional, guppie, very few steroid queens.*

Club Electra. The city's club of the moment offers an urbane disco experience. Many patrons head here after hitting the early evening cocktail bars and later move on to the Copa or Saint; just as many, however, make a night of Club Electra. The light and sound system are first-rate, there's both a high-tech dance floor and a spacious, relaxing patio, and the club is in a touristy section of town. Best of all, the staff is courteous and friendly, with hot bartenders, both male and female. ⊠ *1600 S.E. 15th Ave.,* ☎ *954/764–8447. Crowd: 75/25 m/f, mostly 20s and 30s, slightly upscale, lots of tourists, from guppies to neopunks.*

The Copa. This club just south of the city limits is the most famous in Broward County, partly because it's close to Miami, and partly because it's open until 4 on weekends (two hours later than most competitors). The music here is fabulous; the layout allows room for mingling, cruising, and dancing; and the L-shape patio and cabaret are pleasant (the occasionally awful drag act notwithstanding). People come to have fun and get sleazy (there's a small room with porn flicks to one side). ⊠ *2800 S. Federal Hwy.,* ☎ *954/463–1507. Crowd: 75/25 m/f, 20s to 40s, mixed racially, club gear, flashy attire.*

825. This sprawling stripper-and-hustler joint has two distinct sections: In front you'll find a tired but engaging cocktail lounge and piano bar right out of a B movie; in back is the main event—a lounge with a stage and benches, around which very young men with bulging muscles mix it up alongside older men with bulging wallets. Later (usually around 10), there's lap-dancing, when a more direct examination of the goods occurs. ⊠ *825 E. Sunrise Blvd.,* ☎ *954/524–3333. Crowd: male, under 25 and over 55, rough trade.*

End Up. Because it's west of the city limits, this ramshackle bar serves liquor until 4 AM and is open even later (the doors usually don't even open until midnight). If you haven't figured it out yet, everybody "ends up" here when there's nowhere else to go. It's a favorite haunt of bartenders after they finish their shifts. ⊠ *3521 W. Broward Blvd.,* ☎ *954/584–9301. Crowd: mostly male, all ages, bleary eyed, cruisy, always picking among the leftovers.*

Georgie's Alibi. This slick upscale video bar with a sports theme opened in summer 1997 in Wilton Manors, further establishing the neighborhood as the region's hub of queer nightlife. Georgie's has filled a void in Fort Lauderdale's gay scene, providing a classy but unstuffy space where cruising and casual conversation are equally appropriate. The club is the most crowed between 7 and 11 each night. ⊠ *2266 Wilton Dr.,* ☎ *954/ 565–2526. Crowd: 80/20 m/f, all ages, affable, easy-going, somewhat professional but still diverse in dress and style.*

Moby Dick. Northern Fort Lauderdale's main cruise bar employs a stable of enticing male dancers, has remarkably cheap drink specials, and pulls in a lusty energetic crowd. ⊠ *4200 N. Federal Hwy.,* ☎ *954/568– 2823. Crowd: mostly male, mixed ages, action-oriented.*

Ramrod. The hard-edged, sexy Ramrod is a great leather bar. It's not large, and dim mining lights, chains, candles, and steel bars give it an cozier feel. Gargoyles and Tom of Finland art further enhance the Gothic dungeon aesthetic. There's no dance floor, but patrons cluster in several areas, including a small enclosed space with a pool table and a patio out back. A leather shop sells gay mags, lube, toys, and clothing. ⊠ *1508 N.E. 4th Ave.,* ☎ *954/763–8219. Crowd: mostly male, mixed ages; mostly leather but some rubber, uniforms, and denim; on the make.*

Saint. This major player in the club scene caters to a diverse, although still predominantly male, crowd. The owners spend big bucks on the decor, which they change often. As you enter you'll find a narrow video bar with relatively quiet music and a smoked-glass wall separating it from the rest of the club. A second room has a stage, an eight-seat table designed specifically for table-dancing, another bar, and plenty of room for standing and modeling (which the men do here with great tenacity). The third room, the largest, has a huge dance floor with more dancers strutting their wares on wooden boxes, and yet another bar. ⊠ *1000 State Rd. 84 (S.W. 24th St.),* ☎ *954/525–7883. Crowd: mostly male, mostly 20s and 30s, very mixed in dress and style, from club kid to preppy to leather bear.*

2509 West. This new lesbian disco with pool tables, plenty of lounge space, and a large dance floor opened in early 1998. On busy nights, many women head for the landscaped patio out back. The location, just west of I–95, is a drag, but there's ample secured parking. ⊠ *2509 W. Broward Blvd.,* ☎ *954/791–2509. Crowd: 70/30 f/m, mostly 20s to 40s; more lipsrick than not but with many exceptions; unpretentious.*

Whale and Porpoise. It's all about '50s-inspired kitsch at this drag-and-karaoke mecca that looks something like the VIP lounge you'd expect to find on *The Love Boat.* There are two levels of plush seating, dark-wood railings, low ceilings, brass tables, mirrored walls, and copper reliefs of whales and porpoises—it adds up to a quirky ambience. ⊠ *2750 E. Oakland Park Blvd.,* ☎ *954/565–2750. Crowd: 60/40 m/f, mostly 20s to 40s, local, come as you are.*

Neighborhood Haunts

West of downtown, **Boots** (⊠ 901 S.W. 27th Ave., ☎ 954/792–9177) gets a leather, Levi's, and uniform crowd—seriously cruisy. The **Cubby Hole** (⊠ 823 N. Federal Hwy., ☎ 954/728–9001) is sometimes teased for being a leather-wannabe, but it still draws a loyal following. **Everglades** (⊠ 1931 S. Federal Hwy., ☎ 954/462–9165) attracts less leather and more Levi's; it's best on Sundays, when even nonlocals drop by. As we headed to press, the folks at Everglades were planning to open a new dance club in Wilton Manors beside Georgie's Alibi.

Bushes (⊠ 3038 N. Federal Hwy., ☎ 954/561–1724) is a small, narrow locals bar. Not only is **Tropics** (⊠ 2000 Wilton Dr., ☎ 954/537–6000) a great restaurant (*see* Eats, *above*), it's a nice alternative to some of the rowdier clubs—relax in the cocktail lounge and listen to live piano cabarets. Tropics attracts more women than some of the others.

You never know who you'll run into at the mostly male hustlery **Bus Stop** (⊠ 2203 S. Federal Hwy., ☎ 954/761–1782). Hang out on the semi-enclosed deck with local guys at the **Hideaway** (⊠ 2022 N.E. 18th St., ☎ 954/566–8622) or stay inside for a game of pool and watch the nightly surprises come out on stage. **Johnny's** (⊠ 1116 W. Broward Blvd., ☎ 954/522–5931) has two bars—one for watching and stroking the lap dancers and the other for meeting and groping the lap dancers.

Action

Catalog X (⊠ 850 N.E. 13th St., ☎ 954/524–5050) has 8,000 square feet of videos, toys, and magazines, as well as nonerotic lesbigay books, CDs, and T-shirts. **Club Fort Lauderdale** (⊠ 400 W. Broward Blvd., ☎ 954/525–3344) is a clean facility, extensive fitness areas, a large pool, and plenty of sundecks. **Clubhouse II** (⊠ 2650 E. Oakland Park Blvd., ☎ 954/566–6750) is a hit with bears, leather men, and the over-40 set.

SLEEPS

Fort Lauderdale's accommodations scene has improved vastly over the past decade. Several older resorts have been reinvented by entrepreneurs as predominantly gay resorts. Interior Fort Lauderdale also has about a half dozen gay-oriented guest houses or small resorts. You won't find as many good-quality smaller gay accommodations in Fort Lauderdale as you will in Key West, but you will find lower rates. Several chain resorts along Route A1A, however, have received major renovations as the city's tourist base has matured and improved, and there are nice options in every price category.

For price ranges, *see* lodging Chart A at the front of this guide.

Hotels and Resorts

$$$–$$$$ ▫ **Embassy Suites Hotel.** Rates push this hotel into a high price category, but since rooms are ideally suited for two couples, they offer solid value. Every suite has a kitchenette, a large bedroom (many have water views), and a substantial living room (with a foldout sofa). ⊠ *1100 S.E. 17th St., 33316,* ☎ *954/527–2700 or 800/362–2779,* ✉ *954/760–7202. 361 rooms. Restaurant, pool.*

$$$ ▫ **Radisson Bahia Mar Beach Resort.** This sprawling seaside resort on Route A1A has recently refurbished rooms (most with views either of the ocean or the Intracoastal Waterway), top-notch amenities, lush grounds, and beach access. It's upscale without going over the top. ⊠ *801 Seabreeze Blvd., 33316,* ☎ *954/764–2233 or 800/333–3333,* ✉ *954/523–5424. 300 rooms. Restaurant, pool, health club.*

$$–$$$ ▫ **Doubletree Oceanfront Hotel.** This boxy midrise hotel on the beach has midsized, tastefully decorated rooms with beautiful new bathrooms, some of them with whirlpool tubs. An ocean view room usually costs only about $10 more than a city view. ⊠ *440 Seabreeze Blvd., 33304,* ☎ *954/ 524–8733 or 800/222–8733,* ✉ *954/524–8733. 230 rooms. Restaurant, pool, exercise room.*

$$ ▫ **The Bahama Hotel.** The Bahama probably gets more family than most properties. Smack in the middle of the oceanside action, it's home to the patio restaurant, the Deck, and it has a huge tanning area. Although it looks like just a standard tourist-class hotel from the outside, the Bahama has attractive rooms, many with four-poster beds and large kitchens. ⊠ *401 N. Atlantic Blvd., 33304,* ☎ *954/467–7315 or 800/622–9995,* ✉ *954/467–7319. 70 rooms. Restaurant, pool.*

Guest Houses and Small Resorts

$$$ ▫ **Royal Palms Resort.** Charming proprietor Richard Gray transformed this once-sagging budget motel into one of the nation's top gay get-aways. The secluded complex consists of 12 cheerfully furnished rooms (four are full suites). In addition to climate control, voice mail, and data ports, some rooms have balconies overlooking the pool, VCRs, CD players, and kitchenettes; one even has a fireplace. You can laze around the sparkling, clothing-optional grounds, walk two short blocks to the beach, or arrange for a visit from the talented masseur. Caters to a professional crowd. ⊠ *2901 Terramar St., 33304,* ☎ *954/564–6444 or 800/237–7256,* ✉ *954/564–6443, Web site www.royalpalms.com. 12 rooms with phone, TV, and private bath. Pool. Continental breakfast. Gay male.*

$$ ▫ **The Inn.** This attractive women's compound is in a pretty residential neighborhood a short drive or bike ride from the beach. The friendly innkeepers offer massage, free use of bikes, airport pick-up service, and optional sailing excursions. Everybody is treated like part of the family, and many women come back year after year. Rooms are simple and clean, but most guests prefer to lie out by the heated pool, on the clothing-optional patio. ⊠ *1520 N.E. 26th Ave., 33306,* ☎ *800/881–4814. 4 rooms with TV and private bath. Pool. Continental breakfast. Lesbian.*

$$ ▫ **La Casa del Mar.** This bed-and-breakfast offers the charm of a Cape Cod inn with the tropical feel of a Florida resort. Each room has a different theme: Try the Monet Room, laced with bright blues and yellows, or the Judy Garland Room, accented with rainbows and memorabilia and photos. Some of the largest rooms have kitchens. The inn is a two-minute

walk from the beach as well as several good restaurants. Tasty breakfasts. ✉ *3003 Granada St., 33304,* ☎ *954/467–2037 or 800/739–0009,* FAX *954/467–7439. 10 rooms with phone, TV, and private bath. Pool. Full breakfast. Mixed gay/straight.*

$–$$ 🏨 **The Blue Dolphin.** Yet another successful motel transformation, the Blue Dolphin is a lively social resort for gay men, presided over by friendly hosts. Rooms are simple, contemporary, and spacious (nicer than rooms at costlier chain hotels), with clean bathrooms and, in some cases, kitchens. ✉ *725 N. Birch Rd., 33304,* ☎ *954/565–8437 or 800/893–2583,* FAX *954/565–6015, e-mail 75372.1737@compuserve.com. 16 rooms with phone, TV, and private bath. Pool. Continental breakfast. Gay male.*

$–$$ 🏨 **The Palms on Las Olas.** On a canal by the New River Intracoastal Waterway, the Palms has extensive grounds, along with clothing-optional decks and a nice-size pool. It's a 15- to 20-minute walk from the beach, and also to shops and restaurants on Las Olas. Rooms range from basic and economically priced doubles in a motel-style building (some with kitchens) to a striking suite with a Jacuzzi, separate shower, wet bar, and direct access to the pool. The crowd is young and outgoing, with a mix of both couples and singles. ✉ *1760 E. Las Olas Blvd., 33301,* ☎ *954/462–4178 or 800/550–7656,* FAX *954/463–8544. 14 rooms with phone, TV, and private bath. Pool. Continental breakfast. Gay male.*

$–$$ 🏨 **The Rainbow Sun.** This rambling compound has a strong following among European (particularly German) men. Accommodations come in several configurations, from basic rooms to two-bedroom apartments with full kitchens. The attractive, private grounds are studded with palms, waterfalls, and fountains, and most guests take advantage of the clothing-optional policy. The drawback is the location in a dicey neighborhood in western Fort Lauderdale. ✉ *1909 S.W. 2nd St., 33312,* ☎ *954/462–6035,* FAX *954/522–2764, e-mail mribiza@aol.com. 20 rooms with phone, TV, and private bath. Pool, hot tub, exercise room. Gay male.*

$ 🏨 **Edun House.** The nicest gay budget facility, this small complex has a heated pool and exercise room, clean, contemporary guest rooms (with VCRs), and cheerful grounds. The staff is friendly and laid-back. The only drawback is being a short auto or bike ride from the beach. The name of the inn is an anagram for *nude*—indeed, guests are encouraged to dress (or undress) according to their own level of comfort. ✉ *2733 Middle River Dr., 33306,* ☎ *954/565–7775 or 800/479–1767,* FAX *954/565–7912. 4 rooms with phone, TV, and private bath; 1 apartment. Pool, exercise room. Continental breakfast. Gay male.*

$ 🏨 **Gemini House.** At the Gemini House, clothing is not an option—the resort bills itself a "no clothing zone." In the quiet residential neighborhood of Oakland Park, it is about a 15-minute drive from the beach. Rooms are pleasant and homey, and the well-landscaped grounds offer extra amenities like hammocks, a sundeck, and a poolside library. ✉ *1625 N.E. 33rd St.,* ☎ *954/568–9791 or 800/552–7115,* FAX *954/568–0617, e-mail geminihse@aol.com. 4 rooms with TV and shared bath. Pool, hot tub, exercise room. Full breakfast. Gay male.*

$ 🏨 **King Henry Arms.** Rooms here have the ambience of Lucy and Ricky's apartment—with slightly outdated furnishings—but for this price you won't find a better gay option near the beach. The hosts have created an affordable, unpretentious, and friendly hangout that gives guests the minimum of what they need to enjoy a vacation: great location, a pool and sundeck, and a social atmosphere. ✉ *543 Breakers Ave., 33304,* ☎ *954/561–0039 or 800/205–5464. 11 rooms with phone, TV, and private bath. Pool. Mostly gay male.*

THE LITTLE BLACK BOOK

At Your Fingertips

Broward County Gay Hotline (☎ 954/537–0823). **Broward County Mass Transit** (☎ 954/357–8400). **Center One** (✉ 3015 N. Ocean Blvd., Suite 111, ☎ 954/537–4111 or 800/339–2815) provides resources for persons with AIDS/HIV. **Entertainment and Attractions Hotline** (☎ 954/527–5600). **Gay/Lesbian Community Center** (✉ 1164 E. Oakland Park Blvd., ☎ 954/563–9500). **Gay & Lesbian Switchboard** (☎ 954/563–9500). **Greater Fort Lauderdale Convention & Visitors Bureau** (✉ 200 E. Las Olas Blvd., Suite 1500, Fort Lauderdale, 33301, ☎ 954/765–4466 or 800/227–8669). **Health Link** (☎ 954/565–8284) is a resource line for information on AIDS, cancer, and other health issues. **PWA Coalition of Broward County** (✉ 2302 N.E. 7th Ave., ☎ 954/565–9119). **Women in Network** (☎ 954/564–4946). **XS Magazine** (alternative newspaper with good arts and dining coverage, ☎ 954/523–9797, e-mail xsmag@xso.com). **Yellow Cab** (☎ 954/565–5400).

Gay Media

For the best nightlife coverage, stick with the Fort Lauderdale–based weekly, **Hot Spots** (☎ 954/928–1862), a colorful magazine with listings on South and Central Florida, plus a few gossip columns and news clips. **Scoop** (☎ 954/561–9707, e-mail scoop@scoopmag.com) is Fort Lauderdale's main gay news weekly; it also has extensive bar and cultural coverage. **TWN** (*The Weekly News,* ☎ 305/757–6333, e-mail info@twnmag.com) is a similar option, with weekly gay arts, entertainment, and news; it gives equal coverage to Dade and Broward counties. The monthly magazine **Unique** (☎ 954/463–8640), a high-quality production with color photos, is based in Broward County but also has regional coverage and good articles for and by lesbians and gay men. For news of weekly events and support groups, pick up **The Center Voice** (☎ 954/563–9500), published by the lesbian and gay community center.

BOOKSTORES

Once more of a gay gift and greeting card store, the **Pride Factory** (✉ 710 W. Broward Blvd., ☎ 954/463–6600) has increased its selection of lesbigay books and periodicals and is now one of the best sources for such titles in the region; it's also an excellent source for movies (porn and otherwise). Also with a significant gay and lesbian section is **Borders** (✉ 2240 E. Sunrise Blvd., ☎ 954/566–6335), a branch of the national megachain; it has plenty of friendly employees and a queer-popular café.

WORKING OUT

Even if you don't consider bathhouses to be legitimate workout facilities, you'll like **Club Fort Lauderdale** (✉ 400 W. Broward Blvd., ☎ 954/525–3344). While it has its cruisy sections, it's also a new, clean facility with good fitness equipment. The **Zoo** (✉ 3001 S.E. 5th St., ☎ 954/525–7010), by the beach, gets a mix of straights and gays.

14 *Out in* Houston

AS THE 1970S drew to a close, an oil boom vastly increased Houston's coffers, and it seemed poised to become the most vibrant city in the South. Shimmering new skyscrapers rose one after another, and the ritzy western neighborhood of River Oaks witnessed the construction of one mammoth mansion after another. But the oil bust of the 1980s brought Houston to its knees: The infrastructure crumbled, businesses folded, and Houstonians fled for greener pastures. Only in the early '90s did the Bayou City begin to awaken from its economic doldrums.

Now, with Houston back in full swing, residents seem neither cocky nor contrite. Having lived through the '80s they can beat just about anything, but they also know how quickly the tables can turn.

A hybrid of Southern and Western cultures, Houston is situated at the confluence of the Oak and Buffalo bayous (what better marries the Wild West with the Deep South than the words "buffalo" and "bayou"?) near the Gulf of Mexico. A thriving port city, Houston has a diverse population. Many Cajuns and Creoles live here, as well as significant numbers of Latin Americans, Asians, African-Americans, and Greeks. Outsiders themselves at one time, most residents warm quickly to newcomers and visitors.

In the '70s this spirit of tolerance helped to foster the growth of a gay ghetto—Montrose. During the past 20 years Montrose has grown from a loud, lusty, and in many ways downcast district into a haven of restored homes and trendy restaurants and coffeehouses. Plenty of straights have settled here, too, and gays have begun moving elsewhere. As downtown's old warehouses and defunct office buildings reopen as residential lofts, a good many upwardly mobile gays and lesbians are moving there. And despite a lack of national recognition, Houston's queer community continues to play a vital role in the city's commercial, social, and arts scenes.

THE LAY OF THE LAND

Houston, the fourth-largest city in the United States, is marked by striking contrasts. In many sections it looks as if time stood still in the late '70s. Elsewhere, rows of storefront windows are boarded over, victims of the economic downturn in the '80s. Then there are the pockets that have been developed in the '90s—office buildings and swank shopping plazas. What's odd is that these three urban visions appear in combination anywhere you look. There is no zoning: Skyscrapers rub shoulders with vacant lots; the patio of the trendiest eatery sits across from a Jiffy Lube; and an avenue of stately Colonial Revival homes gives way to tenements. Despite these aesthetic blemishes, Houston has acquired an air of accessibility. All cities regard themselves as melting pots; Houston can truly make this claim.

Montrose

Plenty of gays have settled into less-expensive areas such as the Heights, White Oak Bayou, the Old Sixth Ward, and downtown, but **Montrose** remains ground zero. Montrose is about midway between downtown and the Galleria, with intersecting Westheimer Road and Montrose Boulevard its main commercial spines.

This is a pleasant but hardly swank area—a hodgepodge of restored early 20th-century architecture along with more recent experiments in urban design—some tasteful, some not. Walking along these tree-shaded, quiet streets, you'd never know you're a short drive from downtown. Montrose is low-key and modest in most respects—guppies, artists, professionals, and students live here, and Houston's outgoing and welcoming nature is more than evident.

Along Westheimer Road, from roughly the 1500 block to the 2300 block, is a memorable **antiques row.** The blocks just south of Westheimer Road and east of Montrose make up the **Westmoreland Addition,** plotted in 1902 on a 12-block grid and consisting of hundreds of late-Victorian and Colonial Revival homes.

Nearby cultural sights include the **Menil Collection** (✉ 1515 Sul Ross St., ☎ 713/525−9400), with works by Warhol, Léger, Picasso, Braque, Matisse, and Twombly in a space designed in 1987 by Renzo Piano. The **Rothko Chapel** (✉ 3900 Yupon St., ☎ 713/524−9839) contains 14 large-scale Rothko paintings commissioned for the chapel. A peaceful reflecting pool and plaza are punctuated by Barnet Newman's sculpture *Broken Obelisk*. The **Byzantine Fresco Chapel** (✉ Branard and Yupon Sts., ☎ 713/525−9400) opened in 1997 and showcases two 13th-century frescoes rescued from war-torn Cyprus.

Downtown

The most striking of Houston's downtown office towers is I. M. Pei's 75-story **Texas Commerce Tower** (✉ 600 Travis St.). The blocks immediately north and west are at the center of the neighborhood's comeback, which was first felt on a dramatic scale in 1997. Although it was hard hit by the '80s economy, the area continued to draw people in to Houston's first-rate symphony, opera, ballet, and theaters. Recently, many of the stately warehouses and buildings near this arts district have been converted into residential space. The 1997 condo-refitting of the historic **Rice Hotel** (✉ Main St. at Texas Ave.) has perhaps attracted the most attention; it is where President Kennedy spent the final night of his life, and it stood vacant from 1977 until its makeover.

Bayou Place (✉ 520 Texas Ave., ☎ 713/229−8990) opened in late 1997. This restored building has restaurants, bars, and a theater. This space complements nearby existing entertainment districts like **Market Square** and **Allen's Landing,** site of the city's first settlement and now a complex of restaurants, shops, and bars. Future projects include the proposed construction of a vintage-style stadium for Major League Baseball's Houston Astros and the continued beautification of the **Buffalo Bayou Waterfront,** which will soon be laced with landscaped trails and bike paths.

Sam Houston Park and the Old Sixth Ward

Sam Houston Park (✉ Bagby at Lamar Sts., ☎ 713/655−1912) sits literally in the shadows of downtown. With a fascinating collection of historic buildings moved here from other sites in Houston, the park offers an impression of the city's mid-19th-century beginnings; one-hour tours of the seven homes and one church are available.

Northwest of the park, across I−45, the **Old Sixth Ward** is one of Houston's eight National Historic Districts. Many gays and lesbians have migrated here, attracted by the challenge of restoring small, relatively affordable, Greek Revival and Victorian cottages. Kane Street and Washington Avenue are two of the most picturesque streets.

Museum District and Texas Medical Center

Houston is the most culturally endowed city in the Southwest and the Deep South. The **Museum District,** which is south of downtown, begins at the northern tip of **Hermann Park.** Don't miss the recently expanded **Museum of Fine Arts** (⊠ 1000 Bissonnet St., ☎ 713/639–7300), whose 27,000 works include a concentration of Impressionist, as well as Italian and Spanish Renaissance, pieces. Although it contains no permanent collection, the **Contemporary Arts Museum** (⊠ 5126 Montrose Blvd., ☎ 713/526–3129) hosts important temporary exhibitions.

A few blocks east, the **Holocaust Museum** (⊠ 5401 Caroline St., ☎ 713/789–9898) has a sculpture garden, a memorial area, changing exhibits (which sometimes touch on the persecution of gays and lesbians during World War II), and a theater in which oral histories are powerfully rendered. Just south, at the northern tip of the park, the **Houston Museum of Natural Science** (⊠ 1 Hermann Circle Dr., ☎ 713/639–4600) is the nation's fourth-most-visited museum. Check out the Burke Baker Planetarium, which has a 25,000-square-foot tropical rain forest complete with butterflies. (No joke: Spray Calvin Klein's *Obsession* on your shoulder and the butterflies won't leave you alone!)

The south end of the park is dominated by the **Houston Zoological Gardens** (⊠ 1513 N. MacGregor St., ☎ 713/525–3300), the campus of **Rice University,** and the 650-acre **Texas Medical Center,** the world's largest concentration of hospitals and medical research facilities. A major focus at the center is biotechnology, including cutting-edge AIDS and cancer research. Although you can't tour the Medical Center, consider visiting the **Museum of Health and Medical Science** (⊠ 1515 Hermann Dr., ☎ 713/790–1838), which is near the Museum of Natural Science. The museum recently introduced a permanent exhibit that helps explain the workings of the human immune system and how it's affected by HIV/AIDS and other viruses. Clever exhibits actually allow you to "tour" the human body and learn up close how it works.

River Oaks and the Galleria

Head west of downtown and Montrose via Westheimer Road to reach **Uptown,** which encompasses the **Galleria** and snazzy **Post Oak.** The Galleria is made up of three mammoth shopping malls packed with every type of upscale boutique known to humankind.

Between Uptown and Montrose are **River Oaks** and the mildly cruisy but sometimes dangerous **Memorial Park.** Hang around in the park and you run the risk of being mugged or bumping into former President George Bush in jogging shorts (it's hard to say which is the more terrifying prospect). Longtime resident Miss Ima Hogg—heir to a vast fortune and bearer of a highly embarrassing name—left the public her magnificent River Oaks home, **Bayou Bend** (⊠ 1 Westcott St., ☎ 713/520–2600; reservations required), which sits on a scenic curve along the Buffalo Bayou.

GETTING AROUND

With its maze of freeways and clotted two- and four-lane roads, Houston can be a frustrating place to drive during the workday. Westheimer Road is narrow and overused, particularly in the Montrose district. Nevertheless, an automobile is your best bet. You'll need one to get from your hotel to any of the good bars and restaurants. The city has the third-largest cab fleet in America, and drivers are consistently helpful and reliable.

EATS

Thanks to its southern, Cajun, southwestern, Mexican, and Latin American accents, Houston is a food lover's city. And although all of those regional cuisines are known for heavy and/or spicy fare, light contemporary cuisine is also plentiful. Restaurants in Montrose have a gay following, and those in the downtown theater district, River Oaks, and the Galleria tend to be gay-friendly. Many gay bars serve good, basic pub grub, and most have a weekly "steak out," to which you can bring your own meat (so to speak)—generous sides are usually provided. These are fun, and outsiders are welcome. In addition to the two excellent Mexican eateries reviewed below, **Ninfa's** (✉ 2704 Navigation St., ☎ 713/228–1175) in East Houston cranks queer on Sunday afternoons.

For price ranges, *see* dining Chart B at the front of this guide.

$$$$ ✗ **River Oaks Grill.** Probably the gay-friendliest of the city's top-tier restaurants, this debonair establishment with the feel of a hunt club and the tinkle of piano keys in the air specializes in nouvelle but untrendy American and Continental fare such as red snapper with crab-laced pico de gallo. ✉ 2630 Westheimer Rd., ☎ 713/520–1738.

$$$–$$$$ ✗ **Churrascos.** Though mired in a poorly designed shopping plaza with never enough parking, Churrascos is one of the city's hot spots. Hanging plants, bamboo, dark-wood beams, and clean white walls provide an elegant setting for fine Latin American cuisine, like charcoal-grilled tenderloins with garlic sauce. ✉ 2055 Westheimer Rd., ☎ 713/527–8300.

$$$–$$$$ ✗ **La Griglia.** In chichi River Oaks, La Griglia is part of a local syndicate of exceptional, though pricey, Italian trattorias. The design is as impressive as the food: a cavernous dining room painted with dazzling colors. For dinner, any of the rotisserie chicken dishes or wood-grilled steaks will do the trick. ✉ 2002 W. Gray St., ☎ 713/526–4700.

$$–$$$ ✗ **Boulevard Bistrot.** One of the slickest restaurants in Montrose, the Bistrot sits on a promenade of boutiques and has a bright dining room in which steak, pastas, grilled chicken, salmon, flounder, and other tempting possibilities are jazzed up with chef Monica Pope's nationally acclaimed New American preparations. ✉ 4319 Montrose Blvd., ☎ 713/524–6922.

$$–$$$ ✗ **Café Anthony's.** Yet another spot on Montrose Boulevard serving designer pizzas (though they *are* excellent), Café Anthony's is also distinguished by its fine contemporary seafood dishes. The setting is cheerful, with walls of floor-to-ceiling windows and an outside deck overlooking the homo-happy sidewalk. ✉ 4315 Montrose Blvd., ☎ 713/529–8000.

$$–$$$ ✗ **Café Noche.** Not your ordinary Tex-Mex eatery, Café Noche is a festive Mexican restaurant with a somewhat daring chef (note the Portobello mushroom fajitas). It's best to dine in the mercilessly adorable courtyard out front; a foliage-choked, black-iron gate hides the mundanity of Montrose Boulevard. ✉ 2409 Montrose Blvd., ☎ 713/529–2409.

$$–$$$ ✗ **La Strada.** With an ebullient atmosphere but a serious menu, La Strada serves fine, slightly trendy Italian dishes at dinner, including good steak, chicken, and fish grills. The staff is fey and friendly. This place will get you in the mood for bar-hopping later on. ✉ 322 Westheimer Rd., ☎ 713/523–1014; also ✉ 5161 San Felipe Rd., ☎ 713/850–9999.

$$–$$$ ✗ **Ruggles Grill.** Ruggles is highly popular with the queer community. People come because of the colorful (and pretty) staff and the Italy-meets-New Mexico menu, which includes clever creations like red-snapper and crab chowder, and black-bean pasta. The Sunday brunch is legendary. ✉ 903 Westheimer Rd., ☎ 713/524–3839.

$$ ✗ **Solero.** The culinary cornerstone of downtown's comeback, this elaborately restored high-ceiling space—with 1880s architectural details intact—serves the best (well, actually the only) tapas in Houston. Come either to eat or watch the beautiful people devour white-bean and ham

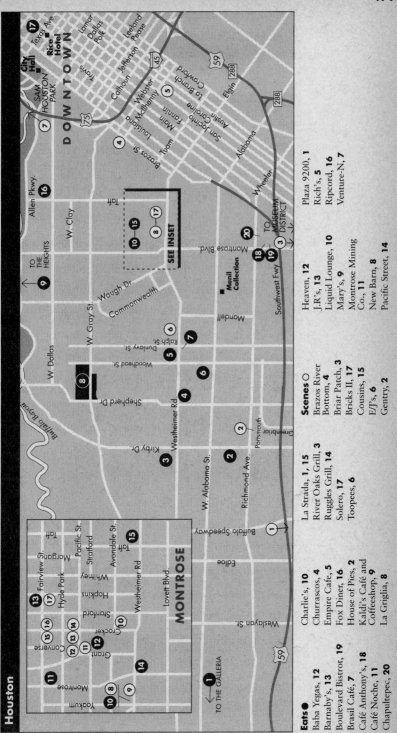

Houston

Eats ●
Baba Yegas, **12**
Barnaby's, **13**
Boulevard Bistrot, **19**
Brasil Café, **7**
Café Anthony's, **18**
Café Noche, **11**
Chapultepec, **20**

Charlie's, **10**
Churrascos, **4**
Empire Cafe, **5**
Fox Diner, **16**
House of Pies, **2**
Kaldi's Café and
Coffeeshop, **9**
La Griglia, **8**

La Strada, **1, 15**
River Oaks Grill, **3**
Ruggles Grill, **14**
Solero, **17**
Toopees, **6**

Scenes ○
Brazos River
Bottom, **4**
Briar Patch, **3**
Bricks II, **17**
Cousins, **15**
E/J's, **6**
Gentry, **2**

Heaven, **12**
J.R's, **13**
Liquid Lounge, **10**
Mary's, **9**
Montrose Mining
Co, **11**
New Barn, **8**
Pacific Street, **14**

Plaza 9200, **1**
Rich's, **5**
Ripcord, **16**
Venture-N, **7**

soup, sliced *Manchego* (Spanish sheep's) cheese with apples, or pan-fried snapper cakes with spicy roasted-pepper sauce. ⊠ *910 Prairie Ave.,* ☎ *713/227–2665.*

$–$$ ✕ **Baba Yegas.** Steps from the queer bar strip, this très gay eatery sprawls with sunny dining rooms and shaded decks, which are constantly abuzz with chatter and gossip. Decent burgers, many veggie items, and other light dishes are served, but the ambience is the big draw. ⊠ *2607 Grant St.,* ☎ *713/522–0042.*

$–$$ ✕ **Fox Diner.** The "New American diner" concept seldom lives up to the tasty success of this queer-popular spot on the northern edge of Montrose. Warm and attentive service, a chic dining room, and sublime creations like warm-grilled tuna steak with tomato-calamata olive relish make for a wonderful dining experience. ⊠ *905 Taft St.,* ☎ *713/523–5369.*

$ ✕ **Barnaby's.** This tatty, down-home diner notable for its rainbow-flag chimney and facade painted with yellow, blue, and red stars is a favorite for casual pub food and filling breakfasts. ⊠ *604 Fairview St.,* ☎ *713/522–0106.*

$ ✕ **Chapultepec.** A popular Montrose hangout, Chapultepec is a cut above most Tex-Mex places in the area—great salsa, chili rellenos, and margaritas that'll purse your lips. The best seating is on the festive but noisy tiled front porch. Open 24 hours. ⊠ *813 Richmond Ave.,* ☎ *713/522–2365.*

$ ✕ **Charlie's.** There are no pretensions at this big ol' diner, just droves of big ol' fags—and butch ones at that. The decor is perfunctory (Tiffany-style lamps are a standout) and the food is so-so, but there isn't a better place on Westheimer to dish with your friends. ⊠ *1100 Westheimer Rd.,* ☎ *713/522–3332.*

$ ✕ **Empire Café.** An old gas station along Westheimer Road's antiques row has been transformed into a hip café offering great pizzas, hearty frittatas, and such breakfast treats as hot polenta with honey-cream and toasted almonds. The cute, curved dining room has high ceilings and funky overhead lamps. ⊠ *1732 Westheimer Rd.,* ☎ *713/528–5282.*

$ ✕ **House of Pies.** This circa-mid-'60s pie diner has, for much of its tenure, been referred to affectionately as "House of Guys." Open 24 hours, it's especially busy after the bars close. Everything is no-frills (meat loaf is a typical special); be sure to order one of the freshly baked pies. ⊠ *3112 Kirby Dr.,* ☎ *713/528–3816.*

Coffeehouse Culture

Brasil Café. The crunchiest of local coffeehouses, this is also an art gallery. You can dine in the tree-shaded courtyard, enjoying such healthful dishes as mesquite-smoked turkey sandwich or baba ganoush. Dozens of vegetable and fruit juice blends are on tap, and there's beer and wine. ⊠ *2604 Dunlavy St.,* ☎ *713/528–1993.*

Kaldi's Café and Coffeeshop. This Heights antiques emporium-cum-restaurant prints its daily menu on brown paper bags and plasters them to the walls. The food itself is somewhat less primitive—sandwiches and salads with gourmet ingredients. Very boho, with poetry readings and open-mike nights. ⊠ *250 W. 19th St.,* ☎ *713/802–2246.*

Toopees. Vinyl booths, Formica tables, and a '60s-looking building belie what is actually a funky coffeehouse with good café fare, exotic beers, and plenty of space for lounging. A nice alternative to the bars, Toopees is especially popular with lesbians. ⊠ *1830 W. Alabama St.,* ☎ *713/522–7662.*

SCENES

Houston has no shortage of bars—nearly 30—most of them small, divey, and catering to a local crowd. The main cluster is in an ordinary-looking residential area east of Montrose Boulevard and north of Westheimer Road; with a few exceptions the bars have predominantly male followings, but the Plaza 9200 complex in southwest Houston is huge and caters largely to women.

Houston bar culture has a raw, gritty character that draws together the city's two strongest (though not mutually exclusive) factions of bar-goers: fans of leather and fans of drag. Many Montrose hangouts still look a lot like they did 15 years ago—dimly lit, the walls coated with chipped paint, the windows shuttered, the floors covered with grubby linoleum. Although bars stop serving liquor at 2 AM, the Montrose Mining Co. and the Ripcord serve coffee and soft drinks until 4 on Friday and Saturday. After-hours clubs pop up frequently; they open, close, but move so rapidly it's impossible to review them. Ask around.

Prime Suspects

Brazos River Bottom (BRB). Hopping for many years and a great place to go if you're new in town, BRB has a good-size bar and two-stepping and line-dancing some nights. On Sunday hundreds cram in for what's arguably the best steakout in town. ⊠ *2400 Brazos St.,* ☎ *713/528–9192. Crowd: mostly male but very female-friendly, all ages and types.*

Briar Patch. The city's main piano bar, this is a nice place to take a date, get to know locals, and flee the intensity of Montrose—it's a 10-minute drive south. It gets campier during the drag shows. The only problem is the soft pink lighting, which gives patrons a sickly salmon complexion. Often thought of as a "wrinkle bar," but young guys like it, too. ⊠ *2294 Holcombe St.,* ☎ *713/665–9678. Crowd: mostly male, generally older, chatty.*

Gentry. This oft-crowded "gentleman's bar" (strip joint) gets busy after work, when suits drop by for a fix of gaiety before heading home to the family. Despite a somewhat sleazy reputation, the bar retains an upscale ambience and the staff is friendly. ⊠ *2303 Richmond Ave.,* ☎ *713/520– 1861. Crowd: male, 30s to 50s, dads and sons, suits and ties, boots and g-strings.*

Heaven. Houston's best small disco has an outstanding lighting and sound system, and huge video screens abound. A second cruise bar off to the side is quieter—a good place to dish. Heaven used to have a more uptight, clonish crowd, but lesbians, alternaqueers, and a more racially diverse set have loosened things up. Watch for the 50-cent drink specials on Sunday. ⊠ *810 Pacific St.,* ☎ *713/521–9123. Crowd: 60/40 m/f, mostly under 30, some stand-and-model, a few goths and grungers, more urban than preppy, plenty of disco bunnies.*

J. R.'s. Like its Dallas namesake, J. R.'s is the quintessential fern bar of the '90s, with hanging plants, Tiffany-style lamps, wood paneling, brass bar fixtures, and nooks and corners for standing around and looking pretty. A flagstone floor leads through an archway to the Santa Fe bar and patio, which is decorated with Navajo tapestries and faux cacti; the patio has a dyke following on Sunday afternoon. ⊠ *808 Pacific St.,* ☎ *713/521– 2519. Crowd: 75/25 m/f, like a J. Crew fashion show with a few cowhands thrown in, young, professional, on the prowl.*

Montrose Mining Co. Once a hard-core leather bar, the Mining Co. now draws bears, Levi's, and even some of the dressy guys from nearby J. R.'s and Heaven. It's dark (they should hand out flashlights at the door) and kind of dingy inside, but there's a nice patio off the back. The club is more mainstream late on weekends, when it's open after hours. ⊠ *805 Pacific St.,* ☎ *713/529–7488. Crowd: male, mostly 30s and 40s, horny and butch, chest and facial hair.*

Pacific Street. Some say this two-story space is merely a quieter, less interesting version of its neighbors on the main bar strip; others say it's more fun than either of them. It has a nice little dance floor, a great balcony overlooking all the action on Pacific Street, and a good game room with pool, pinball, and video games. ⊠ *710 Pacific St.,* ☎ *713/523–0213. Crowd: mostly male, a lot like Heaven's with some of the Mining Co.'s guys thrown in.*

Plaza 9200. The owners emphatically deny that this huge entertainment complex, fashioned ineptly out of a tacky '70s shopping center, is a lesbian bar, but most of its patrons are women. It's a big place with plenty to do and very little attitude, but it's also a haul from Montrose. **Ms. B's,** which looks like a Howard Johnson's cocktail lounge circa 1976, is a conversation/cruise bar; the **Ranch** draws fans of country-western music for dancing and lessons; **XTC** is a weekends-only high-energy disco with the all genders and races (plus quite a few TVs and TSs), and the **Patio** is a fine spot to catch a breath of fresh air and chat up new friends. ⊠ *9200 Buffalo Speedway,* ☎ *713/666–3464. Crowd: 20/80 m/f, all ages and races, dressed-down, butch.*

Rich's. A short drive from Montrose, Rich's is Houston's prime warehouse disco, with a big dance floor and a super sound system. It's only open from Thursday to Saturday. Friday's retro-disco theme is the best of the three nights; Saturday is crowded, though it's still the place to be seen, so most everyone makes an appearance. ⊠ *2401 San Jacinto,* ☎ *713/ 759–9606. Crowd: 80/20 m/f, younger disco bunnies and club kids.*

Ripcord. This is a serious leather bar, with the traditional, mind-numbing black decor and dim lighting (a few preppy boys sneak in for a look every once in a while). It's set in a tan, windowless compound in the heart of Montrose. ⊠ *715 Fairview St.,* ☎ *713/521–2792. Crowd: male, mostly over 35, leather, Levis, uniforms.*

Neighborhood Haunts

Cousins (⊠ 817 Fairview St., ☎ 713/528–9204) is the home of Houston's drag organization. **E/J's** (⊠ 2517 Ralph St., ☎ 713/527–9071) is known for its lively patio grill, nasty but beloved Saturday-night drag shows, and the E/J's Mug Club (you buy a mug and they keep it there for you). **Mary's** (⊠ 1022 Westheimer Rd., ☎ 713/527–9669), one of the oldest bars in town, can get lively from time to time. A seeming exercise in Southern Gothic, **Brick's II** (⊠ 617 Fairview St., ☎ 713/529–4669) is a low, gray house that's spare, trashy, dark, smoky, dirty, and looks almost abandoned. The ultratrendy **Liquid Lounge** (⊠ 220 Avondale St., ☎ 713/ 526–9878) draws a see-and-be-seen hetero/homo crowd for chichi cocktails and posing. The **Venture-N** (⊠ 2923 Main St., ☎ 713/522–0000), just north of Montrose and home to leather-and-Levi's clubs, gets more of the motorcycle crowd than the Ripcord or Mining Co.; it can be very fun late at night. **The New Barn** (⊠ 1100 Westheimer Rd., ☎ 713/521– 9533) is a low-key country-western bar that draws men and women and sometimes has live music.

Action

Club Houston (⊠ 2205 Fannin St., ☎ 713/659–4998) is the city's male bathhouse, with lockers, video rooms, tanning beds, an outdoor pool, and workout equipment.

SLEEPS

Houston's hotel scene is characterized by typical chain properties. Most are downtown or out by the Galleria (Montrose is directly between these two neighborhoods); a smaller, third cluster is in and around the Texas Medical Center. The advantages of the Galleria are its luxe shopping and dining and its location away from the daytime bustle downtown.

For price ranges, *see* lodging Chart B at the front of this guide.

Hotels

Near Downtown

$$$–$$$$ ⊞ **Lancaster.** This is one of only two hotels in Houston that could be said to possess historic character and European charm. A restored 1926 gem, it's equidistant from the theater and financial districts. Rooms have VCRs, CD players, and private fax lines. ✉ *701 Texas Ave., 77002,* ☎ *713/228–9500 or 800/231–0336,* FAX *713/223–4528. 93 rooms. Restaurant, exercise room.*

$$–$$$$ ⊞ **Wyndham Warwick.** The Lancaster's only competitor for charm and style, this newer, slightly less extravagant property is south of downtown in the museum district. Guests appreciate the exquisite public areas and park views. Strong homo following. ✉ *5701 Main St., 77005,* ☎ *713/526–1991 or 800/822–4200,* FAX *713/639–4545. 308 rooms. Restaurant, pool, exercise room.*

$–$$ ⊞ **Allen Park Inn.** The best economy choice within a short drive of Montrose is a typical motor lodge that's cleaner than most and has a nice pool and exercise room. ✉ *2121 Allen Pkwy., 77019,* ☎ FAX *713/521–9321 or 800/231–6310. 249 rooms. Restaurant, pool, exercise room.*

Near the Galleria

$$$$ ⊞ **Sheraton Luxury Collection.** This exclusive and expertly managed property is the hostelry of choice for world leaders and celebrities. Close to Montrose, it has a fabulous rooftop swimming pool and sundeck. ✉ *1919 Briar Oaks La., 77027,* ☎ *713/840–7600 or 800/325–3535,* FAX *713/840–8036. 232 rooms. Restaurant, pool, health club.*

$$–$$$ ⊞ **Westin Oaks.** A frequent host to gay and lesbian events, this 21-story hotel directly above the Galleria Mall has large, contemporary rooms. ✉ *5011 Westheimer Rd., 77056,* ☎ *713/960–8100 or 800/228–3000,* FAX *713/960–6554. 406 rooms. Restaurant, health club.*

Guest Houses and Small Hotels

$–$$ ⊞ **Lovett Inn.** Homey and affordable, this former residence of a one-time Houston mayor has long been the most popular choice of gays and lesbians. Rooms are done with tasteful antiques and reproductions, and in back, a pool and hot tub are given privacy by rows of box hedges. Bars and restaurants are within walking distance. ✉ *501 Lovett Blvd., 77006,* ☎ *713/522–5224 or 800/779–5224,* FAX *713/528–6708, e-mail lovet-tinn@aol.com. 8 rooms with phone, TV, and private bath. Pool, hot tub. Continental breakfast. Mostly mixed gay male/lesbian.*

$ ⊞ **Montrose Inn.** This is the area's most affordable choice, a clean but basic B&B in the heart of Montrose, with friendly hosts and a social, if cruisy, ambience. Rooms have VCRs with adult movies. ✉ *408 Avondale St., 77006,* ☎ *713/520–0206 or 800/357–1228. 5 rooms with phone, TV, some with private bath. Full breakfast. Gay male.*

THE LITTLE BLACK BOOK

At Your Fingertips

AIDS Foundation Houston Hotline (☎ 713/524–2437, Web site www.aid-shelp.org). **Gay and Lesbian Switchboard** (☎ 713/529–3211). **Greater Houston Convention and Visitors Bureau** (✉ 801 Congress Ave., 77002, ☎ 713/227–3100 or 800/365–7575, Web site www.houston-guide.com). **Greater Houston Lesbian and Gay Chamber of Commerce** (☎ 713/523–7576). **Hate Crimes Hotline** (☎ 713/529–9615). **Houston Gay and Lesbian Community Center** (to open some time in 1998, ☎ 713/867–7904). *Houston Press* (☎ 713/624–1400, Web site www.houston-press.com). **Montrose Clinic** (☎ 713/520–2000). *Public News* (☎ 713/520–1520, Web site www.publicnews.com). **Women's Information and Referral Hotline** (☎ 713/528–2121).

Gay Media

Houston has no shortage of gay papers, all of them quite useful and well-written. *Out Smart* (☎ 713/520–7237, Web site www.outsmart-magazine.com) is a monthly news and entertainment magazine, *Houston Voice* (☎ 713/529–8490, Web site www.houstonvoice.com) is a weekly, and *This Week in Texas* (☎ 713/527–9111, e-mail twtmag@aol.com) includes plenty of stuff on Houston. *The Texas Triangle* (☎ 713/521–5822, e-mail txtrihoust@aol.com) is the news-oriented weekly newspaper. Also look out for the helpful weekly newspaper-format *Guide to Gay Houston* (☎ 713/660–6808), which has a handy map, news about upcoming events, and bar and restaurant listings.

BOOKSTORES

Crossroads Market (✉ 1111 Westheimer Rd., ☎ 713/942–0147) is a true community bookstore with mainstream and lesbigay titles; it's upscale and literary. **LOBO Books** (✉ 3939-S Montrose Blvd., ☎ 713/522–5156) has porn and gay books (but not much for dykes), plus framed autographs of gay icons and celebs (from Cher to Walt Whitman) and some first editions and used titles. **Inklings** (✉ 1846 Richmond Ave., ☎ 713/521–3369) has the best selection of feminist and lesbian titles.

Working Out

The big cruising and buffing grounds, for men and women, is the **Fitness Exchange** (✉ 4040 Milam St., No. 100, ☎ 713/524–9932), a huge, well-equipped health club.

15 *Out in Kansas City*

With Lawrence, Kansas, and Eureka Springs, Arkansas

ALTHOUGH IT'S THE CLOSEST MAJOR CITY to the geographic center of America, Kansas City is off the beaten tourist path. Ironically, its centrality obscures Kansas City from the rest of the country. Vacation plans typically begin on either coast and creep inland as far as the Rockies in the West and the Mississippi River in the East. If the United States were a feature film, America's Heartland would be the part where everybody gets up and goes to the bathroom.

This lack of attention seems not to ruffle locals, who are far too busy enjoying themselves to care what coastal snobs think of their fine city. Certain midwestern cities suffer from the so-called "Second City" complex, but Kansas City is far enough out of the loop not to care.

In fact, this is one of the most delightful cities in America. Hilly, green, laced with parks, and with more fountains than any city but Rome, it is blessed with vibrant neighborhoods. The cost of living is not only reasonable, it's shockingly low. Gays and lesbians maintain clear, if not high, visibility in several neighborhoods and are rarely the target of grandstanding right-wing politicians.

Local queers, especially those who have settled here from other parts of the country, complain only that the gay community is too insular. Folks live throughout the city, but there is no gay ghetto or community center. Activists find the community's political edge in need of a good sharpening. This has a lot to do with how mellow everybody is. As one local put it, "If Kansas Citians were any steadier, they'd be dead."

THE LAY OF THE LAND

The metro region is the size of Connecticut, but the chunk of Kansas City you'll want to focus on comprises historic neighborhoods extending south from the Missouri River. Downtown is near the river, and as you head farther south you'll encounter the charming neighborhoods of Westport and the Country Club Plaza. Although part of the metro area falls in Kansas, most of the attractions and amusements are in Missouri.

Downtown and City Market
The southern half of Kansas City, including Westport, has remained fashionable and populated throughout most of this century, but **downtown** has had a rough time since World War II. Only in the past 10 years have there been signs of improvement, but this grid of office buildings encircled by interstate highways is not terribly dynamic.

Take an afternoon, however, to explore the northern tip of downtown, near the Missouri River. A well-preserved warehouse district is anchored by **Old City Market** (✉ 5th St. between Walnut St. and Grand Ave., ☎ 816/842–1271), which has food stalls, cafés, and has the **Arabia Steamboat Museum** (✉ Historic River Market, 400 Grand Ave., ☎ 816/471–4030), a remarkable archaeological find. In 1856, on a mission to deliver supplies to settlers about to begin their migration west, this hulking paddlewheeler sank into the murky depths of the Missouri. For 130 years treasure hunters searched unsuccessfully for the boat until 1988, when a determined team uncovered it in a mausoleum of mud, 40 feet below a farm field (by this time the river had shifted its course considerably). The perfectly preserved contents—including clothing, glassware, tools, and bottled food—are on display at this museum, which also contains a full-size replica of the boat deck.

For a look at a re-created stage coach similar to those used by frontier settlers, drive 10 minutes east of downtown along Independence Avenue to the **Kansas City Museum** (✉ 3218 Gladstone Blvd., ☎ 816/483–8300), a renovated mansion with a planetarium and thousands of artifacts.

A few blocks southeast of downtown, the **18th & Vine Historic District,** which traces the city's rich African-American heritage, has new attractions. Many of the early 20th-century's most talented ballplayers passed through this city to play for or against the Kansas City Monarchs. The **Negro Leagues Baseball Museum** (✉ 1601 E. 18th St., ☎ 816/221–1920) celebrates their legacy and conveys a sense of life in American sports before Jackie Robinson broke baseball's color barrier in 1947.

The Negro Leagues exhibit is the centerpiece of the **Museums at 18th and Vine** (✉ 1501 E. 18th St., ☎ 816/871–3016), which opened in 1997 and also houses a new Jazz Museum, an interpretive center, and a restored theater. The **Black Archives of Mid-America** (✉ 2033 Vine St., ☎ 816/483–1300) contains one of the nation's largest collections of African-American art and artifacts, and a research library.

The neo-Palladian **Folly Theater** (✉ 12th and Central Sts., ☎ 816/474–4444), a salvaged burlesque house, presents a variety of theatrical and musical productions, and is the frequent host to the gay men's chorus. The **Quality Hill Playhouse** (✉ 303 W. 10th St., ☎ 816/474–7529) stages Broadway-style shows.

Midtown
A swath of mixed residential and commercial blocks south of downtown, **Midtown** extends south to Westport and contains a handful of noteworthy sites and neighborhoods.

Crown Center (✉ 2450 Grand Ave., ☎ 816/274–8444), a shopping and entertainment complex with about 80 stores and a pair of hotels, is the headquarters of Hallmark Cards. You can tour the **Hallmark Visitors Center** (✉ third floor, ☎ 816/274–5672), a museum and sentimental superstore. Crown Center fringes historic Union Station and also one of the largest of the city's many fine parks, **Penn Valley.**

The blocks off of Troost Avenue, from about 23rd to 31st streets, are known as **Womyntown,** a feminist and lesbian community that was founded in the 1970s and based on a shared vision of cooperative living (and, of course, monthly potluck suppers). In recent years a few groovy gays and straights have settled here.

Lower Midtown
South of about 39th Street is **lower midtown,** a recently gayifying residential district that includes Westport, the Country Club Plaza, and Brookside Plaza. **Westport** is an artsy, picturesque community with old fashioned lampposts, Victorian buildings, offbeat shops, bars, and neighborhood cafés.

For a colorful stroll, wander along the main drag, **Westport Road,** and explore the adjacent blocks. Go west two blocks on Valentine Road from Summit Street to reach the **Thomas Hart Benton Home and Studio Historic Site** (✉ 3616 Belleview Ave., ☎ 816/931–5722). Check the newspapers to see what's playing at the **Unicorn Theater** (✉ 3820 Main St., ☎ 816/531–7529), one of the Midwest's top venues for alternative plays.

A few blocks south of Westport you'll find America's first planned shopping center, the **Country Club Plaza** (✉ Main St. and Ward Pkwy.), a 55-acre Spanish-style district of ornate buildings patterned after K.C.'s sister city, Seville, Spain. A feast of fountains, sculptures, murals, mosaics, and elaborate archways, the Plaza was designed in 1922 and has been accented with new works of art every few years since. The shops and restaurants are of the high-end chain variety. From Thanksgiving to mid-January the Plaza is decked out with 200,000 holiday lights. The Plaza overlooks **Brush Creek,** a 6-mile-long park with a landscaped promenade on either side and bridges.

Set in luxuriant South Moreland Park, the **Nelson-Atkins Museum of Art** (✉ 4525 Oak St., ☎ 816/751–1278) has works by Rodin, Rubens, Van Gogh, and Rembrandt; one of the best Asian art collections in North America; and the 17-acre Henry Moore sculpture garden.

The blocks south of the Plaza show off the city's wealth of broad, green boulevards, as well as some of Kansas City's fanciest brick and stone mansions. One last patch of boutiques and eateries worth checking out is **Brookside Plaza** (✉ 63rd St. and Wornall Ave.), which anchors another gay-popular residential neighborhood. From here it's a 10-minute drive east to one of the largest chunks of urban greenery in America, **Swope Park.**

Independence
President Harry S Truman hailed from the nearby suburb of Independence. In Independence Square, you'll find the courthouse in which Truman launched his political career. You can also visit the **Truman Library and Museum** (✉ U.S. 24 and Delaware St., ☎ 816/833–1225), which houses a full-scale reproduction of the Oval Office, and the **Harry S Truman Home** (✉ 219 N. Delaware St., ☎ 816/254–9929), where Harry and Bess Truman resided from 1919 until their deaths.

GETTING AROUND

Although you need a car to get around most of the area, Kansas City does have a handy **trolley** service that runs north–south from City Market clear down to the Country Club Plaza, stopping at most major hotels and attractions along the way. The $4 fare entitles you to unlimited travel for the day.

EATS

The city's low cost of living extends to the dining scene, which is characterized by affordable restaurants. Even the new breed of chic eateries sweeping through many neighborhoods respects the general law that Kansas Citians will not spend a ridiculous amount on food.

Known for its steak houses, Kansas City is also internationally famous for barbecue. **Bryant's** (✉ 1727 Brooklyn St., ☎ 816/231–1123) is a long-time favorite of U.S. presidents and celebrities. **Gates & Sons,** with branches all through the metro region, has a tremendous local following. Also highly regarded is **L.C.'s** (✉ 5800 Blue Pkwy., ☎ 816/923–4484, $, no credit cards), a total dive with fantastic brisket and ribs and addictive cut fries.

Another specialty is dirt-cheap, by-the-book Mexican food. You'll find places serving such fare along **Southwestern Boulevard,** near Summit Street.

Many local restaurants have queer followings. Best bets are the patches of funky eateries around the intersection of Westport Road and Broadway, and along the 39th Street corridor, an eight-block stretch of great restaurants extending east from the state line.

For price ranges, *see* dining Chart B at the front of this guide.

Downtown and Midtown

$$$ ✕ **Savoy Grill.** Harry Truman was a kid when this sophisticated Old World restaurant began delighting K.C.'s high society (it later appeared in the film *Mr. and Mrs. Bridge*). The Savoy remains a favorite setting for special occasions. The traditional Continental and American menu holds few surprises, just sublime steaks, seafood, veal, and the like. ⊠ *Hotel Savoy, 219 W. 9th St.,* ☎ *816/842–3890.*

$$–$$$ ✕ **Hereford House.** The 1950s dining room of this revered steak house hasn't caught up with the '90s (or even the '60s), but pound-for-pound it's tough to find better cuts of steak. The epic wine list could keep you busy for hours. The restaurant is a couple of blocks from some of the better gay bars. ⊠ *2 E. 20th St.,* ☎ *816/842–1080.*

$$ ✕ **Velvet Dog.** A chichi supper club with red-brown sponge-painted walls, red velvet seats, and alternative tunes, the Velvet Dog has developed into one of the city's top hipster hangs—gays make up a sizable chunk of the crowd. With a nice wine list and excellent nouvelle fare—salmon cakes with a lemon-herb mayo, grilled chicken bathed in Amaretto—this is more than a place to stand around and look sexy. ⊠ *400 E. 31st St.,* ☎ *816/753–9990.*

$–$$ ✕ **Boulevard Café.** Noisy and festive, this tapas restaurant, with white-tile tables and gorgeous Oriental tapestries offers what appears to be a cheap meal: dozens of under-$10 hot and cold dishes—mouthwatering sardines, smoked meats and sausages, cured olives and peppers, and various dips. Of course, these plates are so good you may end up ordering a half-dozen of them. Jazz musicians perform on most nights and during Sunday brunch. ⊠ *703 Southwest Blvd.,* ☎ *816/842–6984.*

Westport and the Country Club Plaza

$$$ ✕ **Metropolis.** Westport's big-city restaurant has always had a queer following but wins raves from just about everyone. A pressed-tin ceiling, dark lighting, and white linens impart sophistication, and the diverse New American salads and grills are usually tasty. ⊠ *303 Westport Rd.,* ☎ *816/ 753–1550.*

$$–$$$ ✕ **Jazz.** A stone's throw from the Kansas border, Jazz actually feels closer to Bourbon Street, with superb Cajun fare, music-filled dining rooms, and an elaborate balustrade back porch. Riotously noisy and packed to the rafters most nights, the restaurant specializes in crawfish étouffée, oysters, and jambalaya. ⊠ *1823 W. 39th St.,* ☎ *816/531–5556.*

$$ ✕ **Andre's Confiserie Suisse.** An honorary Swiss consulate, Andre's is one of Kansas City's more eccentric eateries: an authentic Swiss pastry shop and tea room that's open for breakfast, lunch, and late-afternoon tea. It's the kind of place you could bring your aunt—or a few drag queens—and have a gay old time. ⊠ *5018 Main St.,* ☎ *816/561–3440.*

$$ ✕ **Fountain Café.** Famous for its upstairs terrace that overlooks one of the Country Club Plaza's ornate fountains, this French-Mediterranean eatery specializes in pastas and grills, including Moroccan chicken with couscous and a delicious cassoulet. This place is more casual than the nearby and similarly good Fedora's and Plaza III, which are owned by the same folks. ⊠ *102 W. 47th St.,* ☎ *816/561–0066.*

Eats ●

Andre's Confiserie
Suisse, **14**
Boulevard Café, **3**
Broadway Café, **12**
Corner Restaurant, **10**
D'Bronx, **8**
Fountain Café, **13**
Hereford House, **2**
Jazz, **6**
Metropolis, **11**
Osteria Il Centro, **15**
Otto's Malt Shop, **9**
Planet Cafe, **5**
Saigon 39, **7**
Savoy Grill, **1**
Sharp's, **16**
Velvet Dog, **4**

Scenes ○

Buddies, **13**
Club Atlantis, **11**
Club Cabaret, **14**
Davey's Uptown
Ramblers Club, **8**
Dixie Bell, **5**
Jamie's, **1**
Mari's, **6**
Missie B's, **10**
Otherside, **9**
Pearl's, **2**
Sidekicks, **12**
Soakies, **3**
Tootsie's, **4**
Velvet Dog, **7**

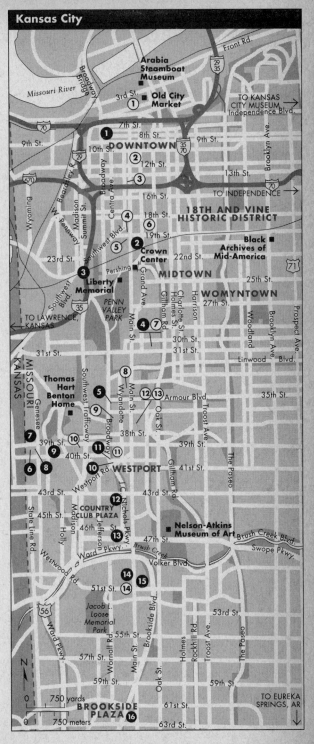

Kansas City

$–$$ ✕ **Osteria Il Centro.** This smart, new, neighborhood Italian eatery, steps from the popular Club Cabaret gay bar, offers filling and sophisticated dishes. Top selections include soft focaccia stuffed with ricotta cheese and Italian sausage, and grilled marinated chicken with roasted vegetables. ⊠ *5101 Main St.,* ☎ *816/561-2369.*

$–$$ ✕ **Saigon 39.** Credit this Vietnamese eatery with redefining the city's standards for Asian cooking. This spiffy little joint serves noodle dishes and stir-fries, plus a bowl of chicken soup with pineapples, tomatoes, and chilies that will bring tears to your eyes (you can request either the mild or spicy version). ⊠ *1806 W. 39th St.,* ☎ *816/531–4447.*

$–$$ ✕ **Sharp's.** This gay-friendly eatery in offbeat Brookside Plaza draws a local crowd three meals a day, as well as for drinks around the antiquey bar. Casual and Italian dishes are the norm—pastas, a mean chili, and good burgers. Cheap and cheerful. ⊠ *128 W. 63rd St.,* ☎ *816/333–4355.*

$ ✕ **Corner Restaurant.** A Westport favorite for breakfast and lunch, the Corner overlooks a busy corner, and so people-watching is a favorite pastime. The usual sandwiches, salads, and pancakes are available, plus hearty potatofuls and eggfuls (you choose your own toppings, and the chef mixes them in with either sautéed potatoes or scrambled eggs). ⊠ *4059 Broadway,* ☎ *816/931–6630. No credit cards.*

$ ✕ **D'Bronx.** Everyone from local power brokers to ordinary Joes flocks to this old-fashioned deli. Antique ceiling fans whir above the counter, and cheerful, un-Bronxlike servers prepare hefty pastrami sandwiches and the best hand-tossed pizzas in the city. ⊠ *3904 Bell St.,* ☎ *816/531–0550.*

$ ✕ **Otto's Malt Shop.** Famously queer-popular and open 24/7, this quirky burger joint along the 39th Street corridor pulls off a fab '50s look with stylish vintage furnishings, light fixtures, and old signs (it's hard to believe the '50s ever looked this good). The food is right out of the era: juicy burgers, sautéed onions, and malts that come in 32-ounce vats. ⊠ *3903 Wyoming St.,* ☎ *816/756–1010. No credit cards.*

Coffeehouse Culture

Broadway Café. This grungy and very gay coffeehouse in Westport is filled with avant-garde artwork, mosaic tables, and big bulletin boards plastered with notices of upcoming events and gatherings. Big windows overlook the busy sidewalk. ⊠ *4106 Broadway,* ☎ *816/531–2432.*

Planet Cafe. The city's newest gay-popular beanery draws a funky crowd for good drinks, light snacks, and cerebral conversation. ⊠ *3535 Broadway,* ☎ *816/561–7287.*

SCENES

Kansas City has about as well-rounded a gay nightlife scene as you'll find in a city this size. As the old cliché goes, there's something for everybody: leather, country-western, drag, cruise, high energy, lesbian, stand-and-model—plus a few cool neighborhood bars. A few straight hangouts have gay nights. The staff and patrons at K.C. bars are uniformly friendly and outgoing, and although folks may not dress to the nines the way they do in L.A. or Dallas, conservative preppy outfits prevail. Westport and a stretch of Main Street south of downtown have the highest concentrations of bars.

Prime Suspects

Club Cabaret. This clean, upscale dance, video, and show bar within walking distance of the Plaza pulls in young guys on their way home from work and a second wave of late-night revelers who come to dance or catch some of the shows. Drag is the norm, but strippers (including touring porn stars) strut their stuff also. There's a casual restaurant. ⊠ *5024 Main St.,* ☎ *816/753–6504. Crowd: 80/20 m/f, under 35, professional, on the make, stand-and-model but not uptight.*

Dixie Bell. The most popular cruise bar in Kansas City, the Dixie Bell fancies itself a leather bar, but only the dark cellar downstairs ever seems to draw a uniformed majority—even that's a bit rare. The DB is a festive stand-and-model bar that happens to show porn on video monitors and have a leather shop on premises. It's an easy place to meet other guys. The ambience is warm and festive; the main room has high ceilings, old-fashioned fixtures, and a small dance floor beyond it. The beer blasts always pack 'em in. ⊠ *1922 Main St.,* ☎ *816/471–2424. Crowd: 85/15 m/f, 20s to 40s, totally eclectic: leather, bears, pretty boys, a few dykes, and even the odd suit-and-tie.*

Missie B's. A popular locals' hangout with lively drag shows, a curvaceous wooden bar, plush rattan armchairs, and an '80s-inspired ambience, Missie B's is a pleasant spot for a cocktail before heading to dinner at one of the trendy restaurants along the 39th Street corridor. ⊠ *805 W. 39th St.,* ☎ *816/561–0625. Crowd: 65/35 m/f, 30s to 50s, chatty, unpretentious, not too cruisy.*

Otherside. The guys at this lounge like to have a good time and welcome strangers (especially younger strangers) with open arms—maybe even a few free drinks. Many folks come here to wind down after a day at the office. The heavy-handed kitsch-glitter decor makes for an unequivocal contrast between work and play. ⊠ *3611 Broadway,* ☎ *816/931–0501. Crowd: 80/20 m/f, late 30s to 60s, professionals, cliquey, catty, flirtatious, and fun.*

Sidekicks. The walls of this bustling country-western dance hall and saloon are so plastered with street and traffic signs it's hard to determine what they're made of. The art of overdecorating works here—all the colors and flashing lights (note the neon cowboy boots pulsing over the doorway) impart plenty of cheer. There are a few rooms, from quiet lounges for chatting and guzzling to a big dance floor usually packed with two-steppers. ⊠ *3707 Main St.,* ☎ *816/931–1430. Crowd: male but very female-friendly, 30s and 40s, urban cowboys in suede and butch rustlers in denim.*

Tootsie's. Not long ago this huge space in a restored building south of downtown was occupied by the Kansas City Eagle leather bar, but since its transformation into a women's disco, Tootsie's has become one of the hottest tickets in town. A big dance floor adjoins the handsome high-ceiling central bar. Other sections have plenty of seating and pool tables, darts, and other games. ⊠ *1822 Main St.,* ☎ *816/471–7704. Crowd: 80/20 f/m, 20s to 50s, completely diverse.*

Neighborhood Haunts

Men and a few women from Sidekicks wander into **Buddies** (⊠ 3715 Main St., ☎ 816/561–2600), the cruisy video bar next door, to shoot pool, mingle, and watch music videos. The bar draws a big crowd for happy hour. **Jamie's** (⊠ 528 Walnut St., ☎ 816/471–2080) is a kinda rowdy dyke bar at the north end of downtown; there's country music most nights. **Mari's** (⊠ 1809 Grand Blvd., ☎ 816/283–0511) may look grim from the outside, but it's a comfy little bar and restaurant (with good but basic Continental and American fare) that's popular with men and women. The staff is one of the friendliest in town.

A famous and lovable old dive in the shadows of downtown's office towers, **Soakies** (⊠ 1308 Main St., ☎ 816/221–6060) has cheap beer, tasty sandwiches, a long counter bar, and a decent-size dance floor. Many African-Americans come here. **Pearl's** (⊠ 1108 Grand Blvd., ☎ 816/421–1082) is a faded bar with a small restaurant serving home-style cuisine; the crowd is older and local.

Hanging with the Hets

The live alternative bands at **Davey's Uptown Ramblers Club** (⊠ 3402 Main St., ☎ 816/753–1909) usually pull in young nongender-specific rockers, hipsters, and the like. Known for its great food, the counterculturally keen **Velvet Dog** (*see* Eats, *above*) is also an ideal spot for a pint of stout before moving on to the late-night bars. Of the megadiscos, **Club Atlantis** (⊠ 3954 Central St., ☎ 816/753–0112) has the strongest homo following, with Thursday night the pinkest.

SLEEPS

If you're on vacation, your best bet is to skip the many business-oriented and pricey chain properties downtown and pick a place near Westport and the Plaza. You'll be close to gay nightlife and within walking distance of good shopping and dining. The city's two gay-hosted inns, though mainstream and open to everybody, tend to draw plenty of family—both are terrific and in great locations.

For price ranges, *see* lodging Chart B at the front of this guide.

Hotels

$$$$ 🏨 **Ritz-Carlton Kansas City.** Less glamorous than other members of the Ritz chain, this high-rise overlooking Brush Creek and the Plaza contains European antiques, formal public areas, and rooms with three phones, marble baths, and the usual deluxe amenities. ⊠ *401 Ward Pkwy., 64112,* ☎ *816/756–1500 or 800/241–3333,* ℻ *816/531–1483. 373 rooms. Restaurant, pool, health club.*

$$$ 🏨 **Raphael.** Less expensive and more understated than its neighbor, the Ritz, this converted 1927 apartment building has the personal ambience and historic elegance of a European boutique hotel. More than half the rooms are suites, and all are done with rich woods, prints, and colors. For such luxury, this is one of the best values in the Midwest. ⊠ *325 Ward Pkwy., 64112,* ☎ *816/756–3800 or 800/821–5343,* ℻ *816/756–3800. 123 rooms. Restaurant.*

$$–$$$ 🏨 **Quarterage Hotel.** A favorite of the community for its Old World ambience, good health club, and proximity to Westport's bars and restaurants, the Quarterage is actually a contemporary structure with modern rooms. The staff is friendly and helpful. ⊠ *560 Westport Rd., 64111,* ☎ *816/931–0001 or 800/942–4233,* ℻ *816/464–5915. 123 rooms. Restaurant, health club.*

$–$$ 🏨 **Holiday Inn Westport.** Convenient to bars and restaurants, this business-oriented property is a deal. Rooms have a slight southwestern influence and are large. ⊠ *801 Westport Rd., 64111,* ☎ *816/931–1000 or 800/465–4329,* ℻ *816/561–0447. 109 rooms. Restaurant.*

$ 🏨 **Budgetel.** It's a 15-minute drive southeast of Westport and slightly farther from downtown and Midtown, but this is a great inexpensive lodging choice. The rooms are clean, the management friendly, the location safe, and access to I–435 is a few hundred yards away. ⊠ *8601 Hillcrest Rd., 64138,* ☎ *816/822–7000 or 800/428–3438,* ℻ *816/822–8488. 107 rooms.*

Guest Houses

$$–$$$ 🏨 **Doanleigh Wallagh Inn.** If you can live without the facilities and large staff of a big hotel, this beautifully restored mansion has some of the most sumptuous rooms in the city; some have fireplaces and most have whirlpool tubs. The women innkeepers have thought of every last detail, including a lovely afternoon wine reception. ⊠ *217 E. 37th St., 64111,* ☎ *816/753–2667,* ℻ *816/531–5185. 5 rooms with phone, TV, and private bath. Full breakfast. Mixed gay/straight.*

$$ 🏨 **Inn The Park.** The slightly more affordable of the city's two gay-popular B&Bs, this German Victorian has a great location by Hyde Park, which is near Womyntown and a short drive from Westport and the Plaza.

The guys who run this place have retained its historic mood while still offering a relaxed and casual accommodation. ⊠ *3610 Gillham Rd., 64111,* ☎ *816/931–0797 or 800/708–6748. 2 rooms with phone, TV, and private bath. Pool. Full breakfast. Mixed gay/straight.*

THE LITTLE BLACK BOOK

At Your Fingertips

Convention and Visitors Bureau of Greater Kansas City (⊠ City Center Square, 1100 Main St., Suite 2550, 66117, ☎ 816/221–5242 or 800/767–7700; also visitor center ⊠ at the Clock Tower, Country Club Plaza, 22 W. 47th St.). *Current News* (☎ 816/561–2679). **Gay Information Hot Line** (☎ 816/753–0700). **Gay Talk Information Crisis Hot Line** (☎ 816/931–4470). **Kansas City Community AIDS Network** (☎ 913/791–8188). **Kansas City Trolley** (☎ 816/221–3399). *PitchWeekly* (☎ 816/561–6061, Web site www.pitch.com). **Yellow Cab** (☎ 816/471–5000).

Gay Media

The statewide, biweekly *News Telegraph* (☎ 816/561–6266, e-mail newstele@aol.com) has offices in St. Louis and Kansas City and provides the scoop on the gay scenes in both cities.

BOOKSTORES

The city has no full-time queer bookstore, but **Larry's Gifts and Cards** (⊠ 205 Westport Rd., ☎ 816/753–4757) has lesbigay titles, plus magazines, cards, and such.

Working Out

The **Gold's Gym** (⊠ 4050 Pennsylvania Ave, ☎ 816/931–9888) in Westport is popular with lesbians and gay men.

LAWRENCE, KANSAS

Long a queer-friendly city with a visible community centered around the politically active University of Kansas, Lawrence (population 75,000) is an appealing side trip from Kansas City—40 minutes away by car. You won't find much nightlife, but you'll see other family roaming around town, hanging out at coffeehouses, and dining at local restaurants.

This is the only city in Kansas with an antidiscrimination ordinance protecting the rights of gays and lesbians, and it's probably a result of the overwhelmingly tolerant population that the queer community has no gathering spots of its own. Most folks in this low-key city prefer to hang out in a mixed environment, and students at groovy KU (or "Gay U" as it's sometimes nicknamed) are progressive.

The city's firm stance on human rights owes something to its origins. Abolitionists from Massachusetts settled Lawrence in the 1850s, after Congress established Nebraska and Kansas as U.S. territories. Kansas was admitted into the Union in 1861 as a free state.

The Lay of the Land

If you suspect that Kansas has a flat, unmemorable landscape, you're partly right—much of the state fits this description. But Lawrence, with its steep, lightly wooded hills, looks more like the New England countryside from whence its founders came (maybe this explains their decision to establish a city here).

KU's campus dominates much of the city, particularly its highest points. Abutting it is a downtown that represents the idealized vision of "Main Street, U.S.A." Businesses thrive along funky Massachusetts Street and neighboring thoroughfares. Day or night, Lawrence has a positive buzz about it. Among the many shops are some fine art galleries—the percentage of full-time artists in Lawrence ranks 12th in the nation.

The university's **Spencer Museum of Art** (✉ Mississippi St., west of the Kansas Union ☎ 785/864–4710) is an outstanding facility with a generous representation of 17th- and 18th-century European artists and a vast contemporary Asian art collection. The acoustically state-of-the-art **Lied Center** (☎ 785/864–3469), built in 1993, contains a performance hall, a dance studio, and a theater. The **Lawrence Arts Center** (✉ 9th and Vermont Sts., ☎ 785/843–2787), which is housed in the city's 1904 Carnegie Library, hosts performing groups and rotating art exhibits. Other first-rate KU attractions include the **Museum of Anthropology** (✉ Spooner Hall, ☎ 785/864–4245) and the not-to-be-missed **Museum of Natural History** (✉ Dyche Hall, ☎ 785/864–4540), the top such facility in this part of the country.

The Native American influence is strong in Lawrence, partly owing to the presence of **Haskell Indian Nations University** (✉ 155 Indian Ave., ☎ 785/749–8404), whose 320-acre campus holds 12 sites on the National Registry of Historic Landmarks.

Getting Around

Although much of the town and campus can be managed on foot, Lawrence is easy to explore by car. Parking on campus is difficult, so find a space downtown and walk to the museums. North–south streets are named after U.S. states from east-to-west in the order in which they were admitted to the Union, so you get a handy lesson in ratification as you drive from one end of town to the other.

Eats

For price ranges, *see* dining Chart B at the front of this guide.

$$–$$$　✕ **Teller's.** Known for its Tuesday-night gay festivities, Teller's is a great spot for drinks, but don't overlook the contemporary American and Italian cuisine. ✉ *746 Massachusetts St.,* ☎ *785/843–4111.*

$$　✕ **Free State Brewery.** Opened in 1989 as the first legal brewery in Kansas in 100 years, this handsome two-level restaurant serves pizzas, salads, sandwiches, cheese dips, and other food that goes with handmade brews. In warm weather you can dine in the outdoor beer garden. On many nights there's live music. ✉ *636 Massachusetts St.,* ☎ *785/843–4555.*

$–$$　✕ **Paradise Café.** Breakfast is a local tradition at this social hub, with everything from pancakes and French toast to fresh salmon grilled with a light lemon-herb butter. Stick to sandwiches and pastas at lunch, and Continental fare like steak au poivre or pasta with artichoke hearts and tomatoes at dinner. ✉ *728 Massachusetts St.,* ☎ *785/842–5199.*

$　✕ **Glass Onion.** A busy student hangout on the edge of campus and close to KU museums, this sunny café specializes in veggie dishes, from black-bean burritos to tofu grain burgers. It's also a good option for espresso and desserts. ✉ *12th and Indiana Sts.,* ☎ *785/841–2310.*

$　✕ **Java Break.** Of the seemingly endless variety of coffeehouses in town, Java Break has the gayest following. It's close to busy Massachusetts Street. ✉ *7th and New Hampshire Sts.,* ☎ *785/749–5282.*

Scenes

Although Lawrence has no shortage of excellent music clubs and bars, the gay scene is in a state of flux. The only gay bar in town closed in 1996, and currently only **Teller's** (*see* Eats, *above*) has a specifically gay event. Tuesday's "family" night attracts queer students, professors, and other locals, who mingle and sip microbrews in this classy converted bank building (the bathrooms are fashioned out of former bank vaults). Mostly straight other nights, Teller's is always gay-friendly. You'll usually spy a few fags at the **Java Break** coffeehouse (*see* Eats, *above*).

Sleeps

Because it's so close to Kansas City, many visitors to Lawrence don't bother spending the night here. But with so much to see and do, and several good restaurants you might consider staying overnight.

For price ranges, *see* lodging Chart B at the front of this guide.

Hotels and Motels

$$–$$$ ☝ **Eldridge Hotel.** This charming redbrick 1920s hostelry is filled with elegant period-style public areas and spacious rooms with modern pieces but a vintage style. Each room has a sitting area, a refrigerator, and a wet bar. ✉ *7th and Massachusetts Sts., 66044,* ☎ *785/749–5011 or 800/527–0909,* ⅢX *785/749–4512. 48 rooms. Restaurant, health club.*

$ ☝ **Super 8 Motel.** Perfectly pleasant, the Super 8 has a cheerful staff and useful amenities like wake-up calls and a laundry. ✉ *515 McDonald Dr., 66044,* ☎ *785/842–5721 or 800/800–8000,* ⅢX *785/842–8243. 48 rooms.*

Guest House

$–$$ ☝ **Halcyon House.** Each room at this restored 1890's cottage has its own unique, and in most cases self-explanatory, theme, such as the Chandelier Room, the Atrium, and the Garden Suite (which has a private patio entrance). Friends traveling together should expect to have a rollicking experience in the Good Times Suite, which has two beds and a fireplace. ✉ *1000 Ohio St., 66044,* ☎ *785/841–0314. 9 rooms, most with private bath. Full breakfast. Mostly straight.*

The Little Black Book

Get information on the region from the **Lesbian, Bisexual, and Gay Services of Kansas** (LesBiGayS– OK, ☎ 785/864–3091, e-mail qanda@raven.cc.ukans.edu), which is a queer student union for the University of Kansas but open to nonstudents and visitors, too; or from the **Lawrence Convention & Visitors Bureau** (✉ 734 Vermont St., Box 586, 66044, ☎ 785/865–4411 or 888/529–5267), which also has a new **Visitors Center** (✉ 402 N. 2nd St., ☎ 785/865–4499) inside a renovated rail depot. On the Internet, check out the city's Web site (www.ci.lawrence.ks.us/ålpl/comguide.html). In addition to consulting the Kansas City gay papers, look to the monthly Wichita-based **Liberty Press** (☎ 316/262–0315, e-mail librtyprs@aol.com) for local queer coverage.

EUREKA SPRINGS, ARKANSAS

How Eureka Springs, the site of the one of the largest free-standing statues of Christ and one of the world's most famous productions of the Passion Play, came to be a haven of gays and lesbians is difficult to pinpoint. As the percentage of the population that is gay continues to grow every year, hundreds of Bible-thumping tourists show up without the slightest inkling that this is the Heartland's main queer resort mecca.

Locals estimate that at least a quarter of the population is gay, but you'd never know this by looking at the crowds milling about the historic district and chugging around town on tour buses. Many locals keep to themselves or live in the splendid countryside, and gays and lesbians strive to blend in as much as possible. Eureka Springs is a live-and-let-live town, where a household of evangelical Christians gets along perfectly well with the lesbian couple next door. People don't always embrace their neighbors' beliefs and lifestyles, but they respect their rights and privacy.

After natural springs believed to have curative powers were discovered in the 1870s, the town developed into a health spa and resort. For the next 40 years businesses prospered, but the rise in popularity of the automobile, which the town's steep narrow streets could not accommodate, threw Eureka Springs into a recession. By the 1950s only 700 full-time residents, many of them artists or societal drop-outs, lived here. The construction in the 1960s of the Christ of the Ozarks statue and the opening of the first six-month-long Passion Play season put Eureka Springs back on the map, but this time as a mecca for Christian families.

It was probably during the mid-20th-century that Eureka Springs developed a gay following. Since the '60s, countless hippies and countercultural types have settled here, and it's still not uncommon to see a car drive by with a rainbow sticker and a Grateful Dead decal on the rear window. The nationally acclaimed Opera of the Ozarks, a two-month-long school of opera (performances run from late June to late July), has brought gay performers through town.

Only in recent years has the local community begun to work in an organized manner to court queer tourists. The Chamber of Commerce, although it's a mainstream organization representing all the town's businesses and interests, could not be more supportive. An effort is under way to establish a weekend or week dedicated to gay tourists.

The Lay of the Land

The region's appeal lies in its remarkable natural beauty, which you can explore simply by hopping into your car and driving 15 miles in virtually any direction—countless ridgeline, mountaintop, and lakeside vistas await you. Of special note, 33-acre **Eureka Springs Gardens** (⊠ Hwy. 62 W, ☎ 501/253–9256) bursts with flowers and gardens from April through November.

The town's historic district is a colorful preserve of Victorian architecture, commercial and residential. Hundreds of meticulously restored wood-frame, brick, and stone houses and buildings cling to Eureka Springs's precipitous slopes, and several are open for touring. The **Queen Anne Mansion** (⊠ Hwy. 62 W, ☎ 501/253–8825), which dates to 1891 is renowned for its hand-carved oak and cherry details. Photos, documents, and artifacts at the **Eureka Springs Historical Museum** (⊠ 95 S. Main St., ☎ 501/253–9417) trace the town's history.

Shops, boutiques, and fine art galleries line downtown's small network of commercial streets, but you'll have to drive 15 minutes to reach one of the region's most innovative arts spaces, **Woman's Work** (⊠ Hwy. 187, ☎ 501/253–4080).

Given the bigotry of many conservative American religious sects, it's not surprising that gays and lesbians have never flocked en masse to religious sites. But Eureka Springs is not like any other community in America, and the nightly **Passion Play** (⊠ Passion Play Rd., off Hwy. 62E, ☎ 800/882–7529), which runs from April to October, draws a few gays and lesbians. With a cast of 250 and a set the size of a small village, this is the largest outdoor drama staged in the country. Homosexuals are also among the 1 million people who come annually to observe the seven-story **Christ of the Ozarks Statue** (⊠ Passion Play Rd., off Hwy. 62E, ☎ 501/253–9200), the world's largest free-standing statue of Christ.

Gays and lesbians have begun to come to Eureka Springs, long a honeymoon capital, in increasing numbers to exchange vows at commitment ceremonies. Contact the local **Metropolitan Community Church of the Living Spring** (✉ 17 Elk St., ☎ 501/253–9337) for advice.

Getting Around

Though not within the immediate vicinity of any major city, Eureka Springs is a day's drive or less from major metropolitan areas, including Little Rock (3 hours), Kansas City (4 hours), Oklahoma City (5 hours), St. Louis (6 hours), Memphis (6 hours), and Dallas (8 hours).

Eureka Springs's winding streets are narrow and hilly. You need a car to get here, but then it's best to park at your inn or hotel and walk or use the local trolley to get around. If you drive down into the commercial district, you'll have to search for a parking space, even in the pay lots. The parking police are very vigilant. Trolleylike trams ($3 for an unlimited day pass) cover downtown and most attractions within 10 miles; they stop near all the hotels and many B&Bs, and run a 5-mile loop through the historic district, as well as to some outlying parking lots.

Eats

For a little town in the mountains, Eureka Springs has a nicely balanced dining scene. Most restaurants outside the historic district cater to families, but downtown has sophisticated and gay-popular options—several are gay-owned. Still, discretion is advised. The staffs at most restaurants are blasé about same-sex couples, but many of the visiting tourists are not.

For price ranges, *see* dining Chart B at the front of this guide.

$$–$$$ ✕ **Chez Charles.** Fresh flowers, white linens, hardwood floors, and contemporary art give this American bistro in the Grand Central Hotel a hip but elegant sensibility—it's one of only a few restaurants where you won't see children racing around. Through the open kitchen you can watch the skillful preparation of rosemary chicken with goat cheese and sundried tomatoes, and pecan pesto–crusted salmon with a subtle lemon-butter sauce. ✉ *37 N. Main St.,* ☎ *501/253–9509.*

$$–$$$ ✕ **Ermilio's.** Set in a majestic Victorian house within walking distance of gay-friendly B&Bs, Ermilio's specializes in homemade semolina wheat pastas, such as gnocchi, spinach-and-cheese ravioli, and linguine. You can pair any pasta with one of several good sauces—the Gorgonzola won't do much for your waistline, but it's one of the best. Traditional Italian seafood, chicken, and steak dishes are also prepared. ✉ *26 White St.* ☎ *501/253–8806.*

$$–$$$ ✕ **Jim and Brent's Bistro.** This romantic dinner-only restaurant is in a picture-perfect yellow house on a bluff just south of downtown. The Continental and American cooking—from beef Stroganoff to spicy jambalaya—rarely disappoints. ✉ *173 S. Main St.,* ☎ *501/253–7457.*

$$ ✕ **Plaza.** On the first floor of this downtown eatery is a cozy timber-beamed room with old-fashioned ceiling fans and hanging plants. Upstairs is an enclosed deck that gets noisy and spirited in warm weather. The menu is varied, with casual American, Continental, and Mexican options. The char-grilled burgers are fantastic, as is orange roughy Cozumel with a lime, garlic, and cilantro sauce. ✉ *55 S. Main St.,* ☎ *501/253–8866.*

$–$$ ✕ **Center Street South.** A gay-popular dance- and live-music club much of the time, Center Street South is a funky Caribbean and Mexican restaurant in the early evening. Specialties such as the chicken breast sautéed in rum and beer and the salmon fillet in a piña colada–like blend of coconut and pineapples suggest the chef loves to get his food pretty drunk before serving it. Fajitas, tacos, and other south-of-the-border favorites round out the menu. ✉ *10 Center St.,* ☎ *501/253–8102.*

$ ✕ **Local Flavor.** With a cheerfully incoherent mix of lava lamps, porcelain figurines, lace curtains, and brass-framed art, this quirky coffeehouse has as much local color as it does flavor (if the campy decor won't do it for you, pick a seat on the deck overlooking the garden). In addition to caffeine brews, you can order beer, wine, and light food, from nachos to sandwiches. Good for breakfast, too. ✉ *71 S. Main St.,* ☎ *501/253–9522.*

$ ✕ **Sonny's Pizzeria.** In a converted yellow cottage downtown, this gay-friendly pizza parlor tosses the best New York–style pies in the area. Great for a light bite or a full meal. ✉ *119 N. Main St.,* ☎ *501/253–2307.*

Scenes

Far less developed than but rather similar to Branson, Missouri, in its variety of wholesome—and in most cases, cheesy—country-music shows and mountain jamborees, Eureka Springs has quite a few nightlife venues where gays and lesbians will find themselves in the extreme minority. Most of these places are on the motel-studded main roads outside of the historic district.

The pubs and saloons downtown tend to be open-minded and ostensibly gay-friendly. **Center Street South** (*see* Eats, *above*) has the strongest community following. The owners bring in some of the best live music in the area, from blues to rock to grunge, and most nights there's dancing. The bar pours 20 varieties of tequila—this is a terrific spot for margaritas. **Chelsea's Corner Cafe** (✉ 10 Mountain St., ☎ 501/253–6753) is a rowdy, mostly straight pub that welcomes gay patrons. It's best to check out the scene before you order a drink. Queerfolk sometimes drop by the bar at the **Crescent Hotel** (*see* Sleeps, *below*).

Sleeps

Inns and hotels in Eureka Springs have about as high a quaint-factor as anywhere in the country. Lace curtains, Victorian antiques, and creaky floorboards are the norm. You won't find a four-star luxury property on the level of what you'd see in Aspen or Key West, but even mid-price properties often have private baths with whirlpool tubs, refrigerators or small kitchenettes, and TVs with VCRs. Virtually none of the properties with fewer than 10 rooms have in-room phones.

More than 100 motels and chain properties are on the main roads leading into town, but none of these are gay, nor are they as interesting as the inns and hotels in the historic district. In a pinch drive along Highway 62 or 23 and you'll find something.

For price ranges, *see* lodging Chart B at the front of this guide.

Hotels

$–$$ ⊞ **Basin Park Hotel.** This six-story structure towers above the historic district, hugging the base of one of Eureka Springs's immense hills. The hotel oozes character, from the rickety elevator to the rooms (12 with Jacuzzi baths), furnished with antiques and reproduction furniture. Though it's not fancy or pretentious, the Basin Park brings to mind a late-19th-century grande dame. ✉ *12 Spring St., 72632,* ☎ *501/253–7837 or 800/ 643–4972,* ℻ *501/253–6985. 61 rooms. Restaurant.*

$–$$ ⊞ **Crescent Hotel.** High on a bluff overlooking part of downtown and miles of rolling hills and sharp ridges, the Crescent was once one of the most luxurious properties in the Ozarks. It had lost some of its spark during the past few decades but was recently purchased by the owners of the Basin Park Hotel (*see above*) and has been extensively refurbished. ✉ *75 Prospect Ave., 72632,* ☎ *501/253–9766 or 800/342–9766,* ℻ *501/ 253–5296. 68 rooms. Restaurant.*

Guest Houses and Small Hotels

$$–$$$ 🏠 **Cliff Cottage & The Place Next Door.** This romantic women-owned complex of two historic houses is decked out in Victorian antiques and sits beside an arbor of fresh flowers—it's a favorite setting for commitment ceremonies, and the owners will happily assist you with planning such an event. Restaurants and bars downtown are minutes away on foot, but this place is well hidden from traffic and tourists. ⊠ *13 Armstrong St., 72632,* ☎ *501/253–7409 or 800/799–7409. 4 rooms with TV and private bath. Full breakfast. Hot tub. Mixed gay/straight.*

$$–$$$ 🏠 **Pond Mountain Lodge & Resort.** Set on the highest parcel of land in the county, this mountaintop resort affords 30-mile views and is only a 10-minute drive from downtown. Many of the rustic but warmly decorated rooms have fireplaces and decks, and a separate cottage has two bedrooms and a Jacuzzi. Enjoy swimming in two large ponds and an outdoor pool, or arrange for horseback riding at the stables. Friendly staff, too. ⊠ *Rte. 1, Box 50, 72632,* ☎ *501/253–5877 or 800/583–8043. 6 rooms with TV and private bath, 1 cottage. Full breakfast. Pool, hot tub. Mixed gay/straight.*

$$–$$$ 🏠 **Rock Cottage Gardens.** Built in the 1930s as a run-of-the-mill motor court, this enchanting compound of stone-faced cottages is extraordinary today. Two friendly innkeepers have worked wonders with the grounds, creating a flower-filled garden abundant with hummingbirds and butterflies. The cottages have been restored with vaulted ceilings, antiques, and whirlpool tubs. ⊠ *10 Eugenia St., 72632,* ☎ *501/253–8659 or 800/624–6646. 5 rooms with TV. Full breakfast. Mixed gay/straight.*

$$–$$$ 🏠 **The Woods.** Clean, light-filled, modern, and tastefully decorated, the four Craftsman-style cottages of this hilltop getaway are among the most comfortable in town. All have kitchens, wicker furnishings, whirlpool tubs, and shaded decks. Though secluded, the property is a short and scenic—but steep—stroll from downtown. ⊠ *50 Wall St., 72632,* ☎ *501/253–8281. 4 rooms with TV and private bath. Continental breakfast. Hot tub. Mixed gay/lesbian.*

$$ 🏠 **Arbour Glen Victorian.** Down a quiet lane off Kings Highway, this cute yellow Victorian is set amid lush grounds. Tall trees shade the property, which is also beside a fish pond with a fountain. Rooms are period decorated, with lace, elaborate wallpapers, and plenty of frill—in particular, the lower garden suite has a cherub theme and appeals especially to romantics. ⊠ *7 Lema St., 72632,* ☎ *501/253–9010 or 800/515–4536. 3 rooms with TV and private bath. Full breakfast. Mixed gay/straight.*

$$ 🏠 **Palace Hotel & Bath House.** The advantage to staying at this intimate European-style hotel is access to a full range of spa treatments, from massage and mineral baths (in vintage claw-foot tubs) to clay facials. Rooms in this 1901 structure have porcelain pedestal sinks, long drapes, Victorian fabrics, and antiques. ⊠ *135 Spring St., 72632,* ☎ *501/253–7474. 8 rooms with TV and private bath.*

$–$$ 🏠 **Cedarberry Cottage B&B.** You'll find cozy but affordable rooms at this top-to-bottom-restored Victorian with whimsical gingerbread trim. Rooms have wet bars and refrigerators, and the vegetarian full breakfast is memorable. ⊠ *3 Kings Hwy., 72632,* ☎ *501/253–6115 or 800/590–2424. 3 rooms with phone, TV, and private bath. Full breakfast. Mixed gay/straight.*

$ 🏠 **Golden Gate Cottage.** A 10-minute drive from downtown, this well-hidden lakeside retreat is open only to female travelers. The grounds are peaceful, and the accommodations simple but well-equipped, especially considering the low rates (although you're on your own for breakfast). Rooms have kitchenettes, air-conditioning, and VCRs. ⊠ *Rte. 5, Box 182, 72632,* ☎ *501/253–5291. 3 rooms with TV and private bath. Hot tub. Women.*

The Little Black Book

You can get information from the town's **Web site** (www.eureka-usa.com) or from the **Eureka Springs Chamber of Commerce** (✉ Box 551, visitors center on Hwy. 62W, 72632, ☎ 501/253–8737). You can book rooms and obtain gay-specific information from **Positive Idea Marketing Plans** (☎ 501/253–2401, Web site www.pimps.com). The **Emerald Rainbow** (45½ Spring St., ☎ 501/253–5445), a funky shop with incense, candles, and New Age material, is an excellent resource; one room has pride items, some lesbigay books, some of the gay newspapers from Kansas City and St. Louis, and the monthly gay *Tulsa Family News* (☎ 918/231–7372, e-mail tulsanews@aol.com).

16 Out in Key West

KEY WEST IS LIKE AN ENTIRE ISLAND of goofy great-uncles and eccentric great-aunts. With a mood that is equal parts American, Caribbean, and bacchanalian, this small city takes great delight in failing to fit in with the rest of the world. In keeping with the town's quirkiness, the most cherished annual event here is Fantasy Fest, a weeklong celebration of all that is wacky and wicked. One year the event was atypically lackluster, which almost everyone blamed on the theme, "Lost in the Sixties." Quipped one local, "For most of us here, 'Lost in the Sixties' isn't fantasy, it's reality. It felt pretty much like any other week in Key West."

Indeed, although Key West has always resisted traditional mores (in part because of its geographical isolation), it wasn't until the '60s that members of various fringe groups began moving here in sizeable numbers, and it wasn't until the mid-'70s that gay guest houses began proliferating. For at least a decade, there were sporadic clashes between the new guard of gayification and the conservative, in some cases homophobic, old guard—but these tensions have all but subsided. Acts of intolerance, typically committed only by the occasional unenlightened tourist, are met with stern disdain by all locals. Residents realize that gays and lesbians have been responsible, in part, for as much as 75% of the restoration of Key West's historic district, and that queers account for a tremendous cut of the city's tourism revenue.

Nineteenth-century New England seafarers built a number of the town's clapboard conch (pronounced "conk") houses, many of which still stand. Subsequent waves of immigrants included persecuted Bahamians, Cuban cigar makers, and anybody with a reason to take flight from the mainland—from bootleggers to run-of-the-mill scofflaws. Wrecking, the salvaging of goods from ships smashed against Key West's dangerous coral reefs, was a popular occupation here for many years, as was the harvest of natural sponges. The city was so prosperous during the late 1800s that for a time it was the wealthiest in all of Florida.

In 1912, railroad magnate Henry Flagler connected Key West to the mainland by building the Overseas Railroad and thereby ushering in a second boom era for the city. But the Depression and a devastating hurricane in 1935 snuffed out the good fortune until 1938, when a highway was built atop the old rail bed, again creating a link to the mainland. The navy, which had earlier taken advantage of the island's strategic position, especially during the Civil War, became a major economic power through the '40s, as did tourism and the ever-popular cigar industry.

Walk through the town today and you'll notice a spirited camaraderie not just among gay men, but among lesbians and gays, and among straights and gays. There is a mischievous gleam in the eyes of most Key Westers. If you spend a week here, you'll leave feeling as though you've befriended half the community. That sounds hokey, but it's true.

THE LAY OF THE LAND

Duval Street and Environs

By day the touristy buzz of **Duval Street** is worth braving if only to observe its diversity: groovy middle-age executives with ponytails and Rolexes; children with ice cream–smeared cheeks; husbands fresh off the cruise ships, dodging furtively in and out of gay peep-show parlors; blue-haired matrons picking voraciously over floral muumuus and seashell jewelry; rippled butch boys in white T-shirts and denim cutoffs snapping photos every 50 feet.

The rule on Duval Street is the smaller the street number (numbering begins at Mallory Square on the north end), the better your chances of running into a small-minded boob with homophobic tendencies. At the north end of Duval are several of the more touristy attractions, among them the predictable **Ripley's Believe It or Not Museum** (✉ 527 Duval St., ☎ 305/293–9686). More interesting is the **Wreckers Museum** (✉ 322 Duval St., ☎ 305/294–9502), which details the city's history of wrecking and contains 18th- and 19th-century antiques.

Many gay bars and gay-popular restaurants are on or just off Duval south of Fleming Street, as are dozens of great shops, mostly notably **Fast Buck Freddies** (✉ 500 Duval St., ☎ 305/294–2007), a department store of glitz and camp. The **Heritage House Museum** (✉ 410 Caroline St., ☎ 305/296–3573), a restored 1830s colonial-Caribbean house filled with period antiques, is just a few doors down from the Virgin Key West resort-wear shop.

Parallel to Duval a block west is **Whitehead Street,** a mostly residential avenue with two great museums. The **Ernest Hemingway House** (✉ 907 Whitehead St., ☎ 305/294–1575), in which the author wrote the majority of his life's work, contains original furnishings. Across the street is the 92-foot-tall **Lighthouse Museum** (✉ 938 Whitehead St., ☎ 305/294–0012), which includes the 1880s house in which the keeper lived, plus a few exhibits. It's worth climbing the 98 steps to the tower, which affords magnificent views of town and of the cute guys sunning themselves around the pool of the Lighthouse Court guest house, next door. At the southern end of Whitehead, where it intersects with South Street, is a marker that incorrectly labels the spot the **Southernmost Point** in the United States—it is actually the southernmost point accessible to civilians; the true location is within Key West's naval base.

Mallory Square and Front Street

Front Street and **Mallory Square,** at the north end of Duval Street, constitute the least gay and most touristy part of Key West. Every night vendors, street artists, and tourists rub shoulders during Mallory Square's sunset celebration. Nearby are the **Harry S. Truman Little White House Museum** (✉ 111 Front St., ☎ 305/294–9911), Truman's vacation home; and the **Mel Fisher Maritime Heritage Society Museum** (✉ 200 Greene St., ☎ 305/294–2633), which contains treasure and artifacts recovered in 1985 from a pair of 17th-century Spanish galleons that sank 40 miles offshore during a hurricane.

Historic District

The blocks east of the action along Duval Street loosely constitute Key West's Historic District. Many of the gay guest houses are here, and plenty of other restored cottages and homes bear examining. Several of Key West's famed gay artists lived in the area, including Tennessee Williams (✉

1431 Duncan St.), Jerry Herman (✉ 701 and 703 Fleming Sts.), and the guy who wrote the "Plop, plop, fizz, fizz . . ." jingle for Alka-Seltzer. At the corner of Margaret and Angela streets, you'll find the **City Cemetery** (☎ 305/292–6718); fascinating guided tours are given three times weekly.

Beaches and Bushes

The **Dick Dock,** at the south end of Reynolds Street, juts rigidly into the Atlantic and is popular with gay sunbathers. It was circumcised a few years back when a ferocious storm passed through. The dock is officially closed at night. Other popular sunning spots, for both gay men and lesbians, are the deck at the **Atlantic Shores Beach Club** (*see* Scenes, *below*)— the only place where you can bare everything legally—and the beach at **Fort Zachary Taylor State Historic Park** (✉ follow the signs from Southard St., ☎ 305/292–6713), which tends to draw more locals than tourists. Fort Taylor Park is a pleasant enough spot for tanning your toned butt, but it's not paradise. You definitely shouldn't plan a trip to Key West solely on account of the beaches.

GETTING AROUND

If you book a couple months ahead, the airfare directly to Key West should-n't be much more than the fare from your original destination to Miami. The most you'd pay on the spot is $200 round-trip. Airlines include **American Eagle, Comair, USAir Express, Gulf Stream** (in partnership with United) and, from Naples and Fort Lauderdale, **Cape Air. Greyhound** (☎ 800/231–2222) comes into town twice weekly, but this is a long ride, and considering how cheaply you can rent a car in Miami, it makes more sense to drive. Heading to Key West on a Friday or back to the mainland on a Sunday can take five or six hours; other times expect a three- to four-hour drive.

Key West has slow, but not impossible, traffic. In high season, parking can be tough. It's best to look on a side street in the historic area—a 15-minute walk from Duval Street. A fleet of pink taxis serves the island. Although you can get around comfortably on foot, the most popular forms of transportation are bicycles, which are available for nominal rental fees from most guest houses, and mopeds, which you can rent from **Keys Moped & Scooter** (✉ 523 Truman Ave., ☎ 305/294–0399) and **Moped Hospital** (✉ 601 Truman Ave., ☎ 305/296–3344).

Many charter boat operations offer sunset cruises or snorkeling excursions. The best—and most gay-friendly—are run by **Sebago** (☎ 305/294–5687), which has catamaran sailing, kayaking, and other great possibilities.

EATS

Key West's culinary standards rise annually, although the influx of cruise ships keeps many tacky, dull, and overpriced restaurants going strong. Every restaurant in Key West is ostensibly gay-friendly, but the touristy ones closest to Mallory Square draw few queers. The culinary emphasis is on fresh seafood and tropical fruits and vegetables, and the phrases "Floribbean" and "Key West regional" are bandied about at some of the more inventive eateries. This blend of culinary cultures may result in creations like conch minestrone or pan-seared grouper with mango chutney. Key West is much closer to Cuba than to the Florida mainland, and the connection to that island's heritage is kept alive in the wealth of good Cuban fare.

For price ranges, *see* dining Chart A at the front of this guide.

$$$$ ✕ **Café des Artistes.** Crisp white table linens, a black-and-white-checkered floor, and smooth, varnished wood—plus some of the best local art of any area restaurant—distinguish this spot's formal, diminutive dining room. The food is French, enhanced by plenty of local ingredients. Try the black grouper braised in champagne and served with lime and tomato butter. ⊠ *1007 Simonton St.,* ☎ *305/294–7100.*

$$$–$$$$ ✕ **Alice's on Duval.** This outstanding eatery scores high marks for attentive, knowledgeable servers, a striking tropical-chic decor, and nonpareil nouvelle Caribbean cuisine. Try such inventive dishes as baked Key West lobster in a Thai red curry sauce and vanilla pan-roasted chicken with seared portobello mushroom–studded mashed potatoes. ⊠ *1114 Duval St.,* ☎ *305/292–4888.*

$$$–$$$$ ✕ **Square One.** A departure from Key West's predominant laid-back tropical look, Square One is a cosmopolitan restaurant done in a bold green-and-white color scheme, with white table linen and fine china. The regional cuisine includes rack of lamb roasted and seasoned with whole-grain mustard and honey-shallot confit. Very gay and very trendy. ⊠ *1075 Duval St.,* ☎ *305/296–4300.*

$$$ ✕ **Keybosh.** One of the island's best-kept secrets, Keybosh is a dapper little storefront café with soft red and yellow lighting and a two-level dining room. The Floribbean menu features such enticing fare as achiote-marinated salmon with fruit salsa and watercress salad with rum-sugared pecans and Gorgonzola. ⊠ *Southard and Duval Sts.,* ☎ *305/294–2005.*

$$–$$$ ✕ **Duffy's.** This très gay steak and seafood restaurant shares its kitchen with the esteemed Café des Artistes (*see above*), so, as you might guess, the food is quite good. What's more, Duffy's is not nearly as expensive as its better-dressed neighbor. Prime rib with Florida lobster tail is enough food for two. ⊠ *1007 Simonton St.,* ☎ *305/296–4900.*

$$–$$$ ✕ **Godfrey's.** It's changed names, styles, and hands a few times during the past decade, but this restaurant at the La Terraza guest house has consistently remained one of the most gay-popular dining options in town. The Continental cuisine is generally good; pan-sautéed semiboneless quail with fresh thyme and rosemary is a standout. ⊠ *1125 Duval St.,* ☎ *305/296–6706.*

$$–$$$ ✕ **La Trattoria.** One of the better Italian restaurants in town, and certainly one of the gayest, La Trattoria has two dining rooms—the smaller one romantic and intimate, the larger better for groups of friends. The straightforward cooking—veal piccata, green and white fettuccine with mushroom and prosciutto cream sauce—draws praise from locals. ⊠ *524 Duval St.,* ☎ *305/296–1075.*

$$–$$$ ✕ **Mangoes.** One of Duval Street's true places to be seen, Mangoes brims with colorful sorts. The designer pizzas, composed salads, pastas, and grills—all with nouvelle Floribbean touches—are commendable. Consider rib eye steak *Caribe* (pan-charred with tamarind steak sauce and yucca). ⊠ *700 Duval St.,* ☎ *305/292–4606.*

$$ ✕ **Blue Heaven.** In the heart of the historic Bahama Village neighborhood, Blue Heaven offers one of the most memorable dining experiences on the island, partly because of the stellar Caribbean and down-home American cooking and partly because the courtyard dining area is presided over by at least two dozen friendly, if overly eager, roosters. Vegetarian black bean soup, tofu burgers, jerk chicken, and fresh grilled fish are among the better dishes. ⊠ *729 Thomas St.,* ☎ *305/296–8666.*

$$ ✕ **Café Karumba.** The owners of the venerable pasta house Mangia Mangia (*see below*) also run this upbeat Caribbean eatery, where you can sip a *mojito* (a Cuban take on a mint julep, consisting of fine white rum, fresh-squeezed lime juice, fresh mint, and a splash of soda) at the bar before heading to your hand-painted table to sample unbelievably tender sautéed conch with coconut, mango, and slivered almonds. ⊠ *1215 Duval St.,* ☎ *305/296–2644.*

Central Key West

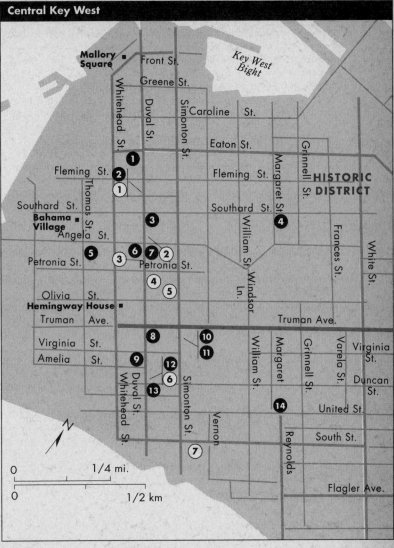

Eats ●

Alice's on
Duval, **9**

Blue Heaven, **5**

Café des
Artistes, **11**

Café
Karumba, **13**

Camille's, **7**

Duffy's, **10**

El Siboney, **14**

Godfrey's, **12**

Keybosh, **3**

La Trattoria, **2**

Mangia
Mangia, **4**

Mangoes, **6**

Sippin', **1**

Square One, **8**

Scenes ○

Atlantic Shores
Beach Club, **7**

Bourbon Street Pub, **3**

Club International, **5**

801 Bar, **4**

Epoch, **2**

One Saloon of
Key West, **1**

Treetop Bar, **6**

$–$$ ✕ **Mangia Mangia.** The slogan here is "pasta to the people," a philoso-
phy reflected by the many varieties of heavenly homemade pasta, all fairly
priced. The painstakingly preserved building has a lovely, quiet garden
and redbrick patio in back. More than 300 choices on the wine list. ✉
900 Southard St., ☎ *305/294–2469.*

$ ✕ **Camille's.** You'll need luck and persistence to get a seat at this small
storefront bistro most nights, but the delightfully dishy atmosphere and
down-home comfort food are worth the trouble. Unusual objets d'art and
vintage photos of movie stars fill the dining room. Expect good salads
and sandwiches, such as Philly cheese steak, and delicious pancakes for
breakfast. ✉ *703½ Duval St.,* ☎ *305/296–4811.*

$ ✕ **El Siboney.** This zero-atmosphere place is the Cuban answer to Deep
South barbecued-ribs joints. Rickety tables are set with plastic tablecloths
and paper napkins. Try such Havana specialties as conch chowder, garlic chicken, stuffed shrimp and crabs, *platanos* (plantains), and a sweet
flan to top it off. ✉ *900 Catherine St.,* ☎ *305/296–4184. No credit cards.*

Coffeehouse Culture

Sippin'. This large coffeehouse a block from Duval Street is the java joint
of choice among most gay locals thanks to fun piped-in music, gilt-frame
posters, queer and straight magazines and newspapers, and plenty of comfy
seating. In addition to coffees, you'll find an extensive selection of specialty teas. ✉ *424 Eaton St.,* ☎ *305/293–0555.*

SCENES

It's surprising that such a small community has so many nightlife options,
particularly when you consider that at least a dozen guest houses have
late-afternoon cocktail hours and bar set-ups around the pool. But of course,
if you're in Key West to socialize, bar-hopping is another way to mingle
with locals as well as with out-of-towners staying at other accommodations. Key West draws a considerably older median crowd (largely ages
35 to 55) than South Beach, and has none of the body-glorification or
standoffishness of some gay resorts. Most of the bar activity is on or just
off Duval Street, from about Appelrouth Lane to Olivia Street. Weeknights,
except during major weeks for tourism, are typically quiet at these bars,
with Fridays and Saturdays the only times you can count on big crowds.

Prime Suspects

Atlantic Shores Beach Club. Key West's essential daytime "sun and be seen"
bar consists of an outdoor deck, pool, and dock jutting into the Atlantic
Ocean from a newly revamped motel complex on South Street. Both boys
and girls lie here all day, often nude, and many more come to watch the
sun set. Sunday's "tea by the sea" dance has been de rigueur for years.
✉ *511 South St.,* ☎ *305/296–2491. Crowd: diverse, mixed m/f.*

Bourbon Street Pub. This is a great, friendly place with a small bar up
front with cocktail tables, a larger central bar in back, and video screens
galore; it's also well lit, and the music isn't ear-splitting. Many nights you
can catch awful (but still entertaining) drag shows on the stage in back,
which, unfortunately, is difficult to see from several parts of the bar. ✉
724 Duval St., ☎ *305/296–1992. Crowd: 75/25 m/f, all ages, amiable
staff, mix of locals and tourists.*

Epoch. Although it draws a mix of gays and straights, Epoch is a spectacular space with a big-city feel, intense sound systems and lighting, and
plenty of space for lounging. The ground floor has a few bars and a big
dance floor; upstairs you can either watch the dancers down below from
a long balcony, or enter a separate cocktail lounge, off which a balcony
overlooks Duval Street. ✉ *623 Duval St.,* ☎ *305/296–8521. Crowd: mixed
gay/straight, 20s to 40s, touristy.*

One Saloon of Key West. What used to be more of a leather bar has gradually become the town's standard cruise bar and small disco. Visitors looking for a cruisy ambience love this place, though relatively few locals bother with it. The dance floor is not especially large, but everyone seems to have a good time. ✉ *1 Appelrouth La.,* ☎ *305/296–8118. Crowd: mostly male, young by Key West standards, a bit stand-and-model, touristy.*

Neighborhood Haunts

Club International (✉ 900 Simonton St., ☎ 305/296–9230) is a cheerful video bar that's popular with both women and men—it has the strongest lesbian following of any bar in town. Some locals are known to pop into the open-air, divey **801 Bar** (✉ 801 Duval St., ☎ 305/294–4737) as often as three times a day to catch up with friends and pitch the dish; the smaller bar in the back gets the town's only leather contingent, and the upstairs is a cabaret lounge. The La Terraza guest house's **Treetop Bar** (✉ 1125 Duval St., ☎ 305/296–6706) consists of a poolside bar, a cocktail lounge, and an intimate piano bar. Less of a dive than most of the local bars, it's still not a place that will leave you feeling underdressed or out of place (the friendly bar staff deserves at least part of the credit for this). The Sunday afternoon tea dance, which precedes the evening tea dance at Atlantic Shores, is a must-do.

Action

Key West has had adult bookstores for years, and some of them have video booths. **Southern Exposure** (✉ 901 Duval St., ☎ 305/292–2171), a bright, modern sex shop, is the newest, and definitely the nicest, of the bunch, but it has no booths.

SLEEPS

Key West has no shortage of rooms, but seasonal events make bookings tight. As with Provincetown or Palm Springs, the gay guest house network here is well developed, and choices abound. Most of the mainstream guest houses here are completely gay-friendly, too, but lack the convivial mood of the all-gay establishments. The bulk of the guest houses—gay and straight—are either in the heart of downtown, along Duval, Whitehead, or Simonton streets, or in the Historic District several blocks east of downtown. The latter accommodations are usually the quietest and most secluded—but nowhere are you too far from the action.

Key West has plenty of great hotels as well, but at any large resort you're paying as much for the extensive staff and facilities as you are for your room. Consequently, comparably furnished and spacious rooms at most guest houses cost from 40% to 60% less than rooms at resorts. Bear in mind that space is tight during the annual **Fantasy Fest** (last week of October), **Women in Paradise** (a.k.a. women's week, mid-July), and the **Key West Theatre Festival** (late September–early October).

For price ranges, *see* lodging Chart A at the front of this guide.

Hotels and Motels

$$$$ ⊞ **Pier House Resort.** Just off Mallory Square, this magnificent hideaway is unaffordable for most mortals. Whirlpool baths, CD players, VCRs, are some of the luxurious touches. There's also a beloved but overpriced restaurant and one of the most impressive health spas on the island. ✉ *1 Duval St., 33040,* ☎ *305/296–4600 or 800/327–8340,* FAX *305/296–7569. 142 rooms. Restaurants, pool, health club.*

$$ ⊠ **Atlantic Shores Motel.** Site of the popular oceanfront bar and grill of the same name, the art deco–inspired Atlantic Shores sports a sleek lavender, turquoise, and yellow exterior. None of the rooms have ocean views, but the pool and deck at the end of the property are on the water. ⊠ *510 South St., 33040,* ☎ *305/296–2491 or 800/526–3559,* FAX *305/294–2753. 72 rooms. Restaurant, pool.*

$–$$ ⊞ **Pegasus International.** Rooms at this art deco property are of the standard hotel variety, but for the price and the convenient location on the corner of Southard and Duval streets, you can't complain. The management is extremely gay-friendly. ⊠ *501 Southard St., 33040,* ☎ *305/294–9323 or 800/397–8148,* FAX *305/294–4741. 30 rooms. Pool.*

Guest Houses

On or Near Duval Street

$$$–$$$$ ⊞ **Heron House.** Heron House ranks among the best of the island's several straight-but-gay-friendly luxury inns. Rooms are clean and luxurious with teak, oak, and cedar walls, granite bathtubs, stained-glass transoms above the French doors, and rich colors and fabrics. Most rooms open onto the central pool. The overall mood is sophisticated and easygoing. ⊠ *512 Simonton St., 33040,* ☎ *305/294–9227 or 800/294–1644,* FAX *305/294–5692, e-mail heronkw@aol.com. 23 rooms with phone, TV, and private bath. Pool. Continental breakfast. Mostly straight.*

$$$–$$$$ ⊞ **Lighthouse Court.** The reputation of the Lighthouse Court has risen in recent years, thanks to several refurbishments. It's intensely social, with its own reception lounge-cum-video bar, a maze of lushly landscaped decks, one of the busiest hot tubs in town, and the most rooms of any guest house compound. Accommodations are large and clean, but spare—you're paying for the atmosphere and the terrific location near downtown. ⊠ *902 Whitehead St., 33040,* ☎ *305/294–9588. 42 rooms with phone, TV, and private bath. Restaurant, pool, hot tub, exercise room. Gay male.*

$$$–$$$$ ⊞ **Pilot House.** The Pilot House, which also operates the Duval Suites a few blocks away, consists of two distinct properties. Choose either the gray gingerbread Victorian with hardwood floors and antiques, or the contemporary poolside cabana house with tile floors, wicker furniture, kitchens, and huge bathrooms with whirlpool tubs and separate showers. Guests at either spot have full use of two pools and the extensive grounds. ⊠ *414 Simonton St., 33040,* ☎ *305/294–8719 or 800/648–3780,* FAX *305/294–9298. 14 rooms with phone, TV, and private bath. 2 pools. Continental breakfast. Mostly straight.*

$$$ ⊞ **Lightbourn Inn.** Charming hosts Scott and Kelly run one of the town's more eccentric inns (which is saying a lot in Key West), a 1903 Queen Anne mansion that was built by a notable cigar manufacturer. Most of the guest rooms surround a pool and sundeck and have fine architectural detailing, antiques, and Oriental carpets. Breakfast is lavish. ⊠ *907 Truman Ave., 33040,* ☎ *305/296–5152 or 800/352–6011,* FAX *305/294–9490. 10 rooms with phone, TV, and private bath. Pool. Full breakfast. Mixed gay/straight.*

$$–$$$$ ⊞ **Big Ruby's.** Qualitatively similar to the Brass Key, Big Ruby's caters to a slightly more singles-oriented set. The resort is secluded and peaceful, with beautiful landscaping, an abundance of sundecks, and an unusual outdoor shower large enough for two. Rooms are sleek, contemporary, spotless, and bright. As for the staff, you won't find a warmer or more professional bunch of guys in Key West. ⊠ *409 Appelrouth La., 33040,* ☎ *305/296–2323 or 800/477–7829,* FAX *305/296–0281. 17 rooms with TV and private bath. Pool. Full breakfast. Mostly gay male.*

$$–$$$$ ⊞ **Duval Suites.** Run by the owners of the Pilot House, but with an even stronger lesbian and gay following, this spacious and clean complex consists of both cottages and suites with either decks or balconies, some over-

looking Duval Street. ⊠ *724 Duval St. Upstairs, 33040,* ☎ *305/294–8719 or 800/648–3780,* ℻ *305/294–9298. 8 suites with phone, TV, and private bath; 1 bungalow. Pool, hot tub. Continental breakfast. Mixed gay/straight.*

$$–$$$ 🏠 **Chelsea House.** A short walk from the action along Duval Street, this enchanting Victorian house is run by some of the friendliest (and cutest) guys in Key West. There are several rooms in the main building; the others are spread among a few small outbuildings, including a cozy pool house with three rooms that open onto the deck. Furnishings are a mix of antiques, four-poster beds, and rattan and wicker. The owners run a similarly nice property, the Red Rooster, next door. ⊠ *707 Truman Ave., 33040,* ☎ *305/296–2211 or 800/845–8859,* ℻ *305/296–4822, e-mail chelseahse@aol.com. 19 rooms with phone, TV, and private bath. Pool. Continental breakfast. Mixed gay/straight.*

$$–$$$ 🏠 **Colours.** Rooms in this stunning 1886 mansion have been restored down to the finest details—ornate carved moldings, elegant wallpaper borders, and fine antiques; many have terraces, and one detached unit opens right onto the pool. Such thoughtful touches as robes and snack baskets are in every room. The grounds are less extensive than at some of the other first-rate gay resorts, but there's still a nice pool and plenty of room to spread out and soak up some rays. ⊠ *410 Fleming St., 33040,* ☎ *305/294–6977 or 800/934–5622,* ℻ *305/292–9030. 12 rooms with phone and TV; 10 with private bath. Pool, hot tub. Continental breakfast. Mostly gay male/lesbian.*

$$–$$$ 🏠 **Rainbow House.** If staying at an all-female house is a priority, Rainbow House is your one choice. A solid resort, this nicely laid-out former cigar factory (circa 1886) has beautiful sundecks, a pretty heated pool, and a personable staff. Rooms are simply decorated with pastel-hued walls and tropical bedspreads and curtains; the bathrooms are large and modern. ⊠ *525 United St., 33040,* ☎ *305/292–1450 or 800/749–6696. 25 rooms with phone, TV, and private bath. Pool, hot tub. Continental breakfast. Lesbian.*

$$–$$$ 🏠 **Sea Isle Resort.** This popular full-scale gay resort is complete with abundant decking and lounge space, a large pool, and a full exercise room. Rooms are of the motor lodge variety, but tile floors, modern baths, pastel walls and fabrics, and minirefrigerators provide all the comfort you'll need. Some have VCRs, separate seating areas, and kitchens. ⊠ *915 Windsor La., 33040,* ☎ *305/294–5188 or 800/995–4786,* ℻ *305/296–7143, e-mail seaislefun@aol.com. 24 rooms with phone, TV, and private bath. Pool, hot tub, exercise room. Continental breakfast. Mostly gay male.*

$$ 🏠 **Merlinn.** This low-key, friendly resort a block from Duval Street has the most tropical atmosphere of any in town, with extensive wooden decking, a large pool, and dense and beautiful foliage. Accommodations include basic economy rooms, spacious apartments with kitchens, and a couple of whimsically decorated suites. ⊠ *811 Simonton St., 33040,* ☎ *305/296–3336 or 800/642–4753. 13 rooms with TV and private bath, 5 apartments. Pool. Continental breakfast. Mixed gay/straight.*

$–$$ 🏠 **Tropical Inn.** Close to bars, the Tropical Inn is one of the best deals in town—a delightfully renovated conch house. Rooms have new furnishings, clean and modern baths, and central air-conditioning; they aren't huge, but some have balconies overlooking the street. Next door are a pair of cottages that share a hot tub and secluded redbrick patio. ⊠ *812 Duval St., 33040,* ☎ *305/294–9977. 5 rooms with TV and private bath, 2 apartments. Hot tub (for apartments). Continental breakfast. Mixed gay/straight.*

Historic District

$$$–$$$$ 🏠 **Brass Key.** This duo of immaculate yellow clapboard buildings contains some of the most elegant rooms on the island, with tropical-print

quilts, high-quality colonial reproductions, and clean, modern baths. Every detail has been thought of—including phones with dataports and voice mail, TVs with VCRs, and a generous cocktail party held each evening around the hot tub. ☒ *412 Frances St., 33040,* ☎ *305/296–4719 or 800/ 932–9119,* FAX *305/296–1994, Web site www.brasskey.com. 15 rooms with phone, TV, and private bath. Pool, hot tub. Continental breakfast. Gay male/lesbian.*

$$$–$$$$ ☷ **Coral Tree.** The owners of the Oasis also run this considerably quieter but similarly inviting establishment across the street. From the antiques-filled lobby to the four-poster beds and private balconies to the lovely redbrick patio and pool out back, this 1892 house is a delight. Guests at either house have access to the public rooms and swimming pools of both. ☒ *822 Fleming St., 33040,* ☎ *305/296–2131 or 800/362–7477,* FAX *305/ 296–2131, ext. 132, e-mail oasisct@aol.com. 11 rooms with phone, TV, and private bath. Pool. Continental breakfast. Gay male.*

$$$ ☷ **Equator.** The hottest new resort on Fleming Street, Equator has plush rooms with wood floors, designer fabrics, feather pillows and comforters, and contemporary Caribbean-influenced furniture; some have whirlpool bathtubs, kitchenettes, and French doors opening onto a porch or deck. The grounds, with a large Jacuzzi, heated pool, and glass-block outdoor showers, are geared toward a fairly social bunch. ☒ *818 Fleming St., 33040,* ☎ *305/294–7775 or 800/278–4552,* FAX *305/296–5765. 15 rooms with phone, TV, and private bath. Pool, hot tub. Full breakfast. Gay male.*

$$–$$$$ ☷ **Alexander's.** A tad less sumptuous than the nearby Brass Key, this popular resort is no less inviting—with abundant tropical flowers, sundecks, rattan and wicker furnishings, and clean tiled bathrooms, some of which are shared. The main 1910 house has been flawlessly restored, and several units were added two years ago. ☒ *1118 Fleming St., 33040,* ☎ *305/294– 9919 or 800/654–9919,* FAX *305/295–0357, e-mail alexghouse@aol.com. 16 rooms with TV, most with private bath. Pool, hot tub. Continental breakfast. Gay male/lesbian.*

$$–$$$$ ☷ **Nassau House.** Rooms at this rambling inn contain a mix of tropical wicker furnishings, attractive antiques, and impressive art; the top-floor suites have separate living rooms and kitchens. In back a small lagoon-inspired pool has spa jets and plenty of room for sunning. ☒ *1016 Fleming St., 33040,* ☎ *305/296–8513 or 800/296–8513. 8 rooms with phone, TV, and private bath. Pool. Continental breakfast. Mixed gay/straight.*

$$–$$$$ ☷ **William Anthony House.** This complex consists of a restored turn-of-the-century house and, five blocks away, a cozy conch cottage with both a two-bedroom suite and an apartment. Although the main house is historic, the six rooms (four of which are spacious full suites with kitchenettes that can sleep up to four) have modern, attractive furnishings, immaculate white-tile baths, and a liveable feel. ☒ *613 Caroline St., 33040,* ☎ *305/294–2887 or 800/613–2276,* FAX *305/294–9209. 6 rooms with TV and private bath; 1 cottage. Hot tub (at both main inn and cottage). Continental breakfast. Mixed gay/straight.*

$$–$$$ ☷ **Curry House.** The oldest exclusively gay guest house on the island, this 1890 house remains a dependable choice. Rooms are clean and bright, with date-palm walls. ☒ *806 Fleming St., 33040,* ☎ *305/294–6777 or 800/633–7439,* FAX *305/294–5322. 9 rooms, most with private bath. Pool, hot tub. Continental breakfast. Gay male.*

$$–$$$ ☷ **Lime House Inn.** This 1850s clothing-optional inn keeps a low profile and draws a nice mix of guys—it's usually quite social, especially around the large pool. Rooms are simple but have such thoughtful touches as coffeemakers and voice mail, and many have kitchenettes. ☒ *219 Elizabeth St., 33040,* ☎ *305/296–2978 or 800/374–4242,* FAX *305/294–5858. 11 rooms with phone and TV, most with private bath. Pool, hot tub. Continental breakfast. Gay male.*

$$–$$$ ▣ **Oasis.** Room for room, the Oasis is still slightly less fancy (and less expensive) than its sister property, the Coral Tree, but the gap between the two is narrowing thanks to constant improvements. The Oasis has three buildings, plenty of decking, a spacious pool and hot tub separated by a gorgeous mosaic wall, an attractive indoor common area, and a diverse, outgoing crowd of single guys and couples. ✉ *823 Fleming St., 33040,* ☎ *305/296–2131 or 800/362–7477,* FAX *305/296–2131, ext. 132, e-mail oasisct@aol.com. 19 rooms with phone and TV; most with private bath. Pool, hot tub. Continental breakfast. Gay male.*

$$ ▣ **Mangrove House.** This smart, small, yellow Bahamian house with thin white columns and a perfectly restored tin roof is one of the most elegant, low-key all-male getaways in town, an ideal retreat for couples. Guests can mingle around the large pool, hot tub, and lounge chairs in the attractively landscaped backyard. ✉ *623 Southard St., 33040,* ☎ *305/294–1866 or 800/294–1866,* FAX *305/294–8757. 4 rooms with phone, TV, and private bath. Pool, hot tub. Continental breakfast. Gay male.*

$–$$$$ ▣ **Coconut Grove.** Next door to the Oasis, this equally social compound has three buildings, most with functional, tropical decor (lots of rattan and wicker) and rooms in a variety of configurations, accommodating from one to six guests. The roof deck is one of the highest points in the Historic District. The evening cocktail hour is one of the best in town. ✉ *817 Fleming St., 33040,* ☎ *305/296–5107 or 800/262–6055. 20 rooms with TV, most with private bath. Pool, hot tub, outdoor exercise room. Continental breakfast. Mostly gay male.*

Rentals

Rental prices have shot up in the past 10 years, but for a group of six to eight, a weeklong stay in a fairly luxurious place still costs a fraction of what you'd pay to stay as couples at one of the better guest houses. Two-, three-, and four-bedroom accommodations in high season start as low as $900 a week but average between $1,800 and $2,400; off-season you can find a small weekly rental for $650 to $700. A few of the better gay-friendly sources are **Greg O'Berry Real Estate** (✉ 701 Caroline St., 33040, ☎ 305/294–6637 or 800/654–2781), **Key West Realty** (✉ 1109 Duval St., 33040, ☎ 305/294–7368 or 800/654–5131, e-mail kwrealty@vacations3.com), **Olde Island Realty** (✉ 525 Simonton St., 33040, ☎ 305/292–7997 or 305/294–6712), and **Rent Key West** (✉ 1107 Truman Ave., 33040, ☎ 305/292–9508 or 800/833–7368).

THE LITTLE BLACK BOOK

At Your Fingertips

AIDS Help Hotline (☎ 305/296–6196 or 800/640–3867). **City of Key West Department of Transportation** (☎ 305/292–8165). **Florida Keys Taxi Dispatch** (☎ 305/296–1800). **General gay/lesbian crisis and referral help line** (☎ 305/296–4357). **Key West Business Guild (gay)** (✉ Box 1208, 33041, ☎ 305/294–4603 or 800/535–7797). **Key West Chamber of Commerce (mainstream)** (✉ 402 Wall St., 33040, ☎ 305/294–2587). **South Florida AIDS Network** (☎ 305/585–7744).

Gay Media

Not one but two gay publications have started up here recently: *Celebrate* (☎ 305/296–1566) is a weekly gay newspaper; *Gay West* (☎ 305/292–1183, Web site www.gaywest.com) comes out twice a month; its Web site is the official one of the Key West Business Guild and provides all sorts of useful information. The monthly *Southern Exposure Guide* (☎ 305/294–6303; Web site www.kwest.com) is a helpful resource for gay and lesbian travelers. The **Key West Business Guild** (☎ 800/535–7797) publishes a useful map and directory of gay-owned or gay-friendly businesses.

Lips (☎ 305/534–4830), a lesbian monthly newspaper out of South Beach, has some Key West coverage.

BOOKSTORES

One of the best bookstores in town, **Flaming Maggie's Books** (⊠ 830 Fleming St., ☎ 305/294–3931) has an excellent selection of gay and lesbian books and magazines, books by or about local authors, and other good literature. There's also a small coffee bar here that serves juices, sodas, and snacks. Another option is **Key West Island Books** (⊠ 513 Fleming St., ☎ 305/294–2904), which has a mix of used and new titles and a nice selection of queer and women's titles. Also check out **L. Valladares & Son** (⊠ 1200 Duval St., ☎ 305/296–5032), the best newsstand in town. The **Leather Master** (⊠ 418A Appelrouth La., ☎ 305/292–5051) carries a small selection of books as well as cards and gay novelties.

Working Out

The larger resorts and a couple of the larger gay guest houses have fitness centers, but most gay men and lesbians work out at **Club Body Tech Health & Fitness** (⊠ 1075 Duval St., ☎ 305/292–9683); weekly memberships are reasonably priced.

17 *Out in Las Vegas*

IN LAS VEGAS you always have time and you always have money. From the perspective of the casinos—and they dictate virtually every city ordinance—it's imperative that you spend your time and money gambling. Only if the average Las Vegas visitor gambles at least a couple of hours a day will the casinos, and therefore Clark County, turn a profit. In 1996, the county alone "won" $5.78 billion in gaming revenue. The casinos themselves raked in billions more.

Day blends imperceptibly into night in Las Vegas. The casinos, which stay open 24 hours, have no windows or clocks to remind you where you are, how long you've been there, or whether other obligations exist. Perhaps the greatest example of timelessness is the trompe l'oeil ceiling above the Forum Shops at Caesars, which are laid out to resemble an ancient Roman city. The ceiling looks like the sky, and the lighting changes subtly but constantly so that one hour the city appears dark, and an hour later it appears light. Spend a few hours here and the distinction between night and day becomes meaningless.

The region has never had a particularly gay following, but this is changing as Las Vegas grows (the population has risen from 125,000 in 1970 to nearly 450,000 today). Transplants, many of them from California, have been drawn by the low cost of living, predictably moderate weather, and job opportunities. The gay newcomers, used to bars, coffeehouses, and enlightened laws, have helped create an active if relatively small community whose pride march gets bigger every year. The conservative Mormon Church still wields considerable political influence in Las Vegas, but many city officeholders are gay-supportive and most big casinos include sexual orientation in their antidiscrimination policies. Las Vegas has become progressive, not necessarily in relation to other major cities but in the sense that so much has been accomplished in such a short period.

THE LAY OF THE LAND

The Strip

Most of the glamorous casinos are along **the Strip,** the nickname for six-lane Las Vegas Boulevard from about Hacienda Avenue north to about Sahara Avenue. Southwest of the Strip, along Paradise Road just below Tropicana Avenue, a small patch of gay bars and businesses has come to be known as the **Gay Quarter,** but there are no specific attractions.

CASINOS

Las Vegas casinos run the gamut from spectacular compounds inspired by theme parks to dives that date from the early '50s. Whether you gamble or not, it's hard not to appreciate their splendor. Below is an entirely random cross-section:

Caesars Palace. Great restaurants, luxurious hotel rooms, a terrific shopping gallery, and a sophisticated atmosphere have made Caesars a favorite among gay travelers. The casino itself has two wings—one for high rollers, the other for low-stakes gamblers. Other compounds blaze with neon and bright lights, but Caesars creates the feeling of ancient Rome with marble columns, archways, and plush design elements. ⊠ *3570 Las Vegas Blvd. S,* ☎ *702/731–7110.*

Flamingo Hilton. There are two reasons not to miss the Flamingo: history and a charming sense of charmlessness. Mobster Bugsy Siegel introduced a "classy" gambling scene to Las Vegas by opening the Fabulous Flamingo in 1947. His mafia cronies exterminated him shortly after the hotel's debut, and as the decades passed, its sophistication waned. The casino's appeal has always depended upon America's relationship to pink flamingos. Today the Flamingo Hilton is back in style—entirely in spite of itself. ⊠ *3555 Las Vegas Blvd. S,* ☎ *702/733–3111.*

Golden Nugget. Most downtown casinos are rough-hewn predecessors of the fabulous wonderlands that dominate the Strip, but the Golden Nugget recalls the days when downtown drew high rollers. Though visitors are spared the radioactive glow of neon, there is more than enough gold to compensate: gold elevators, pay phones, slot machines, and a 63-pound nugget said to be the world's largest. ⊠ *129 Fremont St.,* ☎ *702/385–7111.*

Hard Rock. The surprisingly intimate Hard Rock attracts the young and stylish with indirect lighting, a minimal amount of glitter, slots with guitar-neck handles, and music memorabilia—P.J. Harvey's guitar, the touring costumes of Elton John and Chris Isaak, et cetera. This Hard Rock, very close to the Gay Quarter, avoids the touristy exuberance of the corporation's theme restaurants. ⊠ *4455 Paradise Rd.,* ☎ *702/693–5000.*

Luxor. A sleek pyramid rising high above the Strip, the Egyptian-theme Luxor emits a laser straight into the sky. Unfortunately, the searing glow of every other light in Las Vegas gobbles up the ray: It's barely visible. The casino at Luxor is spacious and less frenetic than some. ⊠ *3900 Las Vegas Blvd. S,* ☎ *702/262–4000.*

MGM Grand. This well-designed Wizard of Oz–theme casino, the world's largest, appeals to all types of people, from high rollers to families with kids. Among the draws are several high-end restaurants and a phenomenal theme park that re-creates Hollywood's back lots and buzzes with rides and attractions. ⊠ *3799 Las Vegas Blvd. S,* ☎ *702/891–1111.*

New York, New York. One of the latest casino-resort complexes to open along the Strip, this remarkably detailed re-creation of Gotham has a rather ordinary casino but is worth touring to catch a glimpse of the Brooklyn Bridge entryway and various Big Apple elements. Don't miss the miniature Greenwich Village, complete with a steaming manhole, newspaper dispensers riddled with graffiti, a great pastry shop, and takeoffs on Sheridan Square and Christopher Place (with, alas, no reference to the Stonewall Inn). Outside, a roller coaster zooms over the mock Manhattan skyline. It's all amazingly authentic—except for the disturbingly perky staff. ⊠ *3790 Las Vegas Blvd. S,* ☎ *702/740–6969.*

AND COMING SOON...
In 1998, the **Bellagio** (⊠ Las Vegas Blvd. at Flamingo Rd.) will open to become one of the ritziest casino resorts in the city, with rooms going for $200 nightly. Soon after, the **Paris Casino Resort** (⊠ Las Vegas Blvd. at Flamingo Rd.) will open, complete with replicas of Parisian landmarks.

Downtown

Formerly the hub of the city's nightlife, **downtown** experienced a decline for many years and has only recently been cleaned up, most notably by the $70 million **Fremont Street Experience,** a covered and landscaped pedestrian mall with shops and casinos. While the Strip grows in popularity, downtown struggles to keep pace, but it's at the center of the action when it comes to pawnshops, among them the **Ace Loan Company** (⊠ 215 N. 3rd St., ☎ 702/384–5771) and **Stoney's Loan and Jewelry** (⊠ 126 S. 1st St., ☎ 702/384–2686).

Wedding Chapel Row

Bette Midler and Richard Gere are just two celebrities alleged to have exchanged vows (not with each other, thankfully) along Las Vegas's handy **Wedding Chapel Row,** which is along Las Vegas Boulevard between Sahara Avenue and Charleston Boulevard. Liberal divorce and marriage laws were instituted in Nevada in 1931 to lure tourists: A man and a woman can get hitched faster than you can fry an egg. Gay weddings are not sanctioned by the state of Nevada, but the **Metropolitan Community Church** (⊠ 1140 Almond Tree La., ☎ 702/369–4380) performs same-sex commitment ceremonies.

Odds and Ends

Set in a small one-story building that looks as though it might once have housed a Chinese fast-food restaurant, the **Liberace Museum** (⊠ 1775 E. Tropicana Ave., ☎ 702/798–5595) is a giddy tribute to the late entertainer, filled with photos, costumes (including Lee's beloved Czar Nicholas uniform), mannequins, and pianos (one was played by Chopin, another by Gershwin). A small gift shop sells Liberace soap, ashtrays, and other colorful mementos.

Among the more than 200 vintage autos at the **Imperial Palace Automobile Museum** (⊠ 3535 Las Vegas Blvd. S, ☎ 702/731–3311) is Adolf Hitler's 1939 Mercedes-Benz touring sedan. On exhibit at the **Debbie Reynolds Hollywood Movie Museum** (⊠ 305 Convention Center Dr., ☎ 702/734–0711) are portions of Ms. Reynolds's $30 million collection of costumes, furnishings, and props. Though not quite as dazzling as Debbie's spread, the **Magic and Movie Hall of Fame** (⊠ 3555 Las Vegas Blvd. S, ☎ 702/737–1343), connected to O'Shea's Casino, contains a splendid assortment of movie, magic, and ventriloquist memorabilia.

The city's arts scene is virtually nonexistent, but all the public libraries have galleries, and the Sahara West branch shares a fine contemporary structure with the **Las Vegas Art Museum** (⊠ 9600 W. Sahara Ave., ☎ 702/360–8000), where the emphasis is on new works.

For the best view of the region, the **Stratosphere** (⊠ 2000 Las Vegas Blvd. S, ☎ 702/380–7777) can't be beat—at 1,149 feet, it's the tallest freestanding observation tower in the country.

Lake Mead

Head east on Lake Mead Boulevard out of north Las Vegas to get to the **gay beach at Lake Mead.** Continue past Hollywood Boulevard and wind through the desert about 5 miles until you reach a stop sign. Turn left and head north toward Overton; 4.8 miles later, make a right onto the road at the 8-mile marker. The ride from town takes about 40 minutes. Keep your pants on at the beach—the cops have been cracking down. Not far from here is the 726-foot-high **Hoover Dam** (⊠ U.S. 93, ☎ 702/294–3523), which has a visitors center and museum and dramatic observation platforms.

GETTING AROUND

You'll need a car, but rentals are cheap and the streets are idiot-proof, laid out in a grid pattern. Las Vegas Boulevard is the main north–south route; it's bisected by several major east–west roads, Tropicana, Flamingo, Desert Inn, and Sahara being the most central. Most attractions, bars, and restaurants are near one another, so cab fares never run high. You can easily hail cabs at hotels and at the airport (but not on the streets). It is possible to take a bus up and down the Strip, but few tourists do.

EATS

Dining in Las Vegas sucked until recently, but celebrity chefs from across the nation have opened some super eateries, mostly inside the newer casinos. Generally, the best *and* worst restaurants are in casinos. Buffets and restaurants at low-stakes casinos can be a fabulous value, but the food ranges from bland to tragic.

For price ranges, *see* dining Chart B at the front of this guide.

In the Casinos

$$$$ ✕ **Emeril's.** Presided over by the charismatic TV chef Emeril Lagasse (star of *Emeril Live* and *The Essence of Emeril*), who's been doing things right in New Orleans for years, this French Quarter–theme seafood restaurant at the MGM Grand excels in freshness and creative presentation. The Alabama rock-shrimp spring-rolls appetizer comes with an Oriental-vegetable salad. Bacon-wrapped monkfish braised in eggplant, olives, tomatoes, and onions is a favorite entrée. ✉ *3799 Las Vegas Blvd. S,* ☎ *702/891–7374.*

$$$$ ✕ **Napa.** World-renowned chef Jean-Louis Palladin opened this contemporary Cal-French restaurant in the already gastronomically stellar Rio Hotel and Casino. Wood-grilled veal chops and eggplant stuffed with lamb are among the specialties. An astounding 240 of the 600 wine selections are available by the glass. ✉ *3700 W. Flamingo Rd.,* ☎ *702/252– 7777.*

$$–$$$$ ✕ **Mortoni's.** With views of the exotic man-made lagoon outside the Hard Rock Hotel, this plant-filled supper club feels very West Hollywood. Expect high-end treats like filet mignon and fresh live lobster, along with more affordable pizzas and pastas. ✉ *4455 Paradise Rd.,* ☎ *702/693–5000.*

$$–$$$$ ✕ **Spago.** The Las Vegas outpost of Wolfgang Puck's L.A. restaurant is at Caesars. An open-terrace café serves light fare (a lamb French dip sandwich with blue-cheese spread and rosemary au jus) to views of a Romanesque streetscape. Inside a formal dining room you can sample the likes of pan-seared monkfish with lobster-potato salad, pancetta, and balsamic aioli. ✉ *3570 Las Vegas Blvd. S,* ☎ *702/369–6300.*

$$$ ✕ **Antonio's.** Locals love the filling northern Italian entrées and desserts prepared at this Rio Suites Hotel eatery. Intimate, with murals, crystal chandeliers, and marble walls, it doesn't feel like a hotel restaurant. For a stellar upscale dining experience in the same hotel, investigate Fiore. ✉ *3700 W. Flamingo Rd.,* ☎ *702/252–7777.*

$$ ✕ **Coyote Café.** Skip the Coyote Café's pricey and uneven Grill Room and consider a meal at the casual Cantina. This MGM Grand eatery's decor is southwestern, as is the inventive menu: You'll find chili rellenos alongside crab cakes, steaks, and tuna, and Nevada's largest selection of tequila. ✉ *3805 Las Vegas Blvd. S,* ☎ *702/891–7349.*

$–$$ ✕ **California Pizza Kitchen.** Las Vegas has two branches of the national chain renowned for its designer pizzas and healthful salads. The restaurant downtown at the Golden Nugget is the better of the two—the one in the Mirage is too loud and too close to the casino action. ✉ *Mirage,*

Eats ●

Antonio's, **8**

Café Copioh, **16**

Café Espresso at Borders Books, **4**

California Pizza Kitchen, **1, 6**

Coyote Café, **20**

Cyber City Café, **13**

Emeril's, **19**

Enigma, **2**

Fog City, **11**

Garlic Cafe, **3**

Gordon Biersch Brewing Co., **12**

Mariposa, **21**

Mediterranean, **14**

Mortoni's, **17**

Mr. Lucky's 24/7, **18**

Napa, **9**

Spago, **7**

Viva Mercado, **10**

Wild Oats, **5, 15**

Scenes ○

Angles, **6**

Backdoor Lounge, **2**

Backstreet, **5**

Badlands Saloon, **3**

Buffalo, **8**

Flex, **1**

Gipsy, **7**

Goodtimes, **11**

Inferno, **4**

Las Vegas Eagle, **9**

Tropical Island, **10**

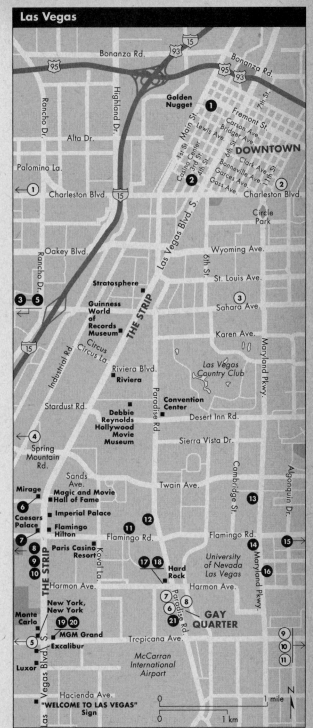

Las Vegas

3400 Las Vegas Blvd. S, ☎ *702/791–7111;* ✉ *Golden Nugget, 129 E. Fremont St.,* ☎ *702/385–7111.*

$ ✗ **Mr. Lucky's 24/7.** The pubby fare—fajitas, burgers, lime chicken, thick milkshakes—at this 24-hour Hard Rock Hotel diner always hits the spot, especially after you've been dancing at the nearby Gipsy disco. ✉ *4455 Paradise Rd.,* ☎ *702/693–5000.*

Outside the Casinos

$$–$$$ ✗ **Garlic Café.** As you might guess, garlic is the common denominator at this cheerful, mural-filled restaurant—it's in every dish, and often used quite inventively. Strangely named favorites include Sy Sperling's Angel Hair Club for Men Pomodoro (with fresh tomatoes, garlic, basil, and marinara) and Suze Wong's Long Garlic Ginger Chicken (sautéed garlic, chicken, bok choy, shiitakes, snow peas, carrots, and jicama over jasmine rice). ✉ *3650 S. Decatur Blvd.,* ☎ *702/221–0266.*

$$–$$$ ✗ **Gordon Biersch Brewing Co.** This postmodern brew pub with high ceilings and huge brass beer vats is a good bet for New American pub grub: a sandwich of rotisserie turkey, green apples, Gorgonzola, and sweet märzen-beer mustard; charred tuna steak with wasabi smashed potatoes and fried sweet-onion strings; and satays, pastas, and pizzas. ✉ *3987 Paradise Rd.,* ☎ *702/312–5247.*

$$ ✗ **Fog City.** Swarms of beautiful people cram into this re-created stainless steel diner that has tile floors and wood trim. Top dishes are Manila clam chowder, snapper po' boys with a kicky remoulade, and a mighty meat loaf. ✉ *325 Hughes Center Dr.,* ☎ *702/737–0200.*

$–$$ ✗ **Viva Mercado's.** These family-run eateries are the best Mexican restaurants in town. Expect potent margaritas, 11 highly charged salsas, and perfectly cooked Mexican dishes, many of them seafood or vegetarian. ✉ *6182 W. Flamingo Rd.,* ☎ *702/871–8826; also* ✉ *4500 E. Sunset Rd.,* ☎ *702/435–6200.*

$ ✗ **Mediterranean.** A landscaped sidewalk and a covered terrace mask Mediterranean's shopping-center location. The tasty Greek and Middle Eastern specialties include *kibbe* (lean ground beef, seasoned with pine nuts, onions, and spices and covered with cracked wheat) with hummus. ✉ *4147 S. Maryland Pkwy.,* ☎ *702/731–6030.*

$ ✗ **Wild Oats.** Las Vegas's contribution to healthful cuisine is set *way* west on Sahara Avenue; a second location is set *way* east on Flamingo Road. Within each bright, cavernous complex are a full grocery store and a café with millet, veggies-and-sprouts sandwiches, and other pure and simple fare. ✉ *6720 W. Sahara Ave.,* ☎ *702/253–7050; also* ✉ *3455 E. Flamingo Rd.,* ☎ *702/434–8115.*

Coffeehouse Culture

Café Copioh. Pensive academics sit around chatting about Proust and the Pet Shop Boys at this Euroboho hangout popular with the gay community and students of the University of Nevada, Las Vegas (UNLV). The best snack food: the gooey pizza bagels. ✉ *4550 S. Maryland Pkwy.,* ☎ *702/739–0305.*

Café Espresso at Borders Books. Poetry readings and musical performances keep things lively at this elegant little café. The yuppiest starched-shirt types, some of them queer, saunter in here for superb sandwiches and desserts. ✉ *2323 S. Decatur Blvd.,* ☎ *702/258–0999.*

Cyber City Café. Open till 3 AM, this espresso bar, juice joint, and beer hall sells cool magazines and has computer terminals for Internet surfing. Queer genXers love the place. ✉ *3945 S. Maryland,* ☎ *702/732–2001.*

Enigma. This lovably strange coffeehouse in a sleepy section of downtown draws tattooed alternateens and soulful intellectuals, all trying to create a countercultural arts scene in a çity that sorely lacks one. ✉ *918½ S. 4th St.,* ☎ *702/386–0999.*

Mariposa. In a shopping center across from the gay bookstore, Get Booked (*see* Gay Media, *below*), and a few of the gay clubs, Mariposa, filled with a comfy blend of retro sofas, chairs, and tables, easily has the strongest late-night (til 3 AM) queer following of coffeehouses. ⊠ *4643 Paradise Rd.,* ☎ *702/650–9009.*

SCENES

People often compare the gay Las Vegas scene to L.A.'s: lots of cliques and plenty of posing—just less of it here. The city's relatively small gay population is a drawback for residents, who quickly get to know each other. (Given all the attention newcomers receive, entering bars they might as well be wearing NEW MEAT signs on their backs.) Most places don't get going until well after midnight, after many actors, waiters, and casino employees finish their shows or shifts. Most bars are open 24 hours. Las Vegas has liberal liquor laws, so beer and liquor busts and drink specials are rampant.

Prime Suspects

Angles. This classic cruise bar has diverse music spanning a couple of decades, a fireplace, slots, and some comfy armchairs and ottomans. Most people pop in here before heading next door to the Gipsy dance club. A second bar in back, Lace, has a large dance floor. It once drew mostly women but the crowd now seems more mixed. ⊠ *4633 Paradise Rd.,* ☎ *702/791–0100. Crowd: 75/25 m/f, mostly 20s and 30s, clean-cut, gym types, a touch of attitude.*

Backstreet. The friendliest bar in town, where the barhands and customers make everyone feel welcome, Backstreet encourages cruising, conversation, and country-western dancing (these men and women know what they're doing). The lighting's good, the western decor attractive. ⊠ *5012 S. Arville Rd.,* ☎ *702/876–1844. Crowd: 60/40 m/f, late 20s to early 40s, starched-shirt cowboys, zero attitude.*

Flex. For many gay men and lesbians who live in northwestern Las Vegas, going to Flex is a twice- or three-times-weekly ritual—it's a cheerful place to mix and mingle. The only hindrance to conversation is the often-throbbing dance music, which seems unnecessary given the tiny dance floor tucked in a corner. A rec room holds two pool tables. ✕ *4371 W. Charleston Blvd.,* ☎ *702/385–3539. Crowd: 65/35 m/f, early 20s to early 40s, mix of locals and tourists, friendly.*

Gipsy. This is the major dance club for the younger set, UNLV students, and guppies. And though it's small, with a tiny dance floor, the music is terrific, the bartenders fun, and the atmosphere vibrant. The cruisy video bar off to one side is a good spot to fill your dance card. Gipsy often presents disco divas, porn stars, and such. ⊠ *4605 Paradise Rd.,* ☎ *702/731–1919. Crowd: mixed m/f, young, cute, and attitude-free.*

Inferno. A big hit when it opened in 1997 while Gipsy was closed for a makeover, Inferno is close to the Strip but can be hard to find. And whether it stays hot remains to be seen. A stylish place with exposed air ducts, it has a dance floor surrounded by a chain-link fence, and other industrial touches; the lighting is colorful and the sound system is positively supersonic. ⊠ *3340 S. Highland Dr.,* ☎ *702/734–7336. Crowd: 80/20 m/f, 20s and 30s, fairly hip, lots of casino workers.*

Tropical Island. Adjacent to the Eagle, this former storefront had been a guys' bar, but in 1997 it reopened for lesbians. The crowd is still thoroughly mixed, though, and everybody gets along well. There's a great jukebox, a pool table, and a cozy bar. Tropical Island is not a big place, so for dancing, women tend to favor Gipsy and Inferno. ⊠ *3430 E. Tropicana Ave.,* ☎ *702/456–5525. Crowd: 60/40 f/m, casual, no attitude.*

Neighborhood Haunts

The engagingly seedy **Backdoor Lounge** (✉ 1415 E. Charleston Blvd., ☎ 702/385–2018) has very friendly barhands. Friday is Latino night. **Badlands Saloon** (✉ 953 E. Sahara Ave., ☎ 702/792–9262) is a decent country-western alternative to the spiffier Backstreet. The bare-bones **Buffalo** (✉ 4640 Paradise Rd., ☎ 702/733–8355)—a large rectangular room with a dirty black linoleum floor, lots of trophies, and three pool tables—draws a cruisy, mostly male, mildly leather-and-Levi's crowd. A low-key cocktail bar most of the time, **Goodtimes** (✉ 1775 E. Tropicana Ave., ☎ 702/736–9494), across from the Liberace Museum, has a near-cult following on Monday night. The **Las Vegas Eagle** (✉ 3430 E. Tropicana Ave., ☎ 702/458–8662) is down-to-earth and very friendly with black walls, dark lighting, and a somewhat cruisy mix of guys in leather, Levi's, and casual attire.

Only in Las Vegas

Kenny Kerr's *Women of Hollywood* is a high-camp drag extravaganza at the **Debbie Reynolds Hollywood Hotel and Casino** (✉ 305 Convention Center Dr., ☎ 702/734–0711); Ms. Reynolds herself delights crowds with *Debbie's Star Theatre,* in which she sings, dances, and shows clips from her old movies. At the **Riviera Hotel** (✉ 2901 Las Vegas Blvd. S, ☎ 702/734–5110), Joan Rivers–impersonator Frank Marino—and a cast of Bettes, Lizas, and Whoopis put on the highly regarded *Evening at La Cage.*

SLEEPS

Nine of the world's 10 largest hotels are here, with the MGM Grand topping the list. When gambling was the city's only draw, hotel rooms were usually drab and unpleasant, the better to keep guests out of their rooms and in the casinos. As the city moved into family-oriented theme-park mode in the '90s, lodgings were quickly whipped into shape, providing guests with all the amenities and perks expected of any top-line destination. Las Vegas is still the land of hotel bargains, but with major conventions in town every other week and a steady inflow of tourists even on weekdays, you'd be wise to book a room several weeks ahead.

For price ranges, *see* lodging Chart B at the front of this guide.

$$$ 🎭 **Mirage.** Arguably the best all-around hotel and casino for value, ambience, size, and amenities, this property shaped by renowned casino developer Steve Wynn has a rain forest with tigers, dolphins, sharks, and more than 3,000 tropical plants. The flamboyant Siegfried and Roy, "Masters of the Impossible," are the house entertainment. ✉ *3400 Las Vegas Blvd. S, 89109,* ☎ *702/791–7111 or 800/627–6667,* 🖷 *702/791–7446. 3,049 rooms. Restaurants, pool.*

$$–$$$ 🎭 **Hard Rock Hotel.** Since its 1995 opening, this chic rocker hotel has been booked solid just about every weekend with L.A. hipsters, grungers, guppies, and yuppies. The Hard Rock's popularity has spurred the construction of another 350 rooms, due for completion in '98. Among the highlights are the florid postmodern rooms bathed in exotic colors, a 1,200-seat concert hall at which top musicians perform, and a faux-lagoon whose pool is fitted with underwater speakers. ✉ *4455 Paradise Rd., 89109,* ☎ *702/693–5000 or 800/473–7625,* 🖷 *702/693–5010. 340 rooms. Restaurants, pool, health club.*

$$–$$$ 🎭 **MGM Grand.** This stupendous 114-acre entertainment megaresort contains several excellent restaurants, an enormous swimming pool and state-of-the-art spa and health club, and an amusement park. The colors of the rainbow illuminate the Oz Casino, the largest in the world. ✉ *3799*

Las Vegas Blvd. S, 89109, ☎ 702/891–1111 or 800/929–1111, FAX 702/891–1030. 5,005 rooms. Restaurants, pool, health club.

$$–$$$ 🏨 **Monte Carlo.** Rooms at the adult-oriented, understatedly elegant Monte Carlo have marble baths and entries, striped Regency-style wallpaper, and polished wood accents. The casino, shops, and restaurants here are rather dull, which seems fine with the laid-back and classy guests. ✉ *3770 Las Vegas Blvd. S, 89109, ☎ 702/730–7000 or 800/311–8999. 3,259 rooms. Restaurants, pools, exercise room.*

$$ 🏨 **Harrah's.** Though garish (it was built during the aesthetically challenged '70s), the New Orleans–style Harrah's actively courts gay business and donated money to help bring the AIDS quilt to Las Vegas. Rooms are simple with darkwood furniture and pastel hues. ✉ *3475 Las Vegas Blvd. S, 89109, ☎ 702/369–5000 or 800/634–6765, FAX 702/369–5008. 1,713 rooms. Restaurants, pool, health club.*

$–$$ 🏨 **Excalibur.** Many families come to this King Arthur–theme complex whose cartoonish facade lights up the sky each evening, but the Excalibur has made a point of marketing to gays and lesbians. The rooms are colorful, and the rates are among the lowest of the city's newer accommodations. ✉ *3850 Las Vegas Blvd. S, 89119, ☎ 702/597–7777 or 800/937–7777, FAX 702/597–7040. 4,032 rooms. Restaurants, pools.*

$–$$ 🏨 **Holiday Inn Emerald Springs.** One of the few nongaming hotels in the area, this terrific property is gay-friendly and small enough so that checking in and out is a painless process. Rooms are tasteful with sedate color; many have whirlpool tubs, and all have refrigerators and coffeemakers. ✉ *325 E. Flamingo Rd., 89109, ☎ 702/732–9100 or 800/732–7889, FAX 702/731–9784. 150 rooms. Restaurant, pool, exercise room.*

$–$$ 🏨 **Riviera Hotel.** The Riviera has long been a hit with gays and lesbians. This centrally located but slightly dated amalgam of towers and wings, one tacked on after another over the past four decades, has spacious guest rooms. ✉ *2901 Las Vegas Blvd. S, 89109, ☎ 702/734–5110 or 800/634–6753, FAX 702/794–9451. 2,159 rooms. Restaurants, pool, health club.*

$ 🏨 **Westward Ho Motel and Casino.** The largest motel in the world has no-frills rooms and a good location along the Strip. Fine only if you don't plan to spend much time in your room. ✉ *2900 Las Vegas Blvd. S, 89109, ☎ 702/731–2900 or 800/634–6803, FAX 702/731–6154. 1,000 rooms. Restaurants, pools.*

THE LITTLE BLACK BOOK

At Your Fingertips

Aid for AIDS of Nevada (☎ 702/382–2326). **CAT—Citizens Area Transit** (☎ 702/228–7433). **City Life** (☎ 702/871–6780, e-mail citylife@vegas.infi.net). **Gay and Lesbian Community Center of Southern Nevada** (✉ 912 E. Sahara Rd., ☎ 702/733–9800). **Las Vegas Convention and Visitors Authority** (✉ 3150 Paradise Rd., 89109, ☎ 702/892–0711, Web site www.lasvegas24hours.com).

Gay Media

The guy-oriented *Las Vegas Bugle* (☎ 702/369–6260, Web site www.lvbugle.com) is quite substantial and has served the community twice monthly for more than two decades. With extensive news and arts coverage for the lesbian and gay male communities, the relatively new *Q Tribe* (☎ 702/871–6981, e-mail qtmagazine@aol.com) has quickly developed a loyal following.

BOOKSTORES

Get Booked (✉ 4640 Paradise Rd., ☎ 702/737–7780) has a small selection of lesbian and gay titles and plenty of magazines and pride items, but with its huge collection of videos, it should really be renamed Get a Movie. The mainstream **Borders Book Shop and Café** (✉ 2323 S. Decatur Ave.,

☎ 702/258–0999) has an outstanding queer section. For the latest "bear-wear," greeting cards, pride gifts, and bondage and fetish gear, drop by **Lock, Stock & Leather** (✉ 4640 Paradise Rd., ☎ 702/796– 9801).

Working Out

The favorite gay gyms, among both men and women, are the trendy **Las Vegas Athletic Clubs** (✉ 1120 Almond Tree La., ☎ 702/798–5822; also ✉ 3830 E. Flamingo Rd., ☎ 702/451–2526).

18 *Out in Los Angeles*

With Laguna Beach

LOS ANGELES'S GAY AND LESBIAN POPULATION—especially in that trendy homo haven West Hollywood—is one of the most image-conscious around. Your status—even as a visitor—is established by, in no particular order, the make of your car, the style of your hair, the designer of your wardrobe, the source of your mineral water, the shape of your nose, the buffness of your body, the location of your home, the breed of your dog, and the influence of your agent. Given that this media mecca's raison d'être is illusion, the emphasis on image is inevitable.

Insofar as it defines your image, being gay also shapes your role in Los Angeles society. Though producing more gay-themed movies than ever, the film industry, for example, still does not encourage its gay stars to live openly so. This is changing. TV star Ellen Degeneres not only came out in 1997, the lead character she portrays on her sitcom, *Ellen,* also came out (and drew fabulous ratings doing so).

The city has an outstanding track record when it comes to gay-related fund-raising, particularly with regard to AIDS causes. The gay and lesbian road to acceptance within Washington legislative circles has been paved largely with L.A. dollars. Perhaps more significant, Hollywood has begun observing an annual "Day of Compassion," when a number of television shows and other events promote AIDS awareness. Activists of Hollywood Supports and other groups have done a remarkable job over the past few years getting the industry to participate in educating the public about gay rights and AIDS and also to provide insurance and other benefits to their lesbian and gay employees' domestic partners.

Los Angeles may be the least-appreciated city in America, its image tarnished by a seemingly ceaseless parade of sensational legal battles, from the O. J. Simpson spectacle to the Menendez murder trials to the case of the "Hollywood madam," Heidi Fleiss. Adding further negativity to the city's image, a major flood, earthquake, fire, mud slide, or combination thereof ruptures L.A.'s infrastructure every year or two. It doesn't cost much more to live here than it does in New York or San Francisco, but the likelihood that your home and your belongings will be destroyed by either natural or human forces adds what you might call a futility surcharge to everything you purchase.

But despite the city's liabilities—did we forget to mention traffic and the sometimes pea-green smog?—it's an exhilarating place. By day you can relive the glamour of Hollywood's past, take in some world-class museums, or hit the surf. By night one of the world's great gay-and-lesbian entertainment districts beckons you.

THE LAY OF THE LAND

The reach of greater Los Angeles is tremendous, but orienting yourself is not impossible. West Hollywood has the densest concentration of gay and lesbian society. To the immediate west are the moneyed and quite-straight communities of Beverly Hills, Westwood, and Bel Air. Santa Monica and Venice (a.k.a. Venice Beach), two coastal towns, have large queer populations. East of Hollywood and north of the largely corporate downtown is one of L.A.'s oldest residential neighborhoods, Silver Lake, which is also one of the West Coast's longest-running gay enclaves. In the San Fernando Valley, quite a few homos call North Hollywood and Studio City home.

Downtown

It's best to come **downtown** during a business day, when you can mingle among a crowd that spans all races and classes. The heart of downtown is just southeast of where the Hollywood and Harbor/Pasadena freeways converge, by Grand Avenue and Temple Street. This section's most significant cultural site is the leviathan **Music Center** (✉ 1st St. and N. Grand Ave., ☎ 213/972–7211), a complex of three performance spaces. The largest venue, the **Dorothy Chandler Pavilion,** often hosts the Academy Awards.

South of here most of the city's newer skyscrapers fall inside downtown's vast **Financial District.** A highlight is the **L.A. Central Public Library** (✉ 630 W. 5th Ave., ☎ 213/228–7000), a graceful 1926 Spanish-style building fitted with an 8-story atrium and surrounded by lush gardens. Up toward the Civic Center is the **Museum of Contemporary Art** (✉ MOCA, 250 S. Grand Ave., ☎ 213/626–6222), whose holdings include works by Mark Rothko, Jackson Pollock, and many others. Nearby is the MOCA-run **Geffen Contemporary** (✉ 152 N. Central Ave., ☎ 213/484–3350). Formerly the Temporary Contemporary (until it was named in 1996 for gay media-magnate David Geffen, a benefactor), this museum presents rotating modern-art exhibitions.

Little Tokyo is east of South Broadway. **Japanese Village Plaza** (✉ 1st and 2nd Sts., between San Pedro St. and Central Ave., ☎ 213/620–8861), the neighborhood's centerpiece, is an impressive mall with shops and restaurants. North of the Hollywood Freeway is **Chinatown,** the commercial spine of which is **North Broadway.**

Los Angeles has a tradition of historic preservation efforts, among them the 1920s movement to save the city's first permanent settlement. The **El Pueblo de Los Angeles Historic Monument** (✉ Visitor Center: 622 N. Main St., ☎ 213/628–1274), a 44-acre park southeast of Chinatown, holds many of L.A.'s oldest structures, some dating as far back as 1781. Bustling **Olvera Street** is the center of the action here.

Southwest of downtown at the intersection of Figueroa Street and Exhibition Boulevard is the immense campus of the **University of Southern California** (USC), home to several historic buildings. The much-delayed move of the **One Institute–International Gay and Lesbian Archive** (☎ 310/854–0271) from West Hollywood to a university-supplied building near campus may have taken place by the time you read this.

Hollywood

Once synonymous with glamour, Hollywood is now simply dowdy. Nonetheless, bits and pieces have been reclaimed in recent years, and a swing toward the hip may be just around the corner.

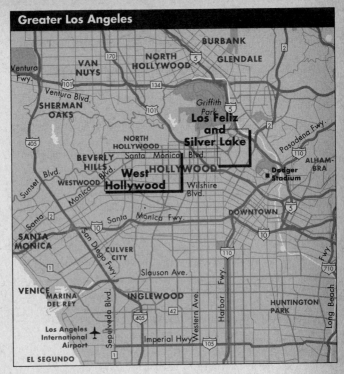

Greater Los Angeles

To the northeast above Beachwood Canyon on the lower slopes of Mount Lee is the immense HOLLYWOOD sign, whose 50-foot letters have graced the horizon for more than 70 years. You can't actually drive up and visit it, but you can tour a number of museums and sights—some tacky, others engaging—along Hollywood Boulevard. At the **Hollywood Wax Museum** (⊠ 6767 Hollywood Blvd., ☎ 213/462–8860), you can admire the wax knockers on "Country's Leading Lady," Dolly Parton, or peek in on Mr. Roarke from *Fantasy Island*. More serious, but still quite fun, is the **Hollywood Entertainment Museum** (⊠ 7021 Hollywood Blvd., ☎ 213/469–9151), which has props and sets from popular TV shows and films.

One of Hollywood's tackiest attractions, and that's saying a lot, is the **Frederick's of Hollywood Museum** (⊠ 6608 Hollywood Blvd., ☎ 213/466–8506), which displays bras, panties, and various undergarments worn by your favorite stars—from Belinda Carlisle's bustier to a corset-like apparatus that once held June Lockhart together on *Lost in Space*.

Hollywood Boulevard itself is a museum of sorts. The beloved **Walk of Fame**—where the names of stars and other entertainment personnel are embedded in the sidewalk—runs from Vine Street to La Brea Avenue. Amid the Walk of Fame is **Mann's Chinese Theatre** (⊠ 6925 Hollywood Blvd., ☎ 213/464–8111), the former "Grauman's Chinese," where more than 160 stars have had their handprints or footprints preserved in cement. The groovy **Capitol Records Building** (⊠ 1756 N. Vine St.) is shaped like a stack of 45s. No trip to Hollywood is complete—if you're a drag queen, anyway—without a visit to the **Max Factor Museum of Beauty** (⊠ 1666 N. Highland Ave., ☎ 213/463–6668). Set inside a grand 1931 art deco building, this over-the-top collection of memorabilia traces the film industry's makeup history.

Los Feliz and Silver Lake

Just east of Hollywood is **Los Feliz,** one of L.A.'s hidden gems, a tidy, attractive neighborhood of hilly lanes tucked beneath the dense greenery of Griffith Park. Home to a mix of old and young home owners, working-class Joes, and yuppies, increasing numbers of gay men, and some lesbians, have been moving here in recent years.

The original Fox Studios was located at Sunset Boulevard and Western Avenue; in the 1920s and the years right before them a number of wealthy residents built their palaces in Los Feliz. Most of the biggest houses are gone, but many outstanding examples of early-20th-century single-family homes and bungalows can be viewed in the gentle hills close to Griffith Park. The most famous is Frank Lloyd Wright's **Hollyhock House** (⊠ 4800 Hollywood Blvd., ☎ 213/662–7272), officially called the Barnsdall House; its early-1920s design mimics the hollyhocks planted on the grounds (note also the moat surrounding the living-room fireplace). Some hot restaurants have opened alongside the neighborhood joints on the main commercial drag, **Hillhurst Avenue,** which runs north–south and is busiest between Los Feliz and Hollywood boulevards. Nearby **Vermont Avenue** is less trendy but has some noteworthy shops and eateries.

Above Los Feliz is 4,213-acre **Griffith Park** (⊠ Enter either off Los Feliz Blvd., east of N. Western Ave., or at Vermont Ave.; ☎ 213/664–1191). Among the better ways to amuse yourself: Drive up to the **Observatory and Planetarium,** around which James Dean, Sal Mineo, and Natalie Wood formed their tragic love triangle in *Rebel Without a Cause.*

The standard joke is that **Silver Lake,** where many gays and lesbians reside, has been an up-and-coming neighborhood for the past 30 years; when it will officially up and come is anybody's guess. The neighborhood contains an impressive concentration of residential architecture and is one of only a handful of places in the region where you'll discover a true sense of community. Although the old homes perched along the hilly streets provide great (albeit perilous) car touring, the area has few sights.

West Hollywood and the Wilshire District

West Hollywood, one of the gayest places in America, remained a working-class community until World War II. Some gentrification took place in the 1950s and '60s, and then retirees and Russian immigrants began to settle here. At the same time many set designers, makeup artists, wardrobe hands, and other behind-the-scenes workers on TV shows and films moved to the area. A decorating and fashion industry grew around the intersection of Melrose Avenue and Robertson Boulevard as skyrocketing rents in nearby Beverly Hills pushed all but the most established designers into unincorporated West Hollywood.

From its earliest days West Hollywood was a major nightlife center. Because it fell outside the jurisdiction of the oppressive L.A. Police Department, strip clubs and peep shows opened along Santa Monica Boulevard, and gay bars ran little risk of being raided. Not only gays but many film celebrities and rock stars had West Hollywood addresses by the '60s. The most dramatic surge in the gay population occurred in the '70s, when Santa Monica Boulevard became a nightlife mecca.

The 2-square-mile city of West Hollywood was officially incorporated in 1984 and now has a population of 37,000, about a third of which is gay. The first mayor, Valarie Terrigno, was openly lesbian, and many of the councilpersons were also gay. Today few homosexuals are involved in city politics, but West Hollywood remains tolerant and queer-friendly—the gay community center here is larger than the new city hall.

Most of the gay action along **Santa Monica Boulevard** lies within "Boys' Town," from Doheny Drive (the Beverly Hills–West Hollywood boundary) east to La Cienega Boulevard. There are gay businesses on Santa Monica clear out to La Brea Avenue, but you'll meet queers who get the shakes once they leave the 310 area code (which ends at La Cienega).

Nevertheless, one of the city's major homo hangouts is just east of Boys' Town. The **French Quarter Market** (⊠ 7985 Santa Monica Blvd.), a small arcade with a huge fountain and a vaguely New Orleans design, is anchored by the often-mobbed French Quarter Market restaurant (*see* Eats, *below*).

The **Mazer Collection** (⊠ 626 N. Robertson Blvd., ☎ 310/659–2478) is one of the nation's only lesbian cultural archives. It holds 3,000 books and a substantial T-shirt collection, plus videos, records, softball uniforms, quite a few misguided psychological studies, some intriguing old pulp novels with wicked portrayals of lesbian love, and 10 file cabinets of articles and clippings.

Since the '30s the hippest, rowdiest nightclubs and music venues have lined **Sunset Boulevard** from Doheny Drive to Fairfax Avenue. Running north of and parallel to Santa Monica Boulevard, the "Sunset Strip" is a touristy, glitzy, and rather straight section of West Hollywood, but most of its clubs and restaurants are gay-friendly. The best place for sidewalk strolling—and celebrity spotting—is Sunset Plaza, a swank stretch of shops and outdoor restaurants.

Melrose Avenue runs parallel to and below Santa Monica Boulevard. The boutiques at this melding of Rome's Via Veneto and New York's Madison Avenue carry everything from avant-garde clothing to futuristic eyewear to kitschy furniture. Also here are coffeehouses, too-fabulous restaurants, and important galleries. At the western end of Melrose Avenue, the striking Cesar Pelli–designed **Pacific Design Center** (⊠ 8687 Melrose Ave., ☎ 310/657–0800) is also known as "the Blue Whale" (in 1988 an also-gargantuan emerald-green annex was erected). PDC has 200 showrooms packed with furniture, textiles, and interior-design accessories. Buying goods here is limited to the "trade"—interior designers, architects, and set designers—but it's easy to get in and stroll around.

West Hollywood and the hills above it contain numerous examples of significant 20th-century residential architecture, including the **R. M. Schindler House** (⊠ 835 N. Kings Rd., ☎ 213/651–1510). Rudolf Schindler's 1922 modernist marvel hosts rotating exhibits, some of which document the architect's many accomplishments.

The nearby **Beverly Center** (⊠ Beverly and La Cienega Blvds., ☎ 310/854–0070) functions as something of an unofficial queer community center. Movie theaters, a pretty decent food court, and all the high-end shops you could ever need are among the draws—not to mention cruisy gay men and chic lesbians flying in every direction.

South and east of West Hollywood, **Farmers Market** (⊠ 3rd St. and Fairfax Ave., ☎ 213/933–9211) offers a true slice of L.A. life. The original market building is a conversational hub for all types—gay, straight, old, young, blue-haired grungers, families with kids. The main building holds souvenir shops, a great newsstand, food stalls (you haven't tasted fresh strawberries until you've eaten them here), and great inexpensive restaurants. KoKoMo (*see* Eats, *below*) has the gayest following.

South of here along **Wilshire Boulevard** is a commercial stretch dubbed the **Miracle Mile** (from La Brea to Fairfax avenues). Curson Avenue intersects Wilshire at **Hancock Park** (not to be confused with the nearby residential neighborhood of the same name). This is the site of the famed and stinky-smelling **La Brea Tar Pits,** from which more than 100 tons of

Pleistocene fossil bones have been excavated. Some are displayed in the adjacent **George C. Page Museum of La Brea Discoveries** (⊠ 5801 Wilshire Blvd., ☎ 213/936–2230). Also at the park is the **Los Angeles County Museum of Art** (⊠ 5905 Wilshire Blvd., ☎ 213/857–6000). LACMA has comprehensive costume and textile exhibits; outstanding Indian, Japanese, and Southeast Asian art galleries; an eclectic 20th-century collection; and two sculpture gardens.

Beverly Hills and Westwood

Here's your chance to buy a map of the stars' homes and putter around looking for the abode of Shirley Jones, Elke Sommer, or Dick Van Patten. Yes, more celebrities—plus quite a few has-beens—live in **Beverly Hills, Brentwood,** and **Bel Air** than anywhere else on the planet. South of Santa Monica Boulevard toward Wilshire Boulevard are the unbelievably chichi shops along **Rodeo Drive.**

Nick at Nite fans will appreciate the most recent Beverly Hills attraction, the **Museum of Television and Radio** (⊠ 465 N. Beverly Dr., ☎ 310/786–1000), an archive of 60,000 radio and TV shows. On display at the nearby **Museum of Tolerance** (⊠ 9786 W. Pico Blvd., ☎ 310/553–8403), next door to the Simon Wiesenthal Center, are original letters from Anne Frank, artifacts from death camps, and dozens of interactive exhibitions that help visitors consider how people have been oppressed on the basis of race, religion, gender, and sexual orientation. Behind the museum is the Memorial Plaza dedicated to the many victims of prejudice over the centuries, including a walkway remembering gays and lesbians.

Westwood, dominated by the campus of the **University of California at Los Angeles** (UCLA), is a haven of yuppies and collegiate types. A thriving café culture centers on Wilshire Boulevard. The **Armand Hammer Museum of Art and Cultural Center** (⊠ 10899 Wilshire Blvd., ☎ 310/443–7000), south of the campus, displays European paintings's greatest hits, from Rubens to van Gogh, plus rare manuscripts. Above the campus is ritzy **Bel Air,** a hilly enclave of mansions. To the west, across the San Diego Freeway, is more modest but still fashionable **Brentwood,** where Joan Crawford raised the ungrateful Christina in a house at 426 North Bristol Circle. The **Getty Center** (⊠ 1200 Getty Center Dr., ☎ 310/440–7300) opened in 1997 on a 110-acre Brentwood hilltop. It houses the Getty collection's vast holdings except for the Greek and Roman antiquities.

Venice, Santa Monica, and Malibu

Hippies, yuppies, retirees, beatniks, in-line skaters, surfer dudes, homeless people, and slackers mill about **Venice**'s boardwalk and run-down streets. This is L.A.'s own East Village or Haight-Ashbury by the sea. Secondhand clothing and music stores, piercing and tattoo parlors, health-food stores, and outdoor markets line the streets near the beach. The streets are narrow and the traffic is heavy on weekends and even sunny weekdays; it's best to park by the beach (don't leave anything valuable in the car) and see the community on foot.

A walk in the north part of Venice along **Main Street** over the border and into **Santa Monica** offers a sharp contrast in styles. Though Santa Monica's Main Street is relatively fancy, it is no less hip, liberal, and gay-friendly than any part of Venice. You'll pass modern-art galleries, several woman-owned and -oriented shops, and some offbeat boutiques. This is one of the most pleasant stretches of sidewalk shopping in Los Angeles.

Several blocks north of the Venice border is one of architect Frank Gehry's most dramatic works, **Edgemar** (⊠ 2415–2437 Main St.), a stark geometric complex of cafés, shops, and courtyards anchored by the **Santa Monica Museum of Art** (☎ 310/399–0433), which hosts changing exhibits of internationally and locally renowned artists.

The **Santa Monica Pier** and the small stretch of Broadway a few blocks east are lined with arcades, gift shops, and colorful, if touristy, diversions. The **Pacific Park** amusement center was added to the pier in 1996. Despite the crowds and occasionally schlocky amusements, Santa Monica's pier and oceanfront make for a good stroll or blade.

Miles of beautiful and relatively undeveloped beaches lie north of Santa Monica. Near Santa Monica's border with **Pacific Palisades,** where San Vicente Boulevard hits the ocean, is an intensely gay and lesbian span of **Will Rogers State Beach** (⊠ 15800 Pacific Coast Hwy., ☎ 310/394–3266). A festive atmosphere prevails on most sunny days—it's a zoo on weekends. The rugged coastline now occupied by **Malibu** wasn't developed until the late '20s. Floods and mud slides have plagued the area in recent years. The **J. Paul Getty Museum** (⊠ 17985 Pacific Coast Hwy.), which contains one of the nation's foremost collections of Roman and Greek antiquities, will be closed for renovations until 2001.

San Fernando Valley

Usually called simply "the Valley," this expanse of bedroom communities northwest of Los Angeles has long been ridiculed for typifying everything that is boring, bland, and banal about suburbia. A decade ago the movie *Valley Girl* lampooned the region; the stereotype has never really died. On the other hand, if image-conscious L.A. starts to wear on your nerves, you might enjoy a visit to the Valley: Though less glamorous, it's far less snooty.

Studio City is home to the Valley's largest gay contingent, some of them employed by the major television and film studios in nearby **Universal City** and **Burbank.** By far the most spectacular attraction is **Universal Studios Hollywood and CityWalk** (⊠ 100 Universal Pl., Universal City, ☎ 818/508–9600), a 420-acre theme park and working studio; you can tour the sets of dozens of famous movies and TV shows. The two-hour tour of **Warner Bros. Studios** (⊠ Hollywood Way and Olive Ave., Burbank, ☎ 818/954–1744) is more production-oriented. Another stop is **NBC Television Studios** (⊠ 3000 W. Alameda Ave., Burbank, ☎ 818/840–3537), where *The Tonight Show,* among other programs, is taped.

GETTING AROUND

Say what you will, L.A.'s fabled freeway system handles the region's several million automobiles with relative ease. If you avoid rush hour and keep an ear out for traffic reports, you should manage quite well. Surface streets are broad and garages and parking lots are easy to find (though you're often forced to deal with the so-called convenience of valet parking). Parking in West Hollywood can be difficult; try the lot at the **Pacific Design Center**—use the entrance off San Vicente Boulevard. The cost is reasonable, and the lot is open until 2 AM.

EATS

The gayest places to dive in Los Angeles are in West Hollywood, especially along Santa Monica and Sunset boulevards. The western part of town, from Beverly Hills to the Pacific Ocean, is a mecca for culinary explorers, though few of the establishments have specifically gay followings. Silver Lake has excellent taquerias and a few greasy spoons that are worth a look, and Los Feliz has lately become a trendy haven. Hollywood has several film-industry watering holes, but many survive on name alone. The **Lesbian Dining Club** (☎ 310/364–4616 to reserve a place) schedules occasional gatherings at one of West Hollywood's better restaurants (or sometimes farther afield). Participants rotate from table to table throughout the three-hour affair; it's a great way to meet a lot of women in one evening.

For price ranges, *see* dining Chart A at the front of this guide.

West Hollywood Vicinity

$$$$ ✕ **fenix.** With fantastic views of both the city and the sleek swimming pool featured in Robert Altman's *The Player,* plus a sophisticated dining room inside the splendid art deco Argyle, fenix warrants a recommendation for its setting alone. As it turns out, the California-French food is among the tastiest fare in WeHo. ✉ *8358 Sunset Blvd.,* ☎ *213/848–6677.*

$$$–$$$$ ✕ **Ago.** A gorgeous Robert DeNiro–backed space, Ago looks like a northern Italian farmhouse. Recipes from Tuscany, Liguria, and Emilia-Romagna are carried out to perfection; the 20-ounce Angus steak cooked in a wood-burning oven is a signature dish. ✉ *8478 Melrose Ave.,* ☎ *213/655–6333.*

$$$–$$$$ ✕ **Cafe La Bohème.** Formal for West Hollywood, La Bohème is truly operatic in its proportions—the dining room is anchored by a huge fireplace and has flowing velvet drapes and other over-the-top furnishings. The incongruous California menu incorporates Mediterranean (try the pasta *pescatore*) and Asian flavors. ✉ *8400 Santa Monica Blvd.,* ☎ *213/848–2360.*

$$$–$$$$ ✕ **Le Colonial.** Warmly lit and decorated with rattan furnishings, this New York import celebrates the sublime cuisine that resulted from the French colonization of Vietnam. Ginger-marinated roast duckling, grilled shrimp wrapped in sugarcane, and other delicacies delight the A-list patrons. ✉ *8783 Beverly Blvd.,* ☎ *310/289–0660.*

$$$–$$$$ ✕ **Spago.** What would the food scene in L.A. be like if Spago had never opened? It's frightening to imagine. The designer pizzas, risottos, and meat grills are sublime. But you may decide—if the maître d' deigns to seat you at a decent table—that Spago is as much a place to see and be seen as it is a cutting-edge restaurant. ✉ *114 Horn Ave.,* ☎ *310/652–4025.*

$$$ ✕ **Georgia.** Catfish and smothered pork chops never tasted so good (or cost so much) west of the Mississippi. This celebrity-studded southern-style restaurant is in a suitably modest building on Melrose, but the kicky food and lively furnishings make quite a splash. Reserve well ahead on weekends. ✉ *7250 Melrose Ave.,* ☎ *213/933–8420.*

$$$ ✕ **Muse.** Postmodern restaurant design is defined by this ultrachic hangout on Beverly Boulevard. Despite the focus on appearances—designer wear is everywhere—the elaborate food is artfully presented and consistently delicious. You might start with a smoked-chicken taco, and then try a spicy entrée of rigatoni with Thai spices and fresh vegetables. ✉ *7360 Beverly Blvd.,* ☎ *213/934–4400.*

$$–$$$ ✕ **Benvenuto.** It's hard to tell that this charming restaurant was once a recording studio. People (including many lesbians, especially on Monday nights) now come to dine on the shady terrace, hemmed in by gardens, vines, and hedges. The food is Italian: traditional pastas, outstanding wood-grilled pizzas, heavenly tiramisu. ✉ *8512 Santa Monica Blvd.,* ☎ *310/659–8635.*

$$–$$$ ✕ **Kass Bah.** This purveyor of so-called California brasserie cuisine is filled with local art, rich mahogany furnishings, and handsome waitrons. Seared ahi tuna with Israeli couscous is a typical dish; burgers, steaks, pastas, and salads are also prepared. ✉ *9010 Melrose Ave.,* ☎ *310/274–7664.*

$$–$$$ ✕ **Melrose Place.** No, this fashionable restaurant near Melrose Avenue shopping is not affiliated with the TV show. It's just a chic, very gay spot for sipping cocktails over fine Pacific Rim cuisine. You might start with shrimp-and-chicken dumplings before moving on to ahi tuna with ginger-garlic soy sauce. ✉ *650 N. La Cienega Blvd.,* ☎ *310/657–2227.*

$$–$$$ ✕ **The Shed.** With fare ranging from Cuban chicken with mojo sauce to stir-fry shrimp with Chinese pepper-salt, this converted carriage house has quickly become a trendy gay-patronized eatery. Watch as it rises to culinary preeminence. ✉ *8474 Melrose Ave.,* ☎ *213/655–6277.*

$$–$$$ ✗ **Tommy Tang's.** The Tuesday-night drag parties are a scream, but this hub of retro-chic twentysomethings is fag-happy just about any day of the week. The food, which ranges from sushi to ginger-plum grilled duck, isn't bad either. ✉ *7313 Melrose Ave.,* ☎ *213/937–5733.*

$$ ✗ **Bossa Nova.** Lauded for its spicy servers and spicy Brazilian food, Bossa Nova is the place to go for rich steaks or lime chicken. The lava-lamp-laden decor is memorable. Request a seat on the patio for extra equatorial ambience. ✉ *685 N. Robertson Blvd.,* ☎ *310/657–5070.*

$$ ✗ **Caioti.** The chef at this Hollywood Hills café trained under Wolfgang Puck and may have bettered the master in creating memorable pizzas. A favorite has wild mushrooms, Gorgonzola, sausage, basil, and pine nuts; also good is the one with shrimp and Thai spices. ✉ *2100 Laurel Canyon Blvd.,* ☎ *213/650–2988.*

$$ ✗ **Chris Michaels.** In a slick space at the fashion-obsessed Pacific Design Center, this new haunt of interior decorators and furniture mavens serves light, healthful breakfasts and lunches plus daily high tea and happy hour. Open on weekdays only, the restaurant closes at 7 PM. ✉ *8687 Melrose Ave.,* ☎ *310/360–7755.*

$$ ✗ **Cobalt Cantina.** Romantic and chic, this branch of the gay-frenzied Silver Lake restaurant has a delightful covered terrace with wrought-iron grillwork around it. The interior is dimly lit, and there's a lounge to the side. Same excellent Cal-Mex menu as the Silver Lake branch. ✉ *616 N. Robertson Blvd.,* ☎ *310/659–8691.*

$$ ✗ **Hugo's.** Power breakfasts have long been associated with this purveyor of carbo-packed morning food; try pumping up with sweet pumpkin pancakes. At night the cavernous dining room serves less-inspired Italian fare—jumbo-shrimp scampi, chicken piccata, and the like. ✉ *8401 Santa Monica Blvd.,* ☎ *213/654–3993.*

$$ ✗ **Mark's.** One of WeHo's most beloved gay eateries offers a strong northern Italian and Californian menu at terrific prices. The fare changes monthly, but typical favorites include lamb sirloin with caramelized blackberry sauce and Maryland crab cakes on a corn puree with a tomato basil sauce. ✉ *861 N. La Cienega Blvd.,* ☎ *310/652–5252.*

$–$$ ✗ **Basix.** A big breakfast crowd heads here for a full meal or the rich coffees; the California-Italian cuisine is healthful and affordable, there's plenty of sidewalk and terrace seating—and how many cafés have valet parking? ✉ *8333 Santa Monica Blvd.,* ☎ *213/848–2460.*

$–$$ ✗ **Figs.** The choice for dykes who lust for home cooking, Figs feels like a neighborhood tavern; it's unpretentious (in a trendy sort of way). In addition to chicken-fried steak and blackened pork chops, you can sample vaguely Continental dishes such as rigatoni with white beans in marinara sauce. ✉ *7929 Santa Monica Blvd.,* ☎ *213/654–0780.*

$–$$ ✗ **Marix Tex-Mex.** The Mexican food here has improved in recent years but, more important, this is a certifiable gay hangout; the patio is especially popular on weekend afternoons. *Huevos chipotle* (eggs with a smoked-pepper sauce), seviche, and chicken-fried steak are among the better offerings. ✉ *1108 N. Flores St.,* ☎ *213/656–8800.*

$ ✗ **Club Cafe.** Beefcakes and muscleheads descend upon this carbo café at the World Gym, in the heart of WeHo. There's a juice bar for smoothies and good-for-you drinks, and a full menu of low-fat sandwiches, salads, and breakfast specialties. ✉ *8560 Santa Monica Blvd.,* ☎ *310/659–6630.*

$ ✗ **French Quarter Market.** Despite the New Orleans decor, the food is upscale diner, from the tuna Manhattan sandwich with cheddar, avocado, and alfalfa to fresh strawberry crepes. It's a scene here any day of the week, especially at breakfast. ✉ *7985 Santa Monica Blvd.,* ☎ *213/654–0898.*

232

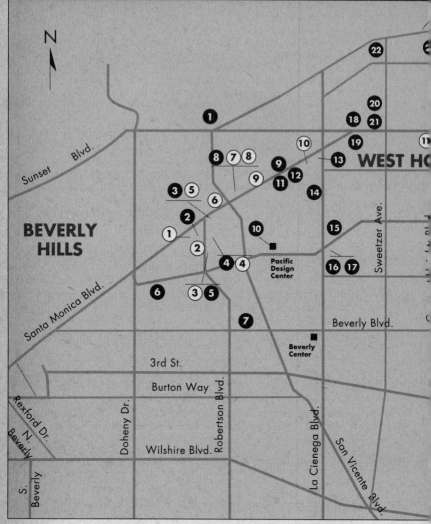

Eats ●

The Abbey, **4**
Ago, **17**
Basix, **21**
Benvenuto, **13**
Bossa Nova, **2**
Cafe La Bohème, **19**
Caioti, **23**
Chris Michaels, **10**
Club Cafe, **12**
Cobalt Cantina, **5**
fenix, **22**
Figs, **25**
French Quarter
Market, **24**
Georgia, **28**
Hugo's, **18**

Kass Bah, **6**
KoKoMo, **29**
Le Colonial, **7**
Little Frida's, **11**
Marix Tex-Mex, **20**
Mark's, **14**
Melrose Place, **15**
Muse, **30**
The Shed, **16**
Spago, **1**
Stonewall Gourmet
Coffee, **9**
Tacos Tacos, **3**
Tommy Tang's, **27**
WeHo Lounge, **8**
Yukon Mining
Co., **26**

Scenes ○

Arena/Circus
Disco, **20**
Axis/Love Lounge, **1**
Club 7969, **14**
Cobalt Cantina, **3**
Firehouse, **4**
Gold Coast, **11**
Hunters, **17**
LunaPark, **2**
Micky's, **7**
Mother Lode, **5**
Mugi, **21**
Numbers, **12**
The Palms, **10**
The Plaza, **18**

Probe, **19**
Rafters, **13**
Rage, **6**
Revolver, **8**
7702, **16**
Spike, **15**
Trunks, **9**

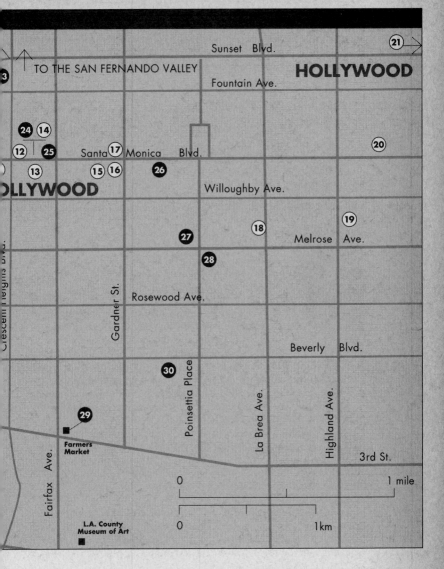

Sunset Blvd.

TO THE SAN FERNANDO VALLEY

Fountain Ave.

HOLLYWOOD

㉑

③

㉔ ⑭

⑫ ㉕ Santa ⑰ Monica Blvd.

⑳

⑬ **OLLYWOOD** ⑮ ⑯ ㉖

Willoughby Ave.

⑲

⑱

㉗ Melrose Ave.

㉘

Gardner St.

Rosewood Ave.

Crescent Heights Blvd.

Beverly Blvd.

㉚

Poinsettia Place

La Brea Ave.

Highland Ave.

㉙

Farmers Market

Fairfax Ave.

3rd St.

0   1 mile

0   1km

L.A. County Museum of Art

$　✕ **KoKoMo.** The best—and gayest—restaurant at the Farmers Market is a deco-style diner with an eclectic New American menu. Break the fast with *huevos rancheros* (eggs with smoked-tomato salsa), stargaze a little, and return later for a plate heaped with apple-wood-smoked chicken salad. ⊠ *6333 W. 3rd St.,* ☎ *213/933–0773. No credit cards.*

$　✕ **Tacos Tacos.** The less-than-inspired name and borderline fast-food setting keep many people from giving this place a chance. It's a shame because the straightforward Mexican food here is spicy, delicious, and inexpensive. Sweet-corn tamales, chicken enchiladas, and the several varieties of salsa (try the smoky roasted tomatillo version) are all excellent choices. ⊠ *8948 Santa Monica Blvd.,* ☎ *310/657–4832.*

$　✕ **Yukon Mining Co.** A major post-club scene, this beloved greasy spoon is open 24 hours. Expect standard diner food. ⊠ *7328 Santa Monica Blvd.,* ☎ *213/851–8833. No credit cards.*

Los Feliz and Silver Lake

$$$　✕ **Katsu.** The first room of this Japanese restaurant is a sleek art gallery—*haute* indeed. It makes for a nice waiting area if there's a seating delay. You dine in a similarly spare rectangular room that's remarkably serene even when packed. The best seats are at the bar in back, from which you can watch the sushi chefs work their wonders. ⊠ *1972 N. Hillhurst Ave., Los Feliz,* ☎ *213/665–1891.*

$$$　✕ **Vida.** Beautiful people swirl around the semicircular bar up front and dine in the postmodern restaurant behind it. Despite the supremely daring (some would call it nutty) menu and stunning digs, Vida is run with a sense of humor—dishes have amusing names (Okra Winfrey Creole Gumbo, Jiffy Pop clams)—and the mood is upbeat. ⊠ *1930 N. Hillhurst Ave., Los Feliz,* ☎ *213/660–4446.*

$$–$$$　✕ **Cha Cha Cha.** This place is often overlooked because of its dicey location southwest of Silver Lake. Yet inventive Caribbean fare like shrimp in a hot *negro* sauce or a starter of black-bean sweet tamales is worth the drive. ⊠ *656 N. Virgil Ave., Silver Lake,* ☎ *213/664–7723.*

$$　✕ **Cobalt Cantina.** Don't let the trendy Cantina's reputation as a drinking spot (*see* Scenes, *below*) fool you: the food is terrific, too. The menu has a variety of southwestern and Mexican dishes, from sweet-potato tamales to more traditional meat grills and enchiladas. The prices are in line with far less-inspired eateries in Los Feliz and Silver Lake. ⊠ *4326 Sunset Blvd., Silver Lake,* ☎ *213/953–9991.*

$　✕ **Astro Family Restaurant.** People come to this diner after the bars close—not so much to eat as to see the hostess, who looks a tad like Alice Ghostley and is usually clad in an inspired and gaudy outfit. A beautiful revolving sign rotates high above the restaurant. ⊠ *2300 Fletcher Blvd., Silver Lake,* ☎ *213/663–9241.*

The Beaches

$$$　✕ **Chaya Venice.** Pretty smashing for beatnik-oriented Venice, everything makes sense when you realize you could toss a sushi roll from your table over the border to ritzier Santa Monica. Whatever the geography, this futuristic-looking sanctuary of the stars has one of the best Pacific Rim menus in southern California. ⊠ *110 Navy St., Venice,* ☎ *310/396–1179.*

$$–$$$　✕ **Border Grill.** Dynamic chefs Mary Sue Milliken and Susan Feniger, stars of the TVFN cooking show *Too Hot Tamales,* travel through Mexico and cull generations-old recipes from locals. Try roasted onion stuffed with Manchego and jack cheeses, or roasted-poblano-chili rellenos. ⊠ *1445 4th St., Santa Monica,* ☎ *310/451–1655.*

$$–$$$　✕ **Warszawa.** One of the most gay-friendly spots in downtown Santa Monica serves authentic filling dishes, including pierogis, stuffed cabbage, and rainbow trout poached in white wine. ⊠ *1414 Lincoln Blvd., Santa Monica,* ☎ *310/393–8831.*

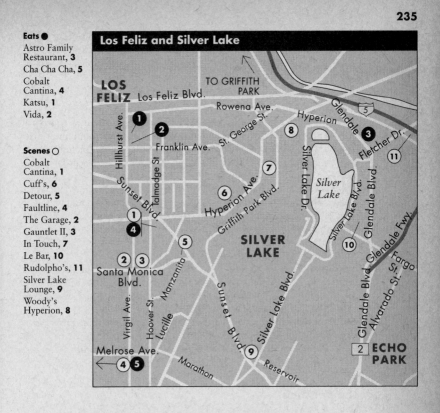

$-$$ ✕ **Rose Cafe.** A cafeteria with ample patio space, this is the most happening of Venice's several near-beach cafés. The crowd is diverse, as is the healthy menu, which includes great swordfish tacos and excellent baked goods. ⊠ *220 Rose Ave., Santa Monica,* ☎ *310/399–0711.*

$ ✕ **Van Go's Ear.** A Venice tradition, Van Go's is a 24-hour café with a '60s ambience and a very today sense of humor: All the dishes are named after shamed or fallen celebrities, such as Freddie Prinze huevos rancheros and Dana Plato (errant child of *Different Strokes*) French toast. Brunching dykes love this place. ⊠ *796 Main St., Venice,* ☎ *310/314–0022. No credit cards.*

San Fernando Valley

$$$ ✕ **Pinot Bistro.** This successful offshoot of Patina and its several L.A. cousins is proof that you don't have to leave the Valley to find world-class cuisine such as grilled sea bass with rock shrimp bolognese, spaghetti zucchini, and olive sauce. ⊠ *12969 Ventura Blvd., Studio City,* ☎ *818/ 990–0500.*

$$ ✕ **Great Greek.** Huge portions of the best Greek food in L.A. County are doled out at this upbeat taverna with pink napery and a warm, outgoing—and singing and dancing—staff. A good bet is the moussaka *Izmir* (baked eggplant with ground beef and béchamel sauce). ⊠ *13362 Ventura Blvd., Sherman Oaks,* ☎ *818/905–5250.*

$$ ✕ **Louise's Trattoria.** One of the ever-expanding chain of high-quality nouvelle-Italian restaurants, this branch is one of the more gay-frequented Valley eateries. Expect great pastas, salads, and pizzas in an atmosphere that's less sterile than that in the competing California Pizza Kitchens. ⊠ *12050 Ventura Blvd., Studio City,* ☎ *818/762–2662.*

$$ ✕ **Venture Inn.** The dark rose-color lighting, heavy '70s decor, and overwhelmingly gay fortysomething crowd will definitely remind you of several restaurants in Palm Springs. This is the Valley's one predominantly gay dining spot, and it's frequented by men and women. The menu is pre-

dictable—steak, chicken marsala, veal cutlets—and the preparation mediocre. ⊠ *11938 Ventura Blvd., Studio City,* ☎ *818/769–5400.*

Coffeehouse Culture

West Hollywood Vicinity

The Abbey. This is *the* gay coffeehouse. Sit cozily inside amid faux-opulent statuary, fountains, and chandeliers, or outside in a courtyard filled with terra-cotta statues and anchored by a gaudy fountain of cast-iron flamingos. Most of West Hollywood and its visitors (including k. d. lang from time to time) wind up here at some point on a Saturday night. ⊠ *692 N. Robertson Blvd.,* ☎ *310/289–8410.*

Little Frida's. You'll find more stylish dykes at this place named for artist Frida Kahlo than at the bars and clubs. Those with tattoos and piercings will feel especially at home. Celeb sightings, ranging from Lily Tomlin to Madonna, are not uncommon. Part of the famous coming-out episode of *Ellen* was set here. Many nights there's live music or a reading. ⊠ *8730 Santa Monica Blvd.,* ☎ *310/854–5421.*

Stonewall Gourmet Coffee. Boys' Town's newest caffeine station has been drawing big crowds to its indoor and outdoor sipping areas. In addition to the usual snacks and desserts this place has gourmet fudge to die for. ⊠ *8717 Santa Monica Blvd.,* ☎ *310/659–8009.*

WeHo Lounge. The former Daily Grind reopened as something more than a run-of-the-mill coffeehouse in 1997. It's now a great place to sip java and is a valuable HIV and AIDS resource center with literature, seminars, and free HIV testing in the back room. ⊠ *8861 Santa Monica Blvd.,* ☎ *310/659–6180.*

The Beaches

Lulu's Alibi. Coastal beat poets and theatergoers stop by this quirky coffeehouse with happy-hour specials on weekday evenings between 5 and 7. ⊠ *1640 Sawtelle Blvd., Santa Monica,* ☎ *310/479–6007.*

SCENES

L.A.'s queer nightlife extends well beyond the clubs along Santa Monica Boulevard in West Hollywood, though for many folks these dozen or so establishments are the only places worth hitting. Fair enough: WeHo's so-called Boys' Town is the glitzy heart of gay Los Angeles. The "industry" crowd parties here, as do most gay tourists. Lesbians frequent this area, but it's dominated by the male bar scene.

Bars stop serving liquor at 2 AM, but many stay open as late as 4. When the bars in West Hollywood close, the blocks between San Vicente and Robertson boulevards, on the north side of Santa Monica, turn into a cruisy sidewalk party. Ask around about after-hours clubs or private parties. Some of the overflow spills into **Pavilions** (⊠ 8969 Santa Monica Blvd.), the 24-hour supermarket down the block, making this an excellent time to do your shopping.

West Hollywood

PRIME SUSPECTS

Axis/Love Lounge. These two clubs are joined but have separate addresses and different parties each night. If you raged in West Hollywood during the '70s and '80s, you'll recognize these spaces as the much-talked-about Studio One. Axis is more of a traditional disco, with several bars on different floors, plenty of places to sit and get cozy, and a room with pool tables. Except on Saturday, the place is open to the over-18 set. The crowd is mixed gay men and lesbians, but on certain nights, dykes rule. Go-go boys and girls frequently perform, and theme nights feature all types of music, including new wave, hi-NRG, tribal, rock, and Latin house. A different promoter takes over the Love Lounge each night, with parties ranging from fetish to retro disco to Asian nights. ⊠ *Axis: 652 N. La Peer Dr.*, ☎ *310/659–0471.* ⊠ *Love Lounge: 657 N. Robertson Blvd.*, ☎ *310/659–0472. Crowd at both: varied but usually under 30, mixed racially, mixed m/f.*

Firehouse. Loud and appropriately red, this disco hosts many theme nights, including the "Men's Room" on Thursday and "Ladies' Night" on Sunday. Every night there's dancing and a sufficiently beautiful bunch of revelers. So far the sound system is earning high marks. ⊠ *696 N. Robertson Blvd.*, ☎ *310/289–1353. Crowd: a cross-section of the usual WeHo bunch.*

Micky's. At first, this place seems the same as Rage, which is down the street. There's a bar in front, a dance floor in back, and lots of room for posing and cruising. People float between the two clubs, but Micky's has an older (except on 18-and-over Tuesdays) more outgoing and diverse crowd. It's known more as a place to get laid. More women come here than to the neighboring guys' clubs. Outstanding drink specials. ⊠ *8857 Santa Monica Blvd.*, ☎ *310/657–1176. Crowd: 80/20 m/f, mostly 20s and 30s, gym boys, plenty of tank tops and ripped jeans, very cruisy, greater racial mix than neighboring bars.*

Mother Lode. This down-to-earth bar famous for its Sunday beer blasts is always a great place to shoot pool or meet friends. The compact tavern has brass light fixtures, polished wood trim, and ornate cast-iron street lamps. Though it's in the heart of Boys' Town, it lacks the intensity of its competitors. ⊠ *8944 Santa Monica Blvd.*, ☎ *310/659–9700. Crowd: mostly male, late 20s to late 30s, jeans and flannel shirts, low-key yet on the make.*

Rage. Among guppies and gym boys, Rage is the preferred nightly gay disco. A midsize club with indoor and sidewalk socializing areas, and it was beautifully redesigned in 1997. The disco has the usual accoutrements (pulsing lasers, strobe lights, a mirror ball), and off to one side is a video lounge where boys exchange vital statistics between stints on the dance floor. ⊠ *8911 Santa Monica Blvd.*, ☎ *310/652–7055. Crowd: 85/15 m/f, young, stand-and-model, shirtless muscle boys, high energy, high attitude.*

Revolver. L.A.'s definitive pretty-boy bar—redolent of cologne, sculpting gel, and Marlboro cigarettes—is friendlier than you might think. You enter through a pair of imposing brass gates. Inside a half-dozen video screens play campy film and music clips. The usual suspects are more often more interested in the monitors than cruising, but it's still an easy place to meet guys. Squeeze your way back to the smaller video bar—it's more conducive to chatting. Open after hours on weekends. ⊠ *8851 Santa Monica Blvd.*, ☎ *310/659–8851. Crowd: mostly male, young, guppies and Twinkies, buffed and bronzed.*

Spike. A harder-action crowd hangs at the Spike, east of Guppie Land where Santa Monica Boulevard begins to turn seedy. Collared shirts appear in spurts at this leather-and-Levi's club, especially on weekends after 2 AM, when this is one of the few places still going (though it serves only coffee and soda). The long narrow bar has three rooms, all dimly lit and minimally decorated. ⊠ *7746 Santa Monica Blvd.*, ☎ *213/656–9343. Crowd: male, mostly thirtysomething, some leather but has drawn more of a jeans-and-T-shirt bunch in recent years, fairly butch.*

NEIGHBORHOOD HAUNTS

Each night at **Club 7969** (⊠ 7969 Santa Monica Blvd., ☎ 213/654–0280) carries a different theme. Often there are strippers (male and female); dancing amid a mixed crowd of gay men, lesbians, and straights; and anything from drag revues to leather and techno parties. Tuesday features the fanatically popular "Michelle's XXX Revue" (*see* Women's Hang-outs, *below*).

Sneeringly nicknamed the "Mold Coast," the **Gold Coast** (⊠ 8228 Santa Monica Blvd., ☏ 213/656–4879) is a cruisy cocktail lounge that draws a mostly thirtysomething dressed-down crowd. A cavernous disco of indirect lighting and mirrored walls, **Numbers** (⊠ 8029 Sunset Blvd., ☏ 213/656–6300) is L.A.'s upscale hustler bar. Similar but more downscale is **Hunters** (⊠ 7511 Santa Monica Blvd., ☏ 213/850–9428); the name says it all. **Rafters** (⊠ 7994 Santa Monica Blvd., ☏ 213/654–0396), across from the French Quarter Market, is a sleepy video bar that has a particularly big following among country-western fans. The nondescript **7702** (⊠ 7702 Santa Monica Blvd., ☏ 213/654–3336) is a usually quiet hang-out for gay men and lesbians that's open after hours on weekends. **Trunks** (⊠ 8809 Santa Monica Blvd., ☏ 310/652–1015), a sports bar, is a nice little place with zero attitude and a friendly older crowd.

HANGIN' WITH THE HETS

Right by Axis/Love Lounge, **LunaPark** (⊠ 655 N. Robertson Blvd., ☏ 310/652–0611) is a thriving restaurant and cabaret that's largely gay. It features everything from drag shows to dancing to comedy acts. **Cobalt Cantina** (⊠ 616 N. Robertson Blvd., ☏ 310/659–8691), an extremely successful spin-off of the like-named restaurant and bar in Silver Lake, is a quietly sophisticated alternative to the raucous clubs elsewhere in WeHo. The much-loved and occasionally celeb-haunted Chinese restaurant **Tommy Tang's** (⊠ 7313 Melrose Ave., ☏ 213/937–5733) hosts **Glenda,** a heel-clicking drag revue, the first Tuesday of every month.

Among the many straight Sunset Strip clubs with gay events and parties are the rock and alternative music club the **House of Blues** (⊠ 8430 Sunset Blvd., ☏ 310/659–3555), which is always very gay-friendly; **Coconut Teaszer** (⊠ 8117 Sunset Blvd., ☏ 213/654–4773 or 213/957–4787), which has live performances and after-hours parties, often queer-themed; and **The Comedy Store** (⊠ 8433 Sunset Blvd., ☏ 213/656–6225), which, by the way, is where the old TV show *77 Sunset Strip* was filmed.

Hollywood

PRIME SUSPECTS

Arena/Circus Disco. These two clubs share adjacent sites with the same address. Arena, which is set inside a 22,000-square-foot former ice factory, draws a throbbing, mostly young gay crowd for deep house. Tuesday and Friday are gay at the largely Latin and African-American Circus Disco; a gay African-American party is held Thursday nights. Music is mostly house and techno, though there's usually mainstream disco in the smaller of the two dance floors. ⊠ *6655 Santa Monica Blvd., ☏ 213/462–0714 for Arena, ☏ 213/462–1291 for Circus Disco. Crowd: mostly male, young; the usual libido-laden, hopped-up club kids.*

NEIGHBORHOOD HAUNTS

Fans of Asian drag flock to the divey **Mugi** (⊠ 5221 Hollywood Blvd., ☏ 213/462–2039), and fans of Latino drag swarm around **The Plaza** (⊠ 739 N. La Brea Ave., ☏ 213/939–0703).

ONE-NIGHTERS, MOVABLE FETES

On Saturday nights, especially after midnight (it's open after hours until 4), the serious dancing and "party" scene centers around **Probe** (⊠ 836 N. Highland Ave., ☏ 213/461–8301), which has been less than friendly in the past toward drag queens and others who don't pass muster with the obnoxious doormen—proceed at your own risk. On Sunday, there's a '70s dance party.

Silver Lake Vicinity

PRIME SUSPECTS

Cobalt Cantina. For several years the hottest gay cocktail bar in Silver Lake has been the Cobalt Cantina's Martini Lounge. The jam-packed room is decorated with huge paintings of celebs. A long bar, zinc cocktail tables, and cobalt drinking glasses (usually filled with either killer margaritas or strong martinis) round out the picture. Weekends or weeknights, the Martini Lounge booms for hours on end. ⊠ *4326 Sunset Blvd.,* ☎ *213/953– 9991. Crowd: mostly gay male but very lesbian- and straight-friendly, distinctly un-L.A., a mix of unpretentious and great-looking guys, 20s– 50s, gym boys mingling with bookish poets, mixed racially, more diverse than the crowd at WeHo's Cobalt Cantina.*

Cuff's. The only visible decor in this dark one-room hangout are a few pilfered street signs and a toilet seat that hangs over the bar. The place's tough blue-collar image seems just that: an image. Many suits-by-day come here to act out their butch fantasies and meet dangerous-looking guys. It's a bar where the hunk in the leather harness turns out to be your accountant. ⊠ *1941 Hyperion Ave.,* ☎ *213/660–2649. Crowd: male, 20s–40s, gruff, horny, wearing lots of leather and denim.*

Gauntlet II. Once strictly a leather bar, the Gauntlet has developed a broader following in recent years yet hasn't really lost its edge. You'll still notice guys with tattoos and piercings, killer leather gear, and *America's Most Wanted* glares. Don't worry: The Gauntlet hasn't gone soft. It's just gone cool—guys tired of WeHo's uniformity stride in here on a regular basis, especially on Saturday nights. ⊠ *4219 Santa Monica Blvd.,* ☎ *213/669– 9472. Crowd: male, somewhat mixed racially, mostly thirtysomething but with plenty of exceptions, half-leather, a quarter grunge, a quarter muscle boy, generally very sexy.*

Woody's Hyperion. The crowd at middle-of-the-road Woody's is rough-edged and down to earth, but the club isn't nearly as seedy as some of its neighbors. There's a small bar up front, a pool table, and a large dance floor. Dance, cruise, or just hang out. ⊠ *2810 Hyperion Ave.,* ☎ *213/ 660–1503. Crowd: 80/20 m/f, mixed Latino and Anglo, mostly of the neighborhood with a smattering of folks from farther afield, diverse in age, friendly, unpretentious, some grunge and alternative, dykes in boots and bras.*

NEIGHBORHOOD HAUNTS

More intensely leather- and bear-oriented than the nearby Gauntlet II, **Detour** (⊠ 1087 Manzanita St., ☎ 213/664–1189) has zero atmosphere and an eclectic following. The **Faultline** (⊠ 4216 Melrose Ave., ☎ 213/ 660–0889) hosts a leather and uniform night on Tuesday and is always extremely butch. Home of the best martini in Silver Lake, the **In Touch** (⊠ 2538 Hyperion Ave., ☎ 213/661–4233) is a handsome piano bar and cocktail lounge with an outgoing crowd and staff. Primarily a Latino club, **Le Bar** (⊠ 2375 Glendale Blvd., ☎ 213/660–7595) welcomes everybody and has terrific music, friendly bartenders, and hot strippers. The **Silver Lake Lounge** (⊠ 2906 Sunset Blvd., ☎ 213/663–9636) is a cruisy club with mostly Latino patrons and great drag shows.

ONE-NIGHTERS, MOVABLE FETES

There are two popular events held at **Rudolpho's** (⊠ 2500 Riverside Dr., ☎ 626/576–0720 or 626/282–0330): **Club Salsa Con Clase** (first, third, and last Saturday of every month) is a mixed lesbian/gay night of salsa, merengue, and Latin house music. Many locals insist that you haven't experienced gay L.A. until you've checked out **Dragstrip 66** (second Saturday of every month), a high-camp affair with a new theme each time—cross-dressing always figures into the equation.

The Garage (✉ 4519 Santa Monica Blvd., ☎ 213/683–3447) is an adult spa with different lesbian and gay dance parties, including **Fuel** (for women) and **Ouch** (more for men), both held on Saturday. Also check out **Sucker** (more for men), on Sunday.

The Beaches

Santa Monica and Venice

PRIME SUSPECTS

Roosterfish. Only a patch of glass brick tempers this cement building's frighteningly bright turquoise paint job. Inside is a small bar with Tiffany-style lamps, a linoleum floor, bits of memorabilia, and a large patio out back. By day the crowd is local; at night—especially on weekends—Metallica fans, Barbra devotees, and poetry slammers all squeeze in for a little peace, love, and understanding. ✉ *1302 Abbot Kinney Blvd., Venice,* ☎ *310/392–2123. Crowd: 80/20 m/f, the most diverse in L.A., popular with aged hippies, retired surfers, and disenchanted West Hollywooders.*

Downtown

PRIME SUSPECTS

Catch One. Gay and straight men and women head to this immense dance club that's not as attitudy as Probe, its major after-hours competitor. Catch One is open until 3 AM most nights, 4 on Friday and Saturday. Strip (male and female) and drag shows are staged, with the performers' gender, dress, and intended audience changing depending on the night of the week. The crowd on Thursday is mostly lesbian. ✉ *4067 W. Pico Blvd.,* ☎ *213/734–8849. Crowd: 60/40 m/f except Thursday (75/25 f/m), youngish, racially and stylistically diverse.*

NEIGHBORHOOD HAUNTS

The downtown dance club **Score** (✉ 107 W. 4th St., ☎ 213/625–7382) caters to a mostly Latino clientele. African-Americans frequent a couple of Inglewood bars: the **Annex Club** (✉ 835 S. La Brea Ave., ☎ 310/671–7323), which has a hopping juke, and the **Caper Room** (✉ 244 S. Market St., ☎ 310/677–0403), which often has strippers. In El Sereno, the **Plush Pony** has an almost exclusively Latin clientele and is best known for its drag shows and dancing. ✉ *5261 Alhambra Ave., ☎ 213/224–9488.*

San Fernando Valley

PRIME SUSPECTS

Apache Territory. This stand-and-model disco and video bar has a small dance floor and is crowded on weekends, especially after hours. Guys who find West Hollywood to be a tease like it here, where everyone is looser. The Apache is a major pick-up scene: easy to bed, easy to rise. Thursday nights are popular. ✉ *11608 Ventura Blvd., Studio City,* ☎ *818/506–0404. Crowd: 80/20 m/f, young, aspiring guppies, many cute Valley boys too lazy to wander over the hills.*

Lodge. The Valley's top workingman's bar is usually packed for happy hour and is always crowded on weekends. The spacious club has abundant diversions—darts, pool, and the like. A friendly crowd always piles around the large central bar. Off that is a dance floor, where you'll hear mostly Top 40 tunes. ✉ *4923 Lankershim Blvd., North Hollywood,* ☎ *818/769–7722. Crowd: male, mixed racially, mostly 30s and 40s, dressed down, low-attitude.*

Oasis. Although the Valley's gay nightlife is often dissed, Oasis may be the coziest, friendliest place in greater L.A. Behind the dull white-concrete facade is a classy piano bar with nightly entertainment, a well-lit pool room, and a cheerful patio. It fills up many nights with an appealing, approachable crowd. ⊠ *11916 Ventura Blvd., Studio City,* ☎ *818/980–4811. Crowd: 80/20 m/f, mostly 30 and up, mellow boys and girls you can take home to the family.*

Oil Can Harry's. It's been around for almost 30 years and continues to be L.A.'s best gay country-western dance club, patronized by men and women of all ages. The attractive interior has video screens, a large central dance floor, and bars at both ends. Two-stepping lessons are given on weekends. ⊠ *11502 Ventura Blvd., Studio City,* ☎ *818/760–9749. Crowd: 70/30 m/f, all ages, gets more non-Valley types than other area bars, insatiable country-western line dancers, very outgoing and fun.*

NEIGHBORHOOD HAUNTS

Bullet (⊠ 10522 Burbank Blvd., North Hollywood, ☎ 818/760–9563) is one of several dreary bars in an industrial neighborhood. The inside is pitch black and smoke-filled; getting to the nice patio in back is like trying to escape from a burning airplane. On Friday is the always-exhilarating "Bear Chest" contest. **Escapades** (⊠ 10437 Burbank Blvd., North Hollywood, ☎ 818/508–7008) is a casual tavern. People used to steal the balls from the pool tables, so now you have to leave your driver's license with the bartender as collateral. Nice.

Gold 9 (⊠ 13625 Moorpark St., Sherman Oaks, ☎ 818/986–0285) is a peculiar bar with a rowdy older crowd; if you're a stranger, just about everybody will notice you—and introduce themselves. In Reseda, **Incognito** (⊠ 7026 Reseda Blvd., ☎ 818/996–2976) is your only option; inside is a small dance floor with mirrored walls, a room with a couple of pool tables, and a cozy video bar. Straights and gays come to see the tired but still funny female impersonators at the **Queen Mary** (⊠ 12449 Ventura Blvd., Studio City, ☎ 818/506–5619) show lounge. The country-western **Rawhide/Shooters** (⊠ 10937 Burbank Blvd., North Hollywood, ☎ 818/760–9798) has a Sunday beer blast, a couple of pool tables, road-house-inspired decor, and a friendly staff.

Women's Bars and Hangouts

Many bars mentioned above, though more than 50% male, have strong lesbian followings, especially the Axis/Love Lounge (women's nights held frequently), Catch One (especially Thursday), Club 7969 (which is called Michelle's XXX on Tuesday, when female dancers perform), Cobalt Cantina (in both Silver Lake and West Hollywood, especially at happy hour), Firehouse (especially on Sunday), Incognito, Micky's, Oasis (especially on Sunday), Oil Can Harry's (especially on Thursday), Plush Pony (mostly Latina), Ripples (especially on Saturday), Rudolpho's (for Club Salsa Con Clase), and Woody's Hyperion (especially on Thursday). Little Frida's is always packed with a hip bunch (*see* Coffeehouse Culture, *above*).

PRIME SUSPECTS

Girl Bar. This glamorous party is thrown at several places; call the information line (☎ 213/460–2531) or check the lesbian rags. In recent years Girl Bar has been held Friday at **Axis** (*see above*) and Saturday at the **Love Lounge** (*see above*). It's occasionally poolside at a fancy hotel, often the Mondrian or the Argyle. These parties draw a modest (usually closeted) celebrity following. *Crowd: mostly mid-20s, hot, stylish, sophisticated, and lively, cruisy, lots of bisexuals.*

The Palms. This pubby bar in the heart of West Hollywood isn't as cruisy as the Girl Bar parties (*see above*) but is more open to out-of-towners than some neighborhood lesbian bars. There's ample seating and standing room; the back section has pool tables, and off that is the Oasis Patio bar. A rocking jukebox, DJs, or live bands power the large dance floor. On Wednesday, when drinks cost a buck, this is the place to be. Sunday's beer blast and barbecue is also popular. ⊠ *8572 Santa Monica Blvd.,* ☎ *310/652–6188. Crowd: 80/20 f/m, highly diverse in age and race, some guppies, some working-class, lipstick, butch—kind of a catchall.*

NEIGHBORHOOD HAUNTS

The Connection (⊠ 4363 Sepulveda Blvd., Culver City, ☎ 310/391–6817), which pulls in the Westside flannel-and-jeans crowd, has live entertainment, pool, campy old videos, and a true retro ambience.
The **Oxwood Inn** (⊠ 13713 Oxnard St., Van Nuys, ☎ 818/997–9666) gets an older suburban crowd (it's nicknamed "Menopause Manor"). An easy place to meet people, it has good music and a fun crowd. Dark, smoky **Rumors** (⊠ 10622 Magnolia Blvd., North Hollywood, ☎ 818/506–9651) has the feel of one of those women-in-prison B movies from the '50s. **Escapades** (⊠ 10437 Burbank Blvd., North Hollywood, ☎ 818/508–7008) has become very dyke-popular. Lesbians of color, especially Latinas, frequent **The Redhead Bar** (⊠ 2218 E. 1st St., downtown, ☎ 213/263–2995).

ONE-NIGHTERS, MOVABLE FETES

A strongly Latina crowd patronizes **Sabor Caliente** (☎ 213/504–4312) at the **Forge** (⊠ 617 S. Brand Blvd., Glendale, ☎ 818/246–1717) on Friday, where DJ Gaye Ann spins the hottest salsa, cumbia, and merengue.

Action

Sex clubs and bathhouses change often. Some standbys: **Basic Plumbing** (⊠ 1924 Hyperion Ave., ☎ 213/953–6731), a Silver Lake bathhouse; the infamous (in a good way) sex club **Zone** (⊠ 1037 N. Sycamore Ave., Hollywood, ☎ 213/464–8881); and **Melrose Baths** (⊠ 7269 Melrose Ave., ☎ 213/937–2122), WeHo's longest-running bathhouse. The neat and tidy **Hollywood Spa** (⊠ 1650 Ivar Ave., Hollywood) and the **North Hollywood Spa** (⊠ 5636 Vineland Ave., North Hollywood) adult-entertainment compounds have special theme nights and DJs that spin tunes in the evening. Call 800/SPA–CLUB for information about either.

SLEEPS

Plenty of establishments are within walking distance of West Hollywood's club scene, but most are pricey. Hollywood has scads of places, but many are motels in questionable areas. Beverly Hills and West Los Angeles have beautiful rooms and exorbitant prices. Downtown isn't a long drive from West Hollywood, and it's close to the Silver Lake restaurants and bars, but most lodgings are characterless business hotels. They're expensive on weekdays but more reasonable on weekends. The retro-looking motor lodges near Farmers Market are convenient to L.A.'s nightlife and are inexpensive and clean.

For price ranges, *see* lodging Chart A at the front of this guide.

Hotels

West Hollywood Vicinity

$$$$ ▦ **Argyle.** The 16-story, 1920s art deco tower, formerly home to glamorous stars like the Gabor sisters and Errol Flynn, contains rooms with stunning period reproductions, VCRs, CD players, and some of the best views in the city. ⊠ *8358 Sunset Blvd., 90069,* ☎ *213/654–7100 or 800/225–2637,* 🖷 *213/654–9287. 64 rooms. Restaurant, pool, health club.*

$$$$ ▦ **Wyndham Bel Age.** Things have improved greatly at this venerable property since Wyndham took over a few years back. The chain has increased the hotel's visibility among gays and lesbians, co-sponsoring the 1996 pride festival. Rooms are spacious and decorated with rich colors and wood

paneling. The on-site Diaghilev is an outstanding Franco-Russian restaurant. ⊠ *1020 N. San Vicente Blvd., 90069,* ☎ *310/854–1111 or 800/996–3426,* ℻ *310/854–0926. 200 rooms. Restaurants, pool, hot tub, health club.*

$$$–$$$$ ☷ **Beverly Prescott.** This discreet 12-story hotel frequented by business travelers and gay and lesbian tourists sits on a hill overlooking Beverly Hills and Century City. Large contemporary rooms have fireplaces and balconies. ⊠ *1224 S. Beverwil Dr., Los Angeles 90035,* ☎ *310/277–2800 or 800/421–3212,* ℻ *310/203–9537. 158 rooms. Restaurant, pool, health club.*

$$$–$$$$ ☷ **Le Montrose.** This secluded all-suites property is just off the Strip and close to Boys' Town bars. Huge rooms have fireplaces, kitchenettes, and private balconies. Enjoy amazing views of the skyline from the rooftop pool and hot tub. ⊠ *900 Hammond St., 90069,* ☎ *310/855–1115 or 800/776–0666,* ℻ *310/657–9192. 125 rooms. Restaurant, pool, health club.*

$$$–$$$$ ☷ **Le Parc.** The low-key rooms here have gas fireplaces, TVs and VCRs, a kitchenette or wet bar, and large sunken living rooms. The boutique hotel is on a quiet residential street, just down the hill from Boys' Town (should you not feel like walking, complimentary limo service is provided within a 3-mile radius). ⊠ *733 N. W. Knoll Dr., 90069,* ☎ *310/855–8888 or 800/578–4837,* ℻ *310/659–7812. 154 rooms. Restaurant, pool, health club.*

$$$ ☷ **Summerfield Suites.** A contemporary all-suites hotel on a sleepy street between Sunset Strip and Boys' Town, the Summerfield attracts business travelers—rooms are equipped with data ports and voice mail and have fireplaces, VCRs, and spacious sitting areas. ⊠ *1000 Westmount Dr., 90069,* ☎ *310/657–7400 or 800/833–4353,* ℻ *310/854–6744. 109 suites. Pool, health club.*

$$–$$$ ☷ **Le Reve.** Another gay-friendly all-suites hotel close to the bars sits high above Santa Monica Boulevard, its rooftop terrace and pool commanding fine views of the area. Rooms (some with kitchenettes) are large, with VCRs, refrigerators, and, in most cases, private balconies. ⊠ *8822 Cynthia St., 90069,* ☎ *310/854–1114 or 800/835–7997,* ℻ *310/657–2623. 88 rooms. Pool, exercise room.*

$$–$$$ ☷ **Ramada West Hollywood.** The famed Ramada is the most gay-popular mainstream hotel in America: It's in the heart of the bar district and has a sleek art deco look and a cruisy pool and sundeck out back. Most of the stylish and spacious suites have sleeping lofts; all have kitchenettes. ⊠ *8585 Santa Monica Blvd., 90069,* ☎ *310/652–6400 or 800/845–8585,* ℻ *310/652–2135. 175 rooms. Restaurant, pool.*

$$ ☷ **Best Western Sunset Plaza Hotel.** Drawing a mix of families and twentysomethings who want to be close to Sunset Strip music clubs without shelling out a fortune, the Sunset Plaza is indeed one of WeHo's top values. Rooms are large and clean. ⊠ *8400 Sunset Blvd., 90069,* ☎ *213/654–0750 or 800/421–3652,* ℻ *213/650–6146. 88 rooms. Pool.*

$ ☷ **Beverly Laurel Motor Hotel.** Attached to the chic little late-night coffee shop Swingers, the Beverly Laurel attracts all manner of visitors—fashionable (but low-budget) genXers, plus families, queers, and budding actors. Each room has a refrigerator. ⊠ *8018 Beverly Blvd., Los Angeles 90036,* ☎ *213/651–2441,* ℻ *213/651–5225. 52 rooms. Pool.*

$ ☷ **Holloway Motel.** This clean and affordable property is in the heart of the gay entertainment strip. Suites have kitchen facilities. ⊠ *8465 Santa Monica Blvd., 90069,* ☎ *213/654–2454. 20 rooms.*

The Beaches

$$$–$$$$ ☷ **Shutters on the Beach.** Not your typical urban hotel experience, Shutters is on Santa Monica's beachfront, only a short blade or bike ride away from the gay beach at Will Rogers State Park. The rooms, spread among three posh buildings, have marble baths with large whirlpool tubs. ✉ *1 Pico Blvd., Santa Monica 90405, ☎ 310/458–0030, FAX 310/458–4589. 198 rooms. Restaurants, pool, health club.*

$$ 🔳 **Pacific Shore.** A block from the Santa Monica beach and a long but scenic walk or short drive to the gay section, the Pacific has bright and simple rooms, and the price is right. ✉ *1819 Ocean Ave., Santa Monica 90401, ☎ 310/451–8711 or 800/622–8711, FAX 310/394–6657. 168 rooms. Restaurant, pool.*

$–$$ 🔳 **Hotel Carmel.** This 1925 hotel is not fabulous, but it's cheap, reasonably clean, and close to the beach. The crowd here is straight, with plenty of Eurotourists. ✉ *201 Broadway, Santa Monica 90401, ☎ 310/451–2469 or 800/445–8695, FAX 310/393–4180. 110 rooms. Restaurant.*

Guest Houses and Small Hotels

$$ 🔳 **Grove Guesthouse.** Couples should consider this romantic small cottage in West Hollywood with a kitchen, a separate living room, and a VCR with a video library. ✉ *1325 N. Orange Grove Ave., West Hollywood 90069, ☎ 213/876–7778. 1 cottage with phone, TV, and private bath. Pool, hot tub. Continental breakfast. Mixed gay male/lesbian.*

$–$$ 🔳 **San Vicente Inn Resort.** This is the quintessential California gay guest house, complete with foliage-choked lanai and buffed and in-the-buff men lying around a pool. All accommodations are either in large suites or detached cottages with tasteful contemporary furnishings. The rates are extremely fair; the friendly owners put a tremendous amount of work into making this one of the best gay places in southern California. ✉ *845 San Vicente Blvd., West Hollywood 90069, ☎ 310/854–6915, FAX 310/289–5929. 19 rooms with phone and TV; most with private bath; some with kitchenette. Pool, hot tub. Mostly gay male.*

THE LITTLE BLACK BOOK

At Your Fingertips

AIDS Hotline of Southern California (☎ 800/922–2437). **Gay and Lesbian Community Center of Los Angeles** (✉ 1625 N. Schrader Blvd., ☎ 213/993–7400). **Gay Men's Activities Hotline** (☎ 213/993–7444). **Hollywood Chamber of Commerce** (✉ 7108 Hollywood Blvd., 90028, ☎ 213/469–8311). **L.A. Weekly** (☎ 213/465–9909, Web site www.laweekly.com). **Los Angeles Convention & Visitors Bureau** (✉ 633 W. 5th St., Suite 6000, 90071, ☎ 213/624–7300 or 800/CATCH–LA). **Los Angeles Visitors Centers** (✉ 685 S. Figueroa St., downtown, ☎ 213/689–8822; ✉ Janes House Square, 6541 Hollywood Blvd., Hollywood 90028, ☎ 213/689–8822). **Metropolitan Transit Authority** (☎ 213/626–4455). **New Times Los Angeles** (☎ 310/477–0403, Web site www.newtimesla.com). **United Independent Taxi** (☎ 213/653–5050). **West Hollywood Convention & Visitors Bureau** (✉ 8687 Melrose Ave., M-26, 90069, ☎ 310/289–2525 or 800/368–6020).

Gay Media

Although its ads are male-oriented, **4-Front Magazine** (☎ 213/650–7772, e-mail the 4front@aol.com) is well written, with a nice balance of sexy and informative coverage for men and women. **Edge Magazine** (☎ 213/962–6994, e-mail edgemag@earthlink.net) provides comprehensive bar and restaurant coverage and has a health-and-fitness bent; it's chatty, full of beefcake, and hard to escape. **Frontiers** (☎ 213/848–2222, Web site www.frontiersweb.com), based in West Hollywood, has news and entertainment features on all of southern California. The **Gay & Lesbian Times** (☎ 619/299–6397), based in San Diego, has information on all of southern California. **California Nightlife** (☎ 213/462–5400) is a standard biweekly entertainment rag with good men's and women's coverage. The small but potent bar rag *Fab!* (☎ 213/655–5716) comes out biweekly and caters mostly to men. The *Orange County Blade* (☎ 949/494–4898, e-mail nfo@ocblade.com) covers the gay scene in Long Beach and Orange County. The *Blk Guide to Southern California* (☎ 310/410–0808, e-mail newsroom@blk.com) covers the area scene for African American lesbians and gay men.

Female FYI (☎ 213/938–5969, e-mail fyizine@aol.com) and *LA Girl Guide* (☎ 310/391–8877, Web site www.girlguide.com) will direct you to lesbian nightlife and fun. The monthly *Lesbian News* (☎ 310/392–8224), founded by Jinx Beers in 1975, carries comprehensive coverage of southern California and lots of news and interviews.

BOOKSTORES
The city's major lesbigay bookstore, **A Different Light** (✉ 8853 Santa Monica Blvd., ☎ 310/854–6601), is in the heart of West Hollywood. **Unicorn Bookstore** (✉ 8940 Santa Monica Blvd., ☎ 310/652–6253) has a more modest array of titles but a good selection of videos, greetings cards, and gifts. You'll find the best erotic videos and magazines at **Drake's** (✉ 7566 Melrose Ave., ☎ 213/651–5600). The excellent **Sisterhood Bookstore** (✉ 1351 Westwood Blvd., Westwood, ☎ 310/477–7300) has been going strong since 1972.

Working Out
The **Sports Connection** (✉ 8612 Santa Monica Blvd., ☎ 310/652–7440) in West Hollywood is one of the gayest gyms on the planet—a major workout and cruise scene for men and women. To come here, you must know a member or be staying at a nearby hotel with guest privileges. The **World Gym West Hollywood** (✉ 8560 Santa Monica Blvd., ☎ 310/659–6630) does not impose such restrictions and has extensive facilities. The above gyms are all lesbian-friendly, but for a women-only environment, head to the **L.A. Women's Gym** (✉ 3407 Glendale Blvd., ☎ 213/661–9456) in Silver Lake.

LAGUNA BEACH

Chic Laguna Beach, the jewel of the so-called California Riviera, has long been a favorite vacation spot of gay men and, to a lesser degree, lesbians. About midway between San Diego and Los Angeles and nicknamed SoHo-by-the-Sea, the area began attracting artists around the turn of the century. A formal art colony was established in 1917.

Lesbian and gay residents and visitors have always maintained a discreet presence. Laguna is, after all, a coastal arm of conservative Orange County. By 1983, though, there were enough politically minded homosexuals to elect the first openly gay mayor in the United States. Laguna later became the only town in Orange County to adopt an antidiscrimination policy that protected the rights of gays and lesbians.

Nevertheless, the formation in 1995 of a gay business alliance brought serious social and political divisions within Laguna to the fore. Both the City Council and the Laguna Chamber of Commerce refused to endorse the annual pride festival in 1995, with the chamber complaining that some of its members had lost straight business during the previous year's event. The festival took place in 1995 without mainstream support, but wasn't held in '96 and '97.

Despite the pride-festival flap, Laguna remains a desirable getaway. The ocean views and landscape are often spectacular, there's good shopping and dining, and party types will find just enough nightlife to keep themselves occupied until another gorgeous day begins.

The Lay of the Land

Broadway intersects with Coast Highway, also called Highway 1, at the oceanside equivalent of a traditional American town green: **Main Beach.** The park has a large sandy beach, tile benches, heavily used volleyball nets and basketball courts, and a small wooden boardwalk. Locals and tourists laze in the sun, their peace interrupted only by the occasional ring of a cellular phone (yuppies abound).

Along **Ocean** and **Forest avenues,** and along **Broadway,** are excellent cafés and some art galleries and boutiques. North of Main Beach past the Cottage Restaurant (*see* Eats, *below*) is Laguna's **Gallery Row,** the most concentrated stretch of art dealing, and also the **Laguna Art Museum** (⊠ 307 Cliff Dr., ☎ 949/494–6531), which houses a small permanent collection of works by local artists and mounts outstanding temporary exhibits.

A five-minute drive south of downtown to where Cress Street, Mountain Road, and Calliope Street intersect with Coast Highway leads to some gay-popular businesses. The anchor is the **Coast Inn** (*see* Sleeps, *below*), which has a large bar and disco and a **gay and lesbian beach** behind it. An alternative to this beach is a short drive south of here. Known as the **West Street Beach** or **Thousand Steps,** the long expanse is off Coast Highway at the end of either Camelpoint Road or West Street.

Driving inland from downtown through Laguna Canyon, you'll pass the **Laguna Moulton Playhouse** (⊠ 606 Laguna Canyon Rd., ☎ 949/497–9244). Laguna's pride and joy and most popular event is its **Festival of Arts** (⊠ Irvine Bowl, 650 Laguna Canyon Rd., ☎ 949/494–1145 or 800/487–3378), which runs from July to August.

Getting Around

Laguna Beach is an easy drive from Los Angeles or San Diego. From L.A. take the San Diego Freeway south to Highway 133 (Laguna Creek Road), which leads directly into downtown Laguna Beach. From San Diego follow the San Diego Freeway north to Highway 1 (Coast Highway). Visitors generally use a car around town, but because most of Laguna Beach's attractions, shopping, and restaurants lie along Coast Highway or in the compact business district, you can do pretty well using Laguna Transit buses. Driving is certainly not impossible, but parking downtown can be tight, especially in summer and on weekends, despite the presence of several municipal lots.

Eats

Laguna's glamorous and artsy aura continues in the decor, presentation, and quality of its restaurants. Outdoor seating, ocean views, and a casual mood are common; seafood is abundant. There's a budding café culture downtown, around Ocean and Forest avenues.

For price ranges, *see* dining Chart A at the front of this guide.

$$–$$$ ✕ **Shame on the Moon.** The Laguna branch of the Palm Springs gay restaurant has black and white photos and other design elements of the original. The hearty Continental fare, such as calves' liver sautéed with mushrooms and bacon, is quite dependable. ⊠ *1464 S. Coast Hwy.,* ☎ *949/497–9975.*

$$–$$$ ✕ **230 Forest Avenue.** One of downtown Laguna's top restaurants wows diners with imaginative New American and West Coast regional cuisine. The emphasis is on seafood: Salmon-and-mussel stew with white beans and smoked bacon is a top starter. Eggplant ratatouille with andouille sausage is one of 10 pasta options. ⊠ *230 Forest Ave.,* ☎ *949/494–2545.*

$$ ✕ **The Cottage.** Although it's touristy, the Cottage has long been a friend of gays and lesbians. The straightforward Continental cuisine is competently prepared—charbroiled lamb with herbs, olive oil, and thyme is a favorite. Sunday brunch is wildly popular. ⊠ *308 N. Coast Hwy.,* ☎ *949/ 494–3023.*

$$ ✕ **Mark's.** A sister to the gay eatery in West Hollywood, this is one spot where the food is truly commensurate with the stylish atmosphere and diva-filled dining room. Top dishes include a grilled pork chop with cranberry-chipotle sauce, and papaya-stuffed quesadillas in melted Brie. Mark's is a big brunch hangout. ⊠ *858 S. Coast Hwy.,* ☎ *949/494–6711.*

$$ ✕ **Viktor Viktoria.** New owners have transformed the former Little Shrimp bar into an excellent restaurant and piano bar, still with a largely gay following. The southern-style American fare is relatively affordable and not as greasy as you might expect. Consider the bourbon-tarragon chicken over pasta. ⊠ *1305 S. Coast Hwy.,* ☎ *949/376–8809.*

$–$$ ✕ **Cafe Zinc.** The ultimate lunch and breakfast spot downtown has outstanding food and a sunny outdoor dining area aglow with greenery and zinc tables. Strengths include the vegetarian chili and the pizzettes (try the Mexican with chipotle and anaheim peppers and several cheeses). ⊠ *350 Ocean Ave.,* ☎ *949/494–6302.*

$ ✕ **Taco Loco.** This self-serve taco joint is one of Laguna's big surfer hangouts. Seating is outside, overlooking the busy highway. Not the most enchanting ambience, but the fish fajitas and tacos are excellent. ⊠ *640 S. Coast Hwy.,* ☎ *949/497–1635.*

Scenes

Laguna's three queer establishments stay lively year-round but are mobbed in summer. All three welcome women (the town has no lesbian bars).

PRIME SUSPECTS

Boom Boom Room. The rambling complex at the Coast Inn is packed, especially on weekends, with tan, toned bodies. The front room has a large central bar, two pool tables, and such embellishments as a pressed-tin ceiling, glass brick, and hurricane shutters. A small room with a pool table connects this bar to the rear one, which has a fabulous 8-foot-long tropical fish tank and soft amber lighting. Off this is the small dance bar. ⊠ *1401 S. Coast Hwy.,* ☎ *949/494–7588. Crowd: 75/25 m/f, varied ages, but mostly under 35 on weekends, touristy, well-heeled, occasionally attitudy but fairly down-to-earth.*

Main Street. With red-leatherette chairs and a mock-Tudor interior, Main Street doesn't look like a typical beach bar. The crowd, however, is southern California all the way: fun-loving, chatty, and bleached blond. People often sing up a storm around the piano. ⊠ *1460 S. Coast Hwy.,* ☎ *949/494–0056. Crowd: 70/30 m/f, a bit older and less touristy than at the Boom Boom Room, but otherwise similar.*

Viktor Viktoria. This squank piano bar and restaurant has high-back oak chairs and navy-blue leather bar stools. Soft lighting and candles create a sophisticated mood. There's also a bar outside on the patio. Weekend afternoons and early on weekday evenings are lively, making this a great stopover before heading out for a night of dancing. ⊠ *1305 S. Coast Hwy.,* ☎ *949/376–8809. Crowd: mostly gay, 70/30 m/f, otherwise diverse.*

Action

Laguna is not a major male cruising scene, but there is one well-lit, relatively safe spot. West of Coast Highway, Mountain Drive becomes little more than a wide driveway bordering the Boom Boom Room. At the end is a staircase that winds down to the beach behind the Coast Inn. Both the beach and the staircase get pretty busy after the bars close. Also along the same small stretch of Mountain Drive there's a tiny store, **Gay**

Mart (☎ 949/497–9108), that sells beachwear, men's clothing, a limited amount of gay erotica, and some gay videos.

Sleeps

There are no gay-exclusive guest houses like you'll find in Palm Springs, but the Coast Inn is a largely gay small hotel, and it's home to the town's most popular gay club. Homos tend to stay at the places below downtown, along South Coast Highway. The knowledgeable folks at the gay-owned **California Riviera 800** (☎ 949/376–0305 or 800/621–0500) reservation service book accommodations from Santa Barbara to San Diego, although they specialize in this area.

For price ranges, *see* lodging Chart A at the front of this guide.

$$$$ 🏨 **Ritz-Carlton Laguna Niguel.** It's stuffy, costly, and a 15-minute drive from downtown Laguna Beach, but the Ritz is also one of the most spectacular resorts along the Pacific coastline: Perched atop a 150-foot cliff, it commands panoramic ocean views. ⊠ *1 Ritz-Carlton Dr., Dana Point, 92629,* ☎ *949/240–2000 or 800/241–3333,* ℻ *949/240–0829. 393 rooms. Restaurant, pool, spa, health club.*

$$–$$$ 🏨 **Best Western Laguna Brisas Spa Hotel.** This cheerful property has a good reputation in the gay and lesbian community. Rooms are done in cool pastels; they're big, comfortable, and have ocean views. The setting is a dramatic hill; rooms tumble down the side of it. ⊠ *1600 S. Coast Hwy., 92651,* ☎ *949/497–7272 or 800/624–4442,* ℻ *949/497–8306. 65 rooms. Pool.*

$$–$$$ 🏨 **Casa Laguna Inn.** This enchanting Spanish Mission–style compound has ocean views, lush gardens and courtyards, and a pool and sundeck shaded by banana and avocado trees. The wide-ranging accommodations include a 1,360-square-foot mission house that sleeps six, a small romantic cottage, and 19 smaller units. ⊠ *2510 S. Coast Hwy., 92651* ☎ *949/494–2996 or 800/233–0449,* ℻ *949/494–5009. 21 rooms. Pool.*

$–$$ 🏨 **Coast Inn.** A full-service gay resort for more than 30 years, the Coast Inn sits right on the beach and has bars, a restaurant, and clean, comfortable rooms. The fanciest accommodations have private sundecks, fireplaces, and wet bars, but you can get simpler ones with ocean views for as little as $60. ⊠ *1401 S. Coast Hwy., 92651,* ☎ *949/494–7588 or 800/653–2697,* ℻ *949/494–1735. 23 rooms. Restaurant.*

The Little Black Book

For more information on Laguna Beach, contact the **Gay and Lesbian Community Center of Orange County** (☎ 714/534–0862; info hot line, ☎ 714/534–3261), **Laguna Beach Chamber of Commerce** (⊠ 357 Glenneyre Ave., 92652, ☎ 949/494–1018), **Laguna Beach Community Clinic** (☎ 949/494–0761), or **Laguna Beach Visitor Information Center** (⊠ 252 Broadway, ☎ 949/497–9229 or 800/877–1115).

The *Orange County Blade* (☎ 949/494–4898, e-mail nfo@ocblade.com), covers Laguna Beach. **A Different Drummer** (⊠ 1294 S. Coast Hwy., ☎ 949/497–6699) specializes in gay and lesbian titles.

19 Out in Memphis

ALTHOUGH IT'S ONE OF the most populous cities in the South, Memphis (population 597,000) is a low-key place, and its lesbian and gay denizens are more closeted and invisible than in most comparably sized cities. Nevertheless, visitors to this Mississippi River metropolis will find that the attractions here (and they're not all about Elvis) merit a few days' exploration. The gay nightlife hasn't the pizzazz of Atlanta's or New Orleans's, but Memphis is party central for queers throughout western Tennessee, eastern Arkansas, and northern Mississippi.

From the day in 1968 that Dr. Martin Luther King, Jr., was felled here by an assassin's bullet until the mid-'80s, Memphis suffered an unrelenting slump—even the city's elegant grande dame, the Peabody Hotel, closed its doors for a time in the '70s. The city began to rebound economically a little more than a decade ago, and its once grim civil rights record has been largely reversed; the impressive civil rights museum that has been fashioned out of the motel in which Dr. King was assassinated is a telling sign of just how far Memphis has come.

As for the queer community, it moves slowly but steadily forward, gradually attaining increased visibility. It's estimated that more than 1,000 attended the Pride March in 1997 in Overton Park; this turnout represents a significant increase over previous years. There aren't many openly gay citizens in Memphis's political or cultural mainstream, but the local P-Flag chapter is one of the South's strongest, and Memphis has a cohesive and well-networked women's community (the city hosted the national NOW conference in 1997).

THE LAY OF THE LAND

Downtown

Elvis Presley wasn't the first, nor was he necessarily the most important, musician to make a name for himself in Memphis. Alabama native W. C. Handy sparked the city's legacy as America's blues capital. The modest wood-frame **W. C. Handy Memphis Home and Museum** (⊠ 352 Beale St., ☎ 901/527–3427) has been moved from its original location to downtown, behind the **Memphis Visitors Information Center** (⊠ 340 Beale St., ☎ 901/543–5333).

Beale Street has plenty of throbbing music clubs and inexpensive but touristy restaurants—much as it did in its heyday; its history of revelry is palpable. The street draws a very straight crowd at night. One favorite stop along here is the original **A. Schwab Dry Goods Store** (⊠ 163 Beale St., ☎ 901/523–9782), which has been running continuously since 1876 and has its own museum; inside you can buy bloomers, incense, top hats, walking canes, harmonicas, and hundreds of other items ranging from the mundane to the bizarre.

Across the street, the free **Center for Southern Folklore** (✉ 130 Beale St., ☎ 901/525–3655) has exhibits on the culture, music, food, and crafts of the Mississippi Delta region. The center can arrange a walking tour of Beale Street (by reservation only). Several blocks east is the **Hunt-Phelan Home** (✉ 533 Beale St., ☎ 800/344–3166), an 1830's restored mansion in which both Ulysses S. Grant and Jefferson Davis once lived (not together, presumably). The rare 1874 Steinway and Sons rosewood piano is a particularly fabulous antique; bibliophiles should check out the library's impressive collection of first editions.

South of downtown is the **Lorraine Motel,** site of Dr. King's assassination on April 4, 1968. The motel has been transformed into the **National Civil Rights Museum** (✉ 450 Mulberry St., ☎ 901/521–9699); exhibits trace the history of the civil-rights movement. There's even a Montgomery, Alabama bus like the one in which Rosa Parks refused to give up her seat, sparking an uprising against segregation.

At the northern end of downtown stands the most distinct component of the city skyline, the glimmering, stainless-steel **Pyramid Arena** (✉ 1 Auction St. at Front, ☎ 901/526–5177), built in 1991. Across a narrow swath of river is **Mud Island** (✉ 175 N. Front St., ☎ 901/576–7241). This 52-acre park and museum, dedicated to the history of the Mississippi River, contains many exhibits about the river's natural history, most memorable of which is a five-block-long scale model of a section of the river, through which 800 gallons of water flow every minute. There are also shops and restaurants; you can easily spend an afternoon here.

One last section of downtown that bears exploring is the 25-block **Victorian Village Historic District** (✉ Adams Ave., from Front St. to Manassas St.). Along this span you'll pass about 20 restored historic homes, of which three are open to the public as museums: **Magevney House** (✉ 198 Adams Ave., ☎ 901/526–4464), **Mallory Neely House** (✉ 652 Adams Ave., ☎ 901/523–1484), and **Woodruff-Fontaine House** (✉ 680 Adams Ave., ☎ 901/526–1469).

As you drive east of downtown along Union Avenue, you'll pass a totally unassuming and relatively small commercial building, **Sun Studio** (✉ 706 Union Ave., ☎ 901/521–0664). Back when this music-recording studio opened in the early '50s, anyone with a few bucks and a love of crooning could stroll in here and cut a demo tape. One such customer was Elvis Presley. If you're a closet diva or a regular at your local karaoke club, take heart. For a nominal fee you, too, can cut your own album here.

Midtown, Overton Park, and Cooper-Young
Most of the city's queer-owned homes and businesses are east of where I–40/I–240 slices through the city center, in **Midtown.** The western and southern edge of Midtown, nearest downtown, is mostly a working-class residential neighborhood, which also claims the bulk of the city's queer neighborhood taverns. Farther east, anchoring Midtown, you'll find **Overton Park,** the name of both an expansive patch of meadows and gardens that's popular with gay sun bunnies, and a stately residential neighborhood. Adjacent to the park are the **Memphis Zoo** (✉ 2000 Galloway St., ☎ 901/276–9453) and the **Memphis Brooks Museum of Art** (✉ 1934 Poplar Ave., ☎ 901/722–3500), an eclectic 7,000-piece collection whose works span eight centuries.

On the east side of Midtown are two small but trendy and fairly queer entertainment districts, **Overton Square** (around the intersection of Madison Avenue and Cooper Street) and, a few blocks south, **Cooper-Young** (around the intersection of Young and Cooper streets). The latter is home to the city's women's bookstore, **Meristem** (*see* Gay Media, *below*), which also has quite a few gay male titles. Between these two neighborhoods, **Cooper Street** is lined with kitschy shops, artsy coffeehouses and the like. Among the several boutiques and stores, **Flashback** (⊠ 2304 Central Ave., ☎ 901/272–2304) is an entire department store of high-quality 1920s to 1960s furnishings.

Graceland

Few attractions are more closely identified with their respective locations than **Graceland** (⊠ 3764 Elvis Presley Blvd. [off 1–55], 12 mi southeast of downtown, ☎ 901/332–3322 or 800/238–2000) is to Memphis. Pronounced "grace-lynn" locally, this campy compound in which the King of Rock and Roll resided upon his rise to mega-stardom contains not only his palatial Colonial-style mansion (filled with many peculiar collectibles and memorabilia, plus a substantial number of Presley's glittery and gaudy costumes), but his custom jets (the *Hound Dog II* and the *Lisa Marie*), a collection of 22 vehicles, and the serene Meditation Garden, where Elvis is buried. The gift shop alone is reason enough to visit. If you're really a die-hard Elvisite, check out the new downtown restaurant **Elvis Presley's Memphis** (⊠ 126 Beale St., ☎ 901/527–6900), which opened in summer 1997 on the 20th anniversary of Presley's untimely demise.

GETTING AROUND

You'll need a car. Downtown Memphis can definitely be explored on foot, but wheels are required to get among the gay-popular bars and restaurants, as well as to several outlying attractions, such as Overton Park and Graceland. Bus routes are geared toward local commuters, but visitors often take the downtown trolley, which runs up and down Front Street.

EATS

Memphis cuisine is influenced by southern, soul, Cajun, and Creole traditions and has become increasingly sophisticated of late. Although the restaurant scene still trails Nashville in creativity and panache, the cost of a meal here is typically quite reasonable. Few of the restaurants downtown are popular with family, but most of those in Midtown draw a steady mix of gay and straight patrons.

For price ranges, *see* dining Chart B at the front of this guide.

$$–$$$$ ✗ **The Peabody Hotel.** The mid-South's most famous historic hotel is home to three excellent restaurants. Dux (☎ 901/529–4199) specializes in international cuisine and has a light casual menu; Mallards (☎ 901/529–4140) has burgers, a raw bar, and other regional favorites (it's more of a sports bar and probably draws the straightest crowd of the three); and formal Chez Phillipe (☎ 901/529–4188) offers a first-rate menu of French and Continental cuisine—the kitchen is presided over by chef José Gutierrez, one of the South's rising culinary stars. ⊠ *149 Union Ave.*

$$$ ✗ **Cafe Society.** A smart nouvelle Continental bistro on the edge of Overton Park, Cafe Society appeals to a stylish crowd, from regulars of the nearby art museum to gaggles of lunching garden-club matrons. The emphasis is on rich cream sauces, but lighter options such as a Caesar salad with lemon thyme–crusted chicken and an always inventive pizza of the day round out the menu. ⊠ *212 N. Evergreen St.,* ☎ 901/722–2177.

$$–$$$ ✗ **Arizona.** This queer-popular newcomer, despite its location in a modest little building on the northern edge of Midtown, has garnered rave reviews for its authentic, and quite inventive, southwestern cuisine. Specialties include grilled chicken with a lime-cilantro cream sauce, and

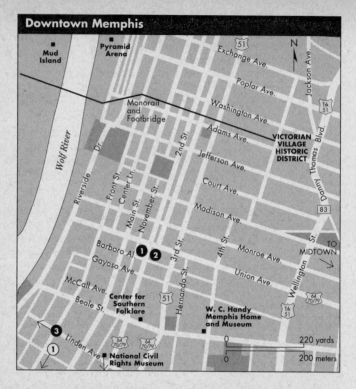

shark with a sharp southwestern rémoulade accompanied by rice and asparagus. ✉ *394 N. Watkins St.,* ☎ *901/272–9000.*

$$–$$$ ✕ **Automatic Slim's Tonga Club.** With all the style and energy of a big-city supper club, this chic downtown favorite dazzles the masses with consistently outstanding nouvelle Caribbean, Latin American, and southwestern cuisine. Sample such complex dishes as salmon with sautéed spinach and cabbage, mango-peanut relish, and coconut milk–roasted pistachio cream sauce. Or just drop by for drinks in the swank cocktail bar. ✉ *83 S. Second St.,* ☎ *901/525–7948.*

$$–$$$ ✕ **Landry's Seafood House.** It's straight, it's touristy, and it has all the intimacy of the Pyramid Arena, but this Memphis outpost of the popular southern chain offers consistently fresh and well-prepared seafood. All of the usual regional suspects—catfish, oysters on the half shell, and gumbo—are available, plus Maine lobster. Try to get a table overlooking the Mississippi River. Reservations aren't accepted, so the wait can exceed an hour. ✉ *263 Wagner Pl.,* ☎ *901/526–1966.*

$$–$$$ ✕ **Maxwell's.** The culinary cornerstone of the funky Cooper-Young district, Maxwell's is a spacious New American eatery that's ideal for a light bite or a full three-course meal. Among the many tasty starters, potato cakes with smoked trout, crème frâiche, capers, and red caviar are a standout. Pecan-crusted chicken pan-sautéed with port wine sauce is a fine entrée. ✉ *948 S. Cooper St.,* ☎ *901/725–1009.*

$$ ✕ **Paulette's.** A local favorite for more than two decades, Paulette's scores high marks for its affordable American cooking and for its festive ambience—on weekends there's a pianist tinkling away at Gershwin standards and Beale Street blues. Crepes are a specialty (try the one with Gulf shrimp in white wine with almonds). Grilled brochettes of chicken with mushrooms, bacon, and scallions grilled on a skewer and served over rice is another strong offering. ✉ *2110 Madison Ave.,* ☎ *901/726–5128.*

$–$$ ✕ **Cafe Olé.** It's a mob scene at happy hour, which can make for fun people-watching, but this funky Cooper-Young restaurant also serves very good Mexican food in a region that's not known for it. The fare ranges from predictable and Americanized (chimichangas, tacos, etc.) to slightly unusual (a black bean enchilada with a robust tomatillo sauce). ✉ *959 S. Cooper St.,* ☎ *901/274–1504.*

$ ✕ **Alternative Restaurant.** This supremely strange café, a trippy living-room-inspired space with pop art on the walls, specializes in affordable home-style southern cooking. Every night there's a two-for-one special, such as chicken and dumplings, that will satisfy any bargain seeker. Desserts such as chess or pecan pies taste better than Mom's. Live music some nights. ✉ *553 S. Cooper St.,* ☎ *901/725–7922.*

$ ✕ **Le Saigon.** This bare-bones Midtown restaurant may not be pretty, but the menu has about 120 enticing Vietnamese specialties, including chicken sautéed with diced water chestnuts, bamboo shoots, mushrooms, celery hearts, and slivers of toasted almond in a piquant sauce. The portions are huge and the prices very low. ✉ *54 N. Cleveland St.,* ☎ *901/276–5326.*

Coffeehouse Culture

The Edge. Definitely the gayest of the few coffeehouses in Midtown, the Edge is a homey place with a spacious deck overlooking delightfully offbeat Cooper Street. It's open late, and draws a diverse mix—from artsy fags to guppies and yuppies. ✉ *532 S. Cooper St.,* ☎ *901/272–3036.*

Java Cabana. This deeply weird Cooper-Young coffeehouse is a shrine to Elvis kitsch (it even has a wedding chapel dedicated to "The King"). The decor is straight out of the 1950s, with Formica tables, gritty linoleum floors, and mismatched chairs. Very popular with students. ✉ *2170 Young Ave.,* ☎ *901/272–7210.*

SCENES

The disco Amnesia is bigger, better-designed, and more interesting than most of the clubs in New York and Los Angeles. Unfortunately for tourists, this is about the only happening venue in the city. A few other bars draw moderately large crowds—one that does is primarily African-American, while a couple others are good choices for lesbians. Most bars are in the western half of Midtown and are usually open till 3; many (including Backstreet, Crossroads, J-Wags, and Pipeline) serve only beer and provide mixers for harder stuff, which you must bring yourself. In the same part of town, the **P&H Cafe** (✉ 1532 Madison Ave., ☎ 901/726–0906) is a busy gay-popular eatery with basic food that's a good place to pop in for a beer or to enjoy the occasional live bands.

Prime Suspects

Amnesia. This slick megaclub is popular with women and men and has a dance floor, several cool lounges, and a very nice lanai and swimming pool (and yes, late on those sultry summer nights, folks do slip into the water to cool off—or heat up). Corridors and doorways connect the one outdoor and three interior spaces, making it very easy to flirt, cruise, ogle, and otherwise chase after the object(s) of your affection. Of the two lounges, one has fairly quiet music and plenty of seating and is ideal for chatting with friends. Show and movie posters line the walls of the second, smaller lounge, where there's a pool table, constant crowds, and campy retro disco blaring. Extremely popular drag and strip shows pack the disco on certain nights; you can take it all in or just catch your breath at one of the bars or the scattered seating areas. Amnesia is set inside a hard-to-see industrial building behind a shopping center on Poplar Avenue, and parking can be tough on weekend evenings. ✉ 2866 Poplar Ave., ☎ 901/454-1366. *Crowd: 70/30 m/f, mostly under 35, gym bodies, guppies, grungers, stand-and-model guys, lots of tourists and visitors from neighboring towns; a pretty spicy bunch on the whole.*

Backstreet. Second in popularity to Amnesia, Backstreet is less attitudy and intense. The cruise factor is especially high late on Friday and Saturday nights. There are two main sections: The first has a bar, tables, and a dance floor, off which is a fenced-in charmless patio that's nevertheless a nice spot for a breath of fresh air. A second room, which is usually open only on weekends, has a stage for drag shows, another pool table, and more lounge space. ✉ 2018 Court Ave., ☎ 901/276–5522. *Crowd: 65/35 m/f, 20s to 40s; very diverse, from professional to working class; somewhat cruisy; fairly approachable.*

C.O.A.D. WKRB, a once-popular but now-defunct dyke bar, recently reopened as C.O.A.D. and continues to draw many of the same women, as well as an increasing number of guys. With new decorations, lighting, and a better sound system, it's a bit flashier than its predecessor, but it's still a fairly run-of-the-mill disco. Country-western Fridays are especially popular. ✉ 1528 Madison Ave., ☎ 901/278–9321. *Crowd: mixed m/f, mostly 30s to 50s, fairly local but some tourists, very down-to-earth.*

J-Wags. This fiercely popular dive has strip shows and a hustlery ambience. J-Wags has two novel things going for it: It's open 24 hours, and the show bar, which is known for its outgoing strippers, is truly one-of-a-kind, consisting of the *actual* set of the Hustler Club used in the film *The People v. Larry Flynt*, which was filmed in Memphis. The owner purchased this and several other pieces from the film set to decorate the bar. A visit here makes for a highly trashy but memorable experience. ✉ 1268 Madison Ave., ☎ 901/725–1909. *Crowd: male, over 35, rowdy, cruisy, butch.*

Madison Flame. A recent addition to Midtown, this lively tavern draws a predominantly lesbian crowd, although everyone is welcome. Dancing, a pool table, sports or videos on the TV, and lots of seating and mingling room keep the assembled occupied. The country-western music many nights (along with lessons and dancing) goes well with all the western paraphernalia on the walls. ⊠ *1588 Madison Ave.,* ☎ *901/278–9839. Crowd: 80/20 f/m, 30s to 50s, similar to the crowd at Secrets (see below) but with country-western attire more common.*

Pipeline. Even though Pipeline is a crowded semi-leather bar, plenty of the guys wear jeans and T-shirts. It has great drink specials, especially on Sunday, and a lushly landscaped two-level deck behind it. With fountains gurgling, incredibly dim lighting, and dense foliage surrounding the deck, the ambience is highly conducive for romance (or at least some good old-fashioned sleaze). Inside is a narrow, long space with a pool table and a bar up front and a tiny dance floor in back. ⊠ *1382 Poplar Ave.,* ☎ *901/ 726–5263. Crowd: male, mostly 30s to 50s, some leather, lots of denim, flannel, tough guys, butch but friendly.*

Neighborhood Haunts

Autumn Street Pub (⊠ 1349 Autumn St., ☎ 901/274–8010) is fun in a cheap-beer-in-a-can kind of way. As the only full-service liquor bar in Midtown, the pub draws a lot of the same guys who frequent J-Wags. A neighborhood lesbian bar east of most of the Midtown action, and not too far from Amnesia, **Changes** (⊠ 2586 Poplar Ave., ☎ 901/327–3175) is a little more butch than Secrets or Madison Flame. **Crossroads** (⊠ 1278 Jefferson Ave., ☎ 901/725–8156) and the adjacent **Club 501** (⊠ 111 N. Claybrook St., ☎ 901/274–8655) are racially mixed Midtown hangouts drawing a mostly over-35 bunch of men. In case the name didn't clue you in, Crossroads has a big following among cross-dressers.

Another mostly-guys bar, **David's** (⊠ 1474 Madison Ave., ☎ 901/278–4313) is a good spot for conversation. Memphis's African-American gay scene is centered around **N-cognito** (⊠ 338 S. Front St., ☎ 901/523–0599), which is down near the water, has a decent size dance floor, and draws a fairly wild crowd on weekends but a mellow one at other times. A shrine to neon beer signage, **One More** (⊠ 2117 Peabody Ave., ☎ 901/278–8015) draws possibly the most diverse crowd in the city: black and white, male and female, gay and straight.

SLEEPS

Many of the city's best and newer chain hotels are well east of downtown, out near the convergence of I–40 and I–240—a quasi-edge city that's a base for many business travelers. Unfortunately, this area's away from gay nightlife and even more of a haul from downtown.

For price ranges, *see* lodging Chart B at the front of this guide.

$$$$ 🏨 **Peabody Hotel.** This landmark Italianate 12-story hotel has anchored the downtown skyline since 1925. The rooms retain the ambience of years past without looking overwrought or passé. The lobby, in whose travertine marble fountain ducks frolic each day from 11 until 5, has been magnificently restored. A class act from top to bottom. ⊠ *149 Union Ave., 38103,* ☎ *901/529–4000 or 800/732–2639,* FAX *901/529–3600. 468 rooms. 4 restaurants, pool, health club.*

$$$–$$$$ 🏨 **Adam's Mark Hotel.** This 27-story cylindrical tower 20 minutes east of downtown is a slick business-oriented property with panoramic vistas and first-class amenities. Rates drop a bit on weekends. ⊠ *939 Ridge Lake Blvd., 38120,* ☎ *901/684–6664 or 800/444–2326,* FAX *901/762–7411. 389 rooms. Restaurant, pool, health club.*

$$-$$$ ⊡ **French Quarter Suites Hotel.** Guest rooms at this New Orleans–style hotel overlook the fabulous atrium lobby; they're decorated with reproduction antiques, and many have two-person whirlpool tubs. Sunday brunch at the hotel's Bourbon Street Cafe has become a ritual in the gay community. ⊠ *2144 Madison Ave., 38104,* ☎ *901/728–4000 or 800/843–0353,* FAX *901/278–1262. 453 rooms. Pool, exercise room.*

$$–$$ ⊡ **Hampton Inn Midtown.** The best thing about this comfortable mid-priced chain hotel is its Midtown location, close to nightlife and to downtown attractions. ⊠ *1180 Union Ave., 38104,* ☎ *901/276–1175 or 800/426–7866,* FAX *901/276–4261. 126 rooms. Pool.*

$$–$$ ⊡ **Wilson World Graceland.** Although it's far from the gay scene, Wilson World does have the advantage of being across the street from Graceland. You can take free popcorn back to your room and munch away to free movies on the Elvis channel. Rooms are equipped with microwaves and refrigerators. ⊠ *3677 Elvis Presley Blvd., 38116,* ☎ *901/332–2107 or 800/945–7667,* FAX *901/366–6361. 134 rooms.*

THE LITTLE BLACK BOOK

At Your Fingertips

Friends for Life AIDS Resource Center (☎ 901/272–0855 or, for 24-hr hot line, ☎ 901/278–AIDS). **Memphis Area Transit Authority** (☎ 901/274–6282). **Memphis Gay & Lesbian Community Center** (different locations depending on the event; switchboard, ☎ 901/728–4297). **Memphis Convention & Visitors Bureau** (47 Union Ave., 38103, ☎ 901/543–5300 or 800/873–6282). *Memphis Flyer* (alternative weekly, ☎ 901/521–9000, Web site www.memphisflyer.com). **Memphis Visitors Information Center** (⊠ 340 Beale St., ☎ 901/543–5333). **Yellow Cab** (☎ 901/577–7700).

Gay Media

The *Triangle Journal News* (☎ 901/454–1411, e-mail tjnmemphis@aol.com), a queer monthly, carries news and entertainment coverage. The statewide gay paper, *Query* (☎ 615/259–4135, e-mail querynews@aol.com), is based in Nashville but has Memphis coverage.

BOOKSTORES

Although Memphis has no queer bookstore, it has a terrific women's store, **Meristem** (⊠ 930 S. Cooper St., ☎ 901/276–0282), which has many gay and general-interest titles; its an excellent community resource. Of general-interest stores, **Davis-Kidd** (⊠ 397 Perkins Rd. Ext., ☎ 901/683–9801) has one of the best selections of queer books.

Working Out

French Riviera Spa (⊠ 1330 Monroe St., ☎ 901/385–1096) is a gay-friendly facility.

20 Out in Miami Beach

MIAMI BEACHERS ARE OBSESSED with preservation. Over the past decade, the median age has dropped from 69 to 44. But more significant than the *actual* difference in age, though, is the *apparent* one: 10 years ago, most of the destitute 69-year-olds in South Beach looked about 89; today, most of the buffed and bronzed 44-year-olds look about 24. In 1513, Spanish explorer Juan Ponce de León poked around South Florida in search of the "Fountain of Youth." It's taken nearly 500 years, but a posse of savvy, queer escapees from New York City seems finally to have found it.

Indeed, the beauty factor is outrageously high. In South Beach, the restored and buzzing southern tip of Miami Beach, people feel a need to look and be hot. The importance of personal preservation notwithstanding, *architectural* preservation has been the backbone of South Beach's transformation from urban blight into beachfront splendor. In 1912, millionaire Carl Graham Fisher and the island's owner, a determined farmer named John Collins, developed what was an anemic spit of sand into America's greatest winter destination. Miami Beach boomed through the early 1920s, was leveled by a 1926 hurricane, and was reinvented in the 1930s by an innovative band of architects, led by Henry Hohauser; their collective aesthetic was defined by sleek, low-slung structures with rounded edges and ornate Egyptian and Aztec influences.

By the mid-'50s, music and film stars mingled and the wealthy lodged and sometimes lived at the magnificent Fontainebleau Hotel. Even in the heavy, humid heat of summer, denizens wore a shirt and tie or a light dress, shopped along swank Lincoln Road—the Rodeo Drive of its time—and entertained often and vigorously. It's difficult to pinpoint when and why the area's popularity flagged, but wealthy snowbirds began to migrate elsewhere, and South Beach's glamorous hotels became apartment houses for retirees. If desertion and neglect weren't harsh enough, the city was besieged by boat lifts; waves of Castro-persecuted Cubans, brought here from that country's prisons, were settled into South Beach's prisonlike apartment buildings and hotels.

At about this time, disenchanted Northeasterners, many of them gay, began to discover the region. Preservationists rallied to have South Beach designated the historic "Deco District." Hard work and a little luck turned South Beach into a glitzy playground—just as it was in the '50s, but without the formality. Film and fashion folk first fell in love with the renovated art deco beauties along Ocean Drive. Several gay discos opened. Enterprising hoteliers refurbished old properties, while young chefs transformed empty storefronts into first-rate eateries.

As both a destination and a place to live, South Beach is now at a crossroads. For much of the past decade all types have lived, worked, and played together in harmony. In 1992 the city passed a human rights ordinance. Throughout the '90s Miami Beach has had a gay-friendly mayor, and gays have been visible on political and social fronts. But as the end of the decade approaches, questions have arisen about the community's place in South Beach's future.

One result of South Beach's renaissance has been its astonishing rise in popularity among those with money to burn. Rents and hotel rates have risen dramatically, and once predominantly gay clubs, restaurants, and hotels have become increasingly straight. Many business owners in the city would love to see a healthy mix of genders, races, and sexual orientations in their establishments, but the mood around town has grown tense, especially between queers and the younger straight teens and twentysomethings who hit South Beach in full force on weekends.

South Beach will no doubt remain hugely gay-popular for years to come. But the bloom is off the rose, and local businesses with long-term hopes of attracting the queer dollar have their work cut out. Once upon a time nobody but gays and lesbians would have anything to do with South Beach. These hard-working visionaries turned a dreary, dilapidated neighborhood into a destination more desirable than they could ever have imagined. As they say, "Be careful what you wish for . . ."

THE LAY OF THE LAND

South Beach is the small, triangular tip of the larger island of Miami Beach (an incorporated city distinct from Miami proper, with a population of 92,000). Only about a mile across at its widest point, South Beach extends about 2 miles from Dade Boulevard (which feeds into the Venetian Causeway and crosses Biscayne Bay to Miami) at its northern end down to South Pointe Park. From South Beach it's about another 7 miles to Bal Harbour at the northern tip of Miami Beach.

Ocean Drive

Ocean Drive once resisted labels of sexual orientation, but it has become increasingly touristy and straight. The most dramatic instances of Deco District revitalization occurred along here—in 1997 a stretch was honorarily renamed Deco Drive. The **Miami Design Preservation League** (☎ 305/672–2014) gives walking tours of Ocean Drive and Collins Avenue on Saturdays at 10:30 AM. Tours depart from the **Art Deco District Welcome Center** (✉ 1001 Ocean Dr., ☎ 305/531–3484). Recent overdevelopment of Ocean Drive hasn't discouraged celebrities, fashion designers, models, and plenty of gays and lesbians from roaming among the stately hotels and landmarks, including the Mediterranean villa at 1114 Ocean Drive, formerly known as **Amsterdam Palace.** The Palace was the home of the late Italian fashion god Gianni Versace, who was gunned down outside its gate on July 15, 1997.

The **gay beach** is at 12th Street and Ocean, but the whole span from 5th to 15th street is clean and inviting and popular with everyone. The Palace Bar and Grill at 1200 Ocean Drive marks the beginning of buff-boy territory. Although boyish poseurs make up the majority along this stretch of the beach, lesbians camp out here, too.

Washington Avenue

Once an ordinary commercial strip where Cuban refugees and financially strapped retirees shopped for groceries, discount clothing, and cheap dry goods, **Washington Avenue** has become increasingly trendy, with fashion boutiques and home-furnishings stores. It's not as pricey as Ocean

Drive or Lincoln Road, though. The pedestrian traffic, made up of poor and rich, gay and straight, young and old, white, black, Latino, and Orthodox Jew, is never dull.

To see the world's most impressive art deco and Art Nouveau artifacts, drop by the **Wolfsonian Foundation Gallery** (✉ 1001 Washington Ave., ☎ 305/531–1001), a research center and museum, with a 60,000-piece collection of decorative and fine arts, designs, and books. Nearby is the recently expanded **Bass Museum of Art** (✉ 2121 Park Ave., ☎ 305/673–7530), a 40,000-square-foot space known for its 16th-century Flemish tapestries and works by Rubens, Dürer, and Toulouse-Lautrec.

Lincoln Road Mall

In the '50s, **Lincoln Road** was a swank avenue dotted with America's top department stores. It died a decade later with the rest of South Beach, despite efforts to turn it into a pedestrian mall. It came roaring back, however, and Lincoln Road is now the city's hottest place to shop. As other parts of South Beach have lost their charm in the wake of rampant development and unfriendly crowds, Lincoln Road remains an attractive, comfortable space where gays and straights mingle easily.

Notable sights along here include the four-story, deco **Old Lincoln Theater** (✉ 541 Lincoln Rd., ☎ 305/673–3331), now home of Michael Tilson Thomas's New World Symphony; the storefront practice space of the **Miami City Ballet** (✉ 905 Lincoln Rd., ☎ 305/532–7713 or 305/532–4880), where on many afternoons, you can watch through big windows as the dancers rehearse; and the **Colony Theater** (✉ 1040 Lincoln Rd., ☎ 305/674–1026), another of the country's great deco theaters, which hosts a variety of performing arts companies. A dozen art galleries line the mall, including the nonprofit **South Florida Arts Center** (✉ 924 Lincoln Rd., ☎ 305/674–8278), which houses 90 artists and is open to the public.

Miami

Miami proper sprawls north, south, and west, with its downtown due west of South Beach across Biscayne Bay. The most visited neighborhoods—Coral Gables, Coconut Grove, and Key Biscayne—follow the coastline for several miles southwest of downtown.

Miami's **downtown** is a busy, commercial, South Florida hub by day and eerily quiet at night. Unless you're here on business, skip it. South of downtown, follow U.S. 1 into **Coconut Grove** and **Coral Gables,** both worth exploring for their beautiful homes and for high-end shopping districts such as **CocoWalk** (✉ 3015 Grand Ave., Coconut Grove, ☎ 305/631–8888) and **The Shops at 550** (✉ 550 Biltmore Way, Coral Gables).

Miami's oldest settlement, Coconut Grove has long had an artsy cachet and a substantial gay following, but as its desirability has increased in recent years, rents have risen and upscale chains and well-heeled yuppies have largely replaced the once-bohemian ambience. Inland several miles from Coconut Grove, Coral Gables was laid out in the early '20s as a lavish community rich in Spanish and Mediterranean architecture. It remains abundant with courtly mansions, many notable buildings, high-end shopping, and dozens of corporate headquarters of important multinational companies.

GETTING AROUND

The lower half of Miami Beach is connected to the city of Miami by three causeways. The Venetian Causeway, the middle one, connects local streets. To and from mainland highways take the Julia Tuttle Causeway (I–195) from points north or the MacArthur Causeway (U.S. 41/Route A1A) from points south; either route is good from the airport. Because

Miami Beach has grown at a pace that has strained its infrastructure, and the island isn't really built for cars, traffic along Ocean Drive comes to a standstill on weekend evenings. Plans are underway to add more parking by the end of the decade, but the city will never be able to handle cars in great numbers.

EATS

Fashion and food have never been strangers, so it's not surprising that South Beach's culinary scene is thriving. Restaurants continue to get better and better, and many have cutting-edge chefs from big North American and European cities. As Ocean Drive's restaurants have increasingly become the domain of straight tourists, gays have flocked to the cafés along Lincoln Road, which have better food and ambience. Washington Avenue's restaurants offer the most culinary bang for your buck (but no sidewalk seating) and are also gay-friendly.

For price ranges, *see* dining Chart A at the front of this guide.

South Beach

$$$$ ✕ **Blue Door.** In the fanatically trendy Delano Hotel (and formerly owned by Madonna), the Blue Door draws very, very important people with fancy credentials who eat here *conspicuously.* George Morrone, the man in the kitchen, produces heavenly New American dishes such as salmon with oysters, leeks, and red wine sauce, or seared duck foie gras over braised chickpeas. ✉ *1685 Collins Ave.,* ☎ *305/674–6400.*

$$$–$$$$ ✕ **Astor Place Bar and Grill.** This exceptional hotel restaurant uses sculpted woods, elaborate chandeliers, and rich colors to capture a pure deco aesthetic. Standouts from the southwest-, Caribbean-, and Asian-influenced menu include curry smoked-chicken wontons and the wild mushroom short stack (grilled Portobellos drizzled with balsamic syrup and sun-dried tomato butter). ✉ *956 Washington Ave.,* ☎ *305/672–7217.*

$$$–$$$$ ✕ **Osteria Del Teatro.** Osteria heralded the new wave of stellar restaurants vital to South Beach's early '90s renaissance. It's watched a lot of neighbors come and go, yet its intimate dining room is still always packed. Salmon with fennel and orange sauce, and chicken sautéed with shallots and sun-dried tomatoes in champagne cream sauce are among the stars. ✉ *1443 Washington Ave.,* ☎ *305/538–7850.*

$$$–$$$$ ✕ **Pacific Time.** Offering a pan-Pacific sampling of succulent and innovative dishes like whole ginger-stuffed yellowtail tempura with steamed ribbon vegetables, this is one of the region's culinary treasures. Enjoy the nonchalant West Coast atmosphere, and dine late for optimal people-watching. ✉ *915 Lincoln Rd.,* ☎ *305/534–5979.*

$$–$$$ ✕ **Chrysanthemum.** A standout among many strong Asian contenders, Chrysanthemum is a classy spot that will tantalize your taste buds with sizzling Szechuan and Peking cooking. Chicken ravioli with a spicy sesame-and-peanut sauce is a signature appetizer. ✉ *1248 Washington Ave.,* ☎ *305/531–5656.*

$$–$$$ ✕ **Jeffrey's.** This gay-operated restaurant just off Lincoln Road keeps a low profile by South Beach standards, but it's always good, and its slightly formal dining room with tall columns is a perfect venue for romantic dining. The bistro menu features pistachio-crusted chicken and plantain-crusted dolphin with roasted red-pepper tartar sauce. ✉ *1629 Michigan Ave.,* ☎ *305/673–0690.*

$$ ✕ **Larios.** Pop diva Gloria Estefan is part-owner of this chic, moderately priced, and consistently good (if middle-of-the-road) Cuban restaurant. Try the tamale platter, chicken with yellow rice, and sweet plantains, and finish it all off with the fresh guava-and-cheese flan. The cutest Cuban-American waiters alive. ✉ *820 Ocean Dr.,* ☎ *305/532–9577.*

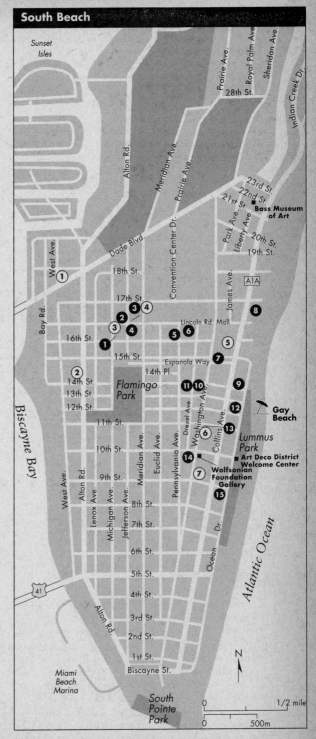

South Beach

$$ ✕ **Van Dyke.** This smart Lincoln Road restaurant, fashioned out of the old Van Dyke Hotel, has plenty of outdoor seating, but the best tables are in the elegant inner dining room. The traditional American food and service are uneven (15% gratuity is included). The salads generally rise above the sandwiches. ✉ *846 Lincoln Rd.,* ☎ *305/534–3600.*

$–$$ ✕ **da Leo Trattoria Toscano** and **Pizza e via da leo.** Across Lincoln Road Mall from each other, these two eateries offer terrific value and dependable northern Italian fare, though the trattoria's menu is somewhat more substantial. The pizza place has great pies and a wildly popular $8.95 lunch buffet. ✉ *819 Lincoln Rd.,* ☎ *305/674–0350.*

$–$$ ✕ **El Rancho Grande.** The food at this Mexican eatery just off Lincoln Road Mall ranges from standard burritos and fajitas to *pescado relleno* (fish fillet marinated and stuffed with shrimp, crab, onions, tomatoes, almonds, green peppers, and raisins, cooked and topped with melted cheese). ✉ *1626 Pennsylvania Ave.,* ☎ *305/673–0480.*

$–$$ ✕ **Toni's.** Most locals agree that Toni's has the area's best sushi. Rolls are fresh and beautifully prepared, and the sushi, sashimi, and shrimp tempura are ideal if you're starving. Be prepared to wait on weekends—but there's enough Buddha statuary around to inspire calm and patience. ✉ *1208 Washington Ave.,* ☎ *305/673–9368.*

$ ✕ **11th Street Diner.** This stainless-steel deco diner serves standard fare, including a great Philly cheese steak and the most voluptuous vanilla malts in South Beach. In the spirit of traditional greasy spoons, service is lousy: pissy to the point that waitpersons actually yell at their patrons. ✉ *11th St. and Washington Ave.,* ☎ *305/534–6373.*

$ ✕ **Front Porch Café.** On the upper stretch of Ocean Drive, the Front Porch fosters a lazy, devil-may-care atmosphere—a far cry from the stand-and-model showdowns a few blocks away. The food is eclectic: Thai noodles, pizzas, overstuffed sandwiches, muffins, breads, and hearty breakfasts. ✉ *1418 Ocean Dr.,* ☎ *305/531–8300.*

$ ✕ **Palace Bar and Grill.** Girls and boys take time out between sun sessions at the gay beach across the street at this open-air hangout. It's a wonderful place for drinks, light food, and breakfast. Better meals of substance—and much better service—can be had elsewhere. Great music. ✉ *1200 Ocean Dr.,* ☎ *305/531–9077.*

Coffeehouse Culture

Papillon. This pretty-peopled café on Lincoln Road has substantial enough fare to qualify as a legitimate restaurant, but it retains a sufficiently loungy ambience to work as a coffeehouse. ✉ *530 Lincoln Rd.,* ☎ *305/ 673–1139.*

SCENES

South Beach's high-profile discos, which resemble New York's and L.A.'s massive warehouse clubs, are the city's main draw. Similar crowds hit the major discos on their "designated" nights—Salvation on Saturdays, Warsaw 2000 on Sundays. The handful of smaller bars vary only in the degree to which they attract the stand-and-model set—Twist leads the pack, though it's still far mellower than the discos. Major circuit-party events are scheduled year-round. Glamorous, mostly straight clubs (most of them along Washington Avenue), as well as terrace bars along Ocean Drive, advertise in gay papers to encourage a mixed hetero/homo crowd. Unfortunately, at most of these places the crowds are young, straight, rowdy, and sometimes hostile (or at least snide) toward gays and lesbians. Even gay clubs are not free from these tensions; on some nights (notably Saturdays) Warsaw 2000 becomes overwhelmingly straight.

South Beach

PRIME SUSPECTS

Equus. South Beach's latest hip supper club opened in fall '97 with a clever lineup of theme nights. Dinner at the adjacent restaurant, which serves Asian-Caribbean fare, is often central to the entertainment. At Thursdays' Café Senju a $10 cover entitles you to an elaborate Japanese buffet, along with Asian beers and drinks. Tuesdays there's a Latin dinner show, Mondays is drag, and other nights feature dancing to house and hip hop. Definitely a club to watch. ⊠ *929 Washington Ave.,* ☎ *305/673–8610. Crowd: mixed gay/straight (depends on night), all ages, stylish, swank.*

Loading Zone. It's several blocks west of the action, but this dark cruise bar with an industrial decorating scheme and a small accessories shop is South Beach's top leather-and-Levi's club. A seat atop a metal oil vat affords a good view of the high testosterone levels. (There's hard-core porn on the TV monitors to help get you in the mood.) For best results, arrive after midnight. ⊠ *1426A Alton Rd.,* ☎ *305/531–5623. Crowd: male, mostly 30s and 40s, leather boys, sleaze hounds, and other raunchy characters.*

Twist. This great little bar has a tiny dance floor upstairs and a pool table; downstairs is a long, traditional bar that's only open when it's crowded. Because it's so dark inside, making eye contact is a challenge—although the open-air porch off the second floor has better lighting. Open until five every night and never a cover charge. ⊠ *1057 Washington Ave.,* ☎ *305/538–9478. Crowd: mostly male and under 35, mixed locals and tourists, cruisy, attractive, more whitebread than the others.*

Warsaw 2000. Though it's popular on Sundays and Fridays, Warsaw has become mostly straight on Saturdays, when the queer masses head to Salvation. Once totally devoid of character—just a big, dark room with a midsize dance floor and a smaller second tier overlooking it—today's Warsaw has classical Italian decorative touches that liven it up. The sound system is still too loud and bassy. ⊠ *1450 Collins Ave.,* ☎ *305/531–4555. Crowd: 80/20 m/f, young, attitudy, hot, strong racial mix.*

ONE-NIGHTERS

Salvation. This Saturday night blowout is a must-attend for the shirtless, tanned, and toned. The lines are long and the cover exorbitant, but for die-hard partyers, there's no substitute. Inside this immense warehouse space is a dark lounge and a small bar off of the enormous dance floor; upstairs a balcony encircles the festivities below and leads to a comfy lounge with sofas and art (for sale) on the walls. ⊠ *1771 West Ave.,* ☎ *305/ 673–6508. Crowd: 85/15 m/f, every brand of club-goer known to the region, dressed to kill.*

NEIGHBORHOOD HAUNTS

There's no sign over the door at **821** (⊠ 821 Lincoln Rd., ☎ 305/531–1188), but this bright storefront space has a long copper bar beside a sitting area with upholstered chairs and swank cocktail tables. Guppies, lipstick lesbians, and pre-Warsaw boys unwind here after a long day working or shopping. **West End** (⊠ 942 Lincoln Rd., ☎ 305/538–9378), a pleasant corner bar and pool hall on Lincoln Road Mall chugs along with a loyal following of older guys with tattoos and muscle shirts, lipstick lesbos, butch pool sharks, and preppy college kids.

Miami

PRIME SUSPECTS

Cactus. The latest queer nightspot to open in Miami is such a hit that even South Beach boys drive over for the crowded but easy-going happy hours and the tasty food served in the adjacent restaurant. Whimsical southwestern furnishings, including strings of cactus and cowboy-boot lights decorate the two video bars and game room. Cactus is just north of the MacArthur Causeway. ✉ *2041 Biscayne Blvd.,* ☎ *305/438–0662. Crowd: 80/20 m/f, 20s to 50s, fairly professional, a few suits at happy hour.*

O'Zone. For meeting cute Latino guys, the O'Zone is far better than any club in South Beach. This large, warehouse-style disco has a video bar, a cruisy industrial bar, an immense dance floor, and a lounge with cushy sofas. It helps to be bilingual, but a number of international gestures and expressions are understood. Sunday salsa nights give South Beach clubs a definite run for their money, and anytime there's a drag show, expect big crowds. ✉ *6620 S. W. 57th Ave. (Red Rd.),* ☎ *305/667–2888. Crowd: male, young, good racial mix, club kids.*

Splash. Near Coconut Grove and Coral Gables, this spacious club has a couple of cocktail bars, a billiards lounge, an outdoor patio, and a disco. You get the feeling that local guys who might regularly venture to South Beach for clubbing come here when they don't feel like making the long drive and want to hang out among friends. The interior is nicely done, the music less intense than at the South Beach clubs. ✉ *5922 S. Dixie Hwy., U.S. 1,* ☎ *305/662–8779. Crowd: mostly male, all ages, not as racially diverse as other Miami clubs, low-attitude; mix of guppies, blue-collar locals, and muscle heads.*

Action

The hot **Beach Head** (✉ 1510 Alton Rd., ☎ 305/534–3788) bathhouse draws guys from all over the region. **The Club Body Center** (✉ 2991 Coral Way, ☎ 305/448–2214) is Miami's popular bathhouse. Fairly clean and well laid out, it has a full gym and sundecks.

SLEEPS

South Florida's top-notch gay reservation service, **Florida Hotel Network** (✉ 521 Lincoln Rd., 2nd floor, 33139, ☎ 305/538–3616 or 800/538–3616, e-mail floridahotels@usa.pipeline.com), lists hotel and guest house accommodations from the Panhandle to Key West, plus many short-term rentals throughout the area.

For price ranges, *see* lodging Chart A at the front of this guide.

South Beach

Hotels and Resorts

$$$$ ⊞ **Delano.** No mere hotel—the Delano is a shrine to pop culture. The restored deco giant is bathed in milky whites: The surprisingly small rooms are white, from the slipcovers to the TV sets. Billowing white draperies hang in the soaring white-columned lobby. The staff of would-be models are clad head to toe in—you guessed it—white. Some call this monochromatic obsession chic and mesmerizing; others observe that the Delano feels a bit like a fancy psychiatric hospital. ✉ *1685 Collins Ave., 33139,* ☎ *305/672-2000 or 800/555–5001,* FAX *305/532–0099. 208 rooms. Restaurant, pool, health club.*

$$$$ ⊞ **Impala.** The finest small hotel in South Florida, bar none. The Impala's greatest strength is its relatively understated elegance—a welcome relief from the over-the-top, harem-inspired decor of certain competitors. Imported cotton linens, Eastlake sleigh beds, and spacious bathrooms with large tubs are ideal for a romantic getaway. State-of-the-art communication and entertainment centers keep business or pleasure close at hand. ✉ *1228 Collins Ave., 33139,* ☎ *305/673–2021 or 800/646–7252,* FAX *305/673–5984. 20 rooms. Restaurant.*

$$$$ 🏨 **Marlin Hotel.** Music industry executives and recording artists favor this small deco gem owned, appropriately, by Island Records mogul Chris Blackwell. A riotously colorful and vibrant Caribbean scheme dominates public spaces and guest rooms. All accommodations have Jamaican bath amenities, batik robes, West Indian art and furnishings, and deluxe entertainment centers. ⊠ *1200 Collins Ave., 33139,* ☎ *305/673–8770 or 800/688–7678,* 𝖥𝖠𝖷 *305/673–9609. 12 rooms. Restaurant.*

$$$–$$$$ 🏨 **Century Hotel.** This ultra–high profile '30s landmark, one of locally renowned architect Henry Hohauser's most acclaimed masterpieces, is a favorite of models—celeb photographers have been known to tap the shoulders of wistful poseurs loitering around the grounds, plucking them from relative obscurity and pasting them across the pages of *GQ* and *Provocateur.* ⊠ *140 Ocean Dr., 33139,* ☎ *305/674–8855,* 𝖥𝖠𝖷 *305/538–5733. 32 rooms. Restaurant, pool.*

$$$–$$$$ 🏨 **Tides.** Cosmetic surgery transformed this derelict 150-room beach property into a 45-room luxury hotel that opened in 1997. The scheme of light woods, beiges, and whites in the lobby and oversize guest rooms has a clean, beachy feel. In-room facilities provide every comfort: down pillows and comforters, safes, minibars, entertainment systems, and telescopes directed seaward. ⊠ *1220 Ocean Dr., 33139,* ☎ *305/604–5000 or 800/ 688–7678,* 𝖥𝖠𝖷 *305/604–5180. 45 rooms. Restaurants, bar, pool, fitness center.*

$$–$$$$ 🏨 **Hotel Astor.** The low-key but luxurious Astor offers the elegance and comfort you'd expect of a high-end property, with neither gimmickry nor attitude. The sedate, classy rooms are done in off-white and beige tones, with muted lighting and marble baths. Three blocks from the ocean and steps from the many bars and clubs along Washington Avenue. ⊠ *956 Washington Ave., 33139,* ☎ *305/531–8081,* 𝖥𝖠𝖷 *305/531–3193. 42 rooms. Restaurant, pool.*

$$–$$$ 🏨 **Kent.** The rates at the historic Kent, once the trendy Island Outpost chain's South Beach bargain option, have crept up since the refurbishment of its rooms, known for their sleek art deco furnishings and hardwood floors. A warm and attractive property with a mellow pace and a fairly gay (heavily European) clientele. ⊠ *1131 Collins Ave., 33139,* ☎ *305/531–6771 or 800/688–7678,* 𝖥𝖠𝖷 *305/531–0720. 54 rooms.*

$$ 🏨 **Beachcomber and Nassau Suite Hotel.** Paul Crowley completely renovated a formerly frumpy hotel and decaying nearby apartment building. The spacious and comfortable hotel rooms have beautiful old hardwood floors and small bathrooms with stylish fixtures. A block away, 22 clean and bright one-bedroom and studio units have fully modernized kitchens, simple but elegant deco furnishings, and plenty of elbow room. ⊠ *1340 Collins Ave., 33139,* ☎ *305/531–3755,* 𝖥𝖠𝖷 *305/673–8609. 32 rooms, 8 apartments. Restaurant.*

$$ 🏨 **Penguin.** This peach-and-red hostelry strikes one of the more inspired poses on Ocean Drive. It has a major gay following, and though fairly basic, rooms are clean, brightly decorated, and outfitted with cable TV and decent-size closets—all the essentials. In the afternoon a local drag queen serves cocktails in the lobby bar. A real bargain on the beach. ⊠ *1418 Ocean Dr., 33139,* ☎ *305/534–9334 or 800/235–3296,* 𝖥𝖠𝖷 *305/ 672–6240. 44 rooms. Restaurant.*

$–$$ 🏨 **Bayliss.** This small 1939 hotel has long been a modest but gay-friendly option a couple of blocks off Washington Avenue. One drawback is the location—this neighborhood is much safer than it looks, but it's still too quiet late at night for total comfort. On the other hand, rooms are surprisingly spacious and attractive given their price; many are efficiencies with kitchens, and some have two bedrooms. ⊠ *504 14th St., 33139,* ☎ *305/531–3755 or 888/305–4683,* 𝖥𝖠𝖷 *305/673–8609. 19 rooms.*

$–$$ ⊡ **Kenmore and Park Washington.** These predominantly gay, jointly owned budget properties take up a prime block of Washington Avenue. Accommodations are clean but plain, with modern baths and minire-frigerators. A major plus are the grounds, which consist of a foliage-enclosed lanai and pool—both of which are clothing optional. ⊠ *Kenmore: 1050 Washington Ave., 33139,* ☎ *305/674–1930,* FAX *305/534–6591. 60 rooms.* ⊠ *Park Washington: 1020 Washington Ave., 33139,* ☎ *305/ 532–1930,* FAX *305/672–6706. 35 rooms. Pool.*

Guest Houses

$$$–$$$$ ⊡ **Lily Guesthouse.** This top-notch women-owned guest house, built in 1936 and stunningly restored, is one of South Beach's best-kept secrets. Rooms have lustrous hardwood floors, fine cabinets and fixtures, and rich marble baths. Other assets: a central location and a spacious sundeck. ⊠ *835 Collins Ave., 33139,* ☎ *305/535–9900,* FAX *305/535–0077. 18 rooms with phone, TV, and private bath. Mixed gay/straight.*

$$ ⊡ **Jefferson House.** Though several blocks from the beach, the Jefferson is the best of South Beach's gay guest houses. All guest rooms are in the two-story building behind a historic 1929 home near Flamingo Park and are furnished with a mix of tropical resort furniture and art deco antiques (they all also have CD players). If you don't feel like beach-going, you can lounge by the pool and patio all day long. ⊠ *1018 Jefferson Ave., 33139,* ☎ *305/534–5247,* FAX *305/534–5953. 7 rooms with phone, TV, and private bath. Continental breakfast. Mostly gay/lesbian.*

THE LITTLE BLACK BOOK

At Your Fingertips

AIDS Hotline (☎ 800/352–2437). **Body Positive Resource Center** (⊠ 175 N.E. 36th St., Miami, ☎ 305/576–1111). **Gay, Lesbian, and Bisexual Hotline** (Miami and Miami Beach) (☎ 305/759–3661.) **Greater Miami Convention and Visitors Bureau** (⊠ 701 Brickell Ave., Suite 2700, Miami, 33131, ☎ 305/539–3063 or 800/283–2707). **Metro-Dade Transit Agency** (☎ 305/638–6700). **Miami Beach Chamber of Commerce** (⊠ 1920 Meridian Ave., Miami Beach, 33139, ☎ 305/672–1270). **Cab Consortium Dispatch Service** (☎ 305/888–4444). *New Times* (alternative weekly, ☎ 305/ 576–8000, e-mail editorial@miami–newtimes.com). **South Beach AIDS Project** (☎ 305/532–1033). **South Beach Business Guild** (gay and lesbian) (☎ 305/534–3336). **Switchboard of Miami** (gay/lesbian referrals) (☎ 305/ 358–4357). **Teen Hotline** (☎ 305/377–8255).

Gay Media

Most of South Florida's gay papers are male- and nightlife-oriented. South Beach's weekly *Wire* (☎ 305/538–3111, e-mail sobewire@aol.com) captures the area's spirit and personality; it's very gay but serves the whole community. *TWN (The Weekly News)* (☎ 305/757–6333, e-mail info@twn-mag.com) has good coverage of local news. *Hot Spots* (☎ 954/928–1862, e-mail info@hotspotsmagazine.com) is a mindless, flashy bar rag packed with provocative bar ads and personals. It's a useful nightlife resource and has fun and bitchy gossip columns. The monthly *Fountain, An Alternative Source for Women* (☎ 954/565–7479) is a cut above any of the male or mostly male South Florida periodicals in terms of both quality and depth.

BOOKSTORES

Books & Books Inc. (⊠ 933 Lincoln Rd., ☎ 305/532–3222), a mainstream general bookstore and café, carries lesbian and gay titles. In Miami, **Lambda Book and Video** (⊠ 7545 Biscayne Blvd., ☎ 305/754–6900) is well-stocked in gay-themed and adult movies and has a small selection of books.

Working Out

The **David Barton Gym** (✉ 1683 Collins Ave., ☎ 305/674–5757), in the Delano Hotel, draws all of the city's glamour boys, who excel not only at working out but at *working* it. Visiting celebs prefer to sweat away their pounds alongside local buff boys at **Club Body Tech** (✉ 1253 Washington Ave., ☎ 305/674–8222), which draws a mixed gay and straight crowd. Serious muscle queens, however, prefer **Idol's Gym** (✉ 1000 Lincoln Rd., ☎ 305/532–0089), which has all the attitude and toned bodies of the city's best gay discos.

21 *Out in Milwaukee*

With Madison

OUTSIDERS ARE QUICK TO ASSOCIATE MILWAUKEE with cheap beer, bowling, motorcycles, *Laverne & Shirley,* socialist labor unions, and kitschy German restaurants with dirndl-clad waitresses and bucket-size beer steins—not that there's necessarily anything wrong with any of that. But the urbanity Milwaukee lacked has begun to develop in recent years. Streets once lined with hardware stores and small groceries are sprouting sidewalk cafés, coffeehouses, the occasional trendy restaurant, and, for better or worse, chain superstores. Young professionals are fixing up houses in once-abandoned neighborhoods, and devotees of queer bar culture have found enough of a cruisy critical mass to keep them happy.

If you're queer and live in this industrious city of 600,000, chances are you came either by way of birth or job opportunity and remain out of an allegiance to something other than the gay scene, which is close-knit and friendly, but quiet. Yet also effective: Queer political, social, and fundraising organizations here are highly successful, and the annual pride celebration is one of only a few in America staged on a city's official festival grounds. A new gay community center is slated to open in 1998.

Milwaukee's demeanor warms even the iciest visitors. Call it a cliché, but this town's greatest commodity is its people. It's no coincidence that the cover of a recent tourist-board guide showed six photographs, not of tall buildings, lakeshore beaches, or sports arenas, but of average citizens.

THE LAY OF THE LAND

Milwaukee is at the confluence of the Milwaukee, Kinnickinnic, and Menomonee rivers, the latter emptying into Lake Michigan's Milwaukee Bay. One strange characteristic of Milwaukee's layout is the way bridges across the aforementioned rivers fail to conform logically with the streets on either side. The city began in the 1840s as three competing settlements: Kilbourntown, now western downtown; Juneautown, now eastern downtown; and Walker's Point, the area south of downtown. The leaders of these three towns refused to cooperate during the early planning stages, and each had bridges constructed to independent specifications. The conflicting system that resulted has never been corrected.

Downtown

A good way to stroll through **downtown** is along colorful **Old World 3rd Street,** near the intersection of State Street, which is lined with many 19th-century cast-iron buildings. You can familiarize yourself with the city's past at the **Milwaukee County Historical Society** (⌧ 910 N. Old World 3rd St., ☎ 414/273–8288). **Usinger's Famous Sausage** (⌧ 1030 N. Old

World 3rd St., ☎ 414/276–9100), a nearly century-old business, makes 75 kinds of links.

Head west a few blocks on State Street and down 7th to reach the **Museum Center** (✉ 7th and W. Wells Sts.), which comprises the interactive **Discovery World Museum** (☎ 414/765–0777), the **Humphrey Imax Dome Theater** (☎ 414/319–4625), and the **Milwaukee Public Museum** (☎ 414/278–2700), which surveys natural history.

State Street leads east from the river to the **Theater District,** whose two anchors are the **Marcus Center for the Performing Arts** (✉ 929 N. Water St., ☎ 414/273–7206) and, just south, the **Milwaukee Repertory Theater** (✉ 108 E. Wells St., ☎ 414/224–1761). Promenades that are part of the new **Riverwalk** pass along the waterfront terraces of trendy restaurants and bars. River tour boats depart regularly from **Pere Marquette Park** (✉ Old World 3rd St. and W. Kilbourn Ave.), where concerts and events are staged.

The **Grand Avenue Retail Center** (✉ 275 W. Wisconsin Ave., ☎ 414/224–0384) is a highlight of downtown shopping. A bonus: You'll have the chance to visit the **International Clown Hall of Fame** (✉ Plankinton Arcade, ☎ 414/319–0848). East of here, new bistros and swank lounges continue to open, especially around grassy **Cathedral Square** (✉ E. Kilbourn Ave. and Jefferson St.).

West of Downtown

Follow Wisconsin Avenue west of downtown and you'll pass through the heart of Jesuit-run **Marquette University** (✉ W. Wisconsin Ave. at 16th St.), whose **Haggerty Museum of Art** (✉ 601 N. 14th St., ☎ 414/288–7039) exhibits old-master and contemporary works. West of campus is the ornate Flemish Renaissance home built in 1893 by local brewing magnate Frederick Pabst, the **Pabst Mansion** (✉ 2000 W. Wisconsin Ave., ☎ 414/931–0808), many of whose intricate interior elements—marble, stained glass, carved woodwork, and panels—were shipped from a 17th-century Bavarian castle.

South across the Menomonee River is the **Mitchell Park Horticultural Conservatory** (✉ 524 S. Layton Blvd., ☎ 414/649–9800), a.k.a. "the Domes," under whose 85-foot glass domes thrive tropical, desert, and other flora.

Miller Brewing Co. is a major contributor to gay causes in Milwaukee and around the nation. Entertaining tours are given daily of the **Miller Brewery** (✉ 4251 W. State St., ☎ 414/931–2467). Adjacent to the brewery is the Bavarian-style Miller Inn, where guests can enjoy free tastings of beer or sodas.

The Lakeshore

Follow State Street east of downtown to **Juneau Park,** a great place to lie around and take in the lake views. From here, Lincoln Memorial Drive leads south by the **Milwaukee Art Museum** (✉ 750 Lincoln Memorial Dr., ☎ 414/224–3200). The striking glassy edifice, which was designed by Eero Saarinen, houses a 20,000-piece collection that spans the past five centuries. Continue south via Harbor Drive to reach **Henry W. Maier Festival Park** (✉ off N. Harbor Dr.), the site of well-attended seasonal events, including German Fest, Irish Fest, African World Festival, Summerfest (the world's largest music festival), and Gay Pride.

North of Juneau Park along Prospect Avenue are some of Milwaukee's most gay-popular districts. **Brady Street,** which intersects Prospect, is the domain of yuppies, skate punks, and elderly Italians who settled here decades ago. Nearby is one of the finest examples of Edwardian architecture and decorating, the **Charles Allis Art Museum** (✉ 1801 N. Prospect

Ave., ☎ 414/278–8295). Prospect then leads into north–south **Downer Avenue,** another strip of funky shops and cafés.

Historic Third Ward and Walker's Point

Head south of eastern downtown, along Broadway and beneath I–794, to reach the **Historic Third Ward,** a patch of renovated warehouses that now hold coffeehouses, antiques shops, and art galleries. Billed as Milwaukee's "Off-Broadway," the district is also home to experimental and cutting-edge theaters, most notably the **Broadway Theater Center** (✉ 158 N. Broadway, ☎ 414/291–7800). Looming over the neighborhood is the world's largest four-face clock, the **Allen-Bradley Co. Clock** (✉ 1201 S. 2nd St.). Bridges lead from here into **Walker's Point,** a neighborhood that draws both gay and straight night crawlers.

GETTING AROUND

Having a car helps for travel between the city's neighborhoods, but once you've arrived, you can park and explore sights or partake of nightlife on foot. Downtown you'll want to use garages. Because gay nightlife is concentrated in a walkable quadrant in Walker's Point, you might want to take a taxi to and from your downtown accommodation.

EATS

Excellent ethnic cuisine and hearty, straightforward American and Continental fare are the mainstays of Milwaukee's casual dining scene. Cutting-edge chefs are moving into town, though, determined to familiarize the general population with field greens, sun-dried cherries, braised fennel, and other edible tools of the New American culinary trade. The best of the gay bars that serve food, Glass Menagerie, is described below.

Milwaukee is also a haven of old-style German cuisine. The two best options are **Karl Ratzch's** (✉ 320 E. Mason St., ☎ 414/276–2720; $$$), which offers the most authentic and tastiest take on German cooking, and flamboyant **Mader's** (✉ 1037 N. Old World 3rd St., ☎ 414/271–3377, $$–$$$), whose floridly Old World decor will immediately set off your kitschometer.

For price ranges, *see* dining Chart B at the front of this guide.

$$$$ ✕ **Sanford.** This restaurant is superior in every regard, from the impeccable decor to the nonpareil New American cuisine. Recent showstoppers on the New American menu have included char-grilled elk loin with corn potato gratin and tart cherry essence, grilled rack of lamb with black-bean flan and chayote, and braised lamb ragout. ✉ *1547 N. Jackson St.,* ☎ *414/276–9608.*

$$$–$$$$ ✕ **Bartolotta's Lake Park Bistro.** A classic French restaurant, great for a special occasion, Bartolotta's takes full advantage of the city's stellar lakeside location. The recipes often include Tuscan overtones. ✉ *3133 E. Newberry Blvd.,* ☎ *414/962–6300.*

$$$–$$$$ ✕ **Boulevard Inn.** Live piano music and a dressed-up crowd suggest a supper club from the 1920s, as do this classy restaurant's mainstays: twin lobster tails, filet mignon, and uncommonly good Wiener schnitzel. Stately setting near the lakefront. ✉ *925 E. Wells St.,* ☎ *414/765–1166.*

$$$ ✕ **Mimma's.** Owned by a woman who treks back to Italy in search of new recipes, this trattoria has been a catalyst for the Brady Street renaissance. Soaring columns, marble accents, and flattering indirect lighting accent tasty fare like porcini ravioli with walnut and marsala cream. ✉ *1307 E. Brady St.,* ☎ *414/271–7337.*

Milwaukee

$$–$$$ ✕ **Lakeside Inn.** Historic and gay-friendly, this restaurant has a formal Continental menu—steak Diane, lemon chicken, whitefish with basil—and a lighter salad and pasta menu. In a wonderful old building close to both downtown and the lakefront, it's a fine option for brunch. ⊠ *800 E. Wells St.,* ☎ *414/276–1577.*

$$–$$$ ✕ **Louise's Trattoria.** When the L.A.-based chain went national, it chose Milwaukee's Cathedral Square as the place to test its first branch. Louise's doles out satisfying portions of Cal-Italian pastas, designer pizzas, calzones, and leafy green salads. ⊠ *801 N. Jefferson St.,* ☎ *414/273–4224.*

$$–$$$ ✕ **Red Rock Café.** A superb, chic restaurant well north of downtown, Red Rock serves internationally influenced seafood fare: sautéed soft-shell crabs, shrimp po'boys, and macadamia-nut-crusted Chilean sea bass with pineapple-mango salsa and Thai red curry. ⊠ *4022 N. Oakland Ave.,* ☎ *414/962–4545.*

$$ ✕ **Glass Menagerie.** Milwaukee's premier gay restaurant—great for a special occasion—serves traditional American and Continental fare. Both the patio and the solarium-style dining room offer warmth and elegance. Popular Sunday brunch. ⊠ *124 N. Water St.,* ☎ *414/347–1962.*

$–$$ ✕ **Coffee Trader's.** This fern-filled establishment is the social center of Downer Avenue. From bar munchies and breakfast favorites to more substantial fare—yellowfin tuna sandwiches, Greek salads, baked Brie—everything here is great except the flaky service. Open till 1 AM. ⊠ *2625 Downer Ave.,* ☎ *414/332–9690.*

$–$$ ✕ **Three Brothers.** An only-in-Milwaukee experience that's as much fun for the delicious food as for the ambience, this century-old tavern serves plates slathered with chicken paprikash, stuffed cabbage, and other Serbian specialties. If you're lucky, you'll hear family members bickering in the kitchen. ⊠ *2414 S. St. Clair St.,* ☎ *414/481–7530. No credit cards.*

$ ✕ **La Fuente.** Festive, gay-friendly La Fuente, in the heart of Walker's Point, serves some of the Midwest's best Mexican fare: spicy garlicky salsa, chicken mole tamales, excellent fresh shrimp dishes, and thirst-quenching margaritas. ⊠ *625 S. 5th St.,* ☎ *414/271–8595.*

$ ✕ **La Perla.** As popular with gays as nearby La Fuente, this place has a more eye-catching decor but more Americanized food. In warm weather, dine on the deck out back. ⊠ *734 S. 5th St.,* ☎ *414/645–9888.*

Coffeehouse Culture

Brewed Awakenings. This funky spot on Brady Street is within a short drive of other queer-friendly favorites. Art exhibitions, an extensive community bulletin board, and great light food (including waffles and veggie chili) are among the draws. ⊠ *1208 Brady St.,* ☎ *414/276–2739.*

Comet. A simple neon sign and a minimalist dining room beckon grungers and artists to this boho, low-key café for coffee and light food. ⊠ *1947 N. Farwell Ave.,* ☎ *414/273–7677.*

SCENES

Milwaukee has more gay bars per capita than most U.S. cities. The upside: In one weekend you won't easily exhaust the two-dozen options, the best-known of which are described below. The downside: Attendance is spotty at many places, especially during the week. Most Milwaukee bars are in a seedy-looking but actually safe section of Walker's Point.

Prime Suspects

Ballgame. It should come as no surprise that the city that organized the nation's first gay softball teams and bowling league has some intense queer sports bars. The guys at the Ballgame definitely know the score and don't hesitate to express their allegiances during televised games. Ballgame's other claim to fame is the longest happy hour in town, daily from

2 to 9 PM. ⊠ *196 S. 2nd St.,* ☎ *414/273–7474. Crowd: mostly male, all ages, baseball caps, jeans and T-shirts, casual, hootin' and hollerin'.*

Boot Camp. Milwaukee has a saucy leather scene, and Boot Camp is its main hub. It's dark in here (surprise!) and crowded on weekends. For a breath of air, or to get a better look at your suitor, head outside to the patio. ⊠ *209 E. National St.,* ☎ *414/643–6900. Crowd: male, mostly mid-30s to mid-50s, butch, leather, bearish.*

Club 219. This mid-size club used to be one of Milwaukee's top stand-and-model discos but it has become more eclectic and less of a scene. The big draws these days are the Saturday night strippers and the Sunday drag shows, but it's still a nice place for dancing. ⊠ *219 S. 2nd St.,* ☎ *414/271–3732. Crowd: 70/30 m/f, 20s to 50s, mixed racially, low-attitude, campy, dishy, fun.*

In Between. A favorite among the young male set (though all are welcome), In Between feels like an Old World saloon. The place is filled with vintage memorabilia, including old Coca-Cola signs, taxi hoods, bicycles, and even a mailbox that's been repainted and rechristened the "male box," where you'll find stacks of free gay newspapers. Lots of fun. ⊠ *625 S. 2nd St.,* ☎ *414/273–2693. Crowd: 80/20 m/f, mostly under 40, a few guppies, lots of regular Janes and Joes.*

Just Us. It's hard to know exactly what to make of this quirky dance and cocktail bar, which tends to draw more women than men (not to mention a few transgenders) and can be fun on certain theme nights. On Thursday more guys come to mingle and ogle, and on other nights the pickings are so slim you could rename the place "Just the Five of Us." ⊠ *807 S. 5th St.,* ☎ *414/383–2233. Crowd: 60/40 f/m, mostly 30s to 50s, some transgenders, otherwise totally diverse.*

La Cage. You're sure to see Milwaukee's die-hard clubbers at brightly lit La Cage on most weekends. Up front is a video bar with stool seating, toward the back is a cozy bar with more video screens and a small dance floor, and in an adjacent room are a larger dance floor and a show stage. If you're hungry, head outside and down a flight of stairs to **Grubb's** (⊠ *807 S. 2nd St.,* ☎ *414/384–8330*), a mellow pub that serves drinks and simple food. ⊠ *801 S. 2nd St.,* ☎ *414/383–8330. Crowd: 50/50 m/f, mostly 20s and 30s, white and blue collar, some club kids and poseurs.*

M&M Club. A stylish bunch heads to this old-fashioned tavern in the Historic Third Ward for cocktails and sometimes dinner at the adjoining Glass Menagerie restaurant (*see* Eats, *above*). The space is beautiful—gilt-frame mirrors, pressed-tin ceilings, tree-shaded deck. There's live piano and cabaret most nights. ⊠ *124 N. Water St.,* ☎ *414/347–1962. Crowd: 50/50 m/f, all ages, slightly upscale, pre- and post-theatergoers.*

This Is It. Around the corner from Cathedral Square, the city's only downtown gay bar has a retro-chic interior that resembles a '60s airport cocktail lounge—complete with vinyl seats and ruby-red walls. One local describes the crowd as a mix of "suits and psychopaths," which might be a little harsh but does hint at the eccentric types you'll bump into. Friendly staff, cheap drinks. ⊠ *418 E. Wells St.,* ☎ *414/278–9192. Crowd: Mostly male, 30s to 60s, guys just off work, colorful.*

Triangle. A consistently crowded cruise and video bar in Walker's Point, this homey tavern has corrugated metal walls, a plant-filled patio, and just enough room for standing and modeling—but no dance floor. There's pool and darts. ⊠ *135 E. National St.,* ☎ *414/383–9412. Crowd: mostly male, 20s and 30s, semiprofessional, lots of jeans and flannel, guy-next-door types, approachable, a bit cruisy.*

Neighborhood Haunts

La Cage and Just Us are arguably the favorite gathering spots for lesbians, but among bars exclusively for women, **Fannie's** (⊠ *200 E. Washington St.,* ☎ *414/643–9633*), which has a rockin' jukebox and a down-to-earth, somewhat butch crowd, is the top choice. As its name suggests, **Kathy's Nut Hut** (✉ 1500 W. Scott St., ☎ 414/647–2673) cultivates a zany yet friendly atmosphere. Diesel dykes favor this place.

Fans of table dancers and female impersonators cram into **C'est La Vie** (✉ 231 S. 2nd St., ☎ 414/291–9600) for nightly shows. **1100 Club** (1100 S. 1st St., ☎ 414/647–9950) is a mellow leather-and-Levi's bar that's good for pool, conversation, and dancing; women are in the minority but welcome. Intensely cruisy, rough-edge **Zippers** (✉ 819 S. 2nd St., ☎ 414/645–8330) serves up cheap booze and light food. Fans of country-western music and dancing flock to **B's Bar** (✉ 1579 S. 2nd St., ☎ 414/672–5580), which has darts and hosts drag pageants.

The **South Water Street Dock** (✉ 354 E. National St., ☎ 414/225–9676) leather bar pulls in many of the guys who frequent Boot Camp. Both men and women favor the curious **Walker's Point Marble Arcade** (✉ 1106 S. 1st St., ☎ 414/384–7999) when seeking an alternative to the standard cruise bars; this place has live entertainment, a bowling alley, and a restaurant that serves light food.

Northeast of downtown, not far from the Brady Street action, is **Mama Roux** (✉ 1875 N. Humbolt St., ☎ 414/347–0344), a male/female hangout with live music some nights. **D's Place** (✉ 4025 N. Port Washington Rd., ☎ 414/962–9487) is a women's bar in northern Milwaukee. In northwestern Milwaukee the **10% Club** (✉ 4332 W. Fond du Lac St., ☎ 414/447–0910) is a lounge with an African-American following.

Hangin' with the Hets

Nomad (✉ 1401 E. Brady St., ☎ 414/224–8111) is an old storefront tavern where you can listen to alternative music, choose from a vast list of beers, and shoot the breeze with gay and straight hipsters, grungers, and yuppies. Snazzy **Elsa's** (✉ 833 N. Jefferson St., ☎ 414/765–0615) and gay-popular **Taylor's** (✉ 795 N. Jefferson St., ☎ 414/271–2855), both downtown, draw local fashion plates and dishy scenesters.

Action

Bathhouses are illegal in Wisconsin, but Milwaukee does have a frisky adult bookstore, **Popular News** (✉ 225 N. Water St., ☎ 414/278–0636), with private video rooms and arcades.

SLEEPS

For price ranges, *see* lodging Chart B at the front of this guide.

$$$$ 🏨 **Pfister Hotel.** This historic confection dazzles guests with its Victorian decor, high-quality 19th-century art, and sterling service. ✉ *424 E. Wisconsin Ave., 53202*, ☎ *414/273–8222 or 800/558–8222*, ℻ *414/273–5025. 307 rooms. Restaurants, pool, health club.*

$$$ 🏨 **Wyndham Milwaukee Center.** A first-rate business hotel in a Flemish Renaissance building, the Wyndham has contemporary rooms done in clubby dark woods and colors. The handsome lobby bar is good spot for a drink. ✉ *139 E. Kilbourn Ave., 53202*, ☎ *414/276–8686 or 800/996–3426*, ℻ *414/276–8007. 221 rooms. Restaurant, health club.*

$$–$$$ 🏨 **County Clare.** This distinctive boutique property, the only true city inn you'll find in Milwaukee, has warmly appointed rooms with four-poster beds and all the amenities you'd expect of a full-service hotel: data ports and fax lines, double whirlpool tubs, and attentive service. ✉ *1234 N. Astor St., 53202*, ☎ *414/272–5247*, ☎ *800/942–5273*, ℻ *414/290–6300. 31 rooms with phone, TV, and private bath. Mostly straight.*

$$–$$$ 🏨 **Milwaukee Hilton.** After a multimillion-dollar overhaul in 1996, this art deco beauty is back in form. The staff is helpful and the management supports gay causes. ✉ *509 W. Wisconsin Ave., 53203,* ☏ *414/271–7250 or 800/445–8667,* ⅎⅅⅩ *414/271–8841. 500 rooms. Restaurant, pool, health club.*

$–$$ 🏨 **Park East Hotel.** Gay-friendly and comfortable, this business hotel is a few blocks from the lakeshore but within walking distance of downtown. ✉ *916 E. State St., 53202,* ☏ *414/276–8800 or 800/328–7275,* ⅎⅅⅩ *414/765–1919. 159 rooms. Restaurant, health club.*

THE LITTLE BLACK BOOK

At Your Fingertips

BESTD Clinic (☏ 414/272–2144). *City Edition* (☏ 414/273–8696). **City Veteran Taxicab** (☏ 414/291–8090). **Gay Information Services** (☏ 414/444–7331). **Gay Youth Milwaukee** (☏ 414/265–8500). **Greater Milwaukee Convention & Visitors Bureau** (✉ 510 W. Kilbourn Ave., 53203, ☏ 414/273–7222 or 800/231–0903, Web site www.milwaukee.org). **Lesbian Alliance of Metro Milwaukee** (☏ 414/264–2600). **Milwaukee County Transit System** (☏ 414/344–6711). **Milwaukee Lesbian and Gay Community Center** (☏ 414/483–4710, Web site www.milwaukeelgbtcenter.com). *Shepherd Express* (alternative weekly, ☏ 414/276–2222, Web site www.shepherd-express.com). **Wisconsin AIDS Line** (☏ 414/273–AIDS or 800/334–AIDS).

Gay Media

In Step Newsmagazine (☏ 414/278–7840, e-mail instepnews@aol.com) and the *Wisconsin Light* (☏ 414/372–2773, Web site www.wilight.com) are two very good statewide biweekly gay newspapers. The more nightlife-oriented *Q Voice* (☏ 414/278–7524, e-mail qvoice@aol.com) and *Quest* (☏ 920/433–0611, Web site www.quest-online.com), an entertaining bar rag, are also helpful.

BOOKSTORES

Afterwords (✉ 2710 N. Murray St., ☏ 414/963–9089), a great little lesbigay bookstore, carries periodicals, videos, and CDs; there's a counter where you can order a cup of coffee and chat with the personable staff or other customers. In the bar district at Walker's Point, **Designing Men** (✉ 1200 S. 1st St., ☏ 414/389–1200) sells cards, leather gear, pride goods, and the like.

Working Out

Body Inspired (✉ 2009 E. Kenilworth Pl., ☏ 414/272–8622) is popular with the community.

MADISON

Madison, population 200,000, is one of the gayest smaller cities in America. It's the capital of Wisconsin, home of Steve Gunderson, the gay former congressman, and part of a state with some of the most gay-positive laws in the nation. Madison is also home to lesbian politician Tammy Baldwin and gay city councilperson Mike Verveer.

The city's good vibes inspired *Money* magazine in 1996 to name Madison as the best place to live in America. Other notable rankings include its selection as one of *Outside* magazine's "Dream Towns," one of *Bicycling* magazine's "Best Bicycling Cities," and one of *Cosmopolitan*'s top cities for finding single men—straight and gay. At the same time, Madison has one of the most unified and visible feminist communities of any U.S. city. Women occupy influential positions in all walks of city life.

Lay of the Land

On the surface, Madison, about 60 miles west of Milwaukee, looks like many other smaller U.S. cities. Its downtown is laid out as a standard grid with the Capitol at its crux and four diagonal streets emanating from Capitol Square. But downtown Madison is atypical in that it occupies an isthmus between two bodies of water—Lake Mendota to the north and Lake Monona to the south. A mere dozen city blocks separate these two lakes at the very center of town.

You'll rarely find a thoroughfare as engaging—and so integral to a city's identity—as **State Street,** the **downtown** transit and pedestrian mall that connects Madison's two most important institutions, the Capitol and the University of Wisconsin. The many murals, mosaics, and marble details in the regal **Capitol** (⊠ 4 E. State St., ☎ 608/266–0382) definitely warrant a tour.

State Street near Capitol Square is largely the domain of suits and politicos, but the mood is consistently more bohemian than in most cities' central business districts. Once you make your way past Gorham Street, you'll begin to detect collegiate energy—cheap ethnic restaurants, bike racks, coffeehouses, and the buzz of academe. Among the gay-popular shops along or near State Street are **Home Environment** (⊠ 216 N. Henry St., ☎ 608/251–4905), which sells eco-friendly clothing and household goods; **Soap Opera** (⊠ 319 State St., ☎ 608/251–4051), a favorite for soaps, fragrances, and oils; **Four Star Video Heaven** (⊠ 315 N. Henry St., ☎ 608/255–1994), one of the best sources of queer-theme and general-interest videos in the Midwest; and several excellent bookstores (*see* Gay Media, *below*).

Six museums in the State Street area constitute Madison's **Museum Mile.** The best are the **State Historical Museum** (⊠ 30 N. Carroll St., ☎ 608/264–6555); the **Madison Art Center** (⊠ Madison Civic Center, 211 State St., ☎ 608/257–0158), whose holdings are chiefly contemporary; and the **Elvehjem Museum of Art** (⊠ 800 University Ave., ☎ 608/263–2246), whose works date from as far back as 2300 BC.

Local boosters may not promote downtown's seventh museum with the same swelled pride as they do the ones above, but the **Madison Museum of Bathroom Tissue** (⊠ 305 N. Hamilton St., ☎ 608/251–8098) is memorable stop. Its noble mission: to display "t.p." from around the world.

The campus of the **University of Wisconsin** is the domain of 40,000 students. You can check out university happenings at the **Wisconsin Union** (⊠ 800 Langdon St., ☎ 608/262–2263). Out back, overlooking Lake Mendota, is dangerously seductive **Memorial Union Terrace,** one of the Midwest's most intellectual pick-up spots, gay or straight.

The **Monona Terrace Community and Convention Center** (⊠ 1 John Nolen Dr., ☎ 608/261–4000), constructed to the late Frank Lloyd Wright's ambitious design, was completed in July 1997. In addition to Monona Terrace, eight Frank Lloyd Wright buildings within a two-hour drive of Madison are open to the public. Well worth a trip is **Taliesin** (⊠ Rte. 23 at Rte. C, Spring Green, ☎ 608/588–7900), a drive of about 45 minutes from Madison. Among Wright's most famous works, the complex consists of the Hillside Home School and the Frank Lloyd Wright Visitors Center, as well as the Taliesin Bookstore.

Getting Around

Madison has all the goods of a big city, and only one of the bads: Finding a parking space downtown can be maddening. And downtown has numerous one-way streets, dead-ends, and busy intersections. Fortunately, the city is highly walkable, or you can tour it by bicycle.

Eats

Ethnic variety is the hallmark of Madison dining. You'll find many Mediterranean, Middle Eastern, and Asian options, either in traditional establishments or at the **ethnic-food stalls** on the UW campus, or lined up along the State Street Mall. Another must-do for gourmands is the Saturday-morning **Dane County Farmers' Market** (⊠ Capitol Square, ☎ 920/563–5037); it's open from late April through October.

For price ranges, *see* dining Chart B at the front of this guide.

$$$–$$$$ ✕ **L'Etoile.** The chefs at L'Etoile have a delightful time dreaming up new ways to show off the region's cornucopia of fine ingredients. The menu changes weekly but might feature sautéed walleye pike with an Italian parsley pesto and celery coulis. ⊠ *25 N. Pinckney St.,* ☎ *608/251–0500.*

$$$ ✕ **Deb and Lola's.** The kitchen here churns out tantalizing international fare such as pan-seared halibut with oven-dried organic tomatoes over grilled onions and fennel. Comprehensive wine list. ⊠ *227 State St.,* ☎ *608/255–0820.*

$$–$$$ ✕ **Coyote Capers.** This handsome bistro on the eastern edge of downtown serves globally charged seasonal fare like Moroccan spice-rubbed game hen, and shrimp and black-bean tamales. ⊠ *1201 Williamson St.,* ☎ *608/251–1313.*

$$–$$$ ✕ **The Opera House.** Dramatic and sleek, the Opera House has a formal New American menu and a simpler bar appetizer list. Options from the main menu include skillet-seared marlin loin served with tangerine vinaigrette, jasmine rice, and lemongrass cucumbers. Stellar wine list. ⊠ *117 Martin Luther King Jr. Blvd.,* ☎ *608/284–8466.*

$$ ✕ **Greenbush Bar.** In the basement of the 1904 Italian Workmen's Club building, "the Bush" is a good place to relax over a microbrew or single-malt whisky or to dine on light pastas and pizzas. ⊠ *914 Regent St.,* ☎ *608/257–2874.*

$$ ✕ **Fyfe's Corner Bistro.** Shrouded within a vintage redbrick factory warehouse on the east side of downtown, bustling Fyfe's draws gays and straights for drinks at its circular bar. The bistro menu—pan-fried trout, stir-fried pasta dishes, and the like—is unpretentious and eclectic. ⊠ *1344 E. Washington Ave.,* ☎ *608/251–8700.*

$$ ✕ **Wild Iris Café.** The owners of nearby Greenbush Bar operate this festive eatery that specializes in traditional Italian cuisine. The burgers are good, too, as are some of the more innovative dishes, like Thai chicken pasta. ⊠ *1225 Regent St.,* ☎ *608/257–4747.*

$–$$ ✕ **Savory Thymes.** A fixture on funky Williamson Street—south of downtown—this vegetarian restaurant is softly lit and decorated in a rich purple and burgundy color scheme. Favorites include winter squash ravioli, Sicilian pizza, and udon noodles with a spicy Thai peanut sauce. ⊠ *1146 Williamson St.,* ☎ *608/255–2292.*

$ ✕ **Monty's Blue Plate Diner.** A home-style diner in eastern Madison, the Blue Plate serves sandwiches, American entrées, and great baked goods and desserts. ⊠ *2089 Atwood Ave.,* ☎ *608/244–8505.*

Coffeehouse Culture

Mother's Fool. Less student-oriented than some of the java joints near campus, this homey Williamson Street coffeehouse captures a true living-room ambience with mismatched furnishings, table lamps, and comfortable seating. ⊠ *1101 Williamson St.,* ☎ *608/259–1301.*

Steep and Brew. This student hangout serves a full range of coffees and teas, good pastries, and light snacks. The buzz of lit crit wafts through the air. ⊠ *544 State St.,* ☎ *608/256–2902.*

Scenes

In addition to the bars below, several of the above-mentioned restaurants—especially Fyfe's and Greenbush Bar—have community cachet. If you're a woman planning to spend an *intime* night in your lodging (with or without company), **A Woman's Touch** (⊠ 600 Williamson St., Gateway Mall, ☎ 608/250–1928) is a great source of erotic and romantic gifts and accessories.

Prime Suspects

Geraldine's. The only gay club not within walking distance of downtown—it's a 10-minute drive east—draws sizable crowds because of a few important attributes: a patio, a volleyball court, a casual restaurant, and the largest dance floor of any club in Madison (gay or straight). Smartly decorated, it's run by an outgoing staff. ⊠ *3052 E. Washington St.,* ☎ *608/241–9335. Crowd: 65/35 m/f, all ages, unpretentious, a mix of students, white collars, and blue collars.*

Manoeuvers. Downtown's most popular full-time dance club is a few blocks southeast of Capitol Hill. Next to a basic dance floor with roaring music is a long bar with video screens overhead. Attached is a smaller, darker, and sexier lounge called MAD (Manoeuvers After Dark), which bills itself as a leather-and-Levi's bar but is actually open to all persuasions. ⊠ *150 S. Blair St.,* ☎ *608/258–9918. Crowd: 85/15 m/f, mostly 20s and 30s, cruisy, lots of UW students, rougher-edge at MAD.*

Neighborhood Haunts

Local guys hang out at **Scandals** (⊠ 121 W. Main St., ☎ 608/251–1030), which has a small dance floor and a cozy fireplace lounge, and **Shamrock** (⊠ 117 W. Main St., ☎ 608/255–5029), a good old-fashioned drinkin' and smokin' bar.

Hangin' with the Hets

Cardinal (⊠ 418 E. Wilson St., ☎ 608/251–0080), a gay-popular mainstream dance club, has a queer night on Thursday. On the ground floor of a restored apartment building, Cardinal has a terrific sound system.

Sleeps

For price ranges, *see* lodging Chart B at the front of this guide.

$$–$$$$ 🖭 **Canterbury Inn.** The rooms at this inn—a former rock club, the place Otis Redding was to have performed the night of his plane crash—are painted with murals based on Chaucer's *Canterbury Tales* and accented with rich golds, greens, and burgundies; all have CD players, high ceilings, and fluffy beds. Some have whirlpool tubs. ⊠ *315 W. Gorham St., 53703,* ☎ *608/258–8899 or 800/838–3850. 6 rooms with TV, phone, and private bath. Continental breakfast. Mixed gay/straight.*

$$–$$$$ 🖭 **Mansion Hill Inn.** Atop a bluff near campus, this Romanesque Revival 1850s mansion is a short walk from Lake Mendota. Many of the lavish rooms have skylights, marble baths, carved marble fireplaces, and antiques. ⊠ *424 N. Pinckney St., 53703,* ☎ *608/255–3999 or 800/798–9070,* FAX *608/255–2217. 11 rooms with phone and private bath, many with TV. Continental breakfast. Mostly straight.*

$$–$$$ 🖭 **The Madison Concourse Hotel.** A lavish refurbishment and high-quality reproduction antiques and fabrics have made this one of Madison's elite hotels. The location is ideal—midway between Capitol Square and State Street. ⊠ *1 W. Dayton St., 53703,* ☎ *608/257–6000 or 800/356–8293,* FAX *608/257–5280. 360 rooms. Restaurants, pool, health club.*

$$–$$$ 🖭 **Sheraton Madison Hotel.** Among contemporary chain properties, this mid-rise a short drive from Monona Terrace wins high praise for its pleasant, efficient service and brightly appointed rooms. ⊠ *706 John Nolen*

Dr., 53713, ☎ *608/251–2300 or 800/325–3535,* FAX *608/251–1189. 236 rooms. Restaurant, pool, health club.*

$–$$ 🛏 **Prairie Garden B&B.** A 30-minute drive north of Madison, this farmhouse sprawls on 20 acres of gorgeous country near lakes, ski slopes, hiking trails, and a nude beach. ⊠ *W. 13172 Hwy. 188, Lodi, 53555,* ☎ *608/592–5187 or 800/380–8427. 4 rooms, some with TV and private bath. Hot tub. Full breakfast. Mixed gay male/lesbian.*

$ 🛏 **University Inn.** For proximity to student life you can't beat the State Street location of this dated-looking motor inn. ⊠ *441 N. Frances St., 53703,* ☎ *608/257–4881 or 800/279–4881. 45 rooms.*

The Little Black Book

At Your Fingertips
Gay and Lesbian Information Line (☎ 608/263–3100, ext. 3333). **Isthmus** (☎ 608/251–5627, Web site www.thedailypage.com). **Lesbian, Gay, and Bisexual Business Alliance** (☎ 608/256–6214). **Madison AIDS Network** (☎ 608/252–6540 or 800/486–6276). **Madison Convention and Visitors Bureau** (⊠ 615 E. Washington Ave., 53703, ☎ 608/255–2537 or 800/373–6376, Web site www.visitmadison.com). **Madison Gay and Lesbian Resource Center and Library** (⊠ 14 W. Mifflin St., Suite 103, ☎ 608/255–0704). **University of Wisconsin Lesbigay Campus Center** (⊠ UW Union, ☎ 608/265–3344). **University of Wisconsin Campus Women's Center** (⊠ 710 University Ave., Room 202, ☎ 608/262–8093). **Wisconsin Women's Network** (☎ 608/255–9809).

Gay Media
The Milwaukee and statewide gay papers (*see* Milwaukee, *above*) cover Madison.

BOOKSTORES
Clean and comfy **A Room of One's Own** (⊠ 307 W. Johnson St., ☎ 608/257–7888) carries many lesbian and feminist titles and has a considerable general gay and gay-male section, too. There's also a fine coffeehouse. The leftist **Rainbow Coop** (⊠ 426 W. Gilham, ☎ 608/257–6050) bookstore has a more politically oriented queer section. Of general-interest stores, **Canterbury Booksellers** (⊠ 315 W. Gorham St., ☎ 608/258–9911) also has lesbian and gay sections. **We Are Family** (⊠ Wilson Hotel, 524 E. Wilson St., ☎ 608/258–9006) carries a few gay books plus pride gear and clothing, and has a coffeehouse. **Pride Gallery and Gifts** (⊠ 229 North St., ☎ 608/245–9229) stocks gay and lesbian gifts and local art.

22 Out in Minneapolis and St. Paul

TO BORROW FROM OSCAR WILDE (sort of), Minneapolis and St. Paul are two cities divided by a common river. Lumped together by most folks as the Twin Cities, these vibrant and gay-friendly getaways have their own distinctive charms. Observers sometimes note that St. Paul shares a close kinship with the nearest major city to the east, Chicago, while Minneapolis has a spirit and aesthetic similar to that of the nearest major city to the west (albeit 1,700 miles away), Seattle.

Despite having been developed originally as a rough and ragged mill town, Minneapolis is the flashier and more cosmopolitan of the two cities. Its residents tend to dress up before heading out to a show, party in large numbers at Warehouse District nightclubs, and dine in see-and-be-seen restaurants. Here you'll find the Twin Cities' pro sports teams and two best art museums. The male-dominated gay scene focuses around cruisy clubs and fashionable coffeehouses, although Minneapolis queers are still less attitudy than most.

The money generated by Minneapolis's early industrial prosperity typically found its way into the banks and white-collar concerns of St. Paul, a city with a subdued Old Money air. Despite this reputation, the city possesses a comfortable, middle-class, almost gritty character today—thanks in part to its abundance of close-knit low-keyed residential neighborhoods dominated by neatly preserved redbrick row houses and subdivided Victorian mansions. Nesting lesbians and lesser numbers of nesting gay men have long been attracted to the city's community spirit and quiet pace, but visitors will find less to see and do here than in Minneapolis.

The unrelenting niceness of Minnesotans causes plenty of visitors and newcomers to groan. People here are friendly and agreeable, but they are also famous for not saying quite what they mean. One East Coast transplant who's lived here for more than 20 years comments, "It's great that everyone here is so polite—drivers wait patiently for pedestrians to cross in front of them, waiters and waitresses insist that their customers have just a *super* day. But where I lived for much of my life, if somebody disagreed with you, they'd tell you to your face. Here, if somebody thinks your point of view is stupid, they say, 'Oh, well now, that's sure a different way of looking at things.'" Nevertheless, if you could bottle and market this region's personality, you'd name it Minnesota Mellow and make a fortune selling it to harried New Yorkers and New Englanders.

THE LAY OF THE LAND

Minneapolis

Downtown

The Mississippi runs through the heart of downtown Minneapolis. About 10 miles west of downtown St. Paul as the crow flies, this walkable city center has a towering modern skyline that suggests prosperity but doesn't quite command the respect of Chicago's or capture the postmodern panache of Houston's. Many of the towers went up during the '50s, '60s, and '70s and reflect that era's banality, such notable exceptions as Philip Johnson's masterful 57-story **IDS Building** (✉ 777 Nicollet Mall) and the elegant 32-story **Foshay Tower** (✉ 821 Marquette Ave. S, ☎ 612/341–2522) notwithstanding. This latter landmark 1929 structure's observation deck is open to the public.

The Foshay Tower is near the geographic center of downtown; linking it to buildings on the 52 surrounding blocks is a 5-mile network of second-story interior **skyways.** If you wonder why, on blustery winter days, you see so few pedestrians dashing along downtown's icy streets, it's because most folks use these climate-controlled glass tubes to work their way around the city. The five miles of downtown skyways lead through the lobbies of several-dozen office buildings and hotels, and provide interior access to hundreds of shops and restaurants. Thanks to these ingenious skyways, many employees can get between home and the office—and eat out for lunch, pick up their dry-cleaning, and drop by the bank—without ever donning a winter coat.

The one street that does typically buzz with colorful street life, especially in warm weather, is **Nicollet Mall,** a 12-block pedestrian-and-bus mall lined with park benches, trees, and sculptures. The mall offers access to some of downtown's best shopping centers. On summer Thursdays there's a farmers' market. A few blocks over, **Hennepin Avenue** is lined with clubs and restaurants and also anchors Minneapolis's **Theater District.**

Warehouse Historic District

The **Warehouse Historic District,** beginning west of Hennepin Avenue, offers the gritty Old World character that downtown lacks. Most of the 150 buildings are on seven blocks just south of the river, along 1st and 2nd avenues, and date from the turn of the century. The ground floors contain shops, restaurants, nightclubs, a few strip clubs and adult bookstores, and art galleries. Most of the upper floors have been reconfigured as loft apartments and design studios. Closest to downtown, around the Target Center (home of the NBA's Minnesota Timberwolves), the streets turn into a lively entertainment scene on weekend nights. Among the most remarkable architectural transformations is the Cass Gilbert–designed Minneapolis Van and Warehouse Company Building, which became the **Theatre de la Jeune Lune** (✉ 105 N. 1st St., ☎ 612/333–6200), the home of a an internationally recognized avant-garde acting company.

St. Anthony Main and the Mississippi

North of downtown, Hennepin Avenue leads across the Mississippi River and over **Nicollet Island,** which is part of the 165-acre **St. Anthony Falls Historic District.** The island is filled with old mills and warehouses and makes for an interesting walk. **St. Anthony Main,** the area immediately north of the island, was once an old Polish neighborhood and, along the river, the city's first African-American enclave. Several new bars and restaurants have opened, and a new wave of younger residents—many of them gay—have begun settling here in recent years. While wandering along cobbled **Main Street** and past the many numerous historic industrial structures, be sure to poke your head inside the bizarre **Museum of**

Questionable Medical Devices (✉ 219 S.E. Main St., ☎ 612/379–4046), an eye-opening tour of implements and remedies that have proven to be ineffective and in many cases injurious.

Loring Park and Lowry Hill

Hennepin Avenue leads southwest from downtown and the Theater District to modest but delightfully inviting **Loring Park.** Here a mix of queers, vagrants, yuppies, and families wander around the grassy, minimally landscaped shore of the park's pond. This is where Mary Richards seems to thank the stars for life in Minneapolis during the opening credits of *The Mary Tyler Moore Show,* and where the gay pride parade commences each year. **Harmon Place,** which fringes the south side of the park, houses some neoboho shops and eateries.

West of the park, across Hennepin Avenue, begins **Lowry Hill,** a mixed-income and fairly gay and artsy residential neighborhood that's home to the country's largest regional theater, the **Guthrie** (✉ 725 Vineland Pl., ☎ 612/377–2224), and one of the top-10 most-visited art museums in the nation, the **Walker Art Center** (✉ Vineland Pl. at Lyndale Ave. S, ☎ 612/375–7622). The nine galleries host top contemporary traveling exhibitions, and the permanent collection represents all the major European and American movements of the past century. Just outside are 11 landscaped acres comprising the **Minneapolis Sculpture Garden,** excellent for an afternoon stroll.

The Chain of Lakes

Lowry Hill leads southwest into fashionable residential neighborhoods that surround three sparkling bodies of water, which make up a significant part of **the Chain of Lakes.** Many of the large mansions have been divvied up into apartments. Such has not been the fate of the imposing private home at 2104 Kenwood Parkway, although its depiction in the opening credits of *The Mary Tyler Moore Show,* as the residence of Mary Richards, might lead you to conclude otherwise. Go ahead and drive by, but don't ask the no-doubt frazzled owners for a house-tour—tourists are said to show up regularly expecting to find it laid out and decorated exactly as it appeared on the show, complete with Rhoda's fabulous beaded doorway. *Duh.*

The Mary house is just a couple of blocks from **Lake of the Isles,** a particularly picturesque member in the Chain of Lakes; it's so named for the two small isles in the center. Due south is **Lake Calhoun,** around which joggers and bladers make their way. The grassy eastern shore, between 33rd and 34th streets, is a popular **gay beach** all summer long.

Uptown and Lyn-Lake

The city's genX alternative scene centers on **Uptown,** a once dowdy neighborhood east of Lake Calhoun and south of downtown via Hennepin Avenue. The area is becoming somewhat more costly, and many indigent artists and wary iconoclasts are moving slightly east into **Lyn-Lake.** The main drags, **West Lake Street** and **Hennepin Avenue,** are loaded with used record stores, vintage clothiers, coffeehouses, and inexpensive eateries. Be sure to scan the papers to see what's playing at the **Uptown** (✉ 2906 Hennepin Ave., ☎ 612/825–4644) and the **Lagoon** (✉ 1320 Lagoon Ave., ☎ 612/825–6006) film theaters, both of which specialize in independent, foreign, and vintage flicks. For live drama, check out the **Jungle Theater** (✉ 709 W. Lake St., ☎ 612/822–7063). Each August, the **Uptown Art Fair** (☎ 612/827–8757) draws about 300,000 visitors to the largest arts and crafts show in the northern Midwest.

Several blocks northeast of Lyn-Lake, midway between it and downtown, is the **Minneapolis Institute of Arts** (✉ 2400 3rd Ave. S, ☎ 612/870–3131), which is housed in a 1915 Beaux Arts building. The 80,000-piece collection includes works by Picasso, O'Keeffe, Grant Wood, Rembrandt, and Titian; a 2,000-year-old mummy; and an exhaustive collection of African masks. Nearby is the **American Swedish Institute** (⊠ 2600 Park Ave., ☎ 612/871–4907), a 1920s mansion with Swedish art, furnishings, and historical documents.

Mall of America

Hailed by some as one of America's greatest man-made wonders, the **Mall of America** (⊠ 60 E. Broadway, I–494 at 24th Ave., Bloomington, ☎ 612/883–8800) is a hulking shrine to middle-class values, containing every mid-range chain store known to man. Additionally, you'll find "unique" local-interest stores like **Lake Wobegon, USA,** and **Northern Lights,** which sell folksy knickknacks and celebrate a time and a world that existed long ago—before we had massive indoor shopping malls.

The 400-store mall is in Bloomington, south of Minneapolis and St. Paul. If you have some time to kill, it's worth popping over here, but in the end it's not such a big deal. It's the equivalent of combining the contents of any four typical American shopping malls under one roof, and throwing in a bunch of ordinary restaurants and a nightclub, a children's amusement park, and a legitimately interesting 1.2-million-gallon aquarium and marine science center. Minnesota has no sales tax on clothing, which also accounts for the mall's raging success: It's by far the most visited attraction in the northern Midwest.

St. Paul

Downtown

St. Paul's workaday **downtown** is centered around the intersection of North Robert and 7th streets, where the **Minnesota Office of Tourism** (⊠ 100 Metro Square, 121 7th Pl. E, ☎ 612/296–5029 or 800/657–3700) runs a visitor center. From here it's about a 10-minute walk northwest to reach the **Science Museum of Minnesota** (⊠ 30 E. 10th St., ☎ 612/221–9488). The museum is not far from the large park anchored by the Cass Gilbert–designed **Minnesota State Capitol** (⊠ Aurora and Constitution Aves., ☎ 612/297–3521), a structure rife with domes, arches, columns, and murals.

Quite likely the most engaging downtown attraction is the **Minnesota History Center** (⊠ 345 Kellogg Blvd. W, ☎ 612/296–6126), whose collection of memorabilia and artifacts captures the region's past, from a replica of an early sod house to an actual costume worn by Prince in *Purple Rain*. A short walk from here is the **Minnesota Museum of American Art** (⊠ 75 W. 5th St., 2nd floor, ☎ 612/292–4380), a modest facility that's strong on American painting, and works from Asia and Africa.

Only southeastern St. Paul, down near the river and known as the **Lowertown Historic District,** is really worth a stroll. This 17-block tract of former warehouses and industrial concerns bears a certain resemblance to Minneapolis's Warehouse District. A key landmark is **Depot Place** (⊠ 214 E. 4th St.), a 1920s rail depot that houses restaurants and boutiques. Nearby is the also interesting **St. Paul Farmers' Market** (⊠ 290 E. 5th St., ☎ 612/227–6856), which is held on weekend mornings.

Summit Hill and Crocus Hill

If you stand on the western edge of downtown and look in a northwesterly direction, high on a hill you'll easily spy the 175-foot-tall **Cathedral of St. Paul** (⊠ 239 Selby Ave., ☎ 612/228–1766). The area near the cathedral contains the most charming historic residential neighborhood in the Twin Cities. Running due west from the Cathedral, **Selby Avenue** is lined with beautifully restored buildings, many of them housing gay-friendly restaurants and shops. **Summit Avenue** runs southwest of the cathedral and is where a young F. Scott Fitzgerald, who lived at No. 599 (a private residence), penned his first novel, *This Side of Paradise*. Continue west on Summit and drop down a block south near Dale Street to **Grand Avenue,** which for the next 10 blocks west is lined with cafés, coffeehouses, antiques shops, and other stores. This spirited and slick but unpretentious strip is the heart of **Crocus Hill,** a desirable neighborhood of Victorian homes and streets lighted with old-fashioned street lamps.

Farther west are two less pricey but equally queer-popular neighborhoods, **Merriam Park** and **Macalester-Groveland.** By the time it crosses Hamline Avenue, Selby is again a main—albeit less impressive—commercial drag, this time in Merriam Park. Along here are good ethnic restaurants and coffeehouses. This is a totally mixed neighborhood of families, young queers, skate punks, retirees, and others: At one house you'll see a rainbow wind chime on the porch, at the next you'll see a Minnesota Vikings football pennant in the window, and at the next you'll see both.

Como Park

The one northwestern St. Paul neighborhood that merits exploration is **Como Park** and the residential blocks around it. It is an area rich with turn-of-the-century residences, the nicest of which are around **Lake Como,** which occupies the eastern edge of **Como Regional Park** (⊠ 1421 N. Lexington Pkwy.) On the grounds of this lush 450-acre park you'll find a **public zoo** (☎ 612/488–5571), with 500 animals, and a glorious glass-enclosed **conservatory** (☎ 612/489–1740).

GETTING AROUND

Although the Twin Cities are laid out in a grid and highways connect the two downtowns, converging freeways, one-way streets, and poor street signage conspire to make driving an adventure for newcomers. In either downtown, parking on the street is usually not possible or advisable, but you'll find dozens of large parking garages (or "ramps," as they're referred to by Minnesotans).

In Minneapolis there are few better ways to get a quick (hourlong) and entertaining sense of the city than by grabbing a ride on the **Minneapolis RiverCity Trolley** (☎ 612/204–0000), which runs daily from mid-May through October and completes a narrated circuit of the city's highlights; a two-hour pass costs $5, or pay an extra buck for an all-day pass.

EATS

Despite the white-bread reputation, Minneapolis and St. Paul have many immigrants of numerous ethnicities, including Mexican, Hmong, Chinese, Vietnamese, and Thai. Inexpensive and generally excellent Mexican and Asian fare is abundant. A particularly good source of cheap ethnic eats is in Minneapolis along **Nicollet Avenue.** Favorites include **Jerusalem's** (⊠ 1518 Nicollet Ave., ☎ 612/871–8883, $–$$) for Middle Eastern; **Ping's** (⊠ 1401 Nicollet Ave., ☎ 612/874–9404, $$) for Chinese; and **Royal Orchid** (⊠ 1835 Nicollet Ave., ☎ 612/872–1938, $–$$) for Thai. Stroll the main drags of the Warehouse District, Loring Park, Uptown and Lyn-Lake, and St. Anthony Main, and you'll easily find a tasty, trendy bite to eat. In St. Paul your best bets are along Selby Avenue west of Cathedral Hill and also in Merriam Park, and along Grand Avenue in Crocus Hill.

For price ranges, *see* dining Chart B at the front of this guide.

Minneapolis

$$$$ ✕ **D'Amico Cucina.** For the finest northern Italian fare in the city head to this Warehouse District eatery. It has a stunning Art Nouveau interior, world-class service, gnocchi to die for, and more than 500 vintages imported from Italy. ⊠ *Butler Sq., 100 N. 6th St.,* ☎ *612/338–2401.*

$$$ ✕ **Bobino's.** This wine bar and café in St. Anthony Main is proof that the old Polish neighborhood has turned a new corner. A former funeral parlor the space is said to be haunted by friendly ghosts, but it's unquestionably the haunt of dapper guppies and yuppies, who come to sample New American winners like roasted mallard duck served on wild-mushroom polenta. ⊠ *222 E. Hennepin Ave.,* ☎ *612/623–3301.*

$$$ ✕ **New French Café and Bar.** Homey and unpretentious, this Warehouse District complex consists of a storefront dining room, a cute bakery, and a mundane bar. Grab fresh breakfast goodies from the bakery, or feast on a dinner of lobster-and-chèvre quesadillas and grilled sea bass with rosemary-roasted eggplant. ⊠ *128 N. 4th St.,* ☎ *612/338–3790.*

$$–$$$ ✕ **Café Un Deux Trois.** With antique mirrors, sparkling chandeliers, and efficient but slightly stiff service, this suave downtown eatery has the whole gay Paris ambience down to a science. Fortunately, the by-the-book bistro fare lives up to the romantic trappings—sample rich pâté *de campagne,* fried steak chips, and sautéed calves' liver with caramelized onions and a mustard demi-glace. ⊠ *Foshay Tower, 114 S. 9th St.,* ☎ *612/673–0686.*

$$–$$$ ✕ **Cafe Havana.** The latest Warehouse District playground for posing, sipping martinis, and smoking cigars has credible Latin American food, including spicy plantain and yucca stew and tender lamb shank braised with tomatoes, rosemary, and sherry. ⊠ *119 N. Washington Ave.,* ☎ *612/338–8484.*

$$–$$$ ✕ **Loring Café.** This chateauesque complex includes an avant-garde theater, a relentlessly countercultural bar and lounge (with its own café menu), and a more formal dining room where you can try New American treats like chilled, seared ahi tuna and Italian bread salad with oven-roasted tomatoes, olives, croutons, greens, and roasted garlic. ⊠ *1624 Harmon Pl.,* ☎ *612/332–1617.*

$$–$$$ ✕ **Lucia's.** Exotic beers and daring but consistently successful takes on American cuisine are the hallmark of this Uptown bistro. Turkey breast marinated in crème fraîche and tarragon is just one of Lucia's tasty experiments. ⊠ *1432 W. 31st St.,* ☎ *612/825–1572.*

$$–$$$ ✕ **Mpls Café.** The long list of pastas, pizzas, and sandwiches at this theater district newcomer is complemented by specialties like a salad of steamed herb-infused mussels, bay shrimp, and clams on a bed of basmati, and couscous with Moroccan olives, raisins, smoked almonds, and vegetables. ⊠ *1110 Hennepin Ave.,* ☎ *612/672–9100.*

$$ ✕ **Caffè Solo.** Good in the early AM for breakfast and in the *very* early AM for après-disco noshing, this cavernous converted warehouse has a full dining room and a mellow coffee bar. About 10 pastas and several pizzas are offered, plus many salads and sandwiches. ⊠ *123 N. 3rd St.,* ☎ *612/332–7108.*

$$ ✕ **Café Brenda.** Slaves to organic cooking never had it so good: This fine purveyor of nouvelle health food whips up pleasing but low-fat creations like smoked trout–risotto croquette, organic-chicken enchiladas, and duck salad without getting too outlandish. ⊠ *300 1st Ave. N,* ☎ *612/342–9230.*

$–$$ ✕ **Mud Pie.** A staple of Lyn-Lake's alternative scene since 1972, this left-of-center vegetarian restaurant specializes in meatless burgers, filling tamale pies, and a terrific rendition of its namesake for dessert. ⊠ *2549 Lyndale Ave. S,* ☎ *612/872–9435.*

$–$$ ✕ **Rock Bottom Brewery.** This brew pub specializes in soul-warming comfort food—burgers, hazelnut chicken, Asiago cheese dip with toasted beer bread—and hearty ales with names such as North Star and Gopher

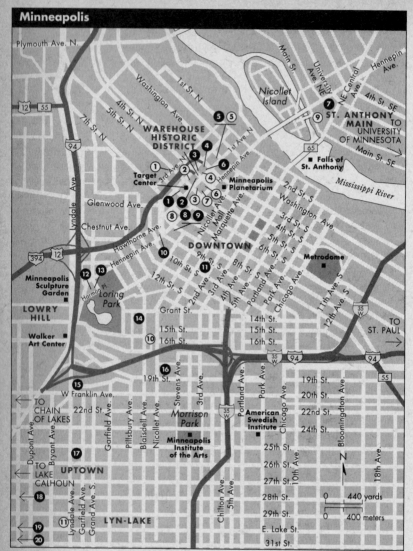

Minneapolis

Eats ●

Bobino's, **7**
Cafe Brenda, **6**
Cafe Havana, **5**
Cafe Un Deux
Trois, **11**
Cafe Wyrd, **19**
Café Zev, **14**
Caffe Solo, **4**
D'Amico Cucina, **1**
Laughing Cup, **16**
Loring Cafe, **12**
Lucia's, **20**
Mpls Cafe, **10**

Mud Pie, **17**
New French Cafe
and Bar, **3**
Pizza Lucé, **2**
Rock Bottom
Brewery, **8**
Ruby's, **13**
Rudolph's
Bar-B-Que, **9, 15**
Uncommon
Grounds, **18**

Scenes ○

Brass Rail, **7**
Bryant Lake Bowl, **11**
Fine Line
Music Cafe, **4**
Gay '90s, **6**
Havana, **5**
The Lounge, **2**
19 Bar, **10**
Saloon, **8**
Sophia, **9**
South Beach, **3**
Tropix, **1**

Gold. Suits prevail early in the evening, but the place loosens up later. ✉ *825 Hennepin Ave.,* ☎ *612/332–2739.*

$ ✕ **Pizza Lucé.** A Warehouse District institution, where fags like to dish over deep dish, this pizzeria is kind of a dive. The pies, which come with a litany of odd toppings, are the main attraction. ✉ *119 N. 4th St.,* ☎ *612/333–7359.*

$ ✕ **Ruby's.** Lesbians favor the cute café attached to the women's bookstore, Amazon (*see* The Little Black Book, *below*). It's open for lunch and breakfast; top offerings include buttermilk pancakes, smoked-turkey sandwiches, and a tasty hummus salad platter. ✉ *1614 Harmon Pl.,* ☎ *612/338–2089.*

$ ✕ **Rudolph's Bar-B-Que.** These queer-popular, late-night ribs joints serve certifiable stick-to-your-innards barbecue. Hot wings, chops, steaks, veal, and seafood come with all the usual sides and fixings. ✉ *1933 Lyndale Ave. S,* ☎ *612/871–8969;* ✉ *815 Hennepin Ave.,* ☎ *612/623–3671.*

St. Paul

$$$–$$$$ ✕ **Vintage Wine Bar and Restaurant.** Inside a stunning redbrick Victorian, the Vintage's cozy dining rooms are warmed by fireplaces—the ambience is comforting on a bitter winter day. Entrées such as rack of lamb with Vidalia onions, couscous, vegetables, and a red-wine pomegranate glaze prove that this is as impressive an eatery as it is a wine bar. ✉ *579 Selby Ave.,* ☎ *612/222–7000.*

$$$ ✕ **W. A. Frost & Co.** This picture-perfect Victorian tavern's straightforward Continental cooking, such as filet mignon with Bordelaise sauce and fusilli with grilled eggplant, is decent but wouldn't stand out if not for this inviting setting. ✉ *374 Selby Ave.,* ☎ *612/224–5715.*

$–$$ ✕ **La Corvina.** The name of this gay-popular hole-in-the-wall means sea bass, so you can be sure the *corvina* inside an enchilada and served with a punchy green tomatillo sauce, black beans, and sweet plantains is worth a visit. The other Mexican and Latin American offerings are also tasty. ✉ *1570 Selby Ave.,* ☎ *612/645–5288. No credit cards.*

$ ✕ **St. Clair Broiler.** With neon flames pulsing above the logo on a sign outside, this retro-trendy home of the charco-burger preserves a slice of St. Paul history. Locals rave about the breakfasts and the sweet offerings from the authentic soda fountain. ✉ *1580 St. Clair Ave.,* ☎ *612/698–7055. No credit cards.*

$ ✕ **White Lily.** Take a break from window-shopping along Grand Avenue with a meal at this Vietnamese restaurant, whose specialties include barbecues, fried fresh bean curd, and sweet-and-sour ground shrimp and pork. ✉ *758 Grand Ave.,* ☎ *612/293–9124.*

Coffeehouse Culture

Café Wyrd. It's almost a bit disappointing that this Uptown favorite of lipstick lesbos isn't as weird as its name might suggest. In a comfy space with a curvaceous espresso bar, tasteful art on the walls, ample seating, and a neoboho mood. ✉ *1600 W. Lake St., Minneapolis,* ☎ *612/827–5710.*

Café Zev. This garagelike space has the cruisy buzz of a gay video bar, without the attitude. Grungers and artsy types favor it, but all drop in periodically for good coffee and baked goods, and perhaps to catch a poetry reading or performance piece. ✉ *1362 LaSalle St.,* ☎ *612/874–8477.*

Cahoots. Gays and lesbians head to this intimate storefront space that has mismatched tables and chairs, potted plants, mags and newspapers, and plenty of reading lamps to illuminate your perusing or cruising. Excellent baked goods and daily coffee drink specials. ✉ *1562 Selby Ave., St. Paul,* ☎ *612/644–6778.*

Laughing Cup. This coffeehouse amid Nicollet's row of ethnic restaurants is busy day and night with Birkenstockers, artists, and other free spirits.

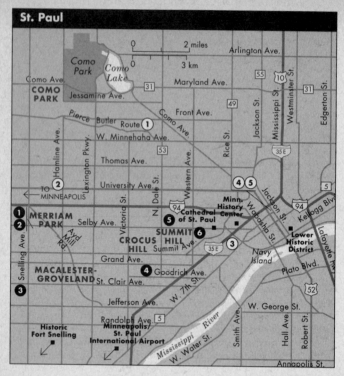

Pizzas, calzones, sandwiches, and salads are among the offerings. ✉ *1819 Nicollet Ave., Minneapolis,* ☎ *612/870–7015.*

Uncommon Grounds. Set inside an elegant house in colorful Uptown, this cozy space is a favorite spot to kick off a first date or laze away a snowy afternoon. In warm weather you can take advantage of the outdoor patio. ✉ *2809 Hennepin Ave., Minneapolis,* ☎ *612/872–4811.*

SCENES

For a couple of highly queer cities, Minneapolis and St. Paul are fairly quiet when it comes to nightlife. The Minneapolis clubs are louder, brasher, sexier, and sleazier—and extremely popular with visitors and guys looking to get laid. Bar owners in St. Paul have made a conscious effort during the past decade to cultivate gay male and lesbian crowds, hoping that casting a wider net would boost revenues. The result has been a friendly, only moderately cruisy, and very laid-back scene.

Minneapolis

PRIME SUSPECTS

Brass Rail. With a blank door and smoked-glass windows, the Brass Rail's exterior is a throwback to the dreary bars of another era. The ambience is dated as well, though the place is fairly upbeat thanks to the chatty patrons and staff and the tavernesque decor. The center of a small dance floor is usually busy with a drag show. A mature crowd prevails, but quite a few younger guys also hang around—perhaps hoping to find some deep pockets to play in. ✉ *422 Hennepin Ave.,* ☎ *612/333–3016. Crowd: mostly male, mostly late 30s to late 50s, drag and karaoke fans, low-key.*

Gay '90s. Many regulars of this high-energy complex are deserting it in the face of an invasion of straight, and in some cases hostile, patrons (and, reportedly, staff). The negative publicity hasn't yet hurt overall attendance; the place is packed most weekends, and those who do come appear to enjoy themselves. ☒ *408 Hennepin Ave.,* ☎ *612/333–7755. Crowd: mixed gay/straight, mixed m/f but most of the women are straight, mostly 20s and 30s, uneasy blend of horny men scoping out the men and women, guppies, tourists, frat boys, jocks, giggling bridal parties (at the strip and drag shows).*

Saloon. This popular and cruisy video bar is tops in Minneapolis on Friday and always fun during the rest of the week. The space is divided into three parts: a large dance floor, a large stand-and-model video bar, and a tavern with a bar, pool table, darts, and some booth seating. ☒ *830 Hennepin Ave.,* ☎ *612/332–0835. Crowd: male, 20s to 40s, somewhat mixed racially, leather some nights, cruisy, beefcakes, guppies.*

NEIGHBORHOOD HAUNTS
Small, mellow **19 Bar** (☒ 19 W. 15th St., ☎ 612/871–5553) is a decent hangout with pool, darts, and a rocking jukebox.

ONE-NIGHTERS
The Warehouse District's **Tropix** (☒ 400 3rd Ave. N, ☎ 212/333–1006) has "Ten Percent" Thursdays that draw gays and lesbians. If you like the tropical bars at Club Med, you'll like this brash dance club.

HANGIN' WITH THE HETS
You can catch local and national acts at **Fine Line Music Café** (☒ 318 1st Ave. N, ☎ 612/338–8100); dance and admire the pretty crowd at **South Beach** (☒ 325 1st Ave., ☎ 612/204–0787); pose with a martini in hand at **The Lounge** (☒ 411 2nd Ave. N, ☎ 612/333–8800); or check out **Cafe Havana** (*see* Eats, *above*). In St. Anthony Main is the jazz and blues club **Sophia** (☒ 65 S.E. Main St., ☎ 612/379–1111).

The fabulous **Bryant Lake Bowl Cabaret Theatre** (☒ 810 W. Lake St., ☎ 612/825–8949) is a not-to-be-missed, "only in Minneapolis" phenomenon, a lesbian, gay, straight, and always chic sports bar with a bowling alley and a theater that presents wildly experimental works. There's also an excellent café with a good wine list and affordable New American cooking. Expect a funky punky crowd and a staff of occasionally snide but usually entertaining aspiring artists, actors, and musicians. Finally: a chance to wear that stained retro bowling shirt you paid $85 for.

St. Paul

PRIME SUSPECTS
Club Metro. What began primarily as a lesbian bar has evolved, on weekends anyway, into the hottest gay nightclub in the Twin Cities. This compound is well northwest of downtown in a nearly desolate warehouse district, and in order to fill the place up the management clearly had to draw as many types of queers as possible (most weekdays a sizable chunk of the club is shut off and the staff reduced). On weekends you'll find a massive dance floor, a patio, and several bars and lounging spaces on the main level. In the basement there's a cruisy, pseudo-leather lounge. Here you can get cozy with a new friend, play pool or air hockey, or just chill out to music videos. Other Club Metro features include GALE (☎ 612/880–3560), a pride shop specializing in clothing and jewelry, and Back in Black (☎ 612/870–2968), which custom-makes leather and fetish gear and outfits. The Sunday tea dances are a lot of fun. ☒ *733 Pierce Butler Rte.,* ☎ *612/489–0002. Crowd: mixed m/f, mostly 20s and 30s, some racial mix, blue and white collar; the lesbian club crowd is mixed with plenty of those fed up with the Minneapolis scene.*

Rumours. It's tough to find a bar anywhere that attracts such a friendly and diverse clientele, and for this reason Rumours stands out as a sort of queer "Cheers" of the Upper Midwest. Walk in, grab a seat, and rather quickly you'll find yourself immersed in conversation. On weekends the pace is a bit faster and folks head out onto the dance floor, but much of the time this is just a mellow lounge. Cool staff. ⊠ *490 N. Robert St.,* ☏ *612/224–0703. Crowd: mixed m/f, all ages, all types, extremely outgoing, low attitude.*

Townhouse. Following a recent and ambitious redesign, this former country-western dance hall has reformatted itself as a theme club, still with excellent two-stepping and line-dancing parties on Thursday and Saturday, but with live piano, cabaret, retro disco, and other themes the rest of the week. In addition to a nice-size dance floor, the club has loads of seating, an inexpensive restaurant serving American chow, and a piano lounge. ⊠ *1415 University Ave.,* ☏ *612/646–7087. Crowd: 50/50 m/f, all ages, very friendly, still country but also a little bit rock 'n' roll.*

NEIGHBORHOOD HAUNTS

Innuendo (⊠ 510 N. Robert St., ☏ 612/224–8996) is a convivial bar next to Rumours. Catch sporting events on TV at **Over The Rainbow** (⊠ 249 W. 7th St., ☏ 612/228–7180), which has good karaoke nights and a somewhat older crowd.

Action

Bathhouses and sex clubs are a no-no in the Twin Cities. Minneapolis does have all-night porn palaces, including **Broadway Books** (⊠ 901 Hennepin Ave., ☏ 612/338–7303) and **Sexworld** (⊠ 241 2nd Ave. N, ☏ 612/672–0556); the latter has buddy booths and a much friendlier staff than the former.

SLEEPS

The region has many very good hotels, ranging from the usual cookie-cutter business properties to some splendid older ones, as well as a few gay-friendly smaller inns.

For price ranges, *see* lodging Chart B at the front of this guide.

Hotels

Minneapolis

$$$$ ☷ **Hyatt Regency Minneapolis.** The top choice among business travelers, the 24-story Hyatt offers some nice weekend deals. It's within walking distance of the Warehouse District. ⊠ *1300 Nicollet Mall, 55403,* ☏ *612/370–1234 or 800/233–1234,* ℻ *612/370–1233. 533 rooms. Restaurant.*

$$$–$$$$ ☷ **Whitney Hotel.** This lavish boutique hotel is ideal for a romantic getaway. Impress your friends by inviting them to meet you in the bold but refined marble lobby, whose highlights include the chandelier and a sweeping staircase. ⊠ *150 Portland Ave., 55401,* ☏ *612/339–9300 or 800/248–1879,* ℻ *612/339–1333. 97 rooms. Restaurant.*

$$$ ☷ **Embassy Suites.** The units at this all-suites atrium property have kitchenettes, VCRs, and highly appealing art deco furnishings. The indoor pool and steam room come in handy during the brutal winters. ⊠ *425 S. 7th St., 55415,* ☏ *612/333–3111 or 800/EMBASSY,* ℻ *612/333–7984. 218 rooms. Restaurant, pool.*

$–$$ ☷ **Best Western Normandy Inn.** Conveniently situated, this chain hotel has a Euro-retro, Normandy-inspired exterior but typical rooms and a well-trained staff. ⊠ *405 S. 8th St., 55404,* ☏ *612/370–1400 or 800/528–1234,* ℻ *612/370–0351. 160 rooms. Restaurant, pool.*

St. Paul

$$$–$$$$ 🏨 **The Saint Paul.** This opulent stone hotel is furnished in the style of the grande dames of yesteryear but has the service and amenities you'd expect of a modern property. The restaurants are superb; the Café serves outstanding bistro fare and meals cost half what they do in the formal dining room. ✉ *350 Market St., 55102,* ☎ *612/292–9292 or 800/292–9292,* FAX *612/228–3810. 254 rooms. Restaurants.*

$ 🏨 **Days Inn.** A mid-rise by the Civic Center, the Days Inn is great if you're looking to save some money but want to be a short drive from St. Paul attractions and nightlife. The bar Over The Rainbow is a short walk away. ✉ *175 W. 7th St., 55102,* ☎ *612/292–8929,* FAX *612/292–1749. 203 rooms. Restaurant.*

Guest Houses and Small Hotels

Minneapolis

$$–$$$ 🏨 **Nicollet Island Inn.** The characterful rooms at this distinctive limestone hotel have reproduction antiques, four-poster beds, French Impressionist prints, and great views of the Mississippi River and downtown. ✉ *Nicollet Island, 95 Merriam St., 55401,* ☎ *612/331–1800 or 800/331–6528,* FAX *612/331–6528. 24 rooms with phone, TV, and private bath. Restaurant. Mostly straight.*

$ 🏨 **Hotel Amsterdam.** This European-style budget property is gay-operated. Created out of a former flophouse, it's still a bit floppy, but the basic rooms are clean. ✉ *828 Hennepin Ave., 55403,* ☎ *612/288–0459 or 800/649–9500. 28 rooms with phone, TV, and shared baths. Restaurant. Mostly mixed gay male/lesbian.*

St. Paul

$–$$ 🏨 **Como Villa.** A quiet and romantic spot for a weekend getaway, this 1870 Victorian has rooms with tasteful antiques. On weekends you can relax over an abundant full breakfast while listening to music from the grand piano. ✉ *1371 W. Nebraska Ave., 55108,* ☎ *612/698–3571. 4 rooms, some with private bath. Full breakfast weekends, Continental on weekdays. Mixed gay/straight.*

THE LITTLE BLACK BOOK

At Your Fingertips

Chrysalis Women's Center (✉ 2650 Nicollet Ave. S, Minneapolis, ☎ 612/871–0118). **City Pages** (☎ 612/375–1015, Web site www.citypages.com). **Gay and Lesbian Community Action Council referral and helpline** (☎ 612/822–8661 or 800/800–0907, e-mail glcacmpls@aol.com). **Greater Minneapolis Convention & Visitors Center** (✉ 4000 Multifoods Tower, 33 S. 6th St., 55402, ☎ 612/348–7000, Web site www.minneapolis.org). **Men's Center** (✉ 3249 Hennepin Ave., Suite 55, Minneapolis, ☎ 612/822–5892; ✉ 986 Forest St., St. Paul, ☎ 612/822–5892). **Metropolitan Transit Commission** (bus system, ☎ 612/349–7000). **Minneapolis Visitor Information Centre** (✉ City Center, Skyway Level, 40 S. 7th St., Suite 230). **Minnesota AIDS Line** (☎ 612/373–2437 or 800/248–2437). **Pride Twin Cities** (☎ 612/362–3680, Web site members.aol.com/mplspride). **Pulse** (☎ 612/824–0000, e-mail pulsetc@aol.com). **District 202 lesbigay youth center** (✉ 1601 Nicollet Ave., Minneapolis, ☎ 612/871–5559). **Quatrefoil Library** (lesbigay library/archive, ✉ 1619 Dayton Ave., St. Paul, ☎ 612/641–0969). **St. Paul Convention and Visitors Bureau** (✉ 102 Norwest Center, 55 E. 5th St., 55101, ☎ 612/297–6985 or 800/627–6101). **Yellow Cab** (☎ 612/222–4433 in Minneapolis, ☎ 612/824–4444 in St. Paul).

Gay Media

Biweekly *Lavender Magazine* (☎ 612/871–2237, Web site www.lavendermagazine.com) gives the scoop on local news, nightlife, and entertainment. *Q Monthly* (☎ 612/375–1015, e-mail adinfo@citypages.com) offers more of the same in a monthly format. *focusPOINT* (☎ 612/288–9008) has weekly coverage of the entire Upper Midwest. The *Minnesota Women's Press* (☎ 612/646–3968) also runs a bookshop and library (✉ 771 Raymond Ave., St. Paul).

BOOKSTORES

A Brother's Touch (✉ 2327 Hennepin Ave., Minneapolis, ☎ 612/377–6279), carries titles for men and women. It's operated by helpful, friendly people. **Amazon Bookstore** (✉ 1612 Harmon Pl., Minneapolis, ☎ 612/338–6560) is an excellent feminist resource. **Rainbow Road** (✉ 109 W. Grant St., ☎ 612/872–8448) stocks gay adult and nonporn movies and magazines, plus pride items, cards, and gifts.

Working Out

In Minneapolis, the **Arena Health Club** (✉ Target Center, 600 1st Ave. N, ☎ 612/673–1200) and **Body Quest** (✉ 245 Aldrich Ave. N, Unit 300, ☎ 612/377–7222) have community followings. St. Paul has no gay-popular gyms, but the **Sweat Shop Health Club** (✉ 167 Snelling, ☎ 612/646–8418) is a good facility.

23 Out in Nashville

IF YOU RATE REGIONS OF THE COUNTRY on the basis of their tolerance of homosexuality, the South, because of its consistently antigay state laws and identification with the religious right, scores low marks. And so it is with trepidation that many gay men and lesbians, especially when traveling as couples, approach a state like Tennessee and a city like Nashville.

To be sure, you'd be wise as a gay couple to conduct yourself differently in Nashville than you might in Key West or West Hollywood. Nashville has no gay ghetto, no street where you're likely to see an unusually high homo presence. If you wish to avoid confrontation, you should, as you would in 98% of America, behave discreetly.

But on the balance, Nashville is quite tolerant. The presence of 16 universities contributes to this general tolerance of sexual, as well as religious and ethnic, diversity. The presence of higher education also keeps a steady flow of twentysomethings passing through town.

AIDS has ravaged every gay community, including Nashville's, and several country-music stars—most notably Garth Brooks and Kathy Mattea—devastated by the loss of friends and crew, responded with fund-raising, as well as consciousness-raising. Country music has hardly "gone gay," but Nashville continues to witness changes.

The emergence of Branson, Missouri, as a major competitor for tourism has fueled Nashville's transformation into a sophisticated and more open-minded city. There now appear to be two distinct camps of country-western entertainment: Nashville appeals to a broader, younger, hipper crowd; Branson pulls in the older, more traditional, and more conservative segment. These two camps overlap, but gays are far more welcome in Nashville than in Branson.

THE LAY OF THE LAND

Downtown

But for the controversial twin-spired **South Central Bell building,** which resembles Batman's pointy-eared logo, little about the downtown skyline stands out. Downtown is set around the courtly Greek Revival **Capitol** (✉ Charlotte Ave., ☎ 615/741–2692), which is perched atop the highest hill in Nashville. Behind here, beyond the north face of the hill, a long, landscaped, **Bicentennial Mall State Park** was constructed in commemoration of the state's 1996 bicentennial. A pretty spot for a stroll, it's filled with fountains, a 200-foot granite map of the state, and several other outdoor exhibits. Nearby is the **Tennessee State Museum** (✉ 505 Deaderick St., ☎ 615/741–2692), which traces the state's history, and the Beaux

Arts–style **Hermitage Suite Hotel** (✉ 231 6th Ave. N, ☎ 615/244–3121), which is where, in 1920, suffragists and antisuffragists from around the country encamped while debating the ratification of the 19th Amendment (which granted women the right to vote). A block over, **5th Avenue** was the site throughout the '60s of civil rights demonstrations, the success of which inspired similar protests throughout the South. Just off 5th, between Union and Church streets, is a restored turn-of-the-century arcade of boutiques and simple eateries.

A few blocks east, toward the Cumberland, is Nashville's old Market Street, now **2nd Avenue,** where a long row of redbrick Victorian warehouses was rescued from neglect in the 1980s and converted into restaurants, music clubs, brew pubs, and specialty shops. **Broadway** between 3rd Avenue and the river has a similar feel, and a few good antiques shops. **First Avenue** is lined on one side with the backs of 2nd Avenue's buildings; across the street is **Riverfront Park,** a long brick promenade with views across the murky Cumberland of the industrial east bank. At the top of the park, just below where Church Street intersects 1st Avenue, is a reproduction of the settlement's first outpost, **Fort Nashborough** (✉ 170 1st Ave. N, ☎ 615/862–8400). The revitalization of this area has been a tremendous success, and though many of the attractions are predictable tourist haunts (the Hard Rock Cafe, Hooters), this is a boisterous, festive neighborhood perfect for wandering on weekend nights.

On 5th Avenue, between Broadway and Commerce Street, stands the **Ryman Auditorium** (✉ 116 5th Ave. N, ☎ 615/254–1445), within whose walls country music transformed Nashville into Music City USA. The ornate Ryman, built in 1892, was the site where the Grand Ole Opry House got its start; an on-site museum chronicles the Ryman's history.

Music Row

Not to be confused with the Opryland section of Nashville, **Music Row** (✉ Demonbreun St. exit off I–40, ☎ 615/256–1639) is the hub of the city's recording industry. The neighborhood is southwest of downtown, where 16th Avenue intersects Demonbreun Street. You can actually tour **Studio B** (✉ 26 Music Square W, ☎ 615/256–1639), where everyone from Elvis to Dolly Parton has recorded. Other attractions here include the **Hank Williams Jr. Museum** (✉ 1524 Demonbreun St., ☎ 615/242–8313), the **Car Collectors Hall of Fame** (✉ 1534 Demonbreun St., ☎ 615/255–6804), and the **Country Music Wax Museum and Mall** (✉ 118 16th Ave. S, ☎ 615/256–2490). The **Country Music Hall of Fame and Museum** (✉ 4 Music Sq. E, ☎ 615/256–1639) abounds with photos, costumes, instruments, and memorabilia.

West End Avenue and Belle Meade

Beyond Music Row, if you follow Broadway southwest until it turns into **West End Avenue,** you'll pass several of the city's schools and medical facilities, including **Vanderbilt University,** and discover many of the city's best (and gay-friendliest) restaurants and shops. Also along West End is the city's most memorable site, the **Parthenon** (✉ West End and 25 Aves., ☎ 615/862–8431), a detailed replica of the one that sits above Athens. Built for the city's 1897 centennial, the Parthenon is in a landscaped park and houses a small collection of American paintings and *Athena Parthenos,* a 42-foot-tall statue.

West End eventually leads into ritzy **Belle Meade,** where many of Nashville's celebrities and politicians reside. There are a couple of mansion-museums in this area, including the Greek Revival **Belle Meade Plantation** (✉ 5025 Harding Rd., ☎ 615/356–0501), once the site of a 5,300-acre Thoroughbred breeding farm, and **Cheekwood** (✉ 1200 Forrest Park Dr., ☎ 615/356–

8000), a 1925 Georgian-style house on whose grounds you'll find the **Tennessee Botanical Gardens & Museum.**

Opryland USA

This 120-acre **theme park** (✉ 2808 Opryland Dr., via Briley Pkwy., ☎ 615/889–6611) is Nashville's most-visited attraction, an amusement park and country-music entertainment compound, with 70 live shows and 30 rides. It's twice the size of Disneyland and nearly as popular. Though it employs many gays and lesbians, Opryland is not a setting where homosexuals will feel comfortable to let loose and be themselves. Admission to the park is $25 per person. On the other hand, touring the grounds of America's most heavily booked hotel, the **Opryland Hotel** (✉ 2800 Opryland Dr., ☎ 615/889–1000), is free and entertaining. Though a bit hokey and overwrought, the Opryland Hotel is no less spectacular for it. The **Grand Ole Opry** (✉ 2804 Opryland Dr., ☎ 615/889–6611), still the hottest ticket in town, has been infused in recent years with a slick roster of today's stars, including Vince Gill, Marty Stuart, Travis Tritt, Alison Krauss, Hal Ketchum, Patty Loveless, and many others.

Metro Nashville

Attractions throughout greater Nashville range from the historic to the outlandishly commercial. Among the former, Andrew Jackson's homestead, **The Hermitage** (✉ 4580 Rachel's La., Hermitage, ☎ 615/889–2941), is the most impressive, with its 28,000-square-foot museum, the original mansion, and many gardens. Among the latter, Johnny Cash's shrine to country music, the **House of Cash** (✉ 700 Johnny Cash Pkwy., Hendersonville, ☎ 615/889–2941), contains many of his personal mementos.

GETTING AROUND

Nashville's downtown is walkable, but only a fraction of the city's notable restaurants, bars, and sights are in this section. Buses are impractical and taxis are worthwhile only in a pinch; it's best to use a car. Garages are cheap and plentiful downtown, and parking is easy elsewhere.

EATS

Of smaller inland southern cities, Nashville has the best culinary reputation. Barbecue is popular throughout the South, and Nashville is no exception, but the residents of no southern city east of Texas are as fond of steak as Nashvillians. The two best local steak-house chains are **Longhorn Steaks** (✉ 110 Lyle Ave., ☎ 615/329–9195, plus four other locations; $$–$$$) and **Outback Steakhouse** (✉ 3212 West End Ave., ☎ 615/385–3440, plus three other locations; $$–$$$). **World's End** (*see* Scenes, *below*) is an excellent queer option for tasty casual American food.

For price ranges, *see* dining Chart B at the front of this guide.

$$$$ ✕ **Arthur's in Union Station.** This supremely elegant French restaurant in the meticulously restored Union Station is replete with polished silver, fine china, and formal linens. The staff verbally presents the seven-course menu, which might include pinwheels of fillet of salmon filled with mousse of lobster. ✉ *1001 Broadway,* ☎ *615/255–1494.*

$$$$ ✕ **Mario's.** The place to go if your goal is to dine among country-music glitterati and hotshot politicos, Mario's serves northern Italian food— veal medallions with roasted peppers and fontina cheese, and duck marsala. ✉ *2005 Broadway,* ☎ *615/327–3232.*

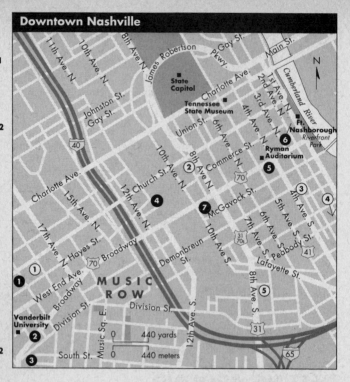

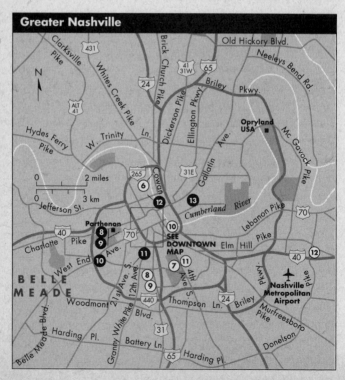

$$$–$$$$ ✕ **Mad Platter.** This is the city's most gay-identified restaurant with serious food, set in a quiet historic neighborhood abutting the Capitol mall. It's a quirky place; one wall of the dining room is lined with shelves of old books. The New Southern cuisine is anything but quaint, however, with bold selections like grilled molasses-and-black-pepper-marinated duck breast. ✉ *1239 6th Ave.,* ☎ *615/242–2563.*

$$$–$$$$ ✕ **Mère Bulles.** Part of 2nd Avenue's big comeback, Mère Bulles is a place to meet for wine, listen to jazz, and dine on fine Continental fare amid clear river views. Specialties include the asparagus salad and shrimp and scallops in a walnut pesto. The old-fashioned brass-and-mahogany bar is a favorite gathering spot. ✉ *152 2nd Ave. N,* ☎ *615/256–1946.*

$$$ ✕ **Merchants.** A $3 million restoration of this 1892 brick building, a former hotel, has given Nashville one of its most cosmopolitan restaurants. Dishes such as coconut chicken with mango guacamole and Louisiana skillet shrimp with linguine, garlic, and seared peppers are standouts on the New American menu. ✉ *401 Broadway,* ☎ *615/254–1892.*

$$–$$$ ✕ **Bound'ry.** Part of a strip of trendy collegiate hangouts off West End Avenue, the Bound'ry is a bright and airy restaurant with French doors opening onto the street. Exotic tapas like lobster-curry flapjacks are served; entrées include paella and vegetarian burritos. ✉ *911 20th Ave. S,* ☎ *615/321–3043.*

$$ ✕ **Way Out West.** Don't be put off by the setting of this popular regional Mexican and southwestern eatery; it's on the ground floor of a dull apartment complex, way west of downtown. Inside is a dining room with festive paintings and decorative arts. Innovative and quite affordable offerings include *pozole verde* (Mexican pork and hominy stew with a broth of toasted pumpkin seeds and tomatillos) and pecan catfish with sweet potatoes and greens. ✉ *3415 West End Ave.,* ☎ *615/298–5562.*

$–$$ ✕ **12th and Porter.** There are a few hip music clubs that double as restaurants around this industrial intersection just west of downtown—a miniature version of Atlanta's Little Five Points. Some of the best food and music are found in the all-black, minimalist interior of this turquoise-and-salmon brick building. Good designer pizzas and pastas. ✉ *114 12th Ave. N,* ☎ *615/254–7236.*

$ ✕ **Cafe Elliston.** On sunny days you're sure to see a mix of family and friends of family nibbling on casual American fare on the spacious front porch of this funky old house around the corner from the Parthenon. It's also a popular spot for ice cream, baked goods, and coffees. ✉ *210 Louise Ave.,* ☎ *615/329–2871.*

$ ✕ **Dancing Bear.** This sunny café next to the lesbigay bookstore Outloud! prepares sandwiches, salads, and pasta dishes. A great option for lunch. ✉ *1805 Church St.,* ☎ *615/963–9900.*

$ ✕ **Mosko's.** This strangely alluring neighborhood deli close to the universities sells magazines, out-of-town newspapers, cigars, cards, mugs, and other oddities. The sandwiches are as much fun to order as to eat: try the "I'll Have What She's Having," with roast beef, bacon, cheddar, and vegetables. Very gay-friendly. ✉ *2204 Elliston Pl.,* ☎ *615/327–2658.*

Coffeehouse Culture

✕ **Bongo Java.** In this turn-of-the-century house, local artists display their art not only on the walls but on the tabletops. Pastries and healthful dishes complement the wide array of coffees. This is a great place to meet locals. Bongo Java earned international infamy as the home of the "nun bun," a cinnamon roll that bears an amazing likeness to Mother Teresa—the Vatican was not amused. ✉ *2002 Belmont Blvd.,* ☎ *615/385–5282.*

✕ **Radio Cafe.** In up-and-coming Edgewood, a historic middle-class residential neighborhood east of downtown, this quirky café fashioned out of an old pharmacy doles out hearty home-style breakfasts and lunches,

as well as the full gamut of designer coffees. There's a big patio, magazines to thumb through, and various antiques and goodies (including a
few pride items) for sale. At night drop by for live blues, country, jazz,
and rock. ⊠ *1313 Woodland St.,* ☎ *615/262–1766.*

SCENES

For a small city, Nashville has a varied and lively gay nightlife that includes two decent lesbian bars, two popular gay discos, and a terrific restau-
rant-cruise bar in the heart of downtown. South of downtown are a slew
of neighborhood hangouts—most of them are pretty rough and rowdy,
but outsiders are always welcome.

Prime Suspects

Chez Collette. Come if only to examine the extensive collection of bras hanging from the several chandeliers. Chez Collette is a trip—sort of a dykey
French burlesque. Proprietress Collette, who still retains her thick native
French accent, greets all and sometimes belts out a tune or two on karaoke
night. Photos of celebs and bar regulars coat the walls, and one section
of this brightly decorated and lighted lounge is furnished with long wooden
tables and chairs, a family-style restaurant. ⊠ *300 Hermitage Ave.,* ☎ *615/
256–9134. Crowd: female, stylish, loud, festive, diverse in age.*

Chute Complex. The Chute offers a little of everything—dancing, a patio,
a sports bar, a piano bar, a restaurant. Before Connection opened this
was the major club in Nashville for many years. The main room has a
bar and a midsize dance floor, off of which are a sports bar and patio.
The Silver Stirrup, a clubby-looking piano bar churns out nondescript
traditional American dishes. There's karaoke and drag some nights. ⊠
2535 Franklin Rd., ☎ *615/297–4571. Crowd: 60/40 m/f, mostly 30s to
50s, friendly, more blue collar than at the Connection.*

Connection. Few would guess that the largest gay club in America—at 40,000
square feet—would be in Nashville, but here it is, a few miles northeast
of town. The parking lot looks as if it could accommodate about 1,000
cars; inside are five bars, a restaurant, a show room with well-known female impersonators, and the best-looking bar hands in Nashville. What's
more, the club is intelligently laid out and well decorated. No matter what
your taste in music, in this club you can always cut loose: two-stepping
on the smaller dance floor in the lounge, and high-energy dancing in the
warehouse-style arena. ⊠ *901 Cowan St.,* ☎ *615/742–1166. Crowd: 75/
25 m/f, diverse, but tending to be under 35.*

The Gaslight. Attached to the historic Savage House Inn, the Gaslight exudes French Quarter charm with its ornate chandeliers, gilt-frame mirrors, and overstuffed armchairs. It's a great space, completely absent of
attitude and contemporary atmosphere. Drag shows are occasionally
presented on a stage up front, and live piano music is featured many nights.
⊠ *167½ 8th Ave. N,* ☎ *615/254–1278. Crowd: 80/20 m/f, mostly mid-
30s and up, local crowd, down-to-earth, some couples.*

Illusions. Nashville's newest gay club, out by the airport, has quickly become a big hit. There's a front bar with country music (plans are underway to add a dance floor), a show lounge with drag on weekends, and
a separate private club ($5 cover for nonmembers), the Men's Room, which
is cruisy and touchy-feely in a tough kind of way. ⊠ *555½ Donelson Pike,*
☎ *615/871–0500. Crowd: 80/20 m/f, (except for the Men's Room), all
ages, fairly butch, wild and diverse.*

World's End. Though it's the closest thing Nashville has to an after-work,
stand-and-model video bar, the World's End is not exactly any of these
things—it just happens to attract that crowd with a pub-style American
menu (burgers, grilled chicken, omelets, pizzas); two bars and a long room
with pool tables and lounge chairs; a large patio; and great alternative

rock, grunge, and dance music. The food is quite good, but many come simply to toss back a few drinks after work, shoot the breeze, and shed the day's stresses. A good place to go before hitting the discos. ✉ *1713 Church St.*, ☎ *615/329–3480. Crowd: mostly gay, mixed m/f, young, guppies mixing with college students, low-key.*

Your Way Cafe. Though small, this is the city's main lesbian dance bar, just south of downtown. It's always jumping around happy hour, and lots of women come here before heading out to dance elsewhere. The decor could best be described as contemporary American roadhouse, with plenty of tables and chairs and a pool table. Check the bar rags for live music performances—they usually happen three or four times monthly. ✉ *515 2nd Ave. S*, ☎ *615/256–9682. Crowd: 75/25 f/m, mixed ages, working class, neighborhoody, a few cowboy hats, some baseball caps, no attitude.*

Neighborhood Haunts

Downtown, **Victoria Victoria's** (✉ 617 7th Ave. S, ☎ 615/244–7256) moved into new digs in 1997 after a fire destroyed its original location; it draws a pretty rough bunch, as does **The Jungle** (✉ 306 4th Ave. S, ☎ 615/256–9411). **Blu's Crazy Cowboy II** (✉ 2311 Franklin Rd., ☎ 615/ 269–5318) gets mostly, as the name suggests, crazy cowboys into its long, dark bar packed with video games and neon signs. **Ynonah's Station Saloon** (✉ 1700 4th Ave. S, ☎ 615/251–0980) bills itself as a sports bar but draws a rowdy crowd (lots of pickup trucks in the lot); there's a nice big patio outside. Near Ynonah's is **TC's Triangle** (✉ 1401 4th Ave. S, ☎ 615/242–8131) which draws a local crowd.

SLEEPS

Nashville's selection of hotels is typical of other small business cities: Only the Opryland Hotel stands out. All of the major chains are represented and none are any more gay-popular than any other. Hotels are generally in three areas: downtown, which puts you within walking distance of several good restaurants and shopping; the Opryland area; and West End Avenue, which puts you near Music Row, Vanderbilt, and Belle Meade.

For price ranges, *see* lodging Chart B at the front of this guide.

Hotels

$$$–$$$$ 🏨 **Loew's Vanderbilt Plaza Hotel.** Slightly removed from downtown, this sleek, luxurious property has dark cherry furniture, a slick white lobby, and first-rate service. This is the top business hotel in the city. ✉ *2100 West End Ave., 37203*, ☎ *615/320–1700 or 800/336–3335*, ℻ *615/320– 5019. 338 rooms. Restaurants.*

$$$–$$$$ 🏨 **Renaissance Nashville Hotel.** Convenient to historic Second Avenue, the Country Music Hall of Fame, and the river taxis to Opryland, this 25-story property has high-end reproduction antiques and great views, but is attached to a convention center and can get chaotic at times. ✉ *611 Commerce St., 37202*, ☎ *615/255–8400 or 800/HOTELS-1*, ℻ *615/ 255–8163. 673 rooms. Restaurant, pool, health club.*

$$$ 🏨 **Westin Hermitage.** One of the better deals downtown is this beautifully renovated, all-suites hotel with elegant period reproductions; it's just steps from the capitol. The New American restaurant is one of the hottest in town. ✉ *231 6th Ave. N, 37219*, ☎ *615/244–3121 or 800/251–1908*, ℻ *615/254–6909. 120 rooms. Restaurant.*

$$–$$$ 🏨 **Union Station Hotel.** The turn-of-the-century railroad terminal is full of character. The lobby contains the station's original clock and furnishings, and the restaurant, Arthur's, is one of the best in the city. ✉ *1001 Broadway, 37203*, ☎ *615/726–1001 or 800/331–2123*, ℻ *615/248–3554. 136 rooms. Restaurant.*

$–$$ ☷ **Ramada Inn.** Just across the street from Opryland, the national chain offers perfectly gracious rooms at a good value. ⊠ *2401 Music Valley Dr., 37214,* ☎ *615/889–0800 or 800/228–2828,* FAX *615/883–1230. 307 rooms. Restaurant, pool.*

$–$$ ☷ **Hampton Inn Vanderbilt.** Another option on West End Avenue is this bright, contemporary, six-story motel with unusually large rooms for such low rates. ⊠ *1919 West End Ave., 37203,* ☎ *615/329–1144 or 800/426–7866,* FAX *615/320–7112. 171 rooms.*

Guest Houses and Small Hotels

$–$$ ☷ **Savage House Inn.** Ragged but comfortable, this inn is the only Victorian town house still standing downtown. With its eclectic smattering of antiques and bric-a-brac, it still feels a bit like the rooming house it was during the mid-1800s. This is a perfectly suitable budget choice, but rooms and baths are slightly threadbare. ⊠ *165 8th Ave. N, 37203,* ☎ *615/254–1277. 9 rooms with TV, some with private bath. Full breakfast. Mixed gay/straight.*

THE LITTLE BLACK BOOK

At Your Fingertips

AIDS Hotline (☎ 800/845–4266). **Gay and Lesbian Community Center and Switchboard** (⊠ 703 Berry Rd., ☎ 615/297–0008). **Allied Cab** (☎ 615/244–7433). **Metropolitan Transit Authority** (☎ 615/862–5950). **Nashville Convention and Visitors Bureau** (⊠ 161 4th Ave. N, 37219, ☎ 615/259–4700). *Nashville Scene* (☎ 615/244–7989, Web site www.nashville.com). *Nashville Women's Alliance* (☎ 615/297–0008). **Positive Voice** (gay health resource, ☎ 615/259–4866, ext. 128).

Gay Media

Nashville has a tiny gay and lesbian newspaper, *Xenogeny* (☎ 615/832–9701, e-mail xenogenyx@aol.com), which comes out weekly. There's also a statewide newsweekly, *Query* (☎ 615/259–4135, e-mail querynews@aol.com), which is based in Nashville.

BOOKSTORES

Outloud! (⊠ 1805-C Church St., ☎ 615/340–0034) is a great little store with books, cards, CDs, and many pride items; a couple of gay restaurants are within walking distance. The three-story **Davis-Kidd Booksellers** (⊠ Grace's Plaza, 4007 Hillsboro Rd., Green Hills, ☎ 615/385–2645) has a good selection of gay and lesbian titles.

Working Out

No gym is a major gay scene, but you'll feel comfortable working out at the huge **Centennial Sportsplex** (⊠ 222 25th Ave. N, ☎ 615/862–8480).

24 Out in New Orleans

IMAGINE SIFTING THROUGH YOUR HOUSE in search of every dust-covered bottle of cleaning agent, paint, grease, lubricant, cooking oil, and flavor enhancer. Now imagine tossing into a bowl a tablespoon of every solution you discovered. In creating New Orleans, the Grand Architect of our Universe conducted just such an experiment. And yet somehow, though its infrastructure decays as though consumed by an invisible toxic sludge, New Orleans is the most magical city in North America, if not the world.

The "Crescent City," the "Big Easy," the "northernmost coast of Central America"—New Orleans is forever nicknamed, forever picked on, and forever adored and abhorred by natives and tourists. For nearly three centuries, immigrants—over the years French, Spanish, African, Caribbean, Irish, Choctaw Indian, Italian, Slavic, Acadian, and Anglo—have mixed and settled and boiled and bubbled here. The experiment has been conducted not in a land with plenty of elbow room and distinct seasons to steady tempers. No, New Orleans is a patch of swamp fringed on one side by a lake and on the other by a mighty river. The climate is hot and sultry most of the year—the humidity level rarely drops below 60%, and even in the dead of winter, temperatures often rise into the mid-60s.

The renowned capacity of New Orleanians for revelry is most apparent during Carnival, the pre-Lenten festival that reaches fever pitch on Mardi Gras (Fat Tuesday), the day before Ash Wednesday. Though parties and balls commence on January 6 (Twelfth Night) and continue through the big day, the festivities really get hopping on the two weekends before Ash Wednesday. It's an official holiday, and everybody but the police, who try desperately to preserve order, comes out to celebrate. (If you're planning ahead: In 1999 Ash Wednesday is on February 16; in 2000, it's March 7.)

New Orleans has long been a city of sin. And because homosexuals are traditionally less persecuted in such environs, the city has collectively accepted gays for as long as just about anyplace in America. Countless queer writers and artists have called the Big Easy home during the past century (most notably Tennessee Williams and Truman Capote), and Mardi Gras has long been perceived as a highly gay event.

In many American cities, the gay community has been accepted by the straight community first as a political force—as men and women fighting for their rights—then later as a social force. In New Orleans, gay men were first accepted—if not celebrated—as a social force, as flamboyant decorations at the city's many wild parties. The gay lifestyle was accepted as another outlandish aspect of life in New Orleans—particularly during Carnival.

Through the '80s, as the number of gay krewes (secret societies that hold parties and processions during Mardi Gras) marching in the parades decreased, owing partly to the death of so many gay men to AIDS, New Orleanians slowly began to think of their gay fellow citizens as real people living real lives. Gays and lesbians began wielding more political clout and showing more interest in activism. In 1992 an ordinance was passed protecting persons from discrimination on the basis of gender, race, ethnicity, religion, or sexual orientation—a remarkable piece of legislation in a part of the country not known for its progressive views.

For tourists, New Orleans remains that same gay playground it was 20 years ago. The bar scene has changed relatively little—the block of Bourbon Street between St. Ann and Dumaine continues to be one of the wildest queer hangouts in America. Gays and lesbians will always be among the most loyal defenders of the city's unofficial motto: *Laissez les bons temps rouler* (Let the good times roll).

THE LAY OF THE LAND

The layout of New Orleans is tricky for newcomers. Locals don't use such directional cues as "east," "west," "south," and "north," so once you finish reading this, put away your compass. The city is sandwiched between Lake Pontchartrain (whose shore runs east–west, forming the city's northern boundary) and the murky Mississippi River (whose shore curves around the city—hence the nickname, the "Crescent City"—but for all practical purposes forms the city's southern boundary).

Canal Street bisects the city, heading northwest from the river to Metarie Road, then turning and traveling due north to the lake. Anything below Metarie Road and to the left of Canal Street is considered Uptown. Uptown streets are, paradoxically, named South. Once they bisect Canal Street, they're considered Downtown and named North. The region just downriver from Canal, on the river side, is the French Quarter. The next two neighborhoods in that direction are Faubourg Marigny and Bywater.

Canal Street heading Uptown passes the Central Business District, the up-and-coming Warehouse District, and eventually the Garden District, the interesting part of Magazine Street, and finally the campuses of Tulane and Loyola universities.

French Quarter

Some of the nation's finest examples of late-18th-century and 19th-century residential architecture line the streets of the **French Quarter.** Yet to the surprise of many first-time visitors, they are neither cute nor sparkling. New Orleans is not an amusement park but an economically unstable, working city that looks a bit like the capital of some Caribbean island. Hopefully, even as the city begins to prosper, the French Quarter will remain as engagingly unkempt and scruffy as it has been for centuries.

New Orleans may be the only major city in America whose primary entertainment district is equally frequented by gays and straights, locals and tourists. Virtually every restaurant in the French Quarter (a.k.a. Vieux Carré, which residents pronounce voo-*cair*-eeh) is gay-popular, as is every hotel and bar or music venue. St. Ann Street acts as something of a dividing line between the predominantly straight *lower* French Quarter and the gay *upper* one. (New Orleanians, ever the contrarians, have named the upriver half of the French Quarter the "lower" one, and vice versa.) Particularly with regard to **Bourbon Street,** just about every establishment between Canal and St. Ann overflows with gaudy signage, noise, and the usual tourists, frat boys, sorority girls, and more than a few "Bubbas" from points intolerant. Once you cross St. Ann Street, however, you'll encounter two of the city's three most popular gay clubs, Oz and the Bourbon Pub; a block later you'll discover the third one, Café Lafitte.

Decatur Street is a better walking thoroughfare than Bourbon; it's less frenetic and more diverse, still touristy, but home to good, cheap eateries and quirky shops. Off Decatur is the entrance to **Jackson Square,** the historic center of the French Quarter. Behind the square is the stunning late-18th-century **St. Louis Cathedral.** William Faulkner once resided at **624 Pirate's Alley,** which is one of two alleys (Père Antoine is the other) that cut beside the cathedral between Chartres and Royal streets. At 632 St. Peter Street, is the house (now private) in which Tennessee Williams lived when he penned *A Streetcar Named Desire.*

Many antiques shops and galleries can be found along **Chartres** and **Royal** streets, as can the wonderful open-air **French Market.** Historic house museums in the area include the **Beauregard-Keyes House** (✉ 1113 Chartres St., ☎ 504/523–7257), the **1850s House** (✉ 523 St. Ann St., at Jackson Sq., ☎ 504/568–6968), and the **Gallier House** (✉ 1132 Royal St., ☎ 504/523–6722). Across from the entrance to Jackson Square are steps leading to the Mississippi River and **Woldenberg Riverfront Park,** which is a relaxing place to explore day or night.

Faubourg Marigny

The neighborhood just downriver from the Quarter—across tree-shaded Esplanade Avenue—is **Faubourg Marigny,** which, because of its high concentration of gays and lesbians, is often dubbed "Fagburg" Marigny. Some of the French-colonial buildings here have been restored. Nearer the Quarter, from about Elysian Fields—south of Burgundy and north of Chartres—more rainbow flags fly than anywhere else in the city. The next neighborhood downriver, **Bywater,** is being swallowed by a new wave of settlers, many of them gay, salvaging more historic homes.

The Central Business District

Modern New Orleans falls within the **Central Business District (CBD).** There are some prime examples of early 20th-century commercial architecture in and around where Perdido Street intersects with Loyola Avenue, but this district looks like any other city's downtown and offers little to the visitor. Toward the river, along Julia Street, is the **Warehouse District,** a formerly industrial section that has become the center of an avant-garde arts scene.

Uptown

From Canal Street, you can take the streetcar along **St. Charles Avenue** for several miles clear out to Carrollton Avenue, where the river once again bends in a northerly direction before leaving the city for good. The tour along here takes in house museums, churches, and the exteriors of beautiful private homes; landmark establishments like the **Commander's Palace restaurant** (*see* Eats, *below*), and the **Pontchartrain Hotel** (✉ 2031 St. Charles Ave., ☎ 504/524–0581); **Audubon Park and Zoo** (✉ 6500 Magazine St., ☎ 504/861–2537); **Loyola** and **Tulane universities;** and the courtly **Garden District.** To see the homes and gardens that give the Garden District its name and allure, alight at the Washington Avenue stop and walk a block down Washington to Prytania Street. Follow Prytania back toward the Quarter all the way to First Street (about five blocks).

Roughly parallel to and about seven blocks closer to the river than St. Charles Avenue is **Magazine Street,** which from about Felicity Street heading upriver to Audubon Park is an outstanding antiques and art-gallery row.

GETTING AROUND

New Orleans is highly walkable, but certain parts are unsafe. As is the case in most big cities, it's necessary to follow a few common-sense rules.

The Quarter itself, especially up around Rampart Street, can be dicey, so it's best to travel in groups (especially at night); avoid any street or situation that arouses a sense of uneasiness.

Roads in these parts are often under construction (or in need of it) and can be confusing to navigate. Walk, take taxis, or ride the streetcar when you can. Once you're in the Quarter or Faubourg Marigny, you can get to most of the important sights on foot. The bus system isn't particularly helpful to tourists, but the historic **St. Charles Avenue Streetcar** heads as far Uptown as you'll likely need to go (from the Quarter, pick it up at the corner of St. Charles Avenue and Canal Street; fare $1.25). Cabs can be a nuisance; although taxis are metered, cabbies will try to trick you, leave you short of your destination, or, on a whim, refuse to take you certain places. Get good directions ahead of time, and make your wishes clear to your cab driver.

EATS

You can count on a few things at most every New Orleans eatery: fresh ingredients, easygoing (i.e., slow) but congenial service, stellar seafood, and outstanding coffee (always chicory-laced) and desserts. That every dish is hot and spicy is something of a myth. Towering *muffuletta* sandwiches (Italian bread with cold cuts, ham, mozzarella, and green olives) are never incendiary. Other food is consistently well seasoned, but only a few traditionally hot dishes (gumbo, jambalaya, étouffée, blackened tuna) need be avoided if fire is your enemy.

There is some crossover between the two, but Cajun and Creole food are two different breeds. Few places actually draw on legitimate Cajun recipes. K-Paul's, with its blackened fish and meats, fried crawfish tails, and sweet potato–pecan pie is the most famous purveyor, but true Cajuns would never serve their families such "fancy" dishes.

The roots of Cajun cuisine are in the Acadian-settled areas of Louisiana, but Creole cooking evolved throughout the Deep South, the Carolinas Low Country, and the Caribbean, influenced by French, Spanish, African, and Native American traditions. Those New Orleans restaurants you've been hearing about for decades (Antoine's, Galatoire's) specialize chiefly in Creole techniques, not Cajun ones. With Creole cooking, expect cream and butter sauces and a menu that's equal parts tame (souffléed potatoes, trout meunière, lamb in béarnaise sauce) and exotic (spicy andouille sausage, saffron-infused bouillabaisse, smoked soft-shell crab).

New Orleans has a reputation for great sandwiches, everything from oyster and shrimp po'boys to thick deli sandwiches to classic muffulettas. In the Quarter, try **Café Maspero** (✉ 601 Decatur St., ☎ 504/523–6250) for gargantuan chili burgers, turkey sandwiches, and the like; **Johnny's Po'boys** (✉ 511 St. Louis St., ☎ 504/524–8129) for outstanding po'boys made on the softest French bread and "dressed" with pickles, tomatoes, and lettuce; or **Central Grocery** (✉ 923 Decatur St., ☎ 504/523–1620) for foot-in-diameter muffulettas.

For price ranges, *see* dining Chart A at the front of this guide.

The French Quarter

$$$$ ✗ **Antoine's.** Oysters Rockefeller was invented here in the 1880s, as was, many argue, New Orleans's marriage of fine French and regional Creole cuisine. Antoine's, set in a former Quarter rooming house, is the longest-running show in town, having opened more than 150 years ago. Pricey, formal, and a bit overrated, it's still a must-do for many. ✉ *713 St. Louis St.,* ☎ *504/581–4422.*

In case you want to be welcomed there.

We're here to see that you're always welcomed at establishments everywhere. That's why millions of people carry the American Express® Card – for peace of mind, confidence, and security, around the world or just around the corner.

do more

In case you're running low.

We're here to help with more than 118,000 Express Cash
locations around the world. In order to enroll, just call
American Express before you start your vacation.

do more

AMERICAN
EXPRESS

**Express
Cash**

And just in case.

We're here with American Express® Travelers Cheques
and Cheques *for Two*® They're the safest way to carry
money on your vacation and the surest way to get a
refund, practically anywhere, anytime.
Another way we help you...

do more®

AMERICAN
EXPRESS

Travelers
Cheques

French Quarter and Faubourg Marigny

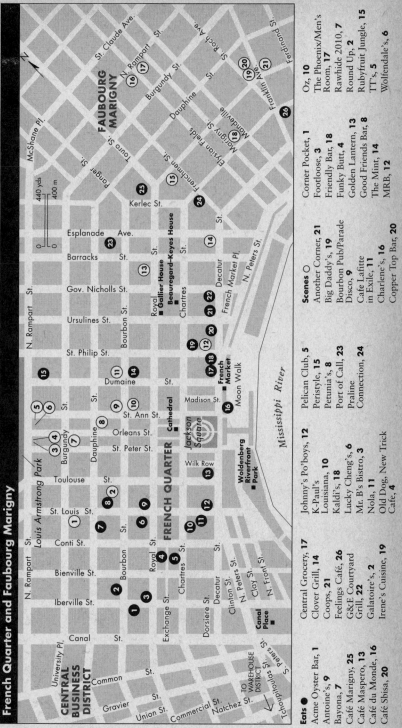

Eats ●

Acme Oyster Bar, 1
Antoine's, 9
Bayona, 7
Café Marigny, 25
Café Maspero, 13
Café du Monde, 16
Café Sbisa, 20
Central Grocery, 17
Clover Grill, 14
Coops, 21
Feelings Café, 26
G&E Courtyard Grill, 22
Galatoire's, 2
Irene's Cuisine, 19
Johnny's Po'boys, 12
K-Paul's
Louisiana, 10
Kaldi's, 18
Lucky Cheng's, 6
Mr. B's Bistro, 3
Nola, 11
Old Dog, New Trick Cafe, 4
Pelican Club, 5
Peristyle, 15
Petunia's, 8
Port of Call, 23
Praline Connection, 24

Scenes ○

Another Corner, 21
Big Daddy's, 19
Bourbon Pub/Parade Disco, 9
Cafe Lafitte in Exile, 11
Charlene's, 16
Copper Top Bar, 20
Corner Pocket, 1
Footloose, 3
Friendly Bar, 18
Funky Butt, 4
Golden Lantern, 13
Good Friends Bar, 8
The Mint, 14
MRB, 12
Oz, 10
The Phoenix/Men's Room, 17
Rawhide 2010, 7
Round Up, 2
Rubyfruit Jungle, 15
TT's, 5
Wolfendale's, 6

New Orleans

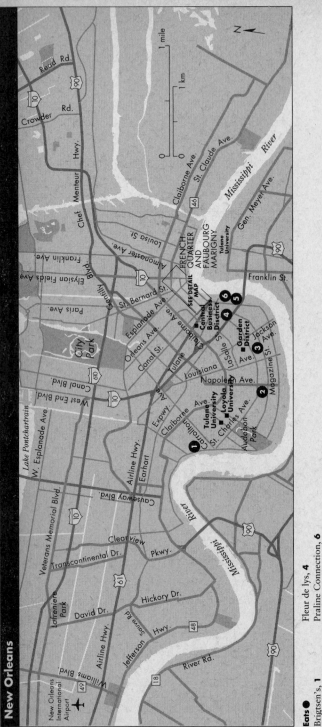

$$$$ ✕ **Peristyle.** In a yellow building near the gate to Louis Armstrong Park—a part of the Quarter that's well off the beaten path—Peristyle is a huge hit with foodies. New American fare like seared grouper medallions with truffle-thyme butter, Yukon gold potatoes, and crispy bacon are consistently remarkable. ⊠ *1041 Dumaine St.,* ☏ *504/593–9535.*

$$$–$$$$ ✕ **Bayona.** Not exactly what you'd expect in the Quarter, Bayona's cuisine is eccentric, almost overwrought, but delectable. Salmon in white wine paired with sauerkraut is a classic that's done to perfection. The building is a quaint, late-1800s Creole cottage, but the dining room is contemporary and refined, with dried flowers and neatly matted photographs. ⊠ *430 Dauphine St.,* ☏ *504/525–4455.*

$$$–$$$$ ✕ **G&E Courtyard Grill.** This Decatur Street favorite seems more San Francisco than New Orleans, with brass, exposed brick, and varnished wood. But local influences creep into California-French–inspired cuisine: The crisp Caesar salad has flash-fried oysters, and the grilled Louisiana shrimp are almond-pepper encrusted. Rotisserie-roasted poussin with browned garlic, balsamic vinegar, fresh mint, pumpkin polenta, and organic arugula is another winner. ⊠ *1113 Decatur St.,* ☏ *504/528–9376.*

$$$–$$$$ ✕ **Galatoire's.** Nearing its first century of operation and showing no signs of slowing down—the place is packed on weekends—chic Galatoire's is done in polished brass, bentwood chairs, and crisp white napery. The long French-Creole menu incorporates traditional dishes like Creole bouillabaisse and fried oysters and bacon in a pastry shell. ⊠ *209 Bourbon St.,* ☏ *504/525–2021.*

$$$–$$$$ ✕ **K-Paul's Louisiana Kitchen.** While we wait for some gay-savvy entrepreneur to open "Roux-Paul's" Louisiana Kitchen, many of us shall continue to stand in long, long lines for a chance to dine at this hallowed dining room presided over by the portly celebrity chef Paul Prudhomme. This is Cajun fare—blackened everything-under-the-sun, spicy gumbos, fried crawfish tails. ⊠ *416 Chartres St.,* ☏ *504/524–7394.*

$$$–$$$$ ✕ **Nola.** Television Food Network celebrity chef Emeril Lagasse serves up his rich, lusty fare in slick surroundings at this Quarter favorite. Try roasted lamb shank in herb-enriched broth with housemade noodles, summer veggies, and Creole tomatoes stuffed with goat cheese. ⊠ *534 St. Louis St.,* ☏ *504/522–6652.*

$$$ ✕ **Café Sbisa.** Tuscan-Provence meets Cajun-Creole on funky Decatur Street, a few blocks down from the crowds in Jackson Square. Among the seafood options are courtbouillon (fresh fish, shrimp, and blue crab meat in a spicy Creole sauce) and trout Eugene (sautéed with shrimp, oysters, sea scallops, and crawfish tails in a light cream sauce). In good weather sit in the patio out back. ⊠ *1011 Decatur St.,* ☏ *504/522–5565.*

$$$ ✕ **Pelican Club.** A good place to dress to the nines and sip cosmopolitans while checking out the ultrachic crowd, this supper club is a throwback to a bygone era. The seafood-oriented Nouvelle Creole menu, though, speaks to '90s tastes; try the pecan-and-coconut-crusted Gulf fish with Gulf shrimp, pineapples, peppers, and onions. ⊠ *312 Exchange Alley,* ☏ *504/523–1504.*

$$–$$$ ✕ **Irene's Cuisine.** This outstanding, gay-frequented hole-in-the-wall is something you would expect to find tucked off a side street in Florence. The decor and food are traditional Italian: Chianti bottles hanging about and chicken marsala or veal-and-mozzarella-stuffed manicotti on the plates. There's a great, moderately priced wine list. The amiable staff borders on being flirtatious. ⊠ *539 St. Philip St.,* ☏ *504/529–8811.*

$$–$$$ ✕ **Lucky Cheng's.** Campy and queer, this New York City import keeps tourists amused with drag waitresses and wild antics. The Asian food isn't bad, though it's nothing to write home about (especially if home is Asia). You will find some interesting options, though, such as lacquered salmon with a satsuma orange glaze over zucchini and yellow squash with jasmine rice. ⊠ *720 St. Louis St.,* ☏ *504/529–2045.*

$$–$$$ ✕ **Petunia's.** This very gay creperie beside the Roundup (*see* Scenes, *below*) is in a pink-stucco 1830s town house. The dining room is softly lit, and the tables, on which fresh flowers are arranged, are covered with pink linen. The Creole and Continental menu has everything from hearty jambalaya to seven crepes, including one filled with ratatouille, shrimp, and crab meat. ⊠ *817 St. Louis St.,* ☎ *504/522–6440.*

$–$$ ✕ **Acme Oyster House.** For oysters on the half shell, not to mention po'boys and red beans and rice, Acme Oyster House is the best—a no-frills cafeteria with linoleum floors, a great jukebox, and low-key service. ⊠ *724 Iberville St.,* ☎ *504/522–5973.*

$ ✕ **Clover Grill.** Pretty boys, leather hunks, and hungry dykes chow down on greasy comfort food—burgers and fries and the like—at this joint across from Café Lafitte. Open all night, the Clover employs the funniest and sauciest waitrons in town. ⊠ *900 Bourbon St.,* ☎ *504/523–0904.*

$ ✕ **Coops.** A small, pubby hangout on Decatur Street, Coops serves many domestic and imported beers and big portions of inexpensive Creole and Cajun food—thick crab cakes, shrimp remoulade, hot gumbos, fried crab claws. ⊠ *1109 Decatur St.,* ☎ *504/525–9053.*

$ ✕ **Old Dog, New Trick Café.** Queer-sensible and politically correct, this smartly decorated vegetarian restaurant has comfy outdoor tables. The kitchen does amazing things with tempeh, vegetarian patties, polenta, and the like. ⊠ *307 Exchange Alley,* ☎ *504/522–4569.*

Faubourg Marigny

$$–$$$ ✕ **Feelings Café.** One of the essential gay restaurants in New Orleans, a long walk or short cab ride east of the Quarter, Feelings is in an old white-stucco building at the corner of Franklin and Chartres streets. Best known for Sunday brunch, it serves good Creole and Continental food at every meal. ⊠ *2600 Chartres St.,* ☎ *504/945–2222.*

$–$$ ✕ **Port of Call.** It won't win any awards for charm, but this faggy dive on the border between Faubourg Marigny and the Quarter serves unbelievably tasty burgers, hefty baked potatoes, and other pub grub. ⊠ *838 Esplanade Ave.,* ☎ *504/523–0120.*

$–$$ ✕ **Praline Connection.** As the Praline Connection has become more touristy, the food has become milder, but the mixed soul-Creole cuisine still hits the spot. Whatever you order, save room for the rich bread pudding or any of the pralines sold in the sweetshop next door. ⊠ *542 Frenchmen St.,* ☎ *504/943–3934; also* ⊠ *901–907 S. Peters St.,* ☎ *504/ 523–3973.*

Elsewhere

$$$$ ✕ **Commander's Palace.** Several national magazines and restaurant surveys have named this Garden District landmark the top eatery in New Orleans and one of the top 10 in America. The menu draws on various non-Creole cultures, resulting in elaborate fare, like the renowned turtle soup and the poached oysters in a cream sauce with caviar. ⊠ *1403 Washington Ave.,* ☎ *504/899–8221.*

$$$$ ✕ **Emeril's.** TV chef Emeril Lagasse's Warehouse District establishment captures the postmodern spirit of the neighborhood with burnished metals, abstract art, brick-and-glass walls, and an open, noisy dining room. Legasse's New American takes on Creole dishes—maybe a corn crepe topped with Louisiana caviar or sautéed crawfish over jambalaya cakes—also challenge tradition. ⊠ *800 Tchoupitoulas St.,* ☎ *504/528–9393.*

$$$ ✕ **Brigtsen's.** This restaurant occupies a simple Uptown cottage that dates from the turn of the century. The eponymous chef is one of the most innovative practitioners of modern South Louisiana cooking, so the food—a cream of oysters Rockefeller soup, robust duck dishes, intense gumbos, and an incredible banana ice cream—is anything but simple. ⊠ *723 Dante St.,* ☎ *504/861–7610.*

$$$ ✕ **Upperline.** A rustic cottage with an art deco–inspired interior houses one of the few gay-popular restaurants outside the Quarter that serves serious food. The creative Nouvelle Creole and Continental dishes include the Portobello mushrooms with wheatberries and goat cheese and the hickory-grilled Gulf fish with warm salad Niçoise. ⊠ *1413 Upperline St.,* ☎ *504/891–9822.*

$$ ✕ **Fleur de lys.** The southern French menu at this CBD restaurant is brief but excellent, offering dishes like braised lamb shanks in a red-wine gravy with saffron orzo and goat cheese, and a spinach-and-leek salad with an andouille vinaigrette. ⊠ *1032 St. Charles Ave.,* ☎ *504/588–2616.*

Coffeehouse Culture

Café du Monde. One late-night New Orleans tradition to which even the most stubborn individualist should conform is enjoying café au lait and beignets at this classic open-air hangout overlooking Jackson Square. ⊠ *French Market, Decatur and St. Ann Sts.,* ☎ *504/525–4544.*

Café Marigny. Smack in the middle of Faubourg in a cute old house, this café is très gay. Leaflets and fliers will clue you in on upcoming events. ⊠ *1913 Royal St.,* ☎ *504/945–4472.*

Kaldi's. The coffeehouse in this century-old building draws an artsy, intellectual bunch. Grab a cappuccino and sit by the huge windows overlooking busy Decatur Street. ⊠ *941 Decatur St.,* ☎ *504/586–8989.*

SCENES

All those tales you've heard from bleary-eyed buddies returning from the Quarter overfed, oversexed, and on the brink of liver failure—well, they're all true. Gay New Orleanians party constantly, though not seriously. They're a laid-back, disheveled set, with not too many stand-and-model types. Most bars are unabashedly cruisy, and even when in the blurriest stupor the average patron remains shockingly polite.

The touristy bars are in the heart of the Quarter, though a few are farther over in Faubourg Marigny. North Rampart Street has a strip of neighborhood bars. It's a dicey thoroughfare, especially at night, so don't wander along here alone. Except for the rough-and-rowdy Phoenix/Men's Room, ol' boys'-oriented Café Lafitte, and Oz, the more popular bars all have a mix of men and women.

French Quarter

PRIME SUSPECTS

Bourbon Pub/Parade Disco. Many people move back and forth between these two bars and Oz. The crowd is more diverse on weeknights and during the afternoon, but on weekend evenings it's almost exclusively young, guppie, stand-and-model types. There's no cover in the Pub. Hurricane doors open onto Bourbon Street, allowing patrons to party in the street. The Parade Disco (above the Pub) is usually open only on weekends and often has a cover. Doors from the dance floor lead onto the exterior wraparound balcony, from which you can gawk at the crowd across the way at Oz. ⊠ *801 Bourbon St.,* ☎ *504/529–2107. Crowd: mostly male in the Pub, 70/30 m/f in the Disco, 20s to early 30s, cruisy, touristy.*

Café Lafitte in Exile. Lafitte's is the grandfather of gay bars—you may even spot a few grandfathers. But you'll see most every other type, too, from club kids on their way up to Oz and Parade to leather bears heading the opposite way toward the Phoenix. Both levels are usually crowded, with more mingling around the first-floor cruise bar and a more cliquey crowd upstairs either playing pool or sitting around the bar. Sexual activity is not unheard of upstairs, and guys sometimes neck on the wraparound balcony overlooking Bourbon Street. A good place to let your hair down, Lafitte's has the friendliest bartenders in New Orleans. ⊠ *901 Bourbon St.,* ☎ *504/522–8397. Crowd: mostly male, mostly ages 30s to 50s, fairly butch, Levi's and T-shirts, looking for action.*

Good Friends Bar. Fireplaces, wood-panel walls, and vases with neon floral designs lend a homey feel to this bar that's less frenetic than its neighbors, Oz and the Bourbon Pub. Upstairs is the cozy Queen's Head Pub, open Thursday to Sunday, which has darts and comfy seating. ⊠ *740 Dauphine St.,* ☎ *504/566–7191. Crowd: 80/20 m/f, mostly 30s and 40s, guys/gals next door, cross-section of locals and tourists, low-key.*

The Mint. This stately building has elaborate moldings, tile floors, and other wonderful architectural details. One of the Quarter's favorite off-the-wall show bars, it draws straight onlookers. The bartenders are cute and sweet, and the drag acts and comedy and cabaret shows are most entertaining. ⊠ *504 Esplanade Ave.,* ☎ *504/525–2000. Crowd: 80/20 gay/straight, mixed m/f, all ages, many tourists, curiosity seekers, outgoing, fun-loving, loud.*

MRB (Mississippi River Bottom). But for a great courtyard out back, MRB is a typical cruise bar—mostly local on weekdays, more popular on weekends. The strip shows are wild and well attended. ⊠ *515 St. Philip St.,* ☎ *504/524–2558. Crowd: 80/20, mostly 30s and 40s, ribald, dishy.*

Oz. The Bourbon Pub's biggest rival has a small dance floor (fun music) encircled by a wrought-iron balustrade balcony that's perfect for people-watching and cruising. Outside is an equally impressive balcony with good views across Bourbon Street to Parade's balcony. Unfortunately, many of the bartenders and bouncers are rude, and the club recently began charging a cover that's higher for women than for guys. What decade are we in? ⊠ *800 Bourbon St.,* ☎ *504/593–9491. Crowd: 75/25 m/f, mostly under 30, somewhat stand-and-model, energetic.*

Rawhide 2010. If you bear in mind that it's difficult to walk into this nearly pitch-black cruise bar and not end up in a compromising position, you'll do fine—novices may want to begin their partying where the guys aren't so revved up. You'll find porn videos, some pool tables, a new steel cage (that's so far underutilized, though it should become more popular as the regulars figure out what to do inside it), and a cute little fireplace. About the only thing you won't find guys doing in the restrooms is resting. ⊠ *740 Burgundy St.,* ☎ *504/525–8106. Crowd: male, all ages, butch, aggressively horny, usually pretty smashed.*

NEIGHBORHOOD HAUNTS

Footloose (⊠ 700 N. Rampart St., ☎ 504/523–2715) has drag shows some nights but is otherwise on the sleepy side. Homely little **Funky Butt** (⊠ 714 N. Rampart St., ☎ 504/558–0872) has strippers and a handful of loyal customers. **TT's** (⊠ 820 N. Rampart St., ☎ 504/523–9521) is skeevy but fun, known for its bartop strippers who have an affinity for heavy-metal music. A mostly African-American clientele patronizes **Wolfendale's** (⊠ 834 N. Rampart St., ☎ 504/523–7764), which is crowded on weekends but quiet the rest of the time.

The frighteningly low-budget **Corner Pocket** (⊠ 940 St. Louis St., ☎ 504/568–9829) may be the only strip bar in America where the go-go dancers must provide their own music by dropping quarters into the jukebox. Most guys hang out at the tiny **Golden Lantern** (⊠ 1239 Royal St., ☎ 504/529–2860) to watch soaps on TV. **Roundup** (⊠ 819 St. Louis St., ☎ 504/561–8340), the city's only true country-western bar, lacks a dance floor and a personality but has a good jukebox.

Faubourg Marigny

Charlene's. The city's catch-all dyke bar is in a pale-yellow corner build-ing across Elysian Fields from the Phoenix. It has shows, dancing, pool tables, and space for mingling. Charlene herself is a local institution. Younger lesbians tend to patronize Rubyfruit and the Parade Disco; the crowd here tends to be older. ⊠ *940 Elysian Fields Ave.,* ☎ *504/945–9328. Crowd: 80/20 f/m, mostly over 30, diverse.*

The Phoenix/Men's Room. The "anything goes" scene here is surprising considering the Phoenix's setting: a cute, fire-engine–red clapboard house. Inside is another story: a dark seedy room that's only slightly more inviting than somebody's garage. The crowd is wound up and wild. The back stairs lead to the Men's Room, something akin to a back room, where things go bump in the night. ⊠ *941 Elysian Fields Ave.,* ☎ *504/945–9264. Crowd: male, all ages, fairly hard-core, leather, bears, motorcycle types, rough-and-ready.*

Rubyfruit Jungle. What began as a lesbian bar has developed into an al-ternative-minded queer bar. Its hip young dykes and fags prefer the retro-lounge environment of this slick Faubourg Marigny hangout to the cruise scene in the Quarter (not to say this place never gets cruisy). ⊠ *640 French-men St.,* ☎ *504/947–4000. Crowd: mixed m/f, mostly under 35, scene-sters, rockers, lounge lizards, self-consciously trendy, a little cliquey.*

Big Daddy's (⊠ 2513 Royal St., ☎ 504/948–6288), one of the warmest bars in the city, is popular with men and women; it has big windows look-ing out onto the street. **Another Corner** (⊠ 2601 Royal St., ☎ 504/945–7006), across the street from Big Daddy's, is in a great old building; it has high ceilings, antique ceiling fans, a long bar of red-vinyl stools, and a mag-nificent exterior balcony. The **Friendly Bar** (⊠ 2301 Chartres St., ☎ 504/943–8929) lacks atmosphere and is set in an unattractive mint-green building with glass brick windows. It attracts a mixed-gender crowd. The **Copper Top Bar** (⊠ 706 Franklin Ave., ☎ 504/948–2300) is worth the trip from the Quarter for its fun beer blasts. It's also the home of the $1 "cocksucker," which is apparently the nickname of a drink and not an employee. Early in the morning, the Copper Top serves a Continental break-fast of coffee, pastries, fresh-squeezed orange juice, and light beer.

Music Clubs

You can eat, drink, listen to alternative rock and blues, cruise, and do your laundry at the French Quarter's **Checkpoint Charlie's** (⊠ 501 Es-planade Ave., ☎ 504/947–0979)—right off the main room is a complete coin-operated laundry. **Pete Fountain's** (⊠ 2 Poydras St., ☎ 504/524–6255) masterful Dixieland jazz is presented several nights a week on the third floor of the New Orleans Hilton. **Preservation Hall** (⊠ 726 St. Peter St., ☎ 504/522–2841), though touristy, is worth visiting to hear jazz. In the Garden District **Tipitina's** (⊠ 501 Napoleon Ave., ☎ 504/897–3943), the former base of the late R&B pianist Professor Longhair, regularly hosts important national and local acts.

Action

Most guys looking for a good time favor **Club New Orleans** (*see* Work-ing Out, *below*), which is also the top gay gym. The main competitor is **Midtowne Spa** (⊠ 700 Baronne St., ☎ 504/566–1442). Another option that's different from your standard sexplex is the **Country Club** (⊠ 634 Louisa St., ☎ 504/945–0742), a daytime-only (from 10 to 6 daily) out-door compound with a big pool, a cabana, a poolside bar, and a racy crowd into sunning and sleazing. In Bywater, a short drive or cab ride from the Quarter, Country Club is closed from November to February.

SLEEPS

This is a great city for B&Bs, but because hotel rates are on the rise, some guest houses charge more than they should given what they offer in return. Many of the best gay-friendly or gay-operated guest houses are listed below, but just as many are small (often renting out one or two rooms) and don't book directly to the public. To find them, call the gay-staffed **French Quarter Reservation Service** (☎ 504/523–1246 or 800/523–9091). If an establishment's gay quotient is less important to you, the mainstream **Bed & Breakfast, Inc.** (☎ 504/488–4640 or 800/729–4640) represents accommodations of all types throughout the city.

For price ranges, *see* lodging Chart A at the front of this guide.

Hotels

French Quarter

$$$–$$$$ 🏨 **Bourbon Orleans Hotel.** This property off St. Ann Street has the gayest clientele of any major city hotel, with a few rooms overlooking the fun at Oz and the Bourbon Pub. The interior is brighter and better maintained but has less character than that of the Royal Sonesta. ⊠ *717 Orleans St., 70116,* ☎ *504/523–2222 or 800/521–5338,* FAX *504/525–8166. 211 rooms. Restaurant, pool.*

$$$–$$$$ 🏨 **Royal Sonesta Hotel.** In the eyes of many, this property that encompasses an entire block is *the* place to stay in the Quarter. The stylish rooms have wrought-iron balconies overlooking either the streets or the lush courtyard. ⊠ *300 Bourbon St., 70140,* ☎ *504/586–0300 or 800/766–3782,* FAX *504/586–0335. 500 rooms. Restaurant, pool, health club.*

$$ 🏨 **Inn on Bourbon Street.** This Best Western property is in the heart of vibrant (and noisy) Bourbon Street. With a courtyard and pool, and reproduction antiques throughout, it looks and feels more charming than most mid-range chain properties. The large rooms contain helpful amenities like irons and blow-dryers. ⊠ *541 Bourbon St., 70130,* ☎ *504/524–7611 or 800/535–7891,* FAX *504/568–9427. 188 rooms. Restaurant, pool, health club.*

$–$$ 🏨 **Le Richelieu.** A favorite bargain property close to the Quarter and Faubourg Marigny, this hotel built in 1854 has big rooms with high ceilings. ⊠ *1234 Chartres St., 70116,* ☎ *504/529–2492 or 800/535–9653,* FAX *504/524–8179. 86 rooms. Restaurant, pool.*

Outside the Quarter

$$$$ 🏨 **Windsor Court.** A contemporary structure that's a 15-minute walk from Jackson Square, the Windsor is among the most sumptuous accommodations in America. The public rooms and restaurants are the finest of any New Orleans hotel. ⊠ *300 Gravier St., 70130,* ☎ *504/523–6000 or 800/262–2662,* FAX *504/596–4513. 324 rooms. Restaurant.*

$$$–$$$$ 🏨 **Fairmont Hotel.** The three connected buildings at the Fairmont hold large guest rooms with down pillows, bathroom scales, and other thoughtful touches. The staff is top-notch and the public areas and restaurants excellent. This is a great choice if you're seeking a classic Old World experience. ⊠ *123 Barrone St., 70140,* ☎ *504/529–7111 or 800/527–4727,* FAX *504/522–2303. 700 rooms. Restaurants, pool.*

$$–$$$ 🏨 **Wyndham Riverfront.** Superb amenities and warmly furnished rooms lure corporate types to this property across from the convention center. The four buildings that compose the hotel were once a rice mill and silo. ⊠ *701 Convention Center Blvd., 70130,* ☎ *504/524–8200 or 800/996–3426,* FAX *504/524–0600. 202 rooms. Restaurant, exercise room.*

$–$$ ⊞ **Prytania Park Hotel.** This multibuilding hotel in the Garden District is a solid choice with an unexciting but reasonably safe location. The nicest rooms are in the 1834 town house. ⊠ *1525 Prytania St., 70130,* ☎ *504/524–0427 or 800/862–1984,* FAX *504/566–1518. 56 rooms.*

Guest Houses and Small Hotels

French Quarter and Vicinity

$$$–$$$$ ⊞ **Hotel de la Monnaie.** Luxurious and gay-frequented, this hostelry has one- and two-bedroom suites with kitchenettes and sofa beds. It's ideal for two, or even three, couples traveling together. ⊠ *405 Esplanade Ave., 70116,* ☎ *504/947–0009,* FAX *504/945–6841. 53 rooms with phone, TV, and private bath. Hot tub. Mixed gay/straight.*

$$–$$$$ ⊞ **Lamothe House Hotel.** Rooms at this small hotel range from fancy to simple, but all are furnished with antiques and fine fabrics. The Lamothe's well-kept grounds are among its greatest strengths. ⊠ *621 Esplanade Ave., 70116,* ☎ *504/947–1161 or 800/367–5858,* FAX *504/943–6536. 20 rooms with phone, TV, and private bath. Continental breakfast. Pool, hot tub. Mixed gay/straight.*

$$–$$$ ⊞ **The Frenchmen.** This salmon-color complex of 1860 town houses has a brick courtyard and pool in back and rooms with Victorian furnishings. Very gay and very charming, it's across the street from the Mint nightclub. ⊠ *417 Frenchmen St., 70116,* ☎ *504/948–2166 or 800/831–1781,* FAX *504/948–2258. 27 rooms with phone, TV, and private bath.*

$$–$$$ ⊞ **Lafitte Guest House.** The truly fabulous, gay or straight, adore this ritzy town house steps from several bars. Rooms are decorated with antiques, flowing drapes, and Oriental rugs; many have fireplaces. ⊠ *1003 Bourbon St., 70116,* ☎ *504/581–2678 or 800/331–7971. 14 rooms with phone, TV, and private bath. Continental breakfast. Mixed gay/straight.*

$$ ⊞ **Ursuline Guest House.** Gas lamps illuminate the exterior of this 18th-century structure, one of the classiest gay-frequented guest houses in the Quarter. Within minutes of the major bars, it has rooms that open onto a brick courtyard with wrought-iron furniture. ⊠ *708 Ursulines St., 70116,* ☎ *504/525–8509 or 800/654–2351,* FAX *504/525–8408. 12 rooms with phone, TV, and private bath. Continental breakfast. Hot tub. Mixed gay/straight.*

$–$$ ⊞ **New Orleans Guest House.** Historic well-kept houses line Ursulines Street, but at night the last few blocks of the walk from the Bourbon Street action to this guest house can be a tad unsettling. The pretty-in-pink hostelry, built in 1848, has plenty of parking, though. ⊠ *1118 Ursulines St., 70116,* ☎ *504/566–1177 or 800/562–1177. 14 rooms with TV, private bath, some with TV. Continental breakfast. Mixed gay/straight.*

$–$$ ⊞ **Rathbone Inn.** Two blocks north of Rampart and up Esplanade Avenue in a mildly dicey section, this courtly two-story inn has terrific accommodations. Behind its handsome, white, Greek-Revival façade are simply but smartly decorated rooms. ⊠ *1227 Esplanade Ave., 70116,* ☎ *504/947–2100 or 800/776–3901,* FAX *504/558–0566. 9 rooms with phone, TV, and private bath. Continental breakfast. Hot tub. Mixed gay/straight.*

$–$$ ⊞ **Rue Royale Inn.** A modest hotel, notable for its quirky decor, kitchenettes in many rooms, and proximity to Jackson Square, the Rue Royale has a gracious (and disproportionately gay) staff. The inn was built in 1830 as a private home. The courtyard units, though small, are among the city's top bargains. ⊠ *1006 rue Royal, 70116,* ☎ *504/524–3900 or 800/776–3901,* FAX *504/558-0566. 17 rooms with TV, private bath, some with phone. Continental breakfast. Mixed gay/straight.*

Outside the French Quarter

$$$$ ☷ **Claiborne Mansion.** For the ultimate in New Orleans opulence, book a room at this stately 1859 yellow mansion that overlooks Washington Park in Faubourg Marigny. The huge rooms have soaring ceilings, priceless antiques, warm fabrics, cushy towels and linens, VCRs, phones with voice mail, marble bathrooms, and top-of-the-line bath amenities. ⊠ *2111 Dauphine St., 70116,* ☎ *504/949–7327 or 800/449–7327,* ℻ *504/ 949–0388. 5 rooms with phone, TV, and private bath. Pool. Continental breakfast. Mixed gay/straight.*

$$–$$$ ☷ **B&W Courtyards.** This upscale but reasonably priced complex of three small buildings has had only three owners since it was built in 1855. The smallish rooms are beautifully furnished, all with private entrances opening onto a landscaped courtyard with a hot tub and a fountain. Expect one of the best Continental breakfasts in the city. ⊠ *2425 Chartres St., 70117,* ☎ *504/949–5313 or 800/585–5731. 6 rooms with TV and private bath. Continental breakfast. Hot tub. Mixed gay/straight.*

$$ ☷ **McKendrick-Breaux House.** Antiques, family heirlooms, and fresh flowers fill the spacious rooms in this restored masonry house in the Lower Garden District, right where Magazine Street begins to get interesting. A first-class operation. ⊠ *1474 Magazine St., 70130,* ☎ *504/586–1700 or 888/570–1700,* ℻ *504/522–7138. 5 rooms with private bath. Continental breakfast. Mixed gay/straight.*

$–$$ ☷ **Macarty Park Guest House.** A delightful gay retreat not far from the French Quarter in Bywater, this Victorian house and its two neighboring cottages contain bright rooms filled with classic and reproduction antiques, distinctive framed photos and reproduction paintings, and plush beds. The grounds are well kept and tropical, complete with a large secluded swimming pool. Even factoring in the cost of cab rides, this place is a tremendous value. ⊠ *3820 Burgundy St., 70117,* ☎ *504/943–4994 or 800/521–2790. 8 rooms with phone, TV, and private bath. Continental breakfast. Pool, exercise room. Mixed gay/straight.*

$ ☷ **St. Charles Guest House.** Students, artists, and folks looking for an affordable yet comfortable way to enjoy the city stay at these adjoining buildings. The inviting hotel is on the edge of the Garden District, an easy streetcar ride form the Quarter. ⊠ *1748 Prytania St., 70130,* ☎ *504/523–6556. 36 rooms, most with private bath, TV, phone. Continental breakfast. Pool. Mixed gay/straight.*

THE LITTLE BLACK BOOK

At Your Fingertips

AIDS Hot Line (☎ 504/944–2437 or 800/992–4379). *Gambit* (alternative weekly, ☎ 504/486–5900). **Lesbian and Gay Community Center of New Orleans** (⊠ 816 N. Rampart St., ☎ 504/522–1103). **New Orleans Metropolitan Convention and Visitors Bureau** (⊠ 1520 Sugar Bowl Dr., 70112, ☎ 504/566–5003 or 800/672–6124, Web site www.neworleanscvb.com). **Regional Transit Authority** (☎ 504/242–2600).

Gay Media

New Orleans has two good gay newspapers, *Ambush* (☎ 504/522–8049, Web site www.ambushonline.com), a tabloid paper with coverage of New Orleans and the Gulf South, and *Impact* (☎ 504/944–6722, Web site www.impactnews.com/eclipse), which carries news and features and also publishes a racy biweekly bar rag, *Eclipse.* You'll also find bar news in the *Weekly Guide* (☎ 504/522–4300).

BOOKSTORES

The gay and lesbian **Faubourg Marigny Bookstore** (⊠ 600 Frenchmen St., ☎ 504/943–9875) stocks books, compact discs, and porn magazines and other periodicals. Of mainstream chain stores, the **Bookstar** (⊠ 411

N. Peters St., ☎ 504/523–6411) in the Quarter carries many gay and lesbian titles, plus gay periodicals. **Gay Mart** (✉ 808 N. Rampart St., ☎ 504/523–6005) sells books, magazines, flags, cards, and gifts. Another good source of queer fashion and gifts is **Alternatives** (✉ 907 Bourbon St., ☎ 504/524–5222). **Chartres St. Conxxxion** (✉ 107 Chartres St., ☎ 504/586–8006) is your 24-hour one-stop for porn mags and videos.

Working Out

The main gay health club (beer is sold, so the place's dedication to fitness is questionable) is **Club New Orleans** (✉ 515 Toulouse St., ☎ 504/581–2402). Guys do work out, in the legitimate sense, but it's also a five-floor bathhouse with lockers and rooms and a sundeck.

25 Out in New York City

IN *GAY NEW YORK,* **A RICH ACCOUNT** of the city's homosexual culture prior to World War II, George Chauncey demonstrates that there was a lively gay presence in the bawdy Bowery during the 1890s and in Greenwich Village, Harlem, and Times Square through the 1920s. Elaborate drag balls attended by gays and curious straights were major to-dos during the late '20s and early '30s. Eventually, high visibility spawned a backlash, which began in the '30s and peaked during the '50s. Homophile organizations began rallying for civil rights during this period, when gay life was forced underground. This nascent activism culminated in the 1969 Stonewall riots: Early on the morning of June 28, police raided a small Greenwich Village gay bar called the Stonewall Inn. Its patrons defied the cops, and the ensuing riot lasted several days. Nowadays thousands of gays and lesbians stroll by the site of the Stonewall, remembering that before 1969 homosexuals could not congregate publicly without fear of police harassment.

The Manhattan of the '90s is largely a tolerant place for gays and lesbians. Its gay community is diverse, creative, and visible throughout the city, particularly in the Village, Chelsea, Hell's Kitchen, and on the Upper West Side. City Council members Tom Duane (Chelsea) and Margarita Lopez (Lower East Side) are openly gay, and Deborah Glick, an out lesbian, represents Greenwich Village in the New York State Assembly. The annual pride parade draws a big crowd each June (a mayoral appearance is a given), turning all of Manhattan into a gay and lesbian mixer for the day. Some of the warmest, loudest cheers are for the gay and lesbian police officers who march; their straight counterparts patrolling the procession are famous for their civility.

But New York is no paradise. It's easy to be put off by the traffic, the panhandling, and the noise. While the city has tens of thousands of hotel rooms, rates are the highest in the nation and can resemble monthly mortgage payments. Much of what there is to see and do comes with a high price tag and a long line. New York is exciting, raw, and full of opportunity; it is also chaotic, dirty, and draining.

And yet locals take it all in stride. They bristle when outsiders disparage the city even as they joke about their dysfunctional relationship with it. But you can be sure they wouldn't live anywhere else.

THE LAY OF THE LAND

Manhattan claims most of the city's popular attractions, restaurants, and hotels and is the gayest of the city's five boroughs. Central Park is Manhattan's geographical center; any of several neighborhoods might be considered its spiritual center. For most visitors it's Midtown, which begins just south of Central Park. North of Midtown are the Upper West and East sides, and above them Harlem, Morningside Heights, Riverside Heights, and Inwood. Below Midtown are, in descending order, Chelsea, the West Village, SoHo, and TriBeCa on the West Side; Gramercy Park, the East Village, the Lower East Side, Little Italy, and Chinatown on the East Side. Finally, at the southern tip of the island, there's Lower Manhattan, also known as the Financial District or simply "Wall Street."

North of 14th Street the city is laid out in a grid pattern. Consecutively numbered streets run east and west (crosstown), while the broad avenues, most of them also numbered, run north (uptown) or south (downtown). The chief exceptions are Broadway (which runs on a diagonal from East 14th to West 79th streets) and the highways that hug the shores of the Hudson and East rivers. Below 14th Street, the monolithic grid gives way to a host of smaller grids that jostle with one another and ultimately dissipate as you move south.

Lower Manhattan

Though relatively few people live in **Lower Manhattan,** which encompasses the southern tip of the island below Chambers Street, this is the area that comprised the original Dutch colony of Nieuw Amsterdam—Wall Street is on the site of the wall that used to form its northern border. The 16-acre **World Trade Center** (☎ 212/323–2340) begins at the intersection of Vesey and Church streets. For the highest vantage point in the city, head to the 107th floor of **2 World Trade Center.**

New Yorkers have turned the 1½-mile **Hudson River Park** due west of here into an in-line-skating paradise. Residents of Chelsea and the West Village frequently blade down here on sunny weekends, making it a cruisy place to walk by the river. The park connects to the **Battery Park City Esplanade,** which curves south to sprawling **Battery Park,** from which ferries (☎ 212/269–5755) leave for both the **Statue of Liberty** (☎ 212/363–3200) and **Ellis Island** (☎ 212/363–3200). Two of America's favorite attractions, they can be mobbed; waits to get up the statue can be particularly horrendous.

Virtually no original Colonial architecture remains in Lower Manhattan, but a few relics still stand, including the **Fraunces Tavern** (✉ 54 Pearl St., ☎ 212/425–1778), which dates from 1719 and now houses a period-furnished museum, restaurant, and bar. Four blocks north of here is **Wall Street,** the heart of the Financial District, and not especially exciting save for the neoclassical **New York Stock Exchange** (✉ 20 Broad St., ☎ 212/656–5165). Visit on a weekday to see trading action.

A few blocks northeast of Wall Street is the 11-block **South Street Seaport Historic District,** an urban entertainment complex fashioned out of a once-deteriorating old seaport. Though popular with tourists, South Street Seaport has never quite lived up to expectations; at night the bars here are taken over by rowdy straights.

SoHo, TriBeCa, and the Lower East Side

Most of **SoHo**'s handsome cast-iron buildings here were built as factories and warehouses in the 1850s and 1860s, but when many these businesses closed during the first half of the 20th century, SoHo died with them. By 1959 the City Club of New York declared the area, then popularly referred to as Hell's Hundred Acres, "an industrial slum without any notable architecture." The "slum" offered a prime opportunity for artists and designers to find stunning as well as practical architecture at rock-bottom prices, and by the late '60s, artists' cooperatives were snapping up entire buildings. SoHo was granted landmark status in 1973—a formal recognition of the elegance and historic significance of its cast-iron buildings, many of which are graced by Corinthian columns,

Palladian windows, and Second Empire dormers. During the next decade antiques shops, fashion boutiques, retail galleries, and smart cafés opened beneath the artists' lofts.

Today SoHo is still exciting but, some say, too fashionable for its own good. Streets are often overrun with flashy big spenders and narcissistic beautiful people. Oddly, for such an artsy neighborhood, SoHo is overwhelmingly straight, although comfortable for gays and lesbians. As for all those chic shops, their success has driven rents to such a point that many artists have packed up and moved to the East Village's Alphabet City, west Chelsea, and Greenpoint, Fort Greene, and Williamsburg in Brooklyn. Many buildings still provide work space for (highly successful) artists; others are commercial outlets specializing in wholesale fabrics, electronic components, and the like.

The best-known galleries (including **Leo Castelli,** the father of pop art, and **O. K. Harris,** the oldest gallery in the neighborhood) are on or near **West Broadway.** Don't confuse West Broadway with **Broadway,** which runs parallel to it two blocks east and is best known for its plethora of both upscale (e.g., **Armani Exchange** at 568) and secondhand clothiers (**Canal Jeans** is at 504 and **Alice's Underground** at 481). Take a break from rifling through hot duds by poking your head into the **Leslie-Lohman Gay Art Foundation** (✉ 127 Prince St., ☎ 212/673–7007), a sub-street-level gallery that mounts group and individual shows of queer, often erotic art.

Three excellent art museums line Broadway in SoHo: the **Guggenheim Museum SoHo** (✉ 575 Broadway, ☎ 212/423–3500), which showcases contemporary art and pieces from its permanent collections; the Maya Lin–designed **Museum for African Art** (✉ 593 Broadway, ☎ 212/966–1313); and the cutting-edge **New Museum of Contemporary Art** (✉ 583 Broadway, ☎ 212/219– 1222).

South of SoHo, concentrated around the intersection of Greenwich and Harrison streets, is trendy **TriBeCa** ("*Tri*angle *Be*low *Ca*nal"), where Robert De Niro has established his **TriBeCa Film Center** (✉ 375 Greenwich St.) above the popular TriBeCa Grill restaurant. There are a few interesting buildings—some of which contain shops and eateries—and a slight spillover of artists who prefer the neighborhood to SoHo, but there's not a whole lot to see and do.

Greenwich Village

You may have heard that **Greenwich Village**—"the Village," to most New Yorkers—is no longer the center of New York's gay community. Life in this historically gay ghetto has definitely changed. The onset of AIDS, the neighborhood's 1980s real estate boom, and an increase in straight tourists and rowdy teens have discouraged new generations of queers from settling here and have driven away some gay-owned businesses. Despite the changes, the West Village and its anchor, Sheridan Square, are still mighty pink.

Greenwich Village has been America's most prolific pocket of bohemian culture for a century. A modest village in the early 1700s, it soon became a rural retreat for New Yorkers fleeing frequent malaria epidemics. For the next century it was a fashionable neighborhood but devolved into a sewer of poverty and seediness. In the early 20th century the Village transformed itself into a spirited art colony, an image it retains. As early as the 1920s, the Village developed a reputation as a discreetly queer gathering spot, with numerous speakeasies and salons catering to deviants unwelcome elsewhere in Manhattan. Over the next 50 years lesbians and gays continued to thrive here, and by the late '60s Greenwich Village had become one of the world's most recognizable gay addresses. The riots outside the former **Stonewall Inn** (✉ 57 Christopher St.) in 1969 propelled both the West Village and the gay rights movement into the international spotlight. The actual Stonewall Inn closed long ago; a neighborhood bar, Stonewall, now stands next door at 53 Christopher (*see* Scenes, *below*).

The Stonewall Riots occurred just off **Sheridan Square** (7th Ave. S and W. 4th St.), the heart of the **West Village**—the maze of quaint, crooked streets comprising the western half of Greenwich Village. This neighborhood is more diverse than it was a decade ago, when it was largely the province of young, white, upwardly mobile gay men. There are still a handful of gay bars near Sheridan Square.

As you move west along **Christopher Street** from Sheridan Square, you'll notice that most bars cater to an older, rougher crowd. Christopher Street is still alive with gay shops and still a tad tawdry—it has some of New York's best adult video parlors. The western edge of Christopher Street, past Hudson Street, is a major gay African-American and, to a lesser degree, Hispanic entertainment district. The streets south of Christopher and east of Hudson have in recent years become a significant lesbian community and playground.

If you don't mind the sometimes excessive crowds, the entire West Village is ideal for sidewalk strolling. **Seventh Avenue South** has dozens of cafés, some small theaters, and a few cabarets—most of them mixed gay/straight. **Bleecker** and **West 4th streets** are lined with unusual boutiques (including that repository of safe sex supplies, **Condomania,** at 351 Bleecker St.), discount dry goods shops, and clothiers. Farther west, **Hudson Street** has dozens of gay-oriented shops and hangouts. **Greenwich Avenue,** which cuts diagonally across the Village in a southeasterly direction, also has plenty of fun shops and cafés.

Every visitor to New York should check out the **Lesbian and Gay Community Services Center** (⊠ 208 W. 13th St., ☎ 212/620–7310, Web site www.gaycenter.org), an outstanding resource that is just off Greenwich Avenue. The Center distributes a hefty free packet of orientation literature and offers walking tours on the queer heritage of several Manhattan neighborhoods, from the Village to Harlem. Tours depart Saturdays from April through October and cost $15 per person; call for themes and exact times.

The central part of Greenwich Village, whose hub, **Washington Square,** is dominated by the Washington Arch (⊠ 5th Ave. and W. 4th St.), is mostly the domain of **New York University.** Jazz clubs, coffeehouses, and funky shops line the area's main commercial drags—most notably Bleecker Street (which is straight and touristy along this span) and the narrow lanes that lead off it. North of the square, saunter by some of the priciest real estate in the city, **Washington Mews** and **MacDougal Alley.**

The East Village

If Chelsea has threatened Greenwich Village's reputation as Manhattan's gay mecca, the **East Village** has threatened its sister neighborhood's reputation as the city's Bohemia, although it, too, is fast gentrifying. Young avant-garde artists who could no longer afford the West Village or SoHo began settling here over the past two decades, and the neighborhood now draws quite a few yuppies in search of slightly more affordable rents and a funky ambience. Indeed, the East Village is the city's center for alternative (not necessarily queer) dress, nightlife, and entertainment. The East Village is neither gay nor straight, but cultivates a mix of ages, races, and orientations. Shaved heads and pierced tongues still dominate much of the local club and café scene, but many neobohos have moved farther east and south, chased by the tidal wave of gentrification.

The East Village has few name attractions, but cheap eateries, iconoclast-meets-slacker bars and lounges, and garage-sale-inspired shops keep a steady stream of tourists and locals slinking along at all hours of the night. One of the best streets for strolling is **St. Marks Place** (the name of 8th Street east of 4th Avenue), which is jammed with divy bars, groovy shops, and cheap restaurants. Just to the north, **East 9th Street,** between 2nd and 1st avenues, has emerged in recent years as a block of small, high-quality home furnishings, antiques, and clothing shops. The city's highest concentration of Indian restaurants and groceries is along **East 6th Street,** between 2nd and 1st avenues. Good shopping, browsing, and people-watching can be had along **2nd and 1st avenues,** where you'll find a similar assortment of stores, most notably **Little Rickie** (⊠ 49½ 1st Ave.), whose peculiar gifts and cards should set off your kitschometer.

Chelsea

As recently as a decade ago, few visitors entered **Chelsea,** though gays have lived in this neighborhood immediately north of the West Village for years. The neighborhood was developed in the 1830s by clergyman Clement Clark Moore, author of "A Visit from St. Nicholas" ("Twas the night before Christmas . . ."), whose family owned most of the area. For many decades Chelsea was a drab lower-income neighborhood where workers at nearby garment factories and river docks lived in cheap boardinghouses and rickety, airless tenements. But as gayification crept in from Greenwich Village in the '70s, gentrification took hold. Today Chelsea is a mix of subsidized housing, artists' spaces, middle-class apartments, and town houses that rival those on the Upper East Side.

Several gay discos and leather bars have been doing business for years in the westernmost reaches of Chelsea. In the mid-'80s a few trendy restaurants, shops, and bars opened along 7th and 8th avenues. **Eighth Avenue** has now eclipsed Christopher Street as *the* hip gay thoroughfare. The street's older bodegas and discount stores have quickly been snapped up by entrepreneurs who have converted them into new eateries, coffeehouses, gyms, and gay-theme shops.

The Flatiron District, Union Square, and Gramercy Park

Named for and concentrated around the distinctive neo-Renaissance **Flatiron Building** (⊠ 5th Ave. and 23rd St.), the **Flatiron District** is a chichi enclave of ornate early 20th-century apartment and office buildings that now house media-related industries, artists' lofts, and design studios. The most interesting streets are **Broadway** and **5th Avenue** south of 23rd Street. Walk south along Broadway to **Union Square,** once the home of Andy Warhol's "Factory." North and east of here is a sight reminiscent of London, **Gramercy Park** (⊠ Lexington Ave. and E. 21st St.). This tiny, dapper park and most of the grand town houses surrounding it date from the 1830s; only residents are furnished with a key to the park.

Midtown

New York City's other major commercial district is **Midtown.** The heart of the neighborhood is **Rockefeller Center,** a collection of 19 buildings between 5th and 7th avenues and 47th and 52nd streets. The 70-story **GE Building** looms above the popular Lower Plaza, whose world-famous ice-skating rink is open from October through April (the rest of the year, it becomes an open-air café). **Radio City Music Hall** (⊠ 6th Ave. and 50th St., ☎ 212/247–4777), also a part of Rockefeller Center, is home to the Rockettes chorus line. For a view of it all, take the elevator to the 102nd floor of the **Empire State Building** (⊠ 350 5th Ave., ☎ 212/736–3100).

Fifth Avenue between 50th and 59th streets has long been the city's most elegant shopping corridor—**Bergdorf Goodman, Takashimaya** (Japan's largest department store chain), **Saks Fifth Avenue, Steuben,** and **Tiffany**

& Co. are a few notables. From Lexington Avenue west to Broadway, **57th Street** has several other famous shops, many galleries, **Carnegie Hall** (⊠ W. 57th St. and 7th Ave., ☎ 212/247–7800), and, more recently, a number of touristy theme restaurants. For a diversion, tour the huge **F. A. O. Schwarz** toy store (⊠ 5th Ave. and 58th St., ☎ 212/644–9400), which has an entire section devoted to Barbie and Ken dolls. One of the Ken dolls is clad in earrings, a tank top, and hot pants, but a spokesperson for the manufacturer insists that the doll is not gay. Perhaps he's bi-curious.

Though Midtown hardly oozes charm, it boasts a few important attractions. The collection of the six-floor **Museum of Modern Art** (MoMA, ⊠ 11 W. 53rd St., ☎ 212/708–9480) emphasizes modern artistic movements from Impressionism onward. Cézanne, Van Gogh, Picasso, and Matisse are all represented here. The relationship between **St. Patrick's Cathedral** (⊠ 5th Ave. and 50th St.) and the gay community is at best tenuous, but you'll be hard-pressed to find a more breathtaking church, inside and out. The **New York Public Library** (⊠ 5th Ave. and 42nd St., ☎ 212/930–0800) is one of the most stunning examples of the Beaux Arts style; it sits in front of **Bryant Park,** Midtown's most glorious oasis; green café chairs dot the broad lawn, the site of an ever-expanding lineup of free entertainment. Nearby **Grand Central Terminal** (⊠ Park Ave. and 42nd St.), another Beaux Arts masterpiece, will soon complete a $175 million restoration. Next door is the unique and magnificent art deco **Chrysler Building** (⊠ Lexington Ave. and 42nd St.). The nearby **United Nations Headquarters** (⊠ 1st Ave. and 46th St., ☎ 212/963–7713) has fascinating multilingual tours of the General Assembly.

The Theater District and Hell's Kitchen

It's almost unheard of to pass through New York City without taking in a show. The most popular options in the **Theater District** are in a 10-block stretch of Broadway between Times Square (⊠ 7th Ave. and 42nd St.) and 53rd Street. It's best to book through **Tele-Charge** (☎ 212/239–6200) or **TicketMaster** (☎ 212/307–4100), both of which add a few dollars' surcharge to the ticket price, or through any of several brokers that mark up tickets but often have last-minute seats to the hottest performances (scan major newspapers or check with your hotel concierge for brokers). The adventurous and those short on funds drop by the **TKTS booth** (⊠ 47th St. and Broadway, ☎ 212/768– 1818), a discount, same-day clearinghouse where tickets to major and lesser-known shows often go for as little as half price (cash only). The booth is open from about four hours before most performances until show time, but lines can be long.

Times Square boasts more signs using an astonishing array of technologies than anywhere else in the U.S; there's so much electronic illumination that it's as bright as day around the clock. Natives actually spend little time here; restaurants and shops are overpriced and a bit too theme-oriented for most local tastes. For years riddled with porn shops, panhandlers, and prostitutes, 42nd Street is in the midst of massive redevelopment and the area is cleaner (in every sense) than it has been in 100 years.

Central Park

Without **Central Park** and its 843 acres of make-believe countryside, the city would simply go mad. Endless meadows, dense forests, comfy lawns, wooded trails, and serene lakes constitute this urban oasis. Most non-residents are unaware of the dozens of wonderful things there are to do and see in the park. As a break from shopping and museum-hopping, you might try the following: Feed the many ducks bumbling around the **pond** (enter from E. 59th St.); peek at the animals in the **Children's Zoo** (off 65th St. at 5th Ave.); pick up brochures and park information at the **Dairy's Central Park Reception Center** (⊠ Midpark, at 65th St., ☎ 212/794–6564); sun yourself amid the throngs of queens—and straights—who take over

Sheep Meadow (enter at W. 67th St.) on warm days; in-line skate, cycle, or jog along the several miles of winding roads (which are closed to auto traffic weekdays 10 AM–3 PM and 7–10 PM, and on weekends and holidays); rent a rowboat ($10) at the **Loeb Boathouse** (☎ 212/517–4723) and paddle yourself and a date around the **lake** (enter at W. 77th St.), site of the magnificent Bethesda Fountain; catch a free summer production of **Shakespeare in the Park** (☎ 212/539–8500) at the enchanting, open-air **Delacorte Theater** (enter at W. 81st St.); or, in winter, rent ice skates and glide for a while around **Wollman Memorial Rink** (enter from Central Park S at 6th Ave., ☎ 212/396–1010).

The **Ramble,** a tortuous tangle of woodland just north of the lake and just south of the **79th Street Transverse** (the easiest access is via **Bow Bridge**), is a notorious (and dicey) cruising ground for gay men.

Upper East Side
The antithesis of hip, the Upper East Side is where 19th-century moguls built their mansions, and where many of the city's wealthiest folks continue to nest. Few establishments cater specifically to homosexuals. Gay residents tend to be older, male, well-off, and discreet (confirmed bachelors, as the saying goes), although a younger wave of fags has recently begun moving here to take advantage of the relatively affordable apartments east of Lexington Avenue and north of 72nd Street. As a general rule, those who appreciate the Upper East Side tend to live here; those who can't stand it live elsewhere and seldom visit. For this reason it has an insularity atypical of other Manhattan neighborhoods.

Madison Avenue from 59th to 79th streets thrives with so many high-end fashion boutiques it now rivals 5th Avenue for serious shoppers' dollars. **Lexington Avenue** has fewer big names but is also posh. Antiques shops are well represented on both avenues. Closer to Midtown are two of the city's most popular department stores, **Barneys** (⊠ 660 Madison Ave., ☎ 212/826–8900) and **Bloomingdale's** (⊠ 1000 3rd Ave., ☎ 212/355–5900). Wide, ritzy, and residential, **Park Avenue** runs parallel to and between Lexington and Madison avenues; it's what Lisa (Eva Gabor) trades for a life of agrarian enchantment on her husband, Oliver's (Eddie Albert's) farm on *Green Acres*. Walk along this tony avenue and wonder what on earth she was thinking.

Between 79th and 104th streets, **5th Avenue** is New York's **Museum Mile.** It would take a month of daily viewing to exhaust the Mile's options. The **Metropolitan Museum of Art** (⊠ 5th Ave. and 82nd St., ☎ 212/535–7710), at 1.6 million square feet, is the largest art museum in the Western Hemisphere. Other top museums include the **Frick Collection** (⊠ 1 E. 70th St., ☎ 212/288–0700), a survey of masterworks assembled by coke-and-steel baron Henry Clay Frick; the **Whitney Museum of American Art** (⊠ 945 Madison Ave., ☎ 212/570–3676), which mounts major temporary exhibits (and the always controversial Whitney Biennial) alongside its own small but esteemed permanent collection; Frank Lloyd Wright's singular **Guggenheim Museum** (⊠ 1071 5th Ave., ☎ 212/423–3500), which houses modern painting and photography; the **Cooper-Hewitt Museum** (⊠ 2 E. 91st St., ☎ 212/860–6868), the former Andrew Carnegie residence and now home to thousands of works in metal, glass, textile, and other media; and the unique **El Museo del Barrio** (⊠ 1230 5th Ave., ☎ 212/831–7272), one of the nation's largest collections of Latin American art and culture—its Puerto Rican holdings are especially important.

Upper West Side and Columbia University
Although the Upper West Side has a sizeable queer contingent, rainbow flags are rare here and the homos harder to distinguish from the hets.

Historically the area has always been middle-class, and over the past 30 years it has attracted increasing numbers of academics, actors, and artists along with advertising, public relations, and publishing types.

This is a terrific walking neighborhood. **Broadway** from Columbus Circle (at 59th Street) up to 125th Street is loaded with everything from tiny boutiques to major chain stores, plus dozens of restaurants and movie theaters. **Central Park West,** from Columbus Circle to 96th Street, is lined with beautiful, often overwrought apartment houses (including the Dakota at 72nd Street, where John Lennon lived and outside of which he was shot). In addition to the **Dakota** (whose residents have also included Lauren Bacall, critic Rex Reed, the late composer Leonard Bernstein, and the late dancer Rudolf Nureyev, and which starred in the film *Rosemary's Baby*), you'll find several other celebrity-ridden addresses along this stretch.

The **Lincoln Center complex** (✉ Broadway between 62nd and 66th Sts., ☎ 212/875–5000), the performing arts anchor of Manhattan, comprises the Metropolitan Opera House, the New York State Theater, Avery Fisher Hall, the Guggenheim Bandshell, the Juilliard School for music and theater, Alice Tully Hall, and the Walter Reade Theater.

The Upper West Side's only must-see museum is the immense **American Museum of Natural History** (✉ Central Park W between 77th and 81st Sts., ☎ 212/769–5920). The adjacent **Hayden Planetarium** is being renovated and will not open until the year 2000.

On both Broadway and Amsterdam Avenue at 116th Street, iron gates mark the entryway to the campus of **Columbia University,** the only Ivy League school in New York City. Across the street is **Barnard College,** the esteemed women's institution. The nearby **Cathedral of St. John the Divine** (✉ 1047 Amsterdam Ave., ☎ 212/316– 7540) is a work in progress; when finished it will be the world's largest cathedral. There's a moving National AIDS Memorial and, in the cathedral's Saint Saviour Chapel, Keith Haring's final work, a three-panel plaster altar.

Harlem
Around the turn of the century, African-Americans began moving to **Harlem,** a country village that had become a suburb of apartment houses and brownstones. In the '20s the Harlem Renaissance took hold, and the area buzzed with jazz clubs and literary salons. One of its most interesting sights is a handsome set of town houses known as **Striver's Row** (W. 138th and W. 139th Sts. between 7th and 8th Aves.), where many of Harlem's elite once lived, including musicians W. C. Handy and Eubie Blake. Major cultural attractions include the **Studio Museum in Harlem** (✉ 144 W. 125th St., ☎ 212/864–4500), which contains historic art and photos depicting the neighborhood; the fully restored **Apollo Theatre** (✉ 253 W. 125th St., ☎ 212/749– 5838); and the **Schomburg Center for Research in Black Culture** (✉ 515 Lenox Ave., ☎ 212/491–2200), a collection of 5 million items relating to black history.

Washington Heights
At the northern tip of Manhattan, in **Washington Heights,** is one of New York City's most enchanting attractions, **The Cloisters** (take either the A train to 190th St. or the M-4 bus from Madison Ave. below 110th St. or from Broadway above it; ☎ 212/923–3700). Atop a hill overlooking the Hudson River are five authentic monastic cloisters and a 12th-century chapter house, moved here from France and Spain.

Park Slope
New York City's queerest neighborhood outside of Manhattan, **Brooklyn's Park Slope** (a.k.a. "Dyke Slope") has been popular with lesbians—and to an increasing degree, gay men—for many years, but lately it has

blossomed with gay bars, coffeehouses, and even a queer bookstore. Here you can check out the **Lesbian Herstory Archives** (☎ 718/768–3953), which contains an exhaustive collection of documents tracing lesbian history.

The Slope's magnificent bow-front brownstone mansions and quiet tree-lined streets border 526-acre **Prospect Park.** The park is adjacent to the acclaimed 52-acre **Brooklyn Botanic Garden** (✉ 1000 Washington Ave., ☎ 718/622–4433), where you'll find the **Steinhardt Conservatory;** the 5,000-bush **Cranford Rose Garden;** and the **Celebrity Path,** stepping stones celebrating the lives of such Brooklyn-born household names as Joan Rivers, Willem DeKooning, Barbara Stanwyck, Walt Whitman, Harvey Fierstein, Barbra Streisand, and Mary Tyler Moore. The **Brooklyn Museum of Art** (✉ 200 Eastern Pkwy., ☎ 718/638–5000) is the second-largest art museum in the city, with excellent sections dedicated to Egyptian, African, and pre-Columbian art, American painting and sculpture, and many other periods and genres. The north end of Prospect Park is dominated by the immense **Brooklyn Public Library** (✉ Grand Army Plaza, ☎ 718/780–7700).

GETTING TO PARK SLOPE FROM MANHATTAN

Take the No. 2 or 3 subway to Grand Army Plaza, the B train to 7th Avenue, or the F train to 7th Avenue/Park Slope. By car, take the Manhattan Bridge and continue straight along Flatbush Avenue, which leads directly into the Slope.

GETTING AROUND

Manhattan is disturbingly huge yet surprisingly easy to navigate. Walking is one of the best forms of transportation. Stick to major avenues and broad, busy cross streets, and take cabs late at night. Check with a local to be sure that the most obvious route is the safest.

The subway is cheap ($1.50 per trip) and for the most part safe. It is the quickest way to get between uptown and downtown and your best bet for exploring Brooklyn. Buses (also $1.50), brighter and cleaner than subway cars, are exceptionally slow. If you need to go crosstown (east and west), they are a convenient option since most of the subway lines only run north–south. Buses and subways are mobbed at rush hour; avoid traveling at this time if you don't want to stand for 40 minutes with somebody's elbow jammed against your kidney. MetroCards have rapidly replaced tokens and allow free transfers from subway to bus or bus to subway within two hours. Cabs are an efficient if sometimes hair-raising way to get around and indispensable late at night.

New York City's crime rate has dropped dramatically over the past few years and is now lower than that of many American cities. Most residents of Manhattan are gay-tolerant, but for some morons, the sight of two boys or girls schmoozing—even in the Village—is an invitation to start trouble. It's a cliché, but if you exercise common sense you'll be fine.

Unless you have a serious death wish, enjoy paying up to $30 a day for parking, and don't value your car and/or any of its contents, you should not bring an automobile into New York City. Very few Manhattanites own cars, let alone keep them in the city—it's rarely worth the hassle.

EATS

Although there are 17,000 options for eating out in New York, it's pretty easy to strike out, even at some of the city's best-known eateries. The touristy restaurants around Times Square and Midtown's corporate-oriented high-end eateries can disappoint. For a more interesting and rewarding meal, try the neighborhood restaurants outside the tourist/corporate loop. Still, the city has its share of nationally acclaimed stars, and contrary to popular belief, most of these culinary shrines treat John Doe from Dubuque as well as they do celebrities and regulars. So if you're dead set on experiencing one of the city's *name* restaurants, by all means do so. But if your goal is simply to find good food, you don't need to stand in line or make reservations, nor must you shell out more than $30 per person—even for a three-course dinner.

In addition to the restaurants reviewed below, consider strolling along some of the city's "restaurant rows." For a good meal in the Theater District, try the diverse grouping along **46th Street** between 8th and 9th avenues or, if you want to stray a bit farther afield, **9th Avenue** from 46th to 57th streets—this is the spine of Hell's Kitchen. Downtown, Chelsea's **8th Avenue** has tons of fair-to-decent gay-popular bistros, the quality of which has improved greatly in recent years. In the Village, **West 4th** and **Bleecker streets** between 6th Avenue and Hudson Street have some of the city's most romantic cafés. The intersection of **Mulberry and Spring streets** is the heart of Little Italy; just to the south along **Mott Street** are many of Chinatown's best restaurants.

For price ranges *see* dining Chart A at the front of this guide.

Below Houston Street

$$$$ ✕ **Nobu.** You may recognize the name if you've been to L.A., where the extraordinary young chef, Nobu Matsuhisa, has revolutionized Japanese cuisine. Nobu and his restaurant have been in Manhattan since 1995, but you still may need to reserve a month ahead. What's all the fuss? Sublime clam skewers, okra tempura, and soft-shell crab rolls. ⊠ *105 Hudson St.,* ☎ *212/219–0500.*

$$$–$$$$ ✕ **Aquagrill.** For seafood connoisseurs this is a shrine. The menu consists entirely of fresh, luscious creatures from the ocean. Sample grilled swordfish with broccoli rabe, bacon, and polenta; wolf down fresh oysters at the impressively stocked raw bar; or savor the faintly sweet bouillabaisse in a garlic-saffron tomato broth. ⊠ *210 Spring St.,* ☎ *212/274–0505.*

$$$ ✕ **Odeon.** Hmmm . . . the Formica, the linoleum floor, the elegantly downcast neighborhood: It's easy to see where the West Village's Florent (*see below*) received its inspiration. At Odeon, however, the food is superior (and pricier). The menu emphasizes French bistro cooking, with world-beat influences. Try sautéed scallops with sun-dried tomatoes and ancho chilies. ⊠ *145 W. Broadway,* ☎ *212/233–0507.*

$$–$$$ ✕ **Da Nico.** Tux-clad owner Nick Luizza, a native Italian, often greets guests at this restaurant, arguably the best and gay-friendliest in Little Italy, with a hearty, "Ciao!" Come for heaping portions of pasta and antipasti, crisp-crust coal-fired pizzas, rotisserie poultry, and suckling pig. ⊠ *164 Mulberry St.,* ☎ *212/343–1212.*

$$–$$$ ✕ **El Teddy's.** This post-mod cantina with an over-the-top decor has the best margaritas in New York: tart, potent, and huge. The Mexican menu is a cut above the ordinary; there's always a nice, smoky, roasted-corn soup and excellent grilled seafood. ⊠ *219 W. Broadway,* ☎ *212/941–7070.*

$$–$$$ ✕ **Trattoria Amici Miei.** Next to the gay-friendly lounge, the Attic, this romantic downtown favorite has a fine variety of pasta, grilled fish, and chicken dishes, a vast wine list, cheerful service, and a festive ambience. ⊠ *475 W. Broadway,* ☎ *212/533–1933.*

$–$$ ✕ **Basset Coffee & Tea Co.** The name suggests merely a quick stop for a caffeine pick-me-up, but this is actually a full-scale restaurant serving homestyle American favorites, such as meat loaf and baked macaroni and cheese. Basset overlooks a pretty-peopled street corner. ⊠ *123 W. Broadway,* ☎ *212/349– 1662.*

Greenwich Village

$$$$ ✕ **Gotham Bar & Grill.** Chef Alfred Portale's culinary creations have knocked the socks off New York's most curmudgeonly food critics and jaded diners. Grilled Atlantic salmon with artichokes, basil, and tomato sauce sounds simple but dazzles when presented with such artful panache. Fantastic wine list. ⊠ *12 E. 12th St.,* ☏ *212/620–4020.*

$$$–$$$$ ✕ **Indochine.** The city's most imaginative Cambodian and Vietnamese menu includes such zesty creations as fried chicken stuffed with rice vermicelli, bean sprouts, carrots, lemongrass, and diced chicken. Palm fronds and dark-green banquettes create a tropical mood. ⊠ *430 Lafayette St.,* ☏ *212/505–5111.*

$$$ ✕ **Mary's.** The intimate dining room with gilt mirrors and ornate chandeliers captures the ambience of a late 19th-century town house. The nouvelle-international cuisine (items like escarole pie and sea scallops with a peanut-sesame sauce), however, is anything but old-fashioned. ⊠ *42 Bedford St.,* ☏ *212/741–3387.*

$$–$$$ ✕ **Grange Hall.** The noisy, well-heeled crowd and elegant art deco decor belie what is actually a down-home dining experience. Herb-crusted organic chicken or lamb roast entrées can be matched with items from a long list of hearty vegetable sides—rosemary potatoes, crunchy green beans, and the like. ⊠ *50 Commerce St.,* ☏ *212/924–5246.*

$$–$$$ ✕ **Lips.** The ultimate in drag dining encompasses two floors of nonstop camp and kitsch. Entrées, salads, and desserts are named for your favorite girls. Sample the Ru Paul (grilled marinated chicken breast) or the Misstress Formika (*new* white meat, with wine and shiitake mushrooms). Violet velvet drapes, animal-print pillows, remnants of drag *her*story, and disco lights set an enjoyably chaotic mood. ⊠ *2 Bank St.,* ☏ *212/675– 7710.*

$$–$$$ ✕ **Paris Commune.** Country-French brunches and romantic candlelit dinners draw delighted gourmands to this narrow storefront bistro. A glass of calvados before the fire takes the edge off a day spent trying on leather culottes. The no-nonsense menu offers grilled loin of pork with a fruit compote and calves' liver with capers and shallots. ⊠ *411 Bleecker St.,* ☏ *212/929– 0509.*

$$–$$$ ✕ **Rubyfruit Bar and Grill.** Frequent women's entertainment—comedy, music, costume parties—makes this a favorite dyke dining spot (but everyone is welcome). Red lights and sapphic-celeb photos line the exposed-brick walls. Traditional American chow is featured—simple but usually pretty tasty. ⊠ *531 Hudson St.,* ☏ *212/929– 3343.*

$$–$$$ ✕ **Universal Grill.** Quite possibly the West Village's merriest gay eatery, Universal is tucked in a tiny amber-lit brick box. Trashy '70s music serves as background for the gregarious waitstaff's antics—a birthday celebration here is deliciously embarrassing. The cuisine is American with a Continental drift; try the corn-and-sage soup, followed by tender pan-fried brook trout with lemon-caper butter. ⊠ *44 Bedford St.,* ☏ *212/989–5621.*

$$ ✕ **Seventh Avenue South.** This cozy dyke favorite has a long, elegant bar and an affordable, eclectic, and not especially foofy menu: individual-size pizzas, hearty salads, and main dishes like chicken marsala and poached salmon with a Pernod-dill sauce. ⊠ *46 Bedford St.,* ☏ *212/647–7636.*

$–$$ ✕ **Florent.** An all-night pageant of drag queens and assorted merrymakers ventures well off the beaten path to this stainless steel retro diner known for its eclectic food—*boudin noir* (blood sausage), vegetarian chili, fresh salads, etc. Open 24 hours on weekends and until the wee hours during the week, and sure to tickle après-bar tastebuds. ⊠ *69 Gansevoort St.,* ☏ *212/989–5779. No credit cards.*

$–$$ ✕ **Manatus.** This diner in the heart of the West Village is informal, affordable, quick, warmly decorated, open 24 hours, and decidedly gay. The food isn't bad, but most come more for one of the above reasons. ⊠ *340 Bleecker St.,* ☏ *212/989–7042.*

$–$$ ✕ **Sarong Sarong.** Gorgeous (and flirtatious) sarong-wrapped waiters whisk about the cozy dining room of this Malaysian eatery on busy Bleecker Street. Regional preparations of squid, shrimp, chicken, and beef can be ordered mild or spicy, but the crowded happy hour is always hot. ✉ *343 Bleecker St.,* ☎ *212/989–0888.*

$–$$ ✕ **Tartine.** You'll probably have to wait 30 minutes for a table at this immensely popular purveyor of hearty French fare—the kind of victuals you'd expect to find in a cozy Parisian bistro: chicken potpie, endive and goat cheese salad, grilled salmon with a citrus vinaigrette. BYOB. ✉ *253 W. 11th St.,* ☎ *212/229–2611. No credit cards.*

$ ✕ **Tiffany Restaurant.** What could be more appropriate than breakfast at Tiffany's after a night of powdering your nose in every disco in town? Detoxifying diner food is served 'round the clock, along with egg creams, cappuccino, and the lightest of cheesecakes. ✉ *222 W. 4th St.,* ☎ *212/ 242–1480.*

East Village

$$$ ✕ **Chez Es Saada.** This ultrachic French-Moroccan newcomer is set in a gorgeous basement space on a quiet East Village street. Take your eyes off the sexy crowd long enough to study the sophisticated menu. Pan-roasted seabass with almonds, haricots vert, chanterelle mushrooms, and harissa vinaigrette is a specialty. ✉ *42 E. 1st St.,* ☎ *212/777–5617.*

$$$ ✕ **Opaline.** The constant chatter and music of this spacious nouvelle French-American spot can make it seem more like a chichi nightclub than a restaurant. But take a bite of duck confit over a frisee salad or sautéed monkfish with braised onions, and you'll know that it has a serious kitchen. ✉ *85 Ave. A,* ☎ *212/475–5050.*

$$–$$$ ✕ **Circa.** The famous, the upper crusty, and the fashion conscious come to the EV to eat and party at this very *in* restaurant. Brick-oven pizzas are a staple on the seasonally changing menu; try pumpkin gnocchi with chanterelles, fresh cream, and toasted pecans. DJs and dancing or theme fetes keep things hopping. ✉ *103 2nd Ave.,* ☎ *212/777–4120.*

$$–$$$ ✕ **Pisces.** This tony seafood house on the western edge of Alphabet City is proof that even the local counterculturists demand good food. Check out chef Keith Rennie's aquatic inspirations, including fennel-fried calamari with marinated tomatoes, and a spicy starter of steamed mussels with rosemary, garlic, and spaetzle. ✉ *95 Ave. A,* ☎ *212/260–6660.*

$$ ✕ **Boca Chica.** Sassy and spirited Boca Chica offers a broad and spicy sampling of Latin American and Caribbean dishes, including jerk chicken, shrimp chipotle, and Cuban sandwiches. The downside: long, long lines on weekend evenings. ✉ *13 1st Ave.,* ☎ *212/473–0108.*

$$ ✕ **85 Down.** This smart but affordable New American bistro on increasingly snazzy Avenue A wows EV devotees with sparkling service and such hearty fare as meatloaf with baby carrots and chive-mashed potatoes, and cedar-plank salmon with a red-pepper coulis, roasted garlic, and spaghetti squash. ✉ *85 Ave. A,* ☎ *212/673–8073.*

$–$$ ✕ **Stingy Lulu's.** This Formica fantasyland is popular for above-average diner food after the bars close. On weekend nights a DJ spins tunes for a dress-to-depress crowd. None of the New American–accented entrées costs more than $12; try the blackened grilled Louisiana catfish in a roasted red-pepper chili sauce with crispy polenta. ✉ *129 St. Marks Pl.,* ☎ *212/ 674–3545. No credit cards.*

$–$$ ✕ **Veselka.** An impressive redesign has brightened this neighborhood staple of eastern European cooking, but luckily the menu hasn't changed. Veselka's cheese blintzes, award-winning borscht, and pierogi prove that cooking from this part of the world doesn't have to leave you feeling as though you've just consumed a pile of grease-soaked sandbags. ✉ *144 2nd Ave.,* ☎ *212/228–9682.*

328

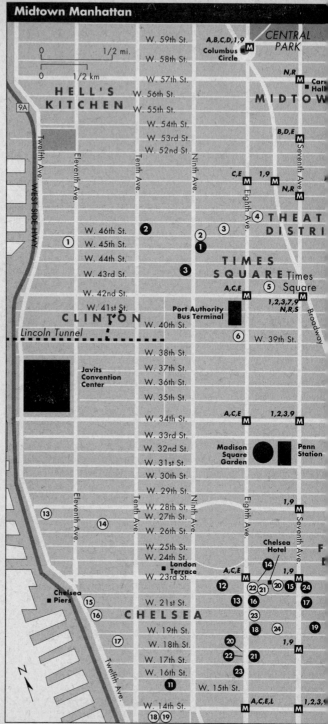

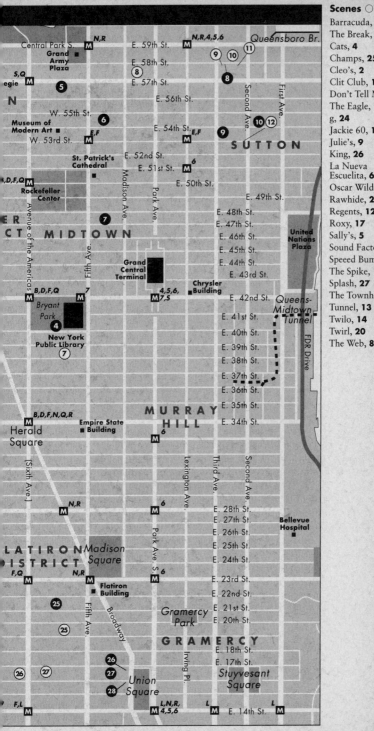

Scenes ○
Barracuda, **21**
The Break, **22**
Cats, **4**
Champs, **25**
Cleo's, **2**
Clit Club, **19**
Don't Tell Mama, **3**
The Eagle, **15**
g, **24**
Jackie 60, **18**
Julie's, **9**
King, **26**
La Nueva
Escuelita, **6**
Oscar Wilde, **10**
Rawhide, **23**
Regents, **12**
Roxy, **17**
Sally's, **5**
Sound Factory Bar, **1**
Speeed Bump, **7**
The Spike, **16**
Splash, **27**
The Townhouse, **11**
Tunnel, **13**
Twilo, **14**
Twirl, **20**
The Web, **8**

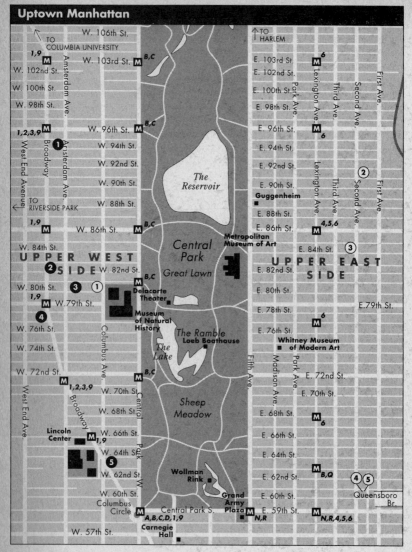

Uptown Manhattan

(map labels, read top to bottom, left to right)

W. 106th St.
TO COLUMBIA UNIVERSITY
1,9
W. 103rd St. **B,C**
W. 102nd St.
W. 100th St.
W. 98th St.
Amsterdam Ave.

TO HARLEM
E. 103rd St. **6**
E. 102nd St.
E. 100th St.
E. 98th St.
E. 96th St. **6**
Park Ave.
Lexington Ave.
Third Ave.
Second Ave.
First Ave.

1,2,3,9
W. 96th St. **B,C**
W. 94th St.
W. 92nd St.
W. 90th St.
W. 88th St.
Broadway
Amsterdam Ave.
West End Avenue

The Reservoir

E. 94th St.
E. 92nd St.
E. 90th St.
Guggenheim
E. 88th St.
E. 86th St. **4,5,6**
Lexington Ave.
Third Ave.
Second Ave.
First Ave.
2

TO RIVERSIDE PARK
1,9
W. 86th St. **B,C**
W. 84th St.

**U P P E R   W E S T
S I D E**
W. 82nd St.
W. 80th St.
1,9
W. 79th St.
W. 76th St.
W. 74th St.
Columbus Ave.

Central Park
Great Lawn
Delacorte Theater
Museum of Natural History
The Ramble
Loeb Boathouse
The Lake

Metropolitan Museum of Art
E. 84th St. **3**
E. 82nd St.
**U P P E R   E A S T
S I D E**
E. 80th St.
E. 78th St. **6**
79th St.
E. 76th St.
Whitney Museum of Modern Art
Fifth Ave.
Madison Ave.
Park Ave.

1
2
3
4
5

W. 72nd St.
1,2,3,9
W. 70th St.
W. 68th St.
W. 66th St.
Lincoln Center
1,9
W. 64th St.
W. 62nd St.
W. 60th St.
Columbus Circle
West End Ave.
Broadway
Central Park W.

Sheep Meadow
Wollman Rink
Grand Army Plaza

E. 72nd St.
E. 70th St.
E. 68th St. **6**
E. 66th St.
E. 64th St.
E. 62nd St. **B,Q**
E. 60th St.
E. 59th St. **N,R,4,5,6**
N,R
4 5
Queensboro Br.

Central Park S.
A,B,C,D,1,9
Carnegie Hall
W. 57th St.

Eats ●

Gabriela's, **1**
Josephina, **5**
La Caridad, **4**
Republic, **2**
Sarabeth's
Kitchen, **3**

Scenes ○

Brandy's
Piano Bar, **3**
Bridge Bar, **5**
Circles, **4**
Toolbox, **2**
The Works, **1**

$ ✕ **Yaffa Café.** Your boho barometer should burst upon strolling into this funky open-all-night restaurant. Lesbian grungettes rub elbows with green-haired boys with pierced extremities and drag queens fighting over the last morsels of the city's best chocolate mud cake. Cheap food, with lots of veggie dishes. ⊠ *97 St. Marks Pl.,* ☎ *212/674–9302.*

Chelsea

$$$–$$$$ ✕ **Chelsea Bistro & Bar.** With a garden in back, a large bar up front, and plenty of dining space in between, there's something for all, groups of friends and solo socializers alike. The Parisian menu—grilled sea scallops and shrimp with leeks, vegetable risotto, and a lemon chive sauce—rarely disappoints. ⊠ *358 W. 23rd St.,* ☎ *212/727–2026.*

$$$–$$$$ ✕ **La Nouvelle Justine.** If you enjoy a touch of domination with your meal, you'll thoroughly appreciate this S/M–theme French restaurant. The food's good—potato-crusted mahimahi with a wild mushroom ragout, roasted garlic, and tomato vinaigrette—but the real draw is the dark seductive interior and the nightly antics. ⊠ *206 W. 23rd St.,* ☎ *212/727–8642.*

$$$ ✕ **Restivo.** With the perfect ambience for first-time dates, this handsome trattoria draws a mix of queers who linger over first-rate Italian cooking. The emphasis is on fresh pasta, salads with rich greens and ripe cheeses, and flavorful grills. ⊠ *209 7th Ave.,* ☎ *212/366–4133.*

$$–$$$ ✕ **Candy Bar & Grill.** This yummy Chelsea confection looks like a queer, '90s update of *Willy Wonka and the Chocolate Factory.* There's no candy on the menu, but the inventive food has plenty of sugary influences: chili-rubbed pork loin with pineapple, red pepper, ginger chutney, and sweet-potato fries. ⊠ *131 8th Ave.,* ☎ *212/229–9702.*

$$–$$$ ✕ **East of Eighth.** Chelsea's latest hot spot for eclectic New American fare is best regarded for its elegant high-ceilinged digs and gracious patio. Typical fare includes grilled pork chops with apple chutney and sun-dried tomato–corn relish. Great brick-oven pizzas, too. ⊠ *254 W. 23rd St.,* ☎ *212/352–0075.*

$$–$$$ ✕ **Meriken.** Drop by for the freshest sushi in the neighborhood, traditional Japanese favorites (chicken teriyaki), or some sublime creations like shrimp, scallops, clams, asparagus, and peppers in a spicy shiitake mushroom sauce on a bed of seaweed noodles. ⊠ *189 7th Ave.,* ☎ *212/620–9684.*

$$–$$$ ✕ **Viceroy.** Try ricotta-filled tortellini with artichoke hearts, sage, tomato, and wild mushroom sauce; or fill up on burgers, salads, or some great sandwiches at this trendy eatery. The service is competent, and the scenery isn't bad either: polished brass, varnished wood, and sculpted men in white muscle Ts. ⊠ *160 8th Ave.,* ☎ *212/633–8484.*

$$ ✕ **Che 2020.** The gay-famous Food Bar reopened in late 1997 as Che 2020 (not, in case you're wondering, because Hugh Downs and Barbara Walters are co-owners). The affordable eclectic American dishes include pan-roasted turkey steak with a mushroom-leek compote. ⊠ *149 8th Ave.,* ☎ *212/243–2020.*

$$ ✕ **Rocking Horse Café.** The Rocking Horse serves some of the most inventive Mexican fare in the city at extremely fair prices. Mussels steamed in a smoky chipotle sauce and tamales in a rich garlic cream sauce are a couple of favorites—the chips and salsa draw raves, too. ⊠ *182 8th Ave.,* ☎ *212/463–9511.*

$–$$ ✕ **Chelsea Market.** This foodies mall opened in spring 1997 in the southwestern corner of Chelsea. Nearly 20 vendors, some with outlets elsewhere in the city, purvey soups, cookies, bread, and every other kind of food imaginable. ⊠ *88 10th Ave.,* ☎ *212/243–5678.*

$–$$ ✕ **Eighteenth & Eighth.** Despite an expansion, everybody's favorite neighborhood hangout is as cramped as ever. Big plates of straightforward high-carbo chow keep the gym queens coming, and plenty of women, too. The grilled salmon special is always a good bet. Long lines, especially on weekends. ✉ *159 8th Ave.,* ☎ *212/242–5000.*

$ ✕ **Bendix Diner.** Despite the uneven service and food, hordes of gays and lesbians convene here for cheap eats and people watching. The standard diner menu is enlivened with several pseudo-Thai dishes (satays, chicken in ginger). Challah-bread French toast is a brunch favorite. ✉ *219 8th Ave.,* ☎ *212/366–0560.* ✉ *also East Village, 167 1st Ave.,* ☎ *212/260–4220.*

The Flatiron District and Gramercy Park

$$$–$$$$ ✕ **Lola.** Yellow walls, candy-stripe upholstery, killer tunes, and the flicker of candlelight make for one of the more exciting (and more expensive) restaurant settings in the Flatiron District. International dishes like pumpkin seed–crusted salmon and mojo-marinated grilled chicken sizzle right off the menu. ✉ *30 W. 22nd St.,* ☎ *212/675–6700.*

$$$–$$$$ ✕ **Union Square Café.** It's among the top restaurants in town (reserve at least a month ahead), yet dinner for two can be had for about $60. And although this kind of New American bistro fare (risotto with spinach, prosciutto, and sage, for example) has been mimicked by competitors, the Café does it best. In summer try for a seat outside looking toward Union Square. ✉ *21 E. 16th St.,* ☎ *212/243–4020.*

$$–$$$ ✕ **The Coffee Shop.** Despite the name, you won't find doughnuts or white ceramic cups and saucers, though there is a small coffee bar. The models and wannabes who flock here like drag queens to a makeup sale at Macy's booze it up at the large main bar and schmooze it up over such well-prepared dishes as latkes with applesauce or coq au vin. ✉ *29 Union Sq. W,* ☎ *212/243– 7969.*

$–$$ ✕ **Republic.** The red-star logo calls to mind Chairman Mao. This spacious and airy Asian restaurant has taken Union Square (and now the Upper West Side) by tsunami. Cheap, tasty, filling fare like seaweed salad (cucumbers, mint, ginger, and tofu with a sesame vinaigrette) is prepared before your eyes. ✉ *37 Union Sq. W,* ☎ *212/627–7172;* ✉ *also Upper West Side, 2290 Broadway,* ☎ *212/579–5959.*

Midtown East

$$$$ ✕ **Lespinasse.** The dining room of the snazzy St. Regis Hotel is stellar in every way. Let the doorman roll out the red carpet and introduce you to the cuisine of chef Gray Kunz: crabmeat with avocado, rice flake–crusted shrimp, and stewed bell peppers; citrus-marinated tuna, fluke, and spinach mackerel in pumpkin seed oil. Start off with cocktails in the hotel's King Cole Bar, popular among gay men in the 1950s. ✉ *2 E. 55th St.,* ☎ *212/ 339–6719.*

$$$–$$$$ ✕ **Vong.** The artfully seductive decor alone makes a trip to this French-Thai restaurant worthwhile: a gold-leaf ceiling, unusual Thai-inspired wooden lamps, shutter doors, wicker chairs, and wood floors. Of course, the fusion cooking is quite remarkable, too. Try Muscovy duck breast roasted with a spicy sesame sauce. ✉ *200 E. 54th St.,* ☎ *212/486–9592.*

$$–$$$ ✕ **Townhouse Restaurant.** One of the city's few gay-dining venues is north of Chelsea—a tad stuffy, and the only one in New York where suits and ties are common—is run by the owners of the nearby Townhouse and Julie's bars (*see* Scenes, *below*). Expect Continental fare such as lobster crab cakes and rack of lamb. ✉ *206 E. 58th St.,* ☎ *212/826–6241.*

$$ ✕ **Regents.** After perusing the generic but decent Italian menu, you may notice that there is more to meet the eye than the food. On the first floor is a cocktail bar and a restaurant serving pastas, salads, and antipasti. On the second floor is a piano bar and lounge, which gets pretty cruisy. The crowd is mixed but mostly gay upstairs—lots of suits. ✉ *317 E. 53rd St.,* ☎ *212/593–3091.*

$–$$ ✕ **Mangia.** Finding a decent, affordable lunch in Midtown is nearly impossible, and although this spot is a bit pricier than an average deli, the quality and variety of food is first-rate. Dozens of Euro-style sandwiches are available, or try the amazing all-you-can-eat antipasto buffet. ⊠ *16 E. 48th St.,* ☎ *212/754–0637.* ⊠ *50 W. 57th St.,* ☎ *212/582–3061.*

Midtown West

$$–$$$$ ✕ **Bryant Park Grill and Café.** Dining at either of these two hot New American eateries will give you a firsthand view of Bryant Park, gloriously restored in the early '90s. The more formal Grill serves uneven cuisine that doesn't always merit the high prices. At the less expensive Café, blissful outdoor seating makes up for food that's nothing special, but be forewarned that noise spills over from the adjacent bar, a prime after-work watering hole. ⊠ *25 W. 40th St.,* ☎ *212/840–6500.*

$$–$$$ ✕ **Revolution.** Locals and tourists jam in around the crowded, homo-popular bar (note the rainbow sticker in the window—rare above 23rd Street). Enjoy the fireplace and busy video screens. The nouvelle-Continental cooking also has plenty to recommend it: Try the pistachio-crusted chicken with curry sauce, grilled polenta, and crispy onions. ⊠ *611 9th Ave.,* ☎ *212/489– 8451.*

$$ ✕ **Mike's American Bar & Grill.** It's scruffy, but the crowd is queer and fun (to say nothing of the staff). Squeeze into this inexpensive option for dependable American food—steaks, burgers, fajitas—and sit bar-style or at almost nonexistent tables. Also a popular hangout for pre- or post-theater drinks. ⊠ *650 10th Ave.,* ☎ *212/246–4115.*

$–$$ ✕ **Cara Mia.** In the heart of booming Hell's Kitchen, this Italian standby excels at appetizers (roasted artichokes are sublime) and fresh, homemade pastas, offered nightly as specials (try the lobster ravioli). The simply decorated, ceramic-tile-floored room is often abuzz before or after the theater. ⊠ *654 9th Ave.,* ☎ *212/262–6767.*

Upper West Side

$$–$$$ ✕ **Josephina.** In a row of Lincoln Center restaurants that range from okay to awful, Josephina is usually good and sometimes outstanding. Continental fare, such as herb-crusted St. Peter's fish with roasted vegetables, is emphasized, and there's a three-part appetizer sampler that changes nightly. ⊠ *1900 Broadway,* ☎ *212/799–1000.*

$$–$$$ ✕ **Sarabeth's Kitchen.** The neighborhood's yuppie central is so popular on weekends (especially for brunch) you may as well forget trying to muscle your way in. Still, the eclectic American food is worth the wait. Try pan-seared salmon with a citrus-curry sauce, potato waffle, and apple-apricot chutney. ⊠ *423 Amsterdam Ave.,* ☎ *212/496–6280.*

$–$$ ✕ **Gabriela's.** A colorful, Aztec-inspired atmosphere and hand-painted murals brighten the otherwise unmemorable coffee-shop decor. The chef taps into family recipes from Guadalajara to create such memorable dishes as shrimp tamales with olives and capers in a roasted tomatillo sauce; and sliced and roasted baby cactus simmered in a cascabel-pepper sauce. ⊠ *685 Amsterdam Ave.,* ☎ *212/961–0574.*

$ ✕ **La Caridad.** Manhattan has several good Cuban-Chinese restaurants, founded by descendants of Chinese laborers who emigrated to Cuba to build its railroads. This no-frills place often has long lines, but when you sit down to a plate of shrimp fried rice, black beans, and sweet plantains, you'll know why. ⊠ *2199 Broadway,* ☎ *212/874–2780. No credit cards.*

Park Slope

$$ ✕ **Max & Moritz.** You'll feel right at home at this stylish but unprepossessing restaurant on 7th Avenue. The food is outstanding: Try roasted duck with a dried fig and orange sauce or lamb shank with a red wine and rosemary reduction and root vegetables. Prices are low, the service sweet, and the dining room warm and jazzy. ⊠ *426A 7th Ave.,* ☎ *718/499–5557.*

$–$$ ✕ **Cornbread Café.** Chef Bettina Harris cooks authentic Southern food accented with nouvelle touches. Try the half-roasted chicken with a sweet andouille sausage and cornbread stuffing or the pan-fried catfish. The long list of sides (choose two with your entrée, such as mashed potatoes and candied yams) makes for monster meals. Very diverse crowd: lesbian moms with kids, art students, and the like. ⊠ *434 7th Ave.,* ☎ *718/768– 3838. BYOB.*

Coffeehouse Culture

Manhattan

Big Cup. This cruisy coffeehouse in Chelsea is a wonderful alternative to the sometimes sullen bar scene. Armchairs and diner-style tables and seats are arranged so that you can't help but chat with the cute caffeine addicts around you. Improvements in the kitchen have resulted in some nice pastries, burritos, and soups, along with okay sandwiches. ⊠ *228 8th Ave.,* ☎ *212/206–0059.*

Caffe dell'Artista. Although this European-style café serves excellent soups, salads, and sandwiches, it's really best for after-dinner coffee and dessert. Dim lighting, mismatched furniture, eclectic and well-chosen art, and upbeat music put everybody in a great mood. Suggestions: Mississippi mud or amaretto cake. ⊠ *46 Greenwich Ave.,* ☎ *212/645–4431.*

Caffe Rafaella. The phrase "strike a pose" might have been coined at this ultrastylish, antique-filled coffeehouse with amazing desserts and some of the best sidewalk seating in the Village. ⊠ *134 7th Ave. S,* ☎ *212/ 929–7247.*

A Different Bite Café. But for a magnificent crystal chandelier looming overhead, this snacking and sipping adjunct to the famously queer A Different Light bookstore is a modest, mellow space. Not surprisingly, it's fairly easy to meet well-read dykes and fags. ⊠ *151 W. 19th St.,* ☎ *212/ 989–4850.*

Limbo. The gayest coffeehouse in the East Village has good sandwiches, dozens of coffee and tea selections, board games, and plenty of gay staff. ⊠ *47 Ave. A,* ☎ *212/477–5271.*

Tea & Sympathy. Anglophiles and other aficionados of clotted cream, scones, and tea cram into this minuscule teahouse on Greenwich Avenue, where the finger sandwiches, sweets, and Earl Grey flow freely. Very civilized and very gay. ⊠ *108 Greenwich Ave.,* ☎ *212/807–8329.*

Park Slope

Rising Café. Next door to Beyond Words bookstore, Rising hosts live music, poetry readings, open-mike gatherings, games nights, and "women's pick-up" mixers. Lounge furniture, unfinished wooden floors, and exposed brick make this half rustic country store and half urban arts space. ⊠ *186 5th Ave.,* ☎ *718/789–6340.*

SCENES

For all of its glamour and panache, New York City's gay nightlife is surprisingly accessible. Contrary to sensationalist rumors, getting into hot discos does not typically require being dressed or looking a certain way— you just have to be willing to pay a $10 to $20 cover and deal with high drink prices. And although it's easy to find attitude at the most "in" spots, Manhattan's bar-goers are an approachable lot. There are at least four or five choices for most brands of gay bar, from leather to piano to stand-and-model to genX to neighborhood. Several smaller gay discos are open seven nights a week, and an equal number of megasize dance clubs have gay nights once or twice a week. The only negative about the city's gay bars is that most are too cramped—an unavoidable result of the city's exorbitant real-estate costs. That said, newer clubs are both larger and more cleverly decorated than their predecessors.

Pick up the phone.
Pick up the miles.

Is this a great time, or what? :-)

Now when you sign up with MCI you can receive up to 8,000 bonus frequent flyer miles on one of seven major airlines.

Then earn another 5 miles for every dollar you spend on a variety of MCI services, including MCI Card® calls from virtually anywhere in the world.*

You're going to use these services anyway. Why not rack up the miles while you're doing it?

Body Positive (☎ 800/566–6599) holds tea dances for men with HIV/AIDS and their friends at various locations. There's always great music, prizes, and a nice crowd.

Greenwich Village

PRIME SUSPECTS

The Lure. This is the only leather club that enforces a dress code, at least on weekends. You may wear a jockstrap; you may not wear knickers. You may wear rubber rain gear; you may not wear clothing whose scent has been enhanced by a fabric softener. You may wear military gear; you may not dress in drag. The bar is cavernous, crowded, and anchored by a dentist's chair. During the week there are theme nights, such as Wednesday's Pork, when drinks are half price and a DJ presides over S/M demonstrations and other wholesome fun. ✉ *409 W. 13th St.*, ☎ *212/741–3919. Crowd: male, all ages, serious leather, bears, butch-chic.*

The Monster. People either love or hate this Sheridan Square institution, and for some New Yorkers it's the only West Village bar they still bother with. On the first floor, the tone-deaf gather and sing around the piano or swill liberally at the large bar; downstairs, the rhythm-impaired gyrate in a campy pitch-black disco. Leave your attitude at the door. ✉ *80 Grove St.*, ☎ *212/924–3558. Crowd: 85/15 m/f, very diverse in age and race, strong Latin and African American following, cruisy, outgoing, fun.*

Stonewall. An odd mix of curious tourists and down-to-earth locals ensures that this place remains untrendy and free-spirited. Channel the spirits of our brothers and sisters who rioted for our rights near this very spot (the original Stonewall Inn was next door). The pool table gets more action than most of the patrons, though lonely hearts can pile into the snug back room to view blue videos. An upstairs dance floor was recently added. ✉ *53 Christopher St.*, ☎ *212/463–0950. Crowd: mostly male, diverse in ages, local, down-to-earth.*

NEIGHBORHOOD HAUNTS

For lounge lizards, the gay-friendly lounge **hell** (✉ 59 Gansevoort St., ☎ 212/727–1666), filled with red drapes, crystal chandeliers, and high-end lounge furniture, appeals to self-consciously stylish, downtown crowd. On the border of SoHo and Greenwich Village, **The Attic** (✉ 77 W. Houston St., ☎ 212/388– 1384) is a mixed gay/straight tapas bar and cocktail lounge with a crowd similar to hell's.

The West Village has quite a few sleepy bars, each with a small but fiercely loyal following: **Boots & Saddle** (✉ 76 Christopher St., ☎ 212/929–9684) and **Ty's** (✉ 114 Christopher St., ☎ 212/741–9641) get more of a butch Levi's crowd; the **Dugout** (✉ 185 Christopher St., ☎ 212/242–9113) aims to be a sports bar but feels more like an Off-Track-Betting parlor; and the **Hangar** (✉ 115 Christopher St., ☎ 212/627–2044) and **Pieces** (✉ 8 Christopher St., ☎ 212/929–9291) are friendly, mellow video bars. **Julius** (✉ 159 W. 10th St., ☎ 212/929–9672), though slightly ragged, has been a West Village landmark since the 1860s and has had a queer following since the 1950s.

The West Village has a racially integrated gay nightlife scene, and most of the above-mentioned bars have a moderate following among men of color. A few others have primarily African-American crowds: **Two Potato** (✉ 143 Christopher St., ☎ 212/255–0286) has go-go boys some nights and a high cruise factor; it's also fairly popular with Latinos. **Sneakers** (✉ 392 West St., ☎ 212/242–9830) is a rickety old dive that gets a mixed race and mixed gender crowd. **Keller's** (✉ 384 West St., ☎ 212/243–1907), which is most popular has been going strong for more than four decades. It shows blaxploitation movies on the monitors, and has friendly bartenders.

The least snobbish parties in Manhattan are the dances held at the **Lesbian and Gay Community Services Center** (⊠ 208 W. 13th St., ☎ 212/620–7310) on the second and fourth Saturday of every month (they go on hiatus in summer, however). Sunday nights the Center hosts the Country Tea Dance, a boot-stomping, two-stepping extravaganza.

On Sunday, consider **Boy's Life** (Life, ⊠ 158 Bleecker St., ☎ 212/420–1999), a recently expanded spot with a midsize dance floor, funky lounges, and an earsplitting sound system. Manhattan's most distinctive weekly event is **Squeeze Box,** held Fridays at Don Hill's in SoHo (⊠ 511 Greenwich St., ☎ 212/334–1390). An ensemble of drag queens burns up the stage with high-decibel renderings of classic and original rock, punk, and heavy metal. Don Hill's also has a retro disco and New Wave fest on Saturdays.

Piano cabarets are numerous in the West Village, especially on Grove Street. Most popular are **Marie's Crisis** (⊠ 59 Grove St., ☎ 212/243–9323), which is extremely shaggy—even dumpy—and strangely lovable; the cozy and queer **Rose's Turn** (⊠ 55 Grove St., ☎ 212/366–5438); and **Eighty-Eights** (⊠ 228 W. 10th St., ☎ 212/924–0088), which has top-notch performers in its upstairs cabaret (where a cover is usually charged) and a laid-back piano scene downstairs. The famous **Duplex** (⊠ 61 Christopher St., ☎ 212/255–5438) has cabaret shows and stand-up comedians, plus a cozy bar upstairs.

East Village

The Bar. This intimate, self-consciously scruffy East Village institution is dressed in black and blessed with an amazing jukebox (mostly rock/punk/grunge) and a slightly worn pool table. Although the cruise factor is high, many people come here to socialize with friends. ⊠ 68 2nd Ave., ☎ 212/674–9714. Crowd: mostly male, college age to thirtysomething, alternative, racially mixed, lots of black jeans and goatees, a bit of an edge.

Boiler Room. A cruisier version of its neighbor, the Bar, this trendy lounge is the neighborhood's hottest fag bar. Armchairs and sofas in two corners make it possible to hold your own salon. There's a mellower local crowd on weekdays, when you can actually make your way from one end of the bar to the other. The numbers swell on Fridays and Saturdays, however. ⊠ 86 E. 4th St., ☎ 212/254–7536. Crowd: 85/15 m/f; mostly under 35, mildly grungy, hip but increasingly mainstream, a few straying Chelsea boys, a real meat market.

Wonder Bar. More swank and sophisticated than other EV bars, this tiny lounge has resfreshingly offbeat DJ-blended music every night, a grown-up selection of beers and cocktails, psychedelic lighting, and a wall of comfy candlelighted sofas. A great place to dish with friends, and for gay guys, dykes, and straight friends to mix it up. ⊠ 505 E. 6th St., ☎ 212/777–9105. Crowd: 70/30 m/f, young with a few latter-day hippies; goatees, tattoos, shabby-chic, low attitude, very anti–pretty boy.

When the Boiler Room and the Bar get overrun with visiting Chelsea boys, locals retreat to **Dick's Bar** (⊠ 192 2nd Ave., ☎ 212/475–2071), a narrow, dark, somber space whose jukebox has the most delightfully obscure tunes—lots of "greatest hits" compilations by bands you never realized had any. Well-heeled yuppies and guppies (crowds are mostly straight except for Sunday, when there's an even mix) congregate at **Liquids** (⊠ 266 E. 10th St., ☎ 212/677–1717) for sake, wines by the glass, microbeers, and colorful mixed drinks (cocktails are no bargain, by the way). Life's always a drag at the mixed gay-straight cross-dressing clubhouse in the basement of **Lucky Cheng**'s (⊠ 24 1st Ave., ☎ 212/473–0516), the touristy pan-Asian restaurant.

ONE-NIGHTERS, MOVEABLE FETES

The grrrl bar **Meow Mix** (*see* Women's Bars, *below*) packs a mixed-gender crowd on Wednesdays and Sundays. **Salon Wednesday** (⊠ 219 2nd Ave., ☎ 212/533–2860) is an I'm-too-slick-for-words, drag-hosted mixer at the chic restaurant Flamingo East that has been pulling in a pretty crowd for some time now. On Friday fags pile into **Pyramid** (⊠ 101 Ave. A, ☎ 212/802–9502) for **1984,** a nostalgic New Wave bash. College boys and the guys who love them can't get enough of Thursday's 18-and-over **Kurfew** (at System, ⊠ 76 E. 13th St., ☎ 888/458–7339). On Friday, everybody piles into **Sunrise** (at Bar 13, ⊠ 35 E. 13th St., ☎ 212/979–6677), an after-hours party that rocks til 10 AM.

Chelsea

PRIME SUSPECTS

Barracuda. Chelsea's artsy (but still cruisy) gay bar has a happily cluttered, cozy rear lounge so filled with dated sofas and couches it could be a Salvation Army furniture showroom. Any day of the week the lounge is an ideal retreat and, thankfully, cute cocktail waiters bring the drinks right to you. A pool table sits in the middle of this funky morass. Up front there's a more intimate bar. ⊠ 275 W. 22nd St., ☎ 212/645–8613. Crowd: mostly male, mostly under 35, hip, stylish, some goatees and piercings.

Champs. Although it bills itself Manhattan's gay sports bar, not a single queen here knows the difference between a javelin and a hockey stick. Still it's a fiercely crowded club in the city, with an acute gotta-get-laid focus. The once-cutesy, faux-phys-ed decorating motif has given way to dim lighting, a few cheap sofas, a busy pool table, and an even busier but generic-looking dance floor. Someone obviously realized that boys come here to look at each other, not the walls, so why dress the place up? ⊠ 17 W. 19th St., ☎ 212/633- -1717. Crowd: male, 20s to 30s, well-built, amazingly high testosterone levels, quite a few blockheads, tight shirts, tight jeans, tight abs.

g. This futuristic guppie boîte feels more like a post-postmodern airport lounge than a gay bar. Striking (some say contrived), the lounge completely shuns the color black; walls are panels of molded blond wood, and the central bar is stainless steel. There are low vinyl seats, a bank of shimmering metal pay phones in one rear corner, a U-shape bathroom with mosaic walls, and a small juice bar in back. The pale, airy design conveys a remarkable sense of relaxation and serenity. ⊠ 223 W. 19th St., ☎ 212/929–1085. Crowd: 80/20 m/f, mostly late 20s to 40s, professional, suits and designer duds, buffed and coiffed, very A-list.

King. This pleasantly decorated space is popular on weekends because it often stays open after hours, but not everybody's thrilled to pay a cover to get in here, and the bitchy staff doesn't help. On the first floor is a standard-issue cruise bar, on the second a dance floor. The top floor is open only on certain nights and offers back-room action. ⊠ 579 6th Ave., ☎ 212/366–5464. Crowd: mostly male, extremely cruisy, a blend of the Champs and Splash crowds.

The Spike. Once the ultimate parade of black leather, chains, and Levi's, the Spike now has a bark that's quite a bit worse than its bite. A couple of rooms are done in the requisite butch motorcycle look, but most guys here are regular old Chelsea fags looking for something a little seedier than the Break but who aren't ready for a full-on leather bar. ⊠ 120 11th Ave., ☎ 212/243–9688. Crowd: male, late 20s to 40s, some leather but more Levi's, a few guppies.

Splash. This long-running good-times bar remains a Manhattan hot spot, owing largely to the management's ongoing improvements that keep the mammoth cruise hall looking spiffy and cutting-edge. The go-go shows are among the most popular in town—the dancers perform in translucent shower cubicles. The basement has a gay gift boutique, a comfy lounge, and porn on the video monitors. Upstairs a midsize dance floor is just large enough for 50 guys to get going. ⊠ *50 W. 17th St.,* ☎ *212/691–0073. Crowd: mostly male, young to middle-age, becoming slightly more diverse racially, generally cute, dapper, touristy.*

Twirl. The newest addition to Chelsea's club-saturated scene. Expect the usual mix of buff locals and dance-mad out-of-towners who are regulars on New York's frenetic follow-the-DJ circuit. There's a different dance fete every night; Saturday **Swirl** is a rage. A games area has Nintendo and Internet surfing. ⊠ *208 W. 23rd St.,* ☎ *212/691–7685. Crowd: mostly male, young, professional club-goers, less attitude than at other superdiscos.*

NEIGHBORHOOD HAUNTS

Once one of Chelsea's hottest cruise scenes, **The Break** (⊠ 232 8th Ave., ☎ 212/627–0072) has become more rough-and-tumble as new guppie and musclehead bars have opened nearby. It now draws a down-to-earth neighborhood crowd—not to mention a few banjee boys and leather men. Patrons of **the Eagle** (⊠ 142 11th Ave., ☎ 212/691–8451) are extremely serious about three things: drinking, glaring, and shooting pool. Lean against the pool table and you'll lose a finger. Much more hard-core than the nearby Spike but not as hip as the Lure, this is the place to break in those chaps you got for Valentine's Day. *Not* the place to show off your bright white Calvins or your Gap anything, **Rawhide** (⊠ 212 8th Ave., ☎ 212/242–9332) is the only Chelsea bar away from 12th Avenue that has any edge to it. It's a small, dark room, whose most distinctive feature is a vent above the front door that blows several cubic tons per second of nasty exhaust onto passing pedestrians.

ONE NIGHTERS, MOVEABLE FETES

The labyrinthine **Tunnel** (⊠ 220 12th Ave., ☎ 212/695–4682) has mixed gay/straight parties on Friday and Saturday that grow progressively faggier as the night goes on and glow pink by morning. Stepping into the 20,000-square-foot glam-filled **Twilo** (⊠ 530 W. 27th St., ☎ 212/268–1600) is like fast-forwarding into the 21st century. The multicolor odd-shape flashing lights and the first-class sound system are almost extraterrestrial. On gay Saturdays, blastoff is at 11 PM; although admission is a hefty $20, this kind of heady dance trip is worth it. Once famous for its blowout Saturday parties, **Roxy** (⊠ 515 W. 18th St., ☎ 212/645–5156) is now mostly straight and only worth a visit for Saturday's gay dance party.

On Tuesdays catch **Jackie 60** (Mother, ⊠ 432 W. 14th St., ☎ 212/677–6060), a freak show jamboree out to shock the masses with performance art and planned and spontaneous acts of mayhem.

Above 23rd Street

PRIME SUSPECTS

La Nueva Escuelita. Midtown's favorite queer Latin club draws big crowds for salsa, merengue, and house music. La Nueva Escuelita looks terrific, and plenty of money and effort have turned this into the hottest gay club in Midtown. The best night is Sunday for Lady Catiria's sequin-disaster drag show. ⊠ *301 W. 39th St.,* ☎ *212/631–0588. Crowd: mostly Latinos and Latinas, but an increasingly mixed bunch.*

The Townhouse. On good nights, it's like stepping into a Ralph Lauren wet dream—cashmere sweaters, Rolex watches, distinguished-looking gentlemen—and it's surprisingly festive. On bad nights, you bump into your sister's husband and he's cruising your boss's son (a lot of these suits have never been out of the closet). The decor recalls a stately Philadelphia hunt club, although the plaid carpeting is more reminiscent of a suburban VFW hall. If it gets a little stuffy here head to the back, where most of the fun guys congregate around the piano. There's also a smoke-free downstairs, which is rare in Manhattan bars. ⊠ *236 E. 58th St.,* ☎ *212/754–4649. Crowd: mostly male, upscale crowd, lots of suits, may be the only bar left in Manhattan where ascots are still fashionable.*

The Works. Gay men who typically suffer nosebleeds north of 23rd Street still flock religiously to this Upper West Side institution for great drink specials. Weekends see a little more bridge-and-tunnel action. There are always a few boys who look like J. Crew models, and the rest of the crowd at least dresses like them. Long and narrow, the place has dim lighting, black walls, lots of video screens, and zero ambience. There's more lounging in the basement. ⊠ *428 Columbus Ave.,* ☎ *212/799– 7365. Crowd: mostly male, late 20s and 30s,, guppie, stand-and-model, very cruisy, some attitude, a mix of collared shirts and muscle T's with a few suits thrown in.*

NEIGHBORHOOD HAUNTS

The Theater District's *other* **Cats** (⊠ 232 W. 48th St., ☎ 212/245–5245) is a skeevy little bar where go-go boys willingly paw at your lap in exchange for certain favors. The only nonsleazy gay bar near Times Square, **Cleo's** (⊠ 656 9th Ave., ☎ 212/307–1503) is a good spot to grab a drink before or after catching a Broadway show. Little **Don't Tell Mama** (⊠ 343 W. 46th St., ☎ 212/757–0788), a mixed gay/straight piano bar and cabaret along Restaurant Row in the Theater District, presents some outstanding acts. **Sally's** (⊠ 252 W. 43rd St., ☎ 212/944–6000, ext. 212) is big with cross-dressers.

The Web (⊠ 40 E. 58th St., ☎ 212/308–1546) is the only gay Manhattan club with any substantial Asian following. This two-tiered basement has dated decor, mediocre music, and rarely draws much of a crowd. **Oscar Wilde** (⊠ 221 E. 58th St., ☎ 212/486–7309) is an after-work suits bar on the pinkest street in Midtown. Consider dropping by **Regents** (⊠ 317 E. 53rd St., ☎ 212/593–3091), a restaurant with a piano and cocktails in a cruisy second-floor lounge.

Brandy's Piano Bar (⊠ 235 E. 84th St., ☎ 212/650–1944) has long had a following with Upper East Side lesbians and gays. This cabaret bar with an old-fashioned feel looks like something you'd find on Grove Street. Right below the tram to Roosevelt Island is the **Bridge Bar** (⊠ 309 E. 60th St., ☎ 212/223–9104), one of the nicest local bars around, with friendly bartenders, plenty of attractive seating, and an upscale but unpretentious feel. **Circles** (⊠ 1134 2nd Ave., ☎ 212/588–0360) is the latest piano cabaret to hit the neighborhood. **Toolbox** (⊠ 1742 2nd Ave., ☎ 212/348–1288) is a generic video bar with Tom of Finland drawings on the walls—it's your only hope of getting laid on the Upper East Side.

ONE-NIGHTERS, MOVEABLE FETES

The **Sound Factory** (⊠ 618 W. 46th St., ☎ 212/643–0728) is back, this time on the far western edge of Hell's Kitchen. Inside you'll discover a three-floor space that some say lives up to the legendary name, but that many fans of the old Sound Factory complain is an inferior version. Saturday is now the main gay night; Fridays are mixed gay/straight. **Speeed Bump** (⊠ 20 W. 39th St., ☎ 212/719–9867) is *the* hottest Sunday-night club event in the city, complete with several bars and dance floors.

Park Slope

The Slope's most popular hangout is hopping **Carry Nation** (✉ 363 5th Ave., ☎ 718/788–0924). The crowd is artsy, sometimes cliquey, and often quite cute—a strong mix of lesbians and gay men, all ages. The front room has a long bar and rocking jukebox; the rear room has some seating and a pool table. A cousin of the East Village women's hangout, Meow Mix, **Sanctuary Lounge** (✉ 444 7th Ave., ☎ 718/832–9800) is interesting and very Gothic; although the crowd is mostly women, men are welcome.

Women's Bars

Alas, relatively few of the bars reviewed above have significant lesbian followings (with the exception of Carry Nation and Sanctuary Lounge, both in Brooklyn's Park Slope; *see above*). Still, women are definitely welcome (if seldom seen) at the East Village bars listed, all the piano bars, and several other boy haunts, including Barracuda, Brandy's, Circles, Cleo's, Crawford's, g, the Monster, Regents, and the Stonewall.

PRIME SUSPECTS

Crazy Nanny's. The biggest dyke bar in the city is painted a striking shade of purple, so you can't miss it. The downstairs video bar rocks only on weekends. An invariably big crowd sashays away on the sizable dance floor upstairs. A no-frills lounge has a bunch of benches against the wall and an extremely popular pool table. Nanny's doesn't get going until after midnight. ✉ *21 7th Ave. S,* ☎ *212/366–6312. Crowd: mostly female (men only with female friends), young, about half African-American and Latina, cruisy, boisterous, fairly working-class, lots of diesel dykes, downtown vagabonds, Sinead O'Connor wannabes, backward baseball caps.*

Henrietta Hudson. The whole place feels like an old ale house, with weathered-wood paneling, hardwood floors, and a classic bar that's usually packed on weekends. A jukebox plays middle-of-the-road dance and pop tunes. Long lines to the bathroom. ✉ *438 Hudson St.,* ☎ *212/924–3347. Crowd: 85/15 f/m, mostly 20s and 30s, white-bread, friendly, down-to-earth, fairly professional.*

Julie's. This classy, popular spot is decorated like somebody's parlor, but the stuffiness stops there: The staff is friendly and outgoing, the patrons outgoing if not downright wild (especially late in the evening). A long bar with stools connects with a small standing area that opens into a larger (but still compact) dance floor. ✉ *204 E. 58th St.,* ☎ *212/688–1294. Crowd: mostly female, mid- 20s to late 30s, well-heeled, professional, Ann Taylor dykes, expensive coifs.*

Meow Mix. You have to love the name of this new dyke hangout on the border between the Lower East Side and the East Village. Here you'll find the best jukebox of any women's bar in Manhattan, a hip downtown crowd, and nightly performances ranging from poetry readings to stand-up comedy. The fashionable hangout, which draws the occasional unannounced celebrity (Courtney Love, Ellen DeGeneres, Ann Heche), starred in the genX love saga *Chasing Amy.* ✉ *269 E. Houston St.,* ☎ *212/254–0688. Crowd: mostly female, young, granny dresses, layered lace, combat boots, cakey white makeup, pierced septums, tarnished silver bangles, cropped hair.*

NEIGHBORHOOD HAUNTS

Drop by the aptly named **Cubbyhole** (✉ 281 W. 12th St., ☎ 212/243–9041) to chat with old friends or to sit around watching the tube—the kind of place where you might bump into your high-school phys ed teacher. The popular cocktail bar at the **Rubyfruit Bar and Grill** (✉ 531 Hudson St., ☎ 212/929– 3343) has become increasingly lesbian over the past couple of years.

ONE-NIGHTERS, MOVEABLE FETES

Friday nights **Clit Club** (⊠ 432 W. 14th St., ☎ 212/529–3300) is the hottest dyke party in the city—a feast of combat boots and black bras. Spicy go-go girls work the sweaty dance crowd upstairs; downstairs women cruise and flirt and others getting hot and heavy in the packed lounge. Very young, very hip. Women only.

Action

Despite the crackdown on bathhouses, sex clubs, X-rated movie houses, video booths, and all-around moral debauchery, there is, at least for the moment, far more sleaze in New York City than Mayor Rudolph Giuliani would like you to believe. (Still, as part of the mayor's wide-ranging so-called "quality of life" campaign, impending zoning changes could close down many of the city's sex-positive venues in one fell swoop.)

One of New York's most action-packed playgrounds, the **Bijou Theater** (⊠ 82 E. 4th St., no phone) gets pretty busy after the East Village bars close. This basement complex (the door is beneath an illuminated sign that says STRADA) comprises a few well-lighted lounges; a bar that distributes free soda, chips, and cookies; a small adult-video theater (be careful, the seats come unhinged easily), and a few dark corridors lined with 20 or so private rooms. Not far away, and attracting many of the same guys, the **All Male XXX Video** (⊠ 14th St. and 3rd Ave., no phone) has 24-hour booths.

Several adult video stores are near the intersection of Christopher and Hudson streets, the best of which are the **Christopher Street Bookshop** (⊠ 500 Hudson St., ☎ 212/463–0657) and **Harmony Video** (⊠ 139 Christopher St., ☎ 212/366–9059). In Chelsea, plenty of fun is only $10 ($8 on weekdays) and a turnstile away at **Unicorn** (⊠ 277C W. 22nd St., ☎ 212/924–2921), a porn video and magazine store with a video arcade.

In Times Square, the **Gaiety** (⊠ 201 W. 46th St., ☎ 212/221–8868) is without question the best place to watch male strippers—it does, after all, feature some of the boys in Madonna's book *Sex*.

Popular saunas include the **East Side Club** (⊠ 227 E. 56th St., 6th floor, ☎ 212/753–2222), the **West Side Club** (⊠ 27 W. 20th St., 2nd floor, ☎ 212/691–2700), and the **Wall Street Sauna** (⊠ 1 Maiden La., ☎ 212/233–8900).

SLEEPS

New York City's hotels are unbelievably expensive—it's virtually impossible to find basic accommodations for less than $100 a night (the standard room rate averages about $200 a night). Operating expenses and customer demand are high, so rates are unlikely to drop soon. Still, the "rack rates" printed on most hotel brochures are anything from 20% to 50% higher than you will *ever* have to pay. For the best deals, scan the travel sections of major newspapers for packages (which often include dinner, tickets to a show, free parking, and/or airport shuttle service), book through a travel agent (who may have a good relationship with a certain property), call as well in advance as possible (the later you call, the less your leverage), and be sure to ask about corporate rates.

Most hotels are in Midtown or the nearby Theater District. There aren't a lot of options in gay neighborhoods, but many of the rooms available in Greenwich Village, SoHo, Chelsea, and on the Upper West Side are comparatively affordable.

For price ranges, *see* lodging Chart A at the front of this guide.

Hotels

Uptown

$$$$ ⊞ **Lowell.** If you must be kept, try to be kept at New York's most dignified and intimate transient address, just a few blocks from the suits-saturated gay nightlife along East 58th Street. Noël Coward once resided at this 1926 hotel, which is decorated with a magnificent mix of art deco and Second Empire antiques; some rooms have wood-burning fireplaces. ⊠ *28 E. 63rd St., 10021,* ☎ *212/838–1400 or 800/221–4444,* 𝔽𝔸𝕏 *212/ 319–4230. 65 rooms. 2 restaurants, health club.*

$$$ ⊞ **Barbizon.** For 50 years this Upper East Side neo-Gothic landmark was a women's residential hotel (Candice Bergen and Grace Kelly both stayed here). The smallish rooms have entertainment armoires with CD stereo systems and large TVs, as well as fully modernized baths. ⊠ *140 E. 63rd St., 10021,* ☎ *212/838–5700 or 800/223–1020,* 𝔽𝔸𝕏 *212/888–4271. 386 rooms. Restaurant, health club.*

$$–$$$ ⊞ **Radisson Empire.** A good bet if you're in town for the Metropolitan Opera, this hotel overlooking Lincoln Center has evolved into one of the city's best in this price range. Rooms are small but have VCRs, CD players, and other high-end amenities. The ground-floor restaurant, Merlot, is highly regarded. ⊠ *44 Broadway, 10023,* ☎ *212/265–7400 or 800/ 333– 3333,* 𝔽𝔸𝕏 *212/315–0349. 373 rooms. Restaurant.*

$ ⊞ **Malibu Studios Hotel.** It isn't fancy, but this gay-friendly hotel has clean rooms with minirefrigerators and hot plates and is ideal if you need a cheap pad close to Columbia University. Rooms have private or shared baths; some have full kitchenettes. ⊠ *2688 Broadway, 10025,* ☎ *212/ 222–2954 or 800/647–2227,* 𝔽𝔸𝕏 *212/678–6842. 150 rooms.*

Midtown

$$$$ ⊞ **Peninsula.** Of 5th Avenue's top-of-the-line hotels, this is the warmest and the most romantic. Unlike the Plaza or even the Pierre, it has a human scale and ultraefficient, unstuffy service. Rooms are big with peaceful decor, marble baths, and some have Jacuzzis. The three-floor, bar-equipped rooftop health club and spa is spectacular. ⊠ *700 5th Ave., 10019,* ☎ *212/247- -2200 or 800/262–9467,* 𝔽𝔸𝕏 *212/903–3949. 250 rooms. Restaurant, pool, health club.*

$$$$ ⊞ **Royalton Hotel.** This playground of visiting fashion, film, and publishing moguls is popular with New York's movers and shakers for its Round Bar and 44 restaurant. The finest of Ian Schrager's three properties, the hotel's haute-decor rooms have cushioned window seats, working fireplaces, and spacious, curvaceous bathtubs. ⊠ *44 W. 44th St., 10036,* ☎ *212/869–4400 or 800/635–9013,* 𝔽𝔸𝕏 *212/869–8965. 168 rooms. Restaurant, health club.*

$$$$ ⊞ **U.N. Plaza–Park Hyatt.** The Park Hyatt surpasses many of the Big Apple's ritziest properties when it comes to service and style. The staff works hard to anticipate the needs of its bigwig clientele—visiting diplomats and dignitaries. Rooms are slick and refined with wood trim and indirect lighting but lack the Old World character of the city's top-of-the-line hotels. ⊠ *1 United Nations Plaza, E. 44th St. and 1st Ave., 10017,* ☎ *212/758–1234 or 800/223–1234,* 𝔽𝔸𝕏 *212/702–5051. 427 rooms. Restaurant, pool, health club.*

$$$–$$$$ ⊞ **Morgans.** The least known—but to many celebs, the most preferred—of Ian Schrager's trendy properties thinks of itself as a discreet home away from home; a turn-on for many of its famed guests: there's not even a sign outside the door. Rooms are futuristic, monochromatic, even bleak. Many have specially commissioned Mapplethorpe photos and CD players. ⊠ *237 Madison Ave., 10016,* ☎ *212/686–0300 or 800/334–3408,* 𝔽𝔸𝕏 *212/779–8352. 112 rooms. Restaurant.*

$$$ ☷ **The Mansfield.** This 1904 hotel, one of the best values in the neighborhood, is ideal if you're looking for the style and panache of the Royalton but unwilling to shell out big bucks. The small but sleek rooms have CD and VCR players, high-tech lighting, and black marble baths. ⊠ *12 W. 44th St., 10036,* ☎ *212/944–6050,* ℻ *212/764–4477. 147 rooms.*

$$–$$$ ☷ **The Beverly.** Despite its drab exterior and public areas, this all-suites hotel is one of Midtown's best options. Most of the midsize rooms were redecorated in 1996–97 and have walk-in closets but dinky bathrooms. Some suites have kitchenettes. ⊠ *125 E. 50th St., 10022,* ☎ *212/753– 2700 or 800/223–0945,* ℻ *212/715–2452. 187 suites. Restaurant.*

$$–$$$ ☷ **Paramount.** Its minuscule rooms draw the ultrachic (but not necessarily ultrawealthy) thanks to designer Philippe Starck's clever touches, like quirky conical stainless-steel sinks. The lobby is filled with Starck's trademark lamps; a staircase leads to a mezzanine restaurant that has taken a backseat to the hotel's newer, hipper eatery, Coco Pazzo Teatro. ⊠ *235 W. 46th St., 10036,* ☎ *212/764–5500 or 800/225–7474,* ℻ *212/354– 5237. 600 rooms. Restaurants, health club.*

$$ ☷ **Travel Inn.** On the western fringe of Hell's Kitchen and the theater district, 20 blocks due north of Chelsea, this budget inn is worthwhile for its generous amenities and relatively low price. Spanking-new rooms occupy four wings that center around an outdoor swimming pool; there's free parking. ⊠ *515 W. 42nd St., 10036,* ☎ *212/695–7171 or 800/869– 4630,* ℻ *212/967–5025. 160 rooms. Pool.*

Downtown

$$$$ ☷ **SoHo Grand.** SoHo's first hotel since the 1800s has quickly established itself as one of the city's finest. The lobby's suspended metal staircase and streamlined postmodern details recall the neighborhood's industrial past. Rooms are minimalist, but a bit cramped—those taller than 6′ 2″ will find the beds too short. The service garners raves. ⊠ *310 W. Broadway, 10013,* ☎ *212/965–3000 or 800/965–3000,* ℻ *212/965–3200. 367 rooms. Restaurant, health club.*

$$–$$$ ☷ **Holiday Inn Downtown.** Near Chinatown, Tribeca, and SoHo, this historic 14-story hostelry has small, clean rooms, a friendly staff, and one of the city's most loyal gay followings. Asian antiques and designs enliven public areas. ⊠ *138 Lafayette St., 10013,* ☎ *212/966–8898 or 800/ 465–4329,* ℻ *212/966–3933. 223 rooms. Restaurant.*

$–$$ ☷ **Chelsea Hotel.** The Victorian-era hotel is much hyped because of its history: Tennessee Williams, Joni Mitchell, Robert Mapplethorpe, and Patti Smith, among many other luminaries, have lived here; Edie Sedgwick and Dylan Thomas died here, and Sid Vicious killed Nancy Spungeon here before killing himself. It's close to things gay and rooms are cheap; it's also a dump. ⊠ *222 W. 23rd St., 10011,* ☎ *212/243–3700,* ℻ *212/243–3700. 300 rooms.*

$–$$ ☷ **Hotel 17.** Slackers, club kids, fashion addicts—the city's trendsetters hole up in this modest budget property near Union Square. Rooms are small and many share baths, but most guests spend little time in their rooms. There's usually a glam soirée going on, attracting a predictable mix of androgynous wannabes. ⊠ *225 E. 17th St., 10003,* ☎ *212/475–2845,* ℻ *212/677–8178. 140 rooms.*

$–$$ ☷ **Washington Square Hotel.** Rooms at this Greenwich Village hotel are unmemorable, but the staff is knowledgeable and helpful. Downstairs are C3, a good value restaurant, and its companion lounge. Best of all, it's only steps from the action of both villages and the NYU scene. ⊠ *103 Waverly Pl., 10011,* ☎ *212/777–9515 or 800/222–0418,* ℻ *212/979– 8373. 160 rooms. Restaurant, exercise room.*

$ ☷ **Carlton Arms.** New York's so-called "art-break hotel" has a cultlike following among its guests, who range from queer club kids to backpacking Europeans. Doors and hallways are cluttered with surreal murals and ultravivid decorations, while each room is decorated in a memorable theme. Since this is a place for *starving* artists, don't expect plush towels, a TV, a phone, or, in many cases, a private bath. ⊠ *160 E. 25th St., 10010,* ☎ *212/684–8337. 54 rooms.*

$ 🏨 **Off Soho Suites.** True to its name, this small all-suites property on the Lower East Side is just outside SoHo, about 10 minutes on foot, similarly close to the East Village. Suites are bright and airy, with basic but contemporary furnishings and full kitchens, and some have marble baths. ⊠ *11 Rivington St., 10002,* ☎ *212/979–9801 or 800/633–8646,* 𝔽𝔸𝕏 *212/979–9801. 37 suites. Restaurant.*

Guest Houses and Small Hotels

The **New York B&B Reservation Center** (☎ 212/977–3512) is a gay and lesbian reservation service that will find you accommodations in any of 80 hosted and unhosted apartments throughout the city. Rates range from $60 to $150 per night.

$ 🏨 **Chelsea Pines Inn.** On the border of the Village and Chelsea, the city's best-known gay accommodation is in an 1850 town house. It's run by a helpful staff and has small but agreeable rooms and a patio and greenhouse garden out back where Continental breakfast is served when the weather cooperates. Some rooms have fireplaces. ⊠ *317 W. 14th St., 10014,* ☎ *212/929–1023,* 𝔽𝔸𝕏 *212/645–9497. 21 rooms with phone, TV, and some with private bath. Continental breakfast. Mostly gay male.*

$ 🏨 **Colonial House Inn.** Set in a historic 1850s brownstone on a spiffy tree-lined Chelsea street, the inn has attractive rooms decorated with art created by the owner. There's also a terrific roof sundeck ideal for nude sunbathing. A wall divides the common breakfast area from a gallery filled with changing exhibits by local gay artists. Some rooms have fireplaces. ⊠ *318 W. 22nd St., 10011,* ☎ *212/243–9669 or 800/689–3779,* 𝔽𝔸𝕏 *212/633–1612. 20 rooms with phone and TV, most with shared bath. Continental breakfast. Mixed gay male/lesbian.*

$ 🏨 **Incentra Village House.** Its great location at the northern tip of the West Village makes this B&B a popular choice. Rooms in these adjoining Victorian town houses are a bit run down, but some have fireplaces and some have kitchenettes. ⊠ *32 8th Ave., 10014,* ☎ *212/206–0007. 12 rooms with phone, TV, bath. Continental breakfast. Mixed gay male/straight.*

Hostels and Dorms

$ 🏨 **Vanderbilt YMCA.** The best of the city's Ys has tiny, bare rooms that accommodate one to four persons. The well-outfitted health club is a big plus, and there's an above-average cafeteria. Convenient Midtown location. ⊠ *224 E. 47th St., 10017,* ☎ *212/756–9600,* 𝔽𝔸𝕏 *212/752–0210. 430 rooms. Restaurant, 2 pools, health club.*

$ 🏨 **West Side YMCA.** Rooms and health club facilities are a bit dowdier than at the Vanderbilt Y, but it's steps from Lincoln Center and Central Park and closer to the subway lines to Chelsea and the West Village. Some rooms have private baths. ⊠ *5 W. 63rd St., 10023,* ☎ *212/787–4400,* 𝔽𝔸𝕏 *212/875–1334. 539 rooms. Restaurant, pool, health club.*

THE LITTLE BLACK BOOK

At Your Fingertips

AIDS Hotline (☎ 718/768–0221). **AIDS Resources Hotline** (NYC Dept. of Health, ☎ 212/447–8200). **Bisexual, Gay, Lesbian, Transgender Youth of New York** (☎ 212/620–7310). **Gay and Lesbian Alliance Against Defamation** (☎ 212/807–1700). **Gay and Lesbian Anti-Violence Project** (☎ 212/807–0197). **Gay and Lesbian Switchboard** (☎ 212/777–1800).

Gay Men's Health Crisis (✉ 119 W. 24th St., ☎ 212/807–6664). **Lesbian and Gay Community Services Center** (✉ 208 W. 13th St., ☎ 212/620–7310). **Lesbian Switchboard** (☎ 212/741–2610). **Metropolitan Transit Authority** (MTA, ☎ 718/330–1234). **New York City Police Department Liaison to the Lesbian and Gay Community** (☎ 212/374–2366). **New York Convention and Visitors Bureau** (✉ 2 Columbus Circle, 10019, ☎ 212/397–8222 or 212/484–1200). *Time Out New York* (☎ 212/539–4444, Web site newyork.citysearch.com). *Village Voice* (☎ 212/475–3300, Web site www.villagevoice.com).

Gay Media

Homo Xtra (*HX*) (☎ 212/627–0747) and *Next* (☎ 212/627–0165), both of which are produced by club promoters and used to advertise their own events, have detailed listings for all bars and gay-popular restaurants. Women can consult *Homo Xtra for Her* (*see* HX, *above*). The biweekly *Lesbian & Gay New York* (*LGNY*) (☎ 212/343–7200, e-mail lgny@aol.com) carries gay and lesbian news, book and movie reviews, and events calendars. *The New York Blade* (☎ 212/268–2711), an offshoot of the *Washington Blade,* began publishing in late 1997. *MetroSource* (☎ 212/691–5127), an exhaustive quarterly directory of community businesses, has articles and entertainment coverage, too.

BOOKSTORES

A Different Light (✉ 151 W. 19th St., ☎ 212/989–4850) is one of the country's best lesbigay bookstores; it has a great café, too (*see* Coffeehouse Culture, *above*). Tiny **Oscar Wilde Bookstore** (✉ 15 Christopher St., ☎ 212/255–8097) has been serving the community since 1967. **Creative Visions** (✉ 548 Hudson St., ☎ 212/645–7573) has a limited number of titles and rents and sells male porn. **Rainbows and Triangles** (✉ 192 8th Ave., ☎ 212/627–2166) has gay cards, gifts, CDs, magazines, and a few books. In Brooklyn's Park Slope, **Beyond Words** (✉ 186 5th Ave., ☎ 718/857–0010) is a cozy store with strong sections on race, women's, and cultural studies.

Coliseum Books (✉ 1771 Broadway, ☎ 212/757–8381), a huge independent bookstore, has great sections on travel, cooking, and the arts. The **Drama Bookshop** (✉ 723 7th Ave., ☎ 212/944–0595) specializes in titles on drama, television, film, and dance. **St. Mark's Bookshop** (✉ 31 3rd Ave., ☎ 212/260–7853), a sleek nest of intellectuals, neo-punks, and philosophers, stocks many queer-theory titles. The self-proclaimed "eight miles of used books" at the **Strand** (✉ 828 Broadway, ☎ 212/473–1452) include a decent queer section. **Untitled—Fine Art in Print** (✉ 159 Prince St., ☎ 212/982–2088) has one of the city's best selections of art books and monographs.

Working Out

Your best deal is at either of these two branches of the **YMCA:** the **Vanderbilt** (✉ 224 E. 47th St., ☎ 212/756–9600), which gets a corporate crowd; and the **McBurney** (✉ 215 W. 23rd St., ☎ 212/741–9210), a dreary facility in glittering Chelsea. **Spa 22?** (✉ 227 E. 56th St., ☎ 212/754–0227) is a members-only spa and fitness center for men, with licensed massage, seaweed body masks, salt glows, and facials. There's also a sauna, steam room, and decent gym. The very professional, young to middle-aged crowd can get a little frisky, for what it's worth. The **Chelsea Gym** (✉ 267 W. 17th St., ☎ 212/255–1150) has been the city's gayest—and cruisiest—gym for more than a decade. The huge, clean **American Fitness Center** (✉ 128 8th Ave., ☎ 212/627–0065) is popular with gay men and lesbians. The spanking-new **New York Sports Club** (✉ 270 8th Ave., ☎ 212/243–3400) attracts many queer locals.

26 Out in Orlando

IT'S HARD TO IMAGINE a city less like feverishly commercial Walt Disney World than Orlando, an amiable and low-key spread of new and historic residential enclaves surrounding one of Florida's few walkable downtowns. If you're visiting the Orlando area, you'd be crazy not to take full advantage of the myriad theme parks southwest of the city, which together compose the world's most dazzling amusements mecca. (You never know whom you'll meet traipsing around the parks—a gay porn star once moonlighted as a costumed cartoon character at Disney's Magic Kingdom.) But even the scores of queers employed by Disney head to Orlando to party and shop.

This city with 170,000 residents is artsy and intellectual, more so than elsewhere in Florida. Cinemas show foreign and independent films, cafés and clubs with mixed gay and straight clienteles sponsor everything from raves to poetry readings, several theaters present experimental and fringe productions, and arts newspapers and 'zines provide the lowdown on these events. The queer scene thrives from November to April, the height of the tourist season, but with more gay men and lesbians settling here permanently, things stay lively year-round.

THE LAY OF THE LAND

Lake-dotted Orlando sprawls in every direction. The city is centered where I–4 crosses the East–West Expressway, several miles north of the Orlando International Airport. Gay businesses exist throughout the city, but many are east and northeast of downtown, in Thornton Park and along Mills Avenue. Disney and the numerous mega-attractions are 10 to 15 miles south of downtown Orlando.

Downtown

Downtown is a tiny quadrant of Orlando proper, which itself is a relatively small chunk of the vast Central Florida region with which it is usually associated. **Church Street Station** (⌧ 129 W. Church St., ☎ 407/422–2434), a restored rail depot, is the only certifiable tourist attraction. Its redbrick buildings are legitimately historic, but the schlocky amusements, dinner shows, and souvenir shops within the complex borrow more than a little from Disney and other area theme parks. Visit after 6 PM and you'll have to cough up about $18. During the day admission is free, and the place actually seems queerer before nightfall. Walk two blocks east across busy Orange Avenue to reach some funkier blocks with a random mix of grunge clothiers, law offices, coffeehouses, discount pharmacies, and nightclubs.

Eola Heights and Thornton Park

Historic **Eola Heights** begins a few blocks east of downtown. Stroll around the grassy oak-shaded perimeter of rippling **Lake Eola** and you'll likely see queerfolk jogging, strolling, and hanging out. Nearby streets hold some of Orlando's earliest homes, but the neighborhood fell on hard times during the second half of the 20th century. Among the first folks to move in and clean it up were gays and lesbians, who later continued east into **Thornton Park.** This area's tree-lined streets and restored clapboard homes have the peaceful grace and artsy accents of Key West's historic district. A few cafés and urbane boutiques, all of them gay-frequented, have enlivened **Washington Street,** Thornton Park's main drag.

Mills Avenue and Loch Haven Park

Mills Avenue (Highway 15) runs north from near Thornton Park to above Colonial Drive; it's lined with gay bars and businesses, including **Out & About** (*see* Bookstores, *below*). Especially around the intersection with Virginia Drive, Mills is the closest thing Orlando has to a gay district.

North of Virginia Drive, Mills Avenue cuts through a dense concentration of lakes. Turn left at Princeton Street to find grassy **Loch Haven Park,** which overlooks Lake Estelle and Lake Rowena and contains a trio of modest but engaging museums. Among the highlights of the **Orlando Museum of Art** (⊠ 2416 N. Mills Ave., ☎ 407/896–4231) are pre-Columbian artifacts collected from Mayan excavations and some worthy 19th- and 20th-century paintings. The **Orange County Historical Museum** (⊠ 812 E. Rollins St., ☎ 407/897–6350) displays photos, documents, and memorabilia. The tactile exhibits at the **Orlando Science Center** (⊠ 810 E. Rollins St., ☎ 407/896–7151) keep the underage set chirping and squirming.

The star of the neighborhood, east of Loch Haven Park via Virginia Drive, is the 56-acre **Harry Leu Botanical Gardens** (⊠ 1920 N. Forest Ave., ☎ 407/246–2620). A tremendous garden of camellias stays in bloom from October to March. You can admire a 50-foot-tall floral clock and tour the century-old, antiques-filled Leu Mansion.

Winter Park

The exclusive town of **Winter Park** lies north of Loch Haven Park. Lake Sue, the northernmost of the several lakes near Mills Avenue, touches the edge of **Mead Gardens** (⊠ S. Denning Ave., ☎ 407/623–3334), a pristine and unkempt cousin of the Leu gardens where a boardwalk cuts through 55 acres of wetlands and wildlife.

Northeast of here along Osceola Avenue (Highway 426) is the gorgeous campus of **Rollins College** (⊠ 1000 Holt Ave., ☎ 407/646–2000), a private liberal arts school that snickering students of rival universities often call "Rollins Country Club." The grounds, replete with fine examples of Spanish Revival and Mediterranean Revival architecture, possess something of the grandeur of a swank resort. The school's **Cornell Fine Arts Museum** (☎ 407/646–2526) often mounts intriguing temporary exhibits, though its permanent collection is unremarkable.

Downtown Winter Park, a short drive north of Rollins College, evokes the grace of Savannah and the glamour of Beverly Hills, albeit on a tiny scale. Chain clothiers, smart boutiques, and tony restaurants line both sides of **Park Avenue,** interrupted only by the positively prissy but pleasant **Central Park.** Queer couples, grunger students, and countercultural types share the downtown streets with the expected yuppies and wealthy snowbirds. The area's leading attraction, the **Charles Hosmer Morse Museum of American Art** (⊠ 445 Park Ave., ☎ 407/645–5311) maintains the largest Tiffany stained-glass collection in the country and has some excellent 19th- and 20th-century American paintings.

Walt Disney World and the Theme Parks

Since **Walt Disney World** (✉ Magic Kingdom: U.S. 192 off I–4, ☎ 407/824–4321) opened in 1971, more than 500 million guests have passed through its gates. Disney has received flack from conservatives for its gay-positive personnel policies, but though the corporation welcomes the annual **Gay Day,** it plays no official role in the event. Begun several years ago as an impromptu romp, Gay Day has blossomed into a fully organized nearly weeklong series of parties and other activities. About 80,000 gay men and lesbians attended in 1997, and over 100,000 are expected in 1998, when the festivities will run from June 3 to June 8. For details check out the event's Web site (www.gayday.com) or contact its official travel packager and tour operator, **Good Time Tours** (☎ 888/429–3527, Web site www.goodtimegaytravel.com).

The theme streets of **Disney–MGM Studios** hold memorabilia and souvenir shops, theaters, rides (a deliciously frightening free-fall begins at the 13-story Twilight Zone Tower), simulated back lots and studios, and the soundstage still used by *Star Search*. **Epcot** reflects on the world—past, present, and future. Pavilions within the **World Showcase** examine the cultures of Canada, France, Japan, Norway, and other nations. The mostly corporate-sponsored pavilions of **Future World,** complete with innovative and thought-provoking explanations of space colonization, environmental preservation, and DNA research, offer a suspiciously rosy take on how technology will propel us blissfully into the next century or two. The educational focus of Epcot ensures a less frenetic atmosphere than at other parts of Walt Disney World. Main Street, U.S.A; Frontierland; Fantasyland; and the other components of the famed **Magic Kingdom** have rides, costumed characters, adult- and kid-oriented amusements and exhibitions, and entertainment pavilions.

Walt Disney World issues **passes** good for one or more days that get you into one or more of its major theme parks and waterparks. Even using the passes, two people can easily blow $200 a day for admission, parking, a couple of basic meals, and a few souvenirs.

At 1,200 acres, **Sea World** (✉ I–4, Exit 28, ☎ 407/351–3600) is the world's largest zoological park, with the expected marine life but also many birds and mammals. Set mostly around a 17-acre lake, the pricey attraction is strictly for those who really dig this sort of thing.

Universal Studios (✉ I–4, Exit 29, ☎ 407/363–8000) follows the basic format of Disney–MGM Studios but has more exciting, sophisticated, and adult-oriented rides, theaters, and other diversions. From a campy tribute to Lucille Ball to a shaky exhibit based on the disaster film *Earthquake* (it involves a ride on a San Francisco BART subway car during an 8.3 Richter-scale quake), this is one wild experience.

Splendid China (✉ U.S. 192 off I–4's Exit 25B, ☎ 407/396–7111 or 800/244–6226), a refreshingly unflashy antidote to the theme parks, re-creates the Great Wall, Dr. Sun Yat Sen's Mausoleum, and other famous structures and landmarks.

GETTING AROUND

Constant construction on roads that were not built to handle heavy traffic causes delays in and around Orlando, as do the many nonlocal drivers, one-way roads, and unpredictable street layouts. Disney is a good 30- to 45-minute drive from downtown Orlando. International Drive (a.k.a. I–Drive), where you'll find many of the area's best hotels, is between the two. It is possible to get around downtown Orlando and even I–Drive by bus, but few tourists rely on the public-transit system. Cabs are even less practical—a ride from I–Drive to downtown, for example, will set you back about $25. A detailed map of Greater Orlando is essential if you plan to explore by car.

EATS

Culinary wastelands a decade ago, Orlando and Winter Park now have fine restaurants, and the prices at even the stylish ones tend to be lower than those at comparable places elsewhere in the United States. Several gay-popular establishments are in Thornton Park or on or near Mills Avenue.

As for options dining near Disney, there are hundreds of touristy chain restaurants along I–Drive, to say nothing of all the restaurants actually inside Disney World. These places don't have gay followings, but the three restaurants at the Orlando Peabody Hotel (*see below*), which hit every price range, are sophisticated, relatively low-key, and offer outstanding food—if in doubt, head here.

For price ranges, *see* dining Chart B at the front of this guide.

Downtown and Thornton Park

$$$–$$$$ ✕ **Le Provence.** One of only a handful of Orlando eateries where you'll have a chance to spend a little money, this splendid French restaurant has a smart but casual ambience. The grilled chicken with a Dijon mustard crust and white-wine coriander sauce and the grilled yellowfin tuna with Portobello mushrooms and a raspberry vinaigrette are typical dishes. ⊠ *50 E. Pine St.,* ☎ *407/843–1320.*

$$–$$$$ ✕ **Straub's.** The TGIF-inspired decor won't win any awards and you won't see too many gay folks, but this restaurant serves the freshest seafood in Orlando. Florida lobster tails, fried oysters, baby back ribs, and shellfish cheese dip are a few of the standouts. ⊠ *743 Lee Rd.,* ☎ *407/628–0067; also* ⊠ *5101 E. Colonial Dr.,* ☎ *407/273–9330.*

$$–$$$ ✕ **Numero Uno.** On every dining critic's short list of favorites, this intimate Cuban restaurant has charming, knowledgeable waiters eager to explain the food to novices. The paella is good, but also consider the mussel soup, shredded flank steak, or shrimp *ajillo* (sautéed in a sauce of garlic, onion, green peppers, and spices). ⊠ *2499 S. Orange Ave.,* ☎ *407/841–3840.*

$$ ✕ **Luciano's.** Redolent with the smell of garlic and oregano, this gay-frequented trattoria serves top-notch pizzas, calzones, and pastas. The small indoor space is fine, but head for the plant-bedecked covered terrace with its gurgling fountains and floral tablecloths. Beware: Eating the fabulous cannoli is the equivalent of reverse liposuction. ⊠ *900 E. Washington St.,* ☎ *407/425–0033.*

$$ ✕ **Union.** A cross between a down-home southern café and a big-city bistro, gay-popular Union is on a sleepy residential street near Thornton Park. The New American chow is inventive and artfully presented. Grilled pork chops come on a bed of garlic-fried red cabbage and corn with cumin-baked red beans. ⊠ *337 N. Shine Ave.,* ☎ *407/894–5778.*

$$ ✕ **White Wolf.** Worldly yet understated, this quirky bric-a-brac emporium serves terrific international fare, from mango-nut-tabbouleh sandwiches to shiitake lasagna. After so enchanting a meal, you might decide to purchase some of the funky furnishings. ⊠ *1829 N. Orange Ave.,* ☎ *407/895–9911.*

$–$$ ✕ **Little Saigon.** Locals cherish compact Little Saigon for its inexpensive lunch specials. The traditional soup of noodles, rice, vegetables, and chicken or seafood is always a winner, as is the char-broiled beef with rice vermicelli and spring rolls. ⊠ *1160 E. Colonial Dr.,* ☎ *407/423–8539.*

$ ✕ **Dexter's.** Sassy and stylish, this restaurant, market, and wine shop behind a black-tile deco facade buzzes with the chatter of Thornton Park's trendiest residents. The delicious Provençal-inspired food—ratatouille

Orlando

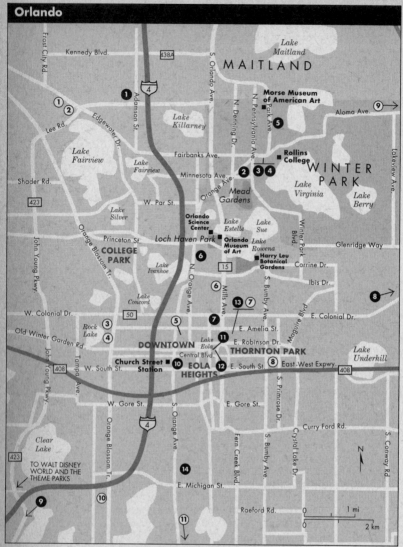

Eats ●

Dexter's, **4, 11**
Le Provence, **10**
Little Saigon, **7**
Luciano's, **12**
Numero Uno, **14**
Orlando Peabody
Hotel, **9**

Park Avenue Grill, **5**
Petit Four, **2**
Straub's, **1, 8**
Taqueria
Quetzelcoatl, **3**
Union, **13**
White Wolf, **6**

Scenes ○

Cactus Club, **6**
Club Firestone, **5**
The Complex, **10**
Crews, **11**
Faces, **2**
Full Moon, **3**
Hank's, **1**
Parliament House, **4**
Phoenix, **9**
Southern Nights, **8**
Union, **7**

Niçoise, pressed roasted duck on French bread with grilled onions and Brie—is available to eat in or take out. ✉ *800 E. Washington St.,* ☎ *407/ 648–2777; also* ✉ *200 W. Fairbanks Ave., Winter Park,* ☎ *407/629–1150.*

Winter Park

$$–$$$ ✗ **Park Avenue Grill.** For a chance to ogle Winter Park's yuppies and guppies, try this courtly bi-level place with arched windows, marble tables, and indirect lighting. The American food is decent, if not particularly daring: bacon-wrapped filet mignon, coconut-fried shrimp, and the like. ✉ *358 Park Ave.,* ☎ *407/647–4556.*

$$–$$$ ✗ **Petit Four.** A promising chef and his talented mom run this airy café and bakery that has high ceilings and vine-stenciled walls. Traditional Continental dishes receive a healthy dose of Old South panache. The rack of lamb comes with a sweet honey-mustard glaze; veal-and-apple scallopini is another favorite. Open till 1 AM on weekends. ✉ *702 Orange Ave.,* ☎ *407/645–0897.*

$ ✗ **Taqueria Quetzelcoatl.** This busy San Francisco–style burrito parlor churns out fresh fish burritos and funky fare like Yucatan sweet-hot quesadillas filled with grilled chicken, caramelized onions, jack cheese, and a tangy secret sauce. Always swarming with revelers at happy hour, the bar stocks several dozen beers. ✉ *350 W. Fairbanks Ave.,* ☎ *407/629–4123.*

International Drive

$$–$$$$ ✗ **Orlando Peabody Hotel.** Few Florida eateries manage the cutting-edge flourish of formal, pricey **Dux.** A typical offering might be grilled breast of young hen with an organic fig and wine-blanched garlic confit, served over ancho-pumpkin rice. Lighter but no less appetizing northern Italian fare is prepared at **Capriccio**—try the mesquite grilled mahimahi with three-vegetable vermicelli, pesto risotto, white beans, and cold-pressed olive oil. For a light but still trendy bite, 24 hours daily, visit the '50s-style **B-line Diner.** ✉ *9801 International Dr.,* ☎ *407/352–4000.*

SCENES

The owners of Orlando's most popular gay nightspots have learned a thing or two from the area's amusement complexes: Two of these clubs are sprawling compounds with several theme bars (and in one case a motor lodge and a restaurant), and another concocts a wild theme party nearly every night of the week. Your other options include neighborhood bars, one major dyke hangout, some leather clubs, and an amusing strip bar. Disney itself, despite the fact that plenty of its 35,000 employees are queer, has no nearby gay clubs.

Prime Suspects

The Complex. It's hard to believe Orlando can support two enormous gay entertainment compounds, but the Complex gives the Parliament House (*see below*) a good run for its money. A meandering corridor that seems to go on forever connects several bars arranged around a central courtyard: a spacious stand-and-model cruise and dance bar with counter dancers and loud music, a smaller bar with pool tables, a cabaret with an impressive stage and frequent drag shows, a country-western dance bar, and a saloonlike lounge beyond that. ✉ *3400 S. Orange Blossom Trail,* ☎ *407/843–6334. Crowd: mostly male (but with some women at the cabaret), mostly over 35 early in the evening—younger as the night progresses, similar to crowd at Parliament House but with fewer tourists.*
Faces. Off the beaten path in northwestern Orlando, this midsize dyke bar, a success since the mid-'70s, has pool tables, a spacious dance floor, and a great landscaped patio off to the side. Weekly events include Sunday cookouts and free pool and darts on Monday and Wednesday. A DJ spins dance tunes most nights. ✉ *4910 Edgewater Dr.,* ☎ *407/291–7571.*

Crowd: female (men welcome if accompanied by a card-carrying lesbian), all ages, very friendly, low attitude, butch, jeans and flannel; lots of Jeeps and pickups in the parking lot.

Full Moon. This country-western and leather dance club (it sounds like an unlikely combo but it works) has an ordinary interior and a central bar with cruisy guys sitting around it, but moss-draped trees droop over a spacious outdoor deck and a grassy lawn filled with picnic tables—a setup that captures the mood of the Deep South better than any club in that region. Boot-stomping line dancing and two-stepping take place on the deck. ⊠ *500 N. Orange Blossom Trail,* ☎ *407/648–8725. Crowd: mostly male, 30s to 50s, mix of leather chaps and cowboy hats, some bears, extremely friendly (and cruisy).*

Parliament House. The considerable legend surrounding Parliament House rivals that of Shangri-la—countless gay men have returned from their vacations in Orlando with tales of a multibar sexplex pulsing with mass debauchery and nonstop revelry. A central building houses a diner, piano and video bars, a disco, and a small lounge in the back that's big with the grungy pierced set. Surrounding this building is a two-story L-shape motel, parts of which have been converted into a porn shop, a country-western saloon, and a weird boutique selling kitschy gifts. The rest of this shabby structure contains motel rooms with outdoor entrances. The standard cruising routine is to saunter past the rooms: Behind partly drawn curtains, guests looking for action typically pose with "come hither" expressions on their faces. (It's sort of like Motel 6 decided to open a bathhouse.) The PH's gigantic outdoor swimming pool is particularly busy during the day. ⊠ *410 N. Orange Blossom Trail,* ☎ *407/425–7571. Crowd: mostly male (except in piano bar, which is 60/ 40 m/f), 20s to 50s, fun-loving, tremendous variety, many tourists, some leather and bears, cruisy and often downright sleazy.*

Southern Nights. Aside from the megacompounds, Parliament House and the Complex, this is the grooviest dancing and cruising space in Orlando. East of downtown, it draws college students and Thornton Park locals. There's a large high-energy disco, a mellower patio, and Spank, a funky mock-pretentious martini lounge where subtitled movies are sometimes screened. Weekly events and theme parties take place; depending on the night there might be a cook-out, Latin music, drag shows, or strip contests. ⊠ *375 S. Bumby Rd.,* ☎ *407/898–0424. Crowd: 65/35 m/f (closer to 50/50 on Saturdays), mostly 20s and 30s, somewhat mixed racially, fairly hip, some stand-and-model.*

Neighborhood Haunts

The **Cactus Club** (⊠ 1300 N. Mills Ave., ☎ 407/894–3041), a tacky but fun guys' strip club, can get crowded on weekends. Spacious but otherwise unremarkable **Phoenix** (⊠ 7124 Aloma Ave., ☎ 407/678–9220), a 10 minute-drive east of downtown Winter Park, has dartboards and pool tables. The diverse crowd is up to 40% women on most nights. The chic counter bar at **Union** (⊠ 337 N. Shine Ave., ☎ 407/894–5778) restaurant (*see* Eats, *above*) attracts trendy gay boys and lipstick lesbians for happy hour and for late-night martinis.

South of downtown, **Crews** (⊠ 4716 S. Orange Ave., ☎ 407/850–6033) is an easy place to meet older guys; strippers and drag artistes perform occasionally. The butch men's bar **Hank's** (⊠ 5026 Edgewater Dr., ☎ 407/291–2399), which is up near the butch women's bar Faces (*see above*), can get rowdy on weekends. **Club Firestone** (⊠ 578 N. Orange Ave., ☎ 407/426–0005), a wild warehouse disco, hosts gay nights on Wednesday and Saturday.

Action

Club Orlando (✉ 450 E. Compton St., ☎ 407/425–5005) is a clean and well-equipped bathhouse and gym. The grounds of **Parliament House** (*see* Scenes, *above*) are famously cruisy. The sidewalk outside the Full Moon and Parliament House is cruisy, but most of the guys who hang around this corner are hustlers.

SLEEPS

If you have only a marginal interest in Disney and the theme parks, stay downtown or in Winter Park, where the rates are reasonable. For easy access to downtown Orlando and the theme parks, consider the I–Drive area, which is lined with chain properties. Because this chapter focuses on the city of Orlando, the Disney properties are not reviewed below.

Orlando and Winter Park

Hotels

$ ▥ **Holiday Inn.** A mid-rise property north of downtown, this Holiday Inn has midsize rooms with functional but pleasant furnishings. It's a short drive from the lesbian bar Faces and from downtown. ✉ *626 Lee Rd., 32810,* ☎ *407/645–5600,* FAX *407/740–7912. 201 rooms. Restaurant, pool, exercise room.*

$ ▥ **Parliament House.** If you don't mind horny men roaming outside your door at all hours, this gay-owned motor lodge and entertainment complex (*see* Scenes, *above*) does have cheap rooms. Basic and a bit dreary, they're nonetheless clean and safe. ✉ *410 N. Orange Blossom Trail, 32805,* ☎ *407/425–7571. 132 rooms. Restaurant, pool.*

Guest Houses and Small Hotels

Two full-service properties are reviewed below, but a third option is to contact the women who own the **Garden Cottage** (✉ 1309 E. Washington St., ☎ FAX 407/894–5395), a charming one-bedroom 1920s structure in Thornton Park with antiques and a kitchenette. Lesbians and gay men are welcome.

$$–$$$$ ▥ **Veranda.** Easily one of the most attractive and well-run queer-friendly inns in Florida, the Veranda may not have the all-gay buzz of comparable properties in Key West, but it matches most of them in character and romantic ambience. A small compound of historic buildings holds rooms of various sizes, all of them with period antiques and some with kitchenettes. ✉ *115 N. Summerlin Ave., 32801,* ☎ *407/849–0321 or 800/420–6822,* FAX *407/872–7512. 11 rooms with phone, TV, and private bath. Continental breakfast. Mixed gay/straight.*

$$–$$$ ▥ **Park Plaza.** Although not very gay, this intimate 1920s hotel is in the heart of Winter Park's shopping and dining district. Many of the antiques- and wicker-filled rooms overlook Central Park and bustling Park Avenue. Enjoy breakfast and afternoon cocktails on a plant-filled balcony. ✉ *307 Park Ave. S, Winter Park, 32789,* ☎ *407/647–1072 or 800/228–7220,* FAX *407/647–4081. 27 rooms with phone, TV, and private bath. Restaurant. Continental breakfast. Mostly straight.*

International Drive

Hotels

$$$$ ▥ **Orlando Peabody.** The Orlando branch of the Memphis grande dame combines the southern charm of its sister property with the modern amenities you'd expect at a resort: great restaurants, a top-notch fitness center, and tennis courts. It's beside the convention center, so the mobs of guests can be an annoyance. But the management is quite gay-friendly,

and the rooms are sumptuous. ⊠ *9801 International Dr., 32819,* ☎ *407/ 352–4000 or 800/732–2639,* FAX *407/351–0073. 891 rooms. Restaurants, pool, health club.*

$$–$$$ ⊡ **Embassy Suites.** The Embassy is a class act. Its spacious rooms have pastel contemporary furnishings, large kitchenettes and bathrooms, and can easily sleep four. Rooms on the upper few floors have views of the Magic Kingdom in the distance. ⊠ *8978 International Dr., 32819,* ☎ *407/352–1400 or 800/433–7275,* FAX *407/363–1120. 244 rooms. Restaurant, pool, health club.*

$ ⊡ **Quality Inn–Plaza.** With 1,000-plus rooms, it's a zoo, but if you're looking to be near Disney and want low rates, you'll do no better than this complex with clean run-of-the-mill rooms. ⊠ *9000 International Dr., 32819,* ☎ *407/345–8585,* FAX *407/352–6839. 1020 rooms. Restaurant, pools.*

THE LITTLE BLACK BOOK

At Your Fingertips

Gay and Lesbian Community Services Center (⊠ 714 E. Colonial Dr., ☎ 407/425–4527, Web site www.glcs.com). **Gay and Lesbian Day at Disney** (Web site www.gayday.com). **LYNX** (bus system, ☎ 407/841–8240). **Metropolitan Business Association** (gay and lesbian business guild, ☎ 407/ 420–2182). **Orlando/Orange County Convention and Visitors Bureau** (⊠ 8723 International Dr., Orlando, 32819, ☎ 407/363–5871). *Orlando Weekly* (☎ 407/645–5888). **Yellow Taxi** (☎ 407/699–9999).

Gay Media

Central Florida's best paper, the biweekly *Watermark* (☎ 407/481– 2243, Web site www.watermarkonline.com) provides insightful news and feature stories about Orlando and Tampa Bay and covers clubs, restaurants, and the arts. The helpful monthly *Triangle* (☎ 407/849–0099) carries community news. Look to the monthly *11 Magazine* (☎ 407/ 896–9067) for alternative and cutting-edge arts news and events listings.

BOOKSTORES

Out & About Books (⊠ 930 N. Mills Ave., ☎ 407/896–0204) is a dependable lesbigay store amid a small row of gift, clothing, and music shops.

Working Out

Two options for men double as bathhouses but also have great workout facilities. The **New Image Fitness Center** (⊠ 3400 S. Orange Blossom Trail, ☎ 407/420–9890) is adjacent to the Complex (*see* Scenes, *above*). **Club Orlando** (*see* Action, *above*) has excellent equipment. There are no gyms in Winter Park or downtown with notable lesbian followings, but both men and women will feel comfortable working out at the **Bally's** (⊠ 4850 Lawing La., ☎ 407/297–8400) near Disney.

27 Out in Palm Springs

IT WAS IN THE 1930S that well-to-do Hollywood types first discovered the virtues of Palm Springs, a lushly landscaped oasis in the heart of the rugged, barren, and dramatic Coachella Valley. Gay people have maintained a steady if discreet presence since the city's beginnings, but only in the early '70s did a specifically gay resort open. In the early '80s several more followed, as did some bars, shops, and restaurants. Development was booming by the late '80s, as Palm Springs reemerged as an exclusive getaway. In the last few years, tourism—gay and straight—has leveled off, but the region's popularity doesn't appear to be in jeopardy. With a higher charge of sexual energy than any other gay resort in the western United States, Palm Springs will always lure fast-lane types.

Palm Springs is a fiery hell much of the year. You'll be assured again and again by locals that "it's a dry heat" and that your blood begins to thin within days. But 110°F is still 110°F—this is a typical high from late May into early October. These months are, not surprisingly, Palm Springs's slowest, but it's a great time to find hotel bargains; just pace yourself and drink plenty of fluids. The most crowded and expensive times to visit are late November (when the gay rodeo comes to town), Christmas, and late March through April (when the dyke-popular Dinah Shore LPGA Championship and guy-oriented White Party come to town).

THE LAY OF THE LAND

Most gay resorts and many businesses are in the southeastern part of Palm Springs proper, with much of the nightlife in the next town over, Cathedral City, a young commercial burg southeast of Palm Springs.

Downtown Palm Springs

North Palm Canyon Drive, the city's commercial spine, used to have the cachet of Beverly Hills's Rodeo Drive, but it's become considerably more pedestrian. But there's still chichi browsing to be done at the **Desert Fashion Plaza** (⊠ N. Palm Canyon Dr. at Tahquitz Canyon Way, ☎ 760/320–8282), an indoor mall with about 50 stores. Gay-popular shops in Palm Springs include **R&R Menswear** (⊠ 333 N. Palm Canyon Dr., ☎ 760/320–3007) and **Gay Mart** (⊠ 305 E. Arenas Rd., ☎ 760/320–0606), an emporium of gay-male gifts, swimwear, gym gear, and sex stuff—including adult videos.

The **Palm Springs Desert Museum** (⊠ 101 Museum Dr., ☎ 760/325–0189) is the area's cultural center. It focuses on western and Native American art. For a simulated version of desert vegetation, visit nearby **Moorten Botanical Garden** (⊠ 1701 S. Palm Canyon Dr., ☎ 760/327–6555). Enjoy phenomenal views of the desert from the **Palm Springs Aerial**

Tramway (✉ Tram Hill Rd., off Hwy. 111, ☎ 760/325–1391), a 20-minute tram ride to the 8,500-foot peak of Mt. San Gorgino.

Farther Afield

The **Indian Canyons** (✉ 38-500 S. Palm Canyon Dr., ☎ 760/325–5673), one of the area's most fascinating attractions, are about 5 miles south of Palm Springs. Here you can view pictographs and hike among four canyons inhabited for centuries by the Agua Caliente Band of Indians. There's more hiking (you did come to P.S. for an outdoorsy experience, didn't you?) at the often-dramatic **Living Desert Wildlife and Botanical Park** (✉ 47-900 Portola Ave., ☎ 760/346–5694). The wildlife includes everything from cheetahs to bighorn sheep. Trails of varying difficulty crisscross desert gardens. For an even longer hike spend a day exploring the half-million-acre **Joshua Tree National Park.** It's an hour's drive from Palm Springs on Highway 62. Information can be obtained from the **Oasis Visitor Center** (✉ 74-485 National Park Dr., Twentynine Palms 92277, ☎ 760/367–7511).

GETTING AROUND

Palm Springs is a straight, though sometimes congested, shot down I–10 from Los Angeles, and an only slightly longer and more convoluted drive from San Diego on I–15 to Highway 60 to I–10. Highway 111 connects the major resort towns. There are few walkable neighborhoods, and most stores are in shopping centers and malls. If you're without a car take advantage of Palm Springs's excellent **Gay Taxi** (☎ 760/864–9357). Another good option is the **Rainbow Cab Co.** (☎ 760/327–5702).

EATS

Steak houses, fast-food franchises, and Italian restaurants dominate the Palm Springs dining landscape. Some of the nicer hotels have good food (notably the Ritz-Carlton), but most of the cuisine is comparatively tame and old-fashioned. The gayest places are in Cathedral City.

For price ranges, *see* dining Chart A at the front of this guide.

Palm Springs

$$$–$$$$ ✕ **Europa Restaurant.** Landscaped gardens and gurgling fountains surround this romantic bungalow, where the Continental specialties include lightly breaded roast rack of lamb with Dijon mustard and minted demi-glace, and stuffed shrimp with deviled crab and warm goat cheese. ✉ *1620 Indian Trail*, ☎ 760/327–2314.

$$–$$$ ✕ **Billy Reed's.** The nice thing about this Palm Springs institution is that lunch entrées can be ordered all day. Just as good as the dinner fare, they're quite a bit cheaper. The place looks like an old brothel and its entertainers impersonate famous stars. The traditional American food is perfectly good but unspectacular. ✉ *1800 N. Palm Canyon Dr.*, ☎ 760/325–1946.

$$–$$$ ✕ **Blue Angel.** Tiger-stripe chairs, lavender napery, and other exotic touches set the mood at this cavernous see-and-be-seen eatery. The Continental and American menu is dependable, offering large portions of classic steak, salmon, and chicken dishes. Cute queerfolk sip drinks at the swank cocktail bar. ✉ *777 E. Tahquitz Canyon Way,* ☎ 760/778–4343.

$$–$$$ ✕ **Blue Coyote.** By Palm Springs standards the southwestern food at this trendy downtown restaurant is good, but it's still decidedly unadventurous. Sautéed chicken marinated in orange juice and served with chipotle peppers is one of the better dishes. Try the outstanding flan for dessert. The setting is charming, with ample courtyard seating and soft lighting. ✉ *445 N. Palm Canyon Dr.*, ☎ 760/327–1196.

Eats

Billy Reed's, **2**
Blue Angel, **7**
Blue Coyote, **3**
Europa Restaurant, **8**
La Taqueria, **5**
Michael's Cafe, **11**
Palmie, **4**
The Red Tomato, **10**
Shame on the Moon, **13**
Triangles, **12**
2095, **1**
Village Pride Coffehouse, **6**
The Wilde Goose, **9**

Scenes

C. C. Construction on Sunrise, **6**
Choices, **8**
Rainbow Cactus Café, **3**
Speakeasy, **1**
Streetbar, **4**
Sundance Saloon, **9**
Sweetwater Saloon, **2**
Tool Shed, **5**
Wolfs Den, **7**

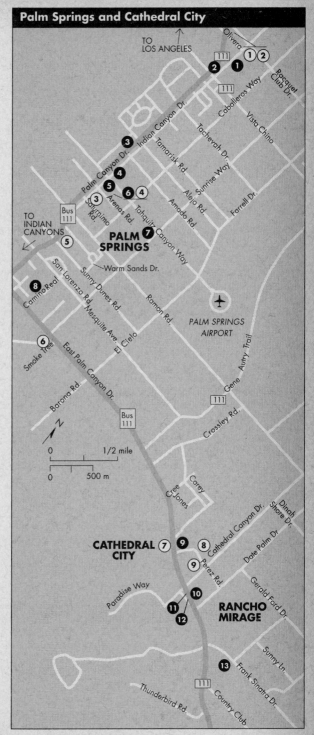

Palm Springs and Cathedral City

$$-$$$ ✗ **Palmie.** It looks decidedly unchic, but you'll find some of the best French cuisine in the desert at Palmie. The standout dishes include a two-cheese soufflé appetizer and the signature entrée, a fish stew in a butter-cream broth. ⊠ *Galeria Henry Frank, 276 N. Palm Canyon Dr.,* ☎ *760/320–3375.*

$$ ✗ **2095.** Inside the swank gay resort of the same name is the classic homo date restaurant, where lovers can nuzzle over a drawn-out four-course dinner without feeling self-conscious. The piano entertainment on weekends adds a spark to the meal. The Continental cuisine is generally quite good. ⊠ *2095 N. Indian Canyon Dr.,* ☎ *760/320–4333.*

$-$$ ✗ **La Taqueria.** This inexpensive Mexican restaurant in the heart of Palm Springs serves veggie dishes, build-your-own tacos, and oversize platters of fresh food. ⊠ *125 E. Tahquitz Canyon Way,* ☎ *760/778–5391.*

Cathedral City

$$$–$$$$ ✗ **The Wilde Goose.** A rare Cathedral City restaurant that draws celebrities down from Palm Springs, this classy spot serves stellar Continental fare in a formal, if stuffy, setting. Five varieties of duck (plus a chilled duck salad), several wild game dishes, and decent lobster are usually offered. ⊠ *67-938 Hwy. 111,* ☎ *760/328–5775.*

$$ ✗ **Triangles.** Cathedral City's latest gay restaurant has two smart, modern dining rooms with black-and-teal color schemes. Asian and Continental influences grace steak and pasta entrées, Thai curries, and noodle dishes. ⊠ *68-85 Hwy. 111,* ☎ *760/324–9113.*

$ ✗ **Michael's Cafe.** A terrific retro diner with stainless steel furnishings and a U-shape counter, Michael's delights patrons with simple, tasty fare and a fabulous collection of Marilyn Monroe commemorative plates. ⊠ *68-665 Hwy. 111,* ☎ *760/321–7197.*

$ ✗ **The Red Tomato.** The name of this pizza parlor celebrates juicy red tomatoes, but it's actually best known for garlicky white pies. All the pizzas are baked to perfection, and the crowd always includes a few cute queens. ⊠ *65-751 Grove St. at Hwy. 111,* ☎ *760/328–7518.*

Rancho Mirage

$$–$$$ ✗ **Shame on the Moon.** The Continental fare at Shame features few surprises but is consistently good—favorites include medallions of pork and fresh seafood with pasta. Bite for bite, it's the best gay-popular restaurant in the valley. ⊠ *69-950 Frank Sinatra Dr.,* ☎ *760/324–5515.*

Coffeehouse Culture

Village Pride Coffeehouse. This cheerful java house in Palm Springs's "Little Castro" has sandwiches, snacks, cards, and gifts. ⊠ *214 E. Arena Rd.,* ☎ *760/323–9120.*

SCENES

The high-season club scene here is not unlike that at Fire Island, Key West, or Provincetown: The biggest discos are packed with every kind of guy and a smaller contingent of women, and each season, specific establishments become *the* places to haunt at particular times of the day or night. In other places some of these bar-scene rituals—like the popular tea dances—take place in scenic spots out of doors. In Palm Springs, however, most dancing and socializing goes on indoors; outdoor patios typically have very little ambience.

Although the majority of the gay guest houses are in Palm Springs, most nightlife is in Cathedral City. There are a few Palm Springs bars, but most are small and neighborhoody—the sorts of places you might check out before hitting one of the Cathedral City discos. The little bars on Palm Springs's Arenas Road, hyperbolically dubbed "Little Castro," are within walking distance of the accommodations in the Warm Sands and San Lorenzo areas and are a great option if you're looking for a quick drink or game of pool.

Cathedral City

PRIME SUSPECTS

Choices. Things have gotten a little quieter at this disco since its former neighbor C. C. Construction Co. relocated to Palm Springs. Choices has a video-game and pool-table area, and a nondescript patio outside. Most visitors include Choices on their barhopping rounds. ✉ *68-352 Perez Rd.,* ☎ *760/321–1145. Crowd: very diverse, more women than at C. C. Construction and other male clubs but otherwise similar.*

Sundance Saloon. Grim and bunkerlike on the outside, the saloon is a rollicking joint inside, with country videos screening above a large dance floor. You can run circles around the central bar, chasing all those cute cowpokes.✉ *36-737 Cathedral Canyon Dr.,* ☎ *760/321–0031. Crowd: 60/40 m/f, mixed ages; denim, flannel, and boots prevail.*

Wolfs Den. Tall blackened-plate-glass windows surround the exterior of this popular butch bar, and the owners have done their best to create a dark macho place. Leather is taken seriously, though guppies are never frowned upon. Check out the on-site leather shop. ✉ *67-625 Hwy. 111,* ☎ *760/321–9688. Crowd: male, ages 35 and up, lots of leather, leatherette, Levi's, and tank tops.*

Palm Springs

PRIME SUSPECTS

C. C. Construction on Sunrise. The desert's most popular gay bar became more so after moving from Cathedral City to Palm Springs. A large disco is open only on weekends (Hi-NRG Friday and Saturday; beer bust, tea dance on Sunday). The main section (open daily, many drink specials) has two bars, big-screen videos, and a pool room. ✉ *Smoke Tree Plaza, 1775 E. Palm Canyon Dr.,* ☎ *760/778–1234. Crowd: mostly male, youngish, some cowboys, mostly disco bunnies.*

Rainbow Cactus Café. A piano bar whose peach walls are festooned with an odd mix of Christmas lights and Native American art, this lively spot is a great alternative to the high-energy dance clubs in the area. ✉ *212 S. Indian Canyon Dr.,* ☎ *760/325–3868. Crowd: 80/20 m/f, mostly older guys, many locals.*

Speakeasy. This popular piano bar in northern Palm Springs is spacious and well decorated. Cabaret acts run the gamut from predictable if well-performed standbys to some quite good stuff. ✉ *2400 N. Palm Springs Dr.,* ☎ *760/322–3224. Crowd: 65/35 m/f, silver haired and silver tongued.*

Streetbar. Lots of guys drop in here for a beer or two before heading to Cathedral City. A simple video bar with pool and pinball, Streetbar has a little terrace out front on the sidewalk. ✉ *224 E. Arenas Rd.,* ☎ *760/ 320–1266. Crowd: mostly male, low-key, as local as at any area bar.*

Sweetwater Saloon. This cheery video bar north of downtown is a spot to make friends or hang; it's not a cruise scene. ✉ *2420 N. Palm Canyon Dr.,* ☎ *760/320–8878. Crowd: 75/25 m/f, mostly over 35, unpretentious.*

Tool Shed. Described in its ads as a "workingman's bar," the Tool Shed is reminiscent of the no-nonsense bars in Long Beach or parts of Phoenix. ✉ *600 E. Sunny Dunes Rd.,* ☎ *760/320–3299. Crowd: male, blue-collar, some leather, lots of facial hair, guys trying to look rough.*

Action

Club Palm Springs (✉ 68-449 Perez Rd., ☎ 760/324–8588) in Cathedral City is the area's only 24-hour, seven-day-a-week bathhouse. On weekends things get pretty steamy around the corner at the **Gravel Pit** (✉ 68-774 Summit Dr., ☎ 760/324–9771). If you're looking for a comfy leather jockstrap or some stainless-steel nipple clamps, stop by either of the two Cathedral City locations of **Black Moon Leather** (✉ Wolfs Den, 67-625 Hwy. 111, ☎ 760/328–2667; ✉ 68-449 Perez Rd., ☎ 760/770–2925). Among the joys at the **Hidden Joy Bookstore** (✉ 68-424 Commercial Rd., Cathedral City, ☎ 760/328–1694) are video arcades and gay porno.

SLEEPS

When it comes to service and in-room amenities, Palm Springs is like no other gay vacation hub in the country. A resort generally won't survive here without at least one pool, a misting machine (indispensable on sundecks, especially from May to October), new furnishings, large guest rooms, and in most cases, in-room VCRs with an extensive adult-video library. But though resorts are consistently plush and clean, the quaintness factor of Key West or Provincetown is absent. If you have an aversion to chrome and mirrors, you may have difficulty with Palm Springs. Finally, as the most hormonally charged resort scene on the planet, at least in season, it's not the ideal destination for a romantic retreat.

Well over half the gay resorts are in two clusters just south of Palm Springs's commercial district. The more upscale accommodations are in the **Warm Sands** area, and the older and more affordable properties are just south in **San Lorenzo.** The remaining properties are scattered among Palm Springs and Cathedral City. You should be able to get a nice one-bedroom unit with a kitchen and a pool view for $80 to $100 a night in season and as little as $60 the rest of the year. Few gay resorts have a mix of men and women, and only two are specifically for lesbians.

For price ranges, *see* lodging Chart A at the front of this guide.

Mainstream Resorts and Motels

$$$$ 🏨 **Ritz-Carlton Rancho Mirage.** Monied queens hold court here. Rooms are fairly ordinary for a luxury resort, but the property's location in the foothills of the Santa Rosa Mountains affords spectacular views. ✉ 68-900 Frank Sinatra Dr., Rancho Mirage 92270, ☎ 760/321–8282 or 800/241–3333, ℻ 760/321–6928. 240 rooms. Restaurants, pool, health club.

$$$ 🏨 **Wyndham Palm Springs.** The host to many gay gatherings has expansive grounds and is within walking distance of several Palm Springs gay bars. The large rooms are brightly furnished. ✉ 888 E. Tahquitz Canyon Way, Palm Springs 92262, ☎ 760/322–6000 or 800/822–4200. ℻ 760/322–5551. 568 rooms. Restaurants, pool, exercise room.

$ 🏨 **Vagabond Inn.** An excellent budget option, this well-run three-story motel is midway between downtown Palm Springs and Cathedral City. Gays and lesbians are always made to feel welcome. ✉ 1699 S. Palm Canyon Dr., Palm Springs 92264, ☎ 760/325–7211 or 800/522–1555, ℻ 760/322–9269. 120 rooms. Restaurant, pool, hot tub.

Gay Resorts and Guest Houses

Palm Springs

WARM SANDS AREA

$$–$$$ 🏨 **Atrium, Mirage, and Vista Grande Villa.** This complex of three neighboring lodgings has a reputation for wild, fun-loving horny guys. All rooms have VCRs, and there's a library of more than 200 adult films—at least one of which was filmed on-site. Guests wander freely among the three properties, whose grounds are gussied up with some fairly campy touches—waterfalls, Flintstones-inspired lagoons, pink flamingos. Rooms are clean, bright, and simple. ⊠ *574 Warm Sands Dr., 92264,* ☎ *760/322–2404 or 800/669–1069,* FAX *760/320–1667. 20 rooms with phone, TV, and private bath. 3 pools, hot tubs. Continental breakfast. Gay male.*

$$–$$$ 🏨 **Desert Paradise.** One of the best pools in town gives this sprawling property the feel of a first-rate resort. Rooms are furnished in contemporary style; all have VCRs and plenty of movie choices. Appeals to a younger crowd. ⊠ *615 Warm Sands Dr., 92264,* ☎ *760/320–5650 or 800/342–7635,* FAX *760/320–0273. 12 rooms with phone, TV, and private bath. Pool, hot tub. Continental breakfast. Gay male.*

$$–$$$ 🏨 **El Mirasol.** This '40s estate was opened in 1974 as the first gay resort in Palm Springs. The grounds are full of native trees, fountains, and beautiful gardens (all visited by dozens of exotic birds), and there are two bright pool areas. ⊠ *525 Warm Sands Dr., 92264,* ☎ *760/327–5913 or 800/327–2985,* FAX *760/325–8931, Web site www.elmirasol.com. 15 rooms with phone and TV; most with private bath. 2 pools, hot tub. Continental breakfast and lunch. Mostly gay male.*

$$–$$$ 🏨 **Hacienda El Mirasol.** If only every resort in Palm Springs was run as efficiently and thoughtfully as this one. Each room has a kitchen, and three on-site pantries are stocked with booze, soft drinks, and hundreds of different foods—simply sign for whatever you want. The front guest rooms with red-tile floors are the nicest, but all are large. ⊠ *586 Warm Sands Dr., 92264,* ☎ *760/327–8111 or 800/359–2007,* FAX *760/327–6026, Web site www.elmirasol.com. 8 rooms with phone, TV, and private bath. 2 pools, hot tub. Mostly gay male.*

$$–$$$ 🏨 **Inndulge.** One of several examples of Palm Springs's predilection for resorts with punny "inn" names, this complex is in the middle of a neighborhood already crammed with guest houses. But the Inndulge stands out: Rooms are spacious and bright, and the pool is one of the best in town. ⊠ *601 Grenfall Rd., 92264,* ☎ *760/327–1408 or 800/833–5675,* FAX *760/327–7273, Web site www.inndulge.com. 18 rooms with phone, TV, and private bath. Pool, hot tub. Continental breakfast. Gay male.*

$$–$$$ 🏨 **InnTrigue.** Of the more social resorts, the neatly landscaped InnTrigue is the most tasteful and down-to-earth. It's run by, and seems to attract, a genuinely nice, fairly young bunch of guys. Having so many rooms puts the place somewhere between a guest house and a small hotel. ⊠ *526 Warm Sands Dr., 92264,* ☎ *760/323–7505 or 800/798–8781,* FAX *760/ 323–1055. 28 rooms with phone and TV; most have private bath. 2 pools, hot tubs. Continental breakfast. Gay male.*

$$ 🏨 **Inn Exile.** With great rates, luscious grounds, sleek southwestern-inspired guest rooms, super public areas and facilities, and complimentary breakfast, lunch, and happy hour, this expansive resort is tops in the Warm Sands area. Many rooms open onto one of the four pools and inviting sunning areas, and some have fireplaces. ⊠ *960 Camino Parocella, 92264,* ☎ *760/327–6413 or 800/962–0186,* FAX *760/320–5745, Web site www.innexile.com. 26 rooms with phone, TV, and private bath. 4 pools, 2 hot tubs, exercise room. Continental breakfast. Gay male.*

$$ 🏨 **Sago Palms.** If you want a kitchen and dining area in your room, the Sago Palms is one of the best deals in town. With just seven rooms, there's never a huge crowd poolside (clothing is optional). Rooms have an eclectic array of Sears-type furnishings, but they're clean and fairly large. ⊠ *595 Thornhill Rd., 92264,* ☎ *760/323–0224 or 800/626–7246,* FAX *760/ 320–3200. 7 rooms, with phone, TV, and bath. Pool, hot tub, outdoor exercise area. Continental breakfast. Gay male.*

$–$$ 🏨 **Alexander Resort.** This solid option is not as fancy or sleek as some of the other Warm Sands resorts, but the owners are friendly, the rates are decent, and many rooms have kitchens. Remodeled and under new ownership since January 1998. ⊠ *598 Grenfall Rd., 92264,* ☎ *760/327–6911 or 800/448–6197. 8 rooms with phone and TVs, most with private bath. Pool, hot tub. Continental breakfast. Gay male.*

$–$$ ⊞ **Mountain Shadows.** This recent addition to Warm Sands Drive is a fine budget option. Though not fancy, the pleasant rooms have East Indian and Asian themes, and the hosts are friendly. Breakfast is served near a gazebo overlooking the pool and sunning areas. ⊠ *568 Warm Sands Dr., 92264,* ☎ *760/322–2324 or 888/563–6646,* FAX *760/322–3982. 15 rooms with phone, TV, and private bath. Pool, hot tub. Continental breakfast. Gay male.*

SAN LORENZO

$$–$$$$ ⊞ **Triangle Inn.** This is one of the better resorts on San Lorenzo Road. Rooms are sumptuous, with such creature comforts as CD players and extensively equipped kitchens. Many suites have two bedrooms. ⊠ *555 San Lorenzo Rd., 92264,* ☎ *760/322–7993 or 800/732–7555,* FAX *760/322–0784. 9 rooms with phone, TV, and private bath. Pool, hot tub. Continental breakfast. Gay male.*

$$–$$$ ⊞ **Chestnutz.** What happens when two guys from Connecticut move to Palm Springs and open their ideal gay resort? The result is a modern take on *Mr. Blandings Builds His Dream House.* Unlike neighboring establishments, this one offers a full country-style breakfast (brought to your room), and the rooms are done in inventive styles, from New England farmhouse to Italian modern. ⊠ *641 San Lorenzo Rd., 92264,* ☎ *760/325–5269,* FAX *760/320–9535. 12 rooms with phone, TV, and private bath. Pool, hot tub. Full breakfast. Gay male.*

$–$$$ ⊞ **Camp Palm Springs.** Rooms at this motel-style resort have standard furnishings but come in varied configurations (it's good for three or four guys traveling together). From the nightly cocktail parties to the continual frolicking around the pool, this place is always abuzz. ⊠ *722 San Lorenzo Rd., 92264,* ☎ *760/322–2267 or 800/793–0063,* FAX *760/322–5699. 20 rooms with phone and TV; many have private bath. Pool, hot tub. Continental breakfast. Gay male.*

$$ ⊞ **Santiago.** Tops among the San Lorenzo area resorts, this motor hotel has large rooms (furnished with contemporary light-wood furniture and VCRs) that overlook a long rectangular pool. Second-floor rooms have mountain views. The crowd is on the young side, and the staff enthusiastic. ⊠ *650 San Lorenzo Rd., 92264,* ☎ *760/322–1300 or 800/710–7729,* FAX *760/416–0347. 23 rooms with phone, TV, and private bath. Pool, hot tub. Continental breakfast and lunch. Gay male.*

$–$$ ⊞ **Avanti.** The run-of-the-mill Avanti has a standard pool, reasonably large rooms (some with kitchens), and VCRs. Very casual. ⊠ *715 San Lorenzo Rd., 92264,* ☎ *760/325–9723 or 800/572–2779,* FAX *760/325–4357. 14 rooms with phone and TV; some with private bath. Pool, hot tub. Continental breakfast. Gay male.*

ELSEWHERE IN PALM SPRINGS

$$$–$$$$ ⊞ **Abbey West.** A luxury gay resort in a quiet Palm Springs neighborhood, the Abbey West has sleek art deco rooms named after celebs (Bogart, Bergman, Garbo, Monroe); they average nearly 500 square feet in size and have kitchenettes and modem hookups. The landscaped grounds are beautiful, and there's a bar on the premises. ⊠ *772 Prescott Circle, 92262,* ☎ *760/416–2654 or 800/223–4073,* FAX *760/322–8534. 17 rooms with phone, TV, and private bath. Pool, hot tub, exercise room. Continental breakfast. Mostly gay male.*

$$$–$$$$ ⊞ **Harlow Hotel.** This is one of the best gay resorts in the country. Every room is done in high-end contemporary pieces and comes with a chilled bottle of chardonnay and snacks. There's a long palm-shaded pool, and you can take your breakfast or lunch in fragrant gardens of gardenias and jasmine. The mood is social; nudity is common on the sundeck and the crowd is a bit younger and more likely to be on the make. ☒ *175 El Alameda, 92262,* ☎ *760/323–3977 or 800/223–4073,* FAX *760/320–1218. 15 rooms with phone, TV, and bath. Pool, hot tub, exercise room. Continental breakfast. Gay male.*

$$$–$$$$ 🏨 **2095.** The guest rooms of this longtime P.S. favorite (formerly known as Casablanca) contain art deco antiques and reproductions and black carpeting; the walls are painted English racing green. Outdoors there's a large diamond-shape pool. The restaurant (*see* Eats, *above*), an homage to '30s glamour queens, hosts cabaret acts and live music. ☒ *2095 N. Indian Canyon Rd., 92264,* ☎ *760/320–4333 or 800/223–4073,* FAX *760/ 323–5719. 12 rooms with phone, TV, and private bath. Continental breakfast. Mostly gay male.*

$$–$$$ 🏨 **Desert Stars Resort.** A bit off the beaten path, this secluded resort is close to C.C. Construction on Sunrise. The best features are the pool and the cruisy landscaped walkway that encircles the grounds. This is a frisky but not sleazy place with personable owners and spacious rooms with refrigerators. ☒ *1491 Via Soledad, 92264,* ☎ *760/325–2686,* FAX *760/ 322–5054. 11 rooms with phone, TV, and private bath. Pool, hot tub. Continental breakfast. Gay male.*

$$ 🏨 **Bee Charmer.** One of the nicest women's resorts you'll find, this sprawling low rise is clean and attractive, with a striking bronze-tile roof and a very private enclosed pool. Rooms have a bright southwestern decor. ☒ *1600 E. Palm Canyon Dr., 92264,* ☎ *760/778–5883, e-mail beecharmps@aol.com. 13 rooms with phone, TV, and private bath. Pool. Continental breakfast. Lesbian.*

$–$$ 🏨 **Canyon Club Hotel.** This is a solid accommodation, with standard rooms and a large pool. With the reasonable rates and a racy atmosphere, you can get plenty of bang (so to speak) for your buck. ☒ *960 N. Palm Canyon Dr., 92262,* ☎ *760/322–4367 or 800/295–2582,* FAX *760/322–4024. 32 rooms with phone, TV, and private bath. Pool, hot tub. Continental breakfast. Gay male.*

Cathedral City

$–$$ 🏨 **Cathedral City Boy's Club.** This is a steamy place, teeming with sexual energy. The 2-acre grounds are landscaped, and the pool is one of the largest around. The steam room, gym, and "bunkhouse" are easy places to become closely acquainted with other guests. Rooms are large and clean but ordinary; many have kitchens. ☒ *68-369 Sunair Rd., 92234,* ☎ *760/324–1350 or 800/472–0836,* FAX *760/324–1269. 40 rooms with phone, TV, and private bath. Pool, hot tub, exercise room. Gay male.*

$–$$ 🏨 **The Villa.** One of the West Coast's largest gay resorts is a secluded, shaded spot run by friendly guys. The Villa draws an older and laid-back bunch. Rooms are spacious, and the rates are extremely fair. ☒ *67-670 Carey Rd., 92234,* ☎ *760/328–7211 or 800/845–5265,* FAX *760/321– 1463, Web site www.thevilla.com. 45 rooms with phone, TV, and private bath. Restaurant, pool, hot tub. Mostly gay male.*

$ 🏨 **Desert Palms Inn.** Behind the Target Shopping Center and Camelot Amusement Park, the Desert Palms has long had a rambunctious following of men and women. It had become a bit of a dump until new owners spruced up the rooms and added a restaurant and bar. Draws a younger crowd. ☒ *67-580 Hwy. 111, 92234,* ☎ *760/324–3000 or 800/801–8696,* FAX *760/770–5031, e-mail dsrtplms@aol.com. 29 rooms with phone, TV, and bath. Restaurant, pool, hot tub. Mixed gay/lesbian.*

THE LITTLE BLACK BOOK

At Your Fingertips

AIDS Assistance Program (☎ 760/325–8481). **Desert Business Alliance (gay)** (☎ 760/324–0178). **Desert Woman's Associations** (☎ 760/363–

7565). **Gay Taxi** (☎ 760/864–9357). **Palm Springs Desert Resorts Convention and Visitors Bureau** (✉ 69-930 Hwy. 111, Rancho Mirage, 92270, ☎ 760/770–9000 or 800/417–3529). **Rainbow Cab Co.** (☎ 760/327–5702). **SunBuss** (☎ 760/343–3451).

Gay Media

Palm Springs has several gay publications, all male-oriented. The **Bottom Line** (☎ 760/323–0552) magazine, which has entertainment listings, comes out twice a month. Also check out **Mega Scene** (☎ 760/327–5178). The Palm Springs Gay and Lesbian Services Center publishes a bar and shopping booklet, the **Desert Daily Guide** (☎ 760/320–3237).

BOOKSTORES

Crown Books (✉ 333 S. Palm Canyon Dr., Palm Springs, ☎ 760/325–1265) has a solid selection of gay and lesbian titles. Although it's an adult bookstore, **Perez Books** (✉ 68-366 Perez Rd., Cathedral City, ☎ 760/321–5597) has a few non-porn publications (such as *The Advocate*). Of vintage stores, **Bloomsbury Books** (✉ 555 S. Sunrise Way, Suite 105, Palm Springs, ☎ 760/325–3862) carries a terrific number of used gay-and-lesbian titles, plus plenty of film, photography, and antiques books.

Working Out

The gayest health club in town is **Gold's Gym** (✉ 4070 Airport Centre Dr., Palm Springs, ☎ 760/322–4653).

28 Out in Philadelphia

With New Hope

FOR A CITY OF 1.6 MILLION PEOPLE, Philadelphia appears, at first glance, to lack the scene evident in other large metropolises. There are only 15 gay bars, recent gay pride parades have been low-key, civil rights protests are few and far between, and in few places are you likely to see a highly visible queer presence.

Few come to Philadelphia to *be* gay the way one might in other large cities; accordingly, the city lacks a large gay ghetto—the community lives throughout the metro area. The city has long been highly tolerant; without the constant threat of homophobia, activists find relatively little around which to mobilize.

This was not always the case. New York, Los Angeles, and San Francisco weren't the only cities to foster a pre-Stonewall homophile movement. In August 1960, New York City's Mattachine Society held a meeting in the Philadelphia suburb of Radnor; the police got wind of the cabal and arrested 84 people, most of them men, for showing gay-theme films. The organizers' aim had been to establish a Philadelphia chapter of the society. They succeeded, and in the mid-1960s, according to local gay historian Marc Stein, Philadelphia emerged with "the most militant female and male wings of the national homophile movement."

From 1965 through 1969, each July 4 was marked at Independence Hall by lesbian- and gay-rights protests. In 1975 the state of Pennsylvania became the first governmental body in the world to establish a committee to address the concerns of sexual minorities. A year later, as America celebrated its bicentennial, Pennsylvania became the first state to establish a gay pride month. The Philadelphia Lesbian and Gay Task Force, formed in 1978, guided passage of the 1982 Philadelphia Fair Practices Act, one of the country's earliest gay civil rights measures, which secured gays the right to fair employment, housing, and public accommodation.

A police-civilian review board was put in place in 1991 to remove gay bashers from police ranks, and all officers receive gay-sensitivity training. The convention and visitors bureau has been a pioneer in courting gay and lesbian tourism; it helped attract the International Gay and Lesbian Travel Association's annual convention in 1997. Lesbians and gays work at senior levels in the mayor's office, which has its own sexual minorities task force, and serve on virtually every city commission.

Many societal wrongs have been righted in the city of brotherly love. But the fight continues for passage of legislation to provide same-sex-couple employment benefits in the public and private sectors.

Philadelphia doesn't usually wow tourists the way Washington, D.C., New York City, and Boston do—the average visitor spends only a half-day here, compared with four days in Boston. But the gay nightlife scene has improved immeasurably, and there is no shortage of engaging museums and historic sites, first-rate eateries, and performing-arts venues. And of cities in the Northeast, you'll not find another whose population and business community so welcomes and respects gay and lesbian visitors.

THE LAY OF THE LAND

The part of the city most visitors see, downtown or Center City, is less defined by neighborhood monikers than is the case in other major metropolises. The tourist area runs east–west between the Schuylkill and Delaware rivers (streets are numbered, going high to low toward the Delaware) and north–south from around Race to South streets. In the northwest, Fairmount Park and the Art Museum also hold great interest.

City Hall and Rittenhouse Row

A good place to begin exploring is **City Hall** (☎ 215/686–9074), which looms 548 feet above the intersection of Broad and Market streets. The ornate structure took 30 years (1871–1900) to build and is the largest and most stunning city hall in America. Nearby is the **Masonic Temple** (✉ 1 N. Broad St., ☎ 215/988–1917), a marvelous 1868 structure that draws from seven architectural styles—Corinthian, Ionic, Italian Renaissance, Norman, Gothic, Oriental, and Egyptian. The rest of this area has attractive and not-so-pretty office buildings, including the deco-inspired 61-story **One Liberty Place** (✉ 1650 Market St.), the first building to rise higher than City Hall.

Two blocks north, stop by the **Pennsylvania Academy of the Fine Arts** (✉ Broad and Cherry Sts., ☎ 215/972–7600), a grandiose High Victorian Gothic structure built in 1876. The late-19th-century artist Thomas Eakins, who is believed to have been gay, was the Academy's director until the 1880s, when his insistence on using nude models in coed classes cost him his job. A few blocks east is the leviathan **Pennsylvania Convention Center,** and beyond that the city's small but lively **Chinatown.**

Broad Street, especially south of City Hall, is the city's "Avenue of the Arts," the site of new or restored theaters and performing-arts spaces, including the **Academy of Music** (home to both the city's orchestra and opera company). (The city's most queer-oriented performance space, the **Painted Bride Art Center** (✉ 230 Vine St., ☎ 215/925–9914), is 15 blocks east of here, just north of Old City.)

The five blocks west of Broad Street between Market and Spruce streets have recently come to be known as **Rittenhouse Row,** after the neighborhood's sophisticated anchor, Rittenhouse Square. Apart from being a high-end residential sector with a significant gay population, this is where you'll find much of the city's best upscale shopping, especially along Chestnut and Walnut streets.

A great spot for lounging around on the grass is **Rittenhouse Square** (✉ between 18th and 19th Sts. at Walnut St.), which is near some outstanding small museums and surrounded by beautiful architecture. It is picturesque, socially diverse, and relatively safe. The Square was once a popular queer pick-up spot.

Off the Square's southeast corner are the **Philadelphia Art Alliance** and the **Curtis Institute of Music** (✉ 1726 Locust St., ☎ 215/893–5261). Walking south and west several blocks you'll hit **Delancey Street,** a beautifully preserved block of row houses. Here the **Rosenbach Museum and Library** (✉ 2010 Delancey Pl., ☎ 215/732–1600), a Victorian town house, has more than 130,000 manuscripts (Joyce's *Ulysses* and several Conrads), and 25,000 rare books.

Fairmount Park and the Schuylkill River

From the corner of 16th and Arch streets, the Benjamin Franklin Parkway runs diagonally toward Fairmount Park, passing first through **Logan Circle,** which is actually a lovely—and sometimes cruisy—square anchored by an Alexander Calder-designed fountain. This area, which deviates from William Penn's original grid plan, was meant—with its expansiveness, stately mansions and museums, and trees and statuary—to recall the Champs Elysées. Notable museums include the **Franklin Institute Science Museum** (⊠ 20th St. and Benjamin Franklin Pkwy., ☎ 215/448–1200); the **Academy of Natural Sciences** (⊠ 19th St. and Benjamin Franklin Pkwy., ☎ 215/299–1020); and the stellar **Auguste Rodin Museum** (⊠ 22nd St. and Benjamin Franklin Pkwy., ☎ 215/563–1948). The **Philadelphia Museum of Art** (⊠ 26th St. and Benjamin Franklin Pkwy., ☎ 215/763–8100) has imposing Greek architecture and 10 landscaped acres. Its contemporary collection has works by Picasso, Braque, and Matisse as well as a number of post–World War II artists. The outstanding Marcel Duchamp collection includes renditions of his *Nude Descending a Staircase* (the "nude," people often overlook, is male). Check out the fine collection of Eakins's photos and paintings of young, virile men crewing and boating on the Schuylkill River. North of the Museum, **Fairmount Park** comprises nearly 9,000 acres of picturesque gardens, walkways, and bike and bridle paths, plus about a dozen historic (mostly Colonial) mansions, which are open to the public. Highlights include **Mt. Pleasant** (☎ 215/763–8100) and **Strawberry Mansion** (☎ 215/228–8364).

Almost anywhere three queens are caught tanning together is dubbed "Judy Garland Memorial Park"—the entire east bank of the Schuylkill River has earned this distinction. Most popular for sunning, and at night, cruising, is **Schuylkill River Park** (where Spruce, Pine, and Lombard streets meet the river). It's also busy along the Schuylkill from below the Philadelphia Museum of Art through Fairmount Park, from Boathouse Row to roughly East Park Reservoir.

The Gay District

The tiny **Gay District** is anchored by the tiny Colonial alley **Camac Street** (pronounced cuh-*mack*) and the quaint blocks near it, between Walnut and Pine streets. In the 19th century this small enclave of historic redbrick mews (or trinities, as they're known here), was the area's red-light district. It later became the site of several artists' clubs and small theaters, and a commercial—though not especially residential—gay scene has since grown up around it. In the heart of the district, gay-male club fashion and accessories are proffered at **Surfaces** (⊠ 206 S. 13th St., ☎ 215/546–5944), down the block from Woody's nightclub, where most of this stuff is worn. Home furnishings junkies should not miss **Pine Street,** which is loaded with antiques shops between 9th and 17th streets.

East of the Gay District, to about Washington Square but south of Walnut Street, also makes for some beautiful sidewalk strolling. Here you'll find **Jewelers' Row** (⊠ the block bounded by Sansom, 8th, Chestnut, and 7th Sts.), the nation's oldest and most prestigious diamond district.

South Street

Philadelphia's grunge, punk, and funk scene glows along **South Street,** from about 10th Street east to near the Delaware River. Many of the unconventional shops, galleries, eateries, performance spaces, and lounges around here are still queer-owned or -frequented. Despite its festive ambience, South Street draws a rowdy suburban crowd on weekends, so exercise caution when displaying affection. Be sure to check out the fabulous **South Street Antiques Market** (⊠ 615 S. 6th St., ☎ 215/592–0256), whose pieces range from authentic Colonial to kitschy.

People like to joke about the neighborhood south of here, **Queen Village.** Despite its name, it's not particularly queeny. It was, however, named in the 18th century for Sweden's Queen Christina, who was said to be a lesbian.

Old City

Historic **Old City** contains the bulk of the city's pre-1800s attractions, most of which are centered around **Independence National Historical Park** (✉ Visitor Center, 3rd and Chestnut Sts., ☎ 215/597–8974). These are usually free and open daily from 9 to 5. Most famous is the **Liberty Bell Pavilion** (✉ Market St., between 5th and 6th Sts.), the glass-enclosed site of America's beloved and cracked 2,000-pound bell. Although commonly and mistakenly thought to have played a significant role in Colonial history, the Liberty Bell actually rose to prominence during the 1830s as a symbol of the movement to abolish slavery.

Independence Hall (✉ Chestnut St., between 5th and 6th Sts.) is where the Second Continental Congress met in 1775, the Declaration of Independence was adopted in 1776, the Articles of Confederation were signed in 1778, and the Constitution was adopted in 1787. It was the site of the city's first major civil rights demonstrations (which included the concerns of lesbians and gays). Nearby is **Old City Hall,** where the U.S. Supreme Court convened until 1800 and where Emma Goldman, one of the nation's first gay-rights advocates, was briefly imprisoned early in this century. Other major sights in the vicinity are the Parthenon-inspired **Second Bank of the United States** (✉ 420 Chestnut St.), which contains an unparalleled collection of political portraiture; **Independence Square** (✉ between 5th and 6th Sts. and Chestnut and Walnut Sts.), where the Declaration of Independence was first read publicly; and the first meeting place of the U.S. Congress, **Congress Hall** (✉ 6th and Chestnut Sts.).

In the northern edge of Old City, you can visit the home of early flag-fashion maven **Betsy Ross** (✉ 239 Arch St., ☎ 215/627–5343) and the **United States Mint** (✉ 5th and Arch Sts., ☎ 215/597–7350), the largest in the world.

Penn's Landing

City father William Penn disembarked in 1682 at what is now known as **Penn's Landing** (✉ Delaware River, from Market to Walnut Sts., ☎ 215/923–8181). Here you'll find shops, hotels, and condos; an amphitheater that hosts major concerts and festivals; the **Independence Seaport Museum** (✉ 211 Columbus Blvd., ☎ 215/925–5439); several historic ships and homes; and the **Riverbus** (☎ 609/365–1400), which runs every 30 minutes across the Delaware to Camden, home of the impressive **New Jersey State Aquarium** (✉ 1 Riverside Dr., ☎ 609/365–3300). The Camden–Philadelphia connection was also a notorious source of controversy: In the early 1950s the Bishop of Camden flipped out upon learning that a new bridge spanning the Delaware would be named after former resident Walt Whitman—a noted deviant. Despite a completely offensive antigay offensive, the Catholic Church failed to sway public opinion. You can visit the **Walt Whitman House** (✉ 330 Nickel Blvd., ☎ 609/964–5383), where the poet lived during the 1880s and entertained a number of kindred spirits, including Edward Carpenter, Oscar Wilde, and Thomas Eakins.

North and West

West of Center City, across the Schuylkill River, is **University City,** which is dominated by the campuses of the **University of Pennsylvania** and **Drexel University.** The neighborhood just southwest of campus, north of Baltimore Avenue between about 38th and 50th streets, has a significant queer population.

Head west via I–76 alongside the Schuylkill River to reach one of Philadelphia's trendiest neighborhoods, **Manayunk,** which was named a National Historic District in 1983. Begun in the 1800s as a mill town and gradually peopled with Irish, German, Italian, and Polish immigrants, Manayunk slid downhill following the Depression. It was reclaimed by preservationists and yuppie entrepreneurs in the early 1980s. Most of its 30 restaurants and 70 boutiques are along picturesque **Main Street,** whose only drawback is limited parking. Although none of its businesses are specifically gay, Manayunk has a community following—especially among moneyed types who take seriously the Lenape Indian translation of the village's name: "Where we go to drink."

Consider a drive northwest of Center City, through the far reaches of Fairmount Park and up into the lesbian- and gay-popular residential neighborhoods of **Germantown** and **Mt. Airy.** Beyond those is the wealthy domain of high-end shops and grass tennis courts, **Chestnut Hill.** Most of the interesting browsing up here is along the main drag, **Germantown Avenue** (U.S. 422).

Philadelphia is within a 30- to 60-minute drive of scenic and culturally rich suburbs. Diversions include Lancaster's Amish Country, New Hope (*see below*) and the rolling hills of Bucks County, and the Brandywine Valley—the setting of mansions and gardens (several of them open to the public) and the inspiration for Andrew Wyeth's (and family) paintings. One must-see is the **Barnes Foundation** (✉ 300 Latches La., Merion, ☎ 610/667–0290), a collection of some of the world's most important Impressionist and Post-Impressionist paintings, including 175 Renoirs, 66 Cézannes, and many works by Matisse, van Gogh, Picasso, and Gauguin. The collection is in the horsey Main Line suburb of Merion, about a 20-minute drive west of Philadelphia.

GETTING AROUND

Drive to Center City, park in a garage, and don't touch your car again until you leave (or take a side trip). Central Philadelphia is small enough to manage on foot, or at worst by cab. Cabs are easy to hail during the day, when they seem to crawl all through Center City. A ride across town shouldn't run you more than $5. At night, as bars are closing, consider phoning for a cab. Although the FBI Crime Index rates the city the safest of the nation's 12 largest metro areas, streets downtown can feel eerie at night; stick to populated routes.

You don't need SEPTA (Southeastern Pennsylvania Transportation Authority) buses, subways, or trains downtown; these are really for running between Philly and the 'burbs. More helpful are the PHLASH minibuses, which make a loop downtown every 10 minutes with stops at major attractions from Logan Circle to the riverfront, including one by the Gay District at 12th and Market streets. Buses run from 10 to 6 (until midnight in summer) and cost $1.50 one-way or $3 for an unlimited day pass.

EATS

Visitors are often surprised by the wealth and sophistication of Philadelphia restaurants. French cuisine is the star; Deux Cheminées (reviewed *below*), Le Bec-Fin, and Chanterelles are tops. Several luxury hotels have nationally renowned restaurants—notably the Four Seasons, the Rittenhouse, and the Park Hyatt. Most of the city's hottest eateries are along Rittenhouse Row, which abuts the Gay District, and all have moderate community followings. South Street also has a bunch of queer-popular spots that tend to have high funk factors, low prices, and decent but not necessarily memorable food. Most of the gay bars have restaurants, which usually serve pub grub (recently paroled from storage freezers). The Venture Inn, Westbury Bar, and Raffles are well regarded; Rodz (reviewed *below*) is the best of them.

For price ranges, *see* dining Chart A at the front of this guide.

Center City

$$$$ ✕ **Deux Cheminées.** Probably the gayest of the stellar restaurants: The nonpareil French cuisine of award-winning American chef Fritz Blank is served in an elegant Frank Furness town house. The rack of lamb with truffle sauce is legendary. Prix-fixe only: Dinner is $68. ⊠ *1221 Locust St.,* ☎ *215/790–0200.*

$$$$ ✕ **Striped Bass.** Fresh seafood and nothing but. This culinary star stands out for its setting: a dramatic space with mahogany ceilings, marble pillars, and an exhibition kitchen. The innovative menu changes daily, but might offer sesame-crusted grouper with black-bean and tomato-coriander vinaigrette. ⊠ *1500 Walnut St.,* ☎ *215/732–4444.*

$$$$ ✕ **Susanna Foo.** In Philadelphia's priciest Chinese restaurant, a renovated former steak house hung with a fortune in art, Chinese food gets a contemporary twist. Eight Treasure Quails, a favorite, has Chinese sausage, lotus seeds, and sweet rice; even the fortune cookies stand out—they're chocolate-dipped. ⊠ *1512 Walnut St.,* ☎ *215/545–2666.*

$$$–$$$$ ✕ **Inn Philadelphia.** Set on the city's tiny queer alley, Camac Street, this suave town house exudes romance. In good weather ask for a seat in the intimate garden; in winter enjoy the interior's five roaring fireplaces. The Continental American menu is first-rate; consider seared sesame-crusted tuna steak with a faintly sweet plum-pear sauce. There's piano music nightly. ⊠ *251–253 S. Camac St.,* ☎ *215/732–2339.*

$$–$$$ ✕ **Astral Plane.** You know it's gay-operated the minute you walk in the door—a parachute wafts against the ceiling overhead, the walls are rubycolor, there's clutter and Victoriana everywhere, and it's dark. The New American food (orange roughy with a piquant tomato-cilantro salsa) is outstanding. The Sunday brunch has a make-your-own Bloody Mary bar. Very romantic. ⊠ *1708 Lombard St.,* ☎ *215/546–6230.*

$$–$$$ ✕ **Circa.** High ceilings, marble accents, and gilt-frame mirrors lend an airy, classical ambience. Feast on tasty world-beat creations like salmon osso buco and fire-grilled lobster tortillas. Late on weekend evenings Circa is transformed into a campy disco, with a significantly gay following. ⊠ *1518 Walnut St.,* ☎ *215/545–6800.*

$$–$$$ ✕ **Judy's Café.** This offbeat minimalist space near South Street is packed with lesbians, gay men, fabulously hip straight people, and gourmands eagerly awaiting plates weighed down with dineresque New American fare. Consider stuffed meat loaf or a more elaborate rainbow trout panfried with a nut flour-caper sauce. ⊠ *3rd and Bainbridge Sts.,* ☎ *215/928–1968.*

$$–$$$ ✕ **Waldorf Café.** You'll find great American and Continental dishes in this small brick house with a blue awning and an elaborately carved gray cornice. Try the sautéed wild mushrooms in cognac sauce or the osso buco with white wine. Background jazz and vintage photos set a refined tone. ⊠ *20th and Lombard Sts.,* ☎ *215/985–1836.*

$$ ✕ **Marco's.** One of the few gay-popular restaurants in the neighborhood has a tapas-style menu that borrows from around the globe. Salmon buckwheat cakes with caviar and shrimp with radicchio over basmati rice are a couple of dandies. BYOB. ⊠ *232 Arch St.,* ☎ *215/592–8887.*

$$ ✕ **Philadelphia Tea Party.** The city's several gay bands and musicians who perform here have made this casual addition to otherwise upmarket Walnut Street into a favorite of bohos and homos. You won't go wrong with the Spanish potato frittata topped with roasted peppers, olives, and feta cheese. What's with the name? Check out the domestic and imported teas. ✉ *1334 Walnut St.,* ☎ *215/732–8327.*

$$ ✕ **Rodz.** Though the traditional American cuisine here is the best of Philly's gay bars, you still come as much for atmosphere and value. Choose from a few dining rooms plus an inviting roof deck with city views. The Sunday brunch draws a convivial crowd. ✉ *1418 Rodman St.,* ☎ *215/735–2900.*

$–$$ ✕ **Latest Dish.** Off South Street on a funky row of tattoo and piercing parlors, this mod lounge with copper-top tables presents a heavily vegetarian menu of far-out world-beat dishes like polenta lasagna. ✉ *613 S. 4th St.,* ☎ *215/629–0565.*

$–$$ ✕ **Opera Café.** Set in an ugly stucco building but with a sleek, contemporary interior, Opera Café is a big hit with everybody but has an especially devout dyke following. The healthful Italian-influenced menu lists creative salads, veggie pastas, and refreshing selections from the juice bar. ✉ *1940 Pine St.,* ☎ *215/545–3543. No credit cards.*

$–$$ ✕ **Reading Terminal Market.** For a century this cavernous food market's 80 stalls have sold food ranging from local produce to exotic dishes from around the world. The regional Mexican fare at **12th Street Cantina** (☎ 215/625–0321) is outstanding; **Salumeria** (☎ 215/592–8150) is a terrific deli. ✉ *12th and Arch Sts.,* ☎ *215/922–2317. Many stalls do not accept credit cards.*

$ ✕ **Cheap Art Café.** The name refers to the changing local-art exhibits, which brighten up this otherwise dreary 24-hour greasy spoon in the heart of the Gay District. The short-order cooking is OK, with the breakfast dishes among the tastiest. Service ranges from flighty to brusque, but for queer people-watching, you won't find a busier venue. ✉ *260 S. 12th St.,* ☎ *215/735–6650.*

$ ✕ **1521 Café Gallery.** Great for brunch, light lunches and dinners, or coffee and desserts, this art-filled airy café serves great pastas, salads, and paninis all day long, until midnight. The snazzy crowd merits some serious ogling, but you'll have to head elsewhere to work up the courage to flirt—there's no liquor. ✉ *1521 Spruce St.,* ☎ *215/546–1521.*

Outside City Center

$$$ ✕ **White Dog Café.** This queer-popular bric-a-brac–filled eatery serves wonderful New American food prepared with farm-fresh ingredients. The vegetarian offerings are among the best; sample balsamic roasted organic mushrooms over baked parmesan polenta with broccoli rabe, sautéed with pine nuts, roasted garlic, red onions, and savory herbs. ✉ *3420 Sansom St.,* ☎ *215/386–9224.*

$$–$$$ ✕ **BLT's Cobblefish.** With due respect to the fine eateries along Manayunk's Main Street, some of the best cooking is about a mile north at this seafood restaurant. The interior's colorful cartoony fish murals will psych you up for such nouvelle-inspired seafood as horseradish-crusted scrod with garlicky Italian greens. There's plenty of parking. ✉ *443 Shurs La.,* ☎ *215/483–5478.*

$$ ✕ **Goat Hollow.** In the very lesbian enclave of Mt. Airy, northwest of City Center, Goat Hollow is a woman-operated restaurant in a restored building on a picturesque street. A big pull is the wide selection of tap and imported beers. Grilled seafood dishes, bountiful salads, and pasta dishes are among the main offerings. ✉ *300 W. Mt. Pleasant Ave.,* ☎ *215/242–4710.*

$ ✕ **Melrose Diner.** *Not* a gay restaurant (so stare at any cute patrons at your own risk), Melrose Diner is a big-hair-and-bangles institution in a working-class South Philly neighborhood with a sea of CHECKS CASHED signs and pawnbrokers. It's best to come after the bars let out, but drive (there's a small lot) or take a taxi. ✉ *1501 Snyder Ave.,* ☎ *215/467–6644.*

Philadelphia

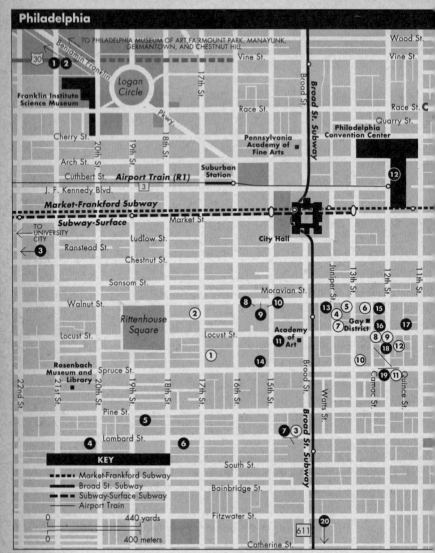

Eats ●

Astral Plane, **6**
BLT's Cobblefish, **1**
Cheap Art Café, **18**
Circa, **8**
Deux Cheminées, **16**
1521 Café
Gallery, **14**
Goat Hollow, **2**
Inn Philadelphia, **19**
Judy's Café, **22**
Latest Dish, **21**
Marco's, **23**
Melrose Diner, **20**
Millennium
Coffee, **15**
More Than Just Ice
Cream, **17**
Opera Café, **5**

Philadelphia Tea
Party, **13**
Reading Terminal
Market, **12**
Rodz, **7**
Striped Bass, **10**
Susanna Foo, **9**
XandO, **11**
Waldorf Café, **4**
White Dog Café, **3**

Scenes ○

Bike Stop, **12**
Key West, **4**
Martini Café, **14**
The Post, **2**
Shampoo, **13**
Rodz, **3**
Sisters, **7**
Sugar Mom's, **15**
12th Street Air
Command, **9**
2–4 Club, **6**
247 Bar, **1**
Uncles, **8**
Venture Inn, **11**
Westbury Bar, **10**
Woody's, **5**

Coffeehouse Culture

Millennium Coffee. This is the unofficial homo coffee shop of Philadelphia, right beside Afterwords (*see* Gay Media, *below*), the unofficial lesbian-and-gay newsstand. In addition to the tables in front (good for people-watching) and in back (good for people-chatting), there's a coffee bar midway (good for people-meeting). Friendly and unpretentious. ⊠ *212 S. 12th St.,* ☎ *215/731–9798.*

More Than Just Ice Cream. This gay-friendly café with wrought-iron chairs and tables moved to a slick new space in late 1997. Along with ice cream and a limited range of coffees, it has great soups and sandwiches and outstanding apple pie. ⊠ *1119 Locust St.,* ☎ *215/574–0586.*

XandO. Ideal for a snack, a shot of java, or a sip of wine (there's a full liquor license) before or after catching a show at one of Broad Street's theaters or performance spaces, this mural-filled espresso bar has great soups and sandwiches. ⊠ *235 S. 15th St.,* ☎ *215/893–9696.*

SCENES

Barflies and conversationalists adore Philadelphia's small but convivial bar scene. Twentysomethings, poseurs, and lonely hearts complain a bit, generally dubbing Woody's and, on Fridays, Shampoo the only "real" games in town. Most of the bars are in the Gay District. The others are close by. On a good night you could hit all of them. Several gay-friendly restaurants around South Street—notably Judy's and the Latest Dish—have active little bars, particularly in the early evening. In Rittenhouse Row the same can be said about Circa and Astral Plane.

Philadelphia crowds are chatty, often older and local, and relatively uninterested in playing musical beds. Bartenders and patrons will strike up a conversation with strangers. Because all these places serve food, a tavernlike atmosphere prevails. To the visitor from other big cities, it will seem quiet—but you'll be made to feel right at home.

Prime Suspects

Bike Stop. Although it's large, with four floors, the Bike Stop retains the ambience of a neighborhood bar. On the ground floor there's a butch bear bar; the sports-theme second floor has darts, pinball, and pool; the third floor has a small dance floor (open on Friday and Saturday); and the basement "Dungeon" is a dark leather bar open from Friday to Sunday. ⊠ *206 S. Quince St.,* ☎ *215/627–1662. Crowd: 70/30 m/f, leather-and-Levi's on first floor and in basement, jocks on second, and a mix on the third.*

Rodz. It's popular for many reasons: a good restaurant, a romantic roof deck with city views, and a classy piano bar. Most nights the several bars draw a down-and-dirty crowd of regulars who come for the banter. Attached is an after-hours dance spot, **Club Tyz,** for which membership is required (you must be sponsored by a member). Tyz has dancing on the top floor; on the lower floor, called Bottoms, there are pool tables and pinball machines. Weekly events, such as jock-strap night, change monthly. ⊠ *1418 Rodman St.,* ☎ *215/735–2900. Crowd: 80/20 m/f (more mixed in the restaurant), otherwise very diverse.*

Sisters. The city's premier lesbian club has three floors, the wildest of which is the top-level disco. Downstairs is a restaurant and low-key cocktail lounge that gets revved up on Friday when bands perform. There's a pool hall in the basement. Popular events include Wednesday for open-mike crooning and the Sunday tea dance, which follows brunch. ⊠ *1321 Chancellor St.,* ☎ *215/735–0735. Crowd: 80/20 f/m (more mixed on Saturday), all ages, eclectic.*

12th Street Air Command. In the space that used to be occupied by Hepburn's, this busy dance and cruise bar is a good place to get warmed up—

either drinking or dancing—before heading on to Woody's. There's a large lounge on the ground floor and a medium-size dance floor upstairs (with usually a small cover to get in). ⊠ *254 S. 12th St., ☎ 215/545–8088. Crowd: Mostly male, 20s to 40s, mixed racially, cruisy, more butch than Woody's but less so than the name might suggest.*

247 Bar. This complex has several rooms and floors, and though none allow sexual activity, the atmosphere is steamy. Some reports of hustlers. Gets a rush after midnight. ⊠ *247 S. 17th St., ☎ 215/545–9779. Crowd: male, mid-30s and older, some leather-and-Levi's.*

Westbury Bar. A neighborhood hangout that's been the *Cheers* of the Gay District since 1987, this is a great place to meet friends before heading elsewhere or just to grab soup and a sandwich. Bartenders are gregarious when it's not too busy. ⊠ *13th and Spruce Sts., ☎ 215/546–5170. Crowd: 80/20 m/f, late 20s to 40s, local, mixed racially, down to earth.*

Woody's. This is easily Philadelphia's most popular club; the first—and often the only—place out-of-towners head. The very people who complain about the scene, the attitude, and the conformity of its clientele hang out here night after night. Its two levels have a spacious disco, two video bars, a game room, and a small restaurant. You can barely move on weekends, which keeps things frisky. Best dance night: Wednesday, when under-21s are admitted for a $3 cover—more women come then, too. The downstairs video bar draws more of a friendly neighborhood bunch than the stand-and-model upstairs one. ⊠ *202 S. 13th St., ☎ 215/545–1893. Crowd: mostly male, 20s and 30s, guppies, gym boys, club kids.*

Neighborhood Haunts

Once a popular disco, guy-oriented and racially mixed **Key West** (⊠ 207 S. Juniper St., ☎ 215/545–1578) is now big only on weekends. **The Post** (⊠ 1705 Chancellor St., ☎ 215/985–9720) is known for its colorful bar staff and Sunday go-go boys. **Uncles** (⊠ 1220 Locust St., ☎ 215/546–6660) is popular with players on Philly's lesbian and gay softball teams. The **Venture Inn** (⊠ 255 S. Camac St., ☎ 215/545–8731), the oldest gay bar in town, is in a historic tavern in the heart of the Gay District.

Late in the evening, locals sometimes head to the private **2–4 Club** (⊠ 1221 James St., ☎ 215/735–5772), which has dancing and nonalcoholic drinks until 5 AM. It costs $15 to join (membership is good for a year), and you must be introduced to become a member. Best bet: Hang out till closing at Woody's, and with enough persistence you'll meet somebody who belongs.

One-Nighters and Movable Fetes

Shampoo. The opening of this huge postmodern warehouse disco, which is mostly gay on Friday and mostly straight on Saturday, may have permanently altered Philadelphia's queer nightlife scene—this place is right up there with the best clubs in Manhattan and D.C. The upper one has most of the action, including two dance floors (the large one plays new stuff; the smaller cramped one, more disco classics), several lounge areas, and numerous nooks and crannies ideal for chatting and making out. Downstairs is a quieter transitional space. Shampoo is several blocks northeast of Center City, so cab it. ⊠ *417 N. 8th St., ☎ 215/922–7500. Crowd: 80/20 m/f, under 35, hip, club kids, high-profile voguers.*

Ladies 2000 (☎ 609/784–8341), based in southern New Jersey, sponsors lesbian parties at dance clubs and bars throughout the region. Depending on the venue, the turnout can be incredible. Call for details.

Hangin' with the Hets

The food at this South Street eatery gets mixed reviews, but the self-consciously hip **Martini Café** (⊠ 622 S. 6th St., ☎ 215/629–0661) is a favorite spot. Gay-friendly and poseur-infested **Sugar Mom's** (⊠ 225

Church St., ☏ 215/925–8219) has a kicking jukebox, pool tables, and decent bar food.

Action

Numerous gay or mixed gay/straight adult bookstores are near the Gay District, several of them north of Walnut Street, along 12th and 13th streets. This is also where you'll find the gay bathhouse, **Club Body Center Gym Philadelphia** (✉ 120 S. 13th St., 2nd floor, ☏ 215/735–9568).

SLEEPS

Philadelphia has some of the most sumptuous luxury hotels in the country, several of which are gay-friendly and close to nightlife. Although pricey, most of these places are business traveler–oriented and slash their rates on weekends. For less expensive options you're better sticking with one of the B&Bs or smaller hotels, of which there are a few affordable options within steps of the Gay District.

For price ranges, *see* lodging Chart A at the front of this guide.

Hotels

$$$$ **The Rittenhouse Hotel.** This hotel is about as gay-oriented a luxury hotel as you're going to find. It has a large queer staff and a concierge with information about gay bars and restaurants. The Rittenhouse treats all its guests like old friends, and movie buffs will appreciate its having hosted the cast of *Philadelphia* during filming. ✉ *210 W. Rittenhouse Sq., 19103,* ☏ *215/546–9000 or 800/635–1042,* FAX *215/732–3364. 98 rooms. Restaurants, pool, health club.*

$$$$ **The Ritz-Carlton.** The Ritz rises 15 stories above a chichi shopping mall, and it's close to Rittenhouse Square and the Gay District. The blocks nearest are a bit bleak, but once inside, the warmth and superior service one expects from a Ritz show through. ✉ *17th and Chestnut Sts., 19103,* ☏ *215/563–1600 or 800/241–3333,* FAX *215/567–2845. 290 rooms. Restaurant, health club.*

$$$–$$$$ **Embassy Suites Center City.** Rates here hover close to those of neighboring luxury hotels, but each of the suites sleeps four and has two balconies with outstanding views and a small kitchenette—a great value for two couples traveling together. ✉ *1776 Benjamin Franklin Pkwy., 19103,* ☏ *215/561–1776 or 800/362–2779,* FAX *215/963–0122. 288 rooms. Restaurant, health club.*

$$$ **Doubletree Hotel Philadelphia.** This contemporary property offers weekend deals; it's close to the bars and in the heart of the performing-arts district. The fitness center is good, and rooms are among the largest in town. Unusual city views. ✉ *Broad and Locust Sts., 19107,* ☏ *215/ 893–1600 or 800/222–8733,* FAX *215/893–1663. 427 rooms. Restaurant, pool, health club.*

$$$ **Holiday Inn Select.** Centrally located, this business hotel is an easy walk to the Gay District, the museums, and 30th Street Station. The entire hotel was revamped top-to-bottom early in 1998, and the management has hosted gay events. ✉ *1800 Market St., 19103,* ☏ *215/561–7500 or 800/465– 4329,* FAX *215/561–2556. 445 rooms. Restaurant, pool, exercise room.*

$$–$$$ **Holiday Inn Express Midtown.** When there are gay events in town this 1960s hotel with drab rooms but fair prices is wall-to-wall homos. It has friendly employees, and is just steps away from the Gay District (and several steamy adult theaters). ✉ *1305 Walnut St., 19107,* ☏ *215/735–9300 or 800/465–4329,* FAX *215/732–2682. 166 rooms. Pool, health club.*

Small Hotels and Guest Houses

$$–$$$ ⌂ **Ten Eleven Clinton.** The elegant apartments in this Federal town house are a better deal than those in the big chain properties. Most units have working fireplaces, and all have private kitchenettes (which are stocked daily with Continental breakfast supplies), VCRs, and fresh flowers. The Gay District is steps away from tree-shaded Clinton Street. ✉ *1011 Clinton St., 19107,* ☎ *215/923–8144,* ℻ *215/923–5757, e-mail 1011@ concentric.net. 7 rooms with phone, TV, and private bath. Continental breakfast. Mixed gay/straight.*

$–$$ ⌂ **Abigail Adams.** This seven-story budget hotel in the heart of the Gay District is one of the best deals in town. The rooms are large and clean, though very plain. ✉ *1208 Walnut St., 19107,* ☎ *215/546–7336 or 800/ 887–1776,* ℻ *215/546–7573. 32 rooms with phone, TV, and private bath. Continental breakfast. Mixed gay/straight.*

$–$$ ⌂ **Uncles Upstairs Inn.** Above the bar of the same name, Uncles Upstairs Inn is the only predominantly gay accommodation in the city. Rooms have period themes. Near the bar scene. ✉ *1220 Locust St., 19107,* ☎ *215/ 546–6660,* ℻ *215/546–1653. 6 rooms with TV and private bath. Continental breakfast. Mostly gay male/lesbian.*

$ ⌂ **Antique Row Bed & Breakfast.** This cozy and warmly decorated European-style B&B is steps from gay nightlife and the dozens of antiques shops along Pine Street, set inside a 1820s town house. The hearty breakfasts are memorable. ✉ *341 S. 12th St., 19107,* ☎ *215/592–7802,* ℻ *215/592–9692. 3 rooms with TV, some with private bath; 1 apartment. Full breakfast. Mixed gay/straight.*

THE LITTLE BLACK BOOK

At Your Fingertips

AIDS Information Network (☎ 215/575–1110). *City Paper* (☎ 215/732–5542, Web site www.citypaper.net). **Gay and Lesbian Counseling Service Hotline** (☎ 215/732–8255). **Gay and Lesbian Switchboard** (☎ 215/ 546–7100). **Philadelphia Convention and Visitors Association** (✉ 1515 Market St., Suite 2020, 19102, ☎ 215/636–3300 or 800/537–7676, Web site www.libertynet.org/phila-visitor). **Philadelphia Lesbian and Gay Task Force Anti-Violence and Discrimination Hotline** (☎ 215/772–2005). **Philadelphia Visitors Center** (✉ 16th St. and John F. Kennedy Blvd., ☎ 215/636–1666). **PHLASH** (☎ 215/4–PHLASH). **Quaker City Cab** (☎ 215/728–8000). **William Way Lesbian, Gay, Bisexual, and Transgender Community Center** (✉ 1315 Spruce St., ☎ 215/732–2220, Web site www.iamproud.comþwaygaycenter).

Gay Media

Philadelphia's main lesbian/gay newspapers are the *Pride Weekly* (☎ 215/790–1179), which began in 1982, and the considerably more substantial *Philadelphia Gay News* (☎ 215/625–8501, e-mail Marco @aol.com). The city's free women's monthly, *Labyrinth* (☎ 215/546–6686, e-mail LTPWN@aol.com), is not gay per se, but has much lesbian-oriented coverage.

BOOKSTORES

Giovanni's Room (✉ 345 S. 12th St., ☎ 215/923–2960), the city's (and one of the nation's) largest gay bookstore, is on the edge of the Gay District. It has two floors of lesbian and gay titles, plus a wealth of feminist material. There are several community bulletin boards, a wide range of periodicals, and porn. The staff is helpful and has a real knack for finding out-of-print, imported, or hard-to-find titles. **Afterwords** (✉ 218 S. 12th St., ☎ 215/735–2393) has a limited gay-oriented selection of books, plus lesbian and gay periodicals, postcards, and greeting cards. It also car-

ries magazines and newspapers from around the world as well as gifts
and T-shirts. It's open late.

Working Out

The **12th Street Gym** (✉ 204 S. 12th St., ☎ 215/985–4092), in the Gay
District, is the city's queerest gym, very guppie and good for women and
men. **Pennsport Athletic Club** (✉ 325 Bainbridge St., ☎ 215/627–4900)
is another gay-popular choice.

NEW HOPE

Compared to other gay-popular resorts in the Northeast, New Hope is
less a place to see and be seen and more a restful weekend hideout for
couples. New Hope, though it has two queer nightspots and several
trendy restaurants, floats along at an unhurried pace. This small riverside hamlet is a mere hour from Philadelphia and 90 minutes from New
York City.

Like the Russian River in California, the New Hope area is that rare breed
of gay resort neither fringed by ocean nor surrounded by desert. The terrain and appeal of both destinations are similar. Each is set in a verdant
river valley traversed by winding rural roads. You can sun for a few hours
back at the inn and tour downtown on foot in an afternoon, but you'll
need to strike out by car or bicycle to appreciate the region's attractions—
its history, country manors, antiques shops, and sylvan vistas.

New Hope does not aggressively market itself as a gay destination. There
are no pride parades, and few gay-specific events. Of the gay-owned accommodations, only one is exclusively gay; by the same token, most
straight-owned inns are amenable to gay guests. Lesbians now own several businesses in town.

Few people think of New Hope as a year-round destination, but only from
January to March are things truly slow. Spring and fall are defined by
warm afternoons and crisp evenings (from mid-October to mid-Novem-
ber is when the foliage is most vibrant, but the crowds keep coming until
Christmas). Summer is hot enough to turn potential visitors toward the
breezy seashore, but it's still a joy. After a winter snowfall the area is stunning. It's never as chilly here as it is in New England, and many of the
inns remain open.

The Lay of the Land

Downtown

New Hope is tiny—roughly 1 square-mile of preserved 18th- and 19th-
century buildings, most of them now inns, restaurants, shops, and private homes. But locals often refer to the three or four miles south, west,
and north of town as New Hope, encompassing the towns bordering the
Delaware River from Morrisville north to Riegelsville.

Main Street runs north-south parallel to and between the river and the
canal and is lined with restaurants, crafts and antiques shops, and galleries. Running perpendicular to Main Street are historic **Mechanic, Ferry,**
and **Bridge** streets. At the corner of Main and Ferry streets is the 1784
Parry Mansion (☎ 215/862–5148), which contains decorative arts and
furnishings from the late Colonial period to the late Victorian era.

The Delaware Canal, though commercially defunct, still trickles through
town. Hour-long, mule-led, historian-narrated **barge excursions** along
the canal are given from April to November (☎ 215/862–2842 or 800/
592–2743); the tour passes old cottages and artists' studios. Covering
more territory is the 9-mile, 50-minute ride aboard an antique steam train

given by the **New Hope and Ivyland Railroad** (⊠ 32 W. Bridge St., ☎ 215/862–2332), year-round but weekends-only from January to March.

Getting Around

The only practical way to reach and explore the New Hope area is by car. I–95 crosses the Delaware River about 10 miles to the south; U.S. 202 crosses the river just to the north. Downtown is easily walkable, although the gay bars are on Bridge Street, a 20- to 30-minute walk west from the heart of things. Parking is tight on summer weekends, but not impossible.

Eats

A number of good restaurants are in New Hope and across the Delaware River in Lambertville, New Jersey, and the prices are lower than at resorts such as Provincetown and Fire Island. Though the Raven and the Cartwheel are the most gay-frequented, every restaurant in town has a noticeable following.

For price ranges, *see* dining Chart B at the front of this guide.

$$$ ✗ **The Raven.** Most nights you'll find dozens of lesbian and gay couples clinking their wine glasses here. The Continental American menu is dependable, if predictable, though you'll find a few unusual offerings, like po'boy pasta with oysters, mushrooms, leeks, and spinach. ⊠ *385 W. Bridge St.,* ☎ *215/862–2081.*

$$–$$$ **Hamilton's Grill Room.** It's a bit tough to find, down a gravel alley in Lambertville, but locals insist this is one of the area's top eateries. The menu specializes in inventive seafood grills and Mediterranean dishes; try couscous with seared duck, green peppercorns, and currants; or braised cod with orange and fresh sage. ⊠ *8 Coryell St., Lambertville,* ☎ *609/397–4343.*

$$–$$$ ✗ **Karla's.** Karla's is a gay-popular place downtown. Eat either on the open terrace with marble-top tables, on the glassed-in porch, or in the formal, intimate dining room. A mix of sophisticated and casual fare is served, from St. Peter's fish with red potatoes to pâté to steak fajitas. ⊠ *5 W. Mechanic St.,* ☎ *215/862–2612.*

$$–$$$ ✗ **The Café.** This funky café in tiny Rosemont, New Jersey, looks and feels like a 1940s general store. Offered are a variety of dishes—pasta with blue cheese and walnuts, a peasant omelet with sour cream and caviar—with an emphasis on farm-fresh ingredients. ⊠ *Rtes. 519 and 604, Rosemont,* ☎ *609/397–4097.*

$$ ✗ **DeAnna's.** Local queers love this pasta house in the heart of downtown Lambertville. The pasta dishes are homemade—try the ricotta gnocchi with marinara sauce. The same owners run a small sandwich and coffeehouse, **Festival** (☎ 609/397–9430), around the corner. ⊠ *18 S. Main St., Lambertville,* ☎ *609/397–8957.*

$$ ✗ **The Landing.** Popular with New Hope's day-trippers and shoppers, the Landing is a red clapboard tavern on the river. The brick patio offers views clear across the Delaware to Lambertville and hosts a friendly, if aggressive, posse of ducks. The quasi–New American food is healthful and light; try the turkey chili. ⊠ *22 N. Main St.,* ☎ *215/862–3558.*

$ ✗ **Wildflowers.** The small, traditional dining room lacks atmosphere, but scoot through to the back and you'll find a shady brick terrace overlooking Ingham Creek. The food is old-fashioned Pennsylvania cooking, such as baked ham and meat loaf. ⊠ *8 W. Mechanic St.,* ☎ *215/862–2241.*

Scenes

Though sneeringly called "No Hope" by city folk disheartened by New Hope's low-key nightlife, the community supports an enormous disco, the Cartwheel, and a gay tavern and video bar. On weekends, especially in spring through fall, your odds of meeting friends and having a blast are very good. Other times the crowds are local and a bit cliquey. Across the river in Lambertville you won't find any gay clubs per se, but local gays and lesbians frequent the **Boathouse,** a curious little shingle house down an alley across from Hamilton's (*see* Eats, *above*). ⊠ *8½ Coryell St., Lambertville,* ☎ *609/397–2244.*

Cartwheel. New Hope's largest club draws huge crowds on weekends. Things don't usually get going here until midnight. Inside is a large disco with great music, a cocktail lounge with a central bar, a room with pool tables, a dark and cruisy basement bar (a.k.a. "the Dungeon"), and, in the club's original historic section, an intimate piano lounge and casual American restaurant, Café Mo (nachos, burgers, etc.). ⊠ *Rtes. 202 and 179,* ☎ *215/862–0880. Crowd: mixed male/female, all ages but on the young side, and diverse in every other regard.*

Raven. There are three good times to come here: during the afternoon to lie out by the pool, in the early evening for cocktails, or later for after-dinner drinks. Off the amber-lit tavern, there's a handsome lounge with a fireplace, chandeliers, and a large video screen. The Raven has a loyal local following. ⊠ *385 W. Bridge St.,* ☎ *215/862–2081. Crowd: mostly male, locals and hotel guests, over 35.*

Sleeps

New Hope and the surrounding area are loaded with inns, several of them gay-operated and virtually all of them gay-friendly.

For price ranges, see lodging Chart B at the front of this guide.

Hotels

$$$ ⊞ **Inn at Lambertville Station.** Among hotel options close to New Hope, this contemporary property (a 10-minute walk by bridge) has the most character. The homey rooms are furnished with antiques and reproductions, and there are great river views. Families and conventioneers stay here, but it's perfectly gay-friendly. ⊠ *11 Bridge St., Lambertville, NJ 08530,* ☎ *609/397–8300 or 800/524–1091. 45 rooms. Restaurant.*

$ ⊞ **New Hope Motel.** This basic, clean motel is within walking distance of gay nightlife. ⊠ *400 W. Bridge St., 18938,* ☎ *215/862–2800. 28 rooms. Pool.*

Guest Houses and Small Hotels

$$$ ⊞ **The Lexington House.** This gay B&B on several serene acres is authentically, though simply, furnished. The stone foundation of an old barn has been transformed into a pool and is surrounded by gardens and a flagstone terrace. ⊠ *6171 Upper York Rd., 18938,* ☎ *215/794–0811. 6 rooms. Pool. Mixed gay/straight.*

$$–$$$ ⊞ **Fox & Hound.** Period antiques fill the homey rooms (each comes with tempting bowls of Hershey's Kisses), and there's a pretty patio outside. A 1997 addition to the rear of the building houses three new rooms. ⊠ *246 W. Bridge St., 18938,* ☎ *215/862–5082 or 800/862–5082. 8 rooms with private bath. Full breakfast. Mixed gay/straight.*

$$–$$$ ⊞ **Victorian Peacock.** This grand B&B in Pipersville, a 15-minute drive northwest of New Hope, is set on five pastoral acres. The three-story Victorian-style mansion is filled with antiques. ⊠ *309 E. Dark Hollow Rd., Pipersville, 18947,* ☎ *215/766–1356, e-mail peacock@epix.net. 5 rooms, 3 with bath. Pool, hot tub. Continental breakfast. Mixed gay/straight.*

$$–$$$ ⊞ **Woolverton Inn.** A 1792 stone manor with a high mansard roof, this inn is set on several pastoral acres with an old stone barn, a carriage house (with several guest rooms), and apple and oak trees everywhere. One of the loveliest settings in the valley—romantic and secluded. ⊠ *6 Woolver-*

ton Rd., Stockton, NJ 08559, ☎ 609/397–0802, ⅎ̅A̅X̅ 609/397–4936. 10 rooms. Full breakfast. Mostly straight.

$$–$$$ 🛏 **York Street House.** This women-operated, three-story, 1909 manor house on a tree-lined side street in Lambertville contains elegant rooms reached via a winding staircase. Public spaces contain tile fireplaces and original Waterford crystal chandeliers. The inn is steps from several great restaurants. ✉ *42 York St., Lambertville, NJ 08530,* ☎ *609/397–3007. 6 rooms with phone, TV, and private bath. Full breakfast. Mixed gay/straight.*

$–$$$ 🛏 **Raven Hall.** West of downtown, near the gay bars, Raven Hall is the only true gay guest house, although it feels more like a small motor lodge. Rooms, most of which have private baths, are basic and set in a Colonial-style, dark blue building, which is a new addition to the original structure. Very social. ✉ *385 W. Bridge St., 18938,* ☎ *215/862–2081. 17 rooms. Mostly gay male.*

The Little Black Book

For general tourism information, contact the **Central Bucks County Chamber of Commerce** (✉ 115 W. Court St., Doylestown, 18901, ☎ 215/348–3913), **Lambertville Area Chamber of Commerce** (✉ 4 S. Union St., Lambertville, New Jersey, 08530, ☎ 609/397–0055), or **New Hope Borough Tourism Information Center** (✉ 1 W. Mechanic St., Box 633, 18938, ☎ 215/862–5880). There are no gay papers in Bucks County, but you'll find some New Hope coverage in Philadelphia's papers. The general-interest store, the **Book Gallery** (✉ 19 W. Mechanic St., ☎ 215/862–5110), has feminist and gay/lesbian titles.

29 Out in Phoenix

With Sedona

PHOENIX IS LIKE Los Angeles dressed in cowboy boots. A highly contemporary metropolis surrounded by mountains and high desert, Arizona's capital is in many ways the last stronghold of the western frontier. But the city has been transformed over the past four decades, its formerly rugged terrain now a mass of tract housing and strip malls, its mountains a cradle for the thick smog that suffuses the valley on most afternoons.

Arizona remained a territory of the United States for nearly 150 years, longer than any of the first 48 states. Perhaps for this reason, its residents harbor a distinct distrust of the federal government or any other external influence that might threaten civil liberty. Adamantly opposed to interference, Phoenicians have created their own paradise, one that rolls along according to the laws of nature rather than those of constitutional democracy. The drawbacks to this approach include unchecked pollution, an unzoned and disjointed landscape, and more than a whiff of corruption. The lack of rules lends the city a *Lord of the Flies* mentality, which has brought out the best and the worst in its residents.

The ninth-largest city in the country, Phoenix lacks a center—even a downtown. Like Los Angeles, it's a sprawling city in a dry climate—only the Sahara Desert is less humid than Phoenix's Sonoran Desert. Southern California's cultural influence can be felt as well: Californians were the first Americans to move to Phoenix in great numbers, in the 1870s, and the city still takes its cues from its neighbor to the west on a host of lifestyle and political issues.

One difference between the two, though, is that in Phoenix the grocery clerk will stop checking items long enough to say hello. The bus driver will pause to offer directions. People move here for the job opportunities—greater Phoenix is the third-largest high-tech center in the country—but also to escape the fast pace and rudeness of other big cities.

Phoenix's population grew to 600,000 by the mid-'70s and has since swelled to more than a million. The population first boomed in the '30s, when air-conditioning became relatively affordable. Most Phoenicians installed these heavenly devices, and living here comfortably year-round became a reality. Further spurring the population explosion was the establishment of Luke Air Force Base during World War II. The aviation enterprises that simultaneously set up shop were the forerunners of the technological ventures that have dominated the commercial landscape for the last half-century.

Voters in Phoenix tend to be deeply conservative. The city has never been especially sympathetic to the plight of minorities, sexual or racial, though the most famous Phoenix conservative, former U.S. Senator Barry Goldwater, espoused a live-and-let-live philosophy. In his later years a defender of the gay community, Goldwater was unable to sway popular opinion in favor of gay-rights initiatives. At best, the average conservative Phoenician believes that consensual acts in the privacy of people's homes are no one else's business.

Until November 1995 this was the largest city in the country without a full-scale gay and lesbian bookstore, and it's still one of the largest without a gay ghetto—or even a strip of gay bars. (It might help if residents walked the streets more, but this is the sort of place where you drive 50 feet to buy a pack of gum.) But the diffusion of gays and lesbians has its advantages: No matter where you tour, you'll come across queerfolk.

THE LAY OF THE LAND

As the policeman shouts to a mob of rubberneckers in every low-budget cops-and-robbers film ever made: "Move along folks . . . there's nothing to see here!" For all of its shops, spas, and good restaurants, Phoenix has relatively few attractions and few remnants of its pre-1900 past. The city's strengths are some interesting examples of 20th-century architecture and a few good museums and galleries.

Downtown and the Cultural Center

Over the past decade Phoenix has revitalized its once barren **downtown,** renovating historic buildings and erecting innovative postmodern structures. The **East End,** which has become somewhat walkable, is home to cultural venues like the restored Spanish Revival **Orpheum Theatre** (⊠ 203 Adams St., ☎ 602/252–9678), which has film festivals and theater productions; the multi-use **Herberger Theater Center** (⊠ 222 E. Monroe St., ☎ 602/252–8497), which hosts dance and theater companies; and the **Symphony Hall** (⊠ 225 E. Adams St., ☎ 602/262–6225), where the Phoenix Symphony and the Arizona Opera perform.

History and preservation buffs could easily spend a day wandering around **Heritage Square** (⊠ Adams and 7th Sts.). Among the century-old homes you can tour here is the Victorian **Rosson House** (⊠ 6th and Monroe Sts., ☎ 602/262–5029), on the south side of the square.

West of the square is the new **Arizona Science Center** (⊠ 600 E. Washington St., ☎ 602/716–2000), whose touch-friendly exhibits are a hit with kids and fun for adults. Also here is the state-of-the-art **Dorrance Planetarium** (☎ 602/716–2079). A block below Heritage Square, the **Phoenix Museum of History** (⊠ 105 N. 5th St., ☎ 602/253–2734), a steel-and-glass structure that opened in 1996, contains exhibits documenting the region. A few blocks west, the small **Museo Chicano** (⊠ 1242 E. Washington St., ☎ 602/257–5536) is a major showcase for contemporary Latin-American art. North of these museums is the **Arizona Center** (⊠ 3rd and Van Buren Sts., ☎ 602/271–4000), with 60 shops and restaurants and a 24-screen cineplex.

North of the mall on and around Central Avenue, the **Cultural Center** contains thought-provoking large-scale contemporary architecture; you'll see buildings shaped like King Tut's tomb and in the form of an inverted pyramid (appropriate given the echoes of ancient Egypt in the city's name). Of particular note is the **Phoenix Central Library** (⊠ 1221 N. Central Ave., ☎ 602/262–4636), a curvaceous copper sheathed wonder meant to evoke the region's red-rock terrain.

The outstanding **Phoenix Art Museum** (⊠ 1625 N. Central Ave., ☎ 602/257–1222), a green-quartz structure, houses 19th-century European paintings, delightful artworks of the American West, and Abstract Expressionist masterworks. Re-created miniature rooms are decorated in architectural styles ranging from 17th-century French to 1930s art deco. Eddie Matney of Eddie's Grill (*see* Eats, *below*) operates **Eddie's Art Museum Café** (☎ 602/257–2191), which overlooks the sculpture garden. Two blocks north of the art museum is the **Heard Museum** (⊠ 22 E. Monte Vista Rd., ☎ 602/252–8840), a 1928 Spanish Colonial Revival house containing the nation's top collection of Native American art and artifacts.

Camelback Road and the Rainbow Zone

In central Phoenix, especially along **Camelback Road,** you will find plenty of excuses to spend money. **Park Central Mall** (⊠ Central Ave. and Earll Dr., ☎ 602/264–5575), less snazzy than some of its newer competitors, is the gayest shopping center in Phoenix. Park Central Mall is in the heart of what's becoming known as the **Rainbow Zone,** a large rectangle bounded by 7th Avenue, Indian School Road, 7th Street, and Bethany Home Road; it's the closest Phoenix comes to having a gay district. There's not much to explore, but many lesbians and gays live, work, and socialize here. The heavily utilized **Gay and Lesbian Community Center** (⊠ 3136 N. 3rd Ave., ☎ 602/234–2752) has a library and hosts various groups. On some nights, there's a lesbian coffeehouse (call for details).

Many a diva whiles away her Saturday afternoon at the **Biltmore Fashion Park** (⊠ 24th St. and E. Camelback Rd., ☎ 602/955–8400), strolling through Polo, Gucci, and other high-end boutiques.

Scottsdale

A cross between Beverly Hills and Santa Fe, **Scottsdale** has hundreds of high-end arts and crafts galleries and specialty shops. Though conservative, locals aren't often freaked out by same-sex couples strolling arm in arm. In this sophisticated community, the laws of morality are superseded only by the laws of discretion: Scottsdale residents may not approve of homosexuals, but they're too refined to notice them and too polite to comment.

The **Scottsdale Fashion Square** (⊠ Scottsdale and Camelback Rds., ☎ 602/941–2140) is an enormous, fancy mall, but *the* place to be seen is definitely the **Borgata** (⊠ 6166 N. Scottsdale Rd., ☎ 602/998–1822), a swank Renaissance-style compound that supposedly resembles an Italian village. Just south of the Fashion Square, **5th Avenue** curves northeast from Indian School Road up to Scottsdale Road. Clothiers, jewelers, and boutiques line this street; tucked off a parking lot behind the shops is the guppyish gay bar BS West (*see* Scenes, *below*). More touristy but still brimming with great shopping is **Old Town Scottsdale,** which is at its best along Main Street between Brown Avenue and 70th Street (Scottsdale Road crosses Main Street midway).

The one nonshopping must-see is **Taliesin West** (⊠ 114th St. and Cactus Rd., ☎ 602/860–2700), architect Frank Lloyd Wright's winter home, built in 1937. Tours of the grounds are conducted daily.

Tempe

One of the few places in the metro area with a sidewalk culture is in the heart of the **Arizona State University** (ASU) campus in **Tempe,** about a 20-minute drive east of central Phoenix (take I–20 to Route 220, or take U.S. 60/89). **Mill Avenue,** which runs just north of University Drive, has dozens of funky shops, restaurants, and hangouts; none are specifically gay-oriented, but most are quite hospitable.

GETTING AROUND

You will need a car in Phoenix—very little is within walking distance of anything else here. Within the city limits, north–south roads are numbered, fanning out from Phoenix's commercial spine, Central Avenue. Every north–south thoroughfare to the east is a "street" (the major ones being

7th, 16th, 24th, and 32nd streets); each one to the west is an "avenue" (the major ones being 7th, 19th, 24th, and 35th avenues). Major east–west roads are named. Following either Indian School Road or Camelback Road east will lead you into Scottsdale.

EATS

Phoenix supports dozens of inventive California-inspired restaurants, and some of southwestern cuisine's major chefs operate restaurants here. Many gay bars have limited menus of blah American food or serve brunch—Charlie's and Wink's are the best.

For price ranges *see* dining Chart A at the front of this guide.

Phoenix

$$$$ ✕ **Christopher's and the Bistro.** A formal French restaurant with beautiful linen and silver and a New American bistro share an open kitchen that turns out impeccable fish and veal dishes. The French menu focuses on contemporary fare with international influences—the lobster with curry risotto and a mild Thai sauce is sublime. The wine list is epic. ⊠ *2398 E. Camelback Rd.,* ☎ *602/957–3214.*

$$$$ ✕ **Vincent Guerithault on Camelback.** Presided over by Vincent Guerithault, considered by many the founder of contemporary southwestern cuisine, this place-to-be-seen has a very L.A. feel—and valet parking, too. Sophisticated French techniques transform regional ingredients into creations like duck tamales and sautéed veal sweetbreads with blue cornmeal. ⊠ *3930 E. Camelback Rd.,* ☎ *602/224–0225.*

$$$–$$$$ ✕ **El Chorro Lodge.** This posh girls' school turned elegant eatery sits snugly between Mummy and Camelback mountains in northern Phoenix. The classic dinner entrées like chateaubriand and rack of lamb are always great, but El Chorro is best known for its lavish Sunday brunches on the festive patio. ⊠ *5550 E. Lincoln Dr.,* ☎ *602/948–5170.*

$$$–$$$$ ✕ **RoxSand.** Larger-than-life decor and culinary chutzpah are the trademarks of Phoenix's most outrageous restaurant. The menu borrows from countries where food reigns supreme: France, Thailand, Jamaica, Greece, Mexico. Let your hair down and dive in to a plate of Chilean sea bass with a bread-crumb and grated-horseradish crust, served with charred eggplant, deep-fried leeks, and artichoke hearts. ⊠ *2594 E. Camelback Rd.,* ☎ *602/381–0444.*

$$$–$$$$ ✕ **Timothy's.** This creeper-covered cottage draws a hip pack of bon vivants who appreciate the live jazz and sophisticated ambience. The food is good, too, with New American specialties like pan-seared ahi with sesame-mustard, wasabi, and ginger sauces, served with a steamed-vegetable compote. ⊠ *6335 N. 16th St.,* ☎ *602/277–7634.*

$$–$$$$ ✕ **Durant's.** A gay-friendly downtown stalwart, Durant's has been pleasing its fans with traditional if predictable fare for more than 50 years. Filet mignon, mesquite-broiled salmon, and prime rib are typical offerings. The dining room is a study in retro-elegance—more Fred and Ethel than Fred and Ginger, but charming nonetheless. ⊠ *2611 N. Central Ave.,* ☎ *602/264–5967.*

$$$ ✕ **Avanti.** This notable Italian mainstay attracts many gays (try to ignore the Charlton Heston photo in the lobby). The striking Art Nouveau decor—black-and-white checkered floor, zebra-stripe banquettes, and *lots* of chrome—sizzles and sparkles. Beluga caviar, grilled lamb chops, and cioppino are among your options. ⊠ *2728 E. Thomas St.,* ☎ *602/956–0900; also* ⊠ *3102 N. Scottsdale Rd., Scottsdale,* ☎ *602/949–8333.*

$$$ ✕ **Eddie's Grill.** One of the most gay-frequented of the city's hot-shot establishments, this Mediterranean-meets-the-Southwest restaurant has a warm and atmospheric dining room. The best bets include shrimp broiled with lime juice, olive oil, peppers, cilantro, and mustard, and the barbe-

388

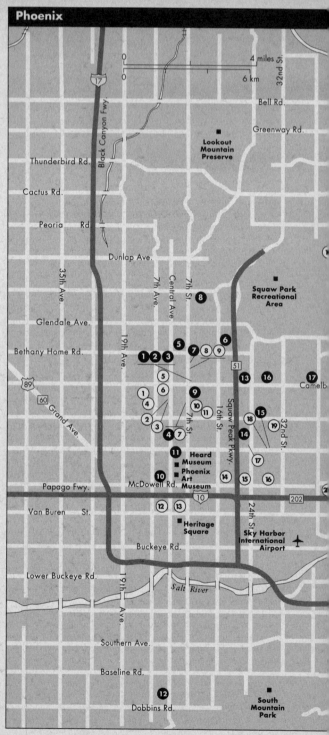

Phoenix

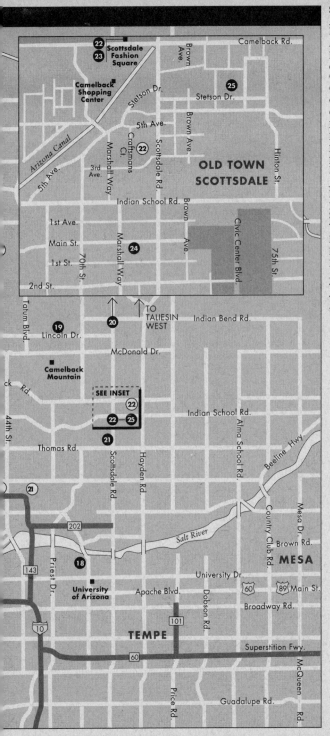

cue chicken on a bed of cinnamon apples, red potatoes, and mustard greens. ✉ *4747 N. 7th St.,* ☎ *602/241–1188.*

$$–$$$ ✗ **Christo's.** Expect no surprises at this slightly formal Italian eatery with Greek undertones. But for the strip-mall location, you'd think you were eating in a place straight out of *The Godfather.* The service is attentive, the decor refined, and the shrimp, chicken, and fresh-fish specials delicious; veal with mushrooms, white wine, cream, and cinnamon is a specialty. ✉ *6327 N. 7th St.,* ☎ *602/264–1784.*

$$–$$$ ✗ **Such Is Life.** The chefs at this Mexican restaurant transform ingredients and preparations from Guadalajara and the Yucatán into dazzling specialties like the chicken Maya (shredded in a piquant achiote sauce) and the adobo pork with an ancho chili sesame-orange sauce. The mood here is sedate and romantic. ✉ *3602 N. 24th St.,* ☎ *602/955–7822; also* ✉ *Scottsdale Promenade, 7000 E. Shea Blvd.,* ☎ *602/948–1753.*

$–$$ ✗ **Los Dos Molinos.** You'll have to drive way south of downtown (nearly to Mexico, complain some locals) to reach this rambling compound of courtyards and a colorful dining room, where yuppies and guppies chatter over live music. The rewards are considerable: the best southwestern cooking in metro Phoenix, using chilies from Hatch, New Mexico (known for their eye-popping potency), and traditional regional recipes. ✉ *8646 S. Central Ave.,* ☎ *602/243–9113.*

$–$$ ✗ **Orbit Restaurant and Jazz Club.** What used to be a hip coffeehouse has evolved into a full-scale restaurant and top-notch live-music club (from salsa to modern jazz). Sample reasonably priced American fare like the pan-roasted sirloin with cracked pepper or the roasted half-chicken with herbs. The lively dining room has leopard-print furnishings and art-covered walls; the patio overlooks a gurgling fountain. ✉ *40 E. Camelback Rd., Ste. 102,* ☎ *602/265–2354.*

$–$$ ✗ **Pookie's.** With white tile floors, potted plants, and cheerful art deco touches, Pookie's feels like an upscale gay supper club. But the restaurant, which draws a diverse crowd of lesbians and gay men, is highly affordable. On the menu are about 20 kinds of burgers and chicken sandwiches, plus salads, steaks and fries, and other straightforward American fare. ✉ *4540 N. 7th St.,* ☎ *602/277–2121.*

$ ✗ **Denny's.** You know what to expect from Denny's: cheap, cholesterol-laden breakfasts and meat-loaf dinners around the clock. After the bars close, this outpost swells with bitchy and butchy queens. ✉ *16 E. Camelback Rd.,* ☎ *602/266–9868.*

$ ✗ **Eggery.** The gayest of a small chain of breakfast hangouts, the Eggery prepares filling and delicious frittatas and several southwestern and Mexican dishes; try the English muffins topped with ham, tomatoes, poached eggs, melted cheese, sour cream, and scallions. ✉ *50 E. Camelback Rd.,* ☎ *602/263–8554.*

$ ✗ **Windsock Deli.** This cute little deli that opened in 1997 has quickly developed a strong following in the community. It's a good bet for salads, burgers, and filling sandwiches. ✉ *5805 N. 7th St.,* ☎ *602/279–6544.*

Scottsdale

$$–$$$ ✗ **Malee's on Main.** Queens just love this place on gallery-studded Main Street in Old Town Scottsdale. Perhaps the signature dish, flaming Cornish hen, marinated and stuffed with ground chicken, water chestnuts, carrots, potatoes, and peas, accounts for this. (Then again, it might be the flaming waiters.) ✉ *7131 E. Main St.,* ☎ *602/947–6042.*

$$–$$$ ✗ **P. F. Chang's.** Part of a growing regional chain of slick pan-Asian restaurants with Americanized but consistently superb food, this cavernous space in Scottsdale Fashion Square has only one major drawback: a two-hour wait on many weekends. Once you're seated, feast on Malaysian chicken with coconut milk, peanuts, onions, and Szechuan-style long beans. ✉ *7014 E. Camelback Rd.,* ☎ *602/949–2610.*

$$ ✕ **Z'Tejas.** Quick service, spicy food, and an engagingly strange postmodern tropical-southwestern decor add up to a memorable dining experience at this trendy haunt. Try the achiote-seared halibut with smoked shiitake mushrooms or the pork tenderloin stuffed with chorizo, jack cheese, grilled onions, and poblano chilies. ✉ *7014 E. Camelback Rd.,* ☎ *602/946–4171.*

$ ✕ **AZ 88.** As with most Scottsdale restaurants, this steel-and-glass dining room near the Civic Center brims with fashion plates and pretty people. What's rare for this part of town is the queer following. Folks come to hobnob over martinis and nosh on excellent updated bar fare—burgers, club sandwiches, Cobb salads, and the like. This is a great late-night option. ✉ *7353 Scottsdale Mall,* ☎ *602/994–5576.*

Coffeehouse Culture

Bean Tree. Plenty of regulars in their 30s and 40s come to the funky Bean Tree for coffee or tea, biscotti and other goodies baked on the premises, and wonderful salads, soups, and sandwiches. Every month the café displays the works of a different Phoenix artist. You can eat inside or on a covered patio with greenery and post-industrial silver chair~ and small tables (stylish but hardly comfy). ✉ *7818 N. 12th St.,* ☎ *602/906–0406.*

Coffee Plantation. Hip and homo-friendly (if predominantly straight), this student hangout is in the heart of ASU's campus. The interior, perky if a trifle too Third World–glib, is done in Caribbean hues, and the coffee preparers toil inside a little Caribbean-style shanty. ✉ *680 S. Mill Ave., Ste. 101, Tempe,* ☎ *602/829–7878.*

Willow House. You'll spot everybody here: lesbians with kids, grungers, students, gay bikers. In addition to being a full deli and coffee joint, the Willow House sells odd jewelry, T-shirts, and gifts. On Thursday evening, it has the best-attended poetry readings in the city. ✉ *149 W. McDowell Rd.,* ☎ *602/252–0272.*

SCENES

Phoenix's bar scene has graduated from mostly down-home neighborhood haunts with more-or-less interchangeable crowds to larger venues with captivating decors and distinct personalities. Despite the changes, local bar culture remains refreshingly free of attitude. Dressing down is still the rule at most places, and western attire is quite common, along with leather and Levi's.

The so-called Rainbow Zone, between 7th Street and 7th Avenue, holds many of the city's bars, but Phoenix has no highly concentrated bar district. Bars close at the annoyingly early hour of 1 AM, although a few places remain open after hours (sans booze), notably Charlie's, Incognito Lounge, Trax, and the Works.

Prime Suspects

Ain't Nobody's Bizness. The largest women's bar in Phoenix is also one of the nicest. It plays Top-40 music, has a big dance floor, and presents live music many weekends. Every weekend the place serves up pretty good (and free) bar food. If you're looking to lasso a sugar mama, this is your best bet, but for the most part the crowd is young, hip, and unpretentious. ✉ *3031 E. Indian School Rd.,* ☎ *602/224–9977. Crowd: mostly female, 20s and 30s, generally professional, guppie, well-heeled.*

BS West. This video bar in Scottsdale is easily the preppiest gay hangout in metro Phoenix—one of the few spots where Polo shirts and dressy jeans are the norm. This amber-lit, festive space has a tiny dance floor and a patio out front with seating. Nice boys come here to pick up other nice boys. ✉ *7125 E. 5th Ave.,* ☎ *602/945–9028. Crowd: mostly male, mid-20s to early 40s, cute, guppie, friendly, white-bread.*

Charlie's. A pretty butch crowd—guys who by night trade in their business suits for 10-gallon hats—patronizes this two-stepping dance club and cruise bar. Dance lessons are given regularly, as are volleyball lessons—Charlie's has a court and regularly stages tournaments. Sunday brunch here is a favorite with locals. On weekends after 1 AM Charlie's re-emerges as the hottest after-hours hangout in the city, spinning cutting-edge dance music and attracting hordes of revelers (there's usually a long line to get in). ✉ *727 W. Camelback Rd.*, ☎ *602/265–0224. Crowd: mostly male, all ages, nicely dressed country-western; after-hours the crowd is younger but otherwise totally diverse.*

Crow Bar. This swank downtown cocktail lounge is the city's latest spot to sip colorful drinks and look sophisticated. It opened in fall 1997 and immediately became a hit with glam boys and club kids. The decor is dramatic and industrial, and there's dancing to the latest tunes. ✉ *702 N. Central Ave.*, ☎ *602/258–8343. Crowd: mostly male, 20s and 30s, guppies, hipsters, the trendy set.*

Desert Rose. No dive, the second-most-popular dyke venue in Phoenix is well lit and nicely decorated, with a decent-size dance floor on which two-stepping lessons are given on Wednesday and Thursday. The Sunday-night $2 steak-fry is a major crowd-pleaser. ✉ *4301 N. 7th Ave.*, ☎ *602/265–3233. Crowd: mostly female, all ages, more butch than lipstick, lots of western attire.*

Foster's. The size and makeup of the crowd at the city's most popular all-around dance and video bar depend almost entirely on the night of the week. Wednesday's drag shows are popular but not too cruisy. Sunday's Trash Disco party is legendary and usually packed with horny retro queens. When Foster's advertises nickel drafts, you can count on a full house. The dance floor is small but potent, with laser beams bouncing off the several disco balls and music blaring at ear-splitting decibels. If the heat's too much for you, seek refuge on the loft high above the action. ✉ *4343 N. 7th Ave.*, ☎ *602/263–8313. Crowd: 75/25 m/f, mostly under 35, cruisy but approachable, blue- and white-collar.*

Harley's 155. What used to be the city's hottest leather venue has become more diverse, attracting a generally edgy and somewhat butch crowd but few guys in all-out leather gear—especially on weekends, when the place is absolutely packed. Harley's even draws a fair share of guppies and fag hags. This is a terrific place to cut loose, with a hot, sweaty, and crowded dance floor and an inviting dark space, decked out in prison paraphernalia, that's called the Cell. Another room has pool tables and a fireplace. There's never a dull moment here. ✉ *155 W. Camelback Rd.*, ☎ *602/274–8505. Crowd: 80/20 m/f, 20s to mid-30s, mixed black, Latin, and white, occasional leather (especially weekdays), lots of denim, muscle Ts, club gear, loud, wild, out to have a great time.*

The Park. Queer locals on Phoenix's east side no longer have to drive 15 minutes to the bars in the Rainbow Zone for late-night socializing. Beautifully decorated, with mirrors, a long bar, and fresh flowers everywhere, the Park has a big stage that hosts cabaret acts. The landscaped patio out back has fountains and pink lighting. ✉ *3002 N. 24th St.*, ☎ *602/957–6055. Crowd: 70/30 m/f, 20s to 50s, very mixed, pretty boys, femmes fatales, neighborhood regulars, longtime couples.*

Roscoe's. A great little sports bar across from Pookie's, Roscoe's has a well-attended happy hour. The music is always at a level that allows conversation, doubtless to accommodate the many darts and pool players, whose zeal (and that of their fans) can be a little scary. ✉ *4531 N. 7th St.*, ☎ *602/285–0833. Crowd: 60/40 m/f, mostly 20s and 30s, cute butch boys and girl jocks, low-key.*

The Wave. The strangely dark and unremarkable show bar here presents drag most nights. A second lounge with darts, a jukebox, and electronic trivia games appeals to a crowd largely uninterested in the shows next door. Sunday attracts the largest following. ✉ *998 E. Indian School Rd.,* ☎ *602/266–5640. Crowd: 70/30 m/f, late 20s to late 40s, neighborhoody, drag queens and their admirers, low attitude.*

Wink's. This is the kind of bar you could bring your mom to—an intimate place alive with holiday lights and mirrors. The entertainment ranges from lounge lizards performing Billy Joel covers to female impersonators to talented piano acts. There's a decent bar-food menu, and Saturday's submarine lunch buffet and Sunday's brunch are popular. ✉ *5707 N. 7th St.,* ☎ *602/265–9002. Crowd: 70/30 m/f, 20s to 80s, disco bunnies on their night off, suits, cowboys, lipstick lesbians, seniors, drag queens, bears, piano-barflies.*

Neighborhood Haunts

Apollo's (✉ 5749 N. 7th St., ☎ 602/277–9373) and the **Country Club** (✉ 4428 N. 7th Ave., ☎ 602/264–4553), a ramshackle piano bar, draw a mostly local crowd. **Johnny Mc's** (✉ 138 W. Camelback Rd., ☎ 602/ 266–0875), which is across from Harley's 155, is favored by the male over-age-40 set. The gay restaurant **Pookie's** (✉ 4540 N. 7th St., ☎ 602/ 277–2121) is a wonderful spot for a cocktail or to enjoy live piano.

The mostly lesbian and Hispanic-patronized **Incognito Lounge** (✉ 2424 E. Thomas Rd., ☎ 602/955–9805), a mellow roadhouse along East Thomas that welcomes all, recently began holding teen nights; the bar pulls in a diverse crowd after hours. **Nasty's** (✉ 3108 E. McDowell Rd., ☎ 602/267–8707) is popular with men and women for karaoke and decent drink specials. The similarly mixed-gender **Cash and Country** (✉ 2140 E. McDowell Rd., ☎ 602/244–9973) attracts members of gay sports teams; country-western tunes fill the air most nights. **TRAX** (✉ 1724 E. McDowell Rd., ☎ 602/254–0231) has become less gay in recent years—it's a fairly rough urban disco.

The **307 Lounge** (✉ 222 E. Roosevelt St., ☎ 602/252–0001), a locals place and sort of divey, hosts fun shows and has friendly staff. Two bars in the southeastern part of town are the **Pumphouse** (✉ 4132 E. McDowell Rd., ☎ 602/275–3509), a dark space with three pool tables, a filthy gray linoleum floor, and zero ambience (but good music); and, out by the airport, the **Nu Towne Saloon** (✉ 5002 E. Van Buren St., ☎ 602/267–9959), which thanks to its discount-drinks parties, is the easiest place to get laid on Sunday or Tuesday.

Action

Phoenix is one of the nation's smuttiest cities. You'll have no trouble at all finding porn—there are adult bookshops, gay and straight, all over town. They're among the cleanest and most consumer-friendly such stores, especially **Castle Boutique** (✉ 5501 E. Washington St.; ✉ 300 E. Camelback Rd.; ✉ 8802 N. Black Canyon Hwy.; ✉ 8315 E. Apache Trail).

Flex (✉ 1517 S. Black Canyon Hwy., ☎ 602/271–9011) provides the latest in bathhouse facilities—waterbeds, a complete gym, a swimming pool, videos, and a massage therapist. Fairly new and also popular is the **Chute** (✉ 1440 E. Indian School Rd., ☎ 602/234–1654).

SLEEPS

Lodgings in Phoenix tend to be corporate—all the usual franchises are represented—but there are a few gay-oriented B&Bs. Scottsdale is known for its luxury resorts, which benefit from the clear, dry climate. The gay-friendly **Bed & Breakfast Inn Arizona** (☎ 602/561–0335 or 800/266–7829) has listings for properties throughout metropolitan Phoenix in every price range and offering virtually every amenity.

For price ranges *see* lodging Chart A at the front of this guide.

Hotels

$$$$ 🏨 **Ritz-Carlton.** This 11-story mock-Federal luxury hotel across the street from the Biltmore Fashion Square captures the chain's typical Old World elegance with British paintings, bone china, and marble baths. Thanks to some reasonable weekend deals, it's not as pricey as you might think. ⊠ *2401 E. Camelback Rd., 85016,* ☏ *602/468–0700 or 800/241–3333,* ℻ *602/468–9883. 281 rooms. Restaurants, pool, health club.*

$$–$$$ 🏨 **Wyndham Metro Center.** A 15-minute drive north of downtown, on the outskirts of the Metro Center Mall, the Wyndham is a contemporary and rather luxurious hotel. ⊠ *10220 N. Metro Pkwy. E, 85051,* ☏ *602/997–5900 or 800/858–1033,* ℻ *602/371–2857. 284 rooms. Restaurant, pool, exercise room.*

$–$$ 🏨 **Ramada Phoenix, Camelback.** Gay-popular and within a short drive of several queer bars and businesses, the Ramada has clean rooms and a landscaped pool area that's stylish enough to make you want to hang out and catch some rays. ⊠ *502 W. Camelback Rd., 85013,* ☏ *602/264–9290 or 800/688–2021,* ℻ *602/264–3068. 166 rooms. Restaurant, pool.*

$ 🏨 **Hotel San Carlos.** One of the few historic buildings in Phoenix, with elegant public areas, the gay-friendly San Carlos offers a healthy dose of charm and rock-bottom rates. The standard rooms are on the small side, but the suites are only slightly more expensive. ⊠ *202 N. Central Ave., 85004,* ☏ *602/253–4121 or 800/678–8946,* ℻ *602/253–6668. 115 rooms. Restaurant, pool.*

Resorts

$$$$ 🏨 **The Boulders.** Twelve miles north of Phoenix in the aptly named town of Carefree, this secluded complex amid massive boulders has the most dramatic setting of all the area's resorts. Rooms are in pueblo-style casitas with beam ceilings, patios, and kiva fireplaces. Horseback riding, golf, and hiking are among the activities you can pursue. It doesn't get much better than this. ⊠ *34631 N. Tom Darlington Dr., Carefree 85377,* ☏ *602/488–9009 or 800/553–1717,* ℻ *602/488–4118. 193 units. Restaurants, pools, exercise room.*

$$$$ 🏨 **The Phoenician.** Everything at this mammoth resort exists on a grand, lavish scale, almost to the point of being overdone. But hey, if swimming in a pool inlaid with mother-of-pearl excites you, it's worth shelling out the big bucks—in fact, you already have: taxpayers picked up a chunk of the tab for this property involved in the savings-and-loan scandal of the 1980s. ⊠ *6000 E. Camelback Rd., Scottsdale 85251,* ☏ *602/941–8200 or 800/888–8234,* ℻ *602/947–4311. 580 rooms. Restaurants, pools, health club.*

Guest Houses

$–$$ 🏨 **Arizona Royal Villa Resort.** Done in the style of the relaxing men's resorts of Palm Springs, this converted motel complex has been reconfigured into an secluded compound with attractive landscaping and rooms set around a central pool. Social butterflies will love it. Even if you're staying elsewhere, drop by for some fun around the pool—day passes are $10. ⊠ *1110 E. Turney Ave., No. 8, 85014,* ☏ ℻ *602/266–6883, e-mail azroyalvil@aol.com. 15 rooms with TV and private bath. Pool, hot tub. Continental breakfast. Gay male.*

$ 🏨 **Arizona Sunburst.** Homey and centrally located, this B&B with a lovely pool and a clothing-optional hot tub is run by two terrific guys who know plenty about area dining and nightlife. ⊠ *6245 N. 12th Pl., 85014,* ☏ *602/274–1474 or 800/974–1474. 7 rooms with TV, some with private bath. Pool, hot tub. Continental breakfast. Gay male.*

THE LITTLE BLACK BOOK

At Your Fingertips

Arizona AIDS Info Line (☎ 602/234–2752, TTY 602/265–9953). **Camelback Business & Professional Association** (lesbigay business guild, ☎ 602/225–8444). **Checker/Yellow Cab** (☎ 602/252–5252). **Gay and Lesbian Community Center and Switchboard** (⌂ 3136 N. 3rd Ave., ☎ 602/234–2752, Web site www.swlink.net/~vsglcc). **Lesbian Resource Project** (☎ 602/266–5542). **Phoenix and Valley of the Sun Convention and Visitors Bureau** (⌂ Arizona Center, 400 E. Van Buren St., Suite 600, 85004, ☎ 602/254–6500). *Phoenix New Times* (☎ 602/271–0040, Web site www.phoenixnewtimes.com). **Project LifeGuard** (AIDS/HIV educational and referral resource, ☎ 602/266–7233). **Scottsdale Chamber of Commerce** (⌂ 7343 Scottsdale Mall, 85251, ☎ 602/945–8481 or 800/877–1117). **Valley Metro** (public transportation, ☎ 602/253–5000).

Gay Media

Echo (☎ 602/266–0550, Web site www.echomag.com), a biweekly gay and lesbian news and entertainment magazine, is distributed throughout the Southwest. *Heatstroke* (☎ 602/264–3646, e-mail reidhead@mail.idt.net), a fine biweekly gay newspaper, carries local features and nightlife coverage. Check out the monthly *Women's Central News* (☎ 602/898–4844, Web site www.swlink.net/~wcnews) for coverage of the lesbian community. *"Transformer"* (☎ 602/864–7682, e-mail gwpublish@psn.net) is a thin bar and resources pamphlet. *X-Factor* (☎ 602/266–0550), Arizona's gay-male adult entertainment biweekly, is filled with classifieds and phone-sex ads. The local AIDS education and support group, Project LifeGuard, publishes a handy and informative monthly 'zine, *For The Boys* (☎ 602/266–7233, Web site www.apaz.org/project.html).

BOOKSTORES

Obelisk Books (⌂ 24 W. Camelback, Unit A, ☎ 602/266–2665), a great shop in the heart of the Rainbow Zone, carries men's and women's titles, plus magazines, music, videos, and cards. **Unique on Central** (⌂ 4700 N. Central Ave., Suite 105, ☎ 602/279–9691) has some gay and lesbian books and quite a few magazines, but specializes in pride gifts and clothing. There's a small coffee bar. The general-interest bookstore at ASU, **Changing Hands** (⌂ Mill Ave. and 5th Ave., Tempe, ☎ 602/966–0203), stocks gay titles and periodicals.

WORKING OUT

Gay-friendly and open 24 hours, **Fitness Planet** (⌂ 7303 E. Earll Dr., Scottsdale, ☎ 602/941–0800) maintains full gym facilities. **Fitness West** (⌂ 1505 E. Bethany Home Rd., ☎ 602/248–8920) also has all the right machines, as well as steam, sauna, pool, and cold-plunge facilities.

SEDONA

Mellow, colorful Sedona has developed a strong following among lesbians and New Agers, who recognize the region as containing some of the Earth's most significant vortices (energy centers). Sedona has definitely succumbed somewhat to the vagaries of zoneless development—such as the rapidly expanding sea of shops hawking T-shirts and pet rocks. But balancing the negatives are Sedona's rippling azure creeks, precious Indian ruins, dark-green patches of pine forest, and majestic red-rock cliffs.

Sedona is clearly—but quietly—open to gay tourism. Though the terms New Age and queer-friendly aren't necessarily interchangeable, tolerance is the rule. Nonetheless, Sedona is as conservative as other northern Arizona towns; the gay community is discreet, if not closeted, especially for men. But it's a perfect destination for a relaxed, romantic interlude.

The Lay of the Land

Sedona's three neighborhoods are loosely separated by the intersection of Route 179 and U.S. 89A. Off 89A west of the intersection is **West Sedona;** it's the least touristy of the three and where most locals hang out and do their shopping. Off 89A east and north of the intersection is **Uptown,** where most of the touristy shops and motor lodges are. The stretch of 179 south of the intersection is the least neighborhood-identified of the three, but after the road crosses Oak Creek it's sometimes referred to as **Bell Rock.** A mile or two later, you enter the village of **Oak Creek,** which contains upscale shops, many of the town's newer homes, and resorts and restaurants.

You won't get bogged down by museums here, and you shouldn't plan to spend much time inside. That is unless shopping is your game, in which case you shouldn't miss stunning **Tlaquepaque** (pronounced tuh-*lah*-cuh-*pah*-cuh) (⊠ Rte. 179, ☎ 520/282–4838), a southwestern-style village of studios where more than 100 artists, including jewelers, painters, sculptors, and potters, sell their goods.

The lesbian-owned **Kachina Stables** (⊠ 5 J La., Lower Red Rock Rd., West Sedona., ☎ 520/282–7252) operates a memorable dinner horse ride down to a creekside. Kachina also fashions custom tours and group events, and though they cater to all, you'll find they have as gay a following as any company in town. **Pink Jeep Tours** (☎ 520/282–5000 or 800/888–9494) and **Sedona Red Rock Jeep Tours** (☎ 520/282–6826 or 800/848–7728) conduct tours that start at about $22 per hour.

U.S. 89A winds west from Sedona for about 30 miles through the Verde Valley and the towns of Cottonwood and Clarkdale to **Jerome,** whose two main drags hold wonderfully offbeat shops and galleries. A breathtaking 27-mile drive north from Sedona leads to **Flagstaff,** whose **Arizona Snowbowl** (☎ 520/779–1951, 602/779–1950 for ski information) ski area offers a tram ride to a height of 11,500 feet in summer. Many people stop in Flagstaff on their way to **Grand Canyon National Park** (☎ 520/638–7888), which is 110 miles northwest of Sedona.

Getting Around

From Phoenix it's a two-hour drive to Sedona—there's no train or bus service. Take I–17 north to Route 179. **Sedona Airport** in West Sedona handles on-demand charter flights from Phoenix on **Scenic Airlines** (☎ 520/282–7935); the cost is $195 for a three-passenger plane each way.

Eats

Sedona's restaurants range from touristy chains and casual American eateries to some quite sophisticated establishments; most are gay-friendly. **New Frontiers** (⊠ 2055 W. U.S. 89A, ☎ 520/282–6311), a New Age deli and market, prepares good sandwiches, salads, smoothies, coffees, and desserts to go or to eat in.

For price ranges, *see* dining Chart A at the front of this guide.

$$$$ ✗ **House of Joy.** Many appetites have been satisfied in this historic Jerome house that was a bordello. Perhaps as a tribute to its sordid history, the two dining rooms are strung with red lights. Dinner is the only meal served here, and only on weekends—you *must* make a reservation well in advance. The traditional Continental fare, such as crab crepes stuffed with a blend of snow crabs, herbs, wine, and cream, or Cornish game hen Kiev, are excellent, but the ambience is the real draw. ⊠ *Hull Ave. off Main St., Jerome,* ☎ *520/634–5339.*

$$$$ ✕ **Yavapai Room.** Tall windows at the main dining room at Enchantment afford stunning views of the red-rock formations surrounding the resort. The Southwest-inspired Continental dishes include molasses-seared loin of elk with a roasted poblano demi-glace, a blackberry-sage compote, and a five-onion polenta cake. ✉ *525 Boynton Canyon Rd., 86336,* ☎ *520/282–2900.*

$$–$$$ ✕ **Heartline Café.** A trendy spot with plenty of gay staff, Heartline has a loyal following. Track lighting, ceiling fans, fresh flowers, and wood trim and beams create a romantic mood, especially in winter. Eclectic pasta, vegetarian, and grilled-meat selections are the menu mainstays. Just about every dish packs a little punch, thanks to an infusion of southwestern spices and ingredients. ✉ *1610 W. Hwy. 89A,* ☎ *520/282–0785.*

$–$$ ✕ **El Rincón.** This Mexican restaurant set in the Tlaquepaque shopping complex has plenty of atmosphere: beam ceilings, arches, a fireplace, and festive carpeting. The hearty Sonoran cuisine is good but predictable— lots of cheese and beans and rich green- and red-chili sauces. ✉ *336 S. Rte. 179, Ste. No. A-112,* ☎ *520/282–4648.*

$–$$ ✕ **Thai Spices.** Cute and quirky, this eatery adjacent to a budget motel has a homey dining room, friendly servers, and fiery, authentic Thai food. Chicken, beef, shrimp, or tofu are prepared dozens of ways, including a sweet and spicy pineapple curry with carrots and coconut milk. Many vegetarian choices, too. ✉ *2986 W. U.S. 89A,* ☎ *520/282–0599.*

$ ✕ **Red Planet.** Alien-like sculptures and otherworldly kitsch fill this lovably strange place that's like a '50s diner set on Mars. Dishes have aptly odd names: the Lunar burger has grilled onions, tomatoes, and Gorgonzola. Also good are the red beans and rice, as well as the several Italian specialties. ✉ *1655 W. U.S. 89A,* ☎ *520/282–0057.*

Scenes

Except for a few straight bars, Sedona has virtually no nightlife. A pleasant enough crowd hangs out at the town's top music venue, **Red, Rock & Blues** (✉ 1730 W. Hwy. 89A, ☎ 520/282–1655). Jerome has two straight but open-minded taverns, the **Spirit Room** (✉ Main St., ☎ 520/634–5792) and **Paul and Jerry's Saloon** (✉ 206 Main St., ☎ 520/634–2603).

Sleeps

Accommodations in Sedona include a few deluxe resorts, some chain hotels, and many B&Bs. There aren't any gay-operated inns or B&Bs in Sedona, but most establishments are family-friendly.

For price ranges, *see* lodging Chart A at the front of this guide.

Resorts and Hotels

$$$$ 🏨 **Enchantment.** Nestled in Boynton Canyon, this retreat has one of the most dramatic settings in the Southwest. Accommodations are set inside casitas on a hillside below the red cliffs. Built as a tennis resort, Enchantment appeals more to the sports enthusiast than to the New Age traveler. ✉ *525 Boynton Canyon Rd., 86336,* ☎ *520/282–2900 or 800/826–4180,* FAX *520/282–9249. 162 rooms. Restaurants, pools, fitness center.*

$$$–$$$$ 🏨 **Los Abrigados.** This gay-friendly resort beside the Tlaquepaque shops is less secluded and luxurious than Enchantment, but it still has great accommodations, each with separate living areas, stocked wet bars, and balconies; some rooms have fireplaces and whirlpools. ✉ *160 Portal La., 86336,* ☎ *520/282–1777 or 800/521–3131,* FAX *520/282–2614. 175 suites. Restaurants, pools, health club.*

Guest Houses and Small Hotels

$$–$$$$ ⊞ **The Lodge at Sedona.** Combining the intimacy of a B&B with the privacy and professional service of a small luxury inn, this lodge has smartly decorated bedrooms and five common rooms with fireplaces. The gourmet breakfast is so filling you can wait until dinner to eat again. ⊠ *125 Kallof Pl., 86336,* ☎ *520/204–1942 or 800/619–4467,* FAX *520/204–2128, e-mail lodge@sedona.net. 13 rooms with phone, TV, and private bath. Full breakfast. Mostly straight.*

$$ ⊞ **Cozy Cactus B&B.** Simple and attractive, this B&B has rooms with various themes. The Wyeth Room has reproductions of Andrew Wyeth works. The Nutcracker Room contains an impressive collection of nutcrackers. An excellent value. ⊠ *80 Canyon Cir., Oak Creek, 86351,* ☎ *520/284–0082 or 800/788–2082. 5 rooms with private bath. Full breakfast. Mostly straight.*

$–$$ ⊞ **Iris Garden Inn.** This budget motor inn within walking distance of the many shops in Uptown has comfy rooms, some with full kitchens. ⊠ *390 Jordan Rd., 86336,* ☎ *520/282–2552 or 800/321–8988,* FAX *520/204–1653. 8 rooms with phone, TV, and private bath. Mostly straight.*

The Little Black Book

For further information on Sedona and the region, contact the **Jerome Chamber of Commerce** (⊠ Box K, 86331, ☎ 520/634–2900) or the **Sedona–Oak Creek Chamber of Commerce** (⊠ 331 Forest Rd., 86336, ☎ 520/282–7722 or 800/288–7336). The **Book Loft** (⊠ 175 Rte. 179, Sedona, ☎ 520/282–5173) is a handsome gay-friendly general-interest store with a coffeehouse.

30 *Out in Pittsburgh*

ONCE THE NATION'S LEADER for mining and metals manufacture, Pittsburgh has reemerged over the past decade as a thriving center of health and medical research, education, and computer software industry. Much of the city's renaissance has centered around the conversion of former industrial concerns into cultural attractions—ranging from the Heinz Regional History Center to the Station Square entertainment complex. The residential and commercial building stock, which dates from the late 1800s, has been remarkably well preserved, and fans of architecture and preservation have learned to take advantage of Pittsburgh's 88 neighborhoods. Gays and lesbians are a marked presence in North Side, South Side, and Shadyside.

The gay scene, although not terribly visible, is well integrated with the mainstream population. Particularly among the under-30 set, gays and straights mix at many bars, restaurants, and coffeehouses. The city has numerous theaters with artsy and gay-themed films and a high appreciation of alternative culture—consider that two of its top attractions are the Mattress Factory contemporary art museum and the Andy Warhol Museum.

THE LAY OF THE LAND

Downtown

Although, **downtown** (a.k.a. "the Golden Triangle") contains only a hint of what greater Pittsburgh has to offer, its handsome contemporary skyline and regal command over the confluence of the Ohio, Allegheny, and Monongahela rivers imbues it with a stately countenance.

For an intimate look at Pittsburgh's relationship to its three now sparkling rivers, walk through the very tip of downtown's landscaped **Point State Park** (☎ 412/471–0235) where Forts Duquesne (pronounced doo-*kane*) and Pitt once guarded the settlement's vulnerable flanks. Today, the **Fort Pitt Museum** (⌧ 101 Commonwealth Pl., Point State Park, ☎ 412/281–9284), which stands on the site of the original garrison, houses exhibits on the city's early history. Standing behind it is the **Fort Pitt Block House** (☎ 412/471–1764), which dates to 1764. At the very tip of the park, a fountain gushes high above the three rivers.

The Golden Triangle comprises Pittsburgh's thriving business district. There are few major attractions here, but the busy streets make for a colorful walk during the day, when you can admire the eclectic architecture and catch a live band performing for lunchtime brown baggers at **Market Square** (⌧ Forbes Ave. and Market St.). The square lies in the shadows of Pittsburgh's most remarked upon building, **PPG Place** (⌧ Stanwix St. and 4th Ave., ☎ 412/434–3131), a neogothic monolith designed by Philip Johnson and glazed with 20,000 panes of reflective glass. (PPG is an acronym for the Pittsburgh Plate Glass company.)

Liberty Avenue runs northeast from near Market Square and claims a few of the city's better-known gay bars (around 8th Street). Liberty and parallel **Penn Avenue** are the spines of a 14-block **Cultural District** (a.k.a. "the Penn/Liberty District"). Its theaters and performance halls house the Pittsburgh Symphony Orchestra (☎ 412/392–4800), the Pittsburgh Ballet (☎ 412/281–0360), the Pittsburgh Opera (☎ 412/281–0912), and various theater companies.

Continue along Penn Avenue and you'll soon reach the historic warehouses and still-operating wholesale markets known as **the Strip.** Many house clubs, hip restaurants, art galleries, and offbeat shops; most businesses here have an artsy and fairly gay following. The Allegheny River side of the Strip centers on **Down by the Riverside Boardwalk,** a $50 million complex with a marina, restaurants, and a floating boardwalk on 13 acres. In the west end of the Strip, a seven-story icehouse has been converted into the **John Heinz Pittsburgh Regional History Center** (✉ 1212 Smallman St., ☎ 412/454–6304), a fantastic museum whose exhibits range from a re-created 1790 log house to a '50s-era dwelling in the 'burbs.

North Side

From downtown, you can easily cross the Allegheny River via any of the close-together bridges, known as the Three Sisters, to reach **North Side,** which is home to the Three Rivers stadium and arts and cultural attractions. This area, part of which is still known as Deutsche Town, is where many Germans (and later Italians and Poles) settled during the late 1800s. Before Pittsburgh annexed it in 1907, it was a separate entity, Allegheny City.

The **Andy Warhol Museum** (✉ 117 Sandusky St., ☎ 412/237–8300) celebrates the life of the late pop art icon, who grew up in nearby Oakland. Created inside the eight-story Frick and Lindsay Building, a 1911 steel supply warehouse, the museum contains 3,000 works, from Campbell's soup cans to countless earlier sketches and drawings, as well as Warhol's time capsules—boxes in which he stuffed each day's receipts, notes, lists, and other ephemera. This is an outstanding, engaging, and often very funny museum, laid out with abundant commentary on Warhol's life (and his homosexuality).

Within walking distance is the **Carnegie Science Center** (✉ 1 Allegheny Ave., ☎ 412/237–3400), which contains the world's most technologically advanced planetarium, an Omnimax theater, and 250 exhibits. Head a few blocks northwest to reach the **National Aviary** (✉ Allegheny Commons W, ☎ 412/323–7235), under whose glass-dome atrium fly Andean condors, hummingbirds, and more than 250 other species.

The northwestern edge of North Side, especially the Victorian **Mexican War Streets,** fell on hard times during the middle of this century but is now gentrifying. Many gays and lesbians have settled in this part of the city, which is also home to the **Mattress Factory** (✉ 500 Sampsonia Way, ☎ 412/231–3169), known for its provocative larger-than-life installations, which are created by visiting artists in residence.

Station Square and Mount Washington

South of downtown, across the Monongahela, the city rises sharply above the river. Several tight-knit communities are on this side of the river, with much of the activity centered on **Mount Washington,** a neighborhood whose commercial drag, **Grandview Avenue,** hugs the ridgeline and offers spectacular views of the downtown skyline.

No visit to Pittsburgh is complete without a ride up the slope to Mt. Washington via **the incline,** or funicular. The **Duquesne Incline** (✉ 1220 Grandview Ave., ☎ 412/381–1665) departs from near the Fort Pitt Bridge, and the **Monongahela Incline** (✉ 2235 Beaver Ave., ☎ 412/442–2000) runs from near the Smithfield Bridge, by Station Square. The Monongahela is more popular, because the station at the top has a viewing platform and a small museum. Mt. Washington itself isn't all that interesting, but there are a few restaurants along Grandview with amazing views, if so-so food.

You can combine your ride on the incline with a visit to **Station Square** (✉ Carson St. at the Fort Pitt Bridge, ☎ 412/261–2811 or 800/859–8959), the redbrick complex at the foot of the Monongahela Incline and on the south side of the **Smithfield Street Bridge.** Formerly the Pittsburgh and Lake Erie Railroad Company's freight yard, this 52-acre riverfront complex has been converted into quirky shops, a Sheraton Hotel (*see* Sleeps, *below*), and some touristy nightclubs and restaurants. Even if you don't eat there, try to poke your head inside the **Grand Concourse** restaurant, in the restored terminal, which has a vaulted stained-glass ceiling.

South Side

Also along the south side of the Monongahela, a short drive east of Station Square, the hip **South Side** is a repository of funky shops, galleries, and restaurants. Once the heart of the city's Lithuanian and Polish communities, **Carson Street** is now lined with music stores, bric-a-brac emporia, coffeehouses, and such on-the-edge galleries as **Women's Work** (✉ 130 S. 18th St., ☎ 412/481–5014), a feminist art gallery with a strong community following. The neighborhood has no queer nightlife per se, but many gayfolk window-shop, dine, or sip martinis at straight but groovy lounges.

Oakland

A few miles east of downtown, **Oakland** has enough offices, hospitals, universities, and businesses to make locals think of the area as its own city. With its own positive energy and few vestiges of the region's blue-collar roots, it seems strangely removed from the rest of Pittsburgh. Oakland was built from the gobs of money generated during Pittsburgh's industrial heyday, and today is the heart of the city's computer software industry. You may know it best as Mister Rogers's "Neighborhood of Make Believe"—the children's show first aired here at WQED, the nation's first public TV station.

Forbes and 5th avenues run through the heart of Oakland, with the **University of Pittsburgh** to the northwest and formidably endowed **Carnegie Mellon University** to the southeast. Collegiate shops and cafés surround these two campuses, both of which have their share of attractions. At CMU, spend a few hours at the **Carnegie Museums of Art and Natural History** (✉ 4400 Forbes Ave., ☎ 412/622–3131). The art museum has well-conceived architectural and decorative arts exhibits. The Natural History museum's great strengths are its cache of artifacts from ancient Egypt and the nation's third-largest dinosaur collection.

Across the street, towering 42-stories above Pitt's campus, is the tallest school building in the western world, the Gothic **Cathedral of Learning** (✉ 5th Ave. and Bigelow Blvd., ☎ 412/624–6000). Head to the 36th-floor observation deck for views of the region, or make your way through the ground-floor's 24 **Nationality Classrooms;** each celebrates the heritage of a particular ethnicity that has settled in Pittsburgh.

Walk for a few minutes south of the Carnegie Museums to gorgeous **Schenley Park,** the highlight of which is the 1893 **Phipps Conservatory** (✉ 1 Schenley Park, ☎ 412/622–6914), a Victorian glass edifice comprising 13 rooms of orchids, palms, bonsai, and other exotic flora.

Shadyside

East of Oakland are **Squirrel Hill,** a now-yuppified neighborhood settled earlier in this century by Russian and Eastern European Jews, and **Shadyside,** a similarly gentrified patch of neatly kept yards and attractive old homes. Although more queers live here than elsewhere in Pittsburgh, it's a mixed neighborhood and not an obvious gay ghetto. Shadyside has two nice spots for sidewalk strolling: **Ellsworth Avenue** (around the 5800 block) has several gay-popular eateries and businesses, including the clothier **Eons** (✉ 5850 Ellsworth Ave., ☎ 412/361–3368). More chichi **Walnut Street** (along the 5500 block) holds mid- to high-end chain stores.

From Shadyside it's a short drive east to **Clayton** (✉ 7227 Reynolds St., ☎ 412/371–0600), the former estate of industrialist Henry Clay Frick that now consists of a magnificent mansion, a carriage house filled with vintage vehicles, a restored 1897 greenhouse, and a café renowned for its afternoon high tea. The top draw here is the **Frick Art and Historical Center,** which has an outstanding collection of Italian, French, and Flemish master paintings.

Fallingwater

Frank Lloyd Wright's most celebrated residential creation, **Fallingwater** (✉ Rte. 381, Mill Run, ☎ 412/329–8501) is worth the 90-minute drive. To reach the house, which is cantilevered precipitously above a rushing waterfall, head southeast about 60 miles on the Pennsylvania Turnpike to Donegal; from here drive 15 miles south on Route 381.

GETTING AROUND

In 1994 Pittsburgh launched the Wayfinder navigating system, in which the city is broken down into five regions, each labeled with street signs of a different color. As ambitious and helpful as this system is, driving remains tricky. Still, a car is the best way to see the sights, which are spread throughout the city. Pittsburgh's subway system, known as the **T,** covers some interesting sights and is free within downtown stops. Buses are another option; No. 51C, which runs between Oakland and downtown, is especially useful. Once you reach a particular neighborhood, you'll find its streets walkable.

EATS

With so many transplants moving to Pittsburgh, the restaurant scene has begun to show surefire signs of trendiness—postmodern influences in the decor, meticulously chosen ingredients, and international flair in the preparation. But the city still retains a no-nonsense working-class spirit, and the trendier a restaurant, the harder time it has appealing to Pittsburgh's old guard. Even more revealing is that the Red Lobster placed second for best seafood restaurant in a recent *Pittsburgh* magazine reader poll. The gay-friendly Burrito Brothers restaurant group has opened some of the hottest eateries in the city.

For price ranges, *see* dining Chart B at the front of this guide.

Downtown, North Side, and South Side

$$$–$$$$ ✕ **Café Victoria.** Run by the same gay-friendly management as the Victoria House B&B (*see* Sleeps, *below*), this romantic North Side New American bistro has lovely service and a frilly old-fashioned dining room, but highly contemporary cooking that rivals any in the city. Consider starting with Gorgonzola, zucchini, and eggplant polenta stacks with fresh mozzarella and smoked-tomato coulis before graduating to grilled lamb chops with rosemary au jus. ✉ *946 Western Ave.,* ☎ *412/323–8881.*

Eats ●

Beehive Coffeehouse and Dessertery, **7**
Café Allegro, **6**
Café Victoria, **1**
City Grill, **8**
Kaya, **5**
Liberty Avenue Saloon, **2**
Mallorca, **10**
Rosebud, **4**
Siena, **3**
Zythos, **9**

Scenes ○

C. J. Deighnan's, **3**
Cairo, **4**
Donny's Place/Prizm, **12**
Heaven, **5**
House of Tilden, **7**
Images, **9**
Liberty Avenue Saloon, **8**
Metropol, **11**
Pegasus, **6**
Pittsburgh Eagle, **1**
Real Luck Café, **10**
Rusty Nail Saloon, **2**

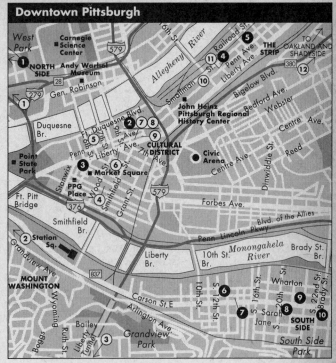

Downtown Pittsburgh

Eats ●

Common Grounds Coffee House, **6**
Elbow Room, **3**
La Feria, **2**
New York, New York, **4**
The Original Hot Dog Shop, **1**
Soba Lounge, **5**

Scenes ○

Holiday Bar, **1**

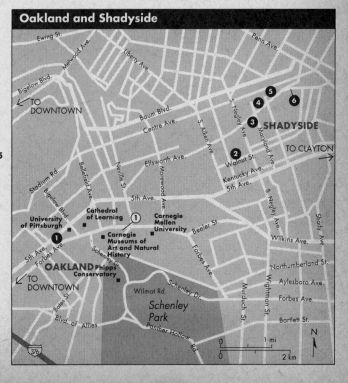

Oakland and Shadyside

$$$–$$$$ ✕ **Siena.** This posh New American restaurant with global culinary aspirations overlooks Market Square and its round-the-clock drama of colorful characters—it's people-watching at its very best. The mood inside this skylighted airy space has plenty going for it, too. Top dishes include chicken–pine nut salad, and pork rib chops with apple and dried-cherry compote. ⊠ *430 Market St.,* ☎ *412/338–0955.*

$$$ ✕ **Café Allegro.** A slice of swank in the grungy South Side, this sleek contemporary restaurant has earned kudos for such Mediterranean Riviera–inspired creations as a mixed grill of market-selected seafood simmered in red wine, scallions, and a peppercorn sauce. ⊠ *51 S. 12th St.,* ☎ *412/481–7788.*

$$–$$$ ✕ **Kaya.** This gay-popular Burrito Brothers restaurant in the Strip presents unusual Caribbean food in a noisy but fun warehouse setting. The small and large plates range from conch fritters with a fiery Yucatán hot bean dip to tropical paella with chicken, chorizo, papaya, calamari, rock shrimp, roasted peppers, snow peas, and mussels. ⊠ *2000 Smallman St.,* ☎ *412/261–6565.*

$$–$$$ ✕ **Mallorca.** With rich murals, warm lighting, and an alluring patio, this traditional Spanish restaurant exudes character. Clams with a garlicky green sauce, baby eels, and veal with lemon-brandy are a few of the consistently first-rate dishes. ⊠ *2228 E. Carson St.,* ☎ *412/488–1818.*

$–$$ ✕ **City Grill.** This queer-popular neighborhood restaurant serves the best burgers in a city that loves them. These juicy patties—along with sirloin steaks, yellowfin tuna, and most every other item on the menu—are hardwood-grilled in an old-fashioned coal-fired oven. Dishy servers add further charm to the experience. ⊠ *2019 E. Carson St.,* ☎ *412/481–6868.*

$ ✕ **Liberty Avenue Saloon.** This Cultural District tavern with a mostly queer following and packed happy hours dishes up reasonably good pizzas (both traditional and white), chicken wings, and addictive cholesterol-laden "Saloon fries" with Monterey jack, cheddar, and bacon, served with Cajun ranch dressing on the side. ⊠ *941 Liberty Ave.,* ☎ *412/338–1533.*

$ ✕ **Zythos.** It could pass for an old Lithuanian social club from the mundane exterior, but the rocking music and cigar smoke bellowing out the front door suggest this South Side boîte's true identity is as a haven for hipsters, neobohemians, and quite a few queers. The great bar has a nice selection of single malts and exotic beers, but don't miss out on the tasty Mediterranean food. A special $3.99 sampler of any three dishes lets you taste such fare as veggie hummus, couscous, and roasted red pepper salad. ⊠ *2108 E. Carson St.,* ☎ *412/481–2234.*

Oakland and Shadyside

$$–$$$ ✕ **Soba Lounge.** Yet another wildly successful Burrito Brothers creation, this funky lounge has live music and dancing later in the evening and a fab patio. The food borrows from various Asian locales, with a pinch of peanut sauce here and a sprig of lemongrass there. Consider honey-hoisin chicken with asparagus, apples, fresh mint, and coconut rice. ⊠ *5847 Ellsworth Ave.,* ☎ *412/362–5656.*

$$ ✕ **New York, New York.** A quintessentially queer restaurant with excellent nightly cabaret, glass-brick walls and tightly packed tables, and a campy fun-loving staff, this purveyor of fairly standard American and Continental chow (pork chops, steaks, and pastas) is a long-standing favorite of the community. ⊠ *5801 Ellsworth Ave.,* ☎ *412/661–5600.*

$–$$ ✕ **La Feria.** This tiny second-floor Shadyside café is a terrific find. Such authentic recipes as *tacu tacu* (black bean and rice casserole baked with hot peppers and served with fried bananas and sweet potato chips), buffalo meat loaf, and spicy deviled eggs show off the variety of Peruvian cooking. ⊠ *5527 Walnut St.,* ☎ *412/682–4501.*

$ ✕ **Elbow Room.** Since around World War II this spirited and spacious Shadyside café has warmed the souls of locals with a long menu of salads, sandwiches, and simple but hearty entrées, including a robust white chili that'll blow you away. Pubby wooden tables and green booths fill the dining rooms, and there's now a trendy cigar room for stogie aficionados. ⊠ *5744 Ellsworth Ave.,* ☎ *412/441–5222.*

$ ✕ **The Original Hot Dog Shop.** Known simply as the "Big O" by the students and locals who pig out here regularly, this shocking shrine to gluttony doles out huge portions of greasy food—fried chicken, shrimp, hot dogs the size of full-grown dachshunds—at rock-bottom prices ($3.99 for a 16-inch pizza). You order and pay at any of several stations—one is dedicated entirely to fries (the kitchen goes through 30,000 pounds of potatoes weekly). ⊠ *3901 Forbes Ave.,* ☎ *412/687–8327.*

Coffeehouse Culture

Common Grounds Coffee House. The queerest coffeehouse in the city, this comfy Shadyside spot has a fireplace, a few lounge chairs, and plenty of lesbian, feminist, and gay literature to thumb through. Quiche, soups, and salads are all served. ⊠ *5888 Ellsworth Ave.,* ☎ *412/362–1190.*

Beehive Coffeehouse and Dessertery. Beside a grunge clothier and Slacker, a piercing parlor, Beehive is indeed a home away from home for alternateens, misfits, literati, music fans, queers, and quite a few slackers. With a manic color scheme and design that rivals Pee-Wee's Playhouse, this java joint is a mainstay of bohemian South Side. ⊠ *1327 E. Carson St.,* ☎ *412/488–4483.*

Rosebud. Adjacent to the groovy live music hall Metropol (*see* Scenes, *below*), Rosebud provides some of Pittsburgh most colorful people-watching day and night, along with tasty breakfasts, sandwiches, and light entrées. ⊠ *1650 Smallman St.,* ☎ *412/261–2221.*

SCENES

Pittsburgh specializes in that brand of neighborhood bar where the staff and patrons know each other's names and newcomers rarely enter unnoticed. Even with the city's transformation into a trendy high-tech city, the gay nightlife scene remains fairly low-key and intimate—maybe a bit too insular for some tastes. This isn't to say the city lacks an edge. Pittsburgh has a strong leather presence, and genXers and artsy students foster a progressive music and social club scene in the Strip, by the universities in Oakland, and in the South Side.

Prime Suspects

Cairo. Pittsburgh's hottest club is set inside an old building whose soaring ceilings, generous use of marble, and elegant lighting fixtures evoke a bank's interior. The place is packed on weekends, often to the point that the friendly but overworked bartenders become unable to manage even simple requests. The dance floor rocks and is usually cramped with hot bodies. What little attitude you'll find in Pittsburgh you'll find here. ⊠ *333 4th Ave.,* ☎ *412/261–0881. Crowd: 75/25 m/f, quite a few straights, mostly under 30, lots of students, stand-and-model, gym kids.*

C. J. Deighnan's. This complex south of downtown via the Liberty Bridge and Liberty Tunnel has a large island bar, a dance floor, and tons of games—minibowling, pool, air hockey, pinball, and plenty of video terminals. Used to draw mostly lesbians but is now quite mixed. ⊠ *2506 W. Liberty Ave.,* ☎ *412/561–4044. Crowd: 60/40 f/m, 30s and 40s, very friendly and outgoing, not cruisy, great place if you're new in town.*

Donny's Place/Prizm. A raucous leather bar in the '70s and '80s, Donny's has diversified and quieted down. The main level is a lively country-western dance bar with a pool hall. Downstairs is a tight basement with a steamy atmosphere; it can get a bit frisky on weekends. A separate entrance leads to a Saturday-only gay youth disco, **Prizm,** which is operated by the Gay and Lesbian Community Center (☎ 412/422–0114) and open only to lesbians, gays, bisexuals, and transgenders 21 and under. ⊠ *1226 Herron Ave.,* ☎ *412/682–9869. Crowd: mixed m/f but more male in basement, mostly 30s to 50s, very diverse, some leather and Levi's, lots of flannels and denim, casual.*

Pittsburgh Eagle. This large, seedy leather bar, similar to other Eagles around the country, hosts various leather and motorcycle clubs and draws crowds for dancing on weekends. The bar, in an industrial part of town, is a little tricky to find: Head to the very end of Eckert Street, directly beneath the Ohio River Boulevard overpass (a 10-minute drive north of downtown). ⊠ *1740 Eckert St.,* ☎ *412/766–7222. Crowd: male, 20s to 40s, leather and Levi's, fairly hardcore (at least during theme parties and on weekends), on the make, hard-drinking, loud, ribald.*

Pegasus. Highly popular but more accessible and easygoing than Cairo, Pegasus has long been the main see-and-be-seen downtown dance-and-video bar, drawing strong crowds every night of the week. The oddly configured basement space has two levels, a central dance floor, and numerous nooks and crannies ideal for cruising and conversing. ⊠ *818 Liberty Ave.,* ☎ *412/281–2131. Crowd: 80/20 m/f, mostly 20s and 30s, somewhat mixed racially, some guppies, fairly professional crowd, very cruisy.*

Neighborhood Haunts

In a run-down, barely marked building near Pitt and CMU, the **Holiday Bar** (⊠ 4620 Forbes Ave., ☎ 412/682–8598) is one of the city's most popular neighborhood bars, drawing a mix of guys of all ages who crowd under the red lights and sip local (and rather foul) Iron City beer while listening to ear-splitting dance music. Fans of karaoke, pool, and zoning out on music videos congregate at **Images** (⊠ 965 Liberty Ave., ☎ 412/391–9990), an unpretentious and pleasantly decorated downtown spot; it's especially busy after work.

A good place for an inexpensive meal (*see* Eats, *above*), the **Liberty Avenue Saloon** (⊠ 941 Liberty Ave., ☎ 412/338–1533) is also a pleasant place for a drink before heading to out for dancing at nearby Pegasus or upstairs to **House of Tilden** (☎ 412/391–0804), a private club that's open for dancing an hour after the other bars have closed at 2 AM. You need to know somebody before you arrive to gain entry to House of Tilden, and there's a $5 cover—it's not really worth the bother for visitors.

Real Luck Café (⊠ 1519 Penn Ave., ☎ 412/837–6614), which more than a few people refer to as the "Hard Luck," sits a short walk from the music clubs and restaurants in the Strip but tends to be fairly quiet most nights. A divey men's and women's bar in blue collar McKees Rocks, southwest of the city, the **Rusty Nail Saloon** (⊠ 704 Thompson Ave., McKees Rocks, ☎ 412/331–9011) is notable for its country-western music on certain nights.

Hangin' with the Hets

The top alternative music venue in a city with an unheralded but impressive scene, **Metropol** (⊠ 1600 Smallman St., ☎ 412/261–2221) has always been a great friend to the gay community, with queer nights on Thursday and a following all the time. A restored historic theater, gay-popular **Heaven** (⊠ 107 6th St., ☎ 412/338–2727) is best-known for its wild cabaret and drag shows on Sunday nights; it's also fun for dancing or to catch live music other nights of the week.

Action

The **Arena Health Club Baths** (⊠ 2025 Forbes Ave., ☎ 412/471–8548) are open 24 hours and always draw a willing crowd.

SLEEPS

Pittsburgh has some excellent gay-friendly inns in some of the city's most charming neighborhoods. Rates are reasonable—only the downtown business properties consistently command more than $140 nightly, and that's only on weekdays. If you find yourself stuck for a room at the last minute, head to nearby Braintree, which has a slew of chain hotels and motels, many with good weekend deals.

For price ranges, *see* lodging Chart B at the front of this guide.

Hotels

$$$ ⊞ **Sheraton Station Square.** The most leisure-oriented of the city's downtown chain properties, the Sheraton is a short walk from downtown and the South Side and a quick tram ride from Mt. Washington. Half the rooms have downtown skyline views; all are spacious and nicely appointed. ⊠ *7 Station Square Dr., 15219,* ☎ *412/261–2000 or 800/255–7488,* FAX *412/261–2932. 293 rooms. Restaurant, pool, health club.*

$$$ ⊞ **Westin William Penn.** A 24-story, 19th-century grande dame, the Westin is the city's most prestigious lodging address. Rooms, although not very large, capture the grace of a bygone era with vintage-style fabrics and colors and reproduction furnishings. ⊠ *530 William Penn Pl., 15219,* ☎ *412/281–7100 or 800/228–3000,* FAX *412/553–5252. 595 rooms. Restaurant, exercise room.*

$$ ⊞ **Holiday Inn Select.** This upscale Holiday Inn in the heart of Oakland has functional rooms geared toward business travelers. ⊠ *100 Lytton Ave., 15213,* ☎ *412/682–6200 or 800/465–4329,* FAX *412/681–4749. 252 rooms. Restaurant, pool, exercise room.*

$–$$ ⊞ **Hampton Inn University.** A pleasant property in Oakland, the Hampton offers proximity to museums and gay scene. Guests have access to the downtown Y's health facilities. ⊠ *3315 Hamlet St., 15213,* ☎ *412/681–1000 or 800/426–7866,* FAX *412/681–3022. 133 rooms.*

Guest Houses and Small Hotels

$$–$$$ ⊞ **Appletree B&B.** Your best bet for convenience to Oakland and the funky shopping and dining along Shadyside's Walnut Street and Ellsworth Avenue, this 1884 house is run by a friendly young couple and filled with family heirlooms and quilts, decorative fireplaces, and antiques. ⊠ *703 S. Negley Ave., 15232,* ☎ *412/661–0631, Web site www.appletreeb-b.com. 4 rooms with TV and private bath. Full breakfast. Mostly straight.*

$$–$$$ ⊞ **Morning Glory Inn.** A delightful urban retreat in South Side, this Victorian inn is filled with memorable touches, from an 1890 grand piano in the music room to late-afternoon wine that you can enjoy on a shaded terrace. Rooms have fine antiques, tasteful fabrics, fully modernized marble baths, and phones with voice mail. ⊠ *2119 Sarah St., 15203,* ☎ *412/431–1707,* FAX *412/431–6106, Web site www.bnb.im.com. 5 rooms with phone, TV, and private bath. Full breakfast. Mostly straight.*

$$–$$$ ⊞ **The Priory.** This highly romantic inn was created out of an 1888 converted home for traveling Benedictine monks and an 1852 German Catholic Church. Filled with Victorian antiques and oozing character, the inn has a well-trained staff committed to first-rate service. ⊠ *614 Pressley St., 15212,* ☎ *412/231–3338,* FAX *412/231–4838. 24 rooms with phone, TV, and private bath. Continental breakfast. Mixed gay/straight.*

$$–$$$ ⊞ **Victoria House B&B.** This North Side redbrick inn is a study in Victorian opulence, with lavishly decorated rooms, colorful gardens, and magnificent public rooms. Most rooms are large, with separate sitting areas. Within walking distance are the Warhol Museum, National Aviary, Mattress Factory, and excellent restaurants. ⊠ *939 Western Ave., 15233,* ☎ *412/231–4948. 5 rooms, most with private bath. Full breakfast. Mixed gay/straight.*

$–$$ ⊡ **Inn on the Mexican War Streets.** This restored town house in North Side's Mexican War Streets neighborhood is ideal for independent travelers, as the hosts pretty much leave guests to their own devices. Kitchenettes and on-site laundry are helpful if you stay long-term. ⊠ *1606 Buena Vista St., 15212,* ☎ *412/231–6544. 4 rooms with phone and TV, some with private bath. Continental breakfast. Mostly mixed gay male/lesbian.*

THE LITTLE BLACK BOOK

At Your Fingertips
Gay and Lesbian Community Center (⊠ 5860 Forward Ave., ☎ 412/422–0114). **Greater Pittsburgh Convention and Visitors Bureau** (⊠ 4 Gateway Center, Pittsburgh, PA 15222, ☎ 412/281–7711 or 800/359–0758, Web site www.pittsburgh-cvb.org). *In Pittsburgh* (☎ 412/488–1212, Web site www.inpgh.com). **Pittsburgh AIDS Task Force** (☎ 412/242–2500). *Pittsburgh City Paper* (☎ 412/560–2489, Web site www.pghcitypaper.com). **Port Authority Transit Information** (☎ 412/442–2000). **Yellow Cab** (☎ 412/665–8100).

Gay Media
Planet Q (☎ 412/683–9741, e-mail planetq@aol.com) and *Out* (☎ 412/243–3350, Web site www.outpub.com) are monthly newspapers.

BOOKSTORES
Technically a general-interest bookstore, the South Side's **Saint Elmo's** (⊠ 2208 E. Carson St., ☎ 412/431–9100) has all the major lesbigay titles and many periodicals. In the same neighborhood, the **Gertrude Stein Memorial Bookstore** (⊠ 1003 E. Carson St., ☎ 412/481–9666) is a fine women's and lesbian bookstore.

Working Out
Club One (⊠ 6325 Penn Ave., ☎ 412/362–4806), one of the city's best gyms, is near the gay-friendly blocks of Ellsworth Avenue. **YMCA of Pittsburgh** (⊠ 330 Blvd. of the Allies, ☎ 412/227–6457) has excellent facilities and a convenient downtown location.

31 *Out in Portland*

PORTLAND DOESN'T HAVE A GAY QUARTER, but just about every section of town has a smattering of homo households. Many queerfolk live in the Northwest (sometimes called Nob Hill). A slightly more bohemian and more lesbian contingent resides in Hawthorne in the southeast. Others have discovered the charms of Broadway and the Hollywood district in the northeast.

Counterculturists have long been attracted to the seclusion, serenity, and rugged individualism of Oregon in general and Portland in particular. But the small-town mentality has also fostered distrust of outsiders. Portlanders act—and react—from a gut level, uninfluenced by external forces, a point repeatedly emphasized by the proponents of the twice-passed referendums legalizing assisted suicide in certain situations. This means that homosexuals and ethnic minorities in Portland find themselves in a precarious position. They possess strength in numbers and sympathy from many politicians. But local hatemongers such as white supremacist Tom Metzger and homophobe Lon Mabon have also found secure and visible platforms from which to spew their bile.

Portland is the sort of city where someone like Kevin Kelly Keith can be seen in a pickup truck outfitted with placards bearing anti-queer slogans. He parks his four-wheel pulpit in high-profile areas and sits in a chair mounted on the roof, overseeing the discomfort and anger he provokes. On the other hand, Portland is also home to defiant people like Billie Lou Kahn. When Ms. Kahn, a 52-year-old lesbian, stumbled upon the controversial pickup truck, she ran inside a nearby variety store, bought a can of black spray paint, and covered Mr. Keith's hateful signs with a message of her own: "Ignorance Kills."

THE LAY OF THE LAND

The heart of Portland lies just below the confluence of the Columbia and the Willamette (pronounced wuh-*lamm*-ett) rivers. The Columbia is the border between Washington and Oregon; from it, the Willamette twists in a southerly direction, bisecting the city center. Portland is divided into four quadrants; the Willamette being the north–south spine and Burnside Street being the east–west spine.

Downtown
Portland has an eye-pleasing, though unspectacular, downtown. The skyline is varied in height, color, and shape, and blocks are small. The bases of all buildings are built out to the sidewalk, and their ground floors are required to have display windows. High-end boutiques border pawn shops, trattorias sit beside burger joints, and postmodern boxes rise

above cast-iron Victorians. A green median of trees graces 12 blocks of Park Avenue—this breadth of nature, known as the Park Blocks, was established in 1852, early evidence of Portland's appreciation for its natural resources. The city center is a planner's dream, a bona fide neighborhood with several fountains, some parks, and an abundance of statuary. The streets are busy with nine-to-fivers all day, and they remain lively into the evening when a flood of teens, genXers, and thirtysomethings descends upon music clubs, cafés, and coffeehouses.

Downtown's boundary is perfectly clear: Burnside Street to the north, the river to the east, and curving I–405 to the south and west. Along the river the **Tom McCall Waterfront Park** stretches for more than a mile, providing a scenic venue for cycling, jogging, blading, and sunning. The park begins along Naito Parkway (still known to locals as Front Avenue) north of the **Oregon Maritime Museum** (⊠ 113 S.W. Naito Pkwy., ☎ 503/224–7724) and terminates at the **RiverPlace Promenade,** a contemporary condo and shopping complex.

The six-block **Yamhill Historic District,** a rectangle of classic Italianate cast-iron buildings that date from the early 1870s, runs from about Taylor Street to Morrison Street close to the waterfront. Brown baggers spend lunch hour at **Pioneer Square,** a tidy redbrick plaza at the intersection of Yamhill Street and Broadway. Many high-end chain stores and shopping centers are clustered here, including **NikeTown** (⊠ 930 S.W. 6th Ave., ☎ 503/221–6453), the unabashedly commercial tribute to the Portland-based maker of athletic wear, and a rather cruisy **Nordstrom** (⊠ 701 S.W. Broadway, ☎ 503/224–6666) department store.

South of Pioneer Square the impressive **Portland Center for the Performing Arts** (⊠ S.W. Broadway and S.W. Main St., ☎ 503/796–9293) presents ballet, opera, and classical music. The **Portland Art Museum** (⊠ 1219 S.W. Park Ave., ☎ 503/226–2811) specializes in Native American, regional contemporary, and graphic arts. The **Oregon History Center** (⊠ 1200 S.W. Park Ave., ☎ 503/306–5198) has the lowdown on what's happened in the stated from prehistoric times to the present. North of Pioneer Square, bounded by 4th and 11th avenues and Oak and Yamhill streets, is the **Glazed Terra-Cotta Historic District,** worth a visit for architecture buffs. Run your eye across the rooflines of these early 20th-century buildings and you'll notice ornate griffins, floral displays, and animal heads.

The Pearl District and Stark Street

The warehouses and defunct rail yards of the **Pearl District,** the center of which is a few blocks east of I–405, north of Burnside Street to about Hoyt Street, are rapidly being developed into condos and businesses; several trendy restaurants have opened here recently. On the south side of Burnside Street lies the city's tiny gay entertainment mecca, the commercial spine of which is **Stark Street.** Though bar-studded Stark Street is slightly seedy it's generally safe and is a short walk from most major downtown hotels. Vintage-clothing, book, and used-record shops line Burnside and Oak streets. The neighborhood's malty smell comes from the **Blitz-Weinhard Brewing Co.** (⊠ 1133 W. Burnside St., ☎ 503/222–4351), producers of a fine local beer; tours are given on weekdays at noon, 1:30, and 3 PM.

Old Town

The oldest commercial part of town begins with the **Skidmore Historic District,** in the blocks immediately south and west of the Burnside Bridge. Buildings are a mix of cast iron and glazed terra-cotta, and though many are restored, the area retains a skid-row atmosphere. You'll find music clubs, restaurants, and galleries here. Continue north above Burnside to reach Old Town's many restaurants and several divey gay bars. This neighborhood is in a state of transition, as is **Chinatown** just to the west.

Northwest

Though it's devoid of gay bars, Portland's **Northwest** is one of the city's prime spots for gay eats and shopping. Technically called (though only occasionally referred to as) Nob Hill, it has some fine Victorian houses. **Northwest 23rd** and **Northwest 21st avenues** are the area's two commercial strips. Both, from about Burnside north to around Thurman Street, are replete with alternative-minded students, yuppies, gay men, lesbians, feminists, and aging hippies.

Southwest

Drive west of downtown via U.S. 26 to reach the **Metro Washington Park Zoo** (✉ 4001 S.W. Canyon Rd., ☎ 503/226−7627), which anchors 322-acre, densely wooded **Washington Park.** On the opposite side of the park, and reached via Burnside Street, sits the **International Rose Test Garden** (✉ 400 S.W. Kingston Ave., ☎ 503/823−3636); 10,000 bushes with more than 500 varieties are displayed within its 4 acres. Just above the test garden is a 5½-acre **Japanese Garden** (✉ 611 S.W. Kingston Ave., ☎ 503/223−4070). Another attraction near Washington Park is the **Pittock Mansion** (✉ 3229 N.W. Pittock Dr., ☎ 503/823−3624), a restored French Renaissance−inspired home filled with art and antiques. The wooded grounds abut the 5,000-acre **Forest Park,** great for hiking and biking.

The Lloyd District and Northeast Broadway

Once a derelict industrial neighborhood on the northeastern shores of the Willamette River, the **Lloyd District** is now anchored by the twin-towered **Oregon Convention Center** and **Rose Garden Arena** (home to the Trail Blazers pro-basketball team). Check out the high-intensity shopping at the 200-store **Lloyd Center** (✉ 2201 Lloyd Center, off N.E. Multnomah St., ☎ 503/282−2511). From here you're a short walk from the **Northeast Broadway** neighborhood. This swiftly emerging business district has deep roots in the queer community. Most of the action is along Broadway from about 18th Avenue to 28th Avenue.

Hawthorne and Sellwood

The **Hawthorne District** in Portland's southeast quadrant is the city's most concentrated lesbian enclave. **Southeast Stark** and **Southeast Belmont streets,** which run north of the Hawthorne District, hold a share of the area's coffeehouses, boutiques, and music clubs. But the main commercial stretch is **Hawthorne Boulevard.** A grittier version of Nob Hill, the Hawthorne District is a great place for Sunday brunch, browsing in bookshops and galleries, avant-garde theater, and listening to poetry readings and folk bands while sipping coffee.

Take Highway 99E south for several miles to reach the **Old Sellwood Antique Row;** it runs along **Southeast 13th Street,** between Bidwell and Sherrett streets. This community of wood-frame Victorians was annexed by Portland in 1893 and contains more than 50 great antiques shops.

GETTING AROUND

Downtown, up to Hoyt Street and then bound by I−405 and the Willamette River, is known as Fareless Square in transit lingo: Within this 300-square-block area, bus, restored trolley, and MAX light-rail travel are free. You'll probably need a car to get to the southwestern hills, Northeast Broadway, and the Hawthorne District.

EATS

Portland has strong Mexican, Eastern European, German, Asian, and Irish communities. The variety is evident in the number of ethnic eateries, and owing to the abundance of freshwater and saltwater seafood, you'll find ample contemporary Pacific Northwest cuisine.

For price ranges, *see* dining Chart B at the front of this guide.

West of the Willamette

$$$–$$$$ ✕ **Paley's Place.** Specializing in Pacific Northwestern cuisine with southern French and northern Italian spins, this intimate chef-owned bistro wows even the most jaded diners with sautéed sweetbreads with baby bok choy and a shiitake-plum sauce, and a knockout rabbit cassoulet. ⊠ *1204 N.W. 21st St.,* ☎ *503/243–2403.*

$$$–$$$$ ✕ **Wildwood.** One of Portland's hottest purveyors of Pacific Northwest cuisine is typically trendy, with postmodern furnishings. The menu changes often but has featured such winners as seared halibut with risotto and Romano beans. ⊠ *1221 N.W. 21st Ave.,* ☎ *503/248–9663.*

$$–$$$ ✕ **Café des Amis.** A romantic and very queer place to take a first date, this elegantly appointed bistro on Nob Hill serves reasonably priced country-French fare—fillet of beef with garlic and port sauce and savory wild-mushroom ravioli. ⊠ *1987 N.W. Kearney St.,* ☎ *503/295–6487.*

$$–$$$ ✕ **Cassidy's.** Power lunchers and moon-eyed lovers have made this old-fashioned restaurant a favorite. The contemporary menu features Pacific Northwest variations on seafood and pasta. Later in the evening actors and stage crews from local theaters stop by for a late meal or coffee. ⊠ *1331 S.W. Washington St.,* ☎ *503/223–0054.*

$$–$$$ ✕ **Hobo's.** The city's one upscale gay restaurant is so popular that straight movers and shakers come here, too. With a classy lounge and piano bar the place has the feel of a big gay supper club. Steak and seafood are the menu's mainstays. ⊠ *120 N.W. 3rd Ave.,* ☎ *503/224–3285.*

$$–$$$ ✕ **Oba.** This wildly popular *Nuevo Latino* restaurant opened in the Pearl District in October 1997. Expect such tempting fare as seared ancho-crusted ahi tuna with matchstick vegetables, crème fraîche, and a boniato mash, and slow rotisserie-roasted prime rib with a horseradish-garlic sauce. ⊠ *555 N.W. 12th Ave.,* ☎ *503/228–6161.*

$$–$$$ ✕ **Papa Haydn.** One of the more yuppified hangouts in northwest Portland is famous for its weekend brunches. For weekday lunches try the overstuffed sandwiches; tasty dinner entrées include chicken marinated in apple brandy. The desserts never disappoint. ⊠ *701 N.W. 23rd Ave.,* ☎ *503/228–7317; also 5829 S.E. Milwaukie Ave.,* ☎ *503/232–9440.*

$$ ✕ **Bridgeport Brew Pub.** This century-old converted warehouse in the northern reaches of the Pearl District is one of the best in town. The pizza, focaccia sandwiches, and salads are excellent. ⊠ *1313 N.W. Marshall St.,* ☎ *503/241–7179.*

$–$$ ✕ **Sauce Box.** This self-consciously hip café delivers tasty multinational fare—veggie samosas, quesadillas, Chinese pot stickers—in an austere dining room. Tripping music, patrons sporting the latest gas-station-attendant uniforms, and flatware that looks stolen from ValuJet heighten the tortured artiste ambience. ⊠ *214 S.W. Broadway,* ☎ *503/241–3393.*

$ ✕ **Pizzicato.** This chic little pizzeria's pies come with any number of toppings—lamb sausage, prosciutto, and eggplant are a few options. Or try one of the focaccia sandwiches. ⊠ *505 N.W. 23rd Ave.,* ☎ *503/242–0023;* ⊠ *2811 E. Burnside St.,* ☎ *503/236–6045, 750 S.W. Adler St.,* ☎ *503/226–1007.*

$ ✕ **The Roxy.** Gay meets grunge in the queer district's 24-hour study in Formica. On any given night you'll see big hair, pierced extremities, lotsa muscle, leather, rubber, drag, you name it. The Roxy is liveliest after the bars close, so expect a wait. ⊠ *1121 S.W. Stark St.,* ☎ *503/223–9160.*

$ ✗ **Shaker's.** Several cuts above your average greasy spoon (the generous use of Formica and knotty pine notwithstanding), this très gay Pearl District favorite is justly renowned for its filling breakfasts (Scottish oats, challah French toast) and lunches where burgers reign supreme (the tuna's pretty memorable, too). ✉ *1212 N.W. Glisan St.,* ☎ *503/221–0011. No credit cards.*

East of the Willamette

$$$–$$$$ ✗ **Genoa.** The city's best northern Italian restaurant has been wowing national culinary magazines since the early 1970s. Seven-course prix-fixe dinners include antipasto, soup, pasta, fish or salad, entrée, dessert, and fruit. ✉ *2832 S.E. Belmont St.,* ☎ *503/238–1464.*

$$–$$$ ✗ **La Catalana.** Hand-painted ceramics and objets d'art fill the romantic, gay-frequented La Catalana. Fresh bass and trout are specialties, as is the appetizer of mussels on the half shell with spinach mousse. ✉ *2821 S.E. Stark St.,* ☎ *503/232–0948.*

$$–$$$ ✗ **28 East.** This festive and unpretentious neighborhood bistro's star is rising rapidly along with the strip of offbeat shops it anchors. Pizzas, grilled sea scallops, and tasty meat, seafood, and poultry grills are menu highlights. ✉ *40 N.E. 28th Ave.,* ☎ *503/235–9060.*

$$ ✗ **Montage.** A teetering redbrick building directly below the Morrison Street Bridge in a slightly dicey warehouse district houses one of Portland's quirkiest taverns. Chic grungers and artistes congregate for sautéed sea bass with crabs, the kitchen's trademark jambalayas, and other diverse fare. ✉ *301 S.E. Morrison St.,* ☎ *503/234–1324. No credit cards.*

$$ ✗ **Wild Abandon.** This dark and intimate restaurant, a great place to bring a date, dishes up eclectic cuisine with new American overtones. Check out the risotto of the day. Sunday brunch is popular. ✉ *2411 S.E. Belmont St.,* ☎ *503/232–4458.*

$–$$ ✗ **Chez José.** You're as likely to find a mom and dad with a zillion children as you are a posse of muscle queens in this cavernous Mexican restaurant with a festive patio out back. ✉ *2200 N.E. Broadway,* ☎ *503/280–9888.*

$ ✗ **Old Wives' Tales.** This healthful, affordable, sunlit café draws plenty of dykes with tykes—and everybody else hankering for terrific Caesar salads, vegetarian burritos, fresh-baked goods, and other simple, wholesome fare. ✉ *1300 E. Burnside St.,* ☎ *503/238–0470.*

$ ✗ **Saigon Kitchen.** For the best spring roll in Portland head over the Broadway Bridge to this bustling Southeast Asian restaurant. The quick service verges on being frantic. ✉ *835 N.E. Broadway,* ☎ *503/281–3669.*

Coffeehouse Culture

West of the Willamette

Coffee People. There are a couple of Starbucks branches on Nob Hill, but the best spot for java is Coffee People, a tiny place with counter seating along the wall and front windows. There's no real food, but you can get great ice cream, shakes, and other sweets. ✉ *533 N.W. 23rd Ave.,* ☎ *503/221–0235; 3500 S.E. Hawthorne Blvd.,* ☎ *503/235–1383.*

East of the Willamette

Cafe Lena. The brash and beatnik Cafe Lena has newspaper clippings and photos of Billie Holiday, Lenny Bruce, and other performers on the walls, disco music blaring when poetry readings aren't being staged, and great sandwiches. ✉ *2239 S.E. Hawthorne Blvd.,* ☎ *503/238–7087.*

Rimsky-Korsakoffee House. This place has no sign out front and is staffed by smart-ass waitrons (the bad service is intentional—apparently a marketing gimmick). The desserts are delicious, though, and folk musicians perform most nights. ✉ *707 S.E. 12th Ave.,* ☎ *503/232–2640.*

414

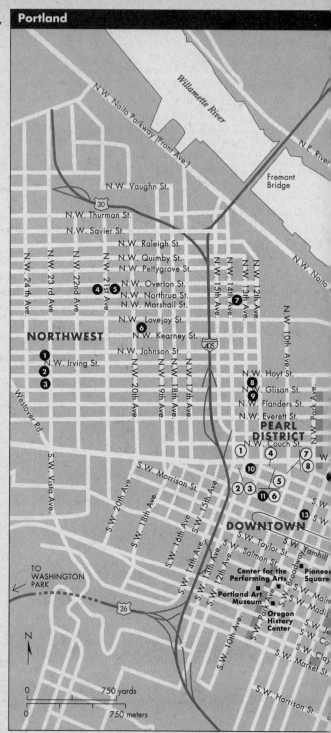

Portland

N.E. Graham St.

N.E. Graham St.

N.E. Russell St.

N.E. Knott St.

N.E. Thompson St

N.E. Thompson St.

N.E. Vancouver Ave.

N.E. Union Ave.

N.E. 9th Ave.

N.E. 15th Ave.

River St.

N.E. Wheeler Ave.

N.E. Hancock St.

N.E. Hancock St.

5

N.E. Interstate Ave.

N.E. Schuyler St.

15

N.E. Broadway

16

14

N.E. 2nd Ave.

N.E. Weidler St.

LLOYD DISTRICT

Broadway
Bridge

**Memorial
Coliseum**

N.E. Halsey St.

N.E. Halsey St.

Naito Parkway (Front Ave.)

N.E. Wasco St.

Lloyd Center

N.E. Multnomah St.

**OLD
TOWN**

Steel
Bridge

N.E. Holladay St.

N.E. 1st Ave.

**Oregon
Convention
Center**

N.E. Lloyd Blvd.

84

N.E. Glisan St.

N.W. Broadway

N.W. 6th Ave.

N.W. 5th Ave.

N.W. 4th Ave.

N.W. 3rd Ave.

11

N.E. Everett St.

N.W. Park Ave.

N.E. Sandy Blvd.

N.W. Davis St

10

12

14

N.E. Everett St.

9

13

Burnside
Bridge

**Chinatown
Gate**

E. Burnside St.

18

W. Burnside St.

S.W. Ankeny St.

S.W. Ankeny St.

17

19

S.W.
Ash
St.

S.E. Ash St.

12

S.W. Pine St.

**Maritime
Center**

S.W. Oak St.

99E

99E

S.W. Stark St.

**Tom McCall
Waterfront
Park**

15

S.E. Stark St.

S.E. 11th Ave.

S.E. 12th Ave.

S.E. 14th Ave.

S.W. Washington St.

S.E. Washington St.

20

S.W. Alder St.

16

S.W. 1st Ave.

Morrison
Bridge

21

17

mhill St.

S.W. 3rd Ave.

S.W. 2nd Ave.

S.E. 7th Ave.

S.E. 8th Ave.

**oneer
quare**

26

N.E. Union Ave.

S.E. Grand Ave.

S.E. Morrison St.

22

Main St.

Willamette River

S.E. Belmont St.

23

S.E. 15th Ave.

Madison St.

Naito Parkway (Front Ave.)

W. Jefferson St.

S.E. Main St.

**TO
HAWTHORNE
DISTRICT**

N. Columbia St.

S.E. Madison St.

Clay St.

**River
Place**

S.E. Hawthorne Blvd.

24

ket St.

Hawthorne
Bridge

S.E. Clay St.

25

S.W. 1st Ave.

5

S.E. Water Ave.

S.E. 1st Ave.

S.E. 2nd Ave.

S.E. 3rd Ave.

S.W. Harbor Way

S.E. Market St.

27

SCENES

Most places draw a decent mix of lesbians and gay men. The popular bars west of the Willamette are on Southwest Stark Street, and the hottest ones on the east side are on Southeast Stark Street. The several other options north of Burnside Street in the Old Town district are convivial neighborhood dives. Portland's taverns are open relatively late by West Coast standards, until 2:30 AM. They can't serve liquor unless they also serve food; many clubs either have (generally unexceptional) restaurants attached, or serve only beer and wine.

West of the Willamette

PRIME SUSPECTS

Boxx's/The Brig. These two connected bars are gay Portland's favorite hangouts. What little stand-and-model action exists in the city you'll find here, though this is still a laid-back place. You enter through Boxx's, a nicely decorated, if typical, video bar. A hallway leads to the Brig, which has the dance floor. You can lean on the railings surrounding the small space and watch everybody wiggle, but the ambience is strangely grim, as though the designers had in mind the recreation room of a nuclear fall-out shelter. ⊠ 1035 S.W. Stark St., ☎ 503/226–4171. Crowd: 75/25 m/f, mostly under 35, some guppies, clean-cut by Portland standards, cruisy.

Eagle PDX. Portland has a good leather scene, and the Eagle is where you'll find the most intense action. The first floor has a dark cruise bar, next to which is a smaller room with a pool table. Upstairs is an open interior balcony, a cozy aerie more conducive to conversation. In addition to the strong leather presence, you're apt to see some guys in creative uniforms. ⊠ 1300 W. Burnside St., ☎ 503/241–0105. Crowd: male, mostly mid-20s to late 30s, mostly leather but some denim.

Embers. This Old Town fixture was *the* hot disco for some time, but in the past couple of years it's begun to slide downhill, almost to the point of sliding back uphill in spite of itself (i.e., going retro). The main reason to come now is to catch one of the drag shows, held in the main disco. ⊠ 110 N.W. Broadway, ☎ 503/222–3082. Crowd: mostly gay but increasingly more straights, mixed m/f, all ages and races, loud and disorderly, some hustlers.

Hobo's. Known more as a restaurant (*see* Eats, *above*), this huge steak house and lounge on the edge of Chinatown has piano music nightly. A large game room has pool tables, video games, and other diversions. ⊠ 120 N.W. 3rd Ave., ☎ 503/224–3285. Crowd: 80/20 gay/straight, mixed m/f, all ages.

Panorama. Despite being in the same overwhelmingly gay complex that houses Boxx's and the Brig, the crowd at Panorama has always been at least 50% hetero. It's a good place to dance, but tension between straights and gays pretty much kills the cruise factor. The crowd is unbelievably young—lots of rebellious kids from the 'burbs. Open weekends until 4 AM. ⊠ 341 S.W. 10th Ave., ☎ 503/221–7262. Crowd: 50/50 gay/straight; mixed m/f; extremely young; serious dancers; poseurs; lots of spiked hair, shaved heads, body piercing.

The Rage. This large, impressive space in the heart of things gay is only open Friday and Saturday, but always draws a huge and varied crowd for dancing, drag shows, and the fag equivalent of American Bandstand (which is usually Friday). ⊠ 13 N.W. 13th Ave., ☎ 503/286–1764. Crowd: 80/20 m/f, young (18 and older permitted), flashy, some stand-and-model.

Silverado. Were it not in the heart of the gay entertainment section, this would be just another hustler bar with strippers. Instead, it's all that and so much more. Inside is a small stage for the (mostly) gangly strippers, with a counter and seats around it on which patrons can rest their asses and their highballs yet still be close enough to stick dollar bills in as many waistbands as possible. A DJ spins mostly dated disco for the small dance floor in the far corner. ⊠ *1217 S.W. Stark St.*, ☎ *503/224–4493. Crowd: mostly male, chickens and chickenhawks, racially mixed, a few drag queens, hard drinkers, rough-and-ready, overall sleazy but kind of fun.*

NEIGHBORHOOD HAUNTS

C. C. Slaughter's (⊠ 413 S.W. 13th Ave., ☎ 503/248–9135), a Portland stalwart, moved into the same block as the Eagle in late 1997. **Darcelle XV** (⊠ 208 N.W. 3rd Ave., ☎ 503/222–5338) is famous among gays and straights for its elaborate drag revues; on nights the gals don't dress up, strippers dress down. Leather bears head to the **Dirty Duck** (⊠ 439 N.W. 3rd Ave., ☎ 503/224–8446), a dirty old pub in an industrial area. The **Fox and Hound** (⊠ 217 N.W. 2nd Ave., ☎ 503/243–5530), in the Old Town district, serves up sandwiches and burgers, karaoke, and a saucy crowd of locals. **Scandals** (1038 S.W. Stark St., ☎ 503/227–5887) is a casual beer-and-wine tavern; on weekends, an adjacent espresso bar and gallery is open. **Three Sisters Tavern** (⊠ 1125 S.W. Stark St., ☎ 503/ 228–0486) is another mellow spot for a beer.

East of the Willamette

PRIME SUSPECTS

J.O.Q.'s. Once a simple blue-collar drinking hole, J.O.Q.'s attracts more diverse patrons these days. Still basically a place where locals dish and rub elbows, it now gets crowded early most evenings; weekends can get downright packed. ⊠ *2512 N.E. Broadway*, ☎ *503/287–4210. Crowd: mostly male, all ages, regulars and newcomers, zero attitude.*

Kokopeli's. Though predominantly lesbian, this chummy pub east of the river welcomes most everyone. The large brightly lit place has two pool tables, a rockin' jukebox, a small dance floor, darts, and a couple of large-screen TVs. There's live music Thursday through Sunday. ⊠ *2845 S.E. Stark St.*, ☎ *503/236–4321. Crowd: mostly gay, 80/20 f/m, all ages, all types.*

NEIGHBORHOOD HAUNTS

Starky's (⊠ 2913 S.E. Stark St., ☎ 503/230–7980), a warm, terrific lounge in eastern Portland, has a restaurant that serves the usual pub fare. Men and women are welcome.

HANGIN' WITH THE HETS

In addition to the specifically queer clubs listed above, **La Luna** (⊠ 215 S.E. 9th Ave., ☎ 503/241–5862) has long been a Portland institution for cutting-edge music and alternative performances. A young crowd of gays and straights filters in here just about every night of the week. Mondays ($5 cover) are queer nights.

Action

Washington Park is called the **Fruit Loop.** As you approach the park from the city, the loop, to which there is no auto access at night, is across from the reservoir. There are a few adult bookshops, but both **Fantasy Video** (⊠ 3137 N.E. Sandy Blvd., ☎ 503/239–6969) stores are open 24 hours, are cruisy, and have busy video arcades. The **Club Portland** (⊠ 303 S.W. 12th Ave., ☎ 503/227–9992) bathhouse is in the heart of the downtown bar strip.

Gay Beaches

Rooster Rock State Park (☎ 503/695–2261), a.k.a. Cock Rock, lies 20 miles east of the city on I–84 in the scenic Columbia Gorge. Nearby mountain ranges form the backdrop. Nudity is permitted at the beach; the gay section is to the right, along the river, about a half mile up. The nude beach at **Sauvies Island** is about 8 miles northwest of Portland on U.S. 30. After taking the bridge to Sauvies Island, turn right onto Northwest Gillihan Loop Road and follow this for some time before making a right onto Northwest Reeder Road. Parking for the gay section is near the end of Reeder Road in the last lot. When you reach the banks of the Columbia River, turn left and walk about 10 or 15 minutes until you start noticing the throngs of queers—the numbers can be very high on sunny weekends. These two beaches go back and forth in popularity, but Rooster Rock definitely has the cruisiest reputation.

SLEEPS

Portland has several outstanding European-style hotels, most in century-old buildings and all within a short walk of the Pearl District's gay bars. Several are high-end, but three excellent ones charge as little as $60 nightly. All the major chain hotels are represented in Portland.

For price ranges, *see* lodging Chart B at the front of this guide.

Hotels

$$$–$$$$ ▥ **Fifth Avenue Suites.** This Kimpton Group property improved on a familiar Portland strategy: Take a classy old building and convert it into a charming hotel. The twist here is that each of the richly decorated rooms is a full suite with a spacious sitting area. A first-rate property all around. ⊠ *506 S.W. Washington St., 97205,* ☎ *503/222–0001 or 800/711–2971,* ℻ *503/222–0004. 221 rooms. Restaurant, exercise room.*

$$$–$$$$ ▥ **Governor Hotel.** Before the 1909 Governor Building was converted into this posh hotel, its gutted interior starred as the home of a raffish posse of ne'er-do-wells and their Faginesque leader in Gus Van Sant's film *My Own Private Idaho.* Public rooms have dark mahogany detailing and a lodgelike rusticity, and the guest rooms are sumptuous and softly lit. ⊠ *6119 S.W. 10th St., 97205,* ☎ *503/224–3400 or 800/554–3456,* ℻ *503/241–2122. 100 rooms. Restaurant, pool, exercise room.*

$$$–$$$$ ▥ **Hotel Vintage Plaza.** A fully restored historic downtown building holds one of the spiffiest properties in the Pacific Northwest. The rooms are large and done in warm colors; many have hot tubs and spiral staircases leading to second-story sleeping lofts. ⊠ *422 S.W. Broadway, 97205,* ☎ *503/228–1212 or 800/243–0555,* ℻ *503/228–3598. 107 rooms. Restaurant, exercise room.*

$–$$ ▥ **Imperial Hotel.** This characterful 1908 hotel is a great budget option. It looks and feels nearly as nice as its luxury-hotel neighbors, and though it lacks some of their amenities, it's a classy property with good-size rooms. ⊠ *400 S.E. Broadway, 97205,* ☎ *503/228–7221 or 800/452–2323,* ℻ *503/223–4551. 136 rooms. Restaurant.*

$ ▥ **Mark Spencer Hotel.** Steps from the gay bars, the Mark Spencer looks unsavory from the outside but is clean and comfortable inside. Basic and dirt cheap (weekly rates are especially good), its rooms come with walk-in closets and kitchens. ⊠ *409 S.W. 11th Ave., 97205,* ☎ *503/224–3293 or 800/548–3934,* ℻ *503/223–7848. 101 rooms.*

Guest Houses and Small Hotels

$–$$ ▥ **MacMaster House.** On swank King's Hill two blocks from Washington Park, this grand turn-of-the-century Colonial Revival home is convenient to the business district. The rooms have a romantic mix of antiques and reproductions, and four have fireplaces. ⊠ *1041 S.W. Vista Ave., 97205,* ☎ *503/223–7362 or 800/774–9523,* ℻ *503/224–8808, Web site www.macmaster.com. 7 rooms, 2 with private bath, all with TV. Full breakfast. Mixed gay/straight.*

$ ▥ **Holladay House B&B.** This 1922 Dutch Colonial in northeast Portland is a short walk from the Lloyd Center mall and also quite close to the burgeoning gay shopping and dining scene on Broadway. Rooms are homey and casual, with a few antiques. ⊠ *1735 N.E. Wasco St., 97232,* ☎ *503/ 282–3172. 2 rooms share a bath. Full breakfast. Mostly straight.*

$ 🏠 **Sullivan's Gulch B&B.** The gay-operated Sullivan's Gulch is in a modest residential neighborhood, near Northeast Broadway. Rooms in the art-filled, 1904 Colonial Revival home are furnished with Western and Native American art; a deck in back overlooks well-tended gardens. ⊠ *1744 N.E. Clackamas St., 97232,* ☎ *503/331–1104,* FAX *503/331–1575. 4 rooms, 2 with private bath, all with TV. Continental breakfast. Mixed gay/straight.*

THE LITTLE BLACK BOOK

At Your Fingertips
Broadway Cab (☎ 503/227–1234). **Cascade AIDS Project** (☎ 503/223–6339, ext. 111). **Gay Resource Connection** (☎ 503/223–2437 or 800/777–2437). **Oregon AIDS Hotline** (☎ 800/777–2437). **Phoenix Rising** (queer youth support, ☎ 503/223–8299). **Portland/Oregon Visitors Association** (⊠ 3 World Trade Center, 97204, ☎ 503/275–9750; events not line, ☎ 503/222–2223). **Tri-Met** (public transportation, ☎ 503/238–7433). **Willamette Week** (☎ 503/243–2122, Web site www.wweek.com).

Gay Media
Just Out (☎ 503/236–1252) is the biweekly gay and lesbian newspaper.

BOOKSTORES
Gai-Pied (⊠ 2544 N.E. Broadway, ☎ 503/331–1125, Web site www .gaipied.com), pronounced gay *pee* ay, a gay-male store, carries books, magazines, videos, and novelties, and there are plans to add a café. **Twenty-Third Avenue Books** (⊠ 1015 N.W. 23rd Ave., ☎ 503/224–5097) has an excellent selection of lesbian and gay titles. **In Other Words** (⊠ 3734 S.E. Hawthorne Blvd., ☎ 503/232–6003) carries feminist and lesbian books and videos, plus many children's titles. This is a great place for lesbians to find resources and social opportunities. **It's My Pleasure** (⊠ 4258 S.E. Hawthorne Blvd., ☎ 503/236–0505) is a fun feminist sex boutique with books, magazines, and movies. **Powell's City of Books** (⊠ 1005 W. Burnside St., ☎ 503/228–4651) has an amazing selection of new and used titles, including lesbian and gay ones.

Working Out
The well-appointed **YWCA** (⊠ 1111 S.W. 10th Ave., ☎ 503/294–7440) gym and swim center is extremely dyke-positive. Downtown gay men and lesbians favor the fancy **Princeton (a.k.a. "Princess") Athletic Club** (⊠ 614 S.W. 11th Ave., ☎ 503/222–2639).

32 Out in Provincetown

AMERICA'S ORIGINAL GAY RESORT developed as an artists' colony at the turn of the century. A young artist and entrepreneur named Charles Hawthorne, charmed by the town's seclusion and magnificent setting, founded the Cape Cod School of Art, one of America's first open-air academies. By 1916 the town's once vibrant fishing industry had slowed, and its whaling industry had died. But a half dozen art schools had opened; the Provincetown Art Association had staged its first exhibitions; and a small band of modernist theater folk—notably the young Eugene O'Neill and Edna St. Vincent Millay—had begun to produce plays on a small wharf in the town's East End.

During the next few decades many leaders of our country's artistic and literary movements spent summers here, but as time passed, the town was identified increasingly for its outrageousness—its willingness to flout convention. By the 1960s Provincetown had become a haven for anyone whose artistic leaning, political platform, social manifesto, or sexual persuasion was subject to persecution elsewhere in America. Today the most visibly gay resort community in the United States, excepting the Pines and Cherry Grove in Fire Island and, possibly, Key West, it is as appealing to artists as it is to gay and lesbian, as well as straight, tourists.

Many P-town loyalists won't set foot here during the frantic, crowded months of July and August, but those are the prime months: If you're looking for nightlife, tea-dances, a good tan, and the height of queer society, brave the crowds and higher prices and jump into the fray. Less hectic May, June, September, and October see generally moderate weather.

THE LAY OF THE LAND

The two main strips in town are **Commercial Street,** which runs east-west the length of the harbor front, and **Bradford,** which parallels Commercial, a block inland. Dozens of short roads intersect the two. The West End includes everything west of about Central Street; the East End takes in points east of about Washington Street. Many of the town's basic services and retail shops, such as grocery stores and laundries, are on Shank Painter Road, a north-south link between Bradford and U.S. 6, the main highway into town. The three-fourths of town north of U.S. 6 encompasses the national seashore property.

Gay-oriented businesses line Commercial Street. To name but a few, **Silk and Feathers** and **Moda Fina** are popular with lesbians for trendy clothing; **All American Boy** is tops with the guys. **Hirsheldons** and **Northern Lights** carry leather goods. **Pride's of Provincetown** sells gay cards and jewelry, and **Womencrafts** has lesbian jewelry, books, music, and crafts.

Only a few attractions in town, most significantly the 252-foot-tall **Pilgrim Monument** (☎ 508/487–1310), commemorate the landing of the Pilgrims in 1620. Climb the steps to the observation deck for amazing views of the entire Cape and South Shore. Another source of local history is the **Provincetown Heritage Museum** (✉ Monument Hill, ☎ 508/487–0666). Exhibits show replicated rooms and shops in Provincetown. The **Provincetown Art Association and Museum** (✉ 460 Commercial St., ☎ 508/487–1750) houses more than 1,500 works and mounts exhibitions year-round. For a break during these explorations, grab a bite at **Snackattack** (✉ 331 Commercial St., ☎ 508/487–4749), a great little stand with meat and veggie burgers, frozen yogurt, and many low-fat and nonfat choices.

Outdoor Diversions

The **Cape Cod National Seashore** (☎ 508/349–3785) extends for about 40 miles, from Chatham, at the Cape's outer elbow, to Provincetown; the visitor center at **Race Point Beach** (☎ 508/487–1256) has trail maps, exhibits, and park rules. Park land includes more than 7 miles of paved bike trails; several dune- and forest-walking trails; and two beaches: **Race Point**, which is on the northern side of town and gets more wind and rougher waters, and **Herring Cove,** which is in the West End and, to the far left, has a crowded gay beach. Parking lots are full at both beaches by late morning in summer; consider walking. There's a small entrance fee.

GETTING AROUND

Provincetown is about a 2- or 2½-hour drive from Boston or Providence. From New York City it's about six hours. There are only two bridges onto the Cape, and both are unbelievably congested on weekends. Bus service is also available from these cities, and from Boston's Logan International Airport, but it's a long ride. From Boston, also consider taking the relaxing passenger ferry (☎ 508/487–9284; once daily; 3 hrs.) from Commonwealth Pier to P-town's MacMillan Wharf. If money isn't an issue, several flights are offered by **Cape Air** (☎ 508/771–6944 or 800/352–0714) daily between Provincetown Municipal Airport and Logan; it's a 20-minute trip that affords breathtaking views.

P-town parking can be a challenge. Some accommodations have ample spaces, but many have either no designated parking or enough for only a few guests. Once in town, find a legal spot for your car (parking rules are enforced vigilantly), then leave it there. You can walk the entire length of Commercial Street in about an hour, and most points in town are within easy walking distance of one another. **Ptown Bikes** (✉ 42 Bradford St. and 306 Commercial St., ☎ 508/487–8735) rents cycles.

EATS

Provincetown dining is typical of Cape Cod—lots of lobster, clams, cod, bluefish, and other indigenous seafood, plus plenty of Italian and Portuguese recipes. Stop by the **Provincetown Portuguese Bakery** (✉ 299 Commercial St., ☎ 508/487–1803) to sample the delicious meat pies, pastries, rolls, and breads. The few restaurants in the West End have the strongest queer followings.

For price ranges, *see* dining Chart A at the front of this guide.

$$$–$$$$ ✕ **Front Street.** Chef-owners Donna Aliperti and Kathy Cotter are renowned for their innovative menus, which change weekly, usually offering dishes with a vaguely Continental spin, such a swordfish-and-shrimp Napoleon with fried chickpeas and asparagus. This bistro, in the brick cellar of an old Victorian home, is an ideal spot for special occa-

sions—one of the few places you might dress to dine. ⊠ *230 Commercial St.,* ☎ *508/487–9715.*

$$$–$$$$ ✕ **Martin House.** A former captain's residence (circa 1750), the Martin House has several intimate dining rooms, many with fireplaces, original wide-plank floors, exposed brick, local paintings, pitched roofs, beamed ceilings and other charming touches—there's also a cheerful redbrick garden terrace in back. Here you'll find some of the fancier food in town: sample pan-roasted striped bass on salted-cod mashed potatoes with a fresh basil beurre blanc. ⊠ *157 Commercial St.,* ☎ *508/487–1327.*

$$–$$$$ ✕ **Mario's.** Popular for its diverse menu, deck seating, and bustling pace, Mario's Mediterranean restaurant has an informal pizza parlor up front (open late), and a full dining room in back, where there's always a daily selection of tapas, plus great vegetable kebabs, seafood *fra diablo* (a spicy tomato coulis), and clam chowder that's as good as you'll find. ⊠ *265–7 Commercial St.,* ☎ *508/487–0002.*

$$–$$$$ ✕ **The Mews.** Home of the best margarita in town and great live entertainment—from open-mike nights to drag shows. The pubby café upstairs has great lighter fare (burgers, salads, etc.), a piano, and a popular bar. The downstairs dining room, with pickled-wood floors, mahogany wainscoting, and stylish sand-color, textured-plaster walls, is more formal. A favorite here is peanut-crusted rack of lamb with chili-hoisin sauce and roasted-garlic mashed potatoes. Both rooms have great harbor views. ⊠ *429 Commercial St.,* ☎ *508/487–1500.*

$$–$$$ ✕ **Bubala's.** Becoming more and more of a late-night fixture (all dishes are served until 11; the bar is open till 1), Bubala's setting, in a roadhouse on Commercial, is more funky than charming but has great bay views. The menu is quite sophisticated, however, with everything from tuna wasabi to native steamers to grilled tofu with Thai curry. ⊠ *183 Commercial St.,* ☎ *508/487–0773.*

$$–$$$ ✕ **Commons Bistro.** This sophisticated space with a bay window overlooking Commercial offers tasty straightforward American fare, such as herb-roasted half-chicken with potato gratin, and excellent inventive pizzas (try the one topped with duck confit, scallions, and wild mushrooms). There are also some creative theme nights, such as Asian nights. Brunch is great, too, with several hearty and creative dishes, including a delicious goat-cheese frittata. ⊠ *386 Commercial St.,* ☎ *508/487–7800.*

$$–$$$ ✕ **Dancing Lobster.** This name of this longtime favorite, which moved from its wharf location to Commercial Street in 1997, suggests a seafood shanty, but it's actually a full-scale restaurant offering an extensive menu of fine Continental cuisine, from hefty lobsters to steak Gorgonzola and grilled salmon with a crisp fennel salad, sun-dried tomatoes, and a balsamic glaze. The flower-filled dining room has glorious bay views. ⊠ *463 Commercial St.,* ☎ *508/487–0900.*

$$–$$$ ✕ **Gallerani's Café.** Gallerani's serves the kind of food you imagine the town's salty and sweaty Portuguese and Italian fishermen devoured after long days at sea: rich chowders, squid stew, and some non–New England dishes such as shrimp stuffed with crawfish, pecans, and lime with a spiced lime butter. Extra points for the homey, untrendy interior, and the fact that many dishes are available in half portions. ⊠ *133 Commercial St.,* ☎ *508/487–4433.*

$$–$$$ ✕ **Grand Central.** Grand Central, indeed—this intimate ivy-draped bistro with an interior right out of England's Cotswolds is directly opposite the hub of gay nightlife, Atlantic House. Tasty fare ranges from Thai burritos to chipotle barbecued pork tenderloin; it's a very eclectic menu. ⊠ *4–6 Masonic Pl.,* ☎ *508/487–7599.*

$$–$$$ ✕ **Lobster Pot.** Don't leave P-town without having a meal at this tried-and-true, family-style tourist mecca overlooking the harbor and MacMillan Wharf. Come here to feast on the best lobster rolls in town, plus steamers, and a few unusual dishes like a tuna sashimi wrap. Unusually

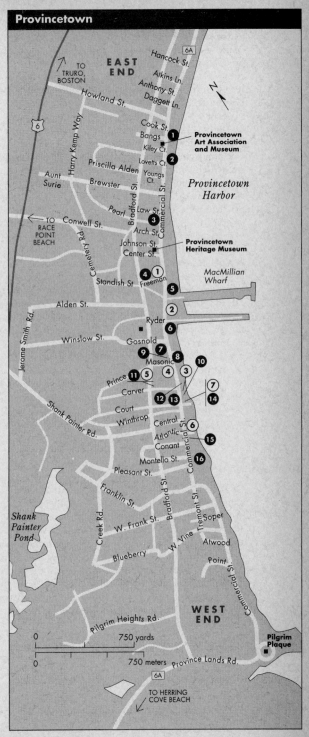

polite service, considering the crowds. ✉ *321 Commercial St.,* ☎ *508/ 487–0842.*

$$–$$$ ✗ **Lorraine's.** For some of the best cooking in Provincetown, and some of the best Mexican food in New England, call well ahead to book a table at this small and intensely popular restaurant. Crab enchiladas and roasted duck are a couple of the artfully presented dishes; the smooth and refreshing margaritas win raves. Friendly service tops it off. ✉ *229 Commercial St.,* ☎ *508/487–6074.*

$$–$$$ ✗ **Napi's.** Napi's has the most exotic menu in town, including such tasty world-beat fare as caponata, hummus, Brazilian steak, chicken teriyaki, Syrian falafel melts, and cod Provençale. There's a long wine list, too. The atmosphere is festive, with old-fashioned laminated wooden tables, stained glass, amber lighting, and Tiffany-style lamps. Lots of lesbians hanging around the bar. ✉ *7 Freeman St.,* ☎ *508/487–1145.*

$$ ✗ **11 Carver.** The ramshackle Gifford House hotel is an unlikely spot for this dapper eatery serving good New American cooking at moderate prices. Dishes like Chilean sea bass and mussels in saffron tomato broth over garlic mashed potatoes rarely disappoint. Great queer first-date setting. ✉ *11 Carver St.,* ☎ *508/487–2119.*

$ ✗ **Café Heaven.** Noted for incredible, filling breakfasts (available all day), this small storefront hangout has long wooden benches, cream-color tables, and pale olive walls that contrast nicely with two huge, bright murals of P-town's beach scene. Come for great omelets, sharp antipasti, or sandwiches like avocado, goat cheese, tomato, and lettuce on French bread. Long lines for brunch. ✉ *199 Commercial St.,* ☎ *508/487–9639.*

$ ✗ **Spiritus.** If not the home of the town's best pizza, it's certainly where you'll find the best people-watching, especially late at night, especially in that golden hour between bar closing and Spiritus's closing (1 AM-2 AM). In addition to a variety of slices (the Greek has Kalamata olives, red onions, spinach, feta, and mozzarella), dozens of coffees and milk shakes are available. The service can be rude and brusque. You can eat inside, but most people grab a slice and sit outside on the steps. ✉ *190 Commercial St.,* ☎ *508/487–2808.*

SCENES

Of all the gay summer resorts, Provincetown has the most varied nightlife scene (Fire Island runs a close second). But even with the diversity of options, several conventions seem to prevail: Most visitors—especially singles—head to the beach in the morning, drop by the Boatslip for the afternoon tea dance, rush home to shower and change, catch the end of the post-tea dance party at the Pied Piper, and then head off to dinner. After that, women generally congregate at the Pied Piper or Vixen, men at the Atlantic House or Union. Bars used to be very male or female; now the scene is quite mixed at most places on most nights, and almost every bar has a women's night once a week. A fire destroyed the Crown & Anchor bar, a longtime P-town haunt, in February 1998. As we headed to press, no plans had been announced regarding its future.

At 1 AM, when the bars close, *everybody* heads to Spiritus (*see above*) for an hour of dishing, posing, and, ideally, discovering where the after-hours parties are. A little persistence is required if you're unfamiliar with the scene, but P-town's many houseboys/girls, waitrons, and retail workers are known to party until dawn. Ask around.

Prime Suspects

Atlantic House. Set inside one of the town's most historically significant buildings, the downstairs bar dates from 1798, and the hotel half was added in 1812. Tennessee Williams and Eugene O'Neill used to stay here. It's the main men's disco, and it has a small dance floor, a terrace out back that's good for talking, and a cozy lounge off the dance floor. The smaller upstairs bar, which has a separate entrance from the street, attracts more of a leather contingent. Of the many theme parties held throughout the summer, the Thursday-night full costume parties are undoubtedly the best. This is the only gay bar open year-round. ⊠ *6 Masonic Pl.,* ☎ *508/487–3821. Crowd in main bar: 80/20 m/f, younger, very stand-and-model; upstairs: older, more leather and Levi's.*

Boatslip. All summer long, the poseurs and party creatures—mostly men but plenty of women, too—mingle and cruise during the Boatslip's legendary tea dances, daily 3:30 to 6:30. The party rocks on the long wooden deck, which has great harbor views, but there's also dancing in the enclosed disco. At night, the younger crowd heads elsewhere, but lots of locals gather in the lobby lounge for quiet chitchat; dance fans head to the downstairs disco for two-stepping (four nights weekly) and ballroom dancing (three nights weekly). ⊠ *161 Commercial St.,* ☎ *508/487–1669. Tea-dance crowd: 70/30 m/f, mixed ages, fresh from the beach. Lobby-bar crowd: older, mixed m/f, more couples, regulars.*

Pied Piper Lounge. This is the best women's disco of any gay resort town in the country. The dance floor is small but has a good sound system, and the intimacy makes it easy to get, well, intimate. Off the dance floor, however, is one of the loveliest decks in town, a great spot to savor the early evening during the Pied Piper's popular after-tea dance, or gaze at the moon later in the evening. ⊠ *193A Commercial St.,* ☎ *508/487–1527. Crowd at after-tea dance: same as at Boatslip tea dance; crowd at other times: 80/20 f/m, very diverse.*

Union. The Gifford House hotel got a terrific boost in 1997 when its somewhat dated Backstreet disco was reinvented as the impressive Union club. This basement space has a small dance floor with fun old-meets-new dance music, a few attractive bars, and a nice little nook filled with shelves of old textbooks (in case you spy some cute college student in need of tutoring). Different theme nights cater to different crowds, and sometimes there's live music. Stairs lead up to the casual Porchside bar, which is open earlier in the evening and caters mostly to hotel guests. ⊠ *Gifford House, 9 Carver St.,* ☎ *508/487–6400. Crowd: generally gay, but otherwise totally varied.*

Vixen. Perhaps a reflection of the degree to which lesbians continue to visit P-town in increasing numbers each year is the fact that the town's most recent addition is a lesbian bar. Vixen is the only gay hangout in the East End, and some of the guys drop by here, too. The attractive bar and dance floor are set back off Commercial; there are live shows on many nights. ⊠ *336 Commercial St.,* ☎ *508/487–6424. Crowd: 70/30 f/m, all ages, fairly similar to the folks at Pied Piper but with more locals.*

Neighborhood Haunts

This tiny front bar at Sebastian's Restaurant, next door to the Boatslip, **Larry's Bar** (⊠ 177 Commercial St., ☎ 508/487–3286) is famous for the ongoing, relentlessly bitchy, irreverent, obnoxious, and genuinely funny commentary and banter of Larry the bartender. Locals and tourists love the cabaret and informal atmosphere of the **Post Office Cafe** (⊠ 303 Commercial St., ☎ 508/487–3892), a great spot for a bite three meals a day, with a low-key bar.

Action

The **Fetish Chest** (✉ 176 Commercial St., ☎ 508/487–1131) has porn movies, CDs, books, and magazines, as well as a wide selection of leather and fetish wear.

SLEEPS

More than 60 of P-town's inns and B&Bs are gay-owned, and others have strong gay followings. The West End is quieter and near the beach; Bradford Street is less scenic, but its higher elevations mean great views and soft breezes; and the East End is the straightest and a long walk from most gay clubs and the beach. The inns on Commercial Street near the center of town are more social, but the area is congested and noisy.

About two-thirds of P-town's gay-oriented lodgings are reviewed below. A handful are upscale , but most B&Bs here are glorified rooming houses. At least a quarter of the town's rooms share baths; most establishments serve scant Continental breakfasts; few places have air-conditioning (although that's rarely needed), private phones, extensive off-street parking, or substantial closet space; many are without TVs and radios. Only a smattering have swimming pools, though several have hot tubs. Many places require four- to seven-night minimums in summer, especially around holidays. All these factors might lead you to suspect that the lodging experience in Provincetown is an unpleasant one. On the contrary: Though accommodations are simple, they're also comparatively inexpensive (a shared bath in high season can be had for as little as $50, a private bath for $70), their atmosphere is casual, their pace is unhurried.

For price ranges, *see* lodging Chart A at the front of this guide.

Hotels and Motels

$$$ 🏨 **Boatslip.** This bayfront compound is ground zero for P-town's frenetic party scene—its daily tea dances are not to be missed. A lounge and a reasonably good restaurant are also on-site. Rooms are of the standard motel ilk: clean, bright, with functional baths. Street-side rooms lack water views but are much cheaper and cozier, with timber ceilings and sloped walls. You're paying for the location and atmosphere. ✉ *161 Commercial St., Box 393, 02657,* ☎ *508/487–1669 or 800/451–7547,* FAX *508/487–6021, e-mail boatslip@provincetown.com. 45 rooms. Restaurant, pool. Mixed gay/straight.*

$–$$ 🏨 **Gifford House.** Decidedly youth- and male-oriented, this grand but tattered Victorian hotel is basically a gay boarding house. Rooms are simple but functional, many with bay or Monument views, but they also have scarred wallpaper and dingy carpeting. The two-bedroom suites are great for four guys on a budget. Friendly staff. Site of the Union nightclub, Porchside cocktail bar, and 11 Carver restaurant. ✉ *9–11 Carver St., 02657,* ☎ *508/487–0688 or 800/434–0130,* FAX *508/487–4918. 25 rooms with private bath. Restaurant. Continental breakfast. Mostly gay male.*

Guest Houses

Central to West End

$$$–$$$$ 🏨 **Brass Key.** Owner Michael MacIntyre further redefined the notion of gay luxury inns by taking over a neighboring guest house and expanding into a full-scale, 33-room resort in 1997. No other property in this market compares. The new rooms are set in a few buildings around a central pool, and every conceivable detail has been considered; furnishings are subtle and elegant New England, and the craftsmanship in the bedrooms and bathrooms is stunning. The original rooms are still wonderful, all with VCRs and many with whirlpool tubs and fireplaces. The inn is done in a colonial folk theme, carried out with original antiques and hand-stenciling; other touches include pickled-wood tables and Hitchcock chairs. The pool, hot tub, and redbrick lanai are among the prettiest in town. Attracts a very professional crowd, 30s to 50s. ⊠ 67 *Bradford St., 02657,* ☎ *508/487–9005 or 800/842–9858,* 𝖥𝖠𝖷 *508/487–9020. 33 rooms with phone, TV, and private bath. Pool, hot tub. Continental breakfast. Mixed gay male/lesbian.*

$$$–$$$$ 🖭 **Land's End Inn.** Atop a bluff in the far West End, Land's End is one of the most unusual buildings in the Cape, and the exotic over-the-top interior of stained glass, Asian wood carvings, and museum-quality antiques is no less memorable. Rooms, suites, and efficiency apartments come in all shapes and sizes, and many command spectacular water views; there's also a wraparound porch facing the bay. ⊠ 22 *Commercial St., 02657,* ☎ *508/487–0706 or 800/276–7088. 17 rooms, 16 with private bath. Continental breakfast. Mixed gay/straight.*

$$$–$$$$ 🖭 **Piaf.** This is the smallest of P-town's luxury inns, a restored 1790s cape hidden down little Prince Street, which is quite charming once you get past the big municipal parking lot. Each of the three rooms shares an elegant European ambience but has its own atmosphere, from the regal *La Vie en Rose* to the sun-filled *Hymne à L'Amour,* with skylights, pitched ceilings, and a kitchenette. This is ideal for couples seeking a quiet retreat. ⊠ 3 *Prince St., 02657,* ☎ *508/487–7458 or 800/340–PIAF,* 𝖥𝖠𝖷 *508/487–8646, e-mail reserve@piaf.com. 3 rooms with phone, TV, and private bath. Continental breakfast. Mixed gay/straight.*

$$–$$$ 🖭 **The Bayberry.** Run as part of the neighboring Beaconlight guest house until summer 1997, this handsome house is filled with eclectic American pieces, many of them antiques. Two rooms have a fireplace, all have VCRs, and the common room is homey and relaxing. ⊠ 16 *Winthrop St., 02657,* ☎ 𝖥𝖠𝖷 *508/487–4605 or 800/422–4605, e-mail bayberry@capecod.net. 6 rooms with TV and private bath. Continental breakfast. Mostly mixed gay male/lesbian.*

$$–$$$ 🖭 **Beaconlight.** Two charming London transplants have brought British elegance to the Beaconlight, thanks to the many antiques from their English home. The building, part of which dates to the 1850s, is one of the most impressive in town: The grounds are lushly landscaped, a piano is often heard from in the living room, an octagonal roof deck affords panoramic views, and the thoroughly plush guest rooms are lavishly furnished and have refrigerators and private baths—several have fireplaces. A hot tub will be added in 1998. ⊠ 12 *Winthrop St., 02657,* ☎ 𝖥𝖠𝖷 *508/487–9603 or 800/696–9603, e-mail beaconlite@capecod.net. 10 rooms with phone, TV, and private bath. Continental breakfast. Mostly mixed gay male/lesbian.*

$$–$$$ 🖭 **Captain & His Ship.** The owners of this stately 1800s sea captain's house have done a fantastic job decorating the high-ceiling rooms with antiques, tasteful fabrics, and many eye-pleasing details. This house is steps from the Boatslip and much of the action on Commercial Street, but it's intimate and quiet enough for those seeking privacy. Very romantic. ⊠ 164 *Commercial St., 02657,* ☎ *508/487–1850 or 800/400–2278. 8 rooms with phone, TV, and private bath. Continental breakfast. Mixed gay/straight.*

$$–$$$ 🖭 **Fairbanks Inn.** This wonderful and historic compound consists of a stately white clapboard colonial—a former captain's house that dates from 1776—a carriage house, and a Victorian next door. The rooms in the main house are cozy and thoughtfully appointed; the two that share a bath are a bargain. Many rooms have working fireplaces, canopy beds, stenciled walls or period papering, and wide-plank floors. There's plenty of homey common space and a beautiful central garden and patio. Great hosts. ⊠ 90 *Bradford St., 02657,* ☎ *508/487–0386 or 800/FAIRBNK,* 𝖥𝖠𝖷 *508/*

487–3540, e-mail fairbank@capecod.net. 14 rooms with TV, most with private bath, 1 apartment. Continental breakfast. Mixed gay/straight.

$$–$$$ 🏨 **Gabriel's.** This is the largest and most social women's guest house. Rooms and apartments (which have full kitchens) are named and themed after famous women: The Georgia O'Keeffe room has southwestern furnishings; the Diane Fosse room has a loft filled with stuffed gorillas. For general use are a large sundeck, two whirlpools, a gym and sauna, and a women's lending library and workshop center. All in all, an excellent, professionally run guest house. ⊠ *104 Bradford St., 02657,* ☎ *508/487–3232 or 800/9MY-ANGEL,* ℻ *508/487–1605, e-mail gabriels@provincetown.com. 20 units with phone and TV, most with private bath. Hot tubs, exercise room. Continental breakfast. Mostly lesbian.*

$$–$$$ 🏨 **Lamplighter Inn.** Friendly and thoughtful hosts Steve and Brent took over this sagging 1830s Federal house in 1995 and have turned it into a terrific guest house. Rooms vary in size but are filled with charming antiques, framed vintage advertisements, and other warm touches. The house sits atop one of the highest points in town, and some rooms—as well as the sundeck—have astounding bay views. The cottage has a full kitchen and sleeps up to four. ⊠ *26 Bradford St., 02657,* ☎ *508/487–2529 or 800/263–6574,* ℻ *508/487–0079, e-mail lamplite@lamplite.com. 9 rooms with phone, TV, and private bath; 1 cottage. Continental breakfast. Mostly mixed gay/lesbian.*

$$–$$$ 🏨 **Sandpiper.** This century-old former boarding house strikes a successful balance between privacy and intimacy. Rooms in this gray, turreted Victorian are warmly appointed, with plenty of hanging plants and large windows; the upper rooms have eaved ceilings and many look over the harbor. Guests have use of the pool, restaurant, and grounds at the Boatslip, next door. ⊠ *165 Commercial St., Box 646, 02657,* ☎ *508/487–1928 or 800/354–8628,* ℻ *508/487–6021, e-mail sandpiper@provincetown.com. 13 rooms with phone, TV, and private bath. Mixed gay/straight.*

$$–$$$ 🏨 **Six Webster Place.** This is one of the town's best-kept secrets. The main 1750s house is one of the oldest in town; it retains the original wide-plank pine floor and wavy-glass windows, and there are fireplaces and antiques everywhere. A second house has apartments, which can be rented by the week. This is a low-key, secluded spot, drawing mostly couples and professionals; Gary, the owner, is a great host. Most rooms have working fireplaces. ⊠ *6 Webster Pl., 02657,* ☎ *508/487–2266 or 800/693-2773.* ℻ *508/487–9242. 7 rooms with TV and private bath, 3 apartments. Hot tub. Continental breakfast. Mostly mixed gay male/lesbian.*

$$–$$$ 🏨 **West End Inn.** Rooms in this Greek Revival may not be the fanciest in town, but they're clean, eclectically decorated, and well looked after; they have peach, pink, and pale-green walls, some papered and some painted. The top-floor suite sleeps four and has a private deck and a half kitchen. Very friendly and professional staff. ⊠ *44 Commercial St., 02657,* ☎ *508/487–9555 or 800/559–1220,* ℻ *508/487–8779. 7 rooms with TV and private bath. Continental breakfast. Mostly mixed gay male/lesbian.*

$$–$$$ 🏨 **White Wind Inn.** This Queen Anne near the Boatslip has comfortable rooms with Berber carpeting, air-conditioning, and, in many cases, four-poster or brass beds, Victorian settees and other period antiques, chandeliers, nautical paintings, fireplaces, and separate entrances. One room has a deck with terrific bay views. ⊠ *174 Commercial St., 02657,* ☎ *508/487–1526,* ℻ *508/487–3985, e-mail wwinn@capecod.net. 11 rooms with TV and private bath. Continental breakfast. Mostly mixed gay male/lesbian.*

$–$$ 🏨 **Ampersand Guesthouse.** This stately white Greek Revival house on a pretty side street in the quiet West End is filled with a mix of tasteful antiques and newer pieces—the rooms are among the best-decorated in town, especially considering the fair rates. The common space is warm and nice for socializing, but guests also enjoy as much privacy as they'd like. The sundeck affords nice views of the bay and this historic neighborhood. ✉ *6 Cottage St., Box 832, 02657,* ☎ *508/487–0959 or 800/574–9645, e-mail ampersan@capecod.net. 12 rooms, most with private bath. Continental breakfast. Mostly mixed gay male/lesbian.*

$–$$ 🖭 **The Bradford-Carver House.** This relatively new guest house, close to nightlife, is one of the best private-bath budget properties, with clean rooms; homey public areas; in-room air-conditioners, refrigerators, and VCRs; use of a substantial video collection, air-conditioning, and congenial laid-back hosts. Some rooms have private entrances. ✉ *70 Bradford St., 02657,* ☎ *508/487–4966 or 800/826–9083,* FAX *508/487–7213. 5 rooms with private bath and TV. Continental breakfast. Mostly mixed gay male/lesbian.*

$–$$ 🖭 **Chicago House.** Near the Pilgrim Monument and steps from the bay, Chicago House is one of Provincetown's original gay guest houses. This pretty white structure is actually two Federal capes joined together. Though it's set on a quiet side street away from the noise of Commercial Street, it's a very social, casual house—the kind of place where you can relax and kick back. A clean, simple interior. ✉ *6 Winslow St., 02657,* ☎ *508/487–0537 or 800/733–7869,* FAX *508/487–6212. 11 rooms, many with TV and private bath, 4 apartments. Continental breakfast. Mostly mixed gay male/lesbian.*

$–$$ 🖭 **Dusty Miller Inn.** A dependable women's choice, this white colonial with black shutters is set near Town Hall on a high hill. It's a homey place, with lots of art, bric-a-brac, pillows, teddy bears, and personal touches. Men may rent any of the rooms with private baths. Adjacent are several nondescript motel units. Gets a young, friendly, social bunch. ✉ *82 Bradford St., 02657,* ☎ *508/487–2213. 13 rooms, some with private bath, 1 apartment. Mostly lesbian.*

$–$$ 🖭 **1807 House.** This is a simple, weathered-shingle cape with several detached apartments (with kitchens) in back. On broad, sweeping grounds with restful gardens and its own gym, this is a good place to chill out and meet fellow guests. Rooms have the ubiquitous blend of Colonial-style furnishings and a few antiques, and four-poster or brass beds. ✉ *54 Commercial St., 02657,* ☎ *508/487–2173, e-mail ptown1807@aol.com. 3 rooms with TV and shared bath, 5 apartments with TV. Mixed gay/straight.*

$–$$ 🖭 **Lady Jane's.** This women's guest house in the West End is one of the best values in town. The cedar-shake guest wing overlooks a garden and contains 10 bright, immaculate rooms, each with bath with blue-tile floor and a selection of walnut and mahogany antiques. Innkeeper Jane Antonil built several of the Adirondack chairs. A popular common room has a VCR and fridge. ✉ *7 Central St., 02657,* ☎ *508/487–3387 or 800/ 523–9526,* FAX *508/487–4259, e-mail ladyjanes@wn.net. 10 rooms with private bath. Continental breakfast. Lesbian.*

$–$$ 🖭 **Revere Guest House.** Of central budget accommodations, this 1830 house is a good bet. Newly furnished and clean, rooms range from small to quite spacious with hardwood floors and a very tasteful mix of antiques. Some of the shared-bath rooms go for as little as $50. ✉ *14 Court St., 02657,* ☎ *508/487–2292 or 800/487–2292, e-mail reveres@tiac.net. 8 rooms, some with TV and private bath. Continental breakfast. Mostly mixed gay male/lesbian.*

$–$$ 🖭 **Watership Inn.** One of the more social guest houses in the neighborhood, the Watership has a large pool and sundeck, is known to host informal parties and mixers from time to time, and has an affable staff. Built in the 1820s and the former home of a prominent sea captain, the house has original floors, beam ceilings, a smattering of antiques, and plenty of character. Rooms are basic but comfy. ✉ *7 Winthrop St., 02657,* ☎ *508/487–0094 or 800/330–9413. 17 rooms, most with TV and private bath. Continental breakfast. Mostly mixed gay male/lesbian.*

$ ☷ **The Ranch.** One of the most social houses in town, the Ranch draws a frisky bunch of younger guys seeking basic but very clean rooms and bathrooms and plenty of camaraderie. It's down the street from the Gifford House, which draws a similar bunch. Some of the lowest rates in town. ☒ *198 Commercial St., 02657,* ☎ *508/487–1542 or 800/942–1542,* ℻ *508/487–3446. 20 rooms with shared bath. Gay male.*

Central to East End

$$$–$$$$ ☷ **Bradford Gardens.** Said to be a favorite hangout of such sapphic celebs as Melissa Etheridge, this is one of the most luxurious gay-frequented inns on the island. Choose from rooms in the 1820s main house, four rose- and wisteria-wrapped cottages, or five two-bedroom town houses—all are set on a hilltop acre of exquisite gardens, noted for their plentitude of Oriental lilies. Even the smaller rooms here are large by Provincetown standards, with private baths, fine antiques, hardwood floors, braided rugs, and classy color schemes. There are also 15 fireplaces set among the several buildings. A delicious full breakfast is prepared daily. ☒ *178 Bradford St., 02657,* ☎ *508/487–1616 or 800/432–2334,* ℻ *508/487–5596, e-mail bradgard@capecod.net. 8 rooms, 4 cottages, 5 town houses, 1 small penthouse. Full breakfast. Mostly mixed gay male/lesbian.*

$$–$$$$ ☷ **Benchmark Inn & Annex.** The folks at the Ranch opened this handsome property in 1997—yet another bit of evidence that P-town's accommodations are becoming increasingly sophisticated. The main inn, a beautifully restored 1840s Greek Revival has rooms with fireplaces, separate entrances, refrigerators, air-conditioning, and VCRs; some have whirlpool tubs, and many have bay views. Rooms next door in the Annex are more basic and less expensive and many share baths; adjacent to the Annex is a large cabana guest room that fronts the common pool and landscaped deck. The whole complex is lovely, with great furnishings and airy rooms. First-class all around. ☒ *8 Dyer St., 02657,* ☎ *508/487–7440 or 888/487–7440,* ℻ *508/487–7442, e-mail benchmark@capecodaccess.com. Inn: 7 rooms with phone, TV, and private bath. Annex: 7 rooms with TV, some with private bath. Pool. Continental breakfast. Mostly gay male.*

$$–$$$ ☷ **Hargood House at Bayshore.** This attractive women-owned apartment complex is one of the best deals in town for long-term visitors—in fact, in high season, only weekly rates are offered. Each unit has a fully equipped kitchen, tasteful furnishings, and plenty of space; most have decks or patios, and many have direct bay views. Guests have use of a private beach and pretty lawn. ☒ *493 Commercial St., 02657,* ☎ ℻ *508/487–9133. 20 units with phone, TV, and private bath. Mixed gay/straight.*

$$–$$$ ☷ **Tradewinds.** Of guest houses with a social reputation, this bustling place is the best of the bunch—attractive individually decorated rooms, outgoing guests, cute houseboys, and not a lot of attitude. Furnishings are contemporary; most rooms have large closets (rare in Provincetown), Berber carpeting, VCRs, refrigerators, and clean tile baths. A lot of care has been put into the inn's upkeep and appearance. There's also a lovely beachfront cottage for rent (sleeps up to four) in the West End. ☒ *12 Johnson St., 02657,* ☎ *508/487–0138 or 800/487–0138,* ℻ *508/487–9484. 16 rooms with TV and private bath, 1 cottage. Hot tub. Continental breakfast. Mostly gay male.*

$$ ☷ **Normandy House.** High on a hill on eastern Bradford Street, this homey spot has VCRs in every room, a sundeck (a bit worn) with great harbor views, and a hot tub in back. There are antiques in some rooms, but decor is mostly a mix of old and new. The third-floor room of this 150-year-old house is sought after for its great views. ☒ *184 Bradford St., 02657,* ☎ *508/487–1197 or 800/487–1197. 8 rooms with TV; most with private bath. Hot tub. Continental breakfast. Mixed gay/straight.*

$$ ⊡ **Tucker Inn.** Katherine Bishop and Denise Karas run this delightfully restored former sea captain's home slightly east of the center of town. The light and spacious rooms are warmly furnished with elegant antiques and handsome bathrooms with tile floors—this place is a real find. ⊠ *12 Center St., 02657,* ☎ *508/487–0381,* ℻ *508/487–6236. 9 rooms with TV, most with private bath; 1 cottages. Continental breakfast. Mostly mixed gay male/lesbian.*

$–$$ ⊡ **Admiral's Landing.** If the feel of yesteryear's Provincetown appeals to you, this a decent choice. Nautically themed art, old tools, antiques, and collectibles fill the common areas and some rooms, which aren't fancy but are full of character. Most have pastel-painted furnishings and walls, and clean baths. Fairly social. ⊠ *158 Bradford St., 02657,* ☎ *508/487–9665 or 800/934–0925,* ℻ *508/487–4437, e-mail adm158@capecod.net. 6 rooms with TV, most with private bath; 2 cottages. Continental breakfast. Mostly gay male.*

$–$$ ⊡ **John Randall House.** This is a terrific inn with extremely reasonable rates and warm attentive hosts—the only slight drawback is the busy location, but the attractive antiques-filled rooms are pretty well-insulated from street traffic. Common amenities include a cheerful garden terrace, a huge movie library, VCRs in every room, and a warm front sunporch. ⊠ *140 Bradford St., 02657,* ☎ *508/487–3533 or 800/573–6700,* ℻ *508/487–3533, e-mail jrhouse@capecod.net. 12 rooms with TV, many with private bath. Continental breakfast. Mixed gay/straight.*

$–$$ ⊡ **Plums.** Run on a small scale but with great attention to detail and guest comforts, this women's house is in a white Victorian with distinctive lavender-and-plum trim and a fence out back covered with dozens of colorful buoys. Rooms are peaceful and have private baths, authentic Victorian furnishings, lace curtains, and flowered wallpaper. ⊠ *160 Bradford St., 02657,* ☎ *508/487–2283. 5 rooms. Full breakfast. Lesbian.*

$–$$ ⊡ **Somerset House.** This courtly 1850 house is one of the nicest of the few gay-popular guest houses in the East End, filled with reproduction and original antiques, pedestal sinks, brass beds, and nautical prints. ⊠ *378 Commercial St., 02657,* ☎ *508/487–0383 or 800/575–1850,* ℻ *508/487–4746, e-mail somrsethse@aol.com. 13 rooms, most with private bath, 1 apartment. Continental breakfast. Mostly mixed gay male/lesbian.*

$–$$ ⊡ **Sunset Inn.** This huge, memorable, white Victorian has a graceful second-floor veranda and a clothing-optional third-floor sundeck. It's a classic New England inn (an Edward Hopper depiction of it hangs at the Yale University Art Gallery). Rooms are bright and cheerful, with hardwood floors, floral bedspreads, pretty but basic furnishings, and local paintings and prints. ⊠ *142 Bradford St., 02657,* ☎ *508/487–9810 or 800/965–1801,* ℻ *508/487–7820. 20 rooms with TV and phone, many with private bath. Continental breakfast. Mixed gay/straight.*

$ ⊡ **Captain's House.** This small old house down an alley off Commercial Street has a surprising number of rooms. It's a budget property through and through, but the friendly owners work hard to keep rooms cheerful and clean (and public areas a bit campy—note the Lucille Ball and Marilyn Monroe memorabilia), and there's a nice little private patio off the side of the house. ⊠ *350A Commercial St., 02657,* ☎ *508/487–9353 or 800/457–8885. 11 rooms with TV, some with private bath. Continental breakfast. Mixed gay/straight.*

$ ⊡ **Heritage House.** The three women who operate this top-notch, affordable accommodation strive to create the sort of friendly atmosphere in which both genders can mingle and have fun. There's lots of common space: The living room is large and bright, with a VCR, sofas, and antiques; and a second-floor veranda has Adirondack chairs and wicker. One drawback: though rooms are simply but smartly decorated, 13 of them share only four baths. ⊠ *7 Center St., 02657,* ☎ *508/487–3692,* ℻ *508/*

487–4776. 13 rooms with shared bath. Full breakfast. Mostly mixed gay male/lesbian.

THE LITTLE BLACK BOOK

At Your Fingertips

Helping Our Women (resource for women with disabilities, ☎ 508/487–4357). **Provincetown AIDS Support Group** (☎ 508/487–9445). **Provincetown Business Guild** (gay/lesbian business and tourism association ✉ 115 Bradford St., Box 421, 02657, ☎ 508/487–2313 or 800/637–8696). **Provincetown Chamber of Commerce** (✉ MacMillan Wharf, 02657, ☎ 508/487–3424).

Gay Media

The Provincetown Business Guild, an alliance of businesses that cater to the gay community, puts out a useful directory detailing its members' services. The weekly, gay-friendly ***Provincetown Magazine*** (☎ 508/487–1000) has restaurant and nightlife listings and articles.

BOOKSTORES

Now, Voyager (✉ 357 Commercial St., ☎ 508/487–0848), an excellent independent bookstore, carries gay and lesbian books and periodicals.

Working Out

Mussel Beach (✉ 35 Bradford St., ☎ 508/487–0001) moved recently into a huge and extremely impressive new facility with plenty of new equipment, aerobics space, and a nice sauna and tanning salon; it remains very queer-popular. The **Provincetown Gym** (✉ 170 Commercial St., ☎ 508/487–2776) is also very nice and gets a broad mix of lesbians and gay men.

33 Out in Rehoboth Beach

THE NATION'S SUMMER CAPITAL," reads the sign that greets you as you enter Rehoboth Beach, largest of the handful of towns along Delaware's 23-mile coast. A flat, 1-mile-square salt-air village, Rehoboth has become the beach resort of choice for gay men and lesbians from Washington, D.C., Baltimore, Philadelphia, and other smaller cities and towns throughout the Mid-Atlantic area.

Most gay resorts grew up around artist colonies, but Rehoboth's roots are religious: In 1873 the Methodists established a summer meeting ground here. A rail line, completed five years later, and steamers shuttling between Cape May and Lewes brought many more visitors, and Rehoboth's popularity as a summertime destination has continued to grow since then. Rehoboth's gay history began during the McCarthy era, when a couple of area bars began developing gay followings. Lesbians and gays continued to settle here in dribs and drabs before 1980, when Glenn Thompson opened a full-scale gay resort, the Renegade. Soon after, the Blue Moon restaurant and bar opened downtown. Both are still going strong. In the mid-1990s, larger numbers of lesbians and gay men began buying homes and opening businesses—shops, real estate agencies, and guest houses, in addition to dozens of restaurants. Today locals speculate that 25% of the town's homes and businesses are lesbian- or gay-owned, and the gay populace now spills beyond Rehoboth's borders to the quieter towns of Milton, Lewes, and Bethany.

Especially on holiday weekends, lesbians and gay men are apparent everywhere in town. They coexist with the families who have traditionally vacationed here, with almost everyone unbegrudgingly accepting the presence of the others. Just about every young dyke and queen within a three-hour drive makes it a point to party here at least once a summer, and many take house shares for the weekends. On some of Rehoboth's streets, every second or third house shows evidence of gay occupancy— a rainbow flag hanging from the front porch or a pink triangle decal on the rear window of a car in the driveway.

To be sure, Rehoboth's transformation into a resort hospitable to queers didn't take place overnight. Antigay violence and harassment have been and continue to be issues, although an activist police chief who came on board in the early 1990s has made it a point to react quickly to antigay violence. In 1997 the Delaware legislature made his job easier when it passed an amendment to the state's hate-crimes law that includes coverage for antigay crimes. The governor signed the amendment into law in Rehoboth, a clear signal that lesbians and gay men are a presence to be reckoned with in the First State—and that Rehoboth is their bastion.

THE LAY OF THE LAND

Beaches

Rehoboth's one-mile-long beach is straight and family-oriented from the northern edge of the Boardwalk down to St. Lawrence Street. The main gay section, **Poodle Beach,** begins south of here, at—appropriately— Queen Street and extends roughly two blocks to Penn Street. Poodle Beach's name allegedly dates to the early 1970s when two gay cousins from Maryland's Eastern Shore would arrive in town on summer weekends in their white Cadillac convertible, two French poodles in tow. On hot summer days this stretch is rife with a tanned and toned posse of mostly male sun worshipers. Most dykes head to the shores of **Cape Henlopen State Park,** a 10-minute drive north of downtown Rehoboth, via Ocean Drive. In season, there's a parking fee ($2.50 for a car with Delaware plates, $5 for out-of-staters). Walk to the beach via the far northern end of the lot; women tend to walk to the right side of the jetty. To the left you'll typically find an older and less body-conscious crowd of guys who favor Cape Henlopen over Poodle Beach.

Downtown

Much of the town's commercial development is along the **Boardwalk,** a hodgepodge of saltwater taffy and pizza parlors, games booths and video arcades, miniature golf courses, and souvenir and surf shops. Many more shops and restaurants line the main drag, **Rehoboth Avenue,** which runs perpendicular to the Boardwalk. A few community-oriented businesses and steadily gay pedestrian traffic notwithstanding, these two thor- oughfares appeal to a predominantly straight crowd.

The two queer shopping and entertainment zones are a block on either side of Rehoboth Avenue. To the north, dozens of boutiques, antiques shops, restaurants, and home-furnishing emporia line **Baltimore Avenue** between First and Second streets, as well as First Street and the mews that connect Baltimore and Rehoboth avenues. To the south, **Wilmington Avenue** has some of the town's trendiest restaurants, most with a gay fol- lowing. It's a 10- to 15-minute walk from these two avenues to Poodle Beach.

For a historic detour, the Boardwalk Plaza Hotel (⊠ Olive Ave. at the Boardwalk), was once the site of Rehoboth's first gay bar, the **Pink Pony,** which stood here through the 1950s. In the two decades prior to the 1980s, several bars opened and closed in this area before things began to boom.

GETTING AROUND

The only practical way here is by car: Airports, train stations, and bus terminals are too far away to justify their use. It's a straightforward three-hour drive from Washington, Baltimore, Philadelphia, or Norfolk, Virginia. From the northeast you can either take the Jersey Turnpike to Wilmington before heading south on U.S. 13/Route 1 (follow the signs for SHORE POINTS). Or, for more scenery in roughly the same amount of time, take the Garden State Parkway to Cape May, New Jersey. Then board the **Cape May-Lewes Ferry** (☎ 800/643–3779; in Delaware: 302/645– 6346 or 302/645–6313; in New Jersey: 609/886–9699; cars cost $18 one-way plus $4.50 for each additional passenger over 12) for Lewes, Delaware, which is 8 mi north of Rehoboth. There are no same-day reser- vations, and there's a $5 reservation fee. The ride takes 70 minutes. The first ferry heads south at 6:20 AM, the last at 7:40 PM.

Once here, almost everything is within walking distance. Taxis are virtu- ally nonexistent. Parking in Rehoboth is tight, although a few accommo- dations have a limited number of spaces. From Memorial Day through

Labor Day, parking permits are required on most streets daily between 10 AM and 5 PM. Permits can be bought for the day ($2 weekdays, $8 weekends), for a three-day weekend ($12), weekly ($20), and for the season (prices vary). You can purchase a permit at two streetside locations as you drive into town: On Rehoboth Avenue between Grove Avenue and State Road (ideal if you're arriving from the north), and on Bayard Avenue just after you cross the bridge into town (if you're arriving from Dewey Beach). Permits are also available at City Hall (⊠ 229 Rehoboth Ave.), the Parking Meter Division (⊠ 30½ Lake Avenue), and at several downtown merchants. If in town for more than a few days, consider renting a bike from **Bob's Rentals** (⊠ First St. and Maryland Ave., ☎ 302/227–7966).

EATS

Rehoboth has two distinct dining scenes. There are dozens of cheap, touristy seafood shanties, pizza parlors, taco joints, and other spots to grab a quick but often mediocre bite, and there are an astonishing number of sophisticated dining rooms with stellar cuisine and prices competitive with Washington's chichiest eateries. At the better restaurants, crowds tend to be mixed gay and straight.

For price ranges, *see* dining Chart A at the front of this guide.

$$$$ ✕ **Fusion.** Floor-to-ceiling windows frame Fusion's four minimalist rooms, an elegant setting for chef Jeffrey Thiemann's fusion of complex East-meets-West cuisine. Expect such rarefied fare as grilled seared rare tuna with sushi rice, tomato-sesame-soy vinaigrette, bean sprouts, snow pea strings, rice sticks, pickled ginger, wasabi coulis, and fermented black beans. ⊠ *50 Wilmington Ave.,* ☎ *302/226–1940.*

$$$$ ✕ **La La Land.** A weathered shingle house with a fanciful blue-and-purple color scheme and dappled chairs makes for an unprepossessing setting, although the service can be haughty. Southwest spiced mahimahi with corn salsa, guacamole, black beans, smoked bell-pepper aioli and fried tortillas exemplifies the New American fare, as does the summery croustade of crab and corn appetizer, served with lemon and chive mayonnaise and marinated cucumber. Very romantic. ⊠ *22 Wilmington Ave.,* ☎ *302/227–3887.*

$$$$ ✕ **Savannah's.** In a contemporary building that has housed several gay-popular restaurants, Savannah's is one of the town's latest hot spots, complete with all the cliched elements of '90s trendiness: cigars, a martini bar, and live jazz. Still, the food is excellent. Try corn and roasted garlic crab cakes, with cilantro and ginger rémoulade and Thai chili-pepper beurre blanc. ⊠ *37 Wilmington Ave.,* ☎ *302/227–1994.*

$$$–$$$$ ✕ **Blue Moon.** The classy Blue Moon, open since 1980, is a superb restaurant and a lively gay bar (*see* Scenes, *below*). Dine either in the airy, open dining room or on the front porch overlooking Baltimore Avenue. Chef Peter McMahon's cutting-edge contemporary cuisine reflects his years cooking in California. Try the shrimp dumplings with a wakame seaweed salad to start, followed by roasted duck breast with Anaheim pepper and sweet potato hash. ⊠ *35 Baltimore Ave.,* ☎ *302/227–6515.*

$$–$$$ ✕ **Cloud 9.** This funky New American restaurant competes favorably with more popular (and expensive) competitors (it doesn't hurt that much of the staff is queer, too). Sixteen or so starters, salads, pastas, and pizzas (try the pie with gulf shrimp, fresh spinach, tomatoes, goat cheese, and pine nuts) are alternatives to the half-dozen main courses, which always include a daily fish special. ⊠ *234 Rehoboth Ave.,* ☎ *302/226–1999.*

$$ ✕ **Iguana Grill.** This old beach cottage on the "gay strip" with a brightly painted wraparound porch and colorful laminated tables has decent southwestern fare, including ten sandwiches, plus calamari, quesadillas, jerk chicken, barbecued ribs, and the like. The busy brunch comes with $1 well drinks. ⊠ *52 Baltimore Ave.,* ☎ *302/227–0948.*

Rehoboth Beach

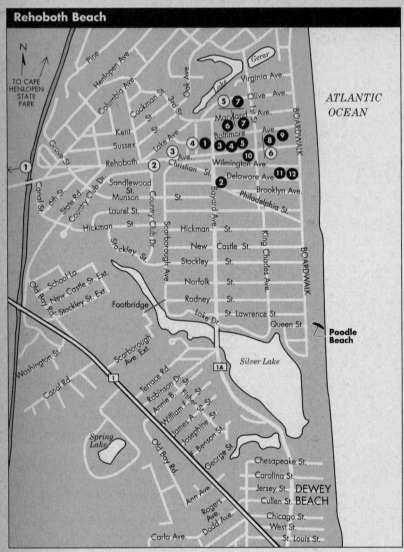

Eats ●

Blue Moon, **7**
Cloud 9, **1**
Coffee Mill, **4**
Dos Locos, **5**
Dream Café, **9**
Fusion, **2**
Iguana Grill, **3**
La La Land, **11**
Lori's, **6**
Mano's, **12**
Plumb Loco, **8**
Savannah's, **10**

Scenes ○

Blue Moon, **5**
Cloud 9, **4**
Oscar's, **3**
Plumb Loco, **6**
Potpourri, **2**
The Renegade, **1**

$$ ✕ **Mano's.** On Rehoboth's premier restaurant row, Mano's has a fairly priced, nothing-fancy menu. The space itself is informal, cheerful, and cavernous, and a vase of sunflowers brightens up each table. Competently prepared and enormously endowed portions of heavenly crab cakes, charcoal-grilled filet mignon, and shrimp and scallop linguine keep the regulars coming back. ⊠ *10 Wilmington Ave.,* ☎ *302/227–6707.*

$–$$ ✕ **Dos Locos.** The best of the few Mexican restaurants in town, Dos Locos serves up nachos, quesadillas, fajitas, burritos, tacos, and chimichangas, as well as specialties such as the kicky Guadalajaran *birria* (chile-and-spice-crusted chicken). Portions are large but excessively pricey ($10.50 for a no-frills burrito?). There's a great patio out back, and it's open late. ⊠ *42½ Baltimore Ave.,* ☎ *302/227–5626.*

$–$$ ✕ **Plumb Loco.** The folks at Dos Locos opened this similarly late-night-oriented restaurant and tavern in 1997. The wood-paneled, nautically themed dining room is cozy, and the casual southwestern fare decent, but Plumb Loco's raison d'être is hanging out with friends. It's quickly established itself as one of Rehoboth's leading dyke hotspots, but all are quite welcome. ⊠ *10 N. First St.,* ☎ *302/227–6870.*

$ ✕ **Dream Café.** Gourmet coffees, rich Belgian waffles, and deli sandwiches (try the provolone with greens and sundried-tomato pesto) are served in this kitschy postmodern building with a huge coffee-cup sculpture perched above the front door—very L.A. looking and very gay. It's also a great place for ice cream and sweets. Closes at 3 PM daily. ⊠ *26 Baltimore Ave.,* ☎ *302/226–2233.*

$ ✕ **Lori's.** This tiny deli in one of the cute mews off of Baltimore Avenue is an ideal place for a take-along lunch for the beach. The hefty sandwiches use very fresh ingredients (one has vine-ripened tomatoes, fresh basil, Vidalia onions, and a smear of mustard on a bagel). Outstanding desserts, too. ⊠ *39 Baltimore Ave.,* ☎ *302/226–3066.*

Coffeehouse Culture

✕ **Coffee Mill.** Amid a row of quaint queer-popular boutiques, this intimate coffeehouse sells great drinks and snacks as well as related gifts and accessories. The owners recently opened a small branch at the Renegade (*see* Scenes, *below*) that'll remain open until 4 AM, well after liquor has been cut off. ⊠ *127B Rehoboth Mews,* ☎ *302/227–7530.*

SCENES

Much of the early-evening socializing revolves around the lounges at several popular restaurants. **Oscar's** (⊠ 247 Rehoboth Ave., ☎ 302/227–0789) and **Potpourri** (⊠ 316 Rehoboth Ave., ☎ 302/227–4227) typically have live piano and cabaret acts. **Cloud 9** (*see* Eats, *above*) has a DJ many nights, and is a great place to cut loose. Otherwise, the long-running **Blue Moon** and **Renegade** (*see below*) remain the region's mainstays. Overall the scene is fairly mellow, with the only high-energy action found at the Renegade. There are no women's bars, but dykes are abundant everywhere men are, though less so at the Blue Moon. Also, the new eatery **Plumb Loco** (*see* Eats, *above*) has made a successful effort to provide a fun and friendly space for dykes.

Blue Moon. A rare gay-owned restaurant-cum-bar that could survive solely on the merit of either venue. The bar here is small but chatty and downright packed on weekends and during the daily late-afternoon tea dances. The tiny inside section is standing room only; the wooden deck out back (watch out for unexpected steps) has a central section that's usually as packed as inside, but the peripheral area is usually quieter. ⊠ *35 Baltimore Ave., 302/227–6515. Crowd: mostly male, mixed ages, very convivial and down-to-earth on weekdays.*

The Renegade. You need a car to reach this classic gay resort, just off Route 1, a ten-minute drive from the center of town (parking is plentiful but chaotic). Inside there's a main cruise bar with a pool table and some video games and beyond it a mid-size dance floor. The music, sound, and lighting are all stellar. One corner of the dance floor always seems to draw a lot of dykes; the rest of it packs in the shirtless pretty boys from D.C. The deck outside gets a much mellower—though still dense—crowd of lesbians and gay men. ⊠ *4274 Rte. 1,* ☎ *302/227–4713. Crowd: 80/20 m/f, mostly under 35, varied, attitudy on the dance floor, friendlier out on the decks.*

SLEEPS

Rehoboth has surprisingly few motels and hotels on the Boardwalk; what few you'll find cater principally to families and straights. If a sea view matters to you, you might consider one of the motels, or consult a rental agent about renting a place. The gay-oriented places are a block or two from the water. Book well ahead, especially if you're trying for one of the relatively few gay-owned guest houses. You'll save 25% to 50% by visiting in spring or fall. If you and a group of friends plan to come for a week or longer, it's generally much more economical to rent a house, which is what the vast majority of the families who vacation here do.

For price ranges, *see* lodging Chart A at the front of this guide.

$$$–$$$$ ⛱ **Brighton Suites.** The spacious rooms at this contemporary sand-color hotel are each done in beachy pinks and teals. They're nothing fancy, but all have a fridge, freezer, and wet bar. Although it caters mostly to families, it's very gay-friendly. ⊠ *34 Wilmington Ave., 19971,* ☎ *302/227–5780 or 800/227–5788,* 𝖥𝖠𝖷 *302/227–6815. 66 rooms with phone, TV, and private bath. Restaurant, pool, exercise room. Mostly straight.*

$$$ ⛱ **Chesapeake Landing.** Just south of Silver Lake and a block from the beach, this stunning three-story inn is one of Rehoboth's most recent additions. The interior sparkles with attractive contemporary furnishings, light-filled rooms, and a secluded deck and pool. An excellent higher-end option. ⊠ *101 Chesapeake St., 19971,* ☎ *302/227–2973,* 𝖥𝖠𝖷 *302/227–0301. 4 rooms with private bath. Continental breakfast. Pool. Mostly mixed gay male/lesbian.*

$$$ ⛱ **Mallard House on Baltimore Avenue.** After suffering through a fire a few years ago, this attractive guest house has been fully refurbished with beautiful antiques and designer fabrics. Two of the rooms have private balconies. In the heart of the action on Baltimore Avenue, it draws a fairly social bunch. A 10-bedroom sister property at 67 Lake Avenue is a short walk away. ⊠ *60 Baltimore Ave., 19971,* ☎ *302/226–3448. 6 rooms with private bath. Continental breakfast. Mostly gay male.*

$$–$$$ ⛱ **At Melissa's.** It isn't fancy, but this woman-operated inn close to the beach and Wilmington Avenue's restaurant row has loads of character and a warm, homey ambience—devotees claim it's like staying with old friends. Guest rooms are done with fun colors, and the front porch has loungy chairs and a pile of board games—ideal for those rainy days. An attic suite can sleep six. ⊠ *36 Delaware Ave., 19971,* ☎ *302/227–7504 or 800/396–8090,* 𝖥𝖠𝖷 *302/227–3628. 6 rooms, some with private bath. Continental breakfast. Mixed gay/straight.*

$$–$$$ ⛱ **Cabana Gardens B&B.** This spanking-new contemporary inn has some of the largest and brightest rooms in town and successfully blends the warmth of a B&B with the privacy and professional look of a small inn. Rooms have a simple uncluttered feel with rattan and wicker resort furniture; all of them open onto balconies, and steps lead to a dramatic roofdeck with views of neighboring Lake Gerar. ⊠ *20 Lake Ave., 19971,*

☎ *302/227–5429,* ₣ᴬˣ *302/227–5380. 5 rooms with TV and private bath. Continental breakfast. Mostly mixed gay male/lesbian.*

$$–$$$ ▪ **Cape Suites.** In the heart of the gay area, this three-story cement structure (think Berlin circa 1960) is impersonal, but rooms are large and clean, have two separate bedrooms, two TVs, a frig and microwave, private entrances, and porches overlooking Baltimore Avenue. For two couples traveling together, it's one of the best deals in town. ⊠ *47 Baltimore Ave., 19971,* ☎ *302/226–3342. 8 suites with phone, TV, and private bath. Mixed gay/straight.*

$$–$$$ ▪ **Guest Rooms at Rehoboth.** Each of the four bedrooms at the charming Guest Rooms at Rehoboth has a different theme: Choose from Shaker, Victorian, art deco, or eclectic. The latter has a cozy sleigh bed that's perfect for snuggling away a rainy Sunday. This small cedar-shake house with peacock trim is in the heart of gay territory. ⊠ *45 Baltimore Ave., 19971,* ☎ ₣ᴬˣ *302/226–2400. 4 rooms with TV, 2 with private bath. Continental breakfast. Mixed gay male/lesbian.*

$$–$$$ ▪ **Mallard House on Lake Street.** The less fancy and more affordable cousin of the Mallard on Baltimore, this place is quiet and secluded—a traditional white-bread-looking '50s summer house that's been chopped up into clean, smartly furnished rooms. It's a 25-minute walk to Poodle Beach, and a 10-minute drive to Cape Henlopen State Park Beach. ⊠ *67 Lake Ave., 19971,* ☎ *302/226–3448. 7 rooms with private bath. Continental breakfast. Mostly gay male.*

$$–$$$ ▪ **Ram's Head.** The explicit brochures for this place capture the intensely sexual atmosphere but fail to convey just how clean, pleasantly decorated, and lushly landscaped this resort is. It's the only all-male resort in Rehoboth, and, indeed, it's an ideal spot if you're looking for action—both the pool and ten-man sauna get pretty frisky. Rooms are quite large (all have VCRs, useful for surfing the extensive [and hot] video library); try to get one of the three new poolside rooms added in 1997. The only drawback is that you'll need a car to get to and from downtown. ⊠ *R.D. 2, Box 509, 19971,* ☎ *302/226–9171, e-mail tworams41@aol.com. 9 rooms with phone and private bath. Continental breakfast. Pool, hot tub, exercise room. Gay male.*

$$–$$$ ▪ **Rehoboth Guest House.** A homey, and at times very social, accommodation, the Rehoboth Guest House is in a white clapboard house with pale blue trim, a 15- to 20-minute walk from Poodle Beach but a block from the gay commercial strip. With very basic furnishings and a nice deck, the place has the feel of a summer rooming house. Recent renovations have included the addition of private baths to most rooms. ⊠ *40 Maryland Ave.,* ☎ *302/227–4117 or 800/564–0493. 12 rooms, most with private bath. Continental breakfast. Mixed gay male/lesbian.*

$$–$$$ ▪ **Silver Lake.** This is one of the nicest of Rehoboth's inns, with friendly and professional innkeepers, and views across Silver Lake and, from some rooms, of the ocean (Poodle Beach is a 10-minute walk). A third floor was added in 1997; the rooms up here are the most impressive, with French doors opening on to private decks. There are also some apartments with kitchens and two bedrooms, ideal for couples traveling together. ⊠ *133 Silver Lake Dr., 19971,* ☎ *302/226–2115 or 800/842–2115,* ₣ᴬˣ *302/226–2732. 13 rooms with TV and private bath, 2 2-bedroom apartments. Continental breakfast. Mostly gay male.*

$$ ▪ **Renegade.** The region's first and only fully gay resort is a 10-minute drive from the beach, near Route 1. Rooms are of the standard, nondescript motel variety. It's worth staying here if everywhere else is booked, or because you want to be where the action is (*see* Scenes, *above*). ⊠ *4274 Rte. 1,* ☎ *302/227–1222,* ₣ᴬˣ *302/227–4281, e-mail renegade@ce.net. 28 rooms with phone, TV, and private bath. Restaurant. Mostly mixed gay male/lesbian.*

$$ ⊞ **Sand In My Shoes.** For those Gidgets who want a homey, beachy feel, this two-story former motel six blocks from the beach offers rooms with private baths and sundecks. It's on a dirt road by the Rehoboth–Lewes Canal, on the edge of town. Guest take advantage of the spacious common area with TV and video library, stereo, and grand piano. ⊠ *6th and Canal Sts., 19971,* ☎ *302/226–2006. 12 rooms. Hot tub. Continental breakfast. Mostly lesbian.*

$$ ⊞ **Shore Inn.** This former mainstream motor lodge has been purchased by two men and is now run as a mostly queer resort, complete with a festive pool, deck, and hot tub. Otherwise standard rooms have been brightened considerably with attractive color schemes and fabrics. It's a bit of a haul from the beach, closer to Route 1 than to downtown Rehoboth. ⊠ *703 Rehoboth Ave., 19971,* ☎ FAX *302/227–8487 or 800/597–8899, e-mail shoreinn@ce.net. 14 rooms with phone, TV, and private bath. Continental breakfast. Pool, hot tub. Mostly gay male.*

THE LITTLE BLACK BOOK

At Your Fingertips
AIDS Hotline of Delaware (☎ 800/422–0429). **Camp Rehoboth** (lesbian/gay community service organization, ⊠ 39 Baltimore Ave., Rehoboth Beach, 19971, ☎ 302/227–5620). **Rehoboth Beach–Dewey Beach Chamber of Commerce** (⊠ 501 Rehoboth Ave., Box 216, Rehoboth Beach 19971, ☎ 302/227–2233 or 800/441–1329, Web site www.dmv.com/business/rehoboth).

Gay Media
The nonprofit group **Camp Rehoboth** (*see above*), an outstanding community resource, publishes a helpful and informative newspaper, **Letters from Camp Rehoboth** (☎ 302/227–5620, Web site www.camprehoboth .com), every two weeks from early March to late November. Copies of the paper are free at many of the establishments it lists. The **Rehoboth Beach Gayzette** (☎ 302/644–1032, e-mail rbg@gayrehoboth.com) is a new monthly rag with news and entertainment coverage about the town's gay community.

BOOKSTORES
Stop by the tiny outpost of the Washington and Baltimore lesbigay bookstore **Lambda Rising** (⊠ 39 Baltimore Ave., ☎ 302/227–6969). The staff is friendly and knowledgeable. It's open daily 10 AM–midnight.

Working Out
Body Shop Fitness Center (⊠ Virginia Ave. at the Boardwalk, ☎ 302/226–0920) is right on the Boardwalk, but it's tiny. Near the Renegade just outside of town, the **Sussex Family YMCA** (⊠ 105 Church St., ☎ 302/227–8018) has a large exercise room and an indoor heated pool.

34 Out in Sacramento

THE CAPITAL OF CALIFORNIA has always been more popular with business travelers than vacationers, perhaps because it lacks certain quintessentially Californian attributes: craggy mountain peaks, sweeping views of the Pacific, dramatically desolate deserts, verdant redwood forests. A river city of politics and commerce, Sacramento is in many ways spiritually closer to Chicago than it is to San Francisco or Los Angeles—the feel here is more friendly Midwest than California chic.

California pioneer John Sutter established a modest frontier outpost in 1839 in what is now Midtown Sacramento. The area remained relatively sedate until 1848, when James Marshall discovered gold while building a sawmill for Sutter on the American River, initiating the famous gold rush of 1849. Sacramento became the state capital in 1854, four years after California was admitted to the Union.

The city of Sacramento has a population of 400,000; a total of 1.5 million people live in its four-county metropolitan area. There are two gay newspapers, an excellent lesbigay bookstore and a long-standing feminist one, and a queer community center that moved into impressive digs in 1996. Local gays have an excellent record of AIDS and community fund-raising and a definite say in city politics. But they're not a conspicuous lot: You won't see many rainbow flags, even in gayified Lavender Heights, and the club scene isn't a cruisy or high-profile one. One recent transplant describes the city as "a nice place to move to when you've already done everything and everybody."

Sacramento is an ideal hub from which to explore northern California; it's within a two-hour drive of Tahoe, Reno, Yosemite, the Gold Country, the Wine Country, the Russian River, and San Francisco. If you're visiting this part of the state for the first time, the city may not be your highest priority. But don't rule it out, especially if California history or the Old West interests you. There's enough here to keep you busy for a long weekend, and you'll find the the scene here more accessible than in the Golden State's gay meccas.

THE LAY OF THE LAND

Relatively flat and laid out on a grid, Downtown and Midtown Sacramento—the two city's two core neighborhoods—are eye-pleasing and walkable. The freshly painted homes that line the tree-shaded residential streets here represent a cross-section of America's architectural history, in particular from the years between 1880 and 1960. Commercial developers have for the most part respected the aesthetics of these historic neighborhoods. Sixteenth Street officially separates commercial Downtown from residential Midtown, but the two halves blend both visually and psychologically. Adjacent to central Sacramento are several more attractive residential areas.

Downtown and Old Sacramento

Downtown begins southeast of the confluence of two broad waterways, the Sacramento and the American rivers. You can explore the restored vestiges of the city's earliest commercial settlement, **Old Sacramento,** which boomed during the gold rush. Constant flooding forced businesses to relocate to slightly higher ground a few blocks east of the river. Old Sacramento's Victorian-era structures fell into a state of disrepair, and the neighborhood's demise was exacerbated in the 1960s by the construction of I–5, which cuts these blocks off from the rest of the city.

In the '70s, preservationists and entrepreneurs recognized Old Sacramento's potential and turned it into the city's most visited attraction. Highly commercial, Old Sacramento is nevertheless an engaging stop. With horse-drawn carriages, frontier-style buildings with wooden balconies and period details, and riverboats tied up along the boardwalk fronting the Sacramento River, this festive district has the feel of a Mississippi River town. The restored Central Pacific Passenger Depot, conversely, recalls a scene out of America's Wild West. Stop by the **Visitor Information Center** (⊠ 2nd and K Sts., ☎ 916/442–7644) to get yourself situated.

In between poking around the trinkets shops and filling up on fudge and ice cream, step inside the one must-see in Old Sacramento, the **California State Railroad Museum** (⊠ 125 I St., ☎ 916/552–5252, ext. 7245). The 21 rail cars at the best such facility in the country detail the state's fascinating relationship with trains and train travel. The bakeries, ethnic food outlets, and meat and produce stalls of the **Old Sacramento Public Market** (⊠ Front and K Sts.) draw a steady stream of local fags. Locals pooh-pooh the cuisine at the restaurant at the **Riverboat Delta King** (⊠ 1000 Front St.), a hotel docked on the Sacramento River, but the bar makes a nice stop for a late-afternoon cocktail. A **water taxi** (⊠ L St. Landing, ☎ 916/448–4333) makes six loops up the river and back and stops at several restaurants along the waterfront.

East of Old Sacramento and I–5 is **Downtown Plaza** (⊠ bordered by 4th, 7th, J, and L Sts.), whose shops, restaurants, and cinemas include a brand-new Hard Rock Cafe. East of here are more shops and businesses along the pedestrian-only **K Street Mall** (⊠ K St., from 7th St. to 13th St.). Head south of the mall to tour Sacramento's most famous structure, the 1874 **State Capitol** (⊠ 10th and L Sts., ☎ 916/324–0333). The domed structure anchors dashing **Capitol Park.** Filled with colorful flora, the park attracts the occasional deranged character (often an elected official). You can also visit the nearby **Governor's Mansion** (⊠ 1526 H St., ☎ 916/323–3047), built in 1877 and home to California's heads of state between 1903 and 1967.

Southwest of the capitol, you can get a real feel for how the wealthy lived in 19th-century California at the **Stanford Mansion State Historic Park** (⊠ 802 N St., ☎ 916/324–0575), the 1856 home of one of the state's first governors. The **Crocker Art Museum** (⊠ 216 O St., ☎ 916/264–5423), the oldest art museum in the West, contains 700 European and American paintings. West of I–5 at V Street, the **Towe Ford Museum of Automotive History** (⊠ 2200 Front St., ☎ 916/442–6802) contains vintage cars and trucks, many of them Fords.

Midtown and Lavender Heights

Midtown, which is due east of Downtown, has few attractions but is an ideal neighborhood for shopping, dining, and admiring numerous examples of Victorian, Craftsman, Arts and Crafts, Spanish Revival, and Colonial

Revival architecture. The section of Midtown between 20th and 29th streets and E and N streets is known to many as **Lavender Heights,** owing to its high number of gay-owned homes and businesses. Some funky shopping can be found along **J Street** and the blocks immediately off it. The intriguing **State Indian Museum** (⊠ 2601 K St., ☎ 916/324–0971) contains arts, crafts, and historical exhibits. At the nearby **Sutter's Fort** (⊠ 2701 L St., ☎ 916/445–4422) is the restored adobe structure in which John Sutter set up his trading post.

Greater Sacramento

The blocks of J Street between 40th and 45th streets, known as the **Fabulous Forties,** contain the city's fanciest mansions. North of Downtown, **Del Paso Boulevard** is fast becoming a second gay district. Many of its formerly dull and decrepit storefronts have been converted into design shops, art galleries, and even a few restaurants and bars. The gorgeous **American River Bike Trail,** which is popular with queers at certain points (particularly at the end of North 10th Street and also at La Riviera Drive), winds for 23 miles from Old Sacramento to Folsom Lake.

GETTING AROUND

You can see most of Sacramento on foot. You may need to park in a garage Downtown, but in Midtown it's easy to find a space on the street. If your feet need a rest, use the free shuttle bus that loops past the convention center, the K Street Mall, Downtown Plaza, and Old Sacramento.

EATS

The tone at Sacramento restaurants is considerably less rushed and more friendly than in San Francisco and Los Angeles. Many of the best places to dine are in Lavender Heights and have decidedly queer followings.

For price ranges, *see* dining Chart B at the front of this guide.

$$$–$$$$ ✕ **1201.** One of the city's few eateries with an equally strong following among local queers and political power brokers, 1201 is a short walk from the capitol. Highlights from the haute world-beat menu include house-smoked quail on braised fennel with a tomato vinaigrette, and sesame-crusted ahi with baby bok choy, asparagus, wasabi crème fraîche, ginger, and cellophane noodles. ⊠ *1201 K St., ☎ 916/444–1015.*

$$$ ✕ **Scorpio's.** Don't be turned off by its location at a Best Western (albeit a nice one): Scorpio's transcends the genre of hotel dining. The subtly elegant space, bathed in muted grays, is redolent of fine Continental-American food, including melt-in-your-mouth pistachio-crusted sea bass and sassy sun-dried-cherry–glazed pork chops. ⊠ *815 11th St., ☎ 916/325– 4949.*

$$–$$$ ✕ **City Treasure.** A culinary treasure indeed, City Treasure is one of several hopping and relatively new purveyors of New World (as in New American but with international panache) cuisine. Among the stars are cioppino with fried polenta, Cajun shepherd's pie, and Caribbean salad with spicy jerk chicken strips. ⊠ *1730 L St., ☎ 916/447–7380.*

$$–$$$ ✕ **Moxie.** Just about every resident of Lavender Heights, not to mention folks from other parts of town, is fussing over the delightful, reasonably priced victuals prepared at this refined and romantic space. Jambalaya, crab pot stickers, and medallions of pork with scallions, ginger, and sesame-seed butter are among the diverse offerings. ⊠ *2028 H St., ☎ 916/443–7585.*

$$ ✕ **Aioli Bodega Español.** Soft lighting and vibrant Spanish-style murals warm the eyes at this chic dining room where the hearty authentic cooking, from mussels in garlic and a sherry-wine cream sauce to white-bean

Sacramento

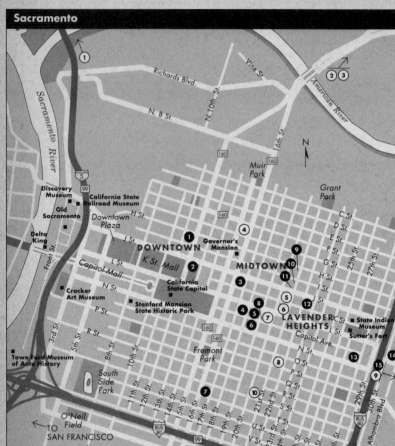

Eats ●

Aioli Bodega
Español, **5**
Barrett's, **14**
Café Bernardo, **13**
City Treasure, **4**
Cornerstone, **12**
Ernesto's, **7**
Hamburger Mary's, **3**
Moxie, **9**

New Helvetia Roasters and
Bakers, **8**
The Open Book, **11**
Paesanos, **6**
Scorpio's, **1**
33rd Street Bistro, **15**
1201, **2**
Weatherstone
Coffee and
Trading, **10**

Scenes ○

Bolt, **3**
Faces, **6**
Garage, **10**
Joseph's, **2**
Mercantile, **7**
Mirage, **4**
Mr. Bojangles, **9**
Townhouse, **8**
Verona Village, **1**
Western Pacific
Depot, **5**
Wreck Room, **11**

casserole with spicy sausage, warms the soul. Aioli Bodega is one of two outstanding tapas restaurants in Lavender Heights. Tapa the World, at J and 21st streets, is the other, should you have trouble getting a table here. ⊠ *1800 L St.,* ☎ *916/447–9440.*

$$ ✕ **33rd Street Bistro.** The staggering popularity of this restaurant east of Midtown sometimes translates into a wait for a table and always entails enduring the din of the crowd, but persevere if at all possible. Outstanding New American fare like the Manila clams and gulf prawns with spinach and prosciutto and a panini of fire-roasted pork loin with Gorgonzola relish, fresh apples, and herb mayonnaise await you. ⊠ *3301 Folsom Blvd.,* ☎ *916/455–2282.*

$–$$ ✕ **Café Bernardo.** Gaggles of local queers crowd the sidewalk tables and Parisian-influenced dining room of this smart Cal-French-Italian eatery. You'll get plenty of bang for your buck feasting on the grilled salmon with roasted new potatoes and a lemon-basil vinaigrette or the stir-fry of hoisin chicken, asparagus, oyster mushrooms, carrots, and noodles. ⊠ *2726 Capitol Ave.,* ☎ *916/443–1180.*

$–$$ ✕ **Ernesto's.** A great spot to sip margaritas and dish with your pals, Ernesto's is a fixture of the queer community, as much for its atmosphere as for its pleasant but standard Mexican fare—carne asada, tamales, enchiladas, and the like. Grab a seat on the sidewalk patio or in the festive dining room with Frida Kahlo prints on the walls. ⊠ *1901 16th St.,* ☎ *916/441–4340.*

$ ✕ **Cornerstone.** Each day, dykes and fags pile inside this frumpy diner for eggs and bacon, hash browns, burgers, and grilled-cheese sandwiches. The waitresses, all of whom look like they could have auditioned for the '70s sitcom *Alice,* gab away with the locals and everybody has a wonderful, artery-hardening time. ⊠ *2330 J St.,* ☎ *916/441–0948.*

$ ✕ **Hamburger Mary's.** The Sacramento branch of the ubiquitous queer franchise is inside a cozy Victorian building, with red leather booths, southwestern-inspired colors and designs, and a popular cocktail bar. Expect the usual burgers (including some veggie versions), nachos, and sandwiches (try the char-broiled mahimahi). ⊠ *1630 J St.,* ☎ *916/441–4340.*

$ ✕ **Barrett's.** This perky, seat-yourself, deco-style café is ideal for breakfast or lunch and is as gay as can be, especially on weekends. Teriyaki burgers, eggs Benedict, and a well-rounded sampling of salads are among the better dishes. ⊠ *1221 Alhambra Blvd.,* ☎ *916/737–0694.*

$ ✕ **Paesanos.** A loud and airy haunt of guppies and yuppies, Paesanos specializes in brick-oven pizzas and pastas but also serves inventive salads and sandwiches, such as oven-baked tri-tip and Italian sausage on sourdough bread with onions, mushrooms, smoked gouda, and Chianti. ⊠ *1806 Capitol Ave.,* ☎ *916/447–8646.*

Coffeehouse Culture

New Helvetia Roasters and Bakers. Named for the Swiss settlement John Sutter established on this site in the 1830s, the New Helvetia is one of the queerest coffeehouses in a city with plenty of terrific options. It's steps from the gay community center inside a warm and appealing converted redbrick firehouse. ⊠ *1215 19th St.,* ☎ *916/441–1106.*

The Open Book. The small informal café attached to Sacramento's lesbigay bookstore frequently stages author readings and other community events. The crowd is diverse in age and attitude. The tight layout encourages mingling. ⊠ *910 21st St.,* ☎ *916/498–1004.*

Weatherstone Coffee and Trading. It's difficult to stroll by this converted redbrick carriage house and not be lured in for a cup of espresso and some intensely interesting people-watching—the mix here is students, professionals, and genXers. Old-fashioned street lamps and wrought-iron fencing and furniture decorate a splendid arbored patio. ⊠ *812 21st St.,* ☎ *916/443–6340.*

SCENES

Couples-oriented Sacramento has a low-key bar scene. Local queers aren't into staying out all night and tend to seek out alternatives to the clubs, which accounts for the high concentration of coffeehouses and the tight network of gay social organizations. Not that you can't have a great night on the town. The choices are becoming more varied, with some new clubs opening recently and some old standbys moving into bigger and better digs. Wherever you go, you'll encounter minimal attitude and a balance of ages, genders, and styles.

Prime Suspects

Bolt. This dark bare-bones leather-and-Levi's bar in Del Paso Heights has a long bar, darts, pool, a small dance floor (the music ranges from alternative to dance), and an intimate patio out back. The place can get crowded on weekends but is pretty much a neighborhood hangout the rest of the week. Very friendly if you fit the look, and cruisy. From Del Paso Boulevard take the first right after El Camino. ⊠ *2560 Boxwood St.,* ☎ *916/649–8420. Crowd: male, 30s and 40s, some leather, butch, bulked up or bearish, goatees.*

Faces. For many years this has been the city's main event for men and women, but the opening of the Garage (*see below*) may diminish the popularity of Faces. The club has become increasingly straight in recent years, a trend some locals speculate may continue. For the moment, everybody here seems to get along. The spaces include a quiet cocktail lounge up front, a cruisy video bar with a show stage, an industrial dance floor with I-beams and strobe lights, and a sprawling covered patio. Some nights feature country-western dancing or are predominantly for dykes. ⊠ *2000 K St.,* ☎ *916/448–7798. Crowd: 65/35 m/f, some straights, all ages, somewhat racially mixed, disco bunnies, gym queens, guppies, lipstick lesbians.*

Garage. This two-level club with a large disco and a balcony looking down on the action opened in early 1998 on the site of the Buffalo lesbian bar. The set-up includes a coffeehouse. The club stays open after hours on weekends. ⊠ *1831 S St.,* ☎ *916/442–1087. Crowd: still evolving, but mixed m/f, all ages, fairly trendy.*

Joseph's. Despite a recent move to Del Paso Boulevard, Joseph's still draws a neighborhood crowd, along with drag queens and devotees of cabaret. The setting, in a vintage redbrick building with peach walls, bentwood chairs, and good but not loud music, is ideal for conversation. The patrons are down-to-earth—definitely not as dressy as the interior. The attached restaurant serves standard American and Continental fare, and there's a cabaret on the second floor. Quite a few women come here now that the city has no official dyke bar. ⊠ *1454 Del Paso Blvd. (take 16th St. north from Midtown),* ☎ *916/922–8899. Crowd: 70/30 m/f, mid-30s and up, low-key.*

Townhouse. An early-in-the-evening hangout, this rollicking bar has a downstairs saloon with a long bar and a few red-vinyl seats. The upstairs space, which has pool, darts, and other games, feels a bit like a frat-house rec room. The karaoke nights are big here. ⊠ *1517 21st St.,* ☎ *916/441–5122. Crowd: 80/20 m/f, 20s to 50s, fairly local, semi-cruisy, an even mix of hunks, chunks, and punks.*

Western Pacific Depot. This longtime neighborhood hangout is looking quite snazzy after a 1997 makeover, and the new management's attempt to capture the ambience of video bars like the Midnight Sun in San Francisco or Revolver in Los Angeles shows potential. Western Pacific is across the street from Faces; plenty of guys (but only a few women) head back and forth between the two. ⊠ *2001 K St.,* ☎ *916/443–9831. Crowd: mostly male, 20s to 40s, some stand-and-model but fairly low-key.*

Wreck Room. When it's still light outside, walking into this pitch-black leather bar on the southern edge of Midtown poses more danger than staring directly into a solar eclipse. Once inside, you'll have to feel your way around to find a bar stool or, failing that, a friendly local familiar enough with the layout to order a drink for you. A second room off the bar is lit better and has pool tables, a leather boutique, and a stage that hosts amateur strip shows, armpit contests, and other crowd-pleasing events. As for the clientele, the big fuzzy stuffed bear sitting above the cigarette machine says it all. Open after hours on weekends. ⊠ *2513 Broadway,* ☎ *916/456–1181. Crowd: male, mostly over 30, leather and Levi's, butch.*

Neighborhood Haunts

The **Mercantile** (⊠ 1928 L St., ☎ 916/447–0792), an edgy, guys-oriented tavern, has a loyal following. The **Mirage** (⊠ 601 15th St., ☎ 916/444–3238) gets a mix of lesbians and gay men after work but quiets down later in the evening. Large, well-lit, and rarely very crowded, it has pool, pinball, and darts. The owner of Faces opened **Verona Village** (⊠ 6985 Garden Hwy., ☎ 916/656–1320 or 800/550–1320) not long ago. This complex on the banks of the Sacramento River has a restaurant, a bar, a piano cabaret, and considerable potential, though it's a good 20-minute drive from Downtown (take I–5 and Highway 99 north; head west on Riego Road and north on the Garden Highway).

Hangin' with the Hets

Mr. Bojangles (⊠ 7042 Folsom Blvd., ☎ 916/382–9882) opened as a gay club, but it's now straight except on Wednesday, when an angst-ridden, hormones-raging posse of 18-and-over gay, bi, or curious suburban kids dances the night away. If you're over 25 and don't own a skateboard, you may feel out of place.

SLEEPS

If you stay near the capitol or Downtown, you'll be within walking distance of Lavender Heights. The city has dozens of chain properties and several nice B&Bs, the best of which happens to be gay-owned.

For price ranges, *see* lodging Chart B at the front of this guide.

Hotels

$$$–$$$$ ⊞ **Hyatt Regency.** Well-run and with spacious, bright, and airy rooms, this modern high-rise towers above Capitol Park. The rates are high on weekdays but sometimes drop on weekends and holidays. ⊠ *1209 L St., 95814,* ☎ *916/443–1234 or 800/233–1234,* ✉ *916/321–6699. 500 rooms. Restaurant, pool, health club.*

$$ ⊞ **Best Western Sutter House.** This owner-managed property maintains a higher standard than most in the chain. The rooms are clean and comfortable, the restaurant is outstanding (*see* Scorpio's *in* Eats, *above*), and the location is equidistant from Lavender Heights, the capitol building, and Old Sacramento. ⊠ *1100 H St., 95814,* ☎ *916/441–1314 or 800/830–1314,* ✉ *916/441–5961. 98 rooms. Restaurant, pool.*

$ ⊞ **Quality Inn.** The rooms and level of service at this basic motor inn are a cut above those at Sacramento's other budget properties, and it's just minutes from gay nightlife. Don't let the dated exterior turn you off: This is a solid option. ⊠ *818 15th St., 95814,* ☎ *916/444–3980 or 800/228–5151,* ✉ *916/444–2991. 40 rooms. Pool.*

Guest Houses and Small Hotels

$$$$ ⊞ **Sterling Hotel.** If money's no object, this dramatic Victorian hotel will suit you nicely. The lavishly decorated rooms have Jacuzzi baths and many business amenities, the staff is first-rate, and the management is gay-friendly.

1300 H St., 95814, ☎ *916/448–1300,* FAX *916/448–8066. 21 rooms with phone, TV, and private bath. Restaurant. Mostly straight.*

$$–$$$ ⊞ **Hartley House.** One of the top gay-operated guest houses on the West Coast, Hartley House is a marvelously restored turn-of-the-century structure with stained woodworking, stained-glass windows, and rooms with first-class amenities like data ports and Neutrogena soap and shampoo. The highly professional staff prepares a delicious full breakfast and can provide a top-notch gourmet dinner with 24-hours notice. ⊠ *700 22nd St., 95816,* ☎ *916/447–7829 or 800/831–5806,* FAX *916/447–1820, Web site www.hartleyhouse.com. 5 rooms with phone, TV, and private bath. Full breakfast. Mixed gay/straight.*

THE LITTLE BLACK BOOK

At Your Fingertips

Lambda Community Center (⊠ 919 20th St., ☎ 916/442–0185, Web site www.midtown.net/lambda). **Lesbian and Gay Business Alliance** (☎ 916/442–0185). **Sacramento AIDS Foundation** (☎ 916/448–2437). **Sacramento Convention and Visitors Bureau** (⊠ 1303 J. St., Ste. 1600, 95814, ☎ 916/264–7777, Web site www.sacto.org/cvb). *Sacramento News & Review* (☎ 916/498–1234, e-mail newsreview@aol.com). **Sacramento Regional Transit** (☎ 916/321–2877). **Sacramento Visitors Information Center** (⊠ 1101 2nd St., ☎ 916/264–7644). **Yellow Cab** (☎ 916/444–2208).

Gay Media

Sacramento has a pair of handy gay and lesbian newspapers, the biweekly *MGW (Mom...Guess What!)* (☎ 916/441–6397, Web site www.mgwnews .com) and the monthly *Outword* (☎ 916/329–9280, Web site www .outword.com).

BOOKSTORES

The terrific lesbigay **Open Book** (⊠ 910 21st St., ☎ 916/498–1004) carries books and magazines and has a comfy coffee bar. Nearby **Lioness Books** (⊠ 2224 J St., ☎ 916/442–4657) stocks feminist, lesbian, and general gay titles. For gifts, postcards, pride items, and cool decorative odds and ends, head to **Postcards Etc.** (⊠ L and 21st Sts., ☎ 916/446–8049).

Working Out

Valenti's (⊠ 921 11th St., ☎ 916/863–9629) is a favorite gym of men and women.

35 Out in St. Louis

S**T. LOUIS IS A BIG BASEBALL** city, a beer city, a working-class city—a place that entertains its visitors without much fanfare. Families vacation here because St. Louis possesses attractions that are perfect for kids: dozens of museums and parks, a restored train station decked with shops and restaurants, and the magnificent St. Louis Arch, which soars gracefully above the banks of the mighty Mississippi. Yet it's their *parents* who enjoy St. Louis. Charmed by the city's embrace of the past, and by its nostalgic styles, tastes, and diversions, adults relate to a place that hasn't had the money or the interest over the past half century to mow down its old neighborhoods in favor of new high-rises. It's had little reason to fund fancy amusements and sightseeing venues. Most of the newer development has occurred west in St. Louis County, in places like Frontenac, Clayton, and West Port. St. Louis is just St. Louis—looking much as it has for three or four decades.

And now, as tourism has begun to improve, as the city begins to pump money into its appearance, preserving the past is *in*. St. Louis continues to spruce up some of its older neighborhoods and landmark buildings, rather than razing them and starting anew. Slowly but surely, the city is again becoming a destination.

For all of their tradition and mainstream values, St. Louisians are fairly accommodating of gays and lesbians. Queers are highly visible, having transformed several neighborhoods, most notably the Central West End, from blighted victims of white flight into desirable blocks of restored homes. The community is large, spread out, and vibrant, with a gay pride festival that's estimated to be among the 10 largest in the country. The community is also a relatively mature one. The several area colleges infuse the city with some younger faces, but most of them graduate and move elsewhere. Remaining are the lifers—lesbians and gays who have been fighting for gay rights for so long they may not realize how much they've accomplished, and how well-adjusted St. Louis's gay community is.

THE LAY OF THE LAND

St. Louis's small downtown hugs the river, and distinctive neighborhoods surround it on all sides: Soulard and Benton Park are to the south, Lafayette Square and Tower Grove to the southwest; the Hill, Dogtown, and the Central West End to the west; and the Ville to the north. The character of downtown neighborhoods changes dramatically from street to street. Though the contrast can be fascinating, also bear in mind that it's easy to amble absent-mindedly into crime-ridden pockets of town.

Downtown and Laclede's Landing

St. Louis's constantly redefining downtown is made up of eclectic buildings that represent the last century in architecture. The area most changed is the **Riverfront,** which has riverboats outfitted with restaurants and casinos where once there were only tankers and tugs. Above the river is the **Jefferson National Expansion Memorial** (☎ 314/425–4465), a rolling green park that acts as a buffer between the city and the river; the park's centerpiece is the 630-foot **Gateway Arch.** The lines here can be a drag (try to go early in the morning), and the visitor center and museum are a bit hokey, but the tram ride to the top of this sleek tribute to westward expansion is memorable. On the west side of the park is St. Louis's oldest church, the **Old Cathedral,** also known as the Basilica of St. Louis, the King (✉ 209 Walnut St., ☎ 314/231–3250), which dates from the 1840s. Two blocks west of here is the green-domed **Old Courthouse** (✉ 11 N. 4th St., ☎ 314/425–4468), site of the infamous case in which Dred Scott unsuccessfully sued for his freedom from slavery.

French furrier Pierre Laclède first disembarked in St. Louis at a point just north of the Jefferson Memorial Park. **Laclede's Landing** later evolved into the city's warehouse district and is now a touristy nine-square-block network of cobblestone streets dotted with gas lamps, bars, restaurants, shops, and a goofy wax museum. Though few gay couples roam these streets today, Pierre Laclède is said to have spent much of his time here in bed with his young footman.

About 20 blocks west of the riverfront, on Market Street, is the restored, century-old **St. Louis Union Station** (✉ 1820 Market St., ☎ 314/421–6655), formerly the world's largest and busiest rail terminal (train service was discontinued in 1979); it now encompasses a collection of shops, restaurants, and the Hyatt Regency Hotel. Just north of the station is the **Drury Inn,** formerly the YMCA. During World War II, troops moving east to west were housed here midway through their journey—many a gay trick is said to have been turned during these stopovers. During the 1950s, Martin's, a gay bar, was run out of the basement.

Just west of downtown is **Grand Center** (✉ Grand Ave. and Lindell Blvd.), the city's theater and performing-arts district. **St. Louis University** abuts Grand Center on its western edge; the university is close to several gay bars. Near here, at 4633 Westminster, is the otherwise ordinary brick apartment building in which Thomas "Tennessee" Williams grew up; it is the setting of *The Glass Menagerie.*

Central West End and U. City Loop

Following the World's Fair of 1904, which was held in Forest Park, the adjacent **Central West End** evolved into St. Louis's most fashionable neighborhood. Enormous mansions still line Hortense and Portland places. In the middle of this century, however, the CWE fell into abandonment and disrepair. Hippies and counterculturists—many of them students and faculty at nearby Washington and St. Louis universities—moved in to the area's undervalued, neglected homes. The CWE became something of a gay ghetto, and during the next couple of decades, the community thrived here. The CWE remains the city's urban anchor, but many of the gay men who revived its fortunes died of AIDS during the '80s, and queerfolk who hoped to settle here found the property values prohibitive. The shops and restaurants along Euclid Avenue now appeal to a broader, although still somewhat bohemian, mix of cosmopolitans.

Gracious **Washington University** is due west; the hub of its campus is at the northern border of 1,300-acre **Forest Park.** This sprawling rectangle has a skating rink, a golf course, a 7-mile jogging and cycling path, and some of the Midwest's best museums, including the **St. Louis Art Museum**

(✉ 1 Fine Arts Dr., ☎ 314/771–0072), the **St. Louis Science Center** (✉ 5050 Oakland Ave., ☎ 314/289–4444 or 800/456–7572), and the **History Museum** (✉ Lindell Blvd. and Debaliviere Ave., ☎ 314/746–4599). Washington University also has an excellent collection of American and European painting at its **Gallery of Art** (✉ Steinberg Hall, 1 Brookings Dr., ☎ 314/935–5490).

A landmark study on cruising for sex, released as the book *Tearoom Trade,* was based allegedly on observations made at tearooms and cruising areas around Forest Park and in many of the buildings at Washington University. It has been noted that Forest Park's cruising activity involved mostly married men and other closeted figures afraid of venturing into gay bars, whereas the transactions in the city's other major venue, Tower Grove Park, involved mostly hustling hoosiers (the local slang for white trash, not to be confused with natives of Indiana!).

East of Washington University, where Skinker runs into Delmar Boulevard, is the **U. City Loop,** a smaller, more alternative, and generally younger version of the restaurant-and-shopping row along the CWE's Euclid Avenue. So named because it's where the streetcar used to loop around before heading back downtown, the Loop's most famous establishment is the nightclub, **Blueberry Hill** (✉ 6504 Delmar Blvd., ☎ 314/727–0880), a lively tribute to American pop culture.

Soulard, Benton Park, and Lafayette Square

St. Louis's richly hued red, orange, and brown bricks are most evident in **Soulard,** a residential row house neighborhood south of downtown that is significantly gay-populated. You can wander among houses, Irish pubs, and bars. At 7th Street and Lafayette is the **Soulard Market** (☎ 314/622–4180), a public food market for more than 200 years. Farther south is the **Anheuser-Busch Brewery** (✉ 12th and Lynch Sts., ☎ 314/577–2626; tours available), and beyond that is the **Chantillon-DeMenil House** (✉ 3352 DeMenil Pl., ☎ 314/771–5828), a Greek Revival mansion with period furnishings. Just south and west of Soulard is **Benton Park,** home to the **Cherokee Antique Row** (✉ Cherokee St. btw. Jefferson Ave. and Lemp St., ☎ 314/879–7344), a six-block expanse lined with 45 shops.

Northwest of Soulard, across I–55 and I–44, **Lafayette Square** is an increasingly gay neighborhood. This was St. Louis's most desirable address until a tornado destroyed many of its most beautiful homes in 1896. Eight years later the World's Fair was staged in Forest Park, drawing most of the city's wealth and prestige into the Central West End. Lafayette Square then languished until the 1970s, when gentrification began. The neighborhood's focal point, **Lafayette Park,** is the oldest park west of the Mississippi (the wrought-iron fence surrounding it is original). The roads fringing the square are lined with historic buildings, some of them restored painted ladies but just as many awaiting face-lifts. Park Avenue, between Mississippi and 18th streets, has a few good restaurants.

Just west of Benton Park, **Grand South Grand** is a short stretch of Grand Avenue between Utah and Arsenal streets, which now has many ethnic restaurants and funky shops. In the past several years, the residential neighborhood just west of here, **Tower Grove** (a.k.a. Dyke Heights), has begun to attract many lesbians. In the adjacent Tower Grove Park is the stellar **Missouri Botanical Garden** (✉ 4344 Shaw Ave., ☎ 314/577–5100), a 79-acre spread created by the allegedly gay Victorian horticulturist, Henry Shaw.

GETTING AROUND

You can cover St. Louis's downtown on foot, but the city's strengths are its colorful neighborhoods, which are most conveniently explored by car.

Meter parking is easy to find outside downtown, and the streets are navigable with relative ease; you will need to garage your vehicle downtown (the fees are reasonable). St. Louis's light-rail system, the MetroLink, is good if you're hopping between some of the tourist sights like Laclede's Landing and Union Station, but it's not a viable means for seeing the whole city. Taxis are neither plentiful nor practical.

EATS

Thanks to its large number of German, Italian, and Irish immigrants, St. Louis is strong on food from those three cultures. Some places around town have spruced up their traditional meat-and-potatoes menus with contemporary touches. St. Louisians are a bit wary of radical foodies, however, so overall expect the emphasis to be on dependably good, well-prepared comfort food. Many sidewalk cafés and pubs line Euclid Avenue in the CWE and Delmar Boulevard in the U. City loop. Downtown has few good restaurants, though the converted Union Station has some notable ones. Grand South Grand has a slew of Chinese, Thai, Indian, and other Asian eateries.

St. Louis's most famous food neighborhood, however, is the Hill, a vibrant Little Italy of authentic pasta joints and food markets west of downtown. **Dominic's** (✉ 5101 Wilson Ave., ☎ 314/771–1632; $$$$) is considered the best and most formal. More affordable are **Bruno's** (✉ 5901 Southwest Ave., ☎ 314/781–5988; $$) and **Zia's** (5256 Wilson Ave., ☎ 314/776–0020; $–$$).

For price ranges, *see* dining Chart B at the front of this guide.

Central West End and Environs

$$–$$$ ╳ **Blue Water Grill.** This snappy contemporary eatery south of the CWE and near the Hill offers Mexican and southwestern takes on fresh seafood. A show stopper is bouillabaisse with green chiles, chorizo, saffron, loads of shellfish, and a light tomato–white wine broth. ✉ *2607 S. Hampton Ave.,* ☎ *314/645–0707.*

$$–$$$ ╳ **Café Balaban's.** The most popular of upper Euclid Avenue's infectiously spirited taverns, Balaban's serves extremely good American food that reflects extensive foreign and contemporary influences. Beef Wellington in a golden raisin sauce is among the tasty dishes. The best seating is on the glassed-in porch. A cozy pub serves a variety of ales and wines. ✉ *405 N. Euclid Ave.,* ☎ *314/361–8085.*

$$–$$$ ╳ **Duff's.** Another of CWE's sidewalk cafés always abuzz with chatter and laughter, this is one of the few places with tables outside, directly on the pavement (as opposed to overlooking it through a glassed-in porch). Interior rooms are pubby and filled with art. A great Continental menu— try the bouillabaisse or chicken marsala. ✉ *392 N. Euclid Ave.,* ☎ *314/ 361–0522.*

$$–$$$ ╳ **Niner Diner.** Attached to Magnolia's bar (*see* Scenes, *below*), this cute hole-in-the-wall serves better fare than most diners: gussied-up American dishes such as chicken magnolia (with artichoke hearts, tomatoes, black olives, and onions) as well as inventive pastas and grills. ✉ *9 S. Vandeventer Ave.,* ☎ *314/652–6500.*

$–$$ ╳ **Brandt's.** College students, self-styled intellectuals, and artistes of every background mingle at this fancy-food market and sidewalk café on the U. City Loop's main drag. The wide-ranging menu includes pizzas, trendy sandwiches, and pastas, plus a vast selection of wines, beers, vodkas, and coffees. ✉ *6525 Delmar Blvd.,* ☎ *314/727–3663.*

$–$$ ╳ **Dressel's.** This Upper Euclid favorite is notable for its warm downstairs tavern, where celeb drawings and opera posters cover the walls, and for the authentic Welsh-style pub upstairs, where a hearty pint of Felio-

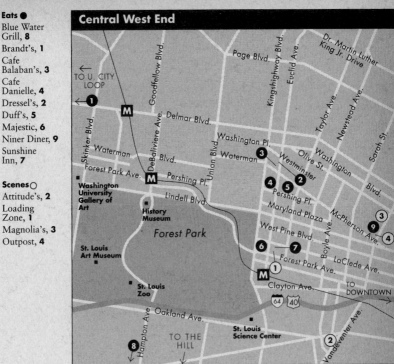

Edel ale always awaits you. Has burgers, diverse veggie dishes, and St. Louis's best chips. ⊠ *419 N. Euclid Ave.,* ☎ *314/361–1060.*

$ ✕ **Majestic.** All the boys take their dates here the morning after, to parade them before the legions of hung-over revelers. The Majestic is a true gay diner, and the Greek fare is above average—wonderful feta omelets, Greek salads, gyros, and flaky baklava. Has a bright streetside patio. ⊠ *4900 Laclede Ave.,* ☎ *314/361–2011.*

$ ✕ **Sunshine Inn.** Another major brunch scene, Sunshine is definitely less cruisy, less showy, and less gay-male than the Majestic. Large plate-glass windows front the several smart bright dining rooms. Juices, apple pancakes, guacamole omelets, and homemade soups fill the restaurant's veggie menu. ⊠ *8½ S. Euclid Ave.,* ☎ *314/367–1413.*

Elsewhere

$$$$ ✕ **Tony's.** Despite protests from skeptics who can't fathom paying $50 for a pasta dinner, this nationally acclaimed downtown trattoria continues to be the first choice for lovers and gourmands celebrating special occasions. Prime steaks, tender veal, and sublime seafood dishes live up to the high praise. ⊠ *410 Market St.,* ☎ *314/231–7007.*

$$–$$$ ✕ **Sidney Street Café.** Antiquing tourists from Cherokee Street rub elbows with workers from the nearby Anheuser-Busch Brewery at this redbrick tavern in Benton Park. Tables are candlelit and green plants hang everywhere. The ever-changing chalkboard menu ranges from fat, juicy burgers to crab cakes to chicken over spinach with prosciutto, artichoke hearts, and goat cheese. ⊠ *2000 Sidney St.,* ☎ *314/771–5777.*

$–$$ ✕ **9th Street Abbey.** Eating in this dramatic 1850 former abbey may make you feel as if you're eating at a church potluck supper. Capellini in fresh tomato sauce, curried chicken salad, and BLT sandwiches typify the fare, which, although decent, tends to be somewhat less memorable than the setting. Very gay following. ⊠ *1808 S. 9th St.,* ☎ *314/621–9598.*

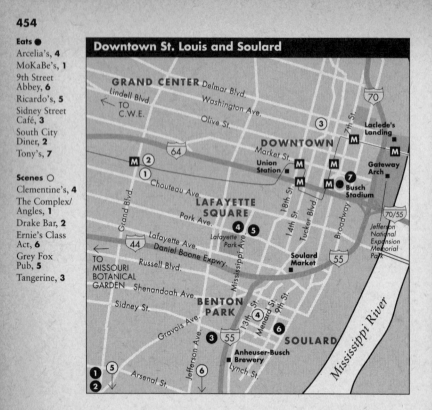

$-$$ ✕ **Ricardo's.** About 30 varieties of pasta are available at this smart Italian café just off Lafayette Park. Through the storefront windows is a classy but informal dining room. One of the more romantic settings in town. ✉ *1931 Park Ave.,* ☎ *314/421–4833.*

$-$$ ✕ **South City Diner.** Amid Grand South Grand's numerous Asian eateries is this traditional late-night greasy spoon. Trendily untrendy, the look is somewhat outdone by the menu, which includes, along with the usual breakfast-any-time and blue-plate specials, several upscale dishes. ✉ *3141 S. Grand Blvd.,* ☎ *314/772–6100.*

$ ✕ **Arcelia's.** The atmosphere is casual; the menu, unusual Mexican. Surrounded by cedar, stucco, exposed brick and, of course, the occasional sombrero, you can feast on *nopales* (stir-fried cactus) or great chicken fajitas. One of the two dining rooms is for smokers; each has a bar. ✉ *2001 Park Ave.,* ☎ *314/231–9200.*

Coffeehouse Culture

Café Danielle. Drop by this café for stimulating conversation and bracing coffees. Light-hued wood furnishings, soft lighting, and large windows opening onto the street create a cheerful ambience. ✉ *399 N. Euclid Ave.,* ☎ *314/367–2233.*

MoKaBe's. This Tower Grove Park space feels half like a typical diner and half like a neighborhood bar—if only more coffeehouses had pool tables. Another plus is the live entertainment offered many weekends. You can sit either at the long bar or at several tables and booths. ✉ *3606 Arsenal St.,* ☎ *314/865–2009.*

SCENES

St. Louis is not exactly abuzz with gay nightlife, as this isn't a town you come to expressly to party. Most of the few good clubs and bars, however, are easygoing and open to new faces. They tend to be either close to the Central West End (younger crowd) or Soulard (older crowd), but St. Louis doesn't have a specifically gay entertainment district. The decor and atmosphere of most bars reflects the city's straightforward, working-class mentality. The average St. Louis gay bar is largely indistinguishable from most of the mainstream Irish pubs and German beer halls around town—the crowd just happens to be gay.

Prime Suspects

Attitude's. The city's most popular dyke bar is in an old brick building in a somewhat seedy area—near where Manchester becomes Chouteau, at the intersection with Sarah Street. You won't see many professionals here; in fact, the crowd's a little rowdy. Darts, pool, a large central bar, and a small dance floor, which has country-western dancing some nights. ⊠ *4100 Manchester Ave.,* ☎ *314/534–3858. Crowd: mostly female, mixed ages, loud, down-to-earth.*

Clementine's. A fixture of historic Soulard, Clementine's is the oldest gay bar in St. Louis, set in a redbrick town house with stained glass windows and original architectural details. Although the crowd at the bar is almost exclusively male, the attached restaurant (it's quite good) is a better mix of lesbians and gay men. ⊠ *2001 Menard St.,* ☎ *314/664–7869. Crowd: mostly male, mostly ages 40s and 50s, some leather but more Levi's, laid-back.*

The Complex/Angles. On weekends, guys go back and forth between this sprawling brick converted warehouse and Magnolia's, a five-minute drive away. The various spaces include a room for drag shows and musical performances, a dance floor, a renowned leather bar, a leather-and-lace boutique, and a patio. It's a bit less stuffy and stand-and-model than Magnolia's, but still has plenty of cute guys. ⊠ *3511 Chouteau Ave.,* ☎ *314/772–2645. Crowd: mostly male, all ages, racially mixed, college students, leather men, drag queens, white collars, blue collars.*

Drake Bar. In an ancient redbrick house on a side street behind the Complex, this lively but quiet pub has room to sit and talk. Coffees are served on one floor; on another there's piano entertainment. Very civilized and not too cruisy—a good place to bring a date. ⊠ *3502 Papin St.,* ☎ *314/ 865–1400. Crowd: mixed m/f, all ages, unpretentious, mellow.*

Loading Zone. This textbook video bar has three floors of patrons staring each other down and making hollow conversation. It's as stand-and-model as anywhere in St. Louis, but still largely free of snootiness. The decor is jet black and nondescript, but video screens hang in every corner. Great happy hour. ⊠ *16 S. Euclid Ave.,* ☎ *314/361–4119. Crowd: 75/25 m/f, young, cruisy, collegiate.*

Magnolia's. Magnolia's is *the* main nightspot—it even gets fairly crowded during the week. The crowded mishmash of rooms, although similar to those at the Complex, are not as distinctly themed here. There's really no leather contingent to speak of either, as most of those guys head to the Outpost down the block. Within view of St. Louis University. ⊠ *5 S. Vandeventer Ave.,* ☎ *314/652–6500. Crowd: mostly male, mixed racially, similar to crowd at Complex but somewhat more professional and buttoned-down, a little cliquey.*

Neighborhood Haunts

If you're spending a lot of time in St. Louis, you might also want to check out one or more of the following downtown bars: **Ernie's Class Act** (⊠ 3756 S. Broadway, ☎ 314/664–6221) is actually not all that classy, but it's a fairly popular, and rowdy, dyke bar; no men. The city's answer to *Cheers*, that quiet neighborhood bar where everybody knows your name (or at least asks), is the **Grey Fox Pub** (⊠ 3503 S. Spring St., ☎ 314/772–2150). Leather hands congregate at the otherwise characterless **Outpost** (⊠ 17 S. Vandeventer Ave., ☎ 314/535–4100), a few doors down from Magnolia's.

Hangin' with the Hets

Downtown along Washington Street has developed into a funky alternative-music club scene, and gays (especially younger artsy types) greatly favor **Tangerine** (⊠ 1405 Washington Ave., ☎ 314/621–7335).

Action

Club St. Louis (⊠ 2625 Samuel Shepphard Dr., ☎ 314/533–3666) is the city's bathhouse and sauna, open 24 hours, with steam room, tanning bed, sauna, gym, lockers, TV lounge, and all the usual fixtures.

SLEEPS

St. Louis was once a grand hotel city, but as the population and popularity of the city waned, many of its finest properties—the Planters House, Chase, and Park Plaza hotels among them—were razed or converted into luxury apartments. A few classics remain, but much of the region's hotel business has moved out to the rather dull suburb of Clayton. In the city itself, most hotels are downtown, with only a few up near Forest Park and the Central West End. The accommodations around Union Station are about equidistant from downtown attractions, Soulard, Lafayette Square, and the CWE.

For price ranges, *see* lodging Chart B at the front of this guide.

Hotels

$$$–$$$$ 🖭 **Hyatt Regency St. Louis.** This distinctive hotel has been fashioned out of the city's former Union Station rail terminal. The lobby was the station's original grand concourse, and the gold-leaf plasterwork, stained glass, frescoes, and barrel-vaulted ceilings are still intact. Beautiful guest rooms. ⊠ *1 St. Louis Union Station, 63103, ☎ 314/231–1234 or 800/233–1234, ℻ 314/923–3970. 538 rooms. Restaurants, pool.*

$$–$$$ 🖭 **Mayfair Grand Heritage Hotel.** One of the most interesting of St. Louis's historic properties, the Mayfair, which opened in 1925, in its heyday hosted Harry Truman, Cary Grant, and many others. Most of the guest rooms (which are quite large) have sitting rooms, and the original, hand-operated elevator is still in use. ⊠ *806 St. Charles St., 63101, ☎ 314/421–2500 or 800/437–4824, ℻ 314/421–0770 184 rooms. Restaurant, exercise room.*

$$ 🖭 **Drury Inn Union Station.** This historic hostelry, the city's former YMCA, is around the corner from the Hyatt Regency. Pleasant rooms, complimentary breakfast, and an indoor pool help make it one of the best values in the city. ⊠ *201 S. 20th St., 63103, ☎ 314/231–3900 or 800/325–8300, ℻ 314/231–3900. 176 rooms. Restaurant, pool, hot tub, exercise room.*

$–$$ 🖭 **Best Western Inn at the Park.** Extremely close to CWE bars and restaurants, as well as Washington University, this is a clean affordable option that's been greatly spruced up in the past two years. ⊠ *4630 Lindell Blvd., ☎ 314/367–7500 or 800/373–7501, ℻ 314/367–9015. 128 rooms. Restaurant, pool, exercise room.*

Guest Houses

$–$$ 🖭 **Napoleon's Retreat B&B.** This mansard-roofed Victorian, painted creamy yellow with burgundy and dark blue trim, is just around the corner from Lafayette Park, about a mile from downtown. The rooms are huge, done with a smattering of antiques and period reproductions, and bright modern baths (one room has a Jacuzzi). Friendly and helpful owners Jeff and Michael can tell you a great deal about the area. ⊠ *1815 Lafayette Ave., 63104, ☎ 314/772–6979 or 800/700–9080, ℻ 314/772–7675. 5 rooms with phone, TV, and private bath. Full breakfast. Mixed gay/straight.*

$ ⊞ **Brewers House.** In the Soulard/Benton Park area, this restored mid-19th-century row house has a secluded garden hot tub and fireplaces in some rooms. Soulard's bars and the antiques shops on Cherokee Street are nearby. ⊠ *1829 Lami St., 63104,* ☎ *314/771–1542. 3 rooms with TV, 1 with private bath. Hot tub. Continental breakfast. Mostly mixed gay male/lesbian.*

THE LITTLE BLACK BOOK

At Your Fingertips
AIDS Hotline (☎ 314/367–8400 or 800/337–2437). **Laklede Cab Co.** (☎ 314/535–1162). **Lesbian and Gay Community Center** (☎ 314/725–3122 or 314/997–9897). **Lesbian and Gay Hotline** (☎ 314/367–0084). **MetroLink** (☎ 314/231–2345). *Riverfront Times* (alternative weekly, ☎ 314/231–6666, Web site www.rftstl.com). **St. Louis Convention and Visitors Bureau** (⊠ 10 S. Broadway, Suite 1000, 63102, ☎ 314/421–1023 or 800/916–0040). **St. Louis Effort for AIDS** (☎ 314/645–6451; information hot line, ☎ 314/647–1144).

Gay Media
Covering the entire state, but focusing chiefly on St. Louis and Kansas City, the biweekly *News-Telegraph* (☎ 314/664–6411, e-mail newstele@aol.com) is the city's queer news source.

BOOKSTORES
St. Louis has a terrific lesbian and gay bookstore, **Our World Too** (⊠ 11 S. Vandeventer Ave., ☎ 314/533–5322), which is tucked between a pair of gay bars, Magnolia's and the Outpost. The store has an extensive section of secondhand titles out-of-state gay papers and magazines, and porn mags. **Left Bank Books** (⊠ 399 N. Euclid Ave., ☎ 314/367–6731) is a terrific independent mainstream bookstore with a significant gay following. Also on Euclid, **Pages, Video & More** (⊠ 10 N. Euclid Ave., ☎ 314/361–3420) has some gay and lesbian titles, plus magazines and video rentals.

Working Out
A gay-friendly gym is the **Maryland Fitness Center** (⊠ 48 Maryland Plaza, ☎ 314/361–3603).

36 Out in Salt Lake

THE HOST CITY OF THE 2002 WINTER OLYMPIC GAMES will soon have the chance to shed its image as a conservative Mormon settlement and publicize its transformation into a high-tech metropolis. With apologies to Denver, Salt Lake (locals never call it Salt Lake City) has the potential to become the social and cultural darling of the Rockies. You'll find plenty to see and do in this city with a metropolitan population of 850,000, whether you're a Mormon or a club-craving queer—or both, as these identities are not mutually exclusive. And for the record, Mormons have not practiced polygamy widely since the 1890s, church missionaries generally will not approach you unless you hang out around Temple Square, and the town is not dry (though its nightclubs are subject to annoying liquor laws).

Salt Lake was founded in 1847 by Mormon pioneers—followers of the Church of Jesus Christ of Latter-day Saints (LDS)—in search of a land where they could practice their religion without threat of persecution. As recently as the 1960s, Salt Lake was 75% Mormon, but the LDS presence is now believed to be less than half the population.

Many gays and lesbians have relocated here in recent years, prompting hostility from the LDS. The church fought to prevent a gay/straight student alliance from forming at a local public high school, and in 1998 mobilized its congregants with lightning speed to repeal the city's gay-rights ordinance, which was scrapped one month after its passage. Still, many Mormons quietly break with the church on the issue of homosexuality and embrace their queer family, friends, and neighbors. And despite, or perhaps because of, the LDS attempts to suppress gay rights, queer visibility in Salt Lake is high. Nightlife is limited to several bars and coffeehouses, but these establishments thrive. You'll see family working in restaurants and hotels downtown, employed by the new high-tech and service-oriented companies, and flitting around more than just the bars—it turns out that the Utah state bird, the California gull, has homosexual tendencies. With the Olympic Games coming to town, gay issues will continue to make headlines. Some locals predict the increased scrutiny will only make Salt Lake more hospitable to gays and lesbians.

THE LAY OF THE LAND

Salt Lake sits at the western base of the Wasatch Range, whose peaks are capped with snow from early fall to late spring. The city itself has a moderate year-round climate, with snow downtown often melting shortly after it falls. There's no predominantly gay neighborhood, but a few bars and gay-popular restaurants are on the western edge of downtown in the Warehouse District. Most attractions are downtown, with several others to the east in the foothills and on the campus of the University of Utah.

Downtown

You may find it too unsettling to visit the grounds of a church that has no respect for gays and lesbians, but the most logical place to begin your exploration of **downtown** is at landscaped, 10-acre **Temple Square.** Admission is free to most of the Mormon sights in the square and its vicinity. The square's centerpiece is the **Salt Lake Temple** (⌧ 50 W. North Temple St., ☎ 801/240–2534), a six-spire, 210-foot-tall work of granite that took 40 years to complete. The Mormon Tabernacle Choir, whose concerts are open to all visitors, performs next door at the domed **Tabernacle** (☎ 800/537–9703 for scheduling information). As you tour the square, at least one member of the church will likely approach you and politely ask if you'd like to learn more about the LDS. Wearing rainbow jewelry and an Act-Up T-shirt won't spare you from such an encounter (though it might help you get a date).

Lineage is of tremendous importance to Mormons. West of Temple Square, the **Family History Library** (⌧ 35 N. West Temple St., ☎ 801/240–2331) contains the world's largest collection of genealogical data. The **Joseph Smith Memorial Building** (⌧ S. Temple and Main Sts., ☎ 801/240–1266), the Mormon community center, contains 200 computers you can use to trace your family's history.

The 26th-floor observation deck of the **LDS Church Office Building** (⌧ 50 E. North Temple St., ☎ 801/240–2452), is open to the public, as is the 1854 **Beehive House** (⌧ 67 E. South Temple St., ☎ 801/240–2671), once the official residence of Salt Lake's early Mormon leader, Brigham Young. His 27 wives and 56 children lived next door.

Lest anybody think conspicuous consumption runs counter to LDS principles, two fabulous shopping malls flank Temple Square to the south. Mormons established the **Zion Cooperative Mercantile Institution (ZCMI)** (⌧ 36 S. State St., ☎ 801/321–8743), which is billed as America's First Department Store, in 1868. Behind the cooperative's 1902 cast-iron facade are countless brand-name clothiers and boutiques. Next door, **Crossroads Plaza** (⌧ 50 S. Main St., ☎ 801/531–1799) has another 140 shops.

The magnificent **Utah State Capitol** (⌧ Capitol Hill, ☎ 801/538–1050) lies north of Temple Square. One of the most impressive Renaissance Revival buildings in the country, the 1912 structure has a 165-foot-tall rotunda under which Work Projects Administration murals depict Salt Lake's early history. A block west, four floors of exhibits at the **Pioneer Memorial Museum** (⌧ 300 N. Main St., ☎ 801/538–1050) celebrate the valor of the settlers who traversed the rugged Rocky and Wasatch mountains throughout the 19th century on the way to Salt Lake.

In sharp contrast to the broad modern streets of most of Salt Lake, the quirky **Marmalade Historic District,** which abuts Capitol Hill's northwestern slope, contains a beautifully preserved cache of Victorian homes, quite a few of them queer-inhabited. Its network of narrow lanes makes for a nice stroll (and a not-bad workout).

In the other direction, a few blocks south of Temple Square, is the **John D. Gallivan Utah Center Plaza** (⌧ 36 E. 200 S, ☎ 801/532–0459), a funky outdoor space with art installations, an amphitheater, an ice rink and pond, and a huge outdoor chess board. The area, which frequently hosts concerts, fairs, poetry readings, and such, will serve as Olympic Plaza during the 2002 games.

Two testaments to Salt Lake's once prodigious rail industry dominate the western edge of downtown. The vacant 1909 **Union Pacific Railroad Depot** (⌧ S. Temple St. and 400 W) is notable for its murals and stained-glass. Amtrak still serves the 1910 **Rio Grande Depot** (⌧ 300 S. Rio Grande

St., ☎ 801/531–0188), which also houses the Utah State Historical Society. These two structures straddle the **Warehouse District.** Several gay bars have been operating for years in this trendy trove of early-20th-century industrial architecture, but rising rents forced the gay Stonewall Community Center (*see* The Little Black Book, *below*) to abandon the Warehouse District for smaller, less-expensive digs.

Northeast of Temple Square is the **Avenues District,** a neighborhood vaguely reminiscent of Seattle's Capitol Hill. The residential architecture here ranges from imposing Italianate Victorians to Arts and Crafts bungalows. As in the Marmalade District, the abundance of once inexpensive fixer-uppers has lured many gays.

University and Foothills

Drive 2 miles east of downtown along South Temple Street, past a few noteworthy and historic non-Mormon churches as well as the **Governor's Mansion** (✉ 603 S. Temple St., ☎ 801/538–1005) to reach the **University of Utah's** hilltop campus. Although founded by the LDS in 1856, the school is no longer affiliated with the church. The institution, whose 27,000 students are collectively as artsy, progressive, and alternative as those in Boulder, Madison, Berkeley, or any other liberal college town, serves as a foil to Brigham Young University (BYU), its buttoned-down, exclusively Mormon rival in nearby Provo.

Worth visiting if only to wander its lush grounds, the University of Utah campus is the home of the **Utah Museum of Fine Arts** (✉ S. Campus Dr., ☎ 801/581–7332), renowned for its Egyptian artifacts, Italian Renaissance paintings, Navajo rugs, and American art dating back four centuries, and the **Utah Museum of Natural History** (✉ President's Circle, ☎ 801/ 581–4303). On the eastern edge of campus at the **Red Butte Garden and Arboretum** (☎ 801/581–5322), pebbled walkways lead from the Walter P. Cottam Visitor Center through 25 acres of trees, shrubs, flowers, waterfalls, and botanical gardens.

Much of the youthful alternative culture is based to the southeast around the intersection of 900 East and 900 South. Amid this burgeoning district of gay-popular businesses are **Cahoots** (*see* The Little Black Book, *below*), a coffeehouse, some cheap eats, a great record store, and a few offbeat haunts. Nearby **Trolley Square** (✉ 600 S. 700 E, ☎ 801/521– 9877), a renovated 1908 redbrick trolley barn, holds movie theaters and more shops and restaurants. On the grounds of 16-acre **Liberty Park** (✉ 700 E. 900 S, ☎ 801/322–2473), two blocks south of Trolley Square, are one of the West's largest aviaries and the Chase Museum of Utah Folk Art.

Great Salt Lake

With no fish, virtually no foliage, and undrinkable water, the surreal **Great Salt Lake** resembles an ocean on a distant planet as much as it does any waterway on Earth (except perhaps the East River in New York City). The lake has no outlet to the sea, so it traps the salts and minerals that countless mountain streams carry into it. As its water evaporates during dry periods, its salinity can reach as high as 28% (nine times greater than in the oceans on Earth). Access to the lake is via **Great Salt Lake State Park/Saltair Beach** (✉ Exit 104 from 1–80), which is 16 miles west of downtown.

Park City and Sundance

From Salt Lake, head south on I–15 to Exit 287 and take Route 92 (also signed as the Alpine Scenic Byway) up into the mountains, winding above 11,750-foot **Mount Timpanogos.** As the road heads back down the mountain, you'll pass by the short road to Robert Redford's **Sundance Ski Resort** and **Sundance Institute** (☎ 801/225–4107 or 800/892–1600). The latter sponsors the queer-friendly **Sundance Film Festival** each January; films are screened in Park City and at the Institute. In summer, the Institute presents first-rate theater on a magnificent outdoor stage. In winter, when the highest part of Route 92 is closed, take I–15 to Exit 275 in Orem, follow Route 52 east to U.S. 189 north, and continue about six miles to reach the accessible part of Route 92 and Sundance. From September to March, snow tires or chains are required along here.

Continue north from Sundance along U.S. 189, passing by rippling **Deer Creek Reservoir.** With its backdrop of sensational mountains, the reservoir is a perfect photo op. In summer, you can take Route 113 north past the reservoir to **Midway;** from here continue along Route 224 north through gorgeous **Wasatch Mountain State Park** to Park City. In winter, continue on U.S. 189 to the nondescript former mining town of **Heber City** and turn left onto U.S. 40, going north through the Heber Valley. A left onto Route 248 will lead you to Park City.

A hip, gay-friendly, but overdeveloped ski community, **Park City** attracts the same Range Rover counterculturalist types as do Aspen and Telluride. In 1993, when many people boycotted Colorado and therefore Aspen's gay ski week, Park City held a similar event. Smaller crowds attended in '94 and '95, and it was discontinued in '96. But Park City remains a popular getaway for couples and friends traveling together (singles may be disappointed, as there's no gay nightlife). Stroll along historic **Main Street,** which holds dozens of upscale restaurants and boutiques. From Park City, Route 224 leads down to I–80, which will get you back to Salt Lake. This entire trip, depending on which routes you choose, can be done in as little as four hours, but try to allot a full day.

GETTING AROUND

Newcomers find Salt Lake's layout confusing, mostly because the streets have been named in an unconventional manner, but the town's grid is easy to master once you've learned the basics. From Temple Square, streets fan out, at right angles, to the north, east, south, and west. What would be South First Street in most places is called 100 South in Salt Lake. If the address you're looking for falls on the west side of the grid (west of State Street), it's called West 100 South (i.e., West South First Street). For example, the gay bar Bricks, at 579 West 200 South, is between the fifth and sixth blocks west of Temple Square, on the second street south of it.

Although it's possible to walk to bars and many restaurants from downtown hotels, most visitors find a car necessary. Traffic is manageable and parking isn't difficult; there are garages near Temple Square and parking lots farther out. Several gay bars are close together in the Warehouse District, so you can take a cab to the first one and another home in lieu of driving. Buses are free within a 15-block area downtown and on Capitol Hill; a ride on most routes is $1.

EATS

Cutting-edge chefs lured by Salt Lake's entrepreneurial climate have vastly improved what was for decades a meat-and-potatoes dining scene. Traditional mountain dishes like brook trout and buffalo are on many menus; southwestern and Mexican cuisine are two of the city's other strengths, and several restaurants prepare nouvelle Italian and Mediterranean fare. Many of the best and most bohemian spots are in the Warehouse District, but quality options can be found throughout the region.

For price ranges, *see* dining Chart B at the front of this guide.

$$$–$$$$ ✕ **Metropolitan Café.** This converted warehouse space has been recognized by the James Beard Society as one of the top restaurant interiors in the nation. The food's nothing to sneeze at, either. A seven-course tasting menu shows off chef Mathias Merges's world-class cooking. You can also opt for less expensive yet still astounding fare like duck confit on a bed of lentils by ordering off the café menu and eating in the urbane bar. ⊠ *173 W. 300 S*, ☎ *801/364–3472.*

$$$–$$$$ ✕ **Santa Fe.** With stunning views of Emigration Canyon and the Salt Lake Valley, this dramatic restaurant, a 10-minute drive from downtown, blends Asian, Cajun, southwestern, and frontier recipes with considerable success. Buffalo steak and brook trout are among the regional specialties. Same-sex couples will feel comfortable holding hands here. ⊠ *2100 E. Emigration Canyon Rd., ☎ 801/582–5888.*

$$$ ✕ **Capitol Café.** A stark postmodern study in glass and concrete beside the ornate Capitol Theatre, this hot spot courts the opera and ballet crowds with subtle contemporary American fare like grilled rib-eye with whipped Yukon gold potatoes, brown buttered spinach, pine nuts, and roasted garlic butter. ⊠ *54 W. 200 S*, ☎ *801/532–7000.*

$$–$$$ ✕ **Baci's.** Amid a riot of bold hues, guppies and yuppies feast on pizzas, pastas (try rigatoni with sweet Italian sausage, eggplant, bell peppers), and northern Italian grills. This is one of several entries in the gay-friendly Gastronomy Inc. group, which converts historic buildings into hip restaurants. ⊠ *134 W. Pierpont Ave., ☎ 801/328–1500.*

$$–$$$ ✕ **Barking Frog Grille.** High ceilings, marble floors, and contemporary abstract desert art contribute to a loud and colorful experience, ideal for a group of friends out for a good time (and less than ideal for a quiet evening with sweetie). Expect robust and kicky southwestern and western dishes such as salmon with garlic–sweet corn polenta and lime-chipotle butter. ⊠ *39 W. Market St.*, ☎ *801/322–3764.*

$$–$$$ ✕ **Market City.** Plan to wait a bit at dinnertime for a table at this wildly popular seafood restaurant. The clam chowder will quell any Yankee's case of homesickness, and there's a long list of nouvelle-inspired fish grills and roasts. Market City's owners, Gastronomy Inc., also run the adjacent Oyster Bar (⊠ *54 W. Market St.*, ☎ *801/531–6044*), which is slightly more upscale. ⊠ *48 W. Market St.*, ☎ *801/322–4668.*

$$–$$$ ✕ **Piña.** It bills itself as a Caribbean restaurant, but Piña presents enticing international dishes whose influences range from Mediterranean to southwestern. You won't go wrong with curry-coconut-crusted mahimahi with a mango–passion fruit sauce, but the simpler sandwiches, pizzas, and pastas taste great, too. ⊠ *327 W. 200 S*, ☎ *801/355–7462.*

$$ ✕ **Bangkok Thai.** A good place to break up a day of shopping at the upscale Foothills Village shopping center, this sedate restaurant serves up the best Thai cooking in the state—even those demanding West Coast transplants seem happy with the fiery green curries, sweetly mild pad thais, and aromatic teas. ⊠ *1400 S. Foothill Dr.*, ☎ *801/583–7840.*

$$ ✕ **Xiao Li.** This newcomer shuns watered-down Americanized cooking and kitschy decorating schemes and offers only authentic, expertly seasoned fare in an elegant, minimalist setting, complete with high-back chairs, traditional screens, and exposed brick walls. Favorites include chicken-and-corn egg-drop soup and spicy Szechuan-style stir-fried green beans. ⊠ *307 W. 200 S*, ☎ *801/328–8688.*

$–$$ ✕ **Rio Grande.** One of the best of several excellent Mexican restaurants in Salt Lake, Rio Grande is set inside the eponymous railway depot near the Warehouse District. Campy decorations keep everybody's spirits high, and the reasonably authentic tamales, enchiladas, and chilies rellenos rarely miss the mark. The bathrooms are a highlight, not because they're cruisy but because they're haunted by a ghost called the Purple Lady. ⊠ *270 S. Rio Grande St.*, ☎ *801/364–3302.*

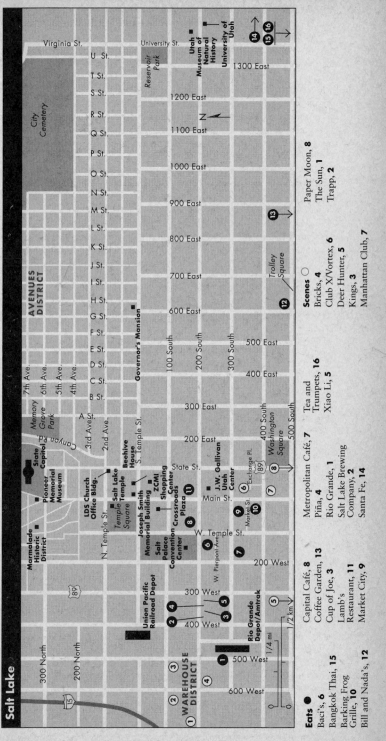

Salt Lake

Virginia St.

University St.

U St.
T St.
S St.
R St.
Q St.
P St.
O St.
N St.
M St.
L St.
K St.
J St.
I St.
H St.
G St.
F St.
E St.
D St.
C St.
B St.
A St.

City Cemetery

Reservoir Park

Utah Museum of Natural History

University of Utah

1300 East
1200 East
1100 East
1000 East
900 East
800 East
700 East
600 East
500 East
400 East

AVENUES DISTRICT

7th Ave.
6th Ave.
5th Ave.
4th Ave.
3rd Ave.
2nd Ave.

Memory Grove Park

Canyon Rd.

State Capitol

Pioneer Memorial Museum

Marmalade Historic District

LDS Church Office Bldg.

Temple Square

Salt Lake Temple

Beehive House

Joseph Smith Memorial Building

ZCMI Shopping Center

Crossroads Plaza

Salt Palace Convention Center

Governor's Mansion

S. Temple St.

State St.

Main St.

Market St.

J.W. Gallivan Utah Center

Exchange Pl.

N. Temple St.

Temple Square

W. Temple St.

W. Pierpont Ave.

100 South
200 South
300 South
400 South
500 South

100 East
200 East
300 East
400 East
500 East

Washington Square

Trolley Square

Union Pacific Railroad Depot

Rio Grande Depot/Amtrak

200 West
300 West
400 West
500 West
600 West

300 North
200 North

WAREHOUSE DISTRICT

1/2 km
1/4 mi
0

Eats ●

Baci's, **6**
Bangkok Thai, **15**
Barking Frog Grille, **10**
Bill and Nada's, **12**

Capital Café, **8**
Coffee Garden, **13**
Cup of Joe, **3**
Lamb's Restaurant, **11**
Market City, **9**

Metropolitan Café, **7**
Piña, **4**
Rio Grande, **1**
Salt Lake Brewing Company, **11**
Santa Fe, **14**

Tea and Trumpets, **16**
Xiao Li, **5**

Scenes ○

Bricks, **4**
Club X/Vortex, **6**
Deer Hunter, **5**
Kings, **3**
Manhattan Club, **7**

Paper Moon, **8**
The Sun, **1**
Trapp, **2**

$-$$ ✕ **Salt Lake Brewing Company.** A hulking complex of century-old buildings on the edge of the Warehouse District houses the city's best and queerest brew pub. The comfort fare here includes Cajun rock-shrimp linguine and a Caesar salad with blackened chicken. Adjoining the cavernous dining room is a space with a few bars and several pool tables that is open long after the kitchen closes. ✉ *367 W. 200 S,* ☎ *801/363–7000.*

$ ✕ **Bill and Nada's.** Workers from the nearby trolley barn used to congregate at this 24-hour diner when it opened many years ago; the crowd has become more trendy and alternative over the years, but this retro greasy spoon hasn't changed. Liver and onions and steak and eggs remain house specialties, and a rickety sign with a few flashing bulbs continues to welcome the hungry masses. ✉ *479 S. 600 E,* ☎ *801/359–6984.*

$ ✕ **Lamb's Restaurant.** Power-lunching politicos favor this restaurant that opened in 1919 and still has much of its original decor, including a fabulous black-marble counter. The dependable meat loaf, leg of lamb, sandwiches, and other American dishes don't appear to have changed much in 80 years, either. ✉ *169 S. Main St.,* ☎ *801/364–7166.*

$ ✕ **Tea and Trumpets.** This charming tea and pastry house prepares great sandwiches, salads, and other treats. If you're looking to stock up on picnic supplies before a drive or hike in the mountains, stop here. T&T is southeast of downtown at the very beginning of the Foothills. ✉ *1515 S. 1500 E,* ☎ *801/487–0717.*

Coffeehouse Culture

Coffee Garden. So named for the floral shop in which it is located, this rambling informal hippie and student hangout serves Seattle's Best Coffee and tasty fare, from burritos and quiche to a heavenly lemon–poppyseed cake. ✉ *900 E and 900 S,* ☎ *801/355–3425.*

Cup of Joe. Probably the queerest of the city's coffeehouses, this high-ceiling warehouse conversion has unfinished wooden floors, raspberry walls and ceilings, tall windows, and plenty of table seating. Peruse the art exhibits, surf for a few hours on the Internet, curl up with a good book, or check out the community bulletin board. Always a scene, day and night. ✉ *353 W. 200 S,* ☎ *801/363–8322.*

SCENES

Despite its conservative reputation, the Salt Lake has several outstanding gay nightclubs—most of them clustered around the Warehouse District—with great music, energetic and unpretentious crowds, and in most cases a welcoming attitude toward women and men. Plenty of Utahns don't partake of bar culture, but it almost seems as though the rest of the population parties doubly hard to compensate. Gays and straights mingle at a few clubs, and raves and indie music performances take place with some regularity. Some of the newer restaurants and microbreweries are sophisticated and tolerant spots for cocktails.

Bars and clubs stay open only until 1 AM, but that's not the only odd facet of the city's liquor laws. Restaurants and hotel lounges may sell alcohol with the purchase of food, but other establishments, including all the gay venues, operate as private clubs. You must purchase a temporary membership (think of it as a cover charge), which typically can used by up to six persons and is valid for up to two weeks.

This is the law, but it's enforced sporadically. Some places have been known to fudge and let visitors in free, especially those who are traveling alone and only in town for the night. Sometimes you'll be asked to sign in; on other occasions you can just wander in. You can also enter free as a guest of a full member. If you hang outside the club of your choice, you may be able to find someone to escort you inside. There's speculation the city will abolish its archaic regulations by the time the Winter Olympics take place, but for the time being, bring along a valid picture ID (preferably a driver's license) and expect to pay $5 to get into each nightspot.

Prime Suspects

Bricks. This enormous club in the heart of the Warehouse District is one of Salt Lake's top nightlife draws, gay or straight. Though it's predominantly a queer scene, the management welcomes everybody, and in recent years the crowd has become more straight—especially when there's live music or drag shows. The mixing has been largely a happy experiment in breaking down social barriers. You enter through a large video lounge staffed by tux-clad cocktail waiters and filled with chatty and cruisy patrons. A short flight of stairs leads into a funky lounge with a bar, some pool tables, and a few cushy sofas. Behind this is a terrific disco with hot music, slick lighting, and intense voguing on the dance floor. Bricks has an 18-and-over policy some nights. ⊠ *579 W. 200 S,* ☎ *801/328–0255. Crowd: 70/30 m/f, 80/20 gay/straight, 20s to early 30s, some racial mix, very diverse in appearance—arrogant gym boys, sneering genXers, sensitive granolas, curious heteros, well-heeled guppies, and down-to-earth students.*

Deer Hunter. As easy as it is to meet people at the bars in the Warehouse District, men looking to get laid usually head to this rambling semileather disco a short drive away. It used to be more hard-core, but all sorts congregate here nowadays, including more than a few women (usually friends of the guys and not necessarily lesbians). The decor is dark and appropriately forbidding, but this place still has most of the same elements of the other clubs in town: pool tables, games, and a large dance floor. ⊠ *636 S. 300 W,* ☎ *801/363–1802. Crowd: mostly male, mostly late 20s to late 40s, some leather and lots of Levi's, butch, bearish, extremely cruisy.*

Kings. As it hasn't a distinct identity and tends to draw mostly locals, you could almost call Kings a neighborhood bar, but for its size. There's a large dance floor, plenty of pool tables, a few bars, and an expansive patio. Theme nights take place from time to time, and the DJ gauges his selections to the crowd's mood. Friday is the most popular night. This is a place where the staff and patrons ask strangers their names and invite them to join in the fun. ⊠ *108 S. 500 W,* ☎ *801/521–5464. Crowd: mixed m/f, all ages, eclectic, low-key, outgoing, very friendly, not especially cruisy.*

Paper Moon. The advertisements for Paper Moon still bill it as the city's only exclusively lesbian bar, but rumors suggest that the management is becoming more open to guys. On weekends, you'll see a slight mix. Nevertheless, this is basically a dyke hangout. Because it's a 15-minute drive south of downtown, the bar generally attracts fewer tourists than the Warehouse District clubs. Among the cool features that make it worth a trip are a good-size dance floor, a well-attended country-western dance on Thursday, and live acoustic music at least once a week. ⊠ *3424 S. State St.,* ☎ *801/466–8517. Crowd: mostly female, all ages, all types, fairly local and neighborhoody, less lipstick and cruisy than at the mixed clubs in the Warehouse District.*

The Sun. Not unlike its neighbor, Bricks, this is a converted warehouse with an old-fashioned bar, a second area with pool tables and seating, and a disco with a large dance floor and stage. Tremendously popular, The Sun is always a lot of fun. The front bar has the quieter music and is better if you're looking to strike up a conversation with one of the countless adorable creatures roaming about. ⊠ *702 W. 200 S,* ☎ *801/531–0833. Crowd: 70/30 m/f, mostly under 30, some racial mix, pretty boys, lipstick lesbians, a few goatees and tattoos, lots of flannel and jeans, less club-kiddy and more casual than at Bricks, especially friendly to out-of-towners.*

Trapp. A favorite of country-western fans, of which there are plenty in Salt Lake, Trapp is in the Warehouse District. You enter a small, narrow tavern and bar with tables; off of that is a dance floor, and beyond that a larger bar with pool tables, darts, and other games. A great asset in warm weather is the deck, which encircles a good bit of the club. ⊠ *102 S. 600 W,* ☏ *801/531–8727. Crowd: 60/40 m/f, mostly 30s, plenty of boots and cowboy hats, friendly, down-home.*

Hangin' with the Hets

Manhattan Club (⊠ 5 E. 400 S, ☏ 801/364–7651) is an alternative-music club with a gay presence. **Club X/Vortex** (⊠ 32 Exchange Pl., ☏ 801/521–9292), another youthful music club, is gay-friendly.

Action

The **14th Street Gym** (⊠ 1414 W. 200 S, ☏ 801/363–2023), a nice bathhouse, stays open until 4 AM. Most of Salt Lake's late-night action occurs on downtown streets, particularly along Exchange Place, where you'll find guys exchanging glances from midnight until dawn almost every night of the week. People generally stay in their cars and drive around until they find somebody interesting or give up and go home empty-handed (as it were). The police are said to avoid confronting those who refrain from public displays of affection, but cruising is illegal and you should consider the potential consequences before participating.

SLEEPS

Salt Lake has all the usual business hotels, most of them in the heart of downtown and within a walk or a short drive of most attractions, restaurants, and the Warehouse District gay bars. More properties are being built in anticipation of the Winter Olympics, so finding a place does not require reservations months in advance. The city has no four-star establishments, and rates are moderate at the chains.

For price ranges, *see* lodging Chart B at the front of this guide.

Hotels

$$$ ⊞ **Wyndham Hotel.** Though it's one of the top properties in town, the Wyndham, which is close to the convention center and Warehouse District, has extremely reasonable weekend rates. The rooms have top-of-the-line bath amenities, coffeemakers, and other nice touches. ⊠ *215 W. South Temple St., 84101,* ☏ *801/531–7500 or 800/996–3426,* ℻ *801/329–1289. 381 rooms. Restaurant, pool, health club.*

$$–$$$ ⊞ **Marriott Residence Inn.** If you're visiting for more than a few days or traveling with friends, these condolike suites near Trolley Square and the University of Utah are ideal. Stocked kitchens, fireplaces in most cases, and free breakfast and evening cocktails are among the pluses. Very popular with skiers as a base for Park City. ⊠ *765 E. 400 S, 84102,* ☏ *801/532–5511 or 800/331–3131,* ℻ *801/531–0416. 128 rooms. Pool, health club.*

$$ ⊞ **Best Western Olympus.** This business property is a few blocks south of Temple Square, convenient to the interstates. The management is extremely gay-friendly. ⊠ *161 W. 600 S, 84101,* ☏ *801/521–7373 or 800/426–0722,* ℻ *801/524–0354. 393 rooms. Restaurant, pool, health club.*

$–$$ ⊞ **Peery Hotel.** As budget hotels go, this is one of the nicest. The restored brick building dates from 1910, and though its guest rooms are basic they have more character than most in this price range. Most of the staff is young, friendly, and relatively hip, and the hotel is steps from good restaurants. ⊠ *110 W. 300 S, 84101,* ☏ *801/521–4300 or 800/331–0073,* ℻ *801/575–5014. 77 rooms. Restaurant, exercise room.*

Guest Houses and Small Hotels

$–$$$ ⚉ **Anton Boxrud.** This gay-friendly historic inn is a half block from the governor's mansion and within walking distance of Temple Square. The rooms have down comforters, leaded-glass windows, handwoven lace, and other Victorian touches. ✉ *57 S. 600 E, 84102,* ☎ *801/363–8035 or 800/524–5511. 7 rooms, some with private bath. Hot tub. Full breakfast. Mixed gay/straight.*

THE LITTLE BLACK BOOK

At Your Fingertips

City Cab (☎ 801/363–5550 or 801/363–5015). *City Weekly* (☎ 801/575–7003, Web site www.slweekly.com). **Salt Lake Convention & Visitors Bureau** (✉ 90 S. West Temple St., 84101, ☎ 801/521–2822 or 800/541–4955, Web site www.saltlake.org). *SLUG* (music and arts weekly, ☎ 801/487–9221, Web site www.slugmag.com). **Utah AIDS Foundation** (☎ 800/FON-AIDS). **Utah Gay and Lesbian Anti-Violence Project** (☎ 801/297–4004). **Utah Stonewall Center** (☎ 801/539–8800, Web site www.stonewall.org). **Utah Transit Authority** (☎ 801/287–4636).

Gay Media

The monthly *Pillar* (☎ 801/265–0066, e-mail pillarslc@aol.com) is the official queer news source.

BOOKSTORES

The front half of **Cahoots** (✉ 878 E. 900 S, ☎ 801/531–6601) is a pride emporium with a few books and many cards, gifts, and home-furnishing items; in back is a small lesbigay bookstore. **A Woman's Place** (✉ 1400 Foothill Dr., Unit 236, ☎ 801/583–6431) is a fine feminist and lesbian bookstore. **Bob's Magazines** (✉ 360 S. State St., ☎ 801/364–1134) has gay periodicals and porn.

Working Out

There are no heavily gay-frequented gyms in Salt Lake.

37 Out in San Antonio

SAN ANTONIO HAS THE LEAST PRONOUNCED gay scene of America's 10 largest cities, but a trip to Texas is not complete without a foray into this Western, multicultural metropolis. The legend of the Alamo, in which nearly 200 settlers sacrificed their lives in a battle with Mexico for independence, will forever symbolize the state's determination and valor. San Antonio is thus the state's spiritual, if not political, capital.

Franciscan Spanish missionaries began attempting to "civilize" the region's Native American population as far back as the 1690s, before establishing a permanent mission, now known as the Alamo, in 1718. After Texas finally secured independence from Mexico, San Antonio developed into a formidable cattle center, and later into a prosperous oil town. San Antonio's economy is now based on tourism, medical research and high-tech industrial concerns, and the military—four Air Force bases and the Army's Fort Sam Houston.

The most-visited city in Texas, San Antonio in many ways captures the essence that outsiders seek but never seem to find in Austin, Dallas, and Houston. For gay and lesbian visitors, discovering a quintessential Texan city may prove to be a mixed blessing. In serious abundance are family-oriented theme parks and touristy dance halls and drinkeries with decidedly straight and conservative clienteles. You're not going to see as many queers checking out the World War II fighter planes on display at Lackland Air Force Base as you might, say, at a museum dedicated entirely to hometown diva Joan Crawford (would that such a shrine existed!).

Queer nightlife centers around a handful of bars, and the city has no gay ghetto. Perhaps because San Antonio is overwhelmingly Catholic and 60% Hispanic, it's never cultivated the free-spirited counterculturalism of California. This city respects traditions and family, and the gays who live here generally embrace such values. Nobody in San Antonio uses sexual orientation as a way to shake up the mainstream population. By the same token, few local civic and religious leaders take aim at the gay community. San Antonians respect each other's cultural and philosophical differences, and the city prospers as a result.

THE LAY OF THE LAND

San Antonio encompasses an enormous area, most of it encircled by Loop 1604 and I–410 and then crisscrossed by highways, all of which skirt downtown. More than half the city's major attractions are downtown, in the only highly walkable neighborhood. Other parks and museums, as well as most gay bars, numerous trendy restaurants, and several picturesque neighborhoods, are north of downtown.

Downtown

Downtown San Antonio has been forever protected by a zealous spirit of historic preservation. At the turn of the century, concerned local citizens fought developers bent on converting the Alamo into a hotel. Similar efforts led to the restoration of the San Antonio River, for which the city is now so famous, and to keeping countless older buildings intact and relatively few newer ones from going up.

Contrary to popular belief, the **Alamo** (⊠ Alamo Plaza, ☎ 210/225–1391) was never a massive fortress, and what remains is even less imposing—only the small chapel whose façade has come to symbolize the pride and independence of Texas, and one of the barracks. The buildings are set within a tranquil walled plaza of lawns and gardens. Inside the chapel are plaques, letters, and artifacts commemorating the lives of the defenders.

The **River Walk** (Paseo del Rio) is one of the most enchanting urban settings in America. The San Antonio River, which is 15 feet below street level, cuts a loop through downtown and is lined with cobbled and flagstone paths, over which hang the drooping branches of cypress and willow trees. During weekdays it makes for a peaceful walk, but on weekends—especially at night—beware the rowdy crowds tanking up on margaritas at the bars and restaurants along the river; this is not an ideal spot for same-sex couples to saunter hand-in-hand.

Built in 1939, the River Walk came into its own during the 1968 World's Fair. River taxis ply the water, offering group tours, during which you'll get a good sense of the architecture and greenery. The taxis depart from a dock at **Rivercenter Mall** (⊠ 849 E. Commerce St., ☎ 210/225–0000), at the east end of the river loop, which has a food court and the usual mid-price to high-end shops.

HemisFair Park (⊠ 200 S. Alamo St., ☎ 210/207–8572), a few blocks south of the mall, contains the remnants of the World's Fair attractions, including the 750-foot **Tower of the Americas** (⊠ 600 Hemisphere Park, ☎ 210/207–8610), the **Mexican Cultural Institute** (⊠ 600 Hemisphere Park, ☎ 210/227–0123), and the **Institute of Texan Cultures** (⊠ 801 S. Bowie St., ☎ 210/458–2300), whose exhibits and programs celebrate the state's rich ethnic heritage. Set aside an hour to visit nearby **La Villita** (⊠ 418 Villita St., ☎ 210/207–8610), a complex of 26 arts and crafts shops. Visit one of the several working artists' studios, such as the **Nueva Street Gallery** (⊠ 507 E. Nueva St., ☎ 210/229–9810), which shows the work of renowned local artist Henry Rayburn.

Head west of the River Walk along Commerce Street, past the magnificent 1749 **Spanish Governor's Palace** (⊠ 105 Plaza De Armas, ☎ 210/224–0601), whose many rooms are decorated in the style of the period. The Palace sits at the eastern edge of **Market Square** (⊠ 514 W. Commerce St., ☎ 210/207–8600), a fun but touristy brick mall of Mexican restaurants and shops, complete with fountains, benches, mariachi bands, and food stalls.

At the far northeastern edge of downtown, about a 15-minute walk from Alamo Plaza, you'll find the **San Antonio Museum of Art** (⊠ 200 W. Jones St., ☎ 210/978–8100), which, in glorious contrast to the more traditional McNay Art Institute (*see* Alamo Heights, *below*), has been created out of the former Lone Star brewery. Inside this maze of glass elevators and skylights is a diverse collection of works from ancient Greece and Rome, as well as numerous ones from Latin America and Asia.

King William Historic District and Southtown

In its early days, San Antonio attracted many German immigrants. The well-to-do merchants among them constructed elaborate Victorian mansions south of downtown, now designated the **King William Historic District.** This area plunged into blight during the middle of this century, but restoration efforts have brought it back to life. The memorabilia and documents at the **Guenther House** (⌧ 205 E. Guenther St., ☎ 210/227–1061), which sits on the river and dates from 1860, document San Antonio's German heritage.

Adjacent to King William is the more modest but up-and-coming **Southtown** neighborhood, in which early 20th-century homes have been bought up and restored during the past few years, and funky shops and businesses have opened. The **Blue Stars Arts Complex** (⌧ Blue Star and S. Alamo Sts., ☎ 210/227–6960), a converted industrial complex of design shops, photo galleries, a contemporary art museum, and a microbrewery (*see* Eats, *below*), anchors Southtown.

The Missions

The chapel that remains of **Mission San Antonio de Valero** (the Alamo; *see* Downtown, *above*) was one of five missions built along the San Antonio River during the 18th century. The other four, which are south of downtown within 6 miles of one another, have been preserved and are open to the public, but you might first stop by the **San Antonio Missions National Historical Park** (⌧ 2202 Roosevelt Ave., ☎ 210/534-8833), which administers them and can provide information on each. If you have time only for one, visit **Mission San Jose** (⌧ 6701 San Jose Dr., ☎ 210/932–1001), which dates from 1777.

Monte Vista and Olmos Park

In the absence of a predominantly queer neighborhood, Monte Vista and Olmos Park—as well as Alamo Heights to the east—have as strong a gay residential following as any. **Monte Vista,** which begins north of U.S. 81/I–35, contains the gay bars along **Main and San Pedro avenues,** as well as the funky coffeehouses, bars, and restaurants along **North St. Mary's Street** (a.k.a. the North St. Mary's Strip). The latter are popular with students at nearby San Antonio College and Trinity University. Northern Monte Vista, where it begins to get hilly, has long been a fashionable place to live, as evidenced by the many courtly Spanish-style mansions and landscaped yards.

Olmos Park is a pleasant, queer-friendly, middle-class suburb north of Monte Vista, with a few gay-popular restaurants. A great throwback to a bygone era, **Olmos Pharmacy** (⌧ 3902 McCullough Ave., ☎ 210/822–3361) is an old-fashioned drug store with a soda fountain serving vanilla malts and decent diner fare.

Alamo Heights

East of Olmos Park, on the other side of U.S. 281, is **Alamo Heights,** a yuppified suburb. The main drag, **Broadway,** also has more than its share of trendy coffeehouses and restaurants. The **Witte Museum** (pronounced witty) (⌧ 3801 Broadway, ☎ 210/820–2181) focuses on regional history but also has exhibits on natural science, ecology, and anthropology; this great museum also presents a film and performing arts series.

The **San Antonio Botanical Gardens** (⌧ 555 Funston St., ☎ 210/821–5115) has 33 acres of gardens and a 90,000-square-foot conservatory—it's one of the nation's best. Just north, the **Japanese Tea Gardens** (⌧ 3800 N. St. Mary's St., ☎ 210/821–3120) have been laid out in a former limestone quarry and consist of winding paths, placid pools, stone footbridges, and a 60-foot waterfall. The **San Antonio Zoological Gardens and Aquarium** (⌧ Brackenridge Park 3903 N. St. Mary's St., ☎ 210/734–7183) is notable for its large bird collection.

Its 23 acres of gardens and paths alone demand a visit, but the **McNay Art Institute** (✉ 6000 N. New Braunfels St., ☎ 210/824–5368) has assembled an acclaimed collection of 19th- and 20th-century art, including European and American drawings, prints, and sculpture. Van Gogh, Picasso, Cézanne, Pollack, and O'Keeffe are among the artists represented inside this Mediterranean Revival mansion.

Theme Parks

The most famous of San Antonio's theme and amusement parks is **Sea World of Texas** (✉ Hwy. 151 at Loop 1604, ☎ 210/523–3000). The other biggie is **Six Flags Fiesta Texas** (✉ I–10 at Loop 1604, ☎ 210/697–5050), which seems about the size of a major city.

GETTING AROUND

Although you can see downtown on foot, you'll need a car to get around the metro area. It's the only way to check out gay nightlife and to visit the missions, parks, and museums. San Antonio's network of highways can be confusing, so get a map. Parking downtown is not difficult; several garages are near the Alamo and River Walk. The city has an extensive bus system but it's mainly useful to residents, although Bus 7/40 loops from downtown to several tourist attractions. Streetcars travel four downtown routes, which hit most of the major sights.

EATS

San Antonio dining is neither as flashy nor quite as accomplished as in other major Texas cities. The region's ubiquitous but rather greasy Tex-Mex cooking has received new life in recent years, as local chefs continue to experiment with regional Mexican and southwestern recipes and ingredients. Steak houses and burger parlors remain a potent force. Chili con carne was invented here in the late 1800s, and you may from time to time stumble upon "chili queens." Not to be confused with "taco queens," the politically incorrect slang for gay gringos with a thing for Hispanic guys, chili queens were the Mexican-American women who for many years hawked hot chili at the city's open-air markets.

Restaurants north of downtown—in Monte Vista, Olmos Park, and Alamo Heights—tend to draw the most same-sexers. With a few exceptions, downtown is the domain of touristy or business-oriented eateries.

In addition to the restaurants reviewed below, a couple of inexpensive and gay-friendly Mexican eateries are downtown, including **Mi Tierra** (✉ 218 Produce Row, ☎ 210/225–1262), which is open 24 hours, and **Rosario's** (✉ 1014 S. Alamo St., ☎ 210/223–1806).

For price ranges, *see* dining Chart B at the front of this guide.

Downtown and South

$$–$$$$ ✗ **Paesanos.** Pretty as it is, the River Walk attracts more than its share of forgettable restaurants. But this water-level, Northern Italian trattoria is outstanding and gay-friendly—and it's one of the few in this area favored by locals. The spinach gnocchi with fresh mozzarella, tomatoes, and roasted garlic, and the grilled amberjack with a Sicilian clam chowder rarely miss the mark. ✉ 111 W. Crockett St., ☎ 210/227-2782.

$$–$$$ ✗ **Blue Star.** Grilled antelope sausage, porterhouse steak, blackened-fish sandwiches, and shrimp-chipotle noodles are among the updated variations on "comfort food" doled out at this hip postindustrial microbrewery at the funky Blue Star Arts Space (*see* Lay of the Land, *above*) in Southtown. ✉ 1414 S. Alamo St., ☎ 210/212–5506.

Eats ●

Blue Star, **3**

Paesanos, **2**

Pecan Street Market, **1**

Scenes ○

Annex, **2**

Bonham Exchange, **6**

Captain's Crew, **7**

El Jardin , **8**

Pegasus, **3**

Rebar, Woody's and Club W, **1**

The Saint, **4**

Silver Dollar Saloon, **5**

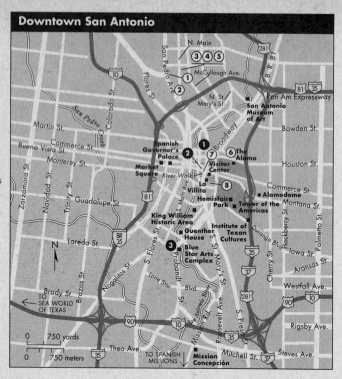

Downtown San Antonio

Eats ●

Barcelona, **5**

Biga, **8**

Camille, **10**

Candlelight, **11**

Earl Abel's, **6**

Freedom, **9**

La Fogata, **1**

Liberty Bar, **12**

Los Barrios, **3**

Madhatters, **7**

Stonewerks at Quarry, **2**

W. D. Deli, **4**

Scenes ○

Eagle Mountain Saloon, **5**

Mick's, **2**

Nexus, **1**

2015, **3**

Tycoon Flats, **4**

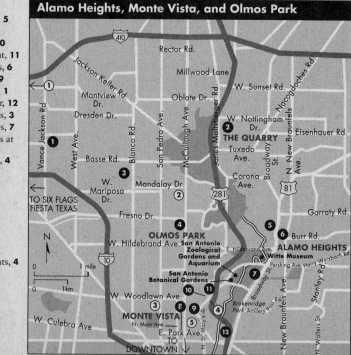

Alamo Heights, Monte Vista, and Olmos Park

$ ✕ **Pecan Street Market.** This favorite downtown lunchery, set on the ground floor of the turn-of-the-century Exchange Building, retains a vintage feel. The sandwiches, soups, and salads are fashioned with considerable New American flair, and the desserts are always a knockout. ✉ 152 E. Pecan St., ☎ 210/227–3226.

Monte Vista, Olmos Park, and North St. Mary's

$$$–$$$$ ✕ **Biga.** The decor inside this turn-of-the-century mansion is Edwardian, but the crowd is cool and sassy, which is also true of the food. Highlights include habanero-spiked swordfish over risotto and game meats (most notably oak-roasted antelope). ✉ 206 E. Locust St., ☎ 210/225–0722.

$$–$$$ ✕ **Camille.** Great for a first date or an anniversary, this terrific purveyor of New American cooking is set in a rustic dining room with wood floors, Renoiresque murals, and antique mirrors. Roasted pork loin on scalloped potatoes with a balsamic-honey glaze is one of many standouts. ✉ 517 E. Woodlawn St., ☎ 210/735–2307.

$$ ✕ **La Fogata.** One of the most famous Mexican restaurants in Texas, "the Flame" is well north of Olmos Park. Despite the sometimes pissy service, it's worth the trip. The menu draws on Texas-influenced and Mexican recipes—a favorite is the smoky and sizzling *chile poblano al carbon* (poblano pepper stuffed with chicken and cheese and cooked under charcoal flame). ✉ 2427 Vance Jackson, ☎ 210/340–1337.

$–$$ ✕ **Liberty Bar.** The Liberty was a German-style beer garden for much of this century. Gay and straight locals drop by to mingle at the bar or nosh on pear and Stilton salad, peppered tenderloin, and venison sausage, plus traditional Mexican favorites. ✉ 328 E. Josephine St., ☎ 210/227–1187.

$–$$ ✕ **Los Barrios.** Not as high-profile as La Fogata, this vast family-run compound built around a former Dairy Queen is a huge favorite of the gay community. Terra-cotta–hued walls, tile floors, hanging plants, and upbeat music complement the tasty fare, including chicken in a piquant mole-poblano sauce and tender Mexican-style chicken-fried steak. ✉ 4223 Blanco Rd., ☎ 210/732–6071.

$ ✕ **W. D. Deli.** A staple of Olmos Park's gay community, this cheerful deli has the best tortilla soup around, and healthful sandwiches (try the spinach-chicken) and salads. The inside dining area has wood floors, floor-to-ceiling windows, and hanging plants. Outside is a tree-shaded patio. ✉ 4227 McCullough Ave., ☎ 210/828–2322.

Alamo Heights and Northeast

$$–$$$ ✕ **Barcelona.** With saltillo-tile floors, Spanish art, wood-beam ceilings, and foliage-choked dining rooms and patios, this tapas restaurant captures the mood of its namesake. The food roams the Mediterranean, with robust and kicky dishes like potato rounds with prosciutto and *Manchego* (Spanish sheep's milk) cheese and duck breast with sun-dried cherry and ancho pepper sauce. ✉ 4901 Broadway, ☎ 210/822-6129.

$$ ✕ **Stonewerks at Quarry.** Across the street from the acutely posh Quarry shopping complex, off U.S. 281 near the airport, Stonewerks is a yuppie haven on weekends, when a taco bar and live music are featured. You'll find tasty pub-style food—burgers, nachos, salads—at this crowded adobe compound and garden. ✉ 7300 Jones Maltsberger Rd., ☎ 210/828–3508.

$ ✕ **Earl Abel's.** This half-century–old tacky diner fills nightly with old ladies with big Texas hair—and quite a few drag queens with big Texas hair. It's sometimes hard to tell them apart. Doting waitresses race around serving plates of cornmeal-battered catfish, fried chicken, and coconut cream pie. ✉ 4200 Broadway, ☎ 210/822–3358.

Coffeehouse Culture

Candlelight. A living-room–like space with settees, arm chairs, and tables on which you can kick up your feet or set up a board game, Candlelight is the perfect blend of a wine bar, coffeehouse, café, and rainy-day hangout. In good weather enjoy the lushly landscaped patio. ⊠ *3011 N. St. Mary's St.,* ☎ *210/738–0099.*

Freedom. A hub of free-thinkers and New Agers, Freedom has food, coffees, and smoothies, but is best-known for its poetry readings, open-mike nights, herbal massage therapy, and other nontraditional services and festivities. ⊠ *2407 N. St. Mary's St.,* ☎ *210/737–3363.*

Madhatters. Attracting a "who's who" of local characters for the weekend jazz brunches, Madhatters is one of the best coffeehouses in Alamo Heights. Great sandwiches and the long list of Benedicts—topped with chipotle Hollandaise sauce and other goodies (grilled artichokes, perhaps)—make for memorable meals. ⊠ *3606 Ave. B,* ☎ *210/821–6555.*

SCENES

Most San Antonio bars are clean and nicely decorated, with down-to-earth and approachable crowds. Many bars are northwest of downtown in Monte Vista, clustered along Main and San Pedro avenues, but a few are scattered elsewhere. There are a few small colleges in San Antonio, but this is not a college town, and under-35 singles—male and female—are less numerous here than in Austin, Dallas, and Houston. The scene is more about socializing and hanging out with friends than about cruising and putting on airs. Drag, which has long played a role in gay Hispanic culture, is a *major* force here. Women are welcome at many of the Monte Vista bars, but the best dyke bar, Nexus, is a half-hour drive northwest of downtown.

Prime Suspects

Annex. Come to Texas expecting every other guy to work on a ranch, drive a Chevy 4-by-4, and smoke unfiltered cigarettes, and you'll be in for a serious disappointment. More of them wear pumps than chaps. What macho dudes you will find favor this low-key bar that's bathed in red light. It's neither a dive nor a hard-core scene, but leather men like it here, and the sexual energy sometimes rises to a fever pitch. Despite the lusty ambience, women do hang here, especially early in the evening. ⊠ *330 San Pedro Ave.,* ☎ *210/223–6957. mostly male, mid-30s and up, some leather, bears, Levi's, cruisy.*

Bonham Exchange. This enormous historic building a few blocks east of the Alamo is the largest queer (technically mixed gay/straight) club in Texas, and when they open the upstairs ballroom (only for special parties and occasions) it's one of the biggest in the country. Open only on Friday and Saturday, the "Bottom Exchange" consists of a cruisy video lounge; a drag/show bar; a pool and games room; a two-level, high-energy disco with catwalks running high above the dance floor; and a pair of cozy lounges steps from the action. ⊠ *411 Bonham St.,* ☎ *210/271–3811. Crowd: mixed m/f, mixed gay/straight, 20s to early 30s, preppy gays, alternative and grungy straights, less of a cruise than at the Saint, upbeat.*

El Jardin. No visitor to San Antonio should miss this idiosyncratic bar that's been serving the community for several decades. All sorts of colorful folks wander in here day and night—including locals who laugh it off as a dive that they swear they'd never be caught dead in. Behind the slightly dingy facade lies a surprisingly cute space with a jukebox outfitted with boppy tunes, a strobe light (but no dance floor), a postage-stamp–size covered patio, and a funny framed caricature of J. Edgar Hoover in drag. ⊠ *106 Navarro St.,* ☎ *210/223–7177. Crowd: 60/40 m/f, mostly over 35, mixed racially, down-to-earth, talkative, dishy.*

Nexus. Northwest of the city, just beyond I–410, Nexus is the main dyke gathering spot on weekends. It's worth the drive if meeting women is your thing. In front is a rec room with plush seating, pool tables, and other games—it's a good spot to check out the crowd and strike up a conversation. There's a large dance floor and video bar, where you will hear the usual dance tunes on weekends and can catch karaoke on some weekdays. Some of the nicest bartenders in Texas. ⊠ *8021 Pinebrook St.,* ☎ *210/341–2818. Crowd: mostly female weekends, 75/25 f/m, weekdays, 20s to 50s, mixed bag, friendly.*

Pegasus. The guys who end up two-stepping next door at the Silver Dollar or voguing at the nearby Saint often begin the evening at this convivial video bar with a tropical-theme patio, swimming pool, beach, and volleyball court out back. On weekend afternoons the crowds enjoy the sand and swimming; late in the evening table-top go-go boys keep the regulars glued to their bar stools. ⊠ *1402 N. Main Ave.,* ☎ *210/299–4222. Crowd: mostly male, mostly 30s and 40s, a few stand-and-model boys, low-key and outgoing, cruisy.*

The Saint. This smartly decorated warehouse disco isn't as large as the Bonham Exchange, but because it's predominantly gay, it's at least as popular and considerably cruisier. Most of the action revolves around a dance floor and surrounding tiered standing areas—ideal for watching cute guys dancing or some of the best drag shows in Texas. All the city's bars are racially diverse, but of the major clubs the Saint has the strongest Hispanic presence. Open weekends only, the club has frequent 18-and-over nights. ⊠ *1430 N. Main Ave.,* ☎ *210/225–7330. Crowd: 80/20 m/f, late teens to 40s, mixed racially, collegiate, well-dressed, disco bunnies, drag queens and their admirers.*

Silver Dollar Saloon. With a great location sandwiched between two of San Antonio's most happening bars, Pegasus and the Saint, this country-western saloon always packs in a decent crowd. Cowboy hats and boots are commonplace, but the prime location also draws quite a few non-country patrons. Good sound system. ⊠ *1418 N. Main Ave.,* ☎ *210/227–2623. Crowd: Mostly male, late 20s and older, clean-cut, friendly.*

Neighborhood Haunts

Steps from the River Walk, the **Captain's Crew** (⊠ 309 W. Market St., ☎ 210/223-0333) is a mellow spot with friendly bartenders and nautical kitsch on the walls. On weekends, **Eagle Mountain Saloon** (⊠ 1902 McCullough Ave., ☎ 210/733–1516) is actually a bit more than a neighborhood bar, drawing drag queens, country-western fans, and regular guys and gals for line dancing and mug hoisting. Tiny **Mick's** (⊠ 5307 McCullough Ave., ☎ 210/828–4222) is big with Olmos Park dykes and fags.

2015 (⊠ 2015 San Pedro Ave., ☎ 210/733–3365) has mirrors, glittery lights, and a show stage—all the right ingredients for drag, but the place isn't a big draw. Although it's a large complex with three distinct bars, the two-level space comprising **Rebar, Woody's, and Club W** (⊠ 820 San Pedro Ave., ☎ 210/271–9663) attracts mostly locals. Woody's has strippers and is kind of sleazy but fun; Rebar, which is upstairs, gets more of a leather and Levi's crowd; and Club W is a drag club with a large dance floor, a central bar, and a couple of pool tables.

One-Nighters

On Wednesday the student-oriented Tex-Mex and burger restaurant **Tycoon Flats** (⊠ 2926 N. St. Mary's St., ☎ 210/737–1929) tosses a wild and well-attended queer party. Out in the courtyard, locally beloved acoustic guitar duo Lenny and Sylvia entertain the chatty crowd, which runs the rainbow gamut: male, female, 20s to 60s, all races, and zero attitude. Don't miss this one.

Action

Of the city's two bathhouses, **Alternative Clubs Incorporated** (✉ 827 E. Elmira St., ☎ 210/223–2177) is the nicer and more popular.

SLEEPS

The dozens of new hotels around the south side of downtown attest to the city's popularity as a leisure and business destination, but shun these cookie-cutter chain lodgings in favor of the many gay-friendly inns and historic hotels. Most of these properties are downtown, within walking distance of major attractions, but they also have the highest rates. For a chance to stay close to gay bars and some good restaurants, consider one of the more affordable B&Bs north of downtown.

For price ranges, *see* lodging Chart B at the front of this guide.

Hotels

$$$–$$$$ **La Mansion del Rio.** Converted into a luxury hotel during the 1968 World's Fair, this former Catholic seminary remains the jewel of San Antonio's hotel scene, replete with wrought-iron balconies, Moorish arches, and numerous Spanish Revival architectural details. Rooms overlook either the River Walk or a landscaped courtyard. ✉ *112 College St., 78205, ☎ 210/225–2581 or 800/292–7300, FAX 210/226–0389. 327 rooms. Restaurant, pool.*

$$–$$$$ **Menger.** The bland rooms in the Menger's 1940s wing are the most affordable, but all guests can enjoy this 1859 charmer's stunning public areas, warm staff, and top-notch facilities. If you are up for a splurge, rooms in the original section exude Victorian charm. ✉ *204 Alamo Plaza, 78205, ☎ 210/223–4361 or 800/345–9285, FAX 210/228–0022. 345 rooms. Restaurant, pool, exercise room.*

$–$$ **Hampton Inn Riverwalk.** If all you require are clean rooms, convenience to downtown, and good value, try this well-managed chain property not far from Rivercenter Mall. ✉ *414 Bowie St., 78205, ☎ 210/225–8500 or 800/426–7866, FAX 210/225–8526. 169 rooms. Pool.*

Guest Houses and Small Hotels

$$$–$$$$ **Arbor House Hotel.** Opened in 1995 by two talented guys with an eye for bold artwork and innovative ideas about restoration, this intimate downtown hotel consists of four turn-of-the-century buildings, each with enormous suites—some with whirlpool baths, kitchenettes, and balconies. Brightly painted southwestern antiques, leopard-print rugs, clawfoot tubs, and a few retro-stylish furnishings salvaged from the old Las Vegas MGM hotel create a memorable yet amazingly tasteful impression. ✉ *339 S. Presa, 78204, ☎ 210/472–2005 or 888/272-6700, FAX 210/472–2007. 16 rooms with phone, TV, and private bath. Continental breakfast. Mixed gay/straight.*

$$–$$$ **Adams House Bed & Breakfast.** Straight-owned but with extremely friendly innkeepers, this 1902 Italianate-inspired mansion sits on a historic street in the heart of King William, just a 15-minute walk from downtown attractions. Rooms have period pieces, and are elegant but not overdone. The breakfasts are quite memorable. ✉ *231 Adams St., 78210, ☎ 210/224–4791 or 800/666–4810, FAX 210/223–5125. 5 rooms with phone, TV, and private bath. Full breakfast. Mixed gay/straight.*

$–$$ **Painted Lady Guest Hotel.** For many years this women-owned 1920s mansion has been a hit with queer travelers, who appreciate its proximity to downtown, reasonable rates, and yellow exterior offset by green balconies and white Doric columns. Rooms are filled with antiques. About the only drawback—at least in summer—is the absence of air-conditioning. Some rooms have kitchenettes. ✉ *620 Broadway, 78215, ☎ 210/220–1092, FAX 210/220–1092. 8 rooms with phone, TV, and private bath. Continental breakfast. Mixed gay/straight.*

THE LITTLE BLACK BOOK

At Your Fingertips

AIDS Information Line (☎ 210/225–4715). **Gay and Lesbian Community Center** (✉ 923 E. Mistletoe St., ☎ 210/732–4300, e-mail trottski@earthlink.net). **Gay and Lesbian Help and Information Line** (☎ 210/734–8648). **Lesbian Information San Antonio** (☎ 210/828–5472). **San Antonio Arts and Cultural Hotline** (☎ 210/207–2166 or 800/894–3819). **San Antonio Convention & Visitors Bureau** (✉ Box 2277, 78298, ☎ 210/270–8700 or 800/447–3372, Web site www.sanantoniocvb.com). **San Antonio Gay Switchboard** (☎ 210/733–7300; for nightlife information, ☎ 210/734–2833). **San Antonio Visitor Information Center** (✉ 317 Alamo Plaza, ☎ 210/270–8748). *This Week* (☎ 210/828–7660, e-mail sacurrent@aol.com).

Gay Media

The city has a monthly gay newspaper, the *San Antonio Marquise* (☎ 210/545–3511, e-mail samarquise@aol.com), and the statewide gay papers (*see* Gay Media in Chapter 2) have some San Antonio coverage.

BOOKSTORES

Textures (✉ 5309 McCullough Ave., ☎ 210/805–TEXT) is a contemporary two-level space with a very good selection of women's and lesbian titles. The quirky **Q Bookstore** (✉ 2803 N. St. Mary's St., ☎ 210/734–4299) carries new and used queer books and porn, plus gifts, stickers, and such. **Encore Video** (✉ 8546 Broadway, ☎ 210/821–5345) and **Zebra'z** (✉ 1216 Euclid St., ☎ 210/472–2800) sell porn, videos, pride items, gifts, and other gay goodies.

Working Out

There are no heavily gay-frequented gyms in San Antonio.

38 Out in San Diego

WESTERN U.S. CITIES ALWAYS SEEM TO GENERATE comparisons: Phoenix to Las Vegas and L.A., L.A. to San Francisco, San Francisco to Seattle, Seattle to Vancouver and Portland. But you rarely hear mention of San Diego in the same breath as another town, except, occasionally, Los Angeles. A tad provincial, California's second-largest city, the sixth-largest in the country, motors along at a comfortable pace, pleasing all who visit but never really knocking anyone's socks off. What gives?

For one thing, San Diego's even keel keeps it out of the public eye; it has a steady, predictable personality, as seen in the resolute cheerfulness of its neighborhoods and its consistently calm and sunny weather. Of California's three children, San Diego behaves like the proper middle child. L.A. plays the oldest child—an arrogant image-conscious dictator of America's styles and trends. San Francisco is the baby—whining about injustice, tattling on the politically incorrect, and basking in its mandate to monitor America's conscience. Mild-mannered, conservative, and willing to take orders, San Diego speaks to America only when spoken to.

By and large San Diegans are a friendly lot. There are few places in America where restaurant servers go to more trouble to check on their patrons' well-being, where shopkeepers utter more heartfelt gratitude, and where locals are quicker to assist visitors. With increasingly active liberals and a conservative majority living in each other's shadows, it's surprising everybody here remains so cordial. Perhaps the pervading civility is owing to the delightful climate and surroundings. In any case, San Diegans truly seem to live under a blissful spell. This as much as anything might explain why visitors find the city so charming and relaxing, if not as memorable as other vacation destinations.

THE LAY OF THE LAND

San Diego's geographic center is leafy 1,400-acre Balboa Park. Downtown abuts the park on the south and west. Several older residential and mixed-use neighborhoods are west and north—including the gay Hillcrest and Uptown districts. Several of the city's most Hispanic and in some cases up-and-coming neighborhoods are east and southeast of the park; of these, Azalea Park and Golden Hill are rapidly becoming gentrified by lesbians and gays. The beach communities of North Island, Coronado, Point Loma, Ocean Beach, Mission Beach, Pacific Beach, La Jolla, and Del Mar are a short drive away.

Hillcrest, the Uptown District, and Environs

Hillcrest, the neighborhood at the northwest tip of Balboa Park, is a greatly toned-down version of San Francisco's Castro. Around its traditional crux, at the intersection of 5th and University avenues, are many bars, restaurants, and shops. In recent years, however, the commercial focus of San Diego's gay community has shifted to the eastern reaches of Hillcrest along the 1000 block of University Avenue. The more gentrified blocks in this area are generally known as the **Uptown District,** but the name technically applies to a cluster of attractive pastel-hue, Spanish-style shopping centers that line the north side of University. On the south side of the street are a strip of gay-oriented shops, eateries, and bars (sometimes called the Rainbow Block). This is one of the prettiest and liveliest gay enclaves in the country.

With Hillcrest's growing popularity, many gays and lesbians are moving east and north of here, to **University Heights, North Park, Normal Heights,** and **Kensington. Adams Avenue** is the small commercial center of Kensington; here you'll find a couple of fun restaurants and the **Ken Cinema** (✉ 4061 Adams Ave., ☎ 619/283–5909), which shows mainly foreign and alternative films, many of them queer-oriented.

Downtown and the Gaslamp Quarter

Downtown San Diego is a grid whose northeast corner touches I–5 and Balboa Park, and whose southwest corner touches San Diego Bay. It's bounded roughly by Cedar Street to the north, 5th Avenue to the east, Market Street to the south, and Harbor Drive to the west. Harbor Drive winds south along San Diego Harbor to **Seaport Village** (☎ 619/235–4014), which anchors the **Embarcadero,** a touristy stretch of shops and restaurants. Farther east is **Horton Plaza** (☎ 619/238–1596), a six-block shopping, dining, and entertainment mall with a **Nordstrom** department store, a farmers' market, the excellent **San Diego Repertory Theater,** and other attractions.

Downtown's renaissance was precipitated by the restoration of the **Gaslamp Quarter,** a 16-block historic district that runs along 4th and 5th avenues from Broadway to Market Street. The city's commercial hub during the late 1800s, the quarter turned into a grim red-light district in the early 20th century. Today it is one of the nation's most successful and aesthetically pleasing urban renovations. The original buildings have been remodeled and reopened as art galleries, coffeehouses, jewelry shops, restaurants, and antiques shops. Several restaurants here are gay-owned and many have gay servers and followings.

Balboa Park

San Diego's major museums and sights are not downtown but almost entirely within the rolling emerald confines of **Balboa Park.** The highest concentration of attractions is in the center of the park along El Prado, which you reach via 6th Avenue. The **Balboa Park Visitors Center** (☎ 619/239–0512) provides general information about park attractions. Must-sees include the **Fleet Space Theater and Science Center** (☎ 619/238–1233); the **San Diego Natural History Museum** (☎ 619/232–3821); the **San Diego Museum of Art** (☎ 619/232–7931); and the smaller **Timken Museum of Art** (☎ 619/239–5548), which houses a collection of 18th- and 19th-century American and earlier European paintings. The world-class **San Diego Zoo** (☎ 619/234–3153) can be explored either on foot (somewhat rigorous), by double-decker bus, or via an aerial tram.

Old Town

San Diego's 18th-century Spanish roots are preserved in **Old Town San Diego State Historic Park,** a quadrant of historic blocks northwest of downtown, just below where I–8 branches off from I–5. Old Town is clean and pleasant for a stroll, but very touristy. **San Diego Avenue,** the main drag, has souvenir stands, crowded Mexican restaurants, and shops selling a mix of legitimate crafts and schlocky reproductions. To orient yourself, stop by the **Robinson-Rose House** (✉ 4002 Wallace St., ☎ 619/220–5422), which doubles as a visitor center.

The hill overlooking Old Town is dotted with hacienda-style homes. Crowning the hill (and it's a steep walk to the top) is green 40-acre **Presidio Park,** where the city's Spanish presidio and mission once stood. A Mission-style 1929 structure at the park's north end holds the **Junípero Serra Museum** (✉ 2727 Presidio Dr., ☎ 619/297–3258), which has artifacts from San Diego's earliest days.

Coronado and the Beaches

The mammoth North Island Naval Air Station at the top of **Coronado Island** (which is really a peninsula) has been a fixture in the region since the beginning of the century. South of the base is the civilian-accessible part of the island. **Orange Avenue** has a stretch of boutiques and restaurants. Also here is the grandiose **Hotel Del Coronado** (✉ 1500 Orange Ave.) where Jack Lemmon, Tony Curtis, and Marilyn Monroe frolicked during the filming of Billy Wilder's 1959 classic *Some Like It Hot.*

You'll find something of a gay following along a funky stretch of **Pacific Beach,** north of Mission Beach, that begins just above the Crystal Pier and extends for a couple of hundred yards. You may or may not see gay couples along the beach, but with the scads of buff surfer boys in tight wet suits and gorgeous women blading along the sidewalk above the beach you'll at least be able to enjoy the scenery.

Black's Beach and La Jolla

Up the coast from Pacific Beach is **La Jolla,** San Diego's most prestigious resort and beach town, a bastion of seaside nobility. Gay folk are not the slightest bit visible in conservative La Jolla, but then neither are homophobes. This is a discreet, civil, and laid-back community—about the only things that excite residents are shopping and eating out.

North of town is **Torrey Pines City Park Beach,** known locally as Black's Beach. This spectacular stretch of sand beneath a steep cliff is the most openly gay of San Diego's beaches. To reach this secluded haven, where nudity is officially not permitted but widely practiced, follow Genesee Avenue west from I–5 to its intersection with Torrey Pines Road. At the light, go straight across the intersection. Make a right turn at the "Torrey Pines Glidersport" sign, and follow this paved road to its end. Turn right into the dirt parking lot, and continue driving across the glidersport runway as far as you can go. Once you've parked, hike down any of the rugged trails to the beach below.

GETTING AROUND

This is an auto-oriented city. I–5 and I–15 are the main north–south routes. I–8 heads east from Mission Bay, Highway 94 from downtown. Once you've reached a desired neighborhood, San Diego becomes more walker friendly. Parking is relatively easy to find, and streets are intelligently laid out and easy to navigate.

The **San Diego Trolley** (☎ 619/233–3004) travels around downtown and to the eastern suburbs, Old Town, and Mission Valley. You can take a trolley to the Mexican border, but a car is more convenient. The **San Diego–Coronado Ferry** (☎ 619/234–4111), an alternative to driving to Coronado, is a terrific way to take in views of the harbor.

EATS

San Diego's dining scene has lately begun catching up with the rest of California. Several extraordinary restaurants stand out among dozens of solid options; the most gay-frequented eateries are around Hillcrest. Gaslamp Quarter restaurants don't have an especially gay following, but they all cater to a trendy, artsy bunch—you'll never feel out of place.

For price ranges, *see* dining Chart A at the front of this guide.

Hillcrest and Environs

$$–$$$ ✕ **California Cuisine.** Minimalist decor and black-and-white photos ensure that nothing distracts from the fabulous California fare at this Rainbow Block establishment. Flashy patrons dine on grilled venison with wild mushrooms and grilled quail with maple-cumin glaze. There's a romantic patio in back. ⊠ *1027 University Ave.,* ☏ *619/543–0790.*

$$–$$$ ✕ **Kemo Sabe.** This "in" spot with the gay community has floor-to-ceiling windows that allow diners to ogle customers passing in and out of the International Male Showroom next door. The fusion menu includes Mexican, southwestern, and Asian dishes, from quail to carpaccio. ⊠ *3958 5th Ave.,* ☏ *619/293–7275.*

$$–$$$ ✕ **Laurel.** One of San Diego's premier restaurants resides about midway between downtown and Hillcrest—appropriately, it draws suits and homos. The French-Mediterranean fare is stupendous. Try roasted breast and confit of guinea hen with apples and balsamic-vinegar-braised red cabbage. ⊠ *505 Laurel St.,* ☏ *619/239–2222.*

$$–$$$ ✕ **Marc's Bar and Grill.** The latest spot for gay dinner dating and piano cabaret, Marc's occupies the top floor of a small office building in Hillcrest. The dining room of chrome, black, and purple is casual but upscale—try for a table on the balcony in good weather. Steaks, pastas, and seafood grills are prepared. Brunch is a big to-do. ⊠ *3940 4th Ave., #200,* ☏ *619/293–0232.*

$$–$$$ ✕ **Montana's American Grill.** A classic art deco building houses one of San Diego's top purveyors of western regional cuisine. Game, smoked fish, grilled-over-hardwood meats, and pastas are menu staples, along with regularly changing microbrewed beers. The restaurant frequently hosts gay fund-raisers. ⊠ *1421 University Ave.,* ☏ *619/297–0722.*

$$ ✕ **Cafe Eleven.** Scenario: You can't spend a lot of money, but you want to take that special someone out for an elegant dinner. The solution is this intimate country-French bistro, where local art brightens the atmosphere and veal sweetbreads or pork chops with a black cherry sauce can be had for a song. ⊠ *1440 University Ave.,* ☏ *619/260–8023.*

$$ ✕ **Mixx.** Fiesta ware, warm lighting, and pretty patrons create a festive ambience at this near-Hillcrest newcomer with a widely regaled international menu. Highlights include chili-roasted pork with a fresh-berry salsa and roasted chicken with a lemon-soy glaze. ⊠ *3671 5th Ave.,* ☏ *619/299–6499.*

$–$$ ✕ **Cafe on Park.** Alternative artsy types and scenesters frequent this offbeat neighborhood café that serves hearty breakfasts and healthful salads, sandwiches, and grills for lunch and dinner. ⊠ *3831 Park Blvd.,* ☏ *619/293–7275.*

$–$$ ✕ **Hamburger Mary's.** Attached to Kickers, the lesbian and gay country-western bar, this branch of the famously queer burger chain is a rollicking party just about any night of the week. The foliage-bedecked patio is the main site for schmoozing and carrying on. The food is okay; come more to socialize, though. ⊠ *308 University Ave.,* ☏ *619/491–0400.*

$–$$ ✕ **Hob Nob Hill.** San Diegans—including those gay navy types—have been coming here since 1944 for the kind of home-style fare you miss when you're on the road. Great pecan rolls, coffee cakes, and other breads and sweets are baked on the premises, and there's a fresh catch of the day. Breakfast is always available. ⊠ *2271 1st Ave.,* ☏ *619/239–8176.*

$ ✕ **Crest Cafe.** A sleek deco diner that's open until midnight and crammed with ogling queers, the Crest Cafe is one of Hillcrest's true culinary and social fixtures. Sorry, Mom: The home-style American chow, from meat

482

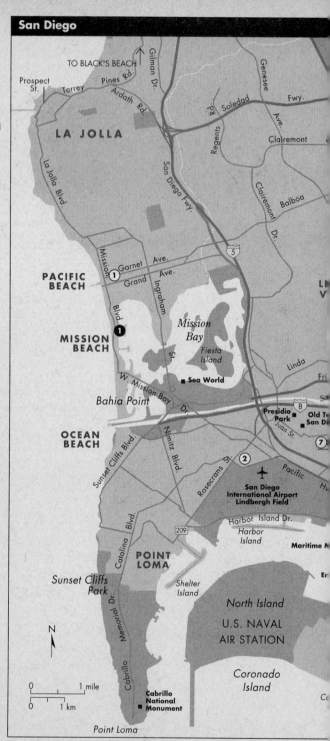

San Diego

loaf to burgers to outstanding homemade pies, may make your children forget about home. ✉ *425 Robinson Ave.,* ☎ *619/295–2510.*

$ ✕ **Topsy's.** This is your standard après-club diner, packed on weekend nights until 4 or 5 in the morning with college kids, green hairs, and sweaty queens. Doting gum-snapping waitresses complete the experience. Open 24 hours. ✉ *1451 Washington St.,* ☎ *619/296–8268.*

$ ✕ **Vegetarian Zone.** The best feature of this health-food café is the New Age store attached to it. Try the curried veggies over brown rice or the five-cheese lasagna. ✉ *2949 5th Ave.,* ☎ *619/298–1559.*

Downtown/Gaslamp Quarter

$$–$$$ ✕ **Café Sevilla.** For Spanish and Latin dining and entertainment, don't miss this place. Feast on *cordero a la cordobesa* (slow-roasted leg of lamb in a mushroom and wine sauce), and partake of sangria and tapas so authentic you may get the urge to don a shawl and mantilla and insist that everyone call you Carmen. ✉ *555 4th Ave.,* ☎ *619/233–5979.*

$$–$$$ ✕ **Croce's Restaurant & Jazz Bar.** In 1985 Ingrid Croce, the widow of folk balladeer Jim Croce, opened a tavern in a seedy section of town—an act that started the renaissance of a historic district and earned her the title of First Lady of the Gaslamp Quarter. Listen to live jazz while dining on great Continental and southwestern fare. ✉ *802 5th Ave.,* ☎ *619/233–4355.*

$$–$$$ ✕ **Fio's.** The best of the trattorias lining 5th Avenue in the Gaslamp Quarter serves up tasty pastas and wood-fired pizzas, along with fish and meat grills like oven-roasted rack of lamb with mustard mashed potatoes and wood-fired root veggies. ✉ *801 5th Ave.,* ☎ *619/234–3467.*

$$ ✕ **Bayou Bar and Grill.** Of Gaslamp Quarter restaurants, this one is the campiest—a tacky plaster fountain festooned with Mardi Gras beads anchors the dining room. The better options include an authentic Cajun version of red beans and rice, wonderful soft-shell crabs, oysters en brochette, and shrimp with Creole spices. ✉ *329 Market St.,* ☎ *619/696–8747.*

$–$$ ✕ **Greek Town.** This informal taverna is often abuzz with plate smashing and live music. The best (and gayest) Greek eatery in a city with several stellar ones, it offers the most for your dollar in the Gaslamp Quarter. ✉ *431 E. St.,* ☎ *619/232–0461.*

Elsewhere in San Diego

$$–$$$ ✕ **Kensington Grill.** This snazzy community-centered restaurant beside the Ken Cinema earns kudos for its healthfully delicious renditions of grilled fish, lamb, duck, and other meats, served with a changing guard of sauces and preparations. ✉ *4055 Adams Ave., Kensington,* ☎ *619/281–4014.*

$ ✕ **Big Kitchen.** For nearly two decades, an eccentric mix of Deadheads, chic lesbians, club kids, and old ladies has headed here for the best breakfasts in San Diego. The chatty servers, headed by Judy the Beauty on Duty, are part of the fun: If you're new, they'll treat you like royalty. If you're a regular, they'll toss the silverware onto the table and treat you like family. ✉ *3003 Grape St., Golden Hill,* ☎ *619/234–5789. No credit cards.*

$ ✕ **El Indio.** You won't find a better place for cheap authentic Mexican food than El Indio. Nothing unusual, just inexpensive fresh tortillas and chips, enchiladas, chicken burritos, and vegetarian dishes. The busiest of several locations is in Middletown, a bit west of Hillcrest. Great for takeout. ✉ *3695 India St., Middletown,* ☎ *619/299–0333; 409 F St., downtown,* ☎ *619/239–8151. No credit cards.*

$ ✕ **Mission Cafe.** This seaside oasis of hipdom pulls in slackers and surf bums. Art on the walls and live music and readings many nights make for an all-around boho atmosphere. The food is cheap, delicious, and eclectic. ✉ *3795 Mission Blvd., Pacific Beach,* ☎ *619/488–9060. No credit cards.*

$ ✕ **Saffron Chicken.** The top Thai eatery in town prepares roasted chicken that comes with any of five hot sauces, including peanut and chili. Some outdoor seating. ✉ *3731B India St., Middletown,* ☎ *619/574–0177.*

Coffeehouse Culture

David's Place. All the proceeds of this nonprofit coffeehouse go to AIDS organizations. David's has garden seating in front and the friendliest crowd in Hillcrest. ⊠ *3766 5th Ave., Hillcrest,* ☎ *619/294–8908.*

Euphoria. Leather chairs, changing artworks, and hot cider are among the offerings at this laid-back java joint. The crowd is trés gay. ⊠ *1045 University Ave., Hillcrest,* ☎ *619/295–1769.*

Extraordinary Desserts. This sweet-tooth's nirvana takes its confections seriously. You can munch on artfully presented cakes, pies, and Danishes— the white chocolate linzer torte is a favorite—either in the indoor dining nook or on the plant-filled terrace off to the side. Best desserts in the region. ⊠ *2929 5th Ave., Hillcrest,* ☎ *619/294–7001.*

Rebecca's. The ever-gaying Golden Hill neighborhood holds this upbeat coffeehouse that serves tasty sandwiches and salads. ⊠ *3023 Juniper St., Golden Hill,* ☎ *619/284–3663.*

The Study. This hangout has a meditative aura about it. Books line the walls, jazz plays in the background, and the lighting is subdued. You'll find soups sandwiches, scones, muffins, Danishes, and—best of all—free refills. ⊠ *401A University Ave., Hillcrest,* ☎ *619/296–4847.*

SCENES

Bars are spread around town, but the highest concentration is in Hillcrest, along 5th and University avenues. Most of the others are east or west of Hillcrest, but almost always north of Balboa Park. San Diego has a good leather scene for men, but not much of one for women.

Hillcrest and Environs

PRIME SUSPECTS

Bourbon Street. You won't often see guys in suits in San Diego, but Bourbon Street usually draws a few. This is the city's most elegant piano bar, a good place to take a date and celebrate with a group of friends. In back is a patio that's meant to recall the jazzy courtyards of New Orleans's French Quarter. ⊠ *4612 Park Blvd.,* ☎ *619/291–0173. Crowd: older, mostly male, smartly dressed, dignified.*

Brass Rail. Devoted club-hoppers stop by San Diego's oldest gay bar for a midweek change of pace, and so do guys who want a night on the town without all the posing. Sort of tired (especially the decor), but fun. The club's Hillcrest Grill is a good bet for casual queer dining. ⊠ *3796 5th Ave.,* ☎ *619/298–2233. Crowd: mostly male, 20s and 30s, regular guys, a few sweater queens, somewhat cruisy.*

The Flame. The city's top lesbian hangout has a large dance floor and several bars. Saturday it's absolutely packed. A mixed bunch comes on Friday night for the drag shows. Tuesday is boys' night, Wednesday is a well-attended Trash disco party, and there's country-western dancing on Thursday. Whenever you come, the music's great and the crowd high-energy. ⊠ *3780 Park Blvd.,* ☎ *619/295–4163. Crowd: 80/20 f/m most nights, stylish, youngish.*

Flicks. Though it's *the* see-and-be-seen video cruise bar in town, Flicks is down-to-earth. The carpeted space is decorated with framed posters of movie stars and the lighting is flattering; music is played at a level that allows conversation. On the yuppie side, but you'll meet nice guys you can take home to Mom. Best on Friday nights. ⊠ *1017 University Ave.,* ☎ *619/297–2056. Crowd: mostly male, young, clean-cut, guppie, cruisy.*

Kickers. As is often the case elsewhere, San Diego's country-western dance hall is the city's friendliest bar. Two-stepping and line-dancing (free lessons most weekday nights) take place in a large, handsomely furnished setting adjacent to Hamburger Mary's restaurant. ⊠ *308 University*

Ave., ☎ *619/491–0400. Crowd: extremely mixed in age, about 60/40 m/f, racially diverse, friendly, country-western, great dancers.*

Number One Fifth Ave. You can kick your feet up and chat with the friendly guys at this casual saloon that has piano entertainment some nights. Everybody-knows-your-name crowd, pop music, videos. No sign over front door. ✉ *3845 5th Ave.,* ☎ *619/299–1911. Crowd: 80/20 m/f, mostly thirtysomething and up, mixed racially, mellow, not so cruisy.*

Numbers. The most distinctive aspect of this video, pool, and sports bar across from the Flame is the no-attitude crowd. A hoppin' dance floor was added in '97. ✉ *3811 Park Blvd.,* ☎ *619/294–9005. Crowd: male, fun T-shirt-and-Levi's boys in their 20s and 30s, casual.*

Rich's. House music dominates at one of the West Coast's hottest gay discos. Up front is a small video bar; the dance floor's in back. Thursdays and Saturdays, everybody stops in. There's a cover most nights. ✉ *1051 University Ave.,* ☎ *619/497–4588. Crowd: young, mostly male, a fair racial mix, buffed, wired, lots of poseurs, serious dancers.*

Tidbits. Look for outstanding drag revues at this huge cabaret. Shows can happen any time from 6 until 1:30, but most begin around 10. The performance area is nicely decorated—not like the usual, cheesy, lost-in-the-'70s drag showcase. Karaoke action takes over many nights. ✉ *3838 5th Ave.,* ☎ *619/543–0300. Crowd: 70/30 gay/straight, diverse but united in their love of singing and campy drag.*

Wolfs. This leather-and-Levi's bar, popular because it's open late (until 4) on weekends, has two large rooms, both very dark. A motorcycle hangs from one ceiling and the usual butch accoutrements adorn the walls. Small leather boutique on premises. ✉ *3404 30th St.,* ☎ *619/291–3730. Crowd: male, mixed ages, as hard-core as leather gets in San Diego.*

NEIGHBORHOOD HAUNTS

The **Caliph** (✉ 3100 5th Ave., ☎ 619/298–9495) is big with chickens and chickenhawks and has piano music. **Club Bombay** (✉ 3175 India St., ☎ 619/296–6789), a mellower (than the Flame) lesbian club, draws a varied local crowd to its small dance floor. Friday is the biggest night. The friendly **Loft** (✉ 3610 5th Ave., ☎ 619/296–6407) attracts an older crowd that you could call inveterate regulars. **Pecs** (✉ 2046 University Ave., ☎ 619/296–0889) gets guys stopping in on the way from or to the nearby F Street Adult Bookstore; lots of leather, facial hair, bears.

The **Eagle** (✉ 3040 North Park Way, ☎ 619/295–8072) is dark, smoky, and cruisy, with lots of leather and facial hair wherever you look. At **Redwing** (✉ 4012 30th St., ☎ 619/281–8700), men and women play pool and watch sporting events on the tube.

As its name suggests, **Shooterz** (✉ 3815 30th St., ☎ 619/574–0744) has many pool tables; it attracts a crowd of varying ages. Shooterz recently opened an adjacent dance bar, **Odyssey** (same phone).

ONE-NIGHTERS

The disco **Club Montage** (✉ 2028 Hancock St., ☎ 619/294–9590), gay on Wednesday and Saturday, is highly popular with club kids male and female.

The Beaches

PRIME SUSPECTS

The Hole. Delightfully offbeat, the Hole has pool tables, a patio, an outdoor stage, and lots of space for mingling. The place is famous for its unbelievable drink specials and unbelievably drunk guys. Sunday nights are best. ✉ *2820 Lytton St., Point Loma,* ☎ *619/226–9019. Crowd: mixed ages, mostly male, butch, low hair-gel factor, lots of tight T-shirts and jeans, navy guys and the men who love them.*

The Matador. This is one of SoCal's best beach bars—the kind of place where men and women hobble in for a beer after a long day sunning or surfing. Not big or memorably decorated, it has a long bar with a juke-box, a few places to sit down, and a patio. ⊠ *4633 Mission Blvd., Pacific Beach,* ☎ *619/483–6943. Crowd: 80/20 m/f, all ages, sun-bleached beach bums, Gidget-dykes, mostly locals.*

Action

Of the 10 **F Street Adult Bookstore** branches, the most convenient are in North Park (⊠ 2002 University Ave., ☎ 619/298–2644), and the Gaslamp Quarter (⊠ 751 4th Ave., ☎ 619/236–0841). **Club San Diego** (⊠ 3955 4th Ave., Hillcrest, ☎ 619/295–0850) is the biggest and most popular bathhouse in town. **Dave's Club** (⊠ 4969 Santa Monica Ave., Ocean Beach, ☎ 619/224–9011) has an outdoor pool and a hot tub. **Mustang Spa** (⊠ 2200 University Ave., ☎ 619/297–1661), several blocks north of Balboa Park, has a 20-man whirlpool.

SLEEPS

The revitalization of downtown and several of its hotels has made it a decent base. To be within walking distance of most gay nightlife, you'll need to stay in Hillcrest, but your options are limited to a few smaller properties.

For price ranges, *see* lodging Chart A at the front of this guide.

Hotels

$$$–$$$$ 🏨 **Marriott Hotel and Marina.** Impersonal and mobbed with conventioneers, the 26-story Marriott has a choice location close to the Gaslamp Quarter and Seaport Village. Rooms are warmly furnished and have views of the bay and Coronado or downtown and Balboa Park. ⊠ *333 W. Harbor Dr.,* ☎ *619/234–1500 or 800/228–9290,* 𝖥𝖠𝖷 *619/234–8678. 1,355 rooms. Restaurant, pool, health club.*

$$$–$$$$ 🏨 **Wyndham Emerald Plaza Hotel.** The Wyndham's distinctive hexagonal towers are visible from all over town. The public areas are handsome and the rooms spacious. The gay-friendly hotel markets directly to the community. ⊠ *400 W. Broadway, 92101,* ☎ *619/239–4500 or 800/996–3426,* 𝖥𝖠𝖷 *619/239–4527. 436 rooms. Restaurant, pool, health club.*

$$$ 🏨 **U.S. Grant Hotel.** This historic property dates from 1910. Every room contains ornate Queen Anne–style reproductions, and the public areas have been handsomely restored. ⊠ *326 Broadway, 92101,* ☎ *619/232–3121 or 800/237–5029,* 𝖥𝖠𝖷 *619/239–9157. 280 rooms. Restaurant.*

$$ 🏨 **Gaslamp Plaza Suites.** Geared to budget travelers who demand cleanliness and charm, the 11-story Gaslamp Plaza Suites was San Diego's first skyscraper. The atmosphere here is a cross between that of a European pension and a beach resort. ⊠ *520 E St., 92101,* ☎ *619/232–9500 or 800/874–8770,* 𝖥𝖠𝖷 *619/238–9945. 65 suites. Restaurant.*

$$ 🏨 **Horton Grand Hotel.** One of the more unusual hostelries on the West Coast is really two Victorian brick properties that were moved to the Gaslamp Quarter and rebuilt in 1986. Rooms have period furnishings and gas-burning fireplaces. High tea here is a much-celebrated event. ⊠ *311 Island Ave.,* ☎ *619/544–1886 or 800/542–1886,* 𝖥𝖠𝖷 *619/239–3823. 132 rooms. Restaurant.*

$–$$ 🏨 **Park Manor Suites.** This all-suites gay-oriented property west of Balboa Park is a 15- to 20-minute walk from most Hillcrest bars. Rooms are large and have dated furnishings, but the ones on the upper floors have good city views; the staff is knowledgeable about the gay scene. ⊠ *525 Spruce St., 92101,* ☎ *619/291–0999 or 800/874–2649,* 𝖥𝖠𝖷 *619/291–8844. 80 rooms. Restaurant.*

Guest Houses and Small Hotels

$$–$$$$ ⊞ **Balboa Park Inn.** It's pricier than other Hillcrest properties, but this classy inn is still less expensive than downtown lodgings. Rooms have individual themes and decors to match. The Tara Suite is right out of *Gone With the Wind*, with sweeping burgundy drapes, a crystal chandelier, a marble fireplace, and a grand canopy bed. ⊠ *3402 Park Blvd., 92103,* ☎ *619/298–0823 or 800/938–8181,* ℻ *619/294–8070. 26 rooms with phone, TV, and private bath. Continental breakfast. Mixed gay/straight.*

$$ ⊞ **Bankers Hill B&B.** This beautifully restored 1912 Craftsman house is on elegant Banker's Hill, within walking distance of Hillcrest nightlife. Rooms have Victorian antiques and amenities like modern baths and phones with fax capability. Lovely grounds. ⊠ *3315 2nd Ave., 92103,* ☎ *619/260–0673 or 800/338–3748. 5 rooms with phone, TV, and private bath. Pool, hot tub, exercise room. Continental breakfast. Mixed gay male/lesbian.*

$$ ⊞ **Blom House.** You'll feel as if you're visiting your groovy Aunt Edna when you stay at this cottage-style home with views of Mission Valley from the 65-foot deck and the living room. Rooms have high ceilings, hardwood floors, and antiques; amenities include VCRs, refrigerators, and irons. ⊠ *1372 Minden Dr., 92111,* ☎ *619/467–0890. 3 rooms with phone, TV, and private bath. Hot tub. Full breakfast. Mixed gay/straight.*

$–$$ ⊞ **Carole's B&B.** An inexpensive option in North Park, this simple bungalow has plain, homey furnishings. Rooms have refrigerators. Separate studios and a furnished apartment are ideal for long-term stays. ⊠ *3227 Grim Ave., 92104,* ☎ *619/280–5258. 8 rooms with TV, most with shared bath; 2 studios, 1 two-bedroom apartment. Pool, hot tub. Continental breakfast. Mixed gay/straight.*

$–$$ ⊞ **Keating House.** This peach-and-sage confection is a short walk west of Balboa Park and a 20-minute walk from Hillcrest; it's one of the most attractive restored Victorians in San Diego. The rooms in the main 1888 house and a cottage are furnished in period style. ⊠ *2331 2nd Ave., 92101,* ☎ *619/239–8585 or 800/995–8644,* ℻ *619/239–5774. 8 rooms, 2 with private bath. Full breakfast. Mixed gay/straight.*

$ ⊞ **Hillcrest Inn.** A cut (and a gay one at that) above a hostel, this inn has simple rooms but a perfect location, within walking distance of bars and restaurants. You get a refrigerator, bar sink, and microwave for an incredibly low rate. Some rooms have private balconies. ⊠ *3754 5th Ave., 92101,* ☎ *619/293–7078 or 800/258–2280,* ℻ *619/293–3861. 45 rooms with phone, TV, and private bath. Mostly gay male.*

THE LITTLE BLACK BOOK

At Your Fingertips

Hillcrest Business Association (☎ 619/299–3330). **International Visitor Information Center** (⊠ 11 Horton Plaza, corner of 1st Ave. and F St., ☎ 619/236–1212). **Lesbian and Gay Community Center** (⊠ 3916 Normal St., Hillcrest, ☎ 619/692–2077). **Metropolitan Transit** (☎ 619/231–1466). **Orange Cab** (☎ 619/291–3333). **San Diego Convention & Visitors Bureau** (⊠ 401 B St., Suite 1400, 92101, ☎ 619/232–3101). **San Diego Visitor Information Center** (⊠ 2688 E. Mission Bay Dr., 92109, ☎ 619/276–8200).

Gay Media

Based in San Diego but covering all of southern California, *Update* (☎ 619/299–0500, e-mail updateed@aol.com) is the weekly news-oriented community paper. The *Gay and Lesbian Times* (☎ 619/299–6397, e-mail gltimes@earthlink.net), a flashier magazine, is more entertainment oriented and has better coverage of San Diego. The city also has a hip new bar 'zine **San Diego Circuits** (☎ 619/291–6690, e-mail sdcircuits@aol.com).

BOOKSTORES

The main lesbigay bookstore is **Obelisk** (⊠ 1029 University Ave., ☎ 619/297–4171), on the Uptown District's Rainbow Block. More general-interest but also with a good selection of feminist, lesbian, and gay titles is **Blue Door Books** (⊠ 3823 5th Ave., Hillcrest, ☎ 619/298–8610). **Gay Mart** (⊠ 550 University Ave., 619/543–1221) sells queer gifts, mags, fashion, and accessories.

Working Out

Bodybuilders Gym (⊠ 3647 India St., ☎ 619/299–2639), at the convergence of downtown, Hillcrest, and Old Town, is for muscle sculptors. **Hillcrest Gym** (⊠ 142 University Ave., ☎ 619/299–7867) is for the see-and-be-seen set (small but clean, more for lifting than for aerobic work).

39 Out in San Francisco

With the Russian River

CLICHÉD AS IT MAY SOUND, San Francisco is *the* gay mecca. Much of what draws gays and lesbians—outstanding performing and visual arts, world-class restaurants, sophisticated shopping, and a manageable layout—makes it a hit with everybody. A case could be made that San Francisco's attractions are more adult-oriented than other hot tourist locations such as Florida and southern California. Relatively few queerfolk travel with families, after all. But there's more to it than that.

The mid-'50s marked the beginning of two tumultuous decades of lesbian and gay-male activism. In 1955 the nation's first major lesbian political organization, the Daughters of Bilitis (DOB), was formed here under the leadership of Del Martin and Phyllis Lyon. Several mostly male-oriented homophile organizations also date from this period. Gays had made sufficient progress by 1959 to provoke the conservative *San Francisco Progress* to whine that "sex deviates" had turned the city into the nation's homosexual "headquarters." Gay and lesbian bars became more commonplace, though their owners had to pay off police to remain in business.

In the early '70s the mostly Irish working-class Castro neighborhood evolved into one of the world's most recognizable gay ghettos. A smattering of gay men, among them the outspoken political activist Harvey Milk, who opened a camera shop on Castro Street, began to settle here. A tidal wave of gay-male—mostly white and middle-class—immigration followed. In Edmund White's *States of Desire,* David Goodstein, the former publisher of the *Advocate,* described the Castro of the late '70s as "essentially a refugee culture made up of gay men, who, in a sense, are convalescing in the ghetto from all of those damaging years in Podunk."

In 1978, Dan White, a disgruntled former city supervisor, assassinated San Francisco's gay-friendly mayor, George Moscone, and supervisor Harvey Milk—who had risen to become the state's first openly gay elected official. Gays rioted in May 1979, White was convicted of manslaughter, courtesy of the famous "Twinkie defense" (that too much junk food had impaired his mental capacity).

The AIDS epidemic hit the city hard in the 1980s—mid-decade estimates put the number of HIV-positive men in the Castro district at above 50%. Opinions vary as to the long-term effects the disease has had on the character and personality of the once-bacchanalian neighborhood. Clearly, life became dramatically more subdued during the '80s, though the Castro is presently enjoying rejuvenation and a renewed trendiness.

The Castro is more diverse than before. People of all colors and classes now settle here, as do many lesbians. By the same token, more gays and lesbians live elsewhere around the city. Perhaps most significant is the emergence of the nation's most visible and powerful lesbian community, which has grown up right beside the Castro, in the lively Mission District.

Lesbians, whose voices were for so many years denied a serious platform, have become organized and vocal. The community supports woman-owned retail shops and restaurants, along with several performance spaces. Tension has always existed between San Francisco's gay men and lesbians—the type of "old-boy" network that often prevented qualified women from advancement in mainstream society operated similarly in the queer community. Tragically, AIDS took the lives of many men who had been at the forefront of San Francisco's gay movement. Lesbians not only picked up the slack, but often took charge. In the last decade, four different lesbians have held seats on the San Francisco Board of Supervisors.

San Francisco strengthened its claim on the title of gayest city in America in late 1996, when the Board of Supervisors passed a regulation that requires all companies and organizations doing business with the city to provide domestic-partner benefits to their employees. There has been intermittent grumbling in the corporate and religious communities, but the supervisors and Mayor Willie Brown were still standing firm on the issue as we headed to press.

THE LAY OF THE LAND

The Castro

The gay community's hub is bounded roughly by Duboce Avenue to the north, Church Street to the east, 21st Street to the south, and Douglass Street to the west, though the surrounding territory is heavily queer as well. The main commercial activity fans out from the intersection of **Castro, 17th,** and **Market** streets to the east and south.

Gay-oriented businesses along Market, 18th, and Castro streets continue to thrive, but new ones are attracting a broader mix of customers. Some favorites include **A Different Light** (⌂ 489 Castro St., ☎ 415/431–0891), the main lesbigay bookstore; **Under One Roof** (⌂ 2362 Market St., ☎ 415/252–9430), which sells gifts and T-shirts to benefit AIDS organizations; **Jaguar** (⌂ 4057 18th St., ☎ 415/863–4777), home to a luscious sampling of sex toys, novelties, lube, and greeting cards; **Does Your Mother Know . . .** (⌂ 4079 18th St., ☎ 415/864–3160), a homo take on a Hallmark store; and the **Harvest Ranch Market** (⌂ 2285 Market St., ☎ 415/626–0805), a well-stocked gourmet and organic market that doubles as a lesbian pickup spot.

The spectacular 1922 **Castro Theatre** (⌂ 429 Castro St., ☎ 415/621–6120) hosts the city's well-attended lesbian and gay film festival each summer; at other times it books first-run art films and many revivals.

Harvey Milk Plaza, above the Castro Muni Metro Station at Market and Castro streets, was dedicated in 1985. The plaque here has a moving inscription. The **Names Project Foundation** (⌂ 2362-A Market St., ☎ 415/863–1966) has a visitor center. The AIDS Memorial Quilt, begun here in 1987, consists of more than 40,000 hand-sewn panels, each a tribute created by the loved ones of a person who has fallen to AIDS. **Hello Gorgeous!!** (⌂ 549-A Castro St., ☎ 415/864–2628) is a full-blown tribute to the career and celebrity of Barbra Streisand. The store-gallery-museum is filled with movie posters, memorabilia, and paintings of the singer-actress-director.

A great way to see the Castro is on the 3½-hour walking tour, **Cruisin' the Castro** (☎ 415/550–8110, e-mail trvrhailey@aol.com), given by Trevor Hailey. She's a delightful speaker and a walking encyclopedia of local lore. The tour includes brunch at Caffe Luna Piena (see Eats, below).

The Mission

The Mission District, due east of the Castro, derives its name from the **Mission Dolores** (✉ Dolores and 16th Sts., ☎ 415/621–8203), which has stood here since 1791. The major commercial blocks of this largely Latino-populated neighborhood are **16th Street** from about Guerrero Street to Mission Street, and **Mission and Valencia streets** from 16th Street to 24th Street. You'll find cheap and tasty ethnic cuisine, left-leaning and lesbian-oriented shops and galleries, and some of the city's queer and women's performance spaces mixed in among the many Latin American and Chinese groceries and dry-goods stores. At **Community Thrift** (✉ 623 Valencia St., ☎ 415/861–4910), the sales of secondhand clothing, shoes, furniture, and household items benefit local queer charities. **Good Vibrations** (✉ 1009 Valencia St., ☎ 415/974–8980), an attractive woman-owned emporium, may be the loveliest erotica boutique you'll ever encounter.

A striking mural illustrating the lives of prominent women over the centuries covers two sides of the **Women's Building** (✉ 3543 18th St., ☎ 415/431–1180). Many feminist and lesbian political and social organizations meet at this terrific resource. If you continue east on 18th Street, you'll reach **Dolores Park,** a gay and lesbian "beach" during the day (the fog rarely affects this neighborhood) that can get dicey at night. East of Mission Street and south of Army Street, the modest residential neighborhood of **Bernal Heights** supposedly has the highest concentration of lesbian-owned houses in the city.

Gayification is rapidly spreading into the **Potrero Hill** district, which is just east of the Mission and shares that neighborhood's fogless climate. Fun shops and a few good restaurants have opened here, mostly along **18th Street.** Artists and young professionals have snapped up newly constructed lofts and apartments on the north slope of Potrero Hill.

Noe Valley

Quiet Noe Valley, with its mixed population of straight yuppies, male couples, and gay women with kids, lies south of the Castro and southwest of the Mission. The commercial strip, **24th Street** between Church and Diamond streets, has several restaurants and bakeries, a well-stocked organic-foods store, a half-dozen coffeehouses, and some shops and galleries. It's a cruisy scene (for gals and guys) but in a folksy way. To the west and high above Noe Valley and the Castro is **Twin Peaks,** a double-hump mountain with sweeping views of the entire city. You can drive up here via Twin Peaks Boulevard, or, from Castro and Market streets, take Muni Bus 37.

SoMa

The artsy **SoMa** district resembles New York City's SoHo district in more ways than one. Here, light industry has been replaced by designer studios and nonprofit galleries. The area is also a major enclave of factory-outlet stores. **Moscone Convention Center** and a couple of large hotels attract immediate attention, but the SoMa showstopper is the **San Francisco Museum of Modern Art** (✉ 151 3rd St., ☎ 415/357–4000), whose permanent collection includes pivotal works by Picasso, O'Keeffe, Kahlo, and Warhol; the museum's holdings in photography and multimedia work are also significant.

Across the street from SFMOMA in the block surrounded by 3rd, 4th, Mission, and Howard streets is **Yerba Buena Gardens,** a broad grassy plot with sculpture (including a waterfall tribute to Martin Luther King Jr.) and promenades. Also here is the **Center for the Arts** (✉ 701 Mission St., ☎ 415/978–2787). The **Ansel Adams Center for Photography** (✉ 250 4th St., ☎ 415/495–7000) exhibits contemporary and historic photography, some of the latter by Adams himself. The **California Historical Society** (✉ 678 Mission St., ☎ 415/357–1848) tends to a half-million photographs, 150,000 manuscripts, and countless paintings, books, periodicals, and documents.

At night SoMa comes alive as San Francisco's major club campus, for gays and straights alike. Gay leather and bear bars have been centered here for years, mostly around 8th and 11th streets. Several big discos pulse with activity around Folsom and Harrison streets. The area has a few great leather shops as well (*see* Action, *below*).

Downtown

Most of the city's hotels and high-end department stores (Neiman-Marcus, Saks, Gump's, Nordstrom) are near or on **Union Square.** The section of **Geary Street** just west of the square constitutes the city's modest Theater Row. **Maiden Lane,** east of the square, holds many high-end boutiques; before the 1906 earthquake it was another of San Francisco's red-light districts. For a fascinating tour of San Francisco's treasured Victorian architecture, take one of Jay Gifford's **Victorian Home Walks** (☎ 415/252–9485, Web site www.victorianwalk.com), which depart daily at 11 AM from Union Square. Gifford's 2½-hour tours (reservations are required), which meander by the most stunning Victorian houses in several great neighborhoods, have a strong gay following.

Northeast of Union Square is the **Financial District,** whose spine, **Montgomery Street,** is often called the "Wall Street of the West." If you head west of the Financial District, you'll approach **Chinatown,** which, for full effect, you should enter via the ornate **Chinatown Gate** at Grant Avenue and Bush Street. This is one of the largest Chinese communities in North America. You're now on the eastern slope of **Nob Hill,** where the city's old money has traditionally come to nest. At the peak of the hill, where California and Mason streets intersect, sit five of the city's most luxurious hotels (the Fairmont, Mark Hopkins, and Huntington among them) and **Grace Cathedral** (✉ 1051 Taylor St.). The congregation's AIDS Memorial Chapel contains a sculpture by the late Keith Haring and always has panels from the AIDS Memorial Quilt on exhibit.

Just northwest of Nob Hill lies **Russian Hill,** with restored Victorians, fancy new high-rises, and the oft-photographed **Lombard Street** (a.k.a. the crookedest street in the world), which switchbacks eight times from its apex at Hyde Street to its base at Leavenworth Street.

North of Nob Hill and Chinatown is the half-yuppie and half-Italian neighborhood of **North Beach,** whose **Columbus Avenue** and **Stockton Street** overflow with pastry shops and boutiques. Gay writers Allen Ginsberg and Gregory Corso were among the Beat Generation artistes who began hanging around North Beach cafés and clubs in the 1950s. The Beats' memory lives on at the **City Lights Bookstore** (✉ 261 Columbus Ave., ☎ 415/362–8193), still the domain of poet Lawrence Ferlinghetti.

If the crowds along Columbus Avenue become overwhelming, take a stroll up **Grant Avenue,** a modest commercial and residential strip with an authentically Italian-American ambience. When Grant hits Filbert Street, walk east to reach **Telegraph Hill** and the steps to 180-foot **Coit Tower,** which yields fine views of San Francisco Bay and Alcatraz Island.

Polk Gulch and the Tenderloin

Polk Street defines "rough trade." Hustlers sit along the curb bumming smokes off passersby. Drunken old men stumble out of some of the city's dreariest gay bars and porn shops at two in the afternoon. Polk Street is actually fashionable up around Russian Hill, but the section that forms the **Polk Gulch** neighborhood, from about Pine Street to McAllister, is on the ratty side. A few blocks east is the infamous **Tenderloin,** home to many gay and straight strip joints and porn emporiums.

Fisherman's Wharf and the Marina District

San Francisco's northern waterfront, from North Beach to the Golden Gate Bridge, contains many touristy attractions. Along much-publicized **Fisherman's Wharf** are several formerly industrial blocks and piers with amusements, schlocky shops, and overpriced restaurants. The action stretches from **Ghirardelli Square,** at the top of Polk Street, to **Pier 39,** home to the tackiest of souvenir stands and the recently opened **Underwater World** (☎ 415/544–9920). From several piers here you can book sightseeing cruises of the bay or excursions to **Alcatraz Island** (☎ 415/705–5555 or 415/773–1188), the infamous prison. Tours of Alcatraz are a must-do—the audio narration by former prisoners and guards is worth the extra fee. Just west of all of this action is the impressive **National Maritime Museum** (⊠ Polk St., at Beach St., ☎ 415/556–3002).

Farther west is the 1,400-acre **Presidio,** now administered as part of the Golden Gate National Recreation Area, and affording dramatic views of the awesome **Golden Gate Bridge.** Abutting the Presidio is **Baker Beach;** its southwesternmost end is sandy and easily accessible. As you hike along the rocky coastline toward the Golden Gate Bridge, you'll find that much of the crowd is sunbathing in the nude (weather permitting), that some of these sunbathers are gay men, and that many of them are a bit frisky. Watch your footing and beware of the dangerous surf.

Southwest of the Presidio is rugged 275-acre **Lincoln Park.** The park's sheer cliffs provide views of the Pacific Ocean, often accompanied by high winds, dense fog, and pounding surf. One of the better vantage points is **Land's End** (parking is at the end of El Camino del Mar). If you've read Armistead Maupin's *Tales of the City,* you'll remember this perch as being fraught with danger (the cliff here is very steep). The beach down below is quite cruisy. Be careful, though—the Park Service patrols this stretch. Swimming is unsafe and not recommended.

If you're in need of a cultural fix while in Lincoln Park, drop into the refurbished **California Palace of the Legion of Honor** (⊠ 34th Ave., off Clement St., ☎ 415/863–3330), which contains several impressive art galleries.

Civic Center

The **Civic Center** is the city's central complex of municipal buildings and cultural institutions. The interior of the **San Francisco Public Library** (⊠ Larkin and Grove Sts., ☎ 415/557–4440) is anchored by a sweeping atrium, off which are 11 special-interest centers that focus on Asian-Americans, African-Americans, the environment, and lesbians and gays. The on-site **James C. Hormel Gay and Lesbian Center** (☎ 415/557–4566), the first of its kind, holds books, periodicals, photographs, and other artifacts of gay life. Exhibits and documents trace local history but also provide an excellent overview of queer culture around the world.

San Francisco's world-class ballet and opera companies perform at the **War Memorial Opera House** (⊠ 301 Van Ness Ave., ☎ 415/861–4008). A block away is the newer **Louise M. Davies Symphony Hall** (⊠ 201 Van Ness Ave., ☎ 415/552–8000). Gay conductor Michael Tilson Thomas leads the band (the San Francisco Symphony). The nearby **San Francisco Performing Arts Library and Museum** (⊠ 399 Grove St., ☎ 415/255–4800) contains a large collection of memorabilia of the city's illustrious performing-arts history.

One by-product of San Francisco's 1989 earthquake was the destruction of a Central Freeway ramp that passed over the **Western Addition,** just west of the Civic Center. The eastern part of this neighborhood, whose commercial heart runs along **Hayes Street,** from Van Ness Avenue to Laguna Street, is known as **Hayes Valley.** Gentrification of this underappreciated district began as soon as the freeway ramp tumbled.

Galleries and funky restaurants now line Hayes Street and the blocks off it.

West of here is **Alamo Square,** at Fulton and Hayes streets. The hilly green slope is surrounded by restored "painted ladies," those colorful Victorian row houses coated with as many as two dozen shades of paint.

The Haight

Haight Street slices through the heart of the **Haight-Ashbury** district, one of the world's most recognizable beds of counterculturalism. During the '50s and early '60s, when the middle class headed for the suburbs, young artists and radical thinkers began taking over, converting the oversize homes into communes or chopping them up into affordable apartments. Progressive rockers such as the Grateful Dead, Janis Joplin, and the Jefferson Airplane lived here, as did their thousands of acid-infused followers. This part of town remains a land of slackers and alternateens, an easy place to find crystal jewelry, incense, vintage duds, and illicit buds. Most of the excessively commercial shops are in the Upper Haight, from about Masonic Avenue to Schrader Street.

The Lower Haight, east of Divisadero and technically outside the Haight–Ashbury proper, resembles the old Haight more than the actual one. The Lower Haight has an authentic struggling-artist mood—it's a good spot to find cheap food and poor students nagging you for spare change.

Beautiful **Buena Vista Park** rises high above the center of the Haight, allowing fabulous views in all directions. This is the city's cruisiest park—no matter what time of day. The police drop by frequently and usually show no mercy.

Golden Gate Park

Golden Gate Park lies between Fulton Street and Lincoln Way, and stretches all the way from Stanyan Street to the Pacific Ocean. Meadows, groves of cypress trees, lakes, and trails meander through the park, a wonderful spot for biking or blading—especially on Sundays when most of its roads are closed to vehicles. The eastern half has several notable attractions, such as the **Strybing Arboretum** (☎ 415/661–1316), the **Asian Art Museum** (☎ 415/668–8921), the **de Young Museum** (☎ 415/863–3330), and the **California Academy of Sciences** (☎ 415/750–7145). The **Japanese Tea Garden** (☎ 415/752–4227) is a serene spot to take tea and a rest from touring.

GETTING AROUND

Up until a few years ago, San Francisco was an easy driving city. It's still not too hard to find parking spaces west of Van Ness Avenue, but downtown as well as points north and south are getting tougher, and parking in most residential areas (including the Castro) for more than two hours requires a permit. Garages downtown are costly, too—the best (and cheapest) bets are the Sutter-Stockton and the 5th and Mission. The main reason to have a car here is to explore the outlying areas; in the city itself, consider relying on mass transit and cabs.

Muni buses are a good way to see the city. From anywhere on Market Street you can pick up Muni Bus 8 to reach the Castro. The fare is $1, and exact change (bills or coins) is required; day passes are available. Muni light-rail cars also stop at Castro and Market.

Cable cars ($2) are fun and exciting, but they only hit a few major sights. **BART** (☎ 800/817–1717) trains (fare varies) are useful for getting to Berkeley and Oakland but are less practical for travel within San Francisco. Taxis are difficult to hail but can be phoned, or picked up at most ho-

tels. A ride from downtown to the Castro shouldn't set you back more
than $8. In SoMa, taxis are usually plentiful after the clubs close; in the
Castro, you can sometimes hail a cab at Castro and Market streets.

EATS

San Francisco may be America's best dining city—it is very difficult to
stumble upon a bad meal. At worst, you'll pay too much in touristy areas,
and the food will be decent but not great. Or in less-expensive neighborhoods, you might sample a mediocre meal, but your financial loss will
be minimal. In any case, disappointments are rare.

The **Castro** went gay in the '70s, but it took nearly two decades for the
neighborhood's greasy spoons and tired Italian, Chinese, and other ethnic eateries—or at least some of them—to give way to more adventurous establishments like Mecca, 2223, and the affordable Fuzio.
Nosh-and-be-noticed bistros continue to pop up in **Hayes Valley,** and the
Mission, always a spot for cheap and delicious fare, has recently sprouted
several trendy yet vaguely boho restaurants. **Noe Valley,** where breakfast
is serious business, holds several upbeat coffeehouses. And although San
Franciscans no longer rush to **SoMa** the minute a new café or supper club
appears, you'll still find formidable purveyors of New American and other
cuisines.

For price ranges, *see* dining Chart A at the front of this guide.

The Castro

$$–$$$ ✕ **Mecca.** Many consider this supper club the true star of Market Street.
Mecca's patrons come to enjoy the stylish decor and Mediterranean-in-
spired cuisine—rare duck breast with a sauce of roasted figs and huck-
leberries. Later in the evening, this place becomes a fiercely hip highly
queer cocktail bar. ✉ *2029 Market St.,* ☎ *415/621–7000.*

$$–$$$ ✕ **2223.** This hopping gay restaurant is alive with gossip, cruising, and
fun, and the air is filled with the aroma of outstanding California cuisine. Roasted monkfish and braised lentils and broccoli rabe with roasted-
red-pepper rouille are among the highlights. On weekends, the brunches
pull in everyone who's anyone. ✉ *2223 Market St.,* ☎ *415/431–0692.*

$$ ✕ **Anchor Oyster Bar.** Meal for meal, this upbeat restaurant is one of the
Castro's most dependable haunts. You'll never be treated to less than won-
derful clam chowder or any of a number of fresh pastas and seafood grills.
✉ *579 Castro St.,* ☎ *415/431–3990.*

$$ ✕ **Caffe Luna Piena.** Trevor Hailey, famous for her queer walking tours
of the Castro, brings her flock to this excellent restaurant for brunch as
part of the trip. You can have brunch or dinner indoors or in a lush garden. ✉ *558 Castro St.,* ☎ *415/621–2566.*

$$ ✕ **Chow.** Right by the newly trendified Pilsner Inn, this frantically pop-
ular eatery serves California-style comfort food: wood-fired pizzas, flame-
broiled burgers, Thai noodles, and light pastas. Chow is less about
chowing than about schmoozing with the cute crowds. ✉ *215 Church
St.,* ☎ *415/552–2469.*

$–$$ ✕ **La Méditerranée.** This eatery serves some of the best under-$10 din-
ners in the city. You'll find all the usual Greek dishes, plus Lebanese *kibbeh*
(ground lamb) and tangy *baba ganoush* (eggplant puree with lemon juice,
olive oil, tahini, and garlic). ✉ *288 Noe St.,* ☎ *415/431–7210; also* ✉
2210 Fillmore St., ☎ *415/921–2956.*

$–$$ ✕ **Patio Café.** Not surprisingly, a pretty garden patio (with faux tropical
birds) provides the setting. This just may be the queerest patio in America: Sunday brunches are usually mobbed with hungover disco queens
dishing the previous night's tricks and treats. The food is just so-so. ✉
531 Castro St., ☎ *415/621–4640.*

The Castro

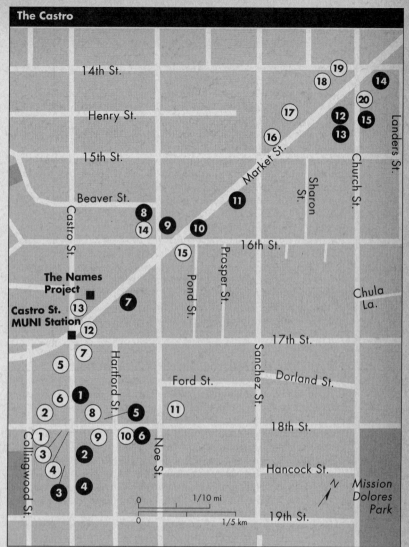

Eats ●

Anchor Oyster Bar, **4**
Bagdad Café, **10**
Cafe Flore, **9**
Caffe Luna Piena, **3**
Castro Country Club, **5**
Chow, **15**
Fuzio, **1**
Hot'n'Hunky, **6**
Just Desserts, **13**

La Méditerranée, **8**
Mecca, **14**
Patio Café, **2**
Pozole, **7**
Sparky's, **12**
2223, **11**

Scenes ○

Badlands, **3**
The Cafe, **12**
Cafe du Nord, **16**
Castro Station, **6**
Daddy's, **5**
Detour, **13**
Edge, **1**
Expansion Bar, **18**
Harvey's, **4**
Josie's Cabaret and Juice Joint, **15**

Lucky 13, **17**
Men's Room, **11**
Metro, **14**
Midnight Sun, **9**
Moby Dick, **10**
Pendulum, **2**
Pilsner Inn, **20**
Transfer, **19**
Twin Peaks, **7**
Uncle Bert's, **8**

$–$$ ✗ **Pozole.** At this lively spot along Market Street, many admire the trompe l'oeil decor and the gorgeous wait staff (few of whom speak any English), known affectionately as the "boys of Pozole." Often overlooked is the cheap and extraordinarily good Mexican food, which emphasizes enchiladas and quesadillas with a mix of traditional and innovative ingredients. ⊠ *2337 Market St.,* ☏ *415/626–2666. No credit cards.*

$ ✗ **Bagdad Café.** Some people call it "the Fag Hag Café," but the crowd—and especially the staff—is lesbo-chic. The food at this 24-hour diner is better and more healthful than that at Sparky's, the Castro's other post-disco nosh pit. But that isn't saying much. ⊠ *2295 Market St.,* ☏ *415/ 621–4434. No credit cards.*

$ ✗ **Fuzio.** This new Mediterranean-meets-Asian noodle house, although owned by the ubiquitous Tex-Mex chain Chevy's, doles out extraordinarily good (and very cheap) food, from simple pasta with meatballs to spicy grilled chicken with hoisin sauce. Fuzio has quickly blossomed into a Castro preclubbing hot spot. ⊠ *469 Castro St.,* ☏ *415/863–1400.*

$ ✗ **Hot 'n' Hunky.** Many people swear by the juicy burgers here; though they're good and have amusing names (e.g., "I wanna hold your ham") they're hardly the stuff of legend. Obviously, the name of the place suggests that you turn your eyes toward the waiters, and they do measure up nicely—not because they're so beefy but rather because they're so fun and dishy. ⊠ *4039 18th St.,* ☏ *415/621–6365.*

$ ✗ **Sparky's.** After the Castro bars close, mostly young, vaguely trendy queens congregate here for filling tuna melts, burgers, fries, and other greasy delights. It's open all night. ⊠ *242 Church St.,* ☏ *415/621–6001. No credit cards.*

Noe Valley, the Mission District, and Potrero Hill

$$$ ✗ **42 Degrees.** A major entrant in San Francisco's supper-club sweepstakes, this two-level converted garage in a desolate section of Potrero Hill oozes postindustrial chic—the patrons look good (and the sexy waiters are downright edible). Stars on the Mediterranean menu run the gamut, from inventive tapas to grills like pancetta-wrapped salmon with a lentil salad and sweet cherry tomatoes. ⊠ *235 16th St.,* ☏ *415/777–5558.*

$$–$$$ ✗ **Firefly.** First dates and long-term lovers will feel equally at home at this understated Noe Valley restaurant. The home-style cooking incorporates a United Nations of ingredients. Crawfish risotto cakes and barbecued Cornish game hen are two favorites that often appear on the menu. ⊠ *4288 24th St.,* ☏ *415/821–7652.*

$$–$$$ ✗ **Mangiafuoco.** Die-hard pasta junkies swear by this bustling but relatively unheralded storefront eatery that serves zesty pastas (including sublime gnocchi) and tender grills. A signature dish is seafood and pasta heated with sauce and herbs in a parchment paper bag. The waiters release the results—and plenty of steam—tableside. ⊠ *1001 Guerrero St.,* ☏ *415/ 206–9881.*

$$–$$$ ✗ **Universal Café.** One of the Mission's rising stars has a striking postmodern dining room set inside a converted turn-of-the-century warehouse. The menu concentrates on French and Italian Mediterranean fare—try the roasted Muscovy duck on spaghetti squash with chanterelle and porcini mushrooms. ⊠ *2814 19th St.,* ☏ *415/821–4608.*

$$–$$$ ✗ **Val 21.** Named for its location at the corner of Valencia and 21st streets, this purveyor of healthful Cal cuisine changes its menu every six weeks. Featured entrées include vegetarian plates, free-range and fish dishes—such as seared ahi on wasabi mashed potatoes—and no red meat. ⊠ *995 Valencia St.,* ☏ *415/821–6622.*

$$ ✗ **Slow Club.** One of the many quasi-tapas pads that have become all the rage in San Francisco, the Slow Club presents a diverse menu of California-inspired small plates. Roasted Yukon potatoes with aioli, and mus-

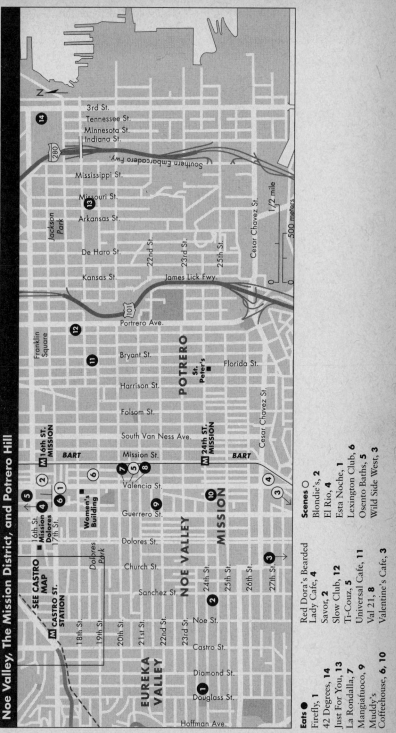

Noe Valley, The Mission District, and Potrero Hill

3rd St.
Tennessee St.
Minnesota St.
Indiana St.

Southern Embarcadero Fwy.

Mississippi St.

Missouri St.

Arkansas St.

Jackson Park

De Haro St.

Kansas St.

22nd St.

23rd St.

25th St.

Cesar Chavez St.

1/2 mile

500 meters

James Lick Fwy.

Portrero Ave.

Franklin Square

Bryant St.

Harrison St.

POTRERO

St. Peter's

Florida St.

Folsom St.

South Van Ness Ave.

BART

Mission St.

24th St. MISSION

BART

16th St. MISSION

Valencia St.

Cesar Chavez St.

Guerrero St.

Women's Building

SEE CASTRO MAP

16th St.
Mission
Dolores
17th St.

CASTRO STATION

Dolores St.

Church St.

Dolores Park

18th St.
19th St.
20th St.
21st St.
22nd St.

Sanchez St.

NOE VALLEY

Noe St.

24th St.

25th St.

26th St.

27th St.

MISSION

23rd St.

Castro St.

EUREKA VALLEY

Diamond St.

Douglass St.

Hoffman Ave.

Eats ●
Firefly, **1**
42 Degrees, **14**
Just For You, **13**
La Rondalla, **7**
Mangiafuoco, **9**
Muddy's
Coffeehouse, **6, 10**

Red Dora's Bearded
Lady Cafe, **4**
Savor, **2**
Slow Club, **12**
Ti-Couz, **5**
Universal Cafe, **11**
Val 21, **8**
Valentine's Cafe, **3**

Scenes ○
Blondie's, **2**
El Rio, **4**
Esta Noche, **1**
Lexington Club, **6**
Osento Baths, **5**
Wild Side West, **3**

sels sautéed in a tarragon-saffron cream sauce are among the highlights. ⊠ *2501 Mariposa St.,* ☎ *415/241–9390.*

$$ ✕ **Valentine's Cafe.** A Mission café with a mission to encourage healthful but robust eating, this diminutive vegetarian restaurant presents world-beat fare, heavy on fresh foods and relatively light on scary meat substitutes, dishes like sweet-potato and chèvre tart with sage pesto and apple relish, and risotto in a port demi-glace with sun-dried tomatoes, fresh garlic, and Swiss chard. ⊠ *1793 Church St.,* ☎ *415/285–2257.*

$–$$ ✕ **La Rondalla.** It's hard to tell whether the food here is truly extraordinary, or whether it simply seems great because all the authentic Mexican kitsch—bright and colorful lights, Christmas paraphernalia, and stuffed birds—distracts you. The food comes in giant heaps. ⊠ *901 Valencia St.,* ☎ *415/647–7474. No credit cards.*

$–$$ ✕ **Ti-Couz.** Lots of cute dykes work at this delightful creperie where you can invent your own crepe or choose from a long list. These Gallic wonders are tasty and reasonably priced. You might also pop in for one of the sweeter dessert creations. ⊠ *3108 16th St.,* ☎ *415/252–7373.*

$ ✕ **Just For You.** East of the Mission in Potrero Hill, this major spot for dykes with tykes has mighty-fine breakfast burritos. ⊠ *1453 18th St.,* ☎ *415/647–3033. No credit cards.*

$ ✕ **Savor.** In a sunny adobe-style courtyard in the heart of Noe Valley, a local blend of neobohos and earnest couples (gay and straight) linger over globally inspired takes on pancakes, crepes, and fresh-baked goods. Orange-ginger pancakes are a favorite. Weekend brunch can be a mob scene. ⊠ *3913 24th St.,* ☎ *415/282–0344.*

SoMa

$$–$$$ ✕ **Bizou.** This chic SoMa café with glowing yellow-and-orange hues offers stellar French-Italian comfort food, including baked *tagliolini* (egg noodle) with lamb sausage and duck-leg confit with curried lentils. ⊠ *598 4th St.,* ☎ *415/543–2222.*

$$–$$$ ✕ **Fringale.** This French Basque–style restaurant is a real find—a bright café with lemon-yellow walls that feels as if it should be out in the countryside, not on a nasty industrial street. People come from all over town for fare that includes Roquefort ravioli and potato and goat-cheese *galettes* (flat round cakes). ⊠ *570 4th St.,* ☎ *415/543–0573.*

$$–$$$ ✕ **Woodward's Garden.** This nine-table hole-in-the-wall tucked under a freeway was begun by Greens and Postrio alums Margie Conard and Dana Tommasino, who present a limited, thoughtful menu of northern California cuisine. Call well ahead for a table. ⊠ *1700 Mission St.,* ☎ *415/621–7122. No credit cards.*

$$ ✕ **South Park Cafe.** A long dining room of closely spaced tables, creamy yellow walls, indirect lights, and flowers galore creates an appropriately Parisian mood for delicious bistro fare. Favorites include savory rabbit stew and grilled chicken with pureed roasted-garlic potatoes, wild mushrooms, and thyme sauce. ⊠ *108 South Park Ave.,* ☎ *415/495–7275.*

$ ✕ **Hamburger Mary's.** This major favorite of SoMa disco bunnies is a colorful burger joint (tofu patties are available) that's open till 1 AM (2 on weekends). ⊠ *1582 Folsom St.,* ☎ *415/626–1985.*

Civic Center and Hayes Valley

$$$$ ✕ **Jardinière.** Award-winning lesbian chef Traci Des Jardins prepares superb French-California cuisine at her chic restaurant just behind the Opera House. The dishes change monthly; Virginia wild striped bass with a lobster saffron broth and potato gnocchi with chanterelles were on a recent menu. ⊠ *300 Grove St.,* ☎ *415–861/5555.*

$$–$$$ ✕ **Carta.** One of the restaurants leading Market Street's culinary renaissance presents a different culture's cuisine each month. The chefs pull it off with aplomb, serving four weeks of Venetian favorites like pan-roasted squab with herb-cream polenta and wild mushrooms, then seamlessly switching gears and delivering authentic Thai curries and satays. ⊠ *1772 Market St.,* ☏ *415/863–3516.*

$$–$$$ ✕ **Hayes Street Grill.** This informal seafood bistro has a dapper dining room with varnished wood tables and soothing walls of cream and forest green. Some of the better entrées include the crispy soft-shell crab meunière and the grilled fresh calamari. Yuppie central. ⊠ *320 Hayes St.,* ☏ *415/863–5545.*

$$–$$$ ✕ **Zuni Café.** Past its prime but still synonymous in San Francisco with upscale gay dining, Zuni gets its share of celebs and movie moguls—you still have to call ahead for a table. A perfect meal: Start with Caesar salad (best on the planet), then sample a dozen oysters (best selection in the city), before moving on to the roast chicken for two (best bargain of the entrées). ⊠ *1658 Market St.,* ☏ *415/552–2522.*

$$ ✕ **Cafe Delle Stelle.** This Hayes Valley pasta house is one of the city's best for a filling, reasonably inexpensive meal. Although you could survive on the rich Tuscan bread that comes with your meal, you'll want to sample the delicious homemade pastas and traditional Italian fare, ranging from porcini gnocchi to veal scallopine with creamy Gorgonzola sauce. ⊠ *395 Hayes St.,* ☏ *415/252–1110.*

$$ ✕ **dame.** This new queer-popular bistro is a fine choice for hearty New American cooking, including delicious tomato-rosemary soup and a main dish of hickory-smoked pork chop with creamy Gorgonzola polenta and sautéed red chard. ⊠ *1815 Market St.,* ☏ *415/255–8818.*

$$ ✕ **Millennium.** Set inside the unassuming Abigail Hotel is one of the city's most creative vegetarian restaurants. All the food is low-fat, organic, and dairy free—the grilled vegetables, polenta, and risotto dishes are terrific. ⊠ *246 McAllister St.,* ☏ *415/487–9800.*

$$ ✕ **Thep Phenom.** Off what unadventurous sorts call a dicey stretch of Lower Haight Street is one of the city's best Thai restaurants, with an elaborate menu, a lavish dining room filled with Thai art and antiques, and warm service. ⊠ *400 Waller St.,* ☏ *415/431–2526.*

$ ✕ **Vicolo.** This noisy dining room churns out the most inventive pizzas in town. The place may be guilty of overkill on the toppings—the "olive" pizza has mozzarella, fontina, red onion, green and Kalamata olives, Parmesan, garlic, and parsley—but everything's delicious. ⊠ *201 Ivy St.,* ☏ *415/863–2382.*

Downtown

$$$$ ✕ **Masa's.** Despite the constant praise this restaurant receives, the service remains refined and its ambience unstuffy. You can opt for the degustation menu or the menu du jour, which is slightly less costly. A sample degustation might include foie gras ravioli in a pheasant consommé with truffles, and a dessert of chocolate-pistachio terrine. ⊠ *648 Bush St.,* ☏ *415/989–7154.*

$$$–$$$$ ✕ **Cypress Club.** This off-the-wall supper club is known for its swank patrons, live jazz entertainment, and freewheeling New American cooking. The lobster soufflé is memorable. The Cypress Club is the brainchild of John Cunin, who opened 2223 in the Castro (*see above*). ⊠ *500 Jackson St.,* ☏ *415/296–8555.*

$$$ ✕ **Postrio.** It's a tad overrated, but this creation and part-time home of celebrity-chef Wolfgang Puck still makes for a memorable dining experience. The crispy Chinese duck is a specialty. Consider saving a few bucks by eating in the bar; its menu shows off Puck's designer pizzas. ⊠ *545 Post St.,* ☏ *415/776–7825.*

$$ ✕ **Café Akimbo.** A certain well-respected dining guidebook describes Café Akimbo as being "popular with ladies who shop." This could not be more true—the place is absolutely crawling with designer fags. Con-

Downtown San Francisco

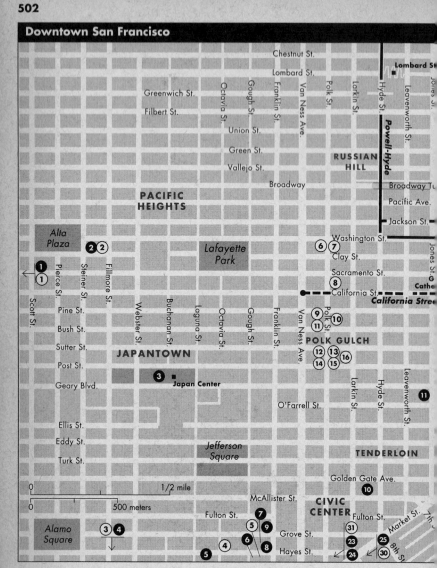

San Francisco Bay

sider such creative seafood fare as spring rolls filled with enoki and shiitake mushrooms in a tangy mango sauce. With many dishes around $10, it's a steal. ⊠ *116 Maiden La.,* ☎ *415/433–2288.*

$–$$ ✕ **North Beach Pizza.** Not only touristy, this place is often populated by slightly horrifying mobs of straight kids from the suburbs. Still, the maroon vinyl booths and green Formica tables are refreshingly ungentrified, and the pizza is otherworldly. The pies are huge—two slices is plenty for most people. ⊠ *1499 Grant Ave.,* ☎ *415/433–2444.*

$ ✕ **Dottie's True Blue Cafe.** It seats perhaps two dozen people and may not look like much, but Dottie's is a San Francisco fixture when it comes to filling breakfast fare and home-style lunches. Pretty gay by Union Square standards. ⊠ *522 Jones St.,* ☎ *415/885–2767.*

West of Van Ness

$$–$$$ ✕ **Alta Plaza.** Chef Amey Shaw has attracted a new following to the restaurant attached to the guppity Alta Plaza bar by cooking up a global storm of tasty cuisine. Favorites include marinated teriyaki-roasted lamb riblets with a spicy mustard sauce and a risotto with golden chanterelle, shiitake, and lobster mushrooms, drizzled with white truffle oil. ⊠ *2301 Fillmore St.,* ☎ *415/922–1444.*

$$–$$$ ✕ **Garibaldi's on Presidio.** Garibaldi's is a bona fide queer-date spot in the heart of Pacific Heights. Even more impressive are the high culinary standards, upheld with such California-Mediterranean dishes as grilled figs stuffed with Stilton and wrapped in prosciutto, and filet mignon flambéed in a faintly sweet butter, brandy, and green-peppercorn sauce. Friendly, knowing service enhances the experience. ⊠ *347 Presidio Ave.,* ☎ *415/563–8841.*

$–$$ ✕ **Mifune.** For fresh, authentic soba and *udon* (white-flour) noodles, head to this Japan Center restaurant where a full dinner typically weighs in at under $6. ⊠ *Kintetsu Bldg., 1737 Post St.,* ☎ *415/922–0337.*

Coffeehouse Culture

The Castro

Cafe Flore. Heading into its third decade of caffeinating the Castro's queers, Café Hairdo (as it's often teased) is San Francisco's gay ground zero. You can come for breakfast, stay through lunch, stick around for afternoon coffee, grab a beer before dinner, eat dinner, and finish things off with cordials and dessert. ⊠ *2298 Market St.,* ☎ *415/621–8579.*

Castro Country Club. This casual spot originated in 1983 as a nonalcoholic alternative to the area's many bars. It remains a pressure-free place for clean-and-sober rendezvous. ⊠ *4058 18th St.,* ☎ *415/552–6102.*

Just Desserts. Chomp on pies, pastries, and heavenly cheesecake at this purveyor of things fattening and delicious. ⊠ *248 Church St.,* ☎ *415/ 626–5774.*

Mission District

Muddy's Coffee House. These lesbian-favored beaneries have a couple of outdoor tables and get a good mix of locals, artists, and queers. Both establishments have bright, airy main rooms with good people-watching vistas. ⊠ *510 Valencia St.,* ☎ *415/863–8006; 1304 Valencia St.,* ☎ *415/ 647–7994.*

Red Dora's Bearded Lady Café. You can get great bagels, veggie burritos, and other meatless fare at this divinely dykey, hip, smoke-free, PC lesbian performance space. The votive candles are a nice touch. ⊠ *485 14th St.,* ☎ *415/626–2805.*

Elsewhere

Caffe Trieste. Beat poet Allen Ginsberg and his pack regularly graced the tables of this North Beach institution. The Giotta family has run the place since it opened in 1956, cultivating a warm but not fancy atmosphere in which to sip a cappuccino. ⊠ *601 Vallejo St.,* ☎ *415/392–6739.*

Chat House. This upbeat SoMa café and espresso bar above the lesbo-chic Co-Co Club prepares healthful salads, sandwiches, and light foods. It's always a scene when the Co-Co Club is hosting a bash, and on Tuesday fans of warrior-princess camp drop by for *Xena* night. ⊠ *139 8th St.,* ☎ *415/255–8783.*

Mad Magda's Russian Tea Room. One of the more eccentric hangouts in Hayes Valley has an unaffected bohemian feel. You can have a tarot card reading while enjoying some of the best sandwiches (like the Fabergé eggplant with mozzarella and basil) in town. Live music many nights. ⊠ *579 Hayes St.,* ☎ *415/864–7654.*

SCENES

By the early '90s the time-honored S.F. fag-bar traditions of lust and licentiousness had lost their vigor. It seemed sometimes as though younger queers, especially male ones, were no longer settling here in great numbers. Recent years have seen more age diversity, and several largely straight clubs and smaller bars have developed mixed followings, with music, fashion, and mood being more the uniting social forces than sexual orientation. That's not to say you can't get laid at these places, only that cruising—the sole priority at many Castro bars—sometimes takes a back seat to mingling. Only one full-time lesbian bar exists—which does seem strange for such a dykey city. Making up for their absence, however, are cafés, weekly roving girl parties, and women's performance spaces—a visiting lesbian can definitely have a good time here.

The Castro and the Mission

PRIME SUSPECTS

Badlands. This is a terrific place for both its eclectic selection of tunes, from oldies to rock to disco, and for its collection of oddly monogrammed license plates. A little larger than its neighbors, the Badlands fills up quickly, especially on Sundays. The decorating scheme is vaguely Southwest—chaps and cattle skulls—and there are pool tables and many pinball machines. Chatty, handsome bartenders. ⊠ *4121 18th St.,* ☎ *415/626–9320. Crowd: mostly male, 20s and 30s, lots of flannel and denim, cruisy, cute but unpretentious.*

The Cafe. The Castro's most—some would say only—happening dance club just gets more and more popular with each passing year. The Cafe opened as a lesbian bar, but pretty soon the boys realized that it's a much nicer space than most of their clubs, so now it's pretty mixed. You enter up a flight of stairs to festive bars, one on your right and another up more stairs to your left. At two always-in-use pool tables, the women generally prove that The Cafe is, in fact, their turf. A tiny dance floor manages to accommodate several dozen hip-shakers. The best mingling space is a wooden deck that's also a good spot to cool off or stargaze with a new friend. ⊠ *2367 Market St.,* ☎ *415/861–3846. Crowd: mixed m/f, baby dykes, club kids, college students, guppies, fashion plates, sometimes a bit too cliquey.*

Detour. Little about the Castro's tried-and-true pickup bar has changed over the years, except that the extensive chain-link fencing may be getting a little rusty (along with a few of the guys). The Detour has precious little open space, which forces guys to brush up against one another. The pool table up front is constantly in use, apparently even when the bar is closed—a couple of years ago Falcon Studios filmed a porn flick on top of it. ⊠ *2348 Market St.,* ☎ *415/861–6053. Crowd: male, mostly under 35, a sea of denim and white T-shirts.*

El Rio. On Sunday afternoons this Mission dive dishes up live salsa music and great food—it's one of the liveliest parties in the city. Queer women of color head to the Saturday-night Red party. The back patio is a great space on warm days. ⊠ *3158 Mission St.,* ☎ *415/282–3325. Crowd: totally mixed gay/straight, male/female; Latino, African-American, white; old, young.*

Esta Noche. A fixture since the '70s, the city's main queer Latin disco still rages. It's a great place to dance, watch the campy drag shows on Wednesday nights, and make a lot of noise. The crowd is young but insular, so don't be shy. ⊠ *3079 16th St.,* ☎ *415/861–5757. Crowd: mostly male, mostly Latino, young, loud, raucous.*

Harvey's. The former Elephant Walk is now named for the late activist Harvey Milk. Appropriately, the walls are covered with memorabilia tracing Milk's life and the history of San Francisco's gay community. Plate-glass windows overlook the cruisy intersection of Castro and 18th. In addition to the usual brews, you can test out hard-to-find wines, vodkas, tequilas, cognacs, single-malt Scotches, and liqueurs. ⊠ *500 Castro St.,* ☎ *415/431–4278. Crowd: mixed m/f, all ages, friendly, low-key, not at all cruisy.*

Metro. It's hard to know what to make of this neon-infused and dated-looking bar. Were it not for its mysteriously mobbed Tuesday karaoke nights and its balcony overlooking Noe, Market, and 16th streets, nobody might venture in here. The weeknight early-evening happy hours and weekend afternoons are also well attended. ⊠ *3600 16th St.,* ☎ *415/703–9750. Crowd: 65/35 m/f, diverse in every other way.*

Midnight Sun. This cruisy midsize video bar is the safest bet for tourists hoping to find boys just like the ones back home. Music videos, campy movie clips, and fag favorites such as *Ab Fab* flicker on TV screens as dance music blares overhead. Has declined slightly in popularity. ⊠ *4067 18th St.,* ☎ *415/861–4186. Crowd: mostly male, young, clean-shaven, professional, like the boys at Alta Plaza but without high-paying jobs.*

Pendulum. This is San Francisco's only African-American bar, though men of color patronize many other spots. Inside, the bar looks like a party room in a frat house, packed with a rowdy, outgoing bunch. Cruisy bathroom. The Pendulum has been around for more than 25 years. ⊠ *4146 18th St.,* ☎ *415/863–4441. Crowd: mostly male, mostly African-American, all ages, all types, very friendly.*

Pilsner Inn. On the increasingly hip eastern edge of the Castro, this former neighborhood dive has developed into a groovy chat-and-cruise bar with a loyal following of artsy, bookish, and brooding sorts. There's a great variety of beers, an always-busy pool table, and a terrific patio out back. ⊠ *225 Church St.,* ☎ *415/621–7058. Crowd: 80/20 m/f, 20s and 30s, friendly, low attitude, sexy without pretense.*

Twin Peaks. Because it attracts many of the Castro's old-timers, bitchy young people often call the Twin Peaks a "wrinkle bar." It's also called a "fern bar," although there are no ferns. In any case, it's a cheerful haunt with Tiffany-style lamps and a crowd that seems to know one another on a first-name basis. Its best attribute is the intimate interior balcony, where lovers who are coping (fighting) often go to process (break up). ⊠ *401 Castro St.,* ☎ *415/864–9470. Crowd: mostly male, 35 to 75, cordial, white-collar, a bit cliquey.*

NEIGHBORHOOD HAUNTS

Long-running Castro hangouts include the mellow and cruisy **Castro Station** (⊠ 456 Castro St., ☎ 415/626–7220), where Tom of Finland-type works line the walls, and **Daddy's** (⊠ 440 Castro St., ☎ 415/621–8732), which draws a bearish leather bunch and frequently plays old campy films on its TV monitors. **The Edge** (⊠ 4149 18th St., ☎ 415/863–4027) draws a eclectic bunch of mostly thirtysomethings. The antique pinball machines are a highlight of the otherwise staid **Expansion Bar** (✉ 2124 Market St., ☎ 415/863–4041). Things don't get much sleepier than they do at the **Men's Room** (✉ 3988 18th St., ☎ 415/861–1310), which behind its cedar-shake exterior has a long bar that's short on customers. **Moby Dick** (✉ 4049 18th St., no phone) is a sleepy but cruisy video bar brightened up a bit with tropical fish tanks. With the emerging cachet of the nearby Pilsner Inn, the sleepy **Transfer** (✉ 198 Church St., ☎ 415/861–7499) may become next year's cool-slacker hangout—then again, it may not. Modest-sized crowds are found at **Uncle Bert's** (✉ 4086 18th St., ☎ 415/431–8616), where they've been known to show televised golf on Saturday nights.

HANGIN' WITH THE HETS

A moody basement of red carpets and dark-wood tables and chairs, **Cafe du Nord** (✉ 2170 Market St., ☎ 415/861–5016) books polished jazz musicians and has great cabaret shows. Self-consciously hip scenesters gravitate to **Lucky 13** (✉ 2140 Market St., ☎ 415/487–1313), where grown-up cocktails and hard-to-find beers flow generously to the sounds of indie rock bands on the CD jukebox. In the Mission, plenty of guys hang with their lesbian buds at **Blondie's** (*see* Women's Bars, *below*), a queer-friendly lounge.

SoMa

PRIME SUSPECTS

Hole in the Wall Saloon. The self-proclaimed "Nasty Little Biker Bar" is aptly named—it's a hellish sliver of a place where they play hard-rock music and the guys throw each other deadly looks. If you're lucky, a fight will break out during your visit. If you want to increase the odds of this happening, wear a polo shirt and plenty of cologne. ✉ *289 8th St.,* ☎ *415/431–4695. Crowd: mostly male, often drunk by noon, lots of leather, piercings aplenty, a smattering of guppies.*

S.F. Eagle. In early 1998, the folks at the Hole in the Wall took over this leather bar but the guys here still take the theme seriously. There's even a great leather shop on the premises, one of the finest you'll find anywhere. Sometimes the place gets dark and cramped, but you can amble out onto the heated outdoor patio. Hmmm. These guys may not be so tough after all. ✉ *398 12th St.,* ☎ *415/626–0880. Crowd: male, leather, brawny, butch, big, rough; he-man central.*

Stud. Yet another of the roving-party venues in SoMa is a tight and compact place with a narrow, crowded dance floor and several areas for mingling. The Stud has been hot for many years. The crowd, ambience, and musical flavor change according to the night, which might feature trip-hop, trash disco, funk, or any other genre you can come up with. ✉ *399 9th St.,* ☎ *415/863–6623. Crowd: depends on the theme but tends to be young, low attitude, mixed genders, multiracial.*

NEIGHBORHOOD HAUNTS

The seedy **Lone Star** (✉ 1354 Harrison St., ☎ 415/863–9999) is called an "ego bar" by some, and that's not because everybody here has a big ego. **My Place** (✉ 1225 Folsom St., ☎ 415/863–2329) is one of the few leather bars in SoMa that still has back-room activity. **Powerhouse** (✉ 1347 Folsom St., ☎ 415/552–8689), once synonymous with hard-core leather, is becoming a hit with the pierced grunge set. The **Rawhide II** (280 7th St., ☎ 415/621–1197) is the city's only full-time queer country-western bar, and it has free dance lessons most nights.

ONE-NIGHTERS, MOVEABLE FETES

The Box. This Thursday-night funk-and-house dance party has been bringin' 'em in for nearly a decade. A room in the front has a balcony with lounge chairs and a small dance floor with great music. The larger dance hall has catwalks, a stage, and that ubiquitous postindustrial black-box-theater look. DJ Page Hodel is a local legend; The Box has always lured a sizable contingent of lesbians. ⊠ *715 Harrison St.,* ☎ *415/647–8258. Crowd: 75/25 m/f, straight-friendly, mostly mid-20s to mid-30s, from hard-core club goers to nostalgia-seeking couples reliving their younger years.*

On Saturday nights the city's wildest, must-do parties are held at **Club Townsend** (⊠ 177 Townsend St., no phone). Most recently the party has been called **Club Universe** (☎ 415/985–5241), but should the name change you'll still be able to count on huge crowds that are young and wired—mostly male but some lesbians and straights. An enormous old warehouse, 177 Townsend has a large dance space and pulsates until 7 AM. Sunday nights, a long-running and largely male tea dance, **Pleasuredome** (☎ 415/985–5256), gets rolling around 10 PM. A women's party, **Club Q** (*see* Women's Bars and Hangouts, *below*), is held here the first Friday of every month. Thursday night's **Anthem** (☎ 415/978–0181) has lured club queers back to the legendary 1015 Folsom Street space.

Featured prominently in *Tales of the City,* and constantly a source of gossip and speculation (Didn't it close? Is it about to close? Have new owners taken over?), the **End Up** (⊠ 401 6th St., ☎ 415/357–0827) has been a San Francisco treat since the early '70s. A throbbing tea dance revs its engine at 5 AM Sunday and rolls along until 2 AM Monday—in good weather most people cut loose on the patio. The mostly male Fag Friday parties roll on until early Saturday morning; a few hours later, G-Spot (*see* Women's Bars and Hangouts, *below*) cranks into action.

Polk Street

PRIME SUSPECTS

Cinch Saloon. Except for the music, which is culled from a hip collection of CDs, this is a Wild West–theme bar—sort of as if Disney had created it, but with the help of a few queens. This may be the easiest place in town to get tanked for under $5. ⊠ *1723 Polk St.,* ☎ *415/776–4162. Crowd: 80/20 m/f, mostly thirtysomething, fun-loving, rowdy.*

The Giraffe. This is the most underrated bar in San Francisco, which means that it can be pretty quiet some nights. On lower Polk Street near all the sleaze, it draws a nice (but still kind of cruisy) guy-next-door crowd. The cute, outgoing bartenders wear white Oxford shirts with snazzy ties. ⊠ *1131 Polk St.,* ☎ *415/474–1702. Crowd: 80/20 m/f, mostly 20s and 30s, mix of working-class and white-collar, slightly rough but congenial.*

N' Touch. A sleek disco where Polk Street begins to get nicer is the hangout of choice for gay Asian men. The narrow bar up front can get claustrophobic on busy nights. The compact dance floor in the back has excellent music; on Thursdays strippers perform before a packed house. ⊠ *1548 Polk St.,* ☎ *415/441–8413. Crowd: mostly male, mostly Asian, young, lively, lots of disco bunnies.*

Polk Gulch. Whew! This place is scary. Rumor has it that not one but *two* men featured on *America's Most Wanted* have hung out at the ole Gulch. Nevertheless, if you want to understand the heart and soul of Polk Street over the past two decades, you should stop by. A good place to perfect your deadly glare. ⊠ *1100 Polk St.,* ☎ *415/771–2022. Crowd: male, mostly 30s and 40s, rough trade, drunk, hustlers.*

QTII. The QT (a.k.a. Quick Tricks) looks like a cross between Studio 54 and a ski lodge. A small elevated stage hosts diverse entertainment, from experimental jazz combos to strippers (amateur contests on Tuesdays are great fun). Several TV screens show vintage music videos, and when there isn't live music, Top 40 classics are piped in. ⊠ *1312 Polk St.,* ☎ *415/ 885–1114. Crowd: 85/15 m/f, diverse in age, bad hair, hairpieces, tourists seeking respite from their dreary hotel rooms at the nearby Leland Hotel, sloppy drunks, many hustlers and dirty old men.*

The Swallow. The gold nameplate outside the front door is a bit much— you'd think you'd stumbled upon the Union Club or something. This is the classiest bar on Polk Street, well north of the shadier places. Every night but Tuesday you can hear some of the community's best piano per-formers—mostly playing show tunes. ⊠ *1750 Polk St.,* ☎ *415/775–4152. Crowd: 85/15 m/f, mostly 40s and up, friendly, lots of ascots and velvet blazers.*

NEIGHBORHOOD HAUNTS

If you're up for more Polk exploring, try **Kimo's** (⊠ 1351 Polk St., ☎ 415/885–4535), which has a show lounge with tired drag acts; the **Moth-erlode** (⊠ 1002 Post St., ☎ 415/928–6006), the city's main transgen-der club, a block east of Polk; the **P.S. Bar** (⊠ 1121 Polk St., ☎ 415/ 885–1448), a dreary piano lounge that's all mirrors and neon, and whose patrons all seem to be named "John"; the **Polk Rendezvous** (⊠ 1303 Polk St., ☎ 415/673–7934), a creepy cocktail lounge that's a good place to rendezvous with your bookie or pimp; and **Reflections** (⊠ 1160 Polk St., ☎ 415/771–6262), a run-down bar with maroon industrial carpeting that adds a certain flavor—or odor—to the place.

Elsewhere in San Francisco

PRIME SUSPECTS

Alta Plaza. Most evenings a gaggle of lawyers and stockbrokers flocks to this oft-teased bar, usually referred to as the "Ultra Plastic." In any other town this guppie bar wouldn't seem so out of place, but San Fran-cisco's gay community is not usually thought to be status-conscious— the sight of guys in Armani suits swarming around a mahogany bar with exotic floral arrangements is a real anomaly. If you want to see the place in full swing, come after work for happy hour. ⊠ *2301 Fillmore St., Pa-cific Heights,* ☎ *415/922–1444. Crowd: mostly male, young, professional, lots of designer duds, sugar daddies, and even some sugar babies.*

Lion Pub. This guppie bar has been in business for more than 25 years, though in the past couple of years the Lion has declined a shade in pop-ularity. It's known for its hunky bartenders and toasty fieldstone fireplace in back. Your parents would be at home amid the clubby decor—Tiffany-style lamps and windows, faux-Corinthian columns, and faux-marble ta-bles. ⊠ *2062 Divisadero St., Pacific Heights,* ☎ *415/567–6565. Crowd: mostly male, young to middle-age guppies, more relaxed than Alta Plaza.*

Mint. Conversation is easy at this clean, bright bar. Regulars and tourists chat with one another, and karaoke is on just about every night of the week—San Francisco appears to be obsessed with this phenomenon. The Mint has been up and running, and gay, since World War II. ⊠ *1942 Mar-ket St., Civic Center,* ☎ *415/626–4726. Crowd: 75/25 m/f, all ages, some suits, friendly, some talented singers, some untalented singers.*

NEIGHBORHOOD HAUNTS

Marlena's (⊠ 488 Hayes St., Hayes Valley, ☎ 415/864–6672) is a mel-low spot popular with TVs and transgenders, as well as old-timers who lived here before Hayes Valley went trendy. A dapper piano bar just off Market Street, **Martuni's** (⊠ 4 Valencia St., Civic Center, ☎ 415/241–0205) has live entertainment nightly. In the Haight-Ashbury, casual **Trax** (⊠ 1437 Haight St., ☎ 415/864–4213) has a good CD jukebox.

The terribly sexy and swank **Red Room** (⊠ Commodore Hotel, 827 Sutter St., ☏ 415/346–7666) lounge pulls in a queer-sensible crowd. With a list of more than 350 vintages, the **Hayes and Vine** (⊠ 377 Hayes St., Hayes Valley, ☏ 415/626–5301) will tickle your inner sommelier. The mood is casual; this is a great place to unwind with friends before hitting one of Market Street's new culinary darlings. North Beach's celebrity (or, more accurately, celebrity-watchers) hangout, **Tosca** (⊠ 242 Columbus Ave., ☏ 415/391–1244), is a straight bar that draws many gays—how could it not with a jukebox that plays only opera selections?

Women's Bars and Hangouts

PRIME SUSPECTS

The Lexington Club. This very cool dyke bar opened in the Mission District in early 1997. A hip grrrl crowd packs the cozy space to hear Joan Jett and Courtney Love tunes on the fierce jukebox. ⊠ *3464 19th St., ☏ 415/863–2052. Crowd: 80/20 f/m, young, stylish, sexy, unpretentious, skater girls, hipsters, and Doc Marten devotees.*

NEIGHBORHOOD HAUNTS

The nonalcoholic **Josie's Cabaret and Juice Joint** (⊠ 3583 16th St., ☏ 415/861–7933) books male and female performers, but often showcases performances by the nation's best-known lesbian comics and musical acts. Many of the dykes who favor the Lexington Club pack into lesbo-friendly **Blondie's** (⊠ 540 Valencia St., ☏ 415/864–2419) to listen to alternative tunes, groove on the postage-stamp-size dance floor, and play pool; Sunday Red party for women of color is the queerest. The owners of Bernal Heights's sleepy **Wild Side West** (⊠ 424 Cortland Ave., ☏ 415/647–3099) don't like to think of this as a lesbian bar, but come see for yourself: There are an awful lot of gay gals in here. **Osento Baths** (⊠ 955 Valencia St., ☏ 415/282–6333), a soothing women's (nonsexual) bathhouse in the Mission, is a relaxing spot to shake off a tense day. Women seeking a raunchier respite head to Power Exchange on Sunday (*see* Action, *below*).

ONE-NIGHTERS, MOVEABLE FETES

The swank and jazzy **Co-Co Club** (⊠ 139 8th St., entrance on Minna St., ☏ 415/626–2337) hosts several happening dyke parties, including a speakeasy with live music on Saturday, dance parties for women of color on Wednesday, open-mike and comedy on Thursday, and "In Bed with Fairy Butch," a risqué cabaret, on Friday. Saturday's **G-Spot** at the **End Up** (⊠ 401 6th St., ☏ 415/337–4962) is one of the city's most glamorous parties. DJs Zanne and Junkyard hold their hip queerclub **Junk** (⊠ Stud, 399 9th St., ☏ 415/863–6623) on the last Saturday of the month. Queers of all colors and genders groove to funk classic, punk, and alternative sounds. The first Friday of each month, don't miss **Club Q** (☏ 415/647–8258) at 177 Townsend, hosted by DJ Page Hodel.

Action

Sex clubs and private parties, as well as video arcades and porn shops, are well attended and widely available in San Francisco. The favorites include **Blow Buddies** (⊠ 933 Harrison St., ☏ 415/863–4323); **Eros** (⊠ 2051 Market St., ☏ 415/864–3767); and the **Black House** (⊠ 633 Castro St., ☏ 415/863–6358). **S.F. Jacks** (☏ 415/267–6999) has parties at different locations but has most recently been settling in at the **Power Exchange Mainstation** (⊠ 74 Otis St., ☏ 415/487–9944), which hosts many other events. On Sundays the **Power Exchange** (⊠ 960 Harrison St., ☏ 415/974–4600) hosts a women-only sex club, complete with slings, showers, and dungeons.

Folsom Gulch (⊠ 947 Folsom St., ☎ 415/495–6402) has a huge selection of videos and mags, and a video arcade. **A Taste of Leather** (⊠ 317A 10th St., ☎ 415/252–9166) is strong on those hard-to-find bedroom necessities—riding crops, slings, slave collars, vacuum pumps, and mouth gags. Dyke-owned **Stormy Leather** (⊠ 1158 Howard St., ☎ 415/626–1672) is good source of women's leather gear.

One of the most famous adult theaters in the country is the **Campus** (⊠ 220 Jones St., ☎ 415/673–3384), in the heart of the Tenderloin. Tickets are on the steep side at $12, but they're good for the whole day (in-out privileges, if you'll pardon the expression). Famous porn stars perform here regularly. The **Gauntlet** (⊠ 2377 Market St., ☎ 415/431–3133) has been the Castro's piercing parlor of choice for more than 20 years.

SLEEPS

No matter what your price range, San Francisco is a marvelous metropolis for accommodations, with luxurious Old World–inspired lodgings on a par with New York's; small hotels rivaled in charm only by those in New Orleans; and the best selection of gay-friendly bed-and-breakfasts anywhere in the country.

If you insist on being within a short walk of the Castro, you'll need to check into one of the area's guest houses. Most of the city's best gay-frequented options are downtown, close to Nob Hill and Union Square. Here, you're a 10-minute cab ride from the Castro and an even shorter ride (or a manageable walk) from the nightclubs in SoMa; you're also close to many of the city's top attractions.

For price ranges, *see* lodging Chart A at the front of this guide.

Hotels

Downtown Vicinity

$$$$ ⊞ **The Clift.** The luxurious Clift, part of the Grand Heritage Hotel chain and convenient to the city's theater district, has earned the respect of the gay community with its support of AIDS and cancer charities. ⊠ *495 Geary St., 94102*, ☎ *415/775–4700 or 800/652–5438*, FAX *415/441–4621. 329 rooms. Restaurant, exercise room.*

$$$$ ⊞ **Ritz-Carlton.** Not just your ordinary Ritz-Carlton, the San Francisco property is one of the top two or three urban hotels in America. Guests inside this gorgeous neoclassical 1920 building enjoy an immense fitness center and two outstanding restaurants. Rooms are large and luxuriously appointed with marble baths, double sinks, and vanity mirrors. ⊠ *600 Stockton St., 94108*, ☎ *415/296–7465 or 800/241–3333*, FAX *415/291–0288. 336 rooms. Restaurant, pool, health club.*

$$$–$$$$ ⊞ **Huntington Hotel.** This Nob Hill hotel is less famous than its neighbors, but it remains one of the top three or four places to stay in San Francisco. The discreet staff aims to please but also respects your privacy. Large elegant rooms reflect a variety of decorating styles. A great hotel, from top to bottom. ⊠ *1075 California St., 94108*, ☎ *415/474–5400 or 800/227–4683*, FAX *415/474–6227. 140 rooms. Restaurant.*

$$–$$$$ ⊞ **Hotel Rex.** This Joie de Vivre hotel adds a touch of Roaring '20s style to Union Square with murals and portraits depicting sophisticated salon society. There's even an antiquarian bookstore on the premises. Rooms continue this theme but also have business amenities like voice mail and computer data ports. ⊠ *562 Sutter St., 94102*, ☎ *415/433–4434 or 800/433–4434*, FAX *415/433–3695. 94 rooms.*

$$$ ⊞ **Hotel Monaco.** The whimsical Monaco's distinctly Parisian flair has made the young hotel the talk of the city. The lobby, with its soaring vaulted ceilings, trompe l'oeil murals, and sweeping staircase, is magnificent. Rooms

are no less captivating, with faux-bamboo writing desks, high-back chairs, four-poster beds, and wallpaper striped in bold colors. ⊠ *501 Geary St., 94102,* ☎ *415/292–0100 or 800/214–4220,* FAX *415/292–0111. 201 rooms. Restaurant, health club.*

$$$ ☷ **Prescott.** A first-rate staff makes this hotel one of the best in the theater district. Guests staying on the concierge level are treated to an evening reception of drinks and pizza from Wolfgang Puck's Postrio restaurant downstairs. Somewhat small rooms are outfitted with sharp cherry-wood furniture and silk wallpaper. ⊠ *545 Post St., 94102,* ☎ *415/ 563–0303 or 800/283–7322,* FAX *415/563–6831. 165 rooms. Restaurant.*

$$–$$$ ☷ **Hotel Triton.** Among the Kimpton Group properties in San Francisco, the Triton is the one that might as well have a pink-triangle welcome mat outside the front door—it markets very openly to the queer community. The seven suites were each decorated by a different celeb designer, from Joe Boxer to Suzan Briganti. ⊠ *342 Grant Ave., 94108,* ☎ *415/394–0500 or 800/433–6611,* FAX *415/394–0555. 140 rooms. Restaurant, exercise room.*

$$–$$$ ☷ **Vintage Court.** This reasonably priced hotel has the atmosphere of a Wine Country inn, and it's among the more queer-friendly downtown properties. Complimentary wine is served each evening in the stately lobby. Even if you don't stay here, you'll want to try Masa's—the city's best French restaurant (*see* Eats, *above*). ⊠ *650 Bush St., 94108,* ☎ *415/392–4666 or 800/654–1100,* FAX *415/433–4065. 107 rooms. Restaurant.*

$$ ☷ **Mosser Victorian Hotel.** This 1913 hotel, just south of Market Street and a short walk from SoMa nightlife—has clean and cheerful rooms furnished with Victorian reproductions. ⊠ *54 4th St., 94103,* ☎ *415/986–4400 or 800/227–3804,* FAX *415/495–7653. 166 rooms, some share bath. Restaurant.*

$–$$ ☷ **Commodore International Hotel.** You won't find better accommodations at these rates so close to Union Square. What the Commodore lacks in elegance it makes up for with hip '40s-style furnishings, spacious rooms, walk-in closets, and an exceedingly artsy but playful personality. Trendoids gather nightly in the Red Room bar (*see* Scenes, *above*) and daily at the Titanic Cafe. ⊠ *825 Sutter St., 94109,* ☎ *415/923–6800 or 800/338–6848,* FAX *415/923–6804. 113 rooms. Restaurant.*

West of Downtown

$–$$ ☷ **The Abigail.** The Joie de Vivre chain's most conventional establishment is an inexpensive Victorian-style hotel with small, modest rooms brightened by down comforters and turn-of-the-century lithographs and paintings. It's midway between the Castro and downtown. ⊠ *246 McAllister St., 94102,* ☎ *415/861–9728 or 800/243–6510,* FAX *415/861–5848. 60 rooms. Restaurant.*

$–$$ ☷ **Atherton Hotel.** This moderately priced choice on the edge of the Tenderloin has a dramatic Mediterranean-inspired lobby with etched glass, marble floors, and carved wood. Guest rooms are simple and small but quite comfortable. The Abbey Bar is fashioned out of pieces from an authentic British abbey. ⊠ *685 Ellis St., 94109,* ☎ *415/474–5720 or 800/ 474–5720,* FAX *415/474–8256. 75 rooms. Restaurant.*

$–$$ ☷ **Phoenix Inn.** This cult favorite bills itself as the city's "creative crossroads." It's also the gateway to the Tenderloin, but don't hold that against it. This '50s motor lodge had become seedy until hotelier Chip Conley converted it into a chic but still affordable lodging. ⊠ *601 Eddy St., 94109,* ☎ *415/776–1380 or 800/248–9466,* FAX *415/885–3109. 44 rooms. Restaurant, pool.*

The Castro

$–$$ ☷ **Beck's Motor Lodge.** This functional '60s motor lodge is a dull but cheap budget (and sometimes cruisy) option in the Castro. ⊠ *2222 Market St., 94114,* ☎ *415/621–8212,* FAX *415/241–0435. 57 rooms.*

Guest Houses and Small Hotels

The Castro and Mission

$$–$$$ ⊞ **Inn on Castro.** This refurbished 1896 house is easily the nicest, though costliest, accommodation in the Castro. The light and airy rooms have a kitschy '50s feel about them. ⊠ *321 Castro St., 94114,* ☎ *415/861–0321. 8 rooms with phone, bath. Full breakfast. Mixed gay male/lesbian.*

$$–$$$ ⊞ **Inn San Francisco.** Feather beds and 19th-century antiques grace the rooms of this pink Italianate Victorian in Mission Hill. You'll find a sunny patio on the roof, and out back there's a lush garden with a redwood hot tub. ⊠ *943 S. Van Ness Ave., 94110,* ☎ *415/641–0188 or 800/359–0913,* FAX *415/641–1701. 22 rooms with phone and TV, most with private bath. Full breakfast. Mixed gay/straight.*

$$–$$$ ⊞ **Parker House.** A splendidly restored 1919 Edwardian residence, Parker House is the Castro's most spectacular inn. Guests make considerable use of the lavish public areas and appreciate the antiques, rich fabrics, and modern conveniences (voice mail, modem hookups) in the sun-filled rooms. Paths wind through extensive gardens and lawns. ⊠ *520 Church St., 94114,* ☎ *415/621–3222 or 888/520–7275,* FAX *415/621–4139, e-mail parkerhse@aol.com. 5 rooms with phone, TV, and private bath. Hot tub. Continental breakfast. Mixed gay/lesbian.*

$$ ⊞ **Black Stallion.** This is a leather-and-Levi's-theme guest house, but don't assume that all the rooms are painted black and have beer stains on the floors (as most leather bars do). Everything here is clean and bright, and if this is your scene, you'll love the friendly owners and patrons. ⊠ *635 Castro St., 94114,* ☎ *415/863–0131,* FAX *415/863–0165. 8 rooms share baths. Mostly gay male.*

$$ ⊞ **House O'Chicks.** What's not to love about the sprightly House O'Chicks, a century-old Victorian whose rooms have VCRs (note the owners' hot collection of "chicks" porn) and CD players. This is a good place to celebrate your anniversary. ⊠ *15th St. near Noe St. (call for details), 94114,* ☎ *415/861–9849,* FAX *415/626–5049. 2 rooms with phone and TV share bath. Lesbian.*

$–$$ ⊞ **Castillo Inn.** At one of the Castro's more modest options, guests have use of refrigerators and microwaves, and a new two-bedroom suite was recently added; it has a full kitchen, deck, and balcony. ⊠ *48 Henry St., 94114,* ☎ *415/864–5111 or 800/865–5112,* FAX *415/641–1321. 4 rooms with phone, TV, and shared baths. Mostly gay male.*

$ ⊞ **Dolores Park Inn.** Not everybody adores the gritty feel of the Mission District, but a visit to the Dolores Park Inn may change your outlook. Antiques fill this 1874 Italianate Victorian, and there's a garden in the back. Good breakfast, too. ⊠ *3641 17th St., 94114,* ☎ FAX *415/621–0482 or 415/861–9335. 4 rooms with phone, TV, and shared baths; carriage house. Continental breakfast. No credit cards. Mixed gay/straight.*

$ ⊞ **24 Henry Street.** This centrally located B&B is bright and cozy, and the two gents who operate it will gladly dispense tips about the Castro and the city. The suites here hold three people and have kitchens. ⊠ *24 Henry St., 94114,* ☎ *415/864–5686 or 800/900–5686,* FAX *415/864–0406. 10 rooms, some with TV, private bath. Mostly gay male.*

East of Van Ness Avenue

$$$–$$$$ ⊞ **Nob Hill Lambourne.** Women executives often choose the sumptuous Lambourne, a cross between an urban spa and a state-of-the-art business center. Guests have access to personal computers and laser printers, but can also partake of an herbal wrap in the on-site spa. Rooms have contemporary furnishings and kitchenettes. ⊠ *725 Pine St., 94108,* ☎ *415/433–2287 or 800/274–8466,* FAX *415/433–0975. 20 rooms with TV, phone, and private bath. Continental breakfast. Mixed gay/straight.*

West of Van Ness Avenue

$$$–$$$$ 🛏 **Anna's Three Bears.** The over-the-top suites in this 1906 gray-and-white inn have fully stocked kitchens, Edwardian antiques, fireplaces, and private decks. This Buena Vista Heights hostelry is especially nice for a longer stay. If you factor in the self-catering option, the weekly rates of $1,000 to $1,400 can be bargains. ⊠ *114 Divisadero St., 94117,* ☎ *415/255–3167 or 800/428–8559,* FAX *415/552–2959. 3 rooms with phone, TV, and private bath. Continental breakfast. Mixed gay/straight.*

$$–$$$$ 🛏 **Archbishops Mansion.** A backdrop for many gay weddings, this Second Empire–style inn, built in 1904 for the city's Catholic archbishop, is one of the most romantic properties in California. Rooms are enormous and filled with Belle Epoque furnishings; many have separate sitting areas and fireplaces. They're each quite special, too; the Don Giovanni suite has a seven-head shower. ⊠ *1000 Fulton St., 94117,* ☎ *415/563–7872 or 800/543–5820,* FAX *415/885–3193. 15 rooms with phone, TV, and private bath. Continental breakfast. Mixed gay/straight.*

$$–$$$$ 🛏 **Chateau Tivoli.** Rodney Karr and Willard Gersbach run this ornate 1892 Victorian, which glows with 22 vibrant colors. If you're impressed by the fanciful exterior, check out the elaborate rooms, decked top to bottom with antiques and collectibles. It's difficult to walk through this museumlike mansion without humming the opening bars to the *Addams Family* theme song. ⊠ *1057 Steiner St., 94115,* ☎ *415/776–5462 or 800/228–1647,* FAX *415/776–0505. 7 rooms with phone, most with private bath. Continental breakfast (full on weekends). Mixed gay/straight.*

$$–$$$ 🛏 **Queen Anne Hotel.** A four-story former girls boarding school built in 1890 houses this top-notch hotel with an extremely helpful staff. Each of the 48 rooms is furnished differently, with a mix of new and antique pieces; many have fireplaces and wet bars. ⊠ *1590 Sutter St., 94109,* ☎ *415/441–2828 or 800/227–3970,* FAX *415/775–5212. 48 rooms with phone, TV, and private bath. Continental breakfast. Mixed gay/straight.*

$ 🛏 **Carl Street Unicorn House.** This small guest house near Buena Vista Park is a safe place for women. The two rooms share one bath, but that's the only drawback. The beautiful 1895 house is filled with owner Miriam Weber's many collectibles. ⊠ *156 Carl St., 94117,* ☎ *415/753–5194. 2 rooms share a bath. Continental breakfast. Mostly women; mixed lesbian/straight.*

THE LITTLE BLACK BOOK

At Your Fingertips

AIDS Hotline (☎ 415/863–2437). **BART** (train service, ☎ 800/817–1717). **Deaf Gay and Lesbian Center** (☎ 415/255–9944, TTY 415/255–9797). **Gay and Lesbian Helpline** (☎ 415/772–4357). **Lavender Youth Recreation Information Center** (⊠ 127 Collingwood St., ☎ 415/703–6150). **Lyon-Martin Women's Health Services** (☎ 415/565–7667). **Muni** (bus system, ☎ 415/673–6864). **San Francisco Convention and Visitors Bureau** (⊠ 201 3rd St., Suite 900, 94103, ☎ 415/974–6900). **San Francisco Gay/Lesbian/Bisexual/Transgender Community Center Project** (☎ 415/864–3733). **"What's Up" Hotline for African-American Lesbians** (☎ 510/835–6126). **Women's Building** (⊠ 3543 18th St., ☎ 415/431–1180). **Yellow Cab** (☎ 415/626–2345).

Gay Media

The two most widely read gay newspapers are the weekly **Bay Area Reporter** (☎ 415/861–5019) and the biweekly **San Francisco Bay Times** (☎ 415/227–0800). The monthly newspaper **Icon** (☎ 415/863–9536) serves as the best resource for lesbians. The biweekly **Frontiers San Francisco** (☎ 415/487–6000; Web site www.frontiersweb.com) runs entertainment and feature stories. **Odyssey** (☎ 415/621–6514, e-mail odyssey@cea.edu) is a handy biweekly fag rag with detailed boys' and girls' club information and lots of fun dish. The new biweekly *Oblivion* (☎ 415/554–0565, Web site www.oblivionsf.com) is an amazingly detailed and dishy chronicle of queer goings-on, dining, and nightlife around the Bay Area. *Q San Francisco* (☎ 800/999–9718), a flashy bimonthly gay news and entertainment magazine, provides excellent bar, restaurant, and arts coverage. The *Bay Guardian* (☎ 415/255–3100, Web site www.sfbg.com) and the *San Francisco Weekly* (☎ 415/541–0700, Web site www.sfweekly.com) are free alternative papers with performing-arts listings and left-of-center political commentary.

BOOKSTORES

A Different Light Bookstore (✉ 489 Castro St., ☎ 415/431–0891), the city's major lesbigay bookstore, is the city's unofficial gay welcoming center. **Books Inc.** (✉ 2275 Market St., ☎ 415/864–6777) is an excellent general independent bookstore in the Castro with a strong lesbigay section. **Bernal Books** (✉ Cortland Ave., ☎ 415/550–0293) is a neighborhood store in Bernal Heights with a sizable lesbigay section. The Civic Center's **A Clean Well-Lighted Place For Books** (✉ 601 Van Ness Ave., ☎ 415/567–6876) has an excellent lesbigay section and is strong on cookbooks and the performing and fine arts. **Get Lost** (✉ 1825 Market St., ☎ 415/437–0529) is a terrific new near-Castro travel bookstore with a great queer section.

Working Out

Gay gyms are easy to find all around town. Some of the most popular include the cruisy **City Athletic Club** (✉ 2500 Market St., ☎ 415/552–6680); the **Muscle System** (✉ 364 Hayes St., ☎ 415/863–4701; ✉ 2275 Market St., ☎ 415/863–4700), a.k.a. "the Muscle Sisters," whose two locations draw buff boys; the coed **Market Street Gym** (✉ 2301 Market St., ☎ 415/626–4488), one of the most crowded and gayest gyms in the city; and the **Women's Training Center** (✉ 2164 Market St., ☎ 415/864–6835), a smaller gym patronized by dykes and straight women that offers personal training and helpful service.

THE RUSSIAN RIVER

The Russian River valley, northern California's premier gay resort, is sleepy, slightly ragged, and blessed with a canopy of redwoods. During this century it's been home to loggers, bikers, hippies, and Mexican immigrants, and before that to Russian fur trappers and the Pomo Indians. After a couple of gay men opened B&Bs in the '70s, the town of Guerneville boomed with activity, and queerfolk replaced families as the River's most visible summertime visitors.

Unfortunately, what inevitably gets billed as the "flood of the century" ravages the area every decade or even less. The most recent deluge struck in 1997. A few restaurants, resorts, and other businesses fold after the floods, but most rebuild better than ever—Russian Riverites are a resilient bunch. The community seems as strong as ever—the gay and lesbian stamp on the area is evident everywhere—and Bay Area residents continue to buy vacation homes or relocate here entirely.

People at the River don't spend huge amounts on fine dining or fancy retreats. This is where you head when big-city living starts to get to you. You'll find enough sundecks and swimming pools to model that figure you've been perfecting, and plenty of fun-loving queens to party with. And don't let stories of torrential rains and flooding put you off—storms come only in winter; the rest of the year can be beautiful.

The Lay of the Land

Quirky **Guerneville** and **Monte Rio,** home to the Russian River's main gay and lesbian resorts, seem almost frozen in time. Guerneville, with 7,000 people, is much larger than Monte Rio, and it's where you'll find the only nightlife and most of the restaurants and accommodations. It's not a shopping mecca, but there are some offbeat stores downtown. **Up the River** (⊠ 16212 Main St., ☎ 707/869–3167) carries both tasteful and unabashedly tasteless cards and gifts. **Memories That Linger** (⊠ 16218 Main St., ☎ 707/869–2971) sells lingerie, clothing, and other fun stuff. The 800-acre **Armstrong Redwoods State Reserve** (⊠ 17000 Armstrong Woods Rd., ☎ 707/869–2015 or 707/865–2391) is home to some of the tallest and oldest trees in northern California. Stop by the visitor center for excellent trail maps and advice. You won't go wrong on any expedition arranged through **Burke's Canoe Trips** (⊠ 8600 River Rd., Forestville, ☎ 707/887–1222). You paddle west with the current, and the company retrieves you and the canoe just east of Guerneville.

If you don't care to drive a long way to taste the grape, there are a few small wineries nearby, including **Mark West Estate** (⊠ 7010 Trenton–Healdsburg Rd., Forestville, ☎ 707/544–4813). For a change of pace from River lounging, take the tour at the **Korbel Champagne Cellars** (⊠ 13250 River Rd., Guerneville, ☎ 707/887–2294), which is headquartered in a century-old, creeper-covered brick building.

Getting Around

You can zip up to the Russian River towns from San Francisco in about 90 minutes by car. Travel along U.S. 101 north through Santa Rosa, getting off at the River Road exit. Follow this west for about 30 minutes to reach Guerneville.

Eats

The Russian River vicinity contains many affordable, often rustic, burger and pasta houses, most of which have a strong lesbian and gay following. Until recently, even gay visitors didn't demand much in the way of San Francisco–influenced nouvelle cooking.

For price ranges, *see* dining Chart A at the front of this guide.

$$–$$$ ✕ **Sweet's River Grill.** This center-of-town eatery is the closest Guerneville has to a see-and-be-seen restaurant. Try the broiled halibut with roasted red pepper and lemon butter or the Thai pasta. Nice beer and wine selection. ⊠ *16251 Main St., Guerneville,* ☎ *707/869–3383.*

$$–$$$ ✕ **Willowside.** When this rustic eatery opened a few years ago, every queer foodie in the region jumped for joy—finally, a restaurant in the woods (about 20 minutes east of Guerneville) worth salivating over. The short California-style menu changes often but might feature orzo with morels, ricotta, and radicchio, or perhaps coriander ahi tuna with similarly enticing accompaniments. ⊠ *3535 Guerneville Rd., Santa Rosa,* ☎ *707/ 523–4814.*

$$ ✕ **Burdons.** This casual roadside restaurant a bit east of downtown Guerneville has been a Russian River standby for years. Expect dependable, old-fashioned Continental fare such as honey lemon chicken and excellent steak. ⊠ *15405 River Rd., Guerneville,* ☎ *707/869–2615.*

$$ ✕ **Chez Marie.** For perhaps the most romantic dinner setting in the Russian River valley, drive 10 minutes east from Guerneville to this storefront French bistro in itsy-bitsy Forestville. The women who run this place are wonderful chefs; try the cassoulet with cannellini beans, confit of duck, and ham. ⊠ *6675 Front St. (Hwy. 116), Forestville,* ☎ *707/887–7503.*

$$ ✕ **Fifes.** Brunch on the deck by the pool is a time-honored Russian River tradition at this gay resort. You can also have lunch or dinner inside or out. The American fare is okay—just okay—but the atmosphere is always saucy. ✉ *16467 River Rd., Guerneville,* ☏ *707/869–0656.*

$–$$ ✕ **Molly's.** The restaurant inside the gay country-western bar of the same name serves dinner late in the evening (until 10 on weekdays and 11 on weekends). Expect well-prepared chicken teriyaki and thick burgers—and plenty of queens in boots and jeans. ✉ *14120 Old Cazadero Rd., Guerneville,* ☏ *707/869–0511.*

$ ✕ **The Hiding Place.** Saturday and Sunday mornings' walking wounded seek solace at this semi-outdoor roadhouse. In addition to sandwiches and typical breakfast foods, you'll find some spicy Mexican fare—burritos, quesadillas, and the like. ✉ *15025 River Rd., Guerneville,* ☏ *707/ 869–2887.*

$ ✕ **Korbel Deli and Microbrewery.** Adjacent to the Korbel Champagne Cellars, this is a delightful spot to take lunch. Excellent salads and sandwiches (try the one with salami, Brie, tapenade, roasted peppers, and greens) and served on a tree-shaded deck. ✉ *13250 River Rd.,* ☏ *707/887–2294.*

Coffeehouse Culture

Brew Moon. One of the few Russian River spots that evokes a cosmopolitan air has an art gallery and fanciful decorating elements like abstract murals and delicate glass tables. There's a substantial menu of barbecue, sandwiches, and sweets, plus an array of coffees. ✉ *16248 Main St., Guerneville,* ☏ *707/869–0201.*

Coffee Bazaar. With the steady trickle of beatnicky locals dropping by all day, a more apt name for this homey java joint might be the Coffee Bizarre. Recently expanded and given a new menu, this is a choice spot for breakfast or lunch. ✉ *14045 Armstrong Woods Rd., Guerneville,* ☏ *707/869–9706.*

Scenes

For a secluded community in the sticks, Guerneville serves up varied nightlife options. Nonguests are perfectly welcome to party at most resort bars. Several gay restaurants have taverns attached, and there are a couple of self-standing clubs. In summer, places stay fairly crowded during the week and are packed on weekends. The rest of the year attendance tends to be sparse. Women and men are welcome at all the places listed, though the Triple R and Rainbow Cattle Company are mostly male.

PRIME SUSPECTS

Fifes. You head up a flight of stairs to the main tavern at this resort; a comfy rec room with large-screen TVs is off to the left. There's live piano music many nights. Out the back door and to the right the sprawling sundeck and pool area is always lively on weekend afternoons. A disco was added in '97. ✉ *16467 River Rd.,* ☏ *707/869–0656. Crowd: 80/20 m/f, all ages but the youngest ones get there early in the day to work on their tans.*

Molly's Country Club. This entertainment adjunct to the western-style restaurant is a casual spot for two-stepping and line-dancing. ✉ *14120 Old Cazadero Rd.,* ☏ *707/869–0511. Crowd: mixed m/f, country-western fans.*

River Business. A dumpy old Mexican restaurant was transformed into this dapper video bar in 1997. It's been welcomed warmly by younger SF tourists who felt that Guerneville lacked an urbane cocktail bar. One room has pool and games and the other cruisy patrons. ✉ *16225 Main St.,* ☏ *707/869–3400. Crowd: 75/25 m/f, mostly 20s to 40s, trendy and almost intense on weekends, laid-back at other times.*

River Theater. This hulking former movie theater is the Russian River's only serious warehouse disco—it ceased being a gay club in '96 but came back in full force recently, drawing big-name DJs on summer weekends. There's a large dance floor, plenty of space to stand and model, and an upper level with a pool table. ⊠ *16135 Main St.*, ☎ *707/869–1400. Crowd: 70/30 gay/straight, mixed m/f, all ages, eclectic.*

NEIGHBORHOOD HAUNTS

Mc T's **Bullpen** (⊠ 16246 1st St., ☎ 707/869–3377), the gay sports bar at Sweet's River Grill, draws men and women, gay and straight, for pool, darts, and televised sports. **The Hiding Place** (⊠ 15025 River Rd., ☎ 707/ 869–2887) in eastern Guerneville is known mostly as a casual restaurant, but fags and dykes also come for cocktails, especially in the early evening. **Rainbow Cattle Company** (⊠ 16220 Main St., ☎ 707/869–0206), a former gambling hall, draws a fairly butch gang of gay guys and a few women, many of whom tumble in after 11 for a nightcap. A good stopover before hitting one of the River's larger clubs is the little video and piano bar at the **Triple R** (⊠ 4th and Mill Sts., ☎ 707/869–0691), where the fireplace and several friendly bartenders keep everybody's spirits up. The crowd is mostly male, but women are welcome.

Sleeps

Russian River gay resorts bear little resemblance to the sleek gay getaways in Palm Springs. Some of the places in Guerneville and Monte Rio can be downright spare. The upside is that you also may fall asleep at night in front of a wood-burning stove while staring through redwoods at a starlit sky.

If you're interested in camping, you'll find sites at Fifes and the Willows (*see below*), and at the **Faerie Ring Campground** (⊠ 16747 Armstrong Woods Rd., Guerneville 95446, ☎ 707/869–2746) and **Schoolhouse Canyon** (⊠ 12600 River Rd., Guerneville 95446, ☎ 707/869–2311).

For price ranges, *see* lodging Chart A at the front of this guide.

Guest Houses and Small Hotels

$$$–$$$$ ⊞ **Applewood.** This posh miniresort is a few minutes from downtown Guerneville. Half the rooms are in the main 1922 Mission Revival house; the others are in a recently built second building done in the same style. All are loaded with antiques and have European down comforters. There's a restaurant attached that's open to nonguests on a space-available basis. ⊠ *13555 Hwy. 16, Pocket Canyon 95446,* ☎ *707/869–9093,* FAX *707/ 869–9170, Web site www.applewoodinn.com. 16 rooms with phone, TV, and private bath. Restaurant, pool, hot tub. Mixed gay/straight.*

$$$ ⊞ **Huckleberry Springs.** You'll discover plenty of elbow room at this women-operated 56-acre tree-studded resort that's high on a hill above the Russian River. Huckleberry Springs has four stunning cottages, each with a skylight and a wood-burning stove. Full massages and four-course dinners are available by reservation only. ⊠ *Box 400, Monte Rio 95462,* ☎ *707/865–2683 or 800/822–2683,* FAX *707/865–1688, e-mail, hucksprings@netdex.com. 4 cottages with private bath. Restaurant, pool, hot tub. Full breakfast. Mixed gay/straight.*

$$–$$$ ⊞ **Highland Dell Inn.** The chalets of Germany's Black Forest were the inspiration for this top-notch 1906 inn. The Highland Dell was largely remodeled after the torrential rains of '97 but retains a warm mix of Victorian and 20th-century antiques in the guest rooms and public areas. Most of the leaded and stained glass, as well as a magnificent wooden chandelier, survived the flood. ⊠ *21050 River Blvd., Monte Rio 95462,* ☎ *707/865–1759 or 800/767–1759, Web site www.highlanddellinn.com. 8 rooms with phone, TV, and private bath. Restaurant. Full breakfast. Mixed gay/straight.*

$$ ⊞ **Paradise Cove.** Rooms at this compound a mile north of downtown Guerneville are unfancy but receive plenty of natural light and have wooden decks; most have cozy wood-burning stoves, and there's a pleasant pool and deck area. ⊠ *14711 Armstrong Woods Rd., Guerneville 95446,* ☎ *707/869–2706 or 800/880–2706. 15 rooms with private bath, most with TV. Pool, hot tub. Continental breakfast. Mostly gay male.*

$–$$ ⊞ **Fifes.** The quintessential rustic resort, Fifes is the largest gay compound in the region, with a restaurant and bar. Cabins and cottages are simple, but many have wood-burning stoves and wet bars. There are also 60 campsites, and guests can roam through the property's 15 acres of rose gardens and wooded trails. ⊠ *16467 River Rd., Guerneville 95446,* ☎ *707/869–0656 or 800/734–3371. 52 cabins with TV and private bath. Restaurant, pool, hot tub, exercise room. Mixed gay male/lesbian.*

$–$$ ⊞ **Highlands.** Modest and low-key, this 4-acre gay resort is a short walk from downtown. Nudity is permitted around the pool and hot tub. Some rooms have kitchens, and there are also cabins with fireplaces. A nice value. ⊠ *14000 Woodland Dr., Guerneville 95446,* ☎ *707/869–0333,* FAX *707/869–0370. 16 rooms, many with private bath. Pool, hot tub. Continental breakfast on weekends. Mixed gay male/lesbian.*

$–$$ ⊞ **The Russian River Resort.** The "Triple R" has a devoted following of guys. The motel-style rooms are small, clean, and affordable; some have wood-burning fireplaces. ⊠ *4th and Mill Sts., Guerneville 95446,* ☎ *707/869–0691 or 800/417–3767,* FAX *707/869–0698. 24 rooms with TV; many have private bath. Restaurant, pool, hot tub. Mostly gay male.*

$–$$ ⊞ **The Willows.** This secluded resort with a sprawling old country lodge and a 60-site tent-and-RV campground sits right on the edge of the Russian River, nestled amid groves of pine and willow trees. Guest rooms in the lodge have dark-wood paneling and VCRs. ⊠ *15905 River Rd., Guerneville 95446,* ☎ *707/869–2824 or 800/953–2828. 13 rooms with phone and TV, 9 with private bath. Hot tub. Continental breakfast. Mixed gay male/lesbian.*

The Little Black Book

The **Russian River Chamber of Commerce** (⊠ 16200 1st St., Guerneville 95446, ☎ 707/869–9000) and the **Russian River Visitors Bureau** (⊠ 14034 Armstrong Woods Rd., Guerneville 95446, ☎ 707/869–9212 or 800/253–8800, Web site www.sonoma.com/rusriver) have plenty of info. **We The People** (☎ 707/573–8896, e-mail WTP pub@aol.com) is the gay-and-lesbian monthly newspaper serving the Russian River. The **River Reader** (⊠ 16355 Main St., ☎ 707/869–2240) is a small independent store with a decent lesbian-and-gay section. You can buy porn and sex stuff at **Sensations** (⊠ 14045 Armstrong Woods Rd., ☎ 707/869–1934).

40 *Out in Santa Fe, Taos, and Albuquerque*

LESS SYNONYMOUS WITH QUEER TRAVEL than party hubs like southern California or the Florida Keys, northern New Mexico has quietly evolved over the past two decades into a gay mecca, particularly among couples in search of romance. Santa Fe, a town of tony galleries and chichi restaurants, has had a discreet gay following for most of this century. Taos, Santa Fe's small and quirky cousin, formerly a crunchy backwater that most travelers visited only briefly, attracts queer devotees who entrench themselves for days and even weeks at a time. And Albuquerque, the state's largest city, once a dusty cultural void whose raison d'être for most visitors to New Mexico was its airport, now has a handful of gay bars and businesses.

The three cities are strung together in a line that extends from Albuquerque (metropolitan area population 600,000), nearly in the center of the state, northeast about 60 miles to Santa Fe (population 60,000), and then north 60 or so more miles to Taos (population 6,000). The scenery becomes more pristine as you travel north, but the entire region is set in high desert. All three destinations are, to varying degrees, popular with New Agers and alternative thinkers, revered by artists and painters, known for skiing and hiking, blessed with great restaurants, and abundant with shops and galleries. A tricultural Hispanic, Native American, and Anglo population calls this wonderful area home.

Northern New Mexico has four distinct seasons. In summer, even on days when the temperature reaches 100°F, nights can be cool enough to require a light jacket. Summer is high season, and, especially in July and August in Santa Fe, hotel rates are among the highest in the nation. Winter is by no means a downtime, however. It snows constantly in the mountains, and though flakes often fall in Taos and Santa Fe, the afternoon sun usually pushes temperatures into the lower 40s. Ski season runs from about Thanksgiving to early April. Fall and spring are beautiful, slightly less crowded and less expensive. There's never a significant shoulder season, but April and November are the quietest.

Getting Around

Santa Fe and Taos have no commercial airports. You must fly to Albuquerque, where you can rent a car and drive the hour to Santa Fe (it's an additional hour to Taos). Greyhound provides bus service from the airport to Santa Fe and Taos. In Albuquerque, you'll need a car to get around—the sights and neighborhoods are far apart. The main plazas of Santa Fe and Taos can easily be toured on foot, but in both places you'll need a car to reach many of the B&Bs and restaurants, not to mention all the region's natural attractions. For information about bus service, contact the appropriate visitors' bureaus (*see* The Little Black Book, at the end of this chapter).

Eats

No southwestern-style restaurant anywhere else in the country does northern New Mexican cooking justice. The regional specialties are lighter, fresher, and better for you than elsewhere. There are dozens of chile (not "chili," as it's spelled in some parts of the country) varieties, and most dishes come with the option of either a green or red chile sauce (the former is the hotter). Blue and red corn are as prevalent as yellow; black beans are as common as pintos. There are plenty of Italian trattorias, western-style steak houses, Asian eateries, and even a few French restaurants. California's influence can be tasted in inventive dishes that combine ingredients and techniques from several cultures.

For the price ranges of all Eats listings in this chapter, *see* dining Chart A at the front of this guide.

Scenes

Don't come to northern New Mexico hoping to party into the wee hours of the morning. Taos has no gay bars and Santa Fe has only one. The half-dozen clubs in Albuquerque make for a pretty good night on the town. They're livelier from September to May, when the nearby University of New Mexico is in session. If you drive down to Albuquerque from Taos or Santa Fe, consider spending the night—incidents of drunk driving are notoriously high in New Mexico; even if you remain sober, you can't count on other drivers.

Sleeps

B&Bs and small inns, most of them in the adobe style of the Indian pueblos, are the region's signature lodgings. Even if you find the personal touch of a small property too personal, consider breaking with tradition. The rates tend to be half the cost of a hotel room, the breakfasts are often so generous you won't need to eat lunch, and privacy is usually not the concern it is elsewhere—at least half the guest-house rooms in Santa Fe have private entrances, and rarely do they lack private baths. Santa Fe has the priciest and most sumptuous lodgings; the ones in Taos tend to have reasonable rates and quite memorable settings. As for Albuquerque, you'll find a handful of excellent small inns along with chain properties.

For the price ranges of all Sleeps listings in this chapter, *see* lodging Chart A at the front of this guide.

The Little Black Book

Information about bookstores and other key resources in Albuquerque, Santa Fe, and Taos is at the end of this chapter.

ALBUQUERQUE

Albuquerque occupies a vast valley at the western base of the Sandia Mountains. From the Sandia foothills, which cradle the city's most expensive homes, Albuquerque's densely settled but low-slung blocks slope gradually for several miles before tapering off around the Rio Grande River. Beyond the river, which loosely the defines the western edge of the city, the land pushes upward again for many miles, culminating in sunburnt mesas and a string of volcanic peaks. Two major interstates, I–40, which runs east–west, and I–25, which runs north–south, meet almost precisely in the center of town. Addresses are divided into four quadrants (NE, SE, SW, NW), which are formed not by the interstates, as one might expect, but by the axis that far predates them, east–west Central Avenue and the north–south rail tracks.

The Lay of the Land

Downtown and Old Town

Most of Albuquerque's **downtown** business district occupies the city's southwestern quadrant. **Old Town,** northwest of downtown, was laid out in 1706. Albuquerque's earliest building, the **San Felipe de Neri Church** (✉ 2005 North Plaza NW, ☎ 505/243–4628), still fronts the north side of the quiet, tree-shaded **Plaza.** The wares for sale at the more than 200 crafts and art galleries and boutiques in the area run the gamut from fine to kitschy. **La Placita** (✉ 208 San Felipe St. NW, ☎ 505/247–2204) and **La Hacienda** (✉ 302 San Felipe St. NW, ☎ 505/243–3131), the old-fashioned New Mexican restaurants on the eastern edge of the Plaza, tone down their food to accommodate the tender taste buds of the many non-locals who visit Old Town, but are atmospheric and inexpensive lunching spots.

A contemporary structure a few blocks north of the Plaza houses the **Albuquerque Museum of Art and History** (✉ 2000 Mountain Rd. NW, ☎ 505/243–7255), whose holdings include the nation's largest collection of Spanish Colonial artifacts. The museum's galleries display traditional and contemporary regional art. Exhibits on geology, volcanoes, and dinosaurs await you across the street at the **New Mexico Museum of Natural History and Science** (✉ 1801 Mountain Rd., ☎ 505/841–2800). Central Avenue travels west from the Plaza to the **Albuquerque Biological Park** (✉ 2601 Central Ave. NW, ☎ 505/764–6200), where there's an aquarium, botanic gardens, and a zoo.

The **Rio Grande Nature Center** (✉ 2901 Candelaria Rd. NW, ☎ 505/344–7240), a 270-acre riverside tract of forest and meadows north of Old Town (head west from Rio Grande Boulevard), contains century-old stands of cottonwood and willow trees. On your way to or from Old Town (head east from Rio Grande Boulevard on Menaul Boulevard) is the **Indian Pueblo Cultural Center** (✉ 2401 12th St. NW, ☎ 505/843–7270), which has a good restaurant and information on the state's 19 Indian pueblos.

Petroglyph National Monument (✉ 4735 Unser Blvd. NW; from downtown, take I–40 west and Coors Blvd. north, ☎ 505/839–4429), a 17-mile black-rock escarpment, runs along the bases of five extinct volcanoes. The monument's 17,000 Indian pictographs are between 400 and 1,000 years old.

Route 66, the University of New Mexico, and Nob Hill

Upon its completion in the late 1930s, **Historic Route 66** was the first continuous blacktop road to span New Mexico. East of Old Town and downtown, after it crosses beneath the I–25 overpass, **Central Avenue** (Route 66's name within Albuquerque proper) begins to take on the retroglamorous aura of the 1940s and 1950s. Countless greasy spoon diners and divey motor hotels, all with monstrous, ultratacky yet eye-catching neon signs, line the highway from here to the eastern foothills.

Central Avenue fringes the southern edge of the **University of New Mexico** (✉ Visitor Information Center, Las Lomas Rd. NE at University Blvd. NE, ☎ 505/277–0111), whose noteworthy attractions include the **Maxwell Museum of Anthropology** (✉ off Roma Ave. NE, ☎ 505/277–4405) and the **University Art Museum** (✉ Fine Arts Center, off Cornell St. NE, ☎ 505/277–4001). The campus's **Jonson Gallery** (✉ 1909 Las Lomas Rd. NE, ☎ 505/277–4967) is a showcase for the works of Raymond Jonson, the late icon of Transcendentalist American art.

South of UNM, several blocks of funky shops and restaurants enliven the stretch along and below Central Avenue. East of UNM is the **Nob Hill Historic District,** which, though hardly a gay ghetto, has the only visible concentration of queer-owned homes and businesses in New Mexico. The blocks between 3000 and 4000 are the best for browsing, noshing, and people-watching.

The Sandia Mountains

The monumental **Sandia Mountains,** rising from the eastern reaches of town, are an easy and rewarding excursion. The quicker, if less spectacular, route to the crest of the mountains is via the **Sandia Peak Aerial Tramway** (⊠ Tramway Loop Rd. NE; from downtown head east on Central Avenue, ☎ 505/856–7325). At the end of the 2.7-mile ride is the **Summit House,** which has observation decks, a small visitors center, and an overpriced restaurant.

Another option is to drive the hour-long scenic route around the rear (eastern side) of the mountain range. Head east on Central Avenue past Tramway Loop Road, beyond the city limits and through Tijeras Canyon. In the village of Tijeras, turn left onto Route 14, which is the beginning of the **Turquoise Trail** (*see below*). Follow this to the village of **San Antonito,** where you'll make a left onto Route 536, the **Crest Highway National Scenic Byway.** The **Sandia Crest House Gift Shop and Restaurant** (☎ 505/243–0605) sits at the mountain's peak. The view from here is comparable to that from Summit House. Trails, from moderate to strenuous, begin in the vicinity.

On the Way to Santa Fe

The most direct route from Albuquerque to Santa Fe is via I–25. A 4½-mile detour west of I–25 leads to **Santo Domingo Pueblo** (⊠ off Rte. 22, ☎ 505/465–2214), where a small arts-and-crafts center sells some of the best jewelry in the region. A more scenic alternative to I–25 is the **Turquoise Trail,** Route 14, which you can access from I–40 heading east out of Albuquerque. If you leave Albuquerque by mid-morning, you can easily visit Sandia Crest, enjoy sights along the trail, and reach Santa Fe in time for chips, salsa, and margaritas at **Tomasita's** (*see* Eats *in* Santa Fe, *below*).

Eats

$$$–$$$$ ✕ **Prairie Star.** North of town off I–25, this Pueblo Revival compound wows diners with its outstanding views, romantic setting, and top-notch service. Southwestern, New American, and Continental accents and ingredients find their way into the dishes, which are sometimes excellent, sometimes a little off the mark, but always inventive. Blue-crusted poblano peppers stuffed with rock shrimp and caramelized onions are a highlight. ⊠ *Jémez Canyon Dam Rd., Bernalillo,* ☎ *505/867–3327.*

$$–$$$ ✕ **Monte Vista Fire Station.** The chefs at this dapper turquoise-trim adobe, a former firehouse, prepare memorable New American entrées like blue-corn-dusted rellenos with poblano pineapple salsa, and served with wild-mushroom tamales and ancho-chile sauce. ⊠ *3201 Central Ave. NE,* ☎ *505/255–2424.*

$$–$$$ ✕ **Scalo.** A noisy see-and-be-seen crowd packs into this Nob Hill restaurant for excellent northern Italian fare such as fillet of beef, with rosemary, green peppercorns, and garlic with a balsamic demi-glace sauce; and marinated half-chicken on oven-roasted potatoes with Kalamata-olives jus and fried red onions. Scala has a romantic loft area and a big patio. ⊠ *3500 Central Ave. SE,* ☎ *505/255–8781.*

$$ ✕ **Café Broadway.** Warmly decorated and with a delightful arbored garden and patio, this Spanish restaurant specializes in traditional tapas, such as cured ham, Manchego cheese, and octopus. Good main dishes include chorizo sandwiches, grilled quail, and a fried breaded pork chop. The paella is great, too. ⊠ *606 Broadway Blvd. SE,* ☎ *505/842–9998.*

Albuquerque

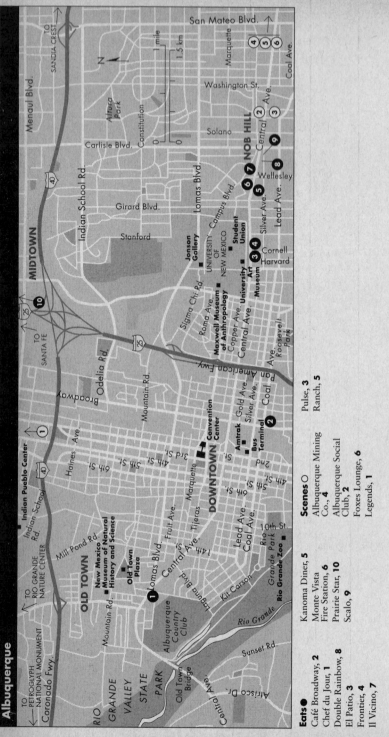

TO PETROGLYPH
NATIONAL MONUMENT
Coronado Fwy.

TO
RIO GRANDE
NATURE CENTER

TO
SANDIA CREST

San Mateo Blvd.

Menaul Blvd.

Altura
Park

Carlisle Blvd.

Indian School Rd.

Girard Blvd.

Stanford

MIDTOWN

Washington St.

Marquette

Coal Ave.

Solano

NOB HILL

Central Ave.

Wellesley

Silver Ave.

Lead Ave.

Cornell
Harvard

**Jonson
Gallery**

**Maxwell Museum
of Anthropology**

**Student
Union**

UNIVERSITY
OF
NEW MEXICO

**University
Art
Museum**

Sigma Chi Rd.

Roma Ave.

Copper Ave.

Central Ave.

Lomas Blvd.

Campus Blvd.

Roosevelt
Park

Indian Pueblo Center

Indian School

Haines Ave.

Mountain Rd.

Broadway

Odelia Rd.

Mill Pond Rd.

OLD TOWN

**New Mexico
Museum of Natural
History and Science**

**Old Town
Plaza**

Lomas Blvd.

Mountain Rd.

Mountain Rd.

6th St.

5th St.

4th St.

3rd St.

Marquette

Fruit Ave.

Tijeras

Central Ave.

DOWNTOWN

**Convention
Center**

Gold Ave.

Silver Ave.

Coal Ave.

Pan American Fwy.

**Amtrak
Bus
Terminal**

2nd St.

4th St.

6th St.

Lead Ave.

Coal Ave.

10th St.

Kit Carson

**Rio
Grande Park**

Rio Grande Zoo

Albuquerque
Country
Club

Rio Grande

Old Town
Bridge

Sunset Rd.

Central Ave.

Atrisco Dr.

**RIO
GRANDE
VALLEY
STATE
PARK**

TO
SANTA FE

N

1 mile

1.5 km

Constitution

Eats ●
Café Broadway, **2**
Chef du Jour, **1**
Double Rainbow, **8**
El Patio, **3**
Frontier, **4**
Il Vicino, **7**
Kanoma Diner, **5**
Monte Vista
Fire Station, **6**
Prairie Star, **10**
Scalo, **9**

Scenes ○
Albuquerque Mining
Co., **4**
Albuquerque Social
Club, **2**
Foxes Lounge, **6**
Legends, **1**

Pulse, **3**
Ranch, **5**

$$ ✕ **Kanoma Diner.** A minimalist postmodern twist on a traditional diner, Kanoma takes patrons on a mouthwatering journey through Asia. Feast on ginger shrimp with green-onion corn cakes, Szechuan peppercorn-crusted pork loin, a wrap of shrimp and lobster with cilantro and mint, and tasty noodle dishes. ✉ *3128 Central Ave. SE,* ☎ *505/265–7773.*

$–$$ ✕ **Chef Du Jour.** This hole-in-the-wall is hidden beside BK's Health Pantry in Old Town. The international menu changes often but might include a spicy Caribbean chicken stew, a BLT made with pancetta, yellow tomatoes, arugula, and grilled sage, or a cardamom plum tart with almond cream for dessert. Chef du Jour only serves lunch on weekdays, but prepares wonderful dinners on Friday and Saturday. ✉ *119 San Pasquale SW,* ☎ *505/247–8998. No credit cards.*

$–$$ ✕ **Il Vicino.** With wood floors, gray tables, and ochre walls, this airy restaurant provides a change of pace from the dowdy student haunts along Central. Inexpensive, it draws an intriguing crowd for wood-fired pizzas and filling calzones. Excellent salads. ✉ *3403 Central Ave. NE,* ☎ *505/266–7855.*

$ ✕ **El Patio.** Few locals agree about what's the best place in town for New Mexican food, but this student hangout near UNM is always part of the debate. The food is authentic and spicy—the green-chile enchiladas will make you cry. Be sure to sample sopaipillas with honey for dessert. The best seating is on the patio, amid trees, birds, and misting machines. ✉ *142 Harvard St. SE,* ☎ *505/268–4245.*

$ ✕ **Frontier.** Something like a Denny's for fags, alternateens, reformed hippies, and drifters, this 24-hour restaurant is famous for its bargain breakfast burritos (the best on the planet). You'll also find good burgers, sandwiches, and basic New Mexican treats. ✉ *Cornell Dr. SE and Central Ave. SE,* ☎ *505/266–0550.*

Coffeehouse Culture

Double Rainbow. The tall windows at Double Rainbow yield optimum views of the curiosities who stroll this stretch of Central Avenue. Yuppies, students, and tourists enjoy iced and hot coffees, delicious baked goods, and some of the best sandwiches and soups in town. ✉ *3412 Central Ave. SE,* ☎ *505/255–6633.*

Scenes

Prime Suspects

Albuquerque Mining Co. Once a hard-driving leather bar, this expansive nightclub caters to a diverse though still butch crowd. The place has several bars, including a cocktail lounge with video screens and a pool table and an enclosed patio with a full volleyball court. The music at the dimly lit, strangely alluring, and often hot and cruisy dance area is loud but catchy. Not as pretty-boyish as Pulse, AMC is a good bet if your primary goal is to hook up with somebody. ✉ *7209 Central Ave. NE,* ☎ *505/255–0925. Crowd: mostly male, 20s to 50s, some leather, diverse.*

Legends. The one Albuquerque bar that's not along Central Avenue, this contemporary dance club in northwestern Albuquerque opened as a lesbian bar. The management welcomes a mixed crowd, but women still predominate. There's a bar, lots of tables and seating, video screens, a central dance floor, and a separate room with a few pool tables. Photos of Barbra, Marilyn, Madonna, and assorted other icons line the walls. Outgoing staff. ✉ *6132 4th St. NW,* ☎ *505/343–9793. Crowd: 75/25 f/m, all ages, low-key, eclectic.*

Pulse. The most happening club in Albuquerque, this disco with a festive patio and a compact but fierce dance floor attracts the few club kids and stand-and-model queens in the area. Odd decorative details like red-vinyl banquettes and a steel cage filled with bowling balls hint that perhaps this building once housed an old steak house or a bowling alley. In any case, the space has certifiable camp appeal. Go-go boys boogying above the masses enhance the sexually charged mood, but the Pulse isn't all that cruisy. And with a goodly number of straights attending, it's not the kind of place where it's easy to tell who's interested in whom. ⊠ *4100 Central Ave. SE,* ☎ *505/255–3334. Crowd: 80/20 gay/straight, 60/40 m/f, young, a few voguers, but laid-back.*

Ranch. Fans of line-dancing and two-stepping head to this club in eastern Albuquerque to take advantage of the enormous dance floor, several bars, and cheerful ambience. Holiday lights drape the DJ booth, which resembles a giant stagecoach. ⊠ *8900 Central Ave. SE,* ☎ *505/275–1616. Crowd: 60/40 m/f, 30s to 50s, lots of 10-gallon hats, low-key.*

Neighborhood Haunts

The **Albuquerque Social Club** (⊠ 4021 Central Ave. NE, ☎ 505/255–0887), a garden-variety video bar across the street from Pulse, attracts a mostly male following; guests are permitted in this private club, but must be introduced by a member, sign in, and purchase a membership (good for one year). The parking lot at the divey **Foxes Lounge** (⊠ 8521 Central Ave. NE, ☎ 505/255–3060) brims with beat-up pickup trucks, giving hints of the rugged, bearish, and horny guys inside. Exotic dancers are the main entertainment. Sleaze-o-rama.

Sleeps

Hotels

$$$ 🏨 **Albuquerque Marriott.** Corporate business travelers frequent this 17-story property close to queer nightlife. Southwestern accents that include kachina dolls and pueblo pottery and art lend warmth to the rooms, many of which have spectacular mountain views. ⊠ *2101 Louisiana Blvd. NE, 87110,* ☎ *505/881–6800 or 800/334–2086,* FAX *505/888–2982. 264 rooms. Restaurants, pool, exercise room.*

$$–$$$ 🏨 **Wyndham Albuquerque Hotel.** This high-rise, a first-class property, has an excellent restaurant and great in-room amenities like irons, dataports, and coffeemakers. All the rooms have private balconies with views. Though the Wyndham is near the airport, it's convenient to downtown and UNM. ⊠ *2910 Yale Blvd. SE, 87106,* ☎ *505/843–7000 or 800/227–1117,* FAX *505/246–8188. 282 rooms. Restaurant, pool, exercise room.*

$–$$ 🏨 **Plaza Inn Albuquerque.** A cheerful mid-price mid-rise, the Plaza Inn is near the intersection of I–40 and I–25. With only 121 rooms and a well-trained staff, it's a great alternative to the large convention zoos. ⊠ *900 Medical Arts NE, 87102,* ☎ *505/243–5693 or 800/237–1307,* FAX *505/843–6229. 121 rooms. Restaurant, pool, exercise room.*

$ 🏨 **Luxury Inn.** Within a short drive of Nob Hill, the gay bars, and the university, this clean motel with spacious rooms and a nice indoor pool and hot tub is tops among the cheap and mostly scuzzy motels on the old Route 66. ⊠ *6718 Central Ave. SE, 87108,* ☎ *505/255–5900,* FAX *505/256–4915. Pool.*

Guest Houses

$$–$$$ 🏨 **Hacienda Antigua.** Claw-foot tubs, wood carvings and Indian art, and beehive-shape kiva-style fireplaces are among the grace notes at this historic women-owned hacienda. Of the area's accommodations with rooms for around $100 nightly, this is one of the best options. ⊠ *6708 Tierra Dr. NW, 87107,* ☎ *505/345–5399 or 800/201–2986. 5 rooms with private bath, 4 with phone. Full breakfast. Pool, hot tub. Mixed gay/straight.*

$$ 🏨 **Casitas at Old Town.** Compact and within walking distance of Old Town attractions and shops, this two-casita compound combines the privacy of an apartment with the charm of a B&B. Each unit has a fireplace, a kitchenette, and southwestern furnishings. A great value. ⊠ *1604 Old Town Rd. NW, 87104,* ☎ *505/843–7479. 2 units with private bath. Mixed gay/straight.*

$$ ⌧ **W. E. Mauger Estate B&B.** Two men from northern New England recently took over this 1897 Queen Anne Victorian on the edge of downtown. A desirable property, it provides a change of pace from the region's many pueblo-style inns. Period antiques, wallpapers, and fabrics decorate the rooms. ⌧ *701 Roma Ave. NW, 87102,* ☎ *505/242–8755,* FAX *505/842–8835. 9 rooms with TV and private bath. Full breakfast. Mixed gay/straight.*

$–$$ ⌧ **Rainbow Lodge.** A 20-minute drive from downtown, this 5,000-square-foot lodge near the foot of the road to Sandia Crest is a perfect choice if you want views of the mountains but also proximity to Albuquerque and the airport. The rooms are comfortable though not fancy; many have fireplaces and all have fantastic vistas. Two suites have full kitchens. ⌧ *115 Frost Rd., Sandia Park, 87047,* ☎ *505/281–7100. 4 rooms with TV and private bath. Hot tub. Continental breakfast. Mostly mixed gay male/lesbian.*

SANTA FE

During the first part of this century, the homosexual sons of wealthy families came to Santa Fe to write or otherwise dabble in the arts and, ideally, stay as far from proper society as possible. Some of these exiles were self-imposed, others enforced, but for some men of this era, Santa Fe represented a cross between a gay summer camp and Devil's Island.

In part because New Mexicans cherish their right to privacy and also because its early members had been banished to the Southwest, the queer community in Santa Fe was discreet, if not downright closeted. This has changed of late. Gay business owners are much more likely to identify themselves as such. And a two-block stretch of Guadalupe Street downtown has developed into a tiny gay district, with a bar, a coffeehouse, and a couple of restaurants big with the community.

The Lay of the Land

Were you to see Santa Fe from only its main thoroughfares, Cerrillos Road and St. Francis Drive, you'd likely leave wondering why on earth anyone would spend more than five minutes here. Much of the greater metropolitan area is a maze of shopping malls and cheap hotels, far too many of them slapped-together, adobe-style stabs at contemporary commercial architecture.

But if you penetrate Paseo de Peralta—the historic ring road encircling the 17th-century city center—you'll discover the Santa Fe of legend. As in Albuquerque, mountains (in this case the Sangre de Cristo range) rise above the city's ritzy residential neighborhoods in the foothills. To the north and west, the terrain is a mix of rolling woodland and stark mesas that extend clear out to the Jémez Mountains, Bandolier National Monument, and the nighttime lights of Los Alamos.

The Plaza

Nearly 400 years ago, Santa Fe's settlers held their military and religious ceremonies in the glorious **Plaza,** a good spot to catch your breath between shopping and museum- or gallery-hopping. At the northern end of the Plaza, the oldest public building in the United States houses the **Palace of the Governors Museum** (⌧ W. Palace Ave., ☎ 505/827–6474), whose many artifacts and decorative arts trace the region's rich history. The Palace is the main and most impressive branch of the **Museum of New Mexico,** a state system that includes five museums in Santa Fe, two of them (the Fine Arts and the Georgia O'Keeffe) close by, and two of them (the International Folk Art and the Indian Arts and Culture) south of the Plaza. For $10 you can buy a five-day pass good for admission to all the museums; otherwise, each one costs $5 to visit.

A block west of the Palace of the Governors, the **Museum of Fine Arts** (⊠ 107 W. Palace Ave., ☎ 505/827–4455) concentrates on southwestern, Mexican, and Native American art. The smallish and somewhat over-hyped **Georgia O'Keeffe Museum** (⊠ 217 Johnson St., ☎ 505/995–0785) houses a permanent collection of several dozen paintings and sculptures, but surprisingly provides little in the way of context for the works or biographical information about the artist.

The city's first Catholic archbishop, Jean Baptiste Lamy, founded the French Romanesque **Cathedral of St. Francis** (⊠ 131 Cathedral Pl., ☎ 505/982–5619), which is east of the Plaza off Palace Avenue. Lamy is the subject of the Willa Cather's novel *Death Comes for the Archbishop*, though the novel depicts his experiences at a church north of Taos. The Zia Indian–inspired **State Capitol building** (⊠ Old Santa Fe Trail and Paseo de Peralta, ☎ 505/986–4589), a few blocks south, was designed to represent the Circle of Life.

Santa Fe's 125 galleries and many sophisticated specialty stores outshine those you'll find in Taos. It's worth poking your head into at least a few of the galleries, many of which are near the Plaza.

The western border of the downtown commercial area is **Guadalupe Street,** once the terminus of the 1,500-mile trade route, El Camino Real, which extended all the way from Mexico City. The street was also the terminus of the Atchison, Topeka, and Santa Fe Railroad. The old depot anchors the **Historic Guadalupe Railyard District.** The **Sanbusco Market Center** (⊠ 500 Montezuma St., ☎ 505/989–9390), a converted century-old freight warehouse, contains galleries, shops, and restaurants. A farmers' market is held in the parking lot on Tuesday and Saturday from June through October. **SITE Santa Fe** (⊠ 1606 Paseo de Peralta, ☎ 505/989–1199), off Guadalupe, presents a biennial exhibition (the next one's in 1999) of provocative international artworks and hosts traveling exhibitions and installations by local and other artists. Many of the funky shops, restaurants and bars on Guadalupe Street north of the Santa Fe River have gay followings.

South and East of the Plaza

Extending south of the Plaza and into the foothills above town, the **Old Santa Fe Trail** leads to the **Museum of International Folk Art** (⊠ 706 Camino Lejo, ☎ 505/827–6350), whose collection of crafts and art spans several centuries and regions of the world. The adjacent **Museum of Indian Arts and Culture** (⊠ 710 Camino Lejo, ☎ 505/827–6344) documents the area's Pueblo, Navajo, and Apache cultures. Also part of this complex is a center of Native American culture and art, the **Wheelwright Museum of the American Indian** (⊠ 704 Camino Lejo, ☎ 505/982–4636).

After a long day of touring, nothing beats a salt glow, herbal wrap, or massage at **Ten Thousand Waves** (⊠ Ski Basin Rd., ☎ 505/982–9304), a Japanese-style spa with private and communal hot tubs.

Tesuque

About 7 miles north of town on U.S. 84/285 are two attractions that have little to do with each other but draw many of the same followers: **Trader Jack's Flea Market** (no phone) and the **Santa Fe Opera** (☎ 505/986–5900 or 800/280–4654). The market, which is open on Friday, Saturday, and Sunday between dawn and dusk from March to November, has incredible bargains and stunning desert views. Browse the 12 acres of wares, and then stop by the nearby Tesuque Village Market for lunch. The world-class opera performs at a 1,200-seat, outdoor amphitheater on a hillside overlooking miles of mesas and the Jémez mountains. The opera's season runs only from late June to late August.

On the Way to Taos

The drive from Santa Fe to Taos can take from 90 minutes to an entire day, depending on which of three routes you take and how much time you spend exploring. The **Low Road** (from Albuquerque, take U.S. 285 to Espanola and turn right onto Route 68) is the quickest route. The **High Road** (take U.S. 285, turn right onto Route 503 before Espanola, head west on Route 76 at Chimaya, turn right on Route 75 at Peñasco, and pick up Route 518 at Placitas) offers the most splendid scenery. The rarely traveled **western route** (via U.S. 285 and U.S. 64) passes the **Ojo Caliente Mineral Springs** (⊠ U.S. 285, ☎ 505/583–2233)—a good place to while away the afternoon—and the majestic **Rio Grande Gorge Bridge.**

Eats

$$$$ ✕ **Hacienda del Cerezo.** This ultraluxurious miniresort serves dinner to the public by reservation only. The several-course prix-fixe New American meal, served with wine, is a bargain at $57.50. Recent offerings have included a seared leek-wrapped scallop tournedo on orange-garlic basmati, and medallions of black Angus beef on a porcini- and field-mushroom potato ragout. ⊠ *100 Camino del Cerezo,* ☎ *505/982–8000.*

$$$$ ✕ **Santacafé.** One of the most romantic spots in Santa Fe, the sparely decorated Santacafé prepares an exotic, outlandish blend of Far Eastern and southwestern cooking. Among the house specialties are duck with maple hoisin sauce and sesame bok choy, and filet mignon with roasted-garlic-and-green-chile mashed potatoes. ⊠ *231 Washington Ave.,* ☎ *505/984–1788.*

$$$–$$$$ ✕ **Geronimo.** The southwestern-influenced international fare at this gay-popular eatery includes oven-roasted halibut wrapped in banana leaf and served with black-bean plantain habañero sauce and tortilla jicama salad. The two dimly lit dining rooms in this 200-year-old adobe building are romantic, but you can also eat in the outdoor courtyard. ⊠ *724 Canyon Rd.,* ☎ *505/982–1500.*

$$$–$$$$ ✕ **Jack's.** Some locals joke that more fags come to Jack's than when this site was the Edge, a gay nightclub. The Continental fare includes mushrooms-and-Brie ravioli with sage cream sauce, and pan-seared Chilean sea bass with roasted sweet-pepper rice, spiced pecans, and citrus beurre blanc. ⊠ *135 W. Palace Ave.,* ☎ *505/983–7220.*

$$$–$$$$ ✕ **Palace Restaurant.** The ruby velvet walls belie the Palace's colorful role in the history of the Wild West—the building has been a whorehouse, a saloon, and a gaming parlor. The place is touristy these days, but it's appealing and very queer. Hefty Caesar salads are prepared tableside; steak, veal, and pasta dishes, none of them spectacular, are also served. ⊠ *142 W. Palace Ave.,* ☎ *505/982–9891.*

$$$–$$$$ ✕ **Pink Adobe.** This downtown pink adobe has been synonymous with Santa Fe dining for 50 years; you're sure to see some of the city's old guard holding court. The generally unimaginative but rich and filling fare includes lamb curry and tournedos bordelaise in a puff pastry. ⊠ *406 Old Santa Fe Trail,* ☎ *505/983–7712.*

$$–$$$$ ✕ **Coyote Café and Cantina.** The café's celebrity chef, Mark Miller, is the man most strongly associated with Santa Fe's brand of New American–inspired southwestern cuisine. The Coyote is loud, expensive, flashy, and prone to pretension, but the food—dishes like buttermilk corn cakes with chipotle shrimp—is always memorable. If the dining room turns you off, head to the rooftop cantina, where the food is half the price and just as good. ⊠ *132 W. Water St.,* ☎ *505/983–1615.*

$$$ ✕ **Paul's.** Guests of local B&Bs get a discount at Paul's, but the savings aside, this storefront dining room is a real find. Grilled ahi tuna with serrano peach chutney and wild-mushroom-and-feta ravioli in a pepper

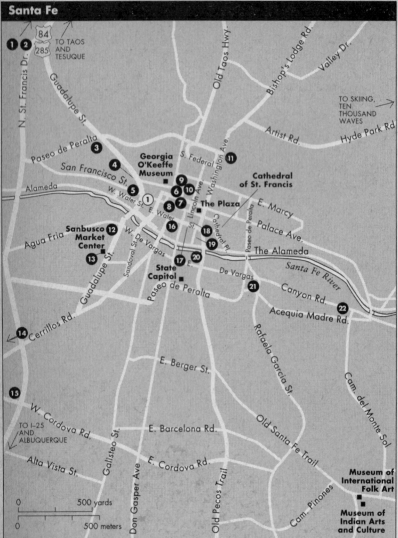

Santa Fe

TO TAOS
AND
TESUQUE

TO SKIING,
TEN
THOUSAND
WAVES

**Georgia
O'Keeffe
Museum**

**Cathedral
of St. Francis**

The Plaza

**Sanbusco
Market
Center**

**State
Capitol**

The Alameda

Santa Fe River

**Museum of
International
Folk Art**

**Museum of
Indian Arts
and Culture**

0   500 yards

0   500 meters

TO I-25
AND
ALBUQUERQUE

Eats ●
Babbo Ganzo
Trattoria, **10**
Blue Corn
Cafe, **14, 18**
Coyote Cafe and
Cantina, **17**
Dana's Afterdark, **4**
Downtown
Subscription, **21**

Galisteo, **16**
Geronimo, **22**
Guadalupe Cafe, **12**
Hacienda del
Cerezo, **2**
India Palace, **19**
Jack's, **6**
Palace Restaurant, **7**
Paul's, **9**
Pink Adobe, **20**

San Francisco Street
Bar and Grill, **8**
Santacafe, **11**
Tesuque Village
Market, **1**
Tomasita's, **13**
Vanessie, **5**
Whistling Moon, **3**
Wild Oats, **15**

Scenes ○
Drama Club, **1**

tomato sauce are two of the favorites on the regionally inspired Continental menu. ⊠ *72 W. Marcy St.,* ☎ *505/982–8738.*

$$–$$$ ✕ **Babbo Ganzo.** A few blocks from the Plaza, this classy northern Italian bistro is known for stellar service, a great wine list, fresh baked breads, and designer pizzas. Not especially Santa Fe, but who cares? The food's top-notch. ⊠ *130 Lincoln Ave., 2nd Floor,* ☎ *505/986–3835.*

$$–$$$ ✕ **India Palace.** When you've overdosed on blue corn and chile sauce, head here for some fine Indian food. Chicken tikka masala and rack of lamb are among the house specialties. There's belly dancing many nights. ⊠ *227 Don Gaspar Ave.,* ☎ *505/986–5859.*

$$–$$$ ✕ **Vanessie.** With one gay bar in town, plenty of folks clink glasses at lodgelike Vanessie, where the air is rich with the sound of piano music and the smell of steaks and ribs. The food is simple and filling—grilled shrimp, rotisserie chicken. The spicy onion loaf is famous. ⊠ *434 W. San Francisco St.,* ☎ *505/982–9966.*

$–$$ ✕ **San Francisco Street Bar and Grill.** A festive late-night cure for the munchies, this casual eatery in the Mercado shopping center has juicy burgers, tempting salads, and excellent sandwiches made with Italian sausages and roasted peppers. ⊠ *114 W. San Francisco St.,* ☎ *505/982–2044.*

$–$$ ✕ **Tesuque Village Market.** A country-deli-cum-café where the Porsches and BMWs in the parking lot flank pickup trucks with muddy golden retrievers in the back, this perfect spot for people-watching is in sleepy Tesuque, 10 miles north of town. Stop by on the weekend after visiting Trader Jack's flea market. The French owners are as proficient in croissant baking and pie making as they are in burrito stuffing. ⊠ *Rte. 591 off U.S. 285, Tesuque,* ☎ *505/988–8848.*

$–$$ ✕ **Whistling Moon.** Très gay and cozy, this café on funky Guadalupe Street serves healthful and tasty Middle Eastern and Mediterranean fare; try Moroccan lamb sausage or any of the bounteous pasta offerings. Cheers to the restaurant's logo: "Celebrating pride, diversity, and falafels." ⊠ *402 N. Guadalupe St.,* ☎ *505/983–3093.*

$ ✕ **Blue Corn Café.** With locations in the Mercado shopping center (by the Plaza) and out on tacky Cerrillos Road (this branch has its own microbrewery), the Blue Corn is an outstanding option for authentic southwestern fare. Always busy, it has a young, outgoing staff and is open for dinner until 11 (the bar closes at 2 AM). Best bets: the chipotle and smoked-corn soup, the veggie tamales, and the margaritas (perhaps the best in town). ⊠ *133 Water St., Plaza Mercado,* ☎ *505/984–1800;* ⊠ *Rodeo and Cerrillos Sts.,* ☎ *505/438–1800.*

$ ✕ **Guadalupe Café.** The breakfast burritos here are tremendous, but nonsouthwestern standbys like raspberry pancakes are also tasty. Basic but great Mexican lunches and dinners are also served. Expect a long wait. ⊠ *313 S. Guadalupe St.,* ☎ *505/982–9762.*

$ ✕ **Tomasita's.** Nowhere in town will you find consistently better and more affordable New Mexican fare than at this always loud and rollicking eatery at the Sanbusco Market Center. If a table isn't immediately available, which is likely, you can munch on chips and salsa and sip fabulous margaritas while you wait. ⊠ *500 S. Guadalupe St.,* ☎ *505/983–5721.*

$ ✕ **Wild Oats.** The Santa Fe branch of this progressive health-market chain is a great place to pick up groceries or delicious prepared foods—the aisles and the café are always packed with dykes and fags. ⊠ *1090 St. Francis Dr.,* ☎ *505/983–5333.*

Coffeehouse Culture

Dana's Afterdark. This new coffeehouse, a short walk from the Drama Club gay bar, opened in summer 1997 and has quickly developed into a queer hangout. There are a few brightly colored rooms, board games and magazines galore, and often a dog or two to play with. Grab a seat on the patio in front and you can watch the world flow by. ⊠ *222 N. Guadalupe St.,* ☎ *505/982–5225.*

Downtown Subscription. Newspaper and magazine racks line three sides of this café that's a good place to cool your heels after touring. Light food and many coffees are served. ⊠ *376 Garcia St.,* ☎ *505/983–3085.*

Galisteo. Sandwiches, good Texas chile stew, and other cheap eats are served at this downtown café whose patio is great for people-watching. ⊠ *201 Galisteo St.,* ☎ *505/984–1316.*

Scenes

Prime Suspect

Drama Club. Snazzy and fun-filled, this is Santa Fe's queer bar of the moment—locals are hoping it won't quickly disappear like so many other nightspots have. The club concocts well-attended country-western, trash-disco, and other theme nights, and also presents excellent live music and comedy. ⊠ *125 N. Guadalupe St.,* ☎ *505/988–4374. Crowd: mixed m/f, all ages, all styles, all types.*

Hangin' with the Hets

Several bars in Santa Fe restaurants, including **Vanessie** and **Geronimo** (*see* Eats, *above*) have queer followings. The owners of Geronimo operate a gay-friendly music club and lounge, the **A Bar** (⊠ 331 Sandoval St., ☎ 505/982–8808), which is attached to a happening restaurant, Cowboy. Another place where you might see family is the **Old House Restaurant** (⊠ El Dorado Hotel, 309 W. San Francisco St., ☎ 505/988–4455). The **Staab House** (⊠ La Posada Hotel, 330 E. Palace Ave., ☎ 505/986–0000) is a great stop for after-dinner drinks.

Sleeps

Hotels

$$$$ ⌂ **Inn of the Anasazi.** This adobe hotel offers a truly luxurious experience. The rooms have kiva fireplaces, four-poster beds, and southwestern furnishings, and there's a library with outstanding history books and local literature. ⊠ *113 Washington Ave., 87501,* ☎ *505/988–3030 or 800/688–8100,* FAX *505/988–3277. 59 rooms. Restaurant.*

$$$$ ⌂ **Inn on the Alameda.** The rooms at this exclusive property on the Santa Fe River are plush yet authentically southwestern, with handmade furnishings and local artworks. ⊠ *303 E. Alameda, 87501,* ☎ *505/984–2121 or 800/289–2122,* FAX *505/986–8325. 66 rooms. Exercise room.*

$$–$$$ ⌂ **Hotel St. Francis.** Classy furnishings like cherry-wood antiques and brass-and-iron beds compensate for the smallish rooms at the centrally located St. Francis, which dates from 1920. ⊠ *210 Don Gaspar Ave., 87501,* ☎ *505/983–5700 or 800/529–5700,* FAX *505/989–7690. 82 rooms. Restaurant.*

$–$$ ⌂ **Comfort Inn.** If you're on a budget, this property on motel-strewn Cerrillos Road is well maintained. ⊠ *4312 Cerrillos Rd., 87505,* ☎ FAX *505/474–7330. 83 rooms.*

Guest Houses and Small Resorts

$$$$ ⌂ **Hacienda del Cerezo.** This stupendous miniresort on 336 acres is about a 30-minute drive north of Santa Fe. The richly appointed hacienda opens onto a striking courtyard and is constructed with saltillo tiles, hand-carved beams, and native building materials; rooms have panoramic mountain views, fireplaces, sitting areas, and enclosed patios. The rate of $600 per couple includes three gourmet meals and complimentary beverages, plus the use of the tennis courts and the stable. ⊠ *100 Camino del Cerezo, 87501,* ☎ *505/982–8000 or 888/982–8001,* FAX

505/983–7162. 10 rooms with phone, TV, and private bath. Full break-fast. Restaurant, pool, exercise room. Mostly straight.

$$$–$$$$ 🏨 **Rancho de San Juan.** A short drive from Ojo Caliente Springs, this gay-operated 225-acre complex is nestled in the mountains north of Es-panola, midway between Santa Fe and Taos. More than half the accom-modations are suites, some of them around the central courtyard and others (the most romantic ones) amid the wilderness. All the rooms have mu-seum-quality southwestern furnishings, CD-stereos, and local artworks; some rooms have fireplaces, Jacuzzi tubs, and full kitchens. The restau-rant—worth a stop, but you have to call ahead—is open to the public from Wednesday to Sunday. There's no smoking anywhere on the com-pound. ✉ *U.S. 285, Espanola (mail: Box 4140, 87533),* ☎ 🖷 *505/ 753–6818 or 800/726–7121. 12 rooms with phone and private bath. Restaurant, hot tub. Full breakfast. Mixed gay/straight.*

$$$ 🏨 **Water Street Inn.** Off a side street a couple of blocks from the Plaza, this gay-run inn has rooms with rustic furnishings and all the conveniences you'd expect of a modern hotel, including VCRs, air-conditioning, and phones with voice mail. Most rooms have fireplaces; three are full suites. The only drawback is the location beside a parking lot, with no real grounds to speak of. ✉ *427 W. Water St., 87501,* ☎ *505/984–1193 or 800/646– 6752. 12 rooms with phone, TV, and private bath. Hot tub. Continen-tal breakfast. Mixed gay/straight.*

$$–$$$ 🏨 **Adobe Abode.** Near the Plaza and with furnishings as impressive as those at any luxury hotel in town, this a great bargain. The Adobe's large rooms have modern baths, upscale amenities, eclectic antiques and folk furniture, and a detailed notebook listing owner Pat Harbour's favorite sights and restaurants. Excellent breakfasts. ✉ *202 Chapelle, 87501,* ☎ *505/983–3133,* 🖷 *505/986–0972. 6 rooms with phone, TV, and pri-vate bath. Full breakfast. Mostly straight.*

$$–$$$ 🏨 **Grant Corner Inn.** This creaky Victorian, an anomaly in adobe-riddled downtown, contains period-furnished rooms whose gentility and ele-gance recalls Savannah or San Francisco. The many thoughtful touches include afternoon refreshments and a common room stocked with snacks, microwave popcorn, and soft drinks. ✉ *122 Grant Ave., 87501,* ☎ *505/ 983–6678,* 🖷 *505/983–1526. 12 rooms with phone and TV, most with private bath. Full breakfast. Mostly straight.*

$–$$$ 🏨 **Preston House.** You can opt for a Victorian or a southwestern expe-rience at this inn that's a 10-minute walk from the Plaza. An 1886 Queen Anne holds quirky rooms, many with brass beds, ceiling fans, and stained-glass windows; in back are two Queen Anne–style cottages with fireplaces. The rooms in the adobe across the street are done in traditional south-western style. ✉ *106 Faithway St., 87501,* ☎ 🖷 *505/982–3465. 15 rooms with phone and TV, most with private bath. Mostly straight.*

$$ 🏨 **Four Kachinas.** California transplants Andrew Beckerman and John Daw built this cozy inn back in 1992, fulfilling a longtime dream to set-tle in Santa Fe. Rooms are clean, crisp, and uncluttered, with saltillo-tile floors and southwestern furnishings; all have a private entrance to which a light breakfast is delivered each morning. There's also a small library with a wood-burning fireplace and sodas and brownies set out for snack-ing. The inn, a 10-minute walk from the Plaza, is off Paseo de Peralta. ✉ *512 Webber St., 87501,* ☎ *505/982–2550 or 800/397–2564. 6 rooms with private bath, most with phone and TV. Continental breakfast. Mostly straight.*

$$ 🏨 **Inn of the Turquoise Bear.** If the walls could talk at the first gay-ori-ented property to open in downtown Santa Fe, some of American his-tory might have to be rewritten. The inn was fashioned out of the 30-room estate of the late gay poet Witter Bynner, who hosted Willa Cather, Stephen Spender, Christopher Isherwood, W. H. Auden, Thornton Wilder, Errol Flynn, and other queer and bisexual figures of his era. Rooms in many shapes and sizes are tastefully and authentically furnished, not lavish but exuding character; most rooms have fireplaces and some open onto private courtyards. Hosts Ralph Bolton and Robert Frost have done a wonderful job of preserving Bynner's legacy and creating a romantic retreat. ⊠ *342 E. Buena Vista St., 87501,* ☎ *505/983–0798 or 800/396–4104,* FAX *505/988–4225, Web site www.turquoisebear.com. 11 rooms with phone, TV, most with private bath. Continental breakfast. Hot tub. Mostly mixed gay/lesbian.*

$–$$　☷ **Hummingbird Ranch.** Set alluringly in the sticks, 7 miles west of town, Cathy Bugliari and Trish Pyke's ranch is an informal place. The main house has two guest rooms, and there's an adjacent casita. A few steps away is a small cottage with a VCR and a stereo, but its guests must use the bathroom in the main house. The location is incredible, with sunset views off the back porch. This is the closest experience to staying with friends that you'll find in Santa Fe. ⊠ *Rte. 10 (mail: Box 111, 87501),* ☎ *505/471–2921. 4 rooms with TV, some with phone and private bath. Mixed gay/straight.*

$–$$　☷ **The Triangle Inn.** The nine adobe casitas at this ranch north of Tesuque are tastefully decorated; with two bedrooms, a VCR, a stereo, and a kitchenette, the largest and nicest of the nine is perfect for two couples. There's a sunning area in the courtyard, and owners Sarah Hryniewicz and Karen Ford are usually around to offer sightseeing advice. ⊠ *Rte. 11, No. 5T, Arroyo Cuyamungue (mail: Box 3235, Santa Fe, 87501),* ☎ *505/455–3375, e-mail trianglesf@aol.com. 9 units with phone, TV, and private bath. Continental breakfast. Hot tub. Mostly gay male/lesbian.*

TAOS

Taos sits at the base of the Sangre de Cristo range, the southernmost extension of the Continental Divide. Looming almost directly above town is 13,161-foot Wheeler Peak, the tallest mountain in the state. To the west, a flat mesa interrupted only by the sharp gorge of the Rio Grande River extends for miles before giving way to gentle mountains. To the north, east, and south, lush aspen- and piñon-coated slopes rise precipitously from the plain. All this beauty will recede in consciousness, though, when you're stuck in summer or weekend traffic on the main road into town, which has been forever marred by overbuilding.

The Lay of the Land

The Plaza

As in Santa Fe, activity in Taos centers around the **Plaza,** in this case a smaller, dustier, but mellower plot of grass surrounded by galleries and shops. Beyond them are more lanes of shops, galleries, and restaurants most of them hawking Native American and southwestern wares and fares. Prices are no longer that much less expensive than those in Santa Fe, however. If there's any difference between the two towns, it's that these days you're apt to find many pieces in Santa Fe that aren't native to the region. Taos, on the other hand, is where generations of craftspeople still weave or whittle together in the same studio. The **Taos Art Association** (☎ 505/758–2052) has information on most of the galleries in town.

Also near the Plaza are the town's two historic hotels: the **Taos Inn,** whose lobby bar is the perfect place for afternoon refreshments, and **La Fonda de Taos Hotel,** where you can view the most disappointing yet fascinating "peep show" in America. A nominal entry fee allows you to survey D. H. Lawrence's erotic paintings, whose content, racy for his era, caused Britain to ban them. Lawrence clearly had a better grasp of the pen than the brush. Much is made of the great poet-novelist's association with Taos; in fact, he spent parts of only three years here in the mid-

1920s. This was toward the end of his life, when he was a frequent guest of the arts patroness Mabel Dodge Luhan. He, his wife Frieda, and their friend, the literary doyenne Lady Dorothy Brett, lived north of Taos at Kiowa Ranch, now known as **D. H. Lawrence Ranch** (*see* Enchanted Circle, *below*), although he never owned it.

Near the Plaza is the **Kit Carson Home and Museum** (⊠ Kit Carson Rd., ☎ 505/758–0505), the 12-room residence of the mountain man who defended Taos from Confederate sympathizers during the Civil War. North of the Plaza is the **Firehouse Collection** (⊠ 323 Placitas Rd., ☎ 505/758–3386), an exhibit in the Volunteer Fire Department of more than 100 paintings by Taos masters. A couple of blocks south of the Plaza are more collections of art from the early Taos colony: the **Blumenschein Home** (⊠ 222 Ledoux St., ☎ 505/758–0505) and the **Harwood Foundation Museum** (⊠ 238 Ledoux St., ☎ 505/758–9826).

Ranchos de Taos
The section of town south of the Plaza, centered at the intersection of Route 68 and Ranchitos Road, is called **Ranchos de Taos.** The town's Spanish roots can be traced through the area's homes and its **San Francisco de Asis Church.** A few miles north on Ranchitos Road (Route 240) is **La Hacienda de Los Martinez** (⊠ Ranchitos Rd., ☎ 505/758–1000), a 21-room adobe residence built in 1804. The fortlike building on the banks of the Rio Pueblo served as the Martinez family's home and as a community refuge against raids by the original inhabitants of the region, the Comanche and Apache. Changing exhibits and demonstrations at the restored house chronicle the Spanish Colonial era.

Taos Pueblo and El Prado
Three miles north of town is the area's most famous attraction, the **Taos Pueblo** (☎ 505/758–9593), the center of a 95,000-acre complex that is the full-time home of roughly 2,000 Native Americans. The largest multistory pueblo structure in the country, it is divided by a creek into two parts, each a seemingly haphazard arrangement of mud-and-straw adobe rectangles atop one another. The pueblo is believed to have housed Taos-Tiwa Indians for as many as 1,000 years.

On your way to the pueblo you'll pass by two unusual museums. What's now the **Fechin Institute** (⊠ 227 Paseo del Pueblo N, ☎ 505/758–1710) was the home and studio of the Russian-born artist Nicolai Fechin; he lived here from 1927 through 1934. The institute displays many of his original woodcarvings, sketches, paintings, and sculptures, but also presents changing exhibits, workshops for artists, and chamber-music recitals. Also on the grounds is the Fechin Inn (*see* Sleeps, *below*). The nearby **Van Vechten–Lineberry Taos Art Museum** (⊠ 501 Paseo del Pueblo N, ☎ 505/758–2690) houses paintings and drawings by the late artist Duane Van Vechten, one of the town's most respected artists and the first wife of the museum's founder, Edwin Lineberry. Also on exhibit are works by many other Taos artists. This museum is impressive for its collection and its 10-acre grounds.

Head north of central Taos along Paseo del Pueblo Norte, and you'll enter the quieter and less developed section of town, **El Prado.** Turning left, shortly before the Texaco gas station—where U.S. 64 and Routes 150 and 522 converge—at the signs for the engrossing **Millicent Rogers Museum** (⊠ Millicent Rogers Museum Rd., ☎ 505/758–2462), the legacy of the eponymous Standard Oil heiress, an avid collector of Native American and Hispanic art. Within the walls of her pueblo home are more than 5,000 pieces—paintings, kachina dolls, rugs, jewelry, and local crafts.

Arroyo Seco and the Taos Ski Valley

At the junction of U.S. 64 and Routes 522 and 150 (a.k.a. "the Blinking Light," although the traffic signal no longer blinks), turn right onto Route 150 to reach the engaging village of **Arroyo Seco,** which has galleries and memorable shops, plus a few cafés. Some of the region's best B&Bs are here (*see* Sleeps, *below*).

This area north of town offers the greatest opportunities for hiking, cycling, horseback riding, llama trekking, snowmobiling, cross-country skiing, and white-water rafting. The **Taos Outdoor Recreation Association** (☎ 505/758–3873 or 800/732–8267) and the **Bureau of Land Management** (☎ 505/758–8851) have information about outfitters and places to go. Follow Route 150 through Arroyo Seco for a 10-mile drive to **Taos Ski Valley** (☎ 505/776–2291, Web site taoswebb.com/skitaos), one of the world's premier resorts. The facility has information about women's ski weeks and weekends, which, though not lesbian, are same-sex friendly.

The Enchanted Circle

Back at the Blinking Light, follow Route 522 to begin the breathtaking 84-mile scenic drive, the **Enchanted Circle,** which passes through the villages of Questa, Red River, Eagle Nest, and Angel Fire. Off this loop are several possible detours, the first of which is north of Taos in the tiny village of **Arroyo Hondo.** As soon as Route 522 crosses a small river, make your first left and follow this road to the soothing natural **hot springs,** a peaceful pair of warm natural pools on the edge of the Rio Grande River. It's a little tricky to find them—check first with locals before setting out—but they're worth the trip, and they're popular with Taos-area gays and lesbians.

Head north of Arroyo Hondo on Route 522, and you'll soon pass the right-hand turn-off for **D. H. Lawrence Ranch** (⊠ Rte. 522, 15 mi north of the Plaza, ☎ 505/776–2245). Several years after Lawrence's death, Frieda had his ashes buried on the ranch's property, in front of a small memorial shrine. Though the buildings at the ranch are not open to the public, you can visit the shrine.

Route 522 next leads to **Questa,** where you'll eventually make a right turn onto Route 38. But first take this rewarding detour: Continue a short way north on Route 522 past the Route 38 junction, turning left onto Route 378, which leads to the **Wild Rivers Recreation Area** (⊠ Rte. 378, ☎ 505/758–8851). Here, at the confluence of the Rio Grande and Red rivers, you can admire the deepest point of the Rio Grande Gorge. Somewhat challenging trails lead down to the river, where you'll find more hot springs. If you're not up for a major hikes, bring along a bite to eat and enjoy lunch at the picnic tables along the rim of the gorge.

Back on Route 38, the Enchanted Circle continues on through **Red River**—a tacky ski town whose lush green terrain bears little resemblance to Taos, which is only 15 miles away as the crow flies. Route 38 then twists through the green pastoral lands of **Eagle Nest** and by the popular boating retreat, **Eagle Nest Lake,** where it joins up with U.S. 64. Continue south past the rapidly developing ski town of **Angel Fire,** over which stands the **Disabled American Veterans Vietnam National Memorial,** a 50-foot-tall monument in the shape of a gull's wing. The road soon climbs back over the mountains, winding back into Taos.

Eats

$$$–$$$$ ✕ **Doc Martin's.** Locals and visitors—gay and straight—congregate at this comfy place. Though pricey, the New American creations like black-bean cakes, pecan-encrusted sea bass, and apple-cider pork tenderloin are as good as any in town. ⊠ *125 Paseo del Pueblo N,* ☎ *505/758–1977.*

$$$–$$$$ ✕ **Stakeout.** People come to this hilltop steak house as much for the views over the mesa west of town as for the thick pepper steaks flambéed in brandy, the grilled Colorado lamb chops with red wine and rosemary, the baked trout with vegetables and herbs, the Alaskan king crab legs, or the fresh oysters (on the half-shell or broiled). ⊠ *Stakeout Dr. off Rte. 68,* ☎ *505/758–2042.*

$$$ ✕ **Marciano's.** Some of the windows at this Italian bistro have views of the Sangre de Cristo range. Pumpkin-orange walls, latilla ceilings, soft music, and mismatched chairs create a slightly quirky atmosphere. The few colorful southwestern touches on the top-notch menu include blue-corn pasta; you'll also find sublime traditional dishes like leek-and-wild-mushroom manicotti. Romantic and gay-popular, Marciano's has a great wine list. ⊠ *La Placita and Ledoux Sts.,* ☎ *505/751–0805.*

$$–$$$ ✕ **Apple Tree.** Taos has only a few restaurants that match Santa Fe's in both price and ambience; the Apple Tree, in an ancient territorial-style house near the Plaza, hits the mark. Straw chairs, beehive-shape kiva fireplaces, and other local touches grace the dining rooms. The food is southwestern eclectic: smoked trout, veggie green curry, mango chicken enchiladas. ⊠ *123 Bent St.,* ☎ *505/758–1900.*

$$–$$$ ✕ **Joseph's Table.** Congenial and unpretentious, this newcomer at the southern end of town draws rave reviews for its fine service, romantic dining room, and delicious, uncomplicated New American fare like baked salmon with roasted-tomato vinaigrette and pizza with caramelized onions, bacon, and Gruyère. ⊠ *4167 Pueblo Sur,* ☎ *505/751–4512.*

$$–$$$ ✕ **Trading Post Café.** This sunny gallery-cum-café is on the approach into town amid a small complex of artisans' studios. The California-style cuisine—Sonoma lamb with mint-tomato salsa, rosemary chicken, pasta dishes, and leafy salads—is tasty and reasonably priced. Some unusual choices punctuate the long wine list. Expect a long wait on weekends. ⊠ *Rte. 68 at Rte. 518,* ☎ *505/758–5089.*

$$ ✕ **Tim's Chile Connection.** The name of this local favorite north of town may conjure up visions of a chain restaurant, but Tim's serves first-rate New Mexican cuisine in rustic dining rooms and open-air patios with great mountain views. The poblano chile relleno stuffed with cheese and served alongside a black-bean tostada and a sweet-corn tamale is a specialty; also consider the tangy shrimp-chipotle enchiladas. ⊠ *Rte. 150, not far after the Blinking Light,* ☎ *505/776–8787.*

$–$$ ✕ **Dolomite Taos.** Forget the location beside an oil-change shop: This casual restaurant has some of the best pizzas, antipasto, and pastas in town, and at reasonable prices. Start with bruschetta with fresh tomatoes, roasted red peppers, herbs, and cheese, then dive into spaghettini with roasted tomatoes, garlic, basil, and pine nuts or one of the made-from-scratch pizzas. ⊠ *812B Paseo del Pueblo N,* ☎ *505/751–4002.*

$ ✕ **Alley Cantina.** Taos is an early-to-bed town, and this is one of your only after-10 o'clock options. The food is okay—burgers, burritos, and the like. Another late-night possibility is **El Pueblo Café** (⊠ 625 Paseo del Pueblo Norte, ☎ 505/751–9817), which is north of the Plaza. ⊠ *121 Teresina La.,* ☎ *505/758–2121.*

$ ✕ **Amigos.** Taos's food co-op has a great little deli. Order a creation from the juice bar to wash down your bean burrito or tofu salad. The bulletin board carries notices for New Age, holistic, outdoors-oriented, arts, and political groups. ⊠ *326 Paseo del Pueblo S,* ☎ *505/758–8493.*

$ ✕ **The Burrito Wagon.** Behind the Central Taos Motorbank (which has a drive-through ATM) is a rusty tan camper known as the Burrito Wagon, from which you can get the finest, cheapest, and most authentic tacos, burritos, and tostadas in town. This place is beyond no-frills: You dine in your car. Closed on weekends. ⊠ *Tiwa La. and Paseo del Pueblo S,* ☎ *505/751–4091. No credit cards.*

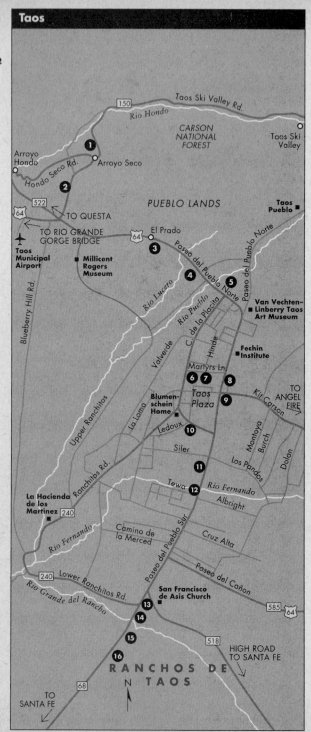

Taos

$ ✕ Casa Fresen. A cross between an upscale café and a laid-back gathering hole, Casa Fresen is officially just a bakery. But along with amazingly good breads, rolls, and pastries, it serves salads, cheeses, and fancy coffees; you can even pick up a box lunch. ✉ *Rte. 150, Arroyo Seco,* ☎ *505/776–2969.*

$ ✕ Eske's Brew Pub. Ski bums head down from the valley to check out the local scene and throw back a few at this lackadaisical brew pub. The crunchy menu includes smoked salmon rolls with spiced carrots and green chile, bangers and mash, green-chile stew (veggie or turkey), and many teas. ✉ *106 Des Georges La.,* ☎ *505/758–1517.*

$ ✕ Orlando's. This pleasant café in El Prado has a bright southwestern decor and delicious but mild New Mexican food (if you want your dishes spicier, just ask). Favorites include shrimp burritos and Frito pie, a casserole-like regional specialty on a crust of broken Fritos (as in the corn chips). The outdoor seating faces Wheeler Peak. BYOB. ✉ *1114 Don Juan Valdez La.,* ☎ *505/751–1450. No credit cards.*

Coffeehouse Culture

Taos Coffee Co. Taos hasn't any gay bars, but on Friday and Saturday this coffeehouse on the southern end of town draws many lesbians and gay guys; the rest of the week it's more mixed, but still very queer. There's live music and readings many nights. ✉ *1807 S. Santa Fe Rd.,* ☎ *505/758–3331.*

Scenes

Hangin' with the Hets

The top hangout for all Taoseños and visitors is the intimate **Adobe Bar** (✉ 125 Paseo del Pueblo N, ☎ 505/758–2233) at the Taos Inn; open-mike Mondays are a hoot. There's country dancing regularly at the **Sagebrush Inn** (✉ S. Santa Fe Rd. [Rte. 68], ☎ 505/758–2254). Few homos have been known to give it a twirl, but it's not likely you'll feel unwelcome. The same goes for the bars up at Taos Ski Valley, which draw a consistently crunchy, open-minded bunch.

Sleeps

Taos Central Reservations (☎ 505/758–9767 or 800/821–2437) handles accommodations at hotels and condos near Taos Ski Valley. Call **Taos Vacation Rentals** (☎ 505/758–5700 or 800/788–8267) for information about long-term rentals in a luxury home or condo.

Hotels

$$$–$$$$ 🛏 Fechin Inn. This romantic inn is set on the grounds of the Fechin Institute (*see* The Lay of the Land, *above*). A couple of blocks north of the Plaza, the six-acre pueblo-style compound has stylish rooms with traditional furnishings, hand-carved woodwork, and prints by Nicolai Fechin; many rooms have kiva fireplaces. ✉ *227 Paseo del Pueblo N, Taos, 87571,* ☎ *505/751–1000 or 800/811–2933,* FAX *505/751–7338. 85 rooms. Exercise room.*

$$$ 🛏 Best Western Kachina Lodge de Taos. Though it's a chain operation, this property a near the Taos Pueblo maintains a southwestern feel, with antique kachina dolls in many of the public areas and traditionally furnished guest rooms. ✉ *413 N. Pueblo Rd.,* ☎ *505/758–2275 or 800/522–4462,* FAX *505/758–9207. 118 rooms. Restuarant, pool.*

$$–$$$ 🛏 Taos Inn. The prize accommodation downtown, this charming adobe structure—parts of which date from the 1600s—is within a block of the Plaza. The rooms are furnished with antiques and bright southwestern bedspreads and fabrics. The service is warm and personable. ✉ *125 Paseo del Pueblo N, 87571,* ☎ *505/758–2233 or 800/826–7466,* FAX *505/758–5776. 39 rooms. Restaurant.*

$ ▢ **El Monte Lodge.** An ideal budget choice a few blocks east of the Plaza, this shaded inn has accommodations in homey casitalike buildings with southwestern furnishings. Many rooms at this fine alternative to area motels have refrigerators and kiva fireplaces. ⊠ *317 Kit Carson Rd., 87571,* ☎ *505/758–3171 or 800/828–8267,* FAX *505/758–1536. 13 rooms.*

Guest Houses

$$$ ▢ **Casa de Las Chimneas.** Susan Vernon's stunning 1912 Spanish-style hacienda, a 10-minute walk from the Plaza, is one of the most luxurious small properties in town. Lush gardens and fountains dot the large grounds. The rooms, decorated with rich fabrics and blankets and filled with writing desks, pewter chandeliers, and other antiques, have southwestern influences but also incorporate European and other American styles. The breakfasts are fabulous. ⊠ *405 Cordoba Rd. (mail: Box 5303, 87571),* ☎ *505/758–4777,* FAX *505/758–3976. 4 rooms with phone, TV, and private bath. Hot tub. Full breakfast. Mostly straight.*

$$–$$$ ▢ **Adobe in the Stars.** This getaway has 360-degree mountain and mesa views from nearly every one of its sun-filled rooms. Accommodations are traditionally decorated, with viga ceilings, kiva or gas fireplaces, and fabulous tile bathrooms, some with double showers or Jacuzzi tubs. ⊠ *Rte. 150 and Valdez Rim Rd., Arroyo Seco (mail: Box 2285, 87571),* ☎ *505/ 776–2776 or 800/211–7076, e-mail stars@taos.newmex.com. 7 rooms with phone and private bath. Full breakfast. Mostly straight.*

$$–$$$ ▢ **Cottonwood Inn.** A grove of cottonwood trees near Arroyo Seco shades this two-story inn that's on the way to the ski valley. Built by an eccentric local artist, Wolfgang Pogzeba, the inn has distinctive rooms with great views and amenities that include, depending on the accommodation you choose, kiva fireplaces, balconies or terraces, and wraparound decks. The honeymoon suite has a huge hot tub in the living room. ⊠ *Hwys. 150 and 230 (mail: HCR 74, Box 24609, El Prado 87529),* ☎ *505/776–5826 or 800/324–7120,* FAX *505/776–1141. 7 rooms with private bath. Full breakfast. Mostly straight.*

$$–$$$ ▢ **Salsa Del Salto.** This Arroyo Seco hostelry offers some of the facilities of a full-scale resort—a tennis court and a pool—but has the ambience and intimacy of a small inn. The rooms are plush and contemporary, with modern handmade southwestern furnishings and views of the mountains or the mesas; some bathrooms have glass-brick walls, heated floors, and whirlpool tubs. Even the smallest rooms are bright and cheerful. ⊠ *Rte. 150, Arroyo Seco (mail: Box 1468, El Prado, 87529),* ☎ FAX *505/ 776–2422 or 800/530–3097, e-mail salsa@taos.newmex.com. 10 rooms with private bath, some with TV. Pool, hot tub. Full breakfast. Mostly straight.*

$$ ▢ **Little Tree.** Built in 1991 by Kay and Charles Giddens, this secluded adobe hacienda is about midway between the ski valley and downtown. Rooms have latilla ceilings, native furnishings, and handmade quilts. With incredible mountain and mesa views from every window and the courtyard, this place has the best star-gazing in town. ⊠ *Hondo-Seco Rd., Arroyo Seco (mail: Drawer II, Taos, 87571),* ☎ *505/776–8467 or 800/ 334–8467,* FAX *505/751–1111, e-mail little@taos.newmex.com. 4 rooms with TV and private bath. Full breakfast. Mostly straight.*

$$ ▢ **Ruby Slipper.** New York City transplants Beth Goldman and Diane Fichtelberg preside over this complex, one of the better deals among the centrally located guest houses. All the rooms have private entrances, tile floors, brightly painted furnishings, and kiva fireplaces. Simple, restful living is emphasized: Hammocks and a hot tub are available in a private backyard, the hearty breakfasts use all-natural ingredients, and there are no TVs. ⊠ *416 La Lomita Rd. (mail: Box 2069, 87571),* ☎ *505/758– 0613, e-mail ruby@taoswebb.com, Web site taoswebb.com/hotel/rubyslipper. 7 rooms with private bath. Full breakfast. Hot tub. Mixed gay/straight.*

$$ ⊞ **Willows Inn.** The rooms at this landscaped adobe compound a few blocks east of the Plaza have varied themes. Steer horns and a soft cowhide rug adorn the Cowboy Room; an artist's studio has a private patio and a whirlpool hot tub. All the rooms have kiva fireplaces and private entrances. ✉ *412 Kit Carson Rd., 87571,* ☎ *505/758–2558 or 800/525–8267,* FAX *505/758–5445, e-mail willow@taos.newmex.com. 5 rooms with private bath. Full breakfast. Mostly straight.*

The Little Black Book

At Your Fingertips

AIDS Helpline (☎ 505/820–2437). **Albuquerque Cab** (☎ 505/883–4888). **Albuquerque Convention & Visitors Bureau** (✉ 20 First Plaza, Galeria level, Box 26866, 87125, ☎ 505/842–9918 or 800/733–9918, Web site www.abqcvb.org). **Albuquerque Lesbian and Gay Chamber of Commerce** (☎ 505/243–6767). *Alibi* (alternative weekly, ☎ 505/268–3456, Web site www.desert.net/alibi). **Capital City Cab Company** (Santa Fe, ☎ 505/438–0000). **City Different–Ciudad Diferente** (the Santa Fe gay business association, ☎ 505/989–2515). **Common Bond Gay and Lesbian Community Center and Info Line** (✉ 4013 Silver Ave. SE, ☎ 505/266–8041). **Faust's Transportation** (Taos-area cab company, ☎ 505/758–3410). **Greyhound** (☎ 800/231–2222). **Santa Fe Convention and Visitors Bureau** (✉ 201 W. Marcy St., 87504, ☎ 505/984–6760 or 800/777–2489, Web site www.santafe.org). **Santa Fe Pride Committee** (☎ 505/988–5703). **Santa Fe Women's Infoline** (☎ 505/438–8503). **Taos County Chamber of Commerce** (✉ Drawer 1, 87571, ☎ 505/758–3873 or 800/732–8267, Web site taoswebb.com/taos). **Women's Resource Center** (✉ Mesa Vista Hall, Room 1160, University of New Mexico, Albuquerque, 87131, ☎ 505/277–3716).

Gay Media

Out! Magazine (☎ 505/243–2540, Web site www.outmagazine.com) is New Mexico's well-written lesbian and gay news monthly.

BOOKSTORES

Albuquerque has the only lesbigay bookstore in New Mexico, **Sisters' and Brothers' Bookstore** (✉ 4011 Silver Ave. SE, ☎ 505/266–7317). Nearby is one of the best feminist bookstores in the Southwest, **Full Circle Books** (✉ 2205 Silver Ave. SE, ☎ 505/266–0022), which carries many lesbian titles and some general gay ones. **Newsland Bookstore and Magazines** (✉ 2112 Central Ave. SE, ☎ 505/242–0694) has a tremendous selection of gay, alternative, and mainstream papers and magazines. In Santa Fe, stop by **She Said...A Women's Bookstore** (✉ 177-B Paseo de Peralta, DeVerges Mall, ☎ 505/986-9196) for feminist titles; **Downtown Subscription** (✉ 376 Garcia St., ☎ 505/983–3085) for periodicals and newspapers, including some gay ones; and **Collected Works** (✉ 208B W. San Francisco St., ☎ 505/988–4226) for the excellent general-interest titles. In Taos, your best options for lesbian and gay material are the **Taos Book Shop** (✉ 122D Kit Carson Rd., ☎ 505/758–3733) and **Moby Dickens** (✉ 124A Bent St., ☎ 505/758–3050).

Working Out

The men-only **Pride Gym** (✉ 1803 3rd St. NW, Albuquerque, ☎ 505/242–7810) is cruisy, but it's a real workout space with all the usual equipment, plus a tanning bed, a steam room, a lounge area, and a health-food bar. The gym at the **Fort Marcy Pool** (✉ 490 Washington Ave., Santa Fe, ☎ 505/984–6725) is gay-friendly. The **Northside Health and Fitness Club** (✉ 1307 Paseo del Pueblo N, Taos, ☎ 505/751–1242) and **Taos Spa and Court Club** (✉ 111 Doña Ana Dr., Taos, ☎ 505/758–1980) are excellent facilities.

41 Out in Seattle

IT'S AWFULLY DIFFICULT NOT TO LOVE SEATTLE. Of course, most locals want their city to be scorned and ridiculed. Travel guides, it is hoped, will assure the world that the place is overrated and nobody need move here. Well, Seattle is a wonderful city, one that's frequently rated in magazine surveys as being among the most livable on earth. But it's also bursting at the seams, its narrow streets unable to handle additional traffic and its cost of living rising sharply. "If you want to visit, fine," seems to be the attitude of most Seattleites. "But for God's sake, don't move here!"

The greatest concentration of gays is in Capitol Hill, but the district is by no means a ghetto. Students, yuppies, latter-day hippies, and young families all live here, the cutting-edge music, liberal politics, coffeehouses and microbreweries, computer technology, and environmentalism among the ties that bind the area's disparate elements.

In this respect Seattle differs from many U.S. cities, particularly those in the Northeast. And Capitol Hill's demography may offer clues to the ways in which urban neighborhoods are changing vis-à-vis sexual orientation. Capitol Hill does not function as a zone into which gay people retreat to find strength and safety in numbers, but rather as a desirable setting, with great shops, clubs, and restaurants, where people accept one another at face value. Were Seattle as a whole less tolerant, a more insular gay neighborhood might be necessary.

THE LAY OF THE LAND

Several bodies of water define Seattle's boundaries. To the west is Puget Sound. Off the sound is Elliott Bay, a snug harbor whose shores constitute the western edge of downtown. To the east is Lake Washington. Snaking across the northern half of Seattle is a stretch of water that begins in the west as the Lake Washington Ship Canal, becomes Lake Union, and continues on as Portage Bay and then Union Bay before finally emptying into Lake Washington. From nearly every elevated point in Seattle—and this is a hilly city—water is visible.

Capitol Hill and Volunteer Park

The western border of **Capitol Hill** begins where I–5 cuts through the city. The neighborhood has few attractions, but several commercial pockets are excellent for shopping, club hopping, cheap dining, and people-watching. **Pine and Pike streets,** which run east–west, Pine one block north of Pike, hold many gay bars, plus some live-music halls and coffeehouses. Also here are few great shops, such as the women's erotica emporium **Toys in Babeland** (✉ 707 E. Pike St., ☎ 206/328–2914) and the thrift and antique clothing store (one of several in this area) **Vintage Voola** (✉ 705 E. Pike St., ☎ 206/324–2808).

Broadway Avenue from Pike about 10 blocks north to Roy Street bustles with a youthful mix of straight and gay-popular businesses. The common denominators are funkiness and thrift, though Broadway is gentrifying as the hippest crowds migrate south toward Pine and Pike. Still, you'll find incredibly cheap food and lots of fun clothing and bric-a-brac. A must-visit is **Broadway Market** (✉ 300 Broadway Ave. E), the largest queer-theme commercial space in America. This three-story atrium mall is loaded with gift shops, stalls, clothing stores, a few restaurants, a gym, a parking garage, and a cinema. Nearby, the **Pink Zone** (✉ 211 Broadway Ave., ☎ 206/325–0050), a much-talked-about salon-cum-boutique, proffers "queer shears and visibly queer gear."

Capitol Hill's other major north–south thoroughfare is **15th Avenue.** From about Madison to Mercer streets it's a tad more upscale and mature than Broadway, with better restaurants, some antiques stores, and **City People's Mercantile** (✉ 500 15th Ave. E, ☎ 206/324–9510), often dubbed Seattle's dyke hardware and household goods emporium.

Volunteer Park, easily entered from 14th Avenue or Highland Drive, is home to the exotic-plant-filled **Conservatory** (☎ 206/684–4743) and a 75-foot water tower from which you can enjoy panoramic city views. The **Seattle Asian Art Museum** (✉ Volunteer Park, 1400 E. Prospect St., ☎ 206/654–3100) has a comprehensive collection. Throngs of queens and lesbians lounge on Volunteer Park's lawns, reading books and each other. At night it can get quite social here (Be warned: It's heavily policed); Seattle, in fact, has an awful lot of cruisy outdoor parks.

Downtown

Downtown Seattle has one remarkable thing going for it: **Pike Place Market** (✉ Pike St. at 1st Ave., ☎ 206/682–7453). The sprawling 1907 structure is abuzz with fishmongers and food marketers of every ilk. Pike Place is on a steep hill; the lower floors hold some genuinely interesting shops, and the ground floor leads under the hideous Highway 99 to the waterfront and its 20 blocks of piers. At Pier 59 is the **Seattle Aquarium** (☎ 206/386–4320). To the north at Pier 66 is the new **Odyssey Contemporary Maritime Museum** (☎ 206/623–2120).

A few blocks south of Pike Place Market is the **Seattle Art Museum** (✉ 100 University St., ☎ 206/654–3100), whose collection emphasizes Asian, Native American, African, and pre-Columbian art.

Pioneer Square and the International District

Many of the buildings in **Pioneer Square** date from just after 1889, the year a fire destroyed most of the city's wood-frame buildings. Technically part of downtown, these blocks around the intersection of 1st and 2nd avenues and Yesler Way composed the city's first business district. At night the square is a mostly collegiate party area; by day it's a good place for wandering through art galleries and the **Downtown Antique Market** (✉ 2218 Western Ave.), which features 70 dealers.

The colorful if hokey, 90-minute **Underground Seattle** (☎ 206/682–1511) tour explores Pioneer Square's original sidewalks and storefronts, many of which still exist intact below ground. South of Pioneer Square and east of the massive Seattle Kingdome sports stadium is the century-old, 12-block **International District,** where many Chinese, Japanese, Laotian, Thai, Vietnamese, and Filipino immigrants live and work. A map available at the fine **Wing Luke Museum** (✉ 407 7th Ave. S, ☎ 206/623–5124) will direct you to all the major sights within the district.

Belltown and the Seattle Center

North of downtown is **Belltown,** a commercial and residential haven of artists, musicians, and bookish yuppies. You'll find great antiques and thrift shops, galleries, restaurants, and some of the city's hottest music clubs, especially along 1st and 2nd avenues. Continue northwest to reach the **Seattle Center,** a 74-acre tract that hosted the 1962 World's Fair. The highlight of this kooky spot is the **Space Needle** (⊠ 5th and Broad Sts., ☎ 206/443–2111) the retro-futurist 600-foot tower visible from most anywhere in the city. You can take an elevator to the top for great vistas (forget the restaurant, it's relentlessly mediocre). The best thing about the view from the Space Needle is that you can't see the Space Needle.

The Lake Washington Shoreline

The east side of Seattle includes the well-to-do enclaves of **Madison Valley** and **Madison Park.** From downtown head east on Yesler Way to **Lake Washington Boulevard,** which skirts the lake's shoreline. Go north a half mile or so to reach **Denny-Blaine Park** (a.k.a. Dyke-kiki, as in Waikiki), a neat but compact lakeside lawn. This is the city's unofficial lesbian tanning salon. Continue north on Lake Washington Boulevard to Madison Street. A right turn leads down the hill to **Madison Park,** a long sandy beach overlooking the lake. North of the lifeguard station the crowd is mostly gay. There's a float out in the water that on hot summer days looks like an ad for Speedo swimsuits.

Take Madison Street back up to Lake Washington Boulevard, hang a right, and follow it to the **University of Washington Park Arboretum** (⊠ 2300 Arboretum Dr. E, ☎ 206/543–8800), a shady public expanse containing more than 5,000 varieties of plants and many winding trails.

The University District, Wallingford, and Fremont

Take I–5 over Lake Union to the Northeast 45th Street exit to reach several personable, untouristy northern Seattle communities, including the University District, Wallingford, and Fremont.

Heading east on 45th Street leads to the **University of Washington's** beautiful, hilly campus. The U. District isn't gay, but it's full of quirky diversions, cheap eats, and vintage clothing stores, especially along the neighborhood's main drag, **University Way.** From I–5 follow Northeast 45th Street west several blocks to its intersection with **Meridian Avenue.** This is the heart of Seattle's most significant lesbian community, low-key **Wallingford.**

Continue west on Northeast 45th Street to Fremont Avenue, then turn left to reach **Fremont,** which is just north of Queen Anne Hill across the Lake Washington Ship Canal. Seattle's hippie haven of the 1960s today hosts a mix of grungers and yuppies. As you enter the neighborhood via the Fremont Bridge, a sign welcomes you to "The Center of the Universe." For some relatively funky window-shopping, check out the intersection of 35th Street and Fremont Avenue. On Sundays vendors show crafts, antiques, and objets d'art at the **Fremont Market,** a two-block plot just off Fremont Avenue.

GETTING AROUND

You enter Seattle by way of I–5 from the north or south, or I–90 from the east or west. You can definitely get around the city without a car, especially downtown and on Capitol Hill. If you're here for more than a few days, however, consider renting a car to see some of the outer neighborhoods. Traffic is a drag: Seattle's dated network of streets is ill-equipped to handle the volume. Buses are fairly practical for getting around even the more remote neighborhoods, and they're free within downtown. It's possible to hail a taxi on the street, but it's best to phone, or, if you're near a downtown hotel, get in line at its cabstand.

EATS

Seattle is an easy place to eat well and cheap. Chefs have continual access to fresh produce, and with all the water you can count on plenty of seafood. And then there is Asian influence, which is reflected in what's come to be known as Pacific Northwest cuisine (which also includes indigenous game and seafood preparations). Authentic Chinese, Thai, and Japanese restaurants are also easy to find. Most of the pricey restaurants are downtown. Everywhere else, especially on Capitol Hill and in the University District, cheap and filling burritos, sushi, veggie platters, pizzas, and *pad thai*, the popular panfried rice-noodle dish, are readily available.

For price ranges, *see* dining Chart A at the front of this guide.

Downtown and Environs

$$$ ✕ **Campagne.** Very chichi but not overdone, this restaurant is a terrific place to celebrate your long-term romance or kick off a new one. The country-French specialties (often game) include a starter of seafood sausage and a cinnamon-roasted quail in a carrot-and-orange sauce. Cafe Campagne serves more affordable bistro fare in a casual atmosphere. ⊠ *86 Pine St.,* ☎ *206/728–2800.*

$$–$$$ ✕ **Dahlia Lounge.** Tom Douglas, an early proponent of Pacific Northwest cuisine, oversees the kitchen at this trendy north-of-downtown restaurant that's decorated with exotic-fish sculpture. The eclectic menu changes often but might include rabbit grilled with roasted garlic or Asian-inspired lobster-and-shiitake-mushroom pot stickers. ⊠ *1904 4th Ave.,* ☎ *206/ 682–4142.*

$$–$$$ ✕ **Flying Fish.** The extensive menu of this contemporary fish house lists small plates, large plates, and platters for sharing. Your party can order mussels with a chili-lime dipping sauce for $7.95 per pound. Or you can try a big dish of crab ravioli with a lemongrass cream sauce. ⊠ *2234 1st Ave.,* ☎ *206/728–8595.*

$$–$$$ ✕ **The Palace.** The retro-chic neon sign may recall a '50s steak house, but the food is strictly au courant at revolutionary restaurateur Tom Douglas's popular venture. There's always a special such as grilled goat cheese with curried sweet potatoes and coriander chutney. ⊠ *2030 5th Ave.,* ☎ *206/448–2001.*

$$–$$$ ✕ **Wild Ginger.** Every critic's short list of top Seattle restaurants includes this sophisticated pan-Asian eatery tucked below Pike Place Market. Seating is in an open dining room with high ceilings and Asian art. Among the fine menu selections is yellowfin tuna wok-fried in a spicy Indonesian candlenut sauce with lemongrass and coconut flakes. ⊠ *1400 Western Ave.,* ☎ *206/623–4450.*

$–$$ ✕ **Wolfgang Puck Cafe.** A hit from the moment it opened in mid-1997, this café across 1st Avenue from the Seattle Art Museum serves pasta and pad thais, pizzas baked in a wood-fired oven, soups and salads, a few entrées, and some fab desserts. And there's a seafood bar. ⊠ *1225 1st Ave.,* ☎ *206/621–9653.*

$ ✕ **Trattoria Mitchelli.** This sprawling publike Italian restaurant off Pioneer Square has great sidewalk seating along Yesler Way, hearty pasta dishes (try the black-bean ravioli), and a huge list of microbrewed beers. A bit touristy and noisy, it's open most nights till 4 AM. ⊠ *84 Yesler Way,* ☎ *206/623–3883.*

Eats ●

B & O Espresso, **11**
Broadway New
American Grill, **19**
Cafe Flora, **25**
Cafe Paradiso, **23**
Cafe Septiéme, **20**
Campagne, **4**
Coastal Kitchen, **17**
Coffee Messiah, **9**
Dahlia Lounge, **3**
The Easy, **22**
Elysian
Brewing Co., **24**
Flying Fish, **1**
Giorgina's, **21**
Gravity Bar, **12**
Hamburger Mary's, **10**
Jack's Bistro, **18**
Julia's, **14**
Machiavelli, **8**
Mae's Phinney Ridge
Cafe, **15**
The Palace, **2**
Simpatico Bistro, **13**
Still Life, **16**
Trattoria Mitchelli, **7**
Wild Ginger, **5**
Wolfgang Puck
Cafe, **6**

Scenes ○

Baltic Room, **5**
C.C. Attle's, **21**
Changes, **8**
The Cuff, **16**
Double Header, **4**
Eagle, **6**
The Easy, **13**
Elite, **9**
Elite II, **7**
Madison Pub, **18**
Mr. Paddywack's, **11**
Neighbours, **12**
R Place, **10**
Re-bar, **2**
Safari Sports
Bar and Grille, **15**
Sea Wolf Saloon, **19**
Sonya's, **3**
Spags, **17**
Thumpers, **20**
Timberline Tavern, **1**
Wildrose, **14**

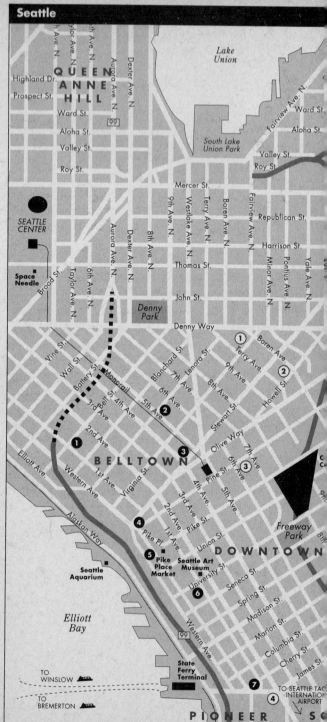

Capitol Hill

$$ ✕ **Broadway New American Grill.** Uneven but reasonably priced American fare marks this major late-night dining option. Some dishes have a nouvelle twist (hence the "New" in "New American") and range from grilled ahi sandwiches to a tasty crab-and-artichoke dip. ⊠ *314 Broadway Ave. E,* ☎ *206/328–7000.*

$$ ✕ **Coastal Kitchen.** Laughing, chattering groups are almost always in residence at this bright white-tile dining room. The cuisine is eclectic, from the rock-shrimp-and-crab cakes to a Caribbean seafood grill to pasta *puttanesca* (tomatoes, garlic, capers, black olives, and anchovies). ⊠ *429 15th Ave. E,* ☎ *206/322–1145.*

$$ ✕ **Elysian Brewing Co.** This two-level relative newcomer to Capitol Hill draws twenty- and thirtysomethings—gayfolk from guppies to drag queens to leather daddies, along with many straights. Vegetarian specialties include fajitas and chili, or you can order inexpensive tapas to go with the fine brews. ⊠ *1221 E. Pike St.,* ☎ *206/860–1920.*

$$ ✕ **Machiavelli.** Set in a large dining room with lots of windows and cheerful red chairs, this poor-man's chic bistro serves decent Italian favorites at reasonable prices. Try the penne with red-pepper pesto, the anchovy pizza, or the eggplant parmigiana. ⊠ *1215 Pine St.,* ☎ *206/621–7941.*

$–$$ ✕ **The Easy.** The good affordable food at the Easy includes a fine Caesar salad with a roasted-garlic-and-anchovy dressing, a smoked-chicken-and-Brie baguette, and rigatoni Siciliano (with Kalamata olives, capers, fresh tomatoes, fresh herbs, and garlic with red wine). ⊠ *916 E. Pike St.,* ☎ *206/323–8343.*

$–$$ ✕ **Jack's Bistro.** Patrons of this peppy Tuscan- and Provençal-inspired restaurant dine in a sunny courtyard, on the sidewalk, or in a cozy storefront eating area. The menu has fine salads and pastas, and interesting starters such as Gorgonzola polenta. Friendly, low-key staff. Live jazz some nights. ⊠ *405 15th Ave. E,* ☎ *206/324–9625.*

$ ✕ **Giorgina's.** One of the classiest Italian restaurants on the hill has been lesbian-owned and gay-frequented for years. The softly lit contemporary dining room is always aglow with smiling patrons sampling designer pizzas (garlic clam is a favorite) and light pasta dishes. ⊠ *131 15th Ave. E,* ☎ *206/329–8118.*

$ ✕ **Gravity Bar.** The postindustrial juice bar in the ultra-faggy Broadway Market is a magnet for cute lesbians. Salads, open-face sandwiches, chapati-bread roll-ups, and rice-and-veggie platters are served under massive chrome air ducts and pipes. And that wheat-grass juice is dee-licious . . . just like Mom's. ⊠ *415 Broadway Ave. E,* ☎ *206/325–7186. No credit cards.*

$ ✕ **Hamburger Mary's.** The fag-happy restaurant chain's Seattle edition looks like a giant fern bar. Tasty burgers and fries are the main offerings, but you might stop in for a late-night banana split. ⊠ *1525 E. Olive Way,* ☎ *206/324–8112.*

Elsewhere in Seattle

$$ ✕ **Cafe Flora.** The most inventive vegetarian restaurant in the city, on the edge of Capitol Hill, welcomes plenty of power dykes and guppies. Munch in the contemporary dining room on veggie vittles like Oaxaca tacos with spicy mashed potatoes, diced peppers, and cheddar and smoked-mozzarella cheeses. ⊠ *2901 E. Madison St.,* ☎ *206/325–9100.*

$$ ✕ **Simpatico Bistro.** This gay-popular Wallingford restaurant never fails. There are booths and tables inside, and also a shaded patio. The food is Italian: Try lamb shank braised in Chianti with garlic and allspice, or the tangy goat-cheese polenta. ⊠ *4430 Wallingford Ave. N,* ☎ *206/632–1000.*

$ ✕ **Julia's.** Straight parents and their kids eat here, but joining them are gay couples (frequently with kids of their own), and folks who just consider one another family. The food is healthful—pasta, veggie dishes, burgers, baked breads, and fresh salads. ⊠ *4401 Wallingford Ave.,* ☎ *206/ 633–1175.*

$ ✕ **Mae's Phinney Ridge Cafe.** Dykes with tykes, alternateens, yuppies— all these and more weekend brunch at this colorful café in Greenwood, just north of Woodland Park. Breakfasts are huge, with memorable cinnamon rolls. You can grab cappuccino in the Mud Room espresso bar. ⊠ *6412 Phinney Ave. N,* ☎ *206/782–1222.*

$ ✕ **Still Life.** One of the best cafés in town has a seating area with yard-sale-quality wooden tables and chairs. The menu at the Fremont eatery is substantial, with corn-tortilla pie, smoked-salmon bagels, and heavenly hazelnut shortbread. ⊠ *705 N. 35th St.,* ☎ *206/547–9850. No credit cards.*

Coffeehouse Culture

B & O Espresso. A fairly bookish and mellow gay crowd—lots of folks chipping away at dog-eared dime novels—hangs out at this Capitol Hill institution. ⊠ *204 Belmont Ave. E,* ☎ *206/322–5028.*

Coffee Messiah. Capitol Hill's newest coffeehouse is an over-the-top shrine—complete with a florid neon crucifix—to the big J.C. ⊠ *1554 E. Olive Way,* ☎ *206/860–7377.*

Cafe Paradiso. What's perhaps the gayest coffeehouse in the city is close to its two lesbian bars. Big windows overlook the action on Pike Street. The crowd is more grunge than guppie but there's plenty of each. ⊠ *1005 E. Pike St.,* ☎ *206/322–6960.*

Café Septième. You can munch on great sandwiches at this huge, dark, intentionally run-down-looking place that's popular with alternateens. ⊠ *214 Broadway Ave. E,* ☎ *206/860–8858.*

SCENES

If Kate Moss is the sort of girl (or boy) you fancy, you'll love Seattle, whose population of gaunt, waiflike, morose-looking young people is probably the highest of any city's in the world (or at least in a developed nation). Transplanted Californians and their love of gyms and tanning salons have made for more buffed-and-bronzed types in recent years, however. At a couple of clubs you'll see guys ripping off their shirts and vogueing, but for the most part Seattleites dress down and behave modestly. Bar goers are surprisingly mellow and polite—even standing single file for drinks— which imparts an oddly formal air to such a countercultural community.

Bars and Clubs

PRIME SUSPECTS

Baltic Room. This gay-friendly upscale lounge (formerly Kid Mohair) has a big after-work following, with live piano many nights. Scenesters come to check out the enticing wine and beer lists and to smoke cigars. Upstairs there's a cozy balcony with a gas-burning fireplace, plush armchairs, and even a reproduction antique pay phone. Surprisingly, the chichi ambience attracts plenty of cute grungers. ⊠ *1207 Pine St.,* ☎ *206/625– 4444. Crowd: mostly mid-20s to late 30s, mixed gay–straight, mixed m/f, some suits, classy but laid-back.*

The Cuff. Now that the Eagle's gone grunge, this is Seattle's only hangout with a significant leather following—but only on weekends. The large room has a central bar with Tom of Finland posters and chains dangling about. It's unusually bright. Off the side of the main room is a narrow patio, the Dog Run. ⊠ *1533 13th Ave. E,* ☎ *206/323–1525. Crowd: male, mostly late-20s and early 30s, low-key, leather but also lots of Levi's.*

Eagle. Like most Eagles, this one began as a leather bar. But perhaps because it's near Capitol Hill's alternative music clubs and several colleges, a young, grungy crowd hangs out here. There's a long dark bar as you enter, a patio out back, an open balcony upstairs overlooking the action, and a smaller cruise bar with pool and pinball. Friendliest bartenders in town. ⊠ *314 E. Pike St.,* ☎ *206/621–7591. Crowd: mostly male, young, a fair racial mix, rough-looking, goatees, a touch of leather, cruisy.*

The Easy. Ever since it expanded with a popular restaurant and a big dance floor, this lesbian hangout has attracted a more diverse crowd. The restaurant-bar area is rustic, with rough-hewn wooden floors where you can mingle and cruise, cuddle with a date, or grab a good meal. The other side of the space has bright lights, high ceilings, and the beat of house music most of the time. Of Seattle's two lesbian bars, this one attracts more men and people of color. ⊠ *916 E. Pike St.,* ☎ *206/323–8343. Crowd: 80/20 f/m, mostly under 35, varies from lipstick to diesel dykes, a lot of energy.*

Neighbours. This is Seattle's big gay disco, and though it's neither better nor worse than similar clubs in other towns, it's disappointingly bland in a city that prides itself on alternative culture and music. The decor is industrial, with exposed piping, corrugated metal, and chain-link fences. The music is house. Although there's lots of cruising and standing space surrounding the dance floor, on Friday and Saturday you can barely move. ⊠ *1509 Broadway Ave.,* ☎ *206/324–5358. Crowd: mostly male but some straight females and even fewer dykes, young, white, guppies in disco duds, attitudy, clonish.*

R Place. Seattle's cruise palace is a smartly furnished fern bar with three floors. A video bar on the first floor has lots of space for mingling. Seating on the second has a view of downstairs, and there are two pool tables (with almost always a line to play). Upstairs from that is a crowded video bar with loud dance music, another pool table, and lots of room to circulate. ⊠ *619 E. Pine St.,* ☎ *206/322–8828. Crowd: mostly male, young, professional, button-down, clean-cut, stand-and-model.*

Re-bar. For some time this tiny disco has been Seattle's hottest. Every night sees a somewhat queer following—the last Saturday of each month gets more dykes but Thursday is officially Queer Disco night, with long cruisy lines. The usually postmodern decor changes often. Some determined dancers climb atop the speakers for more elbow room and a chance to vogue. Music ranges from deep house to older disco. Behave yourself on weekends: The bouncer is an intimidating guy named Isadora. ⊠ *1114 Howell St.,* ☎ *206/233–9873. Crowd: mixed gay/straight; more gay male on Thursdays, but some dykes and groovy straight people; other times young, alternative; Doc Martens and baggy jeans.*

Thumpers. This is the kind of bar that settled professional guys head to, often to enjoy dinner at the terrace restaurant or to catch a cabaret act. Since the place has been around for a long time, it has a comfortable feel. With all these successful mature men standing around you can also expect to see a few younger self-starters looking for somebody with deep pockets. ⊠ *1500 E. Madison St.,* ☎ *206/328–3800. Crowd: mostly male, mostly over 40, casual but well dressed with some suits, very clubby.*

Timberline Tavern. If you think good country music and line dancing are strictly a southern thing, you're mistaken. This bar is renowned throughout the West Coast. A huge pitched ceiling and rustic post-and-beam construction give it the feel of a western hunting lodge—well, one with a disco ball. The crowd is friendly and energetic, though the women seem to keep to the left and the guys to the right. ⊠ *2015 Boren Ave.,* ☎ *206/622–6220. Crowd: 50/50 m/f, all ages, some straights; lots of bolo ties, denim, and cowboy hats.*

Wildrose. This mellow lesbian chat spot has an attractive publike restaurant on one side and a bar with two heavily trafficked pool tables on the other. Big plate-glass windows look onto Pike Street—you can walk by and check out who's inside (too bad more gay bars aren't set up this way). Women often come here before going dancing at the more boisterous Easy across the street. Everyone's welcome if they respect where they are. ✉ *1021 E. Pike St.,* ☎ *206/324–9210. Crowd: mainly lesbian, mostly 20s and 30s, lots of Doc Martens and baseball caps.*

NEIGHBORHOOD HAUNTS
C. C. Attle's (✉ 1501 E. Madison St., ☎ 206/726–0565) looks like an '80s hotel lounge—tinted lights, glass brick, and an awesome tropical fish tank—and draws a casual, mostly over-35 crowd. **Changes** (✉ 2103 N. 45th St., ☎ 206/545–8363), the only gay bar north of Lake Union, up in Wallingford and close to the University District, mainly draws men and women (many of them students) too lazy to drive to Capitol Hill. **Double Header** (✉ 407 2nd Ave., ☎ 206/464–9918) is supposedly the oldest gay bar on the West Coast. **Elite** (✉ 622 Broadway Ave. E, ☎ 206/324–4470), a real old-timer's bar, is just down the street from the Broadway Market. Dykes and guys who play pool hang out at the fun **Elite II** (✉ 1658 E. Olive Way, ☎ 206/322–7334). The former Encore expanded and re-opened in 1997 as the **Safari Sports Bar and Grille** (✉ 1518 11th Ave., ☎ 206/328–4250), with a big new dance floor (the Wednesday drag shows are a hoot), pool and darts, and a friendly mix of women and men of all ages. There's pool at the **Madison Pub** (✉ 1315 E. Madison St., ☎ 206/325–6537), along with a good selection of imported beers. At the cruisy **Mr. Paddywack's** (✉ 722 E. Pike St., ☎ 206/322–4024), you'll find a cadre of male strippers and a diverse, fairly young crowd. The Sunday-night beer bust at the **Sea Wolf Saloon** (✉ 1413 14th Ave. E, ☎ 206/323–2158), always draws a crowd. Things get going early at **Sonya's** (✉ 1532 7th Ave., ☎ 206/624–5377), a serious drinking bar. **Spags** (✉ 1118 E. Pike St., ☎ 206/322–3232) bills itself as "Seattle's Den for Bears and Trappers."

MUSIC CLUBS
Below are a few of the bastions of alternative music, fashion, and culture. They tend to draw on open-minded genXers.

The **Comet Tavern** (✉ 922 E. Pike St., ☎ 206/323–9853), one of the pioneers of grunge music, is almost touristy at this point. Belltown's version of the Comet Tavern, the **Crocodile** (✉ 2200 2nd Ave., ☎ 206/441–5611), is a major concert venue for cutting-edge bands. **The Vogue** (✉ 2018 1st Ave., ☎ 206/443–0673) is a trendy Belltown dance and music club with plenty of bi-curious types racing about.

Action

Favorite Seattle bathhouses include **Basic Plumbing** (✉ 1104 Pike St., ☎ 206/682–8441), which is more of a cruisy sex club than a spa (you don't have to check your clothes); nearby **Club Z** (✉ 1117 Pike St., ☎ 206/622–9958), is most popular between 10 PM and 2 AM.

SLEEPS

A drawback to visiting Seattle is that you can count on good weather only from about June through September. Since most everyone tries to come at this time, it's very hard to find a room, even out by the airport. In-season rates have risen tremendously over the past five years, but there are still places to stay for less than $100 a night. Just book well ahead. The rest of the year, especially in winter, the town is a bargain. Guest houses, which were unheard of 15 years ago, have boomed recently; you'll find plenty of options on Capitol Hill.

For price ranges, *see* lodging Chart A at the front of this guide.

Hotels

$$$$ 🏨 **Alexis Hotel.** Stars and dignitaries often stay at the Alexis, built in 1901 but decorated with postmodern flair. Many suites have wood-burning fireplaces and Jacuzzis, and all rooms are decorated with a mix of antiques and period pieces. ⊠ *1007 1st Ave., 98104,* ☎ *206/624–4844 or 800/426–7033,* ⒡ *206/621–9009. 109 rooms. Restaurant.*

$$$–$$$$ 🏨 **Hotel Vintage Park.** In keeping with Kimpton's reputation, this striking 1922 hotel is intimate, elegant, and professionally managed—the concierge is one of the most knowledgeable in Seattle. Rooms have cherry-wood furniture and rich, dark fabrics; some have fireplaces. ⊠ *1100 5th Ave., 98101,* ☎ *206/624–8000 or 800/624–4433,* ⒡ *206/623–0568. 129 rooms. Restaurant.*

$$$ 🏨 **The Paramount Hotel.** This property has stylish contemporary rooms with state-of-the-art amenities like data ports and movie and game systems. Executive suites cost only a bit more than double rooms and have whirlpool tubs. ⊠ *724 Pine St., 98101,* ☎ *206/292–9500 or 800/426–0670,* ⒡ *206/292–8610. 146 rooms. Restaurant, fitness center.*

$$–$$$ 🏨 **Inn at the Market.** Right across the street from Pike Place Market, this relatively young property has the ambience of a French countryside inn—dine downstairs at the hotel's Campagne (*see* Eats, *above*) restaurant if you're not totally convinced. Many of the good-size rooms have unobstructed views of Elliott Bay. ⊠ *86 Pine St., 98101,* ☎ *206/443–3600 or 800/446–4484,* ⒡ *206/448–0631. 65 rooms. Restaurant.*

$$–$$$ 🏨 **WestCoast Plaza Park Suites.** At the foot of Capitol Hill but still above I–5, this all-suites hotel has a terrific location, spacious accommodations (many with fireplace and kitchen), and provides complimentary Continental breakfast. It caters largely to business travelers but is ideal for anyone planning a stay of a few days or more. ⊠ *1011 Pike St., 98101,* ☎ *206/682–8282 or 800/426–0670,* ⒡ *206/682–5315. 194 rooms. Pool.*

$–$$ 🏨 **WestCoast Camlin.** The Camlin is a reasonably priced, restored, early 20th-century downtown hotel brimming with character. Assets include large closets, a quiet atmosphere, and the Cloud Room, a hip and somewhat gay-popular piano bar and lounge on the roof. ⊠ *1619 9th Ave., 98101,* ☎ *206/682–0100 or 800/426–0670,* ⒡ *206/682–7415. 140 rooms. Restaurant, pool.*

Guest Houses and Small Hotels

$$–$$$ 🏨 **Capitol Hill Inn.** This 1903 Queen Anne home once served as a bordello. The decor is eclectic yet very homey overall. Two rooms have whirlpool tubs, and one has a tub and a fireplace. Upstairs rooms are brighter but smaller. ⊠ *1713 Belmont Ave., 98122,* ☎ *206/323–1955, Web site www.capitolhillinn.com. 6 rooms, most with private bath. Full breakfast. Mixed gay/straight.*

$–$$ 🏨 **Bacon Mansion.** This Edwardian-style Tudor mansion is just east of Broadway. The antiques-filled rooms have lavish architectural details; some have kitchenettes and refrigerators, and one has a two-person soaking tub. ⊠ *959 Broadway Ave. E, 98102,* ☎ *206/329–1864 or 800/240–1864,* ⒡ *206/860–9025. 7 rooms with phone, most with private bath; 1 carriage house. Continental breakfast. Mixed gay/straight.*

$–$$ 🏨 **Gaslight Inn and Howell Street Suites.** The Gaslight is the best of the gay-oriented inns on the Hill, which is saying a lot, as there are a number of great ones. The turn-of-the-century house has arts-and-crafts furnishings and oak paneling. There's a large heated pool outside, along with space for sunning. Next door, accommodations at the more contemporary Howell Street Suites have large sitting areas. ⊠ *1727 15th Ave., 98122,* ☎ *206/325–3654,* ⒡ *206/328–4803, Web site www.gaslight-inn.com. 16 rooms with TV, most with private bath, some with phone. Pool. Continental breakfast. Mixed gay/straight.*

$–$$ ⚲ **Hill House.** This 1903 beauty, purchased recently by Alea and Herman Foster, is another of Capitol Hill's perfectly restored Victorians. Rooms are furnished with antiques and contemporary pieces, lace curtains, and fluffy down comforters. The full breakfast is superb. ⊠ *1113 E. John St., 98102,* ☎ *206/720–7161 or 800/720–7161,* ℻ *206/323–0772, e-mail hillhouse@guesthouses.net. 7 rooms, most with phone, TV, and private bath. Full breakfast. Mixed gay/straight.*

$–$$ ⚲ **Landes House.** The distinctive Craftsman-style Landes House, which was named after the city's only woman mayor, is right off Volunteer Park. Several rooms have decks with views of Puget Sound and the city skyline. Breakfast here is a real treat. ⊠ *712 11th Ave. E, 98102,* ☎ *206/ 329–8781 or 888/329–8781,* ℻ *206/324–0934. 12 rooms with phone and TV, most with private bath. Hot tub. Continental breakfast. Mostly mixed gay male/lesbian.*

THE LITTLE BLACK BOOK

At Your Fingertips
Crisis Clinic Hotline (☎ 206/461–3222 or 800/244–5767). **Graytop Cab** (☎ 206/622–4800). **Lesbian Health Clinic** (☎ 206/461–4503). **Lesbian Resource Center** (⊠ 1808 E. Bellevue St., No. 204, ☎ 206/322–3953). **Metro Transit** (☎ 206/553–3000). **Northwest AIDS Foundation** (☎ 206/ 329–6923). **Seattle Convention and Visitors Bureau** (⊠ 520 Pike St., Suite 1300, 98101, ☎ 206/461–5800). **Seattle Gay Clinic** (☎ 206/461–4540). **Seattle Visitor Center** (⊠ 800 Convention Pl., ☎ 206/461–5840). **Seattle Weekly** (☎ 206/623–0500, Web site www.seattleweekly.com). **The Stranger** (☎ 206/323–7101, Web site www.thestranger.com).

Gay Media
The weekly *Seattle Gay News* (☎ 206/324–4297) is thorough and well written. The *Lesbian Resource Center Community News* (☎ 206/322– 3953), a monthly newspaper, carries news features, community resources, and entertainment notes.

BOOKSTORES
Beyond the Closet (⊠ 518 E. Pike St., ☎ 206/322–4609), a handsome lesbigay store, has a helpful staff and a good selection of porn and mainstream gay and lesbian periodicals. The **Baily-Coy Bookstore** (⊠ 414 Broadway Ave. E, ☎ 206/323–8842) is a great independent in Capitol Hill with a significant gay and lesbian following. The city's oldest independent bookstore, **Red & Black Books** (⊠ 432 15th Ave. E, ☎ 206/322–7323), also has many gay titles. **Elliott Bay Book Company** (⊠ 101 S. Main St., ☎ 206/624–6600), in Pioneer Square, has an extensive lesbian and gay section. Another fine mainstream store downtown, **M. Coy Books** (⊠ 117 Pine St., ☎ 206/623–5354), is close to Pike Place Market.

Working Out
BQ Workout (⊠ Broadway Market, 300 Broadway Ave. E, ☎ 206/860– 3070) has long been popular with lesbians and gays. The *in* muscle shop is the **World Gym** (⊠ 8th Ave. and Pike St., ☎ 206/583–0640) at the Convention Center.

42 Out in Tampa

A BOOM TOWN THROUGHOUT THE '90S, Tampa has grown into a sophisticated, hip, and modern metropolis—the first Florida city that feels and looks as though it could be some place outside of Florida. Disneyesque amusements like Busch Gardens, plus a popular zoo and aquarium, account for the city's tourist appeal, but Tampa has become an increasingly desirable base for Fortune 500 companies. It's the 11th-busiest port in the country, and its high-tech, intelligently designed airport is user-friendly and convenient to downtown.

This city of nearly 300,000 has a large gay community—one that's less transient than those in other Florida cities whose economies depend predominantly on tourism. The gay scene is also younger than in some of the state's retirement-oriented towns, meaning that the 25-to-40 age group is well represented at bars.

If you're not here on business or to visit one of the amusement parks, don't rule out Tampa as a two-day getaway. The city has a lively gay nightlife, some first-rate restaurants, and a restored arts-and-entertainment district fashioned out of what used to be the nation's leading cigar-manufacturing center. And although the beach communities adjacent to nearby St. Petersburg have waned in sophistication and popularity, they can be a nice day trip from Tampa. If you're already planning a visit to Orlando, it's simple to pop over to Tampa. And when winter has you down, a visit here will offer you a mellow pace unattainable along the southeast coast of Florida.

THE LAY OF THE LAND

Tampa's metro area sprawls considerably, but most attractions are in a few pockets, such as downtown, Ybor City, and Hyde Park. The interesting neighborhoods, as well as the most gay-popular ones, are mostly south of Kennedy Boulevard, which cuts across the center of the city. The South-of-Kennedy area fronts two huge bodies of water, Tampa Bay, across which is St. Petersburg, and Hillsborough Bay, over which looms downtown.

Downtown

Downtown streets, while walkable, aren't exactly rife with exciting diversions, but the pedestrianized **Franklin Street Mall** is a hub of engaging shops and eateries.

Locals are justifiably proud of the **Florida Aquarium** (✉ 701 Channelside Dr., ☎ 813/273–4000), the highlight of which is a 60-foot-deep coral reef teeming with marine life. The **Tampa Museum of Art** (✉ 600 N. Ashley Dr., ☎ 813/274–8130), with the top collection of Greek, Roman, and

Etruscan antiquities in the Southeast, deserves a look. The **Museum of African-American Art** (✉ 1308 N. Marion St., ☎ 813/272–2466), which has pieces dating from the early 19th century and quite a few works from the 1920s Harlem Renaissance, is another cultural highlight. Movie buffs shouldn't miss the 1926 **Tampa Theatre** (✉ 711 Franklin St. Mall, ☎ 813/274–8981), which has a dazzlingly ornate design. It's a great place to catch foreign, independent, and classic films.

South Tampa and Hyde Park
The city's growing number of yuppies—along with plenty of guppies—continues to populate **South Tampa.** The most exclusive section, **Hyde Park,** gleams with palm-lined avenues, neatly manicured estates, and a potpourri of Gothic-, Tudor-, Spanish Colonial–, and Moorish-influenced mansions—most of them dating from the city's original heyday, which lasted from about the 1890s to the end of the 1920s. Drive along **South Howard Avenue** to find some of the hottest, and in many cases queerest, restaurants in the city. And spend a few hours wandering through the red-brick complex of shops and cafés known as **Olde Hyde Park Village** (✉ Swann Ave. at Dakota and Snow Sts., ☎ 813/251–3500) if you're looking for an excuse to spend money.

Ybor City
Only a decade ago, **Ybor City** (pronounced *ee*-bor), one of only three historic districts in Florida, was dilapidated and crime-infested. This chunk of hulking redbrick warehouses, balustrade balconies, and cobblestone streets—a short drive northeast of downtown—formed the hub of America's cigar-manufacturing industry from about the late 19th century through the 1940s. Immigrant workers, most of them Cuban but many of them Spanish and Italian, settled here in droves. Production slowed following World War II, and beginning with the U.S. embargo on Cuban products in 1959 the neighborhood plummeted.

Entrepreneurs, many of them artists and gallery owners, began snapping up the dramatic architecture in the '80s. Soon after, a flood of businesses followed. This is the liveliest entertainment district in Central Florida, and scoring a table at any of the several trendy eateries can prove difficult. Although a few clubs continue to hold gay nights once or twice weekly, the discos have become more straight and rowdy.

It's worth coming here for dinner or to experience one of the remaining gay club events. During the mellower daytime consider strolling along the main drags, **7th and 8th avenues,** to check out the galleries and boutiques. Much of the retail and dining action is centered around one former factory, **Ybor Square** (✉ 8th Ave. and 13th Sts., ☎ 813/247–4497). You can examine the neighborhood's rich history at the **Ybor City State Museum** (✉ 1818 9th Ave., ☎ 813/247–6323). Inside a former commercial bakery, it contains reconstructed cigar workers' homes and numerous artifacts.

Greater Tampa
The brash and busy Africa-themed **Busch Gardens** (✉ 3000 Busch Blvd., ☎ 813/987–5082) is Tampa's direct competitor to Disney World. Shopping bazaars proffer trinkets said to be from "the Dark Continent," and some 3,500 exotic animals wander about one region of the park that's meant to give you the sensation of experiencing a safari. The latest draw, a tribute to Egypt, comes complete with a re-creation of King Tut's tomb and an unnerving roller-coaster ride. More rides await you at nearby **Adventure Island** (✉ 4500 Bougainvillea Ave., ☎ 813/987–5660), a 36-acre water park, which is also run by the Anheuser-Busch group (combo tickets are available).

Also above downtown, compact, with about 1,500 animals, the **Lowry Park Zoo** (✉ North Blvd. at Sligh Ave., ☎ 813/935–8552) is one of the best zoos in the Southeast; of particular note is the manatee and aquatic center.

St. Petersburg, Clearwater, and the Beaches

While Tampa has been the Gulf Coast's rising star in the '90s, its across-the-bay neighbor, the once fashionable retirement capital St. Petersburg, has struggled. Despite developing a world-class trio of downtown museums, this city of 250,000 remains fairly depressing. Lesbians, and a smaller number of gay men, have settled in some of the historic neighborhoods north of downtown, and so the city does have a nice network of women's and gay social organizations. But tourists will probably only want to spend an afternoon here.

The highlight downtown is the **Salvador Dalí Museum** (✉ 1000 3rd St. S, ☎ 813/823–3767), with a huge collection of the artist's famed Surrealist works—yes, including many a melting clock. But Dalí's life work is tremendously varied, and this museum offers a glimpse into every medium and genre that was touched by his genius, from holograms to early landscape paintings. Less dramatic but still enjoyable, the Palladian-style **Museum of Fine Arts** (✉ 255 Beach Dr. NE, ☎ 813/896–2667) contains 20 galleries, plus an outdoor sculpture garden. French artists, among them Corot, Cézanne, Monet, and Rodin, are well represented; there's also a fine collection of Steuben glass. Although it has no permanent collection, the **Florida International Museum** (✉ 100 2nd St. N, ☎ 813/822–3693) hosts important exhibitions (a recent one on the life and times of Alexander the Great earned considerable praise).

For a break from museum-hopping have a light meal or coffee and dessert at either **Bay Gables** (✉ 136 4th Ave. NE, ☎ 813/822-0044) or **Benson's** (✉ 244 1st Ave. N, ☎ 813/823–6065), both of which are gay-friendly.

GETTING AROUND

You'll need a car to get around. Local drivers come in two flavors: very slow and very fast. Each camp reviles and fears the members of the other, making driving a challenge. Although you'll need a decent road map to maneuver about Tampa's sprawl, this land of wide roads and shopping centers is abundant with parking and easy to navigate.

EATS

Latin American and Italian restaurants abound in Tampa. Fresh seafood is readily available, often at raw bars or fish shanties. The most gay-frequented establishments are along South Howard Avenue. Ybor City has several eateries popular with the queer community.

For price ranges, *see* dining Chart B at the front of this guide.

$$$$ ✕ **Bern's Steakhouse.** One of America's most revered steak houses, Bern's is famous not merely for its organically grown and raised vegetables, beef, and seafood, but for a wine list almost as long as *War and Peace*. The huge, blank, windowless facade and fancy-schmancy interior convey the retro elegance of an era that predates vegans, chocolate martinis, and sponge-painted walls. ✉ *1208 S. Howard Ave.,* ☎ *813/251–2421.*

$$–$$$ ✕ **Ciccio & Tony's.** This see-and-be-seen favorite prepares dependable pastas, pizzettes, and grills. A favorite is the fusilli *mare verde* (scallops and shrimp tossed with a spinach puree, seafood stock, and a touch of cream, garnished with farm-raised mussels). Try to get a table on the terrace. ✉ *1015 S. Howard Ave.,* ☎ *813/251–8406.*

Tampa

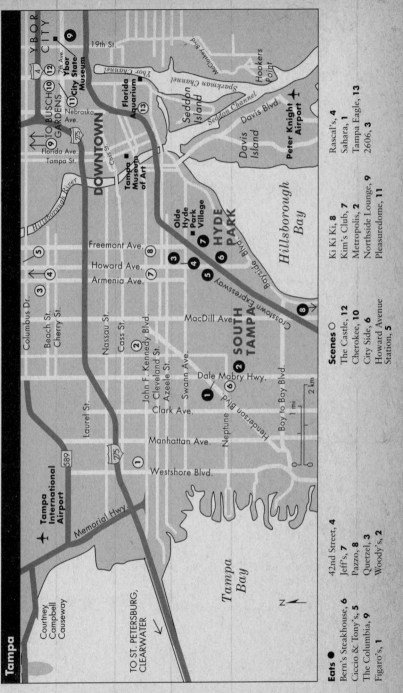

Eats ●
Bern's Steakhouse, 6
Ciccio & Tony's, 5
The Columbia, 9
Figaro's, 1
42nd Street, 4
Jeff's, 7
Pazzo, 8
Quetzel, 3
Woody's, 2

Scenes ○
The Castle, 12
Cherokee, 10
City Side, 6
Howard Avenue Station, 5
Ki Ki Ki, 8
Kim's Club, 7
Metropolis, 2
Northside Lounge, 9
Pleasuredome, 11
Rascal's, 4
Sahara, 1
Tampa Eagle, 13
2606, 3

$$–$$$ ✕ **The Columbia.** What began as a no-frills commissary for Ybor City's cigar workers has grown into an 11-dining-room compound that can seat about 1,700 patrons. A bona fide tourist attraction, the Columbia is not exactly intimate, but elaborate mosaic murals do impart considerable character. ⊠ *2117 E. 7th Ave., Ybor City,* ☏ *813/248–4961.*

$$–$$$ ✕ **42nd Street.** This festive, mural-filled supper club re-creates the ambience of Times Square. The food's seriously delicious, but brace yourself for the goofy menu names like "Tossed in Yonkers," a salad of Italian greens and braised pine nuts, tossed with lemon-garlic dressing and goat cheese croutons; and "Yankee Noodle Dandy" (grilled red snapper, sun-dried tomatoes, garlic, basil, and olive oil tossed over an open flame). ⊠ *516 S. Howard Ave.,* ☏ *813/253–0042.*

$$ ✕ **Pazzo.** A 10-minute drive south of downtown leads to this gay-popular Italian restaurant with some of the finest food in the city. Stars include oak-grilled chicken over angel hair in balsamic broth with goat cheese, and a calzone with spinach, artichoke, sun-dried tomato pesto, ricotta, and mozzarella. ⊠ *5427 Bayshore Blvd.,* ☏ *813/835–7531.*

$ ✕ **Jeff's.** A gay-friendly spot for a hearty lunch—grouper, shepherd's pie, thick deli sandwiches—this café rarely fails to satisfy. High pressed-tin ceilings and elaborate Victorian architectural details are the setting for splendidly artistic desserts, which include a heavenly raspberry white chocolate mousse. ⊠ *815 S. Rome Ave.,* ☏ *813/259–9866.*

$ ✕ **Quetzel.** Quetzel is as appreciated for its wild happy hour (complete with tasty small plates and 70 kinds of beer) as for its affordable fresh burritos, salads, and similarly tasty Cal Mex–inspired cuisine. ⊠ *402 S. Howard Ave.,* ☏ *813/259–9982.*

$ ✕ **Woody's.** In the gay community's—and nearly everyone else's—favorite Tampa sandwich shop, the counter-service–only dining room lacks atmosphere but the food packs plenty of punch. For a bit of local flavor, try the Cuban—with turkey, ham, pork, salami, Swiss, pickle slices, and mustard. ⊠ *1722 S. Dale Mabry Hwy.,* ☏ *813/254–2806.*

Coffeehouse Culture

Figaro's. What could be more appropriate in Tampa than a coffeehouse with a separate cigar room? If you're not a stogie devotee, come for the great sandwiches, coffees, and beautiful cakes and sweets—the Frangelico tart melts in the mouth. ⊠ *1155 S. Dale Mabry Hwy.,* ☏ *813/289–6360.*

SCENES

You'll need a scorecard to keep up with Tampa's nightlife, which seemed to change monthly throughout 1996 and 1997 and is still in transition. Clubs open and close, change names and themes, and pass from gay to straight at an alarming rate. This is partly because Ybor City, which had been a fairly gay entertainment district, has gone more hetero.

Tampa

PRIME SUSPECTS

Cherokee. One of Ybor City's many gorgeous late-Victorian buildings that's been converted into a club, Cherokee is one of the hottest dyke venues in the Southeast—though it's open only on Friday and Saturday. Enter off the quaint cobbled street into the old-fashioned saloon, complete with tile floors, brass details, and many original architectural details. Beyond this room is a dance floor across which you can barely push your way, especially after 11. Drag shows—"Men with great tit jobs doing women," according to one of the amiable bartenders— take place on Friday and Saturday. ⊠ *1320 E. 9th St., Ybor City,* ☏ *813/247–9966. Crowd: 80/ 20 f/m, some straights (especially on Fridays), mostly under 35, mixed* *racially (more so on Fridays), stylish, wild, mix of guppies and working-class women.*

Ki Ki Ki. With jarringly dated colors, strings of blinking lights, and campy furnishings, this long-running queer cocktail lounge has definite retro appeal. Patrons converge nightly around a central bar that's staffed by some of the friendliest bar hands in town. The guys in here definitely like to flirt and have a good time, but it's not a particularly sleazy hangout. Packed on weekends, when a broader mix of ages can be expected. ⊠ *1908 W. Kennedy Blvd.,* ☎ *813/254–8183. Crowd: mostly male, mostly over 35, gregarious, unstuffy.*

Sahara. Sahara draws a steady mix of women. Inside the pink-lit cozy bar, ceiling fans whir above the crowds, and a jukebox churns out popular dance and rock tunes. At happy hour the place rocks (and, despite the fans, fills with smoke). ⊠ *4643 W. Kennedy Blvd.,* ☎ *813/282–0183. Crowd: mostly female, mostly 30s and 40s, down-to-earth, jeans and flannel types.*

Tampa Eagle. The Eagle draws a butch leather-and-Levi's crowd—it's not hard-core by any stretch. The industrial-meets-jailhouse interior has high ceilings, loud music, and a complete prison cell in the center, but the bar's best attribute is the spacious palm-shaded patio. In the southeastern shadows of downtown's skyscrapers, it's a little tricky to find—it's easiest approached by way of Platt Street. ⊠ *302 S. Nebraska Ave.,* ☎ *813/ 223–2780. Crowd: male, 20s to 40s; plenty of leather, tight T-shirts, and denim; more than a few guppies, cruisy.*

2606. At this leather club there's no formal dress code, but preppy or dressy attire is frowned upon. You'll find (but not actually see) hordes of cruisy guys, a couple of bars, and some pool tables and similar such diversions. A trip to the john can be a true adventure. The requisite leather gift shop is on site. ⊠ *2606 Armenia Ave.,* ☎ *813/875–6993. Crowd: male, mostly mid-30s to mid-40s, leather and Levi's, some tattoos, motorcycle gear, kind of sleazy, hard-core.*

NEIGHBORHOOD HAUNTS

City Side (⊠ 3810 Neptune St., ☎ 813/254–6466), which has a strong after-work following, attracts women and men. North of downtown, **Rascal's** (⊠ 105 W. Martin Luther King Blvd., ☎ 813/237–8883) has some of Tampa's best-attended and wildest drag shows. **Kim's Club** (⊠ 2408 W. Kennedy Blvd., ☎ 813/254–4188), a leather guys' bar before fall 1997, now attracts a mostly lesbian crowd, but guys are welcome. The closing of several downtown clubs has given new life to **Metropolis** (⊠ 3447 W. Kennedy Blvd., ☎ 813/871–2410), which presents strippers nightly and cultivates a cruisy somewhat stand-and-model following. Popular with employees from nearby Busch Gardens, the **Northside Lounge** (⊠ 9002 N. Florida Ave., ☎ 813/931–3396) is a festive cocktail bar that's worth a visit if you're in the area.

ONE-NIGHTERS

In recent years, two spaces have offered gay, mixed gay/lesbian, or mixed gay/straight blowouts, though who does what (and when they do it) changes frequently. **Pleasuredome** (⊠ 1430 E. 7th Ave., ☎ 813/247–2711), the latest name on the space that formerly held the disco Tracks, has been having a hot gay night on Tuesday. **The Castle** (⊠ E. 16th St. and 9th Ave., ☎ 813/248–3053), Pleasuredome's nearby competitor, sometimes has gay or gay-friendly nights.

A straight African-American club on most nights, **Howard Avenue Station** (⊠ 3003 N. Howard Ave., ☎ 813/254–7194) opens to the gay community on Friday and Saturday. Whether you're up for dancing, hooking up, or interacting with a diverse cross section of the local guys' scene, this is a good bet. After closing, the parking lot develops into quite a meat market.

St. Petersburg and the Beaches

Back Room. Across the street from the Gulf, the Back Room captures the mood of a laid-back beach bar. Most of the action revolves around an expansive landscaped patio with tables and chairs shaded by beach umbrellas; inside there's an attractive cruise bar with good (but not loud) dance music and more seating. A spacious new bar was added in fall 1997. This is the best nightspot for Tampa queers headed to the beaches. ⊠ *14601 Gulf Blvd., Madeira Beach,* ☎ *813/391–2680. Crowd: mostly male, 30s and 40s, local guys, extremely casual, a bit cruisy.*

Pro Shop. In Clearwater, which is west of Tampa along the Gulf of Mexico, the Pro Shop has been a central fixture of the community since the mid-'70s. Consisting of a patio, a warmly lighted lounge, and a game room (pool table, darts, mini-bowling machine), the Pro Shop feels like any other slightly upscale neighborhood bar. If you're not a regular, the approachable staff will immediately make you feel like one. ⊠ *840 Cleveland St., Clearwater,* ☎ *813/447–4259. Crowd: 70/30 m/f, 30s to 60s, regular folks.*

Vip Lounge and Mexican Food Grill. It's hard not to like this peculiar hangout that's half dated cocktail lounge and half cheap Mexican restaurant— the outgoing staff and patrons clearly seem to enjoy themselves, and you can get a decent plate of tamales or enchiladas while also satisfying your needs to drink, mingle, and take in a mediocre drag show (the latter are offered many nights). ⊠ *10625 Gulf Blvd., Treasure Island,* ☎ *813/360–5062. Crowd: 70/30 m/f, all ages, zero attitude.*

NEIGHBORHOOD HAUNTS

In north St. Petersburg, local dykes and fags head to the **Hideaway** (⊠ 8302 4th St., ☎ 813/570–9025) for drinks and sometimes to see a live band, and to the neighboring **Haymarket Pub** (⊠ 8308 4th St., ☎ 813/577–9621) for a glass of wine, a cup of cappuccino, or to browse the selection of gay-theme greeting cards.

Action

Club Tampa (⊠ 215 N. 11th St., ☎ 813/223–5181) is one of the most popular bathhouses in the state. **Hillsborough Adult Video** (⊠ 5421 W. Hillsborough Ave., ☎ 813/889–9795) has porn and erotica, plus buddy booths.

SLEEPS

These days the nicest accommodations in the Tampa Bay region are downtown or close to the airport, overlooking Tampa Bay. Most of these chain properties cater to business travelers, which means they often have low rates on weekends. In a pinch, consider the budget motels north of the city, near Busch Gardens, but remember that these properties are a good 20-minute drive from downtown and Ybor City.

For price ranges, *see* lodging Chart B at the front of this guide.

Hotels

$$$$ 🖭 **Hyatt Regency Westshore.** The Hyatt tends to attract business travelers and usually offers some nice deals on weekends. Rooms are sumptuous with pastel hues and balconies, many of them looking directly over Tampa Bay and a neighboring 35-acre nature preserve. The location on the western edge of the city is quiet and secluded. Management is very gay-friendly. ⊠ *6200 Courtney Campbell Causeway, 33607,* ☎ *813/874–1234 or 800/233–1234,* FAX *813/281–9168. 445 rooms. Restaurants, pools, exercise room.*

$$$ ☷ **Embassy Suites Hotel–Tampa Airport/Westshore.** Two couples or a few friends traveling together will appreciate this all-suites property near the airport and Tampa Bay—an easy drive from downtown and Ybor City. All rooms have kitchenettes, and the health club is top-notch. ⊠ *555 N. Westshore Blvd., 33609,* ☎ *813/875–1555 or 800/362–2779,* FAX *813/ 287–3664. 221 rooms. Restaurant, pool, health club.*

$–$$ ☷ **La Quinta Inn.** A fine budget option, this cheerfully decorated and efficiently run motel is east of Ybor City, not more than a 15-minute drive from South Tampa nightlife and dining. It's one of the top budget choices in the area. ⊠ *2904 Melbourne Blvd., 33605,* ☎ *813/623–3591,* FAX *813/ 620–1375. 129 rooms. Pool.*

Guest Houses and Small Hotels

$$–$$$ ☷ **Queens Gate Resort.** It's south of Tampa and St. Petersburg, on Anna Maria Island in Bradenton Beach, but this romantic, tropically landscaped miniresort is worth the excursion. The owners often work with the gay-friendly Veranda B&B in Orlando (*see* Chapter 26) to set up vacations where guests can book a few days in each place. The property consists of one- and two-bedroom bungalows with full kitchens, the largest of which can sleep six. ⊠ *1101 Gulf Dr., Bradenton Beach, 34217,* ☎ *941/778–7153 or 800/310–7153. 12 units with phone, TV, and private bath. Mixed gay/straight.*

$–$$ ☷ **Gram's Place B&B.** Named for the mythic rocker Gram Parsons, clearly a favorite of the outgoing owner, this informal resort is in a quiet area north of downtown and the bars. Rooms have kitchenettes and VCRs, and come in a variety of sizes and configurations. This is the sort of place where you can mingle with fellow guests or go off and do your own thing— the mood is very low-key. ⊠ *3109 Ola Ave. N, 33603,* ☎ FAX *813/221– 0596. 12 rooms with phone and TV, some with private bath. Hot tub. Continental breakfast. Mixed gay male/lesbian.*

$ ☷ **Ruskin House.** A three-story tower pokes above the gabled roofline of this fascinating early 20th-century home in a historic part of Tampa— two long porches add further character to this quaint B&B. Rooms, filled with an eclectic assortment of mostly Victorian pieces, create a sense of romance. Very intimate and ideal for couples. ⊠ *120 Dickman Dr. SW, 33570,* ☎ *813/645–3842. 4 rooms with phone and TV, some with private bath. Continental breakfast. Mixed gay/straight.*

St. Petersburg

St. Petersburg has three small women-hosted properties. The largest, the **Barge House** (⊠ Box 46526, St. Petersburg Beach, 33706, ☎ 813/360– 0729, FAX 813/360–8750, $–$$, lesbian) consists of a private cottage and a cabana, each with full kitchen and use of a hot tub; it's just steps from the beach. One-room accommodations, both of which are in pleasant residential neighborhoods in St. Petersburg proper, include **Boca Ciega** (⊠ 3526 Boca Ciega Dr. N, 33710, ☎ 813/381–2755, $, lesbian), which has a kitchenette, TV and VCR, phone, and the use of a pool; and the **Frog Pond** (⊠ 145 29th Ave. N, 33704, ☎ 813/823–7407, $, mixed gay/straight), a tropically furnished room with hardwood floors and the use of a pool table and library.

THE LITTLE BLACK BOOK

At Your Fingertips
Gay and Lesbian Community Center of Tampa (☎ 813/273–8919). **Hillsborough Area Regional Transit** (☎ 813/254–4278). **The Line of Tampa Bay** (lesbigay referrals and information, ☎ 813/586–4297). **Tampa Bay Business Guild** (lesbigay chamber of commerce, ☎ 813/239–1001). **Tampa Bay Visitor Information Center** (⊠ 3601 E. Busch Blvd., ☎ 813/ 985–3601). **Tampa/Hillsborough Convention and Visitors Association**

(✉ 111 Madison St., Suite 1010, 33601, ☎ 800/826–8358). **St. Petersburg/Clearwater Area Convention & Visitors Bureau** (✉ Thunderdome, 1 Stadium Dr., Suite A, 33705, ☎ 813/582–7892). **United Cab** (☎ 813/253–2424). *Weekly Planet* (☎ 813/286–1600).

Gay Media

Central Florida's best gay paper, the biweekly *Watermark* (☎ 407/481–2243, Web site www.watermarkonline.com), provides news and views on Orlando and Tampa Bay, plus good club, arts, and dining coverage. The monthly *Gazette* (☎ 813/689–7566, Web site www.dailyrevolution.com/gazette) covers Gulf Coast news and nightlife. Also useful is the monthly *Stonewall* (☎ 813/832–2878, e-mail stonewal@cyperspy.com). *Encounter Magazine* (☎ 813/877–7913), published twice monthly, consists mostly of ads for Central Florida bars but prints a handful of news stories and light columns.

BOOKSTORES

The lesbigay store **Tomes and Treasures** (✉ 202 S. Howard Ave., ☎ 813/251–9368) carries a fine selection of books, plus mags, movies, and a few gifts. **Oz** (✉ 1142 N. 30th St., ☎ 813/971–9545) carries pride items, incense, jewelry, and smoking stuff. **M/C Film Festival** (✉ 3601 Kennedy Blvd., ☎ 813/870–6233) stocks many gay- and lesbian-theme films. **Affinity Books** (✉ 2435 9th St. N, ☎ 813/823–3662) is St. Petersburg's lesbigay bookstore; it's just north of downtown and has the expected titles, plus many women's and children's books.

Working Out

The premier gay gym, **Metro Flex** (✉ 2511 Swann Ave., ☎ 813/876–3539), has state-of-the-art equipment.

43 *Out in Tucson*

TUCSON IS A CITY WHERE LOCALS NEVER hesitate to say "neat" and "right on"—and when they do, they're being completely genuine. In this sense and in many others, Tucson is unlike most of Arizona—especially its larger sister, Phoenix, 110 miles north. And yet, this is quintessential Arizona: immense stands of saguaro cacti; traditional adobe dwellings mingling with stately, contemporary southwestern structures; a substantial Mexican immigrant population; a sunny, dry-as-death climate; and desert to the nth power.

Tucson is a liberal-leaning, well-educated, and politically active city. Its enlightened mentality derives principally from the presence of the University of Arizona. Its academic base of residents supports a lively arts scene. The city is one of 14 in America with a symphony, opera, theater, and ballet. Underground music, cutting-edge cuisine, and avant-garde arts scenes flourish here. And in much of Tucson, gays, lesbians, and straights eat at the same cafés, walk the same streets, and frequent the same bars.

Few American cities have managed to keep wilderness so close at hand. The precipitous mountain ridges that surround Tuscon afford awesome views, and in a matter of minutes, you can leave the confines of the metro area, drive through a mountain pass, and find yourself in the middle of what appears to be a never-ending tract of desert.

The queer community is less centralized than in many cities, but it is huge and active—more than 10,000 people attend the annual gay pride picnic. The lesbian community is especially strong, and women-owned businesses abound. Tucson is small enough for one woman to start up a social group or develop a particular cause, yet large enough to back her idea and see it through.

THE LAY OF THE LAND

Tucson is low, sprawling, and suburban—an astounding 500 square miles (it can take a good 45 minutes without traffic to drive from corner to corner). Adjacent to its tiny downtown are two small, charming areas: the historic El Presidio district and the 4th Avenue district. Farther east are the campus and environs of the University of Arizona. Beyond these few well-defined neighborhoods residential blocks—broken only by dull strip malls—stretch all the way to the mountains.

The University District
The **University District** is a somewhat left-leaning neighborhood, with the city's highest concentration of homos.

The 325-acre campus of the **University of Arizona** (☎ 520/621–5130) is home to four major cultural institutions. The **Center for Creative Pho-**

tography (✉ 1030 N. Olive Rd., ☎ 520/621–7968) has a vast cache of Ansel Adams's works. The **U of A Museum of Art** (✉ Fine Arts Complex, Bldg. 2, ☎ 520/621–7567) has pieces from the Middle Ages to the present. The **Arizona Historical Society's Museum** (✉ 949 E. 2nd St., ☎ 520/628–5774) traces the state's growth from its Spanish heritage to today. The **Arizona State Museum** (✉ University and Park Aves., ☎ 520/621–6302) focuses on archaeology.

Fourth Avenue, from about 9th to 2nd streets, runs north–south through the western edge of the University District, acting as something of a bohemian Rodeo Drive—a busy stretch of Third World–inspired shops and eateries.

Downtown

Off the southwest corner of the University District, Tucson's compact **downtown** is an amorphous pod of crooked thoroughfares; many lesbians and gays work and socialize here. **Congress Street** has the best shopping. A few galleries and shops are along Pennington Street and Broadway.

El Presidio District

Brushing the northern edge of downtown, the **El Presidio District**'s streets are speckled with colorful vestiges of a rich, 135-year architectural history. El Presidio del Tucson originally stood within this district, an enormous, walled Spanish fortress (1776) that protected the territory of New Spain from "unruly" Native Americans. Notable house museums in the El Presidio, include the **Tucson Museum of Art** (✉ 140 N. Main Ave., ☎ 520/624– 2333); the 1868 **Edward Nye Fish House** (✉ 120 N. Main Ave., ☎ 520/624–2333); the Mission Revival **J. Knox Corbett House** (✉ 180 N. Main Ave., ☎ 520/624–2333); and **La Casa Cordova** (✉ 175 N. Meyer Ave., ☎ 520/624–2333), which houses the fascinating Mexican Heritage Museum. Meyer and Court avenues, which run parallel to Main, are good places to gallery-hop; check out the southwestern pieces in the **Old Town Artisans Complex** (✉ 186 N. Meyer Ave.).

The Mountains and the Desert

Gay sunbathers like to cruise, nap, and relax up at tranquil, rocky **Reddington Pass,** in the Sabino Canyon, where the waterfalls and swimming holes are good places to cool off. From downtown, take Tanque Verde Road, turn left onto Sabino Canyon Road, and follow it into the Santa Catalina foothills to **Sabino Canyon State Park;** at the entrance, beyond which no cars are permitted, is a visitor center (☎ 520/749–8700) where you can get a map and directions.

West of Tucson are some of the most popular sights (take Speedway Boulevard west until it becomes Gates Pass Road; continue over the mountains). Especially if you've never been in a desert before, you oughtn't miss Tucson's best attraction, the world-renowned **Arizona–Sonora Desert Museum** (✉ 2021 N. Kinney Rd., ☎ 520/883–2702). A true outdoor classroom, the museum is home to native wildlife living in its natural habitat, and the exhibits on desert minerals, flora, and other environmental features are worthwhile. Nearby is the western branch of the **Saguaro National Park** (☎ 520/733–5100), which harbors forests of saguaro (pronounced suh-_wahr_-oh) cacti. These jut out of the ground like silly green forks—it takes as long as 15 years for them to grow a foot.

Bisbee

For a colorful excursion, drive 100 miles southeast to **Bisbee** (chamber of commerce ☎ 520/432–5421), a hippified and more recently yuppified haven of artists, dropouts, frayed urbanites, and a fair share of lesbians and gays. The town made a name for itself with copper mining; now it has about 25 restaurants, a dozen historic bed-and-breakfasts (most of them gay-friendly), several excellent antiques stores, numerous galleries, and not a single traffic light; concerts and poetry readings are held frequently. It even has a bar with a gay following, **St. Elmo's** (⊠ 36 Brewery Gulch Ave., ☎ 520/432–5578).

GETTING AROUND

To get anywhere, you'll need a car. Local buses and trolleys are impractical for tourists, as are, except in a bind, taxis, which are unregulated and costly. Many sights are a 10- to 40-minute drive from downtown. In the center of town, streets are numbered in a grid pattern: streets run east–west, avenues north–south. Outside the center but still within the city limits, the streets still run largely in a grid but have names.

EATS

Though Tucson has no ostensibly gay eateries, it ranks among the country's best small cities for innovative and colorful dining—and virtually all the hot restaurants here are patronized by the gay community. Yet despite its sophisticated palate, you'll encounter few pretensions. Meals are rarely served after 10 PM. One surprise: Mexican grub here is not much better than in other near-the-border locales. Tucson's best cooking is southwestern, utilizing local ingredients and borrowing its techniques a bit from Mexico, a lot from California, and to varying degrees from New Orleans, France, Italy, and even Asia.

For price ranges, *see* dining Chart B at the front of this guide.

Central Tucson

$$$-$$$$ ✕ **Janos.** One of Tucson's exemplary southwestern restaurants, trendy Janos is beside the Tucson Museum of Art (but will be moving elsewhere in town when its lease expires in summer '98). Regionally beloved chef Janos Wilder cooks under a French influence; typical are chipotle-roasted rack of lamb or a grilled swordfish in a tomato coulis. ⊠ *150 N. Main Ave.,* ☎ 520/884–9426.

$$-$$$ ✕ **Café Poca Cosa.** Run by a former model from Mexico City, Poca Cosa defies local restaurant stereotypes—that is, the ambience is stylish, the food healthful and creative. The always-changing menu is presented daily on a chalkboard—Cosa's nationally acclaimed mole dishes are always a good bet. ⊠ *88 E. Broadway Blvd.,* ☎ 520/622–6400.

$$-$$$ ✕ **Cottonwood Café.** This converted adobe ranch compound is the latest southwestern eatery to take the city by storm. You might start with the assorted platter of pepper-stuffed shrimp, sweet corn tamales, and pot stickers, before moving on to a truly fiery chicken *diablo* with boar bacon, peppers, onions, and a sherry rosemary jalapeño butter. ⊠ *60 N. Alvernon Way,* ☎ 520/326–6000.

$$-$$$ ✕ **The Dish.** The Rumrunner wine shop doesn't look like much, but push your way into the chic intimate rear dining room where you'll be rewarded with stellar bistro fare. More than 30 wines by the glass complement the New American cuisine such as citrus-glazed salmon with crispy leeks. ⊠ *3200 E. Speedway Blvd.,* ☎ 520/326–1714.

$$-$$$ ✕ **Kingfisher Bar and Grill.** The Kingfisher has charm: the raw bar that offers four kinds of oysters on the half shell plus house-smoked trout; inventive main courses like ahi tuna with green chile avocado cilantro sauce; a menu of about a dozen kinds of small-batch bourbons; and a grazing menu from 10 PM till midnight. ⊠ *2564 E. Grant Rd.,* ☎ 520/323–7739.

$$-$$$ ✕ **Vivace.** This queer-popular restaurant has an upbeat dining room and knowledgeable servers, but it's the superb northern Italian fare that earns it serious raves. Consider filet of beef tenderloin with chianti mushroom sauce with garlic potato puree. ⊠ *Crossroads Plaza, 4811 E. Grant Rd.,* ☎ *520/795–7221.*

Tucson

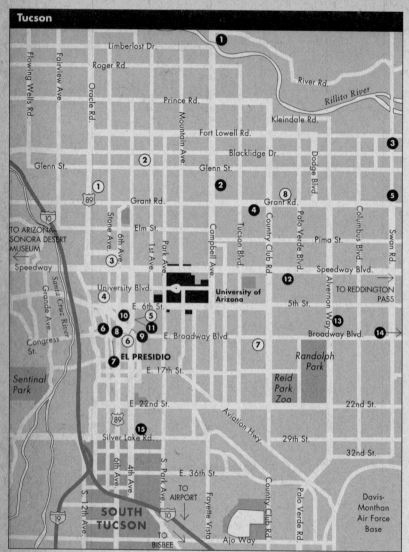

Eats ●

Blue Willow, **2**
Café Magritte, **8**
Café Poca Cosa, **7**
Café Terra Cotta, **1**
Cottonwood Café, **13**

Cup Café and
Library of
Congress, **9**
The Dish, **12**
Firecrackers, **3**
Janos, **6**
Kingfisher Bar
and Grill, **4**

Maralene's Hungry
Fox, **14**
Maya Quetzal, **10**
Mi Nidito, **15**
Rainbow Planet, **11**
Vivace, **5**

Scenes ○

Ain't Nobody's
Bizness, **7**
Boom Boom's, **1**
Club Congress and
the Tap Room at
Hotel Congress, **6**
Graduate, **4**
Hours, **8**
IBT's (It's 'Bout
Time), **5**
Stonewall/Eagle, **2**
Venture-N, **3**

$$ ✕ **Café Magritte.** Very gay, very "in," with decor and atmosphere that are a tribute to the surrealist painter René Magritte. The menu offers such creations as chicken tortilla soup, Caesar salad with the day's seafood, and a number of run-of-the-mill dishes spiced up with southwestern in-. gredients. ✉ *254 E. Congress St.,* ☎ *520/884–8004.*

$$ ✕ **Firecrackers.** Tucson's latest date with Pacific Rim cooking has been met with oohs and aahs. Although some dishes recall the incendiary devices for which the restaurant is named (note the spicy ahi sushi rolls), others such as grilled pork tenderloin with pineapple papaya chutney dazzle the tastebuds without simultaneously charring them. ✉ *2990 N. Swan Rd.,* ☎ *520/318–1118.*

$$ ✕ **Maya Quetzal.** This gay-frequented storefront restaurant is notable for a beautiful mural of El Salvador. Popular dishes include *media lunas* (folded corn tortillas stuffed with spinach and walnuts), and, on Tuesdays, *carne gulsada* (stewed beef flavored with tomatillos, tomatoes, carrots, potatoes, and garlic). ✉ *429 N. 4th Ave.,* ☎ *520/622–8207.*

$ ✕ **Blue Willow.** A favorite breakfast spot among hippies and New Agers, this sprawling café has a funky gift shop, a laidback groovy staff, and a kitchen serving tasty omelets, burritos, and fresh fruit crepes. ✉ *2616 N. Campbell Ave.,* ☎ *520/795–8736.*

$ ✕ **Maralene's Hungry Fox.** When you're feeling homesick and long for your mom's cooking, this is the diner to visit. The food, especially at breakfast, exceeds typical diner fare—try the homemade breads and golden hash browns. The lovable, frumpy waitresses call everyone "honey." *4637 E. Broadway Blvd.,* ☎ *520/326–2835. No credit cards.*

Outer Tucson

$$$ ✕ **Café Terra Cotta.** With a dining room of light woods and bright hues, this exemplary southwestern restaurant establishes a warm, elegant tone for such tantalizing fare as open tomato-basil ravioli with green-lip mussels, sea scallops, and shrimp. ✉ *4310 N. Campbell Ave.,* ☎ *520/577–8100.*

$–$$ ✕ **Mi Nidito.** You'll find all the traditional Sonoran dishes, along with a few attempts at healthful cooking, including a taco jammed with cheese, avocado, tomatoes, onions, and sprouts. The best of the South 4th Avenue Mexican restaurants. ✉ *1813 S. 4th Ave.,* ☎ *520/622–5081.*

Coffeehouse Culture

Cup Café and Library of Congress. Off the lobby of the fabulous, deliriously nonconformist Hotel Congress (*see* Sleeps, *below*), this two-room, coffee-and-sandwiches hangout crawls with waifish Meat Puppets groupies and boys in black mascara. The hotel's latest venture is a cyber space, the Library of Congress, where you can surf the net. ✉ *311 E. Congress St.,* ☎ *520/798–1618.*

Rainbow Planet. This cozy tile-floor coffeehouse with serapes and southwestern colors acts as a perfect complement to the Wingspan queer community center and the hoppin' bar, IBT's (*see* Scenes, *below*), both of which are steps away. There's a nice selection of gay magazines, coffees, and light snacks. ✉ *606 N. 4th Ave.,* ☎ *520/620–1770.*

SCENES

Gay nightlife in Tucson is unflashy but gregarious, small but diverse. The city's small-town flavor keeps the typical bar atmosphere open, chatty, and distinctly uncruisy. Most gay bars have a coed clientele, while several predominantly straight clubs and bars—especially around 4th Avenue and the university—have gay followings. Tucson fosters a strong underground music and arts scene. The under-30 set spends a lot of time, money, and energy trying to look dirty and dated, and, as with most countercultural scenes, nose rings, tattoos, and Day-Glo dyed hair are common.

Prime Suspects

Ain't Nobody's Bizness. This is the snazziest gay bar in the city, with soft lighting, plenty of seating, pool tables, a great dance floor, and go-go dancers on weekends. Most intriguing is a small, soundproof, no-smoking parlor off the main room, done with colonial reproductions; it strongly resembles the lobby of a fancy hotel—and even has a house phone. The staff is amiable and outgoing. ⊠ *2900 E. Broadway Blvd.*, ☎ *520/318–4838. Crowd: 85/15 f/m, stylish, yuppie, lots of lipstick and good hair, mostly under 35.*

Boom Boom's. Tucson's largest and most popular dance club draws the stand-and-model crowd. Devotees like the sprawling layout's of two distinct dance floors, each offering a different style of music or theme of entertainment, depending on the night. Folks mingle in an intimate bar between them. ⊠ *2520 N. Oracle Rd.*, ☎ *520/882– 5799. Crowd: 70/30 m/f, mostly under 35, very mixed racially, club kids, guppies, quite cruisy.*

Club Congress and the Tap Room at Hotel Congress. The gay-friendly Hotel Congress has a small beer tavern, a coffeehouse, and a club with terrific live acts. Most bands are cutting-edge, and plenty of big names come here. The Tap Room has a bar with stools and booths, and it gets a loud, heavy-smoking crowd of all types—gays, straights, Deadheads, punks. Very groovy—kind of like Seattle in the desert. ⊠ *311 Congress St.*, ☎ *520/ 622–8848. Crowd: 85/15 gay/straight; young, wild, and grungy in club; all ages and types but mellower in Tap Room.*

IBT's (It's 'Bout Time). A nice bar to mix with locals, IBT's is amid 4th Avenue's artsy buzz. It has a small dance floor and plenty of seating, and in back a large landscaped and covered patio with a separate bar. It's both atmospheric and unpretentious—with friendly bartenders and a great mix of customers. ⊠ *616 N. 4th Ave.*, ☎ *520/882–3053. Crowd: 70/30 m/f, 20s to 40s, students, artists, singles and couples, a few stand-and-model types.*

Venture-N. Tucson's only rough-and-tough leather bar, Venture-N has a shady atmosphere, with construction signs lining the otherwise dark walls. The staff and patrons, though, are approachable and don't seem to mind people who aren't leather aficionados. A small boutique sells pain-inducing trinkets and tools. ⊠ *1239 N. 6th Ave.*, ☎ *520/882–8224. Crowd: mostly male, 30s and older, leather with a cowboy slant, butch.*

Neighborhood Haunts

The small, dark, smoky, seedy, but fun-filled **Graduate** (⊠ 23 W. University Blvd., ☎ 520/622– 9233) hosts a colorful assortment of guys—many of whom have graduated to social security. **Hours** (⊠ 3455 E. Grant Rd., ☎ 520/327–3390) is a mixed-gay/lesbian, "no bullshit, no attitude" bar, low on ambience. The **Stonewall/Eagle** (⊠ 2921 N. 1st Ave., ☎ 520/ 624–8805), once a leather bar, is now divided in two, being more of a neighborhood place on one side and a dance hall on the other—it has a devoted local following and gets quite crowded on weekends.

Action

There is one sex plex in town, the outrageous and mixed gay/straight **Tropicana Hotel and Adult Bookstore** (⊠ 617 W. Miracle Mile, ☎ 520/622–2289), a ready source of cheap dates, cheap rooms (at hourly rates), and plenty of porn. Open 24 hours.

SLEEPS

Because the city is both a leisure and a business destination, Tucson has a terrific variety of accommodations. You'll find B&Bs, both downtown and in the desert outskirts, plus luxury resorts and the usual city hotels and motor lodges. Unless you're here on business or yearn to see Tucson's urban side, you should spend at least part of your stay in the desert.

For price ranges, *see* lodging chart B at the front of this guide.

Large Hotel and Resorts

Downtown

$$$–$$$$ ▥ **Arizona Inn.** This 1930s 14-acre resort is just east of the U of A and has the most luxurious guest rooms and public areas of any hotel in Tucson proper. Accommodations are large, with patios and fireplaces. ✉ *2200 E. Elm St., 85719,* ☎ *520/325–1541 or 800/933–1093,* FAX *520/881–5830. 86 rooms. Restaurants, pool.*

$$ ▥ **Innsuites Hotel Tucson.** The gayest game in town, this cheerful hotel usually hosts the gay rodeo and actively markets itself to the community. It's just off the interstate, near 4th Avenue's and Congress Street's nightlife and restaurants. ✉ *475 N. Granada St., 85705,* ☎ *520/622–3000 or 800/446–6589,* FAX *520/882–0893. 300 rooms. Restaurant, pool, exercise room.*

$ ▥ **Hotel Congress.** This delightfully peculiar hotel appeals to a decidedly hip budget-oriented crowd of scenesters and students—its coffeehouse, dance club, and bars are legendary. Rooms, though no-frills, have been vastly improved in recent years and offer funky character at bargain prices— some youth dorm beds are also available. ✉ *311 E. Congress St., 85701,* ☎ *520/622–8848 or 800/722–8848,* FAX *520/792–6366, Web site www.hotcong.com. 40 rooms. Restaurant.*

Outer Tucson

$$$$ ▥ **Loews Ventana Canyon Resort.** This desert getaway offers the best southern Arizona resort experience money can buy, but gets a lot of stuffed shirts and dishes out a bit of attitude. Still, it's sumptuous and sensitively designed to blend in with the Coronado National Forest rising up behind it. ✉ *7000 N. Resort Dr., 85750,* ☎ *520/299–2020 or 800/234–5117,* FAX *520/299–6832. 398 rooms. Restaurants, pools, health club.*

Guest Houses

Downtown

$$–$$$ ▥ **Adobe Rose.** A short walk from the U of A campus, this enchanting adobe B&B has the feel of a traditional Santa Fe home—thanks in part to lodge-pole pine furniture, kiva fireplaces, southwestern art and decorative elements. ✉ *940 N. Olsen Ave., 85719,* ☎ *520/318–4644 or 800/328–4122,* FAX *520/325–0055. 3 rooms with TV and private bath. Pool. Full breakfast. Mostly straight.*

$$–$$$ ▥ **Catalina Park Inn.** Hosted by two extremely friendly and knowledgeable guys transplanted from San Francisco, this 1927 Neoclassical Revival inn blends Californian and New Mexican styles and furnishings to create a sophisticated but unpretentious ambience. The house is filled with antiques, Mexican mahogany woodworking, and arts and crafts, art deco, and art nouveau details. ✉ *309 E. 1st St., 85705,* ☎ *520/792–4541 or 800/792–4885,* FAX *520/792–0838. 5 rooms with phone, TV, and private bath. 1 cottage. Full breakfast. Mixed gay/straight.*

$$ ▥ **Casa Alegre.** Phyllis Florek's inn is set in an unfancy yet warm stucco house filled with Craftsman-inspired built-in cabinets, century-old furnishings, and hand-stenciling; each room has a different theme—the Hacienda Room has hand-carved pieces, another has southwestern decor. ✉ *316 E. Speedway Blvd., 85705,* ☎ *520/628–1800 or 800/628–5654,* FAX *520/792–1880. 5 rooms with private bath. Pool, hot tub. Full breakfast. Mostly straight.*

Outer Tucson

$–$$ ⊞ **Casa Tierra.** In case you'd forgotten the definition of remote, this wonderful inn is smack in the middle of the desert, just over the mountains west of Tucson. Rooms surround a lushly landscaped, shady, terraced courtyard, which is steps from an outdoor Jacuzzi. Especially popular with women. ⊠ *11155 W. Calle Pima, 85743,* ☎ FAX *520/578–3058. 3 rooms with private bath. Full breakfast. Mixed gay/straight.*

$–$$ ⊞ **Tortuga Roja.** The only predominantly gay establishment in town, this 1950s adobe-brick home is on the usually dry Santa Cruz River, just north of town. Rooms are large and have tile floors, beam ceilings, and TVs and VCRs. A Jacuzzi and pool are out by the pretty redbrick patio, opposite which is the cottage, which has its own kitchen and fireplace—a great value. ⊠ *2800 E. River Rd., 85718,* ☎ *520/577–6822 or 800/467–6822. 2 rooms with phone, TV, and private bath; 1 cottage. Pool, hot tub. Continental breakfast. Gay male/lesbian.*

THE LITTLE BLACK BOOK

At Your Fingertips

ABC Taxi (☎ 520/623–7979). **Arizona/Sonora Proyecto SIDA** (☎ 520/882–3933). **Gay and Lesbian Information Hotline** (☎ 520/624–1799). **Metropolitan Tucson Convention and Visitors Bureau** (⊠ 130 S. Scott Ave. 85701, ☎ 520/624–1817 or 800/638–8350). **Rape Crisis Line** (☎ 520/327–7273). **Tucson AIDS Project Hotline** (☎ 520/326–2437). **Sun Tran** (☎ 520/792–9222). *Tucson Weekly* (☎ 520/792–3630, Web site tucsonweekly.com). **Wingspan Gay and Lesbian Community Center** (⊠ 422 N. 4th Ave., ☎ 520/624–1779). **Women's Information and Referral Service** (☎ 520/881–1794).

Gay Media

The weekly *Observer* (☎ 520/622–7176, Web site www.bonzo.com/observer) has served the gay and lesbian community since the mid-'70s. All of the Phoenix-based rags also offer limited information on Tucson (*see* Gay Media *in* Chapter 29).

BOOKSTORES

Antigone Books (⊠ 600 N. 4th Ave., ☎ 520/792–3715) is a stellar feminist bookstore, with a wealth of material for lesbians and quite a few general gay titles, too. Women should stop in and leaf through the community resources notebook. Excellent gay-friendly general-interest options include **The Bookmark** (⊠ 5001 E. Speedway Blvd., ☎ 520/881–6350) and **Bookstop** (⊠ 2504 N. Campbell Rd., ☎ 520/326–6661), which specializes in used titles.

Working Out

There isn't a gay gym, but the downtown **YMCA** (⊠ 60 W. Alameda Ave., ☎ 520/623–5200) and the **World Gym** (⊠ 1240 N. Stone Ave., ☎ 520/882–8788) are both very accommodating.

44 Out in Washington, D.C.

IN TERMS OF THE SIZE AND VISIBILITY of its gay population, Washington is one of America's great gay cities. More gay, lesbian, and AIDS organizations have their headquarters here than in any other American city, including the Human Rights Campaign, the National Coalition of People with AIDS, the National Federation of Parents and Friends of Lesbians and Gays (PFLAG), and the National Gay and Lesbian Task Force.

Outsiders may perceive Washington's gays as shaggy throwbacks to '60s grass-roots activists—constantly demonstrating, petitioning, and getting their hands dirty fighting the good fight. The fact is, if you want to fight for gay rights by working within the system, you come to D.C.; activists here are among America's most conservative as far as the means by which they mobilize.

Many of D.C.'s gay residents keep a lid on their sexual orientation—their careers often depend on remaining closeted. But others have carved a livelihood out of their sexual identity, working for think tanks, lobbies, or organizations that exist for gay activism or at least relate to it in a positive way. Or, they might work for the government, in which case being either openly gay or remaining closeted has a significant bearing on their political identity.

Not so long ago the only way you could make progress on behalf of gay rights was to work from outside the system. Now there's incentive to dress the part of an insider, learn the ropes, and work the system. Conforming and assimilating are the keys to success for many. The effects of this "respectable" gay sensibility are obvious in the District. In gay bars you see more collared shirts than leather, drag, or short shorts. And although being open and proud is fashionable, being politically militant or effeminate and campy is frowned upon, ditto for having a pierced septum, or wearing leather chaps or pink-triangle earrings.

THE LAY OF THE LAND

D.C.'s street grid is tricky to navigate. The District is divided into four quadrants: northwest, northeast, southwest, and southeast, with the Capitol Building at the center. Downtown streets run at right angles and come in two flavors: Those that run north–south are numbered; most that run east–west are lettered A through W (J does not exist and I is often spelled "Eye"). Avenues, which are named after states, run in every direction. The same intersection, 4th and D for instance, may appear in all four quadrants; the NE, NW, SE, or SW at the end of the address tells you which quadrant it's in. The street address itself is determined by which streets the building falls between. An address in the 1400s on R street falls between 14th and 15th streets; an address in the 700s on 15th Street falls between G and H streets (the seventh and eighth letters of the alphabet).

Safety is a legitimate concern in Washington. It's best not to stray off the beaten path, particularly in the NE and SE quadrants. At night avoid walking alone. But lesbians and gays will find the city tolerant on the whole. In almost any of the neighborhoods described below, same-sex couples can walk together without much fear of harassment.

Dupont Circle

A few blocks northwest of the White House, Dupont Circle is one of the gayest neighborhoods in the country. Especially nice are Connecticut Avenue north of the circle, 17th Street between P and S streets, and, although a bit dowdier, P Street west of the circle.

Washington is a city of open spaces, parks, statuary, and grand 19th-century architecture, and nowhere is this more evident than around Dupont Circle. After World War II, professionals fled to the suburbs, abandoning the area to hippies, lesbians and gays, and other counterculturalists. Gentrification has reintroduced high rents and a slightly snobby cachet, but the neighborhood remains tolerant and liberal.

The **Phillips Collection** (⊠ 1600–1612 21st St. NW, ☎ 202/387–2151) is the first permanent museum of modern art in the nation; represented are Georges Braque, Pierre Bonnard, Mark Rothko, Paul Klee, and Henri Matisse, as well as gay artists David Hockney, Marsden Hartley, Charles Demuth, and David Hare.

Follow P Street from Dupont Circle a couple of blocks to Rock Creek and you'll discover a large plot of grassy slope and dense shrubbery dubbed, affectionately, the **P Street Beach.** At night this area is somewhat cruisy; by day, in warm weather, it's nature's gay tanning salon.

Extending southeast from Dupont Circle on **Embassy Row** (along Massachusetts Ave. NW) are 150 of the city's foreign embassies.

North and West

An artsy but gentrified set began moving to **Adams-Morgan,** due north of Dupont Circle, in the early '80s. Offbeat shops and hip eateries mix with rows of ethnic restaurants and residential enclaves. Lesbians and gays live, shop, and eat here, but the population is mostly immigrants and young professionals trying to elude the tight grip of conformity in other yuppie neighborhoods.

Adams-Morgan is a popular hunting ground for art deco, Art Nouveau, and other 20th-century furnishings—pieces you might recall from the living rooms of Samantha Stevens and Carol Brady. Most of these spots are along 18th Street between Florida Avenue and Columbia Road. A must-see is the **Brass Knob** (⊠ 2311 18th St. NW, ☎ 202/332–3370), but all of them are great. For Ghanian carvings, clothing, and crafts, check out **Kobos** (⊠ 2444 18th St. NW, ☎ 202/332–9580).

The once slum-infested **U Street Corridor** (around the intersection with 14th Street NW) has become an extension of Adams-Morgan, with the opening of hip, diverse clubs, restaurants, and shops.

West of here in **Cleveland Park,** a neighborhood many D.C. bigwigs call home, you'll find the 160-acre **National Zoological Park** (⊠ 3001 Connecticut Ave. NW, ☎ 202/673–4800 or 202/673–4717).

Georgetown and Foggy Bottom

Straddling the shores of Rock Creek are these two upscale neighborhoods, an easy walk southwest of Dupont Circle. Georgetown has the bulk of Washington's oldest homes, including D.C.'s only pre-Revolutionary building, the **Old Stone House** (⊠ 3051 M St. NW, ☎ 202/426–6851) museum, and the Federal **Dumbarton House** (⊠ 2715 Q St. NW, ☎ 202/337–2288), which is filled with impressive period art and furniture. Walk along the historic **Chesapeake & Ohio Canal,** or shop along **M Street** and **Wisconsin Avenue.**

The Mall and Capitol Hill

The **Mall** and **Capitol Hill** contain many attractions and bustle all day with government and commercial activity. The area quiets down at night. Eastern Capitol Hill, however, especially between **Stanton Park** and **Seward Square,** is booming as gay and straight couples move in and restore the still-affordable 19th-century homes. A few gay bars and restaurants are around the Eastern Market stop of the Metro rapid transit system (*see* Getting Around, *below*).

You can begin your day at the Mall, the eastern half of which is dominated by the **Smithsonian museums** (☎ 202/357–2700)—including the National Air and Space Museum, the National Museum of American History, and the National Galleries of Art. The **U.S. Holocaust Memorial Museum** (⊠ 100 Raoul Wallenberg Pl. SW, ☎ 202/488–0400) distributes a pamphlet, "Homosexuals," that details the plight of gay men and lesbians in Nazi-occupied Europe; gay video testimonies and books are included in the library.

At the eastern end of the Mall are the **U.S. Capitol** (☎ 202/224–3121); the **U.S. Botanic Gardens** (⊠ 1st St. and Maryland Ave. SW, ☎ 202/225–8333); the **Library of Congress** (⊠ Independence Ave. between 1st and 2nd Sts. NE, ☎ 202/707–6400); and the **Supreme Court Building** (⊠ 1st and E. Capitol Sts. NE, ☎ 202/479–3000).

The western half of the Mall contains many of America's most important monuments and memorials, including the **Franklin Delano Roosevelt Memorial** (☎ 202/619–7222); the **Jefferson Memorial** (☎ 202/426–6821); the **Washington Monument** (☎ 202/426–6840); the **Lincoln Memorial** (☎ 202/426–6895); and the **Vietnam Veterans Memorial** (☎ 202/634–1568). The monuments are striking at night when illuminated by spotlights. The **White House** (⊠ 1600 Pennsylvania Ave., ☎ 202/755–7798) is, despite long lines, worth touring.

Nearby are several galleries. The Beaux-Arts **Corcoran Gallery of Art** (⊠ 17th St. and New York Ave. NW, ☎ 202/638–1439) contains more than 11,000 works of art. Several blocks north of the Mall is the **National Museum of Women in the Arts** (⊠ 1250 New York Ave. NW, ☎ 202/783–5000). The **National Portrait Gallery** and the **National Museum of American Art** are housed in the Old Patent Office Building (⊠ 8th and G Sts. NW, ☎ 202/357–2700).

Old Downtown and **Chinatown,** along and south of Massachusetts Avenue between 14th and 6th streets, has undergone a renaissance. To the south, the up-and-coming **Penn Quarter,** which extends along Pennsylvania Avenue between 3rd and 12th streets, has seen the opening of new art galleries and funky cafés and shops.

Arlington

Until 1845 part of the District but now a northern Virginia suburb, **Arlington** has a few attractions but a sizable couples-oriented queer community. The **Arlington National Cemetery** (☎ 703/607–8052) has more than 200,000 graves, including those of John F. Kennedy, Jackie Onassis, Robert Kennedy, and many distinguished war veterans. North of the park, on the southern border of the neighborhood of Rosslyn, is the 78-foot-tall **U.S. Marine Corps War Memorial** (a.k.a. the Iwo Jima Memorial), for years one of the cruisiest spots in D.C.

GETTING AROUND

Washington is a confusing city to drive in, and it's generally hard to find parking. Conditions are a little better around Dupont Circle and Adams-Morgan, where you can sometimes snag a spot on the street, but you're better off parking in a hotel or private lot. Parking rules are strictly and aggressively enforced.

D.C.'s Metro is one of the cleanest and safest mass-transit systems in the country. Though it doesn't reach all the neighborhoods you might want to play in (Georgetown or the southeast), it does run into the Maryland and Virginia 'burbs. New branches are still under construction; the entire system will be completed in 2001. Taking a taxi in the District is a crapshoot. Many drivers are surly and will take advantage of D.C.'s meterless zone system by whisking unsuspecting tourists circuitously to their destination, working up the fare. They'll get you where you're going, and the fare will be less than it is in most major cities, but no two drivers will charge the same fare.

EATS

Politicking involves schmoozing that works best over a bottle of wine and a good meal. Add a stream of hungry tourists, and you can see why the city has so many eateries. More impressive than the quantity of restaurants is the culinary diversity; from Latin American to Central African to East Asian to Central European, every conceivable cuisine is well represented. Most restaurants are gay-friendly, but the queerest spots are around Dupont Circle.

For price ranges, *see* dining Chart A at the front of this guide.

Dupont Circle and Adams-Morgan

$$$$ ✕ **Nora.** This nouvelle organic eatery is a high point among Dupont Circle's many fine restaurants, though the prices run rather steep. For starters consider grilled marinated squid with orange cherry tomatoes and black olives. Popular with foodies. ⊠ *2213 M St. NW,* ☎ *202/797–4860.*

$$$$ ✕ **Obelisk.** The limited prix-fixe menu at this darling of the D.C. dining scene offers a meat, fish, or poultry entrée, always with innovative ingredients and preparation. The setting is a sleek, austere space with tightly squeezed-together tables. ⊠ *2029 P St. NW,* ☎ *202/872–1180.*

$$$–$$$$ ✕ **Vidalia.** Dutch cabinets display antique plates, and dried arrangements of fruits and vegetables serve as wall hangings at this take on a country manor. Indigenous American foods star: Maine oysters, Shenandoah trout, Virginia veal. ⊠ *1990 M St. NW,* ☎ *202/659–1990.*

$$–$$$ ✕ **Cashion's Eats Place.** Rustic and warmly lit, Cashion's has the ambience of a down-home southern restaurant—the chef is from Jackson, Mississippi. The daily-changing American menu borrows as much from France and Morocco as it does from Dixie. Braised duck breast with foie gras, red cabbage, and fresh chestnuts is one specialty of the house; or try the lamb shank with couscous, turnips, pumpkin zucchini, pearl onions, chickpeas, and a harissa sauce. ⊠ *1819 Columbia Rd. NW,* ☎ *202/797–1819.*

$$–$$$ ✕ **Grill from Ipanema.** The hunky waiters account for some of the success of this queer-popular Brazilian restaurant in the District's culinary United Nations, Adams-Morgan. Try the *feijoada* (a traditional stew of black beans

and smoked sausage). Just beware that as few as two *caipirinhas* (a sweet but dangerous Brazilian cocktail) leave most patrons dazed and dizzy—but still rather happy. ⊠ *1858 Columbia Rd.,* ☏ *202/986–0757.*

$$–$$$ ✕ **La Tomate.** You can stare at pretty passersby from Tomate's triangular, arbored patio, which looks south toward Dupont Circle. The chichi French and Italian food—fresh monkfish with grain mustard, shallots, white wine, and a touch of cream—is dependable, the service less so. ⊠ *1701 Connecticut Ave. NW,* ☏ *202/667–5505.*

$$–$$$ ✕ **Mercury Grill.** This classy town house is an ideal rendezvous for predinner drinks or a terrific setting for the main event. New American creations like pan-seared southwestern chicken breast with a tomato-corn relish and sweet-potato puree earn the chefs high marks. ⊠ *1602 17th St. NW,* ☏ *202/667–5937.*

$$–$$$ ✕ **Perry's.** A popular Japanese restaurant with a commendable sushi bar, Perry's is most famous for its Sunday drag brunch—a delightful experience if you don't mind a towering drag queen plopping down on your lap and scrambling your eggs to the disco remix of "Don't Cry for Me, Argentina." The non-Japanese, all-you-can-eat brunch buffet is excellent—raw oysters and mussels, broiled fish, and chicken, all served with spicy Latin-inspired sauces. On warm days you can dine on the roof deck. ⊠ *1811 Columbia Rd. NW,* ☏ *202/234–6218.*

$$–$$$ ✕ **Trumpets.** This favorite of D.C. power fags prepares gutsy, if contrived, New American grub, such as North Carolina barbecue quail on corn-scallion griddle cakes. Artful presentation and swank digs add to the taste-bud-pleasing experience. And when you're finished dining, enjoy drinks in the stylish bar. ⊠ *17th and Q Sts. NW,* ☏ *202/232–4141.*

$$ ✕ **Annie's Paramount Steakhouse.** For years D.C.'s "gay Denny's" has been pleasing late-night disco bunnies with steak and eggs, burgers, and other meat-and-potatoes dishes. A mixed butch crowd tends to hang out at the fairly cruisy bar. The midnight brunch is a popular break from the bars. ⊠ *1609 17th St. NW,* ☏ *202/232–0395.*

$$ ✕ **Il Radicchio.** One of the best and flashiest eateries along 17th Street, Il Radicchio is surprisingly affordable, offering dozens of designer pizzas and lavish salads. Pasta is another specialty; choose from 22 types of homemade sauce. ⊠ *1509 17th St. NW,* ☏ *202/986–2627; in Georgetown,* ⊠ *1211 Wisconsin Ave. NW,* ☏ *202/337–2627; on Capitol Hill,* ⊠ *223 Pennsylvania Ave. SE,* ☏ *202/547-5114.*

$$ ✕ **Sala Thai.** One of D.C.'s best Thai restaurants, this eatery is right along P Street's row of gay bars. Try the shrimp in curry-peanut sauce; when in season the soft-shell crab is as tasty here as anywhere in the city. ⊠ *2016 P St. NW,* ☏ *202/872–1144.*

$$ ✕ **Sol.** Both the service and the food have been uneven, but for the most part this recent addition to cruisy R Street rises above its mediocre neighbors. The food ranges from Caribbean to southwestern to Continental; consider grilled mahimahi with mashed yucca and vegetables with a thyme-shallot sauce. Grab a table on the spacious streetside patio. ⊠ *17th and R Sts. NW,* ☏ *202/232–6965.*

$–$$ ✕ **Café Luna.** This queer eatery serves straightforward pastas, pizzas, and salads (the tuna Niçoise is particularly fine). The prices are reasonable and the food is pretty good, but the main point here is to see and be seen. Video showings and poetry readings are featured on many nights. The same folks run **Skewers** (☏ *202/387–7400*), upstairs, which has kebabs, hummus, and other Middle Eastern specialties. ⊠ *1633 P St. NW,* ☏ *202/ 387–4005.*

$–$$ ✕ **City Lights of China.** D.C.'s top Chinese restaurant is close to Dupont Circle, set in a swank art deco building with period-style decor. Best bets: the fried dumplings or shark-fin soup as a starter, the orange chicken as an entrée. ⊠ *1731 Connecticut Ave. NW,* ☏ *202/265–6688.*

576

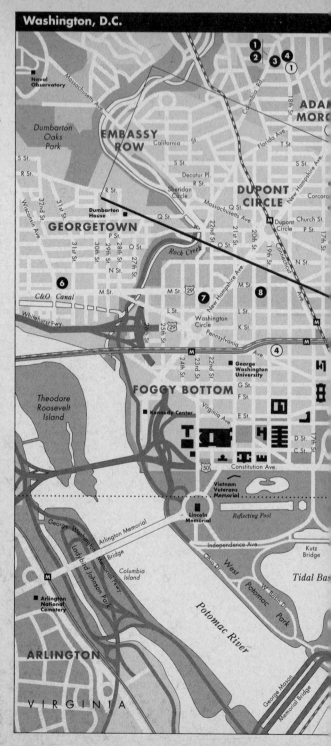

Washington, D.C.

Dupont Circle

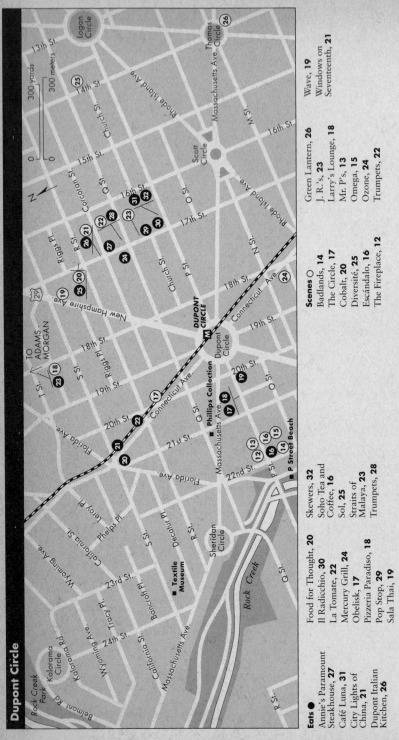

Eats ●
Annie's Paramount
Steakhouse, **27**
Café Luna, **31**
City Lights of
China, **21**
Dupont Italian
Kitchen, **26**

Food for Thought, **20**
Il Radicchio, **30**
La Tomate, **22**
Mercury Grill, **24**
Obelisk, **17**
Pizzeria Paradiso, **18**
Pop Stop, **29**
Sala Thai, **19**

Skewers, **32**
Soho Tea and
Coffee, **16**
Sol, **25**
Straits of
Malaya, **23**
Trumpets, **28**

Scenes ○
Badlands, **14**
The Circle, **17**
Cobalt, **20**
Diversité, **25**
Escándalo, **16**
The Fireplace, **12**

Green Lantern, **26**
J. R.'s, **23**
Larry's Lounge, **18**
Mr. P's, **13**
Omega, **15**
Ozone, **24**
Trumpets, **22**

Wave, **19**
Windows on
Seventeenth, **21**

$–$$ ✕ **Straits of Malaya.** This formal Malaysian restaurant has huge windows looking out onto the street, and a lively bar—many gay folks stop in for drinks before heading elsewhere. A favorite on the menu is the fiery Malaysian beef curry. ⊠ *1836 18th St. NW,* ☎ *202/483–1483.*

$ ✕ **Dupont Italian Kitchen.** Another renowned but unimpressive member of 17th Street's gay-eats row, the Kitchen has a convivial, festive atmosphere with outdoor seats that are perfect for ogling the parade of boys off the Hill. The hearty, heavy Italian cuisine offers no surprises. ⊠ *17th and R Sts. NW,* ☎ *202/328–3222.*

$ ✕ **Fasika's.** It's almost de rigueur among Washingtonians to take out-of-town guests to Adams-Morgan for Ethiopian food, and Fasika's serves some of the best. Meals center around a spicy stew called *watt,* which may contain chicken, lamb, beef, or shrimp. You use no silverware but instead scoop up your food with the aid of *injera,* a spongy flat bread. ⊠ *2447 18th St. NW,* ☎ *202/797–7673.*

$ ✕ **Food for Thought.** A brigade of Birkenstockers descends on this earthy storefront known for folk music (most nights) and a community bulletin board. Among the meatless good-for-you adventures are the Reuben with Russian dressing, sauerkraut, and vegetables on rye, and the legendary black-bean dip. ⊠ *1738 Connecticut Ave. NW,* ☎ *202/797–1095.*

$ ✕ **Pizzeria Paradisio.** The brick-oven wood-fired pizzas have earned Paradisio kudos and long lines (come around 5 to avoid the crowds). The small dining room looks into the open-air kitchen full of cute young chefs preparing these thin-crust wonders. The trompe l'oeil columns and blue sky ceiling are clever, but the acoustics suck. ⊠ *2029 P St. NW,* ☎ *202/223–1245.*

Capitol Hill Environs

$$$–$$$$ ✕ **Red Sage.** George Bush and Bill Clinton have one thing in common: They've both dined amid the barbed wire and lizards in this extravagantly decorated faux adobe warren of dining rooms, the second home of Santa Fe chef Mark Miller. Check out the chile bar upstairs, or go for the artfully arranged fare downstairs (duck breast with habañero peppers and fig sausage, red chile risotto). ⊠ *605 14th St. NW,* ☎ *202/638–4444.*

$$–$$$ ✕ **Café Atlántico.** This hangout for hotshot politicos is notable for its dramatically presented Latino-Caribbean fare: soy-marinated quail with beet sauce and coconut risotto, chicken sausage with pepper coulis and shiitake-coconut polenta. Loud and stylish, Atlántico is in the heart of the trendy Penn Quarter. ⊠ *405 8th St. NW,* ☎ *202/393–0812.*

$$–$$$ ✕ **Two Quail.** This romantic town house in Capitol Hill has long been one of the city's better-regarded eateries, owing to its eclectic Continental and American cuisine—pan-seared tuna with onion marmalade, and chicken stuffed with cornbread and pecans are a couple of faves. ⊠ *320 Massachusetts Ave. NE,* ☎ *202/543–8030.*

$$ ✕ **Banana Café.** Popular for its upstairs piano bar (*see* Scenes, *below*), this is one of the most festive gay haunts on Capitol Hill. Steaks, lime-garlic chicken, plantain soup, and burritos are on the long menu of Latin American specialties. The staff is warm and accommodating, the crowd diverse in age, gender, and style. ⊠ *500 8th St. SE,* ☎ *202/543–5906.*

$$ ✕ **Café Berlin.** If you're in a Christopher Isherwood kind of mood, stop by the Café and fill up on hearty German dishes (such as smoked loin of pork with sauerkraut) and the smiles of cute men. It's beside equally popular Two Quail (*see above*) and has outdoor seating in summer. ⊠ *322-B Massachusetts Ave. NE,* ☎ *202/543–7656.*

$–$$ ✕ **Mr. Henry's.** This Capitol Hill pub, with one of the best (antique) jukeboxes in town, has long been a friend to Washington's lesbian and gay community. The great burgers come with many toppings. Grab a seat on the sidewalk in good weather. Upstairs is a smoke-free cabaret with a mix of piano and folk acts (*see* Scenes, *below*). ⊠ *601 Pennsylvania Ave. SE,* ☎ *202/546–8412.*

Elsewhere in the District

$$ ✕ **Coppi's.** Tops among the scruffy-swank cafés along bohemian U Street, Coppi's is part tapas bar, part pizzeria. Sample sublime escargots; then move on to a hearty portion of whitefish sautéed with black olives, garlic, and anchovies. High ceilings, jazzy tunes, and exotic murals impart the right mood. ⊠ *1414 U St. NW,* ☎ *202/319–7773.*

Coffeehouse Culture

In addition to the full-time venues listed below, the **Coffee House for HIV+ Friends, Family, and Lovers** (⊠ 2111 Florida Ave. NW, ☎ 202/483–3310) is a friendly hangout open on Saturdays from 7:30 PM.

Pop Stop. A hangout for Washington's alternafags, Pop Stop is open all night on weekends. Sometimes cruisier than nearby J. R.'s (*see* Scenes, *below*), it can bristle with attitude. The second floor looks like the lounge of a college dorm—people read in here for hours. ⊠ *1513 17th St. NW,* ☎ *202/328–0881.*

Soho Tea and Coffee. This queer cyber café and java house on the ground floor of a bland apartment complex has art exhibits, live music, and a sexy crowd. ⊠ *2150 P St. NW,* ☎ *202/463-7646.*

SCENES

There's some disagreement as to whether Washington's nightlife is friendly—some say it's unbelievably so, others insist it's chilly—so your results may vary. The city is multiracial with an ethnically diverse gay community; some of the neighborhood bars are predominantly Latin or African-American, but only in recent years have the bars around Dupont Circle begun to draw a less homogeneous crowd. The clubs east of the circle, along 17th Street, tend to attract mostly white-male guppies. Those to the west (as well as The Circle nightclub, just north) get a mix of ages and backgrounds, but very few women. Lesbians often head to Hung Jury in Foggy Bottom and Phase One on Capitol Hill.

Most of the raunchier gay bars and sex clubs are in a rough southeastern Washington neighborhood near the Navy Yard. You should never walk around here at night—even by day it's a little dicey.

Prime Suspects

Badlands. The largest disco near Dupont Circle is in an old brick building. On the main level is a large dance floor, behind which is an alluringly dark video bar with blue lights. Upstairs is a rec room with pool tables and, behind it, a small cabaret with mediocre drag and slightly better karaoke. Though Badlands remains popular, it has has lost some of its edge. ⊠ *1415 22nd St. NW,* ☎ *202/296–0505. Crowd: 80/20 m/f, mostly under 35, clean-shaven, clonish, stand-and-model.*

The Circle. This three-story complex a few blocks north of Dupont Circle is three distinct spaces. The basement and street-level floors contain bars, dance areas, and lounges; one bar has a jukebox, another has pool tables. The top floor has a large video lounge and an outdoor terrace overlooking Connecticut Avenue. The crowd varies depending on the night of the week and the floor you're on; women head for the basement, guys for the terrace, which can be cruisy. This is a low-key hangout that's free of attitude. ⊠ *1629 Connecticut Ave. NW,* ☎ *202/462–5575. Crowd: 60/40 m/f, 20s to 40s, mixed racially, dressed-down, friendly.*

Cobalt. The popularity of this two-level guppie cruise bar means it's impossible to walk the entire place without sidling up to countless strangers, which is okay with most of these guys. Upstairs is split into two spaces, one with a tiny dance floor (but great music), the other with a long bar and lots of standing and modeling. The scene is slightly less chaotic downstairs. The few women who come here seem to be lipstick lesbians or straight. ⊠ *1639 R St. NW,* ☎ *202/232–6969. Crowd: mostly male, young, barely distinguishable from J. R.'s.*

Escándalo. Long and narrow, with brightly colored walls, this is supposed to be a dance spot, though everyone seems happiest crowded around the small bar up front. The drag shows are among the best in the city, and the crowd is diverse and outgoing. ⊠ *2122 P St. NW,* ☎ *202/822–8909. Crowd: 75/25 m/f, mostly 20s and 30s, largely Latino, a fair share of club kids.*

The Fireplace. Guys hit this D.C. standby when they're ready to meet somebody (and it's late, and their standards have dropped a couple of notches). Like a pair of old, comfortable shoes, the Fireplace keeps bringing them back. Downstairs, guys gather around a central bar; upstairs, young men stare at videos and each other. ⊠ *2161 P St. NW,* ☎ *202/293–1293. Crowd: mostly male, 20s to 40s, trashy-preppy, collegiate, racially mixed.*

Green Lantern. This refreshing, unpretentious bar in an old carriage house is a 20-minute walk from Dupont Circle, down an alley behind a Holiday Inn. There's a big, fairly safe parking lot outside with lots of Virginia and Maryland license plates. The split-level first floor has a bar below and a pool table up top. Upstairs, patrons gaze at porn and music videos. ⊠ *1335 Green Ct. NW,* ☎ *202/638–5133. Crowd: mostly male, flannel and Levi's, butch and beefy, late-20s to mid-30s, friendly, casual, on the make.*

Hung Jury. Given that Washington has more women than men and that it has an active lesbian community, it's kind of surprising that there aren't more nightspots for women. This is not to take anything away from the Hung Jury, which is a great club in Foggy Bottom. The only drawback: It's down a hard-to-find alley. Once inside you'll find a large dance floor, loud music, lots of seating, and video games and pool tables. ⊠ *1819 H St. NW,* ☎ *202/785–8181. Crowd: mostly lesbian, mix of lipstick meets soft butch, guppies, wide age range but young on weekends.*

J. R.'s. Welcome to the bar that everybody loves to hate. A work of hunter green, brass, and mirrors, J. R.'s is maligned because it epitomizes the city's standoffish, glaring manner. The ones who dump on it the loudest can't seem to get enough of the place: It's always packed. The bar is long and narrow; upstairs is an even smaller area, from which you can gawk at the crowd below. ⊠ *1519 17th St. NW,* ☎ *202/328–0090. Crowd: male, boys from the Hill, starched collars and stuffed shirts.*

Omega. Formerly the Frat House, the grandpa of Dupont Circle bars, Omega remodeled its downstairs recently; the slick black-tile floor, gilt-frame classical erotica, and improved lighting feel appealingly '80s. The upstairs hasn't changed much: a noisy video bar, a dark room (lots of groping) with one tiny TV showing porn, and a roadhouse-style room with pinball machines, a pool table, and soft music. ⊠ *2123 Twining Ct.,* ☎ *202/223–4917. Crowd: mostly male, 30s and 40s, high testosterone levels, otherwise diverse.*

Ozone. The Ozone is an extremely narrow two-level space with a small, sweaty, but hot dance floor. Behind that is a bar with some mod furnishings, and upstairs is a cozy loft with a balcony overlooking the action below. You have to like tight spaces to appreciate this place, and, judging from the weekend crowds, people do. Fridays are 18 and over. ⊠ *1214 18th St. NW,* ☎ *202/293–0303. Crowd: 80/20 m/f, 20s to early 30s, stylish, trendy, lots of club gear, a bit less suburban than Badlands.*

Remington's. The District's only country-western bar is a spacious club with a green-and-woodtone color scheme, two halves—one of which has a small but potent dance floor—plenty of space for mingling. The crowd is often bigger after work than late at night. You'll find some pool tables, video screens, and a friendly mix of cute southern queens and, increasingly, dykes. Tuesday is specifically for women, who are always welcome. ⊠ *639 Pennsylvania Ave. SE,* ☎ *202/543–3113. Crowd: 65/ 35 m/f, 30s and 40s, some cowboy garb, low attitude.*

Neighborhood Haunts

Bachelor's Mill/Back Door Pub (⊠ 1104 8th St. SE, ☎ 202/544–1931), a sprawling complex in a building near the main gate to the Navy Yard, is an African-American bar and disco. Always packed on weekends, it draws a younger, fast-paced crowd. On the other side of the city, **Nob Hill** (⊠ 1101 Kenyon St. NW, ☎ 202/797–1101) is also mostly African-American, but is quieter. The Circle, Tracks, Phase One (for women), and the Fireplace are popular among African-Americans. Also, in Dupont Circle, cruisy **Mr. P's** (⊠ 2147 P St. NW, ☎ 202/293–1064) draws a racial mix.

Although Hung Jury is bigger and more popular, **Phase One** (⊠ 525 8th St. SE, ☎ 202/544–6831) is a friendly racially mixed dyke bar that fills up on weekends. North of Capitol Hill, the city's tame leather scene centers around the **DC Eagle** (⊠ 639 New York Ave. NW, ☎ 202/347–6025), a dark bar in a bleak neighborhood with two floors of music and lounging.

For a while **Trumpets** (⊠ 1603 17th St. NW, ☎ 202/232–4141) was the city's see-and-be-seen cruise bar; the opening of Cobalt has greatly diminished the crowds, and now this is a mixed gay/straight lounge with good martinis and an upscale ambience. The restaurant is still stellar (*see* Eats, *above*). **Windows on Seventeenth** (⊠ 1635 17th St. NW, ☎ 202/328–0100), a mellow bar with a terrace and plenty of seating, is above Dupont Italian Kitchen. Older (mostly over 35), good-looking suits come here to mingle and network. **Larry's Lounge** (⊠ 1836 18th St. NW, ☎ 202/483–1483), attached to Straits of Malaya (*see* Eats, *above*) is a cheerful Adams-Morgan bar patronized by men and women. Several blocks north, **El Faro** (⊠ 2411 18th St. NW, ☎ 202/387–6554) draws a Latin-American crowd.

One-Nighters

Tracks, the city's largest dance club, has glowed pink on Saturday for many years but has lost its popularity. Some loathe the inconvenient and nasty location, others the obnoxious doormen and often aggressive crowds. Women's nights (once a month, usually on Tuesday or Thursday), however, remain a big deal. Inside are dozens of bars and a couple of dance floors. Tracks is by the Navy Yard Metro station, but consider cabbing it here. ⊠ *1111 1st St. SE,* ☎ *202/488–3320. Crowd: mostly gay and 80/20 m/f on Saturdays, straight and not necessarily gay-friendly other nights; spans genders and races, serious about dancing, wired.*

Hangin' with the Hets

On Capitol Hill, the second floors of the popular restaurants **Mr. Henry's** and the **Banana Café** (*see* Eats, *above*) present cabaret and live music; the latter has a decidedly Latino accent to match the spicy cuisine. Just north of Dupont Circle, the art deco–style **Wave** (⊠ 1731 New Hampshire Ave. NW, ☎ 202/234–3200), in the Carlyle Suites Hotel, is a great place for pre-dinner cocktails.

The hipster-infested U Street Corridor has quite a few clubs with mixed gay/straight followings. The swank **Chi-Cha Club** (⊠ 1624 U St. NW, ☎ 202/234–8400), with its comfy lounge seating, varnished-wood bar, and authentic Andean appetizers, draws as diverse a crowd as you'll find in D.C. **Diversité** (⊠ 1526 14th St. NW, ☎ 202/234–5740) is queerest on Sunday but always draws plenty of family.

Action

La Cage Aux Follies. The best club on D.C.'s infamous and impressive sex block, La Cage is a must for many visitors. Washington is among the few U.S. cities where male strippers shed *all* of their clothes. Guys shake and gyrate out of their scant attire—it's against the law to touch them, but . . . it's amazing what goes on here, and for that matter, what a couple of bucks can get you. Hanging around gay strip clubs is surprisingly acceptable among most circles in D.C.; you're apt to see all kinds of guys. ⊠ *18 O St. SE,* ☎ *202/554–3615. Crowd: male, horny, all ages but tending to the older side, lots of suits on weekdays.*

Near La Cage are several similar clubs, including the **Edge/Wet** (⊠ 56 L St. SE, ☎ 202/488–1200), which has strippers; **Club Washington** (⊠ 20 O St. SE, ☎ 202/488–7317), a gay bathhouse; and **Ziegfeld's** (⊠ 1345 Half St. SE, ☎ 202/554–5141), which has strippers but is better known for drag acts. All are in the Navy Yard neighborhood. Watch your back, your front, and your wallet.

Pride Emporium (⊠ 2147 P St. NW, ☎ 202/822–3984) sells porn, videos, toys, as well as pride goods, clothing, and other queer-positive products. Try the **Leather Rack** (⊠ 1723 Connecticut Ave. NW, ☎ 202/797–7401) for leather goods. The best-known erotica shop in the city (where well-known politicos are said to buy their whips and chains) is the **Pleasure Place** (⊠ 1710 Connecticut Ave. NW, ☎ 202/483–3297).

SLEEPS

D.C.'s hotels—even the major chains—have for years advertised in gay publications and hosted queer conventions. You'll have no trouble finding a friendly accommodation. With countless visiting diplomats and tourists, the city has thousands of hotel rooms. Amenities like full or limited kitchens and separate living rooms are common. If the high cost of hotel rooms bothers you, consider one of the excellent smaller guest houses in D.C., several of which are a short walk from Dupont Circle.

For price ranges, *see* lodging Chart A at the front of this guide.

Hotels

$$$$ 🏨 **Ritz-Carlton Washington.** Just off Dupont Circle, this handsome old property—formerly a luxury apartment building—is where Vice President Al Gore spent his childhood. Small by luxury-hotel standards, the rooms are furnished in the hunt-club motif for which Ritz-Carltons are known. ⊠ *2100 Massachusetts Ave. NW, 20008,* ☎ *202/293–2100 or 800/241–3333,* 📠 *202/466–9867. 206 rooms. Restaurant.*

$$$$ 🏨 **Renaissance Mayflower Hotel.** Of downtown luxury hotels, this is the most impressive—and it's only about a 15-minute walk from Dupont Circle. Many of the 1925 structure's original touches remain, most notably the lavish gilt-trimmed lobby and the nonworking fireplaces in 76 suites. ⊠ *1127 Connecticut Ave. NW, 20036,* ☎ *202/347–3000 or 800/468–3571,* 📠 *202/466–9083. 659 rooms. Restaurant.*

$$$–$$$$ 🏨 **Georgetown Inn.** Across Rock Creek from Dupont Circle, this intimate inn blends the ambience of a small hotel with the amenities of a much larger property. The rooms are outfitted with writing desks, black-lacquer cabinets, French armoires, gilt-frame mirrors, and lavish baths. ⊠ *1310 Wisconsin Ave. NW, 20007,* ☎ *202/333–8900 or 800/424–2979,* 📠 *202/333–8308. 95 rooms. Restaurant.*

$$$–$$$$ 🏨 **Omni Shoreham Hotel.** Though its facade recalls a large city hospital, rooms of this 1930s art deco palace retain a grand, albeit fading, charm—many have fireplaces, and half overlook Rock Creek Park. Close to both Adams-Morgan and Dupont Circle. ⊠ *2500 Calvert St. NW, 20008,* ☎ *202/234–0700 or 800/333–3333,* 📠 *202/332–1373. 770 rooms. Restaurant, pool, exercise room.*

$$$ 🏨 **Radisson Barceló Hotel.** This former apartment house has a dull exterior and perfunctorily furnished rooms, but you can't beat the location—smack in the middle of P Street's bar scene. There's a great restaurant, a chic marble lobby, and a lovely outdoor pool. ✉ *2121 P St. NW, 20037,* ☎ *202/293–3100 or 800/333–3333,* FAX *202/857–0134. 300 rooms. Restaurant, pool, exercise room.*

$$$ 🏨 **Wyndham Bristol.** This European-style hotel is a short walk from Georgetown, the Mall, and Dupont Circle. Rooms are spacious and elegant, with top-notch amenities—suites have small kitchens and separate dining nooks. ✉ *2430 Pennsylvania Ave. NW, 20037,* ☎ *202/955–6400 or 800/996–3426,* FAX *202/955–5765. 240 rooms. Restaurant, health club.*

$$–$$$ 🏨 **St. James.** This all-suites hotel in Foggy Bottom is one of the city's better-kept secrets. The enormous suites have separate living rooms, full kitchens, and are decorated with matching floral-print bedspreads and curtains; there are 10 full studios. ✉ *950 24th St. NW, 20037,* ☎ *202/457–0500 or 800/852–8512,* FAX *202/659–4492. 195 suites. Pool, health club.*

$$–$$$ 🏨 **Carlyle Suites.** A terrific moderately priced option near Dupont Circle with funky art deco touches and a fabulous restaurant, the Carlyle is one of the District's most gay-popular hotels. Rooms have fully equipped kitchens and sitting areas. ✉ *1731 New Hampshire Ave. NW, 20009,* ☎ *202/234–3200 or 800/964–5377,* FAX *202/387–0085. 170 rooms. Restaurant, health club.*

Guest Houses and Small Hotels

$$–$$$$ 🏨 **The Dupont at The Circle.** For a touch of luxury but the coziness of a private home, consider this restored Victorian town house a couple blocks north of the circle. Hosts Alan and Anexora Skvirsky have done a remarkable job decorating. Elaborate moldings, marble baths (some with Jacuzzis), and fireplaces make this an ideal romantic hideaway, but great restaurants and bars are only steps away. Two apartments are also available. ✉ *1606 19th St. NW, 20009,* ☎ *202/332–5251,* FAX *202/408–8303. 6 rooms with TV and private bath, 2 apartments. Continental breakfast. Mixed gay/straight.*

$$ 🏨 **Tabard Inn.** Comprising three adjacent Victorian town houses, this eccentric inn south of Dupont Circle has been operating since the 1920s. Rooms suggest the setting of a Gothic mystery novel, complete with one-of-a-kind antiques, dark-wood paneling, charming bathroom fixtures, tile fireplaces, and other quirky pieces. The equally old-fashioned and very romantic restaurant serves inventive Continental cuisine. ✉ *1739 N. St. NW, 20036,* ☎ *202/785–1277,* FAX *202/785–6173. 40 rooms with phone and TV, many with private bath. Restaurants. Mostly straight.*

$–$$ 🏨 **Brenton.** This three-story Victorian town house with a brownstone and redbrick facade has long been one of the city's most popular gay accommodations. Rooms are decorated with elaborate Victorian antiques and Oriental rugs; beds have feather pillows and bright linens. ✉ *1708 16th St. NW,* ☎ *202/332–5550 or 800/673–9042. 8 rooms, most with shared bath. Continental breakfast. Mostly mixed gay male/lesbian.*

$–$$ 🏨 **Capitol Hill Guest House.** A sign of Capitol Hill's renaissance, this 1893 mansion was converted into a European-style guest house in the late '80s. The location is charming and convenient, a short walk from Union Station, Capitol Hill's many attractions, and a handful of gay bars. Rooms are simple but exude character; each contains at least one furnishing from the house's days as a residence of congressional pages—if only these walls could talk. ✉ *101 5th St. NE, 20002,* ☎ *202/547–1050. 10 rooms, some with private bath. Continental breakfast. Mixed gay/straight.*

$–$$ 🏨 **Kalorama Guest House.** This grouping of four century-old town houses represents one of the top values in the city. Furnishings—from the antique oak tables and chairs to the brass or wooden beds—have a somewhat faded charm. Both properties received major overhauls in '97 and early '98. ⊠ *1854 Mintwood Pl. NW, 20009,* ☎ *202/667–6369,* FAX *202/319–1262; or* ⊠ *2700 Cathedral Ave. NW, 20008,* ☎ *202/328–0860. 50 rooms, many with private bath. Continental breakfast. Mixed gay/straight.*

$ 📷 **The William Lewis House B&B.** From hand-dipped chocolates at night to a sewing-machine stand converted into a writing desk, this inexpensive guest house is filled with homey touches. Though shared, the bathrooms are gorgeous; one has pressed-tin walls. ⊠ *1309 R St. NW, 20009,* ☎ *202/462–7574 or 800/465–7574. 4 rooms with phone and shared bath. Hot tub. Continental breakfast (full on weekends). Mixed gay/straight.*

THE LITTLE BLACK BOOK

At Your Fingertips

AIDS Hotline (☎ 800/342–2437; in Spanish, ☎ 800/344–7432). *City Paper* (☎ 202/332–2100, Web site www.washingtoncitypaper.com). **DC Crisis Hotline** (☎ 202/223–0020). **Gay and Lesbian Information Bureau** (☎ 703/578–4542). **Gay and Lesbian Resources Web site** (www.gaydc.com). Gay Latino Hotline (☎ 202/483–6806). **Lesbian and Gay Switchboard** (☎ 202/833–3234). **Sexual Minority Youth Assistance League** (☎ 202/546–5940). **Washington D.C. Convention and Visitors Association** (⊠ 1212 New York Ave. NW, Suite 610, 20005, ☎ 202/789–7000, Web site www.washington.org). **Whitman-Walker Medical Clinic** (☎ 202/797–3500). **Woman's Monthly** (☎ 703/527–4881).

Gay Media

The city's free bar rag is *Metro Arts & Entertainment Weekly* (☎ 202/344–7640, Web site www.metroweekly.com); in addition to the latest on drink specials, it usually has a few fluffy and fun features on lesbian and gay goings on. The *Washington Blade* (☎ 202/797–7000, Web site www.washblade.com) is one of the most-respected lesbian and gay newsweeklies in the nation. *Off Our Backs* (☎ 202/234–8072) is a feminist news journal, and *Women In The Life* (☎ 202/483–9818) is the city's most widely read lesbian newsletter.

BOOKSTORES

The city's largest gay bookstore, **Lambda Rising** (⊠ 1625 Connecticut Ave. NW, 20009, ☎ 202/462–6969; send $2 for a mail-order catalog), north of Dupont Circle, stocks most lesbian and gay titles in print. **Lammas—Women's Books & More** (⊠ 1607 17th St. NW, ☎ 202/775–8218 or 800/955–2662) has a popular community bulletin board, Sunday readings, and lesbian-oriented books, cards, and music. If you want to find the pulse of the lesbian community, stop here.

Not specifically gay-oriented but definitely gay-frequented, **Vertigo Books** (⊠ 1337 Connecticut Ave. NW, ☎ 202/429–9272) specializes in international studies, African-American titles, and world literature. **Kramer Books and Afterwords** (⊠ 1517 Connecticut Ave. NW, ☎ 202/387–1400) is a comfy independent store with a café, off Dupont Circle.

Working Out

Muscle Beach (⊠ 2007 18th St. NW, ☎ 202/328–5201), in Adams-Morgan, is big with the free-weights crowd, known locally as "the dumb and the buffed." **Results—The Gym** (⊠ 17th and U Sts. NW, ☎ 202/518–0001) is easily the hottest—and spiffiest—health club to take the gay community by storm. The gayest of the **Washington Sports Club** branches is north of Dupont Circle (⊠ 1835 Connecticut Ave. NW, ☎ 202/332–0100). **Bally's Total Fitness** (⊠ 2000 L St. NW, ☎ 202/331–7898) gets a stronger racial mix than the others.

NOTES

NOTES

NOTES

NOTES

NOTES

NOTES

Come out
and play.

WHEREVER YOU TRAVEL, *H*ELP IS NEVER FAR AWAY.

From planning your trip to

providing travel assistance along

the way, American Express®

Travel Service Offices are

always there to help

you do more.

American Express Travel Service Offices are found in central locations throughout the United States. For the office nearest you, please call 1-800-AXP-3429.